For Reference

Not to be taken from this room

The Bowker Annual

Library and Book Trade Almanac™

2002 | 47th Edition

Editor Dave Bogart
Consultant Julia C. Blixrud

 Information Today, Inc.

Published by Information Today, Inc.
Copyright © 2002 Information Today, Inc.
All rights reserved

International Standard Book Number 1-57387-143-5
International Standard Serial Number 0068-0540
Library of Congress Catalog Card Number 55-12434

Information Today, Inc.
143 Old Marlton Pike
Medford, NJ 08055-8750
Phone: 800-300-9868 (customer service)
             800-409-4929 (editorial queries)
Fax: 609-654-4309
E-mail (orders): custserv@infotoday.com
Web Site: www.infotoday.com

Printed and bound in the United States of America

ISBN 1-57387-143-5

$199.00

Contents

Preface..ix

Part 1
Reports from the Field

News of the Year
LJ News Report: Looking Back, Looking Ahead   *John Berry, Eric Bryant,*
Michael Rogers, Andrew Albanese, and *Norman Oder* 3
Facing the Challenges of a New Era in School Librarianship   *Harriet Selverstone*.....9
Publishing in 2001: Shake-Outs, Downsizing, and E-Book Disappointments
Jim Milliot 18

Federal Agency and Federal Library Reports
Library of Congress   *Audrey Fischer* 27
Center for the Book   *John Y. Cole* 40
Federal Library and Information Center Committee   *Susan M. Tarr*.........................44
National Commission on Libraries and Information Science   *Rosalie B. Vlach*........57
National Agricultural Library   *Len Carey* 61
National Library of Medicine   *Robert Mehnert*...66
United States Government Printing Office   *Andrew M. Sherman*............................72
National Technical Information Service   *Linda Davis* 83
National Archives and Records Administration   *Marion H. Vecchiarelli* 93
National Center for Education Statistics Library Statistics Program   *Adrienne Chute*...99
National Library of Education   *Christina Dunn* 108
Educational Resources Information Center   *Christina Dunn*...................................113

National Association and Organization Reports
American Library Association   *John W. Berry*...123
Association of American Publishers   *Judith Platt*..138
American Booksellers Association   *Michael Hoynes* 157
Association of Research Libraries   *Duane E. Webster*...161
Scholarly Publishing and Academic Resources Coalition   *Richard Johnson*...........179
Council on Library and Information Resources   *Kathlin Smith*...............................186

International Reports

International Federation of Library Associations and Institutions *Winston Tabb* ...197
A Canadian-American Librarianship or an American-Canadian Librarianship
in the 21st Century? *William F. Birdsall* 204

Special Reports

Adventures with E-Books: 2001 in Review *Dennis Dillon* 215
Internet Speed, Library Know-How Intersect in Digital Reference
Ilene F. Rockman 234
Libraries, Publishers, Authors, Scholars Jointly Explore Internet Publishing
Boundaries *Edward J. Valauskas* 249
Applying the Principles of Intellectual Freedom: A Cross-Cultural Comparison
Ken Haycock, Michelle Mallette, and *Anne Olsen* 257
Dissemination of Government Information *Harold C. Relyea* 268
Copyright 2001: Exploring the Implications of Technology *Robert L. Oakley* 284

Part 2
Legislation, Funding, and Grants

Legislation

Legislation and Regulations Affecting Libraries in 2001
Emily Sheketoff and *Mary R. Costabile* 301
Legislation and Regulations Affecting Publishing in 2001 *Allan Adler* 312

Funding Programs and Grant-Making Agencies

National Endowment for the Humanities *Thomas C. Phelps* 331
Institute of Museum and Library Services Library Programs *Robert S. Martin*......343

Part 3
Library/Information Science
Education, Placement, and Salaries

Guide to Employment Sources in the Library and Information Professions
Darlena Davis 361
Placements and Salaries 2000: Plenty of Jobs, Salaries Flat
Tom Terrell and *Vicki L. Gregory* 382
Accredited Master's Programs in Library and Information Studies........................396
Library Scholarship Sources 401
Library Scholarship and Award Recipients, 2001 406

Part 4
Research and Statistics

Library Research and Statistics
Research on Libraries and Librarianship in 2001 *Mary Jo Lynch* 427
Number of Libraries in the United States and Canada...440
Highlights of NCES Surveys...443
Library Acquisition Expenditures, 2000–2001: U.S. Public, Academic, Special,
and Government Libraries..453
LJ Budget Report: The New Wariness *Norman Oder* 462
Price Indexes for Public and Academic Libraries *Kent Halstead* 468
Library Buildings 2001: Keep On Constructin' *Bette-Lee Fox*..............................488
Expenditures for Resources in School Library Media Centers, 1999–2000:
New Money, Old Books *Marilyn L. Miller* and *Marilyn L. Shontz*........................503

Book Trade Research and Statistics
Prices of U.S. and Foreign Published Materials *Sharon G. Sullivan* 525
Book Title Output and Average Prices: 200 Final and 2001 Preliminary Figures
Catherine Barr and *Andrew Grabois*..548
Book Sales Statistics, 2001: AAP Preliminary Estimates.......................................553
U.S. Book Exports and Imports: 2001 *Catherine Barr*..555
Number of Book Outlets in the United States and Canada 562
Review Media Statistics...564

Part 5
Reference Information

Bibliographies
The Librarian's Bookshelf *Cathleen Bourdon, MLS* 567

Ready Reference
Publishers' Toll-Free Telephone Numbers and Web Sites 581
How to Obtain an ISBN *Emery Koltay*..633
How to Obtain an ISSN 637
How to Obtain an SAN *Emery Koltay*...639

Distinguished Books
Notable Books of 2001 643
Best Books for Young Adults 645

Quick Picks for Reluctant Young Adult Readers 648
Audiobooks for Young Adults 650
Notable Children's Books 652
Notable Children's Videos 655
Notable Recordings for Children 656
Notable Software and Web Sites for Children..658
Bestsellers of 2001   *Daisy Maryles* and *Laurele Riippa* 659
Literary Prizes, 2001   *Gary Ink* 696

Part 6
Directory of Organizations

Directory of Library and Related Organizations

Networks, Consortia, and Other Cooperative Library Organizations 707
National Library and Information-Industry Associations,
United States and Canada..731
State, Provincial, and Regional Library Associations 792
State and Provincial Library Agencies 805
State School Library Media Associations 810
International Library Associations 818
Foreign Library Associations 826

Directory of Book Trade and Related Organizations

Book Trade Associations, United States and Canada 837
International and Foreign Book Trade Associations...843

NISO Standards 851
Calendar 853
Acronyms 859
Index of Organizations...863
Subject Index..873

Preface

Welcome to the 47th edition of the *Bowker Annual*. Like its predecessors, it is a compilation of practical information and informed analysis of interest to the library, information, and book trade worlds.

We look at a year in which technology—specifically, electronic forms of the printed word—played an ever-growing role, and in which events have made us re-examine the principles of intellectual freedom.

These issues are reflected in our six Special Reports:

- Dennis Dillon reviews a "remarkable" year of ups, downs, and growing pains in the e-book industry.
- Ilene Rockman examines digital reference services and the challenges and benefits they are making for libraries of all types.
- Edward Valauskas looks at the ways in which libraries, publishers, authors, and scholars are exploring the boundaries of Internet publishing.
- Ken Haycock, Michelle Mallette, and Anne Olsen contrast the exercise of intellectual freedom in Canada and the United States in light of the September 11 terrorist attacks and other situations in which the principles of freedom are being tested.
- Harold Relyea examines changes in policy governing the dissemination of government information, another area greatly affected by recent events.
- Robert Oakley reviews the year's developments in copyright with an emphasis on the implications of evolving technology.

Also in Part 1 are reports on the year's activities from federal agencies, federal libraries, and national and international library and publishing organizations.

Part 2 includes detailed examinations of the past year's legislation affecting libraries and publishing, plus reports from major funding and grant-making agencies.

Part 3 contains professional information for librarians: guides to sources of scholarships and employment, our annual look at trends in library placements and salaries, and a list of 2001's major scholarship and award winners.

Research and statistics on libraries and publishing make up Part 4, including reports on current research projects, library acquisition expenditures, book output and price data, and examinations of national and international trends in the publishing trade.

Reference information is found in Part 5: who won the year's top literary prizes; how to obtain an ISBN, ISSN, or SAN; and detailed lists of bestsellers and notable resources for children and young adults.

Part 6 contains our updated directory of library and book trade organizations at the state, national, and international levels. It is followed by detailed indexes and a calendar of information industry events.

The *Bowker Annual* represents the efforts of many people, and gratitude goes to all those who contributed articles, assembled reports, supplied statistics, and responded to our requests for information. Special thanks are due Consultant Editor Julia C. Blixrud and Contributing Editor Catherine Barr.

We believe you will find this edition a valuable and frequently used resource, and—as always—we welcome your comments and suggestions for future editions.

Dave Bogart
Editor

Part 1
Reports from the Field

News of the Year

LJ News Report: Looking Back, Looking Ahead

John Berry
Editor-in-Chief, *Library Journal*

Eric Bryant
Executive Editor, *Library Journal*

Michael Rogers
Senior Editor, *Library Journal*

Andrew Albanese
Norman Oder
Associate Editors, *Library Journal*

The economic repercussions from September 11 are being felt around the country, but that day's effects in library and information-related areas—an erosion of privacy protections libraries once guaranteed patrons, reallocation of scarce funds to beefed-up security and disaster planning, the withdrawal of materials from federal depository library collections, an extension of the moratorium on releasing presidential papers—are only beginning to surface. Observers are still hoping that the new willingness to curb civil liberties and restrict access will be short-lived.

Meanwhile, other, more familiar issues remain at the fore of professional debate. The editors of *Library Journal* (*LJ*) and its sibling outlets—*Library Hotline*, *Corporate Library Update*, *LJ* Academic Newswire, and Library Journal online—sat down to review the most significant of these issues. Here is a recap of the stories from 2001 that will continue to resound in the year to come.

Budget Reversals

A year that began with partisan debate in Washington about the size of coming budget surpluses came to an end with state governments cutting not only next year's budgets but those of the current fiscal year as well. In some cases special circumstances have been at play: In Washington, a referendum trimmed property tax assessments, while New York City libraries were asked to make 15 percent

Adapted from *Library Journal*, December 2001.

cuts along with nearly all other city departments after the World Trade Center attacks. But from Oregon to Arizona, Colorado to Arkansas, Michigan to Tennessee, the reason is simply lower-than-predicted tax revenues, hit first by a slowing economy then by a sharp economic downturn following September 11.

Consequences of the cuts will vary. While many states exempted education from the first round of cuts, university libraries in both Arizona and North Carolina took heavy hits. In South Carolina, State Librarian Jim Johnson told *LJ* that the funds he disperses to public libraries were most commonly used for materials, and he expected the results of his 11 percent cut to be felt there first. In Tennessee, cuts of a similar size were dealt with initially through a halt on grants to the four largest cities, hiring freezes, and travel suspensions.

The source of revenues has taken on greater importance. Some locales draw more heavily from the state, while others depend only on local funds. In addition, property tax revenues should be more stable than sales taxes, which have been devastated in some tourism-dependent regions.

Federal and state aid is expected to remain essentially flat or slightly down for the next fiscal year. So far few municipalities are registering cuts, but those accountings should start to surface shortly, and no one expects good news.

Fighting Back in the Journals Crisis

In the decades-old battle to reclaim scholarly communication for the scholars, 2001 was a breakthrough year. In just three years since the Association of Research Libraries (ARL) launched the Scholarly Publishing and Academic Resources Coalition (SPARC), the library community has become markedly more organized, involved, and innovative in its efforts to control the skyrocketing costs of scholarly journals and monographs. In 2001 librarians saw solid evidence that their efforts were paying off.

A slew of library-friendly, Web-based journals were born. The University of Arizona library even took the extraordinary step of becoming a publisher. Then, in a landmark announcement, the first SPARC-supported journal, *Organic Letters*, exceeded its main commercial competitor (Elsevier's *Tetrahedron Letters*) in impact factor in the subject category of Organic Chemistry after just two years of publication.

But the greatest victory for librarians in 2001 was the realization that their message had finally been heard outside of library walls. In 2001 the Public Library of Science initiative saw more than 27,000 scientists sign a petition stating that they would no longer support, edit, referee for, subscribe to, or submit work to scholarly journals that did not make all of their content available free of charge through the National Institutes of Health's PubMed Central after six months of publication.

Librarians and faculty both are likely to build on the gains realized in 2001. A multitude of nascent Web-based scholarly communication initiatives will be launched. More important than any single initiative will be the long-lasting influence librarians can gain on campus as experts in scholarly communication and information transfer.

Filtering Debate Moves to the Courts

The Children's Internet Protection Act (CIPA), signed into law December 21, 2000, requires libraries and schools receiving E-rate telecomm discounts or Library Services and Technology Act (LSTA) or Elementary and Secondary Education Act (ESEA) funds to filter "harmful to minors" material. Though aimed at protecting children, the law would inevitably impact adults; it also requires that Internet terminals used by adults and staff block obscenity and child pornography, narrow categories that no filter-maker professes to be able to single out.

In March, the American Library Association (ALA) and the American Civil Liberties Union (ACLU) filed tandem lawsuits (since consolidated) to challenge the law. Oral arguments are set to begin before a three-judge panel of the Third Circuit Court of Appeals in Philadelphia; any appeal will go straight to the Supreme Court. A decision should be rendered before July, by which date libraries would have to install filters. However, some libraries have already responded. In Oklahoma City, the Metropolitan Library Commission voted to filter all library computers. In San Francisco, the Board of Supervisors unanimously reaffirmed the library's policy of not filtering for adults or teens and pledged to replace lost funds.

Meanwhile, the Supreme Court heard oral arguments in the government's appeal of the 1998 Child Online Protection Act (COPA). That law would require Web sites publishing "harmful to minors" material to restrict access to minors. The court challenge, led by the ACLU on behalf of online content providers, blocked enforcement. One provision of the law established the COPA Commission, which advised against mandatory filtering.

In May the federal Equal Employment Opportunity Commission (EEOC) offered a preliminary finding, supporting claims by 12 staffers at the Minneapolis Public Library that exposure to heavy porn surfing by patrons constitutes a hostile work environment. While the EEOC suggested that the library pay each employee $75,000 in damages, the library proposed a dialog to address the employees' "nonmonetary concerns."

If the ACLU prevails in both cases, the filtering debates will not disappear, but they may return to the realm of local politics, where individual districts may still be confronted by local pressure groups. Though ALA's hard-line opposition to filters incurred public relations costs, Minneapolis proves that local fights potentially have a very real price tag.

Information Takes the Lead in LIS

The turmoil that has engulfed library education for a decade or more shows signs of quieting. Most of the highly prestigious programs long ago shifted their focus or found new partners and programs to shore up their previously vulnerable positions and low status on the university campus. Much of this has taken them away from librarianship or "library science" to a new conglomeration of information policy and technology librarianship called "library and information studies" (LIS). The shift at the schools has created a rift between them and practicing librarians.

The University of North Carolina, Florida State University, and others have initiated a host of undergraduate programs emphasizing practical skills in information technology to build enrollment and connections to the larger university. At the newly renamed "I School" or Information School at the University of Washington, a dynamic new dean, Mike Eisenberg, has transformed the place while still supporting traditional library studies.

Within ALA, practitioner fears brought about two "congresses" on library education, plus proposals for continuing education and certification programs run by ALA units like the Public Library Association. The most controversial proposal in LIS education is to move the process of accreditation of LIS programs and their degrees out of ALA to a separate federated agency governed by a coalition of library, information, and technology associations. Though this move is very popular with educators looking for new fields for their LIS programs to conquer, ALA remains strongly opposed, based on concerns that ALA will not have authority commensurate with its share of the costs.

The accreditation issue will heat up when a task force chaired by Susan Martin, recently retired university librarian at Georgetown, introduces details of its proposal. This step was recently delayed in order to build support for the idea. A shift back toward practical library instruction might also be spurred by reports that an increasing percentage of LIS programs' master's graduates in 2000 and 2001 went to work in libraries after all.

Digital Copyright

While judicial battles were won, 2001 proved to be a turbulent year in the ongoing development of electronic copyright, and the broader struggle to devise fair and balanced copyright legislation seemed as far from a conclusion as ever. In one of the most pivotal events, the Supreme Court ruled in *Tasini* v. *New York Times* that it is freelance writers, not publishers, who retain electronic rights to published articles included in electronic databases. ALA and ARL filed an amicus brief in favor of Tasini, despite its effect on libraries—the removal of content from licensed digital archives. The book world suffered a similar blow when Random House lost a copyright case against e-book house RosettaBooks, which was producing electronic versions of books by contracted authors in Random's stable. Random cried copyright infringement, but U.S. Judge Sidney Stein disagreed: "[T]he right to print, publish and sell the work[s] in book form does not include the right to publish . . . as the e-book."

In a setback for peer-to-peer network technology, music-share pioneer Napster was shut down by federal judge Marilyn Hall Patel, after an appeals court upheld the judge's injunction charging copyright infringement. Intense lobbying in no small part by librarians successfully stalled the advancement of the Uniform Computer Information Transactions Act (UCITA) in state legislatures. If ratified, UCITA's provisions could dramatically affect the work of libraries, giving software makers the unilateral right to disable networks remotely and codifying through click-on license agreements provisions that essentially override traditional copyright law.

Debate is raging as to how the Supreme Court might view the antidecryption provision of the Digital Millennium Copyright Act (DMCA) in the case of *MPAA v. Corley*, a key digital copyright case in 2000 that is likely to wind up in front of the nine justices. Corley's attorneys contend that the antidecryption provision of the DMCA cannot be applied consistently with the First Amendment. A Supreme Court finding for Corley, also supported by ALA and ARL, could strike down some of the more draconian provisions of the DMCA as unconstitutional.

While most analysts saw passage of the DMCA as yet another victory for the corporations that license and distribute intellectual property, some are discerning a public backlash. The *New York Times* has been criticized for both threatening to yank content from databases and blacklisting authors who participated in the case. The closure of Napster has led a generation to see corporate copyright-holders as the adversary. Most recently, the still-pending criminal prosecution under the DMCA against Russian programmer Dmitry Sklyarov—accused of "trafficking in a copyright circumvention device" for presenting at a conference code that broke Adobe Reader's rights-management software—produced a grass-roots movement in his defense and has been criticized by none other than Adobe itself.

Pushing Portals and Opening Links

Internet- and especially World Wide Web-related goodies continued to be the dominant force in library automation in 2001 and no doubt will remain so for years to come. The most useful tweaking of online resources in 2001 was the release of portal software for libraries by several of the leading vendors. Portals often are attached to the library's online catalog, in essence creating an *über-*OPAC, which in addition to standard listings of author, title, and Dewey number offers author photos, jacket covers, sample pages, reviews, and more.

The portal movement was led by Sirsi's iBistro. The product debuted in 2000 but grew in popularity in 2001. Traditionally, once one vendor offers a successful product, the rest are not far behind, and The Library Corporation/ CARL Corp. (TLC) was in quick pursuit, releasing its YouSeeMore portal product early in 2001. Using YouSeeMore, patrons can submit personal preferences via a simple Web form and in return receive a portal account that delivers recommendations linked to the library's catalog displaying the book jacket image, TOC, reviews, and availability. More recently, VTLS debuted its Chameleon iPortal, which is billed as "an aggregate Web service for libraries that casts a wide net for capturing information via multiple Internet channels and search engines." The product also allows for enhancing the OPAC with the aforementioned extras.

Real gains have recently also been seen in cross-database search systems, which grow out of the same demand for customer-friendly, intuitive tools. While WebFeat may be best known as the company specializing in this product, a variety of vendors now offer similar solutions, from Fretwell-Downing's Zportal, Ex Libris's MetaLib, and Copernic Aggregator to Endeavor's ENCompass and OCLC's SiteSearch.

Expect more enhancements to the portal concept: the latest step in the evolution of automation vendors into service providers, with customization a primary offering. If your vendor of choice currently is not providing a portal, just wait. It will.

Distance Education Moves Ahead

Distance education programs have burgeoned in the last few years at all sorts of academic institutions, placing new demands on libraries. Many librarians find that the sorts of services required by distance ed students—remote access to full-text databases and e-books, electronic reserves—are just as much appreciated by their on-campus cohorts.

LIS distance ed programs have found particular success. They tap growing unrest among support staff, the largest group of library employees and the most fertile ground for recruiting to the profession. The shrinking number of graduate programs has meant that many working in libraries cannot afford the time or travel required to attend programs on campuses. Despite doubts about its rigor and the quality of the student experience, distance LIS is obviously here to stay. The newest program at the University of Pittsburgh has joined dozens of existing distance LIS programs, and it will soon be joined by more.

In the years to come, expect to see real competition and turf wars among the distance LIS programs. The generally unspoken question of whether true rigor and quality will attract more enrollment than a less-rigorous but faster and easier route to the MLS degree may become the subject of recruitment campaigns.

The End of E-Books?

Popular consensus has it that 2001 was a tough year for the e-book. Lowlights— and there were many—include the closing of Random House's atRandom e-book imprint just months after its initial launch, attendance slipping by 50 percent at the fall National Institute for Standards and Technology e-book conference in Washington, D.C., and the continued lack of public interest in any of the available reading devices. But the biggest hit to e-book boosters in libraries was the financial collapse of popular e-book provider netLibrary.

Three years after raising well over $100 million in venture capital to digitize, publicize, and distribute tens of thousands of e-books to thousands of libraries, reality finally caught up with netLibrary's digital dream. Industry watchers thought netLibrary was actually approaching economies of scale to near profitability. Yet the company filed for bankruptcy in November and announced that it would be purchased by OCLC.

Despite setbacks in 2001, e-books have not flopped. Though obscured by the high-profile bursting of the dot-com bubble, the e-book actually made modest gains among users in 2001. "We've reached 6,600 libraries," said netLibrary Senior Marketing Director Marge Gammon. "That tells me we've reached a critical mass. There is certainly not a lack of interest in e-books in the library space."

For e-books to succeed, progress must be made on the very same issues that have plagued the e-book from its inception—the development of a suitable, and sustainable, business model that addresses both fair use for users and piracy concerns for publishers. Additionally, progress must be made on a better reading device. A lower profile for the e-book in 2002 might aid the industry's growth on these fronts, by encouraging small steps rather than all-or-nothing bets. The foundations laid by a more sober industry in 2002 will lead to innovation and eventually to the realization of the e-book's potential in the years to follow.

Facing the Challenges of a New Era in School Librarianship

Harriet Selverstone

The field of school librarianship has changed significantly over the past 30 years, in part because of an exponential increase in information. The introduction of computer technology has resulted in a rapidly changing information world, and information services have become a critical component of our present and future work force. Students must be educated to become actively engaged in creative thinking and problem solving. School library media specialists have been in the forefront of nurturing student learning, by helping them master the concepts and skills of computer and information literacy. In addition, school library media specialists have become full partners with classroom teachers in the instructional lives of our students.

Professional Training

In recent years many library schools have closed their doors. As a result, the number of programs training students to enter the school librarianship field has diminished. In addition, with the infusion of information service professionals in industry, many graduates of library school programs are opting to enter fields that entice candidates with higher paying positions than school systems and public library boards are willing or able to sustain.

Within the graduate library school structure, not all of the programs have school library media specialist components. Many programs direct their students to public library service, academic librarianship, and the more specialized programs like law and medical librarianship. In many of these library fields, additional undergraduate and/or graduate degrees in select fields are prerequisites. The majority of states require those entering the school librarianship field to have at least an undergraduate degree in education since school library media specialists are under teacher contracts and paid on the same salary schedules as teachers.

Given the closure of many graduate library programs, and given the fact that not every current library program has a school librarianship component or strand, many colleges and universities are offering basic courses in school librarianship. Such courses enable students to be state-certified as school library media specialists without receiving an MLS degree. Also, some states, among them Connecticut, have instituted alternative route programs. In Connecticut's program, which operates under the cooperative sponsorship of both the state Department of Education and the only American Library Association-accredited graduate library program in the state, potential school library media candidates must have taught for five years before entering the program. Once enrolled, they are required to take an intensive five weeks of immersion in school library media preparation plus a year of attendance at workshops and conferences.

Harriet Selverstone, MLS, was president of the American Association of School Librarians in 2000–2001. A library media specialist for 29 years at Norwalk (Connecticut) High School, she is an adjunct visiting professor at Pratt Institute School of Information and Library Science.

Staffing Issues

Since there is a dearth of school library media professionals, many elementary and middle school library media centers are now staffed by paraprofessionals. The staffing situation in the high school environment is different, however, since high schools must undergo an accreditation process to maintain their academic status. (Students from a nonaccredited high school often will not be accepted by the more competitive colleges and universities. The armed services, as well, look for recruits from accredited institutions.) Accreditation agencies examine the library media program and its staffing complement. School library media programs have become one of the essential "standards" examined during the accreditation visit and subsequent evaluation. It is imperative that all schools (elementary, middle, and high schools) be adequately staffed with professionally certified library media professionals—people with pedagogical skills in curriculum development and enhancement and with library media background—to instruct and guide students to become information literate and creative problem solvers.

Paraprofessionals complement the services of the professional library media specialist and library media program. At one time, clerical and organizational skills were the only requirements. Now, however, these important assistants must be technologically savvy to assist the professional staff and students with technical needs. They may also be required to understand the workings of electronic resources to maintain the level of searching capability demanded by a technologically advanced student population. School library media professionals collaborate with staff in curriculum design and construction, but the paraprofessional staff provides the necessary backbone to keep the library media program running smoothly and effortlessly. Memos need to be typed, an attractive environment needs to be maintained, supplies need to be accessible, circulation and attendance figures need to be kept up to date, and print collections must be ordered, processed, and shelved. These tasks cannot all be done—along with instruction and professional development for school staff—by a lone school library media specialist.

Collection Development

Collection development has assumed a new meaning with the arrival of electronic resources. Selections for acquisition, whether print or nonprint, are reviewed in professional publications. These reviewing publications devote space to print material—fiction and nonfiction—as well as to Web sites, electronic databases, and hardware to complement the electronic resources. Reviews of Web sites reflect the suitable academic level of the material as well as the applicability of the curricular area(s). Reviews of new hardware appear in monthly issues of these sources. School library media professionals need to update their know-how in order to understand the advances in technology. Reviews also keep the school media specialist apprised of what is worthwhile, what is peripheral, and what will help make their jobs easier and more efficient.

"Cyberlibraries" are slowly making inroads in school library media programs. They will not replace the physical facility and the ongoing library media program, but they will enhance the searching capability and accessibility of resources available for student and staff needs. Remote access to the school library media collection, to online databases, to book lists and bibliographies, to lesson plans, even to help-desk staff can be available on a 24/7 basis.

Responsible collection development also calls for the school library media specialist to create a well-balanced collection. Different viewpoints on topics should be offered to foster students' critical and creative thinking. Media specialists should not proselytize perspectives, but they should provide material with opposing theses. Collections must also support the curriculum, and if new initiatives are planned, new materials must be acquired to enhance these programs. It is also important to consider staff needs and requests when purchasing material. These purchases should be solicited by library media professionals and the staff must be notified once the material is acquired. This procedure enhances and encourages collaboration among staff members.

Budgeting

Budgeting has become an increasing challenge now that new priorities need to be addressed. As indicated earlier, collection development involves greater decision-making efforts. Print collections are aging, and space becomes an issue if a conscientious effort to weed is not pursued. Many vendors offer package deals to purchase materials in both hard-copy and electronic versions. In some instances the electronic versions are more expensive. However, if sources are purchased in electronic format, and if computers are networked within the school, and remote access to materials is available, then the school library media specialist must consider purchasing the electronic versions to enable better access to the resources for staff and students.

Budgets have been reduced, or have not been increased, in many school districts. In order for schools to have what might be referred to as a "state-of-the-art" library media facility in the 21st century, electronic resources must be considered. Capital budgets must also provide for an adequate number of computer terminals to satisfy the ever-growing need for students to do online research and word processing. We must eliminate the "digital divide" and provide equity in educational opportunities. Many students do not have computers at home, and they therefore need to have the chance to work at school. In addition to offering electronic resources, print collections should be kept up to date. Books, newspapers, magazines, supplies, and equipment are big budgetary considerations. Recreational or pleasure reading is still done in the library media center. Hidden expenses are also incurred, including such costs as maintenance of computers and printers and hardware service agreements. These budgetary allowances are handled either by the individual school or the district. If the school has to assume this responsibility, budgeting for other materials is often deferred.

Collaboration

Information Power: Building Partnerships for Learning is the premier joint publication of the American Association of School Librarians (AASL) and the Association for Educational Communications and Technology (AECT). The main premise of this publication is that students' achievement level rises when the library media specialist and the classroom teacher collaborate on instructional units.

There are a number of benefits for the teacher, library media specialist, student, and administrator when all collaborate on the teaching-for-learning process. Students become more involved in the learning process. This engagement often enhances creativity in their work. When teachers and media specialists share ideas, their level of creativity subsequently increases as well. The roles of all concerned in the learning process also tend to change as the collaborative effort is encouraged by administrators and those responsible for curriculum development. When students work on cooperative teams, the teacher assumes the role of resource person and/or facilitator and coach. Students also grow and develop into more sophisticated learners. They begin to interact with people outside the school environment to obtain additional resources and gain clarity of understanding of topics through the interview process. This inquiry-and-response relationship enlarges the student's scope of materials from which to draw in order to complete assignments; this relationship also helps the student develop a respect for the knowledge of others. As the key person in this collaborative effort, the library media specialist gains the professional respect of the staff and administration as the choreographer of this teaching-for-learning model.

Technology in Education

What does "using technology" mean in the educational arena? It means more than students preparing their papers and reports on a word processor. It means more than using the Internet for obtaining both academic and recreational help. It means more than using search engines and electronic databases to locate information. When teachers use technology, the process encompasses more than creating spreadsheets to record student grades or e-mailing students and parents to inform them of class assignments or grades.

For technology to be used effectively in the classroom and/or library media center, it must be fully integrated into the curriculum. Technology enhances learning when teachers and students understand which aspect can assist them in obtaining the information they need, when they need it, and how to analyze the data to determine its credibility, reliability, relevance, and adaptability before presenting the information in a creative manner.

The International Society for Technology in Education has developed standards for students using electronic resources. The library media specialist, in collaboration with the classroom teacher, assumes responsibility for ensuring that students will achieve various technology-related competencies before they leave grade 12. Students need to become comfortable and successful in the use of technology, and they must be responsible users and understand the social, ethical, and cultural issues involved in using technology. They are expected to become adept at evaluating the information they gather to make relevant, informed decisions, and to become effective at communicating their ideas as they learn more in less time through the use of electronic resources.[1]

Information Literacy

Information literacy can be defined simply as knowing how to find information, evaluate it, and use it effectively. AASL has been in the forefront of developing information literacy standards for student learning through its joint publication with AECT, *Information Power: Building Partnerships for Learning.* The nine standards are divided into three major categories: information literacy, independent learning, and social responsibility. Each category is further delineated into concise methods to achieve these standards. Within information literacy, the student must recognize that there is a need for information, frame questions related to that need, decide what sources would be helpful in finding relevant answers, develop the search strategies to obtain the information, and evaluate the information. Within the category of independent learning, the student must show evidence of pursuing learning to benefit his or her own interests (and, therefore, must be self-motivated), develop a creative response with new information achieved, and assess the new product. Under the category of social responsibility, the student must be aware of how important information and information access is to a democratic society, respect all the principles of intellectual freedom, respect copyright laws and not infringe on those rights, and work with others through collaborative and cooperative learning to identify issues, seek solutions, and evaluate the final product or new learning.[2]

Since the time AASL and AECT spearheaded this drive toward information literacy and its attendant standards, the library media specialist has assumed responsibility, in collaboration with the classroom teacher, for encouraging instruction in these standards. Library media specialists should be the professional development instructors in this effort "to ensure that all students and staff are effective users of ideas and information."[3]

Students have often had difficulty with information seeking because they have not understood the information structure. This means they may not know what information is appropriate, relevant, and credible, or what is a primary and secondary resource. Information literacy can be encouraged and fostered by providing students with wide access to multiple resources in the classroom, library media center, and beyond the school walls through print or electronic information. When students become information literate they actually learn how to learn. They will know how information is organized, how to find that information, and how to use that information so others might learn from them. They will then be prepared for lifelong learning and effectuate the AASL slogan that "student achievement is the bottom line."

Intellectual Freedom

School library media specialists have a responsibility to ensure that those they serve have every opportunity to obtain information without constraints. Unimpeded physical and intellectual access to materials and ideas must be supported. School library media specialists may be confronted by those who wish to censor or challenge materials or restrict usage and ideas. We need to confront that censorship to maintain a democratic society that fosters freedom of thought and expression, provides access to materials in all formats, and nurtures inquiry.

Censorship by parent groups, by right-wing organizations, or by teachers and/or administrators has become more prevalent in recent years. School collections, and school library media center collections in particular, have been targets of those who wish to suppress ideas. Books, and now the Internet, have been challenged for issues dealing with sexuality, language that may be offensive to some, political content, teaching of values and self-esteem, drug-abuse prevention programs, creationism vs. evolution, and multicultural education. School library media specialists must be vigilant and sensitive to the methods used by censors to accomplish their aims of suppression. The censors may lobby administrators and school boards to remove material, distribute literature through statewide and national campaigns, mobilize people through religious organizations and churches, attempt to defeat school tax increases, or personally threaten school officials and staff members.

In order to defuse or deal with challenges, school library media specialists must be certain that their boards of education have an approved "selection and reconsideration" policy. A team of administrators, parents, teachers, and students must be formed as a reviewing panel. Community and school support is important as is a planned method for approaching challenges. The material in question ought to be considered on educational/literacy grounds rather than on an ideological or political basis. The media specialist must be ready to articulate the educational value of the material and to contact the local media as soon as a challenge is suspected. The media specialist has an obligation to make thoughtful, defensible collection decisions. A number of groups can assist the school library media specialist in meeting these challenges, by supplying information or sending representatives to a public hearing. Among these groups are ALA's Office for Intellectual Freedom, the National Coalition Against Censorship, and People for the American Way.

The ALA Council adopted a Library Bill of Rights, and its many interpretations, to guide professionals in assuring their constituencies that access to library collections in any format is safeguarded. Materials reflecting opposing viewpoints must be made available, and there should be free access to materials for all, so that no economic barriers are extant.

Research

In the past 35 years more than 60 educational and library research studies have revealed the positive impact of library media specialists and their programs on the academic achievement of students. The research has focused on three main areas: learning and teaching, information access and delivery, and program administration. These areas reflect the roles of the library media specialist within the educational environment as teacher, information specialist, information consultant, and program administrator, as highlighted in *Information Power: Building Partnerships for Learning*.

Within the area of learning and teaching, a positive correlation was found between the teaching role of the library media specialist and the achievement of students. In 1975 S. L. Aaron published research that indicated the importance of including the library media specialist as part of the teaching team, since this inclusion resulted in higher student achievement in language arts, spelling, and computation skills in mathematics.[4] In the 1990s other major studies were conducted to prove that academic achievement was affected by school library media center programs and services, and by adequate professional staffing. This achievement was most evident in a 1993 study where the school library media specialist was part of the instructional team of teachers. That study based its research on the 221 Colorado public schools rather than on individual students, and it demonstrated that funding was a major consideration in fostering higher academic achievement.[5] Funding helped secure larger library print and electronic collections as well as more professional and support staff. Another important factor influencing the academic success of students is the level at which school library media specialists participate in the instructional process—as part of the teaching team or as a participant in curriculum and professional development.

Another study, conducted in 1993 by Stephen Krashen, is described in *The Power of Reading*. His study revealed that free voluntary reading is a major determinant for vocabulary growth and reading comprehension, and that it fosters better spelling and improved students' writing style.[6]

A second Colorado study, *How School Librarians Help Kids Achieve Standards,* was published in April 2000.[7] This study focused less on the library media center as a facility for learning; instead, attention was paid to the school library media specialist and the services he or she offers. This study examined such variables as the collaborative relationships the library media specialist developed with the classroom teacher, whether the library media specialist assumed a leadership role in the instructional process, if the principal was also engaged in the learning and teaching aspect of the library media program, and the part networked computers with licensed databases played in instruction. It was not a surprise to learn that the study found that all of these factors contributed to higher academic achievement.

When considering information access and delivery, increased student visits to the library media center, and, therefore, greater student access to print and electronic resources and more free voluntary reading, have been found to contribute to higher academic achievement.[8]

Research demonstrates, too, that when the library media specialist has strong leadership and library management skills, and when administrative support is strong, greater student learning is the result.[9]

Another study, conducted and published in 1999 in Alaska, reflected the importance of professionally trained library media specialists and the significant contribution they make toward student achievement. *Information Empowered: The School Librarian as an Agent of Academic Achievement in Alaska Schools* indicated that academic achievement was realized when there was a full-time, professionally trained library media specialist, who spent a full day delivering library and information literacy instruction to students, who planned cooperatively with classroom teachers, and who offered professional development programs for teachers. In addition, academic test scores tended to be higher when there was a cooperative relationship between the library media center and the public library, when the library media program provided online access, and when the library media center collection policy included the reconsideration of materials to ensure intellectual and academic freedom.[10]

As discussed earlier in this article, staffing issues are a concern in school librarianship. Recent statistics from the Library Research Service show that the number of school library media positions has not kept pace with the growth in the number of teaching positions. School librarian positions in the United States grew 3.3 percent between 1993 and 1998, but the increase in the number of class-room teachers was about 10 percent.[11] Therefore, recruitment to the profession of school librarianship needs a great deal of attention. Furthermore, the status of the school library media specialty in graduate library education programs and the variability of certification requirements from state to state are areas of concern. If these issues are not addressed, our students will be at risk academically.

National Board Certification and Its Justification

A recent issue facing school library media specialists is that of national certification. We have been concerned about advocacy for our profession and recognition for the important role we play in the education of our students. As noted, studies have been conducted to prove the effectiveness of school library media programming and of professional staffing on the academic achievement of students. However, the process of national certification, just like review processes for schools, indicates the effectiveness of the educational process and offers the school library media specialist an opportunity for self-reflection on topics including where he or she is in the educational process and what he or she wants to accomplish. National certification is not a requirement at this time, but it is an effective way to highlight how school library media specialists contribute to the learning process and it will enhance the standing of media specialists in the eyes of the educational community.

Strategic Planning for the Profession of School Librarianship

AASL, the second-largest division of ALA, spent the academic year 2000–2001 developing a strategic plan to offer responsibility to the field and to its members, to provide outreach to members and to those in the profession of school librarianship, and to maintain the association. This plan was developed after the association distributed a survey to the membership and to those in the field to inquire about association strengths and weaknesses, environmental opportunities, and threats to the association. This survey was deemed vital to helping the association develop a plan to move the profession forward by meeting professional needs of those in school librarianship. As the premier association for the profession, with a national presence and identity, AASL's mission is to "advocate excellence, facilitate change, and develop leaders in the school library media field." To facilitate this mission, the association has developed standards, frameworks, and guidelines; has developed and disseminated theory, best practice, and research to help the field move forward; and has supported the major issues facing school librarianship today: funding, reading, technology, and intellectual freedom. AASL provides opportunities for professional growth through continuing education and it reaches out to other educational associations and constituencies that also affect the quality of school library media programs.

AASL has taken on the responsibility of revising program standards that will drive the profession, investigating funding to conduct action research, providing position papers reflecting the profession, promoting publication of practical titles to aid in the process of school library media program development, encouraging professional development opportunities through regional and national workshops and institutes, and recognizing outstanding leaders and programs in the field (by extending awards and by increasing awareness for school library media programs through collaboration with the ALA Public Information Office's national campaigns, particularly the "@ your library" campaign).

The field of school librarianship has gone through significant changes. School library media specialists face many challenges, including garnering administrative, board of education, parental, faculty, and student support for funding for adequate resources and staff; becoming involved in curriculum planning and implementation; integrating state-of-the-art technology with curriculum; advocating for information literacy training of students and staff; continuing a vigilance for academic and intellectual freedom; and becoming a part of and implementing new research in the field. By facing these challenges, library media specialists can ensure that students receive the best education available to prepare them to be successful and productive members of society. As AASL has promoted, "Student Achievement Is the Bottom Line."

Notes

1. International Society for Technology in Education (ISTE). *National Educational Technology Standards for Students; Connecting Curriculum and Technology* (ISTE, 2000).

2. American Association of School Librarians, Association for Educational Communications and Technology. *Information Power: Building Partnerships for Learning* (ALA, 1998.)

3. American Association of School Librarians, Association for Educational Communications and Technology, *Information Power: Guidelines for School Library Media Programs* (ALA, 1988).

4. S. L. Aaron, "Personalizing Instruction for the Middle School Learner: The Instructional Role of the School Library Media Specialist" (Florida Department of Education, 1975).

5. Keith Curry Lance, Lynda Welborn, Christine Hamilton-Pennell, *The Impact of School Library Media Centers on Academic Achievement* (Hi Willow Research and Publishing, 1993).

6. Stephen Krashen, *The Power of Reading* (Language Education Associates, 1993).

7. Keith Curry Lance, Marcia Rodney, Christine Hamilton-Pennell, *How School Librarians Help Kids Achieve Standards: The Second Colorado Study* (Hi Willow Research and Publishing, 2000).

8. Krashen, 1993.

9. Lance, et al., 2000.

10. Keith Curry Lance, et al., *Information Empowered: The School Librarian as an Agent of Academic Achievement in Alaska Schools* (Alaska State Library, 1999).

11. "Fast Facts: Recent Statistics" (Library Research Service, 2001).

Publishing in 2001: Shake-Outs, Downsizing, and E-Book Disappointments

Jim Milliot

Business and News Editor, *Publishers Weekly*

The hope expressed in 2000 that electronic publishing would quickly take hold throughout the publishing industry gave way to business realities in 2001.

Companies in all aspects of the electronic publishing industry went out of business during the year. Among the casualties were firms that performed data conversion and DRM (digital rights management) functions such as DigitalGoods, Versaware, Reciprocal, and WizeUp. Startups that hoped to supply digital information directly to consumers also fell by the wayside, including Audiohighway.com, Bookface.com, Booktech, Contentville.com, and MightyWords. NetLibrary—one of the highest-profile electronic publishing companies and one that raised about $110 million in venture capital—filed for bankruptcy late in the year but continued to operate as it waited for court approval to be acquired by OCLC.

Several other companies altered their business models during the year in order to remain afloat. Xlibris and iUniverse, both of which began as digital vanity presses, switched their focus to providing back-office digital services for publishers. Ebrary, which had planned to sell online information to students, delayed the launch of its Web site, but began licensing its technology to publishers. Its main rival, Questia.com, did begin selling online material to students in 2001, but the service attracted few subscribers and the company implemented staff cuts throughout the year that dropped the number of employees from 280 to 68.

The publication of e-books by traditional publishing houses did not fare well in 2001. The most ambitious e-book program, Time Warner Trade Publishing's iPublish operation, was closed down in early December when Time Warner executives determined that the unit had no chance to become profitable in 2002. Earlier in 2001 Random House shut down its e-book imprint, AtRandom, which it had launched with great fanfare less than a year earlier. Both Time Warner and Random House said they would continue to publish e-books in cooperation with existing divisions.

The one house that went against the grain of downsizing e-book expectations was HarperCollins, which started the PerfectBound e-book imprint in February 2001. Indeed, the news wasn't all bad on the e-book front. Small, independent e-book publishers, such as Fictionwise.com, Hard Shell, and Word Factory, were making a go of it and even generating profits.

The shake-out in electronic publishing fell most heavily in the second half of the year when the weak economy made it impossible for the start-ups to secure additional financing. In the early part of 2001 the major ongoing story was the consolidation among book retailers. Citing a weak 2000 holiday season, Crown Books, the nation's fourth-largest bookstore chain, filed for Chapter 11 bankruptcy in February and closed its stores several months later. Books-A-Million, the country's third-largest chain, bought 18 Crown outlets. Wallace's Bookstores, one of the country's largest college bookstore chains, also filed for Chapter 11 in

February. Bibelot, a major independent based in Baltimore, filed for Chapter 11 in March, and soon went out of business. In May came the Chapter 11 filing of the children's multimedia chain Zany Brainy; in August Zany Brainy was acquired by Right Start, a chain of specialized educational toy stores. Other multimedia outlets that closed in the year included Store of Knowledge and World of Wonder. The high-end bookstore chain Rizzoli announced in spring 2001 that it was phasing out all but one of its 13 stores over the course of the year. Tower Books cut the number of its standalone bookstores in half, to six, and reduced the size of book departments in its music stores. Late in the year Tower began to expand book departments at selected stores with a new product mix.

Downsizing was not limited to bricks-and-mortar bookstores in 2001. The country's largest online book retailer, Amazon.com, eliminated 1,300 jobs in late January as it began a year-long effort to reach profitability. Although Amazon's books/music/video division had recorded pro forma profits in 2000, company executives promised investors that the entire company would post pro forma profitability by last year's fourth quarter. The e-tailer exceeded its target by not only reporting a pro forma operating profit of $59 million in the quarter, but recording a $5 million profit using generally accepted accounting principles (GAAP). BarnesandNoble.com, the country's second-largest online bookseller, had its own round of layoffs, cutting 350 positions, about 16 percent of its work force. Part of the cuts came from integrating Fatbrain.com, which the company bought in late 2000. Borders.com eliminated 70 jobs in its online division when it decided to outsource the running of its electronic-selling operations to Amazon.

In addition to the electronic publishing and bookselling sectors, consolidation and downsizing hit other industry segments. *Publishers Weekly* reported that more than 460 jobs were eliminated in the distribution area, led by the closing of Ingram warehouses in Chino, California, and Denver. In July, Ingram announced that in the final phase of realigning its distribution network, it planned to open a 665,000-square-foot warehouse in Chambersburg, Pennsylvania, and would close facilities in East Windsor, Connecticut, and Petersburg, Virginia. More than 30 jobs were cut at the LPC Group when the distributor decided to move its warehousing, fulfillment, and distribution functions to Client Distribution Services. Andrews & McMeel began winding down its warehousing operations in preparation for moving its distribution to Simon & Schuster.

In publishing, the struggling direct marketing segment took another big hit as the three largest players in the field all announced dramatic reductions in staffs. Time Life Books announced early in 2001 that it was exiting the direct mail field altogether, a move that eliminated about 100 positions. Late in the year, Rodale cut 148 spots in its direct marketing division as the company continued its efforts to focus more of its resources on trade publishing. Reader's Digest, suffering from disappointing sales in its North American book group, planned to reduce its work force by approximately 380 between October 1, 2001, and June 30, 2002. About 140 positions were cut by the end of 2001.

With the weakening economy hurting sales of expensive illustrated books, art book publishers Harry N. Abrams and Rizzoli announced staff cuts of 25 and eight, respectively, late in 2001. Viking Studio's operations were also scaled down by Penguin.

Two small but well-known publishers went out of business in the year. Fromm International closed its offices on May 31. Zoland Books, publisher of an eclectic list of literary titles, stopped publishing in the fall after 14 years in business.

Mergers and Acquisitions

After several years of brisk acquisition activity that included many mega-mergers, 2001 was a relatively quiet year. Indeed, the largest deal that was completed was one that was announced in 2000: Reed Elsevier's $4.6 billion purchase of Harcourt General and Reed's subsequent sale of some Harcourt assets, including its higher education group, to the Thomson Corporation. The deal was delayed as both American and European regulators examined the purchase for antitrust problems, but was concluded in July with Thomson being forced to sell only a few higher education titles. The only other billion-dollar deal in 2001 was the purchase of Houghton Mifflin by the French firm Vivendi. The purchase was part of Vivendi's strategy of significantly expanding its presence in the American media market. Following the purchase, more than 60 jobs were eliminated in Houghton Mifflin's Boston headquarters.

Financial trouble played a role in the sale of two well-known trade publishers, Golden Books and Hungry Minds. After filing for bankruptcy a second time in two years, Golden Books ended its efforts to remain an independent company and sold its assets for $84 million, plus the assumption of liabilities, to Random House and Classic Media. Random House acquired Golden's book assets, while Classic took home the video properties. The sale ended the comeback bid of Richard Snyder, the former chairman of Simon & Schuster, who led a group that acquired Golden in 1996. John Wiley & Sons paid $90 million in cash plus the assumption of $92.5 million in debt to acquire Hungry Minds in August. Hungry Minds had been put up for sale by its parent company, International Data Group, after falling sales of computer books and disappointing results from its Internet operations buried the company in debt. Wiley followed up its purchase of Hungry Minds with the acquisition of Frank Fabozzi Publishing, a $1 million publisher of finance titles. Earlier in the year Wiley's Australian subsidiary picked up Wrightbooks, a publisher of investment books.

Golden Books was one of three companies Random House acquired in 2001. In the spring, Random House bought Prima Communications for an undisclosed price. Based in Sacramento, California, Prima publishes video and computer game guides, as well as computer books, and books on parenting, natural health, education, business, and current events. After the sale was completed, Random House sold the computer book lines to 22nd Century Inc., a holding company that will publish the Prima titles under the Premier Press imprint. In the fall Random House added the unabridged audio publisher Books on Tape to its spoken word audio holdings. As part of its integration of Prima and Golden into its own operations, Random cut about 120 positions.

Several medium-sized independent publishers looked to add scale to their companies through acquisitions. Travel publisher Globe Pequoth Press bought Lyons Press, which focuses on outdoor titles, in January 2001. At a generally uneventful BookExpo America (BEA), Workman Publishing announced it had acquired Storey Communications, a publisher of illustrated country-living books. Also at BEA, the Perseus Group said it bought the military publisher Combined Publishing. Rowman & Littlefield made a number of purchases in the year, picking up the assets of two Texas units, TaylorWilson Publishing and the trade assets of Taylor Publishing. Following the acquisition, Rowman & Littlefield established a Texas editorial office. In the fall, Rowman & Littlefield acquired the sports publisher Diamond Communications. Religious book publisher Thomas Nelson broadened its program by adding Cool Springs Press, publisher of gardening books. R. R. Bowker, publisher of reference books for the book industry, was sold in the fall by parent company Reed Elsevier to Cambridge Information Group, which then sold about a dozen properties to Information Today.

In deals not involving book publishers, an investor group acquired the small publisher distributor Consortium Book Sales and Distribution. Mark Snow reacquired the 11-store book chain Atlantic Books from Deb Shops for $5 million. SkillSoft paid $32 million to buy Books24x7, a supplier of technology information over the Web.

People

The news in late September that Penguin Putnam President and CEO Phyllis Grann would not renew her contract when it expired at the end of 2001 set off a stream of rumors about where the high-profile executive would land next. The answer came in December when Random House announced that it had appointed Grann vice chairman, effective January 2, 2002. Grann will serve in an advisory capacity to Random House Chairman Peter Olson. Penguin Putnam moved quickly to replace Grann, naming David Shanks, its chief operating officer, to the position of CEO, and appointing Susan Peterson Kennedy, executive vice president, as president. The company also named Carole Baron president of G. P. Putnam's, a hardcover imprint of Penguin Putnam that had been run by Grann. Baron continues to serve as president of the company's Dutton imprint as well. Grann's arrival at Random House touched off speculation about which authors might follow her to her new home. To avoid wholesale defections, Penguin paid Tom Clancy an unspecified sum to remain with the company and signed Patricia Cornwell to two new books.

Grann's appointment was only one of several executive changes at Random House in 2001. In November Joerg Pfuhl, president of Random House publishing development, was named president of the entire company, succeeding Y. S. Chi, who was appointed chairman of Random House Asia. Chi had assumed the Random House presidency in April when Erik Engstrom left the company to join an investment banking firm. Other appointments included the promotion of Don Weisberg to executive vice president and chief operating officer of Random House North America and Edward Volini to executive vice president and chief administrative officer.

Before Grann left Penguin, she hired Bill Shinker to head his own imprint at the house with its first books to be released in fall 2002. Shinker had resigned from the Free Press earlier in the year after a brief eight-month stint. Martha Levin, publisher of Hyperion, was named to succeed Shinker at Free Press.

Grann also spirited Adrian Zackheim away from HarperCollins with the promise of his own imprint; first titles from Zackheim's imprint are due out in early 2003. Shortly after Grann announced her attention to leave Penguin, Stacy Creamer, editor at Putnam, resigned to become executive editor at Doubleday.

Elsewhere, Leona Nevler, longtime editor at Ballantine, left the company to join Berkley Books. NAL President Louise Burke resigned from that post and was appointed executive vice president and publisher of Pocket Books as part of the restructuring of Simon & Schuster's adult publishing program. Little, Brown replaced publisher Sarah Crichton with Michael Pietsch. Literary editor Dan Menaker left Random House to join HarperCollins as executive editor. Donna Hayes was named president of Harlequin Enterprises at year-end, taking over from Brian Hickey, who retired. Amy Rhodes resigned from Harry Abrams to spearhead Rodale's trade publishing program as vice president and publisher of the trade division.

In children's publishing, David Ford was named to succeed John Keller as vice president and publisher of Little, Brown's children's department. Keller had headed the unit for 36 years. Debra Dorfman was named president and publisher of Grosset & Dunlap, succeeding Vivian Antonageli. Danny Gurr resigned as head of DK Publishing as new owner Penguin Putnam integrated DK into its own operations.

With the exception of the personnel shifts at the publishing houses, there were few major changes in other industry sectors. Frank Daly, one-time Baker & Taylor executive, was appointed executive director of the Book Industry Study Group (BISG). He succeeded BISG's longtime director Sandy Paul. Michael Berry, an executive at Disney, was named president of Barnes & Noble Booksellers, replacing Tom Tolworthy, who resigned in January. Craig Richards resigned as CEO of Baker & Taylor early in 2001 and day-to-day responsibilities at the wholesaler were turned over to Gary Rautenstrauch, president and chief operating officer.

Litigation

A number of major legal decisions came down in 2001, although one was highly anticlimactic. After three years of preparation and $18 million in legal fees, the lawsuit by the American Booksellers Association (ABA) against Barnes & Noble and Borders Group was settled out of court after six days of testimony. ABA had charged that the two major bookstore chains coerced publishers into giving B&N and Borders better—and illegal—discounts. ABA settled the case, which was expected to feature a lengthy, bitter courtroom fight, for $4.7 million in exchange for dropping all charges against B&N and Borders. The two chains quickly claimed victory in the lawsuit, noting that they were not required to change any of their business practices. ABA, while acknowledging that it did not achieve all of its goals, said that since the time it filed suit, many of the publishers had altered their pricing policies, giving independent booksellers terms that were closer to those received by the chains.

Another long-running case that was decided in the year was *Tasini* v. *New York Times*. Originally filed in 1993, the lawsuit charged that the *Times* and other major publishers and database publishers violated writers' copyrights when the companies reproduced the writers' work on Web sites and in databases without permission, and without compensating the writers. By a 7-2 vote, the Supreme Court found in favor of the writers.

Copyright was at the heart of two new cases filed in 2001, *Random House* v. *RosettaBooks* and the *Mitchell Estate* v. *Houghton Mifflin.* In late February Random House charged RosettaBooks, an e-book publisher startup, with copyright infringement, claiming that by publishing e-book editions of eight books that Random publishes in print form, Rosetta violated Random's copyright. Random House's bid for a preliminary injunction to prevent Rosetta from distributing the eight titles in question was denied in July by Judge Sidney Stein of the U.S. District Court for the Southern District of New York. In his decision, Stein found that Random House's contracts did not include publication rights for e-books. Authors and agents hailed the ruling as an important victory for the creators of content, while Random House said the decision could slow the growth of e-books even more. Random House appealed the decision and hearings were set for early 2002.

In April executors of *Gone with the Wind* author Margaret Mitchell's estate filed a suit against Houghton Mifflin claiming that a parody of the classic Civil War book, titled *The Wind Done Gone,* by Alice Randall infringed Mitchell's copyright. After a lower court issued an injunction prohibiting the distribution of *The Wind Done Gone,* an appeals court lifted the injunction in late May and Houghton Mifflin rushed the book to stores and immediately went back for a second printing. In finding in favor of *The Wind Done Gone,* the court ruled that the work was protected by the fair-use clause of the copyright act. The Mitchell estate has vowed to appeal the decision all the way to the U.S. Supreme Court if necessary.

September 11

The terrorist attacks of September 11 had both short-term and long-term consequences for the book industry. With the exception of Doug Stone of Odyssey Press, who was killed aboard one of the jets that crashed into the World Trade Center, no one in the industry is believed to have been seriously injured in the assaults. But physical damage was widespread. The Borders bookstore at the World Trade Center was destroyed and a number of publishers in downtown New York suffered severe damage. Abbeville Publishing, an art book publisher located across the street from the World Trade Center complex, was perhaps crippled the most by the attack. Its offices were closed for the remainder of 2001 and Abbeville operated from temporary quarters.

Other short-term issues related to the attacks included the effect on book launches and author tours. A press conference set for September 11 to launch *Jack: Straight from the Gut* by former GE chairman Jack Welch was the most high-profile event to be canceled. Publishers scrambled to get authors who were on tour safely home, and also worked to accommodate media demand for authors who were familiar with terrorism, Afghanistan, Osama bin Laden, and related topics. Coverage of the attack and the subsequent war in Afghanistan, as well as the anthrax scare, made it all but impossible to get most authors exposure on television and radio for much of the fall. Fear of travel kept American attendance significantly down at the Frankfurt Book Fair in October.

The strikes altered the bestseller lists in the weeks immediately after September 11 and during the holidays. The public turned to such titles as *Twin Towers* (Rutgers), *The New Jackals* (Northeastern), *Taliban* (Yale), and *Germs* (Random House) for information immediately after the attacks. Books chronicling the attacks did well later in the fall, among them *One Nation: America Remembers September 11, 2001* (Little, Brown), *New York September 11* (powerHouse), *Brotherhood* (American Express), and *America's Heroes* (Sports Publishing).

Bestsellers

Books related to September 11 as well as religious books, most notably *The Prayer of Jabez* (Multnomah), resulted in 433 books reaching the *Publishers Weekly* bestsellers lists, up from 385 in 2000. But books generally had a shorter stay on the lists in 2001 than in the prior year. Only four hardcover titles, led by John Grisham's *A Painted House* (22 weeks) were on the list for at least 16 weeks. *Who Moved My Cheese?* by Spencer Johnson was on the nonfiction bestseller list for the entire year, and 10 other books had stays of at least 16 weeks. Only two mass market paperbacks—Grisham's *The Brethren* and *The Hobbit* by J. R. R. Tolkien—stayed on the list for at least 16 weeks. Thirteen trade paperback bestsellers stayed on the list for a minimum of 16 weeks.

As usual, Random House placed the most titles on the hardcover and paperback bestsellers lists. Its share of the hardcover list, however, slipped 3 percent in 2001 to 30 percent of all available hardcover slots. Penguin Putnam's market share inched up 0.4 percent to 18 percent and Simon & Schuster's share moved up 1.3 percent to 12.1 percent. In paperback, Random House's share of slots rose 1.8 percent to 26.4 percent, while Penguin Putnam's share increased 6.9 percent to 24.3 percent. Simon & Schuster's share fell 3.8 percent to 9 percent.

Sales

The disappointing 2000 holiday sales season led to higher-than-expected returns in the early part of 2001. For most of 2001 sales were lackluster and, with the economy weakening further after September 11, industry members were bracing for another poor holiday sales period. The industry's jitters were reinforced by repeated statements from Random House executives that consumer book sales were in a slump and that the slump would carry into 2002. Much to the relief of the industry, however, fourth-quarter results from the major chains proved better than expected and sales were up for both Amazon.com and BarnesandNoble.com.

However, the gains in the fourth quarter were not enough to boost sales for the entire year in the trade segment. According to preliminary estimates from the Association of American Publishers, sales in the trade segment fell 2.6 percent in 2001 to $6.37 billion. Adult hardcover sales fell for the second year in a row, declining 2.2 percent in 2001 to $2.63 billion. The trade paperback segment bounced back from a decline in 2000 to post a 1.4 percent sales gain in 2001 to $1.93 billion. Following a terrific year that benefited from the phenomenal sales of *Harry Potter and the Goblet of Fire*, sales in the children's hardcover segment fell 22.7 percent in 2001 to $928.6 million.

Paperback sales, however, had a second solid year with sales ahead 17.9 percent to $887.6 million. In addition to the trade segment, sales were down in the mass market paperback, professional, and mail order segments. The declines in those large segments resulted in sales for the entire book publishing industry inching up only 0.1 percent for the year to $25.36 billion.

Paperback sales fell 0.8 percent in 2001 to $1.55 billion, while sales in the professional segment dropped 7.6 percent to $4.74 billion. After reversing a decade-long sales decline in 2000, sales in the mail order category plummeted 18.0 percent in 2001 to $353.9 million.

The bright spots in the industry were in education. Sales in the school division followed a 13.3 percent gain in 2000 with a 7.8 percent sales increase to $4.18 billion in 2001. Sales in the college segment rose 7.2 percent to $3.47 billion, and sales of standardized tests increased 6.8 percent to $250.1 million.

Other segments that had sales gains in 2001 were religion, with sales up 4.7 percent to $1.30 billion; book clubs, with sales ahead 3.3 percent to $1.33 billion; and university presses, with sales increasing 1.5 percent to $408.2 million.

Federal Agency and Federal Library Reports

Library of Congress

Washington, DC 20540
202-707-5000, World Wide Web http://www.loc.gov

Audrey Fischer
Public Affairs Specialist

The Library of Congress was established in 1800 to serve the research needs of the U.S. Congress. For more than two centuries, the library has grown both in the size of its collection (now totaling more than 124 million items) and in its mission. As the largest library in the world and the oldest federal cultural institution in the nation, the Library of Congress serves not only Congress but also government agencies, libraries around the world, and scholars and citizens in the United States and abroad. At the forefront of technology, the library now serves patrons on-site in its 21 reading rooms in Washington, D.C., and worldwide through its highly acclaimed Web site.

Milestones

Following the celebration of its bicentennial in 2000, the library marked several more milestones in 2001: the centennial of the Cataloging Distribution Service, the 70th anniversary of the National Library Service for the Blind and Physically Handicapped (NLS), the 30th anniversary of the Cataloging in Publication program (CIP), the establishment of the John W. Kluge Center, and the first-ever National Book Festival.

CDS Centennial

The 100th anniversary of the Cataloging Distribution Service (CDS) was observed November 13, 2001, with a forum, "Reshaping Cataloging Distribution for the 21st Century," and an exposition of CDS products and services.

On October 28, 1901, the library announced to some 500 libraries its intention to distribute printed catalog cards, and on June 28, 1902, President Theodore Roosevelt signed the law authorizing the sale of cards and other publications. By the 1960s, CDS had grown to a staff of 600, shipping more than 78 million cataloging cards each year. The Machine Readable Cataloging (MARC) standard made it possible to exchange cataloging data, which CDS distributed on tapes. New information technologies such as CD-ROMs and the Internet took over the labor-intensive job of making printed cards, and CDS published its last cataloging card in 1997.

NLS Anniversary

The National Library Service for the Blind and Physically Handicapped, established by an act of Congress in 1931, has grown to a program that supplies more than 23 million braille and recorded discs to hundreds of thousands of readers through a network of 140 cooperating libraries around the country. Throughout its 70-year history, NLS has continued to harness new technologies, from analog to digital, to better serve its growing constituency. During the year NLS made substantial progress in its goal of developing a digital "talking book" to replace obsolete analog playback equipment.

CIP Milestone

The Cataloging in Publication program began in 1971 as a two-year pilot project funded by grants from the Council on Library Resources and the National Endowment for the Humanities. In its first year, the program created 6,500 pre-publication records to notify book dealers, libraries, and others in the publishing and library communities about forthcoming publications and to facilitate book ordering. The CIP program, which is now fully supported by Library of Congress appropriations, has produced more than 1 million records since its inception. In 1996 the program was expanded to allow publishers to transmit CIP information electronically via the Internet.

Kluge Center

The John W. Kluge Center was established in the fall of 2000 with a gift of $60 million from John W. Kluge, president of Metromedia Company and founding chairman of the James Madison Council, the library's private sector advisory group. Under the library's director for scholarly programs, the center's goal is to bring the best thinkers into residence at the Library of Congress where they can make wide-ranging use of the institution's unparalleled resources to promote scholarship. A Scholars' Council was established during the center's first year. The council held its first meeting in October 2001. As the center's first Distinguished Visiting Scholar, historian John Hope Franklin came to the library to work on his autobiography. Jaroslav Pelikan was appointed the first Kluge Chair in Countries and Cultures of the North. Sylvia Albro, a paper conservator in the library's Conservation Division, was awarded the first Kluge Staff Fellowship for research into Italian papermaking. In association with the Kluge Center, Aaron Friedberg was appointed the first Kissinger Chair in Foreign Policy and International Relations. The center also hosted two visiting International Research Exchange Program Fellows from Russia. With funding from the Mellon and Luce Foundations, seven U.S. post-doctoral scholars were selected through the new Library of Congress International Studies Fellowships program (in cooperation with the American Council of Learned Societies and the Association of American Universities). Competitions were held for the awarding of 12 Kluge Fellowships, two to four Rockefeller Foundation-funded Fellowships in Islamic Studies, and a second year of fellowships under the library's International Fellows program.

National Book Festival

The first National Book Festival was held on September 8, 2001, on the east lawn of the Capitol and in the Thomas Jefferson and James Madison Buildings of the Library of Congress. Hosted by First Lady Laura Bush and sponsored by the library with support from AT&T, the James Madison Council, the *Washington Post,* and other contributors, the festival drew a crowd of approximately 30,000 to the library for readings, book signings, music, and storytelling. The festival began with a special program in the library's Coolidge Auditorium on the evening of September 7 that included readings by David McCullough, John Hope Franklin, Gail Godwin, J. California Cooper, Larry L. King, and Tom Brokaw. President and Mrs. Bush were among the attendees. Sixty nationally known authors and illustrators participated in the day-long event on September 8, along with representatives of the National Basketball Association as part of their "Read to Achieve" national reading campaign. Highlights of the evening program and the Book Festival were broadcast live on C-SPAN.

Response to Terrorist Attacks

The September 11 terrorist attacks had a profound effect on the library as it balanced its mission to serve Congress and the nation with the need to secure its staff, visitors, buildings, and collections. The library asked Congress for an emergency supplemental appropriation of $2.5 million to pay for emergency communications systems, including construction of an emergency management center, and to provide funding for overtime duty by Library of Congress police.

While focusing on important security measures, the library simultaneously provided Congress with timely information on terrorism and related subjects such as immigration policy and documented the events of September 11 and the nation's response to them. For example, the Serial and Government Publications Division began to build a collection of thousands of U.S. and foreign newspapers containing reports and photographs of the tragedy and its aftermath. In addition, the library launched a September 11 Web Archive (http://september11.archive.org) in collaboration with Internet Archives, webArchivist.org, and the Pew Internet and American Life Project. The American Folklife Center also sponsored the September 11, 2001, Documentary Project, which encouraged folklorists across the nation to record on audiotape the national response to the events.

The library also reached out to those directly affected by these events by transferring 183 pieces of furniture valued at $59,900 to New York City through an agreement with the Maryland State Agency for Surplus Property to assist agencies recovering from the September 11 attacks. In addition, the Library of Congress Law Library provided work space and facilities for a member of the Pentagon's library staff who was displaced by the attack on that building.

Budget

Under the Legislative Branch Appropriations Act (H.R. 5657), the Library of Congress fiscal year (FY) 2001 appropriation initially totaled $448,454,000, including authority to spend $36.1 million in receipts. The Consolidated Appropriations Act of 2001 (Public Law 106-554), signed by President Clinton on December 21, 2000, incorporated the provisions of several acts by reference, including H.R. 5657 and the Miscellaneous Appropriations Act (H.R. 5666). H.R. 5666 included a 0.22 percent across-the-board cut in FY 2001 and $100 million for a National Digital Information Infrastructure Program (subsequently reduced to $99.8 million as a result of the cut). The result of both acts was a revised FY 2001 appropriation for the library in the amount of $547,247,401, including authority to spend $36.1 million in receipts. The Supplemental Appropriations Act of 2001 (Public Law 107-20), signed by President Bush on July 24, 2001, provided $600,000 for a collaborative Library of Congress telecommunications project with the United States Military Academy. The 2001 Emergency Supplemental Appropriations Act for Recovery from and Response to Terrorist Attacks on the United States (Public Law 107-38), signed by the president on September 18, 2001, provided $2.5 million for security-related activities. The result of these four acts was a final FY 2001 appropriation for the library in the amount of $550,347,401, including authority to spend $36.1 million in receipts.

The Consolidated Appropriations Act of 2001 (Public Law 106-554) also included third-year funding for the Open World Russian Leadership Program that has brought nearly 4,000 emerging political leaders from the Russian Federation to the United States to observe the workings of U.S. institutions. This same legislation authorized the creation of a Center for Russian Leadership Development in the Legislative Branch, independent of the library, to implement the exchange program in the future.

Legislative Support to Congress

Serving Congress is the library's highest priority. During the year, the Congressional Research Service (CRS) delivered nearly 711,000 search responses to members and committees of Congress. CRS developed two electronic briefing books, "Agriculture and the Farm Bill" and "Welfare Reform." CRS also issued a redesigned, expanded electronic briefing book on terrorism following the September 11 attacks.

Congress turned increasingly to the online Legislative Information System (LIS), as evidenced by a 15 percent increase in system usage from the previous year's level. During 2001 LIS was redesigned to provide easier access and a format that can be expanded to meet Congress's need for information on a wide range of legislative issues. Safeguards were installed to ensure continuous system availability.

The law library kept members of Congress and their staffs informed on developments around the world through the monthly *World Law Bulletin* and the *Foreign Law Briefs,* a research series exclusively for Congress. Law library staff answered more than 2,000 in-person reference requests from congressional users and produced 413 written reports for Congress, including comprehensive multinational studies of the laws of individual nations and regional organizations such as the European Union.

During the year, progress was made on the Global Legal Information Network (GLIN), an online parliament-to-parliament cooperative exchange of laws and legal materials from 46 countries. The law library continued to work in partnership with various institutions to expand and enhance GLIN. An agreement was reached with the National Aeronautics and Space Administration (NASA) to develop an off-site back-up facility for GLIN at NASA's Goddard Space Flight Center in Maryland.

The Library of Congress Copyright Office provided policy advice and technical assistance to Congress on important copyright laws and related issues such as the Digital Millennium Copyright Act (DMCA). In August 2001 the Register of Copyrights delivered to Congress the report required under Section 104 of DMCA. The report evaluated the impact of advances in electronic commerce and associated technologies, as well as the amendments to Title 17 made in DMCA on Sections 109 and 117 of the Copyright Act. The copyright office also responded to numerous congressional inquiries about domestic and international copyright law and registration and recordation of works of authorship.

In addition to assisting members of Congress and their staff in making use of the library's collections, services, and facilities, the library's Congressional Relations Office, along with other library offices, worked with member and committee offices on current issues of legislative concern such as "e-government," digital storage and preservation, and such other projects as documenting the history of the nation's veterans, local community celebrations and milestones, and the institution of Congress itself.

Digital Projects and Planning

Strategic Planning

The Librarian of Congress established the position of Associate Librarian for Strategic Initiatives (ALSI) in 2000 to develop a full range of digital policies and operations for acquiring, describing, and preserving content created and distributed in electronic form. In 2001 the primary focus of the newly appointed ALSI was planning for Congress's FY 2001 appropriation of $99.8 million to develop and implement a congressionally approved strategic plan for a National Digital Information Infrastructure Program. During the year the ALSI initiated a two-tier strategy to develop this national program that focuses on the library's infrastructure and policies as well as addresses the need for the library to collaborate with the public and private sectors. On May 1 the ALSI convened the National Digital Strategy Advisory Board to advise the library on national strategies for the long-term preservation of digital materials, to promote collaboration among diverse stakeholder communities, and to assist in developing a national fund-raising strategy.

Internet Resources

The library continued to expand its electronic services to Congress and the nation through its Web site. During the year 1.4 billion transactions were recorded on all of the library's public electronic systems. The average number of monthly transactions increased by 31 percent. The following are selected resources available on the library's Web site.

American Memory: At year's end 7.5 million American historical items were available on the library's Web site. During the year, 12 new multimedia historical collections were added to American Memory, bringing the total to 102. Ten existing collections were expanded with more than 860,000 digital items. Use of the American Memory collections increased by 50 percent, from an average of 19 million monthly transactions during FY 2000 to 28.5 million per month during FY 2001.

America's Library: Work continued to expand the content and interactive features available in America's Library, an interactive Web site for children and families that draws upon the library's vast online resources. New features added in 2001 included an expanded Explore the States, new educational games, and a jukebox of historic songs. America's Library logged more than 135 million transactions during the year, an average of more than 11 million a month.

THOMAS: The public legislative information system known as THOMAS continued to be a popular resource, with more than 10 million transactions logged on average each month. Public e-mail queries received about the system and its contents were generally answered on the same day as receipt. A new THOMAS Web site design was implemented at the start of the 107th Congress. During the year, the system incorporated legislative information received directly from the House, Senate, the Government Printing Office, and the Congressional Research Service into a new set of information files that were updated several times a day.

International Horizons: As a continuation of the pioneering American Memory project, the Librarian of Congress initiated International Horizons, a project dedicated to fostering international collaboration for joint digitization efforts. At year's end, the project included "Meeting of Frontiers," a bilingual Russian-English Web site showcasing materials from the Library of Congress and partner libraries in Russia and Alaska; and "Spain, the United States and the American Frontier: Historias Paralelas," a bilingual English-Spanish Web site initially including the Library of Congress, the National Library of Spain, and the Biblioteca Colombina y Capitular of Seville.

Online Exhibitions: Six new library exhibitions were added to the Web site in 2001, bringing the total to 34. This feature allows users to view many of the library's past and current exhibitions online.

Web-Braille: At year's end more than 1,600 users were registered for the new Internet service known as Web-Braille that allows access to more than 3,800 digital braille book files. A link to the NLS International Union Catalog allows users to access Web-Braille materials by author, title, subject, language, keyword, and other search parameters. During the year more than 250 music items (music scores and books about music) were added to Web-Braille.

Copyright

The Copyright Office received 590,091 claims to copyright and made 601,659 registrations in FY 2001, including some submitted in FY 2000. The office responded to nearly 340,000 requests from the public for copyright information. The library's collections and exchange programs received 728,034 copies of works from the Copyright Office, including 277,752 items received from publishers under the mandatory deposit provisions of the copyright law.

Collections

During the year the size of the library's collections grew to more than 124 million items, an increase of more than 3 million over the previous year. This figure includes 28.2 million books and other print materials, 55 million manuscripts, 13.3 million microforms, 4.9 million maps, 5 million items in the music collection, and 13.5 million visual materials (photographs, posters, moving images, prints, and drawings).

Integrated Library System

The library implemented all phases of its first integrated library system (ILS) for library functions such as circulation, acquisitions, and serials check-in, and to provide an online public access catalog. The library also continued its conversion into ILS of the 900,000-title Serial Record Division serials holdings manual check-in file that contributes to the library's inventory control and materials security initiatives. In addition, the library used the new system to support its business process improvements.

Arrearage Reduction/Cataloging

At year's end the total arrearage stood at 21.1 million items, a decrease of 53 percent from the 39.7-million-item arrearage at the time of the initial census in September 1989. Staff created cataloging records for 270,801 print volumes and inventory records for an additional 67,837 items. With the library serving as the secretariat of the international Program for Cooperative Cataloging (PCC), approximately 350 PCC member institutions created 143,031 new name authorities, 9,410 series authorities, 2,603 subject authorities, 2,043 LC Classification proposals, 14,445 bibliographic records for serials, and 73,115 bibliographic records for monographs. The library worked with the bibliographic utilities and libraries with large East Asian collections to replace the outmoded Wade-Giles system for romanization of Chinese characters with the more modern pinyin system. After a three-year planning effort, the library began pinyin conversion on October 1, 2000, and completed the project in May 2001.

Secondary Storage

Linked to the library's arrearage reduction effort is the development of secondary storage sites to house processed materials and to provide for growth of the collection through the first part of the 21st century. An architectural team led by Hal Davis of SmithGroup continued to work on the design of the National Audio-Visual Conservation Center at Culpeper, Virginia, on behalf of the library and the Architect of the Capitol (AOC), with funding from the Packard Humanities Institute, the owners of the facility. During the year, the Packard Humanities

Institute entered into an additional contract with BAR Architects to team with SmithGroup. By year's end schematic drawings for a new building and the refurbished existing building were nearly complete. Scheduled to open in June 2004, the facility will house the library's audiovisual materials. The library also continued to work closely with AOC and its contractors in its plans to construct a storage facility at Fort Meade, Maryland.

Important New Acquisitions

The library receives millions of items each year from copyright deposits, from federal agencies, and from purchases, exchanges, and gifts. Notable acquisitions during the year included one of the great treasures of American and world history, the 1507 map of the world by Martin Waldseemüller, the first to refer to the New World as "America." Other major acquisitions included additions to the Jefferson Library Project to reconstruct the collection in the original catalog of Thomas Jefferson's library; a collection of 413 Lontar manuscripts in the traditional Balinese script on palm leaves; three 15th-century books, including an edition of Ovid published by Fasti in Venice, 1482; a first edition of Charles Dickens's *A Christmas Carol*; and 19 rare Persian manuscripts, including *Shams al-Nadar,* the first periodical printed in Afghanistan (1873). Significant new manuscript acquisitions included the papers of Martin Agronsky, radio and television journalist; Clark Clifford, Harry Truman's secretary of defense and Democratic Party elder statesman; Stuart Eizenstat, Jimmy Carter's chief of staff; biologist Lynn Margulis; baseball great Jackie Robinson; Vera Rubin, astronomer; and Malcolm Toon, U.S. ambassador to the Soviet Union. Major additions to these manuscript collections were received: Harry Blackmun, Robert Bork, Ruth Bader Ginsburg, Sol Linowitz, Daniel Patrick Moynihan, Paul Nitze, Eliot Richardson, and Philip Roth.

Reference Service

The library provides reference service to the public in its 21 reading rooms, via telephone, e-mail, written correspondence, and through its Web site. During the year, the library's staff handled more than 500,000 reference requests received on-site, as well as an additional 300,000 requests received via telephone and written correspondence. More than 1.5 million items were circulated for use within the library.

Collaborative Digital Reference Service

Progress was made in 2001 on the Collaborative Digital Reference Service (CDRS), a project to provide professional reference service to researchers anytime, anywhere, through an international, digital network of libraries and related institutions. The service uses new technologies to provide the best answers in the best context, by taking advantage not only of the millions of Internet resources but also of the many more millions of resources that are not online and that are held by libraries. During the year this "library-to-library" network grew to 185 participating institutions.

Publications

In 2001 the Publishing Office produced 24 books, calendars, and other products describing the library's collections, many in cooperation with trade publishers. In collaboration with Harry N. Abrams, the library published *The Floating World of Ukiyo-e: Shadows, Dreams, and Substance,* a companion book to an exhibition. In cooperation with *Congressional Quarterly,* the library published *Democracy and the Rule of Law,* a collection from the bicentennial symposium held at the library in March 2000. With support from the Madison Council, the library continued its series of illustrated guides with the publication of a three-volume set covering the Africana, Hebraic, and Near East collections. At year's end the library published *American Women: A Library of Congress Guide for the Study of Women's History and Culture in the United States,* a resource guide distributed by University Press of New England.

The Library of Congress: An Architectural Alphabet won the "Best in Show" award in the 16th annual Washington Book Publishers Design Effectiveness Competition. The library's new visitor guide book, *The Nation's Library: The Library of Congress, Washington, D.C.,* and the *Charles and Ray Eames 2001 Desk Diary* received design excellence awards from the American Association for Museums. The cumulative index for 25 text volumes of *Letters of Delegates to Congress, 1774–1789* was awarded the H. W. Wilson Award for Excellence in Indexing by the American Society of Indexers and the H. W. Wilson Company.

Exhibitions

The library presented five new exhibitions in 2001, including three that drew on its unparalleled international collections. Most significantly, "World Treasures of the Library of Congress" opened on June 7 in the Northwest Pavilion exhibition gallery of the Thomas Jefferson Building. This continuing exhibition is a companion to the "American Treasures of the Library of Congress" exhibition and presents top treasures from the library's international collections. "The Empire That Was Russia: The Prokudin-Gorskii Photographic Record Recreated" (April 17, 2001, through August 2001) featured unique color images of Russia on the eve of the Russian Revolution (1909–1915). "The Floating World of Ukiyo-e: Shadows, Dreams, and Substance" (September 27, 2001, through February 9, 2002) presented 100 rare and important woodcuts, drawings, and books from the library's extensive collection of Japanese art and literature. "A Petal From the Rose: Illustrations by Elizabeth Green" (June 28, 2001, through September 29, 2001) was displayed in the Swann Gallery of Caricature and Cartoon. "Margaret Mead: Human Nature and the Power of Culture" (November 30, 2001, through May 31, 2002) celebrated the life and work of the noted anthropologist on the 100th anniversary of her birth.

In keeping with conservation and preservation standards, three rotational changes were made in the "American Treasures of the Library of Congress" exhibition and two were made to the "Bob Hope Gallery of American Entertainment." Three major Library of Congress exhibitions that toured nationally and internationally during the year were "The Work of Charles and Ray Eames: A Legacy of

Invention," "Sigmund Freud: Conflict and Culture," and "Religion and the Founding of the American Republic." Six new exhibitions were added to the library's Web site, bringing the total to 34 library exhibitions accessible on the Internet.

Literary Events, Concerts, Symposia

A variety of literary events, lectures, and concerts were held at the library during the year, many of which were cybercast on the library's Web site.

The "Books & Beyond" lecture series centered on the importance of books and readings. The series featured such authors as Sharon Robinson, daughter of Baseball Hall-of-Famer Jackie Robinson, discussing her book *Jackie's Nine: Jackie Robinson's Values to Live By,* and veteran newsman Daniel Schorr, discussing his autobiography, *Staying Tuned: A Life in Journalism.*

On November 10, former Secretary of State Henry Kissinger delivered the inaugural lecture in the Kissinger Lecturer Series. The series was established last year at the Library of Congress as part of the new Henry Alfred Kissinger Chair in Foreign Policy and International Relations.

The 250th anniversary of James Madison's birth was commemorated with an all-day symposium on the nation's fourth president, an exhibition in the James Madison Memorial Building, and a dinner at which Chief Justice William Rehnquist was the principal speaker.

During a two-day program titled "Living the Lore: The Legacy of Benjamin A. Botkin," the library celebrated the 100th anniversary of the birth of Botkin, who headed the Archive of Folk Song from 1941 to 1944. The program included performances by folksinger Pete Seeger and Cherish the Ladies, a traditional Irish band.

The "I Hear America Singing" concert series included a program honoring American composer Irving Fine and an evening devoted to the music of jazz greats Eubie Blake, Duke Ellington, Fats Waller, and others, performed by the New York Festival of Song. The series also presented the world premiere of "From the Diary of Sally Hemings," a new song cycle by composer William Bolcom and playwright Sandra Seaton, featuring mezzo-soprano Florence Quivar.

At the age of 95, Stanley Kunitz held the position of poet laureate consultant in poetry for the 2000–2001 season. In May 2001 Billy Collins was appointed to the position for the 2001–2002 season. At year's end plans were under way for a new Web site called Poetry 180, designed to encourage the appreciation and enjoyment of poetry in America's high schools.

Security

Securing the library's staff members, visitors, collections, facilities, and computer resources continued to be a major priority, and promises to remain so in the wake of the September 11 terrorist attacks. During the year the library made progress in implementing its security enhancement plan, a multiyear program of security upgrades. Under one of the three major components of the plan, the library will consolidate its two police communications centers in the Madison and Jefferson Buildings into one state-of-the-art communications center in the

Jefferson Building. Under the second major component of the plan, the library will expand entry and perimeter security to include additional X-ray machines and detection equipment, security upgrades of building entrances, exterior monitoring cameras and lighting, and garage and parking lot safeguards. The third major component of the plan was completed with the hiring and training of 46 new police officers and five police administrative personnel. This increase brought the number of authorized police positions to 168, the largest police force in the library's history.

The library also continued to review its backup and recovery procedures for its computer systems and determined that remote storage was needed. In the aftermath of September 11, a temporary measure was put in place to house a complete set of backup tapes at a remote location in Virginia in order to safeguard the library's digital collections while working toward procurement of commercial storage services.

Preservation

The library took action to preserve its collections by

- Providing 30,000 hours of preventive and remedial conservation services for items and collections in the custodial divisions
- Establishing new methods for predicting the life expectancies of organic materials
- Successfully integrating its labeling and binding preparation processing into nonpreservation divisions
- Deacidifying 103,522 books and awarding a five-year contract that will enable the library to treat 1 million books and 5 million sheets of unbound materials such as manuscripts
- Increasing public access to Overseas Operations-produced microfilm through the acquisition of 2,086 positive service copies from the New Delhi office and creation of master negative microfilm at a cost of $19 per reel (a cost reduction of $30 per reel)
- Restructuring the Photoduplication Service to meet business requirements and introducing a scan-on-demand service as an adjunct to analog services
- Delivering 18,000 bibliographic records describing foreign newspapers to the Center for Research Libraries' database for the International Coalition on Newspapers (ICON) International Union List of Newspapers

The American Folklife Center continued its mandate to "preserve and present American folklife" through a number of outreach programs, including the White House Millennium Council's "Save America's Treasures" program in concert with the Smithsonian Institution. Known as "Save Our Sounds," the program seeks to preserve a priceless heritage of sound recordings housed at the two institutions. During the year the American Folklife Center received a grant of $40,000 from Michael Greene, president and CEO of the Recording Academy, to support audio and video preservation.

The American Folklife Center also continued to participate in the Veterans History Project. Established by Congress last year, the program was established to record and preserve the first-person accounts of men and women veterans who served during wartime. A project director was appointed in May. In November the American Association of Retired Persons (AARP) became the project's founding private-sector sponsor. A Five-Star Council consisting of prominent leaders (veterans, elected officials, historians, and journalists) will provide leadership and counsel for the project.

The library continued its commitment to preserving the nation's film heritage. The 25 films listed below were named to the National Film Registry in 2001, bringing the total to 325. The library works to ensure that the films listed on the registry are preserved either through its motion picture preservation program headquartered in Dayton, Ohio, or through collaborative ventures with other archives, motion picture studios, and independent filmmakers.

Abbott and Costello Meet Frankenstein (1948)

All That Jazz (1979)

All the King's Men (1949)

America, America (1963)

Cologne: From the Diary of Ray and Esther (1939)

Evidence of the Film (1913)

Hoosiers (1986)

The House in the Middle (1954)

It (1927)

Jam Session (1942)

Jaws (1975)

Manhattan (1979)

Marian Anderson: The Lincoln Memorial Concert (1939)

Memphis Belle (1944)

The Miracle of Morgan's Creek (1944)

Miss Lulu Bett (1921)

National Lampoon's Animal House (1978)

Planet of the Apes (1968)

Rose Hobart (1936)

Serene Velocity (1970)

The Sound of Music (1965)

Stormy Weather (1943)

The Tell-Tale Heart (1953)

The Thin Blue Line (1988)

The Thing from Another World (1951)

Additional Sources of Information

Library of Congress telephone numbers for public information:

Main switchboard (with menu)	202-707-5000
Reading room hours and locations	202-707-6400
General reference	202-707-5522 (TTY 202-707-4210)
Visitor information	202-707-8000 (TTY 202-707-6200)
Exhibition hours	202-707-4604
Research advice	202-707-6500
Copyright information	202-707-3000
Copyright hotline (to order forms)	202-707-9100
Sales shop	202-707-0204

Center for the Book

John Y. Cole
Director, Center for the Book
Library of Congress, Washington, DC 20540
World Wide Web http://www.loc.gov/cfbook

Since 1977, when it was established by Librarian of Congress Daniel J. Boorstin, the Center for the Book has used the prestige and the resources of the Library of Congress to stimulate public interest in books, reading, and libraries and to encourage the study of books and the printed word. With its network of affiliated centers in 42 states and the District of Columbia and more than 90 national and civic organizations, it is one of the Library of Congress's most dynamic and visible educational outreach programs.

The center is a successful public-private partnership. The Library of Congress supports its four full-time positions, but the center's projects, events, and publications are funded primarily through contributions from individuals, corporations, foundations, and other government organizations.

Highlights of 2001

- The addition of two states, Alabama and West Virginia, to the center's national affiliates network

- Major contributions to the success of the first National Book Festival

- The launching of "Telling America's Stories," the Library of Congress's national reading promotion campaign for 2001–2003

- The continued expansion and increased use of the center's Web site (http://www.loc.gov/cfbook)

- The hosting of national family literacy workshops in Montgomery, Alabama, and Albuquerque, New Mexico, both part of the Viburnum Foundation/Center for the Book family literacy project

- Cosponsorship of the publication of *The Rivers of America: A Descriptive Bibliography* by Carol Fitzgerald, edited by Jean Fitzgerald (with Oak Knoll Press), and *A Literary Map of Metropolitan Washington, D.C.* by Martha Hopkins (with the Washington Chapter of the Women's National Book Association)

- Sponsorship of more than 30 programs and events, at the Library of Congress and throughout the country, that promoted books, reading, and libraries

Themes

The Center for the Book establishes national reading promotion themes to stimulate interest and support for reading and literacy projects that benefit all age groups. Used by state centers, national organizational partners, and hundreds of schools and libraries across the nation, each theme reminds Americans of the importance of books, reading, and libraries in today's world.

Librarian of Congress James H. Billington launched "Telling America's Stories," the library's national reading promotion campaign for 2001–2003. First Lady Laura Bush is honorary chair of the campaign, which is being organized primarily by the Center for the Book, with assistance from the American Folklife Center in the Library of Congress.

Reading Promotion Partners

The center's partnership program includes more than 90 civic, educational, and governmental organizations that work with the center to promote books, reading, libraries, and literacy. On March 12, 2001, representatives of many of these organizations gathered at the Library of Congress to share information about their current projects and discuss potential cooperative arrangements. During the year the center cosponsored projects with many of its organizational partners, including the American Library Association, Book Adventure Foundation, Everybody Wins! D.C., Friends of Libraries U.S.A., International Reading Association, KIDSNET, National Book Foundation, National Coalition for Literacy, and Reading Is Fundamental, Inc. More than 60 partners participated in "Great Ideas for Promoting Reading" at the National Book Festival on September 8, 2001.

State Centers

When James H. Billington became Librarian of Congress in 1987, the Center for the Book had 10 affiliated state centers; at the end of 2001 there were 42 states plus the District of Columbia. The newest centers, Alabama and West Virginia, are located, respectively, at the Center for Arts and Humanities at Auburn University and at the West Virginia Library Commission in Charleston. Each state center works with the Library of Congress to promote books, reading, and libraries as well as the state's own literary and intellectual heritage. Each also develops and funds its own operations and projects, using Library of Congress reading promotion themes when appropriate and occasionally hosting Library of Congress-sponsored events and traveling exhibits. When its application is approved, a state center is granted affiliate status for three years. Renewals are for three-year periods. For 2001, renewal applications were approved from Colorado, Connecticut, Georgia, Indiana, Illinois, Louisiana, Maine, Nevada, and Vermont. As part of the renewal process, the Nevada Center for the Book moved from the Nevada State Library and Archives to the Nevada Humanities Council.

On April 30, 2001, representatives of the state centers participated in an idea-sharing session at the Library of Congress. The highlight of the meeting was the presentation of the 2000 Boorstin Center for the Book Award to the Colorado Center for the Book. The Boorstin Award, supported by an endowment established in 1987 by retired Librarian of Congress Daniel J. Boorstin and his wife, Ruth, has been presented annually since 1997 to recognize and support achievements of specific state centers. The Colorado Center for the Book was recognized for the completion of the renovation of its headquarters, the Thomas Honsby

Ferril House in Denver; hosting of the awards ceremonies for the center's "Letters About Literature" and "River of Words" projects at the Governor's Mansion; hosting and organizing the first regional meeting of Centers for the Book in western states; and for its continuing role in organizing and supporting the Rocky Mountain Book Festival and the Colorado Book Awards.

Projects

This was the Center for the Book's fourth year of administering the Viburnum Foundation's program for supporting family literacy projects in rural public libraries. During the year the foundation awarded 45 grants to small rural libraries in ten states. The Center for the Book sponsored regional workshops in Montgomery, Alabama, August 22–24, and in Albuquerque, New Mexico, September 12–14. The workshops provide training for library grant recipients and their community partners.

"Letters About Literature," a student essay contest sponsored with the Weekly Reader Corporation, concluded another record-breaking year. More than 22,000 students wrote letters to their favorite authors and 33 state centers honored statewide winners.

The center's annual "River of Words" project, an environmental art and poetry contest for young people, culminated on April 28, 2001, at the Library of Congress with an awards ceremony and display of the winning art works. The moderator was former Poet Laureate Robert Hass, one of the project's founders.

The Center for the Book made major contributions to the success of the first National Book Festival, which was held September 7–8, 2001, at the Library of Congress and on the East Capitol grounds. First Lady Laura Bush hosted the event, which was organized and sponsored by the Library of Congress. Drawing on its extensive experience in dealing with authors and publishers, the center shaped and carried out a plan that successfully enlisted 60 nationally known authors as festival participants and organized author presentations in the many festival venues. Making use of its national reading promotion organization partners, the center also promoted, organized, and monitored the largest festival pavilion, "Great Ideas for Promoting Reading."

Outreach

The coverage and use of the Center for the Book's Web site continued to expand in 2001. Established and maintained by program officer Maurvene D. Williams, the Web site describes Center for the Book projects, affiliations, and events. It also provides information about organizations that promote books, reading, literacy, and libraries. Access is by subject as well as alphabetical. Most organizational entries are linked to that organization's Web site or to a general descriptive entry about the organization. The Book Events Calendar and Book Fair section were expanded to include more storytelling festivals and more statewide and international literary events. Three new sections were added to the Web site in 2001: guidelines for establishing state Centers for the Book; reading promotion ideas for Telling America's Stories, the new national campaign; and issues of the newsletter *Center for the Book News*. The number of Web site transactions totaled 306,045 in 2001, compared with 240,797 in 2000.

In 2001 the Center for the Book prepared "Read More About It" lists of suggested books for 11 digitized collections on the National Digital Library's Web site and for several Library of Congress exhibitions, including the new permanent installation, World Treasures of the Library of Congress.

C-SPAN2 filmed many of the author presentations at the National Book Festival and eight Center for the Book evening programs for viewing as part of its "Booknotes" and weekend "Book TV" programs.

Five issues of *Center for the Book News* were produced in 2001, along with a new edition of the state center *Handbook*. The Library of Congress issued 36 press releases about Center for the Book activities, and a two-page "News from the Center for the Book" appeared in each issue of the Library of Congress *Information Bulletin*. Center Director John Y. Cole made 17 presentations about the center and its work during visits to 13 states.

Events

Sponsorship of events, symposia, and lectures—at the Library of Congress and elsewhere—is an important Center for the Book activity. Through such special events the center brings diverse audiences together on behalf of books and reading, and publicizes its activities nationally and locally. Among events in 2001 were 19 talks at the Library of Congress by current authors in the center's "Books and Beyond" author series, many of them cosponsored with Library of Congress divisions or offices; a program titled "Celebrating the Children of Our Nation's Capitol" that featured First Lady Laura Bush and was cosponsored with Everybody Wins! D.C.; a symposium, "Private Collectors and Special Collections in Libraries," cosponsored with the Library of Congress's Rare Book and Special Collections Division; cosponsorship with the Folger Institute of "The Transactions of the Book," a scholarly conference at the Folger Shakespeare Library; and cosponsorship, with the American Folklife Center and other organizations, of the Library of Congress conference "Living Lore: The Legacy of Benjamin A. Botkin."

Information about the dozens of events sponsored by affiliated state centers, often in cooperation with the national center, can be found in the Library of Congress *Information Bulletin* or through the national center's Web site.

Federal Library and Information Center Committee

Library of Congress, Washington, DC 20540
202-707-4800
World Wide Web http://lcweb.loc.gov.flicc

Susan M. Tarr
Executive Director

Highlights of the Year

During fiscal year (FY) 2001, the Federal Library and Information Center Committee (FLICC) continued to carry out its mission "to foster excellence in federal library and information services through interagency cooperation and to provide guidance and direction for FEDLINK."

FLICC's annual information policy forum, "Preserving Our Federal Heritage in the Digital Era," focused on the unprecedented challenges facing the federal government with respect to preserving and providing access in perpetuity to authoritative federal information now that so much government information is available only in electronic form and, in the case of some Web sites, can be conveniently modified by any authorized federal worker without regard for the archival record. FLICC also held its annual FLICC Symposium on the Information Professional, this year exploring approaches and tools for measuring federal library and information center performance.

FLICC working groups achieved a broad agenda in FY 2001: the third annual FLICC Awards to recognize the innovative ways federal libraries, librarians, and library technicians fulfill the information demands of government, business, scholarly communities, and the American public; a new working group to focus on emerging federal content management issues; a review of current library science educational programs and opportunities for the future; revisions for the Office of Personnel Management's librarian qualifications requirements; and expanded access to resources through online video broadcasts, distance learning, and the FLICC Web site.

FLICC also continued its collaboration with the Library of Congress General Counsel on a series of meetings between federal agency general counsels and agency librarians. These general counsel forums grew out of the recognition that federal attorneys and librarians face many of the same questions in applying copyright, privacy, Freedom of Information Act (FOIA), and other laws to their agencies' activities in the electronic age—with regard both to using information within the agency and to publishing the agency's own information. These meetings enhanced the relationship between agency attorneys and librarians and helped them develop contacts with their counterparts at other agencies. The 2001 series featured discussions on linking to commercial Web sites and on agency responses and approaches to meet the requirements of Section 508 of the Rehabilitation Act.

Content management and information dissemination were key topics in FY 2001. The FLICC Executive Board advised Sen. Joseph Lieberman's staff on "E-Gov" legislation, and several members joined study panels for the National

Commission on Libraries and Information Science's (NCLIS) "Comprehensive Assessment of Public Information Dissemination."

FLICC's cooperative Federal Library and Information Network (FEDLINK) continued to enhance its fiscal operations while providing its members with $51.7 million in transfer-pay services and $50.5 million in direct-pay services, saving federal agencies approximately $11.6 million in vendor volume discounts and approximately $7 million more in cost avoidance.

FY 2001 saw continued improvements in the efficiency of the FEDLINK program, including new resources and courses on digital libraries, cataloging Internet resources, consortial purchasing opportunities, newly negotiated and substantial vendor discounts, and strategies to replace the FEDLINK financial system. Staff members also sponsored 34 seminars and workshops for 1,600 participants and conducted 74 OCLC, Internet, and related training classes for 588 students.

FEDLINK also continued to customize and configure software and support services for electronic invoicing and to increase online access to financial information for member agencies and vendors. Furthermore, FEDLINK's continuing financial management efforts ensured that FEDLINK successfully passed the Library of Congress's financial audit of FY 2000 transactions.

Following the enactment of the Fiscal Operations Improvement Act of 2000 (P.L. 106-481), which created statutory authority and a revolving fund for FEDLINK's fee-based activities, FEDLINK staff members worked with Library of Congress financial and legal leaders to revise and enhance the FEDLINK program under its new law. The benefits of this new authority include full use of members' fees, no repetitive charging on no-year funds, and more extendable end-of-year spending. In addition, FLICC's executive director, by delegation from the Librarian of Congress, may now sign Interagency Agreements (IAGs), IAG amendments, and Military Interdepartmental Purchase Requests (MIPRs) on behalf of the library. The signatory delegation saves FEDLINK tens of thousands of administrative dollars annually and greatly simplifies and speeds up the IAG process for members.

The new revolving fund requirements also mandated a thorough five-year business plan. FEDLINK managers, with guidance from the FEDLINK Advisory Council (FAC), began analyzing FEDLINK business processes from a new perspective, including reviewing the mission statement, audiences, market position and message, staffing, and resources.

FLICC managers effectively used facilitative leadership (FL) techniques to involve FEDLINK staff and members in the planning process.

FLICC Quarterly Membership Meetings

In addition to regular FLICC working group updates and reports from FLICC/FEDLINK staff members, each FLICC quarterly meeting included a special focus on a new or developing trend in federal libraries. The first FLICC quarterly membership meeting featured William Y. Arms, professor of computer science, Cornell University, on "Strategies for Collecting and Preserving Valuable Materials on the Web at the Library of Congress"; the second meeting included a "Legislative Update: IT Issues in the 107th Congress," presented by Congressional Research Service staff members Harold Relyea and Glenn McLoughlin, and Brooke Dickson, policy analyst, Office of Management and Budget (OMB), gave an OMB Web policy update; and the third meeting featured Jan Herd, business reference librarian, Science, Technology and Business Division, Library of Congress, and her presentation "Taxonomy Creation and Use on the Web." The fourth meeting, scheduled for September 13, 2001, was canceled because of the terrorist attacks on New York and Washington.

FLICC Executive Board

At the July and September FLICC Executive Board meetings, board members considered "content management" from a policy perspective while discussing selected provisions of Senate Bill S. 803, the "E-Gov" legislation, sponsored by Sen. Joseph Lieberman (D-Conn.). Lieberman's committee counsel asked specifically for FLICC's perspective on revisions and refinements to the legislation. The board meeting discussions centered on a centralized Chief Information Officer (CIO) position for federal agencies, a general agency fund for digitization of federal collections, and a process for identifying electronic resources to be cataloged and for coordinating federal cataloging and federal indexing systems. The board concluded that these initiatives would need funding if agencies were to make substantial progress on digitizing, cataloging, and preserving government documents and databases available on the Web.

Two board members and FLICC Executive Director Susan M. Tarr also served on a study panel for the NCLIS "Comprehensive Assessment of Public Information Dissemination." Subsequently, Tarr testified before NCLIS in December urging it to recommend making information dissemination an explicitly budgeted responsibility. With adequate resources, she concluded, information professionals throughout the federal government could help execute the recommendations of the assessment and improve access to government information for both internal and external users.

FLICC Working Groups

FLICC Awards Working Group

To honor the many innovative ways federal libraries, librarians, and library technicians fulfill the information demands of government, business, research, scholarly communities, and the American public, the Awards Working Group administered a series of national awards for federal librarianship. The three awards are:

- Federal Library/Information Center of the Year—to commend a library or information center's outstanding, innovative, and sustained achievements during the fiscal year in fulfilling its organization's mission, fostering innovation in its services, and meeting the needs of its users
- Federal Librarian of the Year—to honor professional achievements during the fiscal year in the advancement of library and information sciences, the

promotion and development of services in support of the agency's mission, and demonstrated professionalism as described in the "Special Libraries Association's Competencies for Special Librarians in the 21st Century"

- Federal Library Technician of the Year—to recognize the achievements of a federal library technician during the fiscal year for service excellence in support of the library or information center's mission, exceptional technical competency, and flexibility in adapting work methods and dealing with change

At the annual FLICC Forum on Federal Information Policies in March 2001, the Librarian of Congress recognized the following winners of the third annual awards:

- Federal Library and/or Information Center of the Year—Scientific and Technical Information Center, U.S. Patent and Trademark Office. (The National Aeronautics and Space Administration's Goddard Space Flight Center Library and the U.S. Agency for International Development Library received honorable mention.)
- Federal Librarian of the Year (tie)—Sherrie M. Floyd, chief, Army Library Program, Vicenza, Italy, and Carlynn J. Thompson, director, Research Development and Acquisition Information Support Directorate, Defense Technical Information Center.
- Federal Library Technician of the Year—Darcy Bates, library technician, Electronic Information Center, U.S. Patent and Trademark Office. (Carolly J. Struck of the U.S. Naval Hospital Medical Library, Great Lakes, Illinois, received honorable mention.)

The award winners each received a certificate and an engraved crystal award in the shape of a book honoring their contributions to the field of federal library and information service, and the institutional winner received a framed, hand-painted certificate for display. The working group then reviewed the program criteria in the spring of 2001 and initiated promotion efforts for the fourth annual awards cycle, including updating the annual promotional brochure with an outside contractor.

Budget and Finance Working Group

The Budget and Finance Working Group developed the FY 2002 FEDLINK budget and fee structure in the winter quarter. Subsequent opinions on FEDLINK's revolving fund authority led to multiple revisions of the budget. Because of timing, the final budget was approved by the executive board late in the summer of 2001. The final budget for FY 2002 kept membership fees for transfer-pay customers at FY 2001 levels: 7.75 percent on accounts up to $300,000 and 7 percent on amounts exceeding $300,000. Direct-pay fees also remained at FY 2001 levels. The Library of Congress approved the budget in September.

Content Management Working Group

In fulfillment of a FLICC member mandate, an ad hoc working group on "content management" formed early in January 2001 and made its report to the board in mid-March. The group recommended that FLICC

- Foster partnerships with other federal stakeholders
- Help coordinate major taxonomies and thesauri
- Expand training on content management topics
- Form a working group to spearhead these efforts

In spring 2001 members of the ad hoc working group met with the chair of the Information Technology Working Group to review their individual charges, missions, goals, and action items. It soon became clear that the two groups should merge. In response to current trends in information science, they decided to call their working group the Content Management Working Group.

Once the merger was complete and approved by the board, the working group initiated efforts to carry out the recommendations. Its first official meeting was held in June. In addition to reviewing and prioritizing its goals and activities, the group finalized preparations for its August discussion series program, "Demystifying Knowledge Management," which focused on the broad view of knowledge management and on attempts to integrate or relate the various perspectives in use by federal knowledge managers. In the summer of 2001 the working group made progress on fostering partnerships by merging with the Special Interest Group on Content Management of the CIO Council's Knowledge Management Working Group.

Education Working Group

During FY 2001 the Education Working Group developed or supported 24 programs for 1,066 participants in the areas of digital imaging, trainer training, legal research, technician training, reference issues, cataloging, and preservation. In addition, the FLICC Orientations to National Libraries and Information Centers series and brown-bag luncheon discussions continued throughout the year.

The working group also explored creating a certificate program for library technicians, reviewed external library science courses and curriculum, and met with a past president of the Special Libraries Association to identify training needs for the future.

Nominating Working Group

The Nominating Working Group oversaw the 2001 election process for FLICC rotating members, executive board members, and FEDLINK Advisory Council. Librarians representing a variety of federal agencies agreed to place their names in nomination for these positions.

Personnel Working Group

The Personnel Working Group made progress in updating the GS-1410 qualification standard for librarians and in expanding and developing core competencies for the professional librarian series. Late in the year, the group began discussions on recruiting new librarians to the federal information community.

Preservation and Binding Working Group

The Preservation and Binding Working Group is planning the creation of a register of endangered rare and historic collections. It is also developing a standard federal conservation/preservation service contract through FEDLINK, and is in the process of completing a statement of work for that initiative and others for rare books, flat paper, preservation, and microfilming.

Publications and Education Office

Publications

In FY 2001 FLICC supported an ambitious publication schedule producing six issues of *FEDLINK Technical Notes* and three issues of the *FLICC Quarterly Newsletter*.

FLICC streamlined and targeted materials to support the FEDLINK program more efficiently, including the FY 2001 *FEDLINK Registration Pamphlet* and six FEDLINK Information Alerts. FLICC also produced the minutes of the four FY 2000 FLICC quarterly meetings and bimonthly executive board meetings and all FLICC Education Program promotional and support materials, including the FLICC forum announcement, attendee and speaker badges, press advisories, speeches and speaker remarks, and forum collateral materials. FLICC produced 31 FLICC meeting announcements to promote FLICC education programs, FEDLINK membership and OCLC users meetings, brown-bag discussion series, and education institutes, along with badges, programs, certificates of completion, and other supporting materials.

FLICC and FEDLINK staff members worked diligently throughout 2001 to continue to expand and update the FLICC/FEDLINK Web site. A series of teleconference meetings with a Web design firm has resulted in a prototype Web page scheduled for a spring 2002 launch. FLICC posted several video series to its Web site, including its awards program and several luncheon discussions. The site also contains a variety of information resources, FEDLINK member information, links to vendors and other members, listings of membership and minutes of various FLICC working groups and governing bodies, access to account data online, awards program information, event calendars, and an online training registration system that is updated nightly. FLICC staff members converted all publications, newsletters, announcements, alerts, member materials, meeting minutes, and working group resources into HTML format, uploading current materials within days of their being printed. Staff members completed an extensive initiative to keep the numerous Web links current throughout the Web site and they now maintain the site's links on a quarterly basis.

Through collaboration with FEDLINK Network Operations staff members, the FLICC Web site continues to expand and offer resources including OCLC Usage Analysis Reports, pricing data, and many new documents, such as the FY 2002 budget materials and training resources. Staff members also worked with the Library of Congress Contracts and Logistics Division to make electronic versions of FEDLINK's requests for proposals (RFPs) available online for prospective vendors.

In FY 2001 staff members also worked with the Member Services Unit to revise and enhance FEDLINK's Online Registration/Online Interagency Agreement (IAG) system and began creating additional FEDLINK forms for members to use to manage their accounts through the online system.

Education

In conjunction with the Education Working Group, FLICC offered a total of 34 seminars, workshops, and lunchtime discussions to 1,600 members of the federal library and information center community. Multiday institutes covered digital imaging, legal research, library technician training, and disaster mitigation; one-day sessions offered hands-on and theoretical knowledge on training trainers, marketing training, reference and reference interviewing, electronic interlibrary loan, knowledge and content management, and developing and managing Web sites. FLICC was also host to two general counsel forums, one on Web linking policies and the other on Section 508 of the Rehabilitation Act.

FEDLINK staff members developed, coordinated, and moderated the 2001 FLICC Symposium on the Information Professional. The theme was measuring library performance, and presenters included Mark Kaprow, webmaster, General Services Administration; Eileen Abels, associate professor, College of Information Studies, University of Maryland; and James Krzywicki, president, North American Operations, RoweCom, Inc.

FLICC continued its commitment to library technicians' continuing education by hosting satellite downlinks to a popular teleconference, "Soaring to . . . Excellence," sponsored by the College of DuPage. Following the success of previous programs, FLICC held the fifth annual Federal Library Technicians Institute, a week-long summer institute that again focused on orienting library technicians to the full array of library functions in the federal context. Federal and academic librarians joined FLICC professionals to discuss various areas of librarianship, including acquisitions, cataloging, reference, and automation.

FLICC also provided organizational, promotional, and logistical support for FEDLINK meetings and events including the FEDLINK fall and spring membership meetings, two FEDLINK OCLC Users Group meetings, and numerous vendor demonstrations.

FLICC continued to improve its multimedia distance-learning initiative, through increased use of upgraded equipment and software, to produce high-quality, edited educational programs. Through its ongoing arrangement with the National Library of Education, FLICC made these videos available for interlibrary loans (ILL) to federal libraries throughout the country and around the world.

Staff members also produced and uploaded downloadable video clips of the FLICC FY 2000 awards ceremony and a series of lunchtime discussions on such topics as Web development, electronic finding aids, digital libraries, and consortium development.

FEDLINK

In FY 2001 FEDLINK gave federal agencies cost-effective access to an array of automated information-retrieval services for online research, cataloging, and ILL. FEDLINK members also procured print serials, electronic journals, books, CD-ROMs, and document delivery via Library of Congress/FEDLINK contracts with more than 100 major vendors. Staff members continued to explore consortial arrangements, both within and across federal agencies.

The FEDLINK Advisory Council met nine times during FY 2001. In addition to general oversight activities, council members advised FEDLINK managers on issues related to implementing FEDLINK's new revolving fund law, options for the FY 2002 budget, and the draft five-year business plan. They also participated in a concept-mapping exercise for the redesign of the FLICC/FEDLINK Web site.

At the annual fall FEDLINK membership meeting, participants learned more about successful federal library programs. John Cole, director of the Center for the Book and co-chair of the Library of Congress bicentennial program, presented a brief history of the Library of Congress and federal libraries. Barbara Christine, chief of the Library Branch, U.S. Army Community and Family Support Center, gave a slide presentation on setting up general libraries for deployed troops in Bosnia. Janice Beattie, director of Central and Regional Libraries, National Oceanic and Atmospheric Administration, highlighted some of that library's award-winning initiatives that led to their selection as the 1999 FLICC Library of the Year. At the spring FEDLINK membership meeting, Donna Scheeder, president, Special Libraries Association, addressed changing competencies in special libraries in the digital age. Carol Bursik of the U.S. Geological Survey and chair of the FLICC Budget and Finance Working Group, presented the proposed FY 2002 budget.

FEDLINK Network Operations

The spring FEDLINK OCLC Users Group meeting included a presentation by George Needham, OCLC vice president for member services, on the OCLC Users Council governance study and on OCLC's strategic plan. He reported on conclusions that indicate OCLC's governance must expand to include more international membership and its current services need to be revised and expanded into new areas, such as digital preservation and the harvesting of metadata, to respond to the growing use of the Web to publish and access systems. FEDLINK staff members continue to support, monitor, and publicize these new developments for their applicability in the federal arena. Two such developments of note include the joint effort of OCLC and the Government Printing Office to support digital archiving by identifying and testing key elements for additional functionality in the Cooperative Online Resources Catalog (CORC) system, and OCLC's support of the Library of Congress's Cooperative Digital Reference Service, both highlighted at OCLC users meetings. FEDLINK staff members supplemented the spring Users meeting with product labs that provided detailed demonstrations of OCLC's current Web products, especially CORC, ILLiad, and WebExpress.

FEDLINK members elected Bursik as the new representative to the OCLC Members (formerly Users) Council.

The FEDLINK OCLC team continued to attend biweekly meetings with OCLC and other networks via the Web and conference calls. Staff members heard briefings on enhancements to CORC and the cataloging MicroEnhancer, on the new ILL Web interface, on improvements to FirstSearch and Electronic Collections Online, and on other services. These updates supplemented semiannual meetings at OCLC and were useful in daily support of members, in writing the OCLC column for *FEDLINK Technical Notes,* and in providing briefings to members at the spring and fall users meetings.

Federal libraries continue to be significant users of CORC. By the end of FY 2001, 21 FEDLINK member libraries were making consistent use of CORC. Suzanne Pilsk, Smithsonian Libraries, was the first chair of the OCLC CORC User Group and hosts the group's Web site.

FEDLINK staff members continued to monitor usage of OCLC, posting usage data to ALIX-FS monthly and working to reduce deficits in OCLC accounts.

Staff members made site visits to ten federal libraries (the National Library of Medicine, the National Agricultural Library, the National Library of Education, National Institutes of Health Library, District of Columbia Public Library, the Naval Research Laboratory Library, the U.S. Naval Academy Library, the Census Bureau Library, the Marine Mammal Commission Library, and the Centers for Medicare and Medicaid Services Library) to discuss ways to improve use of OCLC services.

FEDLINK Training Program

The 2001 FEDLINK training program included technical training classes and customized workshops for members at the FEDLINK training facility and onsite at federal libraries throughout the world. Courses on basic Web searching and finding Web resources on news and current events drew 21 students, while 29 courses on OCLC use drew 174 students. Four of these courses (including advanced cataloging and authorities) were taught by FEDLINK member Robert Ellett, Jr., chief of cataloging at the Armed Forces Staff College. FEDLINK staff members taught 385 students on 13 Air Force and Army bases in the United States and in Guam, Okinawa, Japan, and Korea. Training began but was interrupted on September 11 (by the terrorist attacks on Washington, D.C., and New York City) at Lajes Air Force Base in the Azores. FEDLINK also arranged for a Library of Congress trainer to teach descriptive cataloging to Army catalogers at U.S. Army–Europe headquarters in Germany.

Procurement Program

FEDLINK maintained an open RFP for online retrieval services, which attracted responses from NetLibrary, Skyminder, Factiva, RegScan, and ORS Publications. FEDLINK assisted the Army Library program in establishing a consortium for use of ProQuest, aided the Library of Congress in its renegotiations of consortial purchases from LexisNexis and West services, and worked with individual agencies, such as the Treasury and State departments, to identify similar opportunities.

FEDLINK Fiscal Operations

During FY 2001 FEDLINK processed 8,295 member service transaction requests for current and prior years, representing $51.7 million in current-year transfer pay, $3.7 million in prior-year transfer pay, $50.5 million in current-year direct pay, and virtually zero in prior-year direct-pay service dollars, saving members more than $11.6 million in vendor volume discounts and approximately $7 million more in cost avoidance. Staff members processed 52,087 invoices for payment of current- and prior-year orders and earned $9,997 in discounts in excess of interest penalties for late payment of FEDLINK vendor invoices. FEDLINK also completed FY 1996 member refunds to close out obligations for expired appropriations and remaining account balances and successfully passed the Library of Congress financial audit of FY 2000 transactions performed by Clifton Gunderson, LLP.

During the year FEDLINK worked intently with Library of Congress management, FLICC advisory groups, and the General Accounting Office (GAO) in planning to implement FEDLINK's new revolving fund, effective October 1, 2001. Managers also streamlined the OCLC deficit management process to eliminate problems associated with duplicate communication from FEDLINK units and to link the review and analysis of member deficit status to monthly termination decisions.

FEDLINK began working on developing implementation conventions for processing electronic data invoices by December 31, 2001. The beta application software must still be tested for acceptance of delivery. FEDLINK managers also modified the "vouchering" process for vendor invoices (with special emphasis on publication orders) to accommodate operating in the revolving fund environment.

FEDLINK supported the Library of Congress's procurement planning efforts for a financial management system that will be used by all legislative agencies. Because the replacement legislative financial system is scheduled for implementation in 2004, short-term performance issues concerning SYMIN's Paradox database require FLICC management to look for a replacement local financial management system immediately.

FEDLINK staff members have continued to support reviews of and revisions to the interactive cost-benefit model developed for member agencies to evaluate their FEDLINK procurement decisions. The next step will be to post the model on FLICC's Web site for member agencies to use.

FEDLINK Vendor Services

FEDLINK vendor service dollars totaled $51.7 million for transfer-pay customers and $50.5 million for direct-pay customers. Electronic information retrieval services represented $16.1 million and $37.3 million spent, respectively, by transfer-pay and direct-pay customers. Within this service category, online services comprised the largest procurement for transfer-pay and direct-pay customers, representing $15.2 million and $36.9 million, respectively. Publication acquisition services totaled $28.9 million and $13.0 million, respectively, for transfer-pay and direct-pay customers. Within this service category, serials subscription services comprised the largest procurement for transfer-pay and direct-pay customers, representing $21.8 million and $12.8 million, respectively.

Library support services represented $6.7 million and $74,000, respectively, for transfer-pay and direct-pay customers. Within this service category, bibliographic utilities constituted the largest procurement area, representing $5.0 million and $74,000 spent by transfer-pay and direct-pay customers, respectively.

Accounts Receivable and Member Services

FEDLINK processed 598 signed IAGs for FY 2001 registrations from federal libraries, information centers, and other federal offices. In addition, FEDLINK processed 2,207 IAG amendments (1,031 for FY 2001 and 1,176 for prior years) for agencies that added, adjusted, or ended service funding. These IAGs and IAG amendments represented 8,295 individual service requests to begin, move, convert, or cancel service from FEDLINK vendors. FEDLINK executed these service requests by generating 7,906 delivery orders for the Library of Congress Contracts and Logistics Division to issue to vendors. FEDLINK processed $51.7 million in service dollars for 2,263 transfer-pay accounts and $50.5 million in service dollars for 145 direct-pay accounts. Included in these member service transactions were 640 member requests to move prior-year (no-year and multi-year) funds across fiscal-year boundaries. These no-year and multiyear service request transactions represented an additional contracting volume of $6.5 million comprising 1,027 delivery orders.

The FEDLINK Fiscal Hotline responded to a variety of member questions, ranging from routine queries about IAGs, delivery orders, and account balances to complicated questions regarding FEDLINK policies and operating procedures. In addition, the FLICC Web site and e-mail contacts continued to offer FEDLINK members and vendors 24-hour access to fiscal operations and account data. Staff members also met with many FEDLINK member agencies and FEDLINK vendors to discuss complicated account problems and to resolve complex current- and prior-year situations. FEDLINK's online financial service system, ALIX-FS, maintained current- and prior-year transfer-pay account data and continued to provide members early access to their monthly balance information throughout the fiscal year. FEDLINK also prepared monthly mailings that alerted individual members to unsigned IAG amendments, deficit accounts, rejected invoices, and delinquent accounts, and issued the year-end schedule for FY 2001 IAG transactions.

Transfer-Pay Accounts Payable Services

For transfer-pay users, FEDLINK processed 52,087 invoices for both current- and prior-year orders. Staff members processed these vendor invoices swiftly and efficiently to earn $9,997 in prompt payment discounts in excess of interest penalties for late payments. FEDLINK continued to maintain open accounts for three prior years to pay publications service invoices ("bill laters" and "back orders") for members using books and serials services. Staff members issued 88,553 statements to members (27,537 for the current year and 61,016 for prior years) and generated current fiscal year statements for electronic information retrieval service accounts on the 30th or the last working day of each month, and publications and acquisitions account statements on the 15th of each month.

FEDLINK issued final FY 1996 statements to close obligations for members with expired FY 1996 appropriations and quarterly statements for prior fiscal years. FEDLINK also supported the reconciliation of FY 1997 FEDLINK vendor services accounts and issued the final call to vendors for FY 1997 invoices.

Budget and Revenue

During FY 2001 FEDLINK earned approximately 93 percent of its target FY 2001 operating budget in fee revenue from signed IAGs. Program obligations did not exceed fee projections because of unanticipated attrition and delays in hiring lowered administrative expenditures. As FY 2001 ended, FEDLINK fee revenue was approximately 3.6 percent below FY 2000 levels for the same time period. The decrease in fee revenue was primarily attributed to a 3.4 percent decrease in transfer-pay services compared with the previous fiscal year.

Revolving Fund Implementation

In fall 2000 Congress passed the Fiscal Operations Improvement Act (P.L. 106-481) that provides statutory authority and a revolving fund for FEDLINK's fee-based activities.

Throughout the year, FEDLINK managers focused on developing a sound business model for the revolving fund authority program. The FLICC executive director consulted with key program managers and FEDLINK membership advisory groups on the following:

- Business models for registration/agreement processing and depositing funds in the program
- Use of prior-year obligated balances and their transfer to the revolving fund
- Opportunities to innovate FEDLINK's procurement vehicles
- Fee policies for moving no-year and eligible funds across fiscal-year boundaries

For a thorough interpretation of all of the issues related to initiating and managing a revolving fund program, two months after the new law was enacted FEDLINK managers analyzed and documented issues needing clarification by Library of Congress fiscal and legal experts. After several months of internal analysis and interpretation, FEDLINK managers worked with the library's representatives to contact GAO attorneys to help library staff apply the new authority.

In September the GAO attorneys advised FEDLINK that members working with annual appropriations are still governed by the rules for annual appropriations, even under the FEDLINK revolving fund. In GAO's opinion, ". . . section 103(e) does not clearly indicate that Congress intended unobligated balances of agency advances to be available without fiscal limitation regardless of time restrictions imposed on the appropriation from which the advances were withdrawn." The GAO response also said that "when . . . an agency withdraws funds from its appropriation and makes them available for credit to another appropriation, that amount is available for obligation only for the same time period as the appropriation from which the funds were withdrawn . . . except as specifically provided by law." In addition, ". . . section 103 will not permit the Library to retain any deobligated, unexpended fiscal (or fixed) year appropriations advanced by a customer agency that the Library determines, after filling the customer's order and reconciling the customer's account, is not needed for the costs the Library incurred in filling the order."

At meetings and in publications throughout FY 2001, FEDLINK members were provided detailed updates along with an assessment of the budgetary impact the revolving fund would have on their management-review process. Although the final GAO guidance on P.L. 106-481 was more limited than FEDLINK members had anticipated, the new authority provides a number of benefits, including: (1) full use of members' fees; (2) no repetitive charging on no-year funds; (3) more extendable end-of-year spending; (4) capital cumulation for large expenditures; (5) program stability; and (6) the ability to plan for the long term.

The final budget held member fees constant with unobligated fee revenue from prior years because those funds were eligible for carryover into the FEDLINK administrative operating account. FEDLINK and FSD then documented transaction processing requirements to support the accounting transition to the revolving fund.

The Member Services Unit revised the IAG text to reflect the business model for implementing the revolving fund. Additional changes were also made to the proposed IAG text, including modifying the duration to "indefinite." FEDLINK managers invested significant time and effort in revising the member online program handbook. The revisions reflect the changes in program operations resulting from implementation of revolving fund authority.

National Commission on Libraries and Information Science

1110 Vermont Ave. N.W., Suite 820, Washington, DC 20005-3522
World Wide Web http://www.nclis.gov

Rosalie B. Vlach
Director, Legislative and Public Affairs

The National Commission on Libraries and Information Science (NCLIS) is not a regulatory agency. To carry out its functions, NCLIS conducts hearings, studies, surveys, and analyses of the nation's library and information needs, appraises the adequacies and deficiencies of current library and information resources and research and development activities, and issues publications. These activities support the development of policy advice and recommendations to the president and Congress.

Martha B. Gould continues as NCLIS chairperson. President Clinton made three recess appointments to the commission in late December 2000. Paulette H. Holahan is a former NCLIS commissioner (1980–1985) who has been an active library volunteer for more than 40 years in New Orleans. Marilyn Gell Mason, a consultant on library issues and former director of the Cleveland Public Library, was director of the White House Conference on Library and Information Service in 1979 and 1980. Donald L. Robinson was, when appointed, director of the Washington Internship Program of Boston University and coordinator of the Mickey Leland Congressional Internship Program. As recess appointments, the new members served through the first session of the 107th Congress (through December 2001).

Continuing commissioners in addition to Gould are Rebecca T. Bingham, Joan R. Challinor (vice chair), José-Marie Griffiths, Jack E. Hightower, and Bobby L. Roberts. Members serve for five years; their terms continue until a successor is appointed or until July 19 of the year succeeding the year in which their appointed office expires. The appointed terms for Commissioners C. E. "Abe" Abramson, Walter Anderson, and LeVar Burton expired on July 19, 2000, and no successors were named; therefore, their extension terms, as provided by law, expired on July 19, 2001. Winston Tabb continues to represent James H. Billington, the Librarian of Congress, a permanent NCLIS member. Beverly Sheppard, as acting director of the Institute of Museum and Library Services (IMLS), served until June 2001 as an ex officio member of the commission. At that time Robert S. Martin was named IMLS director and succeeded her.

Robert S. Willard, a former commissioner, is NCLIS executive director, and Judith Russell, whose library career has included time as director of the Federal Depository Library Program, is deputy director. Denise Davis is the director of statistics and surveys and Rosalie Vlach is director of legislative and public affairs.

Highlights of the Year

As part of its responsibility for advising the director of IMLS on policies and financial assistance for library services and for ensuring that IMLS policies and activities are coordinated with other activities of the federal government, NCLIS held several joint meetings with the National Museum Services Board.

NCLIS established a committee to assist IMLS with development of the National Award for Library Service and continues its participation in the cycles of draft, guidelines, plans, feedback, reports, evaluation, and revision for the IMLS federal grants program for libraries and information services.

Support for Executive and Legislative Branches

NCLIS continues to examine government information policy as it relates to the creation, dissemination, and permanent accessibility of electronic government information. Among NCLIS initiatives during 2001 was the completion and delivery of the report *A Comprehensive Assessment of Public Information Dissemination,* recommending policies and procedures for strengthening the dissemination infrastructure of government information. The study was undertaken at the request of Senators John McCain (R-Ariz.) and Joseph Lieberman (D-Conn.). The report, delivered to the president and to Congress, was based on historical research, the oral and written comments of governmental and nongovernmental parties with an interest in the subject, and the recommendations of four panels of experts. [See the Special Report "Dissemination of Government Information" later in Part 1—*Ed.*]

NCLIS continues to work closely with officials of a variety of federal agencies to obtain information and provide timely input on national and international policies affecting library and information services. During 2001 commissioners and staff met with officials of the departments of Education, Labor, Commerce, and State, as well as the Government Printing Office, Library of Congress, National Agricultural Library, National Institute for Literacy, Office of Management and Budget, and Small Agency Council. Meetings also were held with individuals from the Association for Federal Information Resources Management, Federal Depository Library Program, Federal Publishers Committee, Federal Library and Information Center Committee, and the Interagency Council for Printing and Publication Services, among others.

National Information Activities

NCLIS published the report *Library and Information Services for Individuals with Disabilities,* which includes the edited transcript of a commission hearing held at the Kellogg Conference Center of Gallaudet University in Washington, D.C. After reviewing the information presented at the hearing, NCLIS began considering a research and development initiative on library and information services for the disabled.

NCLIS examined the status of school libraries at an April hearing in Cincinnati, Ohio. The school library's role in student achievement and in promoting literacy and information literacy were among the topics examined. The commission also investigated the role of the federal government in supporting school libraries. The transcript of the hearing, *School Librarians: Knowledge Navigators Through Troubled Times,* will be published in 2002.

NCLIS/NCES Library Statistics Program

NCLIS Library Statistics Program collaborative activities during 2001 included the following: annual training workshop and orientation for new state data coordinators, March; steering committee meetings for the Federal-State Cooperative System Survey, March, June, and September; State Library Agency Survey, March; Academic Library Survey advisory committee meeting, January and June; and School Library Media Center Survey task group meetings, January and June.

The year 2001 was the 14th consecutive year of cooperation between NCLIS and the National Center for Education Statistics (NCES). NCLIS advises NCES on policy matters related to libraries, serves as a liaison to the library community, organizes meetings and professional development workshops, supports in-state training and technical assistance, and monitors trends. NCLIS is committed to providing access to the work of all steering committees and task groups associated with the Library Statistics Program (LSP) through its Web site (http://www.nclis.gov/libraries/lsp/statist.html).

NCES and NCLIS continue planning for an expanded library statistics cooperative. The goal is to facilitate work on crosscutting issues without interfering with the ability of existing constituent groups to continue their work on individual surveys. A significant effort during 2001 was the adoption of the state library agency survey of core electronic metrics. These measures come from collaborative work among NCLIS, the Federal-State Cooperative System for collection of public library data, state library agencies, and consultants John Carlo Bertot and Charles R. McClure. The state library agency survey has adopted core network-use measures from that body of work and will begin reporting these with the fiscal year 2001 survey.

In January 2001 NCLIS became the U.S. designee for submitting U.S. library data to the European Union library statistics project, LibEcon. Comprehensive data was submitted for public, academic, and state library agencies for the years 1996–2000 as available. School and national library data will be reported in 2002.

International Activities

An NCLIS and Sister Cities International initiative, Sister Libraries: A White House Millennium Council Project, was completed in 2001. The initial goal was for public and school libraries in the United States to pair with others worldwide, focusing on programs specifically planned for children and teenagers. The project was expanded to include other types of libraries and a wider variety of programs. A total of 143 U.S. libraries in 42 states are designated official Sister Libraries.

NCLIS is actively involved in U.S. international library standards activities. The NCLIS director of statistics and surveys chairs the National Information Standards Organization's Standards Committee Working Group for revision of the Z39.7 library statistics standard. The director also works with the International Standards Organization.

NCLIS also completed its 16th year of cooperation with the Department of State to coordinate and monitor proposals for International Contributions for

Scientific, Educational, and Cultural Activities (ICSECA) funds and to disburse the funds.

The commission continues to be an active participant in the International Federation of Library Associations and Institutions (IFLA). NCLIS commissioners and staff took part in the August 2001 General Conference in Boston and hosted several meetings with UNESCO representatives on topics of mutual interest. NCLIS was an IFLA "international distinguished partner" with a special role in the preparations for the Boston conference.

During the year NCLIS also began preliminary work in preparation for the International Leadership Conference on Information Literacy planned in partnership with UNESCO and the National Forum on Information Literacy.

Publications

Annual Report of the U.S. National Commission on Libraries and Information Science, 1999–2000. GPO, 2001.

A Comprehensive Assessment of Public Information Dissemination. GPO, January 2001.

Library and Information Services for Persons with Disabilities: An NCLIS Hearing in Washington, D.C. GPO, July 2001.

Library Statistics Cooperative Program 2001 (brochure).

Copies of NCLIS print publications are available free in limited quantities from NCLIS until supplies are exhausted. Electronic versions are available on the NCLIS Web site (http://www.nclis.gov). Also on the Web site are selected reports, hearing testimony, comments on various matters before Congress and the administration, news releases, and other items.

National Agricultural Library

U.S. Department of Agriculture, NAL Bldg., 10301 Baltimore Ave.,
Beltsville, MD 20705-2351
E-mail agref@nal.usda.gov
World Wide Web http://www.nal.usda.gov

Len Carey
Public Affairs Officer

The U.S. Department of Agriculture's National Agricultural Library (NAL) is the world's largest and most accessible agricultural research library and the principal source in the United States for information about food, agriculture, and natural resources. The library's expert staff, leadership role in information services and technology applications, and collection of more than 3.5 million items combine to make it the foremost agricultural library in the world. NAL is also actively engaged with agricultural, agricultural research, and agricultural information organizations throughout the world.

Since 1969 NAL has been located in the Washington, D.C., suburb of Beltsville, Maryland, on the grounds of the Henry A. Wallace Beltsville Agricultural Research Center. In 2000 the library's 15-story building was named for Abraham Lincoln, in honor of the president who, in 1862, proposed and signed into law an act of Congress establishing the Department of Agriculture (USDA).

NAL has been established by Congress (7 USCS § 3125a) as the primary agricultural information resource of the United States. Congress assigned to the library responsibilities to

- Acquire, preserve, and manage information resources of agriculture and allied sciences
- Organize agricultural information and information products and services
- Provide agricultural information and information products and services within the United States and internationally
- Plan, coordinate, and evaluate information and library needs related to agricultural research and education
- Cooperate with and coordinate efforts toward development of a comprehensive agricultural library and information network
- Coordinate the development of specialized subject information services among the agricultural and library information communities

NAL is the only library in the United States with the mandate to carry out these national and international responsibilities for the agricultural community.

Collection

NAL manages one of the largest and most accessible collections of information and databases about agriculture in the world. The breadth, depth, size, and scope of the library's collection—more than 3.5 million items on 48 miles of shelves, dating from the 16th century to the present, covering all aspects of agriculture and related sciences, and including rare foreign literature and special "one-of-a-kind" items not available elsewhere—make it a unique and irreplaceable resource for agricultural researchers, policy makers, regulators, and scholars.

With materials in 70 different languages in its collections, the library is relied upon for access to the international literature of agriculture. As the U.S. node of the international agricultural information system, the library serves as a gateway for international agricultural libraries and information centers to U.S. agricultural libraries and resources. Through its gifts and exchange program and its ability to collect information internationally, the library has built a unique collection of international information on agriculture. The NAL collection includes books and journals, audiovisuals, reports, theses, software, laser discs, and artifacts. The library receives more than 25,000 serial titles annually. In addition,

- NAL is valued for its ability to access the "gray literature"—ephemeral information—of agriculture.
- The library's collections include the most extensive accumulation of materials anywhere on the history of agriculture in the United States.
- The library's collections are unique in the aggregate, being the most complete repository of U.S. Department of Agriculture publications in the world.

The NAL staff numbers about 175 librarians, computer specialists, administrators, information specialists, and clerical personnel. A number of volunteers, ranging from college students to retired persons, also work on various programs at the library. NAL has an active visiting scholar program that allows scientists, researchers, professors, and students from universities worldwide to work on projects of joint interest. NAL works closely with land-grant university libraries on programs to improve access to and maintenance of the nation's agricultural knowledge.

Library Services

Through its technology-based services, NAL provides immediate digital access to a widening array and expanding collection of scientific literature, printed text, and images. The NAL Web site (http://www.nal.usda.gov) is its electronic gateway to a wealth of agricultural information resources. In addition to specialized information services available over the Internet, NAL provides traditional library services and products to its customers, including programs that teach patrons how to identify, locate, and obtain needed information. The library works to advance open and democratic access to information about agriculture and to explore emerging technologies with other agricultural libraries and institutions.

NAL's AGRICOLA (AGRICultural OnLine Access) bibliographic database, for example, provided the first opportunities to design and evaluate new techniques for improved organization, linkage, and retrieval of agricultural information. AGRICOLA contains more than 4 million citations of agricultural literature with links to full texts of many articles. AGRICOLA's implementation on the World Wide Web (http://www.nal.usda/gov/ag98) provides a broader base of users with access to this information.

NAL is nationally known as a leader in preservation to ensure long-term access to agricultural information, and has led development of policies and procedures for preserving USDA digital publications. The library is nationally recognized for its expertise in preservation of microform.

NAL's several national information centers are portals to reliable sources of science-based information in key areas of American agriculture. Subjects covered by the information centers include alternative farming systems, animal welfare, food and nutrition, rural information (including rural health), technology transfer, and water quality. These centers provide a wide variety of customized services, ranging from responding to reference requests and developing reference publications to coordinating outreach activities and setting up dissemination networks.

By collaborating with other organizations throughout government, the centers provide timely, accurate, comprehensive, and in-depth coverage in their specialized subject areas. Staff specialists in the centers provide a national information infrastructure in support of the knowledge base for their respective subject areas. The national information centers promote public access to information through training workshops, exhibits, presentations, and other outreach activities.

NAL is also uniquely positioned to innovate in the bibliographic control of agricultural information by developing new intellectual tools, and by promoting new technologies to increase access to critical information resources. By developing the technology and tools to simplify bibliographic and subject descriptions, NAL encourages partnerships among land-grant institutions and other libraries to increase the content of AGRICOLA through distributed input.

NAL's technology leadership in partnership with others can be seen in the newly implemented distributed architecture for providing agricultural information through the Agriculture Network Information Center (AgNIC) alliance, and in the library's exploratory work in merging extensible markup language (XML) and geographic information system (GIS) for the long-term storage of and access to USDA datasets through the AGROS prototype.

Information Management

NAL is the bibliographic authority on managing agricultural information, both nationally and internationally, and an authority on the development and use of controlled vocabulary for agriculture. Its strong foundation and experience in collection development, implementation of bibliographic control standards, and automated systems for information retrieval also leave it uniquely positioned to define and develop new models for identifying, organizing, preserving, and providing access to the vast quantities of raw agricultural information available digitally on the Internet and elsewhere. The collective expertise of the NAL staff and the vast array of print and digital information present in the national collection offer a laboratory for developing and testing innovative methods of creating and linking agricultural research information.

As research libraries are faced with the need to provide permanent access to electronic information, the National Agricultural Library is taking a leadership role in expanding and ensuring permanent access to USDA electronic publications.

Highlights of 2001

Director Andre Retires

NAL Director Pamela Q. J. Andre retired on June 1, 2001. Until a new director is appointed, NAL Deputy Director Eleanor Frierson and Associate Directors Gary McCone, Maria Pisa, and Sally Sinn are taking turns as acting director. NAL expects that the search for a new director will be completed by mid-2002.

Tornado

NAL survived a serious tornado on September 24, 2001. No NAL personnel were killed or injured in the tornado, but the library's Lincoln Building suffered some window breakage and damage to the collection on two stacks floors.

International Symposium on Agricultural Trade

NAL cosponsored an International Symposium on Agricultural Trade, May 14–15, 2001, with the National Center for Agricultural Law, Research, and Information of the University of Arkansas School of Law. Symposium speakers were drawn from law schools in the United States and Britain and other participants from among U.S. and international agricultural trade organizations. The symposium drew about 40 people from agricultural trade associations, foreign agricultural services, and USDA agencies to discussions of legal and socioeconomic aspects of international trade in agricultural and forest products.

Food Safety Research Information Office

In July 2001 the library launched a new Web site (http://www.nal.usda.gov/fsrio/ fsresearchrpts.htm) featuring information on food safety research programs nationwide. The Web site provides detailed information on food safety research priorities, spending, and accomplishments in U.S. federal agencies, as well as links to other important food safety research information. A key component of the Web site is a database of information on food safety research projects dating from 1998. The database describes food safety research done or funded by the USDA Agricultural Research Service; USDA Cooperative State Research, Education, and Extension Service; the Food Safety Consortium (researchers from the University of Arkansas, Iowa State University, and Kansas State University); and the U.S. Department of Health and Human Services' Food and Drug Administration. Also on the Web site are program and planning documents providing detailed information on food safety spending (by federal agency and year); annual reports and program plans describing food safety research efforts; food safety news and important food safety conferences; and more than 100 links to Web-based food safety research information provided by U.S. and foreign governments, and educational and professional organizations.

The new Web site was created by NAL's Food Safety Research Information Office (FSRIO), adding to the library's extensive Web-based information resources on food, nutrition, and food safety.

Interagency Panel for Assessment of the National Agricultural Library

In October 2001 USDA received the report of an Interagency Panel for Assessment of NAL. The panel had been appointed in October 2000 by USDA Under Secretary I. Miley Gonzalez and Deputy Secretary Richard Rominger, and charged ". . . to review the activities of the National Agricultural Library in pursuit of its mandate to serve as the chief agricultural information resource of the United States and make recommendations to the Under Secretary, Research, Education, and Economics, on NAL's management and staff, programs, and operations."

The panel's October report to USDA Under Secretary Joseph L. Jen set forth a broad vision for NAL and 28 specific recommendations. USDA will decide in 2002 how to proceed with each of the recommendations.

National Library of Medicine

8600 Rockville Pike, Bethesda, MD 20894
301-496-6308, 888-346-3656, fax 301-496-4450
E-mail publicinfo@nlm.nih.gov
World Wide Web http://www.nlm.nih.gov

Robert Mehnert

Director, Office of Communications and Public Liaison

The National Library of Medicine (NLM), a part of the Department of Health and Human Services' National Institutes of Health (NIH) in Bethesda, Maryland, is the world's largest library of the health sciences. NLM has two buildings with 420,000 total square feet. The older building (1962) houses the collection, public reading rooms, exhibition hall, and library staff and administrative offices. The adjacent 10-story Lister Hill Center Building (1980) contains the main computer room, auditorium, audiovisual facility, offices, and research laboratories.

NLM continues to evolve from an institution serving primarily health professionals to a source of authoritative health information for all. The library now provides more diverse information to a wider audience than ever before. Polls show that health information is one of the most popular areas of inquiry by the Internet-using public, and that NLM's MEDLINE and MEDLINEplus are heavily used resources. Usage figures continue their steep ascent: the latest statistics show some 400 million searches being done annually, most of them queries to the MEDLINE database via the PubMed access system.

Two Anniversaries and a Funeral

In October 2001 MEDLINE celebrated its 30th anniversary. Its much younger relative, MEDLINEplus, a source of reliable consumer health information available on the World Wide Web, celebrated its third anniversary that month.

The pioneering MEDLINE project, begun in the early 1970s, evolved from the computerized system installed in 1964 to produce the *Index Medicus*. MEDLINE was the first successful marriage of a large reference database to a national telecommunications network. The 1980s saw the introduction of Grateful Med, a software program created by NLM that one could load onto a PC and, equipped with a modem and a password, use to search MEDLINE from one's home, office, or laboratory. Due in large part to outreach efforts by librarians in the National Network of Libraries of Medicine, Grateful Med was eagerly snapped up not only by librarians but also by health professionals, scientists, students, lawyers, medical journalists, and others, who saw the average charge of $2 per MEDLINE search as a bargain. Today, in the age of the Internet and the World Wide Web, the NIH Web site is the second most heavily trafficked federal government site, and MEDLINE and other NLM databases, now free, account for the major share of that use.

MEDLINEplus is NLM's consumer-friendly source of up-to-date health information, with countless resources on health and wellness topics. Consumers and health professionals are using MEDLINEplus as the source of the most reliable and most accurate health information available on the World Wide Web. It receives more than 70 million hits each year.

This year NLM announced that it would cease publishing the *Cumulated Index Medicus (CIM)* with the 2000 edition (volume 41). The publication of the monthly Index *Medicus* is not affected. The production of the first CIM in 1960 was a major achievement of the Index Mechanization Project, which predated the computerized MEDLARS system. For decades, CIM enhanced access to the biomedical literature, but its utility had declined as online access to MEDLINE data increased and sales of *CIM* from the U.S. Government Printing Office decreased; it was no longer economically sensible for NLM to undertake the expense of its creation.

Databases

MEDLINE is the online file of 12 million references to and abstracts of articles from more than 4,500 biomedical serial publications. It covers 1966 to the present, and NLM is now converting printed data from earlier years. In 1997 NLM realized it was not efficient to continue to use keyboarding to add citations and abstracts to MEDLINE. NLM then developed an in-house capability to scan citations and correct any errors by using optical character recognition (OCR) techniques. At the same time, the library developed a standard for accepting electronic submissions directly from publishers. Both these efforts have been successful, and today only 21 percent of MEDLINE data is keyboarded. Fifty-six percent is received electronically from publishers and 23 percent is scanned at NLM. The library is working with the Association of American Publishers to help smaller publishers and those in developing countries who lack the technical skills to supply the data electronically.

PubMed, the free Web-based system for accessing MEDLINE, continues to be improved. For example, it now provides links to some 2,100 of the journals represented in MEDLINE, offering users access to the full text of many articles referenced in the database. Where such links are not available, the PubMed user can invoke the Loansome Doc feature to place an online order via interlibrary loan.

ClinicalTrials.gov became available in February 2000 and hosts more than 5,000 visitors daily. The database is a registry of some 5,700 trials at more than 50,000 locations for both federally and privately funded trials of experimental treatments for serious or life-threatening diseases. Most of the studies are in the United States and Canada, but about 70 countries are represented in all. ClinicalTrials.gov includes a statement of purpose for each study, together with the recruiting status, the criteria for patient participation in the trial, the location of the trial, and specific contact information. NLM is working with the Food and Drug Administration to receive more clinical trial data from pharmaceutical firms and others in the private sector.

In keeping with the emphasis on health information for consumers, NLM this year created a searchable subset of MEDLINE on the subject of complementary and alternative medicine. This subset contains more than 220,000 records and will grow as more articles are published in peer-reviewed journals. Another database introduced in 2001 and aimed at the public, albeit a targeted public, is ArcticHealth. This database provides access to evaluated health information affecting Native American populations of the far North from hundreds of local, state, national, and international agencies, as well as from professional societies and universities. ArcticHealth has sections devoted to chronic diseases, behavioral issues, traditional medicine, pollution, and environmental justice. This is the first in what may become a series of NLM health information Web sites for special populations.

Three Nobel prize-winning scientists have been added to NLM's Web site Profiles in Science. They are biochemist Christian Anfinsen, molecular biologist Marshall Nirenberg, and geneticist Barbara McClintock. Profiles in Science features illuminating correspondence, laboratory notes, unpublished manuscripts, and photographs from outstanding scientific careers. This site, begun in 1998, is now becoming a major online resource for storing the public and private—and sometimes intimate—papers of this century's greatest biomedical scientists. Profiles in Science now features the papers of seven researchers.

PubMedCentral, a digital archive of life sciences journal literature, was announced in 2000 by NLM's National Center for Biotechnology Information. Publishers electronically send peer-reviewed, primary research articles to be included in PubMedCentral. They may also deposit other materials, such as review articles, essays, and editorials. A journal may deposit material as soon as it is published, or it may delay release for a specified period of time. NLM guarantees free access to the material; copyright remains with the publisher or the author. There are, at present, a dozen journals in PubMedCentral, with more soon to come online.

MEDLINEplus

In an effort to arm the public with more useful information about health, NLM in 1998 introduced MEDLINEplus. This is a source of authoritative, full-text health information from the institutes and a variety of nonfederal sources. MEDLINEplus has grown tremendously, both in terms of its coverage of the broad health field and its usage on the Web by the public. As of December 2001 it was being consulted some 6 million times each month. The "health topics," containing detailed consumer information on various diseases and health conditions, have increased from the original two dozen to more than 500. A new addition to MEDLINEplus in 2001 was a series of 60 illustrated, interactive patient tutorials on a variety of commonly encountered medical conditions. They are in language that is accessible to the general public, and some are in Spanish. A popular new feature on MEDLINEplus is a daily news feed from the public media (Associated Press, Reuters, *New York Times*) on health-related topics.

Other information available through MEDLINEplus includes medical dictionaries, an extensive medical encyclopedia written in lay language with thousands of illustrations, detailed information from the *United States Pharmacopoeia* about more than 9,000 drugs (over-the-counter as well as brand name and generic prescription), directories of health professionals and hospitals, and links to organizations and libraries that provide health information for the public. The library is seeking to add more Spanish-language material to MEDLINEplus.

NLM has also learned that health professionals of all kinds find MEDLINEplus to be an excellent source of information. Many physicians use it to keep up-to-date on medical subjects outside of their specialty. Others refer their patients to MEDLINEplus for up-to-date and authoritative information about their health conditions. One reason they feel comfortable in doing this is that they trust the imprimatur of NIH and NLM. They know that NLM information specialists follow strict guidelines to select Web pages that are appropriate to the audience level, well-organized, easy to use, and educational in nature, and that do not sell a product or service. NLM librarians make sure each linked source is dependable (with an advisory board whose names are listed), and is consistently and reliably maintained.

National Network

The goal of the National Network of Libraries of Medicine (NN/LM) is to provide health professionals, researchers, educators, administrators, and members of the general public with timely, convenient access to medical information resources. NN/LM strives to ensure that accurate and up-to-date information is available irrespective of the user's geographic location. The network, created by NLM in the 1960s, today consists of more than 4,700 health sciences libraries, including hospital and academic medical center libraries.

On May 1, 2001, new five-year contracts became effective to operate the eight regional medical libraries. Site visits were done for all regions where more than one institution had submitted a proposal to serve as the regional medical library. The 2001–2006 NN/LM program continues the focus on outreach to health professionals, particularly those serving minority groups and working in rural areas and inner cities, but it also increases the emphasis on outreach to the general public. The goal is to increase partnerships between NN/LM and a range of organizations (including public libraries, state libraries, health departments, tribal colleges, schools, churches, and other community-based organizations) as a means of improving public access to health information. A new category of affiliate NN/LM membership has been defined for organizations that deliver health information but do not have extensive collections of paper-based health information. Also awarded were contracts to operate three special centers—the National Training Center and Clearinghouse, the Outreach Evaluation Resource Center, and the National Outreach Mapping Center.

On January 10–11, 2001, NLM cosponsored a conference focused on helping public library patrons find reliable health information. Organized by NLM, the Medical Library Association, and the Public Library Association, this first-ever conference introduced librarians and library staff to health information resources and collection development and to training in searching health and medical databases.

Research and Development

On February 13, 2001, NLM's National Center for Biotechnology Information (NCBI) announced that the DNA sequence of the human genome is now freely accessible to all, for public or private use, on the Center's Web site. An ongoing research challenge is to piece together and analyze the multitudinous data produced by scientists around the world. NCBI has completed its first assembly of the DNA sequence; the result is an organized and easily accessible resource that includes labels that point to important regions of the sequence, such as those containing genes. Using new search and analysis tools, scientists can, for example, find a gene's location in the genome, find other genes in the same region, correlate diseases and genes, find out if a similar gene exists in another organism, and see genetic variations.

NLM's Lister Hill National Center for Biomedical Communications conducts and sponsors a wide-ranging program of research and development in biomedical communications. One well-known program, the Visible Human Project, is an example of an activity that requires both advanced computing techniques and the capability of the Next Generation Internet if it is to be maximally useful. The Visible Human male and female data sets, consisting of MRI, CT, and photographic cryosection images, were released by NLM as national resources in 1994 and 1995. The data sets are huge, totaling some 55 gigabytes, and are being used in a wide range of educational, diagnostic, treatment planning, virtual reality, artistic, mathematical, and industrial applications by more than 1,700 licensees in 43 countries. The data sets can be obtained over the Internet without charge from NLM and from four mirror sites, two in Asia and two in Europe.

In medical education, the Visible Humans are becoming the touchstone of 21st century anatomy. Projects run the gamut from teaching anatomy to practicing endoscopic procedures to rehearsing surgery. NLM's AnatLine is a Web-based image delivery system that provides retrieval access (even from a home computer) to large anatomical image files of various parts of the Visible Human male thoracic region, such as the heart and stomach, including three-dimensional images. NLM is collaborating with other NIH institutes to develop an extremely detailed, Web-accessible, interactive, three-dimensional, functional anatomy atlas of the head and neck. This atlas will be used both in educational models for the functional processes of facial expression, mastication, deglutition, phonation, hearing, and vision, and for surgical planning by maxillofacial specialists.

The Lister Hill center also has an active program of support for telemedicine. Telecommunications technology is used for medical diagnosis and patient care and as a medium for delivering medical services to sites that are at a distance from the provider. The concept of telemedicine encompasses everything from the use of standard telephone service to the high-speed, wide-bandwidth transmission of digitized signals in conjunction with computers, fiber optics, satellites, and other sophisticated peripheral equipment and software. NLM has used a variety of mechanisms in the past several years to fund innovative telemedicine projects that demonstrate the application and use of the capabilities of the Next Generation Internet. One example is the NLM-supported "A Clinic in Every Home." Building on work successfully done under an existing contract with NLM, this pilot project provides medically underserved rural Iowa residents with access to high-quality health care. The expectation is that using such a system will both raise the quality of health care and lower healthcare costs.

NLM for several years has had a telemedicine/connections program for Native Americans in the Pacific Northwest, conducted through the regional medical library for that area. The project connects tribal educational and health facilities to the Internet and thus relieves this vulnerable population's isolation from quality health information and health care. Many of the involved communities

(16 villages and tribes in Alaska, Washington, Idaho, Montana, and Oregon) are in isolated rural areas. In another project, at the University of Alaska in Anchorage, doctors are using "store and forward" telemedicine technology to assist health aides in isolated Native American frontier villages to diagnose ear infections correctly and thus prevent the overuse of antibiotics. If the village health aide cannot definitively diagnose an ear infection, a full-color digital picture of the eardrum is captured and sent as an e-mail attachment to the specialist at the hospital. The specialist makes the diagnosis, determines the course of treatment, and telephones the health aide with the findings.

The library has a program of grants to fund the development of health information resources in medical institutions and to support medical informatics research and training. In one especially important aspect of this program, NLM has assumed a role in ensuring that the nation's biomedical research enterprise has professionals trained in computational biology, including mathematical modeling in the life sciences, advanced imaging, and molecular biology. The library supports 12 training programs at universities across the nation for the express purpose of training experts to carry out research in general informatics and in the genome-related specialty of bioinformatics.

Administration

The director of the library, Donald A. B. Lindberg, M.D., is guided in matters of policy by a board of regents consisting of 10 appointed and 11 ex officio members. Appointed as regents in 2001 were Richard H. Dean, president, Wake Forest University Health Sciences, and William W. Stead, professor of Biomedical Informatics at Vanderbilt University. The most urgent subject discussed by the regents continues to be the need for more space for the library's increasing collections and the expanding programs associated with the National Center for Biotechnology Information.

Table 1 / Selected NLM Statistics*

Library Operation	Volume
Collection (book and nonbook)	6,204,000
Items cataloged	20,000
Serial titles received	20,300
Articles indexed for MEDLINE	463,000
Circulation requests processed	688,000
For interlibrary loan	339,000
For on-site users	349,000
Computerized searches (all databases)	313,000,000
Budget authority	$250,757,000
Staff	656

*For the year ending September 30, 2001

United States Government Printing Office

North Capitol and H Sts. N.W., Washington, DC 20401
202-512-1991
E-mail asherman@gpo.gov
World Wide Web http://www.gpo.gov

Andrew M. Sherman
Director, Office of Congressional and Public Affairs

The Government Printing Office (GPO) is part of the legislative branch of the federal government and operates under the authority of the public printing and documents chapters of Title 44 of the U.S. Code. Created primarily to satisfy the printing needs of Congress, today GPO is the focal point for printing, binding, and information dissemination for the entire federal community. In addition to Congress, approximately 130 federal departments and agencies—representing more than 6,000 government units—rely on GPO's services. Congressional documents, Supreme Court decisions, federal regulations and reports, IRS tax forms, and U.S. passports are all produced by or through GPO.

Traditionally, GPO's mission was accomplished through production and procurement of ink-on-paper printing. Today, after more than a generation of experience with electronic printing systems, GPO is at the forefront in providing government information through a wide range of formats, including printing, microfiche, CD-ROM, and online technology through GPO Access (http://www.gpo.gov/gpoaccess).

GPO's central office facility is located in Washington, D.C. Nationwide, GPO maintains 14 regional printing procurement offices, six satellite procurement facilities, a field printing office, a major distribution facility in Pueblo, Colorado, a nationwide network of bookstores, and a retail sales outlet at its publications warehouse in Laurel, Maryland.

This report focuses on GPO's role as the disseminator of government information in print and electronic formats.

Superintendent of Documents

GPO's documents programs, overseen by the Superintendent of Documents, disseminate one of the world's largest volumes of informational literature. In fiscal year (FY) 2001 GPO distributed approximately 30 million government publications in tangible print, microform, and electronic formats. In addition, approximately 31 million documents were downloaded each month from GPO Access.

Library Programs Service

Within GPO, the Library Programs Service (LPS) is charged with the administration of the Federal Depository Library Program (FDLP), the Cataloging and Indexing Program, and the distribution component of the International Exchange Program of the Library of Congress. These programs are accomplished through the basic functions of LPS:

- Acquisition, classification, and bibliographic control of government publications in all formats
- Distribution and format conversion of tangible government publications
- Assuring permanent public access to all publications in the 1,313 federal depository libraries, with particular attention to the current and ongoing accessibility of electronic government publications
- Inspection of depository libraries for compliance with statutory requirements
- Provision of continuing education and training initiatives that strengthen the ability of depository library personnel to serve the public

The transition to a more electronic FDLP, begun in 1996 as required by Congress, has continued in line with the overall trends in government publishing. In accordance with recently announced policy, LPS now prefers the electronic version of government publications for FDLP even if the publication originated when the originating agency was still publishing in a tangible format, provided that the electronic version is exactly comparable in content to the printed version and that it is fully accessible.

In FY 2001 about 60 percent of the titles in FDLP were available online. This change has been reflected in the LPS organization. Additional resources have become increasingly necessary for the discovery, classification, cataloging, and archiving of electronic publications.

LPS also began the process of acquiring an up-to-date library cataloging and data management system, typically referred to as an integrated library system (ILS). The system will enhance LPS's ability to perform the statutorily authorized functions of the Cataloging and Indexing Program and FDLP.

FDLP Publication Dissemination

FDLP has become a primarily electronic program. Under policies articulated early in FY 2001, government publications are furnished to federal depository libraries solely in online electronic format unless certain circumstances or criteria exist. As a result, there is now a higher proportion of online-only titles in FDLP than ever before.

Many format changes begun in FY 2000 are now in effect, resulting in a 29 percent reduction in the number of FDLP paper titles. There has been an even sharper reduction in the number of microfiche titles, due in large measure to discontinuing the dissemination of congressional bills in microfiche at the end of the 106th Congress.

In July 2001 a total of 22,865 additional online titles were made available via GPO Access. Overall, 59 percent of the titles disseminated in FY 2001 were online, compared to 53 percent in FY 2000. Table 1 shows the distribution of publications by FDLP in FY 1999, 2000, and 2001.

The downturn in the number of new links to online publications at other agency sites was caused primarily by a reduction in the new additions to the Department of Energy partnership sites, particularly the DOE Information Bridge

Table 1 / Distribution of Publications by FDLP,
FY 1999–2001

Medium	FY 1999	FY 2000	FY 2001
Online (GPO Access)	17,885	11,715	15,235
Online (other agency sites)	14,166	20,951	7,630
Paper (includes USGS maps)	13,103	13,660	9,522
Microfiche	25,740	14,572	4,726
CD-ROM, DVD	682	617	480
Total	71,576	61,515	37,593

(http://www.osti.gov/bridge). LPS operations to identify, catalog, and link to external resources continued at a steady pace.

Policy Guidance Developed

In January 2001 the Superintendent of Documents issued policy guidance, produced with library community input, concerning the distribution of titles in electronic and tangible formats. The resulting document SOD 71, "Dissemination/Distribution Policy for the FDLP," and the related list of "Essential Titles for Public Use in Paper Format" are important working documents for LPS staff to use in acquiring publications for FDLP. SOD 71 and the "Essential Titles" list are available on the FDLP Desktop (http://www.access.gpo.gov/su_docs/fdlp/pubs/estitles.html).

Cataloging Developments

The Cataloging and Indexing Program managed by LPS has an important role in providing access to online resources through bibliographic control. As a center for government publications cataloging, LPS has expanded its cataloging and locator services efforts and moved beyond the traditional *Monthly Catalog* as its principal output.

State Plans Initiative

In August 2001 the Superintendent of Documents asked the directors of depository libraries for their support and assistance in revising the state plans for the delivery of FDLP services. About 20 years ago, many depositories and state library agencies worked together to develop state plans for the delivery of depository services within their states or service areas. Since then, much has changed both in FDLP and in the way libraries receive and deliver information in general. From GPO's perspective, among the benefits of the state plan process is the opportunity to strengthen the relationship among all of the depositories in a state or service area, to coordinate with other library and information planning initiatives, and ultimately to provide improved, cost-effective library services to the citizens. A number of states have begun revising their plans in accordance with current service needs.

Web Document Digital Archive Pilot Project

LPS and OCLC, Inc., are testing the initial release of a system to locate, identify, process, describe, catalog, and archive electronic government publications. The Web Document Digital Archive Pilot Project has recently expanded to include several other partners, including the State Library of Connecticut and the State Library of Ohio. The proposed system will incorporate a mix of new and existing solutions in an effort to refine and integrate LPS workflow and routines for processing and storing e-titles for the long term.

GPO is a full partner in this project and its staff has worked closely with OCLC, providing input in the development process. Archiving functionality will be provided in 2002. In September 2001 ten LPS staff received intensive hands-on training, paving the way for LPS participation in phase one of the project.

LPS's own archive of electronic publications continues to evolve and grow. The highest-priority candidates for this digital archiving remain agency publications that are primarily textual or images of text and that have no tangible counterpart in FDLP. Information about the operation of the FDLP/EC Archive can be found at http://www.gpo.gov/ppa/resources.html.

Systems Modernization

The transition to a more electronic FDLP has given GPO and LPS a distributed library collection of electronic resources to manage and maintain. To meet these requirements, mandated by Chapter 41 of Title 44, LPS is in the process of acquiring an up-to-date library cataloging and data management system that will enhance its ability to perform the statutorily authorized functions of the Cataloging and Indexing Program and FDLP, the type of system known as an integrated library system (ILS). LPS efforts to integrate its technical services operations and to manage and improve public access to electronic resources should improve with the acquisition of an ILS.

LPS Outreach

In 2002 LPS staff will attend American Library Association conferences and Depository Library Council meetings. LPS staff will also make presentations on various aspects of FDLP and the Cataloging and Indexing Program in a variety of other venues relating to government information.

The annual Interagency Depository Seminar, designed for newly appointed staff of federal depository libraries, is held each spring in Washington, D.C. The Federal Depository Conference, which regularly attracts more than 500 information professionals, is held each October.

GPO Access

GPO Access (http://www.gpo.gov/gpoaccess) provides free public access to electronic information products from all three branches of the federal government, as established by the Government Printing Office Electronic Information Access

Enhancement Act of 1993 (P.L. 103-40). GPO Access now contains more than 2,200 separate databases via more than 80 applications. The dynamic collection of GPO Access in its entirety now totals more than 224,000 titles. GPO Access houses more than 130,000 titles on its servers and provides links to more than 94,000 titles on other federal government Web sites.

Improvements to Web Site and Government Information Applications

GPO continues to add new resources and improve the existing resources on GPO Access. The following is a list of enhancements to the Web site that were introduced in FY 2001:

- *Hinds' Precedents of the House of Representatives* is the compilation of Asher C. Hinds's early precedents of the House of Representatives dating from the First Congress. Hinds was Clerk at the Speaker's Table of the House of Representatives from 1895 to 1910. These materials were prepared and published by authority of an act of Congress approved March 4, 1907. The five-volume series provides coverage of the historical origins and evolution of House procedures dating back to 1789.

- Davis-Bacon Wage Determinations contains wage determinations issued by the U.S. Department of Labor under the Davis-Bacon and Related Acts. GPO Access contains the Davis-Bacon Wage Determinations from March 2, 2001, forward.

- A browseable interface to the *Weekly Compilation of Presidential Documents* was released in January 2001. The browse feature allows users to view documents from an HTML-linked table of contents and offers an alternative to using the search function to locate documents. The *Weekly Compilation* contains statements, messages, and other presidential materials released by the White House during the preceding week. GPO Access contains data from January 11, 1993, to the present, with the browse feature available effective with the January 8, 2001, issue.

- A browseable interface to the *United States Code* was released in December 2000. This feature allows users to browse individual titles down to the section level for the latest available edition and supplement.

Finding Aids and Access to Collections of Government Information

GPO Access Finding Aids act as a portal to information available on government Web sites. These tools can be used to conduct government-wide searches, locate government publications both online and in print, and find agency Web sites based on broad subject areas. There were two important enhancements to the finding aids in FY 2001:

- A FirstGov search interface has been added to provide greater accessibility to government information. This tool enables users to search for official federal government information on GPO Access alone or throughout the federal government.

- An Agency Publications Indexes finding aid now allows users to search the indexes created by federal agencies to identify their publications. Some databases provide indexing to related nongovernment literature. Users can retrieve bibliographic citations and, when available, the full text of a document. Many of these indices can trace their origins to printed bibliographic indices that are or were once distributed to federal depository libraries.

New Hosted Web Sites

GPO currently hosts Web sites for 17 federal agencies as well as a number of online federal publications. Recent additions include:

- The U.S. Commission on National Security/21st Century Web site. The purpose of this commission was to provide the most comprehensive government-sponsored review of U.S. national security in more than 50 years. This archived site contains reports, news, and the commission's charter.
- The U.S.-China Security Review Commission Web site. This commission's mandate is to study, investigate, assess, and report to Congress on the economic and security implications of the bilateral economic relationship between the United States and the People's Republic of China. The site contains the commission's charter, information on members, and press releases.

Search Engine Evaluations

One of the most popular ways for users to find the resources available via GPO Access is through major Internet search engines and directories. As a result, GPO is now involved in an ongoing effort to improve the visibility of GPO Access pages in major search engines and directories. The most recent evaluation conducted showed an overall increase in the positioning of GPO Access pages in the 23 search engines studied. The measures undertaken to improve positioning include constant re-evaluation of traditional metatags and inserting Dublin Core metadata into a number of GPO Access pages. (The Dublin Core is an initiative that is attempting to adopt a common set of elements for resource description. It is composed of 15 different elements to be embedded within the HTML metadata of Web pages.) GPO has also procured a software package and subscribed to a fee-based service to assist in the process of URL submission.

GPOLISTSERV

GPOLISTSERV (http://listserv.access.gpo.gov) gives users a quick and easy way to receive up-to-date information on various resources available via GPO Access. Customers can subscribe to e-mail listservs moderated by GPO or hosted on GPO Access for other federal agencies. Current lists available include the *Federal Register* Table of Contents and Merit Systems Protection Board Decisions and Studies Lists. Lists of new products for sale by the Superintendent of Documents are also now available; this service can be found at http://bookstore.gpo.gov/alertservice.html.

Training Classes, Demonstrations, and Trade Shows

The growth of GPO Access continued to generate requests for training classes and demonstrations to help educate users about electronic products and services available through the Superintendent of Documents. During FY 2001 GPO's Office of Electronic Information Dissemination (EIDS) staff conducted 10 hands-on training classes and demonstrations of GPO Access for federal depository librarians, members of Congress, and the general public, both locally and across the country. Recent sessions were conducted in Minneapolis, San Francisco, and Pasadena.

Methods of Access

To serve a large base of users with varying technological capabilities, GPO Access supports a wide range of information dissemination technologies, from the latest Internet applications to dial-up modem access. Methods compatible with technologies to assist users affected by the Americans with Disabilities Act are also available. To accommodate people without computers, more than 1,300 federal depository libraries throughout the country have public-access workstations for GPO Access usage.

Section 508

The Workforce Investment Act of 1998 amended Section 508 of the Rehabilitation Act of 1973 to include accessibility requirements for electronic and information technology. Section 508 now requires that electronic and information technology used by the federal government, including its Web sites, be made as accessible for people with disabilities as it is for people without disabilities. Although Section 508 currently applies only to executive branch agencies, GPO is committed to ensuring that new and existing GPO Access Web pages along with pages on hosted sites meet the standards outlined in Section 508.

GPO Access Usage Statistics

To accurately reflect Web site usage, GPO Access usage statistics are measured in the number of document retrievals. Document retrievals indicate the number of downloads of documents within databases as well as files outside databases that have been identified as containing government information content. More than 26 million retrievals in October 2000 propelled total usage of GPO Access to more than 1 billion documents retrieved since the service premiered in 1994. Today GPO Access customers download more than 31 million documents each month, or approximately 1.5 terabytes of official government information. This equates to about 750 million typewritten pages.

Recognition

The success of GPO Access is visible not only in usage statistics, but also in the numerous awards and commendations that the service has received from organizations, publications, and other Web sites. Highlights for FY 2001 include:

- Lightspan's StudyWeb (http://www.studyweb.com), one of the Internet's premier sites for educational resources for students and teachers, selected the "U.S. Constitution: Analysis and Interpretation" application available via GPO Access as one of the best educational resources on the Web.
- The Public Papers of the Presidents of the United States database was included in the Current Web Contents section of the ISI: Fully Integrated e-Information Solutions Site (http://www.isinet.com/isi/products/cc/cwc/webselect.html).
- The Congressional Bills database on GPO Access was featured in the legislative branch section of GovSpot.com (http://www.govspot.com).
- CBDNet was inserted in the e-government global portal (http://www.egov.it/egovie/index.html).
- The FDLP Desktop site was featured on the Internet Law Web site (http://www.internetlawweb.com/egovernment.htm) under the heading E-Government Law Links.
- LibrarySpot.com (http://www.libraryspot.com), an award-winning library and reference portal, selected the U.S. Supreme Court Web site hosted by GPO Access to be featured among the best and most useful library and reference sites online.
- GPO Access received an E-Gov 2001 Trail Blazer award.

User Support

Customers needing assistance using GPO Access can contact the GPO Access User Support Team. These specialists are available Monday through Friday (except federal holidays) from 7 A.M. to 5:30 P.M. On average, the team receives 6,300 inquiries a month, including approximately 4,100 phone calls and 2,200 e-mail messages. The team can be reached by telephone at 202-512-1530 (Washington, D.C., area), toll-free at 888-293-6498, by fax at 202-512-1262, and by e-mail at gpoaccess@gpo.gov.

Ben's Guide to U.S. Government for Kids

Introduced in December 1999, Ben's Guide to U.S. Government for Kids (Ben's Guide) (http://bensguide.gpo.gov) is the educational component of GPO Access. Using Benjamin Franklin as a guide, the site is designed to teach how the government works, how to use the primary source materials of GPO Access, and how to access information about the activities of the government. The site is broken down into four grade levels: K–2, 3–5, 6–8, and 9–12, and also provides an area for parents and educators. The material in each of these sections is specifically tailored to its intended audience. Ben's Guide includes historical documents and information on the legislative and regulatory processes, elections, and citizenship. The site also features learning activities and a list of federal Web sites designed for children.

Visitors with government-related questions, comments, or suggestions for this site can e-mail askben@gpo.gov and receive a response within 24 hours. Ben's Guide has recorded more than 6.5 million retrievals since its debut.

In May 2001 GPO had the opportunity to gather feedback from students in the first, fifth, and seventh grades on various aspects of Ben's Guide. The focus group was held in conjunction with the Long Island (New York) Library Conference. This was the first time Ben's Guide was the sole subject for a focus group, as well as the first time the site was tested by its target audiences.

For FY 2001, Ben's Guide to U.S. Government for Kids received recognition from Skewl Sites Newsletter, ConnectingStudents.com, SurfNetKids.com, StudyWeb.com, FirstGov.gov, the *Philadelphia Inquirer,* and the *Newsletter of the Documents Interest Group of Oregon* (DIGOR).

Sales

The Superintendent of Documents' sales program currently offers approximately 10,000 government publications on a wide array of subjects. These are sold principally via mail, telephone, fax, electronic, and e-mail orders, as well as through GPO bookstores across the country. The program operates on a cost-recovery basis. Publications for sale include books, forms, posters, pamphlets, maps, CD-ROMs, computer diskettes, and magnetic tapes. Subscription services for both dated periodicals and basic-and-supplement services (involving an initial volume and supplemental issues) are also offered.

Express service, which includes priority handling and Federal Express delivery, is available for orders placed by telephone for domestic delivery. Orders placed before noon Eastern time for in-stock publications and single-copy subscriptions will be delivered within two working days. Some quantity restrictions apply. Call the telephone order desk toll-free at 866-512-1800 (202-512-1800 within the Washington, D.C., area) for more information.

Consumer-oriented publications are also either sold or distributed at no charge through the Consumer Information Center, in Pueblo, Colorado, which GPO operates on behalf of the General Services Administration.

New Sales Program Products

The sales program continued its efforts to conclude cooperative ventures to obtain, promote, and sell products not printed or procured by GPO, as well as products produced by federal agencies in cooperation with other parties. Ongoing projects with the Department of Commerce's Bureau of Export Administration and National Technical Information Service, the Central Intelligence Agency, the Defense Acquisition Agency, the Department of State, the Library of Congress, and the National Imaging and Mapping Agency are continuing. Ventures under development include new partnerships with the General Services Administration.

Product Information

The U.S. Government Online Bookstore (http://bookstore.gpo.gov) is the single point of access for all government information products available for sale from GPO. A search interface with the Sales Product Catalog, a guide to current government information products offered for sale through the Superintendent of Documents (updated every working day), is part of the main page interface.

Advanced search options are also available. Another feature on the main page is a pop-up box that enables customers to browse a topic. This list of topics is based upon the approximately 160 Subject Bibliographies available through the online bookstore. Customers using the Online Bookstore can also browse the "special collections," including CD-ROMs, electronic products, the subscriptions catalog, and the Federal Consumer Information Center. New special collections include a list of emergency-response publications and a catalog of regulatory and legal publications. The Online Bookstore also provides ordering information and information on the locations of GPO bookstores.

Items purchased from the U.S. Government Online Bookstore are now assigned a unique GPO order number, which is useful when contacting GPO's Order Division with questions about an order. A detailed transaction receipt is provided after each order submission, and a copy of the transaction receipt is sent to the customer's e-mail address if provided on the online order form. In addition, customers can now choose the American Express payment option when ordering, in addition to VISA, MasterCard, and Discover/Novus.

GPO publishes a variety of free print catalogs covering hundreds of information products for sale on a vast array of subjects. The free catalogs include

- *U.S. Government Information*—new and popular information products of interest to the general public
- *New Products*—listing of new titles; distributed to librarians and other information professionals
- *U.S. Government Subscriptions*—periodicals and other subscription services
- *Subject Bibliographies* (*SB*s)—approximately 160 lists, each containing titles relating to a single subject or field of interest
- *Subject Bibliography Index*—lists all *SB* subject areas
- *Catalog of Information Products for Business*—GPO's main catalog for business audiences

U.S. Government Subscriptions and Subject Bibliographies are also available via the Internet at http://www.access.gpo.gov/su_docs.

Customers can also register to receive e-mail updates when new publications become available for sale from the Superintendent of Documents through the "New Titles by Topic" e-mail alert service. Anyone can sign up for one or more of the following lists free of charge: Business Publications, Elementary and Secondary Education, Defense and Security, Health Care, Military History, and Travel and Tourism. This service can be accessed at http://bookstore.gpo.gov/alertservice.html.

The sales program also lists its titles on Amazon.com, BarnesandNoble.com, and other online commercial bookselling sites.

GPO Bookstores

Publications of particular public interest are made available in GPO bookstores in major cities throughout the United States. In addition, any bookstore can order any government information product currently offered for sale by the Superintendent of Documents and have it sent directly to a customer. Customers can order from any GPO bookstore by phone, mail, or fax.

An ongoing effort is being made to identify and close GPO bookstores not able to recover their operating expenses. As a result, the bookstores in San Francisco, Boston, Philadelphia, and one of the two stores in Washington, D.C., were closed in FY 2001.

The addresses, hours, and a map of all bookstores currently in operation are available on GPO's Web site.

National Technical Information Service

Technology Administration
U.S. Department of Commerce, Springfield, VA 22161
800-553-NTIS (6847) or 703-605-6000
World Wide Web http://www.ntis.gov

Linda Davis
Marketing Communications

The National Technical Information Service (NTIS) serves as the nation's largest central source and primary disseminator of scientific, technical, engineering, and business information produced or sponsored by U.S. and international government sources. NTIS is a federal agency within the Technology Administration of the U.S. Department of Commerce.

Historical Background

Since 1945, the NTIS mission has been to operate a central U.S. government access point for scientific and technical information useful to American industry and government. NTIS maintains a permanent archive of this information for researchers, businesses, and the public to access quickly and easily. Release of the information is intended to promote American economic growth and development and increase U.S. competitiveness in the world market.

The NTIS collection of approximately 3 million titles contains products available in various formats, including reports describing research conducted or sponsored by federal agencies and their contractors, statistical and business information, U.S. military publications, multimedia training programs, computer software and electronic databases developed by federal agencies, and technical reports prepared by research organizations worldwide. Approximately 60,000 new titles are added and indexed annually.

More than 200 U.S. government agencies contribute to the NTIS collection including the National Aeronautics and Space Agency, the Environmental Protection Agency, the departments of Agriculture, Commerce, Defense, Energy, Health and Human Services, Interior, Labor, Treasury, Veterans Affairs, Housing and Urban Development, Education, Transportation, and numerous other agencies. International contributors include Canada, Japan, Britain, and several European countries.

NTIS now offers a Web-based service for those seeking to access the latest government scientific and technical research information online. Visitors to http://www.ntis.gov can search more than 750,000 database records dating back to 1990, free of charge; download online technical reports, many free of charge, others for $8.95; access links to online documents on other government agency Web sites; and—if the agency removes the report from its Web site—access the permanent NTIS archived copy for a nominal fee.

NTIS Database

The NTIS Database (listings of information products acquired by NTIS since 1964) offers unparalleled bibliographic coverage of U.S. government and world-wide government-sponsored research. Its contents represent hundreds of billions of research dollars and cover a range of important topics that includes agriculture, biotechnology, business, communication, energy, engineering, the environment, health and safety, medicine, research and development, science, space, technology, transportation, and more.

Most records include abstracts. Database summaries describe technical reports, data files, multimedia training programs, and software. These titles are often unique to NTIS and generally are difficult to locate from any other source. The complete NTIS Database provides instant access to more than 2 million records.

Free 30-day trials of the database are available through the GOV.Research_ Center (http://grc.ntis.gov). The database can be leased directly from NTIS; it can also be accessed through the following commercial services: Cambridge Scientific Abstracts, 800-843-7751, http://www.csa.com; DATA-STAR (DIALOG), 800-334-2564, http://www.dialog.com; EBSCO, 800-653-2726, http://www. epnet.com; Knowledge EXPRESS, 800-529-5337, http://www.knowledge express.com; NERAC 860-872-7000, http://www.nerac.com; NISC/NTIS, 800-363-2068; Ovid Technologies, 800-950-2035, http://www.ovid.com; Questel-Orbit, 800-456-7248, http://www.questel.orbit.com; SilverPlatter Information, 800-343-0064, http://www.silverplatter.com; and STN International/CAS, 800-848-6533, http://www.cas.org.

To lease the NTIS Database directly from NTIS, contact the NTIS Subscriptions Department at 800-363-2068 or 703-605-6060. For more information, see http://www.ntis.gov/products/types/databases/ntisdb.asp.

Other Databases Available from NTIS

NTIS offers several valuable research-oriented database products.

FEDRIP

The Federal Research in Progress database (FEDRIP) provides access to information about ongoing federally funded projects in the fields of the physical sciences, engineering, and life sciences. FEDRIP's uniqueness lies in its structure as a nonbibliographic information source on research in progress. Project descriptions generally include project title, keywords, start date, estimated completion date, principal investigator, performing and sponsoring organizations, summary, and progress report. Record content varies depending on the source agency.

There are many reasons to search FEDRIP. Among them: to avoid research duplication, locate sources of support, identify leads in the literature, stimulate ideas for planning, identify gaps in areas of investigation, and locate individuals with expertise. For more information, see http://www.ntis.gov/products/types/ databases/fedrip.asp.

AGRICOLA

The AGRICricultural OnLine Access database (AGRICOLA) is one of the most comprehensive sources of U.S. agricultural and life sciences information. It contains bibliographic records for documents acquired by the National Agricultural Library (NAL) of the U.S. Department of Agriculture. The complete database dates from 1970 and contains more than 3.6 million citations to journal articles, monographs, theses, patents, software, audiovisual materials, and technical reports related to agriculture.

AGRICOLA serves as the document locator and bibliographic control system for the NAL collection. The extensive file provides comprehensive coverage of newly acquired worldwide publications in agriculture and related fields. Subject headings include Agricultural Economics, Agricultural Education, Agricultural Products, Animal Science, Aquaculture, Biotechnology, Botany, Cytology, Energy, Engineering, Feed Science, Fertilizers, Fibers and Textiles, Food and Nutrition, Forestry, Horticulture, Human Ecology, Human Nutrition, Hydrology, Hydroponics, Microbiology, Natural Resources, Pesticides, Physiology, Plant and Animal, Plant Sciences, Public Health, Rural Sociology, Soil Sciences, Veterinary Medicine, Water Quality, and more. For more information on AGRICOLA, see http://www.ntis.gov/products/types/databases/agricola.asp.

AGRIS

The Agricultural Science and Technology database (AGRIS) depends on a cooperative system for collecting and disseminating information on the world's agricultural literature in which more than 100 national and multinational centers take part. References to citations for U.S. publications given coverage in the AGRICOLA database are not included in AGRIS. A large number of citations in AGRIS are not found in any other database. References to nonconventional literature (documents not commercially available) contain information on where a copy can be obtained. The information in AGRIS, much of which can be found nowhere else, includes government documents, technical reports, and nonconventional literature from both developed and developing countries. For more information, see http://www.ntis.gov/products/types/databases/agris.asp.

Energy Science and Technology

The Energy Science and Technology database (EDB) is a multidisciplinary file containing worldwide references to basic and applied scientific and technical research literature. The information is collected for use by government managers, researchers at the national laboratories, and other research efforts sponsored by the U.S. Department of Energy. The results of this research are available to the public. Abstracts are included for records from 1976 to the present. EDB also contains the Nuclear Science Abstracts, a comprehensive abstract and index collection to the international nuclear science and technology literature for the period 1948–1976. Included are scientific and technical reports of the U.S. Atomic Energy Commission, the U.S. Energy Research and Development Administration and its contractors, other agencies, universities, and industrial and research organizations. Approximately 25 percent of the records in the file contain abstracts.

Nuclear Science Abstracts contains more than 900,000 bibliographic records. The entire Energy Science and Technology Database contains more than 3 million bibliographic records. For more information, see http://www.ntis.gov/products/types/databases/engsci.asp.

Immediately Dangerous to Life or Health Concentrations Database

The NIOSH (National Institute for Occupational Safety and Health documentation for the Immediately Dangerous to Life or Health Concentrations database (IDLH) contains air concentration values used by NIOSH as respirator selection criteria. This compilation is the rationale and source of information used by NIOSH during the original determination of 387 IDLHs and their subsequent review and revision in 1994. Toxicologists, persons concerned with the use of respirators, industrial hygienists, persons concerned with indoor air quality, and emergency response personnel will find this product beneficial. This database will enable users to compare NIOSH limits to other limits and will be an important resource for those concerned with acute chemical exposures. For more information, see http://www.ntis.gov/products/types/databases/idlhs.asp.

NIOSH Manual of Analytical Methods

The NIOSH Manual of Analytical Methods database (NMAM) is a compilation of methods for sampling and analysis of contaminants in workplace air and in the bodily fluids of workers who are occupationally exposed to that air. These methods have been developed specifically to have adequate sensitivity to detect the lowest concentrations and sufficient flexibility of range to detect concentrations exceeding safe levels of exposure, as regulated by OSHA and recommended by NIOSH. The Threshold Values and Biological Exposure indices of the American Conference of Governmental Industrial Hygienists are also cited. For more information, see http://www.ntis.gov/products/types/databases/nmam.asp.

NIOSH Pocket Guide to Chemical Hazards

The NIOSH Pocket Guide to Chemical Hazards (NPG) is intended as a quick and convenient source of general industrial hygiene information for workers, employers, and occupational health professionals. The NIOSH Pocket Guide presents key information and data in abbreviated tabular form for chemicals or substance groupings (such as cyanides, fluorides, and manganese compounds) that are found in the work environment. The industrial hygiene information found in NPG should help users recognize and control occupational chemical hazards. The information in NPG includes chemical structures or formulas, identification codes, synonyms, exposure limits, chemical and physical properties, incompatibilities and reactivities, measurement methods, recommended respirator selections, signs and symptoms of exposure, and procedures for emergency treatment. Industrial hygienists, industrial hygiene technicians, safety professionals, occupational health physicians and nurses, and hazardous material managers will find this database a versatile and indispensable tool. For more information, see http://www.ntis.gov/products/types/databases/npgpacts.asp.

NIOSHTIC

NIOSHTIC is a bibliographic database of literature in the field of occupational safety and health developed by NIOSH and has been static since 1988. It contains retrospective information, some dating back to the 19th century. Because NIOSH examines all aspects of adverse effects experienced by workers, much of the information contained in NIOSHTIC has been selected from sources that do not have a primary occupational safety and health orientation. NIOSHTIC subject coverage includes the behavioral sciences; biochemistry, physiology and metabolism; biological hazards; chemistry; control technology; education and training; epidemiological studies of diseases/disorders; ergonomics; hazardous waste; health physics; occupational medicine; pathology and histology; safety; toxicology, and more. For more information, see http://www.ntis.gov/products/types/databases/nioshtic.asp.

Registry of Toxic Effects of Chemical Substances

The Registry of Toxic Effects of Chemical Substances (RTECS) is a database of toxicological information compiled, maintained, and updated by NIOSH. The program is mandated by the Occupational Safety and Health Act of 1970. The original edition, known as the Toxic Substances List, was published on June 28, 1971, and included toxicological data for approximately 5,000 chemicals. Since that time, the list has continuously grown and been updated. RTECS now contains more than 133,000 chemicals as NIOSH strives to fulfill the mandate to list "all known toxic substances . . . and the concentrations at which . . . toxicity is known to occur." RTECS is a compendium of data extracted from the open scientific literature. The data are recorded in the format developed by the RTECS staff and arranged in alphabetical order by prime chemical name. No attempt has been made to evaluate the studies cited in RTECS; the user has the responsibility of making such assessments.

For more information on RTECS, see http://www.ntis.gov/products/types/databases/rtecs.asp. For more information on the databases in general, see http://www.ntis.gov/products/types/databases/data.asp.

Specialized Online Subscriptions

Those wishing to expand their access to subject-specific resources through use of the Internet are likely to benefit from the NTIS online options listed below. Online subscriptions offer quick, convenient online access to the most current information available.

Government Research Center

GOV.Research_Center (GRC) is a collection of well-known, government-sponsored research databases available on the World Wide Web via an online subscription service. Customers can subscribe to a single GRC database product or to several databases. The following databases, made available at GRC by NTIS and NISC, are searchable utilizing NISC's search engine, Biblioline: the NTIS Database, FEDRIP, NIOSHTIC, EDB, AGRICOLA; and RTECS.

NTIS and NISC are constantly improving the content and features of GRC. Users can order documents directly from the NTIS Database by using a credit card or NTIS deposit account. Users can search across all databases within a subscription plan using only one search query. Limited day-pass access to the NTIS Database is available for a nominal fee.

For more information on GOV.Research_Center, see http://grc.ntis.gov.

World News Connection

World News Connection (WNC) is an NTIS online news service accessible via the Internet. WNC provides English-language translations of time-sensitive news and information from thousands of non-U.S. media. Particularly effective in its coverage of local media, WNC provides the power to identify what is happening in a specific country or region. The information is obtained from speeches, television and radio broadcasts, newspaper articles, periodicals, and books, and the subject matter focuses on socioeconomic, political, scientific, technical, and environmental issues and events.

The information in WNC is provided to NTIS by the Foreign Broadcast Information Service (FBIS), a U.S. government agency. For more than 50 years, analysts from FBIS's domestic and overseas bureaus have monitored timely and pertinent open-source material, including gray literature. Uniquely, WNC allows subscribers to take advantage of the intelligence-gathering experience of FBIS.

WNC is updated every government business day. Generally, new information is available within 24 to 72 hours from the time of original publication or broadcast.

Subscribers can conduct unlimited interactive searches and can set up automated searches known as profiles. When a profile is created, a search is run against WNC's latest news feed to identify articles relevant to a subscriber's area of interest. Once the search is completed, the results are automatically sent to the subscriber's e-mail address.

For WNC pricing and subscription information, see http://wnc.fedworld.gov.

U.S. Export Administration Regulations

The U.S. Export Administration Regulations (EAR) provides exporters with the latest rules controlling the export of U.S. dual-use commodities, technology, and software. Step by step, EAR explains when an export license is necessary and when it is not; how to obtain an export license; policy changes as they are issued; new restrictions on exports to certain countries and certain types of items; and where to obtain further help.

This information is now available through NTIS in three formats: looseleaf, CD-ROM, and online. For more information, see http://bxa.fedworld.gov.

Davis-Bacon Wage Determination Database

The Davis-Bacon Wage Determination database subscription product contains wage determinations issued by the U.S. Department of Labor under the mandate of the Davis-Bacon Act and related legislation. The department determines prevailing wage rates for construction-related occupations in most counties in the

United States. All federal government construction contracts and most contracts of more than $2,000 for federally assisted construction must abide by the Davis-Bacon structure. This subscription product offers value-added features such as the electronic delivery of modified wage decisions directly to the user's desktop, the ability to access prior wage decisions issued during the year, extensive Help Desk support, and so forth.

A variety of access plans are available. For more information, see http://davisbacon.fedworld.gov.

Service Contract Act Wage Determination Database

The Service Contract Act Wage Determination database (SCA) contains unsigned copies of the latest wage determinations developed by the U.S. Department of Labor. These wage determinations, issued by the Wage and Hour Division in response to specific notices filed, set the minimum wage on federally funded service contracts. SCA is updated each Tuesday with all wage determinations that were added or revised by the preceding Thursday.

For those federal agencies participating under a memorandum of understanding with the Wage and Hour Division, and meeting all requirements, SCA can be used in the procurement process. For all other users, the wage determinations are for information use only. This data forms a convenient and accurate basis upon which rates can be compared by occupation and geography.

A variety of access plans are available. For more information, see http://servicecontract.fedworld.gov.

Special Subscription Services

NTIS Alerts

More than 1,000 new titles are added to the NTIS collection every week. NTIS Alerts were developed in response to requests from customers to search and tap into this fresh information. NTIS prepares a list of search criteria that is run against all new studies and R&D reports in 16 subject areas. An NTIS Alert provides a twice-monthly information briefing service covering a wide range of technology topics. An NTIS Alert provides numerous benefits: efficient, economical, and timely access to the latest U.S. government technical studies; concise, easy-to-read summaries; information not readily available from any other source; contributions from more than 100 countries; and subheadings designed to identify essential information quickly.

For more information, call the NTIS Subscriptions Department at 703-605-6060 or see http://www.ntis.gov products/types/alerts-printed.asp.

NTIS E-Alerts

NTIS E-Alerts give subscribers online access to the same information as the printed NTIS Alerts. Each week subscribers receive summaries of new titles by e-mail in their choice from one or more of up to 37 subject areas.

For more information, see http://www.ntis.gov/products/types/alerts.asp.

SRIM

Selected Research In Microfiche (SRIM) is an inexpensive, tailored information service that delivers complete full-text microfiche copies of technical reports based upon a customer's needs. Customers choose from Standard SRIM Service (selecting one or more of the 380 existing subject areas) or Custom SRIM Service, which creates a new subject area to meet their particular needs. Custom SRIM requires a one-time fee; otherwise, the cost of Custom SRIM is the same as the Standard SRIM. Through this ongoing subscription service, customers receive microfiche copies of new reports pertaining to their field of interest, as NTIS obtains the reports.

For more information, see http://www.ntis.gov/products/types/srim.asp. Call the NTIS Subscriptions Department at 800-363-2068 or 703-605-6060 to place an order for a SRIM subscription.

Also at NTIS

National Audiovisual Center

The National Audiovisual Center (NAC) makes the U.S. government's collection of federally sponsored or produced audiovisual and multimedia training and educational programs available to state and local governments, businesses, schools, and universities, as well as private individuals.

NAC's collection includes approximately 9,000 active titles covering 600 subject areas from more than 200 federal agencies. Included in the collection are language training materials, occupational safety and health training materials, fire service and law enforcement training materials, drug education programs for schools and industry, fine arts programs, and documentaries chronicling American history.

Call 703-605-6000 for assistance in selecting titles, or visit the NAC Web site http://www.ntis.gov/products/types/audiovisual/index.asp.

Federal Computer Products Center

The Federal Computer Products Center was established at NTIS to provide access to information in electronic formats. The current inventory of computer products includes more than 1,200 titles obtained since 1990 from hundreds of U.S. government agencies. They include datafiles and software on diskette, CD-ROM, and magnetic tape. The products cover a range of topics including banking, business, the environment, health care, health statistics, science, and technology. Most of the center's products are developed or sponsored by the federal government. However, NTIS does announce and distribute products developed by state governments and, in a few cases, by private-sector organizations. Examples include Stream Corridor Restoration, the SSA Death Master File, EPA Water Testing Methods, FDA's Food Code, North American Industry Classification System (NAICS), and the NOAA Dive Manual.

Full descriptions of the software and data available from NTIS can be found on the center's Web site at http://www.ntis.gov/products/types/computer.asp.

NTIS FedWorld

Since 1992 NTIS FedWorld Information Technologies has served as the online locator service for a comprehensive inventory of information disseminated by the federal government. FedWorld helps federal agencies and the public to electronically locate federal government information, both information housed within the NTIS repository and information FedWorld makes accessible through an electronic gateway to other government agencies.

FedWorld is currently meeting the information needs of tens of thousands of customers daily, maximizing the potential of the Internet and the World Wide Web by offering multiple distribution channels for government agencies to disseminate information. Visit FedWorld at http://www.fedworld.gov.

NTIS Customer Service

NTIS's automated systems keep it at the forefront when it comes to customer service. Electronic document storage is fully integrated with NTIS's order-taking process, which allows it to provide rapid reproduction for the most recent additions to the NTIS document collection. Most orders are filled and delivered anywhere in the United States in five to seven business days. Rush service is available for an additional fee.

Key NTIS Contacts for Ordering

Order by Phone

Sales Desk	800-553-6847
8:00 A.M.–6:00 P.M. Eastern time, Monday–Friday	or 703-605-6000
Subscriptions	800-363-2068
8:30 A.M.–5:00 P.M. Eastern time, Monday–Friday	or 703-605-6060
TDD (hearing impaired only)	703-487-4639
8:30 A.M.–5:00 P.M. Eastern time, Monday–Friday.	

Order by Fax

24 hours a day, seven days a week	703-605-6900
To verify receipt of fax, call	703-605-6090
7:00 A.M.–5:00 P.M. Eastern Time Monday–Friday	

Order by Mail

National Technical Information Service
5285 Port Royal Road
Springfield, VA 22161

RUSH Service (available for an additional fee)	800-553-6847
	or 703-605-6000

Note: If requesting RUSH Service, please do not mail your order.

Order Via World Wide Web

Direct and secure online ordering   http://www.ntis.gov

Order Via E-Mail

24 hours a day   orders@ntis.gov.

NTIS understands the concerns customers may have about Internet security when placing an order by e-mail. Customers can register their credit cards at NTIS, thus avoiding the need to send an account number with each e-mail order. To register, call 703-605-6070 between 7:00 A.M. and 5:00 P.M. Eastern time, Monday through Friday.

National Archives and Records Administration

8601 Adelphi Rd., College Park, MD 20740
301-713-6800, World Wide Web http://www.nara.gov

Marion H. Vecchiarelli
Policy and Communications Staff

The National Archives and Records Administration (NARA), an independent federal agency, ensures for the citizen, the public servant, the president, Congress, and the courts ready access to essential evidence that documents the rights of American citizens, the actions of federal officials, and the national experience.

NARA is singular among the world's archives as a unified federal institution that accessions and preserves materials from all three branches of government. NARA assists federal agencies in documenting their activities, administering records management programs, scheduling records, and retiring noncurrent records to federal records centers. The agency also manages the presidential libraries; assists the National Historical Publications and Records Commission in its grant program for state and local records and edited publications of the papers of prominent Americans; publishes the laws, regulations, presidential documents, and other official notices of the federal government; and oversees classification and declassification policy in the federal government through the Information Security Oversight Office. NARA constituents include the federal government, a history-minded public, the media, the archival community, and a broad spectrum of professional associations and researchers in such fields as history, political science, law, library and information services, and genealogy.

The size and breadth of NARA's holdings are staggering. Together, NARA's facilities hold approximately 25.5 million cubic feet of original textual and non-textual materials (more than 7 billion pieces of paper) from the executive, legislative, and judicial branches of the federal government. Its multimedia collections include more than 300,000 reels of motion picture films; 5.5 million maps, charts, and architectural drawings; 257,000 sound and video recordings; nearly 16 million aerial photographs; 35 million still pictures and posters; and 2.3 billion logical data records.

Strategic Directions

NARA's strategic priorities are laid out in *Ready Access to Essential Evidence: The Strategic Plan of the National Archives and Records Administration, 1997–2007,* revised in 2000. Success for the agency as envisioned in the plan will mean reaching four strategic goals:

- Essential evidence will be created, identified, appropriately scheduled, and managed for as long as needed.
- Essential evidence will be easy to access regardless of where it is or where users are for as long as needed.

- All records will be preserved in an appropriate environment for use as long as needed.
- NARA's capabilities for making changes necessary to realize its vision will continuously expand.

The plan lays out strategies for reaching these goals, sets milestone targets for accomplishments through 2007, and identifies measurements for gauging progress. The targets and measurements are further delineated in NARA's Annual Performance Plans.

The Strategic Plan and NARA's Annual Performance Plans and Reports are available on the NARA Web site at http://www.nara.gov/nara/vision or by calling the Policy and Communications Staff at 301-713-7360.

Records and Access

Internet

NARA's Web site provides the most widely available means of electronic access to information about NARA, including directions on how to contact the agency and do research at its facilities; descriptions of its holdings in an online catalog; digital copies of selected archival documents; electronic mailboxes for customer questions, comments, and complaints; an automated index to the John F. Kennedy assassination records collection; electronic versions of *Federal Register* publications; online exhibits; and classroom resources for students and teachers. NARA is continually expanding the kinds and amount of information available on the Web site and evaluating and redesigning the site to make it easier to use.

Electronic Access Project

As a result of the Electronic Access Project, funded through the support of U.S. Senator Bob Kerrey (D-Neb.), anyone, anywhere, with a computer connected to the Internet can search descriptions of NARA's nationwide holdings and view digital copies of some of its most popular documents. This is a significant piece of NARA's electronic access strategy as outlined in its Strategic Plan. The centerpiece of the project is the Archival Research Catalog (ARC)—an online catalog of all NARA holdings nationwide—which will allow the public, for the first time, to use computers to search for information about NARA's vast holdings, including those in the regional archives and presidential libraries. Moreover, anyone will be able to perform these searches through the Internet rather than having to travel to a NARA facility. Development of ARC began with the creation of a prototype catalog, the NARA Archival Information Locator (NAIL), available on the Internet at http://www.nara.gov/nara/nail.html. NAIL contains more than 3,000 microfilm publications descriptions, 607,000 archival holdings descriptions, and 124,000 digital copies of high-interest documents. These represent only a limited portion of NARA's vast holdings; NARA plans to migrate this information to ARC in 2002 and continue to add descriptions to the catalog so that at least 95 percent of the agency's holdings are included in ARC within the next five years.

Renovation and Re-encasement

On July 5, 2001, the Rotunda and exhibit halls of the National Archives Building in Washington, D.C., closed for renovation. When the renovation is completed in about two years, visitors will find the Charters of Freedom (the Declaration of Independence, the Constitution, and the Bill of Rights) displayed in the Rotunda in new, state-of-the-art encasements. The re-encased documents will be easier to view, and the space surrounding and including the Rotunda will be modified to showcase permanent and changing exhibits, educational activities, and public outreach. Research facilities in the building also will be expanded and upgraded with the establishment of a new Genealogy and Community History Research Center. Security for the records and for NARA's visitors will be strengthened. The renovation will open a new window on the National Archives and provide new means to access the history documented in these records.

During the renovation, the research areas of the building will remain open. For more information about the renovation and Charters of Freedom re-encasement, see "The National Archives Experience" at http://www.archives.gov/national_archives_experience/impact.html.

Archives Library Information Center

The Archives Library Information Center (ALIC) provides access to information on ready reference, American history and government, archival administration, information management, and government documents. ALIC is physically located in two traditional libraries, in the National Archives Building in Washington and the National Archives at College Park. In addition, customers can visit ALIC on the Internet at http://www.nara.gov/alic, where they will find "Reference at your desk" Internet links, staff-compiled bibliographies and publications, an online library catalog, and more.

Government Documents

U.S. government publications and publications of individual federal agencies are generally available to researchers at many of the 1,350 congressionally designated federal depository libraries throughout the United States. A record set of these publications also is part of NARA's archival holdings. Publications of the U.S. government (Record Group 287) is a collection of selected publications of U.S. government agencies arranged by the classification system ("SuDoc System") devised by the Office of the Superintendent of Documents, Government Printing Office (GPO). The core of the collection is a library created in 1895 by GPO's Public Documents Division. By 1972, when NARA acquired the library, it included official publications dating from the early years of the federal government and selected publications produced for and by federal government agencies. The collection has been augmented since 1972 with accessions of multiyear blocks of U.S. government publications, selected by the Office of the Superintendent of Documents as a byproduct of its monthly cataloging activity. The collection is estimated at 34,000 cubic feet. Only about one-half to two-thirds of all U.S. government publications are represented in this collection.

NARA Publications

NARA publishes guides and indexes to various portions of its archival holdings, catalogs of microfilmed records, informational leaflets and brochures, and general interest books about NARA and its holdings that will appeal to anyone with an interest in U.S. history; more specialized publications that will be useful to scholars, archivists, records managers, historians, researchers, and educators; and *Prologue,* a scholarly journal published quarterly. Some NARA publications are available through the National Archives Fax-on-Demand System described below. Some are also available on NARA's Web site. The Publications home page (http://www.nara.gov/publications/intro1.html) provides links to information about available publications and ordering details.

Fax-on-Demand

NARA customers can request faxed copies of select informational materials at any time (24 hours a day, 7 days a week, 365 days a year) by calling NARA's interactive fax retrieval system at 301-713-6905. By following the voice-activated instructions—being sure to give their fax number with the area code—customers will receive by fax copies of the materials stored digitally on the hard drive of an agency computer. Among the materials available by fax are brochures regarding NARA internships, NARA and federal government employment, and the semiannual Modern Archives Institute; published General Information Leaflets; other fact sheets about various NARA holdings, programs, and facilities (especially those located in Washington, D.C., College Park and Suitland, Maryland, and at the National Personnel Records Center in St. Louis); instructions, forms, and vendor lists for ordering copies of records; and finding aids for some textual, audiovisual, and micrographic records. Instructions and a listing of currently available documents are found on NARA's Web site at http://www.nara.gov/publications/faxondemand. Except for those customers who are making long-distance calls to Fax-on-Demand, there are no charges for using this service.

Federal Register

The *Federal Register* is the daily newspaper of the federal government and includes proposed and final regulations, agency notices, and presidential legal documents. The *Federal Register* is published by the Office of the Federal Register and printed and distributed by GPO. The two agencies also cooperate to produce the annual revisions of the *Code of Federal Regulations* (*CFR*). Free access to the full text of the electronic version of the *Federal Register* and *CFR* is available through GPO's electronic delivery system, on the Internet at http://www.access.gpo.gov. In addition to these publications, the full text of other *Federal Register* publications is available through GPO Access, including the *Weekly Compilation of Presidential Documents, Public Papers of the President,* slip laws, *U.S. Statutes at Large,* and the *United States Government Manual.* All of these publications also are maintained at all federal depository libraries. Public Law Electronic Notification Service (PENS) is a free subscription e-mail service available for notification of recently enacted public laws. The Federal Register Table of Contents Service (FEDREGTOC) is a free subscription e-mail service available for delivery of the daily table of contents from the *Federal Register.* Publication information concerning laws, regulations, and presidential documents and services is available from the Office of the Federal Register (202-523-5227). Information about and additional finding aids for *Federal Register* publications also are available through the Internet at http://www.nara.gov/fedreg.

Customer Service

Customers

NARA's Customer Service Plan, available free of charge in its research rooms nationwide and on its Web site at http://www.nara.gov/nara/vision/custplan.html, lists the many types of customers NARA serves and describes its standards for customer service. Few archives and records administrations serve as many customers as NARA. In fiscal year 2001 there were more than 313,000 research visits to NARA facilities nationwide, including presidential libraries and federal records centers. At the same time, nearly 477,000 customers requested information by mail and by phone. NARA also served the executive agencies of the federal government, the courts, and Congress by providing records storage, reference service, training, advice, and guidance on many issues relating to records management. Federal records centers replied to nearly 16.5 million requests for information and records, including the nearly 2.4 million requests for information from military and civilian government service records provided by the National Personnel Records Center in St. Louis. NARA also provided informative exhibits in the National Archives Rotunda in Washington, D.C., for more than 745,000 people, and 1.2 million more visited the presidential library museums. NARA's customer service accomplishments are detailed in its Annual Performance Reports.

Customer Opinion

Among the specific strategies published in NARA's Strategic Plan is an explicit commitment to expanding the opportunities of its customers to inform NARA about information and services that they need. In support of that strategy, NARA continues to survey, hold focus groups, and meet with customers to evaluate and constantly improve services. NARA also maintains an e-mail box (comments@nara.gov) for continuous feedback from customers about what is most important to them and what NARA might do better to meet their needs.

Grants

The National Historical Publications and Records Commission (NHPRC) is the grant-making affiliate of NARA. The Archivist of the United States chairs the commission and makes grants on its recommendation. The commission's 14 other members represent the president of the United States (two appointees), the U.S. Supreme Court, the U.S. Senate and House of Representatives, the Departments of State and Defense, the Librarian of Congress, the American Association for State and Local History, the American Historical Association, the Association for Documentary Editing, the National Association of Government Archives and

Records Administrators, the Organization of American Historians, and the Society of American Archivists.

The commission carries out a statutory mission to ensure understanding of our nation's past by promoting nationwide the identification, preservation, and dissemination of essential historical documentation. The commission supports the creation and publication of eight Founding Era documentary editions and basic and applied research in the management and preservation of authentic electronic records; and it works in partnership with a national network of State Historical Records Advisory Boards to develop a national archival infrastructure. NHPRC grants help state and local governments, and archives, universities, historical societies, professional organizations, and other nonprofit organizations to establish or strengthen archival programs, improve training and techniques, preserve and process records collections, and provide access to them through finding aids and documentary editions of the papers of significant historical figures and movements in American history.

Administration

NARA employs approximately 3,000 people, of whom about 2,350 are full-time permanent staff members. For fiscal year 2002 NARA received a budget of $289,826,000, including $6.44 million to support the National Historical Publications and Records Commission.

National Center for Education Statistics
Library Statistics Program

U.S. Department of Education, Office of Educational Research and Improvement
1990 K St. N.W., Washington, DC 20006
World Wide Web http://nces.ed.gov

Adrienne Chute
Elementary/Secondary and Libraries Studies Division

Libraries represent an educational resource available to the public regardless of a person's age, socioeconomic status, or educational background. In an effort to collect and disseminate more complete statistical information about this aspect of the education spectrum, the National Center for Education Statistics (NCES)* initiated a formal library statistics program in 1989 that now includes surveys on academic libraries, public libraries, school library media centers, and state library agencies. The Library Statistics Program is administered and funded by NCES, under the leadership of Jeffrey Williams, Acting Program Director, Library Statistics Program. The National Commission on Libraries and Information Science (NCLIS) and the U.S. Bureau of the Census work cooperatively with NCES in implementing the Library Statistics Program.

The four library surveys conducted by NCES are designed to provide comprehensive national data on the status of libraries. They are used by federal, state, and local officials, professional associations, and local practitioners for planning, evaluation, and making policy, and drawing samples for special surveys. These data are also available to researchers and educators to analyze the state of the art of librarianship and to improve its practice.

The NCES Library Statistics Program is pleased to announce the availability of a greatly enhanced Library Statistics Program Web site, found at http://nces.ed.gov/surveys/libraries. NCES has developed a home page for the program, with links to a calendar of events and links to a page for each of the library surveys. Each of the library survey pages links to survey publications, survey data files, survey contacts, other related Web sites, survey highlights, Web tools (if available), and to "About Survey." "About Survey," in turn, links to the survey questionnaire, the survey definitions, the survey methodology, and the survey manual (if available) for each survey. In this article, the four library surveys are described.

Public Libraries

Descriptive statistics for more than 9,000 public libraries are collected and disseminated annually through a voluntary census, the Public Libraries Survey. The survey is conducted by NCES through the Federal-State Cooperative System (FSCS) for Public Library Data. In 2002 FSCS will complete its 14th data collection.

---

*The authorization for the National Center for Education Statistics (NCES) to collect library statistics is included in the Improving America's Schools Act of 1994 (P.L. 103-382) under Title IV, the National Education Statistics Act of 1994.

Note: Jeffrey Williams and Elaine Kroe of NCES contributed to this article.

The Public Libraries Survey collects identifying information about public libraries and each of their service outlets, including street address, mailing address, city, county, zip code, and telephone number. The survey collects data about public libraries, including data on staffing; type of legal basis; type of geographic boundary; type of administrative structure; interlibrary relationship; type and number of service outlets; operating income and expenditures; size of collection; service measures such as reference transactions, interlibrary loans, circulation, public service hours, library visits, circulation of children's materials, children's program attendance; and other data items. Newer data items on computers and the Internet include

- Does the public library have access to the Internet?
- Is the Internet used by library staff only, patrons through a staff intermediary, or patrons either directly or through a staff intermediary?
- Number of Internet terminals
- Number of users of electronic resources in a typical week
- Does the library provide access to electronic services?
- Number of library materials in electronic format
- Operating expenditures for library materials in electronic format
- Operating expenditures for electronic access

The survey also collects several data items about outlets, including the location of an outlet relative to a metropolitan area, number of books-by-mail-only outlets, number of bookmobiles by bookmobile outlet, and Web address.

Unit response typically has been over 98 percent. The 50 states and the District of Columbia participate in data collection. Beginning in 1993 the following outlying areas joined the FSCS for Public Library Data: Guam, Commonwealth of the Northern Marianas Islands, Republic of Palau, Puerto Rico, and the U.S. Virgin Islands. For the collection of fiscal year (FY) 1999 data, the respondents that provided publishable data were the more than 9,000 public libraries identified by state library agencies in the 50 states and the District of Columbia, the Commonwealth of the Northern Marianas Islands, and Guam.

The first release of Public Libraries Survey data occurs about four months after data collection with the release of the updated Public Library Peer Comparison Tool and the Public Library Locator on the Library Statistics Program Web site. The data used in these Web tools are final, but unimputed (imputation is a statistical means for providing a valid value for missing data). This is followed three months later by the release of an E.D. Tab (an NCES publication that presents data "highlights" followed by a succinct presentation of descriptive statistics, including tables) on the NCES Web site. Within a week of that release, the final imputed data file is released on the Web site. The proportion of data that are imputed in the final file is no more than 2 percent. [For a sampling of content from several recent E.D. Tabs, see "Highlights of NCES Surveys" in Part 4—*Ed.*]

Final imputed data files that contain FY 1998 data on nearly 9,000 responding libraries and identifying information about their outlets were made available in July 2001 on the Library Statistics Program Web site. The FY 1998 data were also aggregated to state and national levels in the E.D. Tab "Public Libraries in the United States: FY 1998" and released in July 2001 on the Library Statistics Program Web site.

Public Libraries Survey data for FY 1999 were collected in December 2000. Final FY 1999 unimputed data were expected to be released as part of the Public Library Peer Comparison Tool and the Public Library Locator (on the Library Statistics Program Web site) in late 2001. Final FY 1999 imputed data are expected to be released in early 2002. Data for FY 2000 were collected in May 2001. Final FY 2000 unimputed data were expected to be released as part of the Public Library Peer Comparison Tool and the Public Library Locator (on the Library Statistics Program Web site) in early 2002. Final FY 2000 imputed data are scheduled for release in winter 2002. Final FY 2001 imputed data are scheduled for release in spring 2003.

The FSCS for Public Library Data is an example of the synergy that results from combining federal-state cooperation with state-of-the-art technology. The Public Libraries Survey was the first national NCES data collection in which the respondents supplied the data electronically. The data can also be edited and tabulated electronically at the state and national levels through NCES-developed software. All public library data collections have been collected electronically. In addition, 49 states and two outlying areas submitted their data via the Internet in 2000.

In 1992 NCES developed the first comprehensive public library universe file (PLUS) and merged it with existing software into a revised software package called DECPLUS. DECPLUS was also used to collect identifying information on all known public libraries and their service outlets. This resource has been available for use in drawing samples for special surveys on such topics as literacy, access for the disabled, and library construction. In 1998 NCES introduced WIN-PLUS, a Windows-based data collection software that retains many key features of DECPLUS but is more user friendly.

Efforts to improve Public Libraries Survey data quality are ongoing. For example, beginning with the FY 1995 data most items with response rates below 100 percent included imputations for nonresponding libraries. NCES also sponsored a series of six studies about the Public Libraries Survey including coverage, definitions, structure and organization, finance data, and staffing data. These studies were conducted by the Governments Division, Bureau of the Census. Over the years the clarity of the Public Libraries Survey definitions, software, and tables has been significantly improved.

At the state level and in the outlying areas, FSCS is administered by data coordinators appointed by each state or outlying area's chief officer of the state library agency. FSCS is a working network. State Data Coordinators collect the requested data from public libraries and submit these data to NCES, and NCES aggregates the data to provide state and national totals. An annual training conference is provided for the State Data Coordinators and a steering committee that represents them is active in the development of the Public Libraries Survey and its data-entry software. Technical assistance to states is provided by telephone and in person by State Data Coordinators, by NCES staff, by the U.S. Department of Commerce's Bureau of the Census, and by NCLIS. NCES also works cooperatively with NCLIS, the Bureau of the Census; the Institute of Museum and Library Services' Office of Library Programs; the Chief Officers of State

Library Agencies (COSLA); the American Library Association (ALA); the U.S. Department of Education's National Institute on Postsecondary Education, Libraries, and Lifelong Learning (PLLI); and the National Library of Education.

Other Completed Public Library Data Projects

In 2001 NCES published a trend analysis report for FY 1992–FY 1996 on 24 key variables from the Public Libraries Survey. As part of this project, FY 1992–1994 Public Libraries Survey data have been imputed for nonresponding libraries and were re-released on the Library Statistics Program Web site in summer 2001 (FY 1995–FY 1996 have already been imputed).

The Public Library Locator tool is now available on the Library Statistics Program Web site. This tool, released in 2000, enables users to locate data about a public library or a public library service outlet in instances where the user knows some but not all of the information about the library. For example, if the user knows the city the library is in but not the library's name, he or she can still locate the library and obtain most of the available Public Libraries Survey data about it including identifying information, organizational characteristics, services, staffing, size of collection, and income and expenditures. To use this tool, visit http://nces.ed.gov/surveys/libraries/liblocator.

The Library Statistics Program has also released a Web-based peer comparison tool on the Library Statistics Program Web site. With this tool, a user can first select a data year (e.g., FY 1998) and a library of interest (their own library for example). Next, the user can search for a peer group by selecting key characteristics to define it, such as total operating expenditures, circulation per capita, and so forth. The user can then view customized reports of the comparison between the library of interest and its peers based on a variety of characteristics he or she selects. These reports include bar charts, pie charts, rankings, data reports, and address/telephone reports. One can also view reports on data for individual public libraries. This tool also features a tutorial. To use this tool, visit http://nces.ed.gov/surveys/libraries/publicpeer.

American Institutes for Research completed a project to develop two indices of inflation, an input cost index and a cost of services index. NCES published a report of the project in 1999. The report presents and compares two approaches to measuring inflation for public libraries. One approach is based on a fixed "market basket" of the prices of library inputs, which yields a public library input cost index. The second approach is based on an econometric model of library services and costs and yields a public library cost of services index.

Questions about public libraries have also been included as parts of other NCES surveys. For example, in 1996 questions about frequency of use and the purposes for which households use public libraries were included on NCES's National Household Education Survey (NHES). More than 55,000 households were surveyed to provide state- and national-level estimates on library items. A Statistics in Brief titled "Use of Public Library Services by Households in the United States: 1996" was released in July 1997 and is available on the NCES Web site. A CD-ROM and User's Manual were also made available in July 1997.

NCES plans to update these data and add some additional survey questions in fall 2002 as part of a Supplement to the Current Population Survey.

Other Planned Public Library Data Projects

NCES has also fostered the use and analysis of FSCS data. The Data Use Subcommittee of the FSCS Steering Committee has been addressing the analysis, dissemination, and use of FSCS data, and several analytical projects recommended by this committee are under way.

NCES is developing a public library geographic mapping tool to be available on the Internet as part of NCES's Decennial Census School District 2000 project. This tool is an interactive online mapping system that integrates 2000 Decennial Census data with school district boundaries and school district data. The library part of this tool will be developed in phases over the next several years. Public library service outlets nationwide will be geocoded (geocodes are latitude and longitude coordinates). In a later phase, the boundaries of the almost 9,000 public library legal service area jurisdictions will be digitized. These will be matched to Census Tiger files and to Public Libraries Survey data files. The project will link census demographic data with Public Libraries Survey data through geographic mapping software. When fully developed, this tool will enable public libraries to identify and map census demographic data within their service boundaries or around their service outlets. For example, a library will be able to identify and map areas with poverty, elderly persons, immigrants, and so forth within its service boundaries so that service delivery can be planned with this awareness. The tool has been designed such that individual privacy with respect to demographic data will be protected. Libraries will also be able to compare their statistics on services with the surrounding demography and present the results in the form of maps.

A fast-response survey on the topic of public library programming for adults, including adults at risk, has been completed. The survey covered programming for adult literacy instruction, family literacy, adults with physical disabilities, the limited English-speaking, homebound adults, the elderly, and parents. The survey also asked about programming offered to adults related to Internet use. Data were collected from a sample of outlets nationwide in 2000 and early 2001 and the response rate was 97 percent. A report is expected to be available in early 2002. Westat, Inc. is conducting the survey. NCES, PLLI, and the National Library of Education are supporting and/or working on this project.

Additional information on Public Libraries data is available from Adrienne Chute, Elementary/Secondary and Libraries Studies Division, National Center for Education Statistics, 1990 K St. N.W., Room 9091, Washington, DC 20006 (telephone 202-502-7328, e-mail adrienne.chute@ed.gov).

Academic Libraries

The Academic Libraries Survey (ALS) provides descriptive statistics on about 3,700 academic libraries in the 50 states, the District of Columbia, and the outlying areas of the United States. NCES surveyed academic libraries on a three-year cycle between 1966 and 1988. From 1988 to 1998, the ALS was a component of the Integrated Postsecondary Education Data System (IPEDS), and was on a two-year cycle. Beginning with FY 2000 the Academic Libraries Survey is no longer a component of IPEDS but remains on a two-year cycle. IPEDS and ALS data can still be linked using the unit identification codes of the postsecondary education institutions. In aggregate, these data provide an overview of the status of academic libraries nationally and by state.

The ALS collects data on the libraries in the entire universe of accredited degree-granting postsecondary institutions and on the libraries in nonaccredited institutions with a program of four years or more.

For a number of years NCES used IDEALS, a software package for states to use in submitting ALS data to NCES. Beginning with the collection of FY 2000 data in fall 2000, the ALS changed to a Web-based data collection system.

The ALS has established a working group comprised of representatives of the academic library community. Its mission is to improve data quality and the timeliness of data collection, processing, and release. NCES also works cooperatively with ALA, NCLIS, the Association of Research Libraries, the Association of College and Research Libraries, and academic libraries in the collection of ALS data.

The ALS collects data on total library operating expenditures, full-time-equivalent library staff, service outlets, total volumes held at the end of the academic year, circulation, interlibrary loans, public service hours, gate count, reference transactions per typical week, and online services. Academic libraries are also asked whether they offer the following electronic services: an electronic catalog that includes the library's holdings, electronic full-text periodicals, Internet access, library reference services by e-mail, and electronic document delivery to patron's account-address. Beginning in FY 2000, questions about consortial services were added to the survey.

The E.D. Tab "Academic Libraries: 1998" was released on the NCES Web site in July 2001. The final ALS FY 2000 file and an E.D. Tab report are scheduled for release in spring 2002.

A descriptive report of changes in academic libraries between 1990 and 1996, "The Status of Academic Libraries in the United States: Results from the 1996 Academic Library Survey with Historical Comparisons," was released in May 2001. A technical report assessing the coverage of academic libraries through the ALS was published in September 1999.

NCES has developed a Web-based peer analysis tool for the ALS. It has a number of features similar to the Public Library Peer Comparison tool and was released in the summer of 2001 with FY 1998 unimputed data.

Several questions about the role of academic libraries in distance education were included as part of another survey sponsored by the U.S. Department of Education's National Institute on Postsecondary Education Libraries and Lifelong Learning. The Survey on Distance Education Courses Offered by Higher Education Institutions was conducted in fall 1995 under NCES's Postsecondary Education Quick Information System (PEQIS). The resulting Statistical Analysis Report, "Distance Education in Higher Education Institutions," was released in October 1997. This report is available on the NCES Web site.

Additional information on academic library statistics is available from Jeffrey Williams, Elementary/Secondary and Libraries Studies Division, National

Center for Education Statistics, Room 9026, 1990 K St. N.W., Washington, DC 20006 (telephone 202-502-7476, e-mail Jeffrey.Williams@ed.gov).

School Library Media Centers

National surveys of school library media centers in elementary and secondary schools in the United States were conducted in 1958, 1962, 1974, 1978, 1986, 1994, and 2000. NCES plans to continue school library data collection once every four years.

NCES, with the assistance of the U.S. Bureau of the Census, conducted the School Library Media Centers Survey as part of the 1999–2000 Schools and Staffing Survey (SASS). The sample of schools surveyed consisted of 9,000 public schools, 3,500 private schools, and the 160 Bureau of Indian Affairs (BIA) schools in the United States. Data from the school library media center questionnaire will provide a national picture of school library staffing, collections, expenditures, technology, and services. These data can also be used to assess the status of school library media centers nationwide, and to assess the federal role in their support. An E.D. Tab and the data file for this survey were planned for release in late 2001. The Bureau of the Census also completed a Technical Report for NCES, an "Evaluation of Definitions and Analysis of Comparative data for the School Library Statistics Program," which was released in September 1998.

NCES has included some library-oriented questions on the parent and the teacher instruments of its new Early Childhood Longitudinal Study, Kindergarten Class of 1998–99. Some of the data from this study were released in 2000. For more information, visit http://nces.ed.gov/ecls.

Additional information on school library media center statistics is available from Jeffrey Williams, Elementary/Secondary and Libraries Studies Division, National Center for Education Statistics, Room 9026, 1990 K St., N.W., Washington, DC 20006 (telephone 202 502-7476, e-mail Jeffrey.Williams@ed.gov).

State Library Agencies

The State Library Agencies (StLA) Survey collects and disseminates information about the state library agencies in the 50 states and the District of Columbia. A state library agency is the official unit of state government charged with statewide library development and the administration of federal funds under the Library Services and Technology Act (LSTA). Increasingly, state library agencies (StLAs) have received broader legislative mandates affecting libraries of all types and are often involved in the development and operation of electronic information networks. The StLAs' administrative and developmental responsibilities affect the operation of thousands of public, academic, school, and special libraries in the nation. StLAs provide important reference and information services to state government and sometimes also provide service to the general public. StLAs often administer the state library and special operations such as state archives and libraries for the blind and physically handicapped, and the state Center for the Book.

The State Library Agencies survey began in 1994 as a cooperative effort between NCES, COSLA, and NCLIS. The FY 2000 StLA survey collected data on 423 items, covering the following areas: direct library services, adult literacy, family literacy, library development services, resources assigned to allied operations such as archive and records management, organizational and governance structure within which the agency operates, electronic networking, staffing, collections, and expenditures. These data are edited electronically, and prior to FY 1999 missing data were not imputed. Beginning with FY 1999 data, however, national totals included imputations for missing data. Another change is that beginning with FY 1999 data the StLA became a Web-based data collection system. The most recent data available are for FY 1999. Two FY 1999 data products were released through the NCES Web site. An E.D. Tab titled "State Library Agencies, Fiscal Year 1999," with 29 tables for the 50 states and the District of Columbia, was released in September 2000. The survey database was also released in September 2000.

An evaluation study of the state library agency survey was released in fall 1999.

Additional information on the State Library Agencies Survey is available from Elaine Kroe, Elementary/Secondary and Libraries Studies Division, Room 9027, National Center for Education Statistics, 1990 K St. N.W., Washington, DC 20006 (telephone 202-502-7379, e-mail patricia.kroe@ed.gov).

How to Obtain Printed and Electronic Products

Under its library surveys, NCES regularly publishes E.D. Tabs that consist of tables, usually presenting state and national totals, a survey description, and data highlights. NCES also publishes separate, more in-depth studies analyzing these data.

Internet Access

Many NCES publications (including out-of-print publications) and edited raw data files from the library surveys are available for viewing or downloading at no charge through the Electronic Catalog on NCES's Web site at http://nces.ed.gov/pubsearch.

Ordering Printed Products

Many NCES publications are also available in printed format. To order one free copy of recent NCES reports, contact the Education Publications Center (ED Pubs) at:

Internet: http://www.ed.gov/pubs/edpubs.html
E-mail: EdPubs@inet.ed.gov
Toll-free telephone: 877-4-ED-Pubs (877-433-7827)
TTY/TDD toll-free telephone: 877-576-7734
Fax: 301-470-1244
Mail: ED Pubs, P.O. Box 1398, Jessup, MD 20794-1398.

Many publications are available through the Educational Resources Information Clearinghouse (ERIC) system. These documents can be ordered from the ERIC Document Reproduction Service (EDRS) in three formats: paper, electronic (PDF), or microfiche. Orders can be placed with EDRS by phone at 800-443-3742 or 703-444-1400, by fax at 703-440-1408, or by e-mail at service@edrs.com. For more information on services and products, visit the EDRS Web site at http://www.edrs.com.

Out of print publications and data files can be available through the NCES Electronic Catalog on the NCES Web site at http://nces.ed.gov/pubsearch or through one of the 1,400 Federal Depository Libraries throughout the United States. Use the NCES publication number to locate items in the NCES Electronic Catalog; use the GPO number to locate items in a Federal Depository Library.

National Education Data Resource Center (NEDRC)

The National Education Data Resource Center (NEDRC) responds to requests for special tabulations of library data and other NCES survey data and provides assistance in obtaining data and publications over the Internet or from the Government Printing Office. These services are free of charge. Contact NEDRC at 1900 N. Beauregard St., Suite 200, Alexandria, VA 22311-1722 (telephone 703-845-3151, fax 703-820-7465, e-mail nedrc@pcci.com).

National Library of Education

U.S. Department of Education
400 Maryland Ave. S.W., Washington, DC 20202
202-401-3745, fax 202-205-6688
World Wide Web http://www.ed.gov/NLE

Christina Dunn
National Library of Education

The National Library of Education (NLE) has been in operation since 1994, the year it was created within the U.S. Department of Education (DOE) by Public Law 103-227.

The legislation gave the library three primary functions:

- To provide a central location within the federal government for information about education

- To provide comprehensive reference services on education issues to employees of DOE and its contractors and grantees, other federal employees, and members of the public

- To promote greater cooperation and resource sharing among providers and repositories of education information in the United States

To carry out these functions, NLE was charged with becoming a principal center for the collection, preservation, and effective utilization of research and other information related to education and to the improvement of educational achievement; ensuring widespread access to the library's facilities and materials, coverage of all education issues and subjects, and quality control; having an expert library staff; and using modern information technology that holds the potential to link major libraries, schools, and educational centers across the United States into a network of national education resources.

Today a major goal of NLE is to establish and maintain a one-stop, central information and referral service, responding to telephone, mail, e-mail, and other inquiries from the public on

- Programs, activities, and publications of DOE
- Research sponsored by DOE
- Statistics from the department's National Center for Education Statistics
- Educational Resources Information Center (ERIC) resources and services, including the ERIC database

Located in the Office for Educational Research and Improvement with a budget of more than $12 million ($10.5 million of which supports ERIC), NLE is organized into three divisions and operates six programs. The Reference and Information Services and Collection Development and Technical Services divisions make up the ED (U.S. Department of Education) Reference Center; the ERIC Program Division oversees all aspects of the ERIC program, including the 16 ERIC clearinghouses; and the Office of the NLE Director oversees the other four programs: National Education Network (NEN), ED Pubs, U.S. Network for Education

Information (USNEI), and the National Clearinghouse for Educational Facilities. ERIC is covered in a separate report; all other programs are described here. [See the following article, "Educational Resources Information Center"—*Ed.*]

ED Reference Center

The ED Reference Center provides general and legislative reference and statistical information services in response to inquiries received by phone, mail, and fax, and, increasingly, via the Internet. Also, it offers interlibrary loan of NLE materials; identifies, selects, and acquires monographs and serials in education and related fields; maintains special collections of resources, such as historical textbooks and DOE documents; provides electronic bibliographic and full-text access to education and related databases, books, and serials; provides orientation and specialized training in the use of NLE and its collections; and serves as a federal depository library in the Government Printing Office Program.

Over the past year, NLE has made a concerted effort to increase the number and variety of instructional opportunities for DOE staff to learn to use the Library's many resources, especially its electronic resources. During that time, the number of training and orientation sessions has more than doubled, from 20 to 50, with most focusing on electronic information sources, especially database use. The increased emphasis on this service area is partly due to the increasing number of electronic resources that are desktop accessible to agency staff.

Collections

NLE's primary collections include its reference, circulating, serials, and microforms collections. While the circulating collection largely includes books in the field of education published since 1965, it also covers such related areas as law, public policy, economics, urban affairs, sociology, history, philosophy, psychology, and library and information science. Current periodicals holdings number more than 800 English-language print and electronic journals as well as a variety of newsletters. The collection includes nearly all of the primary journals indexed by the *Current Index to Journals in Education* (*CIJE*) and *Education Abstracts*. The library subscribes to eight major national newspapers and maintains back issues of four national newspapers, supplemented by electronic access to many others.

The ED Reference Center has been a federal depository library since 1988, and in 1999 it added to its staff a professional government-documents librarian. The librarian—in addition to coordinating the center's participation in the Federal Depository Library Program by organizing and improving access to and awareness of the collection—also is responsible for coordinating the center's collection of DOE publications and its collection of historic legislative materials. The historic legislative materials collection spans more than 100 years, making it a resource covering the history of DOE and its predecessor agencies as well as presenting a useful overview of education in the United States. At present this collection is being reorganized and prepared for digitization.

Other historic collections include a rare-books collection, with titles dating back to the 15th century; early American textbooks; and books about education. Other special collections maintained by the library are documents and archives of the former National Institute of Education and the former U.S. Office of Education (including reports, studies, manuals, and statistical publications, speeches, and policy papers). Of these, the rare-books collection is probably the most unique. It began with the private collection of American schoolbooks belonging to Henry Barnard, first U.S. commissioner of education, was nurtured by Commissioner John Eaton during his tenure (1870–1886), and was further enriched by several private donors.

The ED Reference Center strives to collect copies of all print and digital department publications for permanent access. Digital access is becoming increasingly important as more and more government documents are available in electronic format only. Easy, permanent access to full-text department information on a timely, accurate basis via dependable, low-cost or no-cost channels is an ongoing objective.

In 2001 NLE continued to borrow more items (805) than it loaned to other libraries (686); the totals represented the largest number of items the library has borrowed and loaned in a single year. The increase in the number of borrowed items is due to increased staff use, especially to locate research in education and related topics. During 2001 the library also increased the number of items acquired. There was a concerted effort to locate and catalog older DOE documents not already in the collection. Increased acquisitions and a cooperative venture with the department's Office of Vocational and Adult Education to catalog its collection of research papers increased the number of catalog records entered into OCLC by 16 percent over the previous year.

Services

Reference and Information Services respond to public inquiries, about 90 percent of which are now submitted by e-mail; fewer and fewer questions are received and answered by mail and fax. Of the number of questions received by telephone, most are answered while the caller is on the line. Regardless of the format in which the question is received, the library most often provides guidance to the public in three major areas: the DOE Web site; DOE programs and statistics; and other current education-related issues, such as charter schools, school violence, the educational reform movement, student achievement, and testing. During 2001 the library received more than 20,000 requests for information.

In addition to handling reference inquiries, library staff provide instruction and orientations, prepare pathfinders on current topics of DOE and NLE interest, develop finding aids, locate Web sites for reliable education information, and identify experts on various education research topics. While NLE serves customers from all over the world, major emphasis is on meeting the DOE staff's information needs. The library has enhanced its presence on the department's intranet by adding a number of electronic resources, and is beginning to work on its Internet site. During the past year, the ED Reference Center has continued to cooperate with AskERIC, an Internet-based reference service operated by the ERIC Clearinghouse on Information and Technology at Syracuse University, answering questions on federal education statistics and DOE.

The center can be reached by e-mail at Libraryi@ed.gov or by telephone at 202-205-5015 or 800-424-1616. It is open from 9:00 A.M. to 5:00 P.M. weekdays, except federal holidays.

National Education Network

The mission of the National Education Network (NEN) is to provide and support comprehensive access to education information by promoting effective access for users of education information, leveraging investments in providers and repositories of education information, and sustaining the development and preservation of education information. Sponsored by NLE, NEN is a collaborative partnership of entities that have as part of their mission the collection, production, and/or dissemination of education information. Representatives are from a broad spectrum, including college and university libraries, ERIC and other clearinghouses, publishers of educational resources, K–12 schools, and associations concerned with education.

The NEN Executive Committee, appointed by NLE, meets twice a year to plan and discuss NEN activities. NEN has sponsored forums on the virtual reference desk and preserving education information, and it plans to sponsor additional forums on making education information more accessible, as well as promote pilot preservation projects. In 2001 NEN began developing a Web site to host NEN services, such as an education information materials exchange, allowing institutions to list education-related materials from their collections they want to give away or items they are seeking to add to their collections. Another NEN service will be "Ask NEN," a question-answering service intended primarily for educators, information professionals, and others trying to find information on education at all levels.

ED Pubs

ED Pubs, the one-stop publications distribution center for all of DOE, as well as for seven department-related agencies, originated from the department's desire to get the right information to the right people on time. This program provides the participating agencies with centralized customer service for all of the participating agencies' information products; maintains mailing lists; stores and disseminates products; provides toll-free telephone services and a Web site; and maintains a fully automated, integrated fulfillment system.

Launched in 1998, ED Pubs has continued to grow in popularity with the public, providing easy access to DOE and other federal agency documents through its Web site at http://www.ed.gov/pubs/EDPubs.html and toll-free telephone number at 877-4ED-PUBS (877-433-7827) or TTY/TDD at 877-576-7734, which include Spanish-language service, added in 1999. For all measured activities, ED Pubs continues to receive outstanding customer-satisfaction ratings from the public, including recognition of product quality, ordering ease, timeliness of delivery, and staff courtesy and professionalism.

Since its establishment, the call and distribution center, with a database of more than 700,000 customers, has shipped more than 360 million products and responded to more than 700,000 telephone calls and more than 650,000 electronic requests. During 2001 ED Pubs entered into cooperative service with the U.S. Department of Labor and the National Institute for Literacy to manage a "literacy hotline" for disseminating jointly produced literacy and school-to-work materials.

U.S. Network for Education Information

The U.S. Network for Education Information (USNEI) provides direct, print, and electronic information and referral services to American and overseas customers. The Department of State and the then U.S. Information Agency (now the State Department's Public Diplomacy Branch) approached DOE with the idea in 1996, urged on by national associations in education. USNEI was created to provide a centrally coordinated mechanism for disseminating U.S. education information abroad, and for responding to inquiries concerning international education and U.S. practices and policies in education, including degree equivalency.

Under the requirements of the Lisbon Convention on the Recognition of Qualifications Concerning Higher Education in the European Region, held in 1997, USNEI provides information on both the U.S. education system and foreign systems in respect to issues of mobility, degree equivalency, and information on policies and competent authorities. The service helps Americans needing information on foreign education systems and those who are interested in studying and teaching abroad, as well as foreigners interested in American education or studying or teaching in the United States.

American customers include PK–12 educators and state/local education agencies, parents, students, postsecondary institutions, accrediting associations, corporations, law offices, federal agencies, and U.S. embassies and establishments abroad; overseas customers include international organizations, foreign governments, foreign students, and foreign schools. Monthly, USNEI serves an average of 3,500 U.S. and overseas customers interested in international education opportunities. The USNEI Web site is http://www.ed.gov/NLE/USNEI.

National Clearinghouse for Educational Facilities

The National Clearinghouse for Educational Facilities (NCEF), created in 1997, is an information resource for people who plan, design, build, operate and maintain K–12 schools. Affiliated with ERIC and managed by NLE, NCEF is operated by the National Institute of Building Sciences, a nonprofit, nongovernmental organization authorized by Congress to serve as an authoritative source on building science and technology.

In addition to providing a Web site, the clearinghouse prepares resource lists on key K–12 school facilities issues. Currently the clearinghouse offers more than 25 publications, available in full text, covering such current issues as creating accessible schools, planning school grounds for outdoor learning, science facilities, and teacher workspaces. These annotated bibliographies include links to full-text publications and related Web sites, descriptions of books, studies, reports, and journal articles. The Web site links to a variety of sources of school construction and cost-estimating information. It also lists award-winning school designs and monthly statistics on nationwide school construction activity, and allows customers to request customized searches. The Web site is http://www. edfacilities.org.

Educational Resources Information Center

ERIC Program Office
National Library of Education
U.S. Department of Education
400 Maryland Ave. S.W., Washington, DC 20202

Christina Dunn
National Library of Education

The Educational Resources Information Center (ERIC) program, established by the U.S. Department of Education to increase and facilitate the use of educational research and information to improve American education, is the largest education database in the world, containing more than 1 million bibliographic records. Contributing to the database's development are 16 subject-oriented clearinghouses and three support services—ACCESS ERIC, ERIC Document Reproduction Service (EDRS), and ERIC Processing and Reference Facility. These components, known as the ERIC system, are managed by the National Library of Education's ERIC Program Office.

The ERIC system was reauthorized in 1994 as part of the Educational Research, Development, Dissemination, and Improvement Act. For fiscal year (FY) 2001, the ERIC budget was $10.5 million. Of this amount, 80 percent supported the 16 ERIC clearinghouses; 18 percent went to the three support services; and 2 percent to system improvements, printing, telecommunications, and computer systems.

Since its beginning in 1966, ERIC has been a well-known leader in the dissemination of educational literature, providing education information to teachers, administrators, parents, students, and a broad general public audience. The ERIC database continues to provide journal articles, conference papers, research and technical reports, project descriptions, books, teaching guides, evaluation reports, and many other types of materials. However, the Internet has impacted the dissemination of such resources and the expectations of users. The vision for ERIC is emerging as an information system that is reliable, speedy, usable, and of high quality. Translating this vision into results for ERIC customers has brought about a renewed focus on improving the accessibility and usability of the ERIC database of educational literature. Data quality and speed in data processing deeply affect ERIC's ability to serve its broad customer base, so a recent focus of the ERIC system has been on implementing a new technology infrastructure for processing records for the database.

New developments are under way to improve the timeliness and accuracy of the ERIC database and to include electronic materials in PDF, HTML, XML, video, and audio digital file formats. In addition, the ERIC Processing and Reference Facility is developing an online data entry system, automating data input and validation and streamlining document processing. Clearinghouses will cata-

Note: Much of this report is taken from the *ERIC Annual Report 2001: Summarizing the Recent Accomplishments of the Educational Resources Information Center,* prepared by ACCESS ERIC for the ERIC Program Office. For a copy, call ACCESS ERIC at 800-LET-ERIC (538-3742), send an e-mail request to accesseric@accesseric.org, or visit the ERIC Web site at http://www.eric.ed.gov.

log, abstract, and index directly into this new Web-based system, featuring such advances as error and duplicate checking and online access to descriptors.

ERIC Clearinghouses

ERIC's 16 clearinghouses cover adult, career, and vocational education; assessment and evaluation; community colleges; counseling and student services; disabilities and gifted education; educational management; elementary and early childhood education; higher education; information and technology; languages and linguistics; reading, English, and communication; rural education and small schools; science, mathematics, and environmental education; social studies/social science education; teaching and teacher education; and urban education.

In addition, 12 adjunct clearinghouses and one affiliate clearinghouse have joined forces with the 16 clearinghouses to assist the ERIC system in providing education information. The adjunct clearinghouses focus on child care, clinical schools, educational opportunity, entrepreneurship education, English as a Second Language (ESL) literacy education, international civic education, postsecondary education and the Internet, service learning, test collection, and U.S.-Japan studies, while the affiliate clearinghouse focuses on educational facilities. In an adjunct arrangement, an organization having a special subject interest assists ERIC in covering the literature of that subject by contributing documents, books, and articles to the ERIC clearinghouse with which it is associated at no cost to ERIC. An affiliate is an organization that has an independent existence as an information center in a particular area, that performs many of the same functions as ERIC, and that follows ERIC policies and procedures in performing these functions.

ERIC Support Services

ERIC Processing and Reference Facility

The ERIC Processing and Reference Facility (commonly known as the ERIC Facility) is the centralized database manager for the ERIC system. The main ERIC bibliographic database is maintained and distributed by the facility to online and CD-ROM vendors and interested academic institutions around the world. The Computer Sciences Corporation manages the ERIC Facility contract. In 2000 the facility released its new Web site featuring publicly available, full-text-searchable versions of the *ERIC Thesaurus* and the *CIJE Source Journal Index,* which provides titles, ISSN numbers, and subscription information for the more than 1,000 journals covered by ERIC.

ERIC Document Reproduction Service

The ERIC Document Reproduction Service (EDRS) is the document-delivery arm of ERIC and handles all subscriptions for ERIC microfiche and on-demand requests for paper or electronic copies or microfiche of full-text non-journal documents released for ERIC distribution. The ERIC microfiche collection consists of about 10,000 titles annually on 15,000 fiche cards. An alternative to the microfiche is EDRS's E*Subscribe service, which provides online documents.

In 2000 EDRS installed additional storage devices, servers, and network capacity to support the growing electronic archive and increased demand resulting from the expanding use of its digital document subscription service E*Subscribe and other Web-based services. More than 7,700 new document images were added to the electronic archive in 2000.

ACCESS ERIC

ACCESS ERIC is responsible for maintaining the ERIC systemwide Web site, which provides links to all ERIC-sponsored sites as well as the *ERIC Review, All About ERIC,* and other systemwide materials. In 2000 ACCESS ERIC redesigned the ERIC systemwide Web site (http://www.eric.ed.gov) to provide weekly ERIC news updates and to ease access to the ERIC database and ERIC clearinghouses/Web sites.

ERIC Database

During the last year the ERIC database grew by 32,427 new records—10,268 documents and 22,159 journal articles—bringing the entire bibliographic database to 1,045,081 records. The database is constructed by the 16 ERIC clearinghouses, which acquire and select articles and documents in their scope areas; catalog, abstract, and index them; and send them to the central ERIC Processing and Reference Facility. The facility performs final editing and combines records from all of the clearinghouses into the database.

Journal articles compose about 60 percent of the database, with the clearinghouses currently indexing more than 1,000 journals. While some journals are indexed cover to cover, others are selectively indexed. Documents other than journal articles account for the other 40 percent of the database. The clearinghouses and facility acquire documents from information providers such as universities and other research organizations, associations, commercial publishers, and state and local education agencies, as well as from the U.S. Department of Education. In addition, ERIC aggressively seeks out new education-related resources and accepts unsolicited documents for review. Inclusion of documents in the ERIC database is not automatic; all documents are evaluated by subject-matter experts at the clearinghouses. In addition to being clearly linked to the process or practice of education, every document is evaluated for quality of content, including contribution to knowledge, significance, relevance, newness, innovativeness, effectiveness of presentation, thoroughness of reporting, relation to current priorities, timeliness, authority of source, intended audience, and comprehensiveness. Also, all documents must meet standards for legibility and reproducibility, and must be available from either EDRS or from another source.

ERIC catalogs bibliographic records by describing them according to type of publication. In 2000, the most recent year reported, 90 percent of the documents and articles entered in the database were categorized as research/technical reports, descriptive reports, evaluative/feasibility reports, guides (including administrative and teaching guides), speeches, conference papers, viewpoints, or books. Approximately 14 percent (1,329 documents) of all documents entered during this same year were U.S. Department of Education publications and grantee and contractor reports. The greatest number of document entries came from three scope areas: reading, English, and communication (916 documents); adult, career, and vocational education (916 documents); and elementary and early childhood education (902 documents). The largest number of journal articles processed were in the scope areas of science, mathematics, and environmental education (2,248 articles); information and technology (2,161 articles); and reading, English and communication (1,950 articles).

Database Access

The ERIC database is available free for public use on the Internet and through commercial services—online Internet products from six vendors and CD-ROM products from three vendors, including the ERIC Processing and Reference Facility, which offers a CD-ROM subscription for $100 a year. In addition, the public can search ERIC at more than 1,000 public and university libraries as well as at federal depository libraries.

With the ERIC database accessible from a variety of sources, it is impossible to gather accurate statistics on how many searches are made annually. However, the three ERIC components providing access to the database in 2000—EDRS (http://www.edrs.com/webstore/search.cfm), ERIC Clearinghouse on Assessment and Evaluation (http://searcheric.org), and ERIC Clearinghouse on Information and Technology (http://eric.org/searcheric.html)—reported almost 8.5 million searches conducted, an average of 703,897 a month.

Document Delivery

Access to copies of ERIC documents is provided by EDRS in several different ways. The E*Subscribe subscription service, providing electronic access to ERIC documents, grew from 134 customers at the beginning of 2000 to a year-end total of 438, with 409 U.S. and 29 international subscriptions. This service provides direct access to electronic copies of more than 77,000 publications, representing more than 85 percent of the releasable ERIC documents entered into the ERIC database since 1993. Users at subscribing institutions—mostly academic (84.5 percent of subscribing institutions)—downloaded a total of 192,000 ERIC documents during 2000.

Despite the high interest in electronic document delivery, EDRS filled many on-demand orders for paper and microfiche copies of ERIC documents. In 2000 customers ordered nearly 45,000 copies of ERIC documents, up 51.2 percent from 1999. Of these, 54 percent were paper copies, 28 percent were electronic copies, and 18 percent were microfiche.

Information Sharing

ERIC participates in partnerships for information exchange with other national libraries and sponsors of databases and international collections. For example, ERIC representatives worked with representatives of the Australian Education

Index, British Education Index, and Canadian Education Index to determine additions and changes to the *Thesaurus of ERIC Descriptors*.

ERIC Products

In addition to building the ERIC database, the ERIC clearinghouses create two-page digests that summarize education research, and also produce research reviews, bibliographies, interpretive studies, and other publications to meet user needs. In FY 2000 the clearinghouses produced 536 information products, many the result of collaboration with professional associations, private publishers, academic institutions, and other organizations. All clearinghouse products are reviewed by two subject-matter experts prior to publication.

The *ERIC Annual Report 2001: Summarizing the Recent Accomplishments of the Educational Resources Information Center* identifies bestsellers from the ERIC clearinghouses. They include:

- Adult, Career, and Vocational Education: *Using National and State Skill Standards for Vocational-Technical Education Curriculum Development*
- Assessment and Evaluation: *Multi-Cultural Program Evaluation*
- Community Colleges: *Preparing Department Chairs for Their Leadership Roles*
- Counseling and Student Services: *Cybercounseling and Cyberlearning: Strategies and Resources for the Millennium*
- Disabilities and Gifted Education: *Adapting Curricular Materials* (three-volume set)
- Educational Management: *School Leadership: Handbook for Excellence, Third Edition*
- Elementary and Early Childhood Education: *The Project Approach Catalog 2*
- ESL Literacy Education: *Assessing Success in Family Literacy and Adult ESL*
- Higher Education: *Active Learning: Creating Excitement in the Classroom, Volume 20-1*
- Information and Technology: *Survey of Instructional Development Models*
- Languages and Linguistics: *Making the Connection: Language and Academic Achievement Among African Americans*
- Reading, English, and Communication: *101 Ways to Help Your Child Learn to Read and Write*
- Rural Education and Small Schools: *Next Steps: Research and Practice to Advance Indian Education*
- Science, Mathematics, and Environmental Education: *Proceedings of the 21st Annual Meeting: Psychology of Mathematics Education (PME), Volumes 1 and 2*
- Social Studies/Social Science Education: *Education for Civic Engagement in Democracy: Service Learning and Other Promising Practices*

- Teaching and Teacher Education: *Assessing the Impacts of Professional Development Schools*
- Urban Education: *A Guide to Teaching English and Science Together*

ERIC also produces electronic products such as peer-reviewed electronic journals, virtual libraries, and numerous specialized directories. The clearinghouses collaborate with ACCESS ERIC to produce the *ERIC Review,* a free journal for practitioners that reports critical trends and issues in education. In 2000 issues of the *ERIC Review* focused on school safety, expanding access to higher education, and the developmental path to reading. In 2000 the ERIC clearinghouses produced more than 175 ERIC Digests. These two-page summaries are typically presented in question-and-answer format and list additional resources for research. The complete text of more than 2,300 *ERIC Digests* can be found on CD-ROM versions of the database and on the Web at http://www.ed.gov/data bases/ERIC_Digests/index.

The ERIC support services produce systemwide resources, directories of education-related conferences and information centers; and products to help people use ERIC.

User Services

In concert with its mission to increase and facilitate the use of educational research and information on educational practice, ERIC provides user services to the public, including reference and retrieval services, access to Internet resources, literature searches, bibliographies, identification of popular documents, and referrals to other sources of information. In addition to researchers and graduate students, ERIC serves teachers, policymakers, journalists, parents, students, and the general public. Most users are faculty and students from either K–12 (20 percent) or postsecondary schools (36 percent).

ERIC staff answer requests via a toll-free telephone service, fax, mail, and e-mail, as well as in person at clearinghouses and conferences. According to the *ERIC Annual Report 2001: Summarizing the Recent Accomplishments of the Educational Resources Information Center,* in 2000 ERIC users communicated with ERIC components using a variety of methods.

Method	Number	Percent
E-mail*	109,761	66.3
Phone	35,007	21.1
Letter/fax	15,680	9.5
Visits	5,130	3.1
Total	165,578	100.0

*The e-mail category includes AskERIC e-mail requests.

Since 1992 the AskERIC service has responded to more than 238,000 questions sent via e-mail. Anyone can send an education-related question to askeric@ askeric.org and expect to receive a reply within two business days.

ERIC System Directory

Educational Resources Information Center (ERIC)
National Library of Education, Office of Educational Research and Improvement (OERI)
U.S. Department of Education, 400 Maryland Ave. S.W., Washington, DC 20202-5721
Tel. 800-424-1616; TTY/TDD 800-437-0833
World Wide Web http://www.ed.gov

Support Services

ACCESS ERIC
Aspen Systems Corp., 2277 Research Blvd., 4M
Rockville, MD 20850
Tel. 800-538-3742 or 301-519-5157
E-mail accesseric@accesseric.org
World Wide Web http://www.eric.ed.org

ERIC Document Reproduction Service
DynCorp, Inc.
DynEDRS
7420 Fullerton Rd., Suite 110
Springfield, VA 22153-2852
Tel. 800-443-3742 or 703-440-1400
E-mail service@edrs.com
World Wide Web http://www.edrs.com

ERIC Processing and Reference Facility
Computer Sciences Corp.
4483-A Forbes Blvd.
Lanham, MD 20706
Tel. 800-799-3742 or 301-552-4200
E-mail ericfac@inet.ed.gov
World Wide Web http://ericfacility.org

Clearinghouses

Adult, Career, and Vocational Education
Ohio State University
1900 Kenny Rd.
Columbus, OH 43210-1090
Tel. 800-848-4815 ext. 2-7069 or 614-292-7069; TTY/TDD: 614-688-8734
E-mail ericacve@postbox.acs.ohio-state.edu
World Wide Web http://ericacve.org

Assessment and Evaluation
University of Maryland, College Park
Department of Measurement, Statistics, and Evaluation
1129 Shriver Laboratory
College Park, MD 20742
Tel. 800-464-3742
E-mail ericae@ericae.net
World Wide Web http://ericae.net

Community Colleges
University of California at Los Angeles
3051 Moore Hall
Box 951521
Los Angeles, CA 90095-1521
Tel. 800-832-8256 or 310-825-3931
E-mail ericcc@ucla.edu
World Wide Web http://www.gseis.ucla.edu/ERIC/eric.html

Counseling and Student Services
University of North Carolina at Greensboro
School of Education
201 Ferguson Building
Box 26171
Greensboro, NC 27402-6171
Tel. 800-414-9769 or 336-334-4114
E-mail ericcass@uncg.edu
World Wide Web http://www.ericcass.uncg.edu

Disabilities and Gifted Education
Council for Exceptional Children
1110 North Glebe Rd.
Arlington, VA 22201-5704
Tel. 800-328-0272 or 703-264-9475; TTY/TDD 800-328-0272
E-mail ericec@cec.sped.org
World Wide Web http://ericec.org

Educational Management
University of Oregon
5207 University
Eugene, OR 97403-5207
Tel. 800-438-8841 or 541-346-5043
E-mail eric@eric.uoregon.edu
World Wide Web http://eric.uoregon.edu

Elementary and Early Childhood Education
University of Illinois at Urbana-Champaign
Children's Research Center
51 Gerty Drive
Champaign, IL 61820-7469
Tel. 800-583-4135 or 217-333-1386; TTY/
TDD 800-583-4135
E-mail ericeece@uiuc.edu
World Wide Web http://ericeece.org
(National Parent Information Network http://
npin.org)

Higher Education
George Washington University
Graduate School of Education and Human
Development
1 Dupont Circle N.W., Suite 630
Washington, DC 20036-1183
Tel. 800-773-3742 or 202-296-2597
E-mail eric-he@eric-he.edu
World Wide Web http://www.eriche.org

Information & Technology
Syracuse University
621 Skytop Rd., Suite160
Syracuse, NY 13244-5290
Tel. 800-464-9107 or 315-443-3640
E-mail eric@ericir.syr.edu
World Wide Web http://ericit.org
AskERIC e-mail askeric@askeric.org
AskERIC Web site http://www.askeric.org

Languages and Linguistics
Center for Applied Linguistics
4646 40th St. N.W.
Washington, DC 20016-1859
Tel. 800-276-9834 or 202-362-0700
World Wide Web http://www.cal.org/ericll

Reading, English, and Communication
Indiana University
Smith Research Center
2805 East 10th St., Suite 140
Bloomington, IN 47408-2698
Tel. 800-759-4723 or 812-855-5847
E-mail ericcs@indiana.edu
World Wide Web http://www.eric.indiana.
edu

Rural Education and Small Schools
AEL, Inc.
1031 Quarrier St., Box 1348
Charleston, WV 25325-1348

Tel. 800-624-9120 or 304-347-0400; TTY/
TDD 304-347-0448
E-mail ericrc@ael.org
World Wide Web http://www.ael.org/eric

Science, Mathematics, and Environmental
Education
Ohio State University
1929 Kenny Rd.
Columbus, OH 43210-1080
Tel. 800-276-0462 or 614-292-6717
E-mail ericse@osu.edu
World Wide Web http://www.ericse.org

Social Studies/Social Science Education
Indiana University
Social Studies Development Center
2805 E. 10th St., Suite 120
Bloomington, IN 47408-2698
Tel. 800-266-3815 or 812-855-3838
E-mail ericso@indiana.edu
World Wide Web http://www.ericso.indiana.
edu

Teaching and Teacher Education
American Association of Colleges for Teacher
Education
1307 New York Ave. N.W., Suite 300
Washington, DC 20005-4701
Tel. 800-822-9229 or 202-293-2450
E-mail query@aacte.org
World Wide Web http://www.ericsp.org

Urban Education
Teachers College, Columbia University
Institute for Urban and Minority Education
Main Hall, Rm. 303, Box 40
New York, NY 10027-6696
Tel. 800-601-4868 or 212-678-3433
E-mail eric-cue@columbia.edu
World Wide Web http://eric-web.tc.columbia.
edu

Adjunct Clearinghouses

Child Care
National Child Care Information Center
243 Church St. N.W., 2nd fl.
Vienna, VA 22180
Tel. 800-616-2242; TTY/TDD 800-516-2242
E-mail info@nccic.org
World Wide Web http://nccic.org

Clinical Schools
American Association of Colleges for Teacher
Education
1307 New York Ave. N.W., Suite 300
Washington, DC 20005-4701
Tel. 800-822-9229 or 202-293-2450
World Wide Web http://www.aacte.org/eric/
pro_dev_schools.htm

Early Intervention for Children with Special
Needs
National Early Childhood Technical Assis-
tance Center
137 E. Franklin St., Suite 500
Chapel Hill, NC 27514-3628
Tel. 919-962-7324; TTY/TDD 877-574-3194
E-mail nectas@unc.edu
World Wide Web http://www.nects.unc.edu

Educational Opportunity
National TRIO Clearinghouse
Council for Opportunity in Education
1025 Vermont Ave. N.W., Suite 900
Washington, DC 20005
Tel. 202-347-7430
E-mail clearinghouse@hqcoe.org
World Wide Web http://www.trioprograms.
org/clearinghouse

Entrepreneurship Education
Center for Entrepreneurial Leadership
Ewing Marion Kauffman Foundation
4801 Rockhill Rd.
Kansas City, MO 64110-2046
Tel. 888-423-5233 or 310-206-9549
E-mail celcee@ucla.edu
World Wide Web http://www.celcee.edu

ESL Literacy Education
National Clearinghouse for ESL Literacy
Education
Center for Applied Linguistics
4646 40th St. N.W.
Washington, DC 20016-1859
Tel. 202-362-0700 ext. 200

E-mail ncle@cal.org
World Wide Web http://www.cal.org/ncle

International Civic Education
Indiana University
Social Studies Development Center
2805 E. 10 St., Suite 120
Bloomington, IN 47408-2698
Tel. 800-266-3815 or 812-855-3838
E-mail patrick@indiana.edu

Service Learning
University of Minnesota
R-460 VoTech Building
1954 Buford Ave.
St. Paul, MN 55108
Tel. 800-808-7378 or 612-625-6276
E-mail serve@tc.umn.edu
World Wide Web http://umn.edu/~serve

Test Collection
Educational Testing Service
Princeton, NJ 08541
Tel. 609-734-5689
E-mail library@ets.org
World Wide Web http://ericae.net/testcol.htm

United States-Japan Studies
Indiana University
Social Studies Development Center
2805 E. 10 St., Suite 120
Bloomington, IN 47408-2698
Tel. 800-266-3815 or 812-855-3838
E-mail japan@indiana.edu
World Wide Web http://www.indiana.edu/
~japan

Affiliate Clearinghouse

Educational Facilities
National Institute of Building Sciences
1090 Vermont Ave. N.W., Ste. 700
Washington, DC 20005-4905
Tel. 888-552-0624 or 202-289-7800
E-mail ncef@nibs.org
World Wide Web http://www.edfacilities.org

National Association and Organization Reports

American Library Association

50 E. Huron St., Chicago, IL 60611
312-944-6780, 800-545-2433
World Wide Web http://www.ala.org

John W. Berry
President

Founded in 1876, the American Library Association (ALA) is the oldest, largest, and most influential library association in the world. The ALA membership comprises primarily librarians but also includes library trustees, publishers, and other interested people from every U.S. state and many nations. The association serves public, state, school, and academic libraries, as well as special libraries for people working in government, commerce and industry, the arts, the armed services, hospitals, prisons, and other institutions. Membership in fiscal year (FY) 2001 reached an all-time high of more than 64,000.

The mission of ALA is to provide leadership for the development, promotion, and improvement of library and information services and the profession of librarianship in order to enhance learning and ensure access to information for all. Key action areas include diversity, education and continuous learning, equity of access, intellectual freedom, and 21st century literacy. ALA is a 501(C)(3) charitable and educational organization.

The association has 11 member divisions, each focused on a different area of special interest. They are: the American Association of School Librarians (AASL), the Association for Library Trustees and Advocates (ALTA), the Association for Library Collections and Technical Services (ALCTS), the Association for Library Service to Children (ALSC), the Association of College and Research Libraries (ACRL), the Association of Specialized and Cooperative Library Agencies (ASCLA), the Library Administration and Management Association (LAMA), the Library and Information Technology Association (LITA), the Public Library Association (PLA), the Reference and User Services Association (RUSA), and the Young Adult Library Services Association (YALSA).

ALA is the nation's leading advocate for high-quality library and information services. It maintains a close working relationship with more than 70 library associations in the United States, Canada, and other countries, and works closely with organizations concerned with education, research, cultural development, recreation, and public service.

ALA's headquarters is in Chicago. The association maintains a legislative office and its Office for Information Technology Policy in Washington, D.C., and an editorial office in Middletown, Connecticut, for *Choice,* a review journal for academic libraries.

Diversity, Equity of Access, Education and Continuous Learning

John W. Berry, ALA president for 2001–2002, underscored the relevance of some of ALA's key action areas—diversity, equity of access, and education and continuous learning—during his presidency.

Goals in the area of diversity included:

- Continuing the work begun by the Spectrum Initiative, which was created in 1996 to give $5,000 scholarships each year for three years to 50 minority students to go to library school
- Formulating an action plan to replace numerous retiring colleagues over the next several years
- Expanding recruitment of new professionals to students in community colleges and even at the K–12 level, with a particular emphasis on people of color and those with disabilities

Goals in positioning ALA as a resonant voice for freedom of information and equitable access to information for all people included:

- Developing a clearly articulated public policy agenda in the areas of telecommunications, education, information access, and intellectual property
- Creating new models for library practice that encompass diverse formats, serve all people, and deliver ideas and information to all library and information spaces whether physical or virtual
- Ensuring that ALA services and products are fully accessible to people with disabilities

Goals in the area of building education and continuous learning opportunities for library workers and libraries' larger user communities included:

- Enabling ALA members to participate in ALA meetings and continuing education from their desktops
- Establishing an efficient and effective collaborative structure for delivering continuing education across our diverse association and its units
- Extending learning opportunities that support 21st-century literacy to an expanding global information society

Berry created several presidential task forces to ensure that these areas were given the proper attention. His Task Force on Recruitment and Diversity was charged with developing projects or programs that can be implemented in the broad areas of recruitment, diversity, pay equity, and training. The Presidential

Task Force on Equity of Access/Digital Inclusion focused on library and ALA initiatives that could advance the goal of "full digital inclusion." The Task Force on Electronic Participation concentrated on bringing the areas of equity of access, recruitment, and diversity into the digital age.

@ Your Library

The Campaign for America's Libraries, "@ your library," was publicly launched during National Library Week 2001 with help from First Lady Laura Bush. Also on hand was Mike Bordick of the Baltimore Orioles and other representatives of major league baseball, a founding campaign partner, as well as then-ALA President Nancy Kranich, President-Elect Berry, Immediate Past President Sarah Ann Long, and other leaders in the library community.

The launch was held at the Northeast Neighborhood Library in Washington, D.C., where the first lady described libraries as "community treasure chests." The event received national notice in newspapers and on television and radio, including coverage by the *Washington Post, USA Today,* CNN, and National Public Radio, spreading the word widely about the role that public, school, academic, and special libraries play in their communities.

The campaign is a five-year public education effort. Its key messages are that libraries are changing and dynamic places, places of opportunity, and that libraries "bring you the world." It is the largest public relations and advocacy initiative ALA has ever undertaken. The "@ your library" brand provides libraries with an easy way to customize their marketing efforts to meet their particular needs while being part of a larger national program. It aims to increase awareness and support for libraries and bring renewed energy to the promotion of libraries and librarians.

During National Library Week, 3M Library Systems, a founding partner of the campaign, hosted a Webcast during which 500 librarians around the country logged on to learn how to create five-year marketing plans using the "@ your library" brand. In its first year, national partnerships—which in addition to major league baseball and 3M Library Systems included the Center for the Book in the Library of Congress and Morningstar Foods—reached well beyond the library community with campaign messages. Nationally, libraries began using the campaign as a communications vehicle for everything from developing statewide, multiyear public awareness programs and promoting new services to advocating for new buildings and increased funding. Four Canadian organizations joined the campaign in its first year: the Canadian Library Association, Library Association of Alberta, Ontario Library Association, and Saskatchewan Library Association. For more information on the Campaign for America's Libraries, visit http://www.ala.org/@yourlibrary.

Libraries: Cornerstone of Democracy

The presidential theme of 2000–2001 ALA President Nancy Kranich was "Libraries: The Cornerstone of Democracy," which set the stage for a year of projects related to advocacy, information literacy partnerships, "social capital building," civic forums, emerging democracies, information equity, and bridging the digital divide.

Saying that "libraries are for everyone, everywhere," she called on librarians to seize the unique opportunity to share their knowledge, expertise, and commitment to creating an informed citizenry by making the library a central player in the electoral process. On the ALA Web site, her tipsheet "Smart Voting starts @ your library" (http://www.ala.org/kranich/librariesandelections) provides ideas on how libraries can be an electoral resource for communities and how libraries can use the election season to promote their own issues.

Another key commitment was Kranich's Information Literacy Community Partnerships Initiative, designed to bring together librarians and community members or organizations to help prepare the public to utilize information efficiently and effectively.

Her focus on libraries in emerging democracies culminated in a three-day workshop in Tbilisi in the former Soviet republic of Georgia. "Strengthening Library Associations in the South Caucasus: A Regional Workshop," was held May 5–8 in cooperation with the Armenian Library Association, the Azerbaijan Library Development Association, and the Association of Information Specialists (Georgia). Librarians and library policy makers from these countries met with a contingent of U.S. colleagues including Kranich, former ALA President Ann Symons, and Jordan Scepanski, chair of ALA's International Relations Committee. The Carnegie Corporation of New York, the Open Society Institute, and U.S. State Department programs provided funding for the workshop.

"Equal access to information is a basic tenet in libraries in democratic countries," Kranich commented. "It is vital that libraries in the newly independent states continue to improve their ability to provide access to information to their citizens to help ensure the growth of these fledgling democracies." Complete details on the workshop can be found at http://www.ala.org/work/international/caucasus.

For more information on Kranich and her ALA presidency, visit http://www.ala.org/kranich.

Year of Challenge for Office for Intellectual Freedom

CIPA Lawsuit

On March 20, 2001, ALA, the Freedom to Read Foundation, and other plaintiffs filed a lawsuit on behalf of public libraries and library patrons seeking to overturn the Children's Internet Protection Act (CIPA). CIPA, and the related Neighborhood Children's Internet Protection Act (NCIPA), were signed into law on December 21, 2000, as Public Law 106-554.

The lawsuit asserts that the government cannot constitutionally place restrictions of the type found in CIPA on public libraries. It contends that the law violates the First and Fifth Amendments because it makes access to funding and discounts for Internet use in public libraries contingent on the acceptance of content and viewpoint restrictions on constitutionally protected speech, burdening the right of libraries, their patrons, and those speaking on the Internet to communicate and receive protected speech. When the lawsuit was filed, ALA held simultaneous press conferences at the Free Library of Philadelphia and the New York headquarters of the American Civil Liberties Union (ACLU).

The lawsuit also asserts that under well-established First Amendment principles, the government may not subsidize a forum or a medium of expression, such as the Internet in a public library, and then attempt to suppress a category of protected speech available via that medium based on its disfavored content. The suit seeks a declaration that the law is unconstitutional and an injunction to prevent the government from enforcing its provisions.

On July 27, 2001, ALA gained a preliminary victory. In a one-paragraph decision, a three-judge federal district court panel denied the government's motion to dismiss ALA's case. The suit, *American Library Association, Inc. v. United States,* was scheduled to be heard by the Third Circuit in late March. For the most up-to-date information about CIPA and the litigation, see the Web site http://www.ala.org/cipa, developed by the ALA Office for Intellectual Freedom and the ALA Washington Office.

In order to offset expenses associated with the lawsuit, a first CIPA fund raiser was held at the Union League Club in Chicago on June 6. Hosted by Gerald Hodges, ALA associate executive director for communications and marketing, and ALA member Charles Harmon, the event attracted a diverse crowd of intellectual freedom supporters. ALA's goal for the CIPA fund-raising effort is $1.3 million.

ALA's Development Office worked with the Office for Intellectual Freedom to make ALA members aware of the critical need for funding to combat the act. The Children's Internet Protection Act Legal Fund was launched in March 2001. Online contributions are being accepted at http://www.ala.org/cipalegalfund. html.

Banned Books Week

ALA enjoyed a successful Banned Books Week in 2001. Observed September 23–30, the 19th annual Banned Books Week started with sponsors recognizing children from around the country who had fought censorship by defending the Harry Potter series of books in their schools and communities. The campaign theme, "Fish in the River of Knowledge," highlighted the importance of maintaining access to a wide variety of ideas and information.

Intellectual Freedom Manual Updated

The ALA Office for Intellectual Freedom and the Intellectual Freedom Committee completed the sixth edition of the *Intellectual Freedom Manual,* a thorough update that addresses issues surrounding the Internet and electronic access to information. The manual provides guidance for librarians developing policy, responding to censorship challenges, developing a materials selection program, dealing with pressure groups, and promoting access to all types of information for all types of users in the new millennium. For more information, see http://www.ala.org/alaorg/oif/intellectualfreedommanual.html.

During 2001 the ALA Intellectual Freedom Committee also began drafting an Interpretation of the Library Bill of Rights on the subject of privacy in order to assist librarians in preserving privacy and confidentiality for library users. The draft Interpretation, along with questions and answers on privacy and confidentiality, can be found at http://www.ala.org/alaorg/oif/draftprivacyinterpretation.html.

Busy Year for Washington Office

Nearly 600 people from almost every state traveled to Washington, D.C., on May 1 for the 27th annual National Library Legislative Day, a lobbying event sponsored by ALA and the District of Columbia Library Association. State delegations met with senators, representatives, and their staffs throughout the day, sharing stories and encouraging support for legislation of interest to libraries. Key issues discussed included the reauthorization of the Elementary and Secondary Education Act (ESEA), database protection, funding for library programs and library-related programs, the Library Services and Technology Act (LSTA) reauthorization bill, and e-government legislation. [See "Legislation and Regulations Affecting Libraries in 2001" in Part 2—Ed.]

The ALA Washington Office and Public Information Office participated in LSTA Coalition activities, and with the coalition produced an electronic information brochure available for librarians to distribute in hope of gaining public support for LSTA reauthorization, which is due for congressional action in September 2002. For more information on LSTA and the brochure, visit http://www.ala.org/washoff/lsta.html.

The Washington Office collaborated with the Association of Specialized and Cooperative Library Agencies on LSTA reauthorization efforts by creating an "LSTA Success Stories" database that can be searched by state and congressional district (see https://cs.ala.org/lsta).

The Copyright Education Program continued to focus on three key projects to address libraries' copyright-education needs: the copyright Web site, the UCITA (Uniform Computer Information Transactions Act) online tutorial, and copyright presentations and workshops across the country. The copyright Web site, Copyright, Libraries and the Public (http://www.copyright.ala.org), includes information addressing the most frequently asked questions about copyright and libraries as well as feature articles, essays, and interviews. The UCITA tutorial includes an e-mail feature that sends biweekly messages to members addressing UCITA basics and introductory information on licensing practices and contract law. The tutorial is free of charge and each message is archived on the copyright Web site. For more information, see http://www.ala.org/washoff/ucita.

Staff continued to work over the summer months on S. 803, the E-Government Act of 2001. Sharon Hogan, director of libraries at the University of Illinois in Chicago and chair of ALA's Committee on Legislation, testified on the act July 11 before the Senate Government Affairs Committee. She represented the American Association of Law Libraries (AALL) and the Association of Research Libraries (ARL) as well as ALA. "Our nation's libraries are key access points for the American public," she said, "and already are, and should be, members of e-government teams at the federal, state, and local levels. We cannot have an effective e-government without effective access to government information and coordinated information policies . . . the move to an e-government has not been accompanied by the development of a comprehensive policy framework focusing on the life cycle of electronic government information." The full text of the joint library statement submitted for the record, the verbal testimony given on July 11, and related information are available at http://www.ala.org/washoff/hogantest.pdf and http://www.ala.org/washoff/egovpress.pdf.

Tasini Copyright Case

On June 25, the Supreme Court affirmed copyright privileges of freelance writers in *New York Times* v. *Tasini,* issuing a decision that is considered to be a major pronouncement on issues of copyright law in the digital age. The court ruled that freelance writers can retain copyright privileges on works that were originally published in newspapers and periodicals and then were licensed by the publishers to commercial electronic databases. The court rejected the publishers' argument that a ruling for the authors would have "devastating" consequences.

ALA and ARL had filed a friend-of-the-court brief in support of the freelance writers to help the court understand the practical effect of the issues at stake in this case. The brief suggested that there were constructive ways for the courts to address the issues of the case that would be fair to freelance authors, the commercial database publishers, and the public. The court expressed a similar view, noting that the parties, the courts, and Congress could "draw on numerous models for distributing copyrighted works and remunerating authors for their distribution."

The ALA Office for Information Technology Policy (OITP) sponsored a workshop in Skokie, Illinois, "Developing an Agenda for Libraries and Information Policy Issues." Its purpose was to revise the ALA document *Principles for the Development of the National Information Infrastructure.* Begun in FY 2000–2001, the new document, *Principles for the Networked World,* was adopted in principle at the 2002 Midwinter Meeting. For more information, see http://www.ala.org/oitp/prinintro.html.

Partnerships, New Areas of Interest

Advocacy gained a renewed focus at ALA thanks to a combination of events, including 2000–2001 ALA President Kranich's advocacy initiative, the appointment of an executive director of the Association for Library Trustees and Advocates (ALTA), and appointment of a new staff member dedicated to advocacy within the Public Information Office. ALTA took steps to raise its visibility within ALA, with a redesigned Web site, a revamped newsletter, *The Voice,* and a renewed commitment to relevant and meaningful programming.

LIVE! @ your library continued its two-year initiative of providing grant opportunities and programming support for libraries and partnering organizations to present theme-based cultural programming for adults and family audiences. In 2000–2001, more than $200,000 in LIVE! grants were awarded to 118 libraries and partnering organizations in 39 states and territories. LIVE! @ your library programs were also held at a number of national library and literary events, including an appearance by country music group Paul Burch and the WPA Ballclub at ALA's Midwinter Meeting; readings by Denise Chávez, Dagoberto Gilb, David Haynes, and Gail Tsukiyama at Chicago's Printers Row Book Fair; and performances by such legendary poets as Diane di Prima, Lawrence Ferlinghetti, and Robert Hass on the LIVE! @ your library Reading Stage at the ALA Annual Conference.

LIVE! @ your library is an initiative of the ALA Public Programs Office with major support from the National Endowment for the Arts, the National Endowment for the Humanities, the Wallace-Reader's Digest Funds, and the John S. and James L. Knight Foundation. For more information, see http://www.ala.org/publicprograms/live.

More than 800 public libraries from across the country were selected to receive the Millennium Project for Public Libraries grant. Participating libraries received 50 volumes from the Library of America collection of distinguished books by American authors. The Millennium Project is designed to help libraries enrich their core collections of American literature and provide an opportunity to offer library programs that enhance the public's appreciation of American writing. The participating libraries will host a program or event to increase community awareness of the nature and content of Library of America volumes, encourage patrons to read the books, and promote their long-term use. Smaller libraries participating in the program also received programming stipends to help defray the cost of a program or event.

The Millennium Project is an initiative of the National Endowment for the Humanities, the Library of America, and ALA, with major support from the Carnegie Corporation of New York. For more information, visit www.ala.org/publicprograms/millennium.

PLA is partnering with the National Institutes of Health's National Institute of Child Health and Human Development (NICHD) to facilitate effective early childhood reading instruction. PLA has agreed to help disseminate information contained in the recent National Reading Report and from NICHD research findings on how children learn to read. The two groups will work together to help build public library services for preschool children based on the findings and recommendations of this research and report, and ultimately will create some "best practices" for public libraries to help children start school ready to read.

In June the ALA Tribute Fund was created to allow association members and library supporters to make personal and targeted contributions. Donors can make memorial or honorary gifts, as well as gifts designated to support any specific ALA unit or initiative. Contributions to the ALA Tribute Fund are now being accepted online at https://cs.ala.org/tribute.

At the close of the fiscal year, the Development Office prepared to launch the ALA Planned Giving Program, which gives donors the opportunity to provide for the long-term needs of ALA through estate planning. The program is designed to encourage ALA members and other library advocates to support the ALA unit, program, or area of interest that is most important to them. The program also aims to identify and appropriately recognize members who have already named ALA in their wills by including them in the ALA Legacy Society. For more information or to request an invitation to attend an ALA planned giving seminar, contact the Development Office at development@ala.org.

AASL and 3M continued their partnership for a second year in the 2001 3M Salute to Schools Program; 3M increased its commitment by selecting 104 middle and high schools to receive $1.5 million in security technology to protect their most valuable learning resources, an increase of $500,000 over the previous year. For more information, see http://www.ala.org/aasl/news/3mannounce2001. html.

Workshops, Conferences, and Institutes

Annual Conference

The 2001 Annual Conference in San Franciso was attended by an unprecedented 26,820. Robert B. Reich, secretary of labor during the first Clinton administration, was keynote speaker at the opening general session. Reich is the founder and national editor of *The American Prospect* and Maurice B. Hexter Professor of Social and Economic Policy at Brandeis University and its Heller Graduate School.

The Second Annual Arthur Curley Memorial Lecture featured Lewis H. Lapham, editor of *Harper's* magazine and author. The lecture series honors the late Arthur Curley, a former ALA president and director of the Boston Public Library. Robert D. Putnam, Harvard professor and author of *Bowling Alone: The Collapse and Revival of American Community,* discussed the decline of "social capital" in the United States and explored its impact on society and on democracy. He challenged attendees to create strategies for libraries to play a strong and active role in rekindling civil society.

Singer/songwriter and social activist Buffy Sainte-Marie keynoted the closing session.

Midwinter Meeting

The 2001 ALA Midwinter Meeting in Washington, D.C., in January 2001 saw attendance figures up more than 20 percent over the previous year and exhibitor space up by 10 percent. The President's Program, "The Digital Divide and Information Equity: Challenges and Opportunities for Libraries in the 21st Century," featured several distinguished speakers, led by Larry Irving, who was assistant secretary of commerce for communications and information under President Clinton from 1993 to 1999. The captioned text and audio from the president's program are available at http://www.ala.org/kranich/mw2001_prog.html.

The 2001 Youth Media Awards press conference at the Midwinter Meeting received wide coverage on National Public Radio, in *USA Today,* and on the "Today Show."

IFLA Conference

A record 5,300 participants from 150 countries attended the International Federation of Library Associations and Institutions (IFLA) Conference in Boston August 16–25, 2001. ALA was a major sponsor of the first IFLA conference in the United States in over 15 years.

At the conference, ALA and IFLA unveiled the Campaign for the World's Libraries, a public education effort based on the U.S. @ your library program.

LITA National Forum

LITA held its third National Forum, "High Tech/High Touch: The Human Aspects of Technology" in Portland, Oregon, in November. Attendance at the

LITA Forums has grown from 125 registrations at the first to more than 400 in Portland. LITA sponsored six regional institutes during the year on either data-base-driven Web sites or proxy Web servers and authentication. At the ALA Annual Conference, LITA offered 16 programs and three preconferences on a wide variety of technology topics.

Other Conferences

In January 2001 PLA, the National Library of Medicine, and the Medical Library Association held the Public Library and Consumer Health Conference, a first-of-its-kind collaborative conference, in Washington, D.C. The conference gave librarians and library staff an introduction to health information resources, collection development, and training in searching health and medical information databases.

In March a record 895 people attended PLA's Spring Symposium in Chicago. Workshops included "Emerging Formats, Emerging Challenges: How E-Books, DVDs, and the Internet Are Changing the Publishing and Library World" and "The Early Literacy Initiative."

Also in March, ACRL offered its 10th National Conference in Denver. With the theme "Crossing the Divide," the conference attracted more than 3,300 participants, breaking all attendance records. To increase the availability of professional development opportunities for the membership, ACRL inaugurated Webcasts of selected conference presentations. Videos of various speakers, along with PowerPoint presentations, a bibliography, and discussion questions, are available at a nominal charge that allows access for a limited period of time. For more information, see http://www.ala.org/acrl.

In August the third ACRL/Harvard Leadership Institute was held in Cambridge, Massachusetts. The five-day institute was designed to help library leaders increase their capacity to lead and manage effectively.

ALCTS held a two-day AACR2 and Metadata Institute in Natick, Massachusetts, in August just before the IFLA conference. The 112 attendees heard presentations and discussed cataloging, revisions to the AACR2 cataloging rules, and various ways in which metadata influence their libraries.

Publishing

Choice launched its new Choice Reviewer Web site at http://www.choicemag.org. Using this site, *Choice* reviewers can submit reviews via the Internet and update their *Choice* profile at any time. A new licensing agreement with Syndetic Solutions of Portland, Oregon, allows libraries with one of the new, enhanced Web OPACs being released by the major ILS vendors the option of adding *Choice* reviews to their online card catalog.

American Libraries, published 11 times a year, remains the chief perquisite of ALA membership. The magazine noted an ALA benchmark with its cover story "ALA Celebrates 125 Years" in the June/July 2001 issue. The publication's Web site is http://www.ala.org/alonline.

ALA TechSource introduced two online products: *Library Technology Reports Online,* targeted to libraries that are transferring periodical collections online and to libraries outside the United States, and *Search the Archives,* which lets subscribers search back issues of *Library Systems* newsletter and *Library Technology Reports* by keyword. Subscriptions to both are available through the ALA TechSource Web site, http://www.techsource.ala.org. The site also includes a complimentary editorial product, *The Source Online,* which offers weekly commentary and features from library professionals throughout the United States. The print versions of both *Library Technology Reports* and *Library Systems* introduced redesigns that provide enhanced readability and usefulness for subscribers.

Long regarded as a primary book-selection tool for public and school libraries, *Booklist* now offers, in addition to reviews, a full range of readers-advisory features, including "Read-alike" columns, retrospective bibliographies, top-10 lists of various kinds, and essays about writers and their work. In 2001 every issue of *Booklist* featured a "spotlight" theme, bringing together content aimed at helping librarians not only select books but aid patrons in deciding what to read next. Special issues on types of genre fiction—mysteries, science fiction, romances, and historical fiction—again proved the most popular of the readers-advisory offerings.

Along with expanded content, *Booklist* was active during the year in a variety of ALA-related activities, including serving as sponsor of YALSA's Michael L. Printz award and providing consultants to various ALA committees, including Notable Books, Notable Children's Books, Best Books for Young Adults, Quick Picks, Notable Videos for Adults, and Notable Children's Videos, Recordings, Computer Software and Web Sites. *Booklist*'s Web address is http://www.ala.org/booklist.

Book Links, which spun off from *Booklist* in 1991, welcomed a new editor, inaugurated a new design, introduced a refocused thematic approach, and celebrated its 10th anniversary. Editor Laura Tillotson returned to *Book Links* after an earlier stint as assistant editor. *Book Links* also implemented a back-to-basics thematic approach, highlighting one curricular theme in each issue. The June/July 2001 issue of the magazine culminated a year-long celebration of the 10th anniversary with a special feature by the advisory board and past editors, as well as a new article category, "In the Trenches," describing practical techniques for using children's books in the classroom. *Book Links* is online at http://www.ala.org/BookLinks.

ALA Graphics collaborated with other ALA departments to create numerous products to enhance ALA initiatives, including the @ your library campaign, a National Library Week poster, and other materials using the theme "The Ultimate Search Engine is @ your library." Actors Susan Sarandon and Tim Robbins created public service announcements and READ posters using the @ your library brand. In the most successful Teen Read Week to date, ALA used exclusive images from the movie "Lord of the Rings" for posters and bookmarks. Other teen-related items included "Make Reading a Hobbit" buttons and bracelets. Among additional debut items were a Regis Philbin READ poster, DC Comics superheroes' "The World's Greatest Heroes @ your library," the Tyrannosaurus rex named Sue, civil rights figure Rosa Parks, and basketball star Chamique Holdsclaw.

A READ poster of cellist Yo-Yo Ma was developed in collaboration with the Music Library Association. A member of the U.S. women's soccer team suited up for a READ poster and sex therapist "Dr. Ruth" Westheimer posed behind a huge Curious George book for her READ poster debut.

In a year that exceeded expectations, ALA Editions published a number of strong titles in the association's program priorities, launched the ALA Online Store with ALA Graphics (http://www.alastore.ala.org), continued its successful collaboration with its partners in the ALA divisions with new publications based on PLA's *Planning for Results* and AASL's *Information Power*, and celebrated Michael Gorman's 2001 Highsmith Library Literature Award for *Our Enduring Values.*

Honors

ALSC launched the Robert F. Sibert Informational Book Award, to be presented yearly at the ALA Midwinter Meeting for the most distinguished informational book published during the preceding year. Marc Aronson, author of *Sir Walter Ralegh and the Quest for El Dorado,* was the winner of the first Sibert Award. Four Sibert Honor Books also were named. For more information, visit http://www.ala.org/alsc/sibert01.html.

The Newbery Medal went to *A Year Down Yonder* by Richard Peck, and *So You Want to Be President?* (illustrated by David Small; text by Judith St. George) took the Caldecott Medal. Jacqueline Woodson's *Miracle's Boys* took the Coretta Scott King Book Award. Bryan Collier's *Uptown* won the Coretta Scott King Illustrator Award, and *Kit's Wilderness* by David Almond was the winner of the Printz Award.

John Podesta, former White House chief of staff, received the 12th ALA James Madison Award, which is presented annually on National Freedom of Information Day (March 16) to leaders who have contributed to advancing the principles of equitable access to information and the public's right to know. Rep. Ed Schrock (R-Va.), a former librarian and strong library advocate, was awarded Friends of Libraries U.S.A.'s annual public service award on National Legislative Day.

Arnulfo D. Trejo was awarded honorary membership in the American Library Association "in recognition of his influence on Latino librarianship; his many contributions to library education and recruitment, which enabled him to serve as a role model and mentor to a wide range of library leaders in the Southwest, nationally and internationally; his service as the founder of REFORMA, the National Association to Promote Library and Information Services to Latinos and the Spanish-Speaking; his efforts to increase the availability of Spanish-language materials for libraries; and his long and distinguished career as a librarian, author, scholar and businessman." Trejo received his plaque in a presentation at the opening general session at the 2001 Annual Conference.

[For additional awards, see "Library Scholarship and Award Recipients" in Part 3 and "Literary Prizes" in Part 5—*Ed.*]

Grants

Verizon Communications gave ALA $250,000 to support the continued development of BuildLiteracy.org, an interactive how-to Web site for building and sustaining literacy coalitions, as well as ALA's participation in the Verizon Literacy Network. BuildLiteracy.org was designed to improve the exchange of knowledge, information, and resources between existing literacy coalitions while encouraging the development and growth of new communities across the United States. The Web site is funded by Verizon and administered by ALA's Office for Literacy and Outreach Services.

The Spectrum Initiative awarded 52 scholarships in June 2001. Thanks to the generosity of former ALA President Betty Turock and the Medical Library Association and National Library of Medicine, ALA was able to offer the Betty Turock Spectrum Scholarship and the MLA/NML Spectrum Scholarship in addition to the annual Spectrum awards. For more information on the Spectrum Initiative, visit http://www.ala.org/spectrum.

ACRL received a National Leadership Grant from the Institute of Museum and Library Services for its project "Assessing Student Learning Outcomes in Information Literacy Programs: Training Academic Librarians." The purpose of the project is to give librarians the skills to create baseline data that support the merits of information literacy programs.

The Between the Lions grant was extended to include further community outreach. Agreement was reached with WGBH Educational Foundation to produce a public service announcement that will air on PBS stations in 2002, as well as collateral materials. The collateral will be made available to ALSC members in early 2002.

Westlake Porter Public Library in Ohio was awarded the 2001 Grolier National Library Week Grant, as part of the @ your library campaign. This $4,000 grant is sponsored by Grolier Publishing and administered by the ALA Public Awareness Committee. The library designed a promotions program called "A World of Possibilities @ your library" with an entire week of activities designed around the @ your library brand.

The Chapter Relations Committee was awarded the 2001 World Book/ALA Goal Award for the project Creating Library Leaders. The grant of $10,000 was awarded to enable the committee to hold a full-day preconference at the 2002 ALA Midwinter Meeting to train chapter and other association leaders in ways to maximize their investment in leadership development.

Leadership

John W. Berry was inaugurated as ALA president at the 2001 Annual Conference in San Francisco. Berry is executive director of NILRC: A Consortium of Community Colleges, Colleges, and Universities in River Forest, Illinois.

Maurice J. ("Mitch") Freedman, director of the Westchester (New York) Library System, was elected ALA president for 2002–2003. He will be inaugurated in June at the 2002 Annual Conference in Atlanta. His presidential initiative will focus on the issue of better salaries and pay equity for librarians.

Kent Oliver, Patty Wong, and Barbara Stripling were elected to the ALA Executive Board at the 2001 Midwinter Meeting. Oliver and Wong were elected to three-year terms that began at the end of the 2001 Annual Conference and will run through the 2004 Annual Conference. Stripling was elected to fill the unexpired board term of ALA Treasurer Liz Bishoff, which ends at the conclusion of the 2002 Annual Conference.

Gerald Hodges was appointed ALA's associate executive director of communications and marketing. Karen Muller, executive director of LAMA and ALCTS for more than 10 years, resigned her position to become the new ALA Knowledge Manager, overseeing the ALA Library. Mary Taylor was appointed LITA executive director. Kerry Ward was appointed executive director of ALTA. Charles Wilt was named executive director of ALCTS.

Other Highlights

In April the Library and Research Center (LARC) was dissolved and the ALA Library again became a separately functioning unit. First established in 1924, the library carries out the closely related functions of supporting the information needs of ALA staff as they carry out the work of the association and providing information to members and others who contact ALA with questions about librarianship and ALA programs.

The Office for Research and Statistics (ORS) also became a separate unit again, maintaining its mission to provide leadership and expert advice to ALA staff, members, and the public on all matters related to research and statistics about libraries, librarians, and other library staff; to represent the association to federal agencies on these issues; and to initiate projects needed to expand the knowledge base of the field through research and collection of useful statistics.

Two sections of RUSA celebrated anniversaries in 2001: the Machine Assisted Reference Section (MARS) observed 25 years of service and the History Section celebrated its 40th anniversary.

ASCLA and RUSA established members-only Web sites. Both divisions now offer a variety of full-text databases for members on their Web sites, http://www.ala.org/ascla and http://www.ala.org/rusa.

The Office for Human Resource Development and Recruitment (HRDR) debuted its new Placement Center at the 2001 Midwinter Meeting, including a Career Resource Center with facilities for one-on-one counseling, mini-workshops, and presentations on career development; a resume critiquing service; and pre-arranged interview scheduling. HRDR also has a new Web site at http://www.ala.org/hrdr. The site has several new features including access to information on library careers, ALA scholarships, employment information, and continuing professional development.

ALCTS and LAMA each voted to dissolve their long-standing partnership at the 2001 Midwinter Meeting. For more than 10 years, the two divisions shared a staff and office, but ceased to do so in September.

ALA Council approved the Library Services for People with Disabilities Policy on January 16, 2001. The policy was written by the Americans with Disabilities Act Assembly, a representational group administered by ASCLA. The policy requires that the ALA Web site conform to guidelines for accessibility. As a first step to accomplish this, ALA Web designers participated in accessibility workshops this spring. The full text of the policy is found at http://www.ala.org/ascla/access_policy.html.

At the 2001 Annual Conference, ALA Council adopted a revised preservation policy. The revision was undertaken by the Preservation and Reformatting Section of ALCTS under the leadership of Irene Schubert of the Library of Congress. The policy can be found on the ALCTS Web site, http://www.ala.org/alcts/you/preservation.html.

The Chapter Relations Office continued to expand membership through joint initiatives with various chapters, ALA affiliates, and ALA divisions and round tables. In the past year, new alliances for membership development have resulted in more than 1,000 new members for ALA and for ALA's partner associations. New partner associations in 2000–2001 were Massachusetts Library Association, Georgia Library Association, Hawaii Library Association, California Library Association, Washington Library Association, New York Library Association, Asian/Pacific American Librarians Association, REFORMA, ALTA, ALCTS, RUSA, and the Library Support Staff Interests Round Table (LSSIRT). The 2001 Student Chapter of the Year Award, sponsored by the New Members Round Table, was awarded to the library education program at the State University of New York–Buffalo. Two additional universities have formed ALA student chapters: the University of Toronto and the University of Puerto Rico.

The final product of the Lila Wallace-Reader's Digest Fund/Literacy in Libraries Across America (an ALA initiative) was published. The publication, *Literacy and Libraries: Learning from Case Studies,* edited by GraceAnne DeCandido (ALA Editions) was released in May 2001. Twenty-two library literacy experts contributed to this volume, designed to show how libraries can serve adult learners and educate library school students about the needs, challenges, and rewards of pursuing literacy and outreach as a career.

ALA and the Committee on Accreditation (COA) were recognized by the Council for Higher Education Accreditation (CHEA) as the accrediting agency for library and information studies. Recognition by CHEA, which lasts a period of 10 years, means that ALA and COA meet a set of requirements, best practices, and guidelines that ensure a high-quality review of programs. Meeting these requirements is an indication that ALA's accreditation process respects and protects the rights of institutions, programs, and students, as well as the profession and public at large.

Association of American Publishers

71 Fifth Ave., New York, NY 10010
212-255-0200, fax 212-255-7007
50 F St. N.W., Washington, DC 20001
202-347-3375, fax 202-347-3690
World Wide Web http://www.publishers.org

Judith Platt
Director, Communications/Public Affairs

The Association of American Publishers (AAP) is the national trade association of the U.S. book publishing industry. The association was created in 1970 through the merger of the American Book Publishers Council, a trade publishing group, and the American Educational Publishers Institute, an organization of textbook publishers. AAP's more than 300 corporate members include most of the major commercial book publishers in the United States as well as smaller and medium-sized houses, nonprofit publishers, university presses, and scholarly societies.

AAP members publish hardcover and paperback books in every field including general fiction and nonfiction; poetry; children's books; textbooks; Bibles and other religious works; reference works; scientific, medical, technical, professional, and scholarly books and journals; computer software; and a range of electronic products and services, such as online databases and CD-ROMs.

AAP also works closely with some 2,000 smaller regional publishers through formal affiliations with the Publishers Association of the West, the Publishers Association of the South, the Florida Publishers Association, the Small Publishers Association of North America, and the Evangelical Christian Publishers Association.

AAP policy is set by a board of directors elected by the membership for four-year terms, under a chair who serves for two years. There is an executive committee composed of the chair, vice chair, secretary, and treasurer, and a minimum of two at-large members. Management of the association, within the guidelines set by the board, is the responsibility of AAP's president and CEO, Pat Schroeder.

AAP maintains two offices, in New York and Washington, D.C.

Highlights of 2001

Along with every other segment of American society, the book publishing industry was profoundly affected by the terrorist attacks of September 11. In the immediate aftermath of the attacks, local bookstores around the country reported that they had become de facto community centers crowded with people seeking information, connection, and comfort. As Americans sought to understand, there was a surge in sales of serious books about Islam, religious fundamentalism, terrorism, the Taliban, the Middle East, and biological and chemical warfare. The industry experienced a massive dislocation in the weeks following September 11. Some books slated for fall publication were pushed back to 2002, marketing campaigns were delayed, and Web chat rooms and bulletin boards were being used to compensate for lost face-to-face contact between authors and their readers. By year's end, however, the industry appeared to be weathering the storm and the downturn in the economy; people still seemed to be buying books.

Among the highlights of the year in publishing:

- Book sales totaled more than $25 billion in 2001, according to figures released by AAP in February
- With AAP help, the war on copyright piracy in India escalated to a new level
- Hyperion's Bob Miller began his second year as AAP chairman
- AAP investigations led to the seizure of $14.5 million in counterfeit books in South Korea, the largest raid in global publishing history
- "Get Caught Reading Day" on Capitol Hill attracted more than 90 members of the Senate and House
- Roger Straus, founder and head of Farrar Straus & Giroux, received the Curtis Benjamin Award
- AAP's Diversity Committee intensified its activities, producing a brochure and video to attract a diverse work force to the industry
- AAP took the lead on a friend-of-the-court brief to the U.S. Supreme Court in a challenge to the Children's Online Protection Act (COPA), Congress's second attempt to criminalize constitutionally protected speech on the Internet
- Johns Hopkins University Press received the R. R. Hawkins Award from AAP's Professional/Scholarly Publishing (PSP) Division for *The Bees of the World*
- The Digital Millennium Copyright Act (DMCA) survived two high-profile court challenges
- CBS News anchor Charles Osgood received the year's AAP Honors

Government Affairs

AAP's Washington office is the industry's front line on matters of federal legislation and government policy. The office keeps AAP members informed about developments on Capitol Hill and in the executive branch to enable the membership to develop consensus positions on national policy issues. AAP's government affairs professionals serve as the industry's voice in advocating the views and concerns of American publishers on questions of national policy.

An AAP Government Affairs Council strengthens communications between the Washington Office and the AAP leadership. The council comprises individuals designated by AAP board members to speak on behalf of their houses in formulating positions on legislative issues requiring a rapid response.

Communications/Public Affairs

The Communications and Public Affairs program is AAP's voice, informing the trade press and other media, the AAP membership, and the general public about

AAP's work to promote the cause of American publishing. Through the program's regular publications, press releases, and advisories, op-ed pieces, and other means, AAP expresses the industry's views and provides up-to-the-minute information on subjects of concern to its members.

AAP's public affairs activities include outreach and cooperative programs with such organizations as the Library of Congress's Center for the Book, the Arts Advocacy Alliance (supporting the National Endowment for the Arts and other federal arts programs), PEN American Center and its International Freedom to Write Program, and a host of literacy and reading promotion efforts including an early childhood literacy initiative, Reach Out and Read.

In addition to its traditional print distribution, the AAP newsletter *AAP Monthly Report* is published online at http://www.publishers.org, the association's Web site.

BookExpo America

AAP is a cosponsor of BookExpo America (BEA), the largest book event in the English-speaking world. BookExpo 2001 was held in Chicago June 1–4. Among the outstanding events: a concert by jazz star Wynton Marsalis to benefit the First Amendment work done by the American Booksellers Foundation for Free Expression (ABFFE) and the Get Caught Reading campaign.

At a special Celebration of Books Luncheon at BEA, the Curtis Benjamin Award for Creative Publishing was presented by AAP President Pat Schroeder to Roger Straus, founder of the publishing house Farrar, Straus & Giroux.

AAP joined with ABFFE and the Freedom to Read Foundation to sponsor an important program on media violence and censorship featuring Pulitzer Prize-winning author Richard Rhodes, author Sara Paretsky, and others.

Get Caught Reading

Launching the third year of the Get Caught Reading campaign in May, AAP and the Magazine Publishers of America announced a new partnership as the campaign's cosponsors. On May 9 the two groups organized "Get Caught Reading Day on Capitol Hill," inviting members of Congress to come and have their photos taken "caught reading." The event was a huge success. A total of 96 members of the House and Senate came to be photographed and interviewed by C-SPAN about the importance of reading in their own lives. The interviews ran as part of C-SPAN II's "Book TV" programming throughout the following months.

Among other highlights of Get Caught Reading in 2001:

- Santa Claus, the ultimate Get Caught Reading celebrity, was photographed in a quiet corner with a book taking a break from the holiday rush. Photos ran in *Bookselling This Week* and *Publishers Weekly,* and were distributed to bookstores for holiday displays.
- Get Caught Reading posters were among the most sought-after materials at the first National Book Festival, which was held September 8 on the U.S. Capitol grounds and drew an estimated 25,000 visitors.

- AAP's display of Get Caught Reading materials attracted a lot of attention at the Food Marketers Institute trade show in Chicago in May.
- To broaden the reach of the campaign, a Spanish-language logo was created in 2001.
- The roster of Get Caught Reading celebrities continued to grow. Now appearing on posters are Clifford the Big Red Dog, Donald Duck, Whoopi Goldberg, Derek Jeter, Jake Lloyd, Rosie O'Donnell, Dolly Parton, the Rugrats, Pat Schroeder, Jane Seymour, Sammy Sosa, and Robin Williams (not to mention 96 members of Congress).
- Barnes & Noble displayed Get Caught Reading window banners and signs in all of its stores and in 30 B&N College Stores across the country throughout May. Posters were also displayed in all of the Borders stores.
- The American Booksellers Association sent specially prepared Get Caught Reading Retail Tool Kits to all of its Book Sense stores.
- Follett distributed Get Caught Reading posters to its stores and will use Get Caught Reading buttons, postcards, and T-shirts for store giveaways and contests.
- The campaign got a boost from two new sponsors at the AAP Annual Meeting as Trade Committee Chairman Michael Jacobs (Scholastic) received checks for $25,000 from the National Association of College Stores and $5,000 from Mibrary. The Mibrary check was given in honor of Microsoft, the winner of Mibrary's Alan Kay Award for Ebook Innovation.

As in past years, teachers, librarians, and booksellers across the country creatively used Get Caught Reading materials to stage their own events to encourage their students and patrons to "get caught reading." AAP continues to receive photographs of the events and letters too numerous to count, and continues to support these reading-promotion ambassadors with posters and ideas.

Copyright

The AAP Copyright Committee coordinates efforts to protect and strengthen intellectual property rights and to enhance public awareness of the importance of copyright as an incentive to creativity. The committee monitors intellectual property legislation in the United States and abroad and serves as an advisory body to the board of directors in formulating AAP policy on legislation and compliance activities, including litigation. The committee coordinates AAP's efforts to promote understanding and compliance with U.S. copyright law on U.S. college and university campuses. Lois Wasoff (Houghton Mifflin) chaired the committee in 2001.

Through its involvement in the International Intellectual Property Alliance (IIPA), AAP works with other U.S. copyright industries to mobilize U.S. government support for intellectual property protection among the nation's trading partners.

The Rights and Permissions Advisory Committee (RPAC), which sponsors educational programs for rights and permissions professionals, held a full-day conference in New York in May focusing on Copyright and Permissions in the Digital Age, including a bonus session for small publishers on the basics of granting permissions. The *RPAC Copyright Primer,* one of AAP's most popular publications, has gone back to press for a new printing.

At the direction of the Copyright Committee, AAP provided amicus support in several important copyright cases.

Early in the year AAP joined an amicus brief to the U.S. Court of Appeals for the Second Circuit supporting the copyright industries' views in *Universal City Studios, Inc.* v. *Reimerdes,* a case involving a software utility called DeCSS. Developed to crack the encryption of movies released on digital video discs (DVDs), the DeCSS algorithm was widely disseminated on Internet sites and through other means. The movie studios and the Motion Picture Association of America sued the Web site's operators under the anticircumvention provisions of DMCA, which outlaws devices and services "primarily designed" to circumvent technologies used to protect copyrighted work from unauthorized access. After issuance of a preliminary injunction by a federal judge in New York was upheld by the Second Circuit, the case proceeded to trial, where the plaintiffs prevailed. In his ruling, the judge rejected the defendants' argument that DMCA violates the First Amendment by imposing a prior restraint on protected speech. The case went up on appeal to the Second Circuit and in November the appellate court issued an important ruling that upheld the lower court's finding, rejecting claims that DMCA violates the First Amendment. While acknowledging that a computer program's "capacity to convey information" characterizes its instructions to a computer as "speech" for First Amendment purposes, the court distinguished between the limited scope of First Amendment protection applicable to computer code and the broader protection afforded "pure speech" instructions, such as blueprints or recipes.

Another important DMCA case, *Felten* v. *Recording Industry Association of America* (RIAA), was also decided in November. The suit was brought by Princeton University professor Edward Felten after he successfully responded to an industry-sponsored challenge to crack technologies that were being tested to protect music CDs. Felten and his team planned to publish a paper and make a presentation at an academic conference explaining their success, but were dissuaded from doing so after Felten received a letter in April from RIAA stating that public release of the paper "would be facilitating and encouraging the attack of copyrighted content" outside the boundaries of the authorized challenge and in violation of DMCA. Unable to get the suit voluntarily withdrawn despite repeated assurances that no legal action would be taken against Felten for publishing or presenting his paper, in July RIAA moved to dismiss the suit for lack of subject matter jurisdiction (that is, lack of "case or controversy" and standing). They were subsequently supported in these arguments by the U.S. Department of Justice, which filed its own dismissal motion and noted that, despite his earlier apprehensions, Felten had in fact published and presented his paper at another academic conference while his suit was pending. After listening to brief arguments, a federal district judge dismissed the case on the grounds that no "case or controversy" was actually before the court. The dismissal of the Felten suit, however, does not resolve the underlying premise of the action, which is the claim that the threat of a civil suit or possibly even criminal prosecution under DMCA's anticircumvention provisions is having a "chilling effect" on core activities of the scientific research community that are protected by the First Amendment.

AAP also joined with magazine and newspaper publishers and other media organizations in an amicus brief urging the U.S. Supreme Court to review and reverse an 11th Circuit ruling in *Greenberg* v. *National Geographic,* which held that publication on CD-ROM of photographs that had originally appeared in print infringed the copyrights of the original photographs. At issue were four photo spreads by photographer Jerry Greenberg that had appeared in print editions of *National Geographic* over three decades. In 1997 the photographs were included in a CD-ROM set that reproduced the magazines from 1888 to 1996. The amicus brief argued that the 11th Circuit ruling ran counter to the Supreme Court ruling in *New York Times* v. *Tasini* in which the court held that electronic collective works are permitted as long as the context and position of the photographs and articles remains as they appeared in print, which was the case in the National Geographic CDs. The Supreme Court declined to review the case.

During the past year, the committee continued its function of advising and supporting AAP staff with respect to participation in key proceedings and activities focusing on copyright issues, including congressional testimony on distance education and publisher participation in a wide-ranging distance learning pilot project with the Defense Department.

Enabling Technologies

AAP's Open Ebook Standards Project, which was undertaken in 2000 to facilitate and encourage the development of the electronic book market, was formally completed in January 2001 with presentation of the proposed standards and recommendations at a seminar organized with the help of Accenture (AAP's partner in the project). More than 60 representatives from AAP member companies attended the seminar. With the completion of the project, the AAP Enabling Technologies Committee assumed the responsibility for AAP's ongoing standards efforts. Evelyn Sasmor (McGraw-Hill) serves as chair of the committee.

The Ebook Project teams proposed numerous extensions to ONIX—the industry standard for electronically transmitted product information files describing books—to cover e-book product information, and members of the Enabling Technologies Committee worked to ensure that ONIX version 2.0 (released in the summer of 2001) contained all of the publishers' recommendations.

The committee also supported the Ebook Standards Project's numbering proposal, which consists of a proposed standard using both the DOI (Digital Object Identifier) and the ISBN (International Standard Book Number) to identify e-books. The committee successfully lobbied for the appointment of Content Directions, Inc., as the first U.S. DOI registration agency focused on issuing e-book DOIs.

Later in the year, Learning Objects Network was also approved as a DOI registration agency for U.S. publishers. In June, Learning Objects Network and AAP held a meeting to inform publishers about a new Department of Defense distance-learning initiative to enhance on-the-job performance and provide other Web-based learning opportunities to U.S. military personnel and institutions. The Defense Department envisions enabling the flexible use of what it calls "learning objects," that is, individual content components and associated information tags enabling them to be located, acquired, and tracked. The specification that is being developed as a foundation for the project is called SCORM (Sharable Content Objects Reference Model), an XML specification for tagging content so that it can be shared across numerous hardware and software platforms. The committee successfully advocated implementation of ONIX and the DOI in a project that will provide both field training and education courses to members of the military and their families.

In May committee members met with representatives of retailers, distributors, and other vendors to discuss problems arising from the vendors' practice of assigning stock keeping units (SKUs) that looked like ISBNs to publishers' e-books, risking confusion among consumers. It was pointed out that a consumer might see what appeared to be an ISBN on an online retail site, and then attempt, without success, to use that identifier as an ISBN in ordering the book through a local bookstore; or a librarian might change the book's ISBN in the library's database and then attempt to order additional copies of the book using the invalid ISBN-lookalike. Agreement was reached at the meeting that publishers are solely responsible for assigning ISBNs and vendors need to take appropriate steps to avoid confusing similarity between SKUs and ISBNs.

Throughout 2001 AAP was also active in the Open eBook Forum (OeBF), an international organization of publishers, hardware and software companies, industry associations, and others working on technological standards for electronic publishing. Ed McCoyd, AAP's director of digital policy, was elected to serve on OeBF's board, and the AAP Enabling Technologies Committee established a subcommittee to review and report on OeBF's activities. Liisa McCloy-Kelley of Random House chaired OeBF's Metadata Working Group, and Bob Bolick of McGraw-Hill chaired the organization's Requirements Working Group. The committee also presented publishers' recommendations to OeBF's Rights and Rules Working Group, which is chartered to produce a specification for the interoperability of digital rights management systems. These recommendations included enabling features such as previewing, lending, and donating e-books, along with a variety of business models and usage scenarios.

Diversity

AAP's Diversity Committee works to encourage individuals from a variety of ethnic, racial, and religious backgrounds to seek careers in book publishing and to aid AAP member publishers in attracting and retaining a diverse work force. Ernest Urquhart (Harcourt) chaired the committee in 2001.

In the spring of 2001 the committee completed a new brochure, *Real Careers for Real People: Today's Opportunities in Publishing*. Featuring statements by publishing industry professionals from diverse backgrounds about the value and rewards of working in book publishing, the brochure highlights the wide array of vocational specialties and interests that can be found in publishing. Members of the committee use the brochure on visits to college campuses and copies are distributed at college job fairs.

The committee also coordinated the production of a video designed to inspire young people from diverse backgrounds to become book-publishing professionals. The video features interviews with such respected authors as Maya Angelou, Walter Mosley, and Amy Tan, who talk about the importance of books in their lives. The video is being made available to AAP members and will be distributed to career counselors and placement officers at colleges around the country.

Education Program

AAP's Education program is designed to provide educational opportunities for publishing industry personnel. The most popular of these programs is the intensive "Introduction to Publishing" course designed to give entry-level employees an overview of the industry. Other programs have included seminars on issues related to work-for-hire and contracted services; financial issues for editors; and state, local, and federal tax developments affecting the publishing industry, the Internet, and new media.

Freedom to Read

The AAP Freedom to Read Committee works to protect intellectual freedom and the free marketplace of ideas, serving as the industry's early warning system on such issues as libel, privacy, school censorship, attacks on public libraries, reporters' privilege (confidentiality of source materials), the Internet and filtering technology, sexually explicit materials, third-party liability, and efforts to punish speech that "causes harm." The committee coordinates AAP's participation, as plaintiff or friend-of-the-court, in important First Amendment cases, and sponsors educational programs on free-speech issues of importance to publishers. Jane Isay (Harcourt) chaired the committee in 2001.

The Freedom to Read Committee works closely with allied organizations, notably the Office for Intellectual Freedom of the American Library Association (ALA) and ABFFE. AAP is a founding member of Media Coalition, a group of trade associations working together on censorship issues.

In fulfilling its educational mandate, the committee sponsored a seminar in October entitled "Risky Business: Publishing Exposés in Print and Online." The panel, which included bestselling author James Stewart (*Den of Thieves*), literary agent/attorney Gail Ross, Scribner vice president Lisa Drew, and others, offered a behind-the-scenes look at the decision-making and risk-assessment process involved in publishing works of investigative journalism.

At BookExpo America in June, the committee joined with ABFFE and the Freedom to Read Foundation to cosponsor "Murderous Media? The Debate Over Media Violence." The informative discussion, moderated by author Sara Paretsky, explored the alleged connection between fictional portrayals of violence on film and other media and actual acts of violence. Panelists included Pulitzer Prize-winning author Richard Rhodes, clinical psychologist Ginger Rhodes, psychiatrist Carl Bell, and Brian Wilcox of the University of Nebraska.

The committee was involved in a number of important First Amendment cases during the past year:

- AAP took the lead in filing an amicus brief to the U.S. Supreme Court supporting a challenge to the Child Online Protection Act (COPA). Dubbed "CDA II," COPA was Congress's second attempt to criminalize constitutionally protected speech on the Internet, making an end-run around the Supreme Court's unanimous rejection of the Communications Decency Act as unconstitutional. The AAP brief argues that COPA— which makes it a crime to communicate to minors "for commercial purposes" via the World Wide Web material deemed "harmful to minors"— would wrongly deny adults access to constitutionally protected materials. While the district court found COPA to be unconstitutional on a number of grounds, the Third Circuit affirmed the preliminary injunction on a much narrower basis, focusing on the impossibility of establishing one "community standard" by which Internet speech can be governed. In oral arguments in November, the Supreme Court seemed to focus its attention solely on the community standards question.

- Notwithstanding the fact that state laws banning harmful-to-minors material on the Internet have been held unconstitutional by federal courts in New York, New Mexico, and Michigan, among others, state legislators persist in enacting such statutes and defending them in court. In 2000 AAP joined other members of Media Coalition as a plaintiff in challenging Arizona's statute, and in February 2001 AAP again joined in filing suit, this time in Vermont.

- Charging that the Children's Internet Protection Act (which mandates the use of blocking software on computers in public libraries) is unconstitutional because it restricts library patrons' access to First Amendment-protected material, ALA and the American Civil Liberties Union (ACLU) went to court to challenge the act. Although AAP is not yet involved in the litigation, the committee is closely monitoring the case with an eye to providing amicus support to the plaintiffs at an appropriate time.

- In the spring of 2001 AAP welcomed a ruling by the U.S. Court of Appeals for the Seventh Circuit reversing a lower court and enjoining enforcement of an Indianapolis statute barring access for anyone under 18 to arcade video games containing "graphic violence." AAP was one of a number of friends-of-the-court who asked the appellate court to grant the injunction. Significantly, the Seventh Circuit held that the record contained no proof that video games incite minors to violent behavior.

- AAP joined with other media and civil liberties groups in an amicus brief asking a federal court in California to declare unenforceable in the United States a French court ruling against Yahoo! concerning Internet content. The French court penalized Yahoo! for permitting its auction sites to offer Nazi memorabilia, in violation of French hate-speech laws. Noting specifically that it does not address disputes concerning intellectual property, the amicus brief argued that the French court ruling posed a direct threat to free speech traditions, commenting that "Freedom of expression would be crippled were online speakers in the United States required to conform their speech to the restrictions of foreign nations, which vary widely from country to country and often conflict with core First Amendment principles." The federal district court agreed, and in November ruled that Yahoo! is not bound by the French court ruling. The French groups who brought the original suit against Yahoo! are asking the Ninth Circuit Court of Appeals to review the decision.

- AAP welcomed a ruling by the Ninth Circuit that held that a computer-altered photo of actor Dustin Hoffman that appeared in *Los Angeles Magazine* was not a violation of the actor's rights but an editorial use of his image entitled to full First Amendment protection. AAP was included in an amicus brief asking the Ninth Circuit to reverse the lower court and rule in the magazine's favor.

- AAP, ABFFE, the ALA-affiliated Freedom to Read Foundation, and others joined in filing an amicus brief to the U.S. Supreme Court in *Aschcroft v. Free Speech Coalition,* a challenge to the Child Pornography Prevention Act (CPPA), on appeal from the Ninth Circuit. CPPA broadens the definition of child pornography to criminalize images of adults who "appear to be" minors or images created totally by computer. While remaining sensitive to the underlying serious and legitimate concerns about sexual abuse of children, the brief stresses the constitutional dangers of CPPA and the fact that mainstream works of art are susceptible to prosecution under it.

At year's end, the committee's attention and concern were becoming more and more focused on new censorship challenges and threats to civil liberties growing out of expanded government power in the wake of the September 11 attacks.

The committee was also profoundly disturbed by the Presidential Executive Order signed November 1 by President Bush that allows the incumbent president, former presidents, and even members of their families to indefinitely block the release of presidential papers and tapes. AAP is taking the lead on an amicus brief in support of a legal challenge to the Executive Order brought late in the year.

Higher Education

AAP's Higher Education Committee continues to serve the needs and interests of AAP members that publish for the postsecondary educational market. The Higher Education Committee was chaired by John Isley (Pearson Education) in 2001.

The Higher Education group again coordinated AAP's participation at the National Association of College Stores (NACS) Annual Meeting and Campus Exposition held in Nashville in April, as well as ConTEXT, the NACS trade show for textbooks. The committee continued its outreach to college stores to improve sell-through.

The committee published its annual *AAP College Textbook Publishers Greenbook,* a resource for college-store buyers that provides a wealth of information on the college publishing industry.

International Committee

The International Committee represents a broad cross section of the AAP membership. Deborah Wiley (John Wiley & Sons) chaired the committee in 2001.

This group met twice in 2001 to discuss issues facing the international publishing community. It hosted a strategy meeting with BookExpo America officials, publishing rights staff, agents, and scouts on ways to improve and enhance international attendance at BookExpo America 2002 in New York.

The International Sales Committee (chaired by McGraw-Hill's Chitra Bopardikar) met several times in 2001 to be briefed by AAP staff on global issues of interest to U.S. publishing exporters. The committee hosted events at BookExpo America and the Frankfurt Book Fair.

International Freedom to Publish

AAP's International Freedom to Publish (IFTP) Committee defends and promotes freedom of written communication worldwide. The committee monitors human rights issues and provides moral support and practical assistance to publishers and authors outside the United States who are denied basic freedoms. The committee carries on its work in close cooperation with other human rights groups, including Human Rights Watch and PEN American Center. Nan Graham (Scribner) chaired the committee in 2001.

The committee continued to provide Judith Krug of the ALA Office for Intellectual Freedom with information on book censorship around the world. This listing of books that are banned in their own country but available in the United States forms the new international section of the Banned Books Week resource guide published by ALA.

The committee expressed deep concern to government officials in Iran over harsh sentences handed down by a court against a group of writers, publishers, and rights activists who attended an international conference organized by the Heinrich Böll Foundation in Berlin in the spring of 2000. The defendants were charged with "conspiring to overthrow the system of the Islamic Republic." In separate letters to Iranian Supreme Leader Ayatollah Ali Khamenei, President Mohammad Khatami, and the head of Iran's judiciary, AAP decried the "politically motivated prosecution" of members of the group, including writer/journalist Akbar Ganji, translators Said Sadr and Khalil Rostamkhani, publisher and women's rights advocate Shahla Lahiji, and writer/lawyer/activist Mahrangiz Kar. AAP expressed particular concern about Kar, who had been diagnosed with breast cancer and was forbidden to leave the country for medical treatment. "The Association of American Publishers believes that the charges against these individuals are politically motivated and that their trials violated international standards," the letter stated. Copies of the letters were sent to United Nations Secretary General Kofi Annan.

In letters to Pakistani authorities, AAP expressed concern about the safety of Afghan writer Esmat Qaney and his publisher Mustafa Sahar, who were labeled as "apostates" by Taliban religious leaders and had sought refuge in northern Pakistan. Citing a pattern of harassment and intimidation of Afghan writers and journalists living in exile in Pakistan, the letter noted that "In recent years, more than a dozen Afghan intellectuals living as refugees in Pakistan have been assassinated, and many more have received death threats." AAP urged the government of Pakistan to "take decisive steps to end the harassment and intimidation," in accordance with Article 19 of the Universal Declaration of Human Rights.

AAP sent a strong letter to President Robert Mugabe of Zimbabwe protesting his government's harassment of independent newspapers and journalists, including the *Zimbabwe Standard* and Geoff Nyarata of the *Daily News.* The letter points out that after attending the 2000 Zimbabwe International Book Fair, members of the committee had recommended that AAP members continue to attend future fairs despite a host of serious problems in Zimbabwe, including economic instability, human rights abuses, election fraud, and the government's inadequate response to the AIDS crisis. However, the letter asserts, "this position is untenable in light of your government's continued censorship of pro-democratic voices through intimidation and harassment." Copies of the letter, which was jointly signed by AAP President Schroeder and IFTP Chair Graham, were sent to U.N. Secretary General Annan, U.S. Secretary of State Colin Powell, and a host of human rights and media organizations.

The committee received funding from the Open Society Institute for a project to encourage the publication of Iranian literature in English translation. The project grew out of a meeting with a group of visiting Iranian writers, as well as from a mission to Iran by IFTP in May 2000. Very little Iranian literature is published in the United States. The aim of the project will be to increase understanding of Iran and Iranian culture and to connect relatively isolated Iranian writers with the international literary world.

International Trade Relations/Antipiracy Activities

AAP conducts a vigorous international program designed to combat the worldwide problem of copyright piracy, increase fair access to foreign markets, and strengthen foreign copyright law regimes.

The war on copyright piracy in India escalated to a new level in January 2001 with the seizure by Indian police of thousands of illegal copies of books by some of the world's bestselling authors. The massive raid, which targeted six businesses in the Indian state of Mumbai, netted nearly 20,000 pirated books including trade fiction, nonfiction, and books for young readers, along with a smaller number of scientific, technical, and medical books. The illegal copies included popular works of fiction by Robert Ludlum, Tom Clancy, Len Deighton, Sidney Sheldon, Robin Cook, and Danielle Steele, and best-selling children's books including J. K. Rowling's Harry Potter series and the Nancy Drew and Hardy Boys books. The raid was a direct result of a joint antipiracy initiative undertaken by U.S. and British publishers through their trade associations, AAP and the British Publishers Association, with the support of the Indian publishing industry.

In what is believed to be the largest raid in publishing history, law enforcement officials in South Korea, with the cooperation of AAP, discovered some 600,000 counterfeit English-language books with an estimated value of more than $14.5 million. The books, comprising about 2,000 titles, ran the gamut from popular best-selling fiction to college textbooks to reference and professional works. The dramatic raid, which took place February 26 and was announced in Seoul March 7, was carried out in a warehouse on the outskirts of Seoul belonging to well-established book distributor Han Shin. The quantity of books seized indicates that Han Shin controlled upward of 90 percent of the market for some titles.

Although many illegally produced books seized in past raids in South Korea and elsewhere in the Pacific Rim have been very poor counterfeits meant to sell at substantially lower prices than legitimate copies, many of the books discovered in the February raid were extremely good copies—so good, in fact, that their legitimate publishers needed forensic help, including microscopic analysis, to identify them as forgeries. Despite their appearance, however, and the fact that they were being sold on college and university campuses at or near their full retail price, the counterfeit books were very cheaply made. This reality would only become apparent to the unwitting purchaser after a few months, when the binding glue came undone or the paper disintegrated and the books would literally fall apart, prompting the consumer to complain to the legitimate publisher.

The raid on Han Shin underscores the fact that pirates are no longer fly-by-night operators requiring only a photocopying machine but have evolved into sophisticated, high-tech entrepreneurs requiring substantial capital investment and posing an even greater threat to legitimate publishing interests.

Postal

AAP's Postal Committee coordinates activity in the area of postal rates and regulations, monitors developments at the U.S. Postal Service (USPS) and the independent Postal Rate Commission, and intervenes on the industry's behalf in formal proceedings before the commission. The committee also directs AAP lobbying activities on postal issues. Paul DeGuisti (McGraw-Hill) chaired the committee in 2001.

In May AAP President Schroeder appeared before the House Government Reform Committee to outline AAP's concerns about proposed postal rate increases. She strongly protested the heavy burden placed on "Bound Printed Matter," the mail category used by publishers to ship books to bookstores, schools, and book club members including millions of young members of children's book clubs. Bound printed matter, she pointed out, had seen largest rate increase of any mail category, and by July 1 the cost of mailing a book would have risen more than 18.4 percent on average (and in some cases as much as 36 percent) since the beginning of the year. Publishers were now facing yet another proposed rate increase. Schroeder noted that long-standing congressional policy requires the Postal Service to consider the cultural, informational, and educational value of the material being mailed as a key factor in setting rates, and that this mandate was being ignored in the latest round of rate increases.

In September the Postal Service filed another rate case. However, by year's end AAP and other major players in the mailer community reached a tentative agreement with USPS to settle rather than litigate the pending rate case, essentially agreeing to the rates requested in September and setting June 2002 as their implementation date. The decision to reach a settlement was prompted by the desire to head off a refiling of the rate case, which would be likely to result in much steeper proposed increases prompted by the desperate circumstances in which USPS now found itself. The financially strapped USPS suffered unprecedented drops in mail volume and staggering, unbudgeted security costs in the wake of the September 11 terrorist attacks and the subsequent anthrax mail incidents. However, if the settlement is adopted early in 2002, it will not establish a precedent nor bind any of the parties in future negotiations.

Professional/Scholarly Publishing

The Professional/Scholarly Publishing (PSP) Division is composed of AAP members who publish books, journals, looseleaf products, and electronic products in technology, science, medicine, business, law, humanities, the behavioral sciences, and scholarly reference. Professional societies and university presses also play an important role in the division. Ted Nardin (McGraw-Hill) chaired the division in 2001.

The 2001 PSP Annual Conference "What's Working Now: Professional/ Scholarly Publishing in the 21st Century," featuring guest speakers Alan Lightman and John Gage, was held in Washington, D.C., in February. Prior to the opening of the meeting, the division's Electronic Information Committee sponsored a preconference seminar on "Transformational Publishing: Creating New Identities in the Digital Marketplace." The division sponsors an awards program, open only to AAP/PSP members, to acknowledge outstanding achievements in professional, scholarly, and reference publishing. At the 25th annual PSP Awards, the R. R. Hawkins Award for the outstanding professional/scholarly work of the year went to Johns Hopkins University Press for *The Bees of the World*. In addition, book awards were presented in 33 subject categories, in design and production, and in journal and electronic publishing.

Among the division's educational activities in 2001: PSP's Journals Committee sponsored an intensive, three-day, case-studies approach to journal publishing in Montreal, and the Marketing and Sales Committee held a one-day seminar, "The Basics of Marketing," which addressed a broad range of marketing issues as they apply to professional and scholarly publishing.

School Division

The School Division is concerned with publishing for the elementary and secondary school (K–12) market. The division works to enhance the role of instructional materials in the education process, to maintain categorical funding for instructional materials and increase the funds available for the purchase of these materials, and to simplify and rationalize the process of state adoptions for instructional materials. It serves as a bridge between the publishing industry and the educational community, promoting the cause of education at the national and state level and working closely with an effective lobbying network in key adoption states. Margery Mayer (Scholastic) chaired the division in 2001.

Early in 2001, as the U.S. economy slid toward recession, many states were faced with budget deficits for the first time in years. The economic downturn became a crisis in many states after the tragic events of September 11, and by the end of 2001 cuts in state education spending totaled more than $11 billion by some estimates. Many states had to call their legislatures into special session to deal with their budget crises. Yet—despite the most stringent fiscal conditions in a decade—as the School Division continued to stress the importance of high-quality, up-to-date instructional materials, funding for these materials fared better than most education line items. In Florida, for example, funding for instructional materials was increased by 11 percent or more than $21 million. The Texas legislature fully funded Proclamation 98-99 at a record cost of $570 million. In California, a state hard hit by an energy crisis in addition to the national economic downturn, funding for instructional materials was left uncut. In Utah, AAP helped enact a $24 million one-time supplemental funding for instructional materials.

Another major victory for AAP members was the passage of H.R. 1, President Bush's Education Bill, legislation that will usher in a new era of federal K–12 education reform. Of particular interest for educational publishers is a new requirement that all students in grades 3–8 be tested every year in reading and math. Starting in 2005, science will be added to the testing requirement on a periodic basis. To help states pay to develop and administer these new tests, the federal government will be spending up to $490 million a year.

In addition, H.R. 1 created a major new literacy program called " Reading First." Funded at $900 million annually, the program is designed to help states establish reading initiatives with "scientific research-based materials" in kindergarten through grade 3. It would also provide funds for necessary professional development to help provide effective reading instruction. AAP staff is actively working with the U.S. Department of Education on how best to implement the testing and reading provision of the "Leave No Child Behind Act" of 2001.

In January 2001 the School Division established several committees to focus on key challenges and opportunities facing the educational publishing industry.

The School Division maintains an Accuracy e-line to help publishers continue to monitor and improve the quality of their instructional materials. In addition, the division developed a colorful new brochure to explain *What It Takes to Publish a Quality Textbook,* which lays out, in simple graphics, the intensive effort and commitments of time and resources that go into the process of publishing instructional materials.

In the hope of informing the debate on Capitol Hill and in communities and state legislatures across the nation about the value and role of educational testing, the School Division prepared a new publication, *Education Assessment: A Primer,* to give policymakers and the public information about the role of testing, what tests can do, and how testing systems should be designed, created, and administered. In addition to answering some frequently asked questions about tests and testing, the *Primer* discusses key elements essential to effective testing programs.

After almost 18 months of intense negotiation, the School Division and organizations representing the blind and visually impaired reached agreement on the framework for federal legislation that would establish a national file format and central file depository for electronic files provided by publishers to be used to produce braille and other instructional materials accessible to blind students. If enacted, the Instructional Materials Accessibility Act would create a single nationwide set of rules under which the files would be provided, relieving publishers of the burden and cost of complying with an ever-increasing and confusing array of state and local laws and regulations. Speaking to 3,000 delegates to the 2001 Convention of the National Federation for the Blind on July 6 in Philadelphia, AAP President Schroeder praised the historic agreement, but warned that "passage of the Instructional Materials Accessibility Act won't be easy because it would preempt the vast array of confusing, often conflicting and redundant, state and local laws and regulations." Passage of the bill is essential, she said, "because the status quo is chaos." Expressing her pleasure at being in Philadelphia on the Independence Day holiday, Schroeder said: "If 'Liberty and Justice for All' means anything, it means the right to a high-quality education."

For the second year, School Division lobbying efforts defeated legislation in New Mexico that would have eliminated the state's adoption system for instructional materials as well as set the foundation for eliminating categorical funding for textbooks. AAP lobbying efforts in New York helped defeat legislation that would have put unreasonable restrictions on the use of brand-name or company logos in instructional materials. The School Division was instrumental in helping the New York legislature pass a compromise bill that will improve access to textbooks for disabled students but will keep publisher requirements similar to those in other states.

In June members of the School Division Executive Committee came to Washington, D.C., to lobby key members of Congress and the U.S. Department of Education on the need for an increased federal role in funding instructional materials to overcome the "textbook divide." This was the first time the division has focused lobbying efforts at the federal level. AAP plans a major push in this area in 2002.

Georgia is now the fourth-largest adoption state. However, unlike most adoption states, Georgia funds only a portion of the cost of purchasing state-adopted instructional materials and its replacement time is seven years compared with six in most states. AAP is leading a coalition of Georgia education organizations in a major effort to get the state to increase its funding for textbooks and shorten the replacement cycle to six years. This effort is being well received and will hopefully see positive results in this year's legislative session.

In the fall AAP hosted a highly successful national Math Summit involving nearly 200 publishers and math educators from across the country including U.S. Secretary of Education Rod Paige. The summit brought together many of the leading experts on teaching mathematics to help find better ways to teach math to American students.

The School Division, in conjunction with the National Association of Textbook Administrators (NASTA), held a forum on the size and weight of textbooks. This issue has been getting quite a bit of press attention during the last year and textbook publishers are often blamed as the cause of injury to young students who carry heavy backpacks to and from school each day. This forum gave the industry a chance to set the record straight that the "heavy backpack" problem has multiple causes—including the absence of lockers in schools for security reasons and the practice of carrying backpacks over one shoulder instead of two—most of which are beyond the control of the publishing industry.

At year's end North Carolina established an electronic procurement system for all state purchases that would require publishers to pay a 1.75 percent market fee to participate in the e-procurement process, in addition to the 8 percent discount publishers are already required to provide to fund the state's depository and adoption system. AAP has retained legal counsel in North Carolina to fight this unprecedented double charge for publishers doing business in the state.

Trade Publishing

AAP's Trade Publishing group comprises publishers of fiction, general nonfiction, poetry, children's literature, religious, and reference publications, in hardcover, paperback, and electronic formats. Michael Jacobs (Scholastic) chaired the Trade Publishing Committee in 2001.

Much of the committee's attention in 2001 focused on the Get Caught Reading campaign, which is discussed in detail earlier in this report.

The committee also works on the AAP honors program, nominating and electing a candidate from outside the publishing industry who has helped promote American books and authors. The award is presented at the AAP Annual Meeting.

To deal with what publishers see as an industry crisis—the difficulty of finding and retaining talented employees—the committee created the Recruit and Retain Task Force to target college students approaching graduation, individuals currently working in other industries who would like to change careers, and junior-level publishing employees who may be considering a move to a high-tech industry. The recruitment efforts include college campus career outreach programs in cooperation with the AAP Diversity Committee. The task force works on establishing an industry-wide publishing job board that includes positions in marketing, technology, and sales. The retention effort focuses on a series of bimonthly brown-bag lunches for junior-level employees, hosted by AAP member houses, designed to facilitate networking, encourage a sense of community, and create opportunities for career growth and development. Executives from participating houses are invited to talk about their own work experiences and responsibilities.

2001 Annual Meeting

More than 200 people attended AAP's Annual Meeting in Washington, D.C., Feb. 7 and 8. With the PSP conference and exhibit attracting some 300 attendees earlier in the week, and 100 registrants for the third annual Small and Independent Publishers (SIP) meeting on February 7, the entire week at the Mayflower was taken up with the business of publishing.

A well-timed story in the *Washington Post* on February 7 featuring an interview with AAP President Schroeder stressed the industry's determination to protect the creative rights of authors and publishers in the face of new technological challenges. Responding to the *Post* reporter's interest in the "copyright wars" between publishers and librarians, Schroeder was quick to point out that this was "not exactly breaking news," and that publishers and librarians have long disagreed over the boundaries of fair use although the two communities work together on any number of issues, including literacy and freedom of expression.

The story, which generated much favorable comment, provoked some good-natured ribbing from political satirist Mark Russell, who entertained at dinner.

The tempo of the meeting was generally upbeat, although the need to safeguard intellectual property and other challenges facing the industry provided a constant underlying theme. The darkest note was sounded by SIP luncheon speaker Andre Schiffrin (New Press), reiterating the theme of his book *The Business of Books: How the International Conglomerates Took Over Publishing and Changed the Way We Read* (Verso, 2000) that "big is dangerous to publishers, readers and booksellers." His view of small publishers as an endangered species was challenged, however, by two small publishers in the audience, Lynne Rienner (Lynne Rienner Publishers) and Jed Lyons (Rowman & Littlefield Publishing Group). Peter Chernin, CEO of News Corporation, took direct issue with Schiffrin's viewpoint, asserting that "big is good for publishing." "Thanks to the deep and extensive resources of their parent companies," he said, "a growing variety of publishing houses has been able to thrive—and to produce a wider range of books with greater ambition and confidence than would ever be possible for an independent press." Chernin argued that the guiding principles that have always worked in publishing—the high quality of the work itself, active and productive relationships with authors, and innovative marketing to get books to their readers—are more critical now than ever before. But beyond these the "single most important issue" for publishers is copyright protection, "a fundamental right that has become endangered in the digital age." Without it, Chernin said, "book publishers are in danger of being extinguished in a matter of years."

Christie Hefner, president and CEO of Playboy Enterprises, who was responsible for her company's highly successful electronic expansion, expressed her enthusiasm for the Internet. Hefner said that—contrary to predictions that cyberspace will eliminate the need for publishers and editors—the freewheeling world of the Internet will make editorial judgment and selection more necessary than ever. She admitted, however, that she is not as sanguine about the Internet as an instrument to end censorship and open all borders, citing ample evidence of the ongoing struggle between freedom and state control. The struggle will only intensify as totalitarian governments become more threatened by the free flow of information, and she warned against government attempts to assume a "parental" role in legislating constitutionally protected speech.

Henry Yuen, CEO of Gemstar–TV Guide International, made a pitch for the Gemstar ebook, a device designed for reading without a PC, which would eliminate the incentive for cracking encryption codes because content stored on one device could only be read on that device. Yuen's proposal is based on a "timed release" concept similar to the hardcover/paperback transition in print publishing.

Goldman Sachs investment policy guru Abby Joseph Cohen sounded an optimistic note about an economy that "looks slower than it is." "The time to have worried was a year ago," when the economy was experiencing unsustainable growth, she asserted. Cohen pointed out that changes over the last eight to ten years have strengthened the economic infrastructure in important and fundamental ways. In 1992 the United States was staggering under the largest budget deficit in its history, $300 billion representing 6 percent of the gross domestic product. Labor productivity growth was the slowest in decades, and many U.S. corporations, anticipating increased inflation, were bypassing long-term investment in favor of creating inventory. In the past decade, she said, the United States has instituted the best fiscal policy in its history, controlled inflation, changed the way the future is approached by spending more on research and development instead of inventory, and developed exciting new technologies that have increased productivity significantly.

Two late surprises enlivened the presentation of the AAP Honors to CBS News anchor Charles Osgood. AAP learned just a week before the meeting that Michael Powell, the newly named chairman of the Federal Communications Commission, would be on hand to present the award. Powell called "CBS Sunday Morning," which Osgood hosts, "a precious way to start the day." Osgood had asked that the $5,000 charitable gift that accompanies the AAP Honors go to the Alliance for Lupus Research to fight the disease that had taken his friend and colleague Charles Kuralt. Osgood was surprised by the presentation of a second $5,000 check by Eddie Fritts, president of the National Association of Broadcasters, who joined in honoring Osgood.

Jim Barksdale, managing partner of the Barksdale Group and former CEO of Netscape, reported on a reading initiative he has launched in his home state of Mississippi, which has the lowest per capita income in the country. Through the Barksdale Reading Institute, a joint venture with the University of Mississippi Department of Education, Barksdale and his wife Sally have committed $100 million to fund an early childhood reading program, including equipping whole elementary school libraries. Operating on the philosophy that "what gets rewarded gets done, and what gets measured gets done," participating schools are being given five years to bring up reading scores and qualify for further funding.

Business Meeting

The membership approved an operating budget of $6,343,217 for fiscal year 2000–2001, with $4,319,617 allocated to Core (including the three committees serving the Trade, Higher Education, and International constituencies) and $2,023,600 allocated to the two divisions ($1,376,500 for the School Division and $647,100 for PSP). Included in the Core budget was a funding increase of $224,000 (to $737,700) for AAP's overseas antipiracy activities.

At its March 7 meeting, the AAP board recommended that additional funds be earmarked to address critical postal issues and appointed a special task force to monitor these issues.

Peter Mayer, president of Overlook Press, and Joseph P. Reynolds, president and CEO of Bell & Howell Information and Learning, were nominated to AAP's Board of Directors. Robert L. Faherty, director of Brookings Institution Press, was nominated by AAP's University Press members to represent them on the board.

American Booksellers Association

828 S. Broadway, Tarrytown, NY 10591
914-591-2665, fax 914-591-2724
World Wide Web http://www.bookweb.org
E-mail info@bookweb.org

Michael Hoynes
Senior Marketing Officer

Founded in 1900, the American Booksellers Association (ABA) is a not-for-profit trade organization devoted to meeting the needs of its core members—independently owned bookstores—through advocacy, education, research, and information dissemination. ABA actively supports free speech, literacy, and programs that encourage children to read. The association, headquartered in Tarrytown, New York, also hosts the annual ABA Convention in conjunction with the BookExpo America trade show each spring.

ABA's core member is the independent bookstore with a storefront location, operated by professional booksellers according to sound business principles. Although ABA provides programs and services to others in the bookselling industry, its primary focus is on its core members.

ABA meets the needs of its members by dedicating its resources and staff to the following services:

- *Advocacy.* ABA serves as a national collective voice for independent booksellers. It acts as an advocate for legal trade practices, lobbies on First Amendment issues and legislation important to its members, advocates beneficial and fair practices that are not in conflict with antitrust laws, and supports programs that encourage book buying, literacy, reading, intellectual freedom, and arts and literature.

- *Partnerships and alliances.* ABA engages in partnerships with regional and other bookseller organizations that build on the organizations' knowledge and ABA's national presence and resources. ABA also participates in partnerships, strategic alliances, and dialogues with publishers, wholesalers, and other interest groups when there is shared interest in pursuing mutually beneficial initiatives.

- *Education, training, and skills development.* ABA provides access to competitive retail and business skills in various ways, using the most effective methods and technologies available.

- *Research.* ABA collects, analyzes, disseminates, and provides immediate access to timely information that is critical to the success of independent booksellers, making it an important information resource for the entire book industry.

- *Systems and software development.* ABA facilitates the development and standardization of systems and forms, customer database information, and financial and operational software support, and actively helps booksellers adapt to and take advantage of emerging technologies.

- *Business support services.* ABA facilitates booksellers' access to services such as business insurance, 401K plans, capital providers, financial advisers, and other essential services.

• *New business models.* ABA facilitates development of feasibility studies, pilot projects, and prototypes that help to incubate new competitive models for its members.

Book Sense

Book Sense, an innovative, strategic, marketing, branding, and bookselling campaign created in 1999 for ABA members, is in its third year of operation. There are now more than 1,200 bookstores in the Book Sense program in the 50 states, Puerto Rico, and the Virgin Islands.

An integral part of the Book Sense marketing program is the Book Sense national gift certificate, which allows consumers to purchase a gift certificate in any participating bookstore that is redeemable in all participating bookstores.

The Book Sense brand is supported by a national advertising campaign running in major national magazines, including the *New Yorker, Atlantic Monthly,* and the *Ruminator Review.*

The program has established the Book Sense 76 List, a bimonthly list of books being recommended by independent bookstores across the country, which has become a valuable resource for both bookstores and consumers. Additionally, there are periodic Book Sense 76 Specialty Top-Ten Lists in such subject areas as children's books, mysteries, science fiction/fantasy, teen reading, poetry, and mind/body/spirit. There is also the Book Sense Bestseller List, a weekly list of bestselling books in independent bookstores, which is being cited in various press reports on books and the bookselling industry. Along with the Book Sense 76 List, it has attracted the attention of publishers and motivated them to become Book Sense marketing partners; as the year 2002 began, there were 70 Book Sense "publisher partners" representing some 400 publishers.

Each month Book Sense coordinates a mailing to all participating stores and to the publisher partners composed of materials provided by the publisher partners. These items include advance reading copies, book excerpts, brochures covering upcoming titles and special offers, easelback posters, "shelftalkers," and other promotional items. Response to the mailings has been positive, with booksellers grateful for materials they might not otherwise have access to and publishers thankful for a look at the promotional items other houses are producing.

The Book Sense e-commerce service, BookSense.com (http://www.book-sense.com), allows independent bookstores to give customers a full range of e-commerce services. Customers can search more than 2 million titles, purchase a book online, and either have it sent to them or pick it up at a participating bookstore. They also have the option of gift-wrapping and can purchase national gift certificates. Each bookstore maintains its own local identity and can offer local content on BookSense.com, such as highlighting local bookstore events. More than 240 independent bookstores currently use the BookSense.com service.

In 2001 Book Sense branding activities were incorporated in ABA's Prescription for Reading program, which pairs independent booksellers with health-care providers in an effort to remind parents and caregivers about the importance of reading to very young children. New partnerships with Pizza Hut and Chronicle Books will be part of Prescription for Reading in 2002.

Antitrust Lawsuit

On April 19, 2001, ABA and 26 independent bookstore plaintiffs settled their legal battle with major bookstore chains Barnes & Noble and Borders. ABA and the other plaintiffs agreed to accept the $4.7 million offered by the defendants because the objectives of the litigation had, by and large, been achieved. The scrutiny brought by the suit revealed several practices within the industry that favored the chains and put independent bookstores at a competitive disadvantage. ABA feels the way to address and change the unfair practices that still remain is through negotiation, discussion, and an open airing of issues with publishers, wholesalers, and distributors. However, the settlement makes clear that independent booksellers retain all their options to address their grievances in the future.

Research

A primary source of statistics for the book industry, specifically on trends in market share, has been the Consumer Research Study on Book Purchasing, based on research conducted by IPSOS-NPD (a Chicago market research firm) in conjunction with the Book Industry Study Group (BISG) and ABA. The 2000 study, released in March 2001, revealed no change from 1999 in the market share for independent bookstores, which remained at 15 percent. Other findings highlighted by the study included the steady but not surprising hold popular fiction retained on the adult book market (54 percent).

Following its introduction at BookExpo 2001 in Chicago, ABA officially launched a new Local Marketing Intelligence (LMI) program. The focus of the service is to assist booksellers in their efforts to gain more knowledge about, and insight into, their local market.

ABA also conducted research to see how its membership had fared in the past year and how independent bookstores were succeeding in building their revenue bases. It commissioned other studies to gain additional insight into consumer book-purchasing behavior; one such study looked into the purchasing behavior of grandparents in regard to children's books.

Sales Tax Action

On November 15, 2001, the U.S. Senate approved legislation that provides for a two-year moratorium on any new Internet commerce taxes. As part of the effort against imposition of taxes on Internet commerce, ABA President Neal Coonerty wrote to the nation's governors urging them to equitably enforce all existing sales tax regulations.

Membership

Although there was a decline in total membership, a substantial portion of this decrease came from the associate member category. This category includes representatives from wholesalers, publishers, authors, and others in the book industry. Total membership at the end of 2001 stood at about 3,500.

Affinity Programs

All ABA members have access to a range of business services especially for independent booksellers. Among these are Libris Casualty and Property Insurance, an ABA-owned business insurance program for independent retailers involved in the sale of books and related products; discounted payment processing on most major credit cards; a Merrill Lynch Comprehensive Financial Services program offering such services as business checking, credit facilities, commercial mortgages, and 401Ks; discounts on inbound and outbound small package shipments through FedEx; and discounts on interstate freight shipments of more than 250 pounds.

Foundation for Free Expression

The American Booksellers Foundation for Free Expression (ABFFE) is leading a fight to defend the privacy of bookstore records. In the past two years, there were four attempts to force booksellers to turn over purchasing information about their customers. ABFFE recently helped Books and Books (Coral Gables, Florida), Olsson's Books and Records (Washington, D.C.), and Arundel Books (Los Angeles) successfully fight subpoenas issued in an investigation undertaken by a U.S. Senate committee. ABFFE is also supporting the fight by Tattered Cover Book Store in Denver against a search warrant seeking customer information. The Colorado Supreme Court heard oral arguments in the case in December and was expected to issue an opinion by late spring.

ABFFE has issued a new edition of its pamphlet *Protecting Customer Privacy in Bookstores.* A free copy can be ordered through the ABFFE online store at http://www.abffe.com.

ABFFE is also educating children about the dangers of censorship. Following the success of its efforts to help defend the Harry Potter books, it has launched an anticensorship Web site, kidSPEAK! (http://www.kidspeakonline. org) to help inform young readers about the First Amendment and the importance of fighting censorship. More than 19,000 children, parents, and grandparents have become members of kidSPEAK!

ABFFE was also active in 2001 in helping fight efforts to suppress the novel *The Wind Done Gone*, a parody sequel to *Gone with the Wind,* by filing two amicus briefs supporting author Alice Randall's right to publish the parody. The estate of *Gone with the Wind* author Margaret Mitchell attempted to block publication of the Houghton Mifflin title on the grounds that it violated the copyright protecting the original novel. Although a court ruling was in favor of Randall, the Mitchell interests vowed to appeal the decision.

ABFFE distributed more than 1,000 Banned Books Week kits to booksellers in September. The kits are free to all ABFFE and ABA members. ABFFE membership is $35 for individuals and $100 for bookstores. For more information, call 212-587-4025 or visit the ABFFE online store at http://www.abffe.com.

Association of Research Libraries

21 Dupont Circle N.W., Washington, DC 20036
202-296-2296; e-mail arlhq@arl.org
World Wide Web http://www.arl.org

Duane E. Webster
Executive Director

The Association of Research Libraries (ARL) represents the 123 principal research libraries that serve major research institutions in the United States and Canada. ARL's mission is to shape and influence forces affecting the future of research libraries in the process of scholarly communication. ARL programs and services promote equitable access to and effective use of recorded knowledge in support of teaching, research, scholarship, and community service. The association articulates the concerns of research libraries and their institutions, forges coalitions, influences information policy development, and supports innovation and improvement in research library operations. ARL operates as a forum for the exchange of ideas and as an agent for collective action.

ARL fulfills its mission and builds its programs through a set of strategic objectives. To meet these objectives, ARL resources are organized into a framework of programs and capabilities. Annually the ARL Board of Directors identifies priorities that the association staff and standing committees will address in the coming year. As outlined in the ARL Program Plan, the present priorities are to

- Provide leadership in advocacy and educational efforts within the research and educational community in the areas of information and telecommunications policy, copyright, and intellectual property
- Create and implement cost-effective strategies for managing scholarly communication in partnership with other organizations
- Help research libraries and their constituencies develop new approaches and models for measuring and improving their service effectiveness, diversity, and leadership
- Advance the development, preservation, and accessibility of research collections through local institutional efforts, collaborative library efforts, and the application of networking technologies

Scholarly Communication

The Office of Scholarly Communication (OSC) undertakes to understand and influence the forces affecting the production, dissemination, and use of scholarly and scientific information. OSC seeks to promote innovative, creative, and affordable ways of sharing scholarly findings, particularly through championing evolving electronic techniques for recording and disseminating academic and research scholarship. OSC collaborates with others in the scholarly community to build a common understanding of the challenges presented by electronic scholarly communication and to generate strategies for transforming the system.

A priority of OSC is to explore and promote strategies that have the potential to transform scholarly communication into a system the primary goal of which is to disseminate research findings in support of the public good. OSC is looking at nonsubscription-based economic models that would support scholarly publishing and allow the peer-reviewed results to be available publicly without fee. It continues to work with the Association of American Universities (AAU) to encourage broad dissemination and discussion of the Tempe Principles. OSC also is promoting the Open Archives Initiative (OAI) and the creation of institutional archives to provide broader accessibility to scholarly information. As part of this effort, ARL is working to encourage the development of new methods of peer review in the electronic environment that address evaluation of new genres of scholarly works or have the potential to disassociate the value of a work from the journal in which it is published.

To build broader engagement within the community in its efforts to transform the scholarly communication system, OSC is working with a number of organizations that share its goal. In March 2001 ARL, the National Humanities Alliance (NHA), and the Knight Higher Education Collaborative jointly sponsored the Knight Higher Education Roundtable on Scholarly Communication in the Humanities and Social Sciences. Participants represented faculty, administrators, scholarly societies, scholarly publishers, and librarians. The final report of the roundtable was issued in December 2001 in the form of an essay, "Op. Cit."

Engaging faculty in these discussions is also critical to the success of any effort to change the system of scholarly communication. In May 2000 OSC, the Scholarly Publishing and Academic Resources Coalition (SPARC), and the Association of College and Research Libraries (ACRL) launched the Create Change Web site, a resource that provides information and tools to support library programming on scholarly communication issues and encourage individual faculty action. In addition, OSC has supported the efforts of the Public Library of Science (PLoS), an initiative launched during 2000 by a group of biomedical scientists. These scientists are encouraging their peers to support only those journals willing to make their research articles available in an open, free public archive six months after publication.

Because both the publishing industry and the research community are global, OSC will work with colleagues in the newly formed International Scholarly Communications Alliance (ISCA) to develop an agenda for addressing scholarly communication issues globally. In February 2002 research library associations in Australia, Canada, Europe, Japan, Hong Kong, New Zealand, the United Kingdom, and the United States announced they had formed an action-oriented global network that will collaborate with scholars and publishers to establish equitable access to scholarly and research publications.

To build a better understanding of the evolving publishing environment, OSC continues to track mergers and acquisitions in the scholarly publishing arena and continues its efforts with antitrust authorities to raise awareness of library concerns about the increased consolidation of the publishing industry. OSC is working to build a collaborative capacity for data collection and maintenance that will provide libraries with the information necessary to support antitrust arguments and advance other educational and advocacy initiatives related to scholarly communication.

OSC is working to create a better community understanding of intellectual property and copyright by developing products designed to educate faculty and librarians about copyright (both ownership and use) and its critical connection to the scholarly communication system. It continues to work with the Association of American Publishers (AAP), Copyright Clearance Center (CCC), American Association of University Presses (AAUP), and AAU on the development of a joint booklet about copyright on campus.

Federal Relations and Information Policy

The Federal Relations and Information Policy program is designed to monitor activities resulting from the legislative, regulatory, or operating practices of international and domestic government agencies and other relevant bodies on matters of concern to research libraries. The program analyzes and responds to federal information policies and influences federal action on issues related to research libraries. It examines issues of importance to the development of research libraries and develops ARL positions on issues that reflect the needs and interests of members. Through the Canadian Association of Research Libraries (CARL), the program monitors Canadian information policies. In 2000 the ARL membership endorsed a new tactic that led in 2001 to a direct investment in a Canadian-based advocacy effort jointly with CARL.

The ARL Board of Directors has identified intellectual property and copyright as a defining set of issues for the future of scholarly communications. While these issues have been a priority for several years, activity has been accelerated because of developments in the U.S. Congress, state legislatures, and the courts. As part of ARL's interest in raising library and scholarly community awareness of issues associated with copyright and intellectual property management, the Federal Relations program participates in a number of collaborative efforts to advance its agenda in these critical areas.

The Digital Future Coalition (DFC) is composed of a diverse constituency of library, education, legal, scholarly, consumer, and public-interest associations; hardware and software manufacturers; and telecommunications providers. DFC members share common concerns with copyright and intellectual property legislation and Uniform Computer and Information Transactions Act (UCITA) issues and believe that any legislation must strike a balance between owners, users, and creators of copyrighted works. ARL is also a member of Americans for Fair Electronic Commerce Transactions (AFFECT), formerly 4CITE. This is a broad-based coalition of end users and developers of computer information and technology opposed to UCITA. Although there has been some level of activity on UCITA in 21 states, including introduction of the legislation in 11 states, it appeared to stall in 2001 in comparison to its swift passage in 2000 in Maryland and Virginia.

ARL works with the humanities and social sciences communities through the NHA Committee on Libraries and Intellectual Property to keep those communities informed and mobilized on copyright issues. ARL also works collaboratively with the six major presidential associations—the American Association of Community Colleges (AACC), American Association of State Colleges and Universities (AASCU), AAU, American Council on Education (ACE), National Association of Independent Colleges and Universities (NAICU), and National Association of State Universities and Land Grant Colleges (NASULGC)—on key issues of importance to higher education on national policy governing digital networks, intellectual property, and information technology.

The ad hoc Database Coalition is composed of members of the public and private sectors including portals such as Yahoo!, financial services companies such as Bloomberg Financial Markets and Charles Schwab and Company, telecommunications companies such as AT&T, the leading library associations, and the higher education community. ARL collaborates with a number of these constituencies to address issues relating to database proposals.

ARL continues to work with various agencies and offices on information policy issues including the National Science Foundation, United States Geological Survey, Government Printing Office, Office of Science and Technology Policy, Institute of Museum and Library Services (IMLS), the Office of Management and Budget, and others.

In 2001 the Federal Relations program represented ARL interests in a number of amici curiae briefs that were filed in copyright and intellectual property court cases. ARL and the American Library Association (ALA) filed an amici curiae brief in the case of *New York Times* v.*Tasini* to present the library perspective to the U.S. Supreme Court concerning the practical effects of the issues at stake in the case. The brief refuted a number of inaccurate claims and offered constructive ways to balance the rights of freelance authors, commercial electronic database producers, publishers, and the public. On June 25, 2001, the court issued its decision: in a decisive 7-2 ruling, the justices upheld an appeals court ruling that the reuse of a freelance author's work on CD-ROMs and in commercial electronic databases without the author's permission constituted copyright infringement. ARL continues to monitor the effects of the Supreme Court's ruling in the *Tasini* case and its impact on libraries.

ARL, ALA, the American Association of Law Libraries, and the Medical Library Association filed an amici curiae brief in support of the National Geographic Society (NGS) petition for certioria before the U.S. Supreme Court in the case of *Greenberg* v. *National Geographic Society*. Two photographers claimed that the inclusion of their photographs in NGS's CD-ROM version of *National Geographic* magazine violates certain of their copyright rights and that NGS is not exempt under Section 201(c) of the Copyright Act. This section permits the owner of copyright in a collective work, such as a magazine or encyclopedia, to reproduce and distribute an individual author's freelance contribution "as part of that particular collective work, any revision to that collective work, and any later collective work in the same series." The brief argued that the CD-ROM is fundamentally a mere conversion of the original print periodicals into another medium, analogous to a microfilm collection that is permissible under Section 201(c) and, if the decision stands, it would inhibit the dissemination of collective works via digital and electronic media. The court declined to hear the case.

Several court cases provided visibility to Section 1201 of the Digital Millennium Copyright Act (DMCA), the provision concerning anticircumvention of technical protection measures. The ruling by Judge Kaplan of the U.S. District Court for the Southern District of New York in the case *Universal City Studios* v. *Eric*

Corely et al.—commonly known as the "DVD case"—raised First Amendment and fair-use concerns. These prompted ARL, together with ALA, DFC, the American Civil Liberties Union (ACLU), and others, to file an amici curiae brief. The defendant in this case, *2600: The Hacker Quarterly,* posted a computer program for decrypting and copying movies on DVDs on its Web site. As DVDs are protected by technological protection measures, to some this action seemed to run afoul of anticircumvention provisions in DMCA. The court ruled that the defendants could not post the information that would bypass the protections and link to that information at other sites. The brief argued that DMCA punishes new categories of noninfringing, protected speech and creates new levels of liability for Web users that shrink free-speech rights. The case is on appeal to the Supreme Court.

The Sonny Bono Copyright Term Extension Act extended the term of copyright from life plus 50 years to life plus 70 years. The court case *Eldred* v. *Ashcroft* challenges the constitutionality of the act. The U.S. Supreme Court agreed to hear the case in the next term. The library community will file an amici curiae brief before the court.

Results of the implementation of DMCA demanded considerable attention of the program during 2001. In August the U.S. Copyright Office released the DMCA Section 104 Report on the impact of DMCA and electronic commerce and associated technologies on Sections 109 and 117 of the Copyright Act. In the report, the Register of Copyrights recommended no change in the law, especially with respect to extending the first-sale doctrine into the digital age.

Access and Technology

The Access capability undertakes activities to support resource sharing among research libraries in the electronic environment and to improve access to research information resources while minimizing costs for libraries. This capability works to strengthen interlibrary loan and document delivery performance, interoperability among library systems, cooperative cataloging programs, and policies that increase user access to information both on-site and remotely.

The Scholars Portal Working Group was established in 2000 to advance the concept of a collective research library presence on the Web. The concept was first identified at the 1999 ARL/OCLC Strategic Issues Forum in Keystone, Colorado, and was further articulated by Jerry Campbell in April 2000 in "The Case for Creating a Scholars Portal to the Web: A White Paper." During the first half of 2001, the working group narrowed its focus to the development of specifications (conceptual, functional, and technical) for a "super-discovery tool." This tool would search, aggregate, integrate, and deliver licensed and openly available digital content across a broad range of subject fields and from multiple institutions. Members of the working group agreed early on that it would not be desirable for ARL to develop the tool itself but rather to identify potential partners (commercial and otherwise) with whom to collaborate in the tool's development. The working group conducted an environmental scan that identified a wide range of companies and products that have been described as "portals." Some products were reviewed and determined to be out of scope of the goals of the Scholars Portal; others were of sufficient interest to warrant additional research and contact with the company. The working group also monitors developments in portal services, software, and implementations with the intention of developing a set of "best practices" of the functionality and service options of portal services and software.

The 1996 ILL/DD Performance Measures Study highlighted characteristics of high-performing borrowing and lending operations in research libraries. Techniques to implement these "best practices" were the basis for the "From Data to Action" workshops. More than 400 librarians and representatives from the commercial community attended the 12 workshops offered between October 1998 and March 2001.

In addition, more than 200 librarians and vendors participated in "Shaping Interlibrary Loan/Document Delivery in the 21st Century." Cosponsored by ARL and the University of Michigan and held in Ann Arbor in early November, it was the first national conference devoted to ILL/DD issues. Fifteen ILL/DD leaders gave presentations on such diverse topics as distance education, standards, the new national ILL code, and management software. Ten vendors provided updates on ILL/DD-related products and services. The Research Libraries Group hosted an evening reception to toast 10 years of use of the Ariel document delivery software.

The first Directors Forum on Managing ILL/DD Operations was held in February 1995. The final Directors Forum was held at the ALA Annual Conference in San Francisco in June 2001. Brewster Kahle, director of the Internet Archives, spoke on the legal framework of connecting library users with digital resources including the Internet Archives and other digital repositories.

The Access capability has worked to advance support for implementation of the ISO ILL Protocol for several years. At the 2001 International Association of Library Associations and Institutions (IFLA) General Conference in Boston in August, five vendors exchanged ISO ILL messages to an overflow crowd of more than 70 librarians from more than a dozen countries. This was historic; the first time that more than two vendors exchanged ILL messages. This workshop demonstrated the successful results of many test messages exchanged by these five as well as other members of the ILL Protocol Implementors Group (IPIG).

The Access capability continues to support several projects of the AAU/ARL Global Resources Program. The Japan Journal Access Project supports enhanced document delivery between libraries in Japan, the United States, and Canada. In January 2001 the Conference on Improvement of Academic Information Access between the United States and Japan was held in Tokyo. Participants reviewed the document delivery project between members of the AAU/ARL Global Resources Program Japan Project and members of the Association of National University Libraries (ANUL) and agreed that the pilot on electronic delivery of journal articles was very successful. Participants also agreed to resume "regular ILL" during the remainder of 2001. In early March a delegation from Japan's National Institute for Informatics (NII) visited OCLC to finalize the details of testing and use of the ISO ILL Protocol between Japan's NACSIS ILL system and the OCLC ILL system.

The German Resources Project and Xipolis are interested in making the xipolis.net database of key German research resources available to members of the German Resources Project, one of the projects of the AAU/ARL Global Resources Program. In late 2001 ARL signed a license with Xipolis. Participants will sign an agreement with ARL as they register to access xipolis.net. ARL will serve as the fiscal agent, with participants establishing deposit accounts with ARL.

The Collaborative Digital Reference Service (CDRS) is an initiative of the Library of Congress to provide professional reference service to researchers anytime, anywhere, through an international digital network of libraries and related institutions. Answers to reference questions often result in the submission of ILL requests. Representatives of OCLC, ARL, the National Library of Canada, and the Library of Congress held a series of informal meetings during the spring to identify technical requirements to permit CDRS answers to generate an ISO ILL Protocol-compliant patron request message. The December 2001 issue of *ARL: A Bimonthly Report* includes an article that describes the service: "Libraries Meet the World Wide Web: The Collaborative Digital Reference Service" by Diane Kresh, director of public service collections, Library of Congress.

Collection Services

The Collection Services capability pursues initiatives to assist in developing the collections of member libraries and enhancing access to scholarly resources, regardless of their location. The focus is both local and collaborative, covering a variety of strategies, which include improving the structures and processes for effective cooperative collection development, including access to digital resources; collaborating with other organizations in collections-related projects, both within North America and internationally; addressing collection policies and budget management; promoting government and foundation support for collections and collaborative programs in the United States and Canada; and operating collection management training programs. This program also provides oversight for the AAU/ARL Global Resources Program.

In June 2001 a symposium was held at Brown University to explore the prospects and promise of special collections in the expanding electronic environment. "Building on Strength: Developing an ARL Agenda for Special Collections" brought together ARL directors and heads of special collections, along with invited guests and speakers, to articulate a long-term programmatic agenda for special collections in research libraries. The symposium was especially timely, coming just after the publication of *Special Collections in ARL Libraries,* the results of a 1998 survey of the ARL membership.

A new ARL Special Collections Task Force was formed in late 2001 and charged to engage and advance the agenda that emerged from the "Building on Strength" symposium. This group brings together ARL directors and special collections librarians, including representatives of the ALA Rare Books and Manuscripts Section (RBMS) and the Society of American Archivists (SAA). The task force will develop a report and an action plan that addresses key points in the symposium agenda, including enhancing access to collections and backlogs; coordinating planning for collecting 19th- and 20th-century materials and those in new formats; defining core competencies among special collections librarians and creating training opportunities; and incorporating special collections topics into the agenda of ARL standing committees.

The Forum on Collections and Access for the 21st Century Scholar, sponsored by ARL, was held in October 2001. It gave ARL directors and other library administrators the opportunity to discuss and debate many issues ranging from the architecture of the new library environment to the OAI metadata harvesting protocol, new instructional uses of the Web, and information-seeking behavior of library users. As a result, a Task Force on Collections and Access has been named and asked to work initially for one year to advance the multifaceted agenda that emerged from the forum.

The AAU/ARL Global Resources Program (GRP) was established in early 1997 with funding from the Andrew W. Mellon Foundation. Originally intended to be a three-year grant, the funding has enabled more than five years of activity focused on improving access to international research materials through cooperative structures and the use of new technologies and on generating increased communication with the scholarly community regarding future information needs. In addition, the GRP funding has served as seed money for the regional projects, two of which have received significant additional funding from the U. S. Department of Education's Title VI Program for Technological Cooperation and Innovation for Foreign Information Access (TICFIA). The regional projects sponsored by GRP address seven countries or world areas: Africa, Eastern Europe, Germany, Japan, Latin America, South Asia, and Southeast Asia. Each has developed differently, based on the needs of scholars who use materials from the area and on the perceptions of area specialist librarians of the most pressing challenges for information access. All share a focus on a basic GRP goal: to enhance access through cooperation and new uses of technology.

The African Newspaper Union List Project (AFRINUL) is a multi-institutional project to produce and maintain an electronic union list of sub-Saharan African newspapers. A joint initiative of the Africana Librarians Council (ALC) of the African Studies Association (ASA) and the Cooperative Africana Microform Project (CAMP) of the Center for Research Libraries (CRL), AFRINUL also complements CRL's International Coalition on Newspapers (ICON) project. The database will consolidate holdings information for collections in North America and will later expand to include holdings in Africa, Europe, and elsewhere. The project also has a preservation component and plans to digitize the content of newspapers to facilitate research on African political, economic, and cultural events. AFRINUL currently has 15 participating libraries.

The German Resources Project has working groups that coordinate activities in four areas: collection development, document delivery, digital libraries, and bibliographic control. In collections, a project was launched in early 2002 to enable participating libraries to subscribe corporately to a list of German databases through the xipolis.net online reference service. In document delivery, the emphasis has been in two areas: the promotion and refinement of the GBVdirekt/ North America document delivery service for North American libraries (more than 25 institutions now participate in GBV/NA and the number is increasing), and the establishment of a comparable service to supply documents to libraries in Germany. The mission of the German Digital Library Working Group includes fostering the digitization of research materials, assisting in funding for such projects, and identifying standards. The working group met in Bielefeld at the German Library Association Meeting and at ALA. Four joint German-North American projects are under way. The bibliographic control working group is finalizing the AACR2 German Translation Project as well as developing extensive German and English dictionary tools and word lists devoted to library technical services and cataloging.

The goals of the Japan Journal Access Project are to expand access to research materials published in Japan and to coordinate Japanese collection development initiatives in North American libraries. The North American Coordinating Council on Japanese Library Resources (NCC) is a key cosponsor of the project, and there are 38 project participants. Activities focus on three areas: the Union List of Japanese Serials and Newspapers (ULJSN), document delivery with Waseda University Library, and document delivery with the Association of National University Libraries. This second document-delivery project included ten North American libraries, six Japanese national university libraries, and the National Institute for Informatics (NII). In 2002 six libraries will undertake technical testing between the NACSIS ILL system and OCLC, with production exchange of ILL requests scheduled for spring 2002.

The Latin Americanist Research Resources Project (LARRP), which currently includes 50 members, sponsors several cooperative activities, all aimed at expanding the range of materials available to students and scholars. The LAP-TOC (Latin American Periodicals Table of Contents), the centerpiece of LARRP, is a database that includes tables of contents of more than 700 journals, representing close to 140,000 articles, published throughout Latin America. Distributed resources, through an optional reallocation of funds to deepen existing local strengthens, expands the collective coverage of monographs and other resources produced in Latin America and provides enhanced coverage of non-core materials for the Latin American region. The full texts of presidential messages from Argentina and Mexico are available in digital form on the server at the University of Texas Latin American Networked Information Center (UT-LANIC). LARRP sponsored a case study examining the challenges and effects of specialized collection development, *The University of Florida's Latin American Collection: A Case Study of Unilateral Specialization in Caribbean Material,* prepared by University of Florida economist Jennifer Cobb Adams. Another project component, Latin American Partnerships, has developed a cooperative model that enables Latin American libraries to contribute to the LAPTOC database tables of contents of journals that are not widely held. The newest facet of LARRP for which funding is being sought, Latin American Open Archives Portal, addresses the need for improved control of and access to Latin America's "gray literature"—publications, working documents, and other materials produced by research institutes, nongovernmental organizations, and peripheral agencies, none of which is controlled by commercial publishers.

The Slavic Document Delivery Project is the newest project and is still in the formative stages. The goal is to create a mutually beneficial document delivery system among libraries in Slavic countries and in North America. Initially, six libraries in East Central Europe and the countries of the former Soviet Union will participate and will be provided with Ariel for a one-year trial period, courtesy of the Research Libraries Group. The goal is to have six countries and languages represented.

The Digital South Asia Library (DSAL) and the closely related Digital Dictionaries of South Asia project (DDSA) both originated with the support of the Global Resources Program. Lessons learned under the period of ARL support continue to inform the directions and technology deployed, as the projects continue to expand and to diversify their sources of funding. The resources to which DSAL has dramatically enhanced access include books and journals, dictionaries, bibliographies, images, statistics, and maps.

The Southeast Asia Indexing Project/Thai Journal Index is composed of two parts: a project based at Cornell University Library to enhance the range of materials represented in the *Bibliography of Asian Studies*, and a project based at the University of Washington to provide access to Thai journals, using scanned images of part of the original text and transliterated metadata. Both are cooperative projects sponsored by the Committee on Research Materials on Southeast Asia (CORMOSEA), a subcommittee of the Association of Asian Studies.

Preservation

The Preservation capability pursues initiatives that support member libraries' efforts to provide enduring access to their research collections. Strategies include encouraging and strengthening broad-based participation in national preservation efforts in the United States and Canada, supporting development of preservation programs within member libraries, monitoring copyright and licensing developments to ensure support of preservation activities in the electronic environment, supporting effective bibliographic control of preservation-related processes, encouraging development of preservation information resources, and monitoring technological developments that may have an impact on preservation goals.

The ARL Committee on the Preservation of Research Library Materials held retreats in June 2000 and February 2001 to refocus its agenda. The committee members and institutional liaisons approved a new action plan in May 2001. The priorities focus on strengthening the commitment of ARL members to preserve collections basic to an understanding of our intellectual and cultural heritage through an active stewardship that enables current and future consultation and use of library resources. The preservation program will work to encourage the best use of the array of preservation strategies presently available, to support the development of promising new methods, and to develop preservation staff in ARL institutions.

Nicholson Baker, in his recent book *Double Fold: Libraries and the Assault on Paper,* criticized librarians for destroying newspapers and depending on sometimes unreadable microfilm copies. Baker is convinced that lack of space—not paper deterioration—is the rationale for microfilming. Systematic microfilming and destruction of the original papers, he claimed, has resulted in the loss of both usable and valuable materials. ARL staff, in conjunction with the Preservation Committee, drafted letters-to-the-editor in response to reviews of Baker's book in the *New York Review of Books* and the *New York Times*. Staff also developed a Web page that provides a question-and-answer document and presents other reviews, articles, and library community responses to *Double Fold.*

A survey on preservation and digitizing in ARL libraries was sent to members in June 2000 to help the Preservation Committee identify specific issues that need to be addressed and actions that might be taken by ARL to advance its preservation goals. Eighty-three ARL libraries responded and the results were published in SPEC Kit 262, *Preservation and Digitalization in ARL Libraries* by Janice Mohlhenrich.

ARL staff worked with the Council on Library and Information Resources (CLIR) and other library associations to conduct a survey of member policies on preserving digital information. This information will help inform the Library of Congress as it develops a plan for a National Digital Preservation Program.

The ARL Digital Initiatives Database (DID) is a Web-based registry containing more than 400 descriptions of digital initiatives within or involving libraries. Each record includes a link to the project site. The database can be searched in a variety of ways, including by library function, technical focus, and keyword. Users can browse the database by project name or host institution.

Diversity

The ARL Diversity Program supports and extends efforts within member institutions to promote and develop library staff and leaders who are representative of a diverse population. These efforts include the recruitment and retention of library personnel from a variety of backgrounds—particularly from groups traditionally underrepresented in the academic and research library work force—and the creation of professional development opportunities and networks that enhance climates conducive to diversity and help promote diverse leadership.

The Diversity program administers two national programs: the Initiative to Recruit a Diverse Workforce and the Leadership and Career Development Program (LCDP). Both programs focus on the recruitment and retention of persons from diverse racial, ethnic, and national backgrounds. Since research supports the belief that successful recruitment and retention of minority personnel depends in large measure on the work environment, climate issues must be an ongoing concern for libraries.

The Initiative to Recruit a Diverse Workforce grants stipends to students from minority backgrounds to assist in the completion of their MLS degree. Grantees agree to a minimum two-year working relationship with an ARL library upon graduation. Four stipends were awarded in 2000. In 2001 the program focused on enhancing the base fund by seeking grant funds and other contributions. This activity will continue in 2002 and beyond. In addition, three new grantees will be selected for the 2002–2003 academic year. An advisory group of deans from ARL and other libraries and the ARL Diversity Committee will continue to provide guidance and support for the program.

LCDP prepares talented midcareer librarians of color for leadership roles and positions in the research library community. Since it was launched in 1997–1998, the program has completed two successful offerings with a total of 38 participants. A combination of theory—presented by key leaders in the research library community—and experiential learning opportunities allows for exploration of critical issues facing leaders in the research library and higher education communities. Twenty librarians—representing a variety of library backgrounds, years of experience, and racial and national origins—were selected to participate in the 2001–2002 program class. In June 2001 an organizing meeting was held to introduce the participants to each other, potential mentors and ARL member leaders, and the LCDP faculty.

LCDP participants attend two week-long leadership institutes. The institutes are intensive, curriculum-based programs designed to intellectually engage the LCDP participants. They focus on horizon issues in the library community and expose participants to library and higher education leaders. The Medical Library Association (MLA) has asked to participate in the program and has proposed sponsoring two LCDP participants from the medical library community by providing mentors and financial support.

The Diversity program and the Office of Leadership and Management Services have worked closely to create the Research Library Residency and Internship Program Database. The database lists residency and internship information available on a broad range of career opportunities for future and new professionals. This tool was created to attract new and transitioning professionals who are interested in academic and research library careers.

The ARL Career Resources Online Service was established in 1996 to provide job hunters with an easy-to-use tool for finding positions in ARL member libraries and to assist institutions in attracting a qualified, talented, and diverse applicant pool. It allows users to search a database of current announcements by service category, region, state or province, or institution. Since its inception, the service has hosted more than 2,300 announcements from member and nonmember libraries alike.

Office of Leadership and Management Services

The Office of Leadership and Management Services (OLMS) offers effective strategies to help libraries develop talented staff in a changing demographic environment. OLMS also helps to develop a pool of library leaders who can motivate and direct efforts to adopt new service roles and ensure broad, enduring access to research resources. Central to this effort is defining the core competencies for research library staff and identifying the means by which staff can acquire these skills.

Over the past 30 years OLMS has successfully designed and facilitated effective and well-attended library staff development programs. OLMS offers a suite of Organizational Learning Services that helps library leaders determine their futures through envisioning and assessing the future and develops library staff to pursue the desired future. OLMS products and services help research libraries serve their clientele through the strategic deployment of talented and well-trained individuals and through the use of timely and relevant information.

The OLMS Leadership and Organizational Development Program is the component of Organizational Learning Services that provides in-person training and consulting services to libraries. The program stays abreast of innovations in library services, technologies, and methods while keeping current with the latest research findings in the areas of organizational structure, productivity, learning, and leadership development. Program faculty design and deliver timely, up-to-date, and focused learning events and organizational development support services.

Public workshops provide participants an opportunity to travel away from the workplace and learn in an intensive, retreat-like setting that also provides participants a valuable networking experience. In 2001 OLMS workshops, institutes, and presentations reached nearly 1,200 library staff members. OLMS also consulted with staff and administrators on such activities as organizational climate assessment, organizational redesign, strategic planning, and values clarification. Beginning in 2002, most public institutes will be hosted by ARL member libraries. This will create an opportunity for institute participants to visit various libraries and give member libraries an opportunity to showcase their collections, facilities, and staff.

The OLMS Information Services program maintains an active publications program composed of SPEC Kits and Occasional Papers. Publications are produced by ARL and OLMS staff, consultants, and guest authors from member institutions. The SPEC Kit series focuses on evaluating successful practices in library management and published six issues in 2001 on topics ranging from management of numeric data services to user authentication practices. In 2001 OLMS published Occasional Paper No. 22: *Alumni Outreach by University Libraries* by Richard Meyer and Mary Jane Mayo, which examines alumni outreach initiatives at academic ARL member libraries and how those libraries perceive the role of alumni in the life of the university library.

The Online Lyceum, a collaborative partnership between ARL and the Southern Illinois University–Carbondale Library Affairs Instructional Support Services is the Organizational Learning Services component that provides professional development opportunities via distance-learning technology. The Online Lyceum specializes in the development of interactive, Web-based learning that provides critical content and instruction related to issues and trends in research libraries, including management skills and leadership development. In 2001 nearly 150 library and information technology professionals took advantage of these online learning opportunities. Several new courses have been developed for 2002.

Statistics and Measurement

The Statistics and Measurement program seeks to describe and measure the performance of research libraries and their contributions to teaching, research, scholarship, and community service. Strategies to accomplish the objectives of the program include collecting, analyzing, and publishing quantifiable information about library collections, personnel, and expenditures, as well as expenditures and indicators of the nature of research institutions; developing new ways to describe and measure traditional and networked information resources and services; developing mechanisms to assess the relationship between campus information resources and high-quality research and the teaching and learning experience of students; providing customized, confidential analysis for peer comparisons; preparing workshops regarding statistics and measurement issues in research libraries; sustaining a leadership role in the testing and application of academic research library statistics for North American institutions of higher education; and collaborating with other national and international library statistics programs and accreditation agencies.

In 2001 the Statistics and Measurement program continued the 40-year effort to collect and publish quantitative and descriptive statistics about ARL member libraries. In 1999 member leaders gathered to discuss what ARL could do to assist members in developing new measures that better describe research libraries and their services. As a result, ARL created the New Measures Initiatives, which focused attention on a number of specific topics to measure and describe the library's contribution to teaching and learning and to research. This initiative has identified several research and development projects and secured funding to support two major projects: LibQUAL+, an effort to measure library service quality from the user's perspective, and E-metrics, an effort to explore the feasibility of collecting data on the usage of electronic resources.

LibQUAL+ emerged from a pilot project spearheaded by Fred Heath and Colleen Cook of Texas A&M University Libraries. In October 2000 ARL and Texas A&M were awarded a grant from the Fund for the Improvement of Postsecondary Education (FIPSE) to continue development work on the LibQUAL+ instrument and service for three years. The goals of the project include the development of tools and protocols for evaluating library service quality, development of effective Web-based delivery mechanisms for those tools, identification of best practices in providing library service, and the establishment of an ongoing, cost-recovery, service quality assessment program at ARL. Forty-three university libraries from across the United States and Canada participated in the spring 2001 survey implementation, nearly doubling the project's original goal of attracting 24 participating libraries. A total of 20,416 surveys were completed, with an overall response rate of approximately 25 percent. Participants were given the survey results in June and were also given online access to their data via a password-protected Web site.

An outgrowth of the LibQUAL+ project is the development of a National Science Digital Library (NSDL) user-based assessment protocol. This new project, a collaborative proposal from the Texas A&M University Libraries and ARL, was approved for funding in November 2001 by the National Science Foundation (NSF). Under the grant, ARL and Texas A&M will jointly receive funding over a three-year period to adapt the LibQUAL+ instrument for use in the science, math, engineering, and technology education digital library community.

The ARL E-Metrics project is led by ARL member library directors Sherrie Schmidt (Arizona State University) and Rush Miller (University of Pittsburgh). The project has completed two of three phases: the identification of current activities being undertaken in ARL libraries to support data collection for electronic resources, and the identification of a set of statistics and measures that can be used to describe electronic resources in ARL libraries. Phase III consists of identifying a project to link electronic measures to institutional goals and objectives.

Using the information from the Phase I inventory of data collection activities, participating institutions worked to better understand and refine the processes needed to collect statistics related to networked information resources. In spring 2001, 16 of the participating libraries field-tested a set of proposed measures. Following a meeting with select vendors in March 2001—including representatives of Elsevier/ScienceDirect, netLibrary, OCLC/FirstSearch, JSTOR, Bell & Howell, Ovid, LexisNexis, Gale Group, and EBSCO—12 vendors agreed to participate in the field-testing and eight vendors provided data for the testing.

To minimize the work involved in receiving analyzed data from the vendors, each field-testing library was assigned to work with three or four vendors. The study team compiled and analyzed field-testing data and the libraries' assessments of how difficult it was to gather the data. The study team completed a draft data-collection manual that was sent to all participating members for comment.

To begin to describe how measures for electronic resources can be used to address institutional outcomes (Phase III), the study team prepared a process diagram of library outcomes in the context of a research university. They also engaged the services of Bonnie Gratch-Lindauer to follow up on some of her previous assessment work and conduct a review of relevant accreditation standards. The result of that investigation was a proposal that outlines a project to investigate the relationship of electronic measures to institutional outcomes.

To advance an investigation of the role libraries could play in addressing learning outcomes, Kenneth Smith, Eller Distinguished Service Professor of Economics at the University of Arizona, was hired as a consultant to draft a White Paper suggesting a role for research libraries. His paper, "New Roles and Responsibilities for the University Library: Advancing Student Learning through Outcomes Assessment," outlined a strategy for involving research libraries in campus assessment activities to demonstrate the value of the library to the learning community. To follow up on his recommendations, the Statistics and Measurement program is defining a course of action for libraries on campus in promoting and assessing student learning outcomes and has established a working group representing institutions interested in promoting learning outcomes.

Office of Research and Development

The ARL Office of Research and Development (ORD) consolidates the administration of grants and grant-supported projects administered by ARL. The major goal within this capability is to identify and match ARL projects that support the research library community's mission with sources of external funding. Among the projects underway in 2001 were the following: Knight Collaborative Roundtable, Scholars Portal Project, FIPSE funding for LibQUAL+, NSDL Digital Library Assessment Project, AAU/ARL Global Resources Program, and the ARL GIS Literacy Project.

In addition, a number of research and development projects were completed in 2001. ARL received a grant from the National Science Foundation to support a two-day symposium held in the Presidio of San Francisco in March 2001. This symposium, developed in collaboration with the Internet Archive, achieved its three objectives: to identify and stimulate pilot projects in the collection and use of born-digital material; to build agreement on how to service and use born-digital material; and to write a call to action on the role of born-digital resources in research libraries, including an outline of next steps and identification of the individuals and/or organizations that could take them.

ARL received two grants to support the symposium "Building on Strength: Developing an ARL Agenda for Special Collections" held June 27–29 at Brown University. The Gladys Krieble Delmas Foundation awarded a grant to cover symposium expenses and the Andrew W. Mellon Foundation gave a grant to assist with the costs of publishing a survey of special collections prior to the symposium.

In summer 2000 IMLS awarded LCDP and the Online Lyceum a grant to capitalize on the success of both of these programs by using the Lyceum as a vehicle for the distance education delivery of the new LCDP curriculum. The grant concluded in December 2001.

Another initiative of ORD is the ARL Visiting Program Officer (VPO) program. This program provides an opportunity for a staff member in an ARL member library to assume responsibility for carrying out part or all of a project for ARL. It provides a very visible professional development opportunity for an outstanding staff member and serves the membership as a whole by extending the capacity of ARL to undertake additional activities. Typically, the member library supports the salary of the staff person and ARL supports or seeks grant funding for travel or other project-related expenses. Depending on the nature of the project and the circumstances of the individual, a VPO may spend extended periods of time in Washington, D.C., or may conduct most of the project from his or her home library.

Communications, External Relations, and Publications

The Communications, External Relations, and Publications capabilities are engaged in many activities in support of ARL's objectives. These include acquainting ARL members with current, important developments of interest to research libraries; informing the library profession of ARL's position on these issues; influencing policy and decision makers within the higher education, research, and scholarly communities; educating academic communities about issues related to scholarly communication and research libraries; and providing the library community with information about activities with which research libraries are engaged. External relations with relevant constituencies are also carried out through all ARL programs.

Using print and electronic media as well as direct outreach, the Communications program disseminates information about ARL and its programs, positions, and services. It works to advance the interests of research libraries to the higher education and scholarly communities as well as to ARL member institutions. One of the goals of the program is to promote a better understanding of the issues confronting research libraries in the process of scholarly communication. The capability supports ARL activities by promoting workshops, conferences, and publications, and by responding to requests for information about ARL and research library issues from the press and community at large. The arl-announce listserv provides timely information about ARL and news items about ARL member library activities. ARL sponsors more than 75 electronic discussion lists, both private and public. Archives for the lists are updated monthly and made available on the ARL server.

The Publications program offers a full range of timely, accurate, and informative resources to assist library and higher education communities in their efforts to improve the delivery of scholarly communication. Print and electronic publications are issued from ARL programs on a regular basis. The association makes many of its titles available electronically via the World Wide Web; some are available in excerpted form for preview before purchase and others are available in their entirety.

Six issues of *ARL: A Bimonthly Report on Research Library Issues and Actions from ARL, CNI, and SPARC* were published in 2001. The December issue focused on digital reference services. The October issue contained Jean-Claude Guédon's article "Beyond Core Journals and Licenses: The Paths to Reform Scientific Publishing." In June, William G. Bowen's Oxford University address "At a Slight Angle to the Universe: The University in a Digitized, Commercialized Age" was published. Other issues in 2001 addressed such topics as metadata harvesting and the Open Archives Initiative, the Tempe Principles, SPARC, the *Tasini* v. *New York Times* copyright case, library service quality, and updates on ARL programs and projects.

In addition, three new books were published in 2001. *Special Collections in ARL Libraries: Results of the 1998 Survey Sponsored by the ARL Research Collections Committee* by Judith M. Panitch provides a snapshot of special collections at the end of the 20th century. The data from this survey not only supply information for local decisions about special collections but also identify areas for further investigation.

Electronic Ecology: A Case Study of Electronic Journals in Context by Karla L. Hahn looks at the ecology community in 1998 as two new peer-reviewed journals were starting up in quite similar subject areas: one electronic only and the other publishing both print and electronic versions simultaneously. This study compares and contrasts authors' and editors' views on whether to publish in a print or online journal. It also looks to the future of emerging publishing systems and highlights the importance of some of the functions developing in electronic publishing systems.

Successful Fundraising: Case Studies of Academic Libraries, edited by Meredith Butler, is a guide that offers well-developed case studies written by experienced professionals who have embraced a variety of fund-raising challenges, met with success, and are willing to share their stories with others.

Association Governance and Membership Activities

ARL's 138th Membership Meeting, Creating the Digital Future, was held May 23–25, 2001, in Toronto. A total of 104 member institutions were represented at the meeting, which was held in conjunction with the Canadian Association of Research Libraries and hosted by the University of Toronto Libraries. ARL President Shirley Baker (Washington University, St. Louis) chaired the meeting. The programs focused on how research institutions are developing the infrastructure and expertise necessary to support the processes of scholarly publishing and operate programs that embrace access to born-digital and digitized primary source materials. The Université de Montréal became the newest member of ARL during the meeting upon a vote of the full membership.

The 139th Membership Meeting, held October 17–18, 2001, in Washington, D.C., was also attended by representatives of 104 member institutions. The meeting was structured to allow members to discuss strategic and operational issues of concern to research libraries. On October 18 Paula Kaufman (University of Illinois at Urbana) began her term as ARL president. The board elected Fred Heath (Texas A&M University) as president-elect of the association. Meredith Butler, Kenneth Frazier, Joseph Hewitt, and Carolynne Presser concluded their terms as board members. Joseph Branin, Frances Groen, and Brian Schottlaender were elected to three-year terms. At the October meeting, the ARL membership approved a document, *Principles and Procedures for Membership in ARL,* which combines the statement of membership principles with a revised explanation of qualifications and procedures for considering new members as well as current members that no longer meet the qualifications.

The 140th Membership Meeting was set for May 22–24, 2002, in Los Angeles, hosted by the University of California, Los Angeles, and the University of Southern California. ARL President Kaufman, working with a committee of colleagues, is planning a program that examines two strategic library issues: fund raising and staff recruitment. The fall Membership Meeting is scheduled for October 15–18 in Washington, D.C.

Scholarly Publishing and Academic Resources Coalition (SPARC)

21 Dupont Circle N.W., Suite 800
Washington, DC 20036
202-296-2296, e-mail sparc@arl.org
World Wide Web http://www.arl.org/sparc

Richard Johnson
SPARC Enterprise Director

The Scholarly Publishing and Academic Resources Coalition (SPARC) is a world-wide alliance of research institutions, libraries, and organizations that encourages competition in the scholarly communications market. SPARC introduces new solutions to scientific journal publishing, facilitates the use of technology to expand access, and partners with publishers that bring top-quality, low-cost research to a greater audience. SPARC strives to return scholarship to the scholar, research to the researcher, and science to the scientist. SPARC's memberships, member affiliates, and endorsers can be found in North America, Britain, Ireland, Europe, Asia, Australia, and New Zealand.

SPARC was established in October 1997 as an initiative of the Association of Research Libraries (ARL) to create competition in a dysfunctional scientific publishing market. In its four years of existence, SPARC has demonstrated not only that high-quality, affordable competitors to high-priced commercial journals can be created, but also that educated and motivated authors and editors can be effective agents for change. Today SPARC has more than 200 members, partnerships with 19 different projects in three program areas, and an extensive and effective publicity and education program.

Three strategic thrusts support SPARC's agenda to enhance broad and cost-effective access to peer-reviewed scholarship:

- *Incubation of competitive alternatives to current high-priced commercial journals and digital aggregations.* This is implemented by publisher partnership programs and advisory services that promote competition for authors and buyers, demonstrate alternatives to the traditional journal business model, and stimulate expansion of the nonprofit sector's share of overall scholarly publishing activity.

- *Public advocacy of fundamental changes in the system and the culture of scholarly communication.* This encompasses outreach targeted at various stakeholder groups (for example, librarians, faculty, and editorial boards), as well as ongoing communications and public relations activities that publicize key issues and initiatives. Advocacy leverages the impact of SPARC's publishing partnerships, provides broad awareness of the possibilities for change, and has motivated scholars to act.

- *Education campaigns aimed at enhancing awareness of scholarly communication issues.* This is achieved by supporting expanded institutional and scholarly community roles in and control over the scholarly communication process.

Since its formal launch in June 1998, SPARC has advanced its agenda by

- Demonstrating that new journals can successfully compete for authors and quickly establish quality
- Effectively showing that journal costs can be driven down by market forces
- Creating an environment in which editors and editorial board members claim more prominent roles in the business aspects of their journals
- Stimulating the development of increased publishing capacity in the not-for-profit sector and encouraging new players to enter the market
- Providing help and guidance to scientists and librarians interested in creating change
- Carrying the methods and message of change to international stakeholders

SPARC Publisher Partnership Programs

SPARC's publishing strategy is to partner with traditional scholarly societies and university presses known for their high-quality publications rather than to become a publisher in and of itself. In order to provide an incentive to publishers, SPARC members commit to subscribe to SPARC partner journals as long as the titles fit into their collection profile. As its partnership projects have developed, SPARC has categorized its efforts into three programmatic areas: SPARC Alternatives, SPARC Leading Edge, and SPARC Scientific Communities.

SPARC Alternatives

Since its inception, SPARC has been most closely identified with its Alternatives Program. These are the titles that were established to compete directly with high-priced STM (science, technology, and medicine) titles. The first partnership in this category was with the American Chemical Society, which agreed to introduce three new competitive titles over three years. *Organic Letters,* the first, began publication in July 1999. Another high-profile SPARC Alternative is *Evolutionary Ecology Research (EER)*, a title founded by Michael Rosenzweig, a professor of ecology and evolutionary biology at the University of Arizona. In the mid-1980s, Rosenzweig had founded another title that had been subsequently bought and sold with significant price increases each time. Unhappy with the increases and the refusal of the publishers to take their concerns seriously, the entire editorial board resigned and in January 1999 launched their own independent journal at a fraction of the cost of the original title. Both of these titles have demonstrated that authors are very willing to submit papers to a new journal if it is edited by respected scholars in the field. Other SPARC partnerships are in fields such as geometry and topology, logic programming, and machine learning, and several others are under negotiation. Partner titles have been the result of both new start-ups and the movement of editorial boards to new publishing arrangements.

SPARC Leading Edge

To support the development of new models in scholarly publishing, SPARC's Leading Edge program publicizes the efforts of ventures that use technology to obtain competitive advantage or to introduce innovative business models. Titles in this program include the *New Journal of Physics* (charges fees to authors whose articles are accepted for publication), *Internet Journal of Chemistry* (exploits the power of the Internet and allows data manipulation), *Documenta Mathematica* (free, Web-based journal with liberal policies on copyright and institutional use), and *Journal of Insect Science* (published by a university library).

SPARC Scientific Communities

Scientific Communities projects are intended to support broad-scale aggregations of scientific content around the needs of specific communities of interest. Through these projects, SPARC encourages collaboration among scholars, their societies, and academic institutions. This program also helps to build capacity within the not-for-profit sector by encouraging academic institutions to develop electronic publishing expertise and infrastructure and seeks to reduce the sale of journal titles by providing small societies and independent journals with alternative academic partners for moving into the electronic environment. Projects in this program include *eScholarship* from the California Digital Library, which is creating an infrastructure for the management of digitally based scholarly information; *Columbia Earthscape,* a collaboration among Columbia University's press, libraries, and academic computing services that integrates earth sciences research, teaching, and public policy resources; and *MIT CogNet,* an electronic community for researchers in cognitive and brain sciences that includes a searchable, full-text library of major reference works, monographs, journals, and conference proceedings, as well as job postings and threaded discussion groups. These projects all received funding from SPARC through a competitive awards process. SPARC is also supporting *Project Euclid,* a joint venture between the Cornell University Library and Duke University Press. This project is providing an infrastructure for Web publishing for independent journals in theoretical and applied mathematics and statistics.

An ambitious SPARC project is *BioOne,* a nonprofit, Web-based aggregation of peer-reviewed articles from dozens of leading journals in the areas of biological, environmental, and ecological sciences. It was officially launched in April 2001 and includes access to the current volumes plus one or two back years of more than 40 titles. *BioOne* was conceived as an opportunity for societies, libraries, and the private sector for collaboration. It would offer small, undercapitalized societies, members of the American Institute of Biological Sciences (AIBS), a means to move to electronic publishing while maintaining financial viability. In addition to AIBS, collaborators include Allen Press, the Greater Western Library Alliance (formerly the Big 12 Plus Libraries Consortium), the University of Kansas, and SPARC. The business plan calls for 50 percent of the revenues from sales to be returned to the societies based on an individual journal's relative size and use, with the other 50 percent covering the cost of operations.

Recognition

The positive impact of SPARC's partnership program was recognized in September 2001 when the Association for Learned and Professional Society Publishers selected SPARC to receive its first Service to Not-for-Profit Publishing Award.

Communication

A strong component of success for SPARC has been its ability to bring scholarly communication issues to the mainstream and scientific press. An aggressive media program was established early, and, through it, SPARC has developed key contacts with journalists, has placed targeted stories in a range of media outlets, issues frequent press releases, and responds quickly to information requests. More than 115 articles and news items recorded on the "SPARC In the News" Web page chronicle the work of SPARC and concerns about the issue of scholarly communication.

SPARC staff, steering committee members, and publishing partners travel extensively to speak at local, regional, national, and international meetings and conferences. A speakers' bureau provides SPARC members and others with assistance in arranging speakers for campus or society meeting events.

Other communication channels update members and interested observers with news about SPARC activities. *SPARC e-news* is a bimonthly newsletter that provides information on new partners, innovative developments in scholarly publishing outside SPARC's own programs, industry news, opinion pieces, and reviews of software or tools. A comprehensive Web site provides resources to those interested in scholarly communication issues and SPARC activities. With the Association of College and Research Libraries (ACRL), SPARC hosts a semiannual forum at American Library Association meetings to bring the issues and SPARC's work to a wider library audience. SPARC also exhibits at library conferences and provides materials for society conferences.

Advocacy and Education

In addition to raising awareness through its public relations work, SPARC has been engaged in specific programs and initiatives to encourage librarians and faculty to take an active part in changing the current system of scholarly communication.

Create Change

SPARC's financial support and relationship with ACRL enabled the ARL Office of Scholarly Communications to deploy a Create Change advocacy program quickly, broadly, and with a content-rich Web site. The Create Change campaign is designed to aid faculty and librarians in advocating changes in scholarly communication. The Web site includes descriptive information on scholarly communication issues with supporting data, advocacy planning tools for librarians, and sample letters and copyright agreements for faculty. The site also includes a database of the editors of the 100 most expensive journals. A designed printed brochure is available for purchase, or the text is available on the Web site for local adaptation. Just over 60 percent of SPARC members have begun or are planning to begin a Create Change program on their campus, representing a substantial number of contacts with scholars about the issues.

Declaring Independence

A key SPARC strategy for expanding scientist control over scientific communication is to encourage editorial boards to assert a broader role in determining journal business policies and practices. This is being advanced with the Declaring Independence initiative, launched by SPARC in collaboration with the Triangle Research Libraries Network in January 2001. Declaring Independence encourages journal editorial boards to evaluate their current journals, and, if warranted, either work with the publisher to make changes or move the editorial board to an alternative publisher.

The main vehicles for carrying the Declaring Independence message are an instructive SPARC-developed handbook and corresponding Web site. The handbook was mailed by SPARC to editorial board members of high-priced journals and distributed by library staff to editors as part of their scholarly communications campus outreach activities. The Declaring Independence themes and availability of the handbook and Web site also are promoted widely at meetings and conferences around the world, in SPARC publicity and articles, and at speaking engagements.

Establishment of SPARC Europe

As a means of extending outreach to scholars and libraries, SPARC and several European supporting organizations launched SPARC Europe in July 2001. By a unanimous vote at its annual meeting in July, LIBER (Ligue des Bibliothèques Européennes de Recherche), the principal association of the major research libraries of Europe, agreed to serve as the umbrella organization for SPARC Europe, which will facilitate competition in the European scientific journals marketplace and introduce advocacy initiatives tailored to the European research and library communities. Other organizational sponsors include CURL (Consortium of University Research Libraries), JISC (Joint Information Systems Committee), SCONUL (Society of College, National and University Libraries), and UKB, the Netherlands cooperative of research libraries, in collaboration with IWI, the SURF Foundation program for innovation in scientific information supply.

Open Access

SPARC has emphasized open access as an especially important issue for its members. In its Leading Edge program, SPARC has supported the Open Archives Initiative (OAI), an effort to develop protocols and standards to link distributed electronic archives, and helped underwrite one of the first meetings of the technical experts running e-print servers to discuss issues regarding interoperability. In 2001 SPARC organized a session at the spring Coalition for Networked Information (CNI) meeting featuring institutions that are working to implement e-print services and a metadata-harvesting protocol in the hope of encouraging others to follow.

Since then, both SPARC and SPARC Europe have participated in the creation of the Budapest Open Access Initiative (BOAI) and have signed a founding statement of intent. BOAI aims to accelerate progress in the international effort to make research articles in all academic fields freely available on the Internet. SPARC and SPARC Europe are involved in BOAI because access to knowledge is the central purpose of scholarly communication. A system built on open access offers the prospect of being less expensive to operate and of better serving scholars, the scholarly process, and society. A number of SPARC's publishing partners have already achieved success as peer-reviewed open access journals.

Priorities for 2002

SPARC's priorities for 2002 will continue to focus on enhancing broad and cost-effective access to peer-reviewed scholarship. Specifically, SPARC will support initiatives that encourage development of institution-based repositories for the work of scholars and will work with universities and libraries to organize, support, and publicize new institutional roles in information dissemination (such as institutional and disciplinary servers) and the intellectual property policies necessary for their implementation.

Scholar-led journal publishing initiatives will be another of SPARC's emphases for 2002. When scholars are ready to take action and assert control over scholarly communication, they must have concrete options. SPARC will continue to provide tools and assistance for those editorial boards that are declaring independence from their current publishing relationships, addressing important emerging fields, developing innovative value-added ventures, or experimenting with new economic models.

Finally, SPARC will develop new collaborative digital publishing enterprises and models. The creation of *BioOne* has been a notable success and offers a base of experience applicable to other initiatives. It and other SPARC projects suggest the power of uniting various players in the information chain (societies, libraries, consortia, academic computing centers, university presses) in pursuit of shared goals. In 2002 SPARC will be closely involved in cultivating projects that harness this power to offer scholars better ways of disseminating their research.

Some of the distinct activities planned for 2002 include

- Publishing *Gaining Independence,* an extensive, free Web resource that provides librarians and scholars with a tutorial on creating business plans for electronic publishing initiatives
- Establishment of a consulting group to provide in-depth business, financial, and strategic consulting services on a fee basis to universities and university presses, not-for-profit learned societies, and other academic and not-for-profit organizations
- Exploration of promoting and underwriting the costs of legal services
- Publishing of resource lists and evaluations of software options
- Organizing workshops

Governance

The working group that established SPARC was determined that SPARC be a lean and agile organization. Its focus was to be on developing partnerships and projects, not on issues of governance or membership. However, as it reached a level of maturity and membership, it was agreed that a more formal structure was needed. The appointed SPARC Steering Committee that had guided SPARC since early

1998 decided that it should replace itself with a democratically elected body that would ensure a mechanism for continually renewing its leadership. A new steering committee consisting of seven members with staggered terms was elected in fall 1999 to take office in January 2000. In 2001 the committee adjusted its membership again to ensure that it included official representatives from Canada and SPARC Europe. The steering committee meets at least twice a year in person and conducts other business through regularly scheduled conference calls.

Membership in SPARC is based on a model of founding, full, consortia, and supporting members extending worldwide.

Web Sites

SPARC	http://www.arl.org/sparc
SPARC Europe	http://www.sparceurope.org
Create Change	http://www.createchange.org
Declaring Independence	http://www.arl.org/sparc/DI

Council on Library and Information Resources

1755 Massachusetts Ave. N.W., Suite 500, Washington, DC 20036-2124
202-939-4754, fax 202-939-4765
World Wide Web http://www.clir.org

Kathlin Smith
Director of Communications

The Council on Library and Information Resources (CLIR) is an independent, nonprofit organization dedicated to improving the management of information for research, teaching, and learning. CLIR works to expand access to information, however recorded and preserved, as a public good.

CLIR's agenda is framed by a single, important question: What is a library in the digital age?

Rapid changes in technology, evolving intellectual property legislation, new modes of scholarly communication, and new economic models for information provision have all contributed to a new information environment for libraries. In partnership with other organizations, CLIR helps create services that expand the concept of "library" and supports the providers and preservers of information.

CLIR is supported by fees from sponsoring institutions, grants from public and private foundations, contracts with federal agencies, and donations from individuals. CLIR's board of directors establishes policy, oversees the investment of funds, sets goals, and approves strategies for their achievement. The program staff of CLIR develops projects and programs in response to the broad charges of the board. CLIR's current activities reflect its concern with six themes: resources for scholarship, preservation awareness, digital libraries, economics of information, leadership, and international developments.

Resources for Scholarship

CLIR is working to ensure that libraries of the future will be well positioned to provide researchers with the resources they need. By defining access to research collections as a primary focus of CLIR's activities, the critical functions of acquisition, description, and preservation can be addressed in an integrated way—that is, as a service to scholarship. CLIR's programs are developed to address the following questions:

- How do we ensure scholars' access to resources in the formats that they require?
- How do we describe items and build access systems that can be navigated with ease?
- How do we define texts and other sources in the digital environment?
- How should libraries reposition themselves to best serve the scholar as creator, researcher, and teacher?

The Role of the Artifact in Library Collections

In 1999 CLIR assembled a task force of 15 scholars, librarians, and archivists to investigate the demands for original source materials in scholarly research. In 2001 CLIR published the final report, *The Evidence in Hand.* The chief findings of the report—that scholars will continue to examine original sources for many reasons, and that the broadest-possible access to unreformatted sources therefore best serves scholarship—were by no means controversial. But the breadth of sources identified—from traditional print collections to recorded sound, broadcast media, moving and still images, and all manner of digital information—greatly expanded the universe of materials that libraries, as well as archives, historical societies, and museums, should be collecting and preserving.

Acknowledging that funds for preservation are limited, the task force proposed a number of approaches. Many rely on cooperation among institutions to reduce unnecessary duplication of preservation responsibilities and to engender cost efficiencies. Cooperation ensures the appropriate types of redundancies through distributed repositories of artifactual collections and, when possible, through broadened access to digital and other surrogates.

Public reviews session, conducted on six campuses across the country, confirmed that the task force was addressing issues that the research community deemed critical. The section on digital resources and the novel, often perplexing, responsibilities that face librarians and scholars when creating and using digital sources drew special interest. The task force's recommendations to ensure the creation of preservable digital objects while preserving the sources for digitized materials have already influenced developments at several institutions.

The work of the task force was supported by a grant from the Gladys Krieble Delmas Foundation.

Creating a Test Database for Digital Visual Resources

CLIR and the Coalition for Networked Information (CNI), with support from the Atlantic Philanthropies, are investigating the value and feasibility of developing a test database for digital visual resources that would serve as a means of measuring the capabilities of various technical applications for creating, managing, and exploiting digital image content.

Project staff are preparing scenarios for two approaches to developing the database. In the first approach, the database would be designed to support fundamental long-term research into image retrieval techniques. This would be most useful to computer science researchers interested in content-based retrieval.

In the second approach, the database would be designed to support the assessment of metadata for retrieving and using image files. Special emphasis would be placed on understanding the costs and benefits of investing in metadata creation. This approach would require research into how users are querying image databases. Two test collections would be used in this approach: one in art and another in history or historic photographs. For both types of collections, metadata would be created that could support multidisciplinary use.

CLIR will issue a report, based on these two scenarios, on the resource implications and processes necessary to assemble content and metadata.

Preservation Awareness

Increasingly, libraries and their funding agencies are supporting the creation of digital surrogates as a way of broadening access to collections. At the same time, there is greater awareness of the problems in keeping digital files—whether born digital or reformatted—refreshed and readily accessible using current hardware and software. As a greater portion of library budgets and grant funds goes to digital resources, funding for preservation of nondigital resources remains flat or is shrinking. This trend, if continued, will endanger the well-being of research collections nationwide and may lead to the loss of print and audiovisual collections created in the last two centuries.

The preservation of cultural and scholarly resources is becoming the responsibility of all who have a stake in them—creators, publishers, and users—as well as of the traditional custodians in libraries and archives. Technologists and relevant sectors of industry must be included in efforts to document the need for preservation of nonprint media and create collaborative strategies for action.

While continuing to seek solutions to the challenge of digital preservation, CLIR is framing the following questions related to the preservation of analog media:

- What extraordinary means will be necessary to preserve the deteriorating collections in research libraries?
- Will new models of organization be needed, such as establishing preservation centers to assume the responsibility for preservation on behalf of all?
- What can we learn by reconsidering the full range of preservation methods in collection management?
- Is there merit in establishing emergency procedures for the most important endangered titles?
- Is it time to revisit the conclusions of the original study of brittle books done in 1986, according to the new understandings and assumptions that inform our current approaches to sound collection management?

State of Preservation Programs in American College and Research Libraries

A grant from the Institute for Museum and Library Services is supporting a study to assess preservation programs in nearly 250 college and research libraries. The study is a joint effort involving CLIR, the Association of Research Libraries (ARL), the University Libraries Group (ULG), and the Regional Alliance for Preservation (RAP). The first objective of this project is to conduct a survey of the 123 non-ARL libraries that constitute the membership of ULG, as well as of leading liberal arts colleges and major non-ARL land-grant institutions. This survey will provide documentation on current preservation efforts in these libraries that is comparable to the information available for ARL members. Survey results will be combined with ARL data to launch the second phase of this project, the objective of which is to document preservation needs as opposed to preservation activities. Twenty case studies will be conducted at representative institutions drawn from the membership of ARL, ULG, and other participating institutions. The project will result in a report that documents current conditions and challenges and that suggests new strategies to equip preservation programs for an increasingly complex technical environment. The survey will be completed by August 2002.

Web-Based Tutorial on Preservation and Conservation

The Henry Luce Foundation awarded a grant to CLIR to develop a Web-based tutorial on preservation and conservation for use in Southeast Asia. The tutorial, now in draft form, will enable librarians, archivists, preservation administrators, and other cultural information practitioners to acquire basic and reliable preservation information, and to develop strategies and responses to preservation challenges distinctive to their climate, culture, resources, and content. The initiative is directed by Anne R. Kenney, director of programs at CLIR, and John F. Dean, director of the Department of Preservation at Cornell University Library. The first release of the tutorial is scheduled for summer 2002.

After the tutorial has been implemented and evaluated in Southeast Asia, CLIR expects to adapt it for use in other regions of the world. In addition, CLIR will work with international organizations with similar interests in developing a financial strategy for maintaining the tutorials over time.

National Plan for Preserving Digital Information

In January 2001 the Library of Congress announced that Congress had set aside $100 million to support a national strategy to preserve information in digital form. The library requested assistance from CLIR in producing a plan to be submitted to Congress in spring 2002. CLIR commissioned background papers on the preservation of six formats: large Web sites, electronic journals, electronic books, digital television, digitally recorded sound, and digital film and video. With these papers as context, CLIR convened three meetings of scholars, librarians, technologists, publishers, entertainment industry representatives, creators, authors, lawyers, and representatives of federal agencies. The meetings were designed to elicit these leaders' views about what the national plan should contain, as well as their thoughts about the priorities for preservation.

In 2002 CLIR will work with the Library of Congress to draft a plan that can be reviewed by the interested communities. In addition, a group of digital preservation experts, hosted by the Digital Library Federation (DLF), is meeting periodically to develop recommendations for consideration by the Library of Congress.

Digital Libraries

CLIR is committed to fostering the development of digital libraries as a resource for research and learning. CLIR's aim is to help policy makers, funding organizations, and academic leaders understand the social and institutional investments in digital libraries that are needed to organize, maintain, and provide access to a growing body of digital materials for scholarly purposes.

The Digital Library Foundation, sponsored by CLIR, is CLIR's major effort in digital libraries. DLF is a consortium of 27 leading research libraries that are developing online collections and services. DLF is active in six areas: architecture, collections, preservation, standards and best practices, user support and user services, and roles and responsibilities. In 2001 DLF continued its efforts in these areas while making progress in fulfilling three higher-level purposes:

- Identifying standards and best practices for digital collections and network access
- Coordinating leading-edge research and development in libraries' use of electronic information technology
- Helping start projects and services that libraries need but cannot develop individually

ArtSTOR

Led by Max Marmor of Yale University, a DLF distinguished fellow, DLF created a prototype for the organizational, business, and technical aspects of an image distribution service. This work was instrumental in formulating and launching ArtSTOR, an independent not-for-profit organization that will develop, store, and electronically distribute digital images and related scholarly materials for the study of art, architecture, and other fields in the humanities. ArtSTOR marks a major advance in the development and dissemination of visual image resources that support research and teaching. It has also taken over DLF's work on a shared catalog tool for visual resources.

Open Archives Initiative

Working with CNI, DLF supported the Open Archives Initiative (OAI), which aims to develop and promote interoperability standards to facilitate the efficient dissemination of information content. In doing so, DLF helped create and sustain a protocol upon which the next generation of scholarly Internet portal services is likely to be built. Several DLF members, including Cornell University, Emory University, the University of Illinois at Urbana-Champaign, and the University of Michigan, are helping to develop such portal services. Twelve DLF members have agreed to contribute to portal services the metadata from more than 50 collections representing millions of objects.

Andrew W. Mellon Foundation E-Journal Archiving Program

In early 2000 DLF, CLIR, and CNI began to consider what it will take to create archives of electronic journals, with a view to facilitating practical experimentation in digital archiving. In a series of three meetings for librarians, publishers, and licensing specialists, respectively, the groups managed to reach consensus on the minimum requirements for e-journal archival repositories.

Building on that consensus, the Andrew W. Mellon Foundation solicited proposals from selected research libraries to participate in a process designed to plan the development of e-journal repositories meeting those requirements. Seven major libraries received grants from the Mellon Foundation, including the New

York Public Library and the libraries of Cornell University, Harvard University, Massachusetts Institute of Technology (MIT), the University of Pennsylvania, Stanford University, and Yale University.

Yale, Harvard, and Pennsylvania will work with individual publishers on archiving the range of their electronic journals. Cornell and the New York Public Library will work on archiving journals in specific disciplines. MIT's project involves archiving "dynamic" e-journals, and Stanford's involves the development of specific archiving software tools. DLF supports the program by hosting its Web pages, reporting its progress to the broader community, and encouraging cross-fertilization among its funded participants.

Sustainable Digital Collections

In 2001 DLF completed three studies that report strategies for developing sustainable digital collections. Based on a survey of practice at leading research libraries, the studies recommend strategies for developing collections from commercially supplied electronic content (Timothy Jewell, University of Washington), digitally reformatted content (Abby Smith, CLIR), and links to third-party public domain Internet content (Louis Pitschmann, University of Wisconsin).

Use of Online Services and Collections

Led by DLF distinguished fellow Denise Troll, DLF completed a survey of how leading research libraries assess the use of online collections and services. The survey, published in January 2002, provides an overview and assessment of the newest evaluation methods and how digital libraries can use them. DLF also completed a member survey that identifies the institutional contexts in which digital libraries are being developed. By documenting the different ways in which digital libraries evolve and in which they organize and fund themselves, the survey will inform strategic planning and decision making within digital libraries, provide benchmarks for assessing digital library development, and identify emerging library roles.

Standards and Best Practices

DLF seeks to identify, endorse, and encourage adoption of those standards and practices that support the development of persistent and interoperable online collections and services. In 2001 DLF endorsed a number of standards and best practices while launching new work in other directions. Among the practices it endorsed is LibLicense, a model license agreement for use by libraries and commercial publishers. The model license documents preferred and good practice and serves as a decision tool that is likely to save libraries time and money in negotiating contracts with commercial content providers.

DLF initiated a process to develop a standard for representing structural, administrative, and technical metadata. Such a standard is a prerequisite for the construction of reliable and persistent distributed digital library collections. The DLF standard (known as METS, for "metadata encoding and transmission standard") is in advanced development and available from the Library of Congress Web site.

Economics of Information

As the role of the library is redefined, economic issues take on even greater importance. Economics of information is a theme that cuts across all program activities at CLIR. The costs of library and information services and possible new economic models for those services underlie nearly every project in which CLIR engages. What does it take to create self-sustaining information services while honoring the ethics of the library profession and engaging all of the stakeholders, including publishers and information creators?

More specifically:

- How can we measure the productivity of those scholars and students using information resources?
- How can we assess the value of library and archival collections as heritage assets?
- How can CLIR help provosts and other university administrators measure the costs of information?
- How can CLIR develop business models for new services that grow out of its activities?

Building and Sustaining Digital Collections

In February 2001 CLIR and the National Initiative for a Networked Cultural Heritage (NINCH) cohosted a conference, "Building and Sustaining Digital Collections: Models for Libraries and Museums." The meeting brought together library and museum executives, technologists, entrepreneurs, publishers, and legal experts to discuss how libraries and museums are building digital collections and what business models are available to sustain them. Participants heard presentations about six organizations, both nonprofit and for-profit, that are pioneering different approaches to the financial sustainability of online collections. Among the topics discussed were the circumstances under which a single organization can achieve its goals for online distribution of collections and services and when collaboration is necessary; how an institution can develop the technical, curatorial, legal, and administrative expertise for the variety of challenges that networked collections present; how market demands affect the core cultures of museums and libraries entering the online environment; and how business models can be developed for nonprofits. Participants identified a number of actions to be taken to address these concerns, and they are included in a report on the conference, which CLIR published in May 2001.

The conference, funded by the Institute of Museum and Library Services, was a follow-up to "Collections, Content, and the Web," which CLIR hosted with the Chicago Historical Society in October 1999. A follow-up to the February 2001 meeting is planned for spring 2002.

Leadership

Frye Leadership Institute

Jointly sponsored by CLIR, EDUCAUSE, and Emory University, the annual Frye Institute brings together individuals from libraries, information technology divisions, and faculty departments in all types of academic institutions to focus on changes in higher education and on the role of information services in the academy.

The second Frye Institute was held at Emory University June 3–15, 2001. Fifty-three of the 175 applicants were selected for participation. During the first week, presidents, provosts, business officers, and other administrative officers provided personal views of the contributions and challenges of higher education. In the second week, faculty conducted sessions on such topics as intellectual property and copyright, technological advances in teaching and research, scholarly communication, public policy, and personal leadership styles.

The Robert W. Woodruff Foundation provides the primary support for the Frye Leadership Institute. The Institute of Museum and Library Services and the Andrew W. Mellon Foundation provide supplemental funding. The Patricia Battin Scholarship Fund makes possible participation by individuals whose institutions cannot afford to support their attendance.

Academic Library Advisory Committee

The Academic Library Advisory Committee identified three projects to receive priority in 2001:

- Research on the outsourcing of library functions
- The identification of issues in library and information resources that are of greatest interest to college and university presidents
- A study on the use of course management software and its impact on libraries

A survey by Outsell, Inc., provided answers to the group's questions about libraries' success with outsourcing. After reviewing the results, the committee concluded that it would not be fruitful to develop case studies on this topic.

Committee Chairman David Cohen prepared a paper on the relationship between the vendors of course management software systems and libraries. He noted that because the two groups rarely interact, students and researchers are often unaware of the wealth of information that exists but is not linked to a course Web site. After reviewing the results of in-depth interviews with vendors, the committee agreed to convene an invitational meeting in January 2002 of library directors and vendors to discuss possible approaches that would allow greater representation of library materials through their systems.

CLIR's new publication series, *CLIRinghouse,* was created in response to recommendations by the Academic Library Committee and the CLIR board, and is supported by a grant from the H. W. Wilson Foundation.

International Developments

Recognizing that all of the foregoing areas of interest have international dimensions, CLIR is focused on identifying relevant work being done abroad and convening appropriate groups in the United States with international counterparts to work on problems of common significance.

Translation of Online Tutorial on Digital Imaging

CLIR has supported the Spanish translation of an online tutorial on digital imaging for libraries and archives (http://www.library.cornell.edu/preservation/tutorial). CLIR is considering requests to translate the tutorial into other languages as well.

Access to Manuscripts and Archives

The international community has shown great interest in Encoded Archival Description (EAD), which U.S. archivists are developing to facilitate electronic access to manuscript and archival finding aids. CLIR, together with the German research consortium Deutsche Forschungsgemeinschaft, sponsored the work of a group of German and American archivists to explore the use of EAD as a means of information exchange for German archives. This work has yielded important information about the flexibility of EAD in non-U.S. contexts and how it can, or cannot, be used in countries with different archival traditions.

Partnership with Mortenson Center

CLIR is now an official partner of the Mortenson Center at the University of Illinois. The Mortenson Center, with endowment and foundation funding, has brought more than 500 librarians from 74 countries to take part in management training and development programs. CLIR will work with the Mortenson Center staff to tailor some portions of the Frye Leadership Institute to an international audience.

Publications

Reports

Bridegam, Willis. *A Collaborative Approach to Collection Storage: The Five-College Library Depository* (June 2001).

Brockman, Bill, et al. *Scholarly Work in the Humanities and the Evolving Information Environment* (December 2001).

Council on Library and Information Resources. *Folk Heritage Collections in Crisis* (May 2001).

Council on Library and Information Resources. *Building and Sustaining Digital Collections: Models for Libraries and Museums* (August 2000).

Council on Library and Information Resources. *CLIR Annual Report* 2000–2001. (October 2001).

Council on Library and Information Resources. *The Evidence in Hand: Report of the Task Force on the Artifact in Library Collections* (November 2001).

Jewell, Timothy. *Selection and Presentation of Commercially Available Electronic Resources: Issues and Practices* (July 2001).

Perushek, Diane, ed. *Proceedings of the 2000 Sino-United States Symposium and Workshop on Library and Information Science Education in the Digital Age* (October 2001).

Pitschmann, Louis. *Building Sustainable Collections of Free Third-Party Web Resources* (June 2001).

Smith, Abby. *Strategies for Building Digitized Collections* (September 2001).

Newsletters

CLIR Issues, nos. 19–24.
CLIRinghouse, nos. 1–4.

Scholarships and Awards

Zipf Fellowship

The Zipf Fellowship is awarded annually to the graduate student in some field of information management or systems who best represents the ideals of Al Zipf, for whom the fellowship is named. Kent Smith of the National Library of Medicine chairs the selection committee. Other members are Christine Borgman, Martin Cummings, Billy Frye, and Rena Zipf.

The 2001 A. R. Zipf Fellowship in Information Management was awarded to Terence Kelly, a Ph.D. student in the Department of Computer Science at the University of Michigan. He is the fifth recipient of the Zipf Fellowship. His research focuses on optimal resource allocation in hierarchical caching systems, especially Web caching. He has spoken and written extensively on this topic; his most recent article, "Optimal Web Cache Sizing: Scalable Methods for Exact Solutions," appeared in *Computer Communications* in February 2001.

Patricia Battin Scholarship

The second annual Patricia Battin Scholarship was awarded in June 2001 to Hans Houshower, director of technology at Bluffton College in Bluffton, Ohio. Established in 1999 by friends and family of Patricia Battin, the scholarship provides financial assistance for participants in the Frye Leadership Institute whose institutions cannot afford to support their attendance.

Mellon Fellowships for Dissertation Research

With funding from the Andrew W. Mellon Foundation, CLIR initiated a fellowship program for dissertation research in the humanities in original sources. The program will offer ten competitively awarded grants per year of up to $20,000 each. Selection of the first year's grantees was scheduled for April 1, 2002.

Bill and Melinda Gates Access to Learning Award

CLIR was selected to administer the annual Bill and Melinda Gates Foundation Access to Learning Award beginning in 2002. The award is given to a library, library agency, or comparable organization outside the United States for efforts to expand free public access to information, computers, and the Internet. The award includes a grant of up to $1 million. Applicants will be reviewed by an international advisory committee of library and information technology experts who will consider the applicants' efforts to make technology freely accessible to the public, train the public in using technology, educate staff on technology use, and reach out to disadvantaged communities. The award will be presented at the annual meeting of the International Federation of Library Associations and Institutions (IFLA), which takes place in August.

International Reports

International Federation of Library Associations and Institutions

Box 95312, 2509 CH The Hague, Netherlands
31-70-314-0884, fax 31-70-383-4827, e-mail ifla@ifla.org
World Wide Web http://www.ifla.org

Winston Tabb
Associate Librarian for Library Services, Library of Congress
Chair, IFLA Professional Committee

The International Federation of Library Associations and Institutions (IFLA) is the preeminent international organization representing librarians, other information professionals, and library users. During 2001 IFLA convened its General Conference in the United States for the first time in 16 years; fostered the integration of digital technologies into an enormous range of library activities; launched the new Section on Reference Work; broadened participation in governance of the federation and conducted elections via postal ballot for the first time; promoted worldwide standards for library service; and pursued collaborations with other library institutions and with commercial entities.

67th General Conference

The 67th IFLA Council and General Conference, held in Boston August 16–25, 2001, was the largest in the history of the organization and the first IFLA General Conference to be held in the United States since 1985. More than 5,330 registrants, approximately twice the usual number (including 1,279 who were attending their first IFLA General Conference), traveled to Boston from 150 countries.

The conference theme was "Libraries and Librarians: Making a Difference in the Knowledge Age," and subthemes included "Advancing the Leadership Role of the Librarian in the Knowledge Age," "Managing Information and Technology in the Knowledge Age," "Developing Information Policies for the Knowledge Age," and "Forging Collaborative Partnerships."

At the opening general session, IFLA President Christine Deschamps said, "Dr. Melvil Dewey, *nous voilà* [here we are] . . ." as she noted that it was entirely appropriate for IFLA to convene in the city in which the first public library in the United States was founded and the state in which library pioneer Melvil Dewey developed the Dewey Decimal Classification system while serving as librarian at Amherst College.

Educator/author Jonathan Kozol delivered the keynote address. Guest lecturers included Laurence Prusak, executive director of the Institute for Knowledge Management, speaking on "What Is Knowledge Management and Why Is It Important?"; Librarian of Congress James H. Billington on "Humanizing the Information Revolution"; and Peter Jaszi of the Washington College of Law, American University, on "Defending Balance in Intellectual Property Law: The Challenge for Librarians." A joint guest lecture, "Preservation in the USA: A Case Study in Cooperation," was delivered by Deanna Marcum, president of the Council on Library and Information Resources; George Farr, director, Division of Preservation and Access of the National Endowment for the Humanities; and Ann Russell, executive director of the Northeast Document Conservation Center.

The national organizers of the General Conference were the American Association of Law Libraries (AALL), American Library Association (ALA), Association for Library and Information Science Education (ALISE), Association of Research Libraries (ARL), Medical Library Association (MLA), and the Special Libraries Association (SLA). The co-chairs of the 2001 National Organizing Committee were Gary E. Strong, director, Queens Borough (New York) Public Library, and Duane Webster, executive director, ARL. Other committee members were Carla J. Funk (treasurer), MLA executive director; Roger H. Parent (secretary), AALL executive director; Nancy D. Anderson, University of Illinois at Urbana-Champaign; David R. Bender, SLA executive director; Evelyn Daniel, School of Library and Information Science, University of North Carolina–Chapel Hill; William Gordon, ALA executive director; James G. Neal, director, Eisenhower Library, Johns Hopkins University; Tovah Reis (Local Planning Committee chair), medical library coordinator, Brown University; Sharon J. Rogers, ALISE executive director; and Larry Wenger, director, University of Virginia Law Library.

In conjunction with the General Conference, the publisher of the Dewey Decimal Classification (DDC), OCLC Forest Press, sponsored the commemoration of the 125th anniversary of the first publication of the classification. This celebration took place on the Skywalk of the Boston Prudential Center on August 21. The following spoke: Joan S. Mitchell, OCLC Forest Press executive director and DDC editor-in-chief; Winston Tabb, chair of the IFLA Professional Committee; and Jay Jordan, Online Computer Library Center (OCLC) president and chief executive officer.

As one of its first official acts, the new IFLA Governing Board at the close of the Boston conference approved a statement of "The IFLA Position on the World Trade Organization (2001)," which declared that IFLA was "positioned to advocate at the WTO on behalf of libraries and information services and to ensure that its members are informed in order to be able to advocate effectively at the national level."

Libraries in a Digital Age

The interdependence of libraries with digital (electronic) content was confirmed as never before at many IFLA workshops and programs. The Bibliography Section Open Forum on "Bibliography: Indispensable or Redundant?" featured a presentation on the Library of Congress New Books Project, which will enrich

Library of Congress cataloging with author information, book jacket images, and so forth, and will enable end users to reserve forthcoming books at their local libraries. The Information Technology Section Open Forum attracted more than 300 attendees to discuss "New Information and Communication Technologies for Libraries in the Knowledge Age." The Division of Regional Activities presented an open forum on "Bridging the Digital Divide: Meeting the Challenge of the Knowledge Age in Developing Countries," highlighting South African, Latin American, and Caribbean perspectives; the division's Asia and Oceania Section featured reports from China, Fiji, Malaysia, and New Zealand on the same topic. The Geography and Map Section presented "Digitizing Cartographic Materials," with speakers from the National Archives of Canada, Library of Congress, and Bibliothèque Nationale de France. Even the Section on Library Buildings and Equipment emphasized the digital revolution at its 12th Biannual Seminar, "Future Places: Reinventing Libraries in the Digital Age," held at Northeastern University in Boston August 15–17. This seminar considered how libraries can balance storage needs for their ever-growing print collections with needs for workstations and scanning equipment, and concluded that a flexible approach to space planning was essential.

The new IFLA Section on Reference Work began its work in Boston with an open forum, "How Is Virtual Reference Different from Face-to-Face Reference? Guidelines and New Competencies for Reference Services to the 'Remote User.'" IFLA has long had sections that addressed reference service and collection development for specific types of materials, such as serials and newspapers, rare books, and government information. The new section will consider reference service in general, and will pay special attention to the pressing questions of optimizing and extending electronic reference service, particularly as an international medium.

Satellite Meetings and Workshops

The General Conference afforded an opportunity to offer satellite meetings and workshops to information professionals from around the world, many from countries where the information profession and publishing industry are not well developed or operate under censorship or other government restrictions. The IFLA Sections on Bibliography and on National Libraries cosponsored a workshop, "What Makes a Good National Bibliography Even Better? Current Situation and Future Prospects." With the Art Libraries Society of North America, IFLA held a joint satellite meeting in Boston, August 16–18, "How Do I Find a Picture of . . . ?—The Changing Nature of Image Research," which brought together art librarians from 17 countries. The IFLA Section on Libraries for the Blind held its satellite meeting, "Digital Libraries for the Blind and the Culture of Learning in the Information Age," in Washington, D.C., August 13–15 in collaboration with the Library of Congress National Library Service for the Blind and Physically Handicapped and the Canadian National Institute for the Blind, Library for the Blind. The IFLA Sections on Management and Marketing and on Education and Training—in collaboration with the School of Library and Information Science of the Université de Montréal, the Canadian Social Science and Humanities Research Council, and the Quebec Ministry of International Relations—sponsored the satellite meeting "Education and Research for Marketing and Quality Management in Libraries/La Formation et la Recherche sur le Marketing et la Gestion de la Qualité en Bibliothèques," in Quebec City August 14–16. "Library Consortia: Current Developments and Future Opportunities—An International Perspective" was a satellite meeting at the Boston Public Library August 16–17, cosponsored by IFLA's Division of General Research Libraries and Division of Management and Technology with NELINET (New England Library Network) and the International Coalition of Library Consortia (ICOLC). The IFLA Sections on Classification and Indexing and on Information Technology, in collaboration with OCLC, presented "Subject Retrieval in a Networked Environment" at OCLC headquarters in Dublin, Ohio, August 14–16. "Technology, Globalization, and Multicultural Services in Libraries" was held in Buffalo, New York, August 14–16, under the auspices of the IFLA Sections on Library Services to Multicultural Populations and on Information Technology.

The Fourth Northumbria International Conference on Performance Measurement in Libraries and Information Services, another joint satellite meeting, took place in Pittsburgh August 12–16, sponsored by the IFLA Section on Statistics in collaboration with ARL. The IFLA Round Table on Continuing Professional Education organized the Fourth World Conference on Continuing Professional Education for the Library and Information Professions in Chester, Vermont, August 15–17.

Collaborations

At the Boston conference, IFLA and ALA announced the Campaign for the World's Libraries, a new public outreach campaign based on the five-year ALA Campaign for America's Libraries with its "@ your library" slogan, which also started in 2001. John W. Berry, 2001–2002 ALA president, proposed the new campaign, and the Turkish Librarians Association was the first IFLA institutional member to join the new endeavor. For IFLA's use, ALA designed a special version of its trademarked "@ your library" logo and translated artwork, brochures, and a video into Spanish for use in the campaign. The Campaign for the World's Libraries will raise awareness of the value of libraries with educators, government leaders, funding agencies, the media, and the general public by promoting three core messages: libraries are changing and dynamic places, libraries are places of opportunity, and libraries bridge the world.

IFLA is collaborating with corporate partners and national libraries to maintain programs and opportunities that would otherwise not be possible, especially for librarians and libraries in developing countries. For instance, the IFLA/OCLC Early Career Development Fellowships have been established to bring five library and information science professionals from countries with developing economies who are in the early stages of their careers to the United States for four weeks of intensive experience in librarianship at the Mortenson Center for International Library Programs at the University of Illinois Library at Urbana-Champaign, at ALA headquarters, and at the Library of Congress. The winners of the Bill and Melinda Gates Foundation 2001 Access to Learning Award, the Proyecto Bibliotecas Guatemala (Probigua) and the Biblioteca del Congreso de la Nación Argentina, were also recognized in conjunction with the General Conference. This award of up to one million dollars has been given since 2000 to recognize libraries and other institutions that promote free public access to technology in innovative and useful ways.

Standards

An important aspect of IFLA's work is the promotion of standards for all aspects of library service. The Public Library Section completed *The Public Library Service: The IFLA/UNESCO Guidelines for Development* (Saur, 2001), the completely revised edition of the *IFLA/UNESCO Public Library Guidelines,* in time for publication of the English version in July, which enabled the section to launch the guidelines officially at the Boston conference. Editions in the other IFLA languages are planned. Also in 2001 IFLA's Professional Board, before it was reshaped as the Professional Committee, approved a completely new set of principles and guidelines for International Lending and Document Delivery. The Section on Cataloguing's ISBD Review Group continued a full-scale review of IFLA's family of International Standard Bibliographic Descriptions.

Membership

IFLA has approximately 1,750 members in more than 150 countries. Initially established at a conference in Edinburgh, Scotland, in 1927, it has been registered in the Netherlands since 1971 and has headquarters facilities at the Koninklijke Bibliotheek (Royal Library) in The Hague. Although IFLA did not hold a General Conference outside Europe and North America until 1980, there has since been steadily increasing participation from Asia, Africa, South America, and Australia. The federation now maintains regional offices for Africa (in Dakar, Senegal); Asia and Oceania (in Bangkok, Thailand); and Latin America (in Rio de Janeiro, Brazil). The organization has five working languages— English, French, German, Russian, and Spanish—and offers four membership categories: international library associations, national library associations, institutions, and personal affiliates. In 2001, for a four-year trial period, IFLA began offering student affiliate memberships at reduced rates, with the aim of broadening participation and enhancing the stability and continuity of the organization by attracting affiliate members early in their careers. In addition, more than 30 corporations in the information industry have formed a working relationship with IFLA as "corporate partners," providing financial and in-kind support. The United Nations Educational, Scientific and Cultural Organization (UNESCO) has given IFLA formal associate relations status, the highest level of relationship accorded to nongovernmental organizations by UNESCO.

Personnel, Structure, and Governance

Ross Shimmon became the secretary general of IFLA in May 1999. Sjoerd M. J. Koopman continues as coordinator of professional activities, an IFLA headquarters position.

The current president, Christine Deschamps, director of the Bibliothèque de l'Université Paris V—René Descartes, completed a first four-year term with the

Boston General Conference and was re-elected, unopposed, for a second two-year term that will run through August 2003. Kay Raseroka, director of library services at the University of Botswana, was chosen as president-elect and began her two-year term at the conclusion of the Boston conference. She will succeed Deschamps as president. Derek Law, Information Resources Directorate, University of Strathclyde, Scotland, was elected treasurer.

This was the first time an IFLA slate of officers had been elected by postal or electronic ballot under the revised IFLA statutes and rules of procedure. The revised statutes were adopted by the IFLA Council at the 66th Council and General Conference in Jerusalem in 2000 and took effect at the conclusion of the Boston conference. IFLA's Executive Board and Professional Board were combined in a new Governing Board, which includes all members of the Professional Committee (formerly Professional Board). The council will meet annually with each General Conference, rather than biennially as in the past.

The IFLA Professional Committee monitors the planning and programming of professional activities carried out by IFLA's two types of bodies: Professional Groups—eight divisions, 36 sections, 12 roundtables, and numerous discussion groups—and Core Programs. The professional committee is composed of one elected officer from each division, plus a chair elected by the incoming members. The eight divisions are I: General Research Libraries; II: Special Libraries; III: Libraries Serving the General Public; IV: Bibliographic Control; V: Collections and Services; VI: Management and Technology; VII: Education and Research; and VIII: Regional Activities. Each division has a coordinating board made up of the chairs and secretaries of the sections. The 36 sections include such interest sections as National Libraries, Geography and Maps Libraries, Libraries Serving Children and Young Adults, Statistics, and Library Services to Multicultural Populations. The five Core Programs are Advancement of Librarianship (ALP), Universal Bibliographic Control and International MARC (UBCIM), Universal Dataflow and Telecommunications (UDT), Universal Availability of Publications (UAP), and Preservation and Conservation (PAC).

The Professional Committee's chair is Winston Tabb; the other members of the committee, each representing an IFLA division, are Cristóbal Pasadas Ureña of Spain (Division I), John Meriton of the United Kingdom (Division II), John Day of the United States (Division III), Ian C. McIlwaine of the United Kingdom (Division IV), Mary Jackson of the United States (Division V), Wanda V. Dole of the United States (Division VI), Marian Koren of the Netherlands (Division VII), and Rashidah Begum bt. Fazal Mohamed of Malaysia (Division VIII). In addition, the Professional Committee includes Sjoerd Koopman (representing IFLA headquarters) and elected members of the Governing Board, currently Claudia Lux (Germany) and Jianzhong Wu (China).

The 21-member Governing Board is responsible for the organization's general policies, management and finance, and external communications. The new Governing Board, which was also elected in the federation's first elections by postal ballot, consists of Derek Law (United Kingdom), Sissel Nilsen (Norway), Alex Byrne (Australia), Ana Maria Zimmerman (Argentina), Jianzhong Wu (China), Sally McCallum (United States), and Ellen Tise (South Africa), plus the members of the Professional Committee. Their terms of service also began at the conclusion of the Boston conference and will run for two years. The Governing

Board delegates responsibility for overseeing the direction of IFLA between board meetings, within the policies established by the board, to a six-member IFLA Executive Committee that includes the president, president-elect, treasurer, chair of the Professional Committee, two members of the Governing Board (elected every two years by members of the board from among its elected members), and IFLA's secretary general, ex officio. The first elected Governing Board members of the Executive Committee are Ingrid Parent, Acquisitions and Bibliographic Services, National Library of Canada, and Ellen Tise, University of the Western Cape, South Africa.

The intention of this new structure is to open up the association to the broadest possible participation, with a particular view to improving the federation's service to libraries in developing countries. For the first time in IFLA's history, members who are not able to travel to the annual conferences will be able to have a real voice in the governance of the association. Over time, IFLA believes, these changes will give more people an opportunity to serve in leadership roles and will make the federation more inclusive, more responsive to rapid change, and better able to serve as the global voice of libraries.

A Canadian-American Librarianship
or an American-Canadian Librarianship
in the 21st Century?

William F. Birdsall

Executive Director, Novanet, Inc., and the Council of Atlantic University Libraries/Conseil
des Bibliothèques Universitaires de l'Atlantique

For years the *Bowker Annual* has included an article on the Canadian library
scene. These reports have taken a variety of forms; over the past several years the
focus has been on trends, issues, and innovations during the year under review.
The focus of this year's report is a significant trend in national public policy that
has important implications and consequences for libraries in Canada, including
the extent to which this development creates the potential for the creation of an
American-Canadian librarianship. The essence of this report is that 2001 is note-
worthy for the extent to which Canadian librarians are involved in federal public
policy making. More than ever before, that policy making involves the provision
of federal funding targeted specifically to libraries. A significant consequence of
this greater involvement of librarians in federal policy making is the possibility
of the formulation of an American-Canadian librarianship, in contrast to the traditional Canadian-American librarianship that prevails in Canada.

A Canadian-American Librarianship

Early 19th-century Canadian librarians looked to Europe for professional guidance, but as the 20th century grew nearer they turned increasingly to the United
States, where modern librarianship was taking form. Thus, librarianship in
Canada has been largely a Canadian-American librarianship for most of its history. Coinciding with the advent of the new century is the issue of whether librarianship in Canada will continue as a Canadian-American librarianship, that is, a
librarianship that is essentially American. Or is an American-Canadian librarianship emerging—a librarianship that is essentially Canadian but with an unavoid-
able American flavor?

Most Americans would be unaware of the long debate within Canada
between nationalists and continentalists. Nationalists fear that Canadian sovereignty and cultural identity will be totally absorbed into the United States.
Continentalists argue that Canada needs a North American political and economic strategy that recognizes the import of the American economic market.
Nationalists traditionally favor public policy that strengthens East-West ties,
often making use of various modes of communication to forward this objective.
In the 19th century a coast-to-coast railroad and in the 20th century the trans-
Canada highway, a national airline, and the Canadian Broadcasting Corporation
are examples of such East-West nation building public policy strategies. Continentalists tend to favor public policies that rely more on the market and that
promote a greater North-South orientation. Thus, recent governments have priva-
tized the national railroad and airline. Calls by prominent corporate CEOs for the

adoption of the U.S. dollar by Canada is a recent example of a continentalist point of view. In the opening decade of the 21st century, this longstanding policy tug-of-war is cast as a contest between those who are proglobalization and those who are antiglobalization.

Where do Canadian librarians fit into this nationalist/continentalist polarity? They are supportive of Canadian cultural development through the acquisition of Canadian publications, the collection of archival collections, author readings in libraries, and so forth. They are good nationalists. Nonetheless, as a profession they tend to be continentalists. Initially Canadian librarians looked to both Europe and the United States for professional sustenance. However, they were drawn to the dramatic developments in modern librarianship that emerged in the United States during the closing decades of the 19th century. Canadian library leaders became active members in the American Library Association (ALA), which met several times in Canada.

This U.S. orientation continued throughout the 20th century. Typical structures of a national librarianship were slow in developing in Canada. It was not until 1946 that a Canadian Library Association (CLA) was formed after decades of discussion about the need for such an association. Canadian university libraries were among the founding members of the Association of Research Libraries (ARL) in 1932. However, the Canadian Association of Research Libraries/ Association des Bibliothèques de Recherche du Canada (CARL/ABRC), a Canadian counterpart, was not formed until 1976. Over the years more CARL/ ABRC members have joined ARL. Presently 16 of CARL/ABRC's 29 members are members of ARL (including the National Library of Canada) with more likely to join.

Many of the CLA and CARL/ABRC initiatives are adaptations of programs initiated by ALA and ARL. For example, Canadian librarians were trained in the ALA library advocacy program when the program was incorporated into CLA initiatives. The American Library Association accredits Canadian master's programs in library and information studies. (An effort some years ago by a president of the Canadian Library Association to promote Canadian-only accreditation was soundly defeated.)

Canadian librarians rely heavily on the library literature generated in the United States, as there are few places in Canada to publish library research and best practices. Canadian library leaders remain active in ALA, ARL, and the Association for Library and Information Science Education (ALISE). In 2003 ALA and CLA are to hold a joint conference in Toronto. Canadian libraries eagerly accept funds from the Bill and Melinda Gates Foundation just as they did from the Carnegie Corporation of New York in an earlier era of Canadian library development.

In sum, Canadian librarians practice a Canadian-American librarianship—a librarianship essentially the same on both sides of the border. However, this situation is changing. The Canadian government is giving increasing attention to public policies focusing on promoting economic development in a global market. Many of these policy initiatives, including an opening for the federal government to funnel funds to libraries at the local level, have significant implications for libraries. These government policy initiatives, along with the new sources of funding, draw librarians into a growing involvement in federal policy making.

This involvement in turn creates the potential for Canadian librarians to formulate a distinct Canadian library perspective within the context of a Canadian public policy environment.

Federal Government Policy and Libraries

Librarians in the United States have a long history of advocacy and success in acquiring federal support for libraries. Since the 19th century there has been a federal department concerned with education, including library development. A manifestation of this federal commitment is the establishment of the National Commission for Libraries and Information Science (NCLIS) and its two White House Conferences on Libraries and Information Science. Such a federal structure and commitment have not existed in Canada. The federal government transferred funds to the provinces for education, but the specific allocation of these funds has been the prerogative of the individual provinces. Therefore, unlike in the United States, few federal dollars flow directly to libraries at the local level.

This situation is changing significantly. To promote economic development in a competitive global market, the federal government implemented an information highway strategy to make Canada the most competitive and connected nation in the world. Accordingly, it is promoting the development of telecommunication services as the foundation for a vital e-commerce sector. To promote increased e-commerce, the government is pursuing policy initiatives in such areas as deregulation, privatization, privacy, intellectual property rights, and access to the information highway. These are areas of direct interest to librarians and those they serve.

In support of these policy initiatives, the Canadian government is channeling funds in support of libraries. Taking a cue from the former Clinton administration's "Connecting All Americans" initiative, the Canadian government adopted its policy of "Connecting Canadians." Industry Canada (the federal department mandated to promote the government's information highway policy) implemented a number of programs to get Canadians connected, including SchoolNet, LibraryNet, and the Community Access Program (CAP). These programs look to libraries as links to the Internet for those who cannot afford their own computers and household connections. In addition, the government's economic development objective includes greater support for research and development programs in the university sector, a strategy that has positive spin-offs for academic libraries. All these programs make funding available to libraries.

Making Government Policy

Librarians, primarily through their professional associations, are drawn into federal policy making as they attempt to strengthen and extend these programs as well as influence federal information highway policies. CLA, CARL/ABRC, and other associations have for years given attention to national public policy in such areas as copyright, human resource development, and the construction of the Canadian information highway. However, there numerous recent examples indicative of heightened activity and success in policy making at the federal level.

The Canadian Library Association has long been an active advocate for libraries in Ottawa, through various lobbying initiatives and the submission of briefs to such bodies as the Canadian Radio-Television and Telecommunications Commission (CRTC), which is the Canadian equivalent of the U.S. Federal Communications Commission. More recently these efforts include the hiring of a government relations firm to assist with CLA's lobbying of federal politicians and public servants with its Campaign for Canada's Libraries. The objective of this campaign is to educate government decision makers on the importance of libraries to the government's innovation agenda. It also promotes the formation of a Canadian Council of Libraries, urges the continuation of special postal rates for library materials, expresses concern about the impact of the World Trade Organization General Agreement in Trade in Services, and supports the National Librarian's efforts to get a new building for the National Library of Canada.

These objectives were pursued by teams of CLA Executive Council members through a "Day on the Hill" meeting with key members of Parliament and senior government officials. (This initiative is another example of CLA using an ALA model, in this case the longstanding ALA Legislative Day.) These government representatives were presented with CLA's brief, *The Role of Canadian Libraries in the Canadian Way.* The brief makes the case that Canadian libraries are central to achieving the Canadian government's programs in community development, and youth employment, in connecting Canadians to the Internet, and in the delivery of information services to remote and rural areas. In particular, CLA urges the government to form a Canadian Council of Libraries to identify national priorities and to administer and disburse federal funds for library development programs.

In addition to these initiatives, CLA has submitted a brief to the government's Access to Information Review Task Force, briefs to the House of Commons Finance Committee (*Sustaining Citizen Connectivity to the Internet Through Canada's Public Libraries* and *Investing in Libraries*), and a response to the government's *Consultation Paper on Digital Copyright Issues.* CLA submitted an extensive brief to the Department of Canadian Heritage's consultative process on new directions for cultural heritage policy in Canada. This brief addresses definitions of heritage, global trends impacting Canadian libraries, libraries and cultural diversity, the risks and opportunities confronting libraries, how libraries contribute to advancing Canadian heritage, and a vision of how libraries can contribute to the government's goals.

In June 2001 the government's National Broadband Task Force issued its report advising the government on how to ensure that rural and remote areas have fast broadband access to the information highway. CLA announced its formal support for the government's broadband initiative while emphasizing the critical role public libraries play in providing access to the information highway in small communities. Through these various initiatives CLA is formulating a body of documentation, positions, and arguments presented in a Canadian, rather than an American, public policy context.

The Association pour l'Avancement des Sciences et des Techniques de la Documentation (ASTED), the francophone counterpart to the anglophone CLA, also presents briefs to the government and parliamentary committees. Indeed, both CLA and ASTED, along with the National Librarian, participated in the

House Standing Committee on Canadian Heritage hearings on the Canadian book-publishing industry. As a result, the committee's report, *The Challenge of Change: A Consideration of the Canadian Book Industry* (2000), included an entire chapter on "Libraries, Preservation and Access."

University libraries are also giving greater attention to Canadian national public policy, as indicated by the creation of a Government Policies and Legislation Committee (GPLC) by CARL/ABRC. As well, CARL/ABRC uses the same governmental affairs consulting firm as CLA. Furthermore, in recognition that Canadian research libraries are operating in a different government policy community from their American counterparts, ARL agreed to underwrite in part a joint federal relations initiative with CARL/ABRC. GPLC is charged with anticipating and tracking legislative, regulatory, and programmatic initiatives by government and related organizations in Canada and abroad that can impact research libraries. It is to engage in policy processes related to intellectual property and telecommunications issues, promote funding for organizations that advance member interests, and form alliances with other organizations with which CARL/ABRC shares a common interest.

Like CLA and ASTED, CARL/ABRC presents substantive briefs to federal government committees, such as its *Canada Research Libraries: Funding the Indirect Cost of Research* (2001) submitted to the House of Commons Standing Committee on Finance. It also put forward briefs on copyright reform and the management of government information. In addition, the association drafted a working document on potential research projects preliminary to preparing a proposal to the federal granting agency, the Social Sciences and Humanities Research Council (SSHRC) Research Development Initiative program. This working document identifies 24 issues and potential research questions relating to the research library environment in Canada. The acceptance of such a proposal by SSHRC would signify the recognition by a major federal agency that research libraries are a crucial public policy concern in the government's efforts to promote research and development in Canada.

The Council of Administrators of Large Urban Public Libraries (CALUPL), the public library equivalent of CARL/ABRC in Canada and of the Urban Libraries Council in the United States, is also active at the national level, especially with regard to Industry Canada's LibraryNet. LibraryNet, along with SchoolNet and the Community Access Program (CAP), is one of the government's "Connecting Canadians" programs. CALUPL has submitted proposals to the government on the development of this program and is represented on the LibraryNet Advisory Committee.

These associations are not only involved individually with policy and legislative processes but they increase their leverage by allying themselves with each other and with organizations outside the library field. Along with CLA and others, the Provincial and Territorial Library Associations Council (PTLAC) launched a "Libraries Advance Canada" movement. An inaugural meeting in June 2001 was attended by 37 people representing 27 library associations from across Canada. Those attending identified four issues requiring national advocacy that have widespread support across all sectors of the library community: a new national library building, federal support of libraries, access to government information, and support for digital copyright. This advocacy movement's audience is politicians, councils of ministers, other governmental task forces and advisory bodies, the media, and the general public.

Copyright Reform

The government's continuing effort to reform the copyright legislation is another example of a collaborative strategy among library and other associations. In 2001 the government announced its third major consultation in copyright reform. Phase I of copyright reform was completed in 1988. Phase II was completed in 1997. These two phases focused on the print environment. Phase III of the process shifts to issues arising out of the digital environment. Heritage Minister Sheila Copps and Industry Minister Brian Tobin initiated this third phase with the issuing of the government's *A Framework for Copyright Reform* and a *Consultation Paper on Digital Copyright Issues.* Library associations had been central players in the policy community involved with the first two phases. Again they are active in promoting the needs of libraries and their users.

Consequently ASTED, CALUPL, CARL/ABRC, CLA, and the Canadian Association of Law Libraries (CALL) are members of the 13-member Copyright Forum, a coalition that also includes associations representing community colleges, universities, archivists, university teachers, museums, school boards and teachers, and provincial ministers of education. The Copyright Forum generated the substantial *Discussion Paper on Digital Copyright Issues.* This document served as a basis for the individual briefs prepared by the members of the forum for submission to the relevant bodies of Parliament and the government, including the National Broadband Task Force.

Developing a Canadian Perspective

Copyright is an example of a public policy issue involving libraries where Canadian and American contexts differ. For example, in addition to the economic rights of authors attached to copyright (the primary focus of U.S. copyright law), authors in Canada also possess personal moral rights under copyright legislation. In Canada, authors have moral rights of paternity, integrity, and association that are attached to the author rather than individual works. Indeed, as we have seen, Canadian librarians are taking advantage of the greater opportunity to influence federal government policy-making, including such issues as:

- The need for sustainable funding for Internet access
- The role of libraries in the provision of access to the information highway
- Broadband access to the Internet
- A federal Council for Canadian Libraries
- Canadian culture
- Canadian publishing
- Copyright
- The National Library of Canada

- National library statistics
- Postal rates for library materials
- International trade agreements
- Telecommunications regulation
- Libraries and the indirect costs of research
- National site licensing initiatives

In their reports, briefs, and policy statements, librarians often indicate to policy makers how the Canadian and U.S. contexts differ for libraries. These differences relate to such factors as values, geography, legal and funding structures, the importation of information and publications, size and distribution of population, and so forth. In short, Canadian librarians are defining how Canadian librarianship is distinct from that below the 49th parallel. Encouraging signs of success of these efforts are now appearing. One example is the government's 2001 budget announced by the Hon. Paul Martin, Minister of Finance, in December 2001. CLA was able to point out that, despite the emphasis the federal budget gives to funding for increased security as an aftermath of the September 11 terrorist attacks in the United States, the government is funding programs advocated by the library community. The budget extends LibraryNet and CAP for three more years. It provides funds for expansion of broadband access to the Internet. Funding continues for the government's own information management initiative to put more government information online. As advocated by CARL/ABRC, the December 10 budget provided C$200 million to ease the pressure of the indirect costs of research. In this context, libraries are identified as a key area.

An American-Canadian Librarianship?

At this time we can only speculate whether a genuine American-Canadian librarianship will appear and what it might look like. But one would anticipate that, because librarians are now moving from public policy at the municipal and provincial levels of government to the national level, an American-Canadian librarianship will reflect fundamental Canadian values. As Canadian librarianship becomes more national, it will reflect the national culture in which it is embedded. It will be, surely, to some extent American, just as Canadian culture has its American elements. But it could also reflect characteristics that are distinctly Canadian.

One value that always distinguished Canada from the United States is the Canadian commitment to universalism in its social policies. In the inevitable trade-off in democratic societies between liberty and equality, Canadians tend to favor the latter while Americans tend to favor the former. In contrast to the United States, in Canada more social services are applied universally, the most prominent example being its healthcare system. The willingness to share for the greater good is also reflected in the strong support remaining, despite a decade of government budget cuts, for federal government equalization payments. (This is a longstanding program whereby the federal government transfers tax funds from wealthier to poorer provinces.) In higher education, provinces and universities have resisted implementing out-of-province tuition fees despite a decade of severe budgetary constraint.

Librarianship in both the United States and Canada has always been, of course, committed to universal access to information. However, increasingly we can see this commitment extended in ways Canadian: that is, policies and programs are national, collaborative, and universal. Indeed, two notable examples of these traits that came to fruition in 2001 are the Canadian National Site Licensing Project (CNSLP) and the provision of free access to the National Library's AMICUS database.

Canadian National Site Licensing Project

CNSLP, reported on in the 2001 *Bowker Annual,* is a prime example of how Canadian libraries formulated a unique Canadian response to the current public policy environment. In April 1999, under the leadership of CARL/ABRC, 64 academic libraries in Canada submitted a successful proposal to the federally funded Canada Foundation for Innovation (CFI) to establish pan-Canadian licensing for research content in electronic form, in order to increase capacity for research and innovation in Canada.

CNSLP was established as a C\$50 million, three-year pilot project, and is now in its second year of operation. Of the C\$50 million, C\$20 million in federal funds were awarded through CFI. The participating universities raised the remaining C\$30 million with the assistance of provincial and regional governmental bodies.

CNSLP's specific objectives are to increase the quantity, breadth, and depth of scholarly publications available to Canadian academic researchers, speed the transition to and usage of electronic formats, and leverage Canadian universities' buying power and influence in the international scholarly publishing marketplace.

In its first year of operation, CNSLP initiated a competitive request for proposal process for publishers of electronic scholarly content, developed a model license agreement, and completed negotiations with seven scholarly publishers for national, multiyear access (2001–2003) to their electronic content. As a result, over 650,000 researchers and students at 64 universities, from the smallest institution to the largest throughout Canada, now have equal access to digital copies of approximately 750 specialized journals and databases in the sciences, health sciences, engineering, and environmental studies. The CNSLP model license agreement also secures consistent and advantageous content usage rights for the Canadian academic community, and establishes an access and pricing model appropriate to the Canadian legal and fiscal context.

This project is a significant public policy achievement for the university library community. For the first time, the federal government, through CFI, recognized academic libraries as an essential component of the research infrastructure, and made funds available for the acquisition of recently published research material. Governed by a steering committee and managed by Executive Director Deb deBruijn, CNSLP has been recognized as an outstanding service and business achievement, and in 2001 was awarded the National First Prize of the Quality and Productivity Awards program of the Canadian Association of University Business Officers (CAUBO).

CNSLP is also a uniquely Canadian response to making electronic research material available to the academic research community in Canada. During the development of the CNSLP proposal for submission to CFI national site-licensing initiatives in Britain, the United States, and Australia were examined. However, in the end, CNSLP reflects the Canadian commitment to provide universal access for all researchers regardless of geographic location or size of institution. CNSLP represents a collaborative approach between regional academic library associations, CARL/ABRC, CFI, and the 64 universities to provide universal access to research material.

AMICUS

AMICUS is the catalog of more than 22 million records of the National Library of Canada and the records contributed by 500 Canadian libraries. Until this year, only those libraries that paid a subscription fee could access AMICUS. When newly appointed National Librarian Roch Carrier toured the country meeting librarians, he got the message from coast to coast that AMICUS should be available free of charge not only to libraries but to all citizens. He gave this objective a high public policy priority and was successful in making AMICUS available at no direct cost to users. Consequently, he was able to announce at the CLA annual conference that AMICUS is now available free of charge to all Canadians 24 hours a day, 7 days a week. Any Canadian can locate a title regardless of his or her location or the location of the item sought.

Both the CNSLP and the free access to AMICUS initiatives provide national, collaborative, and universal service. Indeed, it is quintessentially Canadian that they meet the individual needs of all through a national collaborative strategy using the tool of government. These projects are an extension of the long-standing public policy of using the most modern technological communication tools to bind a population dispersed over a vast geographic area.

Conclusion

As the 21st century gets under way, the public policy needle in Canada is swinging from East-West to North-South. The conclusion of a Canada-U.S. free trade agreement at the close of the 1980s followed by the North American Free Trade Agreement (NAFTA) solidified the economic integration of Canada and the United States. A market-driven public policy seems to signal the victory of the continentalists over the nationalists. The steady decline in the value of the Canadian dollar relative to the American dollar, combined with the fact that 87 percent of Canadian exports are to the United States, continues the pressure toward what one politician calls "a truly integrated economic unit" in North America. Canadians are well aware that their economic well-being is dependent on the vitality of the U.S. economy.

However, it is premature to assume that Canadians are ready to embrace a totally North American context that further blurs the 49th parallel. For example, recent polls show that, while Canadians are concerned about the high costs of health care and the level of service provided, they remain overwhelmingly in support of the provision of tax-supported, universal health care. As well, polls consistently indicate that, although Canadians are becoming more comfortable with globalization and greater economic integration with the United States, they are also determined to maintain a Canadian identity and sovereignty. As globalization progresses, Canadian identity actually may be increasing. But some argue that it is a new type of Canadian identity and nationalism.

Traditionally, federal nation-building public policy concentrated on economic tools (for example, protection for Canadian-owned corporations and trans-Canada airlines, railroads, and highways). Some argue that traditional public policy strategy of economic nationalism is no longer viable or supported by the majority of people. As Canadians become more comfortable with the potentialities of economic integration, the old grounds of the debate between nationalists and continentalists seem increasingly to belong to the previous century and not to the new one. Instead, according to pollster Darrell Bricker and journalist Edward Greenspon in their book *Searching for Certainty: Inside the New Canadian Mindset* (Doubleday Canada, 2001), what is emerging is a confident cultural nationalism, a nationalism less tangible than the traditional national economic enterprises but more in tune with the new global environment.

The emergence of a stronger cultural nationalism could have significant implications for libraries and federal policy. Traditionally, cultural policy has focused on publishing, authors, and the mass media. But, as the CLA brief to the Department of Canadian Heritage stresses, libraries have a history of promoting, preserving, and sustaining the cultural legacy of Canada. Clearly, this is an area of public policy where Canadian librarianship can become more active. Also, as in other areas of public policy, it could formulate a distinctive Canadian voice. In contrast to the American emphasis on cultural homogeneity (the melting-pot metaphor) Canada celebrates cultural diversity (the mosaic metaphor). CLA rightly stresses that libraries in Canada have always provided a wide range of services and programs aimed at the needs of a diverse Canadian citizenry.

Certainly there are those who dispute the Bricker and Greenspon analysis. They insist that cultural nationalism and political sovereignty cannot survive when a country is not willing to pay the economic price to maintain its political independence. Yet, pollsters discern trends similar to those identified by Bricker and Greenspon, most significantly, perhaps, that what Canadians value most is not one ideology over another, but rather the preservation of a sovereignty and rights that allow them to make their own choices on specific issues. Thus, Canadians maintain their commitment to collective action through the one thing they all have in common: their federal government. Within Canadian librarianship one could argue that a new type of cultural nationalism, calling upon a role for an activist national government, is reflected in such programs as CNSLP and AMICUS.

It is too early to ascertain whether Canadian librarians will in time formulate a unique American-Canadian librarianship whose essence is distinctly Canadian. And it is possible to argue that, at a time of globalization, worldwide instantaneous telecommunications networks, and transnational media and publishing empires, a national librarianship anywhere is problematic. However, as evidenced in 2001, the growing participation and success of Canadian librarians in national policy processes perhaps signal a significant step in the process of formulating an American-Canadian librarianship, a case perhaps of thinking globally but acting locally. The preparation of association briefs, reports, surveys, position papers, projects, and research agenda creates the foundation for a critical mass of library literature, values, and ideas that contribute to the definition of an American-Canadian librarianship. If there is emerging in Canada a 21st-century cultural nationalism, we may yet see a flourishing American-Canadian librarianship as well.

Note: For their assistance in the preparation of this report, the author is indebted to Deb deBruijn, Executive Director, Canadian National Site Licensing Project; Norman Horrocks, Scarecrow Press and School of Library and Information Studies, Dalhousie University; Tim Mark, Executive Director, Canadian Association of Research Libraries/Association des Bibliothèques de Recherche du Canada; Mary Jane Starr, Director General, Communications Branch, National Library of Canada; and Vicki Whitmell, Executive Director, Canadian Library Association. However, the author is solely responsible for the presentation of the content and views expressed.

Special Reports

Adventures with E-Books: 2001 in Review

Dennis Dillon

Assistant Director for Collections and Information Resources
General Libraries, University of Texas at Austin

The year 2001 was a remarkable one for the e-book. A year rife with business ups and downs, philosophical speculations, unending press commentary, the very visible failure of many well-funded e-book efforts, and the unnoticed success of several small and ill-funded start-ups. At least in regard to e-books, the better capitalized your project, the more likely you were to overreach; and the less money you had to work with, the more likely you were to design a practical business plan with modest expectations and a positive cash flow. If, as William Least Heat-Moon says, "adventure is putting into motion one's ignorance,"[1] then this was a year filled with e-book adventures. Publishers, authors, and librarians all struggled to understand the new opportunities that the e-book presented, discovering in the process both unexpected failures and insights, along with hints that 2002 is likely to hold more of the same.

The year began with a cascade of confident forecasts and corporate announcements, and it ended with a barrage of closures, bankruptcies, and uncertainty.

January found the industry still under the optimistic sway of the dot-com information technologists, and although publishers engaged in superficial soul-searching and panel discussions occasioned by the publication of Jason Epstein's *Book Business: Publishing Past, Present, and Future,*[2] the troubling implications of his observations were easier to ignore than confront. Epstein suggested that the publishing industry was structurally ill equipped to meet the challenges of the digital age effectively, and little that happened in the following months served to dispel that observation.

In general it was a year filled with hyperbole, hope, and lip service, in which people with little gut feeling for publishing, or even a nodding acquaintance with book-reading customers, rushed into the e-book business as if it were the modern equivalent of the 1849 California Gold Rush. Despite heavy promotion and active interest from the press, consumers ignored the commercial e-book, while contrarian authors and libraries quietly began to experiment with, and put money into, niche efforts that went largely unnoticed by the press and public.

As every month passed it became more obvious that high-profile publishers and middlemen were having problems coming to grips with the market, and that few of the industry's richly paid strategists had appropriately considered the need for customers, or even who those customers might be or how the industry could fill their needs.

By the end of the year, the question of whether publishers owned e-rights to their authors' early works was in the courts. The e-book market was not living up to revenue expectations. The arrest of a 26-year-old Russian Ph.D. student for tinkering with e-book software in violation of the Digital Millennium Copyright Act (DMCA) had occasioned worldwide protest. And several high-profile e-book efforts had closed down or were clinging to life, supported by deep-pocket parent companies or by additional rounds of venture capital.

By December it appeared unlikely that a single path forward for the e-book movement would be found anytime soon. A practical, portable, universal e-book reader still appeared years away. Progress on the Open eBook Publication Structure (OEBPS) continued, but given the competing commercial interests involved, advancement was moving at the expected worm's pace. The large commercial publishers appeared to have reached consensus that a mainstream e-book market would be slow to develop and they began to pull back from their earlier overly optimistic e-book plans. Small e-book publishers continued to do well, and were arguably incubating a new publishing model in which they treated the e-book as a different type of commodity than current traditional publishers have treated the printed book. But the profits of the small e-book presses are too low and e-publishers' approach is too different to interest the multinational conglomerates that run mainstream commercial publishing. The companies that supply e-book infrastructural support (such as digital conversion, fulfillment, digital rights management, e-commerce, and print on demand) appeared to be settling into stable niches. The true believers in the practicality of reading e-books on various small gadgets continued to view the future of the e-book through rose-colored space helmets, fueled in part by a steady trickle of e-book sales to users of the current generation of personal digital assistant (PDA) devices.

No single e-book business model prevailed. Every business approach used to market movies and videos to home viewers could also be found within the e-book industry: from outright purchase, to pay-per-view, to subscription to e-book "channel content" such as information technology books. One firm, RosettaBooks, even experimented with a self-destructing e-book where access expired after ten reading hours.

By the end of the year the future appeared to belong to those publishers with realistic and modest growth plans who were willing to invest their own money in the format, and who were willing to stick with the market and understand its evolving needs. In other words, the future of the e-book may very well be found in the past approaches used to market the printed book. Find a specific market, develop authors and readers within that market, treat both your producers and consumers fairly, and build brand awareness and loyalty within this niche.

E-Books: 2001 Timeline

January

- Gemstar's new e-book readers retail for $299 (REB 1100) and $699 (REB 1200).

- Barnes & Noble forms an e-book publishing division, Barnes & Noble Digital, blurring the lines between publishers and distributors.
- Jason Epstein's influential *Book Business: Publishing Past, Present, and Future* is published to widespread industry comment.

February

- Random House announces the formation of AtRandom.com.
- The research firm IDC projects that demand for digital books will build quickly, with revenue reaching $414 million in 2004.
- HarperCollins launches a dedicated e-book imprint, PerfectBound.
- Versaware study says that electronic texts are making strides in America's colleges.
- Ibooks.com cuts 70 percent of its work force.
- Layoffs occur at Xlibris.
- Random House seeks injunction against RosettaBooks for publishing e-books of three Random House authors.
- Association of American Publishers CEO Pat Schroeder says her organization has "a very serious issue with librarians."

March

- EarthWeb discontinues its ITKnowledge e-book service.
- Forrester Research projects that digital delivery of custom-printed books, textbooks, and e-books will account for revenues of $7.8 billion (17.5 percent of publishing industry revenues) in five years.

April

- Franklin Electronic Publishers begins shipping three eBookMan models.

May

- Time Warner launches iPublish.com with expectations that it will "redefine publishing as we know it."

June

- After numerous layoffs throughout the spring, Versaware closes its Web site.
- E-books declared eligible for National Book Awards.

July

- Court denies Random House bid to block RosettaBooks e-books.
- Dmitry Sklyarov is charged with violating the Digital Millennium Copyright Act for revealing how to defeat Adobe's e-book protection scheme.
- Franklin reports lower-than-expected demand for the eBookMan.

- Lightning Source opens new print-on-demand facility in Britain.

August

- Open eBook Forum releases OEBPS 1.01.

October

- Contentville.com shuts down.
- U.S. Copyright Office registers first e-books.
- RosettaBooks publishes first self-destructing, time-limited e-book.
- IUniverse secures more investor capital.

November

- Random House drops AtRandom.com e-book effort.
- NetLibrary files for bankruptcy.
- More layoffs occur, this time at Questia.
- Simon & Schuster opens new e-book store, SimonSaysShop.com.

December

- Time Warner shuts down iPublish.com.
- Layoffs occur at print-on-demand specialist Lightning Source.
- MightyWords closes shop.
- Reciprocal shuts down.
- U.S. government drops charges against Dmitry Sklyarov in exchange for testimony against his Russian employer.
- Gemstar reduces price on REB 1100 to $199 and REB 1200 to $399.
- Princeton University Press drops e-book program.

Market Forecasts

In February IDC's market research report "Electronic Publishing Forecast and Analysis, 2000–2004: Digital Books and Print on Demand" found that digital book revenues would reach $414 million in 2004, while in March *Information Today* reported that Forrester Research had projected that digital delivery of custom-printed books, textbooks, and e-books would account for revenues of $7.8 billion (17.5 percent of publishing industry revenues) in five years. Of this amount, only $251 million was to come from e-books for e-book devices, as publishers were expected to move to a model of multichannel publishing.[3]. While not quite as rosy as the seminal Andersen Consulting study commissioned by the Association of American Publishers (AAP) in mid-2000 that predicted e-books sales of $2.3 billion reaching 10 percent of the market by 2005, these two later studies were nonetheless encouraging.[4] By summer, signs of caution were apparent as the Electronic Document Systems Foundation issued a report saying that "We'll all still be reading paper books 50 years from now, because it's not just the technology that has to change. People have to change."[5] This was quickly followed by a widely publicized *New York Times* story in August headlined "Forecasts of an E-Book Era Were, It Seems, Premature," which reported that almost no one was buying e-books.[6]

Customers

Customers—or, as these illusionary beings were known during 2001, market segments—continued to be imagined as people who would be interested in e-books to be read on dedicated, handheld reading devices; who might be interested in Web-based e-books; and who might want to read e-books using software on their personal computers or PDAs. Unfortunately, paying customers were few, except for libraries, which bought hundreds of thousands of e-books from netLibrary, and the gadgeteers, who were looking for an additional use for their PDAs. Publishers also hoped that customers could eventually be found for electronic textbooks, and print-on-demand operations. Meanwhile a different kind of customer was evolving and being served by a plethora of self-publishing and small press operations, providing a cheap and easy avenue for authors to distribute their works through the Internet without using a traditional publisher.

Online Retailers

Online sales of e-books in 2001 were dominated by BarnesandNoble.com, Amazon.com, Yahoo, and Powells.com. BarnesandNoble.com, Amazon.com, and Yahoo all sold e-books for PCs that required use of the Microsoft Reader or the Adobe Acrobat eBook Reader, as well as e-books for PDAs that run on Pocket PC software. Powells.com sold books for the Gemstar REB 1100 and REB 1200 as well as the Microsoft Reader and Adobe Acrobat eBook Reader. The numbers of titles available in each format were comparable, ranging from 3,500 to 4,500.

E-books could also be purchased from a number of newly formed, small, independent online retailers, as well as through such publishers as Simon & Schuster's online outlet, SimonSays.com, and a proliferating number of newly formed, small online presses. Realizing that the distinction between an e-book publisher and an e-book retailer was a minor one, the giant retailer Barnes & Noble began publishing e-books through Barnes & Noble Digital. This blurring of the distinctions between the publishers, distributors, and retailers of e-books was further compounded by the distribution of Web-based e-books via subscription arrangements in a manner similar to those used for e-journals, thus blurring even the traditional boundaries between a book and a periodical. The increasingly subtle distinctions between e-book publishers and retailers, and between electronic books and electronic serials, can be expected to become more confusing in the future.

Dedicated Reading Devices

Unlike PCs, laptops, and PDAs, dedicated e-book reading devices are suitable for a limited number of functions and are used primarily for one purpose: reading e-books. Consumers have never taken to the devices and sales have never been encouraging. This trend continued in 2001.

Gemstar continued to dominate this market with the re-release of the mono-chrome display REB 1100 retailing at $299 and the color display REB 1200 retailing for $699, with these prices dropping to $199 and $399, respectively, by the end of the year if purchased from Gemstar's Web site.

Franklin's trio of eBookMan readers began shipping in April, ranging in price from $129 to $229. Sales were disappointing, however, and by year's end Franklin was offering rebates of $30 to $50 on the purchase of one of its devices. In October Franklin teamed up with the French software company MobiPocket, which began including its e-book reading software on the eBookMan product line in order to increase the number of e-books that could be read on the device.

Both of these dedicated reading device vendors are harmed by their propri-etary formats and the relative lack of content for their reading appliances. Given the almost universal rejection of current e-book devices, it would seem unlikely that another company would mount a serious challenge to the two leaders in this market, yet the Korean Hiebook at $249 is a serious competitor with numerous additional flexible features built into its reading appliance. It also functions as an MP3 player, and has audio recording capabilities and PDA functions; however, it still suffers from the same lack of e-book content as other dedicated reading devices.

Reader Software

E-book reader software is free and easily installed on the consumer's PC, laptop, or PDA. It allows the consumer to read an e-book, while providing the copyright owner with protection against unlicensed copying.

For all practical purposes, there are now only two significant contenders when it comes to reader software: Microsoft and Adobe. The Microsoft Reader (http://www.microsoft.com/reader) is a free, downloadable program for PCs and handheld PDAs running the Pocket PC operating system. The Adobe Acrobat eBook Reader (http://www.adobe.com/epaper/ebooks/main.html) is also a free downloadable program for PCs, with a special version (http://www.adobe.com/products/acrobat/acrrmobiledevices.html) for PDAs running the Pocket PC or Palm Operating System. Adobe's reader is based on Adobe's proprietary Portable Document Format (PDF). Previously, PDF files, which were virtual pictures of a printed page, could not adapt to the different screen sizes of portable devices. In May Adobe demonstrated new, flowable PDF with XML tags that adapts to any screen size. Microsoft's reader uses the XML-based OEBPS format and includes Microsoft's pixel-borrowing technology, known as ClearType, for improved readability.

E-books read with either software can be annotated, bookmarked, searched, updated via the Internet, and, if the publisher allows, printed, loaned, or even given away. While this was but a blip when compared with overall book sales,

Palm announced at year's end that it had sold 180,000 units of its 3,500 e-book titles designed for use on Palm PDAs, thus demonstrating that there is indeed a small market for e-books to be read on small screens.

Print on Demand

From a production standpoint, the process used to create an e-book in either Adobe or Microsoft format can also be used to create a print-on-demand book. Print-on-demand books can be printed in small batches virtually overnight with an appearance, including cover, that is almost indistinguishable from the original printed book, thus eliminating the need for expensive print runs and warehousing.

Lightning Source, a subsidiary of Ingram Industries, is the dominant resource for commercial print-on-demand titles. They have printed more than 3 million on-demand books for 1,300 publishers and currently print an average of 5,000 books a day, with an average order size of only 1.6 copies. A single 300-page book costs the company $4.80 to print.[7] The print-on-demand revolution is based on technology from Xerox and IBM that can print, glue, and cover a 300-page book in less than a minute. Prototype machines like the smaller and more inexpensive MTI PerfectBook-80 can produce a printed paperback in 12 minutes. Backers hope for a future when such machines are located in neighborhood bookstores and mini-malls. This technology has been instrumental in leading to a host of new companies dedicated to helping authors publish, distribute, and print their titles in ways that bypass the traditional publishing community. These efforts are covered in the section "The New Guard" later in this report.

Web-Based E-books

In terms of titles available and audience reached, Web-based e-books dwarf the other e-book market segments. NetLibrary (http://www.netlibrary.com), with a collection of more than 40,000 titles and a presence in 6,600 libraries, has the best market penetration, while Questia (http://www.questia.com), which markets its service of 70,000 titles directly to students for $19.95 a month, may be the best known due to its aggressive advertising. However, neither of these services has made a profit, unlike Books24X7, which provides 1,700 technical and business e-books to corporations and libraries. In December Books24X7 was acquired by SkillSoft Corporation for $32.4 million.

Web-based e-books are delivered to a consumer's Web browser through a secure connection after the consumer has entered a password or been authorized for use by other means. This ease of delivery makes libraries of Web-based e-books perfect for the educational and corporate market, where the books can be purchased and managed by an institution on behalf of its user base. However, even this market experienced volatility during 2001.

NetLibrary, which raised more than $180 million in venture capital and was once valued at $450 million, filed for Chapter 11 bankruptcy in November 2001. OCLC, a nonprofit cooperative of libraries, offered to purchase the company for $10 million in December. Questia raised more than $150 million in venture capital, but expected student subscriptions never materialized. Between spring and winter Questia cut its work force from 280 to 68. Ibooks.com, which sold computer science and information technology books to the corporate market, folded less than a year after receiving $30 million in second-round financing and reaching agreements with such industry heavyweights as IBM, O'Reilly, and Oracle. ITKnowledge, another computer science and information technology e-book vendor operated by Earthweb, went out of business in February, just weeks after reaching agreement with library consortia throughout the country. Earthweb, which subsequently changed its name to Dice, operated as a technology job site for the remainder of 2001. Ebrary (http://ebrary.com/), with 6,000 titles online, continued to develop its e-book content during 2001 and planned to market a subscription-based product to libraries during 2002.

The business models employed by the distributors of Web-based e-books varied widely in 2001, ranging from making permanent ownership rights available through a one-time purchase of a specific e-book title, to various annual and short-term subscription models that applied to an entire collection of e-book titles.

Traditional Publishers

The response of traditional publishers to the e-book market was a bit schizophrenic, reflecting both a sense of uncertainty about how best to respond to the development of e-books, and a question of whether e-books represented an opportunity or a threat. In general, publishers selected a restricted number of popular fiction titles for release as e-books, and made them available in formats for both the Microsoft Reader and Adobe Acrobat eBook Reader at prices below those of their print counterparts.

Random House brought e-books into the mainstream by forming the AtRandom.com imprint at the beginning of the year, and then shut down the imprint in November, reorganizing its e-books among its many other imprints.

In a challenge to traditional publishers, Barnes & Noble formed an e-book publishing division, Barnes & Noble Digital, promising authors and agents higher royalties and a better split of wholesale revenue.

Time Warner closed iPublish.com, an e-publishing site that solicited new authors and offered 500 original and backlist e-books, 18 months after it was launched to predictions that it would transform publishing.

In contrast, Simon & Schuster opened SimonSaysShop.com in November to sell its e-books online and said that it expected 2001 e-book sales to be double that of 2000.

Meanwhile, Penguin UK began publishing hundreds of both backlist and frontlist e-book titles, and HarperCollins formed a dedicated e-book imprint, PerfectBound, which began releasing ten to 15 titles a month.

These and other responses by traditional publishers were a test of the e-book waters. The question for the traditional publishers, however, is how they will respond to the e-book format over time. As Jason Epstein and others have noted, publishing today is largely controlled by a handful of large multinational corporations that are a result of the business conditions of print-based publishing, and that inspire little author or reader loyalty. The current system is an "over concentrated and inefficient literary marketplace dominated by book chains rooted in the five-hundred-year-old Gutenberg system of centralized manufacture and physical distribution." On the other hand, e-books involve no physical inventory and involve only minor production and delivery costs, meaning, "authors will contribute more to the final value of the product than publishers and can claim a larger share of the proceeds." Because small-press, start-up companies are not burdened with the vast payroll and overhead necessary to sustain print publishing, they can potentially outbid traditional publishers for authors by offering author royalties of 70 percent or more.[8] The disruptive technologies involved with e-books present traditional publishers with a number of challenges, and it would not be surprising to see the large publishers use all the resources at their command to maintain market dominance and to slow the rise of a new guard of small e-book presses and distributors.

The New Guard: Small and Vanity Presses, Independent Retailers

While traditional publishers were reporting that e-book sales were disappointing or downright unprofitable, a host of small start-up publishers were finding profit in newly created niches opened up by the e-book phenomenon. Offering higher royalties, lower retail prices, and better author rights, and sometimes recouping costs by charging authors minimal e-publishing set-up fees, these companies use e-books and print-on-demand technology to reduce both the author's barriers to getting published and the consumer's reading costs. By employing a model that subverts the big traditional publishers and that provides substantial advantages for both the author and reader, they have mixed the new technologies in original ways and come up with an approach to publishing that is part vanity press, part independent bookstore, and part neighborhood niche publisher. Once their books are in the databases of online retailers like Amazon.com or BarnesandNoble.com, these small publishers benefit from the same global market reach as the large traditional publishers. In essence they have put many of the elements of professional publishing into the hands of authors, allowing authors the power to manage the production and distribution of professional-looking books, on demand, in either print or electronic format. The three best known of these companies are iUniverse, Xlibris, and 1stBooks Library.

IUniverse.com (http://www.iuniverse.com) has 8,500 authors and 10,000 titles, and has printed and sold 750,000 books. It caters to self-published or independent authors; the company slogan is "iUniverse takes the dream of publishing and turns it into a reality." For as little as $99, an aspiring author can have iUniverse create a book and set it up for distribution. Its books are distributed through Amazon.com, BarnesandNoble.com, and other independent booksellers and are available in print and e-book formats. In December Lightning Source agreed to make iUniverse titles available in Britain, where they will be printed at the Lightning Source facility in Milton Keynes.

Xlibris.com (http://www.xlibris.com), which is partially owned by Random House, provides similar services, and charges authors anywhere from $500 to $1,600 per title, depending on the desired services. In return, Xlibris processes book orders, provides book fulfillment, pays royalties, and promises the book's indefinite availability. Xlibris's 6,000 titles are available from "Amazon.com,

Borders.com, BarnesandNoble.com, as well as in the Books In Print database, Ingram's catalogue, and many other online outlets."

The amount charged by 1stBooks Library (http://www.1stbooks.com) to format, design, and distribute an author's books is $399. One 1stBooks title, Buddy Ebsen's debut romance novel, *Kelly's Quest,* reached number three on the *Los Angeles Times* bestseller list. The company offers the same services as iUniverse and Xlibris and pays its authors 100 percent for electronic books up to the first $300 in sales (40 percent thereafter) and 30 percent for paperback and hardcover versions.

Other small presses, such as Hard Shell Word Factory (http://www. hardshell.com), do not charge their authors any fees and are selling more than 1,000 titles a week.

Fictionwise.com (http://www.fictionwise.com) reports a similar experience, selling 10,000 titles a month. In yet another bout of e-book experimentation by small presses, RosettaBooks (http://www.rosettabooks.com) brought out the Agatha Christie classic mystery *And Then There Were None* in October, charging $1 for ten hours of reading. After ten hours, the Adobe Acrobat-formatted book self-destructed and readers had the option of purchasing a permanent edition for $4.99.

What is the difference between the e-book experiences of these small presses and that of the big traditional publishers? Mary Wolf of Hard Shell Word Factory says that among the big traditional publishers it "is the quick-buck mentality—nothing is nurtured and allowed to achieve its potential any more. If something doesn't make immediate, compound return on investment, it's road kill in the path to the next glittering opportunity."[9] This view was echoed by others, such as Mike Shatzkin of Idea Logical, who was quoted in *Publishers Weekly* as noting that "book publishers are most likely to be disintermediated by their own unhappy authors." He was also critical of publishers who "want all the rights but aren't doing anything with them. They are disintermediating themselves."[10]

Each of these new companies is seizing an opportunity that didn't exist a few years ago. They have looked at traditional publishing operations and found them to be burdened with bloated operations necessary for the sustenance of print and shackled to the maintenance of high profits expected by corporate ownership. Large traditional publishers have little freedom to maneuver into areas that won't turn quick profits, and little time to devote to the maintenance and care of new authors, or the development of nontraditional customers, or the exploration of new ways of doing business. Weighed down with the heavy overhead costs of traditional publishing, they are reliant on the existing economics of print publishing in order to supply the revenues necessary to continue current operations.

With author royalties running between 20 and 30 percent of a publisher's net revenues, and another 40 percent or so of revenues absorbed by executive, administrative, and overhead costs, traditional publishers are in a poor position to compete for authors. The leaner operations of the new upstart firms can offer author royalties of 70 percent or more—and can establish themselves in niche fields that traditional publishers have neglected because of low sales volume, lack of interest, or substandard profits.[11]

In the new publishing model, an author can supply digital files to a publisher who then adds only minimal editorial and design value to the manuscript, converts it to a secure e-book format, and then sells the e-book or print-on-demand title directly to the customer. In comparison to traditional publishing, this process allows author royalties to be increased, the retail price of the book to the consumer to be decreased, and the publisher's administrative and overhead costs to be reduced. Everybody wins, and that is why small start-up presses are able to make money with e-books when big publishers with traditional operations are not able to see a profit. This analysis does not factor in the long-term, intangible value of future sales that may come from a customer purchasing an e-book directly from the publisher's Web site, and the loyalty that can be the result of building such a relationship among authors and readers.

Fulfillment, E-Commerce, and Digital Conversion

The lack of huge e-book sales among traditional publishers had a deleterious effect on the middlemen who handled the e-book conversion, fulfillment, hosting, encryption, e-commerce, and digital rights management functions for publishers and retailers.

Reciprocal—which supplied rights management, e-commerce, and fulfillment functions for the e-book operations at Time Warner, HarperCollins, Random House, and St. Martin's, among others—went out of business in the fall. The high profile e-publishing and conversion company Versaware (which the previous year had turned down purchase offers of $200 million and at one time had 1,400 employees) failed to find a buyer and closed down operations in April. Among Versaware's clients were McGraw-Hill, Pearson, Taylor & Francis, ABC-CLIO, Lycos, ZDNet, and Simon & Schuster Interactive.

Among the companies that expanded operations during this period was the very aggressive OverDrive (http://www.overdrive.com), which operates digital rights management, hosting, and e-commerce services for McGraw-Hill, Time Warner, Taylor & Francis, Random House, HarperCollins, John Wiley & Sons, Penguin Putnam, and Barnes & Noble, among others. Its clearinghouse for digital content, Content Reserve (http://www.contentreserve.com), handles more than 10,000 digital products from 30 countries and was gearing up during December to host the customer content from the failed MightyWords. Texterity (http://www.texterity.com), an e-book conversion house that distributes electronic files to retailers, also picked up customers during the year, including Penguin Putnam, Time Warner, St. Martin's, McGraw-Hill, Random House, Rough Guides, Scholastic, and HarperCollins. Texterity specializes in XML markup, which is then output into a variety of formats including PDF. Another conversion and infrastructure house that increased its sales was Rovia (http://www.rovia.com), which counted among its customers Vivendi Universal, Houghton Mifflin, Pearson Education, and Thomson Learning. Rovia is concentrating on the textbook market and has products that allow publishers to price content both by time and by chapters. Lightning Source (http://www.lightningsource.com), known for its print-on-demand business, was also active in digital fulfillment, including file conversion, content management and storage, digital rights management, and secure e-book delivery. Lightning Source currently provides digital fulfillment services to Amazon.com and Simon & Schuster's e-book store SimonSaysShop.com.

Libraries

Libraries were cautious e-book customers during 2001, primarily participating in the e-book phenomenon through purchases of Web-based e-books from netLibrary; more than 6,600 libraries purchased e-books from netLibrary's catalog of 40,000 titles. Most of these purchases were by library consortia, with the result that multiple libraries often shared access to a single copy. For example, the public and academic libraries in Texas shared access to a collection of 18,000 netLibrary titles. NetLibrary's bankruptcy in November raised fears throughout the library community of a possible loss of online access to these e-books. OCLC's offer to purchase the company and continue the service eased these fears, but long-term response of library customers to the reconstitution of netLibrary was unknown.

Other significant vendors active in the library market during the year were Books24X7 and ITKnowledge, both of which offered subscription-based access to a collection of Web-based titles related to computer and information technology. After a presentation to the International Coalition of Library Consortia, the OCLC regional network NELINET negotiated terms with ITKnowledge for consortia-based sales. The negotiated price was higher than the sum individual libraries paid before the intervention of NELINET, so the price was later renegotiated and sales to individual libraries were then brokered by the OCLC regional networks. A few months later ITKnowledge announced that it was withdrawing from the library market and refunded libraries their prorated subscription costs. In contrast, Books24X7 was more cautious in selling to consortia and pursued a primary strategy of selling to corporate clients. Of the three Web-based library e-book vendors, Books24X7 was the only one that ended 2001 still solvent and in business, though it did merge with another firm at year's end.

In the "What were they thinking?" category, a handful of public libraries purchased dedicated e-book reading devices from Gemstar, loaded them with e-books, and began circulating them to the public in the same manner as they did other material. At the time of this writing, most of these efforts had been discontinued. The emerging consensus was perhaps best stated by Susan Kent, director of the Los Angeles Public Library, who said, "We are not lending e-books. They are unwieldy and unreadable."[12] This public identification of the e-book with the device with which it is read was common in the media and with readers throughout 2000 and the early part of 2001. The concept of the e-book as a separate file that could be read via the Web or downloaded to multipurpose devices did not become widespread until it was popularized by the PC and PDA software readers for the promoted by the large commercial firms of Microsoft and Adobe and their partners.

In a sign that e-books in one form or another are here to stay, *Library Journal* began a regular e-book review column at mid-year. Oxford University Press polled libraries about a new product to be called Oxford Scholarship Online that would provide online full-text access to the most recent research-level books published by the press. While both Wiley InterScience and Proquest Information and Learning announced new e-book product launches for libraries at year's end, these two new e-book services were to be marketed as annual subscriptions concentrating on scientific, technical, and computer titles.

Challenges to Libraries

E-books pose an interesting challenge to libraries. It is still not clear which business model will enable the e-book vendor to avoid financial difficulty, properly compensate the publisher, and be affordable. NetLibrary's financial difficulty was largely blamed on the added costs incurred during the company's early practice of absorbing the cost of converting printed books into digital form. They later transferred this expense to publishers by requiring the publisher to supply Web-ready e-books.

Compared with consumers, libraries, by their very nature, make different use of e-books and they require a different set of e-book rights and technical functions. With many e-books currently being sold to consumers for as little as $2, it is possible that many library customers will eventually prefer to eliminate the library as an e-book middleman and obtain their e-books directly from Amazon.com and other Internet distributors. In this scenario, the ubiquity and low cost of readily available e-books could have an effect on the usage of libraries, though it is hard to say whether it would drive readers to the library to get a preferred print edition, or away from libraries since consumers could get their e-books through other means.

The minor tension between the aim of publishers (to charge consumers for reading material) and the aim of libraries (to provide reading material for free), was brought back into focus during the year as publishers and librarians considered how each would like to make use of emerging e-book technology. These tensions became more public in February during an interview that Pat Schroeder, president and CEO of AAP, gave to the *Washington Post,* in which she said "We have a very serious issue with librarians."[13] She went on to explain that publishers were concerned about libraries making electronic content freely available to library users. Librarians in turn argued that libraries were not the enemy, and that the new technologies mean that new publishing and copyright models will have to be found that will work for every segment of society.

The different set of e-book needs for libraries and consumers, along with the different aims of publishers and libraries, do raise questions as to how attractive libraries will eventually be as a market for e-book publishers. But it is also notable that many consumers' first exposure to e-books now occurs through the thousands of libraries that have netLibrary e-books (or through student use of netLibrary titles at home), and since book buyers and library users are one and the same, there appears to be rich ground for publishers to build on the experience of these consumers and develop the market by working with libraries to further the e-book experience.

Copyright and E-books

The RosettaBooks Case.

RosettaBooks (http://www.rosettabooks.com), a small New York e-book publisher, purchased e-book rights from authors Kurt Vonnegut, William Styron, and Robert Parker. The authors' previous printed books had been published by Random House. Random House brought suit against RosettaBooks in February, claiming that the word "book" in the old pre-digital author contracts was a term that covered electronic publishing rights. On July 11, 2001, Judge Sidney H. Stein, U.S. District Court for the Southern District of New York, denied Random House's bid for a preliminary injunction that would have prohibited Rosetta-Books from continuing to sell eight titles for which Random House holds print rights. The judge found that the clause "'print, publish, and sell the work(s) in book form . . .' does not include the right to publish the works in the format that has come to be known as the e-book."[14] Random House appealed on September 13, and on September 19 AAP filed an amicus brief in support of Random House's appeal. RosettaBooks replied to the appeal on October 19, and on October 26 the Authors Guild and the Association of Authors' Representatives filed a joint amicus brief in support of RosettaBooks. By the end of the year the three-judge Court of Appeals had not set a date for oral arguments.

If Random House ultimately prevails, then e-book publication rights would be considered to be an implied part of most existing author contracts. If Rosetta-Books prevails, then e-book publication rights would be considered to remain with the original author. Random House is concerned that if it loses, it would have to renegotiate the electronic rights for its entire backlist of books, since those authors signed their contracts before anyone considered the issue of digital rights.

The Sklyarov DMCA Case

Dmitry Sklyarov, a 26-year-old Ph.D. student and programmer for the Russian firm ElComSoft, was arrested July 17 after giving a talk at DefCon, a hacker convention in Las Vegas. His was the first criminal prosecution under the 1998 Digital Millennium Copyright Act (DMCA). He and his employer were charged with releasing a program, legal in Russia, that disables restrictions on Adobe's e-book software. The ElComSoft software, the Advanced eBook Processor, permits e-book owners to translate from Adobe's secure e-book format into the more common PDF. The software only works on legitimately purchased e-books. And according to ElComSoft, "it has been used by blind people to read otherwise-inaccessible PDF user's manuals, and by people who want to move an e-book from one computer to another (just like anyone can move a music CD from the home player to a portable or car)."[15] Worldwide condemnation and outcry against the arrest was immediate, with *Publishers Weekly* noting "a storm of protest in 23 cities around the world."[16]

On December 13 government attorneys announced they would drop the case in exchange for Sklyarov's testimony against his employer. Among other effects, the case provided wide publicity about the weaknesses of Adobe's encryption technology. As the FBI noted in its affidavit, "Any e-book protection based on Acrobat PDF format, as the Adobe e-Book Reader is, is absolutely insecure just due to the nature of this format."[17]

The *Los Angeles Times* went a step further saying that "one reason for the consumer rejection [of e-books] may be all those strict controls the publishers put on their e-books. The controls are backed up by the Digital Millennium Copyright Act." But in the same article, Allan Adler, AAP vice president, legal and government affairs, said, "While publishers are often being portrayed as money-gouging bullies, they're merely trying to stay alive . . . publishers are extremely vulnerable right now."[18]

DMCA was also a topic of heated debate at this year's Seybold Conference in San Francisco. After these exchanges, Leo Dwyer of RosettaBooks said, "The dilemma of rights management comes from trying to emulate the physical book world. If it's priced at $30, you'd better put a lock on it. From the consumer side, most want to read it and throw it away."[19] The underlying and undecided question for publishers remains: How should the e-book be positioned and marketed? Should the e-book be viewed as a digital incarnation of a printed book, or is it an entirely different product that should be handled in new ways? Does the e-book, in order to be ultimately successful, require the forging of a slightly different relationship with authors, readers, and libraries?

Standards

If there is one thing everybody in the e-book universe agrees on, it is that the ultimate success of e-books is heavily dependent on the ability of any e-book to be read on any device. Despite this theoretical agreement, the multiplicity of e-book formats continued during 2001. Work on a universal format inched forward during 2001 with release of Open eBook Forum's (http://www.openebook.org/) Open eBook Publication Structure (OEBPS) specification version 1.0.1. The forum is composed of about 100 members, including industry heavyweights Microsoft, Adobe, Random House, McGraw-Hill, and IBM. Work is currently proceeding on Publication Structure 2.0, which will introduce new features in the areas of presentation, linking and navigation, internationalization, and metadata. While this effort is widely supported in the industry, there is also some skepticism regarding the desire of the competing interests to reach a speedy agreement, since agreement on a standard would suddenly change the e-book playing field— before anyone is sure how the game should be played.

Displays and E-Ink

Displays for reading e-books continue to be only marginally adequate and nowhere approaching print quality. As Jacob Vlades, the developer of Clearview, a competitor of Microsoft's ClearType, put it, "Screen resolution hasn't improved much over the past decade. It is still abysmal. Until it increases another 50 percent or so in each direction—which means about twice as many pixels per square inch—things will not get substantially better."[20] John Dvorak was quoted as saying in the same article that for e-books to be practical, "the display needs to be at least 300 dots per inch with a contrast ratio of 40:1 to 50:1 and it must be readable in the brightest sunlight and the most poorly lit office."

Industry observers have their eyes on electronic ink and paper (actually flexible transistor technology) as presenting the best chance for practical quality e-book displays. E-Ink (http://www.eink.com) and Gyricon Media (http://www.gyriconmedia.com/smartpaper/index.asp) are both working on this technology. Pierre Wiltzius of Bell Labs believes the E-Ink team "might have e-paper with a resolution equivalent to 100 dots per inch" in three to five years.[21] The company hopes to have an initial device with current E-Ink technology and a seven-inch diagonal screen ready for the market in 2003. But Daniel O'Brien, an analyst with Forrester Research, believes that for a practical, low-cost reading device, "the technology is still five to seven years out." [22]

Textbooks

Textbooks are another e-book market that has yet to mature. Notable existing textbook efforts include the McGraw-Hill Learning Network (http://mhln.com), which continues to provide an online platform for interactive textbooks, and Thomson, Houghton Mifflin, and Pearson Education, which have all contracted with Rovia (http://www.rovia.com) to produce online textbooks. Meanwhile Go-Reader (http://www.goreader.com), the electronic reading device for textbooks, is partnering with Harcourt College Publishers, Addison Wesley, Key College Publishing, and the West Group to publish handheld textbooks for the K–12 and college market. Among distributors, Follett's online textbook store, efollett.com (http://www.efollett.com), carries more than 400 textbooks in Microsoft Reader and Adobe Acrobat eBook Reader format. While this market has been slow to take off, Jupiter Research predicts e-books will make up about 6.5 percent of college textbook sales by 2005. [23]

Nonprofits

Progress on the e-book front among nonprofit organizations continued with the Mellon Foundation-funded American Council of Learned Societies History E-Book Project (http://historyebook.org) moving closer to making 500 backlist and 85 frontlist history titles available for subscription in 2002. Michael Jensen reported in the *Chronicle of Higher Education* that the National Academy Press (http://www.nap.edu) strategy of providing free online access to more than 2,500 titles has led to record sales of their print titles. [24] The University of Virginia Electronic Text Center (http://etext.lib.virginia.edu) reached a total of 51,000 texts and 30,000 daily visitors, with 5,000 of their texts being publicly available. There were signs of caution, however, as Princeton University Press, which had aggressively entered electronic publishing a year earlier, decided to do away with its e-book publishing program at the close of 2001.

Other News

The U.S. Copyright Office registered its first full-length e-book deposit over the Internet with two e-books from McGraw-Hill: *The Hitchhiker's Guide to the Wireless Web* and *The Business Week Guide to the Best Business Schools.* The e-books were submitted via the Copyright Office Electronic Registration, Recordation and Deposit System (CORDS), which checks the authenticity and integrity of digital submissions through digital signatures and provides secure storage of digital works. [25]

The first Independent e-Book Awards were given in a well-attended ceremony in Virginia in March 2001 (http://www.e-book-awards.com/indie2002/media/archive/03.24.01.html). Shortly thereafter the National Book Awards announced that e-books published solely in electronic format could be submitted and considered in the traditional four categories of fiction, nonfiction, poetry, and young people's literature.

Key Viewpoints and Publications

Among the thousands of articles on e-books that appeared during the year, those listed below either garnered the most attention or best represented their divergent points of view.

Jason Epstein's influential *Book Business* (Norton, 2001) argues that publishing today has deep structural problems and that the future will inevitably include e-books, print-on-demand, print books, and different publishing models. Epstein's book appeared early in the year and was the source of much soul-searching and commentary in the publishing world. While not solely about e-books, it is an essential starting place for anyone who wants to understand the state of publishing today.

Clifford Lynch's article in the online journal First Monday "The Battle to Define the Future of the Book in the Digital World"[26] focuses on the many unresolved practical and philosophical issues surrounding e-books. Because of Lynch's thorough understanding of digital issues, his article is an excellent accompaniment to Epstein's thorough understanding of the business of publishing. Taken together, these two works suggest that the e-book is likely to have a tumultuous and interesting future.

Harvard professor Marshall Poe discovered that the current publishing model was not working for him, so he took matters into his own hands, as recounted in his prescient article "Note to Self: Print Monograph Dead; Invent New Publishing Model,"[27] which appeared in the *Journal of Electronic Publishing*. Poe's personal experiences strongly echo the ideas discussed by both Epstein and Lynch.

In a *Library Journal* article, "The Other E-Books," Roy Tennant offers a persuasive reminder that the future direction of e-books does not lie solely in the hands of large, well-capitalized commercial entities, as he points to the continuing online e-book successes and innovations of university presses, libraries, and other nonprofit entities.[28]

Finally, 14 very different and interesting articles can be found in a *Library Hi Tech* theme issue on e-books.[29] All of the authors are involved with the creating, selling, purchasing, and promoting of e-books, and they all have experience with e-book consumers. Articles focus on e-book stakeholders, reading devices, underlying technology, practical challenges, different e-book experiences, competition, the nature of reading, e-book formats, metadata, research studies, and copyright issues.

Conclusion

In summary, the extravagant claims, hucksterism, failures, bankruptcies, and false steps that were the most visible residue of the 2001 e-book industry resolved at year's end into a more settled industry with more reasonable expectations. While it is still too early to predict with any certainty the future direction of the e-book, the emerging consensus is that it does have a future and that its effect on publishing will be profound. Its eventual impact on the mass of the reading public, on textbooks, and on booksellers and libraries is less clear. As Groucho Marx reminds us, "Outside of a dog, a book is a man's best friend. Inside of a dog it is too dark to read."[30] At the moment, the future of e-books still lies inside Groucho's dog.

Notes

1. William Least Heat-Moon, *River-Horse: The Logbook of a Boat Across America* (Houghton Mifflin, 1999), 15.

2. Jason Epstein, *Book Business: Publishing Past, Present, and Future* (W. W. Norton, 2001).

3. "Forrester Research Reports on E-Books," *Information Today* 18, no. 3 (March 2001): 43.

4. The Andersen study, "Reading in the New Millennium," can be found at http://www. publishers.org/home/ebookstudy.htm.

5. Christina Wood, "The Myth of E-Books," *PC Magazine* (July 1, 2001): 223.

6. David D. Kirkpatrick, "Forecasts of an E-Book Era Were, It Seems, Premature," *New York Times,* 28 August 2001, p. A1.

7. "Forget E-Books," *Interactive Week* 8, no. 13 (April 2, 2001): 57, and "IUniverse Expands Internationally with Lightning Source," Internet Wire (http://www1.internetwire.com/iwire/ home), December 18, 2001.

8. The quotations and summaries in this paragraph are from Jason Epstein's online commentary, "Reading: The Digital Future," found at http://www.text-e.org/conf/index.cfm? ConfText_ID=13.

9. M. J. Rose, "E-Books Live on After Mighty Fall," Wired News, December 8, 2001, http://www.wired.com/news/culture/0,1284,49184,00.html.

10. Calvin Reid, "Publishers Embrace E-Books at Confab," *Publishers Weekly* 248, no. 12 (March 19, 2001): 25.

11. Figures from Epstein, "Reading: The Digital Future."

12. James Lichtenberg, "Libraries Look for a Niche in Electronic Publishing World," *Publishers Weekly* 248, no. 39 (September 24, 2001): 21.

13. Linton Weeks, "Pat Schroeder's New Chapter: The Former Congresswoman Is Battling for America's Publishers," *Washington Post,* 7 February 2001, p. C01. Also at http://www. washingtonpost.com/wp-dyn/articles/A36584-2001Feb7.html.

14. "Court Denies Random Bid to Block Rosetta E-Books," *Publishers Weekly* 248, no. 29 (July 16, 2001): 67.

15. http://www.freesklyarov.org.

16. Paul Hilts, "Russian Busted for E-Book Hack," *Publishers Weekly* 248, no. 32 (August 6, 2001): 45.

17. Brian Livingston, "Window Manager: Adobe's Copywrongs—Using the FBI Against a Hapless Programmer Won't Improve Weak PostScript-Based E-Books," *InfoWorld* 23, no. 32 (August 5, 2001): 34.

18. David Streitfeld, "E-Book Saga Is Full of Woe—and a Bit of Intrigue," *Los Angeles Times,* 6 August 2001, p. A1.

19. Bridget Kinsella, "Seybold Focuses on Practical E-Book Issues," *Publishers Weekly* 248, no. 41 (October 8, 2001): 12.

20. Stephen Sottong, "E-Book Technology: Waiting for the False Pretender," *Information Technology and Libraries* 20, no. 2 (June 2001): 72.

21. Charles C. Mann, "Electronic Paper Turns the Page," *Technology Review* 104, no. 2 (March 2001): 44.

22. John Aguilar, "E-Book Industry Seeks Standards, Public Acceptance," *Boulder County Business Report,* 2 November 2001, p. 1A.

23. Eryn Brown, "Who's Afraid of E-Books?" *Fortune* 143, no. 3 (February 5, 2001):159.

24. Michael Jensen, "Academic Press Gives Away the Secret of Success," *Chronicle of Higher Education,* 14 September 2001, p. B24.

25. "U.S. Copyright Office Registers First E-Books," *T.H.E. Journal* 29, no. 3 (October 2001): 26.

26. Clifford Lynch, "The Battle to Define the Future of the Book in the Digital World," *First Monday* 6, no. 6 (June 4, 2001), http://firstmonday.org/issues/issue6_6/lynch.

27. Marshall Poe, "Note to Self: Print Monograph Dead; Invent New Publishing Model," *Journal of Electronic Publishing* 7 (December 2001), http://www.press.umich.edu/jep/07-02/poe.html.

28. Roy Tennant, "The Other E-Books," *Library Journal* 126, no. 15 (September 15, 2001): 31.

29. Thomas Peters, theme editor, "Special Section on E-Books," *Library Hi Tech* 19, no. 4 (2001).

30. Groucho Marx, quotation from http://www.quotationspage.com.

Internet Speed, Library Know-How Intersect in Digital Reference

Ilene F. Rockman

The year 2001 saw an accelerated interest in the number and types of libraries offering digital reference services, also known as virtual or real-time reference services. This form of service is a natural extension and outgrowth of the pre-dominantly fact-based, electronic ready-reference service in which a patron e-mails a reference request and typically receives a text response within 24 hours. With improved connectivity, high-speed networks, and a growing consumer interest in convenience, flexibility, and timely access to Web-based information, these services have grown both domestically and internationally. By the end of 2001 "LiveRef: A Registry of Real-Time Digital Reference Services" (http://www.public.iastate.edu/~CYBERSTACKS/LiveRef.htm), compiled and maintained by librarian Gerry McKiernan of Iowa State University, included more than 150 sites reflecting academic, research, government, public, special, and consortia/regional libraries.

Background

According to Wiese and Borgendale (1986), one of the first digital reference services was the Electronic Access to Reference Service (EARS), launched by the University of Maryland Health Sciences Library in 1984. Early offerings of this type of service were not widespread, even with the rise of the Freenet movement (which began in 1984 as a research project at Case Western Reserve University), which permitted individuals to use bulletin board systems or telnet software to connect to various civic networks, linked to public libraries, to ask questions and receive answers.

It was not until the early 1990s—when personal computers became more affordable to the home user and academic technologies became more pervasive—that services to remote users reached a wide, diverse audience. Wasik (1999) notes that successful models of such electronic reference services during this period of time included AskERIC (1992), the Internet Public Library (1995), and KidsConnect (1996). Among academic library models, Ciccione (2001) writes that the Temple University Libraries in 1998 were one of the first academic library adopters of this service.

Concomitant with the explosion of the World Wide Web and improved technologies in the mid-1990s, electronic reference services slowly evolved from a text-based platform to a Web-based one. As a result, libraries began to market professional reference services to users "anywhere, anyplace, anytime," using graphically appealing interfaces and easy-to-complete forms. Some libraries utilized staff expertise to write scripts to gather and tabulate numbers of questions,

Ilene F. Rockman is Editor, *Reference Services Review,* and Manager, Information Competence Initiative, California State University, Office of the Chancellor. She can be reached by e-mail at irockman@calstate.edu.

as well as to mount instructional Web pages, such as frequently asked questions (FAQs) related to the service.

By the end of the 1990s, these text-based Web forms began to move toward a real-time, interactive model utilizing a variety of software products, including some based on and customized from Call Center software used in the commercial sector. Pilot projects trained librarians, either individually or in teams, to respond to patrons' questions. Modified software, enhanced with pre-scripted text messages, directed patrons to appropriate resources. As such services grew nationally and internationally, several listservs were established to share experiences, offer guidance, diagnose problems, and recommend solutions. These listservs and discussion groups included LiveReference, available through Yahoo (http://groups.yahoo.com/group/livereference), and DigRef (which included both live and e-mail reference services) available through the Virtual Reference Desk Web site (http://www.vrd.org/Dig_Ref/dig_ref.shtml).

With the beginning of the 21st century, digital reference services became more commonplace. Some librarians began to use this technology as a way to reach remote users at distant learning sites, while others viewed it as a natural extension of their text-based reference services to provide reference service to wherever their patrons might be located. Still others saw virtual reference services as an innovative service that might help to reverse the decreasing traffic of traditional walk-in or telephone reference service, while promoting digital collections, "pushing" academic content, and marketing the library as a knowledge and service center.

By the end of 2001 early adopters were ready to move beyond the "start-up" implementation phase to discussions of service quality, sustainability, and new features, while libraries still in the exploratory stages were looking for guidance on product selection, implementation strategies, training, marketing, and "best practices" models.

Definition

There are several working definitions of contemporary digital reference services.

The Duke University Libraries define live online reference or virtual reference as a "service that allows librarians and patrons to communicate with each other in real time through the Internet, like chat or instant messaging." Such services are "often better than our phone service because we can also actually show specific Web pages to students, walk them through Web sites or searches, and more" (http://www.lib.duke.edu/reference/liveonlineref.htm).

The Wesleyan University Libraries define their service as live and interactive—"just as though you were in person at the Reference Desk" (http://www.wesleyan.edu/libr/live_ref/live_help.htm).

The Virtual Reference Desk (http://www.vrd.org) Web site defines digital reference, or "Ask A," services as "Internet-based question-and-answer services that connect users with experts and subject expertise." Such services deliver reference service and information over the Internet in real time.

Diane Kresh (2001) of the Collaborative Digital Reference Service launched by the Library of Congress and OCLC (Online Computer Library Center) views the virtual reference service as "providing professional reference service to researchers any time anywhere, through an international, digital network of libraries and related institutions" using "new technologies to provide the best answers in the best context, by taking advantage not only of the millions of Internet resources but also of the many more millions of resources that are not online and that are held by libraries."

It is not uncommon for some definitions to be based on the type of software features the services provide, such as Web-based voice and chat, document and database sharing, instant messaging, co-browsing (allowing a librarian and patron to navigate the Web together), escorting, on-demand Web conferencing, or live interactive communication. Librarian Stephen Francoeur has compiled a list of digital reference services by software capabilities that includes definitions and examples of e-mail, chat, and Web-based products (http://pages.prodigy.net/tabo1/digref.htm.)

Models

Just as there are a variety of definitions for digital reference service, so, too, is there a diversity of models of such services. Some of these models are based on the type of library, while others may be based on geographic location, collaborative partnerships, consortia relationships, or other factors. Models include both single and multiple sites. Some examples are listed below.

Individual Academic Libraries

Institutions offering virtual reference services to their students, faculty, staff, and researchers include large public academic libraries, such as North Carolina State University (NCSU), the University of Minnesota, and the University of Illinois at Urbana-Champaign. Boyer (2001) notes that offering online, real-time reference service is consistent with the NCSU libraries' history of embracing technological innovation, and the need to serve distant learners who often assume that the library's Web site is "the library."

Kibbee, Ward, and Ma (2002) of the University of Illinois at Urbana-Champaign note that a library's extensive digital resources, coupled with its electronic resources delivered through the online catalog, offer incentives to implement a virtual reference service.

Stemper and Butler (2001) suggest that before tackling the technological strategies of implementing a virtual reference service (especially in a large academic research library with many departments and branches), it is first important to address such organizational issues as question referral policies (how and when), and whether such services should be decentralized or centralized.

Thinking ahead and anticipating such issues prior to implementation can save much stress and time once the service is offered. Francoeur (2001) agrees and suggests that libraries develop a clear understanding of user needs and staff capabilities before launching a service.

As appropriate, libraries may also extend digital reference services beyond their primary clientele of students, faculty, staff, and administrators. The Olin and Uris libraries of Cornell University, a large research institution, offer the digital reference service to Cornell's alumni community, as well to its traditional campus-based community.

Regional Multitype Consortia

One of the earliest multitype consortia players in the virtual reference arena was the 24/7 Reference Project of the Metropolitan Cooperative Library System in Southern California (http://www.247ref.org). This group project of public libraries (including Los Angeles Public Library) and academic libraries (including UCLA) was initially funded by a federal grant administered through the California State Library. Since July 2000 it has been offering live reference services to the people of Los Angeles and Orange counties, and since June 2001 the service has been offered 24 hours a day, 7 days a week.

In Northern California, the QandAcafe (http://www.qandacafe.com) began in August 2000. Composed of 25 public and academic libraries (and more than 120 reference librarians), it combines the speed of the Internet with the "smarts" of a librarian. As part of the Bay Area Reference Project and the Golden Gateway Library Network (which covers 300 miles of California coastline), the service includes numerous libraries in the greater San Francisco, Monterey Bay, and North Bay areas. The site's Web page describes it as "a service of your public library" with "librarians inside." The QandAcafe made a strategic decision to focus on late afternoon and early evening hours, typically the time when homework help is needed. The service is available seven days a week from 2 to 9 P.M. It offers live chat as well as digital reference services for people who have left the library for the Internet or who never came to the library in the first place (Henshall, 2001).

Regional Consortia

Eighteen public libraries in Ohio have completed their first year of virtual reference services as part of the Ask Us Questions project (http://www.askusquestions. com) of the NOLA Regional Library System (formerly the Northeastern Ohio Library Association), a dynamic multitype network supporting interlibrary cooperation within seven counties. Its Web page positions itself as an alternative to online fee-based services that may not be staffed by librarians: "Tired of dealing with overwhelming volumes of information? Not sure where to turn for accurate information on the Internet? We're here to help. Our staff of real librarians is trained to help you locate the accurate information you need quickly and effectively—all for FREE!"

Another model is provided by the Ready for Reference virtual reference desk project (http://www.alliancelibrarysystem.com/Projects/ReadyRef/index. html) of the Alliance Library System and the Illinois State Library (using federal LSTA funding). It is a 24/7 online service for students, staff, and faculty of the eight participating university, college, and community college academic libraries. Participants share online reference duty during hours of normal library operation, and use a specific vendor product, eGain Web call center software as modified and marketed by Library Systems and Services (LSSI). Launched in January 2001, the service has been widely publicized by sending brochures and press releases to campus and community media outlets, posters to the dorms, and e-mail to faculty, staff, and students in the eight libraries, and by placing the icon on various Web sites. The project evaluation conducted by Sloan (2001) shows that 50 percent of the questions are asked during working hours (between 8 A.M. and 5 P.M.), and that optimal staffing is for two librarians for each time period.

The Live Librarian project (http://www.suffolk.lib.ny.us/snl) of the public libraries in Suffolk County, New York, offers evening service from 9 to 11 P.M. Monday through Thursday, and from 5 to 11 P.M. on Sunday. The project's Web page includes helpful guidance for students such as how to cite electronic resources, using information from the Internet Public Library.

The ClevNet Library Consortium in Ohio provides KnowItNow (http://www.knowitnow24x7.net) as a live online reference service 24 hours a day, 7 days a week to all residents of Cuyahoga County and the Cleveland area. Launched in June 2001, the free service is provided by the Cleveland Public Library and members of the ClevNet consortium, and it continues to be one of the busiest virtual reference services currently offered.

Statewide Multitype Consortia

The Florida Distance Learning Reference and Referral Center (http://www.rrc.usf.edu/chat) serves students at 73 regionally accredited public and private higher education institutions based in Florida, including 10 state universities, 28 community colleges, and 35 independent academic institutions. Viggiano and Ault (2001) note that the service offers real-time online library instruction, using a chat room as a virtual classroom, as part of the Florida Distance Learning Library Initiative. Both librarians and graduate students, physically located at the University of South Florida in Tampa, staff the service and work flexible hours, including nights and weekends, seven days a week (five of those days until 1 A.M.). The Do's and Don'ts page notes that "the same etiquette used in face-to-face interactions with library staff is expected."

Government

The U.S. Department of Energy (DOE) Library uses the Virtual Reference Desk software developed by LSSI to provide "live reference." The Energy Library is operated under contract by LSSI and serves as a resource for other DOE locations throughout the United States, as well as for the general public. Patterson (2001) notes that reference librarians conduct reference interviews by chat, take the patron to (or send the patron) Web pages, and provide transcripts for patron follow-up. The service has evolved from one of helping DOE headquarters employees who are looking for codes and similar documents, into a service for non-DOE patrons and the general public who are seeking specialized information from the library.

Other government services include those from the National Institutes of Health and the Los Alamos National Laboratories. They both offer virtual reference services to their staffs, as well as for the general public, through the LSSI Virtual Reference ToolKit, a suite of special products and services from the vendor.

International

Kresh (2001) describes the Collaborative Digital Reference Service (CDRS) as a professional reference service for researchers anytime and anywhere through an international, online network of libraries and related institutions.

Launched by the Library of Congress in June 2000, CDRS includes more than 200 member libraries—academic, public, special, and national—throughout the world, and the numbers are growing. The collaboration is beneficial since each library brings its professional experience, knowledge of user behavior and needs, and subject expertise to the service.

Technical and development support to CDRS is provided by OCLC. Such support includes building and maintaining a database of participating institution profiles, building and maintaining a question-and-answer database system that enables CDRS participants to catalog answers and store them in a searchable and browsable database, and providing administrative support for CDRS, including marketing the service, registering new members, and providing training and user support.

Privacy

Since libraries have a long tradition of protecting the confidentiality of patron records, it comes as no surprise that both virtual reference staff and potential users of the service are concerned about user privacy. As noted in the code of ethics of the American Library Association (ALA), libraries "protect each library user's right to privacy and confidentiality with respect to information sought or received and resources consulted, borrowed, acquired, or transmitted." As a result, written privacy policies can be found on several virtual reference Web sites.

Unlike face-to-face or telephone reference services in which the patron can remain anonymous, the virtual reference environment often requires a patron to provide a name, zip code, library bar code number, e-mail address, IP address, or other personal information prior to the start of the service. However, some products are now permitting patrons to remain anonymous.

Moreover, although services may validate and authenticate users by zip code or bar code, they collect IP addresses only for systems administration purposes in order to use secure servers. If users are asked for an e-mail address, it is usually for the delivery of a session transcript and to send additional information to the patron. If the user does not wish to divulge an address, the transcript may be sent to the library for evaluating and improving the service.

The use of cookies, or the ability to disable them and still offer the service, is a topic that libraries will need to discuss prior to implementation. Cookies can be useful for maintaining live connections with users, as well as for automatically accessing a patron's previously stored question(s) in order to deliver more personalized service. However, not all users feel positively about cookies, so libraries are wise to post their privacy statements and specifically address these issues.

Standards

Horn (2001) notes that "there is currently no common denominator to define quality electronic reference service although there has been an attempt to set standards for the Virtual Reference Desk AskA Consortium." Kasowitz (2001) opines that with the growth of digital reference services and collaborative networks, there is a clear need for defined standards to ensure service quality and interoperable technology.

In 2001 the National Information Standards Organization (NISO) held an invitational workshop on networked reference services at the Library of Congress (http://www.niso.org/news/events_workshops/netref.html). The workshop brought together persons experienced and interested in the development of digital reference services to advise NISO on the prospect of successfully introducing standards in this new area of service. Additional issues considered were such related areas as intellectual property rights and privacy.

The development and assessment of measures and quality standards for digital reference services is the focus of research sponsored in part by OCLC and the Digital Library Federation (McClure and Lankes, 2001). In addition, efforts have begun to address such issues as Question Interchange Profile (QuIP) for maintaining, tracking, storing, and sharing digital reference questions and answers (Kasowitz, 2001). Recognizing the importance of metadata and technical standards is an essential ingredient for creating, providing, and sustaining digital reference networks and services.

Training and Education

As with the implementation of any service, training and education are of paramount importance. Libraries often base their reputations on excellent customer service, and this standard extends to the virtual reference environment.

Gross (2001) notes that traditional reference skills are transferable to the needs of digital reference work, but additional procedures, skills, and training are needed in this new environment. Certainly, the complexities of shared databases, authentication, and licensing issues are unique to an electronic environment requiring specialized content knowledge, technical expertise, and the fundamental skills of communication (for example, the reference interview), source knowledge, and service orientation.

Education strategies may include step-by-step training manuals and guides for using specific software products, how to interact efficiently and effectively with virtual patrons, how to address sensitive questions, and how to act quickly in a multitasking environment.

Hands-on training sessions can enrich the general overview training experiences by simulating questions and providing answers. Such sessions can focus on practicing with the software, searching databases efficiently, and staying within prescribed time periods. Such practice sessions help to ensure that consistent service is being provided, and they help to address any uneasiness on the part of the reference librarians so that they are comfortable with offering the service.

Training and education should be ongoing experiences, especially as new software features, enhancements, and upgrades become available to expand functionality. For example, some products now permit librarians to work with more than one patron at a time (just as they would at a physical reference desk), to stop and start the interactive co-browsing features, to highlight text in the patron's browser, or to share prepared slide shows or other documents with the patron. These changes require refresher courses for librarians so that they may seamlessly invoke certain features and take optimal advantage of them, as needed.

Mini-training sessions offered during regularly scheduled staff meetings can be advantageous. Transaction and transcript logs can also be reviewed to determine if there are "soft spots" that need strengthening, if policies need to be developed or revised, if minimum levels of quality service are consistently being met, and if exemplary practices can be adopted as models.

Administratively, training updates should be part of the regular continuing education opportunities offered by the library, and such needs should be accommodated within institutional budgets, whenever possible.

Virtual reference service courses may become more prevalent in graduate schools of library science and information management. In addition to exposing future librarians to these services, such graduate schools may be able to offer continuing education institutes and/or skills development workshops for librarians interested in keeping up with changes and developments in the world of digital reference and instructional services.

Staffing

Staffing the digital reference service will often be based on local needs and staff capabilities. Choosing to staff the service separately and away from public view of the traditional, desk-based reference services should be considered, especially since librarians need to concentrate and focus on providing excellent, efficient, and effective service. Lankes, Collins, and Kasowitz (2000) suggest various staffing models to consider, and Janes (2002) discusses the mix of desk/phone/ other service offerings.

Some libraries elect to double- or triple-staff the service, as they would a traditional reference service. Other libraries have suggested that single-staffing, with the capability to refer questions to others, is an appropriate model to consider.

Either way, desirable librarian skills for providing the service include flexibility, speed and accuracy in keyboarding, ability to multitask (search, think, write, and deal with stress and/or demanding users), and deal with ambiguity and an evolving technology. Although there may not be face-to-face contact with users, communication skills and efficient use of time are also important qualities of a reference librarian providing this service.

Consideration when staffing the service should be given to whether it will be centralized or decentralized within a single building with multiple departments, with multiple branch locations external to the central site, or perhaps with consortia partners geographically spread over many miles. Although service, rather than cost, should drive staffing decisions, Coffman's studies of multiple models (single, centralized, or tiered) may prove to be helpful to decision makers (Coffman, 2002).

Promotion and Marketing

Although some digital reference services may be viewed as temporary pilot projects, it is still important to market and promote them to ensure effective use. Recommendations for doing so include establishing a visible presence on the library's gateway, portal, or main Web page through a specific icon, button, or graphic; developing promotional materials; and engaging users through other strategies. If awareness and visibility are, in fact, key service goals of the library, then direct paper or e-mail marketing strategies may also be employed, along with press releases sent to local community or campus media outlets.

Some residential colleges or universities may choose to target specific campus populations (such as dormitory residents, first-year students, athletes, sororities, graduate students). At the University of Illinois at Urbana-Champaign, flyers were placed strategically around the campus urging students to "Take a Librarian Home Tonight." Other marketing strategies may include outreach programs to campus or community groups, banners, bookmarks, pencils, pens, magnets, key chains, or other inexpensive items to help publicize the service.

Public libraries may be able to send postcards to residents in service areas, or include promotional materials in city mailings, such as utility bills.

Henshall (2001) says that "just putting the technology out there is not enough." It is important to have a recognizable logo, a usable Web site, and a public relations kit with sample press releases and key messages.

Relationship to Information Literacy

Voice and live conferencing software provide additional opportunities to teach and help users develop the information literacy skills, competencies, and abilities of effectively finding, critically evaluating, and ethically using and citing information.

Web portals such as the Librarians Index to the Internet (funded by the Library of California), Infomine (a scholarly Internet resource collection from the libraries of the University of California), and the Internet Public Library's General/Reference Collection can help users see how information is structured and categorized.

PowerPoint presentations, electronic pathfinders, digital FAQs, Web-based instructional guides, citation tools, and streaming video explanations may all help contribute to supporting information literacy goals. In addition, creating market segmentations (such as children, senior citizens, and users from an academic community) will facilitate targeting and handling specific types of questions (such as those in math, science, or health) and may help to educate and serve those users better.

Accessibility

Hudson (2002) notes that federal government standards for accessibility (adjustments for visual, hearing, mobility, and cognitive impairments) apply to electronic information technologies. Designers of Web sites should keep in mind the needs of those users with low vision, hearing disabilities, and other impairments. The use of color, columns, plug-ins, time-outs, and other features should be carefully considered.

Hudson reminds us that "since universities and public libraries can be sued under the Americans with Disabilities Act, conformity with Section 508 standards for Web sites demonstrates our effort to serve all of our patrons equally."

Evaluation

Formal and informal evaluation strategies are important to consider when offering digital reference services to help ensure consistency and quality of service.

In the early stages of implementation, staff should reflect on their experiences and suggest improvements after each session or shift. User feedback can be collected from Web-based surveys strategically placed on Web pages or "pushed" to users after each session. These evaluative comments are important to retain, and can be stored in a database or archived for future viewing and analysis, as needed.

Analysis can include such factors as the average length of time it takes to answer a question (and whether this response time falls within the targeted guidelines established by the library), the volume of questions answered, the types of questions asked, and user satisfaction levels with the answers provided.

As experience grows, the library can move toward more formal evaluation strategies, including the assessment of quality. For example, CDRS has recently developed "Facets of Quality for Digital Reference Services Standards" that can offer useful guidance and direction to libraries.

Since initial evaluation studies are typically descriptive reports that focus on user surveys, costs, staffing needs, or question log analysis, McClure and Lankes (2001) propose a new research agenda to include benchmarks for outcome measures, process measures, economic measures, and user satisfaction measures. With time, these types of studies will prove useful for service improvement, consistency, and longevity.

Software Selection

Each library will need to determine the desired or required software features necessary for delivering desired and successful services, as well as the budget for doing so. Some costs may be associated with beginning the service, and other costs with continuing it (through ongoing software licenses, training, and so forth).

Kimmel and Heise (2001) note that a library can choose to develop and host a software product locally, purchase/license a product from a vendor with local administration, or have a vendor host, manage, and maintain the software for the library.

The Duke University Libraries Live On Line Reference Web page (http://www.lib.duke.edu/reference/liveonline.ref.htm) refers to a number of vendor products with software capabilities, and gives evaluative comments on the advantages and disadvantages of each. This information can be a useful starting point for a library just beginning to discuss the implementation of such services.

At the Information Strategies 2001 conference, Lisa Roberts expanded upon these points and offered a chat reference software checklist (http://www.uncg.edu/~lcrober2/chatsoftware/checklist.html) that included various features such as functionality, price, report capabilities, maintenance issues, and licensing issues.

Stephen Francoeur's Index of Chat Reference Services (http://pages.prodigy.net/tabo1/chatsoftware.htm) lists a variety of software products, followed by the libraries that use them. Products include Anexa, AOL Instant Messenger,

Camden, Chatspace.com, ConferenceRoom, FirstClass, HumanClick, ICQ, In-stantService, Live Assistance, LiveHelper, LivePerson, LSSI (eGain), NetAgent, NetMeeting, OnDemand, and Virtual Reference Librarian. Other products available, although not included on the list, include Digichat, Docutek, HorizonLive, RefDeskLive, and WebLine.

Coffman (2002) offers an excellent list of software features to consider that he presented at the "State of Digital Reference" preconference in conjunction with ALA's 2002 Midwinter Meeting. His "Picking Software" presentation includes descriptions of e-mail, chat, live videoconferencing, and remote control software features, and factors to consider from the perspective of both the librarian and the patron.

The Future

Software

Some products now include videoconferencing, co-browsing (allowing a librarian and patron to navigate the Web together), escorting (permitting a librarian to "lead" the patron around the Web), page pushing (sharing a Web application with a patron), transferring questions to subject specialists, forwarding after-hours calls to other staff, and file (text) sharing. Other features may include built-in knowledge bases to capture and reuse answers efficiently and effectively, archives of searchable questions and answers, and reports and analysis tools to track how the virtual reference desk is being used—and the types of users who find the service helpful—all within privacy and confidentiality guidelines.

As more libraries gain experience with digital reference services, and thus find functional gaps in current software offerings, new enhancements and expanded features will be developed. As a result, software may also be designed specifically for the library market, rather than customized from other sectors, such as the e-business community.

Issues of database authentication for nonprimary clientele, interoperability of productivity and management tools, and patron service immediately upon connection are ripe for future development. In addition, since patron platforms may not be as robust as library platforms, it will be important to consider software that can function in multiple environments as "platform neutral"—that is, accessible to anyone and independent of any specific browser. As future standards are developed, such advancements will be easier to achieve.

New Technologies

As local infrastructures improve (and Internet2 becomes a reality for many academic institutions and localities), the use of such new technologies as Voice Over Internet Protocol (VoIP), allowing browsing and talking at the same time, and streaming video integrated into virtual reference services may become more commonplace.

For the average patron who may still use and rely on dial-in modem connections (rather than high-speed digital connections), the use of new technologies may not always be appropriate or feasible. But for those users who have high-speed connections, such advanced technologies as streaming video can be delivered virtually anywhere over the Internet as an excellent tool for educating patrons.

Facilities

Often virtual reference services are added without the ability to redesign physical space. As these services become more than pilot or experimental projects within libraries, planners and designers will benefit from incorporating the needs of virtual reference staff into building plans and space layouts. Facilities designed and constructed for maximum flexibility, integrating such services, will greatly enhance the capabilities of the library to offer a diversity of services in the future, especially as live desktop videoconferencing becomes more pervasive.

Standards

The issue of standards will continue to be important. Libraries should follow the deliberations of major standards organizations closely, especially if some vendor products rely on browser capabilities to support certain third-party products, such as plug-ins.

Since the Open Archive Initiative (OAI) supports the sharing of metadata, standards for the interoperability of content will become more important, especially as new forms of digital scholarship emerge and databases become more interconnected.

The ability to access and deliver content from local collections (for example, digitized archival material, photographs, sound files, and historical images) in multiple formats (such as JPEG, TIFF, and PDF) will continue to drive the need for standards and protocols. Also worth watching are the emerging e-book standards, especially those related to digital audio formats and digital rights management.

Cooperation

As practitioner experiences and research data reach critical mass, the virtual reference community looks forward to implementing additional strategic ventures using recommended "best practices." These ventures may include alliances, partnerships, or collaborative activities with libraries, museums, vendors, research institutes, and/or government agencies to provide the smoothest, fastest, and most efficient service available within an economically feasible and technologically robust environment.

Research Studies

To learn more about the measurement and evaluation of virtual question answering, benchmark data, and statistical profiles, practitioners (librarians and vendors) are being joined by university faculty members to explore research questions and provide guidance and assistance.

At the beginning of 2002 LSSI announced the appointment of John V. Richardson, professor in the UCLA Graduate School of Education and Information Studies, as a Presidential Scholar of Virtual Reference Services to assist the company and its clients during a nine-month sabbatical leave.

Charles McClure, director of the Information Use Management and Policy Institute at the School of Information Studies at Florida State University, reported at the third annual Virtual Reference Desk (VRD) Conference that, after studying seven libraries that offer digital reference services, a study team of researchers recommends the development and implementation of improved assessment and evaluation methods. McClure notes that library administrators need strong, grounded metrics and commonly understood data to support digital reference services, assess their successes, determine resource allocations, and determine a means for constant improvement (http://quartz.syr.edu/quality/Overview.htm).

Conclusion

Based on the diversity of libraries involved in providing digital reference services over the past few years, it appears that these services are "catching hold." Their success depends on institutional support, effective products, well-trained and confident staff in sufficient numbers, strong marketing campaigns, and sound assessment practices. As these services mature in the coming years, and as staff become more proficient, so, too, will the sophistication of the products, thus leading to increased patron use, satisfaction, and demand.

Resources

Webcast Transcripts

"Virtual Reference Services" (http://www.learningweek.com/112801.html). Broadcast November 28, 2001.

Registries, Bibliographies, and Indexes

"Digital Reference Services: A Bibliography," compiled by Bernie Sloan (http://www.lis.uiuc.edu/~b-sloan/digiref.html).

"Index of Chat Reference Services," compiled by Stephen Francoeur (http://pages.prodigy.net/tabo1/chatsoftware.htm).

"A Registry of Real-Time Digital Reference Services," compiled by Gerry McKiernan (http://www.public.iastate.edu/~CYBERSTACKS/LiveRef.htm).

Web Pages

Alliance Library System. "Ready for Reference" Virtual Reference Desk (http://www.rsa.lib.il.us/ready).

Code of Ethics of the American Library Association (http://www.ala.org/alaorg/oif/ethics.html).

Coffman, Steve. "The Cost of Virtual Reference." Presentation given at the ACRL preconference "Digital Reference Trends, Techniques, and Changes," American Library Association Midwinter Meeting, New Orleans, January 18, 2002 (http://quartz.syr.edu/ACRL/cost_files/v3_document.htm).

Freenets and Community Networks (http://www.lights.com/freenet).

Gross, Melissa. "Assessing Quality in Digital Reference Services: Overview of Key Literature on Digital Reference." Prepared in association with Charles R. McClure and R. David Lankes. November 2001 (http://dlis.dos.state.fl.us/bld/Research_Office/BLD_Research.html).

Henshall, Kay. "QandACafe.com: The Bay Area Reference Project." Presentation given at "Going Where the Students Are: A Symposium on Live Reference in the California State University (CSU)" sponsored by the CSU Council of Library Directors. California State Polytechnic University, May 10–11, 2001 (http://www.csupomona.edu/~kkdunn/LiveRef/Henshall%20Summary.htm).

Infomine (http://www.infomine.ucr.edu).

Internet Public Library (http://www.ilp.org).

Kasowitz, Abby S. "Trends and Issues in Digital Reference Services." November 2001 (http://www.ericit.org/digests/EDO-IR-2001-07.shtml).

Kresh, Diane Nester. "Libraries Meet the World Wide Web: The Collaborative Digital Reference Service." ARL Bimonthly Report 219 (December 2001): 1–3 (http://www.arl.org/newsltr/219/cdrs.html).

Librarian's Index to the Internet (http://www.lii.org).

McClure, Charles R., and David R. Lankes. "Assessing Quality in Digital Reference Services: A Research Prospectus." 2001 (http://quartz.syr.edu/quality).

Roberts, Lisa. "Choosing a Chat Reference Solution: The Devil Is in the Details." A presentation given at the Information Strategies 2001 Conference, Fort Myers, Florida, November 15, 2001. (http://www.uncg.edu/~lcrober2/chatsoftware/checklist.html).

Sloan, Bernie. "Ready for Reference: Academic Libraries Offer Live Web-Based Reference." Preliminary Report, May 25, 2001 (http://www.lis.uiuc.edu/~b-sloan/ready4ref.htm); Final Report, July 11, 2001. (http://www.lis.uiuc.edu/~b-sloan/r4r.final.htm).

Wesleyan University Libraries. ReferenceNow! (http://www.wesleyan.edu/libr/live_ref/live_help.htm).

Thematic Journals

Information Technology and Libraries 20, no. 3 (September 2001). Special thematic issue on virtual reference services.

Reference and User Services Association Quarterly, 38, no.1 (1998). Special issue on the Reference Service in a Digital Age Institute held June 1998 at the Library of Congress.

Reference Services Review 29, no. 3 (2001). Special thematic issue on reference and instructional services in an electronic environment.

Books

Janes, Joseph. *Introduction to Reference Work in the Digital Age.* Neal-Schuman, 2002.

Lankes, R. David, John Collins, and Abby S. Kasowitz. *Digital Reference Service in the New Millennium: Planning, Management, and Evaluation.* Neal-Schuman, 2000.

Lipow, Anne Grodzins, and Steve Coffman. *Establishing a Virtual Reference Service.* Library Solutions Press, 2001.

Articles

Boyer, Joshua. "Virtual Reference at North Carolina State: The First One Hundred Days." *Information Technology and Libraries* 20, no. 3 (September 2001), 122–128.

Ciccione, Karen. "Guest Editorial: Virtual Reference Today and Tomorrow." *Information Technology and Libraries* 20, no. 3 (September 2001), 120–121.

Francoeur, Stephen. "An Analytical Survey of Chat Reference Services." *Reference Services Review* 29, no. 3 (2001), 189–203.

Horn, Judy. "The Future Is Now: Reference Service for the Electronic Era." *Proceedings of the Tenth National ACRL Conference,* March 15–18, 2001, in Denver. ACRL, 2001, 320–327.

Hudson, Laura. "A New Age of Accessibility." *Netconnect* (supplement to *Library Journal* and *School Library Journal*) (Winter 2002), 19–21.

Kibbee, Jo, David Ward, and Wei Ma. "From Desk to Desktop: A Real-Time On-line Reference Pilot." *Reference Services Review* 31, no. 1 (2002), in press.

Kimmel, Stacey, and Jenne Heise. "Being There: Tools for Online Synchronous Reference. *Online* 25, no. 6 (November/December 2001), 30–39.

Patterson, Rory. "Live Virtual Reference: More Work and More Opportunity." *Reference Services Review,* 29, no. 3 (2001), 204–209.

Stemper, James A., and John T. Butler. "Developing a Model to Provide Digital Reference Services." *Reference Services Review* 29, no. 3 (2001), 172–188.

Viggiano, Rachel, and Meredith Ault. "Online Library Instruction for Online Students." *Information Technology and Libraries* 20, no. 3 (September 2001), 135–138.

Wiese, F. O., and M. Borgendale. "EARS: Electronic Access to Reference Service." *Bulletin of the American Library Association* 74, no. 4 (October 1986), 300–304.

Wasik, Joann M. "Building and Maintaining Digital Reference Services." ERIC Clearinghouse on Information and Technology, Syracuse University. 1999 *ERIC Digest.* ED 427794.

Libraries, Publishers, Authors, Scholars Jointly Explore Internet Publishing Boundaries

Edward J. Valauskas

Chief Editor, *First Monday* (http://firstmonday.org)

Although paper will not vanish, electronic publishing may in the long run evolve to something radically different from what we know today. Though pluralistic, competitive, and economical, like print, it may differ markedly in content from what is now found in magazines, newspapers, and books. Automobiles looked like horseless carriages at the start but not forever; it may be the same with electronic publishing.

—Ithel de Sola Pool[1]

A New Ecology of Scholarly Cyberspace

According to one source, 1,260 different Internet-based journals, magazines, and newsletters appeared in 2001.[2] These journals range from the entirely new and independent entities like *8-Track Heaven* (which can be found at http://www.8trackheaven.com/index2.html and describes itself as "digital online but analog at heart") and *POL.it Psychiatry online Italia* (at http://www.pol-it.org) to publications with a long and illustrious history in print, such as the *American Midland Naturalist* (founded in 1909, at http://www.nd.edu/~ammidnat) and the journal of the Royal Society of Chemistry, *Dalton Transactions* (at http://www.rsc.org/is/journals/current/dalton/dappub.htm). The contents of all of these new Internet journals appear in various combinations of formats, from HTML to PDF and plain text, with access varying from completely open and free to fee-based, bound by passwords, IDs, and proper IP addresses. This abundance of content and sheer variety of style and formats clearly points to an enthusiastic celebration of the Internet as a medium for scholarship and communication.

Some have argued that the terrorist attacks of September 11 put a chill on the Internet as a content provider and medium for communication. Some operations, such as The Motley Fool (at http://www.motleyfool.com), CNET (http://www.cnet.com), and the New York Times Digital (http://www.nytdigital.com), saw drops in revenue from online ads and other sources of income.[3] But it would be difficult to blame the terrorist attacks for all ills in Internet publishing and economy. Some sites responded quite well to the events of September 11, proving the flexibility, responsiveness, and resiliency of the medium.[4] As a result, some Web sites for online journals saw enormous leaps in traffic as a direct result of September 11, not the reverse.[5] These recent trends, tied to the abundance of Internet journals, magazines, and newsletters, point to a rapidly evolving information ecology, where publishers, libraries, authors, scholars, and readers are exploring all of the possible niches of this environment, now a decade old.[6]

Authors, scholars, publishers, and libraries all publicly and privately battle over cyberspace, adjusting to the new niches in this information ecology. Often, their motives are driven by ignorance and fear regarding a still-evolving environment.[7] Nevertheless, if we accept the premise that an information ecology is "a system of people, practices, values, and technologies in a particular environment . . . [and that] the spotlight is not on technology, but on human activities served by technology,"[8] there must be some reasonable way to assess some of the activities and events for the year 2001, as a guide to what may—or may not—happen in 2002 and beyond.

Using the word "ecology" to describe the dynamic and unpredictable Internet publishing scene may be dangerous, given that ecology is fraught with so many meanings. In its simplest meaning, ecology can be viewed as a measure of energy in a system; changes in the energy of the system disrupt an ecology from its conservative state.[9] We could regard information in all of its variety as the "energy" in this ecology. One estimate indicates that one to two billion gigabytes of information are produced annually, some 250 megabytes for every human,[10] with about 5 percent of that total translated into printed journals, magazines, and newsletters. If we specifically focus on World Wide Web-based information, a White Paper by Cyveillance[11] pegs Web growth at 7.3 million pages per day. For lack of a better estimate, suppose we guess that 5 percent of those 7.3 million pages represent Internet serials in all of their variety; hence, some 365,000 Web pages would be created on a daily basis by all of the Internet journals, magazines, and newsletters in the world. If each page contains 14 kilobytes of information, then 4,990 megabytes are created each day, or 1,779 gigabytes annually. Print journals, magazines, and newsletters create a little more than 12 compressed terabytes of information each year,[12] so Internet publishing, which by this crude estimate equals about 2 terabytes, is not yet challenging traditional publishing in terms of sheer quantity. Nevertheless, Internet publishing is perhaps one indicator of the changes in store for the global information economy and ultimately points the way in which all information will be created and consumed in the near future.

With some measure of the amount of information generated by Internet publishing, we can begin to look at the consumers and producers in this information ecology. Defining the consumers and producers in Internet publishing for 2001 is not an easy task, for many of the "species" in this ecology—authors and scholars, traditional publishers, and libraries—played multiple roles. By examining their actions—dedicated to the creation, distribution, and consumption of information—some understanding will emerge that could explain the events in Internet publishing in 2001, and point to trends for the near future.

Authors and Scholars

[In scholarly publishing] there are four principal groups of players. The first one consists of scholars as producers of the information that makes journals valuable. The second consists of scholars as users of that information. However, as users, they gain access to journals primarily through the third group, the libraries. Libraries purchase journals from the fourth group, the publishers, usually in response to requests from scholars. These requests are based overwhelmingly on the perceived quality of the journals, and price seldom plays a role . . .

—Andrew M. Odlyzko[13]

Certainly, no journal would exist without its authors and contributors, and that axiom absolutely applies to Internet serials. However, in 2001 scholars increasingly have been demonstrating flexibility (in a willingness to experiment with their opera in Internet journals not tied to a specific traditional publisher, academic institution, or professional society), determination (in patiently awaiting court decisions affirming the rights of authors in this digital medium), and innovation (taking advantage of software and hardware as vehicles to express complex ideas and projections). We might call authors and scholars a keystone species —that is, a species upon which the entire system depends[14]—in an information ecology of Internet journals and scholarship.

Odlyzko noted that "Scholars as writers of papers determine what journals their work will appear in, and thus how much it will cost society to publish their work. However, scholars have no incentive to care about those costs. What matters the most to them is the prestige of the journals they publish in."[15] In 2001 Internet serials seem to gained the right "prestige" in tenure decisions. Thanks to logs on Web servers, scholars and their tenure committees can examine actual data on access and use of scholarly publication, without the tedious gymnastics of citation analysis. For example, logs for the journal *First Monday* provide exact details on the most-read contributions published in 2001. Among 78 articles published in 12 issues, the top five papers were the following:

1 Richard W. Wiggins, "The Effects of September 11 on the Leading Search Engine," *First Monday,* volume 6, number 10 (October 2001), at http://firstmonday.org/issues/issue6_10/wiggins.

   Number of downloads in 2001: 31,078

   Hyperlinks to article (per Google link check): 154 (as a measure of "citations")

2 Andrew M. Odlyzko, "Content Is Not King," *First Monday,* volume 6, number 2 (February 2001), at http://firstmonday.org/issues/issue6_2/odlyzko.

   Number of downloads in 2001: 30,161

   Hyperlinks to article (per Google link check): 172

3 Clifford Lynch, "The Battle to Define the Future of the Book in the Digital World," *First Monday,* volume 6, number 6 (June 2001), at http://firstmonday.org/issues/issue6_6/lynch.

   Number of downloads in 2001: 29,295

   Hyperlinks to article (per Google link check): 148

4 David Ronfeldt and John Arquilla, "Networks, Netwars, and the Fight for the Future," *First Monday,* volume 6, number 10 (October 2001), at http://firstmonday.org/issues/issue6_10/ronfeldt.

   Number of downloads in 2001: 11,998

   Hyperlinks to article (per Google link check): 46

5 David Lancashire, "Code, Culture and Cash: The Fading Altruism of Open Source Development," *First Monday,* volume 6, number 12 (December 2001), at http://firstmonday.org/issues/issue6_12/lancashire.

   Number of downloads in 2001: 11,246

   Hyperlinks to article (per Google link check): 52

Logs, rather than citation reports, will prove a more exacting measure of communication and scholarly utility.

On several fronts, authors and scholars have scored significant gains. With the U.S. Supreme Court upholding the rights of freelance authors to their works in databases and the U.S. District Court affirming the electronic rights of authors in *Random House* v. *RosettaBooks*,[16] there will be an increasing trend for Internet journals to allow contributors to retain the rights to their works. This trend will mean that scholars will be able to "recycle" their works as they see fit, in courses, translations, excerpts, and expansions into books and other works. By not turning over all rights to publishers, the flow of information from research to application to classroom should be accelerated. It will be interesting to see how quickly traditional publishers move to a more enlightened copyright policy as Internet journals take advantage of this issue to encourage contributors to send their work to digital rather than paper media.

Scholars also have to thank Stephen King for proving in 2001 the rewards of micropayments, a model that more Internet serials will adopt over time (abandoning subscriptions and ties to paper-based mirrors). With micropayments predicted to amount to $200 billion by 2005,[17] authors, with their rights firmly in hand, see Internet publishing as a way to cash in on their works without inference. Stephen King's successful experiments[18] will certainly make Internet publishers, especially those independent of conglomerates, professional associations, and other formal ties, consider micropayments, with a significant portion of the proceeds heading to contributors.

Finally, scholars have exerted enormous pressure on traditional publishing habits and patterns in 2001, with protests, complaints, strikes, and boycotts. From physicists protesting the firing of Jeff Schmidt from the American Institute of Physics for his book *Disciplined Minds*[19] to the Public Library of Science's boycott of journals that do not provide open access to recently published scholarship,[20] scholars are realizing that there are opportunities for constructive change in formal communication and a rich variety of means to influence the future of publishing. The events of 2001 are merely the opening salvo of a campaign that will only grow more heated and controversial as all members of this information ecology struggle to define new niches.

Independently of these very public events, the digital medium has provided the means for scholars to communicate in ways unimagined a decade ago. From organizing research on earthquakes in remote corners of the world[21] to managing massive databases of astronomical, biological, chemical, and other information,[22] the Internet has become the vehicle for innovative communication strategies that simply address the needs of scholars for speed, processing strength, and connectivity.

Publishers

In our examination of this digital information ecology, publishers continue to play a primary role in creating and distributing information on a global basis. Indeed, publishers are taking their role more seriously in this networked time by examining new ways to make scholarship even more accessible. SciDev.Net is probably one of the best efforts in 2001 in addressing the needs of the developing world for access to scholarship from premiere journals. Funded by agencies and publishers in Europe and North America, SciDev.Net is the first serious step in reducing barriers effectively with existing technologies to journals like the *British Medical Journal, Journal of the American Medical Association, Nature, Science,* and others.[23]

Besides these efforts to make scholarship more widely available via the Internet, publishers worked feverishly in 2001 on three fronts. First, they have been mobilizing greater resources to convert paper-based backfiles into digital form, as HTML and PDF. Second, they have been working with diverse groups to develop better instruments to measure the use of Internet-based resources within organizations. Finally, there are signs of innovation in terms of combining existing electronic resources in different ways to make digital content more accessible and relevant.

It has not taken publishers long to realize the market value of increased back runs of journals in Web-sympathetic forms. Access to historically important content encourages the broad and long-term use of a given title, and provides an important marketing tool to space-deprived libraries. For example, Elsevier's ScienceDirect has been promoting its efforts to make available all backfiles of some 1,200 journals, an effort that will be completed in 2003. These files are being organized into specific subject disciplines (the chemistry backfile is now available from ScienceDirect) with unlimited access based on a single payment rather than an annual fee. The Institute of Physics has been hard at work on approximately 500 volume years of journals, with an aim to complete the effort by the end of 2002. In January 2002 the American Institute of Physics extended access to some 40,000 articles, dating back to 1985, in its ongoing historical efforts. These digital projects, in combination with relatively low access fees, have provided a tangible benefit to scholars and their institutions, facing both financial and physical limits.

The use of digital scholarship is of vital concern to publishers and their clients, such as libraries. Given licensing costs and restrictions, as well as privacy concerns and concerns over traditional citation methodologies,[24] it is not surprising that in 2001 libraries and publishers developed guidelines for measuring usage. These guidelines are a first but important step in tempering the demands for accurate reporting and license management with privacy and discretion.[25]

With increasing new content available, along with backfiles, in Internet form, it is not surprising that publishers are working to create new combinations of products that meet the needs of scholars while providing additional new revenue streams. Some of the most innovative experiments in this area have emerged from the physics community, such as the Deutsche Physikalische Gesellschaft and Institute of Physics's *New Journal of Physics* and the American Institute of Physics's Virtual Journal Series.[26] These efforts will continue to flourish in 2002 and beyond, because they provide increased access to scholarship while providing publishers with credentials as innovators and partners with all members of a digital information ecology.

Libraries

Rather than be marginalized in this information ecology, libraries have been expanding their roles in several ways. First, libraries have acted as a catalyst for change with both publishers and scholars by increasingly demanding more interactivity and utilization of new technologies; second, they have encouraged the development of standards to locate information in an information-rich environment.

On change, the Scholarly Publishing and Academic Resources Coalition (SPARC) has been leading efforts to make scholarship available more widely via the Internet. For example, *BioOne* appeared in March 2001 and by September had licensed 46 journals to make available more broadly to scholars and libraries.[27] The effectiveness of a consortium like *BioOne* will need to be measured in both its utility and in the kinds of new consortia it in turn inspires. [See the article "Scholarly Publishing and Academic Resources Coalition" earlier in Part 1—*Ed.*]

Given the sheer quantity of Internet-based information, libraries are playing an increasing role in navigation and will continue to do so in the near future. The release of ANSI/NISO Z39.85, the Dublin Core Metadata Element Set, in November 2001[28] will assist in this process, if the proposed 15 metadata elements are utilized both in content and in search engines. Some studies have pointed to the utility of metadata in the application of Z39.85, but only if search engines are ready to take advantage of it.[29] Libraries have been playing and will continue to play an important role in metadata application and search mechanics. These efforts will earn libraries enormous support from a diverse community of scholars and publishers as Internet-based resources continue to grow at an enormous rate.

Conclusion

The year 2001 saw dramatic developments on a number of fronts as authors and scholars, publishers, and libraries all worked to sustain and create niches in a digital information ecology. Scholarly publishing on the Internet is rapidly creating diverse and fascinating combinations as the former boundaries between all of the participants fade and change over time. The fundamental trends seem to be increased access to scholarship at rapidly decreasing costs, greater assertion of the rights of authors and scholars to control their words and works, and increasing cooperation between libraries and publishers on several fronts to make information more accessible as it becomes more abundant and diverse. Only time will tell if these trends will hold and the fragile but important self-interests of all parties continue to motivate cooperation.

Notes

1. Ithel de Sola Pool, 1983, *Technologies of Freedom.* Belknap Press of Harvard University Press, pp. 212–213.

2. Based on an analysis of all titles reported for the year 2001 on the NewJour archive, a list of "new journals and newsletters available on the Internet," at http://gort.ucsd.edu/newjour. The archive is provided by the University of California at San Diego Libraries.

3. L. Scott Tillett, 2001. "Bad News for Online Media Sites," *InternetWeek,* special issue for December 17, p. 26.

4. See, for example, Rich Wiggins's assessment of Google in Richard W. Wiggins, 2001. "The Effects of September 11 on the Leading Search Engine," *First Monday,* volume 6, number 10 (October), at http://firstmonday.org/issues/issue6_10/wiggins.

5. The Web site for the *Bulletin of the Atomic Scientists* saw an enormous increase in traffic after September 11. "Since September 11, visitors to our World Wide Web site—www.thebulletin.org—have jumped . . . from just over 73,000 to a whopping 200,000 a month. Page views—a measure of what those visitors are reading—soared . . . to nearly 356,000 a month." Letter from Stephen Schwartz, publisher of the *Bulletin of the Atomic Scientists,* undated, but envelope postmarked 4 December 2001, p. 3.

6. On dating the origins of Internet scholarly publishing, see Steve Hitchcock, Leslie Carr, and Wendy Hall. "A Survey of STM Online Journals 1990–95: The Calm Before the Storm," at http://journals.ecs.soton.ac.uk/survey/survey.html.

7. Carol Tenopir and Donald W. King, 2001, "Lessons for the Future of Journals," *Nature,* volume 413, number 6857 (18 October), pp. 672–674.

8. Bonnie Nardi and Vicki O'Day, 1999, *Information Ecologies: Using Technology with Heart.* MIT Press, p. 49.

9. Anna Bramwell, 1989, *Ecology in the 20th Century: A History.* Yale University Press, p. 4.

10. Peter Lyman and Hal R. Varian, 2000, "How Much Information?" at http://www.sims.berkeley.edu/research/projects/how-much-info.

11. Cyveillance, 2000, "Sizing the Internet," White Paper, at http://www.cyveillance.com/; also cited at Peter Lyman and Hal R. Varian, 2000. "How Much Information? Internet—Summary," at http://www.sims.berkeley.edu/research/projects/how-much-info/internet.html.

12. Peter Lyman and Hal R. Varian, 2000, "How Much Information?" at http://www.sims.berkeley.edu/research/projects/how-much-info.

13. Andrew M. Odlyzko, 1997, "The Economics of Electronic Journals," *First Monday,* volume 2, number 8 (August), at http://www.firstmonday.org/issues/issue2_8/odlyzko.

14. "An ecology is marked by the presence of certain keystone species whose presence is crucial to the survival of the ecology itself." Nardi and O'Day, op. cit., p. 53.

15. Odlyzko, op.cit.

16. Summary in Laura Gasaway, 2001, "The Case That Will Not Die!" *Information Outlook,* volume 5, number 10 (October), pp. 44–45. The Ontario Superior Court of Justice supported the electronic rights of authors in an October 2001 decision in *Robertson* v. *Thomson Corp.*; see Gail Dykstra, 2001, "Canadian Court Rules in Favor of Freelance Authors," *Information Today,* volume 18, number 10 (November), pp. 1, 62.

17. Robert McGarvey, 2001, "Wireless Micropayments: Big Barriers for Small Change," *mbusiness* (May), p. 66.

18. "In August, King posted the first 6,000 words of his new novel, *The Plant.* He asked readers for $1 (processed by Amazon) and pledged that as long as 75% of those who downloaded it paid for it, he would put up the next installment. More than 100,000 people grabbed the story the first day, and some paid $10 or $20 to make up for the freeloaders." From http://www.time.com/time/digital/reports/digital12/08.html.

19. See, for example, http://www.lns.cornell.edu/spr/2001-08/msg0035101.html.

20. At http://www.publiclibraryofscience.org/plosFAQ.htm, accessed 22 February 2002; for an alternative view, see Andrew M. Odlyzko, 2001, "The Public Library of Science and the Ongoing Revolution in Scholarly Communication," at http://www.nature.com/nature/debates/e-access/Articles/odlyzko.html.

21. Eugene S. Schweig, Joan Gomberg, Paul Bodin, Gary Patterson, and Scott Davis, 2001, "The Internet: Shaking Up Scientific Communication," at http://www.nature.com/nature/webmatters/equake.

22. For example, the National Virtual Observatory will be the means for the astronomy community to handle and process massive datasets; see "Building the Framework for the National Virtual Observatory," at http://www.us-vo.org/nvo-proj.html.

23. See http://www.scidev.net/, accessed 22 February 2002, and "Welcome SciDev.Net," *Nature,* volume 414, number 6864 (6 December 2001), p. 567.

24. On concerns over citations, see "Errors in Citation Statistics," *Nature,* volume 415, number 6868 (10 January 2002), p. 101.

25. "Guidelines for Statistical Measures of Usage of Web-Based Information Resources," at http://www.library.yale.edu/consortia/2001webstats.htm, and Elsevier's press release on the guidelines, at http://www.library.yale.edu/~llicense/ListArchives/0201/msg00034.html.

26. *New Journal of Physics* at http://njp.org; see, for example, the *Virtual Journal of Quantum Information* at http://www.vjquantuminfo.org.

27. http://www.bioone.org.

28. http://www.niso.org/standards/resources/Z39-85.pdf.

29. See, for example, Robin Henshaw and Edward J. Valauskas, 2001, "Metadata as a Catalyst: Experiments with Metadata and Search Engines in the Internet Journal, First Monday," *Libri,* volume 51, number 2 (June), pp. 86–101.

Applying the Principles of Intellectual Freedom: A Cross-Cultural Comparison

Ken Haycock

Michelle Mallette

Anne Olsen

School of Library, Archival and Information Studies,
University of British Columbia, Vancouver

The terrorist attacks of September 11, 2001, have brought to light once again the discomfiting issues of censorship and challenges to intellectual freedom by government.

At the time of this writing, laws have been enacted or are under discussion that will place limits on access to information that was freely available prior to the attacks on the Pentagon and the World Trade Center. Recent legislative efforts to prevent terrorism in the United States have included the so-called USA Patriot Act (Uniting and Strengthening America by Providing Appropriate Tools Required to Intercept or Obstruct Terrorism) and the Combating Terrorism Act. In Canada, similar anti-terrorist legislation has been proposed and debated as the Public Security Act, Bill C-42. On both sides of the border, these laws have caused concern for civil liberties because of the potential limits placed on freedoms each country holds fundamental to democracy, including freedom of speech and expression. Clearly, censorship as a tool of government still exists, and it may be justified in certain instances. However, as a general rule in a democracy, "the people are best served by being informed, and . . . informed people make the best choices."[1]

Intellectual freedom is fundamental to the operation of a democratic nation, and protection of that freedom is imperative. As John Stuart Mill has said,

> . . . there needs protection also against the tyranny of the prevailing opinion and feeling; against the tendency of society to impose, by other means than civil penalties, its own ideas and practices as rules of conduct on those who dissent from them.[2]

While both Canada and the United States are democratic nations, there is not a parallel in the two countries' understanding of "intellectual freedom." Neither the legislation nor the practice of intellectual freedom is identical; indeed, there are major differences in the way the two countries each approach and apply the principle of intellectual freedom. This article examines the differences and similarities in both legislation and practice in these two closely intertwined societies, with a focus on the impact on libraries and librarians.

Political History

The political histories of Canada and the United States differ significantly, and this difference has led to divergent attitudes, understandings, and legislation about intellectual freedom. The United States was born of a revolution; Canada, of negotiation and agreement. The American motto is that of "life, liberty, and the pursuit of happiness." Canadians hold to the principles of "peace, order, and good government." These disparate histories have created distinct cultures and political ideologies, and importantly, differing attitudes toward government and by government. It is not a stretch to say that the American people have a distrust of big government, preferring a laissez-faire attitude. Canadians, by contrast, expect a great deal of their governments, and—while never welcoming of bureaucracy or red tape—may be considered by Americans to be remarkably tolerant of what might be considered government interference.

Historical Development

United States

Historical examination reveals significant differences between Canada and the United States when it comes to the ideal of intellectual freedom. (As U.S. law is better known, greater attention will be paid here to the Canadian situation.)

The First Amendment to the U.S. Constitution guarantees its citizens freedom of speech. The Constitution was ratified in 1787 only after a promise was extracted that a guarantee of Americans' civil rights would be appended. In 1791 a collection of amendments known as the Bill of Rights was adopted, including the famous First Amendment:

> Congress shall make no law respecting an establishment of religion, or prohibiting the free exercise thereof; or abridging the freedom of speech, or of the press; or the right of the people peaceably to assemble, and to petition the Government for a redress of grievances.[3]

And while Americans generally consider the First Amendment to be "inalienable" and unequivocal, in fact Congress "has never accepted the First Amendment prohibitions as either absolute or inviolate"; the Sedition Act of 1798, the Alien Registration Act (Smith Act) of 1940, and the Subversive Control Act (McCarran Act) of 1950 all "violate the absolute prohibition against the enactment of laws limiting freedom of speech."[4]

Canada

The history of intellectual freedom law is significantly different in Canada. Confederation of the first four Canadian provinces dates back only to 1867, when the British North America (BNA) Act (Canada's first Constitution, even though the document's home was in Britain) was adopted. The BNA Act outlined the rules of government for Canadians, both legislative and executive power, and divided powers of jurisdiction between federal and provincial governments. However, it did not provide Canadians with any protection of their civil liberties.

Because the Canadian constitution draws on the British model, the concept of "unwritten law," or what is known as common law, plays a much larger role in Canada than it does in the United States. Common law is judge-made law, which is based on precedents in courts, rather than in the legislative chambers of government. *Black's Law Dictionary* defines common law as the "body of law derived from judicial decisions, rather than from statutes or constitutions."[5] Thus common law is distinct from statutory law, which is law made by legislators and written in the laws of the area under jurisdiction.

Intellectual freedom in Canada fell under common law because the laws pertaining to it were understood rather than spelled out. As the BNA Act did not specifically provide protection for Canadians' civil liberties, "the federal parliament and the provincial legislatures were free to do what they wanted as long as each acted within its own jurisdiction. The real limit on the power of government was the fear of defeat in an election."[6] A Bill of Rights was adopted by the Canadian government in 1960, but this federal statute had no jurisdiction in the provinces. In addition, it merely "recognized and declared rights already in existence in Canada."[7]

Not until the adoption in 1982 of the Canada Act, which replaced the BNA Act as Canada's repatriated Constitution and included the Canadian Charter of Rights and Freedoms, did Canadians have a written document, with jurisdiction in all provinces, outlining the freedoms guaranteed to all Canadians. Under the charter, intellectual freedom is guaranteed as a fundamental freedom. Section 2(b) reads as follows:

> 2. Everyone has the following fundamental freedoms:
> (b) freedom of thought, belief, opinion and expression, including freedom of the press and other media of communication.

Although "expression" extends beyond solely "speech," it is worth noting that Canadians do not have an "inalienable" right to these freedoms. Section 1 of the charter makes this clear: "The Canadian Charter of Rights and Freedoms guarantees the rights and freedoms set out in it subject only to such reasonable limits prescribed by law as can be demonstrably justified in a free and democratic society." These "reasonable limits" have been interpreted to include "the laws dealing with libel and slander, censorship, and sedition."[8]

Access

The other side of the intellectual freedom coin is, of course, access to information and ideas. Without access, the principle of intellectual freedom is "virtually meaningless."[9] And while the right to access, obtain, or receive information is not specifically articulated in the First Amendment to the U.S. Constitution, "this right is so essential to its fullest exercise that it must be considered a necessary penumbral right."[10] This has been the position of the U.S. Supreme Court: In the 1965 decision in *Lamont* v. *Postmaster General,* Justice Brennan stated:

> The dissemination of ideas can accomplish nothing if otherwise willing addressees are not free to receive and consider them. It would be a barren marketplace of ideas that only had sellers and no buyers.[11]

Government involvement in this issue is necessarily tied to access, and thus in this area lies another method by which to compare and contrast the American and Canadian situations.

Canada

Canadian law as it pertains to intellectual freedom makes clear the tensions that exist between the need to guarantee freedom of expression, and the need for the state to impose "reasonable limits" on that freedom. But, in keeping with the Charter of Rights, any limit "must rest, at least in part, on the presence of exceptional conditions or circumstances that undermine the audience's ability to freely or rationally assess the views expressed."[12] Those conditions, however, are not easy to determine, and the Canadian courts have opted to avoid drawing a line between rational (acceptable) and manipulative (unacceptable) expression. Instead, they have chosen to ask whether the expression in question "causes harm to the interests of another, including harm to reputation, business operations, and public order."[13] Some have labeled this "freedom from oppression."

An example of this approach lies in the Canadian restriction on "wilful promotion of hatred against an identifiable group," which is covered by criminal law. Similar bans on hate speech exist in federal and provincial human-rights codes. "Both forms of regulation have been challenged in the courts and upheld as justified limits on freedom of expression."[14]

The hate laws in Canada are covered under the Criminal Code of Canada. Section 319 makes it illegal to promote hatred against an identifiable group "if such hatred is incited by the communication, in a public place, of words likely to lead to a breach of peace." A second offense consists of "the wilful promotion of hatred against an identifiable group through the communication of statements other than in private conversation. This offence may only be prosecuted with the consent of the Attorney-General."[15]

The laws received nationwide attention in 1990 when the Supreme Court considered the Keegstra case. Jim Keegstra, a teacher in the province of Alberta, taught his students "about an all-encompassing conspiracy on the part of Jews to undermine Christianity and control the world."[16] When his teachings were made public, he was dismissed, and a year later, in 1984, he was charged with willful promotion of hatred under Section 319(2) of the Criminal Code of Canada. His challenge of the constitutionality of the law went to the Supreme Court of Canada, which ruled that the law's restriction on free expression was justified, asserting that laws against hate "are directed at a special category of expression which strays some distance from the spirit of S. 2(b) [of the Canadian Charter of Rights]" (*R. v. Keegstra* [1990], 3 S.C.R., 766).

What is pertinent about this decision is that, in a sense, it was not the content of the message Keegstra was conveying that was ruled to be illegal, but rather the impact of that message (causing harm to an identifiable group). Indeed, the Supreme Court ruled that the protection of freedom of expression under the charter is "irrespective of the particular meaning or message sought to be conveyed" (*Keegstra* 1990, 729). Over time, the court has ruled repeatedly "that it will not exclude an act of expression from the scope of the freedom simply because it is thought to be without value."[17]

United States

There is currently no similar law in the United States, but the debate over the need for a federal hate crime law was reignited following the highly publicized killing of Matthew Shepard in Wyoming in 1998. At least two federal bills were proposed—the Hate Crimes Prevention Act of 2001 (H.R. 74), which was referred to the House Subcommittee on Crime in early 2001, and the Local Law Enforcement Enhancement Act of 2001 (S. 625), which was passed by the Senate Judiciary Committee in mid-2001 and awaits debate by the Senate.[18] The second bill would provide federal assistance to local law officials when crimes are motivated by hate on the basis of sex, sexual orientation, or disability. Currently, race, religion, and national origin are protected.[19] The limit here is on physical assault and, unlike in Canadian law, does not extend to speech.

Library Meeting Rooms

Hate crime legislation in Canada has become particularly important and relevant to libraries in situations where groups suspected of or accused of hate crimes attempt to book meeting rooms at public libraries. The Criminal Code of Canada makes it illegal to promote hatred against an identifiable group "if such hatred is incited by the communication, in a public place, of words likely to lead to a breach of peace."[20] The American Library Association (ALA) has a written policy defining the use of public library meeting rooms, as outlined in its Library Bill of Rights.[21] Canadian libraries, on the other hand, develop individual policies for meeting room use, adapted to the specific aims and intentions of each organization. Those libraries that endorse an open policy for the use of their meeting rooms—viewing them as an extension of library policies promoting intellectual freedom and a site for the expression of a wide range of opinions and points of view—have also made themselves the target of heated debate over the role of public space. The use of meeting rooms in both Victoria and Vancouver, in the province of British Columbia, have been the grounds for recent controversy when groups accused of promoting hatred have gathered in these public areas.

The situation involving the Greater Victoria Public Library arose in the fall of 1996 when it was revealed that a group known as the Canadian Free Speech League had been using meeting rooms in the Central Library in downtown Victoria for a number of years. This organization had received publicity in the past for its far-right political opinions and for statements made, under the auspices of free speech, against "Jews, non-white immigrants, native Indians, and homosexuals."[22] The group had not been booking a public library meeting space specifically to attract publicity, but because it was an economical space in a central location rented to it at the nonprofit rate for room bookings according to the library's policy.[23] Certain anti-racism organizations in the community, when they became aware of this situation, felt that it was inappropriate for this group to meet at a public library, citing its allegedly racist agenda and claiming that the library should not condone such groups by granting them meeting space. An appeal was made to the city council of Victoria, which resulted in a resolution that read, in part:

> . . . [P]ublic space, facilities and property within the jurisdiction of the Capital Regional District, the Library Board, Police Board . . . and other governing bodies in which the City of Victoria has participation will not be made available or accessible to any individual or group that promotes views and ideas which are likely to promote discrimination, contempt or hatred

to any person on the basis of race, national or ethnic origin, colour, religion, age, marital status, family status, sexual preference or disability.[24]

The overarching issue in this situation became one of jurisdiction over the public library's meeting rooms, with the Greater Victoria Public Library Board making a formal statement that the board, and not the City of Victoria, held sole responsibility for the meeting rooms. In a subsequent library board meeting, there was a unanimous vote to retain the open-door meeting room policy but to add a clause stating that groups using the rooms must "agree to abide by the provisions of the Criminal Code of Canada."[25]

Controversy arose again in June of 1998, when the Canadian Free Speech League booked two meeting rooms for dates that coincided with the Canadian Library Association (CLA) annual conference, which was being held in Victoria that year. Once again, the Greater Victoria Public Library allowed the meetings to take place, despite considerable public outcry and a media campaign that portrayed the library's position as one that promoted intolerance.[26] In this instance, CLA had an opportunity to act unequivocally in support of the Greater Victoria Public Library's policy, stating that any legally constituted group, regardless of political position, would be allowed to assemble in library meeting rooms and that no library would "act in place of duly authorized political and police authorities to initiate actions leading to curtailment of basic civil liberties."[27]

The situation at the Central branch of the Vancouver Public Library, in 1999, involved the same Canadian Free Speech League. Again, the library upheld both its own open policy on meeting room use and CLA's statement on intellectual freedom. This meeting was organized by the Canadian Free Speech League to raise support and funding for a court challenge of the constitutionality of British Columbia's anti-hate laws by Doug Collins, a controversial columnist for the *North Shore News,* a community newspaper in the city of North Vancouver. Four specific articles written by Collins for the paper had been identified by the British Columbia Human Rights Tribunal as having the "cumulative effect of exposing Jewish people to hatred and contempt."[28] Several groups, including the Canadian Jewish Congress and the Vancouver Association of Chinese Canadians, planned a peaceful protest at the library while the meeting was going on; this followed their claim that the library had heard but not acted upon their assertions that the library had a responsibility to deny access to its facilities by groups promoting hatred. The protest ended up being anything but peaceful, requiring the dispatch of police to restore order and resulting in the closure of the library in order to maintain public safety. The police considered billing the library to recover costs incurred, holding the library the "party responsible for making the decision to rent public space to certain kinds of groups." Several library board members telephoned the library director the next day to ensure the issue of free speech and room rentals was on the agenda for the next board meeting.[29]

After an open forum, "Public Meetings in Public Places," was held by the Vancouver Public Library Board in April 2000, the board changed the meeting room policy wording, stating that groups renting the room must not contravene the Human Rights Act of British Columbia and the Criminal Code of Canada.[30] The Vancouver Public Library has maintained its policy of open access to its rental facilities by any lawful group, even those whose values and viewpoints may be objectionable to society at large.

Although hate crime legislation exists in Canada, it has been the recent practice of public libraries to uphold the principles of freedom of speech when it comes to the use of meeting rooms, unless or until specific groups have actually been found guilty of a crime. As long as a group is not in violation of the Criminal Code of Canada, libraries and librarians will not become interpreters of what is or is not acceptable and "ask[ing] a library to extend restrictions on speech and assembly beyond those which our courts and legislatures are willing to do strikes at the heart of what a library is and is certainly a complete negation of the Statement on Intellectual Freedom of the Canadian Library Association . . . "[31]

The development of written policy statements by library associations regarding the use of meeting rooms, including those policies endorsed by CLA, has followed a path similar to the entrenchment of personal freedoms in the Canadian Constitution. Compared with the United States, intellectual freedom policies are both "young," having been developed within the last 30 years, and few in number. The situation in Canada is similar to that in Australia, New Zealand, and Britain, obviously reflecting common tradition and law. However, the slow development of written statements does not imply that intellectual freedom has not always been a central tenet of the profession.

Homolka-Bernardo Trials

The trials of Karla Homolka and Paul Bernardo (also known as Karla and Paul Teale), a husband and wife who were responsible for the murders of two teenage girls in the Ontario town of St. Catharines, presented a particular challenge to librarians attempting to uphold intellectual freedom in Canada after an Ontario judge ordered a publication ban during the trial of Karla Homolka. In order to ensure a fair trial for Bernardo and to avoid the risk of a mistrial, testimony and evidence given in the Homolka case, which preceded Bernardo's, was not to be published or broadcast anywhere in Canada. The judge felt that the importance of ensuring a fair trial for Bernardo superseded the public's right to know the specifics of the crimes and the intricacies of the first (Homolka) trial. To American audiences and media, this was a blatant, unacceptable, and "bizarre" case of censorship.[32] The specific wording of the order, imposed on July 5, 1993, by Ontario Justice Francis Kovacs, was:

> There will be no publication of the circumstances of the deaths of the victims referred to during the trial and they shall not be revealed directly or indirectly to a member of the foreign press.[33]

Since the criminal justice system in Canada has a federal jurisdiction, the provincial ban set by the Ontario Court applied to the entire country, requiring the media in all provinces and territories to comply. Canadian media, in print and electronic form, obeyed the ban and did not reveal details that emerged during the trial. The defendant's right to a fair trial was deemed to have precedence over access to information.

However, access to information about the Homolka trial was available through American media sources, including newspapers, cable television channels, and the then relatively new Internet newsgroups, which were beyond Canadian jurisdiction. The existence of this information in foreign sources created a difficult situation for libraries, which collect and disseminate U.S. publications. Despite the additional barring of U.S. media from the courtroom, stories still appeared in several formats, including newspaper articles in the *Washington Post* and *USA Today* and radio and television broadcasts from U.S. stations that could be received in Canada. Magazines and newspapers were seized at the Canada/ U.S. border and U.S. television and radio programs were blacked out by cable companies in Canada in an attempt to comply with the publication ban.[34]

Librarians at both the Vancouver Public Library and the Toronto Public Library, two large urban systems, were compelled, on the advice of legal counsel, to censor American newspapers that had arrived in libraries despite the ban by cutting out articles related to the case. In Vancouver, a statement reading "[a]s a result of an opinion from the City of Vancouver legal department, we have temporarily removed an article dealing with the contents of the Karla Homolka case in Ontario" was inserted where the articles had been removed.[35] According to the director of the Vancouver Public Library, librarians were deeply troubled by the actions they were required to take, saying "[t]his is the antithesis of everything we do in life. We're all about enabling people to get information. We hate this." Some librarians refused to perform the task.[36]

The situation in many academic institutions and libraries was similar. Most computer services departments took action to block access to computer bulletin boards and newsgroups carrying information about the trial that had been leaked to sources in the United States. Academic librarians cut out articles from newspapers and attached notices indicating that the material had been removed due to a court ban.[37] The situation at the McGill University Libraries in Montreal varied somewhat. The computer services department at the university felt it was required to block computer newsgroups after a legal adviser had defined "publication" to mean "the dissemination of information to any number of individuals in whatever form and through any medium."[38] Librarians, however, were advised not to "jump to the conclusion that merely receiving printed publications in the normal course of activities was a criminal act"; the "concepts of publication and distribution, implicit in the decision regarding the withdrawal of the newsgroup by the Computing Centre, were not assumed to transfer directly" to library materials and print publications.[39] The ban was specifically targeted at the publication and distribution of information about the trial, but the legal adviser for the McGill University Libraries did not extend the ban to mere possession of information. As a result, librarians at McGill did not censor in any way those library materials that included American coverage of the case.

Conclusion

These examples in no way cover the full range of challenges to intellectual freedom that have been faced in Canada and Canadian libraries. They simply highlight the ways in which the laws and policies governing intellectual freedom are interpreted differently, due to the nature of the practice of common law. Seminal legal cases and key situations continue to shape and influence the law, debating and defining the issues in the public realm. And in the shadow of September 11, laws are being proposed that will place limits on freedoms in both Canada and the United States. Thus, the point at which freedom of expression pushes up against freedom from oppression varies, as does understanding of "intellectual freedom" across the as-yet longest undefended border in the world.

Notes

1. Tryon, J. (1994). *The Librarian's Legal Companion.* G. K. Hall and Maxwell Macmillan Canada, 117.

2. Mill, J. S. *On Liberty.* Edward Alexander, ed. Broadview Press, 47.

3. National Archives and Records Administration (2002). *The U.S. Bill of Rights.* Retrieved January 10, 2002, from http://www.nara.gov/exhall/charters/billrights/billmain.html).

4. Bielefield, A., and L. Cheeseman (1995). *Library Patrons and the Law.* Neal-Schuman, 22.

5. Garner, B. (Ed.) (1999). *Black's Law Dictionary* (7th ed.). West Publishing, 270.

6. Jennings, W., T. Zuber, D. Zuber, and J. Zuber (1991). *Canadian Law* (5th ed.). McGraw-Hill Ryerson, 33.

7. Jennings et al., 33.

8. Jennings et al., 45.

9. Office for Intellectual Freedom, American Library Association (2002). *Intellectual Freedom Manual* (6th ed.). American Library Association, xiii.

10. Bielefield and Cheeseman, 33.

11. Bielefield and Cheeseman, 36.

12. Moon, R. (2000). *The Constitutional Protection of Freedom of Expression.* University of Toronto Press, 5–6.

13. Moon, 36.

14. Moon, 131.

15. Cleaver, B., M. A. Wilkinson, G. Liew, J. Campbell, and G. Sperryn (1992). *Handbook Exploring the Legal Context for Information Policy in Canada.* Faxon Canada, 120.

16. Cleaver et al., 131.

17. Cleaver et al., 34.

18. Bill summary and status for the 107th congress, H.R. 74. (2002). Retrieved January 2, 2002 from http://thomas.loc.gov/cgi-bin/bdquery/z?d107:HR00074:@@@L&summ2=m&

19. Clymer, Adam (2001, July 27). "Senate Panel Backs Hate-Crime Coverage for Gays." *New York Times* (East Coast ed.), A13.

20. Cleaver et al., 120.

21. American Library Association (2002). "Meeting Rooms: An Interpretation of the Library Bill of Rights." Retrieved January 3, 2002, from http://www.ala.org/alaorg/oif/meet_rms.html.

22. Brook, P. (1999, October 6). "Limits on Free Speech a Double-Edged Sword." *Vancouver Sun,* A19.

23. Williams, N. (1998). "Intellectual Freedom—Who Can Use the Meeting Room." *Feliciter,* 44 (10), 27.

24. Williams, 27.

25. Williams, 27.

26. Kester, N. G. (1999). "The Freedom We Fight For." *Feliciter,* 45 (1), 12.

27. Schrader, A. (1999). "Intellectual Freedom and Access to Information in Canada: 1998 in Review." *Feliciter,* 45 (1), 33.

28. Fong, P. (1999, September 30). "Library Won't Ban Collins Speech." *Vancouver Sun,* B4.

29. Brook, A19.

30. Vancouver Public Library (2001). *Annual Report 2000.*

31. Williams, 29.

32. *New York Times* editorial reprinted in the December 7, 1993, *Vancouver Sun,* A15.

33. Groen, F. K. (1995). "Electronic and Print Information: Active Distribution and Passive Retention in Relation to a Murder—A Case Study." *College & Research Libraries,* 56 (4), 326.

34. Bell, S. (1993, December 7). "Librarians Censor Teale Material." *Vancouver Sun,* A3.

35. Bell, A3.

36. Mason Lee, R. (1993, December 8). "Vancouver Ambivalent About Teale Case. *Vancouver Sun,* B4.

37. Groen, 328.

38. Groen, 326.

39. Groen, 328.

Appendix

Canadian Library Association Position Statements

Subject: Statement on Intellectual Freedom
Approved by: Executive Council
Date approved: June 27, 1974; Amended November 17, 1983, and November 18, 1985

All persons in Canada have the fundamental right, as embodied in the nation's Bill of Rights and the Canadian Charter of Rights and Freedoms, to have access to all expressions of knowledge, creativity and intellectual activity, and to express their thoughts publicly. This right to intellectual freedom, under the law, is essential to the health and development of Canadian society.

Libraries have a basic responsibility for the development and maintenance of intellectual freedom.

It is the responsibility of libraries to guarantee and facilitate access to all expressions of knowledge and intellectual activity, including those which some elements of society may consider to be unconventional, unpopular or unacceptable. To this end, libraries shall acquire and make available the widest variety of materials.

It is the responsibility of libraries to guarantee the right of free expression by making available all the library's public facilities and services to all individuals and groups who need them.

Libraries should resist all efforts to limit the exercise of these responsibilities while recognizing the right of criticism by individuals and groups.

Both employees and employers in libraries have a duty, in addition to their institutional responsibilities, to uphold these principles.

Subject: Code of Ethics Position Statement
Approved by: Annual General Meeting
Date approved: June 1976

Members of the Canadian Library Association have the individual and collective responsibility to:

1 Support and implement the principles and practices embodied in the current Canadian Library Association Statement on Intellectual Freedom
2 Make every effort to promote and maintain the highest possible range and standards of library service to all segments of Canadian society
3 Facilitate access to any or all sources of information which may be of assistance to library users
4 Protect the privacy and dignity of library users and staff

Dissemination of Government Information

Harold C. Relyea

Congressional Research Service
Library of Congress, Washington, DC 20540

In the United States, government information is available to the public from federal entities through various access and dissemination arrangements. Access is requester-initiated; dissemination is government-initiated. Certainly a major change in dissemination arrangements that has occurred since this subject was discussed in these pages less than a decade ago is the widespread digitization of information and making it publicly available on Web sites via the Internet.[1] This development, among other effects, has reinforced the reality that information, because it is not always reliable or credible, is not knowledge.

Such electronic dissemination of government information is being performed, in part, to supplement access arrangements. Access was largely realized during the first 150 years of the federal government through letters of request to public officials, who provided either an opportunity to inspect pertinent materials or copies of responsive documents. With the rise of the administrative state and the concurrent expansion of the federal bureaucracy during the 20th century, such inquiries came to be ignored, frustrated by assertions of official protection, or given greatly delayed response. To rectify the situation, formal information access procedures were legislated with the Freedom of Information Act (FOIA) and the Privacy Act.[2] Amendments to FOIA in 1996 mandated the creation of electronic reading rooms where agency officials could place records of high interest to the public, as well as resource materials on using FOIA, for easy access via the Internet.[3]

Dissemination was largely realized during the first 200 years of federal operations through *publication*—ink on paper printing and, true to the Latin root of the word, distribution of the resulting document to "all of the people." Distribution included free provision, public sale, and depository library availability. Agencies were well aware that appropriated funds should be used carefully and responsibly for their publication activities and that they could incur congressional enmity if they appeared to be engaging in persuasive public relations or propaganda campaigns.[4] More recently—as many federal agencies were statutorily authorized to *disseminate* information, with traditional publication being one option—the distinction between dissemination and publication, never sharply delineated, has blurred as government information increasingly is produced and distributed to the public in electronic form and formats. One danger in this development is the lure of public relations—in brief, putting "spin" on a volume of inexpensive electronic information products to persuade people about a policy or an administrative view. Without a catalog of such products, such concerted efforts at persuasion may pass undetected by overseers.

Another danger is the changed character of some information when offered in electronic form or formats. The matter initially arose in 1998 when the Environmental Protection Agency (EPA), pursuant to the Clean Air Act, was preparing to make publicly available industry-prepared accident prevention plans concerning worst-case scenarios for chemical facilities in the case of a spill or other major environmental problem. EPA decided not only to make copies of these plans and related documents accessible to the public, but also to create a worst-case scenario database containing this information and make it available via the Internet. This latter intention drew opposition from the Federal Bureau of Investigation, the Central Intelligence Agency, and some congressional overseers who contended that the database could be used by terrorists as a targeting tool. In November, after much debate and discussion, EPA finally abandoned its plan to make the worst-case scenario database accessible via the Internet. Nonetheless, the strong possibility existed that the database and the records to create such a database might be accessible to the public under FOIA. Ultimately, legislation was crafted, on a bipartisan basis, balancing security, entrepreneurial, and public information interests concerning so-called consequence analysis information.[5] More recently, with the September 11, 2001, terrorist attacks on the World Trade Center and the Pentagon, information deemed to be in some way potentially useful to terrorists has been removed from various federal Web sites.

Finally, any consideration of contemporary federal arrangements for publishing and disseminating government information must acknowledge the crumbling condition of some of the longest-enduring institutions of relevance— notably, the Joint Committee on Printing and the Government Printing Office —and the problems their decline creates and perpetuates. Certainly the rise of the electronic information phenomenon, the erosion of the Government Printing Office's authority to supervise the public printing system, related constitutional clashes, and—against a background of budget reduction and government downsizing—desires for greater efficiency and economy in the production and dissemination of government information products have contributed to the situation. However, so, too, has prevailing indifference about creating improved structural, organizational, and managerial conditions for the production and dissemination of government information.

Historical Background

That government dissemination of official information to the public is a basic value of democracy is evident, in the American experience, in the constitutional requirements that each house of Congress publish a journal of its proceedings, that a regular statement and account of the receipts and expenditures of all public money be published, and that each state shall give full faith and credit to the acts, records, and judicial proceedings of every other state, which arguably assumes some publication effort. By the time the nation erupted in civil war in April 1861, Congress had a well-established record on the publication of federal laws and ratified treaties;[6] the printing and distribution of the House and Senate journals;[7] the routine printing of all congressional reports, special documents, and bills;[8] and the publication of contemporaneous accounts of floor proceedings, beginning with the *Register of Debates* in 1825. In 1860 it mandated the Government Printing Office (GPO) to produce congressional literature and to serve the printing needs of the executive branch as well.[9] The Joint Committee on Printing, chartered in 1846, closely monitored GPO operations and printing activities throughout the federal establishment.[10]

The Printing Act of 1895 centralized government printing and publication at GPO and affirmed its monopoly on the performance of these functions.[11] It also relocated the Superintendent of Public Documents from the Department of the Interior, where the position had been initially established in 1869,[12] to GPO.[13] The Superintendent managed the depository library program, inaugurated in 1813 with regard to congressional materials and extended in 1857 to include other federal literature.[14] The 1895 act also vested the Superintendent with responsibility for the sale of documents and the preparation of periodic indices of GPO printed products. In 1904 he was authorized to reprint departmental publications, with the consent of the pertinent Secretary, for public sale.[15] Comparable discretion to reproduce congressional documents for sale was provided in 1922.[16]

The rise of the administrative state during the second decade of the 20th century soon resulted in a crisis in government information availability. Increased federal regulatory activity occurred with the establishment of an autonomous Department of Labor and the Federal Reserve System in 1913, the Federal Trade Commission the following year, and a variety of wartime agencies in 1917. With the return to peace in 1918, this government expansion slowed momentarily, but began again with the onset of the Great Depression and the arrival of the New Deal.

As federal regulatory powers and administrative entities grew dramatically during the 1930s, there was a concomitant increase in both the number and variety of controlling directives, regulations, and requirements. While a contemporary observer characterized the situation in 1920 as one of "confusion,"[17] another described the deteriorating conditions in 1934 as "chaos."[18] During the early months of the New Deal, administrative law pronouncements were in such disarray that, on one occasion, government attorneys arguing a lawsuit before the Supreme Court were embarrassed to discover that their case was based on a nonexistent regulation;[19] at another time, they discovered that they were pursuing litigation under a revoked executive order.[20]

To improve information availability, Congress authorized an executive branch gazette, the *Federal Register,* in 1935.[21] Produced in a now-familiar magazine format, it contained various presidential directives and agency regulations, and came to be published each workday. In 1937 Congress inaugurated the Code of Federal Regulations, a useful codification of regulations initially produced in the *Register.*[22] Containing almost all operative agency regulations, the Code is now updated annually. Subsequently, the Federal Register Act of 1935 was relied upon as a dissemination authority for the publication of the *United States Government Manual,* which has been available to the public since 1939; the *Public Papers of the Presidents,* which were first produced in 1960; and the *Weekly Compilation of Presidential Documents,* which was begun in the summer of 1965.

In the years after the conclusion of World War II, authority for the proactive dissemination of government information was regarded as adequate. The emerging information policy issue of the 1950s and 1960s was public access to unpublished information—initially, unpublished records and, subsequently, also oral policy deliberations. Legislative responses included the Freedom of Information Act in 1966,[23] the Federal Advisory Committee Act in 1972,[24] the Privacy Act of 1974,[25] and the Government in the Sunshine Act of 1976.[26]

Shortly thereafter, Congress laid the foundation for improved, comprehensive management of government information throughout the federal executive branch with the somewhat misnamed Paperwork Reduction Act of 1980.[27] The statute specifically vested the director of the Office of Management and Budget (OMB) with responsibility to coordinate, develop, and implement government-wide policies, principles, standards, and guidelines concerning the dissemination of statistics and statistical information and to promote the use of automatic data processing and telecommunications equipment by the federal government "to improve the effectiveness of the use and dissemination of data in the operation of Federal programs."[28] Each agency was required to periodically review its information management activities involving, among other efforts, the dissemination of information.[29]

Amendments to the Paperwork Reduction Act in 1986 reaffirmed the responsibility of the director of OMB concerning the dissemination of statistics and statistical information, and gave the agencies the additional requirement of implementing applicable government-wide and agency information policies, principles, standards, and guidelines with respect to, among other activities, the dissemination of information.[30]

Dissemination received much more detailed attention in the 1995 recodification of the Paperwork Reduction Act. Among the purposes of the new statute were ensuring "the greatest possible public benefit from maximiz[ing] the utility of information . . . disseminated by or for the Federal" government; minimizing the cost to the federal government of the dissemination of information; providing for "the dissemination of public information on a timely basis, on equitable terms, and in a manner that promotes the utility of the information to the public and makes effective use of information technology;" and ensuring that, among other activities, the dissemination of information by or for the federal government "is consistent with applicable laws, including laws relating to . . . privacy and confidentiality, . . . security of information, . . . and . . . access to information."[31] The responsibilities of the director of OMB and the agencies regarding information dissemination were expanded in detailed terms.[32]

Recent Challenges and Issues

A pioneering, comprehensive assessment of the collection and dissemination of information by federal agencies, issued by the House Committee on Government Operations in 1986, observed that "Increasing amounts of information . . . are being maintained in electronic data bases" and surmised that this "trend will continue and will accelerate"[33] A positive response to this assessment, in the context of information dissemination, was the Government Printing Office Electronic Information Access Enhancement Act of 1993, which directed the Superintendent of Documents to provide a system of online access to the *Congressional Record* and the *Federal Register* by June 1994. The Superintendent was given discretion to make available other appropriate publications, and responsibility for maintaining an electronic directory of federal electronic information as well as for operating an electronic storage facility for federal electronic information.[34] In addition to the online Congressional Record and Federal Register, GPO also created a congressional bills database containing all published versions of House and Senate proposals introduced since the 103rd Congress.

The statute mandated free online access for all depository libraries and for cost recovery based upon the marginal cost of dissemination for all others. Subsequently, however, GPO opened access by making arrangements with a number of libraries around the country to offer "gateway" access to the GPO databases via the Internet or through a local telephone call. In December 1995 GPO announced the GPO Access service was directly available over the Internet at no cost. Thus, since 1996 GPO has been bearing the costs of operating an electronic information access system that competes with its document sales program, a situation that certainly has contributed to GPO's financial difficulties.

GPO's exclusive mandate was also coming under fire from various quarters. The General Accounting Office reported in April 1994 that, "for all practical purposes, the framework of laws and regulations used to manage many aspects of government publishing has become outdated" as a consequence of the emergence and use of various new electronic information technologies. GPO was regarded to be ill-equipped to continue to assert monopoly control over agency printing-like operations. Moreover, "some agencies want to publish their work independent of GPO involvement" and can do so as a "result of significant advances in publishing technologies."[35]

Earlier, in its initial September 1993 report to the president, the National Performance Review (NPR) had recommended ending the GPO monopoly on government printing.[36] Two months later, the House approved an omnibus bill implementing various recommendations and containing committee amendments that, while continuing the GPO monopoly on printing, would have downsized GPO, transferred the functions and resources of the Superintendent of Documents to the Library of Congress, closed most agency printing facilities, and directed that public printing "maximize competitive procurement from the private sector." The Senate did not consider the proposal prior to the final adjournment of the 103rd Congress.

Several months later, President Bill Clinton, when signing the Legislative Branch Appropriations Act of 1995, took exception to provisions expanding the definition of *printing* and requiring the agencies to obtain a certification from the Public Printer before procuring the production of certain official documents from sources other than GPO. To minimize what he called "the potential constitutional deficiencies" of the legislation, the president indicated that "the exclusive authority of the Government Printing Office over 'the procurement of any printing related to the production of Government publications' will be restricted to procurement of documents intended primarily for distribution to and use by the general public."[37] By mid-August GPO reportedly was incurring deficits approaching $5 million due to the loss of printing that federal agencies were procuring from other sources.[38] A month later, in a memorandum to federal department and agency heads, OMB Acting Director Alice M. Rivlin indicated that, because an agreement had been reached with congressional leaders to seek comprehensive printing reform during the next year, "the status quo regarding present printing and duplicating arrangements" would be maintained for the remainder of the fiscal year. A few weeks later, when the president's political party lost majority control of both houses of Congress, plans for printing reform disappeared.

Crumbling Structures

Two years later, shortly after the convening of the 105th Congress, Sen. John Warner (R-Va.), newly installed chairman of the Committee on Rules and Administration and the Joint Committee on Printing (JCP), initiated an effort to develop a public printing reform bill. While addressing the various technological, managerial, and constitutional challenges, opportunities, and problems confronting the public printing system, the resulting proposal was to be designed to garner broad support within Congress as well as the approval of the Clinton administration. In April 1997 a legislative working group was formed, consisting of staff from the Committee on Rules and Administration, JCP, and OMB. The group met regularly during the spring, summer, and fall months. Some of its members also held discussions with representatives of various organizations having a direct interest in public printing policy and practice. As a draft bill began to take shape, various agency representatives were consulted to obtain their reactions to the reform measure, as were House and Senate officials who would be affected by the new arrangements. The process was slow and meticulous; much time was consumed and numerous compromises were made.

The resulting reform bill was introduced by Sen. Warner on July 10, 1998, as S. 2288, the Wendell H. Ford Government Publications Reform Act of 1998.[39] Referred to the Committee on Rules and Administration, the bill was discussed at a July 29 hearing when testimony was received from the Public Printer and various library organization, trade group, organized labor, and public interest group representatives. Some witnesses offered recommendations for refining the legislation; all of them expressed support for the bill.[40]

Thereafter, more compromises and adjustments were made. For some, the bill was becoming unwieldy; for others, its basic premises were objectionable. At a second committee hearing on September 16 these latter views were aired by a Xerox corporation executive appearing on behalf of the Information Technology Industry (ITI) Council representing leading American providers of information technology products and services. He expressed dismay that the legislation "continues to vest a central entity, indeed a monopoly, with full responsibility and authority to approve or disapprove the procurement and production of all Government publications and printing." In his view, "S. 2288 perpetuates a model already judged by Congress as ill-suited to the information age." His reference was to information technology management and procurement legislation enacted by Congress very early in 1996 that came to be known as the Clinger-Cohen Act.[41] Concluding, he remarked:

> As currently written, S. 2288 relies on the failed model of a central monopoly wielding absolute authority over the manner and method that Government publications are procured and disseminated. Instead, ITI believes Clinger-Cohen and other recent reforms provide a model for a competitive Government publication procurement process guided by the principle of best value to the Government. GPO should be restructured to focus on the value it brings to the overall printing needs of the Government within a new, competitive and decentralized method. Through the use of information technology, the Superintendent of Documents should be given the capacity to make certain that Government publications are fully accessible through print and electronic means.[42]

That the bill was in trouble had become evident when the committee could not obtain a quorum for a September 10 markup. Meeting next on September 28, the panel approved a modified version of the bill, which was substituted in the legislation, and the amended measure was favorably ordered to be reported.[43] The reported bill would have abolished JCP and transferred many of its responsibilities to the House Committee on House Oversight (House Administration) and the Senate Committee on Rules and Administration or to the Public Printer, who was designated the administrator of the Government Publications Office, the latter being the new denomination of GPO. All federal government publications production, regardless of form or format, would have been centralized in the new Government Publications Office, except such production required by the Supreme Court and certain national security entities. A presidentially appointed Superintendent of Government Publications Access Programs would have assumed the duties of the current Superintendent of Documents, administering the GPO sales, depository libraries, and GPO electronic documents access programs. The House and the Senate, at the outset of each Congress, each would have determined the style, form, manner, and quantity of publications to be produced for them. Throughout the bill, the term "publication" was used in lieu of "printing" to indicate that both traditional paper and new electronic forms and formats were included under the former term. Also, a general thrust of the legislation was to restrain the quantity of government documents being printed without harm to the conduct of official business and the public's right to know about the activities and operations of government—online depository library access to government documents constituting major safety nets in this regard.

The reform bill reached the Senate floor on October 16, resulting in no opportunity for its consideration prior to the October 21 final adjournment of the 105th Congress. Due to leadership changes—Sen. Warner left the chairmanship of the Committee on Rules and Administration to head the Committee on Armed Services—this omnibus reform effort was not renewed in the 106th or 107th Congresses.

The failure of the reform effort also left JCP in difficult circumstances. A 1983 decision by the Supreme Court, requiring that the exercise of legislative power follow the constitutionally prescribed lawmaking process of bicameral consideration and presentation of a bill or joint resolution to the president for his signature or veto, had severely constrained JCP's exercise of its long-standing remedial powers, including the issuance and enforcement of the Government Printing and Binding Regulations.[44] With the convening of the 104th Congress, economy-minded House Republicans demonstrated an active interest in abolishing JCP and transferring its functions to the committees having jurisdiction over House and Senate administrative matters. Rep. Bill Thomas (R-Calif.), JCP chairman, sought no fiscal year (FY) 1996 operating funds for the panel and urged that it be eradicated.[45] Although House appropriators and members agreed with Rep. Thomas, Senate appropriators opposed this action and allocated $1,164,000 for JCP.[46] Conferees cut the JCP allocation to $750,000, which both houses accepted.[47]

A few years later, anticipating that Sen. Warner's omnibus printing reform bill would be enacted prior to the conclusion of the 105th Congress, the Senate, on September 25, 1998, cleared for the president's signature the conference committee version of an FY 1999 legislative branch appropriations bill that provided sufficient amounts to meet the JCP payroll only through the remaining three months of the year and an additional, small transition allowance.[48] Consequently, with the convening of the next Congress, JCP continued to have responsibility for many administrative tasks assigned by provisions of Title 44, but had no staff or offices of its own. To relieve JCP of some of this responsibility, Sen. Warner, the panel's departing chairman, requested, in a December 17, 1998, letter to the Public Printer, that that official carry out certain of the committee's Title 44 authorities; review agency reports and plans required under the government printing and binding regulations; grant agency waivers to enable direct procurement of printing, binding, and blank-book work; continue GPO procurement of printing, binding, and blank-book work from the private sector; and report to JCP regularly on these matters.[49] During the 106th Congress, JCP was supported part time by a few staff members of the Committee on House Administration.

During the closing weeks of the 106th Congress, conferees on the FY 2001 legislative branch appropriations bill agreed to an amended House provision that, as modified, authorized the appropriation to the Clerk of the House of such sums as may be necessary for congressional printing and binding services for the House of Representatives during FY 2001; the preparation of estimated expenditures and proposed appropriations for congressional printing and binding services by the Clerk of the House in accordance with Title 31, United States Code, beginning with FY 2003; and, during FY 2001, the conduct by the clerk of a comprehensive study of the needs of the House for congressional printing and binding services during FY 2003 and succeeding years, including an analysis of the most cost-effective program or programs for providing printed or other media-based publications for House uses. The required study, upon completion, was to be submitted to the Committee on House Administration for review and the preparation of such regulations or other arrangements as considered appropriate to enable the clerk to carry out congressional printing and binding services for the House.[50] The original House provision would have applied to both the Clerk of the House and the Secretary of the Senate, but the Senate declined to follow this course.[51]

Conferees on the legislative branch appropriations bill also modified language in the House report directing the Congressional Research Service to conduct a study concerning the transfer of the functions of the Superintendent of Documents from GPO to the Library of Congress.[52] In their report, the conferees directed GAO to "conduct a comprehensive study of the impact of providing documents to the public solely in electronic format." Continuing, the report said:

The study shall include: (1) a current inventory of publications and documents which are provided to the public, (2) the frequency with which each type of publication or document is requested for deposit at nonregional depository libraries, and (3) an assessment of the feasibility of transfer of the depository library program to the Library of Congress that: Identifies how such a transfer might be accomplished; Identifies when such a transfer might optimally occur; Examines the functions, services, and programs of the Superintendent of Documents; Examines and identifies administrative and infrastructure support that is provided to the Superintendent by the Government Printing Office, with a view to the implications for such a transfer; Examines and identifies the costs, for both the Government Printing Office and the

Library of Congress, of such a transfer; Identifies measures that are necessary to ensure the success of such a transfer.[53]

President Clinton vetoed the legislative branch appropriations bill on October 30, 2000, for reasons not pertinent to the matters discussed above. The text of the measure was subsequently included in the Consolidated Appropriations Act, 2001, which cleared Congress on December 15 and was signed into law by President Clinton on December 21.[54]

As statutorily required, GAO submitted the completed study to the Committee on House Administration and the Senate Committee on Rules and Administration on March 30, 2001.[55] The report cautioned that, while the electronic dissemination of government documents offered the opportunity to reduce the costs of dissemination and make government information more usable and accessible, some formidable challenges would need to be overcome in the event documents were to be disseminated solely in electronic format. These challenges, said the report, include ensuring that documents are authentic, permanently maintained, and equally accessible to all individuals. It was also recognized that certain cost issues, including the effect of shifting printing costs to depository libraries and end users, would have to be addressed.

Regarding the feasibility of transferring the depository library program to the Library of Congress, the report foresaw both advantages and disadvantages. The program was seen as appropriate for the library to administer, and its relocation to the library, said the report, "could facilitate the development of government-wide solutions to issues surrounding the acquisition, management, and dissemination of electronic documents." Indeed, it was thought that three other GPO programs closely linked with the depository library program—cataloging and indexing; GPO Access, including the depository library program's electronic collection; and the international exchange service—might also be considered for transfer. Among the disadvantages cited by the report were "potential negative effects on public access to information and concern about the availability of funds to maintain the current program." The report acknowledged the numerous concerns offered by the Public Printer and the Librarian of Congress concerning its content (letters from both officials commenting on the draft report were included in appendices), as well as the concerns raised by library organizations and GPO employee unions. It was proffered that these issues might be addressed by a joint GPO/Library transition team "to develop appropriate strategies" and "a detailed transition plan including a schedule and detailed cost estimates."

As the 106th Congress moved toward final adjournment, the National Commission on Libraries and Information Science (NCLIS) issued a November 27 discussion draft of *A Comprehensive Assessment of Public Information Dissemination*.[56] The assessment had initially been requested by Sen. John McCain (R-Ariz.), the chairman of the Senate Committee on Commerce, Science, and Transportation, in mid-June as a follow-up on assistance the commission had provided to his committee regarding the future of the National Technical Information Service of the Department of Commerce.[57] In his letter to NCLIS, Sen. McCain recalled testimony received by his committee "on the need for a formal study on the proposed organizational changes to the National Technical Information Service (NTIS) and overall government information dissemination policy."

In making his request for "a review of the reforms necessary for the federal government's information dissemination practices," Sen. McCain asked that the study "include assessments of the need for:"

- Proposing new or revised laws, rules, regulations, missions, and policies
- Modernizing organization structures and functions so as to reflect greater emphasis on electronic information planning, management, and control capabilities, and the need to consolidate, streamline, and simplify missions and functions to avoid or minimize unnecessary overlap and duplication
- Revoking [the] NTIS [financial] self-sufficiency requirement
- Strengthening other key components of the overall federal information dissemination infrastructure.

A month later, in a mid-July letter, Sen. Joseph I. Lieberman (D-Conn.), the ranking minority member of the Senate Committee on Governmental Affairs, joined Sen. McCain's request, and suggested two additions to the NCLIS study: "Include . . . any relevant sections of the Paperwork Reduction Act that may need revision, because [the Governmental Affairs] Committee will be considering the law's reauthorization next Congress," and "consider the viability of maintaining NTIS as a centralized fully electronic repository of federal scientific and technical information, accessible via the Internet and equipped with search and retrieval capabilities."

The November 27 discussion draft of *A Comprehensive Assessment of Public Information Dissemination* began with a working definition of "public information as information created, compiled and/or maintained by the federal government. We assert," the report continued, "that public information is information owned by the people, held in trust by their government, and should be available to the people except where restricted by law." These restrictions, it was stated, are "stipulated in various statutes such as the Freedom of Information Act, the Privacy Act, national security legislation, and a few other laws."[58]

The definition included the information holdings of all three branches of the federal government, and, while recognizing that restrictions on the public availability of some types of information existed, tended to regard these restrictions as being only statutorily prescribed and few in number. Such a view neglected the nonstatutory authority of congressional bodies, the president, and federal judges to limit information availability. It also appeared to be uninformed regarding the numerous instances when Congress has legislated provisions protecting information from disclosure. The Commission on Federal Paperwork reported in July 1977 that it had identified "approximately 200 statutes concerning confidentiality [of information], about 90 of which relate to the disclosure of business or commercial data."[59] A 1984 survey conducted by the American Society of Access Professionals identified 135 statutory provisions cited by a total of 40 federal executive agencies during 1975–1982 in conjunction with the FOI Act exemption recognizing statutory protection of various kinds of information.[60] Also, in addition to the Privacy Act, there are at least two dozen additional statutory provisions restricting the disclosure of personally identifiable information by executive agencies. The NCLIS report offered numerous findings, conclusions, and recommendations, and some statements of findings appeared to be expressed in terms of a recommendation. Major recommendations proffered by the report included the following:

- Formally recognizing and affirming the concept that public information is a strategic national resource, with the president issuing a directive to the heads of executive departments and agencies designating government "knowledge holdings" as a strategic national asset and emphasizing the importance of agency proactive initiatives in making their information resources accessible to all Americans
- Creating, as a new independent executive agency, a Public Information Resources Administration to provide overall policy leadership, management, oversight, and accountability for public information resources, with both new relevant authorities and responsibilities and transfers of existing relevant authorities and responsibilities from extant government entities
- Transferring NTIS to the new Public Information Resources Administration once it is established
- Requiring an Information Dissemination Budget line item at the individual agency level and establishing an overall Information Dissemination Budget line item in the president's budget that aggregates individual agency requirements with those of the new Public Information Resources Administration
- Enacting the draft Public Information Resources Reform Act of 2001 to provide a new statutory foundation for the formal establishment of government's "knowledge holdings" as a strategic national asset
- Establishing a new Congressional Information Resources Office, incorporating the Government Printing Office, to execute programs necessary to support legislative branch public information resources management responsibilities
- Establishing a new Judicial Information Resources Office within the Administrative Office of the U.S. Courts to execute programs necessary to support judicial branch public information resources management responsibilities
- Supporting NTIS information collection, editing, and related tasks with appropriated funds
- Updating NTIS revenue sources to include appropriated funds, sales income, and reimbursements from other agencies for services provided

In general, the report sought formal recognition and affirmation of the concept that public information is a strategic national resource, although many would contend that this objective had already been met with the Paperwork Reduction Act of 1995. Many of its findings and recommendations promoted proactive agency information dissemination activities and practices. These efforts, as the commission was warned, "could result in a misuse of agency resources to promote the agency and generate propaganda," a caution the report dismissed as "unreasonable fears."[61] Nonetheless, longstanding congressional displeasure with zealous information activities was benchmarked almost a century ago with the Gillett Act prohibition on using appropriated funds to pay a publicity expert, unless specifically provided for that purpose.[62]

Finally, three new information resources offices and funding NTIS, in part, with appropriated monies were recommended. These proposals, however, were offered in a climate of opinion supportive of government downsizing, cost reduction, and decentralized administration, the Internet, for some, making the latter particularly attractive regarding information dissemination. In the view of one veteran information policy expert, NCLIS "squandered an opportunity to effect a major impact on federal information policy" with a report that went "wildly off the rails," the future of NTIS becoming "a minor consideration, lost in a much grander and wholly naive scheme." Creating a Public Information Resources Administration (PIRA) was characterized as "a triumph of 1960s political ideology," discarded long ago when it was "realized that creating new government agencies only creates new problems rather than solving old ones." Indeed, it was observed, "NCLIS' report never says how PIRA would overcome the deficiencies of existing government programs that deal in information dissemination because the report does not state how PIRA relates to the existing power structure in the executive branch of government." If created, PIRA "would probably be a tiny agency, chronically underfunded and understaffed, and completely removed from the policy decisions that affect information dissemination programs." In brief, "PIRA would be another NCLIS."[63]

In the end, the NCLIS report was ignored and NCLIS escaped eradication when Congress provided FY 2002 operating funds that the Bush Administration pointedly did not request. However, the NCLIS report well may have contributed to the climate of indifference that has prevailed during the past few years regarding the future of JCP, GPO, NTIS, and improved government information dissemination arrangements. Furthermore, the events of September 11 have seemingly resulted in a national policy agenda affording little opportunity for the consideration of these matters in the immediate future.

Ripple Effects

Terrorist attacks on the World Trade Center and the Pentagon have had wide-ranging effects on a number of aspects of information dissemination. The security of government information technology (IT), which, by one congressional estimate, had fallen from an overall grade of D- to an F for 2001, suddenly has become the single most important aspect of federal IT operations.[64] However, improved and added IT security may result in difficulties at federal Web sites, such as slowing the downloading of documents. Issues of who visits such Web sites, with what frequency, to view what information, and what other Web sites they visit may be reopened.[65] Moreover, in the aftermath of the terrorist attacks, several agencies have removed information seemingly of potential value to terrorists, such as the location and operating status of nuclear power plants, maps of the American transportation infrastructure, and chemical industry shortcomings in preparing for a possible terrorist attack.[66]

These actions also have implications for FOIA operations, including requests involving copies of records and the placement of records of high public interest in electronic reading rooms on agency Web sites. According to the most recent data available, 25 major federal agencies—which, together, handle 97 percent of FOIA requests government-wide—processed in FY 1999 about 1.9 million such requests, providing records in full for 82 percent. For 23 of these agencies, "1.6 million requests were processed with median times of 20 days or fewer, while 140,000 were processed with median times over 20 days." Furthermore, 22 of 24 agencies maintained electronic reading rooms of frequently requested records, while 13 of 25 agencies enabled the electronic submission of FOIA requests.[67] A month after the World Trade Center and Pentagon terrorist attacks, Attorney General John D. Ashcroft advised federal department and agency heads "to carefully consider" interests and values protected under the statute, including "safeguarding our national security" and "enhancing the effectiveness of our law enforcement agencies." "Any discretionary decision by your agency to disclose information protected under the FOIA," he advised, "should be made only after full and deliberate consideration of the institutional, commercial, and personal privacy interests that could be implicated by disclosure of the information."[68] The memorandum, at best, would not appear to encourage agency leaders to be proactive in selecting records and placing them in electronic reading rooms.

Finally, the recent terrorists attacks and the national agenda they have generated may result in continued neglect of federal Web site management. Early in 2001 a guide to federal Web sites repeated the conservative estimate that "the government has created more than 20,000 Web sites containing more than 100 million pages."[69] By the end of the year, a federal webmaster was complaining about the existence of "more than 110,000 Web pages that listed federal jobs—some 52,000 at .gov sites and 60,000 at .mil."[70] In the interests of promoting efficient and economical use of agency resources, facilitating OMB oversight, and assuring that agency information practices do not exceed statutory limitations, several minimal requirements might be set for federal Web sites. For example, agencies might be required to register with, or otherwise report to, the director of OMB all existing Web sites they maintain and subsequently create. Beyond this requirement, agencies might be obligated to obtain OMB approval of new Web sites they propose to create. The director of OMB might be authorized to issue explicit Web site management guidelines for agency compliance. Such guidelines might be required to specify basic expectations concerning Web site accessibility to the public, content, organization and layout, and information security and personal privacy.

Perhaps even more important is establishing the length of time documents or data are available on a Web site and their subsequent retrieval from archival status through the Web site. OMB Web site management guidelines might address this issue. The continued availability of Web site documents or data, including retrieval from archival status through the Web site, is information provision consistent with the E-FOIA Amendments of 1996 and, increasingly, is information dissemination as we know it in the Information Age.

Notes

1. See Harold C. Relyea, "Dissemination of Government Information," in Dave Bogart, ed., *The Bowker Annual Library and Book Trade Almanac*, 41st edition, 1996 (R. R. Bowker, 1996), pp. 220–235.

2. Initially enacted in 1966, the Freedom of Information Act may be found at 5 U.S.C. 552; the Privacy Act, adopted in 1974, is located at 5 U.S.C. 552a.

3. 110 Stat. 3048, text incorporated in 5 U.S.C. 552 (2000 ed.).

4. See the Gillett Act of 1913, found at 5 U.S.C. 3107.

5. See *Congressional Record,* v. 145, July 21, 1999, pp. H6082–HH6089 (daily edition); 113 Stat. 207.

6. See, for example, 1 Stat. 68, 443, 519, 724; 2 Stat. 302; 3 Stat. 145, 439, 576.

7. 3 Stat. 140.

8. 9 Stat. 113.

9. 12 Stat. 117.

10. 9 Stat. 114.

11. 28 Stat. 601.

12. See 11 Stat. 379; 15 Stat. 292.

13. 28 Stat. 610.

14. See 3 Stat. 140; 11 Stat. 253; 38 Stat. 75; 76 Stat. 352; 44 U.S.C. 1901–1916.

15. 33 Stat. 584.

16. 42 Stat. 541.

17. John A. Fairlie, "Administrative Legislation," *Michigan Law Review,* v. 18, January 1920, p. 199.

18. Erwin N. Griswold, "Government in Ignorance of the Law—A Plea for Better Publication of Executive Legislation," *Harvard Law Review,* v. 48, December 1934, p. 199.

19. *United States* v. *Smith,* 292 U.S. 633 (1934), appeal dismissed on the motion of the appellant without consideration by the Court.

20. *Panama Refining Company* v. *Ryan,* 293 U.S. 388 (1935).

21. 49 Stat. 500.

22. 50 Stat. 304.

23. 80 Stat. 250; 5 U.S.C. 552.

24. 86 Stat. 770; 5 U.S.C. App.

25. 88 Stat. 1896; 5 U.S.C. 552a.

26. 90 Stat. 1241; 5 U.S.C. 552b.

27. 94 Stat. 2812; 44 U.S.C. 3501–3520.

28. 94 Stat. 2816–2817.

29. 94 Stat. 2819.

30. 100 Stat. 3341-336, 3341-338; due to an enrolling error (see 100 Stat. 3341-388 note), these provisions duplicate those at 100 Stat. 1783-336, 1783-338.

31. 109 Stat. 163–164.

32. See 109 Stat. 167–168, 171–175.

33. U.S. Congress, House Committee on Government Operations, *Electronic Collection and Dissemination of Information by Federal Agencies: A Policy Overview,* 99th Congress, 2nd session, H. Rept. 99-560 (Washington: GPO, 1986), p. 10.

34. 107 Stat. 112; 44 U.S.C. 4101–4104.

35. U.S. General Accounting Office, *Government Printing: Legal and Regulatory Framework Is Outdated for New Technological Environment,* GAO/NSIAD-94-157 (Washington: April 1994), pp. 2–3.

36. Office of the Vice President, *From Red Tape to Results: Creating a Government That Works Better & Costs Less, Report of the National Performance Review* (Washington: GPO, 1993), pp. 55–56.

37. *Weekly Compilation of Presidential Documents,* v. 30, July 29, 1994, pp. 1541–1542.

38. Bill McAllister, "Competition Sets GPO Into a Tide of Red Ink," *Washington Post,* Aug. 17, 1994, p. A17.

39. *Congressional Record,* v. 144, July 10, 1998, pp. S7953–S7955 (daily edition).

40. U.S. Congress, Senate Committee on Rules and Administration, *The Wendell H. Ford Government Publications Act of 1998,* hearings, 105th Congress, 2nd session, July 29 and Sept. 16, 1998 (Washington: GPO, 1998), pp. 1–49.

41. 110 Stat. 642-698; 110 Stat. 3009-393.

42. U.S. Congress, Senate Committee on Rules and Administration, *The Wendell H. Ford Government Publications Act of 1998,* pp. 72–73.

43. See U.S. Congress, Senate Committee on Rules and Administration, *Wendell H. Ford Government Publications Reform Act of 1998,* 105th Congress, 2nd session, S. Rept. 105-413 (Washington: GPO, 1998).

44. See *INS* v. *Chadha,* 462 U.S. 919(1983); the remedial powers of the JCP are prescribed at 44 U.S.C. 103.

45. Gabriel Kahn, "Thomas, Joint Committee on Printing's New Chairman, Wants to Abolish His Own Panel," *Roll Call,* Feb. 23, 1995, p. 10.

46. See U.S. Congress, House Committee on Appropriations, *Legislative Branch Appropriations Bill, 1996,* 104th Congress, 1st session, H. Rept. 104-141 (Washington: GPO, 1995), pp. 17–18; U.S. Congress, Senate Committee on Appropriations, *Legislative Branch Appropriations, 1996,* 104th Congress, 1st session, S. Rept. 104-114 (Washington: GPO, 1995), p. 28.

47. See U.S. Congress, House Committee of Conference, *Appropriations for the Legislative Branch for the Fiscal Year Ending September 30, 1996, and for Other Purposes,* 104th Congress, 1st session, H. Rept. 104-212 (Washington: GPO, 1995), p. 9; due to a larger budgetary dispute, the president vetoed this appropriations bill (H.R. 1854) on October 3, 1995; see *Weekly Compilation of Presidential Documents,* v. 31, Oct. 9, 1995, p. 1762; subsequently, Congress approved a legislative branch appropriations bill (H.R. 2492) identical to the earlier conference version.

48. 112 Stat. 2430, at 2440.

49. U.S. Congress, Joint Committee on Printing, letter from John Warner, Chairman, to Michael DiMario, Public Printer, Washington, D.C., Dec. 17, 1998 (copy in the possession of the author).

50. U.S. Congress, Conference Committees, *Making Appropriations for the Legislative Branch for the Fiscal Year Ending September 30, 2001, and for Other Purposes,* 106th Congress, 2nd session, H. Rept. 106-796 (Washington: GPO, 2000), pp. 19–20, 43.

51. U.S. Congress, House Committee on Appropriations, *Legislative Branch Appropriations Bill, 2001,* 106th Cong., 2nd sess., H. Rept. 106-635 (Washington: GPO, 2000), p. 22.

52. Ibid., pp. 27–28.

53. H. Rept. 106-796, p. 46.

54. 114 Stat. 2763.

55. See U.S. General Accounting Office, *Information Management: Electronic Dissemination of Government Publications*, GAO-01-428 (Washington: March 2001).

56. The report and related documents were available initially at the NCLIS Web site: http://www.nclis.gov/govt/assess/assess.html.

57. In mid-August 1999 the Secretary of Commerce announced his intention to close NTIS and transfer its holdings to the Library of Congress. Self-supporting through the public sale of scientific and technical reports sponsored by federal agencies, NTIS, according to the Secretary, was experiencing rapidly declining revenues due to the free availability of its salable information via the Internet.

58. U.S. National Commission on Libraries and Information Science, *A Comprehensive Assessment of Public Information Dissemination; First Draft* (Washington: Nov. 27, 2000), p. 6.

59. U.S. Commission on Federal Paperwork, *Confidentiality and Privacy: A Report of the Commission on Federal Paperwork* (Washington: July 29, 1977), p. 26.

60. American Society of Access Professionals, "The (b)(3) Project: Citations by Federal Agencies (1975–1982)" (Washington: American Society of Access Professionals, 1984); the FOIA exemption may be found at 5 U.S.C. 552(b)(3).

61. U.S. National Commission on Libraries and Information Science, *A Comprehensive Assessment of Public Information Dissemination; First Draft*, p. 33.

62. 5 U.S.C. 3107.

63. J. Timothy Sprehe, "NCLIS' Wasted Motions," *Federal Computer Week,* March 26, 2001, available at http://www.fcw.com/fcw/articles/2001/0326/pol-sprehe-03-26-01.asp.

64. William Jackson, "Government Gets a Collective F for Its IT Security," *Government Computer News,* Nov. 19, 2001, p. 12.

65. See Sue Anne Pressley and Justin Blum, "Hijackers May Have Accessed Computers at Public Libraries," *Washington Post,* Sept. 17, 2001, p. A4; David E. Rosenbaum, "Competing Principles Leave Some Professionals Debating Responsibility to Government," *New York Times,* Nov. 23, 2001, p. B7.

66. See Guy Gugliotta, "Agencies Scrub Web Sites of Sensitive Chemical Data," *Washington Post,* Oct. 4, 2001, p. A29; Dawn S. Onley, " . . . While Webmasters Pull Sensitive Information Off Web Sites," *Government Computer News,* Nov. 5, 2001, p. 10; Robin Toner, "Reconsidering Security, U.S. Clamps Down on Agency Web Sites," *New York Times,* Oct. 28, 2001, p. B4.

67. U.S. General Accounting Office, *Information Management: Progress in Implementing the 1996 Electronic Freedom of Information Act Amendments,* GAO-01-378 (Washington: March 2001), pp. 8, 12, 21, 23.

68. U.S. Office of the Attorney General, Memorandum for Heads of All Federal Departments and Agencies, "Freedom of Information Act," Washington, D.C., Oct. 12, 2001, available at http://www.usdoj.gov/04foia/011012.htm.

69. Peter Hernon, Robert E. Dugan, and John A. Shuler, *U.S. Government on the Web: Getting the Information You Need,* 2nd edition (Libraries Unlimited, 2001), p. 1, citing William Matthews, "Access Denied," *Federal Computer Week,* May 29, 2000, p. 21.

70. Walter Houser, "Isn't 110,000 Job Sites Too Much?" *Government Computer News,* Nov. 19, 2001, p. 22.

Copyright 2001:
Exploring the Implications of Technology

Robert L. Oakley

Director, Law Library, and Professor of Law
Georgetown University Law Center

In the years since the adoption of the WIPO treaty and the Digital Millennium Copyright Act (DMCA),[1] there has been a substantial increase in public awareness about copyright and intellectual property. Copyright, in fact, has been headline news as lawsuits have been initiated by some of today's hottest bands, largely because their young fans are taking advantage of new technologies to copy and distribute their recordings. These contrary actions have aroused both anger and support from the technologically savvy part of the population. As a result of this high-profile struggle, almost everyone is aware of the tension between content owners and the users of new technology.

These conflicts and the rapid pace of technological change are challenging the legal system to sort out the balance of rights among the interested parties in the new electronic environment. The Napster case, for example, concerning the free distribution of music over the Internet, was headline news. But even though the legal challenges eventually led to the demise of Napster as we knew it, other newer technologies have sprung up to take its place, including some that are even more powerful and support the distribution of movies as well as music. As a result, for now at least, the free distribution of entertainment materials over the World Wide Web continues largely unchecked. At the same time, content owners are imposing new technological controls on CDs, DVDs, and other new media to prevent just such copying and distribution. Yet the imposition of technological protection has generated some consumer backlash and resistance,[2] and in some ways it is beginning to seem as though this is now a competition between technologies in the context of a legal system that can't keep pace.

In large measure, of course, the legal system has sided with the content owners by banning the devices that allow a user to defeat a technological protection device, even for a legitimate purpose. Nonetheless, the situation remains unsettled, and 2001 was a year in which these issues began to be explored more fully in the legal system. Some of that exploration took place in Congress and the Copyright Office, but much of it took place in the courts, and this article will devote more space than usual to a consideration of those court cases.

Setting the Stage: Prohibition on Circumvention Takes Effect

As 2000 was winding down, the Copyright Office issued its ruling on circumvention of technological protection devices, permitting circumvention in only the narrowest of cases. With that ruling, DMCA took full effect, technological protection gained the protection of law, and it became a foregone conclusion that there would soon be a much wider deployment of such devices.

As background to the ruling of the Copyright Office, it should be remembered that when DMCA was passed there was concern that the increased use of technological protection measures would not only prevent unlawful uses but would also prevent lawful ones, such as fair use. Moreover, since the new systems could not lawfully be circumvented, they could also be used to protect material that was not protectable under copyright at all. In response to these concerns, the effective date of DMCA was delayed two years to allow the Copyright Office to study the matter and determine whether or not there were certain classes of works that ought to be exempted from the anticircumvention provision of the law in order to permit legitimate uses.

> The primary goal of the rulemaking proceeding is to assess whether the prevalence of these technological protections, with respect to particular categories of copyrighted materials, is diminishing the ability of individuals to use these works in ways that are otherwise lawful.[3]

In its submission to the Copyright Office on this rulemaking, the library community urged a broad exemption in support of library uses and preservation. The Copyright Office rejected that approach, however, saying that a definition based on uses does not define a particular class of copyrighted work.[4] Two specific issues raised by the library community were cases where a technological protection measure was being used to protect information that might not qualify for copyright—such as facts or government documents—and cases where the information was only available from a single source, so that a user could not go to a traditional print source in a library to get the information. Again, the Copyright Office rejected these concerns, saying that they did not define particular classes of works and that there had not been a sufficient showing of the need for an exemption.

Instead, the Copyright Office permitted an exemption in only two of the narrowest possible cases: cases where the technological protection measure was not functioning properly and was denying access even to authorized users, and cases where decryption was necessary to gain access to a list of Web sites blocked by filtering software. The first was seen as necessary to allow users access to information for which they had already been authorized. The second was appropriate both for people to understand what particular filtering programs did and for the purpose of reviewing that software.

Except for those two exceptionally narrow exemptions, the Copyright Office rejected all other claims, and the ban on circumvention of technological protection measures went into effect. The Copyright Office will conduct another similar review in 2003.

Copyright Office Rejects Amendments to Provisions Related to First Sale and Incidental and Backup Copying

Shortly after the report on exemptions to the ban on circumvention was issued, the Copyright Office held a hearing on another study, this time on the effect of DMCA on the First Sale Doctrine (which allows libraries and others to lend, sell, or otherwise dispose of works that they have lawfully acquired) and on Section 117 of DMCA, which permits the making of copies incidental to the use of the work and the making of backup copies. Both of these provisions are important to libraries and to individual users, and when DMCA was passed there was a concern that technological protection devices could be used to defeat them. If a library cannot buy and lend an electronic book, for example, then that format is peremptorily eliminated from the library's collection. Similarly, such technology could prevent individuals from lending CDs or movies to one another. If incidental and backup copies cannot be made, then a user may lose software and other data he or she has paid for. It may also become difficult to migrate software from one computer to another when upgrading hardware.

The Copyright Office agreed that there could be problems such as these. However, it also decided that there had not been a sufficient demonstration that these were actually significant problems in the real world. As a consequence, the report concludes that although such results are possible, nonetheless, with one exception, it was premature to decide that these were, in fact, problems in need of a solution. With that one exception, therefore, the Copyright Office declined to make recommendations for amendments to Sections 109 and 117,[5] leaving libraries and others uncertain about the operation of these sections in the new environment and subject to the whims of whatever technological protection measures they may encounter.

The one area where the Copyright Office did make a legislative recommendation was to support the use of streaming audio over the Web. In that case, there is a demonstrable need for buffer copies to be made in order to keep the music smooth and uninterrupted. Although the report found that fair use probably would apply in such a circumstance, the Copyright Office also felt that fair use was too uncertain to permit the development of an economically sound Web-based music distribution system. As a consequence, the Copyright Office proposed a narrowly constructed amendment to remove the uncertainty.

Congress scheduled hearings on this report for the fall of 2001, but the terrorist attacks of September 11 caused them to be postponed. When the hearings are eventually held in 2002, the library community will, no doubt, stress that these are real-world problems, and need a solution. They are likely to say that with its report, the Copyright Office missed an important opportunity to address some of the complex and interesting questions created by the development of new technology.

Court Decisions Continue Consideration of Rights in the Digital Environment

Many of the most interesting developments in copyright law in 2001 occurred in the context of litigation as the courts continued to explore the length of the copyright term, the balance of rights between authors and publishers, the impact of DMCA, and the development of new technologies for the distribution of information over the Internet.

Term Extension

Eldred v. *Ashcroft*

In 1998 Congress resolved a long-fought battle by extending the term of copyright by another 20 years, from life of the author plus 50 years to life of the author plus 70 years. This law effectively put a 20-year moratorium on any new works coming into the public domain, thus preventing today's creators from building upon the works of their predecessors for the creation of new works. This extra-long copyright term is particularly problematic now, since many of today's innovators are involved in the creation of digital multimedia projects and would like to be able to incorporate some of those earlier works into their new compilations. The law did contain a limited exemption for libraries, but many librarians have found the exemption to be confusing and unworkable.

Eric Eldred and several other plaintiffs filed suit against the Attorney General of the United States to obtain a declaration that the term extension act is unconstitutional, violating both the First Amendment and the copyright clause of the Constitution. Among the plaintiffs were a nonprofit association that distributes free electronic versions of books in the public domain over the Internet; a company that reprints rare, out-of-print books that have entered the public domain; a vendor of sheet music and a choir director, who respectively sell and purchase music that is relatively inexpensive because it is in the public domain; and a company that preserves and restores old films.

The District Court ruled in favor of the government and dismissed the case. Plaintiffs appealed, repeating their constitutional claims before the Court of Appeals. On July 13, the Court of Appeals for the D.C. Circuit affirmed the lower court decision, holding that neither the First Amendment nor the "limited times" provision of the copyright clause of the Constitution created a barrier to the extension of the term in this case.[6] A petition for rehearing *en banc* was denied, and the case appeared to be over.

In a very interesting development, however, just as this article was being completed, the Supreme Court agreed to review the case. The *New York Times* reported that this challenge to the term extension act, "which many had regarded as a fanciful academic exercise, suddenly looked very different once the Supreme Court declared its interest."[7] Without any doubt, the library community and many others will file amicus briefs with the court, arguing that the extension of the copyright term should not be upheld. The oral argument will not be held until at least fall 2002, so it is likely to be more than a year before it is finally resolved.

Rights of Authors and Publishers

New York Times v. *Tasini*

Jonathan Tasini is a freelance writer who took a case to the Supreme Court that could have far-reaching implications for libraries. Tasini and the other plaintiffs in the case wrote articles that were originally published in the *New York Times, Newsday,* and *Time.* Later, when those publications were added to LexisNexis and other databases, Tasini's articles were included as part of the collection. Tasini objected, saying that although he had been compensated for the use of the article in the print publication, he had not been compensated for its republication in a new form with a new market.

The publishers countered, saying that under the Copyright Act (Section 201(c)), they had the right to republish the collective work. They reasoned that this republication was no different from republishing the work on microfilm, and no one had ever objected to that.

The library community found this to be a very difficult case and could see arguments on both sides. On the one hand, they felt that the purpose of copyright was to protect authors, and if new markets were being opened, the authors should share in those. On the other hand, the libraries could also understand the analogy to microfilm, and many libraries were now relying on the online databases instead of microfilm for access to the historical record. A decision that either threatened the integrity of the database or raised its cost would be a problem for libraries. In the early stages of the case, the major library associations all remained neutral. When it reached the Supreme Court, however, two of them— the American Library Association and the Association of Research Libraries— decided to weigh in on behalf of authors. The other library associations continued to see both sides and maintained their posture of neutrality.

The District Court ruled in favor of the publishers, finding that since all the articles were included in the database, and since the issue and page numbers were preserved, the original selection and organization remained evident, even in the online version. The authors appealed, and the Second Circuit reversed, saying that databases were not covered by Section 201(c) in the same way that microfilm is covered. The Second Circuit found that since the articles were individually retrievable in the online database, it amounted to the sale of individual articles, rather than the sale of a true collective work. This the publishers do not have the right to do under the Copyright Act.

In a ruling on June 25, 2001, the Supreme Court agreed with the Second Circuit.[8] The court looked closely at the way the information in the database was stored, retrieved, and presented, and they found significant differences between the database version and the version as originally published, differences that did not apply to the microfilm version. The court was particularly swayed by the fact that in two of the databases at issue, the article did not preserve even the original graphics or layout, let alone the other surrounding material. One of the databases presented an image of the article but did not show the other material on the same page. This lack of the original context persuaded the court that the articles were being presented in isolation, not as part of a collective work, as required by the statute. Microfilm, of course, presents the work exactly as it appeared in the original publication.[9] Two justices dissented, finding that the complete work was preserved, since the entire editorial content—together with appropriate source and page references—is stored in the database. Nonetheless, the court finally ruled in favor of Tasini and against the publishers.

As the case progressed through the courts, the publishers sent a warning about the consequences of a final ruling for Tasini. They said that it would be cost prohibitive for them to seek out all their freelance authors and negotiate a new arrangement for the inclusion of those articles in the online database. Publishers said that because of this they would be forced to remove all of the implicated articles from the database. Tasini indicated that he believed that this could be handled more easily than they had suggested, and the court indicated that there were other possibilities for collective agreements or blanket licensing that would make such an impact on the database unnecessary. Nonetheless, almost immediately after the decision was handed down, articles reportedly began to be removed from the online databases and from some microfilm collections as well. On January 25, 2002, the *Chronicle of Higher Education* reported that there had been massive redactions to the databases. The *New York Times* pulled 100,000 articles but restored 15,000 of them after negotiating with authors. They say they hope to get all of them back online eventually, but it's not clear when that will be or what it will take to accomplish it. On the other hand, the Knight Ridder papers have purged more than 800,000 articles and have no plans to restore them. A spokesman said: "We're not going to be renegotiating any past work."[10] Although the final tally is not known, because of these changes to the content of the online databases, the Tasini decision will have a major impact on libraries and their users.

National Geographic Society v. Jerry Greenberg and Idaz Greenberg

Shortly before *Tasini* was handed down by the Supreme Court, a related case was decided in Florida. The new case, however, involved freelance photographers and *National Geographic* magazine. More importantly, it involved a CD-ROM that presented the issues of the magazine in an image-based format exactly as they had been published originally. It included not only the text of the articles, but also the photographs and even the ads in the same order they appeared in the magazine. For all practical purposes, it was exactly like the microfilm, except it was on a computer disk. A search engine was added to permit a user to find particular articles, and the CD-ROM started up with a changing collage of photographs, one of which was taken by one of the plaintiffs in the case. On its face, this case appears to be different from *Tasini,* since unlike *Tasini,* the *National Geographic* CD shows the articles in their original context.

Despite this important difference, the Court of Appeals for the 11th Circuit followed the Second Circuit opinion in *Tasini* and ruled against *National Geographic.*[11] In this case, however, the court found that the inclusion of a computer program to make the data available made this a new, and therefore infringing, work, not just a revision of the original.

The library community was not divided on this case at all and joined in an amicus brief to support the appeal to the Supreme Court. The library community noted that the Copyright Act is medium-neutral, and they asked the court to ensure that publishers could take advantage of new technologies to preserve and distribute creative works to the public. Regrettably, but not surprisingly, the court declined to hear the case.

Taken together, the *Tasini* case and the *National Geographic* case represent something of a setback to the efforts to use digital technologies to preserve and distribute information to the public. Following those cases, the leaders of projects like JStor, Project Muse, Hein Online, and others, need to assure themselves that the authors of all the articles in all the publications they are making available have granted sufficient rights in their work to allow the digital conversion and distribution to occur. Without that assurance, they are exposing themselves to further challenges.

Random House, Inc. v. RosettaBooks, LLC

Is an e-book a book? Shortly after *Tasini* and *National Geographic* were decided, another case dealt with the respective rights of authors and publishers, this time in the context of e-books. In this case, RosettaBooks, an e-book publisher, made arrangements with several authors, including William Styron, Kurt Vonnegut, and Robert Parker, to publish some of their works, including such important titles as *Sophie's Choice, The Confessions of Nat Turner,* and *Slaughterhouse Five,* in an e-book format. Believing they had the exclusive publication rights to those works, Random House sought a preliminary injunction to prevent their electronic publication.

The contract between the authors and Random House gave the publisher "the right to 'print, publish, and sell the work[s] in book form.'"[12] RosettaBooks responded that the rights transferred by the authors to Random House did not include the electronic rights. "Relying on the language of the contracts and basic principles of contract interpretation, the court [found] that the right to 'print, publish, and sell the work[s] in book form' . . . [did] not include the right to publish the works in the format that has come to be known as the e-book."[13] In reaching this conclusion, the court found that e-books contain a number of features that are not found in traditional books, such as the ability to search for specific words, to highlight passages of text, to change the font size, to obtain a definition or pronunciation of a word, or to include hyperlinks between various parts of the work. They also permit a user to type in electronic notes that can be automatically indexed, sorted, and filed.

These special features of e-books, together with the specific language of the contracts, caused the court to conclude that the authors' granting Random House the right to publish their works "in book form" did not include the right to publish them in e-book form. As a result, the court denied the request from Random House for a preliminary injunction. The decision has been appealed to the Second Circuit.

Distribution of Music and Other Online Entertainment

Using innovative peer-to-peer sharing technologies, Napster wrought a revolution in the mechanisms for the free distribution of music over the Web. This technology allowed individual users who stored music on their computer to share that music with anyone else on the Internet who was also a Napster user. In a suit that progressed through the courts in 2000, the judge rejected an argument of fair use and ordered the system to be shut down immediately or find a way to prevent its users from trading any music copyrighted by the 18 record companies suing for copyright infringement.[14]

Napster appealed to the Ninth Circuit, but in a decision on February 12, 2001, the appeals court agreed with the court below that Napster was liable for vicarious and contributory copyright infringement based on the direct infringements of its users.[15] The court did say, though, that the injunction granted was too broad because Napster needed notice of specific infringing files and an opportunity to remove them. Within a few weeks, the lower court issued a new order, giving Napster 72 hours to block specific song titles that the record companies identified as copyrighted.

After a period of time in which Napster tried unsuccessfully to block the files on which it had received notice, the judge ordered the service shut down until it could comply. Meanwhile, Napster entered into settlement talks with individual artists and with the recording industry. On September 24, a $26 million settlement was announced. Although Napster still faced a number of additional proceedings, nonetheless, at about the same time the settlement was announced,

Napster also announced that henceforth it would be working with the music industry and paying royalties to the artists. The "New Napster" would provide a mechanism both for the distribution of music over the Internet and for the payment of royalties. According to the Napster Web site,[16] the new Napster would be launched early in 2002 with a very different look and feel from the old version. In so doing, of course, it may lose the loyalty of the millions of dedicated Napster users from the Old Napster era.

In the meantime, other services have sprung up for the free distribution of music and movies over the Web. Each of these services creates new problems for the entertainment industry, and the industry is moving vigorously to shut them down. Nonetheless, the amount of entertainment material distributed free over the Web continues at unprecedented levels.

Free Speech Issues Raised Under DMCA

Not only does DMCA prohibit the circumvention of technological protection measures, it also provides that "no person shall make, import, or traffic in any technology that is primarily designed for circumventing such technological access controls."[17] This section covers both hardware and software and is designed to make it both difficult and unlawful for people to acquire the means to decrypt a work. A series of cases have begun to explore the limits of this language and its relationship to the First Amendment.

Academic Freedom: *Felton* v. *RIAA*

Edward Felton is a professor at Princeton University who did research into copy-protection systems and uncovered some of their weaknesses. He planned to present the results of his research at an academic conference, but when word of what he was doing got out, the Recording Industry Association of America (RIAA) sent a letter allegedly threatening litigation if he published or otherwise made that information available. Although he was not, himself, making any circumvention technology, RIAA apparently felt that by exposing the weaknesses of their systems he would facilitate the creation of such devices by others. Upon receiving the letter from RIAA, Felton withdrew his paper and brought an action for a declaratory judgment that action under DMCA could not be taken against him for publishing research that revealed the weaknesses of copy protection technologies.[18]

RIAA's action generated an outcry from the academic and scientific communities, who felt that it created a substantial chilling effect on academic freedom. RIAA eventually backed down, saying that it had not intended to interfere with Felton's presentation. It moved to dismiss the case, saying there was no longer any controversy. In November the motion was granted and the case was dismissed, leaving unresolved the important question Felton had raised.

Posting Decryption Information on a Web Site: *Universal City Studios Inc.* v. *Corley*

Most DVD movies are encrypted using a technology known as CSS. Once that system was released, defendants developed a means, DeCSS, to break through the encryption system, which they made available on their Web site. Use of DeCSS would allow CSS-protected motion pictures to be copied and played on devices that lack the licensed decryption technology. The movie studios sued, and in a lengthy opinion the District Court granted an injunction directing the removal of the code from the Web.[19]

Defendants appealed, and the Second Circuit Court of Appeals upheld the earlier decision in a ruling handed down on November 28, 2001.[20] Defendants argued that the prohibition was a violation of their free-speech rights and that it effectively eliminated their fair-use rights. The court rejected both arguments.

The court reasoned that although computer code is protected speech, it is different from "pure speech":

> Unlike a blueprint or a recipe, which cannot yield any functional result without human comprehension of its content, human decision-making, and human action, computer code can instantly cause a computer to accomplish tasks and instantly render the results of those tasks available throughout the world via the Internet. These realities of what code is . . . require a First Amendment analysis that treats code as combining nonspeech and speech elements, i.e., functional and expressive elements.[21]

The court then concluded that this distinction justified the injunction despite the First Amendment, because the act concerns the capacity to instruct a computer to decrypt CSS, a functional capacity that is not within the meaning of the First Amendment. The court also rejected the fair-use claim, saying that although fair use was a part of the Copyright Act, "We know of no authority for the proposition that fair use . . . guarantees copying by the optimum method or in the identical format of the original."

Criminal Responsibility: *U.S.* v. *Elcom and Sklyarov*

In another controversial case, 26-year-old Dmitry Sklyarov, a Russian programmer and Ph.D. student, was arrested and jailed following a hackers conference in Las Vegas for trafficking in a technology that was primarily designed to circumvent the Adobe Acrobat eBook Reader. An indictment against Sklyarov and his company, Elcom, followed on August 28. This case was the first criminal indictment under DMCA and again caused significant concern among the networking community. Although Adobe decided to withdraw its support for the criminal complaint, the charges against Sklyarov were not dropped. As this article was being completed, the Electronic Frontier Foundation was pressing forward with a motion to dismiss.

Legislative Issues Make Little Progress

There was little progress on the legislative agenda in 2001. Those issues that were moving through were largely derailed by the events of September 11, which preoccupied Congress in the fall, and the Enron scandal, which took up a great deal of legislative time in early 2002.

The TEACH Act

The Technology, Education, and Copyright Harmonization (TEACH) Act would amend a provision (17 U.S.C. Sec. 110(2)) of the copyright law to allow performances and displays of copyrighted works in digital distance education. Existing law has a limited exemption for transmissions into classroom settings but not beyond. This proposal would make two changes to the existing law. First, it would broaden the area of potential transmission by removing the requirement that the transmission be made to classrooms. This change would allow distance education over computer networks to be received in the home or office or library. Second, the bill expands the scope of what may be transmitted to include "reasonable and limited portions" of movies, videotapes, or performances of plays. Previously, the privilege was extended only to nondramatic literary or musical works, a serious limitation on the type of material that could be used.

The bill requires that such transmissions be made only from copies of a work that have been lawfully acquired and limits the transmissions to those that are part of a mediated instructional experience analogous to what would be used in a live classroom setting. It also requires the use of technological measures to prevent retention of the work by recipients for longer than the class session and to prevent unauthorized further transmission or copying. It is a compromise bill ultimately supported by both the education and publisher communities.

The TEACH Act emerged from the recommendations of the Copyright Office in a study mandated by DMCA and completed in 1999. It was introduced as S. 487 by Senators Orrin Hatch (R-Utah) and Patrick Leahy (D-Vt.) on March 7, 2001, and passed the Senate on June 7. A similar bill was introduced in the House as H.R. 2100 by Representative Rick Boucher (D-Va.). It was approved by the House Subcommittee on Courts, the Internet and Intellectual Property on July 11 but never reported out for action by the full House.

Database Protection

Database protection continues to be stalled in the House.[22] It was the subject of intense negotiations through the first eight months of the year, and resolution—if not agreement—appeared to be imminent by the end of August. The events of September 11, however, pushed this issue to the back burner, and as of this writing it had not been revived.

UCITA

The Uniform Computer Information Transactions Act (UCITA) is a proposal for state legislation from the National Conference of Commissioners on Uniform State Laws. Technically, it is not a copyright law at all but a law that would govern contracts or licenses for information and software. Nonetheless, it has aroused concern from consumer groups for many of its provisions and from libraries because of the ability it would create for licensors of information to limit a user's rights under copyright by means of a shrink-wrap or click-on license.

The concern about this legislation has been widespread, and despite relatively quick passage in Maryland and Virginia, no other state has passed it. Most of those states that have looked at it have either tabled it or referred it for further study. In 2001 the American Bar Association (ABA) appointed a special committee to review the proposal and make recommendations. That committee met with some members of the drafting committee (known as the UCITA Standby Committee) and other interested parties in November. Shortly thereafter, the drafting committee adopted some further amendments to UCITA, but the ABA committee issued a report that declined to endorse the proposal.

> . . . the Working Committee is concerned that UCITA, as presently drafted, would not achieve the principle objective that a uniform law is expected to achieve, namely, the establishment of a high level of clarity and certainty in a particular area of the law. To the contrary, the Working Group is concerned that if UCITA, in its present form, goes forward, there would be considerable controversy and litigation over what its various "rules" really mean . . . the Working Group believes that UCITA should be redrafted . . . [23]

As of this writing, it did not appear that adoption of UCITA had a lot of forward momentum.

International Issues Raise Some New Concerns

Over the last several years, international issues have become more prominent in copyright discussions as copyright law has begun to evolve from a system of national legislation, protecting local authors within a system of national policies, into an instrument of international trade. These trends have led directly to such issues as term extension, database protection, and the Digital Millennium Copyright Act. As a consequence, it behooves us now to stay aware of issues developing among the important international organizations.

WTO Declares a Provision of the U.S. Copyright Act Inconsistent with International Treaties

In a seminal case, the World Trade Organization (WTO) in 2000 reviewed one of the exceptions granted under the United States Copyright Act and found it to be inconsistent with international copyright treaties. Although this decision was handed down in the year prior to the year of coverage of this report, it has not previously been reported in these pages, and since it may be of singular importance in the future, it is being included in this report for 2001.

Section 110(5) of the Copyright Act provides an exemption for the owners of small restaurants or bars to play a radio or TV in their place of business, but not for larger establishments that install commercial sound systems and can afford to subscribe to a commercial background music service. The challenge to this provision was brought under the Berne Convention and the TRIPS agreement. Article 11bis(1) of the Berne Convention provides in relevant part that:

> Authors of literary and artistic works shall enjoy the exclusive right of authorizing:
> (iii) the public communication by loudspeaker or any other analogous instrument transmitting, by signs, sounds or images, the broadcast of the work.

The United States argued that despite this language in the treaty, this particular situation fell under a recognized doctrine of "minor exceptions." WTO disagreed and concluded that

> Section 110(5) of the U.S. Copyright Act contains exceptions that allow use of protected works without an authorization by the right holder and without charge. Whether these excep-

tions meet the United States' obligations under the TRIPS Agreement has to be examined by applying Article 13 of the TRIPS Agreement.[24]

Among other things, Article 13 of the TRIPS agreement provides that limitations on the rights of copyright owners:

(1) be confined to certain special cases, (2) do not conflict with a normal exploitation of the work, and (3) do not unreasonably prejudice the legitimate interests of the rights holder.[25]

After a lengthy analysis, WTO concluded that this particular exemption did not meet this test and declared it to be in conflict with both Berne and TRIPS. As a consequence of this decision, the issue has been referred back to the United States for the U.S. Congress to take action to remedy the conflict. No action on this issue had been taken as of this writing.

As may be apparent, this case does not directly affect libraries. However, it could have enormous significance in the future, since it signals a willingness on the part of WTO to look at the individual copyright exemptions provided in U.S. law. If the standard being applied is that a given exemption should "not interfere with the normal exploitation of a work," how would WTO respond to challenges to the United States' fair-use provision, which is somewhat different from the more typical "fair dealing" provision of other countries? How would it look at the first-sale doctrine, which permits free library circulations? The interlibrary loan provisions? And so on. There is nothing happening now with WTO and libraries, but this case concerning music in restaurants and bars could be an important precursor of things to come.

IFLA Adopts Positions on Copyright in the Digital Environment and on Licensing

The International Federation of Library Associations and Institutions (IFLA) Copyright and Other Legal Matters Committee developed policies on Copyright in the Digital Environment[26] and on Licensing.[27] Both of these policies were adopted by the IFLA Executive Board and published in time for the IFLA General Conference in 2001.

The IFLA statement on copyright indicates that IFLA supports a copyright system that supports the needs of library patrons to gain access to copyrighted works in addition to respecting the needs of copyright owners to obtain a fair economic return on their intellectual property. But, IFLA says, "overprotection of copyright could threaten democratic traditions and impact on social justice principles by unreasonably restricting access to information and knowledge." Further, it indicates that "digital is not different." IFLA is concerned that with greater enforcement in the digital environment, "there is a danger that only those who can afford to pay will be able to take advantage of the benefits of the Information Society." Some of the trends highlighted earlier in this report suggest that this is a real danger.

The document on licensing is a valuable reference point for all librarians involved in licensing arrangements on behalf of their libraries. It sets out a series of 32 principles of which librarians should be cognizant when they are involved in negotiations.

Looking Forward

There are many copyright issues remaining to be resolved in 2002 and beyond. The impact of the Digital Millennium Copyright Act continues to be felt and explored in the courts. There is also some evidence of consumer backlash against technological protection devices, so it remains to be seen how the marketplace will respond. The Supreme Court will deal with term extension, but the case will probably not be resolved until 2003. Database protection and UCITA will continue to be issues as well, until they are either passed in some form or die. In the meantime, there continue to be developments internationally, particularly with regard to database protection and the public lending right, that librarians should remain aware of. This is a particularly important time in the development of copyright law, as society works through the difficult and often conflicting areas of balancing, in the digital environment, a creator's rights to benefit from his creation against a user's rights for access to information. As the law continues to evolve, librarians need to remain vigilant and attentive to these issues.

Notes

1. For a discussion of WIPO and the Digital Millennium Copyright Act, see "Copyright 1996: Fleshing Out the Issues," by Robert L. Oakley, *Bowker Annual Library and Book Trade Almanac,* 1997, 229 at 236 et seq., and "Copyright 1998: Recalibrating the Balance," by Robert L. Oakley, *Bowker Annual Library and Book Trade Almanac,* 1999, 282 at 284 et seq.

2. "Because the lawyers hate SONICblue's new Replay TV 4000-series digital video recorder, I was predisposed to like it . . . And, unless you are a broadcast-industry lawyer or TV advertiser, you'll probably like it too . . . Let's hope the lawyers don't kill it." "TV Made Better," *Fortune* January 21, 2002, at 125.

3. Report of the Commerce Committee on the Digital Millennium Copyright Act, H.Rpt. 105-551, Part 2, p. 37.

4. 65 Fed. Reg. 64556 at 64562 and 64571-64572 (2000).

5. *DMCA Section 104 Report: A Report of the Register of Copyrights Pursuant to Section 104 of the Digital Millennium Copyright Act.* U.S. Copyright Office, August 2001.

6. *Eldred* v. *Ashcroft,* 239 F. 3d 372, 380 (February 16, 2001), rehearing denied 255 F.3d 849 (July 13, 2001).

7. "Justices to Review Copyright Extension, *New York Times,* February 20, 2002, p. C1 et seq.

8. *New York Times Co., Inc. et al.* v. *Tasini et al.,* 533 U.S. 483; 121 S. Ct. 2381; 150 L. Ed. 2d 500; 2001 U.S. (2001).

9. Ibid.

10. "Once-Trustworthy Newspaper Databases Have Become Unreliable and Frustrating," *Chronicle of Higher Education,* January 25, 2002, A29 at A30.

11. *Greenberg* v. *National Geographic Society,* 244 F. 3d 1267 (11th Cir. 2001).

12. *Random House, Inc.* v. *RosettaBooks, LLC,* 150 F. Supp. 2d 613 (USDC SDNY, 2001).

13. Ibid.

14. *A&M Records, Inc.* v. *Napster, Inc.,* 114 F. Supp. 2d 896 (August 10, 2000).

15. *A&M Records, Inc.* v. *Napster, Inc.,* 239 F. 3d 1004 (February 12, 2001).

16. See http://www.napster.com.

17. 17 USC 1201(a)(2).

18. 62 *BNA Patent Trademark and Copyright Journal* 411 (August 31, 2001).

19. *Universal City Studios, Inc.* v. *Reimerdes,* 111 F. Supp.2d 294 (2000) and 111 F. Supp.2d 346 (2000).

20. See generally *Universal City Studios, Inc.* v. *Corley,* 273 F. 3d 429 (November 28, 2001).

21. Ibid. at 451.

22. For more background see Oakley, "Copyright 1998: Recalibrating the Balance" nt. 1, supra., at 290.

23. American Bar Association Working Group Report on the Uniform Computer Information Transactions Act ("UCITA"), http://www.abanet.org/leadership/ucita.pdf, pp. 8–9 (January 30, 2002).

24. See World Trade Organization, United States—Section 110(5) of the U.S. Copyright Act, Report of the Panel, Document No. WT/DS160/R at http://www.wto.org (June 15, 2000).

25. Ibid.

26. See http://www.ifla.org/III/clm/p1/pos-dig.htm

27. See http://www.ifla.org/V/ebpb/copy.htm

Part 2
Legislation, Funding, and Grants

Legislation

Legislation and Regulations Affecting Libraries in 2001

Emily Sheketoff

Executive Director, Washington Office, American Library Association

Mary R. Costabile

Associate Director, Washington Office, American Library Association

The year 2001 began with optimism in the first blush of a new administration. At the outset, President Bush signaled that he intended to finish the Elementary and Secondary Education Act (ESEA) reauthorization and presented to Congress the No Child Left Behind draft bill. He further outlined a plan for a major tax-cut proposal. The budget resolution that Congress passed in the spring outlined a conservative approach to spending for the year.

By August recess, Congress had passed the tax-cut legislation and was well on the way to finishing appropriations bills. The major ESEA reauthorization bills, H.R. 1 and S. 1, had been passed by House and Senate and sent to a conference committee to work out the differences. The first meeting of that committee had been held in July.

The tragic events of September 11 changed the nation's priorities and created a whole new agenda for Congress that included increased expenditures for defense and war, an airline emergency-relief package, and "homeland security" measures. The anthrax virus found in the U.S. mail and in House and Senate offices required the closure of congressional offices and sent many Senate staff to off-site locations where they conducted business without key materials left behind in the Hart Senate Office Building and other House office buildings. As a result of September 11 and succeeding events, the USA Patriot Act (P.L. 107-56) was speedily passed in late October.

Congress managed to complete and pass the major education bill, H.R. 1, and finish all appropriations bills by the December 21 adjournment date. The president signed remaining bills in January.

Meanwhile, the slightly rosy economic picture of the spring had become a full recession, with the president and Congress ending the year discussing needed stimulus packages but finding no common ground for legislation.

Members of the American Library Association staff who contributed to this article included Lynne Bradley, director, Office of Government Relations; Patrice McDermott, assistant director; Miriam Nisbet, legislative counsel; and Claudette Tennant, Internet policy specialist, Office of Information Technology Policy.

Funding

The Bush administration's fiscal year (FY) 2002 budget request included an approximately 4.2 percent increase in discretionary spending. But by year's end, with much attention focused on the reauthorization of the massive ESEA, pressure from authorizers forced the numbers up to a new high in spending for education—$48.9 billion, a $6.7 billion increase over the previous year. Appropriators waited until the week after H.R. 1, the No Child Left Behind bill, was passed to complete the FY 2002 Labor, Health and Human Services, and Education Appropriations bill.

Both House and Senate had funded the Library Services and Technology Act (LSTA) at the same level, $168,078,000, but the conference on the FY 2002 Labor, Health and Human Services, and Education Appropriations bill funded LSTA at $197,602,000 and included a large number of set-asides.

ESEA Title VI has been changed to a new Title, Title V, which offers many new choices for the block grant but still includes library and instructional materials as one of the choices. However, the Reed school library amendment in H.R.1, the Literacy Through School Libraries program (Title I, Part B, Subpart 4, sec. 1251), authorizes funding for school library media resources at the $250 million level for FY 2002, and "such sums" for the next four years. This will be administered as a competitive grant program through the Department of Education until funding reaches $100 million, when the program is to become a state formula grant program.

Appropriators funded the Literacy Through School Libraries line item at $12.5 million for FY 2002. This is the first time since the original Title II school library program in 1965 that both legislation and funding have been dedicated specifically to school library resources.

The Federal Depository Library Program (FDLP) and the Government Printing Office were funded at the higher of the two levels in House and Senate—$29,639,000 for the Superintendent of Documents. The previous year's budget cuts adversely affected the ability of FDLP to provide services (no-fee public access to government information is ensured through the operations of FDLP).

The Legislative Branch Appropriations bill would allow $452 million for the Library of Congress, including $81 million for the Congressional Research Service (CRS).

The National Commission on Libraries and Information Science (NCLIS) was funded at $1 million. Since its establishment in 1970 as an independent agency within the executive branch, NCLIS has carried out its founding purpose to "advise the President and the Congress on the implementation of national policy" by holding hearings, issuing reports and studies, and assessing the library and informational needs of the nation. Funding for NCLIS in FY 2001 was $1.5 million.

Funding for the National Endowment for the Arts (NEA) and the National Endowment for the Humanities (NEH) was increased to $115.2 million and $124.5 million, respectively, and by year's end, Congress had approved new heads for the two agencies. Michael Hammond, dean of the Shepherd School of Music at Rice University, became NEA chair, while Bruce Cole, an art historian, was named chair of NEH.

Table 1 / Funding for Federal Library and Related Programs, FY 2002
(amounts in thousands)

	FY 2001	Final FY 2002
GPO Superintendent of Documents	27,954	29,639
Library of Congress	547,247*	452,000
Library Services and Technology Act	207,219	197,602
National Agricultural Library	20,400	20,000
National Commission on Libraries and Information Science	1,495	1,000
National Library of Medicine (includes MLAA)	246,801	277,658
Library-Related Programs (reflects changes in programs because of ESEA reauthorization)		
Department of Education		
Adult Education and Literacy	560,000	591,060
ESEA Title I, Education for Disadvantaged	9,664,000	10,350,000
ESEA Title I-B, Even Start	250,000	200,000
Improving Teacher Quality State Grants	n.a.	2,850,000
ESEA Title II-B, Eisenhower Professional Development (see Improving Teacher Quality State Grants)	485,000	n.a.
ESEA Title II-D, Enhancing Education Through Technology, State and Local Grants	872,096	700,500
Part A: Technology Literacy (Consolidated) Challenge	450,000	n.a.
Part B: Star Schools**	59,318	28
ESEA Title VI, Innovative education program strategies (State Grants) **	385,000	385,000†
ESEA Title X-I, 21st Century Community Learning Centers	845,600	1,000,000
Special Education (IDEA) State Grants	6,340,000	8,335,533
Educational Research	185,567	121,817
Educational Statistics	80,000	85,000
Educational Assessment	40,000	111,000
HEA Title III, Institutional Development	392,500	438,625
HEA Title IV-C, College Work-Study	1,011,000	1,011,000
HEA Title VI, International Education	78,022	98,500
HEA Title X-A, Postsecondary Education Improvement Fund	146,687	180,922
Inexpensive Book Distribution (RIF)	23,000	25,000
Reading Excellence Act	286,000	n.a.
Reading First State Grants §	n.a.	900,000,000
Literacy Through School Libraries §	n.a.	12,500,000
IMLS Museum Grants	24,907	26,899
NTIA Information Infrastructure Grants (TOP)	45,500	15,503
National Archives and Records Administration	209,393	244,247
National Endowment for the Arts	102,656	115,234
National Endowment for the Humanities	115,656	124,504
National Historical Publications and Records Commission	6,450	6,436

* The budget request adds $35.8 million in authority to use receipts.
**Now Title V in new ESEA.
† Consolidated into a block grant with a number of other programs.
§ New program in ESEA reauthorization

ESEA Reauthorization (P.L. 107-110)

The Bush administration began activities for the Elementary and Secondary Education Act by forwarding a draft bill titled No Child Left Behind to Congress. The bill included Reading First and Early Reading First initiatives and compressed many of the programs in this major education bill into large block grants. The House bill, H.R. 1, was introduced on March 22 and introduction of the Senate version followed on March 28. In the Senate, floor action took place throughout May and into June, and on May 16 the Reed school library amendment was added to the bill by a vote of 69-30.

On May 24 Sen. Jim Jeffords of Vermont changed his party affiliation from Republican to Independent, giving Democrats the Senate majority. Jeffords's party switch resulted in changes in the chairmanships and majority membership numbers of all Senate committees; this action made Sen. Ted Kennedy (D-Mass.) chair of the Senate Health, Education, Labor and Pensions Committee, and Kennedy became one of the main negotiators affecting the necessary compromises to pass the legislation.

Following a three-year effort, the final conference on the ESEA reauthorization took place on December 11. Staff had been working throughout the August recess and after the terrorist attacks of September 11, albeit under difficult circumstances, to finish the legislation. The afternoon meeting was awash with good feeling and mutual congratulations. While members of House and Senate Committees were quick to claim large increases in program levels, those committees do not set the actual funding, so many members of the public were confused when, a week later, the appropriators did not allocate the same level of funding as that suggested by the authorizers. Many difficult compromises between House and Senate and the president were achieved to create the final bill, with some observers expecting deliberations to continue to flow into 2002.

A major victory for school library supporters as well as for Sen. Jack Reed (D-R.I.) and other Senate sponsors was the inclusion of Reed's school library amendment in the final version of the bill. The amendment now appears in the legislation as Title I, Part B, Subpart 4, section 1251—Improving Literacy Through School Libraries. The amendment had been added on the Senate floor to the Senate bill, but did not appear in the House bill. However, Rep. Major Owens (D-N.Y.), and Rep. Dale Kildee (D-Mich.) had been sponsors of a previous House bill on the same subject.

The president's Reading First and Early Reading First initiatives were major areas of emphasis in the new bill. The 21st Century Community Learning Centers program, which had been initiated during the Clinton administration and limited to local educational agencies as the administrative bodies, was expanded to allow community organizations to be lead agencies. This program was funded for FY 2002 at $1 billion.

The several sections in ESEA dealing with technology were consolidated into a block grant. School library media personnel are among those eligible for professional development. Included in the new ESEA Title III—Technology is a restatement of the filtering language passed by Congress in 2001.

E-Rate

As President Bush took office in January 2001, one of the first education-related proposals his administration made was to transform the E-rate (which provides discounted telecommunications rates to libraries and schools) into a block grant and to expand its use to a host of additional activities. Not only would this plan have endangered the revenue source for the E-rate; it would have overburdened whatever funding was made available to the point of severely limiting the program's impact. In time, as a greater understanding of the workings of the E-rate program was gained by administration officials, and possibly because of the program's vast popularity, the administration backed off this proposal.

There was one serious threat to the E-rate program in Congress in 2001. A large House telecommunications bill, the Internet Freedom and Broadband Deployment Act of 2001 (H.R. 1542), contained a measure that would allow incumbent local exchange carriers (mostly Bell companies) to provide high-speed Internet and data services while exempting them from fees, such as those that fund universal service or the E-rate. H.R. 1542 was reported unfavorably by the House Committee on Energy and Commerce on May 9, 2001. The bill was also referred to the full House Judiciary Committee, and on June 18, 2001, that committee also reported adversely on the bill. As of early 2002, it remained to be seen if the bill would be seriously considered by the full House during 2002.

April 20, 2001, marked the effective date for the Children's Internet Protection Act (CIPA). Libraries and schools receiving E-rate discounts were required to certify by October 28, 2001, that they were in compliance with CIPA's requirements. This compliance could either be "undertaking actions" or actually meeting the "Internet safety policy" requirements in the law. CIPA is being challenged in the courts by ALA and the American Civil Liberties Union (ACLU).

Postal Update

Completing its work on the Emergency Supplemental Appropriations bill, Congress approved the details of a $20 billion bill. This was the last component of the $40 billion emergency supplemental bill approved on September 14. The $20 billion provides $3.5 billion for defense, $8.3 billion for "homeland defense," and $8.2 billion for recovery in areas directly affected by the September 11 terrorist attacks. Included in the bill is a one-time expenditure of $500 million for emergency expenses for the U.S. Postal Service for repair of facilities destroyed in the attacks and to mitigate current and future biohazard threats.

The U.S. Postal Service testified before Congress early in the fall about its widening deficit, caused by increased gasoline prices and, after September 11, anthrax-by-mail hazards. The postal rate case was shortened by discussions among all parties hoping to lead to an early settlement. This change in procedures will save time and funds for those involved. Rate changes will be announced late in June.

USA Patriot Act (P.L. 107-56)

The USA Patriot Act (Uniting and Strengthening America by Providing Appropriate Tools Required to Intercept or Obstruct Terrorism), enacted in late October, is a unique, lengthy, and complicated law. Passed under most unusual circumstances, it raises numerous questions for the library community. By the end of the legislative process, the two key issues on which ALA focused related to (1) access to business records, including library, student, and healthcare records, and (2) computer trespassing, including the definition of "authorized user."

The complexities of the act and its intersection with other federal and state laws make it difficult to obtain a comprehensive analysis. This is made more difficult by the fact that there were no hearings, and hence essentially no legislative record. Soon after the September 11 attacks, Attorney General John Ashcroft asked Congress for additional powers he said would assist the government in fighting domestic terrorism. There was immediate agreement in Congress that the administration should be given such assistance quickly. In barely six weeks of activity, Congress completed passage of legislation only modestly changed from that originally proposed by Ashcroft immediately following September 11. The USA Patriot Act became law when President Bush signed the bill on October 26.

ALA's activities regarding the legislation focused on its possible impact on the library community and library users. As soon as the "unofficial" draft was available, the ALA Office of Information Technology Policy (OITP) convened a group of library and university technology experts to begin analyzing the proposed legislation and identifying key issues. The discussion identified three fundamental areas of concern: (1) the broad definition of *terrorist* to include any "cyber crime"; (2) government access to library records; and (3) use of library systems for active surveillance and wiretapping. Included in the meeting were representatives of the American Association of Law Libraries (AALL) and the Association of Research Libraries (ARL), and chairs of the ALA Committee on Legislation and the OITP Advisory Committee, as well as several librarians, technology specialists, and legal advisers.

Several main concerns emerged that were the focus of subsequent activities reflected in ALA's letters and statements. These concerns, mainly around the issues of privacy and the confidentiality of library and other records, included:

- Expansion of pen register and trap-and-trace devices to the Internet
- Expansion of access to business records
- Expansion of access to educational institution records
- Expansion of the definition of terrorism
- New mandates for technology

The Senate and the House entered into separate and parallel negotiations with the Justice Department, which had the lead for the Bush administration although others in the administration were involved. Numerous changes to the proposed legislation appeared contradictory and unclear, and each new change meant a new legal analysis and discussions of the section in question. Sometimes there were several changes a day.

During this period ALA and its fellow library associations worked closely with the Center for Democracy and Technology (CDT) and the broad coalition of organizations brought together by ACLU under the title of the In Defense of Freedom Coalition (IDOF). On October 2 ARL, AALL, and ALA released a joint public statement, signed by their respective government relations staffs, on each organization's Web site. Subsequently all of the associations signed onto the IDOF statement (http://www.ala.org/washoff/terrorism.pdf).

ALA's main efforts in the House focused on the House Judiciary Committee, which appeared to be developing a bill that included a sunset provision and generally was more responsive to some of the civil liberties concerns. Late on October 3 the committee passed H.R. 2975 unanimously. There were numerous amendments made during the markup, and many of the changes the library community and others would have liked did not become official amendments.

The Senate passed its version of the antiterrorism bill late on October 11. The following morning, the House substituted the Senate language for the original House language during a procedural move in the House Rules Committee. There was no time or opportunity to work for amendments or to get the House to reconsider, and some representatives complained on the floor that they had not even had time to read the bill. The House passed the "new" H.R. 2975 with the Senate language basically intact in a vote of 337-79 late on the afternoon of October 12.

There was considerable uproar from some members of the House because of the unusual process in passing the bill and the failure to have commitments honored. Two changes in the final language include a sunset on the electronic surveillance provisions and a provision for judicial oversight of the use of the FBI's Carnivore system, a government electronic surveillance system.

The library associations and coalition colleagues also focused on trying to make changes to the Senate bill, S. 1510. As the Senate proceeded in its behind-the-scenes discussions, it became apparent that Senator Russ Feingold (D-Wis.) would be willing to work on certain amendments to the Senate version during floor debate.

Two key Feingold amendments involved

- Business records (to avoid preemption of existing privacy laws for medical, library, and other records, and possibly to limit the scope to "agents of a foreign power," as the Foreign Intelligence Surveillance Act statute had previously done)
- Computer trespassing (to make it clear that "unauthorized user" does not include people with an existing "user" relationship, and limiting the communications intercepted to those related to trespassing)

Two additional Feingold amendments addressed roving wiretaps and secret searches. All these amendments were defeated in a procedural move to table them.

The Senate passed S. 1510 by a 96-1 vote late on October 11, and President Bush signed the bill on October 26.

E-Government Act of 2001

On May 1, 2001, Senators Joseph Lieberman (D-Conn.) and Conrad Burns (R-Mont.) introduced S. 803, the E-Government Act of 2001. Nancy Kranich, then president of ALA, presented remarks at the introduction of the bill on May 1, 2001. On July 11, Sharon Hogan, director of libraries at the University of Illinois in Chicago, testified before the Senate Government Affairs Committee on the bill. Hogan represented ALA as well as AALL and ARL.

S. 803 would provide for better accessibility, usability, and preservation of federal government information, build toward improved access to federal judicial records, require "privacy impact assessments" of new systems and collections of information, and create an e-government fund to promote interagency cooperation on e-government efforts. Additionally, the bill addresses the life cycle management of government information and calls for permanent public access initiatives to be developed. A Senate staff outline of the bill is available at http://www. senate.gov/~gov_affairs/egovoutline.pdf. Negotiations were under way in early 2002 between Sen. Lieberman's staff and the administration on specific provisions of the bill. Action on this legislation was deferred in large part because of Congress's work on antiterrorism legislation after September 11.

FirstGov

FirstGov.gov, a Web-based government information service, was launched in September 2000. It calls itself "the only official U.S. Government portal to 47 million pages of government information, services, and online transactions." ALA and others in the library community have followed this service closely because it has implications for all library users seeking access to federal government information and e-government transactions. Many librarians have provided feedback on the site as it has evolved. FirstGov was included in President Bush's "budget blueprint" as a key building block to cross-agency electronic government.

NTIS

The National Technical Information Service (NTIS) continues to experience funding difficulties and continues to receive no appropriated funds for its essential indexing and abstracting activities. NTIS plans to launch a new Web site in 2002 that will provide electronic access to hundreds of thousands of documents. When available, a document summary will link the user to the full text of the publication that is stored on a government Web site. When the document is not available from a government Web site, an electronic version (in PDF format) will be downloadable directly from the NTIS Web site for a fee (downloads of reports 20 pages or less will be free). The latter option includes most publications sent to NTIS since 1997. [See the report "National Technical Information Service" in Part 1—*Ed.*]

'Leaks' Criminalization (Official Secrets Act)

"Leaks" criminalization was part of the Intelligence Authorization Act for FY 2001, and the entire bill was vetoed by President Clinton in November 2000 because of this provision. It would have made it a felony for any former or current government employee to purposely reveal "classified information." In 2001 the primary proponent of this provision, Sen. Richard Shelby (R-Ala.), indicated his intention to attach it to the 2002 Intelligence Authorization Act. ALA, working in conjunction with public interest and press organizations, succeeded in convincing Sen. Bob Graham (D-Fla.), chairman of the Senate Select Committee on Intelligence, that the provision should not be allowed in the 2002 act. It is anticipated that the issue will return, possibly in the 2002 session.

Presidential Records Act

Executive Order 13233, issued November 1, greatly expands the asserted constitutional privileges of the incumbent president and former presidents—or a "representative designated by a former president or his family"—to prevent release of records to the public. It allows a former vice president to assert constitutionally based privileges to bar release of records, and requires that a party seeking access to presidential records must assert a "demonstrated, specific need" for those records. The executive order effectively denies the public's legitimate right of access under the Presidential Records Act (PRA) by giving an incumbent or former president veto power over any public release of materials by the Archivist of the United States even after the 12-year restriction period has expired.

Rep. Stephen Horn (R-Calif.) held a hearing on the order on November 6, and the American Historical Association and others opposed to it filed suit against the National Archives on November 28, 2001. ALA anticipates that legislation will be introduced in 2002 to address the executive order's impact on PRA.

Post-Sept. 11 Restrictions on Access to Government Information

In the aftermath of the September 11 terrorist attacks, agencies at both the federal and state levels began to take a series of actions that limited or prevented public access to previously available government information. Such actions have included the U.S. Geological Survey ordering the Government Printing Office to instruct FDLP libraries to destroy a CD-ROM; the National Archives and Records Administration (NARA) issuing guidance to its regional archives to screen requests for some types of records; and the Nuclear Regulatory Commission shutting down its entire site. It should be noted that none of these actions has been taken at the direction of the Bush administration, but for this reason there is also no central inventory, no direction on ensuring the permanence and integrity of the information restricted, and no guidance on weighing the known benefits of public access with the conceivable use of the information by potential terrorists.

ALA, AALL, ARL, and other public-interest organizations have been in communication with the administration about these concerns and have urged the Office of Management and Budget to encourage federal agencies to engage their publics in ongoing discussion about these issues. [See the Special Report "Dissemination of Government Information" in Part 1—*Ed.*]

Distance Education

A bill to update copyright law for online distance education passed in the Senate in June 2001, but has been pending since then in the House. The bill, S. 487, called the Technology Education and Copyright Harmonization (TEACH) Act, is intended to update the distance-education provisions of the Copyright Act to account for advancements in digital transmission technologies that support distance learning. S. 487 is supported by the higher education community and the content community.

The full Senate passed S. 487 on June 7 with changes to the bill that were developed through extended discussions among the various stakeholders following the bill's introduction in March. In the House of Representatives, on July 11, the Courts, Internet, and Intellectual Property subcommittee of the House Judiciary Committee approved the Senate bill. ALA anticipated that the full Judiciary Committee would mark up the TEACH Act shortly thereafter, but that did not happen. Libraries and educational institutions hope to see the legislation move forward and become law in 2002. [See the Special Report "Copyright 2001: Exploring the Implications of Technology" in Part 1—*Ed.*]

Database Protection Legislation

Database protection legislation remains a priority issue for libraries. Proponents have been urging Congress for several years to pass legislation that attempts to control downstream access to database information, and there were aggressive efforts in 2001 to pass a bill that would have been detrimental to libraries. Although these efforts were unsuccessful, there is every reason to expect the proponents to renew their push in 2002. ALA and the other library associations supported a database protection bill in a previous Congress, but it is ALA's position that any database protection bill must allow "fair use" of databases comparable to that under copyright law and permit downstream, transformative use of facts and government-produced data contained in a database.

First-Sale Legislation

The U.S. Copyright Office issued a report at the end of August 2001 that had been mandated by the Digital Millennium Copyright Act (DMCA) of 1998. That law directed the Copyright Office and the National Telecommunications and Information Administration (NTIA) to make a report to Congress "no later than 24 months after the enactment of DMCA" (October 2000) on the effects on the "first-sale doctrine" of DMCA and the development of electronic commerce.

NTIA released its report in March 2001, concluding that it was "premature to draw any conclusions or make any legislative recommendations at this time."

The main question for the Copyright Office was whether it should recommend legislation to expand the first-sale doctrine to permit digital transmission of lawfully made copies of copyrighted works. The office acknowledged that the library community had raised "potentially valid concerns," such as the ability to make interlibrary loans and to offer off-site accessibility that "may require further consideration at some point in the future." However, the Copyright Office recommended no change to the copyright law at present.

The House Judiciary Committee held two hearings on the Copyright Office report in December 2001.

Legislation and Regulations Affecting Publishing in 2001

Allan Adler

Vice President, Legal and Governmental Affairs
Association of American Publishers
50 F St. N.W., Suite 400, Washington, DC 20001

The First Session of the 107th Congress had two distinct segments that were strongly influenced by events that occurred outside the House and Senate chambers. The first half of the session, which began in January 2001, was dominated by the official debut of the Bush administration, following the U.S. Supreme Court's controversial but historic resolution of the contested presidential election. Then, in the second week of September, when Congress traditionally resumes its work after a long summer recess, the terrorist attacks on the twin towers of the World Trade Center and the Pentagon changed the congressional agenda as swiftly as it changed numerous aspects of life throughout the nation.

As the Second Session of the 107th Congress gets under way, Association of American Publishers (AAP) members can now review some of the significant legislative activities that AAP's Washington Office either monitored or participated in on their behalf. At the same time, this report provides a timely opportunity to alert publishers to some of the public policy issues that can be expected to require AAP's attention during the remainder of the 107th Congress.

This report focuses on legislative actions that affect book and journal publishing interests primarily concerning (1) intellectual property protection, (2) freedom of expression, (3) new technologies and "e-commerce," and (4) educational funding. However, we also report on significant developments regarding (5) tax and (6) postal matters.

A summary, text, and status report for each piece of referenced legislation, whether enacted or not, can be found online in the Congressional Legislative Reference Service of the Library of Congress at http://thomas.loc.gov. Simply look under the Legislation heading at either Bill Summary or Bill Text, click on the icon labeled 107th Congress, and follow the instructions from there.

No Child Left Behind Act

(H.R. 1, enacted as Public Law 107-110, January 8, 2002)

One of the biggest accomplishments of the first session of the 107th Congress was the No Child Left Behind Act (H.R. 1), a compromise education bill, which reauthorized the Elementary and Secondary Education Act (ESEA). President Bush signed this historic bill into law on January 8, 2002, after months of negotiations between both Republicans and Democrats and senators and representatives. As a result of the act, federal education funding reached a historic high with the fiscal year (FY) 2002 authorization level hitting approximately $26.3 billion, $13.5 billion for Title I.

Overall, the act is designed to help educationally disadvantaged children achieve the same high state academic achievement standards as all other students. H.R. 1 is the most significant attempt to date to hold states and local school districts accountable for federal education funds, particularly Title I funds that provide education services to disadvantaged students. H.R. 1 will have a substantial impact on American students, teachers, parents, and publishers, particularly those in the testing arena. The act mandates annual testing in reading and mathematics at grades 3–8 as well as corrective actions for schools that fail to make "adequate yearly progress." Under the reauthorization, states will be required to create new tests and refine existing assessment programs. AAP's Government Affairs Division and School Division were involved in advocating a number of important programs in the bill. Below is a brief summary of the portions of the bill that will have the most impact on publishers.

Assessment and School Improvement Provisions

Authorization period. The act sets an authorization period of six years. The first year of the authorization period will be FY 2002 (October 1, 2001–September 30, 2002) and the last year will be FY 2007. Most of the act's assessment provisions are in Title I, Part A.

Overall funding. The act authorizes $26.5 billion in education spending for grades K–12 for FY 2002. This represents an $8 billion increase over the previous year.

Annual assessments. H.R. 1 requires states to have annual reading and math assessments for grades 3–8. States—not Congress or the U.S. Department of Education—will select and design tests of their choice. State assessments must be aligned with state academic standards, and they must allow achievement to be comparable from year to year.

Implementation of annual tests. States will have until the 2005–2006 school year to develop and implement math and reading assessments. States must develop science standards by the 2005–2006 school year and then implement science assessments by the 2007–2008 school year in one grade in each grade span of 3–5, 6–9, and 10–12.

Use of NAEP as a verification assessment. The act requires state tests to be verified by the National Assessment of Educational Progress (NAEP). Verification of state tests will occur every other year at the fourth- and eighth-grade levels. A sample of students in each state will be assessed as part of the verification process.

Funding for annual testing. The act authorizes $490 million for states to develop and administer annual assessments at grades 3–8. It includes an appropriations "trigger" to ensure that federal funds are available to develop and implement the tests. A state may postpone the start of testing for one year for each year that funds do not reach the set amount. But a state must continue to develop its assessments and it must continue to comply with current (1994) law by administering assessments in reading and math in one grade in each grade span of 3–5, 6–9, and 10–12. The trigger amounts are: $370 million for FY 2002, $380 million for FY 2003, $390 million for FY 2004, and $400 million for FY 2005–2007.

Adequate yearly progress. H.R. 1 specifies that states must make "adequate yearly progress" in improving the performance of disadvantaged students. Each state must now have a definition of adequate yearly progress that applies to disadvantaged students as well as to the overall student population. The act requires states to

- Define adequate yearly progress so that all students achieve at the state's "proficient" level on state reading and math academic assessments within 12 years
- Set the achievement bar to reach 100 percent proficiency. States may choose where to set the initial bar based on the lowest-achieving schools in the state or the lowest-achieving demographic subgroup (whichever is higher). The state must "raise the bar" gradually in equal increments to reach 100 percent proficiency.
- Use one other academic indicator. For secondary schools, the indicator will be graduation rates. Each state will choose the indicator for elementary schools.

School improvement and corrective actions. The act sets the following schedule of corrective actions for schools that fail to make adequate yearly progress:

- Schools that have not made state-defined adequate yearly progress for two consecutive school years will be identified by the school district as needing improvement. These schools will receive assistance to improve performance. They must also develop a two-year plan for improvement. Districts must offer public school choice (unless prohibited by state law) to students in the failing school. Districts must provide transportation for public school choice.
- Schools failing to make adequate yearly progress for three consecutive years must offer school supplemental educational services such as tutoring. The schools must also continue to offer public school choice.
- Schools failing to make adequate yearly progress for four consecutive years must take corrective actions such as replacing staff or implementing a new curriculum. They must also continue to provide public school choice and supplemental services.
- Schools failing to make adequate yearly progress for five consecutive years must implement alternative governance actions such as a state takeover, the hiring of a private management contractor, conversion to a charter school, or staff restructuring. Public school choice and supplemental services continue to be required.
- Corrective actions are not required once the school makes adequate yearly progress for two consecutive years.

Report cards. The act requires states and school districts to report disaggregated data in annual public "report cards" beginning with the 2002–2003 school year.

Toned-Down "Student Privacy" Measure

The final version of the No Child Left Behind Act contains a toned-down version of the proposed Student Privacy Protection Act, legislation jointly sponsored by

Senators Christopher Dodd (D-Conn.) and Richard Shelby (R-Ala.) to increase parental involvement in school activities that include collection of personal information from students for use by third-party commercial interests.

As originally introduced in the last Congress, the Dodd-Shelby legislation, like a similar House bill introduced by Rep. George Miller (D-Calif.), would have required parental consent before schools could allow third-party commercial interests to conduct any personal data-collection activities involving students in the classroom. Prior to the introduction of a revised version of the Dodd-Shelby bill in the Senate earlier this year, AAP worked with Dodd's staff to exempt from the parental consent requirement any personal information collection from students that was conducted in connection with either (1) the "development, evaluation, or provision of educational products or services" (including book clubs and curriculum and instructional materials used by schools to teach) or (2) the "development and administration of tests and assessments used by elementary and secondary schools."

After its inclusion in the Senate version of the overall education reform bill earlier this year, the Dodd-Shelby provisions were revised by House and Senate conferees to eliminate the parental consent requirement, which had been vigorously opposed by a variety of commercial interests and many local school authorities as unjustified, administratively unworkable federal interference with educators' efforts to make up for budgetary shortfalls through cooperative programs with local businesses.

Instead of the parental consent requirement, the conference-approved version requires local educational agencies that receive program funding under the overall legislation to adopt and notify parents of specific policies regarding parental rights to inspect (1) any third-party "survey" to be administered or distributed by a school to a student; (2) any instructional material used as part of the educational curriculum; or (3) any "instrument" to be used in the collection of personal information from students for the purpose of marketing or selling such information (or otherwise providing such information to others for that purpose). Such policies must also address agency arrangements to protect student privacy in connection with certain types of surveys; the administration of physical examinations or screenings conducted on students; and the collection, disclosure, or use of personal information collected from students for the purpose of marketing or selling such information (or otherwise providing that information to others for that purpose).

Reading First and Early Reading First Programs

One of the administration's top priorities in the No Child Left Behind Act is the president's Reading First Initiative. The goal of the initiative is to ensure that every child can read by the third grade.

Reading First provides grants to states and local districts to establish reading programs, based in scientific research, for all children in kindergarten through third grade. The program builds on conclusions issued in a report by the National Reading Panel in April 2000 that effective reading programs include teaching children about phonemic awareness, phonics, guided oral reading, and practice.

The final bill triples federal literacy funding from the present $300 million in FY 2001 to $900 million in FY 2002.

Under the program, states will be awarded six-year funding grants. Once a state is awarded a grant it must expend at least 80 percent of the amount of funds in competitive subgrants to eligible local educational agencies. Local educational agencies will administer screening, diagnostic, and classroom-based instructional reading assessments to determine which students in kindergarten through third grade have below-average reading skills. A percentage of the grant money may also be used to provide professional development for teachers of kindergarten through third grade to prepare them in all the essential components of reading instruction.

Early Reading First is a new $75 million initiative that allows states participating in the Reading First program funds to implement research-based pre-reading methods in preschool programs. Particularly, the program targets children ages 3 through 5 in high-poverty areas where there is a high number of children not reading at grade level. The purpose of the program is to integrate scientific reading-based instructional materials and literacy activities with existing programs in preschools, childcare agencies, or Head Start centers, which would help prepare children for formal reading instruction in kindergarten and first grade. The program is designed to provide the critical early identification and early reading interventions to assist young children in attaining the fundamental skills necessary for optimal reading development. One purpose of the new program is to ensure that children develop automatic recognition of letters of the alphabet, knowledge of letter sounds, and the use of increasingly complex vocabulary.

Final Version Includes Funding for School Libraries

The final version of the No Child Left Behind Act contains a version of the proposed Improving Literacy Through School Libraries Act of 2001 introduced by Sen. Jack Reed (D-R.I.). The line item authorizes $250 million for school library resources and is included as part of President Bush's Reading First Initiative.

Federal research indicates that well-stocked and well-staffed school libraries encourage literacy and learning. Unfortunately, direct funding for school libraries was eliminated in 1981, which has resulted in all-time-low levels of school library funding. Currently, the average cost of a new library book is $16, but the average amount school districts spend per student for books is $6.75 in elementary school, $7.30 in middle school, and $6.25 in high school, enough to buy less than half a book. Due to this lack of funding, school libraries have an insufficient number and variety of books. Many of the books they do have are outdated and contain "facts" that were debunked decades ago, as well as offensive stereotypes of women and minorities.

As originally introduced, the bill would have authorized the appropriation of $475 million for fiscal year 2002 and "such sums that may be necessary" for FY 2003 through FY 2006. In the Senate version, the Reed Amendment provided $500 million to local school libraries to purchase new books, to provide advanced technology training for librarians, and to allow school libraries to remain open longer. The House and Senate conferees reduced the authorization to $250 million for fiscal year 2002 and such sums as may be necessary for each of the five succeeding fiscal years. The funds will be made available to school libraries for the purchase of books and up-to-date technology for media centers and for the hiring of professionally certified school library media specialists. The funding would also enable students to access school libraries on weekends, during summer vacation, and before and after regular school hours. The legislation is targeted toward school libraries with the greatest need.

Department of Education Appropriations Act
(Title III of H.R. 3061, enacted as P.L. 107-116, January 10, 2002)

The Department of Education Appropriations Act, usually a contentious part of the controversial Labor/HHS appropriations bill, moved through the legislative process easily last year. Early agreements between the White House and congressional appropriators on issues that proved contentious in previous years helped speed up the process.

Overall, the House and Senate versions contained $123.4 billion in discretionary spending, a $14 billion increase over FY 2001. Among the line items of possible interest to publishers are the following:

- A total of more than $48.9 billion is provided in the Conference Report for education programs. This is $4.4 billion more than the president's request and $6.7 billion more than the previous year.
- There is a $3.4 billion increase for President Bush's education initiatives authorized in the No Child Left Behind Act 2001 (H.R. 1, enacted as P.L. 107-110), bringing total funding for these programs to $29.6 billion, an increase of $4.6 billion over last year's level. (See separate synopsis of H.R. 1 above.)
- More than $10.3 billion is appropriated for Title 1 programs to aid states and localities in assisting disadvantaged children to achieve the same academic performance as other students, a $1.6 billion increase over the requested amount.
- The Reading First program is funded at $975 million. (See separate synopsis of H.R. 1 above.)
- A total of $387 million will fund the cost of developing annual state assessments of students reading and math skills. (See separate synopsis on H.R. 1 above.)
- State grants for improving teacher quality are funded at $2.85 billion. It is a new program that consolidates existing professional-development programs and provides states and school districts with tools to ensure classrooms have qualified teachers.
- Reading Is Fundamental, the federal government's "inexpensive book distribution" program under ESEA, receives $24 million, a $1 million increase over last year's amount.
- Even Start child literacy programs get $250 million.
- Literacy Through School Libraries is funded at $12.5 million to provide students with up-to-date school library materials, and well-equipped, tech-

nologically advanced school library media centers. (See separate synopsis H.R. 1 above.)

- Education technology state grants are funded at $700.5 million. Under the ESEA reauthorization, several technology programs, including the Technology Literacy Challenge Fund, were consolidated into a state-based grant program to target specific needs of individual schools. The funds may be used to (1) promote innovative state and local initiatives using technology to increase academic achievement; (2) increase access to technology, particularly in schools with a high need; (3) improve and expand teacher professional development in technology.

- A total of $22 million is appropriated for the "Ready to Learn" television program, which develops educational programming for preschool and early elementary school children, but also allows grants to be used to produce printed materials.

USA Patriot Act of 2001

(H.R. 3162, enacted as P.L. 107-56, October 26, 2001)

Immediately following the September 11 terrorist attacks on the World Trade Center and the Pentagon, Congress rushed to give the Bush administration sweeping new authority to investigate, arrest, detain, and prosecute suspected terrorists. Unfortunately, in the process of attempting to provide greater security to the American people, Congress has, in the view of many, also undermined important protections for civil liberties.

Much of the criticism leveled at the USA Patriot Act (Uniting and Strengthening America by Providing Appropriate Tools Required to Intercept or Obstruct Terrorism) by civil libertarians, including a number of members of Congress, focused on amendments to the Foreign Intelligence Surveillance Act (FISA) and other provisions that have blurred distinctions between the federal government's authority to conduct criminal investigations and its authority to pursue intelligence-gathering "national security" investigations in its efforts to combat terrorism. Judicial review requirements—along with other safeguards and accountability mechanisms designed to prevent abusive use of wiretaps, electronic surveillance, secret searches, and other investigative tools by the government—have been substantially diluted, while authority to target, arrest, and detain individuals suspected of being connected to terrorist activities have been substantially expanded.

Some of the most questionable provisions of the new act broaden or establish criminal offenses and expand related government law enforcement and intelligence-gathering powers in ways that could potentially threaten even U.S. publishers, authors, and bookstores based on their involvement with the works or activities of foreign authors and organizations that the U.S. government may consider to be targets in terrorism investigations. For example:

- Expansive definitions of "domestic terrorism," "terrorist organization," and "terrorist activity" create the potential for conspiracy or "guilt-by-association" suspicion and targeting in connection with the solicitation of funds or membership or other material support for certified "terrorist organizations" and even for certain organizations not designated as "terrorist organizations." Such groups, according to some critics, might even include World Trade Organization (WTO) protesters, Greenpeace, or People for the Ethical Treatment of Animals (PETA) on the basis of their minor acts of violence or vandalism. They might also include foreign political organizations, as well as their leaders and supporters, if they act and speak in ways the U.S. government deems supportive of suspected terrorists, terrorist activity, or terrorist organizations. Non-U.S. citizens who are not terrorists may be subject to indefinite detention by the federal government for minor visa violations under certain circumstances.

- In connection with investigations of individuals, activities, or organizations falling within the scope of these expansive definitions, the FBI now has broad authority to access sensitive business records of third parties (including, for instance, book purchases or library loans); to use intelligence investigative authority to intercept Internet-based and other electronic communications (including, for instance, identification of visited Web sites); and to conduct secret searches.

- Similarly, the act permits the FBI to share wiretap and grand jury information, as well as other sensitive information ostensibly collected as part of a criminal investigation, with the CIA, the National Security Agency (NSA), Immigration and Naturalization Service (INS), and Secret Service for intelligence purposes without judicial review. Individual credit reports and other sensitive personal information in the possession of financial institutions are now also subject to easy access and sharing by law enforcement and intelligence agencies.

Intelligence Authorization Act for FY 2002

(H.R. 2883, enacted as P.L. 107-108, December 28, 2001)

Like the dog that did not bark in the famous Sherlock Holmes story, what did not happen with this year's intelligence authorization legislation was of greater interest to publishers than what did. Specifically, enactment of the legislation without the inclusion of a highly controversial criminal "leak" statute has apparently put off once again a major legislative (and potential court) battle over First Amendment protections that some members of Congress deem to be in conflict with national security needs.

At the end of the previous Congress, then-President Bill Clinton had vetoed an initial version of the FY 2001 intelligence authorization legislation because it contained a provision, sponsored by Sen. Richard Shelby (R-Ala.), then chairman of the Senate Select Committee on Intelligence, that would have made virtually any unauthorized disclosure of classified national security information a federal felony punishable by up to three years in prison. In response to vigorous opposition to the provision from media organizations (including AAP), civil liberties advocates, and government "watchdog" groups, President Clinton concluded that the proposed statute, though well intentioned, was overbroad and could "unnecessarily chill legitimate activities that are at the heart of a democracy."

Noting that Congress had passed the proposed criminal statute without the benefit of any public hearings, President Clinton's veto statement echoed the criticisms in many newspaper and broadcast editorials in stating that the legislation "might discourage government officials from engaging even in appropriate public discussion, press briefings, or other legitimate official activities," and could "unduly restrain the ability of former government officials to teach, write, or engage in any activity aimed at building public understanding of complex issues." In the belief that "incurring such risks is unnecessary and inappropriate in a society built on freedom of expression and the consent of the governed and is particularly inadvisable in a context in which the range of classified materials is so extensive," President Clinton vetoed the authorization bill and encouraged Congress to "pursue a more narrowly drawn provision tested in public hearings."

When it became clear last summer that Shelby and other supporters of the "leak" statute were preparing to resurrect the discredited proposal, the same cries of opposition arose and the newly installed Bush administration was courted by both supporters and opponents of the measure. With the House Judiciary Committee making clear its intention to assert legislative jurisdiction over any proposed criminal "leak" statute, the Senate Intelligence Committee was informed by Attorney General John Ashcroft in early September that the administration needed more time to study Shelby's proposed measure and was not prepared to present testimony at a planned hearing on the issues it raised.

The Bush administration's signal that it was not prepared to engage in a major public brawl over the issue took the steam out of Shelby's effort to resurrect the criminal "leak" statute in the present Congress. As a compromise, the intelligence authorization legislation advanced through Congress with a requirement for the attorney general, in consultation with other senior executive branch officials, to "carry out a comprehensive review of current protections against the unauthorized disclosure of classified information" and to submit a report to Congress no later than May 1, 2002, describing the findings of the review and any recommendations for legislative or administrative action.

Cybercrime and Intellectual Property Provisions of Commerce, Justice, State Appropriations Act of 2001

(H.R. 2500, enacted as Public Law 107-77, November 28, 2001)

Unlike past years, the Commerce, Justice, State Appropriations Act sailed through Congress while appropriating $41.6 billion for FY 2002, a $1.9 billion increase over FY 2001. Among other things, legislators once again recognized the importance of ensuring adequate funding to address cybercrimes, including those that target intellectual property.

In the final version of the legislation, House and Senate conferees provided a total of $10 million to the U.S. Attorneys Office for cybercrime and intellectual property enforcement. The conferees directed the U.S. Attorneys to report to the House Appropriations Committee on the number of copyright prosecutions undertaken in the proceeding year, including those under the No Electronic Theft

(NET) Act, by type and location, no later than April 30 of this year. The FBI is required to report to the Senate Appropriations on the number of copyright law investigations that led to prosecutions in the preceding year, including those under the NET Act, by type and location, no later than June 30, 2002.

In addition to providing funding for enforcement of federal copyright laws, House and Senate conferees provided additional funding for promotion of the importance of protecting intellectual property. Under funding for the Patent and Trademark Office, the conference agreement allocated not less than $1 million to the International Intellectual Property Institute "to promote sustainable development in developing countries and to promote business interest by assisting in the establishment of intellectual property legal frameworks." The committee also provided $750,000 to the National Academy of Sciences for a study to develop long-term strategies to address global intellectual property counterfeiting and piracy that threatens U.S. economic strength.

Emergency Postal Funds in Department of Defense Appropriations Act for FY 2002

(Div. B, Title IX, Chap.12 of H.R. 3338, enacted as P.L. 107-117, January 10, 2002)

The U.S. Postal Service (USPS) was already in the midst of a deepening financial crisis, as evidenced by its preparations to file yet another round of proposed rate increases barely six months after the second of two earlier rounds of increases had gone into effect, when it was further traumatized by the events of September 11 and the anthrax-tainted mail crisis that followed in the aftermath.

Emergency expenses relating to the urgent need to protect USPS employees and the public from isolated but unresolved incidents of biohazardous material in the mailing system, along with those relating to the replacement or repair of USPS facilities destroyed or damaged in terrorist attacks in New York City, became a funding priority on top of growing financial crisis arising out of USPS's regular mail operations. But where would the money come from?

Mailers were already being hammered by a series of rate increases sought by USPS to balance its rising costs and falling revenues. Despite AAP's best efforts in the earlier rate case litigation, book publishers, who primarily utilize the mail subclassification known as bound printed matter (BPM), had already taken an extraordinary hit in the form of a nearly 18 percent rate increase for BPM last spring when it became clear that USPS's rising red ink would require additional proposed rate increases in the fall averaging about 9 percent for all subclasses, including BPM.

With efforts for legislative postal reform at a standstill, the acting chairman of the Postal Rate Commission urged settlement of the looming rate case, rather than the usual prolonged 10 months of litigation that had produced such unsatisfactory results for publishers and others in the previous rate case, so that USPS could realize the benefits of the new rate increases as soon as possible. The mailing community grumbled, but—acknowledging the emergency circumstances confronting the USPS—agreed to a settlement that would impose the new rate increases at least four months sooner than would ordinarily occur if the rate case were to be fully litigated. In return, they received a tentative commitment from

USPS to avoid further rate increases before October 2002. The settlement process is expected to be completed in time for the new rates to become effective at the end of June.

Meanwhile, USPS, supported by the mailing community, appealed to Congress for the funding to meet its emergency needs. Initial requests for more than $1.5 billion were ignored as both Congress and the Bush administration grappled with the need to fund the war on terrorism, provide homeland security, and redress the human and property losses of September 11 within some plan of fiscal rationality.

Finally, just before the Congress adjourned in late December, an agreement was reached to include $500,000 for emergency expenses in the Postal Service Fund as part of the defense appropriations legislation. The statement of the House and Senate conferees on that legislation is noteworthy and instructive regarding the inexplicable nonchalance that seems to characterize the overall congressional reaction (or lack thereof) to the USPS's burgeoning problems.

The conferees made it clear that in providing the $500,000 for emergency expenses, Congress intended the funds to be used only to enable USPS to protect postal employees and customers from exposure to biohazardous material, to sanitize and screen the mail, and to replace or repair destroyed or damaged USPS facilities in New York City. However, regarding the task of sanitizing and screening the mail, Congress barred any expenditure of the funds for that purpose until USPS submits to designated congressional committees "an emergency preparedness plan" to combat the threat of biological and chemical substances in the mail, along with a plan for spending the allocated funds in support of that plan.

Moreover, the conferees noted that USPS had not received a direct appropriation for operations for nearly two decades and that, in providing the emergency funds for the "extraordinary circumstances" confronting USPS, they "do not intend to set a precedent for operational subsidies of the Postal Service" because they "continue to support current law requirements that the Postal Service operate on a self-sustaining basis."

PubSCIENCE and Technical Information Management Provisions of the Energy and Water Development Appropriations Act, 2002

(H.R. 2311, enacted as P.L. 107-66, November 12, 2001)

As federal agencies continue to exploit their Internet Web sites as an increasingly important means for communicating with, and distributing materials to, key agency constituencies and the general public, concerns have arisen in some quarters of the private sector—including book and journal publishing—regarding the potentially unfair consequences of such activities that may constitute government competition with commercial business enterprises. In one case this year, these concerns attracted congressional attention.

Since its inception in October 1999, PubSCIENCE has raised complaints among some publishers of scientific journals and, in particular, publishers of abstract and indices services related to such journals. The service, which was developed and administered under the auspices of the Office of Scientific and Technical Information (OSTI) of the Department of Energy (DOE), offers free public online search and access capabilities across a large database of abstracts and citations from journal articles in the physical sciences and other disciplines of interest to DOE researchers. Although PubSCIENCE provides hyperlinks from abstracts to the publisher's server for purposes of obtaining access to the full-text article, it does not provide access to the article unless the user or his or her organization has a subscription to the journal in which the article appears. If the user lacks such a subscription, access to the full-text article can be obtained by pay-per-view, by special arrangement with the publisher, by library access, or through commercial providers. In these and other respects, PubSCIENCE is based, at least in part, on PubMed, a medical sciences service that is funded and operated by the National Institutes of Health.

Although it reportedly obtains abstracts and citations from more than 1,200 journals through the cooperation of some 35 participating publishers (as well as through OSTI's DOE Energy Science and Technology database of journal citations), PubSCIENCE has been criticized by some publishers as constituting unfair government competition to private enterprises that provide essentially the same services on a commercial basis.

This sentiment surfaced in the report of the House Appropriations Committee regarding legislation to fund the FY 2002 budget for DOE's Technical Information Management program, which provides funding for OSTI and, consequently, PubSCIENCE. The committee noted its concern that "the department is duplicating technical information services that are already available from the private sector" and instructed the department to "carefully review its information services such as PubSCIENCE to be sure that such efforts remain focused on appropriate scientific journals and do not compete improperly with similar services available from the private sector."

Internet Tax Nondiscrimination Act

(H.R. 1552, enacted as P.L. 107-75, November 28, 2001)

On October 21, 2001, the Internet Tax Freedom Act (ITFA) expired. The act had prohibited state and local governments from imposing any new taxes on "Internet access services" or any "multiple or discriminatory taxes on electronic commerce" for three years. Although the House of Representatives acted before ITFA's expiration to extend the Internet tax moratorium for another two years, the bill was delayed in the Senate and it was not until a month after ITFA expired that the Senate passed the House bill and sent it to the president to be signed into law.

Originally, H.R. 1552, as introduced by Rep. Christopher Cox (R-Calif.), would have placed a permanent moratorium on taxing Internet access and extended for an additional five years the moratorium on multiple and discriminatory taxes on electronic commerce. Under this legislation, states would have been required to simplify their sales tax system before seeking ratification from Congress.

One of the most controversial issues regarding the extension was the debate surrounding the states' ability to collect sales tax on Internet purchases. As the debate continued, support for a permanent or five-year extension of the moratorium waned. In the House Judiciary Committee, H.R. 1552 was amended to extend the Internet tax moratorium for only two years, until November 1, 2003. This scaled-back version of the original bill passed the full House on October 16, 2001, and was sent to the Senate in the hope it would take up the bill and pass it before the moratorium expired. The debate in the Senate took a lot longer than originally anticipated, with a number of senators supporting the states' request to start collecting sales tax revenues on purchases made over the Internet. On the other side of the issue, the high-tech industry was lobbying the Senate to adopt a straight extension of the moratorium.

On October 18, 2001, Senators Mike Enzi (R-Wyo.) and Byron L. Dorgan (D-N.D.) introduced the Internet Tax Moratorium and Equity Act (S. 1567). If enacted, S. 1567 would have permanently banned Internet access taxes and barred multiple and discriminatory Internet taxes until December 31, 2005. The bill would have also encouraged states to simplify their uniform sales tax systems by authorizing states to enter into an Interstate Sales and Use Tax Compact that streamlines sales and use tax systems. If 20 states entered into the compact, it would be sent to Congress for approval, and, if approved, states could begin to tax online sales. The Senate took up S. 1567 as an amendment to the House-passed bill, but it failed on a 57-43 vote.

Although the moratorium was extended for another two years, the states are working hard to develop a uniform tax system, so we can expect to see the issue of Internet taxation arise in Congress before the extended moratorium expires.

Non-Enacted Legislation

Technology, Education, and Copyright Harmonization (TEACH) Act (S. 487)

After weeks of intensive negotiation during which AAP and other copyright industry organizations, representatives of the education community, and U.S. Copyright Office officials sought a consensus compromise on a digital distance-education bill, a revised version of S. 487 was reported by the Senate Judiciary Committee in May 2001 and passed by the Senate in June.

The Senate-approved version of the TEACH Act, which would broaden the existing copyright exemption for instructional broadcasting to encompass distance education delivered via digital networks, addresses the concerns voiced by AAP at Senate hearings in March regarding the original version of the legislation, which was introduced by Senators Orrin Hatch (R-Utah) and Patrick Leahy (D-Vt.) based on recommendations contained in a study that was conducted and issued by the Copyright Office under a mandate in the Digital Millennium Copyright Act (DMCA).

Although the House Judiciary Subcommittee on Courts, the Internet and Intellectual Property quickly approved the Senate-passed bill following a hearing in July, the legislation has remained stuck in the full House Judiciary Committee since that time. AAP staff have been told that the holdup on moving the bill to the House floor has nothing to do with its substance but is part of a dispute between the leaders of the House and Senate Judiciary Committees regarding the latter committee's failure to take up a number of House-passed measures that originated with the former. It is expected that the bill will be reported by the House committee and passed by the House later this year.

Music Online Competition Act ("MOCA") (H.R. 2724)

On August 2, 2001, Representatives Rick Boucher (D-Va.) and Chris Cannon (R-Utah) introduced the Music Online Competition Act (MOCA) of 2001, H.R. 2724. The bill did not receive much attention in the House in the first session of the 107th Congress, but may see more action in the coming months with a possible hearing and subcommittee mark-up.

Although the bill directly affects the delivery of music online, proposed changes to the Copyright Act regarding ephemeral copies and incidental and archival copying raise concerns among all interested copyright industries. The bill would expand the existing ephemeral recording exemption for broadcasters to include Webcasters and allow them to make multiple in-house copies. The multiple copies would be used to accommodate different bit rates, different formats, and caching throughout the network. The bill would extend the ephemeral recording exemption to include individual song recordings, and would address incidental and archival copying in two particular situations that affect Internet technology. The bill would also exempt from copyright liability buffer copies made in the course of browsing or Webcasting, based on the claim that the buffer copies are "mere technical incidents" that have no economic value. The bill would also permit consumers to make archival copies of lawfully acquired music to protect their collections against hard drive crashes and other damage.

Other changes proposed in the bill:

- *Direct payment to artists:* This would require that royalty payments be shared equally between performing artists and recording companies, and require direct payment to the artists or to a collective organization representing the artists.
- *Nondiscriminatory licensing to affiliated and nonaffiliated music distribution:* The bill would extend the nondiscrimination provision enacted by Congress in 1995 regarding cable and satellite subscription services by requiring vertically integrated companies that own both content and distribution services to offer nondiscriminatory licensing to similar distribution services.
- *Study and report on programming restrictions:* The Copyright Office and Department of Commerce would be required to conduct a joint study focusing on the effect sound recording statutory license programming restrictions have on digital music services, copyright owners, and consumers. The report would include legislative recommendations.
- *Administration of statutory licensing:* Under the bill, users would be permitted to notify the Copyright Office of the use of a statutory license; royalty payments and accounting information would be deposited with the Copyright Office; and the Copyright Office would develop an electronic filing system to receive notices, replacing the paper filing system used now.
- *"In-store sampling" exemption:* The bill would expand the current exemption in copyright law for "brick-and-mortar" music retailers that

record CDs on a server for customers to sample in stores, extending it to include online retail establishments that offer music samples.

National Digital Libraries Legislation (H.R. 1858 and S. 803)

Two pieces of legislation pending before Congress continue a trend toward the creation of "national digital libraries" to provide the public with free online access to certain specified materials. Although the establishment of such libraries may generally be viewed as beneficial to the public, publishers are concerned that the proponents of such libraries often fail to address whether they will contain copyrighted materials and, if so, how the interests of copyright owners will be protected in making such materials freely accessible online.

One pending example of such legislation is Title II of the proposed National Mathematics and Science Partnerships Act (H.R. 1858), which would establish a National Science, Mathematics, Engineering, and Technology Education Digital Library to provide public access to an Internet-based repository of curricular materials, practices, and teaching modules, as well as other information relating to the improvement of elementary and secondary teaching in these subjects. This legislation has passed the House with an amendment intended to protect the rights of copyright owners.

Another pending example is Section 204 of the proposed "E-Government Act of 2001" (S. 803), which would establish an Online National Library providing public access to "an expanding database of educational resource materials, including historical documents, photographs, audio recordings, films, and other media, as appropriate, that are significant for education and research in United States history and culture." This legislation has been the subject of a Senate hearing, but has seen no further legislative action thus far.

Dot Kids Domain Name Act of 2001 (H.R. 2417)

In June 2001 Representatives John Shimkus (R-Ill.) and Edward Markey (D-Mass.) introduced legislation that would direct the Internet Corporation for Assigned Names and Numbers (ICANN) to create a "kids-friendly" top-level Internet domain (TLD) in order to provide a safe online environment for children, one free of material that may be harmful to minors.

Since the bill's introduction, and its controversial reception at a House hearing, Representatives Shimkus and Markey have proposed a substitute bill that would require the National Telecommunications and Information Administration (NTIA) to create a secondary domain within the national "usTLD," such as "kids.us." The new domain would be available for voluntary use and would contain only material that is considered suitable for minors. However, the proposed substitute bill raises some serious concerns for all providers of content.

AAP is concerned with a number of issues in the proposed substitute, particularly the section dealing with civil liability. Liability protection under the bill would be afforded to anyone acting in good faith to restrict access through the new domain to material that a person or entity considers "harmful to minors, obscene, lewd, lascivious, filthy, excessively violent, harassing, or otherwise objectionable, whether or not such material is constitutionally protected." This is an entirely subjective standard that is not based on established criteria. AAP is also concerned that a person or entity whose material is constitutionally protected would not be allowed to seek an injunction or other relief against restriction because the liability standard in the bill would extend to constitutionally protected content. Another concern with the proposed substitute is its lack of specificity in establishing criteria and standards. The criterion for accepting registrants in the new ccTLD would be developed by an "independent board, with diverse membership," but the legislation does not specify how the board will be selected or how the criterion for selection will be developed.

The House Commerce Committee has suspended any further action on this bill and has directed NTIA to try to resolve the issue of "kids.us."

Anti-Spamming Act of 2001 (H.R. 718)

The "spam" bill introduced by Rep. Heather Wilson (R-N.M.) was referred both to the House Energy and Commerce Committee and the House Judiciary Committee. Separate committee mark-ups have created two competing versions of H.R. 718, which would both place restrictions on the transmission of unsolicited commercial e-mail. Although the bill was scheduled for floor action in the House last September, in the week leading up to the vote the House leadership requested that the chairmen of the two committees work out a compromise bill; a compromise had yet to be produced at the time of this writing.

Both versions of the bill would make it illegal to send unsolicited commercial e-mails from a false return e-mail address. The Judiciary bill, however, is much narrower and less restrictive than the Commerce bill. The Commerce version would create a private right of action, giving consumers the right to sue for damages if they receive spam after they have requested it not be sent to their address. The Judiciary version makes it illegal to send fraudulent e-mails.

Rep. Bob Goodlatte (R-Va.) of the House Judiciary Committee and Rep. Wilson have been meeting to negotiate the differences between the two versions of H.R. 718. They hope to reach agreement so the bill can be moved to the House floor. On the Senate side, no action had been taken by early 2002 on the issue of unsolicited commercial e-mail.

Access to Books for Children (ABC) Act (H.R. 1849)

With the support of AAP, Rep. Carolyn Maloney (D-N.Y.) has reintroduced legislation that would amend the 1966 Child Nutrition Act to provide vouchers for the purchase of educational books for infants and children participating in the WIC program (the special supplemental nutrition program for women, infants and children). The ABC Act would authorize the expenditure of $10 million over three fiscal years to enable participating local agencies to distribute book vouchers worth up to $5 to women participating in the program. The bill was referred to the House Education and the Workforce Subcommittee on Education Reform.

Book Stamp Act (H.R. 116)

On January 3, 2001, with the support of AAP, Rep. Rush Holt (D-N.J.) reintroduced legislation to establish a grant program through the secretary of health and human services to promote child literacy and improve children's access to books at home and in early learning and childcare programs. The grant program would provide books for children participating in specified programs and would also establish special postage stamps for child literacy to generate additional funding for literacy programs. The stamps would be of an image relating to a character in a children's book or cartoon, and the rate of the stamps would be the price of a first-class stamp plus a differential amount. The U.S. Postal Service would pay Health and Human Services the money raised by the stamps for child literacy promotion activities. Although the bill has 35 cosponsors and has been referred to the House Education and the Workforce Committee and the House Government Reform Committee, no further action had been taken to advance it through the House, and no Senate counterpart to the bill had been introduced by early 2002.

Contributions of Book Inventory (S. 1415)

One of the biggest partisan battles in the first session of the 107th Congress was the president's tax-cut bill, the Relief Act of 2001. This landmark legislation provided the largest tax cut in 20 years and was designed to provide tax relief over the next decade to most Americans regardless of income. It also included a tax break for publishers, which was dropped from the final legislation but might resurface later in 2002.

On the final day the bill was debated in the Senate, a group of noncontroversial amendments were included in a manager's amendment that passed the full Senate by voice vote. Included in the manager's amendment was the Contributions of Book Inventory Amendment, sponsored by Sen. Hatch. The amendment was designed to enhance the incentives for book publishers to contribute excess book inventory to educational organizations. It provided companies with an enhanced tax deduction for the contributions of book inventory to particular educational organizations.

Under the amendment, eligible educational organizations for donations are defined as (1) educational organizations that normally maintain a regular faculty and curriculum and normally have a regularly enrolled body of pupils or students in attendance at the place where its education activities are regularly carried on (schools); (2) charities organized primarily for purposes of supporting elementary and secondary education; and (3) charities organized primarily to make books available to the general public at no cost or to operate a literacy program. Unfortunately, the Senate amendment was not included in the final bill sent to the president.

Although the amendment was not included in the tax bill, there was an enormous amount of interest raised in the Senate on legislation aimed at increasing book-inventory donations by publishers. The amendment was limited in scope and did not address the disincentives that are often created because the current tax law does not allow deductions to be taken for the full market value. Sen. Hatch has reintroduced his proposal as a stand-alone bill, S. 1415. It is estimated by Congress's Joint Committee on Taxation that the additional tax deduction if the bill were enacted would be about $246 million for deductions of books over the next ten years. AAP is working with the senator's staff to expand his proposal to allow book publishers to deduct the full market value.

Deductions for Teachers for Professional Development Expenses and Credits for Classroom Materials (S. 495)

Two other amendments of possible interest to AAP members were adopted by the Senate in the manager's amendment to the Relief Act: (1) Deduction for Qualified Professional Development Expenses of Elementary and Secondary School Teachers, and (2) Credit for Classroom Materials. Although neither amendment was ultimately included in the final act sent to the president, both amendments passed the full Senate, and a number of senators showed interest in pursuing these goals in other legislation. AAP will support both provisions if another opportunity for passage arises.

The Deduction for Qualified Professional Development Expenses of Elementary and Secondary School Teachers amendment would have permitted teachers an above-the-line deduction for up to $500 for qualified professional development expenses. The deduction would have been available to kindergarten through 12th grade teachers, instructors, and other staff who work 900 hours during a school year in an elementary or secondary school. The deductible expenses included tuition, fees, books, supplies, and equipment.

The Credit for Classroom Materials amendment would have provided a nonrefundable personal credit not to exceed $250 in any year. The credit would have been available to kindergarten through 12th grade teachers, instructors, and other staff who work 900 hours during a school year in an elementary or secondary school. The credits were for books, supplies, computer equipment (software), and supplementary materials.

Although the amendments did not make it into the final act, Sen. Hatch has introduced similar legislation in the Senate. The Tax Equity for School Teachers Act (S. 495) allows eligible kindergarten, elementary, and secondary school teachers and instructors the opportunity to deduct for certain professional development expenses and an unlimited deduction for out-of-pocket expenses for classroom supplies.

Online Privacy (S. 1055)

At the beginning of the 107th Congress, online privacy appeared to be one of the hot-button issues. But as the session progressed, action on privacy bills has been slow, with just a few hearings being held. Many still ask whether the industry's continued self-regulation is enough or whether it needs to be supplemented with federal legislation designed to protect the privacy interests of individual users. Although the online privacy issue is complex and multifaceted, constant public discussion has reduced the major issues to five basic principles of "notice," "disclosure," "access," "choice" ("opt-in" versus "opt-out"), and "security." Each of these issues raises a variety of subissues, which makes reaching consensus on an overall statutory approach to online privacy a difficult task.

In the past, the Federal Trade Commission (FTC) has sought increased authority to address and regulate online privacy. In May 2000, for example, FTC released a report concluding that legislation to ensure a minimum level of privacy protection by incorporating the basic principles mentioned above, coupled with continued industry self-regulation, would increase consumer confidence in e-commerce. Recent changes in the FTC leadership and staff, however, have shifted the focus away from support of online privacy legislation.

On November 7, 2001, Timothy J. Muris, the new FTC chairman, testified before the House Energy and Commerce Subcommittee on Commerce, Trade and Consumer Protection that the majority of FTC does not support enactment of online privacy legislation. Instead, Muris stated, FTC is now focusing on the enforcement of existing consumer privacy laws, additional rulemaking, and continued education for both the consumer and business.

Last June, Sen. Dianne Feinstein (D-Calif.) introduced the Privacy Act of 2001, S. 1055, comprehensive legislation to address the increased theft of personal information and other privacy abuses on the Internet and through other media. The bill would set up a two-tiered system where customers would be allowed to "opt out" of sharing nonsensitive information and "opt in" to the sale of sensitive personal information. Under the legislation, companies that wanted to collect and then sell a customer's nonsensitive information (for example, address or phone number) would be required to offer the customer the opportunity to opt out of the sale. If the company would like to sell, license, or rent sensitive personal information (for example, Social Security numbers, driver's license numbers, and financial and health data), the bill would require the individual whose personal information is for sale to opt in to the sale. Although the Senate Judiciary Subcommittee on Technology, Terrorism, and Government Information held a hearing, at this writing no further action had been taken to advance the bill through the Senate, and no House counterpart had been introduced.

Funding Programs and Grant-Making Agencies

National Endowment for the Humanities

1100 Pennsylvania Ave. N.W., Washington, DC 20506
202-606-8400, 800-634-1121
World Wide Web http://www.neh.fed.us

Thomas C. Phelps

Democracy demands wisdom and vision in its citizens
—National Foundation on the Arts and Humanities Act of 1965

The Humanities

The humanities are the many voices that shape our lives. They are the voices of our parents and grandparents heard over dinner. They are also the historic voices from the fields of literature, history, and philosophy, voices of Plato and Shakespeare, of Abraham Lincoln and Martin Luther King, of Mark Twain and Frederick Douglass.

A strong nation requires an educated citizenry, a people who understand their roots and who can envision their future. For more than three decades the National Endowment for the Humanities (NEH) has protected both the United States' past and its future. Each of the NEH core programs has given critical support to the nation's educational and cultural life. The Research and Education Divisions support summer seminars and research for teachers that enrich the classroom experience for hundreds of thousands of students each year. Public Programs supports high-quality television and radio programs and museum exhibits; the Challenge Grants Division helps build endowment for educational programs; Preservation and Access has saved hundreds of thousands of brittle books and newspapers; and state councils help enrich grassroots humanities programs throughout the nation.

The National Endowment for the Humanities

The act that established the National Endowment for the Humanities says

The term "humanities" includes, but is not limited to, the study of the following: language, both modern and classical; linguistics; literature; history; jurisprudence; philosophy; archaeology; comparative religion; ethics; the history, criticism, and theory of the arts; those aspects of social sciences which have humanistic content and employ humanistic methods; and the study and application of the humanities to the human environment with particular attention to reflecting our diverse heritage, traditions, and history and to the relevance of the humanities to the current conditions of national life.

This act, adopted by Congress in 1965, provided for the establishment of the National Foundation on the Arts and the Humanities, which would promote progress and scholarship in the humanities and the arts. It declared the findings and purposes of the endowments as follows:

- The arts and the humanities belong to all the people of the United States.
- The encouragement and support of national progress and scholarship in the humanities and the arts, while primarily a matter for private and local initiative, are also appropriate matters of concern to the federal government.
- An advanced civilization must not limit its efforts to science and technology alone, but must give full value and support to the other great branches of scholarly and cultural activity in order to achieve a better understanding of the past, a better analysis of the present, and a better view of the future.
- Democracy demands wisdom and vision in its citizens. It must therefore foster and support a form of education, and access to the arts and the humanities, designed to make people of all backgrounds and wherever located masters of their technology and not its unthinking servants.
- It is necessary and appropriate for the federal government to complement, assist, and add to programs for the advancement of the humanities and the arts by local, state, regional, and private agencies and their organizations. In doing so, the government must be sensitive to the nature of public sponsorship. Public funding of the arts and humanities is subject to the conditions that traditionally govern the use of public money. Such funding should contribute to public support and confidence in the use of taxpayer funds. Public funds provided by the federal government must ultimately serve public purposes the Congress defines.
- The arts and the humanities reflect the high place accorded by the American people to the nation's rich cultural heritage and to the fostering of mutual respect for the diverse beliefs and values of all persons and groups.

About NEH

Over the past 36 years, the endowment has reached millions of Americans with projects and programs that preserve and study the nation's cultural heritage while providing a foundation for the future.

The endowment's mission is to enrich American cultural life by promoting the study of history and culture. NEH grants typically go to individuals and cultural institutions such as museums, archives, libraries, colleges, universities, and historical societies, and public television and radio stations. The grants

- Preserve and provide access to cultural and educational resources
- Strengthen teaching and learning in schools and colleges
- Promote research and original scholarship
- Provide opportunities for lifelong learning
- Strengthen the institutional base of the humanities

What NEH Grants Accomplish

Interpretive Exhibitions

Interpretive exhibitions provide opportunities for lifelong learning in the humanities for millions of Americans. Since 1967 NEH has made more than 2,400 grants totaling nearly $190 million for interpretive exhibitions, catalogs, and public programs, which are among the most highly visible activities supported by the agency. All 50 states and the District of Columbia will host more than 122 exhibitions over the next two years. They range from the Newberry Library's exhibition about King Arthur to an exhibition based on Mary Shelley's *Frankenstein* that will travel to 40 libraries throughout the country.

Renewing Teaching

Over the years, more than 20,000 high school teachers and nearly 30,000 college teachers have deepened their knowledge of the humanities through intensive summer study supported by NEH; it is estimated that more than 140,000 students benefit from these better-educated teachers in the first year alone.

Reading and Discussion Programs

Since 1982 NEH has supported reading and discussion programs in the nation's libraries, bringing people together to discuss works of literature and history. Groups are facilitated by scholars in the humanities who provide thematic direction for the discussion programs. Using well-selected texts and themes such as Work, Family, Diversity, and Not for Children Only, these programs have attracted more than 1 million participants.

Preserving the Nation's Heritage

The United States Newspaper Program is rescuing a piece of history by cataloging and microfilming 57 million pages from 133,000 newspapers dating from the early days of the republic. Another microfilming program has rescued the content of more than 860,000 brittle books.

Stimulating Private Support

More than $1.3 billion in humanities support has been generated by NEH's Challenge Grants program, which requires most recipients to raise $3 or $4 in nonfederal funds for every dollar they receive.

Presidential Papers

Ten presidential papers projects are underwritten by NEH, from George Washington to Dwight David Eisenhower. The Washington and Eisenhower papers have each leveraged more than $1.4 million in nonfederal contributions.

New Scholarship

Endowment grants enable scholars to do in-depth study. Jack Rakove explored the making of the Constitution in his *Original Meanings,* while James McPherson chronicled the Civil War in his *Battle Cry of Freedom.* Both won the Pulitzer Prize.

History on Screen

Thirty-eight million Americans saw the Ken Burns documentary *The Civil War,* and 750,000 people bought the book. Through other films such as *Liberty!, Jazz,* and *The Invisible Man,* and film biographies of presidents Theodore and Franklin Roosevelt, philanthropist Andrew Carnegie, and Gen. Douglas MacArthur, Americans learn about the events and people that shaped the nation.

Library of America

Two million books have been sold as part of the Library of America series, a collection of the riches of our literature. Begun with NEH seed money, the 122 published volumes include the writings of Henry Adams, Edith Wharton, William James, Eudora Welty, and W. E. B. DuBois, as well as 19th- and 20th-century American poets. Recently, a $1 million gift to NEH from the Carnegie Corporation of New York enabled 800 public libraries throughout the United States to add 50 of the latest volumes of the Library of America to their collections.

Science and the Humanities

The scientific past is being preserved with NEH-supported editions of the letters of Charles Darwin, the works of Albert Einstein, and the 14-volume papers of Thomas A. Edison.

The Sound of Poetry

One million Americans use cassettes from the NEH-supported Voices and Visions series on poets. As a telecourse, Voices reached more than 200 colleges, 2,000 high schools, and 500 public libraries.

Learning Under the Tent

From California to Florida, state humanities councils bring a 21st century version of Chautauqua to the public, embracing populations of entire towns, cities, even regions. Scholars portray significant figures such as Meriweather Lewis, Sojourner Truth, Willa Cather, Teddy Roosevelt, and Sacagawea, first speaking as the historic character and later giving audiences opportunities to ask questions. The give and take between the scholar/performer and the audiences provides an entertaining, energetic, and thought-provoking exchange about experiences and attitudes in the present and the past.

Special Initiatives

Public/Private Partnerships

The Enterprise Office raises funds for endowment activities, creates partnerships with other federal agencies and private organizations, implements endowment-wide special initiatives, and explores leadership opportunities for the agency. Below are NEH projects developed through public/private partnerships.

A Core Collection for America's Libraries—The Millennium Project for Public Libraries. Millions of Americans will soon have access to writings by many of this country's greatest authors through a national library initiative. More than 800 libraries will receive the 50 most recently published volumes of the distinguished American literature series of the Library of America (LOA).

NEH has been awarded a $1 million grant by the Carnegie Corporation of New York to help budget-strapped public libraries add high-quality literary editions to their collections and expand opportunities for educational programs within their communities. Other partners in the initiative include LOA and the American Library Association (ALA). Libraries that receive the 50 most recent LOA editions will be selected in an open competition administered by NEH.

My History Is America's History. This is a nationwide initiative of the National Endowment for the Humanities, in partnership with the White House Millennium Council, the President's Committee on the Arts and the Humanities, Genealogy.com, PSINet Inc., National Association of Broadcasters, U.S. Department of Education, Heritage Preservation, FamilyFun, and Houghton Mifflin Company.

The project outlines 15 things individuals can do to save America's stories in the My History guidebook, Web site, and poster, and includes simple, easy-to-follow steps to preserve stories and treasures. Among the tools are sample questions for drawing out relatives' memories; tips on preserving family treasures such as photographs, furniture, and videotapes; and classroom and family projects to give children a personal connection to American history. A listing of national and local resources such as historical sites and societies, exhibits, and genealogical groups is also provided. The My History Web site is found at http://www.myhistory.org.

Regional Centers. NEH has launched a competition to create Regional Humanities Centers in ten regions of the United States. Twenty institutions are currently in their planning phase and will compete for implementation grants. The centers are intended to become cultural hubs for the support of research on regional topics; the documentation and preservation of regional history and cultural resources; collaboration with teachers, schools, and colleges; public programming; and resources for cultural tourism.

EDSITEment. This joint project to share the best humanities Web sites with teachers and students was launched in 1997 by NEH, the Council of the Great City Schools (CGCS), and MCI (now MCI WorldCom). Users of EDSITEment (http://edsitement.neh.gov) have access to more than 100 high-quality humanities sites, representing more than 50,000 files searchable through the EDSITEment search engine, http://www.edsitement.neh.gov.

Extending the Reach

A priority of NEH is to make the power and inspiration of the humanities accessible to all Americans. Extending the Reach is a new series of funding opportunities directed at selected jurisdictions and constituencies throughout the United States. During 2000 and 2001 NEH offered three new grant programs targeted to the underserved jurisdictions listed below: Consultation Grants for public programs, Preservation Assistance Grants, and Humanities Scholar in Residence. These jurisdictions are Alabama, Alaska, Florida, Idaho, Louisiana, Missouri, Montana, Nevada, North Dakota, Ohio, Oklahoma, Puerto Rico, Texas, Washington, and Wyoming.

As a special response to three presidential directives, NEH offers two grant programs intended to strengthen the humanities at Historically Black, Hispanic Serving, and Tribal Colleges and Universities around the nation.

Federal/State Partnership

The Office of Federal-State Partnership links NEH with the nationwide network of 56 humanities councils, which are located in each state, the District of Columbia, Puerto Rico, the U.S. Virgin Islands, the Northern Mariana Islands, American Samoa, and Guam. Each humanities council funds humanities programs in its own jurisdiction. A contact list for all the councils can be found at the end of this article.

NEH Overview

Division of Preservation and Access

Grants are made for projects that will create, preserve, and increase the availability of resources important for research, education, and public programming in the humanities.

Projects may encompass books, journals, newspapers, manuscript and archival materials, maps, still and moving images, sound recordings, and objects of material culture held by libraries, archives, museums, historical organizations, and other repositories.

Preservation and Access Projects

Support may be sought to preserve the intellectual content and aid bibliographic control of collections; to compile bibliographies, descriptive catalogs, and guides to cultural holdings; to create dictionaries, encyclopedias, databases, and other types of research tools and reference works; and to stabilize material culture collections through the appropriate housing and storing of objects, improved environmental control, and the installation of security, lighting, and fire-prevention systems. Applications may also be submitted for national and regional education and training projects, regional preservation field service programs, and research and demonstration projects that are intended to enhance institutional practice and the use of technology for preservation and access.

Proposals may combine preservation and access activities within a single project. Historically Black Colleges and Universities (HCBUs) with significant institutional collections of primary materials are encouraged to apply.

Eligible applicants:	Individuals, nonprofit institutions and cultural organizations, state agencies, and institutional consortia.
Application deadline:	July 1
Contact:	202-606-8570, e-mail preservation@neh.gov.

Division of Public Programs

The Division of Public Programs fosters public understanding and appreciation of the humanities by supporting projects that bring significant insights about these disciplines to general audiences of all ages through interpretive exhibitions, radio and television programs, lectures, symposia, multimedia projects, printed materials, and reading and discussion groups.

Public Programs

Grants support consultation with scholars and humanities programming experts to shape an interpretive project; the planning and production of television and radio programs in the humanities intended for general audiences; the planning and implementation of exhibitions, the interpretation of historic sites, and the production of related publications, multimedia components, and educational programs; and the planning and implementation of projects through the use of books, new technologies, and other resources in the collections of libraries and archives in formats such as reading and discussion programs, lectures, symposia, and interpretive exhibitions of books, manuscripts, and other library resources.

Eligible applicants:	Nonprofit institutions and organizations including public television and radio stations and state humanities councils.
Application deadlines:	Planning, scripting, implementation, production, February 1; Consultation grants, April 16 and August 26.
Contact:	202-606-8267, e-mail publicpgms@neh.gov.

Division of Research Programs

Through fellowships to individual scholars and grants to support complex, frequently collaborative, research, the Division of Research Programs contributes to the creation of knowledge in the humanities.

Fellowships and Stipends

Grants provide support for scholars to undertake full-time independent research and writing in the humanities. Grants are available for a maximum of one year and a minimum of two months of summer study.

Eligible applicants:	Individuals.
Application deadlines:	Fellowships, May 1; Summer Stipends, October 1.
Contact:	202-606-8466 for Fellowships for University Teachers, 202-606-8467 for Fellowships for College Teachers and Independent Scholars, 202-606-8551 for Summer Stipends; e-mail: fellowships@neh.gov (for Fellowships), stipends@neh.gov (for Summer Stipends).

Research

Grants provide up to three years of support for collaborative research in the preparation for publication of editions, translations, and other important works in the humanities, and in the conduct of large or complex interpretive studies including archaeology projects and the humanities studies of science and technology. Grants also support research opportunities offered through independent research centers and international research organizations.

Eligible Applicants:	Individuals, institutions of higher education, nonprofit professional associations, scholarly societies, and other nonprofit organizations.
Application deadlines:	Collaborative Research and Fellowships at Independent Research Institutions, September 1.
Contact:	202-606-8200, e-mail research@neh.gov.

Division of Education

Through grants to educational institutions, fellowships to scholars and teachers, and through the support of significant research, this division is designed to strengthen sustained, thoughtful study of the humanities at all levels of education and promote original research in the humanities.

Education Development and Demonstration

Grants, including "next semester" Humanities Focus Grants, support curriculum and materials development efforts; faculty study programs within and among educational institutions; and conferences and networks of institutions. NEH is interested in projects that help teachers use the new electronic technologies to enhance students' understanding of humanities subjects.

Eligible applicants:	Public and private elementary and secondary schools, school systems, colleges and universities, nonprofit academic associations, and cultural institutions such as libraries and museums.
Application deadlines:	National Education Projects, October 15; Humanities Focus Grants, April 15.
Contact:	202-606-8380, e-mail education@neh.gov.

Schools for a New Millennium

Grants enable whole schools, in partnership with colleges and communities, to design professional development activities integrating digital technology into the humanities classroom.

Application deadlines:	Implementation Grants, October 1.
Contact:	202-606-8380, e-mail education@neh.gov.

Seminars and Institutes

Grants support summer seminars and national institutes in the humanities for college instructors and schoolteachers. These faculty development activities are conducted at colleges and universities across the country.

Eligibility:	Individuals, and institutions of higher learning.
Application deadlines for seminars:	Participants, March 1 for summer seminars; Directors, March 1 for summer seminars the following year.
Contact:	202-606-8463, e-mail sem-inst@neh.gov.
Application deadline for national institutes:	March 1.
Contact:	202-606-8463, e-mail sem-inst@neh.gov.

Office of Challenge Grants

Nonprofit institutions interested in developing new sources of long-term support for educational, scholarly, preservation, and public programs in the humanities may be assisted in these efforts by an NEH Challenge Grant. Grantees are required to raise $3 or $4 in new or increased donations for every federal dollar offered. Both federal and nonfederal funds may be used to establish or increase institutional endowments and thus guarantee long-term support for a variety of humanities needs. Funds may also be used for limited direct capital expenditures, where such needs are compelling and clearly related to improvements in the humanities.

Eligible applicants:	Nonprofit postsecondary, educational, research, or cultural institutions and organizations working within the humanities.
Application deadline:	May 1.
Contact:	202-606-8309, e-mail challenge@neh.gov.

Directory of State Humanities Councils

Alabama Humanities Foundation

205-558-3980, fax 205-558-3981
E-mail ahf@ahf.net
http://www.ahf.net

Alaska Humanities Forum

907-272-5341, fax 907-272-3979
E-mail info@akhf.org
http://www.akhf.org

Arizona Humanities Council

602-257-0335, fax 602-257-0392
E-mail dan.shilling@asu.edu
http://www.azhumanities.org

Arkansas Humanities Council

501-221-0091, fax 501-221-9860
E-mail ahc@aristotle.net
http://www.arkhums.org

California Council for the Humanities

415-391-1474, fax 415-391-1312
E-mail info@calhum.org
http://www.calhum.org

Colorado Endowment for the Humanities

303-894-7951, fax 303-864-9361
E-mail info@ceh.org
http://www.ceh.org

Connecticut Humanities Council

860-685-2260, fax 860-704-0429
E-mail brucefraser@cthum.org
http://www.cthum.org

Delaware Humanities Forum

302-657-0650, fax 302-657-0655
E-mail dhfdirector@dca.net
http://www.dhf.org

Humanities Council of Washington, D.C.

202-347-1732, fax 202-347-3350
E-mail hcwdc@humanities-wdc.org
http://www.humanities-wdc.org

Florida Humanities Council

813-272-3473, fax 813-272-3314
E-mail fcary@flahum.org
http://www.flahum.org

Georgia Humanities Council

404-523-6220, fax 404-523-5702
E-mail ghc@emory.edu
http://www.georgiahumanities.org

Hawaii Council for the Humanities

808-732-5402, fax 808-732-5402
E-mail hch@aloha.net
http://www.planet-hawaii.com/hch

Idaho Humanities Council

208-345-5346, fax 208-345-5347
E-mail rickihc@micron.net
http://www2.state.id.us/ihc

Illinois Humanities Council

312-422-5580, fax 312-422-5588
E-mail ihc@prairie.org
http://www.prairie.org

Indiana Humanities Council

317-638-1500, fax 317-634-9503
E-mail ihc@iupui.edu
http://www.ihc4u.org

Humanities Iowa

319-335-4153, fax 319-335-4154
E-mail info@humanitiesiowa.org
http://www.humanitiesiowa.org

Kansas Humanities Council

785-357-0359, fax 785-357-1723
E-mail kshumcoun@aol.com
http://www.ukans.edu/kansas/khc

Kentucky Humanities Council

606-257-5932, fax 606-257-5933
E-mail vgsmit00@pop.uky.edu
http://www.kyhumanities.org

Louisiana Endowment for the Humanities

504-523-4352, fax 504-529-2358
E-mail leh@leh.org
http://www.leh.org

Maine Humanities Council

207-773-5051, fax 207-773-2416
E-mail info@mainehumanities.org
http://www.mainehumanities.org

Maryland Humanities Council

410-771-0650, fax 410-771-0655
E-mail mhcwebpage@aol.com
http://www.mdhc.org

Massachusetts Foundation for the Humanities

413-536-1385, fax 413-534-6918
E-mail tebaldi@mfh.org
http://www.mfh.org

Michigan Humanities Council

517-372-7770, fax 517-372-0027
E-mail mihum@voyager.net
http://mihumanities.h-net.msu.edu

Minnesota Humanities Commission

651-774-0105, fax 651-774-0205
E-mail mnhum@thinkmhc.org
http://www.thinkmhc.org

Mississippi Humanities Council

601-432-6752, fax 601-432-6750
E-mail barbara@mhc.state.ms.us
http://www.ihl.state.ms.us/mhc/index.html

Missouri Humanities Council

314-781-9660, fax 314-781-9681
E-mail mail@mohumanities.org
http://www.umsl.edu/community/mohuman

Montana Committee for the Humanities

406-243-6022, fax 406-243-4836
E-mail lastbest@selway.umt.edu
http://www.humanities-mt.org

Nebraska Humanities Council

402-474-2131, fax 402-474-4852
E-mail nehumanities@juno.com
http://www.lincolnne.com/nonprofit/nhc

Nevada Humanities Committee

775-784-6587, fax 775-784-6527
E-mail winzeler@scs.unr.edu
http://www.unr.edu/nhc

New Hampshire Humanities Council

603-224-4071, fax 603-224-4072
E-mail nhhum@nhhc.org
http://www.nhhc.org

New Jersey Council for the Humanities

609-695-4838, fax 609-695-4929
E-mail njch@njch.org
http://www.njch.org

New Mexico Endowment for the Humanities

505-277-3705, fax 505-277-6056
E-mail nmeh@unm.edu
http://www.nmeh.org

New York Council for the Humanities

212-233-1131, fax 212-233-4607
E-mail hum@echonyc.com
http://www.culturefront.org

North Carolina Humanities Council

336-334-5325, fax 336-334-5052
E-mail nchc@gborocollege.edu
http://www.nchumanities.org

North Dakota Humanities Council

701-255-3360, fax 701-223-8724
E-mail council@nd-humanities.org
http://www.nd-humanities.org

Ohio Humanities Council

614-461-7802, fax 614-461-4651
E-mail ohc@ohiohumanities.org
http://www.ohiohumanities.org

Oklahoma Humanities Council

405-235-0280, fax 405-235-0289
E-mail okhum@flash.net
http://www.okhumanitiescouncil.org

Oregon Council for the Humanities

503-241-0543, fax 503-241-0024
E-mail och@oregonhum.org
http://www.oregonhum.org

Pennsylvania Humanities Council

215-925-1005, fax 215-925-3054
E-mail phc@pahumanities.org
http://www.pahumanities.org

Rhode Island Committee for the Humanities

401-273-2250, fax 401-454-4872
E-mail kelly@etal.uri.edu
http://www.uri.edu/rich

South Carolina Humanities Council

803-691-4100, fax 803-691-0809
E-mail bobschc@aol.com
http://www.schumanities.org

South Dakota Humanities Council

605-688-6113, fax 605-688-4531
E-mail sdhc@ur.sdstate.edu
http://web.sdstate.edu/humanities

Tennessee Humanities Council

615-320-7001, fax 615-321-4586
E-mail robert@tn-humanities.org
http://tn-humanities.org

Texas Council for the Humanities

512-440-1991, fax 512-440-0115
E-mail postmaster@public-humanities.org
http://www.public-humanities.org

Utah Humanities Council

801-359-9670, fax 801-531-7869
E-mail buckingham@utah_humanities.org
http://www.utahhumanities.org

Vermont Council on the Humanities

802-888-3183, fax 802-888-1236
E-mail info@vermont_humanities.org
http://www.vermonthumanities.org

Virginia Foundation for the Humanities

804-924-3296, fax 804-296-4714
E-mail rcv@virginia.edu
http://www.virginia.edu/vfh

Washington Commission for the Humanities

206-682-1770, fax 206-682-4158
E-mail wch@humanities.org
http://www.humanities.org

West Virginia Humanities Council

304-346-8500, fax 304-346-8504
E-mail wvhuman@wvhc.com
http://www.wvhc.com

Wisconsin Humanities Council

608-262-0706, fax 608-263-7970
E-mail whc@danenet.org
http://www.danenet.org/whc

Wyoming Council for the Humanities

307-766-6496, fax 307-742-4914
E-mail hummer@uwyo.edu
http://www.uwyo.edu/special/wch

Amerika Samoa Humanities Council

684-633-4870, fax 684-633-4873
E-mail ashc@samoatelco.com
(No Web address)

Guam Humanities Council

671-646-4461, fax 671-646-2243
E-mail ghc@kuentos.guam.net
http://www.guam.net/pub/guamhumanities

Northern Mariana Islands Council for the Humanities

670-235-4785, fax 670-235-4786
E-mail ron.barrineau@saipan.com
http://cnmi.humanities.org.mp

Fundación Puertorriqueña de las Humanidades

787-721-2087, fax 787-721-2684
E-mail fph@caribe.net
http://www.fprh.org

Virgin Islands Humanities Council

340-776-4044, fax 340-774-3972
E-mail vihc@viaccess.net
(No Web address)

Institute of Museum and Library Services Library Programs

1100 Pennsylvania Ave. N.W., Washington, DC 20506
202-606-5527, fax 202-606-1077
World Wide Web http://www.imls.gov

Robert S. Martin
Director
Institute of Museum and Library Services

The Library Services and Technology Act (LSTA), Subchapter II of the Museum and Library Services Act of 1996, changed the federal administration of library programs by moving programs from the Department of Education (DOE) to the newly formed Institute of Museum and Library Services (IMLS). The first LSTA grants were made in 1998. A total of $207,469,000 was available for library programs in fiscal year (FY) 2001. LSTA funds are administered by the Office of Library Services. The Office of Museum Services administers grants to museums.

The purposes of LSTA are

- To consolidate federal library service programs
- To stimulate excellence and promote access to learning and information resources in all types of libraries for individuals of all ages
- To promote library services that provide all users access to information through state, regional, national, and international electronic networks
- To provide linkages between and among libraries
- To promote targeted library service to people of diverse geographic, cultural, and socioeconomic backgrounds, to individuals with disabilities, and to people with limited functional literacy or information skills

Within IMLS, the Office of Library Services is responsible for the administration of LSTA. It is composed of the Division of State Programs, which administers the Grants to States Program, and the Division of Discretionary Programs, which administers the National Leadership Grant Program, the Native American Library Services Program, and the Native Hawaiian Library Services Program.

State-Administered Programs

Approximately 90 percent of the annual federal appropriation under LSTA is distributed through the State Grant Program to the state library administrative agencies according to a population-based formula. The formula consists of a minimum amount set by the law ($340,000 for the states and $40,000 for the Pacific Territories) and supplemented by an additional amount based on population. For 2001, the State Grant Program appropriation was $148,939,000 (Table 1).

State agencies may use the appropriation for statewide initiatives and services. They may also distribute the funds through competitive subgrants or cooperative agreements to public, academic, research, school, or special libraries.

For-profit and federal libraries are not eligible applicants. LSTA State Grant funds have been used to meet the special needs of children, parents, teenagers, the unemployed, senior citizens, and the business community, as well as adult learners. Many libraries have partnered with community organizations to provide a variety of services and programs, including access to electronic databases, computer instruction, homework centers, summer reading programs, digitization of special collections, access to E-books and adaptive technology, bookmobile service, and development of outreach programs to the underserved. The act limits the amount of funds available for administration at the state level to 4 percent and requires a 34 percent match from nonfederal state or local funds. Grants to the Pacific Territories and Freely Associated States (FAS) are funded under a Special Rule (20 USCA 9131(b)(3)) that authorizes a small competitive grants program in the Pacific. There are six eligible entities in two groups: the Pacific Territories (Insular areas) consisting of Guam, American Samoa, and the Commonwealth of Northern Mariana Islands; and the FAS, which includes the Federated States of Micronesia, the Republic of the Marshall Islands, and the Republic of Palau. The funds for this grant program are taken from the allotments for the FAS (Federated States of Micronesia, Republic of Marshall Islands, and Palau), but not from the allotments to the territories. The three territories (Guam, American Samoa, and the Commonwealth of Northern Mariana Islands) receive their allotments through the regular program and in addition may apply for funds under this program. Five entities (Guam, the Commonwealth of Northern Mariana Islands, the Federated States of Micronesia, the Republic of Marshall Islands, and Palau) received a total of $222,821 in FY 2001. This amount included the set-aside of 5 percent because Pacific Resources for Education and Learning

Table 1 / Funding for LSTA State Programs, FY 2001
Total Distributed to States: $148,939,000[1]

State	Federal Allocation[2] 66%	State Matching Fund 34%	Total
Alabama	$2,376,626	$1,224,322	$3,600,948
Alaska	627,114	323,059	950,173
Arizona	2,689,661	1,385,583	4,075,244
Arkansas	1,564,329	805,866	2,370,195
California	15,852,102	8,166,234	24,018,336
Colorado	2,309,836	1,189,916	3,499,752
Connecticut	1,899,637	978,601	2,878,238
Delaware	698,863	360,020	1,058,883
Florida	7,659,404	3,945,754	11,605,158
Georgia	4,089,127	2,106,520	6,195,647
Hawaii	894,844	460,980	1,355,824
Idaho	932,588	480,424	1,413,012
Illinois	6,027,628	3,105,142	9,132,770
Indiana	3,124,662	1,609,674	4,734,336
Iowa	1,680,160	865,537	2,545,697
Kansas	1,571,207	809,410	2,380,617
Kentucky	2,190,997	1,128,695	3,319,692
Louisiana	2,386,644	1,229,483	3,616,127

Maine	923,873	475,935	1,399,808
Maryland	2,765,617	1,424,712	4,190,329
Massachusetts	3,247,678	1,673,046	4,920,724
Michigan	4,891,481	2,519,854	7,411,335
Minnesota	2,592,960	1,335,767	3,928,727
Mississippi	1,642,760	846,270	2,489,030
Missouri	2,902,423	1,495,188	4,397,611
Montana	753,176	388,000	1,141,176
Nebraska	1,123,702	578,877	1,702,579
Nevada	1,255,136	646,585	1,901,721
New Hampshire	905,949	466,701	1,372,650
New Jersey	4,193,496	2,160,286	6,353,782
New Mexico	1,173,063	604,305	1,777,368
New York	9,030,594	4,652,124	13,682,718
North Carolina	4,026,321	2,074,165	6,100,486
North Dakota	634,107	326,661	960,768
Ohio	5,539,365	2,853,612	8,392,977
Oklahoma	1,920,286	989,238	2,909,524
Oregon	1,906,888	982,336	2,889,224
Pennsylvania	5,964,319	3,072,528	9,036,847
Rhode Island	820,096	422,474	1,242,570
South Carolina	2,177,370	1,121,675	3,299,045
South Dakota	685,694	353,236	1,038,930
Tennessee	2,945,505	1,517,381	4,462,886
Texas	9,889,449	5,094,565	14,984,014
Utah	1,362,718	702,006	2,064,724
Vermont	618,823	318,788	937,611
Virginia	3,581,727	1,845,132	5,426,859
Washington	3,039,314	1,565,707	4,605,021
West Virginia	1,168,162	601,780	1,769,942
Wisconsin	2,796,387	1,440,563	4,236,950
Wyoming	566,136	291,646	857,782
District of Columbia	601,984	310,113	912,097
Puerto Rico	2,143,161	1,104,053	3,247,214
American Samoa	69,972	36,046	106,018
Northern Marianas	72,933	37,572	110,505
Guam	112,156	57,777	169,933
Virgin Islands	95,969	49,439	145,408
Pacific Territories[3]	222,821	114,787	337,608
Total	$148,939,000	$76,726,150	$225,665,150

1 The amount available to states is based on the balance remaining after enacted allocations have been subtracted from the total appropriation as follows:

Library allocation, FY2001	$207,469,000
Native Americans, Native Hawaiians	$2,940,000
National Leadership Grants	$50,550,000
Administration	$5,040,000
Total Distributed to States	$148,939,000

2 Calculation is based on minimum set in the law (P.L. 104-208, as amended by P.L. 105-128 111 Stat 2548) and reflects appropriations enacted by P.L. 106-554. Data for the District of Columbia and the 50 states are from Bureau of Census (BOC) estimates as of April 1, 2000, which were made available by BOC December 28, 2000. For the continental United States, BOC data can be accessed at the BOC Web site: http://www.census.gov/population/cen2000/tab02.xls. Data for the Marshall Islands, Federated States of Micronesia, Puerto Rico, American Samoa, the Northern Marianas, Guam, the Virgin Islands, and Palau areas are available from the BOC international database: http://www.census.gov/cgi-bin/ipc/idbrank.pl. Data are also available by phone at 301-457-2422. It is important to use the most recent data available at the time distributions are made because BOC estimates sometimes change.

3 Total allotment (including administrative costs) for Palau, Marshall Islands, and Micronesia. Funds are awarded on a competitive basis and administered by Pacific Resources for Education and Learning.

(PREL), based in Hawaii, facilitated the competition. PREL received the set-aside amount to administer parts of the program.

Priorities for funding that support the goals of LSTA are set by the individual State Library Administrative Agencies (SLAAs) based on needs they identify in the five-year plans they are required to submit to IMLS. Currently, SLAAs are evaluating the use of LSTA funds for the first five years of the program; new five-year plans are due to IMLS by July 31, 2002.

Discretionary Programs

In 1998 IMLS also began administering the discretionary programs of LSTA. In FY 2001 $53,490,000* was allocated for the National Leadership Grant Program, the Native American Library Services Program, and the Native Hawaiian Library Services Grant Program. This includes $39,469,000 for directed grants.

The Native American Library Services program provides opportunities for improved library services for an important part of the nation's community of library users. The IMLS Native American Library Services program offers three types of support to serve the range of needs of Indian tribes and Alaska Native villages. The Native Hawaiian Library Services program provides opportunities for improved library services to Native Hawaiians through a single award. The National Leadership Grant program provides funding for innovative model programs to enhance the quality of library services nationwide. National Leadership Grants are intended to produce results useful for the broader library community.

The FY 2001 Congressional appropriation for discretionary programs includes the following:

- National Leadership Program: $11,081,000 for competitive programs
- Native American Library Services Program: $2,520,000
- Native Hawaiian Library Services Program: $420,000

National Leadership Grant Program

In 2001 IMLS awarded 49 grants totaling $11,116,150 for National Leadership Grants using FY 2001 funding. This figure represents 3.75 percent of the LSTA appropriation for competitive programs, plus $1,000,000 from the IMLS Office of Museum Services to supplement funding for library and museum collaborations. A total of 132 applications requesting more than $28,480,571 were received. The projects funded were selected as innovative model projects in the field of library and information science in education and training, research and demonstration, creation and preservation of digital media, and library and museum collaborations (Table 2).

The FY 2001 priorities for National Leadership Grant funding are

Education and Training

- Projects to help libraries take a leadership role in the education of lifelong learners in the 21st century

---

* Includes $1,000,000 from the IMLS Office of Museum Services to supplement LSTA funding for library and museum collaborations.

- Projects to attract individuals from diverse cultural backgrounds to the field of librarianship and information science
- Projects that implement innovative approaches to education and training and enhance the availability of professional librarians with advanced skills and specializations
- Projects that train librarians to enhance people's ability to use information effectively
- Projects that train librarians in outcome-based evaluation techniques

Research and Demonstration

- Projects to help libraries take a leadership role in the education of lifelong learners in the 21st century
- Projects that conduct research and/or demonstrations to enhance library services through the effective and efficient use of new and appropriate technologies
- Projects that conduct research and/or demonstrations to enhance the ability of library users to make more effective use of information resources
- Projects that conduct research and/or demonstrations that will assist in the evaluation of library services, including economic, social, and cultural implications of services and other contributions to a community
- A project for development of a metadata agent to collect and broker metadata to other service providers in accordance with the Open Archives Initiative protocol
- Projects to add value to already-digitized collections as a demonstration of interoperability with the National Science Foundation's National Science Digital Library Program

Preservation or Digitization of Library Materials

- Projects to help libraries take a leadership role in the education of lifelong learners in the 21st century
- Projects that address the challenges of preserving and archiving digital media
- Projects that preserve and enhance access to valuable library resources useful to the broader community
- Collaborative projects to increase access to related collections, that provide evidence of good stewardship of materials in all formats, and that exemplify or help to develop standards and best practices for the creation and management of digital collections

Library and Museum Collaborations

- Projects to help museums and libraries take a leadership role in the education of lifelong learners in the 21st century
- Projects that develop, document, and disseminate model programs of cooperation between libraries and museums, with emphasis on how technology is used, education is enhanced, or the community is served

- Projects that support research and other activities to enhance interoperability, integration, and seamless access to digital library and museum resources

(text continues on page 354)

Table 2 / National Leadership Grant Awards, FY 2001

Education and Training: Projects that attract individuals from diverse cultural backgrounds to the field of librarianship and information science; implement innovative approaches to education and training and enhance the availability of professional librarians with advanced skills and specializations; or train librarians to enhance people's ability to use information effectively. Education and Training projects include traineeships, institutes, graduate fellowships and other programs.

*University of Arizona School of Information Resources and Library
Services (SIRLS), Tucson, Arizona* $492,708

In this two-year project, the school will create the Knowledge River Institute, an educational program to attract Native Americans and Hispanics to the field of library and information science. The Institute will offer a master's degree program tailored to the needs of Native Americans and Hispanics as learners and to the information needs of the communities they represent.

University of Denver Penrose Library, Denver, Colorado $233,204

The Colorado Digitization Project consortium will work with the Rocky Mountain Public Broadcasting Network in a two-year project to develop a statewide model program for school librarian and teacher training, incorporating digital primary source material into curricular materials and linking them to the Colorado Education Standards.

Urban Libraries Council (ULC), Evanston, Illinois $500,000

The council, a national association of more than 140 public libraries, will collaborate with the University of Maryland's National Leadership Institute and an advisory committee of ULC directors and trustees, in a three-year project to complete development and initiate two pilot classes of an Executive Leadership Institute. The institute will create a national leadership track in public librarianship, providing recognition and support for new leaders, opportunities for upcoming leaders to acquire new skills and essential perspectives, and a model for action learning within the library profession.

Indiana University, Indianapolis $73,005

This project will support the 2002 Treasure Mountain Research seminar series by advertising the seminar to a wide audience, providing scholarships to recruit a diverse representation of participants, and sponsoring sessions on research opportunities and work in progress. The Treasure Mountain series promotes research in school library media and student achievement.

University of Kentucky School of Library and Information Science, Lexington $329,427

In this two-year project, the University of Kentucky School of Library and Information Science will work with the Jefferson County Public Schools to develop an innovative job-sharing program to encourage certified teachers to complete a master's degree in library science and school media certification, and will disseminate information about the program to the educational community.

Johns Hopkins University, Baltimore $214,839

This two-year project, to be carried out in collaboration with IMLS, will support the Web-Wise Conference on Libraries and Museums in the Digital Age in 2002 and 2003.

Mansfield University of Pennsylvania $356,491

The university will carry out an innovative three-year project to address a critical shortage of school library media specialists by offering a Web-based master of education degree program in School Library and Information Technologies; engaging school principals in addressing recruitment, training, and incentives issues; and disseminating the results to the broad educational community.

Table 2 / National Leadership Grant Awards, FY 2001 *(cont.)*

Texas Woman's University School of Library and Information Studies,
Denton, Texas $77,520

The school will conduct a series of institutes over a two-year period to train librarians from small academic libraries throughout the state in three critical areas: user education, digital service management, and community information needs analysis.

North Harris Montgomery Community College District—Montgomery College,
Houston, Texas $268,491

North Harris Montgomery Community College will work with the University Center of the North Harris Montgomery Community College District over a two-year period to develop and implement a combination of on-site and distance-learning training programs that will prepare professional librarians and library technicians to respond to the needs of off-campus students. The program will offer distance-learning certification for librarians and certificates in library and information technology for technicians.

Research and Demonstration: Model projects that conduct research and/or demonstrations to enhance library services through the effective use of new and appropriate technologies; enhance the ability of library users to make more effective use of information resources; or assist in the evaluation of library services, including the economic implications of services and other contributions to a community.

Council on Library and Information Resources, Washington, D.C. $71,930

The council, with the Association of Research Libraries, University Libraries Group, and Regional Alliance for Preservation, will research and document current conditions and challenges in preservation programs in American college and research libraries and suggest new strategies for an increasingly complex technical environment.

Illinois State Library, Springfield $246,025

Preserving Electronic Publications is a one-year project of the Illinois State Library, State Library of Ohio, Illinois State Archives, and the University of Illinois in Urbana-Champaign's Graduate School of Library and Information Science to develop a framework for monitoring and evaluating changes made to electronically published state government documents to ensure permanent public access.

University of Illinois, Champaign $250,000

In this demonstration project, the Illinois-North Carolina Collaborative Environment for Botanical Resources, in partnership with the University of North Carolina at Chapel Hill, will develop "polyclave" keys for species identification and will train and observe nonprofessionals in their use. This project will provide Web access to a use-based array of botanical resources developed from a collaborative collection and digitization plan.

Indiana University, Indianapolis $249,998

The university, in collaboration with the Mathers Museum in Bloomington and the Indiana State Museum, will create a digital library of cultural treasures from Chichen Itza and Uxmal, Mexico, and Angel Mounds in Southern Indiana. This one-year demonstration project will develop techniques for the integration of state-of-the-art library and museum compliant data of cultural treasures with new media applications to collect, index, and archive data.

University of Michigan School of Information, Ann Arbor $249,949

This two-year demonstration project will train librarians to build interactive multimedia Web sites for library user education and to evaluate these sites to determine their effectiveness for conveying user education content. Participating libraries include Earlham College, Notre Dame University, Purdue University, and the University of Illinois at Chicago.

St. Louis Public Library, St. Louis, Missouri $261,575

Building on a previous project for large urban libraries, this two-year demonstration project will develop a methodology and standardized software to value and communicate the economic benefits of services provided by America's medium-size and small public libraries.

Table 2 / National Leadership Grant Awards, FY 2001 *(cont.)*

University of Wisconsin–Milwaukee $52,250

This research project will identify factors that impact search engine optimization, analyze their impacts on the major search engines on the Internet, recommend applicable and practical methods for improving search engine optimization, and enable libraries and museums to better place their Web sites in end-user searchers' result lists.

Preservation or Digitization: Projects that preserve and enhance access to unique library resources useful to the broader community; address the challenges of preserving and archiving digital media; or that lead to the development of standards, techniques, or models related to the digitization and management of digital resources.

Network of Alabama Academic Libraries, Montgomery $493,480

In the two-year Cornerstone Project—a collaborative statewide initiative to make historical treasures from Alabama's archives, libraries, museums, and other repositories electronically accessible—the Network of Alabama Academic Libraries, Alabama Department of Archives and History, Auburn University, and University of Alabama will establish a Web-based digital collection of documents, images, recordings, maps, and multimedia documenting U.S. and Alabama history.

University of Arizona Library, Tucson $123,672

This Geographic Information Systems (GIS)-based, two-year digitization project will create the Arizona Electronic Atlas, a dynamic Web-based interactive state atlas accessible to all levels of users. In partnership with the Arizona Department of Library, Archives and Public Records and the State Cartographer's Office, the project will develop a model workflow and methodology that other organizations can use to develop their own Web-based atlases and other products using appropriate GIS technologies, and will broaden the collaboration between the state's libraries and other state government agencies.

Broward County Library, Fort Lauderdale, Florida $70,551

The Bienes Special Collections and Rare Book Library of the Broward County Library will digitize its unique collection of Museum Extension Project objects and text produced during the New Deal by the Works Progress Administration from 1935 to 1943.

Northwestern University, Evanston, Illinois $136,367

This two-year project will make the entire text of *The North American Indian* by Edward S. Curtis available on the Web in digital format, converted and indexed to facilitate use and capitalize on the unique breadth and richness of the original publication.

Enoch Pratt Free Library, Baltimore $84,058

The goal of this two-year project is to produce 20 multimedia storytelling performances of multicultural stories that will be featured on the library's Web site and distributed to area schools, Maryland library systems, and other institutions.

Maryland Historical Society, Baltimore $88,318

The society's library will digitize photographs, manuscript sheet music, audio portions of music, and other items from its collection of materials of jazz pianist and composer Eubie Blake.

Washington Research Library Consortium, Upper Marlboro, Maryland $233,420

This consortium of seven university libraries in the Washington, D.C., metropolitan area will develop a collaborative digital production center to promote the development of digital collections among its member libraries. The two-year project will provide staff and systems organized to plan and manage digitizing projects, scan materials, and design and enter metadata developed in conjunction with library staff.

Northeast Document Conservation Center, Andover, Massachusetts $170,000

In this two-year project, Northeast Document Conservation Center and Amigos Library Services will produce teaching tools on preservation planning in several media, including a workbook on how to assess the preservation needs of a library, a video production illustrating major points of the workbook, and a Web publication incorporating clips from the video to illustrate the text.

Table 2 / National Leadership Grant Awards, FY 2001 *(cont.)*

WGBH Educational Foundation Archives, Boston $165,145

The Ten O'Clock News project will digitize and make available on the Web a video archive of the history and culture of Boston's African American community from 1974 to 1991. This one-year project will also create an innovative Web guide to the tapes.

Springfield College, Babson Library, Springfield, Massachusetts $92,780

Babson Library will digitize a historical collection of photographs, lantern slides, photo albums, and other pictorial resources related to the history of the Young Men's Christian Association (YMCA) in the United States.

Brandeis University Libraries, Waltham, Massachusetts $205,097

During this two-year project, the university libraries will digitize the original lithographs created by caricaturist Honore Daumier (1808–1879) and will make descriptions and translated captions of each lithograph searchable in their online catalog.

Michigan State University, East Lansing $249,783

In this two-year project, Michigan State University Library and the university's museum will digitize and make available online 75 of the most important American cookbooks published between 1798 and 1923 and accompanying interpretive materials describing their historical significance.

University of Minnesota, Minneapolis $275,077

In this two-year project, the university libraries and the Minneapolis Public Library will scan and make available and searchable on their Web sites posters from World War I and World War II held by both institutions.

University of Southern Mississippi, Hattiesburg $204,687

The Civil Rights in Mississippi Digital Archive project will result in the creation of an Internet-accessible, fully searchable database of digitized versions of rare library and archival resources on race relations in Mississippi. This two-year project will enhance access to primary source material and create a model for handling copyright and privacy issues associated with digitizing archival collections.

Brooklyn Public Library, Brooklyn, New York $239,412

The two-year Eagle Online–Phase 1 project will digitize, from microfilm, the *Brooklyn Daily Eagle* from 1841 to 1902. Pioneering the use of a new optical character recognition (OCR) software program optimized for historic newspapers, the project will provide Web-based access and full-text searching.

Cornell University Library, Cornell Institute for Digital Collections,
Ithaca, New York $297,083

In this two-year project, the Cornell Institute for Digital Collections will preserve and digitize a collection of ephemera, published materials, and artifacts from U.S. national political campaigns (1800–1976) and make the information available and searchable on the Web.

St. John's University, Kathryn and Shelby Cullom Davis Library, New York $145,435

This two-year project will create and make available on the Internet digital images—linked to indexes, bibliographies and finding aids—of insurance policies issued between 1682 and 1936 and other unique materials related to the history of insurance.

University of Tennessee, Knoxville $238,512

With this two-year project, the university will create a full-text, searchable database of original manuscripts, visual images, and publications documenting the history of Tennessee. This database, composed of searchable transcriptions and OCR'ed texts linked to digital facsimiles, will supplement traditional textbooks on Tennessee history currently used by K–12 teachers and students.

Library and Museum Collaborations: Projects that take a leadership role in educating lifelong learners in the 21st century; or model how museums and libraries can work together to expand their service to the public with emphasis on how technology is used, education is enhanced, or the community is served.

Table 2 / National Leadership Grant Awards, FY 2001 *(cont.)*

Richmond Public Library, Richmond, California $199,325

The WWII Richmond, California, Home Front Digital Project is a two-year project of the Richmond Public Library, the Richmond Museum of History, and John F. Kennedy University's Department of Museum Studies to bring together text and images from their collections into a single Web site. The digital collection will be accessible through the new Rosie the Riveter/World War II Home Front National Park located in the city's harbor area and will include Web-based instructional programming developed in collaboration with teachers and students that address state teaching standards.

University of Denver Seminary, Penrose Library, Denver, Colorado $498,637

This two-year project in partnership with representative museums and libraries from Kansas, Nebraska, Wyoming, and Colorado will explore the degree to which the Colorado Digitization Project (CDP) model for collaboration can be used in other states; explore the issues related to the development of infrastructure for a Digital Library of Western Heritage; test development of a collection of digital primary source materials on Western Trails owned by the participating institutions; and provide the general public with access to this virtual collection and findings to the library and museum community.

Florida Museum of Natural History, Gainesville $244,073

An innovative partnership formed by the Florida Museum of Natural History, Alachua County Library District, and the School Board of Alachua County will provide a literature-based science program for more than 1,200 low-income, predominantly African American preschool children (ages 3–4) enrolled in more than 50 Head Start classrooms. In the two-year project, Marvelous Explorations Through Science and Stories (MESS) will develop a foundation for the children's future academic success by promoting literacy in general and science literacy in particular.

Eastern Iowa Community College District, Davenport $229,972

This two-year project, led by the district, will demonstrate an innovative, collaborative effort among museums, libraries, and schools utilizing emerging information technologies and the unique resources of local museums and libraries to create learning spaces that are an integral part of the core learning of students. Five learning modules, formatted for Web-based or CD-ROM delivery, will be based on exhibits at the museum and focused on a common theme of the environment of the Mississippi River.

Chicago Horticultural Society/Chicago Botanic Garden, Glencoe, Illinois $101,827

This two-year project by the Chicago Horticultural Society/Chicago Botanic Garden, in collaboration with the Library of the University of Illinois at Chicago, will evaluate commercially available plants, including both old "standards" and the latest hybrids, and will inform the horticulture industry, academic and governmental researchers, gardeners, and other plant enthusiasts about the best plants for midwestern and equivalent climates. The Web site will feature annually updated profiles on approximately 1,000 different plants undergoing trials in the garden's plant evaluation program, presenting information on the plant's performance in a nontechnical and searchable format.

Boston Public Library $499,357

The Sargent Murals Restoration Project is a two-year model program of conservation and education bringing together the Boston Public Library and Harvard University Art Museums Straus Center for Conservation in a project to conserve the Boston Public Library's rare and valuable murals by John Singer Sargent and to document the conservation effort as well as engage the community in the process through interactive educational programs.

Discovery Center of Springfield, Springfield, Missouri $182,983

In a two-year project, the Discovery Center of Springfield, in partnership with the Springfield-Greene County Library System, will use state-of-the-art technology and equipment as well as more traditional approaches to increase literacy among children and adults by linking programming efforts of the two centers with families and schools of Springfield and the Ozarks region. Programs will involve the exploration of science, math, health, and the environment.

University of Nebraska–Lincoln $168,688

This is a collaborative two-year research project involving the university libraries, the University of Nebraska State Museum, the Nebraska Historical Society, and members of the

Table 2 / National Leadership Grant Awards, FY 2001 *(cont.)*

Omaha Tribe to locate and catalog Omaha artifacts and photographic images scattered in museums, libraries, and private collections throughout the world. Key to this project is the development and implementation of a Web site to make the resulting database of Omaha artifacts and an online gallery of Omaha images accessible to tribal members, educators, students, and the general public.

Brooklyn Public Library, Brooklyn, New York $175,654

Worklore: Brooklyn Voices Speak brings together the Brooklyn Public Library and the Brooklyn Historical Society to explore the subject of working in Brooklyn as experienced by 18th-, 19th-, and 20th-century residents. The two-and-one-half-year project includes free public programs and lectures; curriculum guides for fourth, seventh, eighth, and 11th grades; marketing and outreach materials; and the creation of a Worklore Web site to provide online access to exhibition text, images, educational materials, and lectures, as well as historic narratives and contemporary oral histories.

Cherokee National Historical Society, Tahlequah, Oklahoma $249,977

This project brings together the Cherokee Heritage Center and the Eastern Oklahoma District Library System to create eight traveling "Cherokee-themed" exhibits, coupled with programming packages that will rotate to each of the 14 participating libraries throughout a two-year time frame. The project will work to make both the museum and the library system active centers for learning in the local communities of small, rural, and underserved populations.

Inter American University of Puerto Rico, San Juan $333,692

This two-year collaborative project between Ponce Historical Archives (PHA), the Ponce Museum of History (PMH), and the Inter American University of Puerto Rico will integrate the historical resources of the three by digitizing materials and providing Internet access and training for teachers and other personnel. The training will use information technology and the integration of primary sources into the history curriculum as a strategy for developing information literacy in students.

American Association for State and Local History, Nashville, Tennessee $187,150

The goal of this two-year project by the American Association for State and Local History, in collaboration with the Michigan Historical Center, the Ohio Historical Society, and the New York State Archives, is to improve management of and access to historical records by providing online continuing education for individuals working in museums, libraries, historical societies, and related organizations with responsibility for archival and manuscript materials.

Washington State University, Pullman $197,371

The Library and Information Services group at Washington State University–Vancouver and the Center for Columbia River History will partner with the Washington State Historical Society, Oregon Historical Society, Washington State University–Pullman, and Idaho State Historical Society in the creation of a digital library that educates the underserved general public in the Pacific Northwest. The two-year collaboration will develop a digital archive that highlights the hidden ethnic histories of the region, provides tutorials on how to research and interpret library and museum collections, and will encourage public discussion of critical historical and contemporary issues.

Museum of History and Industry, Seattle $334,400

Over a two-year period, the museum and the University of Washington Libraries will collaborate with the Association of King County Historical Organizations to select, scan, and create metadata for 12,000 historic images. The project will address collaboratively the challenges of preserving collections and providing community access.

Cable Natural History Museum, Cable, Wisconsin $72,755

This partnership between the Cable Natural History Museum, the Drummond Public Library, Forest Lodge Library, Hayward Carnegie Library, Lac Courte Oreilles Ojibwa Community College Library, and WOJB-FM, a public radio station owned and operated by the Lac Courte Oreilles Band of the Ojibwa, will promote environmental stewardship in rural northern Wisconsin. In a two-year project, the partnership members will offer the opportunity for 12 people—both Native Americans and non-Native Americans—to become new voices for the environment through paid internships in journalism and literary nonfiction.

(continued from page 348)

Native American Library Services Program

In 2001 IMLS distributed $2,520,000 in grants for American Indian tribes and Alaska Native villages.

The Native American Library Services Program provides opportunities for the improvement of library services to Indian tribes and Alaska Native villages, the latter coming under the definition of eligible Indian tribes as recognized by the secretary of the interior. The program offers three types of support:

- Basic Library Services Grants, in the amount of $4,000, support core library operations on a noncompetitive basis for all eligible Indian tribes and Alaska Native villages that apply for such support. IMLS awarded Basic Grants to 220 tribes in 26 states in 2001.
- Professional Assistance Grants, in the amount of $2,000, heighten the level of professional proficiency of Indian tribal library staff. It is a non-competitive program to support assessments of library services and provide advice for improvement. IMLS awarded Professional Assistance grants to 62 tribes in 17 states in 2001.
- Enhancement Grants support new levels of library service for activities specifically identified under the LSTA purposes. In 2001 these competitive awards ranged from $20,000 to $149,760 (Table 3).

Of the 46 applications received, IMLS awarded 13 Enhancement Grants for a total of $1,516,000.

Native Hawaiian Library Services

The Native Hawaiian Library Services Program provides opportunities for improved library services for an important part of the nation's community of library users through a single grant to a Native Hawaiian organization, as defined in section 9212 of the Native Hawaiian Education Act (20 U.S.C. 7912).

In 2001 the Native Hawaiian Library Services Grant was awarded to ALU-LIKE, Inc. of Honolulu, a private, nonprofit organization serving the Native Hawaiian community, in the amount of $420,000.

Evaluation of IMLS Programs

IMLS has taken a leadership role in evaluating the value of its programs through incorporating outcome-based measurement as a tool to document effectiveness of funded projects. Within the state-administered programs, IMLS has provided training in outcome-based evaluation for 26 states. In addition, IMLS is currently training all new National Leadership Grant recipients in outcome-based evaluation and is presenting information about evaluation at state, regional, and national professional meetings. LSTA requires that each SLAA independently evaluate its

(text continues on page 356)

Table 3 / Native American Library Services Program: Enhancement Grants, FY 2001

Central Council Tlingit and Haida Indian Tribes

Juneau, Alaska $149,760

This one-year project will support a joint effort of the tribe, its library, and the United Way to develop a database of social services and educational resources that will be available via the Internet and on CDs to assist the residents of Native Southeast Alaska villages in identifying available services.

Chilkoot Indian Association

Haines, Alaska $127,333

This two-year project, a cooperative effort between the Chilkoot Indian Association and the Haines Borough Public Library, will upgrade computer resources, increase accessibility to those resources, and improve technology literacy by recruiting teenagers to receive training on automated library resources so that they can train other library users, especially elders.

Confederated Salish and Kootenai Tribes of the Flathead Reservation

Pablo, Montana $107,508

This one-year project will increase tribal access to the library's collections by providing document delivery and remote satellite circulation sites to the surrounding communities, joining a university shared catalog system, and enhancing the library Web site.

Eastern Band of Cherokee Indians

Cherokee, North Carolina $148,596

This two-year project will expand services in a newly renovated library by automating access to the collection; purchasing furniture, equipment, and materials for the general library and archives; and upgrading technology resources.

Fort Peck Assiniboine and Sioux Tribes

Poplar, Montana $122,581

This one-year project includes a number of activities, among them upgrading the materials, technology resources, and furniture in the children's collection; providing a children's summer reading program; expanding the archival collection; and improving the Web site.

Igiugig Village

Igiugig, Alaska $62,150

This one-year joint school-library project will organize, increase, and automate the collection of materials; train the staff; provide outreach to elders and the homebound; and upgrade computer resources.

Iowa Tribe of Oklahoma

Perkins, Oklahoma $128,902

This two-year project will increase the hours of the tribal library/archives by hiring a library assistant, upgrade the library's furniture and equipment including the circulation system, and provide supplies for the computer lab.

Lac Courte Oreilles Band of Lake Superior Chippewa

Hayward, Wisconsin $145,140

This two-year project will couple lifelong learning with education and cultural awareness by offering reading enrichment for preschool children and youth; expanding outreach programs for elderly, disabled, preschool, school-aged, and home-schooled populations; implementing a community history/genealogy resource center; sponsoring oral history and genealogy workshops; and promoting the usage of the Ojibwe language in the library and the larger community.

Table 3 / Native American Library Services Program: Enhancement Grants, FY 2001 *(cont.)*

Miami Tribe of Oklahoma

Miami, Oklahoma $124,314

This one-year project will continue and expand services to seven tribal communities through the CHARLIE (Connecting Help and Resources Linking Indians Effectively) Network by improving their joint Web site; purchasing materials for each library; expanding the Books for Babies program; and employing two circuit-rider librarians, one to provide reading enrichment activities to daycare sites and the second to offer training and professional services such as cataloging to the network libraries.

Saginaw Chippewa Indian Tribe of Michigan

Mount Pleasant, Michigan $121,208

This two-year project will target services to children and youth by incorporating Ojibwe culture in library programming, creating a dedicated space for children and youth, expanding technology resources, offering literacy programming, and increasing the collection.

Sealaska Corporation

Juneau, Alaska $20,000

This one-year grant will support staff training and project planning to preserve and digitize a collection of culturally significant audio and video tapes.

Washoe Tribe of Nevada and California

Gardnerville, Nevada $147,825

This two-year project will bring together the environmental resource department, the tribal language immersion school, the tribal education department, the tribal senior center, and the tribal library to help preserve the cultural heritage of the tribe by producing cultural information packets to be disseminated throughout the tribal communities.

Yurok Tribe

Klamath, California $110,683

This two-year project supports the expansion of the archival collections of tribal documents, materials concerning the cultural sites in the surrounding areas, and oral history videos; the digitization of some of those materials; and preparation of an educational packet about the tribe.

(continued from page 354)

LSTA activities prior to the end of the five-year plan. In preparation for this evaluation, IMLS has offered training workshops in outcome-based evaluation to state library staff. Evaluation of their current five-year plan activities can assist SLAAs in determining their priorities for the new five-year plans due July 31, 2002.

In order to assure that it is meeting current public and professional needs in library services, IMLS routinely seeks advice from diverse representatives of the library community, carries out studies of library practice, and evaluates its programs with the assistance of external consultants. In 2001 IMLS carried out a broad study to characterize digital activities in libraries and museums nationwide.

IMLS Conferences

IMLS hosted a conference in 2001 for SLAAs (November 14–16) focusing on the theme of planning. IMLS also hosted two conferences to promote discussion of important issues facing both libraries and museums: "Web-Wise: The Digital

Divide" (February 12–14), and "The 21st Century Learner" (November 7–9). Web-Wise conference papers were published in *First Monday*, a peer-reviewed e-journal (found at http://www.firstmonday.org). A report from the 21st Century Learner Conference appears on the IMLS Web site.

IMLS Web Site

The IMLS Web site (http://www.imls.gov) provides information on the various grant programs, national awards for library and museum service, projects funded, application forms, and staff contacts. It also highlights model projects developed by libraries and museums throughout the country. Through an electronic newsletter, *Primary Source*, IMLS provides timely information on grant deadlines and opportunities. Details on subscribing to the IMLS newsletter are found on the Web site.

National Awards for Museum and Library Service

The National Award for Library Service is a new IMLS award first given in FY 2000. It honors outstanding American libraries that have made a significant and exceptional contribution to their communities, seeking to recognize libraries that demonstrate extraordinary and innovative approaches to public service, reaching beyond the expected levels of community outreach and core programs generally associated with library services. The principal criterion for selection is evidence of the library's systematic and ongoing commitment to public service through exemplary and innovative programs and community partnerships.

Six awards were announced in September 2001. The recipients of the National Awards for Library and Museum Service in 2001 were the Alaska Resources Library and Information Service, Anchorage, Alaska; the Children's Discovery Museum of San Jose, San Jose, California; the Hancock County Library System, Bay St. Louis, Mississippi; the Miami Museum of Science, Miami, Florida; the New England Aquarium, Boston; and the Providence Public Library, Providence, Rhode Island.

Information about the award and upcoming deadlines appears on the IMLS Web site.

Part 3
Library/Information Science Education, Placement, and Salaries

Guide to Employment Sources in the Library and Information Professions

Darlena Davis

Office for Human Resource Development and Recruitment, American Library Association
World Wide Web http://www.ala.org/hrdr

This guide updates the listing in the 2001 *Bowker Annual* with information on new services and changes in contacts and groups listed previously. The sources listed primarily give assistance in obtaining professional positions, although a few indicate assistance with paraprofessionals (see Council on Library/Media Technicians, Inc., under "Specialized Library Associations and Groups" below). Paraprofessionals, however, tend to be recruited through local sources.

General Sources of Library and Information Jobs

Library Literature

Classified ads of library vacancies and positions wanted are carried in many of the national, regional, and state library journals and newsletters. Members of associations can sometimes list "position wanted" ads free of charge in their membership publications. Listings of positions available are regularly found in *American Libraries*, *Chronicle of Higher Education*, *College & Research Libraries News*, *Library Journal*, and *Library Hotline*. State and regional library association newsletters, state library journals, foreign library periodicals, and other types of periodicals carrying such ads are listed in later sections.

Newspapers

The *New York Times* Sunday "Week in Review" section carries a special section of ads for librarian jobs in addition to the regular classifieds. Local newspapers, particularly the larger city Sunday editions, such as the *Washington Post*, *Los Angeles Times*, and *Chicago Tribune* often carry job vacancy listings in libraries, both professional and paraprofessional. The online versions of these newspapers also are useful.

Internet

The many library-related electronic listservs on the Internet often post library job vacancies interspersed with other news and discussion items. A growing number of general online job-search bulletin boards exist; these may include information-related job notices along with other types of jobs. This guide includes information on electronic access where available through the individual organizations listed below.

Among useful resources are "Making Short Work of the Job Search" by Marilyn Rosenthal, *Library Journal*, September 1, 1997, and "Job Opportunities Glitter for Librarians Who Surf the Net" by A. Paula Azar, *American Libraries*, September 1996.

"Winning Résumé," by Scott Grusky in *Internet World*, February 1996, and "Riley's Guided Tour: Job Searching on the Net," by Margaret Riley, et al., *Library Journal*, September 15, 1996, pp. 24–27, offer guidance on databases that might lead to library and information-related position listings.

Some library-related job search Web links include:

- Ann's Place—Library Job Hunting Around the World
  (http://www.uic.edu/depts/st_empl/)
- Finding Library Jobs on the WWW
  (http://toltec.lib.utk.edu/~tla/nmrt/libjobs.html)
- Job and Career Information
  (http://www.peachnet.edu/galileo/internet/jobs/jobsmenu.html)
- Job Opportunities—Librarians and Library Science Net Links
  (http://librarians.about.com/msubjobs.htm)
- Library and Information Science Jobs
  (http://www.fidnet.com/~map/default4.htm)
- The Librarian's Job Search Source
  (http://www.zoots.com/libjob/libjob.htm)
- Library Job Hunting on the Internet
  (http://www.lisjobs.com/jefflee.htm)
- Library Jobs on the Net
  (http://wings.buffalo.edu/sils/alas/usamap)
- The Networked Librarian Job Search Guide
  (http://pw2.netcom.com/~feridun/nlintro.htm)

Library Joblines

Library joblines or job "hotlines" give recorded telephone messages of job openings in a specific geographical area. Most tapes are changed once a week, although individual listings may sometimes be carried for several weeks. Although the information is fairly brief and the cost of calling is borne by the individual job seeker, a jobline provides a quick and up-to-date listing of vacancies that is not usually possible with printed listings or journal ads.

Most joblines carry listings for their state or region only, although some will occasionally accept out-of-state positions if there is room on the tape. While a few will list technician and other paraprofessional positions, the majority are for professional jobs only. When calling the joblines, one might occasionally find a time when the telephone keeps ringing without any answer; this will usually mean that the tape is being changed or there are no new jobs for that period. The classified section of *American Libraries* carries jobline numbers periodically as space permits. The following joblines are in operation:

Jobline Sponsor	Job Seekers (To Hear Job Listings)
Arizona State Library, Archives and Public Records (Arizona libraries only)	602-275-2325
British Columbia Library Association (B.C. listings only)	604-683-5354
California School Library Educators Association	650-697-8832
Connecticut Library Association (24 hours)	860-889-1200
Delaware Division of Libraries (Delaware, New Jersey, and Pennsylvania listings)	302-739-4748 in state 800-282-8696
Drexel University College of Information Science and Technology	215-895-1048
Kansas State Library Jobline (includes paraprofessional and out-of-state)	785-296-3296
Kentucky Job Hotline (24 hours)	502-564-3008
Library Jobline of Illinois (cosponsored by the Maryland Library Association, 24 hours)	410-947-5094
Medical Library Association Jobline (24 hours)	312-553-4636
Nebraska Job Hotline (Nebraska and other openings, regular business hours)	402-471-4019 800-307-2665
New England Library Jobline (24 hours, New England jobs only)	617-521-2815
New York Library Association	518-432-6952, 800-252-NYLA
Ohio Library Council (24 hours)	614-225-6999
Oklahoma Department of Libraries Jobline (5 P.M–8 A.M., seven days)	405-521-4202
Pennsylvania Cooperative Job Hotline (sponsored by Pennsylvania Library Association; accepts paraprofessional out-of-state listings)	717-234-4646
Pratt Institute SILS Job Hotline	718-636-3742
Special Libraries Association	202-234-4700
Special Libraries Association, Illinois Chapter, and Illinois Library Association	312-409-5986
Special Libraries Association, New York Chapter	212-439-7290
Special Libraries Association, Southern California Chapter	818-795-2145
State Library of Florida	904-488-5232
State Library of Iowa (professional jobs in Iowa; regular business hours)	515-281-7574
University of North Texas	940-565-2445
University of South Carolina College of Library and Information Science (no geographic restrictions)	803-777-8443
University of Toronto Faculty of Information Studies	416-978-7073
University of Western Ontario Faculty of Communications and Open Learning	519-661-3542

Specialized Library Associations and Groups

ACCESS, 1001 Connecticut Ave. N.W., Suite 838, Washington, DC 20036, 202-785-4233, fax 202-785-4212, e-mail commjobs@aol.com, World Wide Web http://www.communityjobs.org/access: Comprehensive national resource on employment, voluntary service, and career development in the nonprofit sector. Promotes involvement in public issues by providing specialized employment publications and services for job seekers and serves as a resource to nonprofit organizations on recruitment, diversity, and staff development.

Advanced Information Management, 444 Castro St., Suite 320, Mountain View, CA 94041, 650-965-7900, fax 650-965-7907, e-mail aimno.aimusa@juno.com, World Wide Web http://www.aimusa.com/hotjobs.html: Placement agency that specializes in library and information personnel. Offers work on a temporary, permanent, and contract basis for both professional librarians and paraprofessionals in the special, public, and academic library marketplace. Supplies consultants who can work with special projects in libraries or manage library development projects. Offices in Southern California (900 Wilshire Blvd., Suite 1424, Los Angeles, CA 90017, 213-489-9800, fax 213-489-9802) as well as in the San Francisco Bay Area. There is no fee to applicants.

American Association of Law Libraries Career Hotline, 53 W. Jackson Blvd., Suite 940, Chicago, IL 60604, 312-939-4764: Ads can be viewed online at http://www.aallnet.org/.

American Libraries "Career LEADS," c/o *American Libraries*, 50 E. Huron St., Chicago, IL 60611: Classified job listings published in each monthly issue of *American Libraries* (*AL*) magazine, listing some 100 job openings grouped by type, plus Late Job Notices added near press time as space and time permit. Contains subsections: Positions Wanted, Librarians' Classified, joblines, and regional salary scales. Also contains ConsultantBase (see below) four times annually.

American Libraries ConsultantBase (Cbase): A service that helps match professionals offering library/information expertise with institutions seeking it. Published quarterly, CBase appears in the Career LEADS section of the January, April, June, and October issues of *AL*. Rates: $5.50/line classified, $55/inch display. Inquiries should be made to Jon Kartman, LEADS Editor, *American Libraries*, 50 E. Huron St., Chicago, IL 60611, 312-280-4211, e-mail careerleads@ALA.org.

American Library Association, Association of College and Research Libraries, 50 E. Huron St., Chicago, IL 60611-2795, 312-280-2513: Classified advertising appears each month in *College & Research Libraries News*. Ads appearing in the print *C&RL News* are also posted to C&RL Newsnet, an abridged electronic edition of *C&RL News* accessible on the Web at http://www.ala.org/acrl/c&rlnew2.html.

American Library Association, Office for Human Resource Development and Recruitment (HRDR), 50 E. Huron St., Chicago, IL 60611, 312-280-4281, World Wide Web http://www.ala.org/hrdr/placement.html: A placement service is provided at each Annual Conference (June or July) and Midwinter Meeting (January or February). Register online at the Web address above.

In addition to the ALA conference placement center, ALA division national conferences usually include a placement service. See the *American Libraries*

Datebook for dates of upcoming divisional conferences, since these are not held every year. ALA provides Web site job postings from *American Libraries*, C&RL NewsNet, LITA Job Site, and its conference placement services on its library education and employment menu page at http://www.ala.org/education.

American Society for Information Science and Technology, 1320 Fenwick Lane, No. 510, Silver Spring, MD 20910, 301-495-0900, fax 301-495-0810, e-mail asis@asis.org, World Wide Web http://www.asis.org: An active placement service is operated at ASIST Annual Meetings (usually October; locales change). All conference attendees (both ASIST members and nonmembers), as well as ASIS members who cannot attend the conference, are eligible to use the service to list or find jobs. Job listings are also accepted from employers who cannot attend the conference. Interviews are arranged. Throughout the year, current job openings are listed in *ASIST JOBLINE*, a monthly publication sent to all members and available to nonmembers on request (send a stamped, self-addressed envelope).

Art Libraries Society/North America (ARLIS/NA), c/o Executive Director, 329 March Rd., No. 232, Kanata, ON A2K 2E1, Canada, 800-817-0621, fax 613-599-7027, World Wide Web http://www.arlisna.org: Art information and visual resources curator jobs are listed in *ARLIS/NA UPDATE* (six times a year) and a job registry is maintained at ARLIS/NA headquarters. Any employer may list a job with the registry, but only members may request job information. Listings also available on the ARLIS-L listserv and Web site. Call ARLIS/NA headquarters for registration and/or published information.

Asian/Pacific American Libraries Newsletter, c/o Wilfred Fong, School of Library and Information Science, University of Wisconsin–Milwaukee, Box 413, Milwaukee, WI 53201-0413, 414-229-5421, fax 414-229-4848, e-mail Fong@slis.uwm.edu: This quarterly includes some job ads. Free to members of Asian/Pacific American Librarians Association.

Association for Educational Communications and Technology, 1800 N. Stonelake Dr., Suite 2, Bloomington, IN 47404, 812-335-7675, fax 812-335-7678, e-mail aect@aect.org, World Wide Web http://aect.org: Maintains a placement listing on the AECT Web site and provides a placement service at the annual convention. Free to all registrants.

Association for Library and Information Science Education, 11250 Roger Bacon Dr., Suite 8, Reston, VA 20190-5202, 703-243-4146, fax 703-435-4390, World Wide Web http://www.alise.org: Provides placement service at Annual Conference (January or February) for library and information studies faculty and administrative positions.

Association of Research Libraries, 21 Dupont Circle N.W., Washington, DC 20036, 202-296-2296, World Wide Web http://www.arl.org/careers/vacancy.html. Posts job openings at ARL member libraries.

Black Caucus Newsletter, c/o Greta Lowe, BCALA Editor, Box 1738, Hampton, VA 23669, 757-727-5561, fax 757-727-5952, e-mail greta.lowe@hamptonu.edu: Lists paid advertisements for vacancies. Free to members, $10/year to others. Published bimonthly by Four-G Publishers, Inc. News accepted continuously. Biographies, essays, books, and reviews of interest to members are invited.

C. Berger Group, Inc. (CBG), Box 274, Wheaton, IL 60189, 630-653-1115, 800-382-4222, fax 630-653-1691, e-mail c-berg@dupagels.lib.il.us, World Wide Web http://www.cberger.com: CBG conducts nationwide executive searches to fill permanent management, supervisory, and director positions in libraries, information centers, and other organizations nationwide. Direct-hire and temp-to-hire services are also available. Other employment services include supplying professional and support-staff-level temporary workers and contract personnel for short- and long-term assignments in special, academic, and public libraries in Illinois, Indiana, Georgia, Texas, Wisconsin, and other states. CBG also provides library and records management consulting services and direction and staff to manage projects for clients both on-site and off-site.

Canadian Library Association, 328 Frank St., Ottawa, ON K2P 0X8, Canada, 613-232-9625, World Wide Web http://www.cla.amlibs.ca: Publishes career ads in *Feliciter* magazine.

Carney, Sandoe & Associates, 136 Boylston St., Boston, MA 02116, 800-225-7986, fax 617-542-9400, e-mail recruitment@carneysandoe.com, World Wide Web http://www.carneysandoe.com: An educational recruitment firm that places teachers and administrative personnel in private, independent schools across the United States and in other countries.

Catholic Library Association (CLA), 9009 Carter St., Allen Park, MI 48101, e-mail cla@vgernet.net: Personal and institutional members of the association are given free space (35 words) to advertise for jobs or to list job openings in *Catholic Library World* (four issues a year). Others may advertise. Contact advertising coordinator for rates.

Chinese-American Librarians Association Newsletter, c/o Lan Yang, Sterling C. Evans Library, Texas A&M University, College Station, TX 77843-5000: Job listings in newsletter issued in February, June, and October. Free to members.

Cleveland (Ohio) Area Metropolitan Library System Job Listing Service, 20600 Chagrin Blvd., No. 500, Shaker Heights, OH 44122, World Wide Web http://www.camls.org.

Council on Library/Media Technicians, Inc. (COLT), c/o Membership Chair Julia Ree, Box 52057, Riverside, CA 92517-3057, World Wide Web http://library.ucr.edu/COLT/: *COLT Newsletter* appears bimonthly in Library Mosaics (World Wide Web http://www.librarymosaics.com).

Independent Educational Services (IES), 1101 King St., Suite 305, Alexandria, VA 22314, 800-257-5102, 703-548-9700, fax 703-548-7171, World Wide Web http://www.ies-search.org: IES is a nonprofit faculty and administrative placement agency for independent elementary and secondary schools across the country. Qualified candidates must possess an MLS degree and some experience in a school setting working with students. Jobs range from assistant librarians and interns to head librarians and rebuilding entire libraries/multimedia centers. Regional offices in Boston and San Francisco.

Labat-Anderson, Inc., 8000 Westpark Dr., No. 400, McLean, VA 22102, 703-506-9600, fax 703-506-4646: One of the largest providers of library and records management services to the federal government. Supports various federal agencies in 27 states, with many positions located in the Washington, D.C., Atlanta, and San Francisco areas. Résumés and cover letters will gladly be accepted from librarians with an ALA-accredited MLS and from records managers, or from applicants with library and/or records management experience, for full- and part-time employment.

The Library Co-Op, Inc., 3840 Park Ave., Suite 107, Edison, NJ 08820, 732-906-1777 or 800-654-6275, fax 732-906-3562, e-mail librco@compuserve.com: The company is licensed as both a temporary and permanent employment agency and supplies consultants to work in a wide variety of information settings and functions from library moving to database management, catalog maintenance, reference, retrospective conversion, and more. Recent developments include the forming of two new divisions, ABCD Filing Services and LAIRD Consulting. The latter provides a full range of automation expertise for hardware, software, LANS, and WANS. Reseller of INMAGIL software The company also has hired two specialists in space planning.

Library Management Systems, Corporate Pointe, Suite 755, Culver City, CA 90230, 310-216-6436 or 800-567-4669, fax 310-649-6388, e-mail LMS@ix.netcom.com; and 3 Bethesda Metro Center, Suite 700, Bethesda, MD 20814, 301-961-1984, fax 301-652-6240, e-mail LMSDC@ix.netcom.com: LMS has been providing library staffing, recruitment, and consulting to public and special libraries and businesses since 1983. It organizes and manages special libraries; designs and implements major projects (including retrospective conversions, automation studies, and records management); performs high-quality cataloging outsourcing; and furnishes contract staffing to all categories of information centers. LMS has a large database of librarians and library assistants on call for long- and short-term projects and provides permanent placement at all levels.

Library Mosaics, Box 5171, Culver City, CA 90231, 310-645-4998, World Wide Web http://www.librarymosaics.com: *Library Mosaics* magazine is published bimonthly and will accept listings for library/media support staff positions. However, correspondence relating to jobs cannot be handled.

Medical Library Association, 65 E. Wacker Pl., Suite 1900, Chicago, IL 60601-7298, 312-419-9094, ext. 29, World Wide Web http://www.mlanet.org: *MLA News* (10 issues a year, June/July and November/December combined issues) lists positions wanted and positions available in its Employment Opportunities column. The position available rate is $2.80 per word. Up to 50 free words for MLA members plus $2.45 per word over 50 words. Members and nonmembers may rerun ads once in the next consecutive issue for $25. All "positions available" advertisements must list a minimum salary; a salary range is preferred. Positions wanted rates are $1.50 per word for nonmembers, $1.25 per word for members with 100 free words; $1.25 will be charged for each word exceeding 100. MLA also offers a placement service at the annual meeting each spring. Job advertisements received for *MLA News* are posted to the MLANET Jobline.

Music Library Association, c/o Elisabeth H. Rebman, MLA Placement Officer, 1814 Pine Grove Ave., Colorado Springs, CO 80906-2930, 7619-475-1960, e-mail erebman@library.berkeley.edu, World Wide Web http://www.music libraryassoc.org: Monthly job list ($20/year individuals, $25 organizations), from: MLA Business Office, Box 487, Canton, MA 02021, 781-828-8450, fax 781-828-8915, e-mail acadsvc@aol.com.

Ohio Library Council, 35 E. Gay St., Suite 305, Columbus, OH 43215, World Wide Web http://www.olc.org.

Pro Libra Associates, Inc., 6 Inwood Pl., Maplewood, NJ 07040, 201-762-0070, 800-262-0070, e-mail prolibra-2@mail.idt.net. A multi-service library firm specializing in personnel placement (permanent and temporary), consulting, management, and project support for libraries and information centers. Has for more than 24 years provided personnel services to catalog, inventory, rearrange, and staff libraries and information centers in corporate, academic, and public institutions.

REFORMA, National Association to Promote Library Service to Latinos and the Spanish-Speaking, Box 832, Anaheim, CA 92815-0832, World Wide Web http://www.reforma.org: Those wishing to do direct mailings to the REFORMA membership of 900-plus may obtain mailing labels arranged by zip code for $100. Contact Al Milo, 714-738-6383. Job ads are also published quarterly in the *REFORMA Newsletter*. For rate information, see the Web site.

Society of American Archivists, 527 S. Wells St., 5th fl., Chicago, IL 60607-3922, fax 312-347-1452, e-mail info@archivists.org, World Wide Web http://www.archivists.org: *Archival Outlook* is sent (to members only) six times a year and contains features about the archival profession and other timely pieces on courses in archival administration, meetings, and professional opportunities (job listings). The Online Employment Bulletin is a weekly listing of professional opportunities posted on the SAA Web site. The *SAA Employment Bulletin* is a bimonthly listing of job opportunities available to members by subscription for $24 a year and to nonmembers for $10 per issue. Prepayment is required.

Special Libraries Association, 1700 18th St. N.W., Washington, DC 20009-2508, 202-234-4700, fax 202-265-9317, e-mail sla@sla.org, World Wide Web http://www.sla.org: SLA maintains a telephone jobline, SpeciaLine, 202-234-4700 ext. 1, operating 24 hours a day, seven days a week. Most SLA chapters have employment chairs who act as referral persons for employers and job seekers. Several SLA chapters have joblines. The association's monthly magazine, *Information Outlook*, carries classified advertising. SLA offers an employment clearinghouse and career advisory service during its annual conference, held in June. SLA also provides a discount to members using the résumé evaluation service offered through Advanced Information Management. A "Guide to Career Opportunities" is a resource kit for $20 (SLA members, $15); "Getting a Job: Tips and Techniques" is free to unemployed SLA members. The SLA Job Bulletin Board, a computer listserv, is organized by Indiana University staff. Subscribe by sending the message *subscribe SLAJOB (first name, last name)* to listserv@iubvm.ucs.indiana.edu.

TeleSec CORESTAFF, Information Management Division, 11160 Veirs Mill Rd., Suite 414, Wheaton, MD 20902, 301-949-4097, fax 301-949-8729, e-mail library@corestaff.com, World Wide Web http://www.corestaff.com/searchlines: Offers a variety of opportunities to start a library career in the Washington, D.C., area, through short- and long-term assignments in federal agencies, law firms, corporations, associations, and academic institutions.

Tuft & Associates, Inc., 1209 Astor St., Chicago, IL 60610, 312-642-8889, fax 312-642-8883: Specialists in nationwide executive searches for administrative posts in libraries and information centers.

Wontawk Gossage Associates, 25 W. 43 St., New York, NY 10036, 212-869-3348, fax 212-997-1127; and 304 Newbury St., No. 314, Boston, MA 02115, 617-867-9209, fax 617-437-9317, e-mail swarner@wontawk.com, World Wide Web http://www.wontawk.com: Executive search firm specializing in recruitment of library directors and other library/information-handling service providers. Temporary, long-term and temporary-to-permanent assignments in the NY/NJ/CT and the Boston metropolitan areas in all types of libraries and information management firms, professional and support, all levels of responsibility, all skills.

State Library Agencies

In addition to the joblines mentioned previously, some state library agencies issue lists of job openings within their areas. These include: Colorado (weekly, sent on receipt of stamps and mailing labels; also available via listserv and Access Colorado Library and Information Network—ACLIN; send SASE for access); Indiana (monthly on request) 317-232-3697, or 800-451-6028 (Indiana area), e-mail ehubbard@statelib.lib.in.us; Iowa (Joblist, monthly on request), e-mail awettel@mail.lib.state.ia.us; Mississippi (Library Job Opportunities, monthly); and Nebraska.

State libraries in several states have electronic bulletin board services that list job openings. They include the following:

Colorado http://www.aclin.org (also lists out-of-state jobs)

District of Columbia (Metropolitan Washington Council of Government Libraries) http://www.mwcog.org/ic/jobline.html

Florida http://www.dos.state.fl.us

Georgia http://www.public.lib.ga.us/pls/job-bank

Idaho http://www.lili.org/staff/jobs.htm

Indiana http://www.statelib.lib.in.us

Iowa http://www.silo.lib.ia.us

Kentucky http://www.kdla.state.ky.us/libserv/jobline.htm

Louisiana http://www.state.lib.la.us/publications/jobs.htm

Massachusetts http://www.mlin.lib.ma.us

Mississippi http://www.mlc.lib.ms.us/job

Montana http://www.jsd.dli.state.mt.us

Nebraska http://www.nlc.state.ne.us/libjob

New Hampshire http://www.state.nh.us

New York Library Association http://www.nyla.org

North Carolina http//:www.ncgov.com/html/basic/index.html (professional and paraprofessional positions)

Oklahoma http://www.odl.state.ok.us

South Carolina http://www.state.sc.us

Tennessee http://www.lib.utk.edu

Texas http://www.tsl.state.tx.us

Virginia http://www.lva.lib.va.us

Washington http://www.statelib.wa.gov

In Pennsylvania, the listserv is maintained by Commonwealth Libraries. Arizona offers a jobline service at the e-mail address tcorkery@lib.az.us.

On occasion, the following state library newsletters or journals will list vacancy postings: Alabama (*Cottonboll*, quarterly); Alaska (*Newspoke*, bimonthly); Arizona (*Arizona Libraries NewsWeek*); Indiana (*Focus on Indiana Libraries*, 11/year; Iowa (*Joblist*); Kansas (*Kansas Libraries*, monthly); Louisiana (*Library Communique*, monthly); Minnesota (*Minnesota Libraries News*, monthly); Nebraska (*NCompass*, quarterly); New Hampshire (*Granite State Libraries*, bimonthly); New Mexico (*Hitchhiker*, weekly); Tennessee (*TLA Newsletter*, bimonthly); Utah (*Directions for Utah Libraries*, monthly); and Wyoming (*Outrider*, monthly).

Many state library agencies will refer applicants informally when vacancies are known to exist, but do not have formal placement services. The following states primarily make referrals to public libraries only: Alabama, Alaska, Arizona, Arkansas, California, Louisiana, Pennsylvania, South Carolina (institutional also), Tennessee, Utah, Vermont, and Virginia. Those that refer applicants to all types of libraries are: Alaska, Delaware, Florida, Georgia, Hawaii, Idaho, Kansas, Kentucky, Maine, Maryland, Mississippi, Montana, Nebraska, Nevada (largely public and academic), New Hampshire, New Mexico, North Carolina, North Dakota, Ohio, Pennsylvania, Rhode Island, South Dakota, Vermont, West Virginia (on Pennsylvania Jobline, public, academic, special), and Wyoming.

The following state libraries post library vacancy notices for all types of libraries on a bulletin board: California, Connecticut, Florida, Georgia, Hawaii, Illinois, Indiana, Iowa, Kentucky, Nevada, New Jersey, New York, Ohio, Oklahoma, Pennsylvania, South Carolina, South Dakota, Texas, Utah, and Washington. [Addresses of the state agencies are found in Part 6 of the *Bowker Annual* and in *American Library Directory—Ed.*]

State and Regional Library Associations

State and regional library associations will often make referrals, run ads in association newsletters, or operate a placement service at annual conferences, in addition to the joblines sponsored by some groups. Referral of applicants when jobs are known is done by the following associations: Arkansas, Delaware, Hawaii, Louisiana, Michigan, Minnesota, Nevada, Pennsylvania, South Dakota, Tennessee, and Wisconsin. Although listings are infrequent, job vacancies are placed in the following association newsletters or journals when available: Alabama (*Alabama Librarian*, 7/year); Alaska (*Newspoke*, bimonthly); Arizona (*Newsletter*, 10/year); Arkansas (*Arkansas Libraries*, 6/year); Connecticut (*Connecticut Libraries*, 11/year); Delaware (*Delaware Library Association Bulletin*, 3/year); District of Columbia (*Intercom*, 11/year); Florida (*Florida Libraries*, 6/year); Indiana (*Focus on Indiana Libraries*, 11/year); Iowa (*Catalyst*, 6/year); Kansas (*KLA Newsletter*, 6 issues/bimonthly); Minnesota (*MLA Newsletter*, 6 issues/bimonthly); Missouri (bimonthly); Mountain Plains (*MPLA Newsletter*, bimonthly, lists vacancies and position wanted ads for individuals and institutions); Nebraska (*NLAQ*); Nevada (*Highroller*, 4/year); New Hampshire (*NHLA Newsletter*, 6/year); New Jersey (*NJLA Newsletter*, 10/year); New Mexico (shares notices via state library's *Hitchhiker*, weekly); New York (*NYLA Bulletin*, 10/year; free for institutional members; $25/1 week, $40/2 weeks, others); Ohio (*ACCESS*, monthly); Oklahoma (*Oklahoma Librarian*, 6/year); Oregon (*OLA Hotline, 24/year);* Rhode Island (*RILA Bulletin*, 6/year); South Carolina (*News and Views*); South Dakota (*Book Marks*, bimonthly); Tennessee (*TLA Newsletter*); Vermont (*VLA News*, 6/year. Mailing address: Box 803, Burlington, VT 05402); Virginia (*Virginia Libraries*, quarterly); and West Virginia (*West Virginia Libraries*, 6/year).

The following associations have indicated some type of placement service, although it may only be held at annual conferences: Alabama, California, Connecticut, Georgia, Idaho, Indiana, Iowa, Kansas, Kentucky, Louisiana, Maryland, Massachusetts, New England, New Jersey, New York, North Carolina, Ohio, Pacific Northwest, Pennsylvania, South Dakota, Southeastern, Tennessee, Texas, Vermont, Wisconsin, and Wyoming.

The following have indicated they have an electronic source for job postings in addition to voice joblines: Alabama, allaonline@mindspring.com; California, http://cla-net.org/jobmart; Connecticut, http://www.lib.uconn.edu/cla; Illinois, http://www.ila.org; Kansas, http://skyways.lib.ks.us/KLA/helpwanted (no charge to list job openings); Michigan, http://www.mla.lib.mi.us; Minnesota, http://www.libmankato.musu.edu:2000; Missouri, http://www.mlnc.com/~mla; Nebraska, http://www.nlc.state.ne.us/libjob/libjob.html; New Hampshire, http://www.state.nh.us/nhsl/ljob.htm; New Jersey Library Association, http://www.njla.org; Ohio, http://www.olc.org/jobline.html; Oklahoma, http://www.state.ok.us/~odl/fyi/jobline.htm (e-mail bpetrie@oltn.odl.state.ok.us); Oregon, http://www.olaweb.org; Pacific Northwest Library Association, e-mail listserv@wln.com or listserv@ldbsu.idbsu.edu; Texas, http://www.txla.org/jobline/jobline.txt; Virginia, http://www.vla.org; Wisconsin, http://www.wla.lib.wi.us/wlajob.htm.

The following associations have indicated they have no placement service at this time: Colorado, Middle Atlantic Regional Library Federation, Mississippi, Montana, New Mexico, North Dakota, Utah, and West Virginia. [State and regional association addresses are listed in Part 6 of the *Bowker Annual.—Ed.*]

Library and Information Studies Programs

Library and information studies programs offer some type of service for their current students as well as alumni. Most schools provide job-hunting and résumé-writing seminars. Many have outside speakers representing different types of libraries or recent graduates relating career experiences. Faculty or a designated placement officer offer individual advising services or critiquing of résumés.

Of the ALA-accredited library and information studies programs, the following handle placement activities through the program: Alabama, Albany, Alberta, Buffalo (compiles annual graduate biographical listings), British Columbia, Dalhousie, Dominican, Drexel, Hawaii, Illinois, Kent State, Kentucky, Louisiana, McGill, Missouri (College of Education), Pittsburgh (Department of Library and Information Science only), Pratt, Puerto Rico, Queens, Rhode Island, Rutgers, Saint John's, South Carolina, Syracuse, Tennessee, Texas–Austin, Toronto, UCLA, Western Ontario, Wisconsin–Madison, and Wisconsin–Milwaukee.

The central university placement center handles activities for the following schools: California–Berkeley (alumni) and Emporia. However, in most cases, faculty in the library school will still do informal counseling regarding job seeking.

In some schools, the placement services are handled in a cooperative manner; in most cases the university placement center sends out credentials while the library school posts or compiles the job listings. Schools utilizing one or both sources include: Alabama, Albany, Arizona (School of Information Resources and Library Science maintains an e-mail list: jobops@listserv.arizona.edu), Buffalo, Catholic, Dominican, Florida State, Indiana, Iowa, Kent State, Long Island, Maryland, Michigan, Montreal, North Carolina–Chapel Hill, North Carolina–Greensboro, North Carolina Central, North Texas, Oklahoma, Pittsburgh, Queens, Saint John's, San Jose, Simmons, South Florida, Southern Connecticut, Southern Mississippi, Syracuse, Tennessee, Texas Woman's, Washington, Wayne State, and Wisconsin–Milwaukee. In sending out placement credentials, schools vary as to whether they distribute these free, charge a general registration fee, or request a fee for each file or credential sent out.

Schools that have indicated they post job vacancy notices for review but do not issue printed lists are: Alabama, Alberta, Arizona, British Columbia, Buffalo, Catholic, Clark Atlanta, Dalhousie, Drexel, Florida State, Hawaii, Illinois, Indiana, Kent State, Kentucky, Long Island, Louisiana, McGill, Maryland, Missouri, Montreal, North Carolina–Chapel Hill, North Carolina–Greensboro, North Carolina Central, Oklahoma, Pittsburgh, Puerto Rico, Queens, Rutgers, Saint John's, San Jose, Simmons, South Carolina, South Florida, Southern Mississippi, Syracuse (general postings), Tennessee, Texas Woman's, Toronto, UCLA, Washington, Wayne State, Western Ontario, and Wisconsin–Madison.

In addition to job vacancy postings, some schools issue printed listings, operate joblines, have electronic access, or provide database services:

- Albany: Job Placement Bulletin free to SISP students; listserv@cnsibm.albany.edu to subscribe
- Arizona: listserv@listserv.arizona.edu to subscribe
- British Columbia: uses BCLA Jobline, 604-430-6411, and BCLA job page at http://bcla.bc.ca./jobpage
- Buffalo: Job postings for alumni at http://www.avpc.buffalo.edu/hrs/vacancies
- California–Berkeley: Weekly out-of-state job list and jobline free to all students and graduates for six months after graduation; $55 annual fee for alumni of any University of California campus; 510-642-3283
- Clarion: http://www.clarion.edu/academic/edu-humn/newlibsci/jobs
- Dalhousie: listserv for Atlantic Canada jobs, send message saying *sub list-joblist* to mailserv@ac.dal.ca
- Dominican: Placement News every two weeks, free for six months following graduation, $15/year for students and alumni; $25/year others
- Drexel: http://www.cis.drexel.edu/placement/placement.html
- Emporia: weekly bulletin for school, university, public jobs; separate bulletin for special; $42/6 months; Emporia graduates, $21/6 months

- Florida State
- Hawaii
- Illinois: Free online placement JOBSearch database available on campus and via telnet (alexia.lis.uiuc.edu/gslis/people/students/jobs.html#head; or carousel.lis.uiuc.edu/)
- Indiana: http://www.slis.indiana.edu/21stcentury
- Iowa: $15/year for registered students and alumni
- Kentucky: http://www.uky.edu/CommInfoStudies/SLIS/jobs.htm
- Maryland: send *subscribe* message to listserv@umdd.umd.edu
- Michigan: http://www.si.umich.edu/placement
- Missouri: http://www.coe.missouri.edu/~career
- North Carolina–Chapel Hill: listserv@ils.unc.edu to subscribe, or http://www.ils.unc.edu/ils/careers/resources
- Oklahoma
- Pittsburgh: http://www.sis.pitt.edu/~lsdept/libjobs.htm
- Pratt: free to students and alumni for full-time/part-time professional positions only
- Rhode Island: monthly, $7.50/year
- Rutgers: http://www.scils.rutgers.edu or send *subscribe* message to scils-jobs@scils.rutgers.edu
- Saint John's: Send notices to libis@stjohns.edu or fax to 718-990-2071; lists job postings for United States, Canada, and abroad
- Simmons: http://www.simmons.edu/gslis/jobline.html; Simmons also operates the New England Jobline (617-521-2815), which announces professional vacancies in the region
- South Carolina: http://www.libsci.sc.edu/career/job.htm
- South Florida: in cooperation with ALISE
- Southern Connecticut: http://www.scsu.ctstateu.edu/~jobline; printed listing twice a month, mailed to students and alumni free
- Syracuse: sends lists of job openings by e-mail to students
- Texas–Austin: Weekly Placement Bulletin $16/6 mos., $28/yr. by listserv, $26/6 mos., $48/yr. by mail (free to students and alumni for one year following graduation); Texas Jobs Weekly, $16/6 months or $28/year, or see http://www.gslis.utexas.edu/~careers/)
- Texas Woman's: http://www.twu.edu/slis/
- Toronto: http://www.fis.utoronto.ca/news/jobsite
- Western Ontario: http://www.uwo.ca/adminservices/employment/resources; to list positions call 519-661-2111 ext. 8495
- Wisconsin–Madison: sends listings from Wisconsin and Minnesota to Illinois for JOBSearch
- Wisconsin–Milwaukee: send *subscription* message to listserv@slis.uwm.edu

Employers will often list jobs with schools only in their particular geographical area; some library schools will give information to non-alumni regarding their specific locales, but are not staffed to handle mail requests and advice is usually given in person. Schools that have indicated they will allow librarians in their areas to view listings are: Alabama, Albany, Alberta, Arizona, British Columbia, Buffalo, California–Berkeley, Catholic, Clarion, Clark Atlanta, Dalhousie, Dominican, Drexel, Emporia, Florida State, Hawaii, Illinois, Indiana, Iowa, Kent State, Kentucky, Louisiana, McGill, Maryland, Michigan, Missouri, Montreal, North Carolina–Chapel Hill, North Carolina–Greensboro, North Carolina Central, North Texas, Oklahoma, Pittsburgh, Pratt, Puerto Rico, Queens, Rhode Island, Rutgers, Saint John's, San Jose, Simmons, South Carolina, South Florida, Southern Connecticut, Southern Mississippi, Syracuse, Tennessee, Texas–Austin, Texas Woman's, Toronto, UCLA, Washington, Wayne State, Western Ontario, Wisconsin–Madison, and Wisconsin–Milwaukee.

A list of ALA-accredited programs with addresses and telephone numbers can be requested from ALA or found elsewhere in Part 3 of the *Bowker Annual*. Individuals interested in placement services of other library education programs should contact the schools directly.

Federal Employment Information Sources

Consideration for employment in many federal libraries requires establishing civil service eligibility. Although the actual job search is your responsibility, the Office of Personnel Management (OPM) has developed the "USA Jobs" Web site (http://www.usajobs.opm.gov) to assist you along the way.

OPM's Career America Connection at 912-757-3000 or (TDD Service at 912-744-2299) is "USA Jobs by Phone." This system provides current worldwide federal job opportunities, salary and employee benefits information, special recruitment messages, and more. You can also record your request to have application packages, forms, and other employment-related literature mailed to you. This service is available 24 hours a day, seven days a week. Request Federal Employment Information Line factsheet EI-42, "Federal Employment Information Sources," for a complete listing of local telephone numbers to this nationwide network.

USA Jobs Touch Screen Computer is a computer-based system utilizing touch-screen technology. These kiosks, found throughout the nation in OPM offices, Federal Office Buildings, and other locations, allow you to access current worldwide federal job opportunities, online information, and more.

Another federal jobs site is http://www.fedworld.gov/jobs/jobsearch.html.

Applicants should attempt to make personal contact directly with federal agencies in which they are interested. This is essential in the Washington, D.C., area where more than half the vacancies occur. Most librarian positions are in three agencies: Army, Navy, and Veterans Administration.

There are some "excepted service" agencies that are not required to hire through the usual OPM channels. While these agencies may require the standard forms, they maintain their own employee-selection policies and procedures. Government establishments with positions outside the competitive civil service include: Board of Governors of the Federal Reserve System, Central Intelligence Agency, Defense Intelligence Agency, Department of Medicine and Surgery, Federal Bureau of Investigation, Foreign Service of the United States, General Accounting Office, Library of Congress, National Science Foundation, National Security Agency, Tennessee Valley Authority, U.S. Nuclear Regulatory Commission, U.S. Postal Service, Judicial Branch of the Government, Legislative Branch of the Government, U.S. Mission to the United Nations, World Bank and IFC, International Monetary Fund, Organization of American States, Pan American Health Organization, and United Nations Secretariat.

The Library of Congress, the world's largest and most comprehensive library, is an excepted service agency in the legislative branch and administers its own independent merit selection system. Job classifications, pay, and benefits are the same as in other federal agencies, and qualifications requirements generally correspond to those used by the U.S. Office of Personnel Management. The library does not use registers, but announces vacancies as they become available. A separate application must be submitted for each vacancy announcement. For most professional positions, announcements are widely distributed and open for a minimum period of 30 days. Qualifications requirements and ranking criteria are stated on the vacancy announcement. The Library of Congress Human Resources Operations Office is located in the James Madison Memorial Building, 101 Independence Ave. S.E., Washington, DC 20540, 202-707-5620.

Additional General and Specialized Job Sources

Affirmative Action Register, 8356 Olive Blvd., St. Louis, MO 63132, 314-991-1335, 800-537-0655, e-mail aareero@concentric.net, World Wide Web http://www.aar-eeo.com: The goal is to "provide female, minority, handicapped, and veteran candidates with an opportunity to learn of professional and managerial positions throughout the nation and to assist employers in implementing their Equal Opportunity Employment programs." Free distribution of a monthly bulletin is made to leading businesses, industrial and academic institutions, and over 4,000 agencies that recruit qualified minorities and women, as well as to all known female, minority, and handicapped professional organizations, placement offices, newspapers, magazines, rehabilitation facilities, and over 8,000 federal, state, and local governmental employment units with a total readership in excess of 3.5 million (audited). Individual mail subscriptions are available for $15 per year. Librarian listings are in most issues. Sent free to libraries on request.

The Chronicle of Higher Education (published weekly with breaks in August and December), 1255 23rd St. N.W., Suite 700, Washington, DC 20037, 202-466-1055; fax 202-296-2691: Publishes a variety of library positions each week, including administrative and faculty jobs. Job listings are searchable by specific categories, keywords, or geographic location on the Internet at http://Chronicle.com/jobs.

Academic Resource Network On-Line Database (ARNOLD), 4656 W. Jefferson, Suite 140, Fort Wayne, IN 46804: This World Wide Web interactive database (http://www.arnold.snybuf.edu) helps faculty, staff, and librarians to identify partners for exchange or collaborative research.

School Libraries: School librarians often find that the channels for locating positions in education are of more value than the usual library ones, for instance, contacting county or city school superintendent offices. Other sources include university placement offices that carry listings for a variety of school system jobs. A list of commercial teacher agencies may be obtained from the National Association of Teachers' Agencies, Dr. Eugene Alexander, CPC, CTC, Treas., c/o G. A. Agency, 524 South Ave. E., Cranford, NJ 07016-3209, 908-272-2080, fax 908-272-2080, World Wide Web http://www.jobsforteachers.com.

Overseas

Opportunities for employment in foreign countries are limited and immigration policies of individual countries should be investigated. Employment for Americans is virtually limited to U.S. government libraries, libraries of U.S. firms doing worldwide business, and American schools abroad. Library journals from other countries will sometimes list vacancy notices. Some persons have obtained jobs by contacting foreign publishers or vendors directly. Non-U.S. government jobs usually call for foreign language fluency. *Career Opportunities for Bilinguals and Multilinguals: A Directory of Resources in Education, Employment and Business* by Vladimir F. Wertsman (Scarecrow Press, 1991, ISBN 0-8108-2439-6, $35) gives general contacts for foreign employment and business resources. "International Jobs" by Wertsman (*RQ,* Fall 1992, pp. 14–19) provides a listing of library resources for finding jobs abroad. Another source is the librarian job vacancy postings at http://bubl.ac.uk/news/jobs, a listing of U.S. and foreign jobs collected by the Bulletin Board for Libraries.

Council for International Exchange of Scholars (CIES), 3007 Tilden St. N.W., Suite 5M, Washington, DC 20008-3009, 202-686-7877, e-mail cies1@ciesnet. cies.org, World Wide Web http://www.cies.org: Administers U.S. government Fulbright awards for university lecturing and advanced research abroad; usually 10–15 awards per year are made to U.S. citizens who are specialists in library or information sciences. In addition, many countries offer awards in any specialization of research or lecturing. Lecturing awards usually require university or college teaching experience. Several opportunities exist for professional librarians as well. Applications and information may be obtained, beginning in March each year, directly from CIES. Worldwide application deadline is August 1.

Department of Defense, Dependents Schools, Recruitment Unit, 4040 N. Fairfax Dr., Arlington, VA 22203, 703-696-3068, fax 703-696-2697, e-mail recruitment@odeddodea.edu: Overall management and operational responsibilities for the education of dependent children of active duty U.S. military personnel and Department of Defense civilians who are stationed in foreign areas. Also responsible for teacher recruitment. For complete application brochure, write to above address. The latest edition of *Overseas Opportunities for Educators* is available and provides information on educator employment opportunities in more than 165 schools worldwide. The schools are operated on military installations for the children of U.S. military and civilian personnel stationed overseas.

International Schools Services (ISS), Box 5910, Princeton, NJ 08543, 609-452-0990: Private, not-for-profit organization founded in 1955 to serve American schools overseas other than Department of Defense schools. These are American, international elementary and secondary schools enrolling children of business and diplomatic families living abroad. ISS services to overseas schools include recruitment and recommendation of personnel, curricular and administrative guidance, purchasing, facility planning, and more. ISS also publishes a comprehensive directory of overseas schools and a bimonthly newsletter, *NewsLinks*, for those interested in the intercultural educational community. Information regarding these publications and other services may be obtained by writing to the above address.

Peace Corps, 1990 K St. N.W., No. 9300, Washington, DC 20526: Volunteer opportunities exist for those holding MA/MS or BA/BS degrees in library science with one year of related work experience. Two-year tour of duty. U.S. citizens only. Living allowance, health care, transportation, and other benefits provided. Write for additional information and application or call 800-424-8580.

Search Associates, Box 922, Jackson, MI 49204-0922, 517-768-9250, fax 517-768-9252, e-mail JimAmbrose@compuserve.com, World Wide Web http://www.search-associates.com: A private organization composed of former overseas school directors who organize about ten recruitment fairs (most occur in February) to place teachers, librarians, and administrators in about 400 independent K–12 American/international schools around the world. These accredited schools, based on the American model, range in size from under 40 to more than 4,000 and serve the children of diplomats and businessmen from dozens of countries. They annually offer highly attractive personal and professional opportunities for experienced librarians.

Overseas Exchange Programs

International Exchanges: Most exchanges are handled by direct negotiation between interested parties. A few libraries have established exchange programs for their own staff. In order to facilitate exchange arrangements, the *IFLA Journal* (issued January, May, August, and October/November) lists persons wishing to exchange positions outside their own country. All listings must include the following information: full name, address, present position, qualifications (with year of obtaining), language, abilities, preferred country/city/library, and type of position. Send to International Federation of Library Associations and Institutions (IFLA) Secretariat, c/o Koninklijkebibliotheek, Pn Willem-Alexanderhof S. 2595 BE, The Hague, Netherlands, fax 31-70-3834827, e-mail ifla@nlc-bnc.ca, World Wide Web http://www.ifla.org.

LIBEX Bureau for International Staff Exchange, c/o A. J. Clark, Thomas Parry Library, University of Wales, Aberystwyth, Llanbadarn Fawr, Ceredigion SY23 3AS, Wales, 01970-622417, fax 01970-622190, e-mail parrylib@aber.ac.uk, World Wide Web http://www.inf.aber.ac.uk/tpl/Libex/intro.asp. Assists in two-way exchanges for British librarians wishing to work abroad and for librarians from the United States, Canada, EC countries, and Commonwealth and other countries who wish to undertake exchanges.

Using Information Skills in Nonlibrary Settings

A great deal of interest has been shown in using information skills in a variety of ways in nonlibrary settings. These jobs are not usually found through the regular library placement sources, although many library and information studies programs are trying to generate such listings for their students and alumni. Job listings that do exist may not call specifically for "librarians" by that title so that ingenuity may be needed to search out jobs where information management skills are needed. Some librarians are working on a freelance basis, offering services to businesses, alternative schools, community agencies, legislators, etc.; these opportunities are usually not found in advertisements but created by developing contacts and publicity over a period of time. A number of information-brokering businesses have developed from individual freelance experiences. Small companies or other organizations often need "one-time" service for organizing files or collections, bibliographic research for special projects, indexing or abstracting, compilation of directories, and consulting services. Bibliographic networks and online database companies are using librarians as information managers, trainers, researchers, systems and database analysts, online services managers, etc. Jobs in this area are sometimes found in library network newsletters or data processing journals. Librarians can also be found working in law firms as litigation case supervisors (organizing and analyzing records needed for specific legal cases); with publishers as sales representatives, marketing directors, editors, and computer services experts; with community agencies as adult education coordinators, volunteer administrators, grants writers, etc.

Classifieds in *Publishers Weekly* and the *National Business Employment Weekly* may lead to information-related positions. One might also consider reading the Sunday classified ad sections in metropolitan newspapers in their entirety to locate descriptions calling for information skills but under a variety of job titles.

The *Burwell World Directory of Information Brokers* is an annual publication that lists information brokers, freelance librarians, independent information specialists, and institutions that provide services for a fee. There is a minimal charge for an annual listing. The Burwell Directory Online is searchable free on the Internet at http://www.burwellinc.com, and a CD-ROM version is available. Burwell can be reached at Burwell Enterprises, 5619 Plumtree Dr., Dallas, TX 75252-4928, 972-732-0160, fax 972-733-1951, e-mail burwellinfo@burwellinc. com. Also published is a bimonthly newsletter, *Information Broker* ($40, foreign postage, $15), that includes articles by, for, and about individuals and companies in the fee-based information field, book reviews, a calendar of upcoming events, and issue-oriented articles. A bibliography and other publications on the field of information brokering are also available.

The Association of Independent Information Professionals (AIIP) was formed in 1987 for individuals who own and operate for-profit information companies. Contact AIIP Headquarters at 212-779-1855 or visit the organization's Web site at http://www.aiip.org.

A growing number of publications are addressing opportunities for librarians in the broader information arena. Among these are:

- "Careers in Libraries: A Bibliography of Traditional and Web-based Library Career Resources," compiled by Jan E. Hayes and Julie Todaro for the American Library Association Office for Human Resource Development and Recruitment, August 2000 (call 800-545-2433 ext. 4282 to request a copy).
- "You Can Take Your MLS Out of the Library," by Wilda W. Williams (*Library Journal*, Nov. 1994, pp. 43–46.
- "Information Entrepreneurship: Sources for Reference Librarians," by Donna L. Gilton (*RQ,* Spring 1992, pp. 346–355.
- *The Information Broker's Handbook* by Sue Rugge and Alfred Glossbrenner (Windcrest/McGraw-Hill, 1992, 379p. ISBN 0-8306-3798-2), which covers the market for information, getting started, pricing and billing, and more.
- *Opening New Doors: Alternative Careers for Librarians*, edited by Ellis Mount (Washington, D.C.: Special Libraries Association, 1993), which provides profiles of librarians who are working outside libraries.
- *Extending the Librarian's Domain: A Survey of Emerging Occupation Opportunities for Librarians and Information Professionals* by Forest Woody Horton, Jr. (Washington, D.C.: Special Libraries Association, 1994), which explores information job components in a variety of sectors.
- *Careers in Electronic Information* by Wendy Wicks (1997, 184p.) and *Guide to Careers in Abstracting and Indexing* by Wendy Wicks and Ann Marie Cunningham (1992, 126p.), available from the National Federation of Abstracting & Information Services, 1518 Walnut St., Philadelphia, PA 19102, 215-893-1561, e-mail nfais@nfais.org, World Wide Web http://www.nfais.org.
- The American Society of Indexers, 11250 Roger Bacon Dr., Suite 8, Reston, VA 20190-5202, 703-234-4147, fax 703-435-4390, e-mail info@asindexing.org, World Wide Web http://www.ASIndexing.org, which has a number of publications that would be useful for individuals who are interested in indexing careers.

Temporary/Part-Time Positions

Working as a substitute librarian or in temporary positions may be considered to be an alternative career path as well as an interim step while looking for a regular job. This type of work can provide valuable contacts and experience. Organizations that hire library workers for part-time or temporary jobs include Advanced Information Management, 444 Castro St., Suite 320, Mountain View, CA 94041 (650-965-7799), or 900 Wilshire Blvd., Suite 1424, Los Angeles, CA 90017 (213-489-9800); C. Berger and Company, 327 E. Gundersen Dr., Carol Stream, IL 60188 (630-653-1115 or 800-382-4222); Wontawk Gossage Associates, Inc., 25 W. 43 St., New York, NY 10036 (212-869-3348) and 304 Newbury St., Suite

304, Boston, MA 02115 (617-867-9209); Information Management Division, 1160 Veirs Mill Rd., Suite 414, Wheaton, MD 20902 (301-949-4097); The Library Co-Op, Inc., 3840 Park Ave., Suite 107, Edison, NJ 08820 (908-906-1777 or 800-654-6275); Library Management Systems, Corporate Pointe, Suite 755, Culver City, CA 90230 (310-216-6436 or 800-567-4669) and Three Bethesda Metro Center, Suite 700, Bethesda, MD 20814 (301-961-1984); and Pro Libra Associates, Inc., 6 Inwood Place, Maplewood, NJ 07040 (201-762-0070).

Part-time jobs are not always advertised, but often found by canvasing local libraries and leaving applications.

Job Hunting in General

Wherever information needs to be organized and presented to patrons in an effective, efficient, and service-oriented fashion, the skills of librarians can be applied, whether or not they are in traditional library settings. However, it will take considerable investment of time, energy, imagination, and money on the part of an individual before a satisfying position is created or obtained, in a conventional library or another type of information service. Usually, no one method or source of job-hunting can be used alone. *Library Services for Career Planning, Job Searching, and Employment Opportunities,* edited by Byron Anderson (Haworth Press, 183p., 1992) includes bibliographical references.

Public and school library certification requirements vary from state to state; contact the state library agency for such information in a particular state. Certification requirements are summarized in *Certification of Public Librarians in the United States*, 4th ed., 1991, from the ALA Office for Library Personnel Resources. A summary of school library/media certification requirements by state is found in *Requirements for Certification of Teachers, Counselors, Librarians and Administrators for Elementary and Secondary Schools*, published annually by the University of Chicago Press. "School Library Media Certification Requirements: 1994 Update" by Patsy H. Perritt also provides a compilation in *School Library Journal*, June 1994, pp. 32–49. State supervisors of school library media services may also be contacted for information on specific states.

Civil service requirements on a local, county, or state level often add another layer of procedures to the job search. Some civil service jurisdictions require written and/or oral examinations; others assign a ranking based on a review of credentials. Jobs are usually filled from the top candidates on a qualified list of applicants. Since the exams are held only at certain time periods and a variety of jobs can be filled from a single list of applicants (e.g., all Librarian I positions regardless of type of function), it is important to check whether a library in which one is interested falls under civil service procedures.

If you are looking for a position in a specific subject area or in a particular geographical location, remember your reference skills and ferret information from directories and other tools regarding local industries, schools, subject collections, etc. Directories such as the *American Library Directory*, *Subject Collections*, *Directory of Special Libraries and Information Centers*, and *Directory of Federal Libraries*, as well as state directories or directories of other special subject areas can provide a wealth of information for job seekers. "The Job Hunter's

Search for Company Information" by Robert Favini (*RQ,* Winter 1991, pp. 155–161) lists general reference business sources that might also be useful for librarians seeking employment in companies. Some state employment offices will include library listings as part of their Job Services department.

Some students have pooled resources to hire a clipping service for a specific time period in order to get classified librarian ads for a particular geographical area.

Other Internet sources not mentioned elsewhere include http://www.careerpath.com.

For information on other job-hunting and personnel matters, or a copy of this guide, contact the ALA Office for Human Resource Development and Recruitment, 50 E. Huron St., Chicago, IL 60611, 800-545-2433, World Wide Web http://www.ala.org/hrdr.

Placements and Salaries 2000: Plenty of Jobs, Salaries Flat

Tom Terrell

Assistant Professor, School of Library and Information Science
University of South Florida, Tampa

Vicki L. Gregory

Director and Professor, School of Library and Information Science
University of South Florida, Tampa

In a year of widespread economic downturn, graduates of American Library Association (ALA)-accredited library and information science (LIS) schools found plenty of jobs and overall (though small) salary increases. The average beginning salary for 2000 LIS graduates was $34,871, a 2.63 percent increase over the 1999 average ($33,976). This increase lags about 30 percent behind inflation (3.8 percent) and does not continue the trend of the previous two years, when LIS starting salaries easily beat inflation.

The year's salary leaders, including many of the high-tech and dot-com positions filled by LIS graduates, were not immune to the fall of the high-tech sector. This trend took a toll on both number of jobs and salary ranges. One bright note: minority graduates posted an 11 percent salary gain in 2000, the best in years.

Reversing a trend, the average salary for women rose 3.18 percent in 2000 while that for men increased only 0.57 percent. This is severely down from the 12 percent increase for men last year, but men still earn nearly 5 percent more than women in this field.

Job Trends

Table 1 shows the job status—both by region and in total—of those 1,234 graduates (of 1,392 total) who reported their job status. Of those 1,234 graduates, 1,210 (98.1 percent) were employed in some library capacity.

Of those 1,210 graduates employed in libraries, 1,142 (94.4 percent) are in permanent or temporary professional positions, with the rest in nonprofessional positions. The percentage for temporary professional jobs remains consistent. The 1,029 graduates working in full-time permanent professional positions represent 85 percent of those employed in libraries, as compared with 1,226 (83.5 percent) in 1999, and 1,590 (81.5 percent) in 1998.

Salaries Rise Slowly

Table 7 shows placements and full-time salaries of reporting 2000 graduates on a school-by-school basis. An analysis of aggregate data reported in Tables 5 and 2 reveals that the average 2000 professional salary for starting library positions increased by $925 over 1999.

(text continues on page 388)

Adapted from *Library Journal*, October 15, 2001.

Table 1 / Status of 2000 Graduates, Spring 2001

| Region | Number of Schools Reporting | Number of Graduates | Graduates in Library Positions | | | | Graduates in Nonlibrary Positions | Unemployed or Status Unreported |
			Permanent Professional	Temporary Professional	Non-professional	Total		
Northeast	13	555	407	38	31	476	12	67
Southeast	8	257	202	20	11	233	—	24
Midwest	8	245	183	18	8	209	7	29
Southwest	3	90	72	5	3	80	1	9
West	5	206	141	21	15	177	4	25
Canada	2	39	24	11	—	35	—	4
Total	39	1,392	1,029	113	68	1,210	24	158

Table based on survey responses from schools and individual graduates. Figures will not necessarily be fully consistent with some of the other data reported that came from individual graduates. Tables do not always add up, individually or collectively, since both schools and individuals omitted data in some cases.

Table 2 / Placements and Full-Time Salaries of 2000 U.S. Graduates/Summary by Region

| Region | Number of Placements | Number of Reported Salaries | | | Low | | High | | Average | | | Median | | |
		Women	Men	Total	Women	Men	Women	Men	Women	Men	All	Women	Men	All
Northeast	434	354	73	427	$7,488	$15,000	$68,280	$80,000	$35,037	$37,554	$35,475	$34,122	$35,000	$34,500
Southeast	212	163	49	212	10,200	22,390	75,000	74,250	33,008	33,864	33,207	32,000	32,000	32,000
Midwest	180	146	31	177	16,000	17,500	60,000	60,000	33,864	35,494	34,142	32,700	36,000	33,550
Southwest	76	65	11	76	20,000	28,000	64,000	48,000	33,820	34,336	33,896	32,744	34,000	32,988
West	148	113	30	143	18,000	29,500	68,000	70,000	37,154	40,072	37,783	35,500	37,600	36,000
Canada/Intl.*	36	10	3	13	23,441	26,240	31,254	31,254	26,904	29,583	27,531	27,347	31,254	27,347
Combined **	1,050	851	194	1,035	7,488	15,000	75,000	80,000	$34,555	36,331	34,871	33,500	35,000	34,000

* All international salaries converted to American dollars based on conversion rates for August 1, 2001.
**U.S. results.

Table 3 / 2000 Total Graduates and Placements by School*

Schools	Graduates			Employed			Unemployed			Students		
	Women	Men	Total	Women	Men	Total	Women	Men	Total	Women	Men	Total
Alabama	81	14	95	27	9	36	2	—	2	—	—	—
Arizona	40	16	56	17	8	25	5	3	8	—	—	—
British Columbia	28	7	35	13	3	16	—	1	1	—	—	—
California (UCLA)	—	—	17	14	2	16	2	0	2	—	—	—
Clarion	42	7	49	17	3	20	3	0	3	—	—	—
Dominican	—	—	79	65	7	72	4	3	7	—	2	2
Drexel	64	16	80	30	6	36	5	3	8	—	—	—
Indiana	123	47	170	26	5	31	2	0	2	—	—	—
Iowa	30	7	37	22	2	24	4	1	5	—	—	—
Long Island	124	26	150	39	5	44	1	4	5	—	1	1
Louisiana State	49	18	67	23	6	29	4	0	4	1	—	1
Maryland	—	—	12	8	2	10	2	—	2	—	—	—
Missouri	41	12	53	15	6	21	—	—	—	—	—	—
N.C. Central	50	6	56	—	—	—	—	—	—	—	—	—
N.C. Chapel Hill	43	11	54	17	5	22	2	—	2	—	—	—
Oklahoma	42	5	47	19	1	20	—	—	—	—	—	—
Pittsburgh	61	21	82	—	—	—	—	—	—	—	—	—
Pratt	—	—	40	28	7	35	2	1	3	—	—	—
Puerto Rico	18	4	22	—	—	—	2	—	—	—	—	—
Rhode Island	—	—	17	13	3	16	1	—	0	—	—	—

Rutgers	90	24	114	24	6	30	1	2	3	—	—	—
St. John's	22	5	27	9	2	11	—	1	1	—	1	1
San Jose	191	49	240	52	13	65	6	—	6	1	—	1
Simmons	—	—	199	150	31	181	12	1	13	1	—	1
South Carolina	135	29	164	37	10	47	5	—	—	—	—	—
South Florida	77	25	102	16	10	26	—	1	—	—	—	—
Southern Connecticut	65	14	79	24	1	25	3	2	4	—	—	—
Southern Mississippi	32	10	42	12	3	—	—	—	2	—	—	—
SUNY-Albany	—	—	39	29	6	35	4	2	4	—	—	—
SUNY-Buffalo	—	—	45	33	7	40	2	1	4	—	—	—
Syracuse	—	—	25	15	3	18	1	1	2	—	—	—
Tennessee	73	13	86	30	2	32	5	1	6	1	—	1
Texas (Austin)	117	32	149	38	11	49	3	1	4	1	1	1
Texas Woman's	102	9	111	20	3	23	5	—	5	—	—	—
Toronto	53	33	86	—	—	—	—	—	—	—	—	—
Washington	49	18	67	12	7	19	3	1	4	—	—	—
Wayne State	12	1	13	12	1	13	—	—	—	—	—	—
Western Ontario	19	7	26	—	—	23	—	—	3	—	—	—
Wisconsin (Madison)	43	14	57	31	6	37	4	2	6	—	—	—
Wisconsin (Milwaukee)	46	19	65	17	3	20	3	—	3	—	—	—
Total**	1,962	519	2,954	954	205	1,167	96	31	124	5	4	9

* For schools that did not fill out the institutional survey, data were taken from graduate surveys.

**Totals are greater than gender components as some schools and individuals did not provide gender information.

Table 4 / Placements by Type of Organization

Schools	Public			Elementary & Secondary			College & University			Special			Government			Library Co-op./Network			Vendor			Other			Total		
	Women	Men	Total	Women	Men	Total	Women	Men	Total	Women	Men	Total	Women	Men	Total	Women	Men	Total	Women	Men	Total	Women	Men	Total	Women	Men	Total
Alabama	4	2	6	15	1	16	4	5	9	—	1	1	2	—	2	1	—	1	—	—	0	2	—	2	28	9	37
Arizona	7	2	9	5	—	5	4	4	8	—	—	0	—	1	1	—	—	0	—	—	0	5	4	9	21	11	32
British Columbia	5	1	6	—	—	0	1	1	2	2	—	2	2	2	4	—	—	0	—	—	0	3	—	3	13	4	17
California (UCLA)	3	—	3	—	—	0	6	—	6	4	—	4	—	—	0	—	—	0	—	1	1	1	1	2	14	2	16
Clarion	7	—	7	5	—	6	3	2	5	4	—	4	—	—	0	—	—	0	—	—	0	—	—	0	17	2	20
Dominican	32	1	33	11	2	13	11	3	14	7	1	8	1	—	1	2	—	2	1	—	1	—	—	0	65	7	72
Drexel	7	—	7	6	—	6	9	3	12	6	2	8	—	—	0	—	—	0	2	1	3	—	—	0	30	6	36
Indiana	7	—	7	5	—	5	11	1	12	2	—	2	—	—	0	—	—	0	1	—	1	2	1	3	28	2	30
Iowa	6	—	7	4	1	6	7	1	9	3	—	3	1	—	1	1	—	1	1	—	1	—	—	0	23	2	28
Long Island	17	—	17	12	1	13	4	2	6	4	1	5	—	—	0	—	—	0	1	—	1	2	—	2	40	4	44
Louisiana State	8	2	10	4	—	4	7	3	10	2	—	2	1	1	2	—	—	0	—	—	0	—	—	0	22	6	28
Maryland	2	1	3	1	1	2	1	—	1	3	—	3	1	—	1	—	—	0	—	—	0	—	—	0	8	2	10
Missouri	5	—	5	3	1	4	3	1	4	1	4	5	1	—	1	—	—	0	2	—	2	—	—	0	15	6	21
N.C. Chapel Hill	4	—	4	1	—	1	8	4	12	2	—	2	—	1	1	1	—	1	1	—	1	—	—	0	17	5	22
North Texas	—	—	0	—	—	0	—	—	0	—	—	0	—	—	0	—	—	0	—	—	0	—	—	0	0	0	0
Oklahoma	4	—	4	11	—	11	2	—	2	1	—	1	1	1	2	—	—	0	—	—	0	—	—	0	19	1	20
Pittsburgh	4	1	5	4	—	4	9	5	15	5	2	7	2	—	2	—	—	0	—	—	0	2	—	2	26	8	35

Pratt	12	1	13	2	1	3	6	—	6	4	3	7	1	—	1	—	—	—	2	1	3	1	—	1	28	6	34
Rhode Island	5	—	5	5	—	5	1	3	4	—	—	—	2	—	2	—	—	—	—	—	—	—	—	—	13	3	16
Rutgers	4	2	6	6	—	6	3	3	6	2	1	4	1	—	1	2	—	2	2	—	2	2	1	3	23	6	29
St. John's	3	—	3	1	—	0	1	—	1	—	—	4	—	—	0	—	—	0	—	—	0	—	—	0	7	1	8
San Jose	18	5	23	8	1	9	13	3	16	9	2	11	1	2	3	—	—	0	1	1	1	4	2	6	50	13	63
Simmons	36	2	38	12	—	12	49	13	65	41	10	53	—	—	6	5	—	0	5	1	6	—	2	0	147	28	180
South Carolina	10	3	13	11	1	12	15	5	20	1	1	2	—	—	0	—	—	0	—	—	0	—	—	0	37	10	47
South Florida	5	4	9	5	1	6	5	3	8	1	—	1	1	2	1	—	—	0	—	1	0	1	2	2	16	10	26
S. Connecticut	8	2	10	7	—	7	7	—	7	2	1	3	1	—	1	—	—	0	—	—	0	—	—	1	25	3	28
S. Mississippi	1	2	3	2	—	2	8	1	9	—	—	3	—	—	0	—	—	0	—	—	0	—	—	0	12	3	15
SUNY-Albany	5	—	5	12	—	13	7	4	11	2	1	3	1	—	1	—	—	0	—	—	0	1	—	1	28	6	34
SUNY-Buffalo	10	1	11	8	4	12	10	1	11	3	1	3	1	—	1	1	—	1	1	—	1	—	—	0	33	7	40
Syracuse	3	1	6	4	1	6	9	1	3	2	1	3	3	—	3	—	—	0	—	—	1	1	—	1	15	4	22
Tennessee	7	1	8	9	—	9	9	7	9	4	1	5	—	—	0	—	—	0	1	—	1	4	1	4	30	2	32
Texas (Austin)	7	2	9	6	—	11	11	7	18	4	—	4	3	1	4	—	—	0	4	—	0	—	—	0	35	10	45
Texas Woman's	7	3	10	10	—	10	—	—	0	2	1	2	1	1	1	—	—	0	—	—	0	—	—	0	20	3	23
Washington	7	2	9	—	—	0	2	1	3	3	2	5	1	1	1	—	—	0	—	—	0	1	—	1	12	7	19
Wayne State	7	—	7	3	—	3	1	—	1	3	—	0	—	—	0	—	—	0	—	—	0	—	1	1	12	0	12
Western Ontario	—	—	6	—	—	1	12	—	9	3	—	3	3	—	3	—	—	1	1	—	1	2	—	0	0	0	23
Wisc. (Madison)	8	1	9	3	1	4	12	4	18	3	—	3	2	—	2	—	—	0	—	—	0	—	—	3	30	6	39
Wisc. (Milwaukee)	4	—	4	1	—	1	9	2	11	3	1	3	1	—	0	—	—	0	1	—	1	—	—	0	17	3	20
Total	289	42	340	201	18	223	261	86	363	134	35	174	29	10	42	7	0	7	21	4	26	34	13	48	976	208	1,223

Table 5 / Average Salary Index
Starting Library Positions, 1990–2000

Year	Library Schools*	Average Beginning Salary	Dollar Increase in Average Salary	Salary Index	BLS-CPI**
1990	38	$25,306	$725	143.03	130.7
1991	46	25,583	277	144.59	136.2
1992	41	26,666	1,083	150.71	140.5
1993	50	27,116	450	153.26	144.4
1994	43	28,086	970	158.74	148.4
1995	41	28,997	911	163.89	152.5
1996	44	29,480	483	166.62	159.1
1997	43	30,270	790	171.05	161.6
1998	47	31,915	1,645	180.38	164.3
1999	37	33,976	2,061	192.03	168.7
2000	37	34,901	925	197.26	175.1

*Includes U.S. schools only

** U.S. Department of Labor, Bureau of Labor Statistics, Consumer Price index, All Urban Consumers (CPI-U), U.S. city average, all items, 1982–1984=100. The average beginning professional salary for that period was $17,693.

(continued from page 382)

The salary increase in 2000 (2.72 percent) tapers off from the previous two years (6.5 percent and 5.4 percent increases), returning to the numbers in 1997 and 1996 (2.7 percent and 1.7 percent). While the Consumer Price Index increased in 2000 by 6.4 (or 3.8 percent), the *Library Journal* Salary Index rose 5.23 (or 2.72 percent).

Geography continues to influence salaries, with higher average salaries reported for the West and the Northeast in traditional library positions (public, school, academic, special), as Table 8 indicates. Average salaries for the West are significantly higher for all types of libraries, notably school libraries. The Northeast is a consistent second in most categories except colleges and universities, where the Midwest offers a higher average salary.

In all but three areas, men had higher average salaries by an aggregate of 8.9 percent. However, women led men in average salary in special libraries $37,913 to $37,495 (1.1 percent). Also, there were no reported placements for men in networks/cooperatives.

Most interesting were the changes in the high-tech "other" area. In 1999 the average salary for men in this category increased 31 percent, to $48,082 from $36,750, while that for women went up 8.3 percent, to $38,826 from $35,853. In 2000 the salaries for men dropped 4.4 percent, to $46,000, while those for women rose 4.5 percent, to $40,426. Though this contributed to the significant slowdown in the rise of men's salaries, it did not change the overall disparity between men and women. The number of placements and percent of total placements in this area have dropped dramatically in the last three years, from 108 (7.6 percent) in 1998 to 79 (5 percent) in 1999 to 48 (4 percent) in 2000.

Of those who got full-time permanent jobs, 11.5 percent identified themselves as members of a minority group. The largest group (32.5 percent) found

Table 6 / Salaries of Reporting Professionals by Area of Job Assignment*

Assignment	Number	Percent of Total	Low Salary	High Salary	Average Salary	Median Salary
Acquisitions	19	2.06	$17,500	$48,000	$31,286	$32,000
Administration	50	5.42	19,005	80,000	39,720	37,000
Archives	48	5.20	18,000	55,000	32,844	31,500
Automation/Systems	19	2.06	29,000	68,000	40,042	37,000
Cataloging & Classification	60	6.50	15,600	75,000	33,669	34,254
Circulation	12	1.30	21,250	45,000	31,392	32,500
Collection Development	15	1.63	24,950	44,000	31,938	31,625
Database Management	9	0.98	25,800	50,000	36,728	33,000
Government Documents	3	0.33	30,800	44,796	36,310	33,333
Indexing/Abstracting	3	0.33	32,000	40,000	36,600	37,800
Info Consultant	13	1.41	35,000	50,000	43,833	45,000
Instruction	6	0.65	27,347	38,000	32,545	32,288
Interlibrary Loans	7	0.76	17,560	33,100	25,880	26,000
LAN Manager	3	0.33	23,500	60,000	40,500	38,000
Media Specialist	173	18.74	10,200	65,000	36,682	35,000
Reference/ Info Services	311	33.69	7,488	65,000	33,757	33,000
Research	3	0.33	30,000	52,000	39,533	36,600
Solo Librarian	65	7.04	23,000	65,678	36,553	35,000
Tech Services/ Serials	5	0.54	29,000	34,000	31,500	31,500
Telecomm.	4	0.43	34,000	42,000	38,546	39,091
Youth Services	73	7.91	18,000	42,000	30,525	31,000
Webmaster	22	2.38	27,478	62,000	38,247	36,000
Total	923	100	7,488	80,000	34,843	34,000

*Does not include those graduates who did not specify a principal job assignment.

jobs in public libraries, followed by 30.9 percent in academic libraries, 18.7 percent in special libraries, and 13 percent in K–12 media centers. For minority graduates, salaries rose 11.1 percent ($3,636, to $36,482), which is well above the 6.1 percent rise for 1999 and perhaps attributable to a greater percentage of placements in academic and special libraries. Special libraries provide the highest average salary for minority graduates ($42,665), well above the national average for all special libraries ($37,849).

Salaries vary widely by institution type. Public libraries, in spite of a healthy 6.7 percent increase, still offer the lowest average salary ($31,656, compared with $29,643 in 1999), followed by academic libraries ($33,380, compared with $32,837 last year, up less than 2 percent). Government libraries ($36,720) averaged only a 1.5 percent increase over last year's $36,165. Library cooperatives/networks ($37,617, up a significant 13.6 percent) and school libraries ($36,718, up 3.4 percent) offered a considerably higher average salary than did public libraries, but still lower than those at special libraries ($37,849, up 2.4 percent).

Last year's leader, the Other category, included many of the high-tech and dot-com positions filled by LIS graduates. These graduates were not immune to

(text continues on page 394)

Table 7 / Placements and Full-Time Salaries of Reporting 2000 Graduates

Schools	Placements	Salaries Reported			Low Salary		High Salary		Average Salary			Median Salary		
		Women	Men	Total	Women	Men	Women	Men	Women	Men	All	Women	Men	All
Alabama	35	26	9	35	$19,700	$23,000	$38,000	$41,000	$31,864	$33,288	$32,241	$32,800	$35,000	$32,950
Arizona	20	13	7	20	23,400	26,240	48,000	42,054	31,093	32,214	31,619	30,000	31,254	30,000
British Columbia	15	13	2	15	23,441	40,000	65,000	40,600	34,453	40,300	35,289	27,430	40,300	29,366
California (UCLA)	14	12	2	14	29,000	29,500	68,000	70,000	41,755	49,750	42,985	36,500	49,750	36,500
Clarion	19	17	2	19	20,000	45,000	54,000	52,000	32,162	47,667	34,488	29,500	46,000	30,700
Dominican	55	50	5	55	24,000	40,000	44,000	75,000	34,373	52,303	35,726	35,000	47,105	35,000
Drexel	27	21	6	27	25,000	44,000	80,000	60,000	37,058	51,200	39,777	35,500	50,000	36,200
Indiana	28	24	4	28	27,000	48,000	60,000	52,000	34,364	50,500	36,846	32,000	51,000	34,500
Iowa	23	18	2	20	20,000	38,000	42,500	38,000	31,112	38,000	31,440	30,250	38,000	30,500
Long Island	38	34	4	38	18,000	33,000	55,000	40,000	38,509	35,750	38,219	40,053	35,000	39,500
Louisiana State	28	21	6	27	10,200	41,000	39,500	41,000	28,110	41,000	28,670	29,100	41,000	29,200
Maryland	6	4	2	6	21,000	46,000	41,000	63,000	27,950	54,500	36,800	24,900	54,500	33,400
Missouri	19	13	6	19	26,000	17,500	36,912	36,000	32,139	27,750	31,106	31,500	28,750	31,200
N.C. Chapel Hill	21	16	5	21	23,040	32,000	42,000	36,000	31,289	34,800	32,125	30,000	36,000	32,000
Oklahoma	20	19	1	20	17,560	37,500	40,000	37,500	30,515	37,500	30,864	31,000	37,500	31,500
Pittsburgh	35	26	8	34	20,000	22,500	39,000	44,000	31,809	33,188	32,124	31,500	33,250	32,000
Pratt	34	27	7	34	23,000	32,000	65,000	65,678	37,611	54,446	41,094	35,000	55,000	36,000

Rhode Island	15	13	2	15	28,000	34,000	68,280	43,000	37,973	38,500	38,049	34,200	38,500	34,700
Rutgers	27	21	6	27	29,000	38,972	42,742	44,000	35,144	40,595	36,402	34,000	39,550	35,598
St. John's	10	6	2	8	18,000	42,000	60,000	48,000	39,409	45,000	40,425	36,400	45,000	36,500
San Jose	48	38	10	48	25,000	32,000	55,000	40,000	39,665	35,250	39,244	39,000	34,500	38,542
Simmons	165	132	29	161	7,488	15,000	68,000	55,000	34,456	35,963	34,808	35,000	36,500	35,000
South Carolina	45	35	9	44	15,600	22,390	51,000	74,250	31,866	34,667	32,439	31,000	28,000	30,900
South Florida	24	16	8	24	25,000	27,000	37,000	66,000	30,494	35,663	32,292	31,000	32,000	31,000
S. Connecticut	21	19	2	21	19,000	37,819	49,000	45,000	35,655	42,240	36,150	35,000	43,900	35,000
S. Mississippi	13	10	3	13	22,000	26,000	46,318	35,000	32,394	29,333	31,559	31,500	27,000	31,000
SUNY-Albany	28	23	5	28	20,000	34,857	35,000	42,000	29,253	37,586	30,294	30,000	35,900	30,000
SUNY-Buffalo	31	24	7	31	23,500	27,000	43,500	68,000	32,794	47,317	35,699	33,000	44,950	33,490
Syracuse	20	19	3	22	25,000	38,000	55,500	40,000	37,146	39,333	37,474	36,000	40,000	37,250
Tennessee	29	27	2	29	24,939	31,800	52,149	32,000	33,616	31,900	33,497	33,000	31,900	33,000
Texas (Austin)	47	35	12	47	15,000	27,800	64,000	48,000	35,371	34,046	35,032	33,011	34,000	34,000
Texas Woman's	21	18	3	21	22,000	43,000	55,000	44,000	35,141	43,500	35,937	32,000	43,500	33,000
Washington	12	6	6	12	31,992	36,000	48,000	44,000	39,415	40,167	39,791	39,000	40,000	40,000
Wayne State	8	8	0	8	27,500	—	43,600	—	33,770	—	33,770	32,450	—	43,600
Western Ontario	26	19	7	26	—	—	—	—	—	—	—	—	—	41,500
Wisc. (Madison)	34	26	6	32	24,500	29,000	55,000	41,000	33,660	34,071	33,759	31,500	34,000	32,000
Wisc. (Milwaukee)	17	15	2	17	23,000	21,250	46,000	55,000	32,601	38,125	33,291	33,907	38,125	33,907

Table 8 / Comparison of Salaries by Type of Organization

	Total Placements	Salaries Reported		Low Salary		High Salary		Average Salary			Median Salary		
		Women	Men	Women	Men	Women	Men	Women	Men	All	Women	Men	All
Public Libraries													
Northeast	90	81	9	$7,488	$26,500	$68,280	$39,000	$31,112	$31,727	$31,174	$31,500	$31,500	$31,500
Southeast	46	33	13	19,000	26,000	40,000	74,250	28,312	37,672	30,957	28,000	31,000	28,350
Midwest	55	53	2	20,000	29,000	52,000	34,000	31,019	31,500	31,037	30,000	31,500	30,000
Southwest	17	14	3	22,000	28,000	36,278	35,500	29,860	32,833	30,384	29,982	35,000	30,000
West	39	30	7	25,000	34,000	44,178	45,764	34,660	40,281	35,019	34,774	40,000	35,000
All Public	247	211	34	7,488	26,000	68,280	74,250	31,072	35,845	31,656	31,000	33,370	31,200
School Libraries													
Northeast	86	78	8	20,000	31,000	65,000	55,500	36,915	37,951	37,011	35,506	34,350	35,250
Southeast	49	45	4	10,200	28,000	52,149	63,000	34,591	39,600	35,000	33,000	33,700	33,000
Midwest	30	27	3	27,500	29,000	54,000	42,000	36,874	37,000	36,886	35,000	40,000	35,000
Southwest	27	27	—	24,500	—	51,000	—	34,793	—	34,793	35,000	—	35,000
West	14	13	1	27,900	55,000	65,678	55,000	43,457	55,000	44,281	40,000	55,000	45,000
All School	206	190	16	10,200	28,000	65,678	63,000	36,527	39,734	36,718	35,000	35,000	35,000
College/University Libraries													
Northeast	99	71	28	15,600	15,000	48,000	55,000	33,153	34,670	33,582	33,750	34,000	34,000
Southeast	76	55	21	15,000	22,390	49,210	48,109	32,265	31,389	32,023	31,000	32,288	31,313
Midwest	46	34	12	16,000	18,000	48,000	48,000	33,816	35,208	34,179	33,907	36,500	34,300
Southwest	19	13	6	20,000	29,000	42,000	39,500	31,908	33,533	32,421	31,500	33,000	32,000
West	40	32	8	22,000	30,000	60,000	37,200	35,318	34,112	35,077	35,000	35,000	35,000
All Academic	280	205	75	15,000	15,000	60,000	55,000	33,266	35,406	33,380	33,000	34,000	34,000
Special Libraries													
Northeast	72	57	15	18,000	20,000	62,000	80,000	37,554	40,800	38,230	38,000	38,000	38,000
Southeast	20	15	5	17,560	23,000	75,000	40,000	38,377	32,400	36,883	38,000	32,000	36,000
Midwest	18	12	6	26,000	17,500	52,000	37,081	37,425	28,222	34,357	37,050	28,750	36,000
Southwest	7	7	—	30,000	—	50,000	—	37,286	—	37,286	36,000	—	36,000

West	27	20	7	25,000	34,000	55,000	60,000	38,933	43,143	40,024	35,000	40,000	36,500
All Special	144	111	33	17,560	17,500	75,000	80,000	37,913	37,495	37,849	36,600	36,000	36,550
Government Libraries													
Northeast	6	4	2	28,781	40,750	45,000	51,000	36,195	45,875	39,422	35,500	45,875	38,375
Southeast	14	10	4	25,800	26,640	53,261	37,500	36,982	32,285	35,640	34,877	32,500	33,127
Midwest	5	5	—	28,000	—	38,500	—	32,440	—	32,440	31,200	—	31,200
Southwest	2	2	—	32,988	—	34,256	—	33,622	—	33,622	33,622	—	33,622
West	9	5	4	32,640	36,000	46,000	44,796	39,239	40,199	39,666	39,000	40,000	39,000
All Government	36	26	10	25,800	26,640	53,261	51,000	36,163	38,169	36,720	35,000	37,750	36,000
Library Cooperatives/Networks													
Northeast	3	3	—	32,000	—	34,700	—	33,400	—	33,400	33,500	—	33,500
Southeast	1	1	—	36,500	—	36,500	—	36,500	—	36,500	36,500	—	36,500
Midwest	1	1	—	52,000	—	52,000	—	52,000	—	52,000	52,000	—	52,000
Southwest	—	—	—	—	—	—	—	—	—	—	—	—	—
West	1	1	—	37,000	—	37,000	—	37,000	—	37,000	37,000	—	37,000
All Co-op./Networks	6	6	0	32,000	0	52,000	0	37,617	—	37,617	35,600	—	35,600
Vendors													
Northeast	16	14	2	30,000	38,000	55,000	42,500	41,429	40,250	41,281	41,000	40,250	41,000
Southeast	—	—	—	—	—	—	—	—	—	—	—	—	—
Midwest	7	6	1	25,000	60,000	46,000	60,000	31,167	60,000	35,286	28,250	60,000	28,500
Southwest	2	1	1	64,000	48,000	64,000	48,000	64,000	48,000	56,000	64,000	48,000	56,000
West	5	3	2	35,000	30,000	68,000	70,000	49,333	50,000	49,600	45,000	50,000	45,000
All Vendors	30	24	6	25,000	30,000	68,000	70,000	40,792	48,083	42,250	38,500	45,250	41,000
Other Organizations													
Northeast	12	9	3	30,000	48,000	65,000	68,000	42,000	57,333	45,833	35,000	56,000	43,000
Southeast	—	—	—	—	—	—	—	—	—	—	—	—	—
Midwest	7	3	3	38,182	43,500	60,000	48,000	47,061	45,500	44,097	43,000	45,000	43,500
Southwest	1	—	1	—	30,000	—	30,000	—	30,000	30,000	—	30,000	30,000
West	4	3	1	30,000	29,500	43,000	29,500	37,000	29,500	35,125	38,000	29,500	34,000
All Other	24	15	8	30,000	29,500	65,000	68,000	40,426	46,000	41,778	38,000	46,500	38,091

(continued from page 389)

the turmoil of the high-tech companies, and the Other category was the only one to lose ground, dropping $78 (less than 0.2 percent) to an average of $41,778. The number of reported placements dropped from 52 in 1999 to 24 in 2000, though some of that may be a result of limited responses to our survey. Vendors offered the highest average salary in 2000 at $42,250, up from $36,947 last year, a hefty increase of more than 14 percent. Additionally, the number of graduates reporting vendor placements went from 22 in 1999 to 30 in 2000, an increase of 36 percent, despite fewer responses to the survey.

Placements Remain Strong

About two-thirds of the schools responded to inquiries about the availability of job openings: 15 reported an increase in the number of positions, two experienced a decrease, and the rest reported the number as unchanged. The reported number of available positions listed at individual schools or their placement offices ranged from a low of 150 to a high of 8,867 potential jobs.

Four schools indicated that in 2000 they had experienced less difficulty placing their graduates than during 1999; none reported that it was harder to do so, and 23 said the situation was unchanged. Several schools indicated that they experienced no noticeable increase or decrease by type of library or position.

Table 4 reflects 2000 placements by type of organization. The response rate to this survey question was down from last year (1,223 responses vs. 1,569 in 1999). Reported college and university library placements (363) were down substantially from 1999 (439). Public library placements (340) also fell in 2000, compared with 1999 (458) and 1998 (435). Elementary and secondary library placements (223) continued down from 1999 (271) and 1998 (330). Some of these changes may be simply a result of limited responses.

The Graduates Speak

Asked about the placement process and the preparation they received in library school, 39 students—about half of those contacted—responded. New graduates must have technology skills, but they must also work on a team and interact well with clients. "Based on the interview for my current job, it was very important to have technical skills as well as the ability to communicate ideas and concepts to others," said one.

Keys to Unlocking a Successful Future

Cataloging and collection development were again identified as key areas. Several students felt unprepared for public and school libraries due to the emphasis on Library of Congress cataloging at the expense of Dewey. One new public librarian said, "We as librarians need to be more understanding instead of (as I've found) short-tempered with the teenagers who have never used LC."

Most employers still seek staff with technology and computer skills. One graduate said, "In my last few interviews (public libraries), potential employers have been initially interested in not only my librarian skills (reference, collection development, etc.) but my customer skills (difficult people/patrons, phone voice, etc.). After a good look at my résumé, they nearly salivate at my technical/geek skills. I have a significant background in the Web and Web design. . . . I understand computers, and I'm not afraid of them. That has become one of my most valuable assets."

Technophobia seems to no longer have a place in the work force. Another graduate said, "The employers I interviewed with were interested in basic archival skills (arrangement and description, etc.), as well as new, 'cutting-edge' skills like digitization. My strength, according to my current employer, is that I possessed the traditional skills as well as the newer electronic skills (or at least an understanding of those newer skills)."

Salary negotiations generated a range of responses. Those working at public and school libraries generally face a predetermined salary schedule, while vendors and other private companies offer some room to negotiate. Wrote one student, "The proposed salary for my position was definitely negotiable, although I wouldn't have known this if I hadn't tried. I strongly encourage everyone to negotiate—librarians are in demand! I researched regional salaries for comparable positions, which were generally higher than what I was offered. I wrote a letter asking for an offer closer to the average (very carefully worded, of course) and was very pleased with the response."

Accredited Master's Programs in Library and Information Studies

This list of graduate programs accredited by the American Library Association was issued in February 2002. The list of accredited programs is issued early in each calendar year and is available from the ALA Office for Accreditation. More than 200 institutions offering both accredited and nonaccredited programs in librarianship are included in the 54th edition of *American Library Directory* (Information Today, Inc., 2001).

Northeast: Conn., D.C., Md., Mass., N.J., N.Y., Pa., R.I.

Catholic University of America, School of Lib. and Info. Science, Washington, DC 20064. Peter Liebscher, Dean. 202-319-5085, fax 202-219-5574, e-mail cua-slis @cua.edu, World Wide Web http://slis.cua.edu. Admissions contact: Jason Papanikolas.

Clarion University of Pennsylvania, Dept. of Lib. Science, 840 Wood St., Clarion, PA 16214-1232. Bernard F. Vavrek, Chair. 814-393-2271, fax 814-393-2150, e-mail vavrek@clarion.edu, World Wide Web http://www.clarion.edu/libsci.

Drexel University, College of Info. Science and Technology, 3141 Chestnut St., Philadelphia, PA 19104-2875. David E. Fenske, Dean. 215-895-2474, fax 215-895-2494, World Wide Web http://www.cis.drexel. edu. Admissions contact: Anne B. Tanner. 215-895-2485, e-mail info@cis.drexel.edu.

Long Island University, Palmer School of Lib. and Info. Science, C, W. Post Campus, 720 Northern Blvd., Brookville, NY 11548-1300. Michael E. D. Koenig, Dean. 516-299-2866, fax 516-299-4168, e-mail palmer@cwpost.liu.edu, World Wide Web http://www.liu.edu/palmer. Admissions contact: Rosemary Chu. 516-299-2487, fax 516-299-4168.

Pratt Institute, School of Info. and Lib. Science, Info. Science Center, 200 Willoughby Ave., Brooklyn, NY 11205. Anne Woodsworth, Dean. 718-636-3702, fax 718-636-3733, e-mail infosils@pratt.edu, World Wide Web http://www.pratt.edu/ sils. Admissions contact: Larry Kroah. E-mail lkroah@pratt.edu.

Queens College, City Univ. of New York, Grad. School of Lib. and Info. Studies, 65-30 Kissena Blvd., Flushing, NY 11367. Marianne Cooper, Dir. 718-997-3790, fax 718-997-3797, e-mail gslis@qcunixl.qc. edu, World Wide Web http://www.qc.edu/ GSLIS. Admissions contact: Virgil L. P. Blake. E-mail Virgil_Blake@qc.edu.

Rutgers University, School of Communication, Info., and Lib. Studies, 4 Huntington St., New Brunswick, NJ 08903-1071. Gustav W. Friedrich, Dean. 732-932-7917, fax 732-932-2644, e-mail scilsmls@sclis. rutgers.edu, World Wide Web http://www. scils.rutgers.edu. Admissions contact: Betty Turock. 732-932-5001, e-mail bturock @scils.rutgers.edu.

Saint John's University, Div. of Lib. and Info. Science, 8000 Utopia Pkwy., Jamaica, NY 11439. James A. Benson, Dir. 718-990-6200, fax 718-990-2071, e-mail libis @stjohns.edu, World Wide Web http:// www.stjohns.edu. Admissions contact: Patricia Armstrong. 718-990-2028, fax 718-990-5827.

Simmons College, Grad. School of Lib. and Info. Science, 300 The Fenway, Boston, MA 02115-5898. James M. Matarazzo, Dean. 617-521-2800, fax 617-521-3192, e-mail gslis@simmons.edu, World Wide Web http://www.simmons.edu/programs/ gslis. Admissions contact: Judith Beals. 617-521-2801, e-mail jbeals@simmons. edu.

Southern Connecticut State University, School of Communication, Info., and Lib. Science, 501 Crescent St., New Haven, CT 06515. Edward C. Harris, Dean. 888-500-7278 (press 4), 203-392-5781, fax 203-392-5780, World Wide Web http://www.

southernct.edu/departments/ils. Admissions contact: Mary E. Brown.

State University of New York at Albany, School of Info. Science and Policy, 135 Western Ave., Albany, NY 12222. Philip B. Eppard, Dean. 518-442-5110, fax 518-442-5367, e-mail infosci@albany.edu, World Wide Web http://www.albany.edu/sisp. Admissions contact: e-mail infosci @albany.edu.

State University of New York at Buffalo, Dept. of Lib. and Info. Studies, Box 1020, Buffalo, NY 14260-1020. Judith Robinson, Chair. 716-645-2412, fax 716-645-3775, e-mail UB-LIS@buffalo.edu, World Wide Web http://informatics.buffalo.edu/lis/index.htm.

Syracuse University, School of Info. Studies, 4-206 Center for Science and Technology, Syracuse, NY 13244-4100. Raymond F. von Dran, Dean. 315-443-2911, fax 315-443-5806, e-mail vondran@syr.edu, World Wide Web http://istweb.svr.edu.

University of Maryland, College of Info. Services, 4105 Hornbake Lib. Bldg., College Park, MD 20742-4345. Bruce Dearstyne, Interim Dean. 301-405-2033, fax 301-314-9145, World Wide Web http://www.clis.umd.edu. Admissions contact: Vicky H. Reinke. 301-405-2038, e-mail clisumpc@umdacc.umd.edu.

University of Pittsburgh, School of Info. Sciences, 505 IS Bldg., Pittsburgh, PA 15260. Toni Carbo, Dean. 412-624-5230, fax 412-624-5231, World Wide Web http://www2.sis.pitt.edu. Admissions contact: Ninette Kay. 412-624-5146, e-mail nkay@mail.sis.pitt.edu.

University of Rhode Island, Grad. School of Lib. and Info. Studies, Rodman Hall, Kingston, RI 02881, W. Michael Havener, Dir. 401-874-2947, fax 401-874-4964, e-mail gslis@etal.uri.edu, World Wide Web http://www.uri.edu/artsci/lsc. Admissions contact: Donna Gilton.

Southeast: Ala., Fla., Ga., Ky., La., Miss., N.C., S.C., Tenn., P.R.

Clark Atlanta University, School of Lib. and Info. Studies, 300 Trevor Arnett Hall, 223 James P. Brawley Dr., Atlanta, GA 30314.

Arthur C. Gunn, Dean. 404-880-8697, fax 404-880-8977, e-mail agunn@cau.edu, World Wide Web http://www.cau.edu. Admissions contact: Doris Callahan.

Florida State University, School of Info. Studies, Tallahassee, FL 32306-2100. Jane B. Robbins, Dean. 850-644-5775, fax 850-644-9763, World Wide Web http://www.lis.fsu.edu. Admissions contact: Kathleen Burnett. 850-644-8124, e-mail burnett@lis.fsu.edu.

Louisiana State University, School of Lib. and Info. Science, 267 Coates Hall, Baton Rouge, LA 70803. Beth M. Paskoff, Dean. 225-578-3158, fax 225-578-4581, e-mail slis@lsu.edu, World Wide Web http://slis.lsu.edu. Admissions contact: Nicole Rozas.

North Carolina Central University, School of Lib. and Info. Sciences, Box 19586, Durham, NC 27707. Benjamin F. Speller, Jr., Dean. 919-560-6485, fax 919-560-6402, e-mail speller@slis.nccu.edu, World Wide Web http://www.slis.nccu.edu. Admissions contact: Lionell Parker. 919-560-5211, e-mail lparker@slis.nccu.edu.

University of Alabama, School of Lib. and Info. Studies, Box 870252, Tuscaloosa, AL 35487-0252. Joan L. Atkinson, Dir. 205-348-4610, fax 205-348-3746, e-mail info@slis.ua.edu, World Wide Web http://www.slis.ua.edu.

University of Kentucky, College of Communications and Info. Studies, School of Lib. and Info. Science, 502 King Library Building S, Lexington, KY 40506-0039. Timothy W. Sineath, Dir. 859-257-8876, fax 859-257-4205, e-mail tsineath@pop.uky.edu, World Wide Web http://www.uky.edu/CommInfoStudies/SLIS. Admissions contact: Jane Salsman.

University of North Carolina at Chapel Hill, School of Info. and Lib. Science, CB 3360, 100 Manning Hall, Chapel Hill, NC 27599-3360. Joanne G. Marshall, Dean. 919-962-8366, fax 919-962-8071, e-mail info@ils.unc.edu, World Wide Web http://www.ils.unc.edu. Admissions contact: Lucia Zonn. E-mail zonn@ils.unc.edu.

University of North Carolina at Greensboro, Dept. of Lib. and Info. Studies, School of Education, Box 26171, Greensboro, NC 27402-6171. Lee Shiflett, Chair. 336-334-3477, fax 336-334-5060, World Wide Web http://www.uncg.edu/lis. Admissions contact: Jim V. Carmichael. 910-334-3478, e-mail Jim_Carmichael@uncg.edu.

University of Puerto Rico, Graduate School of Info. Science and Technologies, Box 21906, San Juan, PR 00931-1906. Consuelo Figueras, Dir. 787-763-6199, fax 787-764-2311, e-mail 73253.312@compuserv.com. Admissions contact: Migdalia Dávila. 787-764-0000 ext. 3530, e-mail m_davila@rrpad.upr.clu.edu.

University of South Carolina, College of Lib. and Info. Science, Davis College, Columbia, SC 29208. Fred W. Roper, Dean. 803-777-3858, fax 803-777-7938, World Wide Web http://www.libsci.sc.edu. Admissions contact: 803-777-5067, fax 803-777-0457, e-mail bbailey@gwm.sc.edu.

University of South Florida, School of Lib. and Info. Science, 4202 E. Fowler Ave., CIS 1040, Tampa, FL 33620-7800. Vicki L. Gregory, Dir. 813-974-3520, fax 813-974-6840, e-mail dbejaran@chumal.cas.usf.edu, World Wide Web http://www.cas.usf.edu/lis. Admissions contact: Sonia Ramirez Wohlmuth. E-mail swohlmut@chuma.cas.usf.edu.ml.

University of Southern Mississippi, School of Lib. and Info. Science, Box 5146, Hattiesburg, MS 39406-5146. Thomas D, Walker, Dir. 601-266-4228, fax 601-266-5774, World Wide Web http://www-dept.usm.edu/~slis.

University of Tennessee, School of Info. Sciences, 804 Volunteer Blvd., Knoxville, TN 37996-4330. Elizabeth Aversa, Dir. 865-974-2148, fax 865-974-4967, World Wide Web http://www.sis.utk.edu. Admissions contact: Kristie Atwood. 423-974-5917, e-mail katwood@utk.edu.

Midwest: Ill., Ind., Iowa, Kan., Mich., Mo., Ohio, Wis.

Emporia State University, School of Lib. and Info. Management, Box 4025, Emporia, KS 66801. Robert Grover, Dean. 316-341-5203, fax 316-341-5233, World Wide Web http://slim.emporia.edu. Admissions contact: Mirah Dow. E-mail Dowmirah@emporia.edu.

Indiana University, School of Lib. and Info. Science, Main Library 011, 1320 E. 10th St., Bloomington, IN 47405-3907. Blaise Cronin, Dean. 812-855-2018, fax 812-855-6166, e-mail slis@indiana.edu, World Wide Web http://www.slis.indiana.edu. Admissions contact: Rhonda Spencer.

Kent State University, School of Lib. and Info. Science, Box 5190, Kent, OH 44242-0001. Richard Rubin, Dir. 330-672-2782, fax 330-672-7965, e-mail rubin@slis.kent.edu, World Wide Web http://web.slis.kent.edu. Admissions contact: Marge Hayden. E-mail mhayden@slis.kent.edu.

Dominican University, Grad. School of Lib. and Info. Science, 7900 W. Division St., River Forest, IL 60305. Prudence W. Dalrymple, Dean. 708-524-6845, fax 708-524-6657, e-mail gslis@email.dom.edu, World Wide Web http://www.dom.edu/academic/gslishome.html. Admissions contacts: Elisa Topper (Dominican Univ.), Mary Wagner (College of St. Catherine).

University of Illinois at Urbana-Champaign, Grad. School of Lib. and Info. Science, 501 E. Daniel St., Champaign, IL 61820. Linda C. Smith, Interim Dean. 217-333-3280, fax 217-244-3302, World Wide Web http://alexia.lis.uiuc.edu. Admissions contact: Valerie Youngen. 800-982-0914, 217-333-7197, e-mail vyoungen@alexia.lis.uiuc.edu.

University of Iowa, School of Lib. and Info. Science, 3087 Library, Iowa City, IA 52242-1420. Joseph K. Kearney, Interim Dir. 319-335-5707, fax 319-335-5374, e-mail joe-kearney@uiowa.edu, World Wide Web http://www.uiowa.edu/~libsci. Admissions contact: Ethel Bloesch. E-mail ethel-bloesch@uiowa.edu.

University of Michigan, School of Info., 550 E. University Ave., Ann Arbor, MI 48109-1092. John L. King, Dean. 734-763-2285, fax 734-764-2475, e-mail si.admissions@umich.edu, World Wide Web http://www.si.umich.edu. Admissions contact: Yvonne Perhne.

University of Missouri–Columbia, School of Info. Science and Learning Technologies, 303 Townsend Hall, Columbia, MO 65211. John Wedman, Dir. 573-882-4546, fax 573-884-2917, World Wide Web http://

www.coe/missouri.edu/~sislt. Admissions contact: Paula Schlager. 573-884-2670, e-mail sisltnfo@coe.missouri.edu.

University of Wisconsin–Madison, School of Lib. and Info. Studies, 600 N. Park St., Madison, WI 53706. Louise S. Robbins, Dir. 608-263-2900, fax 608-263-4849, e-mail uw_slis@slis.wisc.edu, World Wide Web http://www.slis.wisc.edu. Admissions contact: Barbara Arnold. 608-263-2909, e-mail bjarnold@facstaff.wisc.edu.

University of Wisconsin–Milwaukee, School of Info. Studies, Bolton Hall 510, 3210 N. Maryland, Milwaukee, WI 53211. Mohammed M. Aman, Dean. 414-229-4707, fax 414-229-6699, e-mail info@sois.uwm.edu, World Wide Web http://www.sois.uwm.edu. Admissions contact: Angela Pope Margerum. 414-229-5027.

Wayne State University, Lib. and Info. Science Program, 106 Kresge Library, Detroit, MI 48202. Dian Walster, Dir. 313-577-1825, fax 313-577-7563, World Wide Web http://www.lisp.wayne.edu. Admissions contact: Yolanda Reader. E-mail af7735@wayne.edu.

Southwest: Ariz., Okla., Texas.

Texas Woman's University, School of Lib. and Info. Studies, Box 425438, Denton, TX 76204-5438. Keith Swigger, Dean and Dir. 940-898-2602, fax 940-898-2611, e-mail kswigger@twu.edu, World Wide Web http://www.libraryschool.net.

University of Arizona, School of Info. Resources and Lib. Science, 1515 E. First St., Tucson, AZ 85719. Brooke Sheldon, Dir. 520-621-3565, fax 520-621-3279, e-mail sirls@u.arizona.edu, World Wide Web http://www.sir.arizona.edu.

University of North Texas, School of Lib. and Info. Sciences, Box 311068, NT Sta., Denton, TX 76203. Philip M. Turner, Dean. 940-565-2445, fax 940-565-3101, World Wide Web http://www.unt.edu/slis. Admissions contact: Herman L. Totten. E-mail totten@lis.unt.edu.

University of Oklahoma, School of Lib. and Info. Studies, 401 W. Brooks, Norman, OK 73019-0528. Danny P, Wallace, Dir.

405-325-3921, fax 405-325-7648, e-mail slisinfo@lists.ou.edu, World Wide Web http://www.ou.edu/cas/slis. Admissions contact: Maggie Ryan.

University of Texas at Austin, Grad. School of Lib. and Info. Science, Austin, TX 78712-1276. Mary Lynn Rice-Lively, Assistant Dean. 512-471-3821, fax 512-471-3971, e-mail info@gslis.utexas.edu, World Wide Web http://www.gslis.utexas.edu. Admissions contact: Julie Hallmark. 512-471-3720, e-mail gradadv@glis.utexas.edu.

West: Calif., Hawaii, Wash.

San Jose State University, School of Lib. and Info. Science, 1 Washington Sq., San Jose, CA 95192-0029. Blanche Woolls, Dir. 408-924-2490, fax 408-924-2476, e-mail office@wahoo.sjsu.edu, World Wide Web http://slisweb.sjsu.edu.

University of California at Los Angeles, Grad. School of Education and Info. Studies, Mailbox 951521, Los Angeles, CA 90095-1521. Michele V. Cloonan, Chair. 310-825-8799, fax 310-206-3076, e-mail info@gseis.ucla.edu, World Wide Web http://is.gseis.ucla.edu. Admissions Contact: Susan Abler. 310-825-5269, fax 310-206-6293.

University of Hawaii, Lib. and Info. Science Program, 2550 The Mall, Honolulu, HI 96822. Peter Jacso, Program Chair. 808-956-7321, fax 808-956-5835, e-mail lischair@yahoo.com, World Wide Web http://www.hawaii.edu/slis.

University of Washington, The Info. School, Box 352840, Seattle, WA 98195-2840. Michael B. Eisenberg, Dir. 206-543-1794, fax 206-616-3152, World Wide Web http://www.ischool.washington.edu. Admissions contact: 206-543-1794, e-mail info@ischool.washington.edu.

Canada

Dalhousie University, School of Lib. and Info. Studies, Halifax, NS B3H 3J5. Bertrum H. MacDonald, Dir. 902-494-3656, fax 902-494-2451, e-mail slis@is.dal.ca,

World Wide Web http://www.mgmt.dal.ca/slis. Admissions contact: Shanna Balogh. 902-494-2453, e-mail shanna@is.dal.ca.

McGill University, Grad. School of Lib. and Info. Studies, 3459 McTavish St., Montreal, PQ H3A 1Y1. Jamshid Beheshti, Dir. 514-398-4204, fax 514-398-7193, e-mail ad27@musica.mcgill.ca, World Wide Web http://www.gslis.mcgill.ca. Admissions contact: Dorothy Carruthers.

Université de Montréal, Ecole de Bibliothéconomie et des Sciences de l'Information, C.P. 6128, Succursale Centre-Ville, Montreal, PQ H3C 3J7. Carol Couture, Dir. 514-343-6044, fax 514-343-5753, e-mail carol.couture@umontreal.ca, World Wide Web http://www.fas.umontreal.ca/EBSI/. Admissions contact: Diane Mayer. E-mail diane.mayer@umontreal.ca.

University of Alberta, School of Lib. and Info. Studies, 3-20 Rutherford S., Edmonton, AB T6G 2J4. Alvin Schrader, Dir. 780-492-4578, fax 780-492-2430, e-mail slis@ualberta.ca.

University of British Columbia, School of Lib., Archival, and Info. Studies, 1956 Main Mall, Room 831, Vancouver, BC V6T 1Z1. Ken Haycock, Dir. 604-822-2404, fax 604-822-6006, e-mail slais@interchange.ubc.ca, World Wide Web http://www.slais.ubc.ca. Admissions contact: Admissions Secretary. 604-822-2404, e-mail slais.admissions@ubc.ca.

University of Toronto, Faculty of Info. Studies, 140 George St., Toronto, ON M5S 3G6. Lynne C. Howarth, Dean. 416-978-8589, fax 416-978-5762, World Wide Web http://www.fis.utoronto.ca. Admissions contact: Pamela Hawes. E-mail Hawes@fis.utoronto.ca.

University of Western Ontario, Grad. Programs in Lib. and Info. Science, Middlesex College, London, ON N6A 5B7. Catherine Ross, Professor and Acting Dean. 519-661-3542, fax 519-661-3506, e-mail fimsdean@julian.uwo.ca. Admissions contact: 519-661-2111, e-mail mlis@uwo.ca.

Library Scholarship Sources

For a more complete list of scholarships, fellowships, and assistantships offered for library study, see *Financial Assistance for Library and Information Studies*, published annually by the American Library Association.

American Association of Law Libraries. (1) A varying number of scholarships of a minimum of $1,000 for graduates of an accredited law school who are degree candidates in an ALA-accredited library school; (2) a varying number of scholarships of varying amounts for library school graduates working on a law degree, non-law graduates enrolled in an ALA-accredited library school, and law librarians taking a course related to law librarianship; (3) the George A. Strait Minority Stipend of $3,500 for an experienced minority librarian working toward an advanced degree to further a law library career. For information, write to: Scholarship Committee, AALL, 53 W. Jackson Blvd., Suite 940, Chicago, IL 60604.

American Library Association. (1) The Marshall Cavendish Scholarship of $3,000 for a varying number of students who have been admitted to an ALA-accredited library school; (2) The David H. Clift Scholarship of $3,000 for a varying number of students who have been admitted to an ALA-accredited library school; (3) the Tom and Roberta Drewes Scholarship of $3,000 for a varying number of library support staff; (4) the Mary V. Gaver Scholarship of $3,000 to a varying number of individuals specializing in youth services; (5) the Miriam L. Hornback Scholarship of $3,000 for a varying number of ALA or library support staff; (6) the Christopher J. Hoy/ERT Scholarship of $3,000 for a varying number of students who have been admitted to an ALA-accredited library school; (7) the Tony B. Leisner Scholarship of $3,000 for a varying number of library support staff; (8) Spectrum Initiative Scholarships of $5,000 for 50 minority students admitted to an ALA-accredited library school. For information on all ALA scholarships, write to: ALA Scholarship Clearinghouse, 50 E. Huron St., Chicago, IL 60611. Application can also be made online; see http://www.ala.org/work/awards/scholars.html.

ALA/American Association of School Librarians. The AASL School Librarians Workshop Scholarship of $2,500 for a candidate admitted to a full-time ALA-accredited MLS or school library media program. For information, write to: ALA Scholarship Clearinghouse, 50 E. Huron St., Chicago, IL 60611, or see http://www.ala.org/work/awards/scholars.html.

ALA/Association for Library Service to Children. (1) The Bound to Stay Bound Books Scholarship of $6,000 each for two students who are U.S. or Canadian citizens, who have been admitted to an ALA-accredited program, and who will work with children in a library for one year after graduation; (2) the Frederic G. Melcher Scholarship of $6,000 each for two U.S. or Canadian citizens admitted to an ALA-accredited library school who will work with children in school or public libraries for one year after graduation. For information, write to: ALA Scholarship Clearinghouse, 50 E. Huron St., Chicago, IL 60611, or see http://www.ala.org/work/awards/scholars.html.

ALA/Association of College and Research Libraries and the Institute for Scientific Information. (1) The ACRL Doctoral Dissertation Fellowship of $1,500 for a student who has completed all coursework and submitted a dissertation proposal that has been accepted, in the area of academic librarianship; (2) the Samuel Lazerow Fellowship of $1,000 for a research, travel, or writing project in acquisitions or technical services in an academic or research library; (3) the ACRL and Martinus Nijhoff International West European Specialist Study Grant, which pays travel expenses, room, and board for a ten-day trip to Europe for an ALA member (selection is based on proposal outlining purpose of trip). For information, write to: Meredith Parets, ACRL/ALA, 50 E. Huron St., Chicago, IL 60611.

ALA/Association of Specialized and Cooperative Library Agencies. Century Scholarship of up to $2,500 for a varying number of disabled U.S. or Canadian citizens admitted to an ALA-accredited library school. For information, write to: ALA Scholarship Clearinghouse, 50 E. Huron St., Chicago, IL 60611, or see http://www.ala.org/work/awards/scholars.html.

ALA/International Relations Committee. The Bogle Pratt International Library Travel Fund grant of $1,000 for a varying number of ALA members to attend a first international conference. For information, write to: Michael Dowling, ALA/IRC, 50 E. Huron St., Chicago, IL 60611.

ALA/Library and Information Technology Association. (1) The LITA/Christian Larew Memorial Scholarship of $3,000 for a student who has been admitted to an ALA-accredited program in library automation and information science; (2) The LITA/GEAC Scholarship in Library and Information Technology of $2,500 for a student who has been admitted to an ALA-accredited program in library automation and information technology; (3) The LITA/OCLC Minority Scholarship in Library and Information Technology of $2,500 for a minority student admitted to an ALA-accredited program; (4) The LITA/LSSI Minority Scholarship of $2,500 for a minority student admitted to an ALA-accredited program. For information, write to: ALA Scholarship Clearinghouse, 50 E. Huron St., Chicago, IL 60611, or see http://www.ala.org/work/awards/scholars.html.

ALA/New Members Round Table. EBSCO/NMRT Scholarship of $1,000 for a U.S. or Canadian citizen who is a member of the ALA New Members Round Table. Based on financial need, professional goals, and admission to an ALA-accredited program. For information, write to: ALA Scholarship Clearinghouse, 50 E. Huron St., Chicago, IL 60611, or see http://www.ala.org/work/awards/scholars.html.

ALA/Public Library Association. The New Leaders Travel Grant Study Award of up to $1,500 for a varying number of PLA members with MLS degrees and five years or less experience. For information, write to: Scholarship Liaison, PLA/ALA, 50 E. Huron St., Chicago, IL 60611.

American-Scandinavian Foundation. Fellowships and grants for 25 to 30 students, in amounts from $3,000 to $18,000, for advanced study in Denmark, Finland, Iceland, Norway, or Sweden. For information, write to: Exchange Division, American-Scandinavian Foundation, 58 Park Ave., New York, NY 10026.

Association for Library and Information Science Education. A varying number of research grants of up to $2,500 each for members of ALISE. For information, write to: Association for Library and Information Science Education, Box 7640, Arlington, VA 22207.

Association of Jewish Libraries. The May K. Simon Memorial Scholarship Fund offers a varying number of scholarships of at least $500 each for MLS students who plan to work as Judaica librarians. For information, write to: Sharona R. Wachs, Association of Jewish Libraries, 1000 Washington Ave., Albany, NY 12203.

Association of Seventh-Day Adventist Librarians. The D. Glenn Hilts Scholarship of $1,000 to a member of the Seventh-Day Adventist Church in a graduate library program. For information, write to: Ms. Wisel, Association of Seventh-Day Adventist Librarians, Columbia Union College, 7600 Flower Ave., Takoma Park, MD 20912.

Beta Phi Mu. (1) The Sarah Rebecca Reed Scholarship of $1,500 for a person accepted in an ALA-accredited library program; (2) the Frank B. Sessa Scholarship of $750 for a Beta Phi Mu member for continuing education; (3) the Harold Lancour Scholarship of $1,000 for study in a foreign country related to the applicant's work or schooling; (4) the Blanche E. Woolls Scholarship for School Library Media Service of $1,000 for a person accepted in an ALA-accredited library program; (5) the Doctoral Dissertation Scholarship of $1,500 for a person who has completed course work toward a doctorate; (6) The Eugene Garfield Doctoral Dissertation Scholarship of $3,000 for a person who has approval of a dissertation topic. For information, write to: Jane Robbins, Executive Director, Beta Phi Mu, Florida State University, SLIS, Tallahassee, FL 32306-2100.

Canadian Association of Law Libraries. The Diana M. Priestly Scholarship of $2,500 for a student with previous law library experience or for entry to an approved Canadian law school or accredited Canadian library school. For information, write to: Jane Taylor, Ministry of the Attorney General, Box 9280, Sta. Provincial Government, Victoria, BC V8W 9L7, Canada.

Canadian Federation of University Women. (1) The Alice E. Wilson Award of $2,100 for two students enrolled in graduate studies in any field, with special consideration given to candidates returning to study after at least three years; (2) the Margaret McWilliams Fellowship of $10,000 for a full-time student who has completed one full year of study at the doctoral level; (3) the CFUW Memorial/Professional Fellowship of $5,000 for a student enrolled in a master's program in science, mathematics, or engineering; (4) the Beverly Jackson Fellowship of $3,000 for a student over age 35 enrolled in graduate work at an Ontario University; (5) the 1989 Polytechnique Commemorative Award of $2,800 for a student enrolled in graduate studies related particularly to women; (6) the Bourse Georgette LeMoyne award of $2,100 for graduate study at a Canadian university where one of the languages of administration and instruction is French; (7) the Dr. Marion Elder Grant Fellowship of $10,000 for a full-time student at the master's or doctoral level (preference will be given to holders of an Acadia University degree). For information, write to: Canadian Federation of University Women, 251 Bank St., Suite 600, Ottawa, ON K2P 1X3, Canada (e-mail cfuwfls@home.com, World Wide Web http://www.cfuw.org).

Canadian Health Libraries Association. The Student Paper Prize, a scholarship of $300 to a student or recent MLIS graduate or library technician; topic of paper must be in health or information science. For information, write to: Student Paper Prize, Canadian Health Libraries Association/ ABSC, Box 94038, 3332 Yonge St., Toronto, ON M4N 3R1, Canada.

Canadian Library Association. (1) The World Book Graduate Scholarship in Library and Information Science of $2,500; (2) the CLA Dafoe Scholarship of $1,750; and (3) the H. W. Wilson Scholarship of $2,000. Each scholarship is given to a Canadian citizen or landed immigrant to attend an accredited Canadian library school; the World Book scholarship can also be used for an ALA-accredited U.S. school; (4) the Library Research and Development Grant of $1,000 for a member of the Canadian Library Association, in support of theoretical and applied research in library and information science. For information, write to: CLA Membership Services Department, Scholarships and Awards Committee, 328 Frank St., Ottawa, ON K2P 0X8, Canada.

Catholic Library Association. (1) The World Book, Inc., Grant of $1,500 is divided among no more than three CLA members for continuing education in children's or school librarianship; (2) The Rev. Andrew L. Bouwhuis Memorial Scholarship of $1,500 for a student accepted into a graduate program in library science. For information, write to: Jean R. Bostley, SSJ, Scholarship Chair, Catholic Library Association, 100 North St., Suite 224, Pittsfield, MA 01201-5109.

Chinese American Librarians Association. (1) The Sheila Suen Lai Scholarship; (2) the C. C. Seetoo/CALA Conference Travel Scholarship. Each scholarship offers $500 to a Chinese descendant who has been accepted in an ALA-accredited program. For information, write to: Meng Xiong Liu, Clark Library, San Jose State University, 1 Washington Sq., San Jose, CA 95192-0028.

Church and Synagogue Library Association. The Muriel Fuller Memorial Scholarship of $115 plus cost of texts for a correspondence course offered by the University of Utah Continuing Education Division.

Open to CSLA members only. For information, write to: CSLA, Box 19357, Portland, OR 97280-0357.

Council on Library and Information Resources. The A. R. Zipf Fellowship in Information Management of $8,000 is awarded annually to a U.S. citizen enrolled in graduate school who shows exceptional promise for leadership and technical achievement. For information, write to: Council on Library and Information Resources, 1755 Massachusetts Ave. N.W., Suite 500, Washington, DC 20036.

Sandra Garvie Memorial Fund. A scholarship of $1,000 for a student pursuing a course of study in library and information science. For information, write to: Sandra Garvie Memorial Fund, c/o Director, Legal Resources Centre, Faculty of Extension, University of Alberta, 8303 112th St., Edmonton, AB T6G 2T4, Canada.

Manitoba Library Association. (1) John Edwin Bissett Memorial Fund Scholarships. Awards of varying amounts for a varying number of University of Manitoba graduates who are enrolled full-time in a master's program in library and information science; (2) Jean Thorunn Law Scholarship. An award of a varying amount for a student enrolled in a full-time master's program in library and information who has a year of library experience in Manitoba. For information, write to: Manitoba Library Association, CE Committee, 416-100 Arthur St., Winnipeg, MB R3B 1H3.

Massachusetts Black Librarians' Network. Two scholarships of at least $500 and $1,000 for minority students entering an ALA-accredited master's program in library science, with no more than 12 semester hours toward a degree. For information, write to: Pearl Mosley, Chair, Massachusetts Black Librarians' Network, 27 Beech Glen St., Roxbury, MA 02119.

Medical Library Association. (1) The Cunningham Memorial International Fellowship of $6,000 plus travel expenses; (2) a scholarship of $5,000 for a person entering an ALA-accredited library program, with no more than one-half of the program yet to be completed; (3) a scholarship of $5,000 for a minority student for graduate study; (4) a varying number of Research, Development and Demonstration Project Grants of $100 to $1,000 for U.S. or Canadian citizens who are MLA members; (5) Continuing Education Grants of $100 to $500 for U.S. or Canadian citizens who are MLA members. For information, write to: Development Department, Medical Library Association, 65 E. Wacker Pl., Suite 1900, Chicago, IL 60601-7298.

Mountain Plains Library Association. (1) A varying number of grants of up to $600 each and (2) a varying number of grants of up to $150 each for MPLA members with at least two years of membership for continuing education. For information, write to: Joseph R. Edelen, Jr., MPLA Executive Secretary, I. D. Weeks Library, University of South Dakota, Vermillion, SD 57069.

REFORMA, the National Association to Promote Library Services to Latinos and the Spanish-Speaking. A varying number of scholarships of $1,000 to $2,000 each for minority students interested in serving the Spanish-speaking community to attend an ALA-accredited school. For information, write to: Ninta Trejo, Main Library, University of Arizona, 1510 E. University, Tucson, AZ 85721.

Society of American Archivists. The Colonial Dames Awards, two grants of $1,200 each for specific types of repositories and collections. For information, write to: Debra Mills, Society of American Archivists, 521 S. Wells St., 5th fl., Chicago, IL 60607.

Southern Regional Education Board. For residents of Louisiana, a varying number of grants of varying amounts to cover in-state tuition for graduate or postgraduate study in an ALA-accredited library school. For information, write to: Academic Common Market, c/o Southern Regional Education Board, 592 Tenth St. N.W., Atlanta, GA 30318-5790.

Special Libraries Association. (1) Three $6,000 scholarships for students interested in special-library work; (2) the Plenum Scholarship of $1,000; (3) the ISI Scholarship of $1,000, each also for students interested in special-library work; (4) the Affirmative Action Scholarship of $6,000 for a minority student interested in special-library work; and (5) the Pharmaceutical Division Stipend Award of $1,200 for a student with an undergraduate degree in chemistry, life sciences, or pharmacy entering or enrolled in an ALA-accredited program. For information on the first four scholarships, write to: Scholarship Committee, Special Libraries Association, 1700 18th St. N.W., Washington, DC 20009-2508; for information on the Pharmaceutical Stipend, write to: Susan E. Katz, Awards Chair, Knoll Pharmaceuticals Science Information Center, 30 N. Jefferson St., Whippany, NJ 07981.

Library Scholarship and Award Recipients, 2001

Library awards are listed by organization. For information on awarding organizations, see the preceding article, "Library Scholarship Sources."

American Association of Law Libraries (AALL)

AALL Scholarships. Offered by: AALL; LexisNexis; West Group. *Winners*: (Library Degree for Law School Graduates) Merrill Chertok, Lisa Wagenheim, Andrew Larrick; (Library School Graduates Attending Law School) Rae Ellen Best; (Library Degree for Non-Law School Graduates) Mary McGraw, Maureen Dunnigan, Krista Lindhard, Rachelle Pacchiano, Sarah Yates; (Library School Graduate for Non-Law School Degree) Greta Boeringer; (George A. Strait Minority Stipend) Tanya Cain, Veronica Foster, Kristy Moon.

American Library Association (ALA)

ALA/Information Today Library of the Future Award ($1,500). For a library, consortium, group of librarians, or support organization for innovative planning for, applications of, or development of patron training programs about information technology in a library setting. *Donor*: Information Today, Inc. *Winner*: Richard College Library, Dallas, Texas.

ALA Research Grant (up to $25,000). To support problem-based research for the library and information science profession. *Donor*: ALA. *Winner*: Virginia A. Walters and Cynthia L. Mediaville, University of California, Los Angeles, for "Models for Homework Center Outcomes."

Hugh C. Atkinson Memorial Award ($2,000). For outstanding achievement (including risk-taking) by academic librarians that has contributed significantly to improvements in library automation, management, and/or development or research. *Offered*

by: ACRL, ALCTS, LAMA, and LITA divisions. *Winner*: Larry Frye.

Carroll Preston Baber Research Grant (up to $7,500). For innovative research that could lead to an improvement in library services to any specified group(s) of people. *Donor*: Eric R. Baber. *Winner*: Ruth V. Small School of Library and Information Studies, Syracuse University.

Beta Phi Mu Award ($500). For distinguished service in library education. *Donor*: Beta Phi Mu International Library Science Honorary Society. *Winner*: Lotsee Patterson.

Bogle/Pratt International Library Travel Fund Award ($1,000). To ALA member(s) to attend their first international conference. *Donor*: Bogle Memorial Fund. *Winner*: Harriet Lightman.

Bill Boyd Literary Award ($5,000). To an author for a military novel that honors the service of American veterans. *Donor*: William Young Boyd. *Winner*: Brig. Gen. (Ret.) Edwin Simmons for *Dog Company Six*.

David H. Clift Scholarship ($3,000). To worthy U.S. or Canadian citizens enrolled in an ALA-accredited program toward an MLS degree. *Winners*: Elizabeth M. Anstak, Jennifer L. Ogrodowski, Marc C. Tiar, Erica Jo Wilder.

Melvil Dewey Award. To an individual or group for recent creative professional achievement in library management, training, cataloging and classification, and the tools and techniques of librarianship. *Donor*: OCLC/Forest Press. *Winner*: Herman L. Totten.

Tom and Roberta Drewes Scholarship ($3,000). To a library support staff person pursuing a master's degree. *Winner*: Alison J. Ince.

Equality Award ($500). To an individual or group for an outstanding contribution that promotes equality of women and men in the library profession. *Donor*: Scarecrow Press. *Winner*: Doris Seale.

Freedom to Read Foundation Roll of Honor Award. *Winner*: John K. Horany.

Elizabeth Futas Catalyst for Change Award ($1,000). To recognize and honor a librarian who invests time and talent to make positive change in the profession of librarianship. *Donor*: Elizabeth Futas Memorial Fund. *Winner*: Maxine H. Reneker.

Loleta D. Fyan Public Library Research Grant (up to $10,000). For projects in public library development. *Winner*: Parsippany-Troy Hills Public Library, Parsippany, New Jersey.

Gale Group Financial Development Award ($2,500). To a library organization for a financial development project to secure new funding resources for a public or academic library. *Donor*: Gale Group. *Winner*: Tompkins County Public Library, Ithaca, New York.

Mary V. Gaver Scholarship ($3,000). To a library support staff member specializing in youth services. *Winner*: Jennifer L. Hart.

Grolier Foundation Award ($1,000). For stimulation and guidance of reading by children and young people. *Donor*: Grolier Education Corporation, Inc. *Winner*: Julie Cummins.

Grolier National Library Week Grant ($4,000). To libraries or library associations of all types for a public awareness campaign in connection with National Library Week in the year the grant is awarded. *Donor*: Grolier Educational Corporation. *Winner*: Westlake (Ohio) Porter Public Library.

Honorary ALA Membership. Arnulfo D. Trejo.

Miriam L. Hornback Scholarship ($3,000). To an ALA or library support staff person pursuing a master's degree in library science. *Winners*: Jane E. Hamilton, Cynthia A. Gibbon.

Paul Howard Award for Courage ($1,000). To a librarian, library board, library group, or an individual who has exhibited unusual courage for the benefit of library programs or services. *Donor*: Paul Howard. *Winner*: Douglas A. Henderson.

Christopher J. Hoyt/ERT Scholarship ($3,000). To worthy U.S. or Canadian citizens enrolled in an ALA-accredited program toward an MLS degree. *Winner*: Melissa H. Gotsch, Dawn M. Thornton.

John Ames Humphry/OCLC/Forest Press Award ($1,000). To an individual for significant contributions to international librarianship. *Donor*: OCLC/Forest Press. *Winner*: Norman Horrocks.

Tony B. Leisner Scholarship ($3,000). To a library support staff member pursuing a master's degree program. *Winner*: Christina L. Deyton.

Joseph W. Lippincott Award ($1,000). To a librarian for distinguished service to the profession. *Donor*: Joseph W. Lippincott, Jr. *Winner*: Patricia Glass Schuman.

Marshall Cavendish Excellence in Library Programing Award. ($5,000). Recognizes either a school library or public library that demonstrates excellence in library programming by providing programs that have community impact and respond to community need. *Winner*: Friends of the St. Paul (Minnesota) Public Library.

Marshall Cavendish Scholarship ($3,000). To a worthy U.S. or Canadian citizen to begin an MLS degree in an ALA-accredited program. *Winner*: Kathyn A. Parker.

SIRSI Leader in Library Technology Grant ($10,000). To a library organization to encourage and enable continued advancements in quality services for a project that makes creative or groundbreaking use of technology to deliver exceptional services to its community. *Donor*: SIRSI Corporation. *Winner:* Long Island (Maine) Community Library.

Spectrum Initiative Scholarships ($5,000). Presented to 50 minority students admitted to an ALA-accredited library school. *Winners*: Rhonda Allende, Camille E. Andrews, Cecilia Barber, Bernadette Beredo, Nathalie Bouillon, Stacey Brown, Randi Carreno, Felecia Clark, Jose Cordova, Malynda Dalton, An-Chi Dianu, Tracy Ducksworth, Cynthia Elizondo, Alicia Ellis, Nance Espinosa, Hoa Flanagan, Trina Ford, Amy Gonzalez, Helen Gonzalez, Xan Goodman, Lillian Hoffecker, Todd Honma, Petrina Jackson, Michael

Johnson, Portia E. Johnson, Willie J. John-
son, Jr., Shannon Jones, Chungsil Kim,
Gail King, Beverly Ku, Carolyn Lei-lani-
lau, Benjamin Longoria, Monica Lopez,
Tamika Maddox, Carmen Markham, Leon
Matthias, Sr., Kassundra Miller, Petra
Morris, Renee Newry, Sandy Pon, Alexan-
dra Rivera-Rule, LeVera Rose, Nicholas
Saunders, Felicia Smith, Crystal Smith,
Joanne Suzara, Darren Sweeper, Teri
Tada, Harry Ting, Elizabeth "Chisa"
Uyeki, Lin-Pyng "Lucy" Wang, Linda C.
White.

Virginia and Herbert White Award for Promoting Librarianship ($1,000). Honors a
significant contribution to the public
recognition and appreciation of librarianship through professional performance,
teaching, and writing. *Winner*: Ken Haycock.

H. W. Wilson Library Staff Development
Award ($3,500). To a library organization
for a program to further its staff development goals and objectives. *Donor*: H. W.
Wilson Company. *Winner*: Sarasota County (Florida) Library System.

World Book–ALA Goal Grant (up to $10,000).
To ALA units for the advancement of pub-
lic, academic, or school library service and
librarianship through support of programs
that implement the goals and priorities of
ALA. *Donor*: World Book, Inc. *Winner*:
ALA Chapter Relations Committee for
"Creating Library Leaders."

American Association of School Librarians (AASL)

AASL ABC/CLIO Leadership Grant (up to
$1,750). For planning and implementing
leadership programs at state, regional, or
local levels to be given to school library
associations that are affiliates of AASL.
Donor: ABC/CLIO. *Winner*: Educational
Media Association of New Jersey.

AASL Collaborative School Library Media
Award ($2,500). For expanding the role of
the library in elementary and/or secondary
school education. *Donor*: Sagebrush Corporation. *Winner*: Marilyn Rothberg, Sugar-

town Elementary School, Malvern, Pennsylvania.

AASL Crystal Apple Award. To an individual or group that has had significant
impact on school libraries and students.
Winner: 3M Library Systems.

AASL/Frances Henne Award ($1,250). To a
school library media specialist with five or
fewer years in the profession to attend an
AASL regional conference or ALA Annual Conference for the first time. *Donor*:
Greenwood Publishing Group. *Winner*:
Katherine Grant Cadden.

AASL/Highsmith Research Grant (up to
$5,000). To conduct innovative research
aimed at measuring and evaluating the
impact of school library media programs
on learning and education. *Donor*: Highsmith, Inc. *Winner*: Not awarded in 2001.

AASL School Librarian's Workshop Scholarship ($3,000). To a full-time student
preparing to become a school library
media specialist at the preschool, elementary, or secondary level. *Donor*: Jay W.
Toor, President, Library Learning Resources. *Winner*: Darlene Wilson.

Distinguished School Administrators Award
($2,000). For expanding the role of the
library in elementary and/or secondary
school education. *Donor*: SIRS-Mandarin,
Inc. *Winner*: Kathleen D. Smith, Cherry
Creek High School, Englewood, Colorado.

Distinguished Service Award, AASL/Baker
& Taylor ($3,000). For outstanding contri-
butions to librarianship and school library
development. *Donor*: Baker & Taylor
Books. *Winner*: Hilda L. Jay.

Information Technology Pathfinder Award
($1,000 to the specialist and $500 to the
library). To library media specialists for
innovative approaches to microcomputer
applications in the school library media
center. *Donor*: Follett Software Company.
Winners: Secondary, Ann Bell; Elementary, Beverly Smith-Edwards.

Intellectual Freedom Award ($2,000, and
$1,000 to media center of recipient's
choice). To a school library media specialist who has upheld the principles of intellectual freedom. *Donor*: SIRS-Mandarin.
Winner: Dianne McAfee Hopkins.

National School Library Media Program of the Year Award ($3,000). To school districts and a single school for excellence and innovation in outstanding library media programs. *Donor*: AASL and Follett Library Resources. *Winners*: Large school district, DeKalb (Georgia) County School System; Single school, Corbett Elementary School, Tucson, Arizona.

Association for Library Trustees and Advocates (ALTA)

ALA Trustee Citations. To recognize public library trustees for individual service to library development on the local, state, regional, or national level. *Winners*: Ruth Newell, Virginia McCurdy.

ALTA/Gale Outstanding Trustee Conference Grant Award ($750). *Donor*: Gale Group. *Winners*: Margaret J. Danhof, Charles R. Myers.

ALTA Literacy Award (citation). To a library trustee or an individual who, in a volunteer capacity, has made a significant contribution to addressing the illiteracy problem in the United States. *Winner*: Lucille Cole Thomas.

ALTA Major Benefactors Honor Award (citation). To individual(s), families, or corporate bodies that have made major benefactions to public libraries. *Winner*: Not awarded in 2001.

Association for Library Collections and Technical Services (ALCTS)

Hugh C. Atkinson Memorial Award. *See under* American Library Association.

Paul Banks and Carolyn Harris Preservation Award ($1,500). To recognize the contribution of a professional preservation specialist who has been active in the field of preservation and/or conservation for library and/or archival materials. *Donor*: Preservation Technologies. *Winner*: Sarah Buchanan.

Best of *LRTS* Award (citation). To the author(s) of the best paper published each year in the division's official journal. *Winner*: Sherry L. Vellucci.

Blackwell's Scholarship Award ($2,000 scholarship to the U.S. or Canadian library school of the recipient's choice). To honor the author(s) of the year's outstanding monograph, article, or original paper in the field of acquisitions, collection development, and related areas of resource development in libraries. *Donor*: Blackwell/North America. *Winners*: Joseph Branin, Frances Groen, and Suzanne Thorin for "The Changing Nature of Collection Management in Research Libraries" in *Library Resources & Technical Services*.

Bowker/Ulrich's Serials Librarianship Award ($1,500). For demonstrated leadership in serials-related activities through participation in professional associations and/or library education programs, contributions to the body of serials literature, research in the area of serials, or development of tools or methods to enhance access to or management of serials. *Winner*: Not awarded in 2001.

First Step Award (Wiley Professional Development Grant) ($1,500). For librarians new to the serials field to attend ALA's Annual Conference. *Donor*: John Wiley & Sons. *Winner*: Allen B. Ashman.

Leadership in Library Acquisitions Award ($1,500). For significant contributions by an outstanding leader in the field of library acquisitions. *Donor*: Harrassowitz Company. *Winner*: Karen Schmidt.

Margaret Mann Citation ($2,000 scholarship to the U.S. or Canadian library school of the winning author's choice). To a cataloger or classifier for achievement in the areas of cataloging or classification. *Donor*: Online Computer Library Center. *Winner*: Brian E. C. Schottlaender.

Esther J. Piercy Award ($1,500). To a librarian with fewer than ten years' experience for contributions and leadership in the field of library collections and technical services. *Donor*: Yankee Book Peddler. *Winner*: Oya Yildrim Rieger.

Association for Library Service to Children (ALSC)

ALSC/Book Wholesalers Summer Reading Program Grant ($3,000). To an ALSC member for implementation of an outstanding public library summer reading program for children. *Donor*: Book Wholesalers, Inc. *Winner*: Lester Public Library, Two Rivers, Wisconsin.

ALSC/Econo-Clad Literature Program Award ($1,000). To an ALSC member who has developed and implemented an outstanding library program for children involving reading and the use of literature, to attend an ALA conference. *Donor*: Econo-Clad Books. *Winner*: Ashley Fowlkes.

ALSC/REFORMA Pura Belpré Award. To a Latino/Latina writer and illustrator whose work best portrays, affirms, and celebrates the Latino cultural experience in an outstanding work of literature for children and youth. *Winner*: Not awarded in 2001.

May Hill Arbuthnot Honor Lectureship. To invite an individual of distinction to prepare and present a paper that will be a significant contribution to the field of children's literature and that will subsequently be published in *Journal of Youth Services in Libraries*. *Winner*: Philip Pullman.

Mildred L. Batchelder Award. See *Literary Prizes, 2001* by Gary Ink.

Louise Seaman Bechtel Fellowship ($4,000). For librarians with 12 or more years of professional level work in children's library collections, to read and study at the Baldwin Library/George Smathers Libraries, University of Florida (must be an ALSC member with an MLS from an ALA-accredited program). *Donor*: Bechtel Fund. *Winner*: Jane Marino.

Bound to Stay Bound Books Scholarships (three awards of $6,000). For men and women who intend to pursue an MLS or advanced degree and who plan to work in the area of library service to children. *Donor*: Bound to Stay Bound Books. *Winners*: Rebecca Ruth Borup, Jennifer Ann Reichert, Gwendolyn Yarborough Smith.

Caldecott Medal. See *Literary Prizes, 2001* by Gary Ink.

Andrew Carnegie Medal. To the U.S. producer of the most distinguished video for children in the previous year. *Donor*: Carnegie Corporation of New York. *Winner*: Paul R. Gagne for Weston Woods Studio, producer of *Antarctic Antics*.

Distinguished Service to ALSC Award ($1,000). To recognize significant contributions to, and an impact on, library services to children and/or ALSC. *Winner*: Margaret Mary Kimmel.

Frederic G. Melcher Scholarship ($6,000). To two students entering the field of library service to children for graduate work in an ALA-accredited program. *Winners*: Rachael L. Bohn, Angela Joyce Grandstaff.

John Newbery Medal. See *Literary Prizes, 2001* by Gary Ink.

Penguin Putnam Books for Young Readers Awards. To children's librarians in school or public libraries with ten or fewer years of experience to attend the ALA Annual Conference for the first time. Must be a member of ALSC. *Donor*: Penguin Putnam. *Winners*: Joel Bangilan, Dana Bjerke, Robin L. Gibson, Kate Houston Mitchoff.

Robert F. Sibert Informational Book Award. To the author of the most distinguished informational book published during the preceding year. *Donor*: Bound to Stay Bound Books. *Winner*: Marc Aronson for *Sir Walter Ralegh and the Quest for El Dorado* (Clarion Books).

Laura Ingalls Wilder Medal. To an author or illustrator whose works have made a lasting contribution to children's literature. *Winner*: Milton Meltzer.

Association of College and Research Libraries (ACRL)

ACRL Academic/Research Librarian of the Year Award ($3,000). For outstanding contribution to academic and research librarianship and library development. *Donor*: Baker & Taylor. *Winner*: Larry Hardesty.

ACRL Doctoral Dissertation Fellowship ($1,500). To a doctoral student in the field of academic librarianship whose research has potential significance in the field. *Donor*: Institute for Scientific Information. *Winner*: Laurie J. Bonnici.

ACRL EBSS Distinguished Education and Behavioral Sciences Librarian Award (citation). To an academic librarian who has made an outstanding contribution as an education and/or behavioral sciences librarian through accomplishments and service to the profession. *Winner:* Charles B. Thurston.

ACRL WSS/Greenwood Career Achievement in Women's Studies Librarianship ($1,000). Honors distinguished academic librarians who have made outstanding contributions to women's studies through accomplishments and service to the profession. *Donor:* Greenwood Publishing Group. *Winner:* Sarah Pritchard.

ACRL WSS/Routledge Award for Significant Achievement in Women's Studies Librarianship ($1,000). *Winner:* Marilyn Dunn.

Hugh C. Atkinson Memorial Award. *See under* American Library Association.

Miriam Dudley Instruction Librarian Award ($1,000). For contribution to the advancement of bibliographic instruction in a college or research institution. *Donor:* Elsevier. *Winner:* Patricia Iannuzzi.

EBSCO Community College Learning Resources Leadership Award ($500). *Donor:* EBSCO Subscription Services. *Winner:* Cary Sowell.

EBSCO Community College Learning Resources Program Award ($500). *Donor:* EBSCO Subscription Services. *Winner:* Tompkins Cortland Community College, Fort Pierce, Florida.

EBSCO Conference Sponsorships. *Donor:* EBSCO Subscription Services. *Winners:* John Kyle Banerjee, Deborah Barristi, Kirstin M. Dougan, Catherine A. Harmon, Sue Hunter, Sarah M. Killoran, Angela Leeper, Jennifer Mott, Sanya P. Oldland, Dauphin County Library System, Gina C. Williams.

Excellence in Academic Libraries Awards ($3,000 plus travel expenses).To recognize an outstanding community college, college, and university library. *Donor:* Blackwell's Book Services. *Winners:* Austin (Texas) Community College, Earlham College (Richmond, Indiana), University of Arizona/Tucson.

Instruction Section Innovation in Instruction Award ($3,000). Recognizes and honors librarians who have developed and implemented innovative approaches to instruction within their institution in the preceding two years. *Donor:* LexisNexis. *Winner:* University of Hawaii at Manoa for its University Library's LIS 100 course, "Libraries, Scholarship and Technology."

Instruction Section Publication of the Year Award (citation). Recognizes an outstanding publication related to instruction in a library environment published in the preceding two years. *Winner: Reference Service Review* special issue, "A LOEX 25-year Retrospective."

Marta Lange/CQ Award ($1,000). Recognizes an academic or law librarian for contributions to bibliography and information service in law or political science. *Donor: Congressional Quarterly. Winner:* Cheryl Nyberg.

Samuel Lazerow Fellowship for Research in Acquisitions or Technical Services ($1,000). To foster advances in acquisitions or technical services by providing librarians a fellowship for travel or writing in those fields. *Sponsor:* Institute for Scientific Information (ISI). *Winner:* Adam Chandler.

Katharine Kyes Leab and Daniel J. Leab Exhibition Catalog Awards (citations). For the best catalogs published by American or Canadian institutions in conjunction with exhibitions of books and/or manuscripts. *Winners:* (Category I–Expensive) *Ulysses in Hand: The Rosenbach Manuscript.* The Rosenbach Library; (Category II–Moderately Expensive) *Word and Image: Samuel Beckett and the Visual Text.* Emory University Robert W. Woodruff Library and Institut Mémoires de l'Édition Contemporaine, Paris; (Category III–Inexpensive) *Curious George Comes to Hattiesburg: The Life and Work of H. A. and Margaret Rey,* University of Southern Mississippi Libraries, de Grummond Children's Literature Collection; (Category IV–Brochures). *So Fairly Bound: Fine Twentieth-Century Bookbindings and Illuminated Manuscripts from the Edward R. Leahy Collection,* University of Scranton, Harry and Jeanette Weinberg Memorial Library.

Martinus Nijhoff International West European Specialist Study Grant (travel funding for up to 14 days' research in Europe). Supports research pertaining to West European studies, librarianship, or the book trade. *Sponsor*: Martinus Nijhoff International. *Winner*: Sue Waterman.

Oberly Award for Bibliography in the Agricultural Sciences ($350). Biennially, for the best English-language bibliography in the field of agriculture or a related science in the preceding two-year period. *Donor*: Eunice R. Oberly Fund. *Winner*: *Biodiversity Studies: A Bibliographic Review* by Charles H. Smith.

K. G. Saur Award for Best *College and Research Libraries* Article ($500). To author(s) to recognize the most outstanding article published in *College and Research Libraries* during the preceding year. *Donor*: K. G. Saur Publishing. *Winner*: Thomas E. Nisonger.

Association of Specialized and Cooperative Library Agencies (ASCLA)

ASCLA Century Scholarship (up to $2,500). For a library school student or students with disabilities admitted to an ALA-accredited library school. *Winner*: Simon John Maxwell Healey.

ASCLA Exceptional Service Award. *Winner*: Linda Lucas Walling.

ASCLA Leadership Achievement Award. To recognize leadership and achievement in the areas of consulting, multitype library cooperation, and state library development. *Winner*: Not awarded in 2001.

ASCLA/National Organization on Disability Award for Library Service to People with Disabilities ($1,000). To institutions or organizations that have made the library's total service more accessible through changing physical and/or additional barriers. *Donor*: National Organization on Disability, funded by Aetna U.S. Healthcare. *Winner*: Cleveland (Ohio) Public Library.

ASCLA Professional Achievement Award. To recognize professional achievement within the areas of consulting, networking, statewide service, and programs. *Winner*: Charles Ewick.

ASCLA Service Award (citation). For outstanding service and leadership to the division. *Winner*: Frederick Duda.

Francis Joseph Campbell Citation. For a contribution of recognized importance to library service for the blind and physically handicapped. *Winner*: Barbara Mates.

Ethnic and Multicultural Information and Exchange Round Table

EMIERT/Gale Group Multicultural Award ($1,000). For outstanding achievement and leadership in serving the multicultural/multiethnic community. *Donor*: Gale Group. *Winner*: Queens Borough (New York) Public Library Workteam for Children and Teens.

Exhibits Round Table

Friendly Booth Award (citation). *Cosponsor*: New Members Round Table. *Winners*: First place, ProQuest; second place, Culture Co-op; third place, Publishers Marketing Association.

Christopher J. Hoy/ERT Scholarship ($3,000). To an individual or individuals who will work toward an MLS degree in an ALA-accredited program. *Donor*: Family of Christopher Hoy. *Winners*: Melissa H. Gotsch, Dawn M. Thorton.

Kohlstedt Exhibit Award (citation). To companies or organizations for the best single, multiple, and island booth displays at the ALA Annual Conference. *Winners*: Single, Zoo Books; Multiple, Demco; Island, Library of Congress.

Federal and Armed Forces Librarians Round Table (FAFLRT)

Federal Librarians Achievement Award. *Winner*: Not awarded in 2001.

Adelaide del Frate Conference Sponsor Award. To encourage library school students to become familiar with federal librarianship and ultimately seek work in federal libraries; for attendance at ALA Annual Conference and activities of the Federal and Armed Forces Librarians Round Table. *Winner*: Jennifer Peterson.

Distinguished Service Award (citation). To honor a FAFLRT member for outstanding and sustained contributions to the association and to federal librarianship. *Winners*: Andrea Morris Gruhl, Jane T. Sessa.

Gay, Lesian, Bisexual, and Transgendered Round Table (GLBT)

GLBT Book Awards. To authors of fiction and nonfiction books of exceptional merit relating to the gay/lesbian experience. *Winners*: Sarah Waters for *Affinity* (Riverhead Books), William N. Eskridge for *Gaylaw: Challenging the Apartheid of the Closet* (Harvard University Press).

Government Documents Round Table (GODORT)

James Bennett Childs Award. To a librarian or other individual for distinguished lifetime contributions to documents librarianship. *Winner*: Myrtle Bolner.

CIS/GODORT/ALA Documents to the People Award ($2,000). To an individual, library, organization, or noncommercial group that most effectively encourages or enhances the use of government documents in library services. *Donor*: Congressional Information Service, Inc. (CIS). *Winner*: Sheila McGarr.

Bernadine Abbott Hoduski Founders Award (plaque). To recognize documents librarians who may not be known at the national level but who have made significant contributions to the field of state, international, local, or federal documents. *Winner*: Maryellen Trautman.

Readex/GODORT/ALA Catharine J. Reynolds Award ($2,000). Grants to documents librarians for travel and/or study in the field of documents librarianship or area of study benefiting performance as documents librarians. *Donor*: Readex Corporation. *Winner*: Debora Cheney.

David Rozkuszka Scholarship ($3,000). To provide financial assistance to an individual who is currently working with government documents in a library while completing a master's program in library science. *Winner*: Kristine Kasianovitz.

Intellectual Freedom Round Table (IFRT)

John Phillip Immroth Memorial Award for Intellectual Freedom ($500). For notable contribution to intellectual freedom fueled by personal courage. *Winner*: Linda Hughes.

Eli M. Oboler Memorial Award ($1,500). Biennially, to an author of a published work in English or in English translation dealing with issues, events, questions, or controversies in the area of intellectual freedom. *Donor*: Providence Associates, Inc. *Winner*: Not awarded in 2001.

SIRS State and Regional Achievement Award ($1,000). To the intellectual freedom committee of a state library, state library media association, or a state/regional coalition for the most successful and creative project during the calendar year. *Donor*: Social Issues Resource Series, Inc. (SIRS). *Winner*: Intellectual Freedom Committee, West Virginia Library Association.

Library Administration and Management Association (LAMA)

Hugh C. Atkinson Memorial Award. *See under* American Library Association.

Certificate of Achievement. *Winner*: Not awarded in 2001.

John Cotton Dana Library Public Relations Awards. To libraries or library organizations of all types for public relations programs or special projects ended during the preceding year. *Donor*: H. W. Wilson Company. *Winners*: Bellingham (Washington) Public Library; Denver (Colorado) Public Library; Dr. Eugene Clark Library, Lockhart, Texas; Friends of the Pikes Peak Library District, Colorado Springs, Colorado; King County Library System, Issaquah, Washington; Metropolitan School District of Washington Township, Indianapolis, Indiana; New Mexico State University Library, Las Cruces, New Mexico; Phoenix (Arizona) Public Library; West Bloomfield (Michigan) Township Public Library.

LAMA/AIA Library Buildings Award (citation). A biennial award given for excellence in architectural design and planning by an American architect. *Donor*: American Institute of Architects and LAMA. *Winners*: Steven Ehrlich Architects of Los Angeles for the Robertson Branch Library in Los Angeles; Carlson Architects of

Seattle for the North Mason Timberland Library in Belfair, Washington; Michael Graves & Associates of Princeton, New Jersey, in association with Klipp Colussy Jenks DuBois Architects of Denver, Colorado, for the Denver Public Library; Elliott & Elliott Architecture of Blue Hill, Maine, for the Friend Memorial Library in Brooklin, Maine; Helfand Myerberg Guggenheimer of New York, for the Rhys Carpenter Library, Bryn Mawr College, Bryn Mawr, Pennsylvania; Fletcher Farr Ayotte of Portland, Oregon, in association with Hardy Holzman Pfeiffer Associates of Los Angeles for the Multnomah County Central Library in Portland; Thomas Hacker and Associates Architects of Portland, Oregon, for the Woodstock Branch Library in Portland; Graham Gund Architects of Cambridge, Massachusetts, for the Dimond Library, University of New Hampshire, Durham.

LAMA Cultural Diversity Grant (up to $1,000). To support creation and dissemination of resources that will assist library administrators and managers in developing a vision and commitment to diversity. *Winner*: Richland County Public Library, Columbia, South Carolina, and Oklahoma Library Association.

LAMA President's Award. *Winner*: 3M Library Systems.

LAMA Recognition of Group Achievement Award. To honor LAMA committees or task forces, recognizing outstanding teamwork supporting the goals of LAMA. *Winner*: LAMA National Planning Committee.

LAMA/YBP Student Writing and Development Award. *Winner*: Not awarded in 2001.

Library and Information Technology Association (LITA)

Hugh C. Atkinson Memorial Award. *See under* American Library Association.

LITA/Christian Larew Memorial Scholarship ($3,000). To encourage the entry of qualified persons into the library and information technology field. *Donor*: Electronic Business and Information Services (EBIS). *Winner*: Ohla Olekandrivna Buchel.

LITA/Endeavor Student Writing Award ($1,000). For the best unpublished manu-

script on a topic in the area of libraries and information technology written by a student or students enrolled in an ALA-accredited library and information studies graduate program. *Winner*: Peter Murray.

LITA/Gaylord Award for Achievement in Library and Information Technology ($1,000). *Donor*: Gaylord Bros., Inc. *Winner*: Louise Addis.

LITA/GEAC Scholarship in Library and Information Technology ($2,500). For work toward an MLS in an ALA-accredited program with emphasis on library automation. *Donor*: GEAC, Inc. *Winner*: Farah Gheriss.

LITA/Library Hi Tech Award ($1,000). To an individual or institution for a work that shows outstanding communication for continuing education in library and information technology. *Donor*: MCB University Press. *Winner*: Digital Imaging and Preservation Research Unit, Cornell University Library.

LITA/LSSI Minority Scholarship in Library and Information Science ($2,500). To encourage a qualified member of a principal minority group to work toward an MLS degree in an ALA-accredited program with emphasis on library automation. *Donor*: Library Systems & Services, Inc. *Winner*: Marla Peppers.

LITA/OCLC Frederick G. Kilgour Award for Research in Library and Information Technology ($2,000 and expense-paid attendance at ALA Annual Conference). To bring attention to research relevant to the development of information technologies. *Winner*: Marcia Bates.

LITA/OCLC Minority Scholarship in Library and Information Technology ($3,000). To encourage a qualified member of a principal minority group to work toward an MLS degree in an ALA-accredited program with emphasis on library automation. *Donor*: OCLC. *Winner*: Marisa Duarte.

Library History Round Table (LHRT)

Phyllis Dain Library History Dissertation Award ($500). To the author of a dissertation treating the history of books, libraries, librarianship, or information science. *Winner*: Mildred L. Jackson for *Do What You*

Can: Creating an Institution, Ladies' Library Associations in Michigan, 1850–1900.
Donald G. Davis Article Award (certificate). For the best article written in English in the field of U.S. and Canadian library history. Winner: Not awarded in 2001.
Justin Winsor Prize Essay ($500). To an author of an outstanding essay embodying original historical research on a significant subject of library history. Winner: Not awarded in 2001.

Library Research Round Table (LRRT)

Jesse H. Shera Award for Distinguished Published Research ($500). For a research article on library and information studies published in English during the calendar year. Winner: Not awarded in 2001.
Jesse H. Shera Award for Excellence in Doctoral Research ($500). For completed research on an unpublished paper of 10,000 words or less on library and information studies. Winner: Not awarded in 2001.

Map and Geography Round Table (MAGERT)

MAGERT Honors Award (citation and cash award). To recognize outstanding contributions by a MAGERT personal member to map librarianship, MAGERT, and/or a specific MAGERT project. Winner: Christopher Baruth.

New Members Round Table (NMRT)

NMRT/EBSCO Scholarship ($1,000). To a U.S. or Canadian citizen to begin an MLS degree in an ALA-accredited program. Candidates must be members of NMRT. Donor: EBSCO Subscription Services. Winner: Barbara Davidson.
NMRT/3M Professional Development Grant. To NMRT members to encourage professional development and participation in national ALA and NMRT activities. Donor: 3M. Winners: Deborah K. Balsamo, Sally Leahey McAuthur, MaryAnn Lis-Simmons.
Shirley Olofson Memorial Award ($500): To an individual to help defray costs of attending the ALA Annual Conference. Winner: Diane Ross.

Public Library Association (PLA)

Advancement of Literacy Award (plaque). To a publisher, bookseller, hardware and/or software dealer, foundation, or similar group that has made a significant contribution to the advancement of adult literacy. Donor: Library Journal. Winner: Providence (Rhode Island) Journal.
Baker & Taylor Entertainment Audio Music/Video Product Grant ($2,500 worth of audio music or video products). To help a public library to build or expand a collection of either or both formats. Donor: Baker & Taylor Entertainment. Winner: Rio (Wisconsin) Community Library.
Demco Creative Merchandising Grant ($1,000). To a public library proposing a project for the creative display and merchandising of materials either in the library or in the community. Donor: Demco, Inc. Winner: Val Verde County Library, Del Rio, Texas.
Excellence in Small and/or Rural Public Service Award ($1,000). Honors a library serving a population of 10,000 or less that demonstrates excellence of service to its community as exemplified by an overall service program or a special program of significant accomplishment. Donor: EBSCO Subscription Services. Winner: Alpine (Arizona) Public Library.
Highsmith Library Innovation Award ($2,000). Recognizes a public library's innovative achievement in planning and implementation of a creative program or service using technology. Winner: Bartlesville (Oklahoma) Public Library.
Highsmith Library Literature Award ($500). For an outstanding contribution to library literature issued during the three years preceding the presentation. Winner: Michael Gorman for Our Enduring Values: Librarianship in the 21st Century (ALA Editions).
Allie Beth Martin Award ($3,000). Honors a librarian who, in a public library setting, has demonstrated extraordinary range and depth of knowledge about books or other library materials and has distinguished ability to share that knowledge. Donor: Baker & Taylor Books. Winner: Nancy Pearl.

New Leaders Travel Grant (up to $1,500). To enhance the professional development and improve the expertise of public librarians by making their attendance at major professional development activities possible. *Donor*: GEAC, Inc. *Winner*: Kevin Barron.

NTC Career Materials Resource Grant ($500 and $2,000 worth of materials from NTC Publishing Group). To a library proposing a project for the development of a career resources collection and program for a target audience either in the library or in the community. *Donor*: NTC Publishing Group. *Winner*: Johnson County Public Library, Overland Park, Kansas.

Charlie Robinson Award ($1,000). Honors a public library director who, over a period of seven years, has been a risk-taker, an innovator, and/or a change agent in a public library. *Donor*: Baker & Taylor Books. *Winner*: Glen Holt.

Leonard Wertheimer Award ($1,000). To a person, group, or organization for work that enhances and promotes multilingual public library service. *Donor*: NTC Publishing Group. *Winner*: Montgomery County Public Libraries, Rockville, Maryland.

Publishing Committee

Carnegie Reading List Awards (amount varies). To ALA units for preparation and publication of reading lists, indexes, and other bibliographical and library aids useful in U.S. circulating libraries. *Donor*: Andrew Carnegie Fund. *Winners*: Not awarded in 2001.

Carnegie-Whitney Awards (up to $5,000). For the publication of bibliographic aids for research. *Donor*: James Lyman Whitney and Andrew Carnegie Funds. *Winners*: Not awarded in 2001.

Reference and User Services Association (RUSA)

Virginia Boucher-OCLC Distinguished ILL Librarian Award ($2,000). To a librarian for outstanding professional achievement, leadership, and contributions to interlibrary loan and document delivery. *Winner*: Lynn Wiley.

BRASS Thomson Financial Student Travel Award ($1,000). For a student enrolled in an ALA accredited master's degree program to attend the ALA Annual Conference. *Donor*: Thomson Learning/Gale Group. *Winner*: Susan Alice Shultz.

Dartmouth Medal. For creating current reference works of outstanding quality and significance. *Donor*: Dartmouth College, Hanover, New Hampshire. *Winner:* Women in World History (Gale Group).

Denali Press Award ($500). For creating reference works of outstanding quality and significance that provide information specifically about ethnic and minority groups in the United States. *Donor*: Denali Press. *Winner*: Macmillan Encyclopedia of Native American Tribes (Gale Group).

Dun & Bradstreet Public Librarian Support Award ($1,000). To support the attendance at the ALA Annual Conference of a public librarian who has performed outstanding business reference service and who requires financial assistance. *Winner*: Lisa Holbrook.

Dun & Bradstreet Award for Outstanding Service to Minority Business Communities ($2,000). *Winner*: June Evans.

Facts on File Grant ($2,000). To a library for imaginative programming that would make current affairs more meaningful to an adult audience. *Donor*: Facts on File, Inc. *Winner*: Howard County (Maryland) Library.

Gale Group Award for Excellence in Business Librarianship (BRASS) ($3,000). To an individual for distinguished activities in the field of business librarianship. *Donor*: Gale Group. *Winner*: Karen Chapman.

Gale Group Award for Excellence in Reference and Adult Services. To a library or library system for developing an imaginative and unique library resource to meet patrons' reference needs ($3,000). *Donor*: Gale Group. *Winner*: University Library, University of Nebraska at Omaha.

Genealogical Publishing Company/History Section Award ($1,500). To encourage and commend professional achievement in historical reference and research librarianship. *Donor*: The Genealogical Publishing Company. *Winner*: Margaret Ann Reinert.

Margaret E. Monroe Library Adult Services Award (citation). To a librarian for impact on library service to adults. *Winner*: Not awarded in 2001.

Bessie Boehm Moore/Thorndike Press Award ($1,000). To a library organization that has developed an outstanding and creative program for library service to the aging. *Winner*: Pasadena (Texas) Public Library.

Isadore Gilbert Mudge–R. R. Bowker Award ($5,000). For distinguished contributions to reference librarianship. *Winner*: Carol Leita.

Reference Service Press Award ($2,500). To the author or authors of the most outstanding article published in *RUSQ* during the preceding two volume years. *Donor*: Reference Service Press, Inc. *Winners*: Donald G. Frank, Katharine L. Calhoun, W. Bruce Henson, M. Leslie Madden. and Gregory K. Raschke for "The Changing Nature of Reference and Information Services: Predictions and Realities" in *RUSQ* 39:151–57, Winter 1999.

John Sessions Memorial Award (plaque). To a library or library system in recognition of work with the labor community. *Donor*: AFL/CIO. *Winner*: Duane G. Meyer Library, Southwest Missouri State University.

Louis Shores–Oryx Press Award ($3,000). To an individual, team, or organization to recognize excellence in reviewing of books and other materials for libraries. *Donor*: Oryx Press. *Winner*: Mary Ellen Quinn.

Social Responsibilities Round Table (SRRT)

Jackie Eubanks Memorial Award ($500). To honor outstanding achievement in promoting the acquisition and use of alternative media in libraries. *Donor*: AIP Task Force. *Winners*: Franklin and Penelope Rosemount, and Carlos Cortez/Kerr Publishing.

Coretta Scott King Awards. See *Literary Prizes, 2001* by Gary Ink.

Coretta Scott King/John Steptoe Award for New Talent (formerly the Genesis Award) ($3,000). For an outstanding book designed to bring visibility to a black writer or artist at the beginning of his or her career. *Winner*: Not awarded in 2001.

Young Adult Library Services Association (YALSA)

Alex Awards. *Winners*: Darin Strauss for *Chang and Eng* (Dutton), Larry Colton for *Counting Coup* (Warner), Juliet Marillier for *Daughter of the Forest* (Tor), Alan Watt for *Diamond Dogs* (Little, Brown), James Bradley and Ron Powers for *Flags of Our Fathers* (Bantam), Tracy Chevalier for *The Girl with a Pearl Earring* (Plume), Nathaniel Philbrick for *In the Heart of the Sea: The Tragedy of the Whaleship Essex* (Viking), Ben Sherwood for *The Man Who Ate the 747* (Bantam), Gillian Bradshaw for *The Sand Reckoner* (Tor/Forge), and June Jordan for *Soldier: A Poet's Childhood* (Basic Books).

Baker & Taylor Conference Grants ($1,000). To young adult librarians in public or school libraries to attend an ALA Annual Conference for the first time. Candidates must be members of YALSA and have one to ten years of library experience. *Donor*: Baker & Taylor Books. *Winners*: Not awarded in 2001.

Book Wholesalers, Inc./YALSA Collection Development Grant ($1,000). To YALSA members who represent a public library and work directly with young adults, for collection development materials for young adults. *Winners*: Kevin Scanlon and Rachel E. Kovacs.

Margaret A. Edwards Award ($2,000). To an author whose book or books have provided young adults with a window through which they can view their world and which will help them to grow and to understand themselves and their role in society. *Donor: School Library Journal. Winner*: Robert Lipstyle.

Great Book Giveaway (books, videos, CDs and audio cassettes valued at a total of $25,000). *Winner*: Hialeah (Florida) Public Libraries.

Frances Henne/YALSA/VOYA Research Grant ($500 minimum). To provide seed money to an individual, institution, or group for a project to encourage research on library service to young adults. *Donor: Voice of Youth Advocates. Winner*: Patrick Jones.

Michael L. Printz Award. See *Literary Prizes, 2001* by Gary Ink.

YALSA/Sagebrush Award ($1,000). For an exemplary young adult reading or literature program. *Donor*: Sagebrush Corporation. *Winner*: Phyllis Saunders.

American Society for Information Science and Technology (ASIS&T)

ASIS&T Award of Merit. For an outstanding contribution to the field of information science. *Winner*: Patrick G. Wilson.

ASIS&T Best Information Science Book. *Winner*: Christine L. Borgman.

ASIS&T/ISI Outstanding Information Science Teacher Award ($500). *Winner*: Barbara Kwasnik.

ASIS&T Research Award. For a systematic program of research in a single area at a level beyond the single study, recognizing contributions in the field of information science. *Winner*: Paul Kantor.

ASIS&T Special Award. To recognize long-term contributions to the advancement of information science and technology and enhancement of public access to information and discovery of mechanisms for improved transfer and utilization of knowledge. *Winner*: Not awarded in 2001.

ASIS&T/UMI Doctoral Dissertation Award. *Winner*: Allison Powell.

James Cretsos Leadership Award. *Winner*: Allison Kopcznski.

ISI Citation Analysis Research Grant. *Winners*: John Budd, MaryEllen Sievert, Gabriel M. Peterson, Ku Chuin Su.

ISI Doctoral Dissertation Proposal Scholarship ($1,500). *Winner*: Alesia A. Zuccala.

Pratt Severn Best Student Research Paper. *Winner*: Brian Hilligoss.

Watson Davis Award. *Julie Hurd.*

Art Libraries Society of North America (ARLIS/NA)

John Benjamins Award. To recognize research and publication in the study and analysis of periodicals in the fields of the fine arts, literature, and cross-disciplinary studies. *Winner*: Not awarded in 2001.

Andrew Cahan Photography Award ($750). To encourage participation of art information professionals in the field of photography through reference, research, or bibliographic work. *Winner*: Rebecca Simmons.

Distinguished Service Award. Not awarded in 2001.

Melva J. Dwyer Award. To the creators of exceptional reference or research tools relating to Canadian art and architecture. *Winner*: Kathy Zimon, for *Alberta Society of Artists: The First Seventy Years* (University of Calgary Press, 2000).

Getty Trust Publications/Avery Index Attendance Award ($500). To encourage conference attendance by ARLIS/NA members. *Winner*: Not awarded in 2001.

Howard and Beverly Joy Karno Award ($1,000). To provide financial assistance to a professional art librarian in Latin America through interaction with ARLIS/NA members and conference participation. *Cosponsor*: Howard Karno Books. *Winner*: Beatriz MacGregor.

David Mirvish Books/Books on Art Travel Award ($500 Canadian). To encourage art librarianship in Canada. *Winner*: Irene Puchalski.

Gerd Muehsam Award. To one or more graduate students in library science programs to recognize excellence in a graduate paper or project. *Winner*: Not awarded in 2001.

Puvill Libros Award ($1,000). To encourage professional development of European art librarians through interaction with ARLIS/NA colleagues and conference participation. *Winner*: Anna Dahl.

Research Libraries Group Asia/Oceania Award ($1,000). To encourage professional development of art information professionals who reside in Asia/Oceania through interaction with ARLIS/NA colleagues and conference participation. *Winner*: Catherine Hammond.

Research Libraries Group Travel Award ($1,000). To promote participation in ARLIS/NA by supporting conference travel for an individual who has not attended an ARLIS/NA Annual Conference. *Winner*: Catherine Cooney.

Thames and Hudson Conference Attendance Award ($500). *Winner*: Sarah McClesky.

H. W. Wilson Foundation Research Award. To support research activities by ARLIS/NA members in the fields of librarianship, visual resources curatorship, and the arts. *Winners*: Jonathan Franklin for *The Art Auction Catalogue: A Bibliographical Study*, Lamia Doumato for *Illuminated Manuscripts of the Crusader Era: A Bibliography*.

George Wittenborn Memorial Book Award. For outstanding publications in the visual arts and architecture. *Winners: The Complete Jacob Lawrence* by Peter T. Nesbett and Michelle DuBois (University of Washington Press, 2000); *The Hours of Henry VIII: A Renaissance Masterpiece* by Jean Poyet, Roger S. Wieck, William M. Voelkle, and K. Michelle Hearne (George Braziller Publisher in association with the Pierpont Morgan Library, 2000); *Women Designers in the USA 1900–2000: Diversity and Difference*, Pat Kirkham, editor (Yale University Press, 2000).

Worldwide Books Publications Award. *Winners*: Paula A. Baxter for *Encyclopedia of Native American Jewelry: A Guide to History, People, and Terms*, Peter Erickson for *Early Modern Visual Culture: Representation, Race, and Empire in Renaissance England*, Kathy Zimon for *Alberta Society of Artists: The First Seventy Years*.

Asian/Pacific American Librarians Association (APALA)

Asian/Pacific American Librarians scholarships ($300 and $500). To enable LIS students to attend the organization's national conference. *Winners*: ($500) M. Jean Williams Adams, Rita Cacas, Antony Cherian, Bei-Hwa Ma, Abike Eyo, Teresa Y. H. Lee, Lee McQueen, Phuoc Nguyen, Joyce Nishioka, Mary Jane Pettman, Mary Y. F. Tao, S. Raymond Wang; ($300) Corey Schultz, Ye Dianna Xu, Mimi Lee, Sue Ann Yanagida, Hardeep Kaur Sareen, Becky Imamoto, Weimin Zhang, Delphine Allen, Beatrice Baptista, Xiping Liu, T. J. Chang, Tracey Y. Y. Tseung, Eleanor Thoe Lis-

ney, Yi Hong, Jeong Him, Haiying Qian, Xiaojun Yuan, Rose Roberto, Pauline Swartz, Yasmin Jamal.

Association for Library and Information Science Education (ALISE)

ALISE Doctoral Student Dissertation Awards ($400). To promote the exchange of research ideas between doctoral students and established researchers. *Winner*: Patricia Coit Murphy for "What a Book Can Do: Silent Spring and Media-Borne Public Debate."

ALISE Methodology Paper Competition. To stimulate the communication of research methodology. *Winners*: Barbara M. Wildemuth and Diane H. Sonnenwald for "Investigating Information-Seeking Behavior Using the Concept of Information Horizons."

ALISE Research Paper Competition. For a research paper concerning any aspect of librarianship or information studies by a member of ALISE. *Winners*: George D'Elia, Corinne Jorgensen, Joseph Woelfel, and Eleanor Jo Rodger for "The Impacts of the Internet on Public Library Use: An Analysis of the Current Consumer Market for Library and Internet Services."

ALISE Research Grant Awards (one or more grants totaling $5,000): *Winners*: Ingrid Hsieh-Yee for "A Delphi Study on Metadata: Curriculum Implications and Research Priorities."

Association of Jewish Libraries (AJL)

AJL Bibliography Book Award. *Winner*: David Assaf for *Bratslav: An Annotated Bibliography* (Merkaz Zalman Shazar, 2000).

AJL Reference Book Award. *Winner*: Shimeon Brisman for *A History and Guide to Judaica Dictionaries and Concordances* (KTAV, 2000).

Special Body of Work Citation. *Winner*: Not awarded in 2001.

Sydney Taylor Children's Book Award. *Winner*: Elsa Okon Rael for *Rivka's First Thanksgiving* (illustrated by Maryann Kovalski) (Margaret K. McElderry/Simon & Schuster).

Sydney Taylor Manuscript Award. *Winner*: Not awarded in 2001.

Sydney Taylor Older Children's Book Award. *Winner*: Catherine Reef for *Sigmund Freud: Pioneer of the Mind* (Clarion).

Beta Phi Mu

Beta Phi Mu Award. *See under* American Library Association.

Beta Phi Mu Doctoral Dissertation Scholarship ($1,500). *Winner*: Laura Slaughter.

Eugene Garfield Doctoral Dissertation Fellowships ($3,000). *Winners*: Eun G. Park, Laura Slaughter, Tony Tse, Kiduk Yang.

Harold Lancour Scholarship for Foreign Study ($1,000). For graduate study in a foreign country related to the applicant's work or schooling. *Winner*: Zewdie Gudeta.

Sarah Rebecca Reed Scholarship ($1,500). For study at an ALA-accredited library school. *Winner*: Christine Thomas.

Frank B. Sessa Scholarship for Continuing Professional Education ($750). For continuing education for a Beta Phi Mu member. *Winner*: Not awarded in 2001.

E. Blanche Woolls Scholarship ($1,000). For a beginning student in school library media services. *Winner*: Vicki L. Ellers.

Bibliographical Society of America (BSA)

BSA Fellowships ($1,000–$2,000). For scholars involved in bibliographical inquiry and research in the history of the book trades and in publishing history. *Winners*: Joseph Black, Patrick Cheney, Cyndia Susan Clegg, Robert L. Dawson, Jared N. Day, Melissa A. Dinverno, Kelly Denise Fuller, John J. McCusker, Lisa Pon, Phillip H. Stump, Pierre A. Walker.

Canadian Library Association (CLA)

Olga B. Bishop Award. *Winner*: Not awarded in 2001.

CLA Award for the Advancement of Intellectual Freedom in Canada. *Winner*: Not awarded in 2001.

CLA Elizabeth Dafoe Scholarship ($3,000). *Winner*: Kim Feltham.

CLA Echo Award Program. *Winners:* Sarah Bonato, Gwen Schmidt.

CLA/Information Today Award for Innovative Technology. *Donor*: Information Today, Inc. *Winner*: Waterloo (Ontario) Regional Library.

CLA Outstanding Service to Librarianship Award. *Donor*: R. R. Bowker. *Winner*: Ernie Ingles.

CLA Research and Development Grant ($1,000). *Winners*: Ross Gordon, and Ray Doiron and Marlene Asselin.

CLA/RoweCom Canada Faxon Marketing Award. *Winner*: Windsor (Ontario) Public Library.

CLA Student Article Award. *Winner*: Wanda Haayen.

CLA/3M Award for Achievement in Technical Services. *Winner*: Simon Fraser University Library, Burnaby, British Columbia.

OCLC/CLA Award for Promoting Library and Information Technologies. *Winner*: Not awarded in 2001.

William C. Watkinson Award. *Winners*: Jeffrey Simpson, Doug Hull.

H. W. Wilson Scholarship ($2,000). *Winner*: Kirsten Wurmann.

World Book Graduate Scholarship in Library Science ($2,500). *Winner*: Omolola Salami.

Canadian Association of College and University Libraries (CACUL)

CACUL Award for Outstanding Academic Librarian. *Winner*: Alexander Slade.

CACUL/CTCL/Micromedia Award of Merit. *Winner*: Not awarded in 2001.

CACUL Innovation Achievement Award ($1,500). *Winner*: University of Winnipeg.

Canadian Association of Public Libraries (CAPL)

CAPL/Brodart Outstanding Public Library Service Award. *Winner*: Ken Roberts.

Canadian Association of Special Libraries and Information Services (CASLIS)

CASLIS Award for Special Librarianship in Canada. *Winner*: Pat Routledge.

Canadian Library Trustees Association (CLTA)

CLTA/Stan Heath Achievement in Literacy Award. For an innovative literacy program by a public library board. *Donor*: ABC Canada. *Winner*: Pictou-Antigonish Regional Library Award, New Glasgow, Nova Scotia.

CLTA Merit Award for Distinguished Service as a Public Library Trustee. For outstanding leadership in the advancement of public library trusteeship and public library service in Canada. *Winner*: Mary Totman.

Canadian School Library Association (CSLA)

National Book Service Teacher-Librarian of the Year Award. *Winner*: Kay Treadgold.

Margaret B. Scott Award of Merit. For the development of school libraries in Canada. *Winner*: Not awarded in 2001.

Chinese-American Librarians Association (CALA)

CALA Distinguished Service Award. To a librarian who has been a mentor, role model, and leader in the fields of library and information science. *Winner*: Eugene Wu.

CALA President's Recognition Award. *Winner*: Judy Yung.

Sheila Suen Lai Scholarship ($500). To a student of Chinese nationality or descent pursuing full-time graduate studies for a master's degree or Ph.D. degree in an ALA-accredited library school. *Winner*: Amy J. Chow.

C. C. Seetoo/CALA Conference Travel Scholarship ($500). For a student to attend the ALA Annual Conference and CALA program. *Winner*: S. Raymond Wang.

Church and Synagogue Library Association (CSLA)

CSLA Award for Outstanding Congregational Librarian. For distinguished service to the congregation and/or community through devotion to the congregational library. *Winner*: Harriett Dallas.

CSLA Award for Outstanding Congregational Library. For responding in creative and innovative ways to the library's mission of reaching and serving the congregation and/or the wider community. *Winner*: Rev. Arthur H. Pace Library, Washington, D.C., Virginia Moore, Librarian.

CSLA Award for Outstanding Contribution to Congregational Libraries. For providing inspiration, guidance, leadership, or resources to enrich the field of church or synagogue librarianship. *Winner*: Betty Stone.

Muriel Fuller Scholarship Award. *Winner*: Not awarded in 2001.

Helen Keating Ott Award for Outstanding Contribution to Congregational Libraries. *Winner*: Holly Bea.

Pat Tabler Memorial Scholarship Award. *Winner*: Not awarded in 2001.

Council on Library and Information Resources

A. R. Zipf Fellowship in Information Management ($5,000). Awarded annually to a student enrolled in graduate school who shows exceptional promise for leadership and technical achievement. *Winner*: Terence Kelly.

Gale Group

ALTA/Gale Outstanding Trustee Conference Grant Award. *See under* American Library Association, Association for Library Trustees and Advocates.

Gale Group Award for Excellence in Business Librarianship; and Gale Group Award for Excellence in Reference and Adult Services. *See under* American Library Association, Reference and User Services Association.

Gale Group Financial Development Award. *See under* American Library Association.

International Federation of Library Associations and Institutions (IFLA)

Hans-Peter Geh Grant. To enable a librarian from the former Soviet Union to attend a conference in Germany or elsewhere. *Winner*: Andrei Massevitch.

Medical Library Association (MLA)

Estelle Brodman Award for the Academic Medical Librarian of the Year. To honor significant achievement, potential for leadership, and continuing excellence at mid-career in the area of academic health sciences librarianship. *Winner*: T. Scott Plutchak.

Lois Ann Colaianni Award for Excellence and Achievement in Hospital Librarianship. To a member of MLA who has made significant contributions to the profession in the area of overall distinction or leadership in hospital librarianship. *Winner*: Carole M. Gilbert.

Cunningham Memorial International Fellowship ($6,000). A six-month grant and travel expenses in the United States and Canada for a foreign librarian. *Winner*: Kgaladi Kekana.

Louise Darling Medal. For distinguished achievement in collection development in the health sciences. *Winner*: Not awarded in 2001.

Janet Doe Lectureship. *Winner*: Betsy L. Humphreys.

EBSCO/MLA Annual Meeting Grant ($1,000). *Winners*: Mary Shultz, Everly Brown.

Ida and George Eliot Prize. For an essay published in any journal in the preceding calendar year that has been judged most effective in furthering medical librarianship. *Donor*: Login Brothers Books. *Winner*: Michael R. Kronenfeld.

Murray Gottlieb Prize. For the best unpublished essay submitted by a medical librarian on the history of some aspect of health sciences or a detailed description of a library exhibit. *Donor*: Ralph and Jo Grimes. *Winner*: Not awarded in 2001.

Hospital Libraries Section/MLA Professional Development Grants. *Winners*: Misa F. Mi, Tamara Rader.

ISI/MLA Doctoral Fellowship ($2,000). To encourage superior students to conduct doctoral work in an area of health sciences librarianship or information sciences. *Winner*: Not awarded in 2001.

Joseph Leiter NLM/MLA Lectureship. *Winner*: Anthony J. Shuker.

Lucretia W. McClure Excellence in Education Award. To an outstanding eduator in the field of health sciences librarianship and informatics. *Winner*: Julie J. McGowan.

John P. McGovern Award Lectureship. *Winner*: Dixie B. Baker.

MLA Award for Distinguished Public Service. *Winner*: Not awarded in 2001.

MLA Career Development Grant ($1,500). *Winner*: Susan London.

MLA Scholarship (up to $5,000). For graduate study in medical librarianship at an ALA-accredited library school. *Winner*: Beverlee Warren.

MLA Scholarship for Minority Students (up to $5,000). *Winner*: Felicia Smith.

Marcia C. Noyes Award. For an outstanding contribution to medical librarianship. The award is the highest professional distinction of MLA. *Winner*: Alison Bunting.

Rittenhouse Award. For the best unpublished paper on medical librarianship submitted by a student enrolled in, or having been enrolled in, a course for credit in an ALA-accredited library school or a trainee in an internship program in medical librarianship. *Donor*: Rittenhouse Medical Bookstore. *Winner*: Marlo Maldonado Young.

Frank Bradway Rogers Information Advancement Award ($500). For an outstanding contribution to knowledge of health science information delivery. *Donor*: Institute for Scientific Information (ISI). *Winner*: Kathryn E. Kerdolff.

K. G. Saur (Munich, Germany)

K. G. Saur Award for Best *College and Research Libraries* Article. *See under* American Library Association, Association of College and Research Libraries.

Society of American Archivists (SAA)

C. F. W. Coker Prize for Finding Aids. *Winners*: Waverly Lowell and Kelcy Shepherd for *Standard Series of Architecture and Landscape Design Records: A Tool for Arrangement and Descriptions of Archival Collections.*

Colonial Dames Scholarship. *Winners*: Laura Polo, John Martinez.

Council Exemplary Service Award. *Winner*: Carroll Dendler.

Distinguished Service Award. Recognizes outstanding service and exemplary contribution to the profession. *Winner*: Ohio Historical Society, Archives/Library Division.

Fellows Posner Prize. For an outstanding essay dealing with a facet of archival administration, history, theory, or methodology, published in the latest volume of the *American Archivist*. *Winner*: Philip C. Bantin for "The Indiana University Electronic Records Project Revisited."

Philip M. Hamer–Elizabeth Hamer Kegan Award. For individuals and/or institutions that have increased public awareness of a specific body of documents. *Winner*: Shelly Henley Kelly for *Through a Night of Horrors: Voices from the 1900 Galveston Storm.*

Oliver Wendell Holmes Award. To enable overseas archivists already in the United States or Canada for training to attend the SAA annual meeting. *Winner*: Eun G. Park.

J. Franklin Jameson Award. For an institution not directly involved in archival work that promotes greater public awareness, appreciation, and support of archival activities and programs. *Winner*: Not awarded in 2001.

Sister M. Claude Lane Award. For a significant contribution to the field of religious archives. *Winner*: Kinga Perzynska.

Waldo Gifford Leland Prize. For writing of superior excellence and usefulness in the field of archival history, theory, or practice. *Winners*: Anne R. Kenney and Oya Y. Rieger for *Moving Theory into Practice: Digital Imaging for Libraries and Archives* (Research Libraries Group, 2000).

Minority Student Award. Encourages minority students to consider careers in the archival profession and promotes minority participation in the Society of American Archivists with complimentary registration to the annual meeting. *Winner*: Rose Roberto.

Theodore Calvin Pease Award. For the best student paper. *Winner*: James M. Roth for "Serving Up EAD: An Exploratory Study on the Deployment and Utilization of Encoded Archival Description Finding Aids."

Preservation Publication Award. Recognizes an outstanding work published in North America that advances the theory or the practice of preservation in archival institutions. *Winner*: Gregory S. Hunter for *Preserving Digital Information: A How-To-Do-It Manual* (Neal-Schuman, 2000).

SAA Fellows. Highest individual distinction awarded to a limited number of members for their outstanding contribution to the archival profession. *Honored*: Valerie Gerrard Browne, Peter Hirtle, Randall Jimerson, Deborah Skaggs, Peter Wosh.

Special Libraries Association (SLA)

Mary Adeline Connor Professional Development Scholarship ($6,000). *Winner*: Laura Jean Smart.

John Cotton Dana Award. For exceptional support and encouragement of special librarianship. *Winner*: David R. Bender (former SLA Executive Director).

Dow Jones 21st Century Competencies Award. *Winner*: Not awarded in 2001.

Factiva Leadership Award. To an SLA member who exemplifies leadership as a special librarian through excellence in personal and professional competencies. *Winner*: Carol L. Ginsburg.

Steven I. Goldspiel Research Grant. *Sponsor*: Disclosure, Inc. *Winner*: Mark Rorvig for "Exploiting Image Content Features for Image Index Term Assignment."

Hall of Fame Award. To a member or members of the association at or near the end of an active professional career for an extended and sustained period of distinguished service to the association. *Winners*: Judith R. Bernstein, Roger K. Haley, Fred W. Roper.

Honorary Membership. *Winner*: Anthony Oettinger.

Innovations in Technology Award ($1,000). To a member of the association for innovative use and application of technology in a special library setting. *Winner*: Susan Fifer Canby.

International Special Librarians Day (ISLD) Award. *Winner*: Nancy Stewart.

SLA Affirmative Action Scholarship ($6,000). *Winner*: Jennifer Ann Alcoset.

SLA Diversity Leadership Development Award. *Winners*: Jacquelyn P. Cenacveira, Irene Cordova, Sandra A. Marshall, Jeanette M. Regan.

SLA Fellows. *Honored*: Cynthia V. Hill, Sharyn J. Ladner, Joanne Gard Marshall, Nigel Oxbrow, Ethel M. Salonen.

SLA President's Award. *Winner*: Susan O'Neill Johnson.

SLA Professional Award. *Winner*: Eric A. Brewer.

SLA Public Relations Media Award. *Winner*: Jennifer Arend.

SLA Student Scholarships ($6,000). For students with financial need who show potential for special librarianship. *Winners*: Merrill D. Chertok, David Hurley, Joe Purtell.

Rose L. Vormelker Award. *Winner*: Judith J. Field.

H. W. Wilson Company Award. For the most outstanding article in the past year's *Information Outlook*. *Donor*: H. W. Wilson Company. *Winner*: Helene Kassler for "Competitive Intelligence on the Internet—Going for the Gold" (February 2000).

Part 4
Research and Statistics

Library Research and Statistics

Research on Libraries and Librarianship in 2001

Mary Jo Lynch

Director, Office for Research and Statistics, American Library Association

The year 2001 will be remembered by all Americans for the tragic events of September 11. For leaders in the research community, the terrorist attacks and their aftermath raised concerns about the long-awaited Library Research Seminar II scheduled for November 2–3 at the University of Maryland. Despite those concerns, the seminar was a great success. A total of 107 people attended some or all of the seminar, "Partners and Connections: Research Applied to Practice."

The group was an interesting mix of practitioners, experienced academic researchers, doctoral students, and government officials. The program consisted of invited speakers on three topics and 25 juried papers chosen by the seminar planning committee from a pool of 50 responses to a call for papers. In addition, there were four panels on various topics and a grant application workshop conducted by the Institute of Museum and Library Services (IMLS). The invited speakers and their topics were:

- Yvonna Lincoln (Texas A&M University), "Insights on Library Services and Users From Qualitative Research"
- Phyllis Dain and Kathleen Molz (Columbia University, retired), "Tracking a Moving Target: Research on Public Libraries"
- Ben Schneiderman (University of Maryland, College Park), "Visualization for Digital Libraries"

Juried papers varied widely. The complete program is available at the LRS II Web site (http://www.dpo.uab.edu/~folive/LRSII/index.htm). Proceedings will not be published, but authors have been encouraged to publish and the LRS II Web site will list publications as they become available.

Academic Libraries

Most of the research activity in 2001 took place in the academic library sector. Two major Association of Research Libraries (ARL) projects, which began in 2001 and were described in the 2001 edition of the *Bowker Annual,* moved into new territory. In spring 2001 the Lib Qual+ project, a 56-item protocol developed to measure the quality of library services, was completed by 20,416 participants at 43 campuses, 35 of them members of ARL. Library users in 170 institutions will participate in Phase Two (2001–2002). For additional information, go to http://www.arl.org/libqual.

In October 2001 the project team at Florida State University's Information Use Management and Policy Institute compiled "Measures and Statistics for Research Library Networked Services: Procedures and Issues: ARL E-Metrics Phase II Report" (http://www.arl.org/stats/newmeas/emetrics/index.html). Based on substantial field testing, the team recommended 16 statistics (items to count) and three performance measures (ratios using the statistics and others commonly collected). The recommended network statistics and performance measures, either independently or in some combination, can assist research libraries in describing a number of aspects of their networked resources and service. There is a section in the report that provides libraries with some guidance regarding the use to which the network statistics and measures can be put. At this writing, it is not yet known how ARL will use these measures in its regular data collection efforts.

Several major new projects were started in 2001. The Andrew W. Mellon Foundation awarded funds to the Digital Library Federation for a study of how faculty and students at universities and colleges use the academic library and how they perceive the library within the larger scholarly information environment. The study, "Dimensions and Use of the Scholarly Information Environment," was to be conducted by Outsell, Inc., a research and advisory firm that focuses on the information-content industry. The findings will help libraries and universities plan information services that match the current and emerging needs of their faculty and students. A keener sense of user needs will also help publishers and content providers that serve the education market to create better information products. The study was scheduled to be completed in April 2002.

The Andrew W. Mellon Foundation also awarded $755,000 to the Penn State University Libraries to support an extensive study of digital image delivery. Project partners include the School of Information Sciences and Technology (IST), Center for Education Technology Services, and the Center for Quality and Planning, Library Computing Services. The Visual Image User Study will examine the use of digital pictures at Penn State in the disciplines of the arts, environmental studies, and the humanities. The project includes the development and testing of a prototype digital library system for image delivery. Phase one of the project will employ a variety of needs assessment methods and information retrieval studies to analyze the current and future needs of teachers, learners, and archival managers. The second phase, based on the results of phase one, will create the design and content of the prototype system. Activities were to begin in May 2001 and continue for 26 months. A summary of the project is found at http://www. libraries.psu.edu/crsweb/vius.

Another Mellon Foundation grant ($150,000 for a one-year planning effort) will go to Cornell University Libraries to explore the idea of creating permanent digital archives for scholarly journals, with the goal of setting up a pilot archive of agricultural journals. While not research in the sense of gathering and analyzing data, "Project Harvest" will answer a number of critical questions, such as

- Will the collective be a "living archive" that scholars can access or a "dark archive" that simply preserves journals against the possibility that they are needed in the future?

- Will the scholarly community feel sure the archive will be available in the future?
- Should there be a procedure for "certification" of an archive to assure users it is reliable?
- Should everything be converted to one standard format, or should the formats used by individual publishers be retained?
- How do librarians ensure that stored material will be readable as technology evolves?
- What assurances are there that digital texts will not be altered?
- Should there be multiple copies in different locations?
- Who will pay for long-term maintenance of the archive?

Project Harvest will create a development team with representatives from a small pilot group of interested publishers. Later, other publishers will be invited to participate. Cornell hopes to secure further funding next year to purchase hardware and create the actual archive.

The National Science Foundation awarded University of Tennessee's Carol Tenopir a $251,961 grant for studying electronic journal use by undergraduates. Her study, "Increasing Effective Student Use of the Scientific Journal Literature," is part of a broad initiative by the National Science Foundation. The research is part of a multidisciplinary effort to create a national science, mathematics, engineering, and technology digital library (NSDL), which will make collections of high-quality scientific resources available for teaching at all levels. The new digital library will also develop communication networks to facilitate interactions and collaborations among educators, researchers, and students. Tenopir, the principal investigator, will begin the two-year research project by identifying, implementing, and testing software features that will promote the sustained use of digital libraries by undergraduate student users. Once the software features have been prioritized as to their effectiveness, professors Peiling Wang and Richard Pollard, also of the University of Tennessee's School of Information Sciences, will construct and manage user testing with the support of the Department of Energy's Office of Scientific and Technical Information.

IMLS awarded a grant to the Council on Library and Information Resources (CLIR) for a study of preservation programs in American college and research libraries. The study, "The State of Preservation Programs in American College and Research Libraries," will be undertaken jointly with ARL, the University Libraries Group (ULG), and the Regional Alliance for Preservation. The partners will assess preservation efforts and concerns in the nearly 250 college and research libraries that constitute the membership of ARL and ULG, as well as in leading liberal arts colleges and major non-ARL land-grant institutions. In addition to documenting current conditions and preservation needs, the study will suggest new strategies to equip preservation programs for an increasingly complex technical environment.

Academic libraries will also be a part of the Heritage Health Index, a cooperative effort by IMLS, Heritage Preservation, and the Getty Grant Program. This is a very broad survey of museums, libraries, archives, and historical societies that will provide a general picture of the conditions of cultural collections nationwide. All kinds of libraries are included. For more information, see http://www. heritagepreservation.org/PROGRAMS/HHIhome.htm.

E-books

Academic librarians have been active in action research on e-books. The Vol. 1, No. 1 issue of the journal *portal: Libraries and the Academy,* which started publication in 2001, featured an article on "E-books: Some Concerns and Surprises" by Susan Gibbons, digital initiatives librarian at the University of Rochester. Recently, she was director of the Electronic Book Evaluation Project funded by the Library Service and Technology Act (LSTA) (see http://www.lib.rochester. edu/main/ebooks/studies/grant.htm). The purpose of the grant was to evaluate the uses and feasibility of electronic books in various types of libraries. Two academic libraries, two public libraries, and two school libraries, all in New York State, participated in the first year of the grant. The grant focused on two portable, dedicated e-book readers: NuvoMedia's Rocket eBook and the SoftBook Reader by SoftBook, Inc. Each library received five electronic readers. Every patron and librarian who used an e-book reader was asked to complete an Electronic Book Evaluation Survey form, and focus groups of patrons, librarians, and educators were held to supplement the survey data. The main surprise Gibbons describes in her article is that patrons reacted positively to the e-book technology. Her major concern, however, is that e-book readers are not library-friendly for a number of reasons.

The second year of the grant focused on netLibrary and audio e-books. Data on the latter were not good enough to allow conclusions, but a report on the use of netLibrary e-books at the University of Rochester has been posted on the Web (see http://www.lib.rochester.edu/main/e-books/studies/pdf). The two studies in this report were conducted over the spring 2001 semester. The first study examined use of the overall netLibary e-book collection and compared that to the use of the paper editions of those same titles. The second study focused on the use of e-books for course reserves. In both cases, core statistics were kept and patrons were asked to complete Web-based surveys.

University of Rochester Libraries has shared ownership of a collection of 3,613 netLibrary e-book titles purchased by a consortium. In addition, the Management Library participated in the netLibrary trial, thus providing access to an additional 618 e-book titles within the fields of management, business, and economics, and bringing the total number of e-books available to members of the University of Rochester community to 4,231. For the second study, an additional 17 books were purchased. The conclusion from the first study (general use of e-books) was positive, though it did lead to recommendations for change—five for the library and one for netLibrary. The conclusions of the second study (e-books for reserve) were less positive for reasons involving the cost and functionality of e-books.

As noted above, the audio book component of the LSTA project in New York State was not successful. Another experiment with audio books, funded by a grant from a local foundation and other gifts, was attempted by the Kalamazoo (Michigan) Public Library with more success. The project began in March 2001 with the purchase of 20 Diamond Rio 500 MP3 players and a one-year contract with Auditile.com to purchase titles. At this writing, two quarterly reports had been posted on the library's Web site (http://www.kpl.gov/av/audible.html). Results so far were positive.

Another academic project, "Academic Libraries Take an E-Look at E-Books," was funded by an "Educate and Automate" grant from the Illinois State Library and evaluated by Thomas Peters, director, Center for Library Initiatives, Committee on Institutional Cooperation. Two undergraduate English classes at two Illinois colleges participated. The primary objective was to learn what happens when a college library provides preloaded course-related content on handheld, portable e-book devices directly to the hands of undergraduate students and their professors for their use in actual course-related readings. After integration of these devices into the classroom and the library, the experiences, impressions, and suggestions of students, professors, and librarians were collected and analyzed. The project team was interested not only in the overall acceptance and usefulness of the e-book devices but also in the use of specific features and the real-life challenges of using e-books in higher education environments. The evaluation report concluded that the project was successful from a pedagogical perspective, but using library-owned e-book devices in college classrooms raises several logistical and policy challenges for academic libraries (see http://www.geocities.com/lbell927/eBkFinal).

Another test of e-books in an academic setting was conducted by the University of Virginia Library's Electronic Text Center and described briefly in the July/August 2001 issue of *C&RL News*. Students in an English class and a religious studies class used compact, handheld personal computers to read most of their assigned reading materials as e-books. The library's Electronic Text Center worked with Microsoft Corp. and electronic course material publisher XanEdu to give the students the tools they needed to read their materials as interactive e-books using Microsoft Reader software. The project sought to gather feedback from the students and professors on how well the e-books integrated into their curriculum. This included the students' reactions to having most of the course materials on one device. Project staff also wanted to understand whether such technology changes teaching and learning, and, if so, how.

The library and Microsoft are evaluating results and at least one article was being prepared for publication at this writing. Several advantages of e-books are already apparent, according to Electronic Text Center Director David Seaman. For example, using the original writings as e-books allowed the students instant, direct access to the primary sources, so they could form their own opinions about the work. Another e-book advantage is that one easy-to-carry handheld device contained most of the course material, giving students the freedom and convenience of accessing their readings whenever and wherever they pleased.

Public Libraries

In a previous edition, this article mentioned an IMLS National Leadership Grant to the St. Louis Public Library to develop methodology large public libraries could use to gather data that will demonstrate the economic value of public library service. Results of that work will be available in 2002. Meanwhile, IMLS awarded a 2001 National Leadership Grant to the same study team to develop a similar methodology for use by medium-size and small public libraries.

Results of a 1999 National Leadership Grant for a project entitled "Counting on Results: New Tools for Outcome-Based Evaluation of Public Libraries" were posted on the Web in late 2001 (http://www.lrs.org/html/about/CountingOn Results.htm). Directed by Keith Curry Lance of the Colorado State Library, the goals of the project were to develop and demonstrate the potential utility of new tools for outcome-based evaluation of public library services. One of the tools was customizable software for Palm personal digital assistants (PDAs) that facilitates collecting standardized data on conventionally recorded library outputs (for example, visits, circulation, reference questions) as well as observable patron activities in the library. The second tool was a set of standardized questionnaires eliciting reports of the outcomes of public library service directly from patrons.

The project developed these tools and demonstrated their use by 45 public libraries representing 20 states and all four major regions of the United States (Northeast, South, Midwest, and West). In addition to reporting data on conventional library service outputs, the project generated data on the observed library activities of more than 40,000 patrons and reports of the outcomes of library services from more than 5,500 patrons. Thus, this project completed the largest, most comprehensive, and most detailed multistate data collection of this type attempted to date. Several articles on this project will be published in 2002.

School Libraries

In previous editions, this article has called attention to a series of studies under the direction of Keith Curry Lance that have demonstrated a correlation between strong library media center programs and student achievement. The first such study was done in Colorado in 1993. That work was repeated in 2000, with similar results. The correlation also held true for studies in Pennsylvania and Alaska. During 2001 studies in Oregon (see http://www.oema.net/Oregon_Study/OR_Study.htm) and Texas (http://www.tsl.state.tx.us/ld/pubs/schlibsurvey/index/html) yielded similar results. In addition to determining the impact of school library media programs on student achievement, the Texas study (done by Ester Smith of EGS Research and Consulting) also examined school library resource service and use in the light of existing state standards and guidelines for school library media programs.

The recent Lance study in Oregon and one under way in New Mexico were the focus of one program at the November 2001 conference of the American Association of School Librarians (AASL) in Indianapolis. The two other research programs focused on information literacy. One was sponsored by the AASL Research and Statistics Committee to honor the recently deceased Judy Pitts. The committee sent out a call for proposals for the Judy Pitts Research Forum and selected a paper by Leslie S. J. Farmer that described a school-wide action research study that investigated ways to improve student information literacy competencies through identifying needed skills, assessing present skill levels, mapping information literacy, identifying gaps in learning, designing interventions, and assessing results.

In a related program on "New Research About Information Literacy," David Loertscher and Blanche Woolls reviewed studies that were done after publication of their 1999 book *Information Literacy: A Review of the Research* (Hi Willow Research & Publishing).

People and Places

In July Lorcan Dempsey was named vice president of the OCLC Office of Research. Since June 2000 Dempsey has been director of Distributed National Electronic Resource (DNER), King's College, London, a British initiative to provide a coherent information environment for higher education communities. From 1994 until joining DNER, he was director of the Office for Library and Information Networking, a research and policy unit at the University of Bath (England). Jay Jordan, CEO of OCLC, describes Dempsey's background as combining "the practical and the theoretical with an important global perspective. He has been extensively involved in applied research and development, with the aim of informing policy and influencing practice."

Two new places to report on and monitor research in progress were unveiled in 2001. *Library Hi-Tech News* (*LHTN*) No. 3 announced a new column, "Research in Progress," to be coordinated by Philip Calvert, co-editor of *LHTN*. The announcement notes that scholars and researchers everywhere want to spread the news about their latest work. Prior to the formal reporting stage, however, there is very little opportunity to tell colleagues and peers about research in progress. Scholars everywhere are invited to contribute reports, especially in the high-tech aspects of libraries and information management. Calvert can be reached at philip.calvert@vuw.ac.nz.

Another place to use and watch is CAROL (Collections and Organizations Research Online). This is a Web database where researchers in any area of library collections or acquisitions can log a description of their research and locate other researchers active in areas of interest to them. The purpose of CAROL is to encourage research by providing a central source of information about ongoing work. Researchers who are not already in CAROL create a researcher record with their name, the names of any co-researchers, their institution, e-mail address, and fax and phone numbers. Then, for each project that they want to list, they create a project record in which they provide the title of the project, a brief description, publication plans if any, and a tentative timetable. As a project develops, the researchers can access their original record in CAROL and update the project status. Users can also query CAROL and in a matter of seconds retrieve a list of research projects of interest.

The idea for CAROL arose from American Library Association (ALA) committee work among members of the Collection Management and Development Section (CMDS) of the Association for Library Collections and Technical Services They encourage all librarians and students carrying on systematic research in any area of collections or acquisitions, whether intended for publication, for a conference, or for use within a library operation, to log their research on CAROL, which can be accessed at http://128.253.121.98/carol/start.htm.

A new source of research began in 2001, the EDUCAUSE Center for Applied Research (ECAR). This center was formed to provide educational leaders with high-quality, well-researched, timely information to support institutional decision making. Although academic libraries are not mentioned in a major way on the ECAR agenda, one of the four components of that agenda is "Teaching and Learning Issues" and one of the topics under that heading is "The Implementation and Socialization of E-Books in Higher Education." For more information, see http://www.educause.edu/ECAR.

Awards That Honor Excellent Research

All active awards are listed, along with the amount of the award, the URL for the award (if available), and the 2001 winners. If the award is annual but was not given in 2001, that fact is noted. General ALA awards are listed first, followed by units of ALA in alphabetical order, followed by other agencies in alphabetical order.

American Library Association

Library and Information Technology Association (LITA)

Frederick G. Kilgour Award (with OCLC) ($2,000 plus expense-paid trip to ALA Annual Conference)
Winner: Marcia J. Bates, University of California, Los Angeles
Rationale: Bates has a 30-year record of research, teaching, and scholarship in search strategies, information-seeking behavior, subject access, user-centered design of information retrieval systems and interfaces, and science and technology information services. Several of her publications have become seminal papers in our field. Her work carries on the tradition of Frederick Kilgour in its recognition of the centrality of the user in the design of response information systems.

Library History Round Table (LHRT)

Donald G. Davis Article Award
http://www.ala.org/alaorg/ors/davis.html
Not given in odd-numbered years.

Justin Winsor Prize ($500)
http://www.ala.org/alaorg/ors/winsor.html
Not given in 2001.

Library Research Round Table (LRRT)

Jesse H. Shera Award for Distinguished Published Research ($500)
http://www.ala.org/alaorg/ors/shera1.html
Not given in 2001.

Jesse H. Shera Award for Excellence in Doctoral Research ($500)
http://www.ala.org/alaorg/ors/shera2.html
Not given in 2001.

Association of College and Research Libraries

One award given by ACRL annually, but not always for research, was given for research in 2001. The **K. G. Saur Award for the Most Outstanding Article in** *College & Research Libraries* (*C&RL*) went to Thomas E. Nisonger for "Use of Journal Citation Reports for Serials Management in Research Libraries: An Investigation of the Effect of Self-Citation on Journal Rankings in Library and Information Science and Genetics," published in the May 2000 issue of *C&RL*. The award committee noted that Nisonger's article "adds to the literature on citation analysis and fully explores the trend of self-citation and its impact. Work like Nisonger's promotes the use of tools like the *Journal of Citation Reports*, and helps refine the interpretative results. The research is carefully done, and the article is well written." The cash award of $500 is funded by K. G. Saur publishing company.

ACRL also gave a new award in 2001 in connection with the ACRL National Conference in Denver (March 15–18). Linda Marion, a doctoral student at Drexel University, was the recipient of the **ACRL Student Paper Award**, which encourages leadership in academic librarianship research. Marion's paper, "Digital Librarian, Cybrarian, or Librarian with specialized Skills: Who Will Staff Digital Libraries?" was presented at the conference. The paper explores the territory of digital librarianship and examines the skills employers are seeking in new hires when filling technologically orientated jobs. Marion's presentation contains a content analysis of job ads to provide a map describing the domain of digital librarianship. She received $500 and complimentary registration to the conference.

American Society for Information and Technology (ASIST)

ASIST Research Award
Winner: Paul Kantor (Rutgers University, School of Communication, Information, and Library Studies)
Rationale: Kantor is an internationally known researcher in the areas of mathematical modeling and information system evaluation, and the author of scores of publications in these areas. His work has included the application of Markov models, Bayesian decision theory, lattice theory, and the calculus of variations, among others, to a variety of questions in the areas of information searching, retrieval, and library costing.

ASIST/UMI Doctoral Dissertation Award
Winner: Allison Powell (University of Virginia)
Project: This dissertation deals with the general problem of choosing the database(s) to which a user's query should be sent. Its primary goal was to "enhance the understanding of the overall multi-collection retrieval problem, including the potential that introducing multiple collections when a single one is possible may become advantageous." In a laboratory environment, Powell created conditions that allowed her to compare and evaluate the performance of different multi-collection information retrieval algorithms methodically and comprehensively.

Pratt-Severn Best Student Research Paper Award
Winner: Brian Hilligoss (University of North Carolina at Chapel Hill)

Project: This paper received high marks in the areas of technical competence, information science, significance of findings, and originality. The findings support some past conclusions, question others, and emphasize the significance of the author's work as well as the need for continued research on the impact of Web page information elements on user-site orientation.

Association for Library and Information Science Education (ALISE)

ALISE Methodology Paper Award
Winners: Diane H. Sonnenwald and Barbara M. Wildemuth
Project: "Investigating Information-Seeking Behavior Using the Concept of Information Horizons"

ALISE/Bohdan S. Wynar Research Paper Award
Winners: George D'Elia, Corinne Jorgensen, and Joseph Woelfel
Project: "The Impacts of the Internet on Public Library Use: An Analysis of the Current Consumer Market for Library and Internet Services"

Eugene Garfield/ALISE Doctoral Dissertation Award ($500 for travel expenses plus 2001 conference registration and membership in ALISE for 2000–2001)
Winner: Patricia Coit Murphy, University of North Carolina at Chapel Hill
Project: "What a Book Can Do: *Silent Spring* and Media-Borne Public Debate"
   Certificates of recognition were given to the following:

Daniel G. Dorner, "Determining Essential Services on the Canadian Information Highway: An Exploratory Study of the Public Policy Process," Faculty of Graduate Studies, University of Western Ontario, 1999

J. Stephen Downie, "Evaluating a Simple Approach to Music Information Retrieval: Conceiving Melodic N-Grams as Text," Faculty of Graduate Studies, University of Western Ontario, 1999

Richard William Kopak, "A Taxonomy of Link Types for Use in Hypertext," Faculty of Information Studies, University of Toronto, 2000

Grants that Support Research

All active awards are listed, along with the amount of the award, the URL for the award (if available), and the 2001 winners. If the award is annual but was not given in 2001, that fact is noted. General ALA awards are listed first, followed by units of ALA in alphabetical order, followed by other agencies in alphabetical order.

American Library Association

ALA Research Grant ($25,000)
Winner: Virginia A. Walter and Cynthia L. Mediavilla, University of California, Los Angeles
Project: This project, "Models for Homework Center Outcomes," will develop evaluation models that can be used by any public library to determine the effectiveness of its homework centers as measured by the positive impact on the teenagers using them. Model A will be relevant to homework centers in which

teenagers participate as the homework-assistance providers; Model B will be relevant to homework centers in which teenagers are the recipients of homework assistance. The research will build on Mediavilla's study of successful homework centers nationwide, which is described in *Creating the Full-Service Homework Center in Your Library,* available from ALA Editions.

Carroll Preston Baber Research Grant ($7,500)
http://www.ala.org/alaorg/ors/baber.html
Winner: Ruth V. Small, Syracuse University
Project: "Motivational Aspects of Information Literacy Skills Instruction in Community College Libraries." Research in information literacy skills instruction has largely focused on process or learning outcomes, with little attention paid to the motivational presentation methods that stimulate and encourage curiosity, information seeking, and exploration. The proposed research, building on earlier work by Small at the K–12 level, seeks to identify instructional motivators used by community college librarians that promote students' task engagement and enjoyment of the research process.

American Association of School Librarians (AASL)

AASL/Highsmith Research Grant ($5,000)
http://www.ala.org/aasl/awardapps/highsmith.html
Not given in 2001.

Association of College and Research Libraries (ACRL)

ACRL/ISI Doctoral Dissertation Fellowship ($1,500)
http://www.ala.org/acrl/doctoral.html
Winner: Laurie Bonnici, Florida State University
Project: "An Examination of Categorical Attributions Through the Lens of Reference Group Theory"

Samuel Lazerow Fellowship for Research in Acquisitions or Technical Services in an Academic or Research Library ($1,000)
http://www.ala.org/acrl/lazerow.html
Winner: Adam Chandler, Cornell University
Project: "An Application Profile and Prototype Metadata Management System for Licensed Electronic Resources"

Martinus Nijhoff West European Specialists Study Grant (10,000 Dutch guilders)
http://www.ala.org/acrl/nijhoff.html
Winner: Sue Waterman, Johns Hopkins University
Project: "Collecting the Nineteenth Century: The Book, the Specimen, the Photograph as Archive"

Young Adult Library Services Association (YALSA)

Francis Henne/YALSA/VOYA Research Grant ($500)
http://www.ala.org/yalsa/awards/hennewinner2001.html
Winner: Patrick Jones, Connectingya.com

Project: "Buyer Beware: Investigating the Quality of Customer Service to Young Adults in a Major Urban Public Library"

American Society for Information Science and Technology (ASIST)

ISI/ASIST Citation Analysis Research Grant ($3,000)
http://www.asis.org/awards/citation.isi.htm
Winners: John Budd, Mary Ellen Sievert, Gabriel M. Peterson, Ku Chuin Su (University of Missouri-Columbia, School of Information Science and Learning Technologies)
Project: Their proposal, "Errors and Corrections in the Biomedical Literature," takes research that has already demonstrated that retracted articles continue to be cited well after retraction statements appear and extends it to a study of other types of anomalies in the literature. This work intends to demonstrate the potential impact of anomalous publications on future research and communication in biomedicine and to alert both end users and librarian-intermediaries to the nature and extent of these problematic publications.

ISI Information Science Doctoral Dissertation Proposal Scholarship ($1,500 plus $500 toward travel or other expenses)
Winner: Alesia A. Zuccala (University of Toronto, Faculty of Information Studies)
Project: Zuccala plans to study the invisible college of singularity theory researchers, viewing it as both an intellectual structure of communication and social process of information sharing. She will use both bibliometric methods (examining the products of communication) and ethnographic data (examining the process of communication) to shed new light on how a small invisible college operates. Thus, the dissertation will make a unique contribution to information science by providing dual perspectives (structural/bibliometric and social/ethnographic) on the nature of invisible colleges.

Association for Library and Information Science Education (ALISE)

OCLC/ALISE Research Grant ($10,000 each)
http://www.oclc.org
Winner: Anna Perrault, University of South Florida
Project: "Global Collective Resources: WorldCat as the Foundation for International Library Cooperation." Perrault's research is a bibliometric study to profile the monographic contents of WorldCat (the OCLC Online Union Catalog) by subject and language parameters using the OCLC/WLN iCAS software. The profile will detail the contents of global publication made accessible through the OCLC international network. The results of this research can foster international resource sharing and cooperative collection development.
Winner: Hong Xie, University of Wisconsin–Milwaukee
Project: "Ease of Use Versus User Control: Desired Interface Models and Functionalities for Web-Based Databases." This study will explore users' perceptions of ease of use versus user control and their preferences for desired interface models and functionalities in searching Web-based online databases. The results will lead to the identification of desired interface models and functionalities and further development of interface prototypes for Web-based online databases to support ease of use without compromising user control.

Winners: Hong Xu and Arlene Taylor, University of Pittsburgh
Project: "Identification of Resource Types of Web Accessible Information." This study will examine a sample from OCLC's Web Characterization Project to determine distribution of resource types, an element of the Dublin Core, among subject areas. In the process it will test the efficacy of various existing lists of resource types.

Research Grant Award (one or more grants totaling $5,000)
http://www.alise.org/nondiscuss/Research_grant.html
Winner: Ingrid Hsieh-Yee, Catholic University of America
Project: "A Delphi Study on Metadata Curriculum Implications and Research Priorities"

Council on Library and Information Resources (CLIR)

A. R. Zipf Fellowship
http://www.clir.org/fellowships/zipf/zipf.html
Winner: Terence Kelly, Department of Computer Science, University of Michigan
Rationale: Kelly's research focuses on optimal resource allocation in hierarchical caching systems, especially Web caching.

Medical Library Association (MLA)

ISI/MLA Doctoral Fellowship ($2,000)
http://mlanet.org/awards/grants/doctoral.html
Not given in odd-numbered years.

MLA Research, Development, and Demonstration Project Grant
http://mlanet.org/awards/grants/research.html
Winners: Mary C. Congleton, Southern Kentucky Area Health Education Center, and Shelley Paden, University of Tennessee Medical Center
Project: Survey of the successes and problems associated with Loansome Doc (an interlibrary loan feature on the National Library of Medicine's MEDLINE Web service) in order to further the understanding of implementing a Loansome Doc program in a library, providing instruction for its use, and the types of delivery methods that libraries offer.

Special Libraries Association

Steven I. Goldspiel Memorial Research Grant (up to $20,000)
http://www.sla.org/content/memberservice/researchforum/goldspiel/index.cfm
Winner: Mark Rorvig, University of North Texas
Project: "Exploiting Image Content Features for Image Index Term Assignment." The primary objective of Rorvig's project is to determine the degree to which content-based feature extraction may support index term assignment. More specifically, to discover the degree to which the similarity of image content measures implies the inheritability of terms; to determine if there is a threshold of similarity beyond which image content similarity has little or no meaning for term assignment; to propose specific uses of the techniques; and to implement the techniques on a trial basis in a special library indexing environment to understand conditions of their acceptability to working staff.

Number of Libraries in the United States and Canada

Statistics are from the 54th edition of the *American Library Directory* (*ALD*) 2001–2002 (Information Today, Inc., 2001). Data are exclusive of elementary and secondary school libraries.

Libraries in the United States

Public Libraries	16,512 *
Public libraries, excluding branches	9,415 †
Main public libraries that have branches	1,358
Public library branches	7,097
Academic Libraries	3,406 *
Junior college	1,084
Departmental	177
Medical	4
Religious	6
University and college	2,322
Departmental	1,535
Law	146
Medical	225
Religious	181
Armed Forces Libraries	335 *
Air Force	94
Medical	13
Army	148
Medical	32
Navy	91
Law	1
Medical	14
Government Libraries	1,376 *
Law	415
Medical	216
Special Libraries (excluding public, academic, armed forces, and government)	9,763 *
Law	1,123
Medical	1,862
Religious	604

Note: Numbers followed by an asterisk are added to find "Total libraries counted" for each of the three geographic areas (United States, U.S.-administered regions, and Canada). The sum of the three totals is the "Grand total of libraries listed" in *ALD*. For details on the count of libraries, see the preface to the 54th edition of *ALD—Ed.*

† Federal, state, and other statistical sources use this figure (libraries *excluding* branches) as the total for public libraries.

Total Special Libraries (including public, academic, armed forces, and government)	11,017
Total law	1,686
Total medical	2,366
Total religious	1,126
Total Libraries Counted(*)	31,392

Libraries in Regions Administered by the United States

Public Libraries	30 *
Public libraries, excluding branches	10 †
Main public libraries that have branches	3
Public library branches	20
Academic Libraries	35 *
Junior college	8
Departmental	4
Medical	0
University and college	27
Departmental	22
Law	2
Medical	1
Religious	1
Armed Forces Libraries	2 *
Air Force	1
Army	1
Navy	0
Government Libraries	10 *
Law	4
Medical	2
Special Libraries (excluding public, academic, armed forces, and government)	19 *
Law	6
Medical	4
Religious	0
Total Special Libraries (including public, academic, armed forces, and government)	29
Total law	12
Total medical	7
Total religious	2
Total Libraries Counted(*)	96

Libraries in Canada

Public Libraries	1,697 *
Public libraries, excluding branches	706 †

Main public libraries that have branches	124
Public library branches	991
Academic Libraries	326*
Junior college	83
Departmental	21
Medical	0
Religious	2
University and college	243
Departmental	204
Law	10
Medical	19
Religious	25
Government Libraries	364*
Law	24
Medical	5
Special Libraries (excluding public, academic, armed forces, and government)	1,311*
Law	125
Medical	240
Religious	32
Total Special Libraries (including public, academic, and government)	1,396
Total law	159
Total medical	264
Total religious	99
Total Libraries Counted(*)	3,698

Summary

Total U.S. Libraries	31,392
Total Libraries Administered by the United States	96
Total Canadian Libraries	3,698
Grand Total of Libraries Listed	35,186

Highlights of NCES Surveys

Public Libraries

The following are highlights from *E.D. Tab: Public Libraries in the United States: Fiscal Year 1998*. The data were collected by the National Center for Education Statistics (NCES). For more information on NCES surveys, see the article "National Center for Education Statistics Library Statistics Program" in Part 1.

Number of Libraries, Population of Legal Service Area, Service Outlets

- There were 8,964 public libraries (administrative entities) in the 50 states and the District of Columbia in fiscal year (FY) 1998.
- Eleven percent of the public libraries served 72 percent of the population of legally served areas in the United States. Each of these public libraries had a legal service area population of 50,000 or more.
- Ninety-seven percent of the population had access to public library services, and three percent did not.
- A total of 1,513 public libraries (17 percent) had one or more branch library outlets, with a total of 7,293 branches. The total number of central library outlets was 8,887. The total number of stationary outlets (central library outlets and branch library outlets) was 16,180. Nine percent of public libraries had one or more bookmobile outlets, with a total of 933 bookmobiles.
- Eighty percent of public libraries had one single direct service outlet (an outlet that provides service directly to the public). Twenty percent had more than one direct service outlet.

Legal Basis and Interlibrary Relationships

- Fifty-three percent of public libraries were part of a municipal government, 12 percent were part of a county/parish, 1 percent were part of a city/county, 6 percent had multijurisdictional legal basis under an intergovernmental agreement, 11 percent were nonprofit association or agency libraries, 3 percent were part of a school district, and 8 percent were separate government units known as library districts. Seven percent reported their legal basis as "other."
- Seventy-three percent of public libraries were members of a system, federation, or cooperative service, while 23 percent were not. Four percent served as the headquarters of a system, federation, or cooperative service.

Operating Income and Expenditures

- Seventy-eight percent of public libraries' total operating income of about $6.7 billion came from local sources, 13 percent from the state, 1 percent from federal sources, and 9 percent from other sources, such as gifts and donations, service fees, and fines.

- Nationwide, total per capita operating income for public libraries was $26.02. Of that, $20.18 was from local sources, $3.28 from state sources, 21 cents from federal sources, and $2.35 from other sources.
- Per capita operating income from local sources was under $3.00 for 11 percent of public libraries, $3.00 to $14.99 for 43 percent of libraries, $15.00 to $29.99 for 30 percent of libraries, and $30.00 or more for 17 percent of libraries.
- Total operating expenditures for public libraries were $6.2 billion in FY 1998. Of this, 64 percent was expended for paid staff and 15 percent for the library collection. Thirty-five percent of public libraries had operating expenditures of less than $50,000, 39 percent expended from $50,000 to $399,999, and 25 percent expended $400,000 or more.
- The average U.S. per capita operating expenditure for public libraries was $23.92. The highest average per capita operating expenditure in the 50 states and the District of Columbia was $42.31 and the lowest was $10.43.
- Expenditures for materials in electronic format were 1 percent of total operating expenditures for public libraries. Expenditures for electronic access were 3 percent of total operating expenditures.

Staff and Collections

- Public libraries had a total of 123,443 paid full-time-equivalent (FTE) staff in FY 1998, or 11.9 paid FTE staff per 25,000 population. Of these, 23 percent or 2.7 per 25,000 population were librarians with an MLS degree from an ALA-accredited program, and 10 percent were librarians by title but did not have the ALA-MLS. Sixty-seven percent of the staff were in other positions.
- Nationwide, public libraries had 739 million books and serial volumes in their collections, or 2.9 volumes per capita. By state, the number of volumes per capita ranged from 1.6 to 5.4.
- Nationwide, public libraries had collections of 28 million audio materials and 17 million video materials.
- Nationwide, public libraries provided 4.4 materials in electronic format (e.g., CD-ROMS, magnetic tapes, and magnetic disks) per 1,000 population.

Library Services

- Nationwide, 88 percent of public libraries had access to the Internet (a 9 percentage point increase since FY 1997). Almost 72 percent of all public libraries made the Internet available to patrons directly or through a staff intermediary, almost 9 percent of public libraries made the Internet available to patrons through a staff intermediary only, and almost 8 percent of public libraries made the Internet available only to library staff.
- Ninety-three percent of the unduplicated population of legal service areas had access to the Internet through their local public library.
- Nationwide, 74 percent of public libraries provided access to electronic services.

- Total nationwide circulation of public library materials was 1.7 billion, or 6.6 materials circulated per capita. The highest circulation per capita in the 50 states and the District of Columbia was 12.5 and the lowest was 2.7.
- Nationwide, 13.5 million library materials were loaned by public libraries to other libraries (an increase of 15.0 percent since FY 1997).
- Total nationwide reference transactions in public libraries totaled 292 million, or 1.1 reference transactions per capita.
- Total nationwide library visits in public libraries totaled 1.1 billion, or 4.2 library visits per capita.

Children's Services

- Nationwide, circulation of children's materials was 612 million, or 36 percent of total circulation.
- Attendance at children's programs was 46 million.

Academic Libraries

The following are highlights from *E.D. Tab Academic Libraries: 1998*, based on information from the 1998 IPEDS Academic Libraries Survey.

Services

- In 1998, 3,658 of the 4,141 two-year and four-year degree-granting postsecondary institutions in the United States reported that they had their own academic library. Of these 3,658 academic libraries, 97 percent responded to the survey.
- In FY 1998 general collection circulation transactions in the nation's academic libraries at degree-granting postsecondary institutions totaled 175.4 million. Reserve collection circulation transactions totaled 40.7 million.
- In FY 1998 academic libraries provided a total of about 9.2 million interlibrary loans to other libraries (both academic libraries and other types of libraries) and received about 7.7 million loans.
- Overall, the largest percentage of academic libraries (42 percent) reported having 60 to 79 hours of public service per typical week; 38 percent provided 80 or more service hours per typical week during the academic year. The percentage of institutions providing 80 or more public-service hours ranged from 6 percent in less than four-year institutions to 75 percent in doctorate-granting institutions. Twenty libraries reported that they were open 168 hours a week (24 hours 7 days a week).
- Taken together, academic libraries reported a gate count of about 16.2 million visitors per typical week (about 1.6 visits per total full-time equivalent [FTE] enrollment).
- About 2.1 million reference transactions were reported in a typical week.
- Over FY 1998 about 438,000 presentations to groups serving about 7.4 million were reported.

Collections

- Taken together, the nation's 3,658 academic libraries at degree-granting postsecondary institutions held a total of 878.9 million paper volumes (books, bound serials, and government documents) at the end of FY 1998.
- The median number of paper volumes held per FTE student was 53.7 volumes. Median volumes held ranged from 18.5 per FTE in less than four-year institutions to 119.8 in doctorate-granting institutions.
- Of the total paper volumes held at the end of the year, 43 percent (376.0 million) were held at the 125 institutions categorized under the Carnegie Classification as Research I or Research II institutions. About 55 percent of the volumes were at those institutions classified as either Research or Doctoral in the Carnegie Classification.
- In FY 1998 the median number of paper volumes added to collections per FTE student was 1.5. The median number added ranged from 0.7 per FTE student in less than four-year institutions to 2.9 in doctorate-granting institutions.

Staff

- There was a total of 96,709 FTE staff working in academic libraries in 1998. Of these, 30,041 (31 percent) were librarians or other professional staff; 38,026 (39 percent) were other paid staff; 270 (less than one-half of 1 percent) were contributed-services staff; and 28,373 (29 percent) were student assistants.
- Excluding student assistants, the institutional median number of academic library FTE staff per 1,000 FTE students was 5.6. The median ranged from 3.6 in less than four-year institutions to 9.1 in doctorate-granting institutions.

Expenditures

- In 1998 total expenditures for libraries at the 3,658 degree-granting post-secondary institutions totaled $4.6 billion. The three largest expenditure items for all academic libraries were salaries and wages, $2.31 billion (50 percent); current paper and electronic serial subscription expenditures, $974.9 million (21 percent); and paper books and bound serials, $514.0 million (11 percent).
- The libraries of the 570 doctorate-granting institutions (16 percent of the total institutions) accounted for $2.924 billion, or 64 percent of the total expenditure dollars at all academic libraries at degree-granting postsecondary institutions.
- In 1998 the median total operating expenditures per FTE student was $301.25 and the median for information resource expenditures was $84.98.

Electronic Services

- In FY 1998, 84 percent of degree-granting postsecondary institutions with an academic library had access from within the library to an electronic catalog of the library's holdings, 95 percent had Internet access within the library, and 54 percent had library reference service by e-mail both within the library and elsewhere on campus. Ninety-two percent had instruction by library staff on the use of Internet resources within the library.

- In FY 1998, 44 percent had technology within the library to assist persons with disabilities and 34 percent of academic libraries had access to this service from elsewhere on campus. Sixty-five percent provided services to distance education students.

- Almost three-fourths (71 percent) had computers not dedicated to library functions for patron use inside the library. Fewer institutions (12 percent) had video/desktop conferencing by or for the library within the library, and 19 percent had access from elsewhere on campus. Seventeen percent had satellite broadcasting by or for the library within the library and 23 percent had access from elsewhere on campus.

- Just under one-third (30 percent) had electronic document delivery by the library to a patron's account or address from within the library.

State Library Agencies

The following are highlights from *E.D. TAB State Library Agencies: Fiscal Year 2000*, a statistical profile of state library agencies in the 50 states and the District of Columbia.

Governance

- Nearly all state library agencies (47 states and the District of Columbia) were located in the executive branch of government. In three states (Arizona, Michigan, and Tennessee), the agency is located in the legislative branch.

- Of the state library agencies located in the executive branch, almost two-thirds (31 states) are part of a larger agency, most commonly the state department of education (12 states). Six other state library agencies have direct connections to education through their locations within departments or agencies that include *education, college, university,* or *learning* in their titles.

Allied and Other Special Operations

- State library agencies in 14 states reported having one or more allied operations. Allied operations most frequently linked with state library agencies are the state archives (10 states) and the state records management service. Expenditures for allied operations totaled $23.4 million, or 2.3 percent of total expenditures.

- State library agencies in 15 states contracted with public or academic libraries in their states to serve as resource or reference/information service centers. State library agencies in 21 states hosted or provided funding for a State Center for the Book.

Electronic Networks, Databases, and Catalogs

- Almost all state library agencies (48 states and the District of Columbia) planned or monitored the development of electronic networks. State library agencies in 42 states and the District of Columbia operated electronic networks. State library agencies in 46 states and the District of Columbia supported the development of bibliographic databases via electronic networks, and state library agencies in 44 states and the District of Columbia supported the development of full-text or data files via electronic networks.

- Almost all state library agencies (49 states) provided or facilitated library access to online databases through subscription, lease, license, consortial membership, or agreement.

- State library agencies in 42 states and the District of Columbia facilitated or subsidized electronic access to the holdings of other libraries in their states through Online Computer Library Center (OCLC) participation. Over half provided access via a Web-based union catalog (30 states) or Telnet gateway (26 states).

- State library agencies in 46 states had combined expenditures for statewide database licensing of over $32.4 million. Of these, Texas had the highest expenditure ($3.1 million) and South Dakota the lowest ($5,000). All state library agencies with such expenditures provided statewide database licensing services to public libraries in their states, and at least two-thirds provided statewide database licensing services to each of the following user groups: academic, school, and special libraries; library cooperatives; and other state agencies.

- Over two-thirds (68.0 percent) of the total expenditures for statewide database licensing were from state funds; 31.8 percent were from federal sources. Of the states reporting statewide database licensing expenditures, 16 states funded this activity with state dollars only, 16 states used federal dollars only, and 13 states used multiple funding sources.

Internet Access

- All state library agencies facilitated library access to the Internet in one or more of the following ways: training or consulting state or local library staff or state library end users in the use of the Internet; providing a subsidy to libraries for Internet participation; providing equipment to libraries to access the Internet; providing access to directories, databases, or online catalogs; and managing gopher/Web sites, file servers, bulletin boards, or listservs.

- Nearly all state library agencies (48 states) had Internet workstations available for public use, ranging in number from 2 to 4 (17 states); 5 to 9 (14 states); 10 to 19 (seven states); 20 to 29 (seven states); and 30 or more (three states). Louisiana reported the largest number of public-use Internet terminals (53).

- State library agencies in 32 states and the District of Columbia were applicants to the Universal Service (E-rate discount) Program established by the Federal Communications Commission (FCC) under the Telecommunications Act of 1996 (P.L. 104-104).

Library Development Services

Services to Public Libraries

- All state library agencies provided the following types of services to public libraries: administration of Library Services and Technology Act (LSTA) grants; collection of library statistics; continuing education programs; and library planning, evaluation, and research. Nearly all state library agencies (49 to 50) provided consulting services, library legislation preparation or review, and review of technology plans for the E-rate discount program.
- Services to public libraries provided by over three-quarters of state library agencies (41 to 47) were administration of state aid, interlibrary loan referral services, literacy program support, reference referral services, state standards or guidelines, statewide public relations or library promotion campaigns, and summer reading program support. About three-quarters of state library agencies (38) provided union list development.
- Two-thirds of state library agencies (33) provided OCLC Group Access Capability (GAC).
- Twelve state library agencies reported accreditation of public libraries, and 22 reported the certification of public librarians.

Services to Academic Libraries

- Over three-quarters of state library agencies (39 to 43) provided the following services to academic libraries: administration of LSTA grants, continuing education, and interlibrary loan referral services.
- Over two-thirds of state library agencies (36) provided reference referral services, 30 agencies provided consulting services, and 31 agencies provided union list development.
- No state library agency accredits academic libraries; only the state library agency of Washington State reported the certification of academic librarians.

Services to School Library Media Centers

- Over three-quarters of state library agencies provided continuing education (39 agencies) or interlibrary loan referral services (41 agencies) to school library media centers (LMCs).
- At least two-thirds of state library agencies provided administration of LSTA grants (35 agencies) or reference referral services (34 agencies) to LMCs, and over half of the agencies (30) provided consulting services.
- No state library agency accredits LMCs or certifies LMC librarians.

Services to Special Libraries

- Over three-quarters of state library agencies (40 to 42) served special libraries through administration of LSTA grants, continuing education, and interlibrary loan referral.
- Over two-thirds of state library agencies (37) provided reference referral services to special libraries.

- About two-thirds provided consulting services (34 agencies) or union list development (33 agencies).
- Over half of state library agencies (26) provided library planning, evaluation, and research.
- Only the Nebraska state library agency accredits special libraries, and only Indiana, Nebraska, and Washington State reported certification of librarians of special libraries.

Services to Systems

- About two-thirds of state library agencies (33 to 36) provided the following services to library systems: administration of LSTA grants; consulting services; continuing education; interlibrary loan referral; library legislation preparation or review; and library planning, evaluation, and research.
- Over half of state library agencies (26 to 29) served library systems through administration of state aid, collection of library statistics, reference referral, state standards or guidelines, statewide public relations or library promotion campaigns, union list development, and review of technology plans for the E-rate discount program.
- Six state library agencies reported accreditation of library systems, and five reported certification of systems librarians.

Service Outlets

- State library agencies reported a total of 151 service outlets—53 main or central outlets, 77 other outlets (excluding bookmobiles), and 21 bookmobiles. The user groups receiving library services through these outlets, and the number of outlets serving them, included the general public (106 outlets); state government employees (101 outlets); blind and physically handicapped individuals (58 outlets); residents of state correctional institutions (34 outlets); and residents of other state institutions (22 outlets).

Collections

- The number of books and serial volumes held by state library agencies totaled 25.6 million.
- Three state library agencies had book and serial volumes of over 2 million each: Tennessee and New York had 2.5 million volumes each, and Michigan had 2.3 million volumes. The number of book and serial volumes held by other state library agencies were 1,000,000 to 1,999,999 (four states), 500,000 to 999,999 (10 states), 200,000 to 499,999 (10 states), 100,000 to 199,999 (nine states), 50,000 to 99,999 (seven states); and under 50,000 (six states). The state library agencies in Maryland and the District of Columbia do not maintain collections.
- The number of serial subscriptions held by state library agencies totaled over 98,000, with New York and Indiana holding the largest number (over 11,000 each), followed by Connecticut (over 10,000). The number of serial subscriptions held by other state library agencies were 5,000 to 9,999

(three states), 2,000 to 4,999 (five states), 1,000 to 1,999 (11 states), 500 to 999 (13 states), 100 to 499 (11 states), and under 100 (three states). The state library agencies in Maryland and the District of Columbia do not maintain collections.

Staff

- The total number of budgeted full-time-equivalent (FTE) positions in state library agencies was 4,053. Librarians with MLS degrees from ALA-accredited programs (ALA-MLS) accounted for almost 1,262 of these positions, or 31.1 percent of total FTE positions; other professionals accounted for 18.8 percent of total FTE positions; and other paid staff accounted for 50.0 percent. Rhode Island reported the largest percentage (55.0 percent) of ALA-MLS librarians, and Virginia reported the smallest (12.5 percent).
- Most of the budgeted FTE positions (56.9 percent) were in library services; 16.5 percent were in library development; 11.5 percent were in administration; and 15.1 percent were in other services such as allied operations. Over two-thirds of the library development positions were for public library development.

Income

- State library agencies reported a total income of over $1 billion in FY 2000. Most income was from state sources (84.6 percent), followed by federal sources (13.7 percent), and other sources (1.8 percent).
- State library agency income from state sources totaled $872.9 million, with over two-thirds ($592.4 million) designated for state aid to libraries. In 10 states, over 75 percent of the state library agency income from state sources was designated for state aid to libraries, with Massachusetts having the largest percentage (96.8 percent). Six states (Hawaii, Idaho, New Hampshire, South Dakota, Vermont, and Wyoming) and the District of Columbia targeted no state funds for aid to libraries.
- Federal income totaled $141.1 million, with 94.7 percent from LSTA grants.

Expenditures

- State library agencies reported total expenditures of over $1 billion in FY 2000. Over four-fifths (84.6 percent) of these expenditures were from state funds, followed by federal funds (14.0 percent) and funds from other sources (1.4 percent).
- In six states, over 90 percent of total expenditures were from state sources. These states were Massachusetts (95.3 percent), Georgia (93.6 percent), Maryland (92.7 percent), New York (92.2 percent), and Rhode Island and Pennsylvania (91.0 percent each). The District of Columbia had the smallest percentage of expenditures from state sources (47.4 percent), followed by Utah (57.5 percent).

- Financial assistance to libraries accounted for 68.6 percent of total expenditures of state library agencies, and over two-thirds of such expenditures were targeted to individual public libraries (46.9 percent) and public library systems (21.6 percent). Most of these expenditures were from state sources (87.9 percent); 11.9 percent were from federal sources.
- Thirteen state library agencies reported expenditures for allied operations. These expenditures totaled $23.4 million and accounted for 2.3 percent of total expenditures of state library agencies. Of states reporting such expenditures, Virginia reported the highest expenditure ($5.1 million) and West Virginia the lowest ($12,000).
- Thirty-five state library agencies had a combined total of $21.9 million in grants and contracts expenditures to assist public libraries with state or federal education reform initiatives. The area of adult literacy and family literacy accounted for 85.0 percent of such expenditures, and prekindergarten learning accounted for 15.0 percent. Expenditures were focused exclusively on prekindergarten learning projects in five states (Kentucky, Louisiana, Maryland, North Carolina, and Vermont) and exclusively on adult literacy and family literacy projects in eight states (California, Illinois, Indiana, Michigan, New Jersey, Rhode Island, West Virginia, and Wyoming).

Library Acquisition Expenditures, 2000–2001: U.S. Public, Academic, Special, and Government Libraries

The information in these tables is taken from the 54th edition of the *American Library Directory* (*ALD*) (2001–2002). The tables report acquisition expenditures by public, academic, special, and government libraries.

The total number of libraries in the United States and in regions administered by the United States listed in the 54th edition of *ALD* is 31,488, including 16,542 public libraries, 3,441 academic libraries, 9,782 special libraries, and 1,386 government libraries.

Understanding the Tables

Number of libraries includes only those U.S. libraries in *ALD* that reported annual acquisition expenditures (4,203 public libraries, 1,877 academic libraries, 590 special libraries, 221 government libraries). Libraries that reported annual income but not expenditures are not included in the count. Academic libraries include university, college, and junior college libraries. Special academic libraries, such as law and medical libraries, that reported acquisition expenditures separately from the institution's main library are counted as independent libraries.

The amount in the *total acquisition expenditures* column for a given state is generally greater than the sum of the categories of expenditures. This is because the total acquisition expenditures amount also includes the expenditures of libraries that did not itemize by category.

Figures in *categories of expenditure* columns represent only those libraries that itemized expenditures. Libraries that reported a total acquisition expenditure amount but did not itemize are only represented in the total acquisition expenditures column.

Table 1 / Public Library Acquisition Expenditures

State	Number of Libraries	Total Acquisition Expenditures	Books	Other Print Materials	Periodicals/ Serials	Manuscripts & Archives	AV Equipment	Microforms	Electronic Reference	Preservation
Alabama	69	6,716,227	5,226,962	188,019	562,660	0	205,523	308,395	273,072	9,423
Alaska	27	2,593,016	1,054,409	57,900	662,037	0	13,207	13,055	140,190	2,350
Arizona	50	15,599,772	10,779,168	276,656	1,615,216	0	529,454	98,650	1,586,119	214,641
Arkansas	31	6,245,898	2,230,969	7,000	269,583	250	89,279	57,400	1,062,389	31,497
California	128	117,668,156	45,983,198	825,945	7,413,804	48,422	2,813,039	1,142,815	5,455,382	595,853
Colorado	46	13,098,442	5,881,774	700	732,788	100	231,029	124,922	405,491	10,163
Connecticut	114	15,453,995	7,191,228	944,376	1,018,139	4,557	419,555	155,040	1,185,256	20,852
Delaware	14	1,177,073	673,349	8,032	94,280	0	41,300	14,143	14,652	0
District of Columbia	2	11,548,248	1,582	1,539	466	0	0	0	0	0
Florida	77	42,463,822	22,117,566	260,630	2,568,260	4,700	1,423,014	355,712	4,088,936	38,330
Georgia	33	23,331,305	7,925,285	4,265	268,400	720	218,845	64,837	492,605	22,256
Hawaii	2	2,400,529	1,749,579	0	429,154	0	0	0	0	0
Idaho	37	2,786,355	1,514,520	32,212	107,928	0	42,264	8,356	685,643	3,372
Illinois	301	60,391,735	21,535,007	641,813	2,779,562	27,084	1,858,761	655,821	2,739,035	111,685
Indiana	133	39,110,908	18,098,895	273,040	2,345,902	0	1,057,048	592,316	1,225,162	168,085
Iowa	231	13,538,713	4,909,212	121,426	733,223	2,555	338,010	82,395	652,109	3,395
Kansas	94	12,772,155	6,561,508	68,487	2,252,036	400	795,780	21,914	688,663	2,750
Kentucky	54	15,869,884	4,088,358	19,551	421,673	0	358,055	47,303	287,191	8,955
Louisiana	35	20,546,785	7,288,162	78,410	1,164,905	1,300	1,141,454	126,505	33,100	41,801
Maine	82	2,421,744	1,594,567	8,399	269,869	1,121	102,454	22,585	168,278	5,441
Maryland	25	42,489,162	14,088,528	17,500	738,016	1,200	240,193	131,432	2,877,232	696
Massachusetts	195	31,551,356	11,224,441	518,552	1,493,354	1,400	1,098,878	271,319	718,619	20,360
Michigan	194	40,297,177	14,613,457	936,733	2,259,783	82,842	844,098	391,024	1,285,009	66,468
Minnesota	83	17,861,239	8,172,894	112,279	858,986	0	300,757	7,646	425,268	6,326

State	Count									
Mississippi	32	6,304,357	2,616,360	13,252	339,106	0	111,889	120,153	2,061,563	6,936
Missouri	65	25,249,359	16,576,846	48,428	2,319,456	200	1,647,303	306,399	1,761,051	75,321
Montana	37	1,590,738	1,162,539	0	118,934	0	5,316	6,559	70,217	14,211
Nebraska	61	4,138,015	2,554,140	26,148	322,274	0	342,379	21,574	127,664	7,167
Nevada	13	8,000,711	2,121,906	5,505	502,253	0	39,890	58,379	42,500	995
New Hampshire	97	3,390,456	2,000,946	26,264	225,675	3,583	111,547	63,204	96,867	11,950
New Jersey	164	32,150,213	17,683,800	74,999	2,615,780	6,500	774,527	376,961	1,268,145	34,245
New Mexico	26	4,747,964	1,645,883	37,641	395,872	0	9,601	18,583	133,231	8,200
New York	313	104,069,754	41,998,618	467,849	7,397,129	13,300	1,394,460	786,703	2,951,197	175,335
North Carolina	78	19,270,717	9,802,210	37,200	733,147	21,171	366,226	223,957	372,763	12,439
North Dakota	19	1,254,863	613,057	8,479	146,431	0	29,650	14,100	155,800	2,500
Ohio	141	107,839,669	39,854,765	1,282,799	7,367,680	18,862	3,153,858	1,552,661	3,441,917	1,001,763
Oklahoma	35	6,896,918	5,074,653	119,908	1,059,793	0	451,663	67,617	119,857	19,000
Oregon	69	27,128,943	6,874,033	44,809	1,107,658	0	1,502,578	7,276	539,697	83,357
Pennsylvania	202	24,689,751	12,600,819	116,899	1,389,800	10,100	728,811	1,014,373	485,486	88,766
Rhode Island	23	3,873,009	1,295,944	4,560	207,059	1,500	121,998	22,942	139,810	10,935
South Carolina	29	11,055,413	7,139,095	48,179	893,720	0	613,938	182,197	822,073	52,695
South Dakota	32	1,789,340	1,070,542	923	192,432	0	111,951	26,967	175,462	600
Tennessee	46	11,305,293	5,133,561	94,032	856,637	8,000	536,474	95,174	130,061	75,767
Texas	209	47,828,191	19,657,180	229,354	3,162,564	1,000	647,942	523,693	1,560,683	74,189
Utah	22	10,082,615	6,972,169	61,739	666,210	0	1,426,035	22,700	513,900	15,400
Vermont	71	1,271,458	936,623	0	77,702	120	18,047	680	36,723	4,156
Virginia	63	27,006,477	16,569,931	96,293	2,786,794	152,000	601,998	1,366,939	648,742	525,050
Washington	41	16,889,130	8,571,406	409,339	998,414	0	713,712	1,060	401,075	2,210
West Virginia	36	3,317,442	2,234,413	45,701	210,800	0	50,617	26,300	147,844	12,827
Wisconsin	202	17,602,343	9,806,482	249,064	2,465,773	0	1,240,714	122,721	499,596	20,624
Wyoming	19	1,200,880	752,481	4,285	74,978	1,105	15,500	5,953	117,871	2,947
U.S. Virgin Islands	1	20,000	19,000	0	1,000	0	0	0	0	0
Total	4,203	1,087,897,715	467,844,020	8,957,113	69,695,095	414,092	30,930,621	11,729,410	45,311,196	3,724,284
Estimated % of Acquisition Expenditures			43.00	0.82	6.41	0.04	2.84	1.08	4.17	0.34

Table 2 / Academic Library Acquisition Expenditures

State	Number of Libraries	Total Acquisition Expenditures	Books	Other Print Materials	Periodicals/ Serials	Manuscripts & Archives	AV Equipment	Microforms	Electronic Reference	Preservation
Alabama	32	36,370,799	5,887,970	131,453	11,247,397	24,066	177,002	378,623	578,223	270,490
Alaska	4	1,500,951	434,041	28,513	535,994	0	12,569	76,321	262,974	64,755
Arizona	20	12,100,324	3,778,293	598,233	5,098,134	41,500	174,750	277,323	2,121,482	91,115
Arkansas	16	9,047,179	2,144,412	7,030	5,498,536	0	98,908	257,430	609,407	149,198
California	132	125,713,068	26,936,561	1,822,129	67,363,492	1,143	826,937	2,402,502	5,685,588	1,449,234
Colorado	22	16,983,399	3,270,818	13,810	8,254,174	0	38,134	969,739	344,598	45,854
Connecticut	27	29,598,260	7,865,834	5,558,695	13,969,033	1,000	49,284	304,588	1,436,444	284,933
Delaware	4	5,458,827	1,994,101	16,000	3,122,980	0	0	20,072	33,500	0
District of Columbia	14	19,673,955	3,110,296	951,528	7,766,521	1,613	0	49,523	0	3,047,337
Florida	54	49,655,110	9,176,850	4,001,421	17,080,270	8,165	503,298	6,934,811	2,558,075	716,109
Georgia	46	37,318,075	9,940,734	1,409,066	18,139,338	35,200	80,487	1,275,757	1,674,646	203,719
Hawaii	8	5,966,306	1,850,830	0	3,829,759	0	19,955	49,930	67,693	20,550
Idaho	7	9,902,605	2,630,212	0	6,530,398	1,000	270,083	51,600	90,763	328,549
Illinois	82	105,375,382	16,214,976	2,306,338	31,581,501	34,318	647,568	621,608	3,873,764	1,173,991
Indiana	45	40,168,514	9,487,584	897,914	22,471,343	876,739	238,401	285,069	994,225	399,663
Iowa	39	18,862,898	4,221,012	336,304	8,164,115	3,363	185,046	862,033	1,199,616	156,849
Kansas	32	6,299,694	2,063,598	27,655	3,164,359	0	45,845	111,934	478,090	102,070
Kentucky	31	27,391,835	6,868,327	60,114	15,003,433	105,974	85,303	869,311	1,220,567	494,238
Louisiana	18	16,354,016	2,406,018	151,184	8,707,005	6,152	99,157	185,851	1,172,582	96,158
Maine	18	10,298,053	2,341,121	1,250	4,887,193	10,247	11,290	176,698	281,136	232,016
Maryland	38	23,979,943	5,846,939	156,143	11,721,872	30,000	331,955	415,566	1,072,473	384,174
Massachusetts	64	84,489,219	14,407,319	1,755,121	30,753,421	12,000	419,821	1,389,305	5,724,341	761,024
Michigan	59	64,813,809	16,711,408	3,438,636	34,382,700	120,850	1,110,773	758,619	6,088,590	1,330,993
Minnesota	35	24,692,080	5,053,770	450,723	6,365,939	1,600	106,518	306,039	1,220,581	269,337
Mississippi	16	11,530,050	913,513	1,148	4,078,911	1,600	122,024	156,802	249,709	161,607
Missouri	48	31,934,212	6,286,865	379,718	18,195,333	8,037	202,040	537,534	2,363,711	513,215

Montana	16	2,564,904	697,989	0	1,150,643	0	27,000	5,060	102,530	3,528
Nebraska	21	17,930,527	1,940,666	148,043	4,578,702	300	110,309	95,000	540,300	134,407
Nevada	6	7,926,564	2,543,788	0	3,819,713	0	58,502	104,332	1,222,894	177,335
New Hampshire	13	5,390,101	1,245,175	43,833	2,905,865	0	39,100	53,688	224,625	78,800
New Jersey	27	27,545,419	10,526,962	276,689	7,737,798	8,000	115,905	4,637,032	1,337,528	157,478
New Mexico	19	11,992,371	3,560,438	179,813	6,154,923	0	207,351	166,561	966,140	218,930
New York	127	115,255,197	22,384,316	1,936,950	43,960,068	13,735	734,614	2,266,836	5,336,816	2,114,019
North Carolina	74	58,697,958	15,625,159	84,183	27,953,116	7,069	917,074	1,308,856	2,790,243	545,827
North Dakota	12	5,429,853	888,482	74,400	3,572,899	0	37,188	99,172	196,630	50,964
Ohio	74	73,915,355	14,870,161	515,414	29,497,245	31,528	640,258	846,083	1,378,984	1,166,133
Oklahoma	29	17,826,741	2,205,810	41,608	6,502,950	7,100	119,730	194,492	299,417	148,061
Oregon	33	20,348,617	5,445,357	231,454	10,724,173	500	361,328	504,100	1,267,249	197,320
Pennsylvania	97	105,907,413	22,243,521	333,906	41,160,035	56,406	533,967	2,138,330	3,882,909	1,158,904
Rhode Island	9	9,634,845	2,371,748	156,774	6,324,570	7,261	16,972	131,215	168,246	311,678
South Carolina	30	18,733,996	3,630,165	46,944	7,134,622	5,000	232,464	364,617	1,164,937	205,293
South Dakota	12	4,373,568	831,997	0	2,222,929	0	43,291	44,976	571,620	69,331
Tennessee	48	34,003,153	7,841,628	972,008	21,531,742	4,550	250,623	681,852	1,448,792	419,750
Texas	111	137,880,827	27,184,745	1,676,195	52,246,687	100,911	1,181,049	1,782,883	8,388,011	1,752,665
Utah	12	21,693,187	4,066,978	11,363	5,787,216	20,578	100,988	53,260	767,193	205,130
Vermont	15	7,787,519	2,090,372	18,500	4,640,112	700	74,770	161,540	438,497	163,296
Virginia	53	45,721,025	12,196,909	254,890	24,134,682	48,151	367,160	1,083,590	2,589,399	790,367
Washington	35	18,025,700	4,336,202	93,967	9,956,779	2,500	201,355	275,726	781,396	213,367
West Virginia	22	4,721,726	1,138,033	14,891	1,932,283	12,493	192,546	246,392	597,800	74,274
Wisconsin	47	18,600,186	5,537,529	28,908	8,637,245	7,868	355,475	428,920	1,609,833	236,119
Wyoming	5	3,210,840	788,854	11,933	2,412,544	0	0	0	0	71,916
American Samoa	1	5,000	1,000	0	3,000	0	0	0	0	0
Guam	2	704,652	205,221	0	420,781	0	12,090	43,210	0	0
Puerto Rico	15	14,848,990	2,045,190	3,045	6,060,981	53,500	141,569	33,500	629,000	73,520
U.S. Virgin Islands	1	112,968	0	0	0	0	0	0	0	0
Total	1,877	1,636,267,765	350,287,797	31,655,837	711,077,454	1,712,717	12,929,826	37,478,311	80,103,767	23,485,590
Estimated % of Acquisition Expenditures			21.41	1.93	43.46	0.10	0.79	2.29	4.90	1.44

Table 3 / Special Library Acquisition Expenditures

State	Number of Libraries	Total Acquisition Expenditures	Books	Other Print Materials	Periodicals/ Serials	Manuscripts & Archives	AV Equipment	Microforms	Electronic Reference	Preservation
									Categories of Expenditure (in U.S. dollars)	
Alabama	3	16,965	2,850	0	1,215	0	9,000	3,500	0	1,000
Alaska	1	10,000	3,000	1,700	3,000	0	250	0	500	0
Arizona	14	151,147	42,068	7,700	71,235	535	1,500	900	0	7,350
Arkansas	1	0	870	0	0	0	0	0	0	0
California	51	2,824,869	557,433	53,250	674,917	20,550	22,500	32,535	79,000	219,652
Colorado	13	107,802	39,284	0	23,976	0	6,158	500	500	3,600
Connecticut	12	405,827	35,784	24,000	111,364	12,000	0	1,000	184,263	6,200
Delaware	2	25,300	10,020	10,000	5,030	0	0	0	0	250
District of Columbia	17	101,015,707	243,384	100	311,745	200	500	30,100	74,700	16,503
Florida	28	1,116,861	208,887	37,400	355,566	8,000	6,600	18,500	27,000	10,450
Georgia	8	219,950	64,400	4,000	117,200	0	3,400	0	23,500	0
Hawaii	3	101,800	14,000	2,500	84,000	200	1,000	0	0	100
Idaho	3	582,463	352,000	30,000	150,250	0	0	0	50,000	0
Illinois	43	4,879,754	1,022,090	53,542	848,704	9,771	17,133	36,292	399,426	97,044
Indiana	9	181,202	75,450	18,300	43,002	0	0	7,850	4,000	0
Iowa	9	608,228	84,518	6,000	39,924	0	0	200	300	2,962
Kansas	6	159,430	37,030	250	94,450	250	1,225	14,000	9,600	2,275
Kentucky	3	9,424	4,575	0	2,649	0	0	0	0	1,200
Louisiana	4	27,600	6,900	0	0	0	0	0	0	0
Maine	5	35,287	7,752	2,954	7,267	1,000	0	0	0	1,300
Maryland	20	931,555	89,434	56,750	267,912	7,550	7,396	1,000	57,000	9,313
Massachusetts	33	3,976,403	506,982	18,285	330,895	8,500	960	31,842	225,386	39,017
Michigan	14	1,196,798	125,982	21,500	539,397	3,000	250	15,574	35,551	7,069
Minnesota	11	10,798,045	3,800,241	875,337	2,159,523	540,119	481,150	338,292	2,593,933	2,850

Mississippi	2	194,600	4,500	0	190,000	0	0	0	0	100
Missouri	13	3,191,409	471,349	1,139	2,342,521	720	200	204	8,554	89,461
Montana	4	69,335	6,200	1,233	53,541	4,000	561	0	1,000	0
Nebraska	7	109,668	23,251	325	8,915	4,000	0	70,102	0	0
Nevada	1	5,470	1,750	0	220	0	1,000	0	500	2,000
New Hampshire	7	682,900	15,000	4,000	5,000	5,000	8,000	2,000	0	15,000
New Jersey	9	2,185,488	166,790	3,400	158,275	0	6,550	20,000	5,000	8,500
New Mexico	7	86,625	31,850	0	16,145	0	3,200	500	0	3,000
New York	66	5,207,542	950,915	36,608	2,098,639	52,020	48,430	700	52,300	75,680
North Carolina	11	244,235	44,550	2,000	146,500	0	0	185	0	0
North Dakota	1	13,398	8,001	0	4,973	0	0	0	0	425
Ohio	31	2,265,883	410,794	23,399	888,274	2,000	30,707	7,537	79,151	26,524
Oklahoma	4	470,345	62,537	0	252,308	0	2,000	0	152,000	1,500
Oregon	8	91,300	33,200	0	48,750	0	0	50	10,000	0
Pennsylvania	30	3,862,658	176,955	33,930	126,413	17,468	800	5,225	6,369	68,333
Rhode Island	4	65,825	48,095	0	15,000	0	0	0	0	2,430
South Carolina	4	220,300	55,000	0	30,000	0	0	0	0	0
South Dakota	0	0	0	0	0	0	0	0	0	0
Tennessee	6	394,700	135,500	0	87,000	0	2,000	32,500	47,000	1,100
Texas	13	1,803,949	249,785	4,300	103,834	4,800	8,314	14,100	154,000	13,000
Utah	3	4,400	50,400	2,100	10,200	2,100	10,600	500	5,500	2,000
Vermont	3	110,868	6,521	0	62,708	1,874	0	0	0	3,763
Virginia	20	1,595,178	220,200	4,425	66,844	28,403	26,000	10,087	18,000	117,433
Washington	9	203,638	39,800	6,000	131,492	14,500	1,500	0	9,546	800
West Virginia	2	166,800	10,000	3,000	151,600	0	0	2,000	0	200
Wisconsin	9	598,037	186,150	17,900	178,000	7,000	8,595	138,000	60,000	100
Wyoming	0	0	0	0	0	0	0	0	0	0
Puerto Rico	3	257,150	34,800	4,600	85,250	0	8,000	0	8,000	500
Total	590	153,484,118	10,778,827	1,371,927	13,505,623	755,560	725,479	835,775	4,381,579	859,984
Estimated % of Acquisition Expenditures			7.02	0.89	8.80	0.49	0.47	0.54	2.85	0.56

Table 4 / Government Library Acquisition Expenditures

State	Number of Libraries	Total Acquisition Expenditures	Books	Other Print Materials	Periodicals/ Serials	Manuscripts & Archives	AV Equipment	Microforms	Electronic Reference	Preservation
Alabama	4	677,071	311,070	2,209	92,422	0	900	7,322	231,625	4,432
Alaska	4	56,050	19,800	5,000	26,250	0	10,000	0	0	0
Arizona	3	290,946	9,427	3,000	258,249	0	0	0	8,270	0
Arkansas	3	644,465	78,598	0	316,761	0	0	0	65,000	0
California	29	4,680,658	1,280,653	586,746	853,340	0	36,500	78,987	52,578	11,183
Colorado	6	276,315	33,259	200	168,667	0	7,552	8,200	37,737	0
Connecticut	1	22,000	0	0	0	0	0	5,000	0	0
Delaware	0	0								
District of Columbia	18	7,376,752	342,600	46,000	788,552	200	50,000	78,150	260,500	110,250
Florida	7	879,000	413,730	1,400	376,800	5,000	0	30,000	20,000	500
Georgia	0	0								
Hawaii	3	922,139	275,336	0	591,403	0	0	3,300	21,840	260
Idaho	1	60,000	4,000	0	36,000	0	0	0	0	0
Illinois	6	4,949,266	8,949	0	100,451	0	0	0	5,000	0
Indiana	3	193,000	0	0	77,000	0	0	0	0	0
Iowa	1	28,000	8,000	0	13,000	0	400	0	2,500	0
Kansas	2	855,527	309,840	181,246	162,156	0	0	0	0	0
Kentucky	1	7,500	3,500	0	4,000	0	0	0	0	11,285
Louisiana	5	3,118,433	15,673	0	123,100	0	0	0	27,660	0
Maine	2	308,892	4,000	0	50,000	0	0	0	4,000	0
Maryland	10	4,563,542	588,000	0	1,739,900	0	306,197	0	521,000	60,000
Massachusetts	9	597,612	251,899	100	166,600	0	3,500	9,236	30,000	500
Michigan	3	109,291	41,405	7,501	59,096	0	739	100	450	500
Minnesota	6	1,284,300	58,000	227,000	819,600	0	0	33,500	35,700	12,000

Categories of Expenditure (in U.S. dollars)

Mississippi	3	212,000	2,500	0	0	0	0	0	0	0
Missouri	2	410,000	200,000	0	0	0	0	0	20,000	0
Montana	5	812,097	45,210	0	229,848	0	0	985	6,454	0
Nebraska	2	25,000	200	0	800	0	0	0	0	0
Nevada	4	1,077,407	577,732	0	195,763	0	0	7,201	165,841	6,590
New Hampshire	0	0	0	0	0	0	0	0	0	0
New Jersey	3	2,900	17,200	0	1,700	0	0	0	420,000	30,000
New Mexico	2	1,232,000	50,000	480,000	246,000	0	0	2,000	98,807	15,300
New York	12	2,220,454	1,570,208	0	368,648	0	41,891	2,900	14,000	0
North Carolina	3	692,700	412,000	600	21,600	0	0	4,500	0	0
North Dakota	1	2,200	500	0	1,500	0	0	0	0	200
Ohio	5	923,124	213,719	8,051	655,427	0	0	0	9,500	0
Oklahoma	1	24,922	1,345	14	19,423	0	0	0	3,000	1,140
Oregon	3	56,835	59,463	2,000	228,126	0	0	0	2,000	0
Pennsylvania	12	1,297,889	1,455,237	0	106,500	0	0	0	106,000	8,000
Rhode Island	2	820,428	616,557	0	56,754	0	1,334	4,000	142,421	0
South Carolina	2	44,644	0	0	47	0	250	0	0	0
South Dakota	1	12,039	5,531	0	2,171	0	0	0	0	0
Tennessee	2	379,316	278,382	0	25,734	0	0	14,200	0	134,314
Texas	6	629,284	407,546	0	96,507	234	0	0	1,500	5,842
Utah	2	168,732	28,610	0	126,858	0	0	0	0	0
Vermont	0	0	0	0	0	0	0	0	0	0
Virginia	5	403,578	39,794	500	170,290	0	820	0	0	0
Washington	3	166,213	17,704	0	38,373	0	0	3,603	0	0
West Virginia	3	271,036	27,661	2,860	59,155	150	1,500	10,500	5,000	2,500
Wisconsin	6	327,752	42,887	3,500	159,094	0	0	0	36,657	0
Wyoming	2	254,500	211,000	1,000	27,000	500	0	10,000	0	5,000
Puerto Rico	2	603,560	180,000	4,000	284,060	2,000	25,000	0	107,500	1,000
Total	221	44,971,369	10,518,725	1,562,927	9,944,725	8,084	486,583	313,684	2,462,540	420,296
Estimated % of Acquisition Expenditures		23.39		3.48	22.11	0.02	1.08	0.70	5.48	0.93

LJ Budget Report: The New Wariness

Norman Oder

Senior Editor, News & Features, *Library Journal*

Public libraries, like several other sectors of government, faced a double whammy in the last quarter of 2001; not only did a recession squeeze public funds, the terrorist attacks of September 11 shifted priorities to public safety and cut further into available funds.

Total budgets (see Table 1) are up 3.9 percent, while salary and materials budgets are up 5.07 percent and 3.1 percent, respectively. That 3.9 percent figure is a decline from last year's increase of 6.5 percent and the previous year's figure of 7.5 percent.

Some of the 355 libraries responding to the *Library Journal (LJ)* Budget Report 2002 survey reported solid budget increases, thanks to a robust local economy or a strong funding mechanism. But most librarians' comments indicate a widespread wariness about their institutions' financial future, with some bracing for further cuts.

That's not to say that burdens are equal. Especially vulnerable were libraries in New York City, which faced a 10 percent budget cut in fiscal year (FY) 2002, and in states dependent on tourism sales tax revenues, such as Florida. Even Ohio, a paragon of library support, froze funding this year. Ohio libraries, though still comparatively well funded, now must pay for the Ohio Public Library Information Network (OPLIN), which was previously paid for out of the general fund.

Also, in a notable shift, libraries reported a substantial decrease in the amount of donations received in 2001, an average of $482,000 vs. $571,000 in the previous year. That can be attributed not only to the economic downturn but also to the substantial charitable focus on the victims of September 11. Some smaller libraries (serving populations under 100,000) actually increased their fund raising in 2001.

Per Capita Funding Up Slightly

Per capita funding continued its steady increase, projected at $34.90 for FY 2002, up more than $1 per capita from FY 2001's $33.68. Seventy-one percent of libraries projected an increase in per capita funding, while 9 percent projected no change.

Compared with budgets from five years ago, medium and larger systems (50,000 population and above) averaged increases of 40 percent or more, while the budgets of smaller libraries grew more slowly. Also over five years, the net increase for materials (39.5 percent) exceeded the increase for salaries (36.8 percent), with the largest libraries (serving one million or more) reporting the most growth in materials budgets. That trend is likely to reverse, as libraries faced with tightened budgets often opt to adjust their materials budgets rather than lay off staff.

Adapted from *Library Journal*, January 2002

Table 1 / Projected Library Budgets for Fiscal Year 2002*

Population Served	Total Budget 2001	Total Budget 2002	Change in Total Budget	Materials Budget 2001	Materials Budget 2002	Change in Materials Budget	Salary Budget 2001	Salary Budget 2002	Change in Salary Budget
Total sample (weighted)	$6,095,000	$6,333,000	3.90%	$838,000	$864,000	3.10%	$3,671,000	$3,857,000	5.07%
Under 10,000	197,000	206,000	4.57	33,000	32,000	-3.03	102,000	106,000	3.92
10,000 to 24,999	568,000	608,000	7.04	88,000	91,000	3.41	325,000	346,000	6.46
25,000 to 49,999	1,612,000	1,674,000	3.85	224,000	228,000	1.79	951,000	1,004,000	5.57
50,000 to 99,999	2,443,000	2,584,000	5.77	365,000	385,000	5.48	1,456,000	1,547,000	6.25
100,000 to 499,999	6,265,000	6,497,000	3.70	848,000	868,000	2.36	3,636,000	3,878,000	6.66
500,000 to 999,999	28,489,000	29,685,000	4.20	4,012,000	4,235,000	5.56	16,528,000	17,583,000	6.38
1 million or more	58,907,000	60,831,000	3.27	7,473,000	7,602,000	1.73	36,580,000	37,174,000	1.62

*LJ mailed out 2000 questionnaires to public libraries in October 2001, with 355 responding, for a response rate of 18%

Then again, of those libraries receiving grant monies in FY 2002, 46 percent said they would use those funds for books/materials. Smaller percentages will use grants for technology (44 percent), literacy (30 percent), and Internet/Web (19 percent). Among the largest libraries (serving 500,000 or more), 69 percent will use grant money for books.

Funding and Technology

While state governments remain the largest source of grants, half the libraries reported receiving money from the Gates Learning Foundation, with an average grant of $88,000. Larger libraries (serving 50,000 and above) were most likely to receive Gates funding. For almost two-thirds of those libraries, the funding will run out this year, while another quarter have already expended their funds. Well over half the libraries aim to replace the Gates grants by increasing their budgets; time will tell if they have the capacity to do so.

Internet-related expenses still represent a very small portion of a library's total budget, but that proportion has almost doubled—from 2.2 percent to 4.2 percent—since 1998. The cost is projected to go up modestly, to 5 percent, in FY 2002. The major Internet-related cost is access, especially for those libraries serving smaller populations, followed by staffing, new hardware, and upgrades/maintenance. Fewer than one in five libraries has had to cut spending to pay for technology; in those cases, nearly all (90 percent) have targeted the materials budget.

The E-rate remained a significant source of funding, as two-thirds of libraries said they had applied for telecomm discounts, a slight drop-off from previous years. Perhaps reflecting the burden of filling out the forms, larger libraries (serving 100,000 and over) were most likely to apply for the E-rate.

Meanwhile, online use continues to grow, by 40.3 percent. Per capita circulation, however, rose only modestly, to an estimated 8.29 for FY 2001 from 8.06 in FY 2000.

Some 43 percent reported filtering Internet use, a jump from previous years (31 percent in 2001, 25 percent in 2000). Of those filtering the Internet, 96 percent filter all their children's terminals. About half of those filtering also filter adult terminals. Perhaps because of the cost of filtering, smaller libraries (under 25,000 population) were least likely to use filters. The average cost was $1,722

Table 2 / Fund Raising Dips

Population Served	Average Amount Raised in		
	1996	2000	2001
Total sample	$384,000	$571,000	$482,000
Under 10,000	4,000	22,000	24,000
10,000 to 24,999	61,000	24,000	41,000
25,000 to 49,999	22,000	88,000*	58,000*
50,000 to 99,999	438,000	136,000	170,000
100,000 to 499,999	122,000	553,000	388,000
500,000 or more	2,009,000	2,402,000	1,776,000

*One library with anomalously high fundraising was eliminated from these averages

per library system, but smaller libraries (serving under 50,000) spent an average of $360 or less.

Local Progress Reports

Here is a fiscal snapshot of how public libraries are faring nationwide. Dollars represent total FY 2002 budget.

Serving fewer than 10,000

Prairie du Chien Memorial Library, WI
($292,212, up 2.2%)

The library credits a supportive board and city council for steady funding. It will be budgeting and fund raising for a building addition in 2003.

Douglas Library, Hebron, CT
($318,000, up 4.3%)

Previously an association library, Douglas became a town library last July. School construction, however, may limit funding for its growth. The library's expansion in 2000 led to more funding for staff but not materials.

Silver Creek Library, NE
($8,500, up 6.3%)

This tiny township library, serving a population of 435, only recently gained a computer. It's open 15 hours a week.

Sutton Public Library, WV
($32,262, up 7.9%)

Dependent on state funds for two-thirds of its budget, the library, which has raised only $700 in the past two years, has started a campaign to construct a new building this year.

Gay-Kimball Public Library, Troy, NH
($69,993, up 3%)

The library was renovated and expanded three years ago. Per capita spending is $26, and trust funds support 12 percent of the budget.

Serving 10,000–24,999

McPherson Public Library, KS
($525,600, up 4.6%)

With a per capita expenditure nearing $37, the library benefits from a city government

and business community that recognize "the importance of a quality public library" both for citizens and to attract new business.

Wead Library, Malone, NY
($386,952, up 5%)

This library, near the Canadian border, fears contraction in the post–September 11 economy. Its $18,427 Gates grant runs out this year, and it must scramble to replace that funding.

Spencer Public Library, IA
($381,771, up 6.4%)

The library relies mostly on local funding (95 percent) and expects the city's contribution to stay consistent. Per capita spending is nearly $33.

Holbrook Public Library, MA
($345,474, up 2.1%)

Due to cuts in both state and local revenue, the library's materials budget is on hold, and "we won't see increases in our budget for two or more years."

Serving 25,000–49,999

Bozeman Public Library, MT
($1.1 million, up 5.2%)

The library has been unable to keep up with the area's 40 percent growth in the past 20 years. It must raise $4 million for a new building, as the city's bonding capacity can only cover one third of the cost.

Wallingford Public Library, CT
($1.9 million, up 5.3%)

The library's modest budget increase represents a cut from its original request, a consequence of a "huge increase in medical benefits" for both the library and the city. The library has saved thousands of dollars in electronic/Web-based services thanks to the state-funded Connecticut Digital Library.

Morley Library, Painesville, OH
($2.75 million, up 5.4%)

Though state funding (69 percent of support) has been cut over a three-year period, the library reports that grants and local funding have increased. Voters in November approved an $11.5 million bond issue for a new, larger building. Per capita spending is $64.

Princeton Public Library, NJ
($2.83 million, up 7%)

The library's budget has increased steadily; per capita spending is $93.53, up $16 in two years. A $9.8 million capital campaign over two years, which will finance an expansion, shows support for the library at an all-time high.

Brookings Public Library, SD
($711,512, up 1.1%)

On top of a static materials budget, the library faces possible cutbacks in hours or services during FY 2003. With 96.5 percent of funding coming from the city, the library (per capita spending $25) may put its long-range plans on hold.

Serving 50,000–99,999

Sandusky Library, OH
($3.4 million, down 5.6%)

Like most Ohio libraries, this is well supported (per capita funding is nearly $70). It will cope with a 15 percent cut in revenue (including a 5 percent state cut) by using funds carried over from FY 2001.

Williamsburg Regional Library, VA
($4.7 million, up 6.8%)

After seeing a 145 percent increase over five years (to a per capita spending level of $71), growth is expected to slow, as municipal funding is dependent on tourism and state aid is uncertain, but the library's major funding, based on property taxes, should be solid.

Columbia County Public Library, Lake City, FL
($1 million, down 2.7%)

State budget cuts are expected to affect both aid to libraries and county budgets. New strains on counties have led to a local freeze on hiring, travel, and capital outlays. The library gets 56 percent of its budget from the county and 40 percent from the state.

Jackson/Madison County Library, Jackson, TN
($903,394, up 0.8%)

With a per capita under $10, and static budget appropriations, the forecast is "not positive" in this economically strained region. The materials budget has declined 7.35 percent over the last five years.

Altoona Area Public Library, PA
($1.04 million, up 4%)

The area economy has "taken a huge hit" as industries have closed. Municipal revenue is down, and state aid—41 percent of support in the recently revamped state funding structure—is expected to level off. Per capita spending is under $17.

Serving 100,000–499,999

Omaha Public Library, NE
($9.76 million, down 6%)

Cuts in tax-supported funding will lead to fewer hours and materials. Because "technology funding is difficult to retain in budget allocations," the library will begin leasing one-third of its computers this year.

Cumberland County Public Library & Information Center, Fayetteville, NC
($6.67 million, unchanged)

The library's county funding (84 percent of total) is jeopardized by decreased sales tax revenue caused by the faltering economy and military relocations. Per capita expenditure is $22.

Pueblo City-County Library District, CO
($6 million, up 8.1%)

Though the local economy has grown uncertain in this well-funded district (per capita spending is $43.8), the library has managed to garner a $4 million gift for the new main library, which will open in 2003.

Chula Vista Public Library, CA
($5.5 million, up 1.2%)

The city is prepared to maintain current funding levels and the library will increase operating hours this year. It hopes to pay for half of a new $12.6 million library with funds from the state's $350 million bond issue approved in 2000.

Broome County Public Library, Binghamton, NY
($2.66 million, up 5.6%)

While circulation is low (2.44 per capita), it has been boosted by a new central library. Still, library service is not a local priority, and state budget support is expected to drop.

Serving 500,000–999,999

DeKalb County Public Library, GA
($12.1 million, up 3.4%)

A fiscal tightening this year is expected to be temporary, but long-term growth prospects are "considered good." Older computer workstations will be replaced in 2003 and 2004.

Tampa-Hillsborough County Public Library, FL
($36.3 million, up 7.7%)

The state's massive revenue shortfall will eventually cut into the library's 7.4 percent state funding share, but the local taxing district that funds library operations (per capita spending is $35) should remain strong.

Tucson-Pima Public Library, AZ
($18 million, down 8.6%)

Though it won a $5.5 million bond issue in

2000, the library is preparing for a nearly 10 percent budget cut for FY 2002–2003 as a downturn in tourism has led to cuts in local revenues. The immediate future "looks uncertain to bleak."

Seattle Public Library
($34.4 million, up 0.9%)

Though the library has raised some $27 million in its capital campaign during the past two years, the recession and a citizen initiative have stalled its operating budget, leading to two planned week-long closures this year.

Serving 1,000,000 or more

Fairfax County Public Library, VA
($27.8 million, up 1.1%)

Though the library's budget has increased by 50 percent over the past five years, the forecast is "not promising," as county agencies have been asked to cut their budgets 5 percent in FY 2002.

San Diego Public Library
($32.8 million, up 18.4%)

The library received a large increase in FY 2002 (to a per capita spending level of $26), with a commitment to continue that increase for three years. However, the economic downturn may delay or eliminate future increases.

Houston Public Library, TX
($37.44 million, up 0.9%)

The library, dependent totally on local funding, will not expend the current year's budget fully and expects a reduced budget next year. A $40 million bond issue passed in November.

Chicago Public Library
($90 million, up 1%)

While 2002 will be a stable fiscal year, the library will continue to spend bond issue funds to build new branches. The library expects more money for personnel and materials in 2003.

Price Indexes for Public and Academic Libraries

Research Associates of Washington
1200 North Nash St., No. 1112, Arlington, VA 22209
703-243-3399
World Wide Web http://www.rschassoc.com

Kent Halstead

A rise in prices with the gradual loss of the dollar's value has been a continuing phenomenon in the U.S. economy. This article reports price indexes measuring this inflation for public libraries, and for college and university academic libraries. (Current data for these indexes are published by Research Associates of Washington. See *Inflation Measures for Schools, Colleges and Libraries, 2001 Update.*) Price indexes report the year-to-year price level of what is purchased. Dividing past expenditures per user unit by index values determines if purchasing power has been maintained. Future funding requirements to offset expected inflation may be estimated by projecting the indexes.

A price index compares the aggregate price level of a fixed market basket of goods and services in a given year with the price in the base year. To measure price change accurately, the *quality* and *quantity* of the items purchased must remain constant as defined in the base year. Weights attached to the importance of each item in the budget are changed infrequently—only when the relative *amount* of the various items purchased clearly shifts or when new items are introduced.

Public Library Price Index

The Public Library Price Index (PLPI) is designed for a hypothetical *average* public library. The index together with its various subcomponents are reported in Tables 2 through 6. The PLPI reflects the relative year-to-year price level of the goods and services purchased by public libraries for their current operations. The budget mix shown in Table 1 is based on national and state average expenditure patterns. Individual libraries may need to tailor the weighting scheme to match their own budget compositions.

The Public Library Price Index components are described below together with sources of the price series employed.

Personnel Compensation

PL1.0 Salaries and Wages

PL1.1 *Professional librarians*—Median salary of professional librarians at medium and large size libraries. Six positions are reported: director/dean, deputy/ associate/assistant director, department heads/coordinator/senior management, managers/supervisors, librarian non-supervisory, beginning librarian.

(text continues on page 474)

Note: Publication rights for the public and academic library price indexes reported here are for sale. The sale package consists of copyrights; computer software; written data collection, compilation, and layout instructions; and mailing lists. Interested parties are requested to call 703-243-3399.

Table 1 / Taxonomy of Public Library Current Operations Expenditures by Object Category, 1991–1992 estimate

Category	Mean	Percent	Distribution
Personnel Compensation			64.7
PL1.0 Salaries and Wages		81.8	
PL1.1 Professional librarians	44		
PL1.2 Other professional and managerial staff	6		
PL1.3 Technical staff (copy cataloging, circulation, binding, etc.)	43		
PL1.4 Support staff (clerical, custodial, guard, etc.)	7		
	100		
PL2.0 Fringe Benefits		18.2	
		100.0	
Acquisitions			15.2
PL3.0 Books and Serials		74.0	
PL3.1 Books printed	82		
PL3.1a Hardcover			
PL3.1b Trade paper			
PL3.1c Mass market paper			
PL3.2 Periodicals (U.S. and foreign titles)	16		
PL3.2a U.S. titles			
PL3.2b Foreign titles			
PL3.3 Other serials (newspapers, annuals, proceedings, etc.)	2		
	100		
PL4.0 Other Printed Materials		2.0	
PL5.0 Non-Print Media		22.0	
PL5.1 Microforms (microfiche and microfilm)	21		
PL5.2 Audio recordings (primarily instructional and children's content)	17		
PL5.2a Tape cassette			
PL5.2b Compact disk			
PL5.3 Video (TV) recordings (primarily books & children's content)	58		
PL5.3a VHS Cassette			
PL5.3b Laser disk			
PL5.4 Graphic image individual item use	2		
PL5.5 Computer files (CD-ROM, floppy disks, and tape)	2		
	100		
PL6.0 Electronic Services		2.0	
		100.0	
Operating Expenses			20.1
PL7.0 Office Operations		27.0	
PL7.1 Office expenses	20		
PL7.2 Supplies and materials	80		
	100		
PL8.0 Contracted Services		38.0	
PL9.0 Non-capital Equipment		1.0	
PL10.0 Utilities		34.0	
		100.0	100.0

Table 2 / Public Library Price Index and Major Component Subindexes, FY 1992 to 1999

1992=100 Fiscal year	Personnel Compensation		Acquisitions				Operating Expenses				Public Library Price Index^ (PLPI)
	Salaries and wages (PL1.0)	Fringe benefits (PL2.0)	Books and serials (PL3.0)	Other printed materials (PL4.0)	Non-print media (PL5.0)	Electronic services (PL6.0)	Office operations (PL7.0)	Contracted services (PL8.0)	Non-capital Equipment (PL9.0)	Utilities (PL10.0)	
1992	100.0	100.0	100.0	100.0	100.0	100.0	100.0	100.0	100.0	100.0	100.0
1993	102.5	104.8	102.0	102.9	75.3	101.9	99.2	102.6	101.8	101.5	101.6
1994	105.8	107.9	103.5	105.5	65.8	104.8	100.8	105.1	103.6	105.8	104.1
1995	110.5	110.6	105.6	107.7	64.8	108.5	102.6	107.7	105.7	103.8	107.3
1996	112.3	113.9	107.3	111.3	67.8	110.3	113.9	113.3	108.5	100.0	109.6
1997	114.6	116.1	111.1	118.5	69.5	110.3	113.3	114.1	110.3	113.7	112.7
1998	119.4	118.1	117.5	122.7	67.2	115.5	112.3	118.0	111.9	119.1	116.8
1999	123.6	121.4	118.0	125.7	68.8	119.2	110.4	121.4	113.5	107.7	118.9
1993	2.5%	4.8%	2.0%	2.9%	-24.7%	1.9%	-0.8%	2.6%	1.8%	1.5%	1.6%
1994	3.2%	3.0%	1.4%	2.5%	-12.6%	2.8%	1.6%	2.4%	1.7%	4.2%	2.5%
1995	4.4%	2.5%	2.1%	2.1%	-1.5%	3.5%	1.7%	2.5%	2.1%	-1.9%	3.0%
1996	1.6%	3.0%	1.6%	3.3%	4.7%	1.7%	11.1%	3.3%	2.6%	-3.6%	2.1%
1997	2.1%	1.9%	3.5%	6.5%	2.5%	0.0%	-0.5%	2.6%	1.7%	13.7%	2.9%
1998	4.2%	1.7%	5.7%	3.5%	-3.3%	4.7%	-0.9%	3.4%	1.4%	4.7%	3.6%
1999	3.5%	2.8%	0.4%	2.4%	2.3%	3.2%	-1.7%	2.9%	1.4%	-9.5%	1.8%

^ PLPI weightings: See text.
Sources: See text.

Table 3 / Public Library Price Index, Personnel Compensation, FY 1992 to 1999

1992=100 Fiscal year	Salaries and Wages							Fringe benefits index (PL2.0)
	Professional librarians			Other professional & managerial (PL1.2)	Technical staff (PL1.3)	Support staff (PL1.4)	Salaries & wages index* (PL1.0)	
	Medium size library~	Large size library~	Index^ (PL1.1)					
1992	100.0	100.0	100.0	100.0	100.0	100.0	100.0	100.0
1993	105.0	99.5	102.3	102.8	102.7	102.8	102.5	104.8
1994	109.2	102.7	106.0	105.7	105.7	106.0	105.8	107.9
1995	115.5	106.9	111.2	109.5	110.1	109.1	110.5	110.6
1996	113.7	108.9	111.3	112.9	113.2	112.1	112.3	113.9
1997	119.2	112.0	115.6	115.6	113.6	113.9	114.6	116.1
1998	123.2	118.2	120.7	121.3	118.1	117.9	119.4	118.1
1999	124.9	125.2	125.1	125.0	122.2	121.9	123.6	121.4
1993	5.0%	-0.5%	2.3%	2.8%	2.7%	2.8%	2.5%	4.8%
1994	4.0%	3.2%	3.6%	2.8%	2.9%	3.1%	3.2%	3.0%
1995	5.8%	4.1%	5.0%	3.6%	4.2%	2.9%	4.4%	2.5%
1996	-1.6%	1.9%	0.1%	3.1%	2.8%	2.7%	1.6%	3.0%
1997	4.8%	2.8%	3.9%	2.4%	0.4%	1.6%	2.1%	1.9%
1998	3.4%	5.5%	4.4%	4.9%	4.0%	3.5%	4.2%	1.7%
1999	1.4%	5.9%	3.6%	3.1%	3.5%	3.4%	3.5%	2.8%

~ medium size libraries have service areas from 25,000 to 99,999 population; large libraries, 100,000 or more.

^ Professional librarian salary weights: 50% medium libraries + 50% large libraries.

* Salaries and wages index weights: 44% professional librarians + 6% other professional + 43% technical staff +7% support staff.

Sources: See text.

Table 4 / Public Library Price Index, Books and Serials, FY 1992 to 1999

Books and Serials

1992=100 Fiscal year	Books printed — Hardcover Price^	Hardcover Index (PL3.1a)	Trade paper Price^	Trade paper Index (PL3.1b)	Mass market Price^	Mass market Index (PL3.1c)	Books printed index* (PL3.1)	Periodicals — United States Price^	U.S. Index (PL3.2a)	Foreign Price^	Foreign Index (PL3.2b)	Periodicals index~ (PL3.2)	Other serials (newspapers) Price^^	Newspaper Index (PL3.3)	Books & Serials index** (PL3.0)	Other printed materials index (PL4.0)
1992	$12.55	100.0	$8.49	100.0	$3.40	100.0	100.0	$45.18	100.0	$117.71	100.0	100.0	$222.68	100.0	100.0	100.0
1993		101.5		102.1		103.4	101.6	48.12	104.0	125.70	105.1	104.1	229.92	103.3	102.0	102.9
1994		102.5		104.4		106.5	102.8	47.19	104.4	133.50	113.4	105.5	261.91	117.6	103.5	105.5
1995		103.9		107.1		108.8	104.3	48.36	108.8	143.78	122.6	110.5	270.22	121.3	105.6	107.7
1996		104.2		109.3		113.7	104.8	50.58	114.2	153.34	134.8	116.7	300.21	134.8	107.3	111.3
1997		107.1		116.1		126.7	108.3	52.76	118.9	164.46	144.5	122.0	311.77	140.0	111.1	118.5
1998	$12.55	114.0	$8.49	120.5	$3.40	135.5	115.0	54.79	123.3	174.05	153.2	126.9	316.60	142.2	117.5	122.7
1999	12.60	114.4	8.57	121.6	3.50	139.5	115.6	56.94	123.3	185.97	153.2	126.9	318.44	143.0	118.0	125.7
1993		1.5%		2.1%		3.4%	1.6%		4.0%		5.1%	4.1%		3.3%	2.0%	2.9%
1994		1.0%		2.2%		3.0%	1.2%		0.4%		7.9%	1.3%		13.9%	1.4%	2.5%
1995		1.4%		2.6%		2.2%	1.5%		4.2%		8.1%	4.7%		3.2%	2.1%	2.1%
1996		0.2%		2.1%		4.6%	0.5%		5.0%		10.0%	5.6%		11.1%	1.6%	3.3%
1997		2.8%		6.2%		11.4%	3.3%		4.1%		7.2%	4.5%		3.9%	3.5%	6.5%
1998		6.4%		3.8%		6.9%	6.2%		3.7%		6.0%	4.0%		1.5%	5.7%	3.5%
1999		0.4%		0.9%		2.9%	0.5%		0.0%		0.0%	0.0%		0.6%	0.4%	2.4%

^ Book and periodical prices are for calendar year. *Books printed index weights: 89.5% hardcover + 8.2% trade paper + 2.3% mass market.
~ Periodical index weights: 87.9% U.S.titles + 12.1% foreign titles.
^^Other serials prices are for calendar year.
** Books & serials index weights: 82% books + 16% periodicals + 2% other serials.
Sources: See text.

Table 5 / Public Library Price Index, Non-Print Media and Electronic Services, FY 1992 to 1999

				Non-Print Media										
	Microforms (microfilm)	Audio recordings					Video			Graphic image	Computer files (CD-ROM)		Non-print media index*	Electronic services index
		Tape cassette		Compact disc		Audio recordings index*	VHS cassette		Video index					
1992=100														
Fiscal year	Index (PL5.1)	Price^	Index (PL5.2a)	Price^	Index (PL5.2b)	(PL5.2)	Price^	Index (PL5.3a)	(PL5.3)	(PL5.4)	Price^	Index (PL5.5)	(PL5.0)	(PL6.0)
1992	100.0	$12.18	100.0			100.0	$199.67	100.0	100.0	100.0	$1,601	100.0	100.0	100.0
1993	104.3	11.73	96.3			96.3	112.92	56.6	56.6	97.3	1,793	112.0	75.3	101.9
1994	107.9	8.20	67.3	$13.36	67.3	67.3	93.22	46.7	46.7	108.4	1,945	121.5	65.8	104.8
1995	110.6	8.82	72.4	14.80	74.6	73.5	84.19	42.2	42.2	111.3	1,913	119.5	64.8	108.5
1996	128.0	7.96	65.4	14.86	74.9	70.1	83.48	41.8	41.8	114.5	1,988	124.2	67.8	110.3
1997	132.9	8.13	66.7	16.43	82.8	74.8	82.10	41.1	41.1	126.5	2,012	125.7	69.5	110.3
1998	138.9	8.31	68.2	14.35	72.3	70.3	72.31	36.2	36.2	129.1	2,007	125.4	67.2	115.5
1999	142.9	8.20	67.3	12.65	63.7	65.5	77.85	39.0	39.0	124.5	2,007	125.4	68.8	119.2
1993	4.3%		-3.7%			-3.7%		-43.4%	-43.4%	-2.7%		12.0%	-24.7%	1.9%
1994	3.5%		-30.1%			-30.1%		-17.4%	-17.4%	11.4%		8.5%	-12.6%	2.8%
1995	2.5%		7.6%		10.80%	9.2%		-9.7%	-9.7%	2.7%		-1.6%	-1.5%	3.5%
1996	15.7%		-9.8%		0.04%	-4.6%		-0.8%	-0.8%	2.9%		3.9%	4.7%	1.7%
1997	3.8%		2.1%		10.60%	6.6%		-1.7%	-1.7%	10.5%		1.2%	2.5%	0.0%
1998	4.5%		2.2%		-12.70%	-6.0%		-11.9%	-11.9%	2.1%		-0.2%	-3.3%	4.7%
1999	2.9%		-1.3%		-11.80%	-6.7%		7.7%	7.7%	-3.6%		0.0%	2.3%	3.2%

^ Prices are for immediate preceding calendar year, e.g., CY 1993 prices are reported for FY 1994.

* Audio recordings index weights: 50% tape cassette + 50% compact disk. Non-print media index weights: 21% microforms + 17% audio recordings + 58% video + 2% graphic image + 2% computer files.

Sources: See text

Table 6 / Public Library Price Index, Operating Expenses, FY 1992 to 1999

1992=100 Fiscal year	Office Operations		Office operations index^ (PL7.0)	Contracted services index (PL8.0)	Noncapital equipment index (PL9.0)	Utilities index (PL10.0)
	Office expenses (PL7.1)	Supplies and materials (PL7.2)				
1992	100.0	100.0	100.0	100.0	100.0	100.0
1993	103.1	98.3	99.2	102.6	101.8	101.5
1994	107.3	99.2	100.8	105.1	103.6	105.8
1995	111.1	100.4	102.6	107.7	105.7	103.8
1996	117.8	112.9	113.9	111.3	108.5	100.0
1997	120.0	111.6	113.3	114.1	110.3	113.7
1998	123.1	109.5	112.3	118.0	111.9	119.1
1999	124.2	106.9	110.4	121.4	113.5	107.7
1993	3.1%	-1.7%	-.8%	2.6%	1.8%	1.5%
1994	4.1%	1.0%	1.6%	2.4%	1.7%	4.2%
1995	3.5%	1.2%	1.7%	2.5%	2.1%	-1.9%
1996	6.1%	12.4%	11.1%	3.3%	2.6%	-3.6%
1997	1.8%	-1.2%	-0.5%	2.6%	1.7%	13.7%
1998	2.6%	-1.9%	-0.9%	3.4%	1.4%	4.7%
1999	0.9%	-2.4%	-1.7%	2.9%	1.4%	-9.5%

^ Office operations index weights: 20% office expenses + 80% supplies and materials.
Sources: See text.

(text continued from page 468)

Source: Mary Jo Lynch, *ALA Survey of Librarian Salaries*, Office for Research and Statistics, American Library Association, Chicago, IL, annual.

PL1.2 *Other professional and managerial staff* (systems analyst, business manager, public relations, personnel, etc.)—Employment Cost Index (ECI) for wages and salaries for state and local government workers employed in "Executive, administrative, and managerial" occupations, *Employment Cost Index*, Bureau of Labor Statistics, U.S. Department of Labor, Washington, DC.

PL1.3 *Technical staff* (copy cataloging, circulation, binding, etc.)—ECI as above for government employees in "Service" occupations.

PL1.4 *Support staff* (clerical, custodial, guard, etc.)—ECI as above for government employees in "Administrative support, including clerical" occupations.

PL2.0 Fringe Benefits

ECI as above for state and local government worker "Benefits."

Acquisitions

PL3.0 Books and Serials

PL3.1 *Books printed*—Weighted average of sale prices (including jobber's discount) of hardcover (PL3.1a), trade paper (PL3.1b), and mass market paperback books (PL3.1c) sold to public libraries. Excludes university press publications and reference works. Source: Baker & Taylor Books.

PL3.2 *Periodicals*—Publisher's prices of sales of approximately 2,400 U.S. serial titles (PL3.2a) and 115 foreign serials (PL3.2b) sold to public libraries. Source: *Serials Prices*, EBSCO Subscription Services, Birmingham, AL.

PL3.3 *Other serials* (newspapers, annuals, proceedings, etc.)—Average prices of approximately 170 U.S. daily newspapers. Source: Genevieve S. Owens, University of Missouri, St. Louis, and Wilba Swearingen, Louisiana State University Medical Center. Reported by Adrian W. Alexander, "Prices of U.S. and Foreign Published Materials," in *Bowker Annual*, R. R. Bowker.

PL4.0 **Other Printed Materials** (manuscripts, documents, pamphlets, sheet music, printed material for the handicapped, etc.)

No direct price series exists for this category. The proxy price series used is the Producer Price Index for publishing pamphlets and catalogs and directories, Bureau of Labor Statistics.

PL5.0 Non-Print Media

PL5.1 *Microforms*—Producer Price Index for micropublishing in microform, including original and republished material, Bureau of Labor Statistics.

PL5.2 *Audio recordings*
PL5.2a *Tape cassette*—Cost per cassette of sound recording. Source: Dana Alessi, Baker & Taylor Books, Bridgewater, NJ. Reported by Alexander in *Bowker Annual*, R. R. Bowker.

PL5.2b *Compact disk*—Cost per compact disk. Source: See Alessi above.

PL5.3 *Video (TV) recordings*
PL5.3a. *VHS cassette*—Cost per video. Source: See Alessi above.

PL5.4 *Graphic image* (individual use of such items as maps, photos, art work, single slides, etc.). The following proxy is used. Average median weekly earnings for the following two occupational groups: painters, sculptors, craft artists, and artist printmakers; and photographers. Source: *Employment and Earnings Series*, U.S. Bureau of Labor Statistics

PL5.5 *Computer files* (CD-ROM, floppy disks, and tape). Average price of CD-ROM disks. Source: Martha Kellogg and Theodore Kellogg, University of Rhode Island. Reported by Alexander in *Bowker Annual*, R. R. Bowker.

PL6.0 Electronic Services

Average price for selected digital electronic computer and telecommunications networking available to libraries. Source: This source has requested anonymity.

Operating Expenses
PL7.0 Office Operations

PL7.1 *Office expenses* (telephone, postage and freight, publicity and printing, travel, professional fees, automobile operating cost, etc.)—The price series used for office expenses consists of the subindex for printed materials (PL4.0) described above; Consumer Price Index values for telephone and postage; CPI values for public transportation; the IRS allowance for individual business travel as reported by Runzheimer International; and CPI values for college tuition as a proxy for professional fees.

PL7.2 *Supplies and materials*—Producer Price Index price series for office supplies, writing papers, and pens and pencils. Source: U.S. Bureau of Labor Statistics.

PL8.0 Contracted Services (outside contracts for cleaning, building and grounds maintenance, equipment rental and repair, acquisition processing, binding, auditing, legal, payroll, etc.)

Prices used for contracted services include ECI wages paid material handlers, equipment cleaners, helpers, and laborers; average weekly earnings of production or non-supervisory workers in the printing and publishing industry, and the price of printing paper, as a proxy for binding costs; ECI salaries of attorneys, directors of personnel, and accountants, for contracted consulting fees; and ECI wages of precision production, craft, and repair occupations for the costs of equipment rental and repair.

PL9.0 Non-Capital Equipment

The type of equipment generally purchased as part of current library operations is usually small and easily movable. To be classified as "equipment" rather than as "expendable utensils" or "supplies," an item generally must cost $50 or more and have a useful life of at least three years. Examples may be hand calculators, small TVs, simple cameras, tape recorders, pagers, fans, desk lamps, books, etc. Equipment purchased as an operating expenditure is usually not depreciated. Items priced for this category include PPI commodity price series for machinery and equipment, office and store machines/equipment, hand tools, cutting tools and accessories, scales and balances, electrical measuring instruments, television receivers, musical instruments, photographic equipment, sporting and athletic goods, and books and periodicals.

PL10.0 Utilities

This subindex is a composite of the Producer Price Index series for natural gas, residual fuels, and commercial electric power, and the Consumer Price Index series for water and sewerage services. Source: U.S. Bureau of Labor Statistics.

Academic Library Price Indexes

The two academic library price indexes—the University Library Price Index (ULPI) and the College Library Price Index (CLPI)—together with their various subcomponents are reported in Tables 8–12A. The two indexes report the relative year-to-year price level of the staff salaries, acquisitions, and other goods and services purchased by university and college libraries respectively for their current operations. Universities are the 500 institutions with doctorate programs responding to the National Center for Education Statistics, U.S. Department of Education, *Academic Library Survey*. Colleges are the 1,472 responding institutions with master's and baccalaureate programs.

The composition of the library budgets involved, defined for pricing purposes, and the 1992 estimated national weighting structure are presented in Table 7. The priced components are organized in three major divisions: personnel compensation; acquisitions; and contracted services, supplies, and equipment.

The various components of the University and College Library Price Indexes are described in this section. Different weightings for components are designated in the tables "UL" for university libraries, "CL" for college libraries, and "AL" for academic libraries (common for both types). Source citations for the acquisitions price series are listed.

UL1.0 and CL1.0 Salaries and Wages

AL1.1 *Administrators* consists of the chief, deputy associate, and assistant librarian, e.g., important staff members having administrative responsibilities for management of the library. Administrators are priced by the head librarian salary series reported by the College and University Personnel Association (CUPA).

AL1.2 *Librarians* are all other professional library staff. Librarians are priced by the average of the median salaries for circulation/catalog, acquisition, technical service, and public service librarians reported by CUPA.

AL1.3 *Other professionals* are personnel who are not librarians in positions normally requiring at least a bachelor's degree. This group includes curators, archivists, computer specialists, budget officers, information and system specialists, subject bibliographers, and media specialists. Priced by the Higher Education Price Index (HEPI) faculty salary price series as a proxy.

AL1.4 *Nonprofessional staff* includes technical assistants, secretaries, and clerical, shipping, and storage personnel who are specifically assigned to the library and covered by the library budget. This category excludes general custodial and maintenance workers and student employees. This staff category is dominated by office-type workers and is priced by the HEPI clerical workers price series reported by the BLS Employment Cost Index.

AL1.5 *Students* are usually employed part-time for near minimum hourly wages. In some instances these wages are set by work-study program requirements of the institution's student financial aid office. The proxy price series used for student wages is the Employment Cost Index series for non-farm laborers, U.S. Bureau of Labor Statistics.

AL2.0 Fringe Benefits

The fringe benefits price series for faculty used in the HEPI is employed in pricing fringe benefits for library personnel.

UL3.0 and CL3.0 Books and Serials

UL3.1a *Books printed, U.S. titles, universities.* Book acquisitions for university libraries are priced by the North American Academic Books price series reporting the average list price of approximately 60,000 titles sold to college and university libraries by four of the largest book vendors. Compiled by Stephen Bosch, University of Arizona.

CL3.1a *Books printed, U.S. titles, colleges.* Book acquisitions for college libraries are priced by the price series for U.S. College Books representing approximately 6,300 titles compiled from book reviews appearing in *Choice* during the calendar year. Compiled by Donna Alsbury, Florida Center for Library Automation.

AL3.1b *Foreign Books.* Books with foreign titles *and* published in foreign countries are priced using U.S. book imports data. Bureau of the Census, U.S. Department of Commerce.

AL3.2a *Periodicals, U.S. titles.* U.S. periodicals are priced by the average subscription price of approximately 2,100 U.S. serial titles purchased by college and university libraries reported by EBSCO Subscription Services, Birmingham, AL.

AL3.2b *Periodicals, Foreign.* Foreign periodicals are priced by the average subscription price of approximately 600 foreign serial titles purchased by college and university libraries reported by EBSCO Subscription Services.

AL3.3 *Other Serials* (newspapers, annuals, proceedings, etc.). Average prices of approximately 170 U.S. daily newspapers. Source: Genevieve S. Owens, University of Missouri, St. Louis, and Wilba Swearingen, Louisiana State University Medical Center. Reported by Bill Robnett, "Prices of U.S. and Foreign Published Materials," in *Bowker Annual*, R. R. Bowker.

AL4.0 Other Printed Materials

These acquisitions include manuscripts, documents, pamphlets, sheet music, printed material for the handicapped, and so forth. No direct price series exists for this category. The proxy price series used is the Producer Price Index (PPI) for publishing pamphlets (PC 2731 9) and catalogs and directories (PCU2741#B), Bureau of Labor Statistics, U.S. Department of Labor.

AL5.0 Non-Print Media

AL5.1 *Microforms.* Producer Price Index for micropublishing in microform, including original and republished material (PC 2741 797), Bureau of Labor Statistics.

AL5.2 *Audio recordings*
AL5.2a *Tape cassette*—Cost per cassette of sound recording. Source: Dana Alessi, Baker & Taylor Books, Bridgewater, NJ. Reported by Alexander in *Bowker Annual*, R. R. Bowker.
AL5.2b *Compact Disc*—Cost per compact disc. Source: See Alessi above.

AL5.3 *Video (TV) recordings*
PL5.3a *VHS cassette*—cost per video. Source: See Alessi above.

AL5.4 *Graphic image* (individual use of such items as maps, photos, art work, single slides, etc.). No direct price series exists for graphic image materials. Average median weekly earnings for three related occupational groups (painters, sculptors, craft artists; artist printmakers; and photographers) is used as a proxy. these earnings series are reported in *Employment and Earnings Series*, U.S. Bureau of Labor Statistics.

AL5.5 *Computer files* (CD-ROM floppy disks, and tape). Average price of CD-ROM disks; primarily bibliographic, abstracts, and other databases of interest to academic libraries. Source: Developed from *Faxon Guide to CD-ROM* by Martha Kellogg and Theodore Kellogg, University of Rhode Island. Reported by Alexander in *Bowker Annual*, R. R. Bowker.

AL6.0 Electronic Services

Average price for selected digital electronic computer and telecommunications networking available to libraries. The source of this price series has requested anonymity.

AL7.0 Binding/Preservation

In-house maintenance of the specialized skills required for binding is increasingly being replaced by contracting out this service at all but the largest libraries. No wage series exists exclusively for binding. As a proxy, the Producer Price Index (PPI) for bookbinding and related work (PC 2789) is used. Source: Bureau of Labor Statistics, U.S. Department of Labor.

AL8.0 Contracted Services

Services contracted by libraries include such generic categories as communications, postal service, data processing, and printing and duplication. The HEPI contracted services subcomponent, which reports these items, is used as the price series. (In this instance the data processing component generally represents the library's payment for use of a central campus computer service.) However, libraries may also contract out certain specialized activities such as ongoing public access cataloging (OPAC) that are not distinctively priced in this AL8.0 component.

AL9.0 Supplies and Materials

Office supplies, writing papers, and pens and pencils constitute the bulk of library supplies and materials and are priced by these BLS categories for the Producer Price Index, Bureau of Labor Statistics, U.S. Department of Labor.

AL10.0 Equipment

This category is limited to small, easily movable, relatively inexpensive and short-lived items that are not carried on the books as depreciable capital equipment. Examples can include personal computers, hand calculators, projectors, fans, cameras, tape recorders, small TVs, etc. The HEPI equipment price series has been used for pricing.

Table 7 / Budget Composition of University Library and College Library Current
Operations by Object Category, FY 1992 Estimate

Category	University Libraries		College Libraries
	Percent Distribution		Percent Distribution
Personnel Compensation			
1.0 Salaries and wages. 43.4			47.2
1.1 Administrators (head librarian)		10	25
1.2 Librarians		20	15
1.3 Other professionals^		10	5
1.4 Nonprofessional staff		50	40
1.5 Students hourly employed		10	15
		100.0	100.0
2.0 Fringe benefits 10.6			11.5
Acquisitions			
3.0 Books and Serials. 28.5			24.8
3.1 Books printed		35	47
3.1a U.S. titles	80		95
3.1b Foreign titles	20		5
3.2 Periodicals		60	48
3.2a U.S. titles	80		95
3.2b Foreign titles	20		5
3.3 Other serials (newspapers, annuals, proceedings, etc.)	5		5
		100.0	100
4.0 Other Printed Materials* 1.2			0.7
5.0 Non-Print Media 1.6			3.3
5.1 Microforms (microfiche and microfilm)		45	45
5.2 Audio recordings		5	5
5.2a Tape cassette			
5.2b Compact disc (CDs)			
5.3 Video (TV) VHS recordings		15	15
5.4 Graphic image individual item use~		5	5
5.5 Computer materials (CD-ROM, floppy disks, and tape)		30	30
		100.0	100.0
6.0. Electronic Services^^ 4.0			3.5
Contracted Services, Supplies, Equipment			
7.0 Binding/preservation. 1.3			0.8
8.0 Contracted services** 4.4			3.1
9.0 Supplies and materials 3.1			2.6
10.0 Equipment (non-capital)# 1.9			2.5
		100.0	100

^ Other professional and managerial staff includes systems analyst, business manager, public relations, personnel, etc.
* Other printed materials includes manuscripts, documents, pamphlets, sheet music, printed material for the handicapped, etc.
~ Graphic image individual item use includes maps, photos, art work, single slides, etc.
^^Electronic services includes software license fees, network intra-structure costs, terminal access to the Internet, desktop computer operating budget, and subscription services.
**Contracted services includes outside contracts for communications, postal service, data processing, printing and duplication, equipment rental and repair, acquisition processing, etc.
Relatively inexpensive items not carried on the books as depreciable capital equipment. Examples include microform and audiovisual equipment, personal computers, hand calculators, projectors, fans, cameras, tape recorders, and small TVs.
Source: Derived, in part, from data published in *Academic Libraries: 1992*, National Center for Education Statistics, USDE.

Table 8 / University Library Price Index and Major Component Subindexes, FY 1992 to 1999

1992=100 Fiscal year	Personnel Compensation		Acquisitions					Operating Expenses			University Library Price Index ULPI
	Salaries and wages (UL1.0)	Fringe benefits (AL2.0)	Books and serials (UL3.0)	Other printed materials (AL4.0)	Non-print media (AL5.0)	Electronic services (AL6.0)	Binding/preservation (AL7.0)	Contracted services (AL8.0)	Supplies and material (AL9.0)	Equipment (AL10.0)	
1992	100.0	100.0	100.0	100.0	100.0	100.0	100.0	100.0	100.0	100.0	100.0
1993	103.2	105.4	105.4	102.9	98.7	101.9	100.5	102.6	98.3	101.8	103.7
1994	106.5	110.5	111.4	105.5	100.8	104.8	101.2	106.2	99.2	103.6	107.7
1995	110.0	114.2	115.6	107.7	101.5	108.5	102.9	108.4	100.4	105.7	111.3
1996	113.4	115.8	122.3	111.3	108.9	110.3	107.1	112.4	112.9	108.5	115.8
1997	117.0	117.0	136.8	118.5	113.3	110.3	108.9	114.8	111.6	110.3	121.8
1998	120.7	122.1	144.4	122.7	115.3	115.5	112.8	118.6	109.5	111.9	126.7
1999	125.1	123.4	154.1	125.7	117.3	119.2	115.0	121.5	106.9	113.5	131.8
1993	3.2%	5.4%	5.4%	2.9%	-1.3%	1.9%	0.5%	2.6%	-1.7%	1.8%	3.7%
1994	3.1%	4.8%	5.7%	2.5%	2.1%	2.8%	0.7%	3.5%	0.9%	1.8%	3.9%
1995	3.4%	3.4%	3.8%	2.1%	0.7%	3.5%	1.7%	2.1%	1.2%	2.0%	3.3%
1996	3.2%	1.4%	5.8%	3.3%	7.3%	1.7%	4.1%	3.7%	12.5%	2.6%	4.0%
1997	3.1%	1.0%	11.8%	6.5%	4.0%	0.0%	1.7%	2.1%	-1.2%	1.7%	5.2%
1998	3.2%	4.4%	5.6%	3.5%	2.0%	4.7%	3.6%	3.3%	-1.9%	1.5%	4.0%
1999	3.6%	1.1%	6.7%	2.4%	1.4%	3.2%	2.0%	2.4%	-2.4%	1.4%	4.0%

Sources: See text.

Table 9 / College Library Price Index and Major Component Subindexes, FY 1992 to 1999

1992=100 Fiscal year	Personnel Compensation		Acquisitions					Operating Expenses			College Library Price Index CLPI
	Salaries and wages (CL1.0)	Fringe benefits (AL2.0)	Books and serials (CL3.0)	Other printed materials (AL4.0)	Non-print media (AL5.0)	Electronic services (AL6.0)	Binding/ preser- vation (AL7.0)	Contracted services (AL8.0)	Supplies and material (AL9.0)	Equip- ment (AL10.0)	
1992	100.0	100.0	100.0	100.0	100.0	100.0	100.0	100.0	100.0	100.0	100.0
1993	103.5	105.4	107.1	102.9	98.7	101.9	100.5	102.6	98.3	101.8	104.2
1994	106.5	110.5	112.8	105.5	100.8	104.8	101.2	106.2	99.2	103.6	107.9
1995	110.0	114.2	114.9	107.7	101.5	108.5	102.9	108.4	100.4	105.7	110.9
1996	113.8	115.8	118.7	111.3	108.9	110.3	107.1	112.4	112.9	108.5	114.7
1997	117.5	117.0	131.2	118.5	113.7	110.3	108.9	114.8	111.6	110.3	119.9
1998	120.9	122.1	138.1	122.7	115.6	115.5	112.8	118.6	109.5	111.9	124.3
1999	125.1	123.4	146.6	125.7	117.3	119.2	115.0	121.5	106.9	113.5	128.8
1993	3.5%	5.4%	7.1%	2.9%	-1.3%	1.9%	0.5%	2.6%	-1.7%	1.8%	4.2%
1994	2.9%	4.8%	5.3%	2.5%	2.1%	2.8%	0.7%	3.5%	0.9%	1.8%	3.6%
1995	3.3%	3.4%	1.8%	2.1%	0.7%	3.5%	1.7%	2.1%	1.2%	2.0%	2.7%
1996	3.5%	1.4%	3.3%	3.3%	7.3%	1.7%	4.1%	3.7%	12.5%	2.6%	3.5%
1997	3.2%	1.0%	10.6%	6.5%	4.0%	0.0%	1.7%	2.1%	-1.2%	1.7%	4.6%
1998	2.9%	4.4%	5.2%	3.5%	2.0%	4.7%	3.6%	3.3%	-1.9%	1.5%	3.6%
1999	3.5%	1.1%	6.2%	2.4%	1.4%	3.2%	2.0%	2.4%	-2.4%	1.4%	3.7%

Sources: See text.

Table 10 / Academic Library Price Indexes, Personnel Compensation, FY 1992 to 1999

1992=100 Fiscal year	Administrators (head librarian) (AL1.1)	Librarians (AL1.2)	Other professional (AL1.3)	Non-professional (AL1.4)	Students hourly employed (AL1.5)	Salaries and Wages Indexes		Fringe benefits index (AL2.0)
						Universities* (UL1.0)	Colleges^ (CL1.0)	
1992	100.0	100.0	100.0	100.0	100.0	100.0	100.0	100.0
1993	105.0	102.6	102.5	103.2	102.7	103.2	103.5	105.4
1994	107.3	106.0	105.6	106.6	105.4	106.3	106.5	110.5
1995	110.6	110.2	109.3	110.1	108.5	110.0	110.0	114.2
1996	116.3	113.6	112.5	113.3	111.8	113.4	113.8	115.8
1997	120.2	116.5	115.8	117.0	115.6	117.0	117.5	117.0
1998	121.6	120.1	119.7	121.2	119.9	120.7	120.9	122.1
1999	125.6	124.5	124.1	125.8	123.6	125.1	125.1	123.4
1993	5.0%	2.6%	2.5%	3.2%	2.7%	3.2%	3.5%	5.4%
1994	2.2%	3.3%	3.0%	3.3%	2.6%	3.1%	2.9%	4.8%
1995	3.1%	4.0%	3.5%	3.3%	3.0%	3.4%	3.3%	3.4%
1996	5.2%	3.1%	2.9%	2.9%	3.0%	3.2%	3.5%	1.4%
1997	3.4%	2.6%	3.0%	3.2%	3.4%	3.1%	3.2%	1.0%
1998	1.2%	3.1%	3.4%	3.6%	3.7%	3.2%	2.9%	4.4%
1999	3.3%	3.7%	3.6%	3.8%	3.1%	3.6%	3.5%	1.1%

* University library salaries and wages index weights: 10 percent administrators, 20 percent librarians, 10 percent other professionals, 50 percent nonprofessional staff, and 10 percent students.
^ College library salaries and wages index weights: 25 percent administrators, 15 percent librarians, 5 percent other professionals, 40 percent nonprofessional staff, and 15 percent students.
Sources: See text.

Table 11 / Academic Library Price Indexes, Books and Serials, FY 1992 to 1999

<table>
<tr><td rowspan="3">1992=100</td><td colspan="8">Books Printed</td></tr>
<tr><td colspan="2">North American</td><td colspan="2">U.S. college</td><td colspan="2">Foreign books</td><td colspan="2">Book indexes</td></tr>
<tr><td>Price~</td><td>Index (UL3.1a)</td><td>Price~</td><td>Index (CL3.1a)</td><td>Price</td><td>Index (AL3.1b)</td><td>University* (UL3.1)</td><td>College^ (CL3.1)</td></tr>
<tr><td>Fiscal year</td><td></td><td></td><td></td><td></td><td></td><td></td><td></td><td></td></tr>
<tr><td>1992</td><td>$45.84</td><td>100.0</td><td>$44.55</td><td>100.0</td><td>n.a.</td><td>100.0</td><td>100.0</td><td>100.0</td></tr>
<tr><td>1993</td><td>45.91</td><td>100.2</td><td>47.48</td><td>106.6</td><td></td><td>98.9</td><td>99.9</td><td>106.2</td></tr>
<tr><td>1994</td><td>47.17</td><td>102.9</td><td>48.92</td><td>109.8</td><td></td><td>96.7</td><td>101.7</td><td>109.2</td></tr>
<tr><td>1995</td><td>48.16</td><td>105.1</td><td>47.93</td><td>107.6</td><td></td><td>105.0</td><td>105.0</td><td>107.5</td></tr>
<tr><td>1996</td><td>49.86</td><td>108.8</td><td>48.17</td><td>108.1</td><td></td><td>108.3</td><td>108.7</td><td>108.1</td></tr>
<tr><td>1997</td><td>52.24</td><td>114.0</td><td>50.44</td><td>113.2</td><td></td><td>106.6</td><td>112.5</td><td>112.9</td></tr>
<tr><td>1998</td><td>53.12</td><td>115.9</td><td>51.33</td><td>115.2</td><td></td><td>99.9</td><td>112.7</td><td>114.5</td></tr>
<tr><td>1999</td><td>54.24</td><td>118.3</td><td>52.72</td><td>118.3</td><td></td><td>105.7</td><td>115.8</td><td>117.7</td></tr>
<tr><td>1993</td><td></td><td>0.2%</td><td></td><td>6.6%</td><td></td><td>-1.1%</td><td>-0.1%</td><td>6.2%</td></tr>
<tr><td>1994</td><td></td><td>2.7%</td><td></td><td>3.0%</td><td></td><td>-2.2%</td><td>1.8%</td><td>2.8%</td></tr>
<tr><td>1995</td><td></td><td>2.1%</td><td></td><td>-2.0%</td><td></td><td>8.6%</td><td>3.3%</td><td>-1.6%</td></tr>
<tr><td>1996</td><td></td><td>3.5%</td><td></td><td>0.5%</td><td></td><td>3.1%</td><td>3.5%</td><td>0.6%</td></tr>
<tr><td>1997</td><td></td><td>4.8%</td><td></td><td>4.7%</td><td></td><td>-1.6%</td><td>3.5%</td><td>4.4%</td></tr>
<tr><td>1998</td><td></td><td>1.7%</td><td></td><td>1.8%</td><td></td><td>-6.3%</td><td>0.2%</td><td>1.4%</td></tr>
<tr><td>1999</td><td></td><td>2.1%</td><td></td><td>2.7%</td><td></td><td>5.8%</td><td>2.8%</td><td>2.8%</td></tr>
</table>

~ Prices are for previous calendar year, e.g., CY 1993 prices are reported for FY 1994.
* University library books printed index weights: 80 percent U.S. titles, 20 percent foreign titles.
^ College Library books printed index weights: 95 percent U.S. titles, 5 percent foreign titles.
Sources: See text.
n.a. = not available

Table 11A / Academic Library Price Indexes, Books and Serials, FY 1992 to 1999

1992=100 Fiscal year	Periodicals U.S. titles Price~	Index (AL3.2a)	Foreign Price~	Index (AL3.2b)	Periodical indexes University* (UL3.2)	College^ (CL3.2)	Other Serials (newspapers) Price~	Index (AL3.3)	Books and Serials Indexes University** (UL3.0)	College^^ (CL3.0)	Other printed materials index (AL4.0)
1992	$125.86	100.0	$341.02	100.0	100.0	100.0	$222.68	100.0	100.0	100.0	100.0
1993	136.33	108.3	377.48	110.7	108.8	108.4	229.92	103.3	105.4	107.1	102.9
1994	145.64	115.7	408.70	119.8	116.5	115.9	261.91	117.6	111.4	112.8	105.5
1995	152.88	121.5	411.32	120.6	121.3	121.4	270.22	121.3	115.6	114.9	107.7
1996	159.46	126.7	475.94	139.6	129.3	127.3	300.21	134.8	122.3	118.7	111.3
1997	185.52	147.4	559.75	164.1	150.7	148.2	311.77	140.0	136.8	131.2	118.5
1998	201.37	160.0	599.35	175.8	163.1	160.8	316.60	142.2	144.4	138.1	122.7
1999	219.67	174.5	642.83	188.5	177.3	175.2	318.44	143.0	154.1	146.6	125.7
1993		8.3%		10.7%	8.8%	8.4%		3.3%	5.4%	7.1%	2.9%
1994		6.8%		8.3%	7.1%	6.9%		13.9%	5.7%	5.3%	2.5%
1995		5.0%		0.6%	4.1%	4.7%		3.2%	3.8%	1.8%	2.1%
1996		4.3%		15.7%	6.6%	4.9%		11.1%	5.8%	3.3%	3.3%
1997		16.3%		17.6%	16.6%	16.4%		3.9%	11.8%	10.5%	6.5%
1998		8.5%		7.1%	8.2%	8.5%		1.5%	5.6%	5.2%	3.5%
1999		9.1%		7.3%	8.7%	9.0%		0.6%	6.7%	6.2%	2.4%

~ Prices are for previous calendar year, e.g., CY 1993 prices are reported for FY 1994.
* University library periodicals index weights: 80 percent U.S. titles, 20 percent foreign titles.
^ College library periodicals index weights: 95 percent U.S. titles, 5 percent foreign titles.
** University library books and serials index weights: 35 percent books, 60 percent periodicals, 5 percent other serials.
^^College library books and serials index weights: 47 percent books, 48 percent periodicals, 5 percent other serials.
Sources: See text.

Table 12 / Academic Library Price Indexes, Non-Print Media and Electronic Services, FY 1992 to 1999

1992=100 Fiscal year	Microforms (microfilm) Index (AL5.1)	Audio Recordings						Video	
		Tape cassette		Compact disc		Audio recordings index* (AL5.2)	VHS cassette		Video index (AL5.3)
		Price~	Index (AL5.2a)	Price~	Index (AL5.2b)		Price~	Index (AL5.3a)	
1992	100.0	$12.18	100.0	n.a.		100.0	$199.67	100.0	100.0
1993	104.3	11.73	96.3	n.a.		96.3	112.92	56.6	56.6
1994	107.9	8.20	67.3	$13.36	67.3	67.3	93.22	46.7	46.7
1995	110.6	8.82	72.4	14.80	74.6	73.5	84.19	42.2	42.2
1996	128.0	7.96	65.4	14.86	74.9	70.1	83.48	41.8	41.8
1997	132.9	8.13	66.7	16.43	82.8	74.8	82.10	41.1	41.1
1998	138.9	8.31	68.2	14.35	72.3	70.3	72.31	36.2	36.2
1999	142.9	8.20	67.3	12.65	63.7	65.5	77.85	39.0	39.0
1993	4.3%		-3.7%			-3.7%		-43.4%	-43.4%
1994	3.5%		-30.1%			-30.1%		-17.4%	-17.4%
1995	2.5%		7.6%		10.8%	9.2%		-9.7%	-9.7%
1996	15.7%		-9.8%		0.4%	-4.6%		-0.8%	-0.8%
1997	3.8%		2.1%		10.6%	6.6%		-1.7%	-1.7%
1998	4.5%		2.2%		-12.7%	-6.0%		-11.9%	-11.9%
1999	2.9%		-1.3%		-11.8%	-6.7%		7.7%	7.7%

~ Prices are for previous calendar year, e.g., CY 1993 prices are reported for FY 1994.
* Audio recordings index weights: 50 percent tape cassette, 50 percent compact disc.
Sources: See text.
n.a. = not available

Table 12A / Academic Library Price Indexes, Non-Print Media and Electronic Services, FY 1992 to 1999

1992=100 Fiscal year	Non-print Media			Non-print media index#	Electronic services index	Total Acquisitions Indexes		
	Graphic image (AL5.4)	Computer files (CD-ROM) Price~	Index (AL5.5)	(AL5.0)	(AL6.0)	University*	College^	All Institutions**
1992	100.0	$1,601	100.0	100.0	100.0	100.0	100.0	100.0
1993	97.3	1,793	112.0	98.7	101.9	104.6	105.6	104.9
1994	108.4	1,945	121.5	100.8	104.8	110.0	110.6	110.1
1995	111.3	1,930	120.5	101.5	108.5	113.9	112.7	113.5
1996	114.5	1,913	119.5	108.9	110.3	120.0	116.6	119.1
1997	126.5	1,988	124.2	113.3	110.3	132.2	126.9	130.7
1998	129.1	2,012	125.7	115.6	115.5	139.2	133.0	137.4
1999	124.5	2,007	125.4	117.3	119.2	147.5	140.2	145.5
1993	-2.7%		12.0%	-1.3%	1.9%	4.6%	5.6%	4.9%
1994	11.4%		8.5%	2.1%	2.8%	5.1%	4.7%	5.0%
1995	2.7%		-0.8%	0.7%	3.5%	3.6%	1.9%	3.1%
1996	2.9%		-0.9%	7.3%	1.7%	5.4%	3.5%	4.9%
1997	10.5%		3.9%	4.0%	0.0%	10.1%	8.8%	9.8%
1998	2.1%		1.2%	2.0%	4.7%	5.3%	4.9%	5.2%
1999	-3.6%		-0.2%	1.4%	3.2%	6.0%	5.4%	5.9%

~ Prices are for immediate preceding calendar year, e.g., CY 1993 prices are reported for FY 1994.

Non-print media index weights: 45 percent microforms, 5 percent audio recordings, 15 percent video, 5 percent graphic image, 30 percent computer materials.

* University total acquisitions 1992 weights: 81 percent books, 3 percent other printed material, 5 percent non-print media, and 11 percent electronic services.

^ College total acquisitions 1992 weights: 77 percent books, 2 percent other printed material, 10 percent non-print media, and 11 percent electronic services.

** All institutions total acquisitions weights: 72 percent university acquisitions, 28 percent college acquisitions.

Sources: See text.

Library Buildings 2001: Keep On Constructin'

Bette-Lee Fox

Managing Editor, *Library Journal*

Building a future for our citizens would seem of paramount importance in light of recent events. The nation's public and academic libraries are doing their part, with continued energy and an influx of huge sums of money. These current projects (completed between July 1, 2000 and June 30, 2001) are a reminder that now more than ever we depend on information and the libraries and librarians who make it available to us.

This year's 80 new structures and 132 additions/renovations comprise 4,140,250 square feet and cost more than $686 million. In terms of land and lucre, that is a tremendous investment. Interestingly enough, most of that money (95 percent) came from local governments/library budgets (including bonds and banks) and contributions, with federal and state coffers ponying up a smaller percentage of funding than it seems they ever have. Our people and our communities are standing behind libraries, even if our legislatures are not.

The Cost of Growth

Some of the larger new projects include the Fort Smith (Arkansas) Public Library, at $13.9 million, the Southwest Regional Library of the Broward County Library, Pembroke Pines, Florida, at $14 million, and the Des Plaines (Illinois) Public Library, at $15.6 million. But one project that eclipses them all is the new Main Library of the Nashville (Tennessee) Public Library, encompassing 300,000 square feet and costing $83 million. The substantial additions/renovations include the African American Museum and Library at the Oakland (California) Public Library, $11.2 million, and the Thomas Crane Public Library in Quincy, Massachusetts, $16.6 million.

Of the 42 academic projects, there are two new buildings at Howard University in Washington, D.C. (total $51 million), the Ferris Library for Information & Technology Education at Ferris State University in Michigan ($39 million), and the Harold B. Lee Library at Brigham Young University, Provo, Utah ($51 million).

The Big Picture

Many of the building projects incorporated new and additional technology, more wide-open spaces, and better access to all library materials. Library architects are depending on input from librarians and community groups before setting pencil to paper and pickax to pavement. The combination will make libraries more responsive to the needs of those they serve. And isn't that our primary goal?

Adapted from the December 2001 issue of *Library Journal,* which also lists architects' addresses.

Table 1 / New Academic Library Buildings, 2001

Name of Institution	Project Cost	Gross Area (Sq. Ft.)	Sq. Ft. Cost	Construction Cost	Equipment Cost	Book Capacity	Architect
Ferris Library for Info & Technology Education, Ferris State University, Big Rapids, MI	$39,200,000	173,000	$161.85	$28,000,000	$5,300,000	440,000	Neuman Smith; Gwathmey Siegel
Louis Stokes Health Sciences Library & LRC, Howard University, Washington, DC	25,730,000	80,000	250	20,000,000	2,620,000	400,000	The Hillier Group
Allen Mercer Daniel Law Library, Howard University, Washington, DC	25,730,000	76,000	263.16	20,000,000	n.a.	215,000	Baker Cooper/ Kallmann McKinnell Wood
Penn State Harrisburg Library, Pennsylvania State University, Middletown	14,600,000	115,000	85.04	9,780,000	1,650,000	500,000	Hayes Large/ Shepley Bulfinch...
Dennis F. & Elsie B. Kinlaw Library, Asbury College, Wilmore, KY	14,110,000	79,237	135.69	10,750,000	1,800,000	235,000	Woollen, Molzan
Hamersly Library, Western Oregon University, Monmouth	13,265,000	80,238	120.18	9,643,045	377,435	400,000	WE Group
O'Grady Library, St. Martin's College, Lacey, WA	11,700,000	41,000	224.39	4,200,000	801,375	130,000	Michael Graves & Assocs.
Waggoner Library & Center for Instructional Tech., Trevecca Nazarene University, Nashville	10,500,000	62,750	131.62	8,259,118	2,240,882	129,530	Earl Swensson Assocs.
Stokes Library, Wallace Hall, Princeton University, Princeton, NJ	4,374,650	12,927	274.8	3,552,325	402,162	n.a.	Bohlin Cywinski Jackson
Preservation & Access Center, Colorado Academic Libraries (PASCAL), Aurora	4,099,650	18,466	144.9	2,675,695	720,615	1,600,000	Bennett, Wagner & Grody
New Hampshire Technical Inst. Library, Concord	3,157,497	23,629	116.89	2,762,000	158,000	45,000	Frederick L. Matuszewski
Reese Resource Center, Central Christian College of the Bible, Moberly, MO	700,000	6,181	70	432,670	n.a.	50,000	McElwee Assocs.

Table 2 / Academic Library Buildings, Additions and Renovations, 2001

Name of Institution	Status	Project Cost	Gross Area	Sq. Ft. Cost	Construction Cost	Equipment Cost	Book Capacity	Architect
Harold B. Lee Library, Brigham Young University, Provo, UT	Total	$51,130,000	315,000	$111.11	$35,000,000	n.a.	5,100,000	FFKR Architecture
	New	44,500,000	235,000	131.92	31,000,000	n.a.	2,200,000	
	Renovated	6,630,000	80,000	.50	4,000,000	n.a.	2,900,000	
Pattee Library & Paterno Library, Pennsylvania State University, University Park	Total	34,510,000	389,000	80.75	31,410,000	$3,100,000	3,200,000	CelliFlynnBrennan
	New	29,010,000	139,000	190	26,410,000	2,600,000	2,000,000	
	Renovated	5,500,000	250,000	20	5,000,000	500,000	1,200,000	
El Pomar Center & Kraemer Family Library, University of Colorado, Colorado Springs	Total	28,143,000	153,396	119.92	18,396,000	6,150,000	450,000	H+L Architecture; Shepley Bulfinch...
	New	n.a.	102,841	n.a.	n.a.	n.a.	n.a.	
	Renovated	n.a.	50,555	n.a.	n.a.	n.a.	n.a.	
Vassar College Libraries, Poughkeepsie, NY	Total	22,000,000	140,000	107.14	15,000,000	300,000	775,000	Hardy Holzman Pfeiffer
	New	n.a.	30,000	n.a.	n.a.	n.a.	n.a.	
	Renovated	n.a.	110,000	n.a.	n.a.	n.a.	n.a.	
James Ross McCain Library, Agnes Scott College, Dectur, GA	Total	19,701,000	76,000	176.08	13,382,000	1,131,000	250,000	Perry Dean Rogers; Thompson, Ventulett...
	New	n.a.	46,000	n.a.	n.a.	n.a.	n.a.	
	Renovated	n.a.	30,000	n.a.	n.a.	n.a.	n.a.	
Edith Garland Dupré Library, University of Louisiana at Lafayette	Total	14,000,000	255,000	52.49	11,810,000	n.a.	1,500,000	Architects Southwest
	New	5,000,000	88,000	n.a.	n.a.	n.a.	n.a.	
	Renovated	9,000,000	137,000	n.a.	n.a.	n.a.	n.a.	
Penrose Library, Whitman College, Walla Walla, WA	Total	11,100,000	100,000	75.43	7,543,000	680,000	590,000	Thomas Hacker & Assocs.
	New	4,400,000	20,000	113.15	2,263,000	204,000	140,000	
	Renovated	6,600,000	80,000	66	5,280,000	476,000	450,000	
John Dewey Boyd Library, Alcorn State University, MS	Total	n.a.	100,664	96.05	9,669,178	n.a.	500,000	Foil Wyatt Architects
	New	n.a.	50,268	n.a.	n.a.	n.a.	n.a.	
	Renovated	n.a.	50,396	n.a.	n.a.	n.a.	n.a.	
W.B. Roberts Library, Delta State University, Cleveland, MS	Total	9,000,000	91,100	81.17	7,394,752	1,605,248	485,000	Dale & Assocs.
	New	5,776,366	36,400	129.01	4,696,034	1,08,332	n.a.	
	Renovated	3,223,634	54,700	49.34	2,698,718	524,916	n.a.	
Buswell Library, Covenant Theological Seminary, St. Louis	Total	4,420,200	39,392	105.5	4,155,671	264,529	136,500	St. Louis Design Alliance
	New	3,068,062	27,342	104.09	2,846,033	222,029	92,520	
	Renovated	1,352,138	12,050	108.68	1,309,638	42,500	43,980	
Sidney Cox Library of Music & Dance, Cornell University, Ithaca, NY	Total	4,241,022	24,667	135.36	3,338,992	550,000	281,396	Shepley Bulfinch...
	New	1,737,878	6,264	204	1,277,856	n.a.	n.a.	
	Renovated	2,503,144	18,403	112	2,061,136	n.a.	n.a.	
Van Pel-Dietrich Library Center, University of Pennsylvania, Philadelphia	Total	1,862,805	14,610	78.57	1,147,913	521,613	27,680	Bower Lewis Thrower; Formworks Design
	New	1,521,580	12,490	73.79	921,613	433,493	10,080	
	Renovated	341,225	2,120	106.75	226,300	88,120	17,600	

Table 3 / Academic Library Buildings, Renovations Only, 2001

Name of Institution	Project Cost	Gross Area	Sq. Ft. Cost	Construction Cost	Equipment Cost	Book Capacity	Architect
Delmar T. Oviatt Library, California State University, Northridge	$23,560,000	240,712	$69.87	$16,818,720	n.a.	500,000	George W. Kelly
CLICS: Center for Library & Instructional Computing Svcs., University of California, San Diego, La Jolla	5,260,000	35,890	104.76	3,760,000	$1,500,000	5,000	Dougherty & Dougherty
Northwestern University Library, Evanston, IL	4,823,144	35,900	67.40	2,419,620	374,407	259,494	Ross Barney + Jankowski
Lucille Caudill Little Fine Arts Library & Learning Center, University of Kentucky, Lexington	2,995,347	40,455	49.39	1,998,170	303,498	120,000	Pearson/Bender Assocs.
Claremont (CA) School of Theology Library	2,400,000	31,800	36.24	1,152,323	469,100	200,000	LPA
Leon S. McGoogan Library of Medicine, University of Nebraska Medical Center, Omaha	2,212,458	41,810	52.92	1,886,358	326,100	255,000	Barry M. Ward
King Library, Miami University, Oxford, OH	1,930,000	43,080	30.94	1,332,940	275,000	198,588	Thomas Sens, BHDP
Nantucket Historical Assn., MA	1,800,000	4,000	400.00	1,600,000	10,000	32	Botticelli & Pohl
Taubman Medical Library, University of Michigan, Ann Arbor	1,500,000	35,000	37.14	1,300,000	200,000	658,000	David Milling & Assocs.
Mathematics Library, University of Notre Dame, IN	1,061,409	9,393	n.a.	n.a.	n.a.	60,000	Mathews-Purucker-Anella
University of New Hampshire–Manchester Library	959,788	9,691	51.80	502,000	457,788	60,000	Lavalee Breninger
Everett Library, Queens College, Charlotte, NC	816,000	2,800	n.a.	n.a.	n.a.	n.a.	Jenkins Peer
Library/LRC, Gateway Technical College Kenosha, WI	650,000	10,225	39.12	400,000	250,000	40,000	Partners in Design
George & Leona Lewis Library, Albany College, of Pharmacy, Albany, NY	480,000	9,510	48.69	463,000	17,000	10,000	Brandt & Poost
Musselman Library, Gettysburg College, Gettysburg, PA	473,681	4,410	107.41	436,008	37,673	4,300	Lawrence D. McEwen
Abell Library Center, Austin College, Sherman, TX	320,000	1,818	139.09	252,879	67,121	8,400	Page Sutherland Page
Carter Music Resources Center, Louisiana State University, Baton Rouge	244,610	1,660	84.90	140,927	103,683	n.a.	none
Purdue University Calumet Library, Hammond, IN	95,000	8,200	11.58	95,000	0	n.a.	not reported

Table 4 / New Public Library Buildings, 2001

Community	Pop. ('000)	Code	Project Cost	Const. Cost	Gross Sq. Ft.	Sq. Ft. Cost	Equip. Cost	Site Cost	Other Costs	Volumes	Federal Funds	State Funds	Local Funds	Gift Funds	Architect
Alabama															
Auburn	43	M	$3,700,000	$2,715,500	24,065	$112.84	$287,000	$500,000	$197,500	80,000	$0	$0	$3,700,000	$0	Williams-Blackstock
Mountain Brook	20	M	8,263,793	5,597,213	40,434	138.43	917,918	460,000	1,288,662	121,285	0	0	1,460,000	6,803,793	HKW
Orange Beach	14	M	1,425,000	700,000	11,000	63.64	150,000	375,000	200,000	60,000	12,238	0	1,392,762	20,000	not reported
Alaska															
Elim	1	M	121,964	104,088	1,200	86.74	0	17,876	0	7,000	71,028	39,664	11,272	0	Independent Lumber
Arizona															
Wellton	2	B	352,523	230,600	4,150	55.57	0	Leased	121,923	n.a.	135,000	0	216,523	1,000	DeWald Architects
Arkansas															
Fort Smith	80	M	13,994,000	10,931,000	67,000	163.15	1,243,000	600,000	1,220,000	325,000	0	0	13,969,000	25,000	Meyer, Scherer…
California															
Mariposa	14	M	2,134,500	1,495,000	8,120	184.11	192,000	256,000	191,500	4,491	296,473	0	1,764,027	74,000	DuPertuis Scott
Potrero	2	B	573,995	380,825	2,500	152.33	100,081	10,251	82,838	10,000	358,000	0	208,495	7,500	Nicoloff & Assocs.
Studio City	43	B	5,115,600	3,350,778	11,500	291.37	207,500	1,270,000	287,322	45,000	0	0	4,845,600	270,000	City of Los Angeles
Wildomar	33	B	1,385,200	878,127	5,000	175.62	125,000	84,700	297,373	15,000	0	0	1,385,200	0	Gary Miller
Colorado															
Lakewood	78	B	7,418,000	5,200,000	31,500	165.08	988,000	500,000	730,000	151,000	0	0	7,038,000	380,000	David C. Anderson
Florida															
Coral Springs	282	B	14,101,200	11,938,894	72,000	165.81	1,806,000	Owned	356,306	170,000	0	0	14,101,200	0	Wolfberg Alvarez Architects in Assn.
Daytona Beach	11	B	1,350,000	773,000	5,886	131.33	106,000	Owned	471,000	23,000	0	300,000	1,000,000	50,000	Barany Schmitt…
Lehigh Acres	40	B	8,253,071	5,893,467	40,000	147.34	2,043,034	Owned	316,570	110,000	0	300,000	7,953,071	0	Haskell Co.
Pembroke Pines	141	B	14,101,200	11,931,200	78,000	152.96	1,826,000	Owned	344,000	175,000	0	0	14,101,200	0	Dow Howell Gilmore
Stuart	29	B	2,893,000	2,291,000	15,500	147.81	200,000	Leased	402,000	45,000	0	400,000	2,093,000	400,000	Gee & Jenson
Tampa	134	B	7,631,766	3,139,891	25,000	125.6	2,040,112	2,323,310	128,453	130,632	500,000	0	7,131,766	0	Stellar Group
Tampa	261	B	5,388,365	3,439,000	25,000	137.56	408,365	1,466,000	75,000	80,040	0	400,000	1,909,365	3,079,000	
Georgia															
Atlanta	n.a.	B	1,990,000	723,950	7,500	96.53	354,250	110,000	801,800	40,000	0	0	1,990,000	0	Cheeks/Hornbein
Cumming	45	B	4,109,368	2,260,002	20,500	110.24	759,791	205,000	884,575	96,000	0	0	4,109,368	0	John Heard Assocs.

Symbol Code: B—Branch Library; BS—Branch & System Headquarters; M—Main Library; MS—Main & System Headquarters; S—System Headquarters; n.a.—not available

Location		Code													Architect
Illinois															
Chicago	9	B	2,100,437	1,854,818	5,600	331.22	91,540	Owned	154,079	28,000	0	240,750	1,859,687	0	Antunovich Assocs.
Des Plaines	59	M	15,629,810	13,500,000	82,000	164.63	1,789,778	Leased	340,032	290,000	0	250,000	15,242,852	136,958	Floyd Anderson
East St. Louis	42	M	5,203,200	4,085,000	18,000	226.94	266,000	125,000	727,200	70,000	0	0	5,203,200	0	Kennedy Assocs.
Indiana															
Mulberry	1	B	828,090	610,075	4,800	127.10	145,949	45,000	27,066	15,578	0	50,000	258,316	519,774	H.L. Mohler & Assocs.
Nashville	15	M	3,855,346	2,948,000	18,500	159.35	260,346	477,000	170,000	80,000	0	0	2,450,000	1,405,346	Ratio Architects
Iowa															
Urbandale	29	M	8,588,356	6,986,943	56,000	124.77	644,825	Owned	956,588	173,042	0	0	7,900,000	688,356	Engberg Anderson
Kansas															
Olathe	100	B	3,048,291	1,889,166	12,062	156.62	295,817	Owned	863,308	50,000	0	5,360	2,999,836	43,095	Kenneth O. von Achen
Overland Park	70	B	5,984,814	3,520,698	24,071	146.26	1,972,221	Owned	491,895	120,000	0	0	5,984,814	0	Gould Evans…
Kentucky															
Lexington	63	B	4,101,943	3,032,116	21,600	140.38	485,120	199,788	384,919	150,000	0	150,000	3,903,947	47,996	Brandstetter Carroll
Louisiana															
Baker	25	B	3,606,992	2,739,464	16,583	165.20	308,183	220,000	339,345	89,250	0	0	3,606,992	0	Stephen P. Jackson
Maryland															
Lonaconing	3	B	1,180,000	n.a.	6,400	n.a.	80,000	Owned	n.a.	14,000	293,000	500,000	600,000	80,000	Grimm & Parker
Massachusetts															
Boston	24	B	8,629,500	6,300,000	20,000	315.00	475,000	1,398,000	456,500	37,000	0	0	6,938,500	1,398,000	Machado & Silvetti
Byfield	7	M	3,217,189	2,248,475	16,747	134.26	377,990	60,000	530,724	42,315	0	984,216	1,933,414	299,559	Stephen Hale
Rutland	7	M	3,088,200	2,693,500	16,625	162.02	154,500	Owned	240,200	45,700	0	200,000	2,700,000	188,200	Wilson H. Rains
Michigan															
Grand Rapids	n.a.	B	2,343,638	1,230,468	10,000	123.05	172,258	766,660	174,252	n.a.	0	0	2,343,638	0	David Clark
Monroe	15	B	1,142,000	940,000	7,250	129.65	112,000	Owned	90,000	52,000	0	0	1,142,000	0	Michael F. Pogliano
Ortonville	18	M	4,408,060	3,289,897	19,264	170.78	233,691	175,000	709,472	78,000	0	0	4,183,060	225,000	David W. Osler
Washington	27	M	5,166,997	3,591,006	24,100	149.00	635,221	500,000	440,770	94,500	0	0	4,488,797	678,200	Harley Ellis
Whitehall	11	M	2,101,807	1,737,638	11,765	147.70	148,327	85,000	130,842	41,000	0	0	1,877,366	224,441	Design Works A/E
Minnesota															
Anoka	60	B	5,755,800	3,600,000	30,150	119.40	490,000	Owned	1,665,800	130,000	0	0	5,755,800	0	Boarman, Kroos…
North Mankato	12	M	761,844	532,877	4,900	108.75	74,305	Owned	154,662	20,000	0	0	761,844	0	Vetter Johnson

Symbol Code: B—Branch Library; BS—Branch & System Headquarters; M—Main Library; MS—Main & System Headquarters; S—System Headquarters: n.a.—not available

Table 4 / New Public Library Buildings, 2001 (cont.)

Community	Pop. ('000)	Code	Project Cost	Const. Cost	Gross Sq. Ft.	Sq. Ft. Cost	Equip. Cost	Site Cost	Other Costs	Volumes	Federal Funds	State Funds	Local Funds	Gift Funds	Architect
Missouri															
Stanberry	6	M	593,526	520,852	14,950	67.00	18,766	16,000	37,908	52,000	0	0	456,000	144,765	Jos. Cheesebrough
Nebraska															
Springfield	5	M	621,139	463,926	4,860	95.45	43,000	50,000	64,213	19000	127,404	0	0	493,735	Peters & Assocs.
New Jersey															
Atco	59	B	3,117,368	2,505,577	21,500	116.54	329,201	Owned	282,590	75,000	0	0	3,117,368	0	Michael Piatetsky
New York															
East Greenbush	15	M	4,602,105	3,328,974	22,000	151.32	534,000	325,949	413,182	80,000	0	0	4,502,105	100,000	Lepera & Ward
Port Washington	27	M	5,968,960	3,989,960	47,500	84.00	540,000	Owned	1,439,000	300,000	0	9,000	5,719,960	240,000	Donald & Liisa Sclare
Southampton	14	M	7,291,766	5,202,169	21,500	241.96	1,416,296	Owned	673,301	110,000	0	0	5,926,273	1,365,493	Beatty Harvey
Town Of Greece	90	M	4,000,000	3,197,000	34,568	92.48	0	Owned	803,000	250,000	0	0	4,000,000	0	Macon Chantreuil...
Ohio															
Akron	25	B	2,348,477	1,603,520	12,000	133.63	151,415	207,542	386,000	68,500	0	0	2,348,477	0	Braun & Steidl
Bridgeport	5	B	706,580	510,608	4,208	121.34	86,761	18,102	91,109	18,000	230,508	0	255,358	220,714	Beck & Tabeling
Richfield	25	B	2,144,032	1,617,820	12,000	134.82	133,212	Leased	393,000	68,500	0	0	2,144,032	0	Spice Costantino
Oregon															
Stanfield	3	M	408,200	325,200	2,900	112.14	18,000	40,000	25,000	14,950	100,000	0	0	308,200	Gail Sargent
Pennsylvania															
Brodheadsville	29	M	3,146,315	2,394,296	29,460	81.27	357,427	194,355	200,237	85,000	0	300,000	1,350,000	1,496,315	Robert E. Strunk
Camp Hill	74	M	6,425,821	4,621,370	37,200	124.23	624,185	594,341	585,925	115,000	0	250,000	0	6,175,821	H2L2
Quarryville	34	M	1,860,000	1,266,000	12,200	103.77	125,600	154,000	314,400	33,000	296,000	725,000	9,000	830,000	Beers, Schillaci...
Tunkhannock	28	M	1,622,362	1,132,118	12,500	90.57	149,763	175,000	165,481	40,000	17,500	0	175,000	1,442,141	Thomas C. Horlacher
South Carolina															
Anderson	166	MS	13,500,000	10,300,000	96,000	107.29	1,600,000	Owned	1,600,000	220,000	0	0	13,500,000	0	Craig, Gaulden...
Green Sea	4	B	521,808	354,417	3,691	96.02	111,000	Owned	56,391	18,000	0	0	461,808	60,000	PMHA
Lake City	15	B	2,067,274	1,214,491	11,300	107.48	218,546	200,000	434,237	36,600	0	995,014	361,665	710,595	LS3P Assocs.
Pelion	14	B	730,298	589,850	6,000	98.31	87,608	10,000	42,840	40,000	0	0	730,298	0	James, DuRant...

Symbol Code: B—Branch Library; BS—Branch & System Headquarters; M—Main Library; MS—Main & System Headquarters; S—System Headquarters; n.a.—not available

Tennessee															
Hermitage	24	B	5,865,456	3,371,631	25,330	133.11	2,223,748	Owned	270,077	110,000	0	0	5,865,456	0	Moody/Nolan
Knoxville	30	B	1,775,048	1,236,800	8,520	145.16	120,114	185,000	233,134	30,000	0	0	1,775,048	0	Goodstein Architects
Knoxville	43	B	2,274,924	1,854,907	12,985	142.85	183,707	70,715	165,595	45,000	0	0	2,274,924	0	Goodstein Architects
Madison	32	B	3,981,601	2,401,438	20,680	116.13	1,180,000	Owned	400,163	90,000	0	0	3,831,601	150,000	Gobbell Hays
Nashville	51	B	6,122,005	3,032,825	25,160	120.55	2,225,000	564,265	299,915	110,000	0	0	6,122,005	0	Tuck Hinton
Nashville	21	B	6,983,707	3,231,805	25,540	126.54	1,445,000	1,887,660	419,242	110,000	0	0	6,805,707	178,000	Earl Swensson
Nashville	570	BS	83,089,043	51,660,962	300,000	172.21	11,410,210	11,881,000	8,136,871	1,000,000	0	0	81,439,043	1,650,000	Robert A.M. Stern
Texas															
Austin	15	B	2,375,000	1,402,330	8,630	162.49	149,674	218,844	604,152	65,000	0	0	2,375,000	0	Bethany Raney; Hatch
Mansfield	28	M	2,035,299	1,618,560	15,000	107.91	243,081	Owned	173,658	90,000	200,000	29,984	1,750,223	55,092	Schutts Magee
Plano	35	B	4,183,699	3,406,781	30,148	113	394,433	Owned	382,485	110,300	0	0	4,183,699	0	Phillips Swager
Virginia															
Edinburg	36	M	1,197,500	854,000	12,000	71.17	165,000	83,500	95,000	75,000	0	200,000	740,500	269,000	Jones & Jones
Fairfax County	106	B	7,085,367	2,980,000	13,000	229	379,367	3,000,000	726,000	68,600	0	0	7,085,367	0	Lukmire Partnership
Hague	5	B	505,000	340,000	3,052	111.4	100,000	35,000	30,000	20,000	0	0	440,000	65,000	Rick Funk
Stephens City	95	B	4,941,858	4,209,610	35,000	120.27	360,658	Owned	371,590	110,000	0	0	4,350,783	591,075	Lukmire Partnership
Virginia Beach	5	B	463,595	369,600	4,412	83.77	83,000	Owned	10,995	26,000	0	0	463,595	0	Parsons Brinckerhoff...
Washington															
Maple Valley	23	B	4,000,000	2,000,000	10,200	196.08	165,000	600,000	1,235,000	80,000	0	0	4,000,000	0	Johnston Architects
West Virginia															
Marlinton	3	M	775,677	652,501	7,612	85.72	59,562	Owned	63,614	30,000	50,000	242,223	259,196	224,258	Clayton L. Carter
Sissonville	9	B	1,419,653	1,083,000	6,700	161.64	105,653	169,000	62,000	40,000	0	125,000	1,009,653	285,000	N Visions
Wisconsin															
Madison	15	B	2,140,500	995,413	12,000	82.95	609,657	465,818	69,612	85,000	0	0	1,649,000	491,500	Kubala Washatko
Waterford	10	M	2,902,254	2,260,648	19,970	113.2	331,196	Owned	310,410	40,000	0	0	2,571,058	331,196	Uihlein/Wilson

Symbol Code: B—Branch Library; BS—Branch & System Headquarters; M—Main Library; MS—Main & System Headquarters; S—System Headquarters; n.a.—not available

Table 5 / Public Library Buildings, Additions and Renovations, 2001

Community	Pop. ('000)	Code	Project Cost	Const. Cost	Gross Sq. Ft.	Sq. Ft. Cost	Equip. Cost	Site Cost	Other Costs	Volumes	Federal Funds	State Funds	Local Funds	Gift Funds	Architect
Alabama															
Hoover	63	MS	$6,528,484	$5,379,339	47,532	113.17	$574,333	Owned	$574,812	134,500	$45,328	$0	$6,483,156	$0	Evan Terry Assocs.
Arizona															
Phoenix	100	B	1,334,031	900,663	10,000	90.06	165,858	Owned	267,510	80,000	0	0	1,309,031	25,000	Architekton
Arkansas															
Jonesboro	56	MS	923,280	651,560	9,747	66.85	195,354	Owned	76,366	29,127	0	0	840,105	83,175	Brackett-Kennerich
Springdale	65	M	4,446,482	3,315,231	43,800	75.69	759,893	Owned	371,358	175,000	0	0	4,381,482	65,000	David Powers
California															
Hemet	31	B	626,114	509,123	5,000	101.82	116,991	Owned	0	18,000	0	0	626,114	0	Holt Architects
Los Angeles	31	B	551,600	342,500	5,125	66.83	23,900	Owned	185,200	54,000	75,000	0	476,600	0	Charles Walton
Oakland	419	B	11,200,000	9,250,560	17,947	515.43	229,167	Owned	1,720,273	15,000	4,000,000	0	7,200,000	0	Michael Willis
Torrance	140	M	1,038,000	813,000	15,000	54.2	195,000	Owned	30,000	39,000	0	226,000	762,000	50,000	Deems Lewis…
Colorado															
Cortez	24	M	1,650,932	1,504,932	18,600	80.91	146,000	Owned	0	90,000	0	300,000	1,282,600	70,000	R. Michael Bell
Littleton	44	M	2,075,515	1,667,393	39,000	42.75	115,150	Owned	292,972	180,000	0	0	2,060,365	15,150	Michael Brendle
Monte Vista	8	M	661,879	589,760	3,420	172.44	15,000	Leased	57,119	30,000	150,225	184,349	327,305	0	Belinda Zink
Delaware															
Rehoboth Beach	7	M	1,536,248	1,421,248	11,000	129.2	35,000	Owned	80,000	35,858	0	700,000	0	836,248	Mike Sing
Florida															
Boynton Beach	55	B	1,745,432	1,216,057	17,770	68.43	324,096	Owned	205,279	94,415	0	0	1,745,432	0	MPA Architects
Citrus Ridge	5	B	392,451	70,935	6,000	11.82	191,235	Leased	130,281	25,000	0	0	392,451	0	Rispoli-Sosa
Dania Beach	25	B	390,000	175,800	12,276	14.32	190,000	Leased	24,200	43,000	0	0	390,000	0	none
Ft. Lauderdale	13	B	95,550	42,170	3,900	10.81	46,550	Leased	6,830	16,000	0	0	95,550	0	Frimet Design
Pinellas Park	45	M	3,181,771	2,350,150	31,283	75.13	378,160	Owned	453,461	157,000	0	300,000	2,777,110	104,661	Harvard Jolly Clees…
Sorrento	4	B	388,736	98,479	5,000	19.7	153,035	Leased	137,222	18,000	0	0	388,736	0	none
Illinois															
East Moline	20	M	40,300	33,800	598	56.52	2,500	Owned	4,000	2,100	0	0	37,800	2,500	Kelly & Assocs.
Woodstock	31	M	5,838,200	4,456,700	43,487	102.48	550,700	151,700	679,100	159,000	0	31,000	5,650,200	157,000	Frye Gillan Molinaro

Symbol Code: B—Branch Library; BS—Branch & System Headquarters; M—Main Library; MS—Main & System Headquarters; S—System Headquarters; n.a.—not available

Location															Architect
Indiana															
Francesville	2	M	1,098,329	815,239	6,034	135.1	141,411	Owned	141,679	2,707lf.	0	500,000	588,808	9,521	H.L. Mohler & Assocs.
Frankfort	33	M	543,746	331,650	10,000	33.17	192,096	Owned	20,000	55,887	0	116,500	316,951	110,295	H.L. Mohler & Assocs.
Nappanee	7	M	2,457,136	1,912,156	22,300	85.75	270,311	Owned	274,669	67,560	0	100,000	2,342,136	15,000	Morrison Kattman…
Plainfield	23	M	8,750,000	6,253,249	58,800	106.35	769,244	509,000	1,218,507	170,000	0	0	8,750,000	0	K.R. Montgomery
Iowa															
Keokuk	38	M	176,500	160,000	8,000	20	0	Owned	16,500	73,400	0	0	0	176,500	OPN Architects
Kansas															
Wellington	9	M	55,000	42,500	110	386	0	Owned	12,500	n.a.	0	0	0	55,000	Duane Hickerson
Kentucky															
Bowling Green	90	B	535,478	36,786	8,000	4.6	415,280	Leased	83,412	5,000	300,000	800,000	83,750	0	HNTB Corp.
Louisiana															
Rodessa	1	B	75,400	72,800	838	86.87	2,600	Owned	0	7,500	0	0	75,200	200	none
Maine															
Belfast	12	M	2,700,000	2,300,000	20,200	113.86	0	Owned	400,000	45,500	0	0	400,000	2,300,000	Scholz & Barclay
Massachusetts															
Boston	555	M	6,423,000	6,100,000	50,400	121.03	0	Owned	323,000	n.a.	0	2,239,800	614,000	3,569,200	Shepley Bulfinch…
Carlisle	5	M	2,384,455	2,248,225	11,900	188.93	93,574	Owned	42,656	62,000	0	919,388	1,489,067	360,000	Richmond French
Newburyport	17	M	8,050,000	6,222,163	38,325	162.35	500,000	Owned	1,327,837	105,000	0	2,202,096	4,447,904	1,400,000	Finegold Alexander
Norwood	29	M	4,091,332	3,102,493	24,820	125	181,940	Owned	806,899	118,000	0	1,088,696	2,802,636	200,000	Childs Bertman…
Quincy	88	M	16,668,847	12,843,228	78,000	164.66	1,019,701	985,126	1,820,792	19,620lf.	0	3,595,291	12,153,556	920,000	Childs Bertman…
Springfield	8	B	1,862,807	1,527,965	10,480	145.8	162,083	Owned	172,759	27,080	0	145,000	1,350,000	367,807	Caolo & Bienek
Michigan															
Dearborn	98	B	2,123,460	1,763,502	13,000	135.65	185,102	Owned	174,856	45,120	1,763,460	0	355,000	5,000	Giffels Consultants
Grand Rapids	n.a.	B	627,033	483,898	3,800	127.34	71,142	Owned	71,993	n.a.	0	0	627,033	0	David Clark
Grand Rapids	n.a.	B	1,449,143	1,127,338	11,000	102.49	142,677	Owned	179,128	n.a.	0	0	1,449,143	0	David Clark
Marquette	36	M	9,044,272	6,386,466	63,000	101.37	934,875	485,216	1,237,715	200,000	300,000	0	5,497,737	3,246,535	Frye Gillan Molinaro
Mt. Pleasant	52	MS	135,000	80,000	1,000	80	40,000	Owned	15,000	150,834	50,000	0	85,000	0	David Milling
Minnesota															
New Prague	5	B	942,883	613,549	7,076	86.71	128,159	Owned	201,175	25,000	0	150,000	678,883	114,000	Meyer, Scherer
St. Paul	287	S	1,180,445	962,600	8,034	119.82	88,650	Owned	129,195	0	0	0	1,180,445	0	Meyer, Scherer

Symbol Code: B—Branch Library; BS—Branch & System Headquarters; M—Main Library; MS—Main & System Headquarters; S—System Headquarters; n.a.—not available

Table 5 / Public Library Buildings, Additions and Renovations, 2001 *(cont.)*

Community	Pop. ('000)	Code	Project Cost	Const. Cost	Gross Sq. Ft.	Sq. Ft. Cost	Equip. Cost	Site Cost	Other Costs	Volumes	Federal Funds	State Funds	Local Funds	Gift Funds	Architect
Mississippi															
Georgetown	1	B	64,532	60,032	2,400	25.01	2,000	Owned	2,500	10,000	0	28,548	32,188	3,806	Carl Nobles
Tunica	9	B	1,618,927	1,330,692	13,320	99.9	165,000	Owned	123,235	45,000	0	500,000	1,118,927	0	Doug Thornton
Missouri															
New Madrid	5	B	349,053	303,063	1,600	189.41	27,678	Leased	18,312	25,000	0	0	349,053	0	Bell Architecture
Springfield	48	B	824,645	726,830	19,670	36.95	40,663	Owned	57,152	100,000	0	0	623,145	201,500	Laura Jean Derrick
Nebraska															
Omaha	448	MS	1,286,847	1,113,238	84,600	13.16	127,487	Owned	46,122	n.a.	0	0	1,407,683	9,696	Schemmer Assocs.
New Hampshire															
Barrington	8	M	131,800	100,000	3,740	26.74	30,000	Owned	1,800	30,000	0	0	126,500	5,300	none
Nottingham	3	M	342,237	311,110	5,168	60.2	7,386	Owned	23,741	15,000	0	0	320,000	22,237	Shelter Enterprises
Tilton/Northfield	9	M	1,221,421	1,010,533	7,200	140.35	81,891	Owned	128,997	40,000	0	0	1,150,000	71,561	Sheerr McCrystal...
New Jersey															
Bridgewater	162	BS	3,992,147	3,556,000	50,989	69.74	219,147	Owned	217,000	215,000	0	0	3,992,147	0	Faridy Veisz Fraytak
Brielle	5	M	189,944	154,381	1,240	124.5	23,000	Owned	12,563	60,000	0	0	166,944	23,000	Arcari & Iovino
Leonia	9	M	568,816	351,411	12,636	27.81	179,785	Owned	37,620	61,211	0	0	350,000	218,816	Arcari & Iovino
Tenafly	14	M	669,703	536,106	9,677	55.4	71,038	Owned	62,559	103,689	0	0	0	669,703	Arcari & Iovino
New York															
Bohemia	40	M	3,000,000	2,300,000	20,800	110.58	n.a.	Owned	n.a.	104,370	n.a.	n.a.	n.a.	0	Ron Benedict
Brooklyn	n.a.	B	1,099,000	748,000	12,360	60.52	200,000	Owned	151,000	n.a.	0	75,221	1,023,779	0	Allanbrook, Benic...
Castile	3	M	434,723	397,711	3,625	109.7	15,394	Owned	21,618	30,000	0	40,000	94,723	300,000	Rick Hauser
Hopewell Jct.	25	M	1,055,150	853,000	12,400	68.79	79,150	Owned	123,000	60,000	0	0	1,055,150	0	Tinkelman Architects
Islip	18	M	3,320,913	2,238,943	18,950	118.15	379,460	Owned	702,510	179,841	0	5,000	3,315,913	0	Beatty Harvey
Ithaca	75	M	9,725,333	5,066,253	69,000	73.42	1,350,280	2,515,000	793,800	56,000	0	123,500	6,695,833	2,906,000	Quinlivan Pierik...
Jackson Heights	100	B	580,000	470,000	17,100	27.49	0	Owned	110,000	251,500	0	0	580,000	0	Ehasz Giacalone
Poestenkill	4	M	383,556	221,871	2,100	105.65	50,000	61,000	50,685	17,500	0	30,000	249,973	103,583	TAP, Inc.
Quogue	4	M	1,124,743	980,479	5,800	169.05	90,842	Owned	53,422	25,000	0	0	0	1,124,743	Jay Lockett Sears
Wayland	4	M	536,000	500,000	2,350	18.5	15,000	Owned	21,000	15,000	0	32,000	204,000	300,000	Anne Hersh

Symbol Code: B—Branch Library; BS—Branch & System Headquarters; M—Main Library; MS—Main & System Headquarters; S—System Headquarters; n.a.—not available

Location															Architect
North Carolina															
Burlington	131	MS	3,540,696	2,705,306	27,620	97.94	358,062	250,000	227,328	95,535	0	0	3,190,696	350,000	J. Hyatt Hammond
Charlotte	100	B	1,680,628	1,314,628	10,000	131.46	246,000	Leased	120,000	100,000	0	0	1,680,628	0	Gantt Huberman
Greenville	127	MS	6,248,625	5,092,778	60,500	84.18	600,000	52,000	503,847	275,000	0	0	6,248,625	0	Calloway Johnson…
Randleman	24	M	152,976	130,000	1,500	86.67	8,626	Owned	14,350	2,400	0	0	90,000	63,000	Dean Spinks
Wilmington	60	B	5,226,480	1,472,392	33,500	43.95	542,225	3,001,801	210,062	105,000	24,500	60,000	4,048,544	1,093,436	Smith Gage
Ohio															
Amherst	25	M	598,788	379,839	14,000	27.13	165,431	Owned	53,518	13,000	0	0	598,788	0	Vector Group
Camden	7	B	108,221	42,608	2,432	17.52	65,613	Leased	0	23,000	0	0	108,221	0	not reported
Cincinnati	n.a.	B	636,685	570,461	7,050	80.92	17,274	Owned	48,950	20,950	0	0	636,685	0	Gartner Burdick…
Columbus	55	B	120,000	85,000	3,280	25.92	35,000	Leased	0	n.a.	0	0	120,000	0	none
Crestline	24	M	237,555	213,180	5,030	42.38	2,150	Owned	22,225	1,386	0	0	237,555	0	Marr Knapp Crawfis
Eaton	15	B	299,882	108,681	8,300	13.1	190,601	Owned	600	60,100	0	0	0	299,882	not reported
Gratis	1	M	40,199	9,989	250	39.96	20,210	Leased	10,000	26,000	0	0	40,199	0	not reported
Kinsman	8	M	77,900	68,300	5,400	12.65	0	Owned	9,600	n.a.	0	0	77,900	0	Baker, Bednar
Madison	22	M	3,390,434	2,208,185	24,463	90.27	361,567	Owned	820,682	125,000	0	0	3,390,434	0	Beck & Tabeling
Marietta	n.a.	B	479,669	261,100	2,400	108.79	78,952	110,000	29,617	n.a.	0	0	477,194	2,475	Stephen Hughes…
Maumee	18	B	2,727,003	2,327,251	20,220	115.1	238,292	Owned	161,460	117,127	0	0	2,527,003	200,000	Buehrer Group
New Paris	3	B	78,204	25,375	1,484	17.1	52,829	Owned	0	13,500	0	0	78,204	0	not reported
Oak Harbor	10	M	1,064,474	868,125	3,877	223.92	68,133	Owned	128,216	48,000	1,064,404	0	0	70	Munger Munger
Scio	3	B	352,993	154,429	3,200	48.25	9,483	170,000	19,081	12,000	0	0	310,278	42,715	HRJL Architects
Tallmadge	25	B	1,805,473	1,261,037	12,000	105.09	168,145	Leased	376,291	68,500	0	0	1,805,473	0	Braun & Steidl
Thornville	6	B	719,295	423,124	3,000	141.05	39,778	165,000	91,393	n.a.	0	0	719,295	0	Phillip Markwood
Toledo	462	MS	45,173,840	33,641,479	265,910	126.51	2,286,753	3,560,822	5,684,786	1,248,335	0	0	41,673,840	3,500,000	Munger Munger
Washington Ct. Hse.	28	M	401,778	371,778	n.a.	n.a.	n.a.	Owned	30,000	n.a.	25,000	0	376,778	0	Historical Design
West Alexandria	8	B	119,776	52,238	2,992	17.46	67,538	Leased	0	23,000	0	0	119,776	0	not reported
West Elkton	2	B	41,891	14,371	960	14.97	27,520	Leased	0	7,500	0	0	41,891	0	not reported
West Manchester	2	B	49,499	12,980	950	13.66	36,519	Leased	0	9,500	0	0	49,499	0	not reported
Xenia	32	BS	1,799,661	1,336,588	25,000	53.46	230,000	Owned	233,073	n.a.	0	0	1,799,661	0	Widener & Posey
Oregon															
Portland	n.a.	B	2,217,005	1,527,582	4,921	310.42	71,374	Owned	618,049	25,000	0	0	2,217,005	0	Thomas Hacker
Portland	n.a.	B	1,359,896	882,362	6,458	136.63	108,494	Owned	369,040	30,000	0	0	1,359,896	0	Thomas Hacker
Portland	n.a.	B	3,758,839	2,001,111	5,466	366.1	95,516	600,000	1,062,212	30,000	0	0	3,758,839	0	Thomas Hacker
Portland	50	M	1,807,569	1,447,569	23,400	61.86	325,000	Leased	35,000	180,000	0	0	1,542,569	265,000	Robert Klas

Symbol Code: B—Branch Library; BS—Branch & System Headquarters; M—Main Library; MS—Main & System Headquarters; S—System Headquarters; n.a.—not available

Table 5 / Public Library Buildings, Additions and Renovations, 2001 *(cont.)*

Community	Pop. ('000)	Code	Project Cost	Const. Cost	Gross Sq. Ft.	Sq. Ft. Cost	Equip. Cost	Site Cost	Other Costs	Volumes	Federal Funds	State Funds	Local Funds	Gift Funds	Architect
Pennsylvania															
Ligonier	16	M	1,365,285	917,601	13,000	70.58	269,984	Owned	177,700	80,000	0	5,000	0	1,360,285	Lettrich Group
Philadelphia	69	B	856,771	500,636	8,550	58.55	259,529	Owned	96,606	37,011	n.a.	n.a.	n.a.	n.a.	Vitetta
Philadelphia	39	B	584,661	248,226	9,600	25.86	225,751	Owned	110,684	48,359	n.a.	n.a.	n.a.	n.a.	Vitetta
Philadelphia	27	B	699,157	340,794	10,396	32.78	245,623	Owned	112,740	23,890	n.a.	n.a.	n.a.	n.a.	Vitetta
Philadelphia	46	B	849,825	494,705	9,712	50.94	217,820	Owned	137,300	32,380	n.a.	n.a.	n.a.	n.a.	Vitetta
Philadelphia	37	B	n.a.	1,024,000	6,000	170.67	n.a.	Leased	n.a.	26,714	n.a.	n.a.	n.a.	n.a.	Wallace Roberts ...
Philadelphia	25	B	n.a.	639,900	7,736	82.72	n.a.	Leased	n.a.	26,000	n.a.	n.a.	n.a.	n.a.	Urban Consultants
Pocono Pines	11	M	550,690	487,791	4,000	121.95	16,116	Owned	46,783	42,000	0	0	540,690	10,000	Robert Lack
Telford	41	M	372,644	325,082	4,393	74	11,402	Owned	36,160	n.a.	0	0	0	372,644	J.D. Delp Carpentry
Rhode Island															
Newport	26	M	7,243,200	5,510,900	47,459	116.12	451,500	Owned	1,280,800	175,000	0	3,270,000	175,000	3,800,000	Hammond, Beeby...
South Carolina															
Fort Mill	40	B	3,104,396	2,054,839	20,440	100.53	140,918	750,000	158,639	68,000	0	0	2,354,396	750,000	Craig, Gaulden...
Hartsville	30	B	602,002	383,257	4,187	91.53	146,569	Owned	72,176	30,000	0	100,000	53,400	448,602	James, Durant...
Tennessee															
Collinwood	3	M	198,000	135,000	1,700	79.41	12,000	35,000	16,000	600lf.	0	75,200	87,800	35,000	Barge, Waggoner...
Mount Juliet	22	M	612,000	465,701	4,000	116.42	0	115,000	31,299	75,000	150,000	10,000	440,000	12,000	Koatz, Binkley...
Nashville	31	B	342,983	255,748	4,451	57.46	34,302	Owned	52,933	16,000	0	0	342,983	0	Woodson Gilchrist
Nashville	51	B	410,333	311,875	5,501	56.69	41,925	Owned	56,533	40,000	0	0	410,333	0	Woodson Gilchrist
Tiptonville	5	M	131,598	106,623	3,025	35.25	1,516	Owned	23,459	15,000	40,000	0	7,000	84,598	MMH Hall Architects
Texas															
Austin	37	B	474,000	285,292	8,000	35.66	25,608	97,161	65,939	65,000	0	0	474,000	0	Suzan Nyfeler
Austin	33	B	372,000	218,185	8,000	27.27	31,443	Owned	122,372	50,000	0	0	372,000	0	Suzan Nyfeler
Cedar Park	27	M	3,356,000	2,286,000	17,700	129.15	370,000	500,000	200,000	150,000	0	100,000	2,756,000	500,000	Phillips Swager
East Bernard	3	B	494,519	379,088	5,000	75.81	82,194	Owned	33,237	15,000	0	0	234,800	259,719	DiStefano/Santopetro
Garland	51	B	4,176,304	1,507,708	36,920	40.84	432,913	1,151,112	1,084,571	85,590	0	0	4,138,649	37,655	Phillips Swager
West Lake Hills	21	M	2,180,891	1,664,377	15,821	105.2	297,004	Leased	219,510	95,000	0	135,282	1,584,191	461,418	Tim Aynesworth

Symbol Code: B—Branch Library; BS—Branch & System Headquarters; M—Main Library; MS—Main & System Headquarters; S—System Headquarters; n.a.—not available

Utah																
Bountiful	78	B	289,998	230,095	4,242	54.24	28,615		Owned	31,288	42,000	0	0	289,998	0	Cooper-Roberts....
Salt Lake City	23	B	1,469,000	1,076,000	9,100	118.24	121,000		Owned	272,000	69,000	0	0	1,469,000	0	Myron Richardson
Vermont																
Woodstock	6	M	4,760,000	4,191,000	15,000	279.4	75,000		Owned	494,000	52,830	0	20,000	0	4,740,000	Mitchell Assocs.
Virginia																
Dinwiddie Ct. Hse.	12	B	238,747	181,429	2,000	90.71	30,358		Leased	26,960	6,170	0	50,000	41,852	146,895	John G. Lewis Jr.
Winchester	95	B	482,273	242,346	12,000	20.2	193,521		Owned	46,406	60,000	0	0	482,273	0	Universal Design
Washington																
Aberdeen	20	B	2,031,282	1,343,405	17,051	78.79	322,701		Owned	365,176	115,000	0	0	1,391,282	640,000	Street Lundgren...
Lopez Island	2	M	1,000,259	810,375	6,370	127.22	96,922		Owned	92,962	25,000	0	0	613,259	387,000	Buffalo Design
Olympia	n.a.	B	467,070	246,570	20,000	12.33	198,000		Owned	22,500	160,000	0	0	427,070	40,000	Nelson Architecture
Poulsbo	8	B	1,508,851	1,339,542	13,558	98.8	n.a.		Owned	169,309	42,090	0	0	1,292,851	216,000	Steve Myrvang
West Virginia																
Shady Spring	14	B	203,500	157,000	1,900	82.63	30,000		Owned	16,500	10,000	0	110,000	0	93,500	SEM
Wisconsin																
Madison	17	B	514,942	392,812	8,000	49.1	122,130		Leased	0	50,000	0	0	505,117	9,825	Strang Inc.
Milwaukee	940	M	3,397,651	2,833,741	49,500	57.25	348,151		Owned	215,759	541,000	0	0	795,969	2,601,682	Uihlein/Wilson
Wyoming																
Burns	2	B	467,800	211,700	4,500	47.04	43,100	200,000	Owned	13,000	12,500	0	0	227,800	240,000	Noel Griffith Jr.

Symbol Code: B—Branch Library; BS—Branch & System Headquarters; M—Main Library; MS—Main & System Headquarters; S—System Headquarters; n.a.—not available

Table 6 / Public Library Buildings, Six-Year Cost Summary

	Fiscal 1995	Fiscal 1996	Fiscal 1997	Fiscal 1999*	Fiscal 2000	Fiscal 2001
Number of new buildings	99	100	97	77	114	80
Number of ARRs[1]	124	145	128	118	127	132
Sq. ft. new buildings	2,102,851	2,002,067	2,153,203	1,555,583	1,752,395	1,924,548
Sq. ft. ARRs	2,469,345	2,315,523	2,710,599	2,188,221	2,272,684	2,215,702
New Buildings						
Construction cost	$232,050,462	$286,141,319	$227,740,506	$192,319,192	$232,832,870	$275,404,635
Equipment cost	28,239,712	57,222,035	35,983,384	25,382,314	36,127,111	51,445,962
Site cost	31,406,749	16,391,748	33,630,070	22,634,855	28,655,584	33,375,676
Other cost	42,946,629	49,498,901	40,060,597	43,631,263	39,878,940	39,511,803
Total—Project cost	334,643,552	409,254,003	337,414,557	283,967,624	331,345,167	400,838,076
ARRs—Project cost	281,750,499	314,191,342	324,762,086	280,604,091	301,200,950	285,583,407
New & ARR Project Cost	616,394,051	723,445,345	662,176,643	564,571,715	632,546,117	686,421,483
Fund Sources						
Federal, new buildings	10,532,079	17,719,253	4,572,130	7,655,690	7,598,492	2,687,151
Federal, ARRs	3,292,272	13,771,483	7,698,270	9,268,183	2,600,334	6,959,013
Federal, total	13,824,351	31,490,736	12,270,400	16,923,873	10,198,826	9,646,164
State, new buildings	31,051,654	32,089,611	73,081,134	17,122,988	12,456,471	6,696,211
State, ARRs	28,482,199	21,212,540	62,169,948	21,677,529	36,982,165	19,396,775
State, total	59,533,853	53,302,151	135,251,082	38,800,517	49,438,636	26,092,986
Local, new buildings	268,609,523	301,996,679	228,793,054	226,616,333	287,118,370	356,563,114
Local, ARRs	227,108,845	182,163,428	233,525,418	201,166,513	220,776,786	211,059,513
Local, total	495,718,368	484,160,107	462,318,472	427,782,846	507,895,156	567,622,627
Gift, new buildings	25,433,205	57,478,470	31,168,178	32,563,613	26,544,144	34,923,118
Gift, ARRs	23,951,472	97,019,403	21,345,010	48,614,252	33,309,803	43,344,138
Gift, total	49,384,677	154,497,873	52,513,188	81,177,865	59,853,947	78,267,256
Total Funds Used	$618,461,249	$723,450,867	$662,353,142	$564,685,101	$627,386,565	$681,629,033

[1] Additions, rmodelings, and renovations.
* Summary statistics were not kept for Fiscal 1998.

Expenditures for Resources in School Library Media Centers, 1999–2000: New Money, Old Books

Marilyn L. Miller

Professor Emeritus and Former Chair, Department of Library and Information Studies
University of North Carolina, Greensboro

Marilyn L. Shontz

Associate Professor, Library Education Program
Rowan University, Glassboro, New Jersey

After a few years of stagnation, spending on school library resources has risen for the past four years, and especially in the past two. But the increase seems to have done more to help libraries expand their electronic resources than to update book collections, according to our most recent biennial survey of school library expenditures and resources.

Between 1999 and 2000 median library spending from all sources was up 15 percent, to $14,047 per school. Yet in 2000 median per-pupil spending on books was only $8.09, not even enough to pay for the average trade paperback. Moreover, nearly half the librarians surveyed reported that somewhere between 11 to 30 percent of their books were out of date.

Still, it is significant that most new money came from local districts, as opposed to from gifts, fund raising, or the federal government. This shows that school districts are at least making an effort to improve support for school libraries.

Here are some other key findings from our survey:

Technology ascendant. There's been a striking rise in spending for what we've termed "Web-based products," that is, online subscriptions and other fee-based Web resources. Spending on this category now overshadows expenditures for all other resources except books. Moreover, in the 1999–2000 school year, media specialists spent nearly half as much money on CD-ROMs, software, and Web resources as they did on books.

A lack of certified librarians. Only 61 percent of media specialists hold a degree in school library media. Sixteen percent have no training beyond an undergraduate degree.

Increased automation. Ninety percent of school libraries have an automated circulation system. Eighty-two percent have an online catalog.

Dwindling number of library directors. More than half of the districts surveyed have no district-level director of library media centers.

More books for the West. In the last two years, media specialists in the western United States added more books to their collections than those in other regions.

Planning time is linked to library schedules. Those with a flexibly scheduled library were significantly more likely to plan instruction with teachers than those with a fixed schedule.

Adapted from *School Library Journal*, October 2001.

Growth of regional networks. The use of state or regional library databases increased significantly in the past two years.

Few library Web pages. Though 55 percent of schools have Web pages, only 27 percent of school libraries have their own Web presence.

The purpose of our survey, begun in 1983, is to provide an up-to-date account and longitudinal view of national trends in school library spending so that readers can compare local data with national norms. The survey also seeks information about the kinds of programs and services provided by media specialists. In addition, each biennial survey collects data that focuses on one or more previously unstudied aspects of school library media programs. This time we provide a more detailed look at high school expenditures (Table 8), as well as the increased acquisition and use of technology in media centers.

Funding Sources and Expenditures

Most money for school library resources comes from local school districts (Table 1). The rest, more than a third, comes from federal funding, gifts, and fundraising. On the spending side, money for print resources—books, periodicals, and microforms—continues to outstrip other allocations.

After a dip in 1995–1996, local funding of media centers increased steadily for the past four years. The biggest jump came in the past two years: median local funding per school was $11,923 in 1999–2000, up from $9,500 in 1997–1998. While the increase barely accounts for inflation, it does show continued effort on the part of many school districts.

Table 3 looks at local spending for various library resources, from books to periodicals to Web resources. As you'll see, there are large discrepancies between mean (or average) and median (or midpoint) expenditures. For instance, mean book spending in 1999–2000 was $8,454, while the median level was only $5,957. This discrepancy reflects a few respondents reporting extremely high spending in some categories, such as books. Because such spending skews the

Table 1 / Mean and Median Expenditures for All Resources, All Funding Sources

1999–2000	Number Responding	Mean	Median
Funding			
Total All Local Funds	558	$18,596	$11,923
Total All Federal Funds	170	$5,473	$2,632
Total All Gifts/Fundraising	330	$2,937	$1,305
Expenditures (All Funds)			
Books	540	$10,305	$7,000
Periodicals	533	$1,500	$1,030
Microforms	55	$1,729	$900
AV Resources/Equipment	460	$3,256	$2,000
Computer Resources/Equipment	428	$8,891	$3,010
Total Expenditures	566	$21,740	$14,047

Table 2 / Mean and Median Expenditures for All Resources, All Funding Sources

	1993–1994			1995–1996			1997–1998			1999–2000		
	Number Responding	Mean	Median	Number Responding	Mean	Median	Number Responding	Mean	Median	Number Responding	Mean	Median
Funding												
Local Funds	590	$12,950	$9,587	575	$12,575	$9,080	524	$15,918	$9,500	558	$18,596	$11,923
Federal Funds	213	$3,569	$2,000	208	$3,588	$1,979	144	$3,669	$2,594	170	$5,473	$2,632
Gifts/Fundraising	330	$2,675	$1,125	347	$3,398	$1,200	356	$3,701	$1,200	330	$2,937	$1,305
Expenditures (All Funds)												
Books	576	$6,299	$5,000	556	$6,415	$5,165	504	$7,279	$6,000	540	$10,305	$7,000
Periodicals	568	$1,529	$1,000	536	$1,308	$900	502	$1,422	$1,000	533	$1,500	$1,030
Microforms	130	$1,380	$990	93	$1,200	$806	62	$1,451	$750	55	$1,729	$900
AV Resources/Equipment	498	$3,209	$2,000	450	$2,834	$1,700	430	$3,036	$1,525	460	$3,256	$2,000
Computer Resources/Equipment	447	$5,423	$2,800	41	$7,429	$3,090	413	$7,697	$2,700	428	$8,891	$3,010
TOTAL EXPENDITURES	590	$15,499	$11,745	580	$15,707	$11,144	532	$19,300	$12,185	566	$21,740	$14,047

Table 3 / Mean and Median Expenditures per School for LMC Resources
Local Funds Only

1999–2000			
Books			$8,454
n=525			$5,957
AV	$1,745		
n=392	$1,000		
Microforms	$1,715		
n=53	$800		
Periodicals	$1,496		
n=517	$1,000		
CD-ROMs and Software	$1,349		
n=233	$675		
WWW Resources	$3,542		
n=202	$2,000		

Mean · Median

$0 $2,000 $4,000 $6,000 $8,000 $10,000

mean upward, the median is often a more reliable figure for all schools (for details, see "Behind the Data").

There's a similar discrepancy in per-pupil spending on resources (Table 5), where the mean spending on books is $11.41, versus a median level of only $8.09. In an age when the importance of reading is given more and more credence by teachers and researchers, one can infer from these numbers that some schools are receiving a lot of money for books. But, with median per-pupil spending at only $8.09, one can also infer there are more schools not meeting the challenge of providing adequate book collections.

The amounts spent on other print and nonprint resources have remained noticeably unchanged. But there have been marked changes in technology spending. For instance, in the 1999–2000 school year, media specialists spent nearly half as much money on CD-ROMs, software, and Web resources as they did on books (Table 4). There has also been a shift in spending away from the CD-ROM format and toward Web-based resources. In 2000 librarians spent $2.46 per pupil on online products and other Web-based resources (Table 6), but only 94 cents per pupil on CD-ROMs and software combined. In fact, expenditures for Web-based resources, which appear separately for the first time in this report, now overshadow expenditures for all other resources except books.

For this report, we also asked if media specialists were purchasing DVDs for their collections, and we found that few schools are purchasing these resources in significant numbers (Table 7). But media specialists at all grade levels continue to find microforms useful in the collection.

Table 4 / Median Expenditures per School for LMC Resources
Local Funds Only

1999–2000

Legend: 1990, 1992, 1994, 1996, 1998, 2000

Books	$3,000; $3,632; $4,000; $4,000; $5,000; $5,957
AV	$1,000; $983; $1,000; $850; $800; $1,000
Periodicals	$800; $987; $1,000; $900; $1,000; $1,000
Microforms	$1,000; $800; $977; $828; $600; $800
Software	$406; $500; $510; $700; $650
CD-ROMs	$650; $600; $700
CD-ROMs Software	$675
WWW Resources	$2,000

Axis: $0; $1,000; $2,000; $3,000; $4,000; $5,000; $6,000; $7,000

Table 5 / Mean and Median Expenditures per Pupil for LMC Resources
Local Funds Only

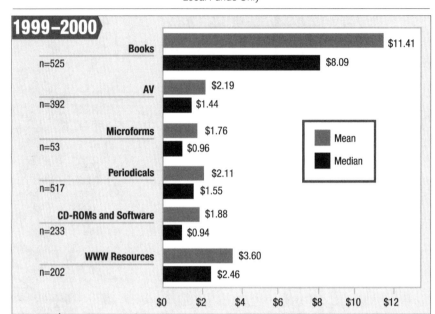

The size of school library collections varies by grade level. The median size of elementary school book collections is 10,096, and the mean is very close, at 10,922 books. Mean and median figures for book collections in middle/junior high schools are identical, at 11,973 books. High school collection sizes are larger than other grade levels in this report—a mean of 15,156 and a median of 13,201—perhaps because of the higher number of high school media specialists responding to the survey and increased expenditures reported in the West.

High School Spending by Region

This year we took a closer look at spending in high schools. High school libraries in the West stand out this year for adding the most new books to their collections, an average of 1,444 and a median of 569 (Table 8). Western high schools also showed higher spending overall than they have in the past. This could reflect the fact that California media centers have received vastly improved book budgets over the past few years, thanks to new appropriations from the state assembly. Also affecting the positive picture from the West might be the high number of respondents from California and this year's increased reporting from high schools.

Though western high schools added the most books to their collections, high school libraries in the Northeast still provide the highest number of books per pupil (Table 8). Northeast media specialists also spent the most money on periodicals and, along with schools in the South and North Central regions, spent sig-

(text continues on page 513)

Table 6 / Median Expenditures per Pupil for LMC Resources
Local Funds Only

1990–2000

Legend: 1990, 1992, 1994, 1996, 1998, 2000

Category	1990	1992	1994	1996	1998	2000
Books	$5.48	$5.88	$6.80	$6.73	$7.35	$8.09
AV	$1.69	$1.52	$1.73	$1.42	$1.24	$1.44
Periodicals	$1.40	$1.51	$1.65	$1.50	$1.60	$1.55
Microforms	$1.08	$1.15	$1.26	$1.04	$1.32	$0.96
Software	$0.81	$0.87	$1.10	$1.14	$0.88	
CD-ROMs				$1.17	$1.15	$1.07
CD-ROMs and Software						$0.94
WWW Products						$2.46

Table 7 / LMC Collection Size and Local Expenditures by School Levels

1999–2000	Elementary n=199		Middle/Jr. High n=142		Senior High n=214		K-8, K-12, and Other n=54	
	Median	Mean	Median	Mean	Median	Mean	Median	Mean
Collections:								
Size of Book Collection	10,096	10,922	11,973	11,973	13,201	15,156	12,125	14,090
Number of Books per Pupil	20	22	15	17	14	15	22	26
Volumes Added	500	602	500	709	473	770	500	721
Volumes Discarded	116	288	200	413	200	475	200	351
Size of Video Collection	200	252	250	319	376	528	200	327
Videos per Pupil	0.40	0.52	0.32	0.46	0.35	0.52	0.42	0.60
Videos Added	20	31	20	44	25	62	20	32
Videos Discarded	0.00	4.00	0.00	6.00	0.00	8.00	0.00	4.00
Size of DVD Collection	0.00	1.16	0.00	1.53	0.00	1.10	0.00	0.46
DVDs Added	0.00	0.18	0.00	0.33	0.00	0.42	0.00	0.00
DVDs Discarded	0.00	0.00	0.00	0.00	0.00	0.00	0.00	0.00
Size of Audio CD Collection	0.00	12.00	0.00	14.00	0.00	17.00	0.00	20.00
Audio CDs Added	0.00	1.30	0.00	3.23	0.00	3.82	0.00	2.44
Audio CDs Discarded	0.00	0.12	0.00	0.60	0.00	0.26	0.00	0.00
Size of Software Collection	1.00	26.00	0.00	21.00	0.00	10.00	0.00	14.00
Software Added	0.00	4.38	0.00	1.93	0.00	1.44	0.00	1.62
Software Discarded	0.00	4.14	0.00	0.77	0.00	3.06	0.00	2.85
Size of CD-ROM Collection	20.00	62.00	15.00	34.00	10.00	21.00	6.00	45.00
CD-ROMs Added	0.00	8.81	0.00	4.65	0.50	3.86	0.00	1.66
CD-ROMs Discarded	0.00	0.51	0.00	2.43	0.00	0.90	0.00	0.91

Table 7 / LMC Collection Size and Local Expenditures by School Levels (*cont.*)

1999–2000	Elementary n=199		Middle/Jr. High n=142		Senior High n=214		K–8, K–12, and Other n=54	
	Median	Mean	Median	Mean	Median	Mean	Median	Mean
Expenditures:								
Books	$4,500.00	$5,330.00	$6,000.00	$8,279.00	$8,000.00	$11,492.00	$5,000.00	$8,087.00
Books per Pupil	$8.44	$10.53	$9.00	$12.01	$7.35	$11.51	$9.00	$12.80
Periodicals	600.00	713.00	1,060.00	1,328.00	1,800.00	2,241.00	1,270.00	1,761.00
Periodicals per Pupil	1.25	1.42	1.65	2.04	1.84	2.59	1.99	2.91
Microforms	350.00	425.00	1,100.00	1,489.00	670.00	1,734.00	3,075.00	3,538.00
Microforms per Pupil	0.74	0.76	1.68	2.49	0.58	1.28	3.93	4.48
Audiovisual Resources	600.00	980.00	1,164.00	1,684.00	1,470.00	2,480.00	500.00	1,048.00
Audiovisual Resources per Pupil	1.54	2.00	1.61	2.64	1.38	2.17	1.17	1.55
Software and CD-ROM Resources	530.00	964.00	500.00	1,036.00	1,000.00	1,671.00	500.00	1,932.00
Software/CD-ROM Resources per Pupil	1.13	2.02	0.91	1.63	1.00	1.85	0.72	2.34
WWW-Based Products	500.00	759.00	1,185.00	1,923.00	3,000.00	4,757.00	2,700.00	5,215.00
WWW-Based Resources per Pupil	0.94	1.65	1.74	2.62	2.94	4.20	6.11	6.73
*Total Materials Expenditures (TME)	$10,475.00	$12,925.00	$14,600.00	$22,150.00	$22,250.00	$30,636.00	$13,137.00	$17,698.00
TME per Pupil	$20.80	$25.29	$19.61	$31.24	$21.85	$32.15	$20.94	$28.61

Table 8 / High Schools: LMC Collection Size and Local Expenditures by Region

1999–2000	Northeast n=46		South n=74		North Central n=61		West n=33	
	Median	Mean	Median	Mean	Median	Mean	Median	Mean
Collections:								
Size of Book Collection	14,000	17,290	12,700	14,544	1,300	14,115	14,905	15,369
Number of Books per Pupil	17	18	11	13	15	17	12	15
Volumes Added	487	628	500	735	375	526	569	1,444
Volumes Discarded	237	706	250	440	101	251	214	600
Size of Video Collection	200	467	500	707	420	470	213	319
Videos per Pupil	0.26	0.47	0.44	0.61	0.43	0.55	0.19	0.35
Videos Added	5	28	36	81	25	48	20	89
Videos Discarded	0	5	2	10	0	9	0	4
Size of DVD Collection	0	1.20	0	1.67	0	.67	0	0.48
Size of Audio CD Collection	0	21	0	18	0	11	0	14
Size of Software Collection	0	8	2	13	0	10	0	6
Size of CD-ROM Collection	10	20	13	25	6	15	12	25
Expenditures:								
Books	$9,750.00	$12,839.00	$8,174.00	$10,359.00	$6,700.00	$8,406.00	$7,112.00	$17,545.00
Books per Pupil	$10.19	$14.72	$6.00	$9.64	$7.69	$9.67	$7.80	$14.68
Periodicals	2,464.00	2,978.00	1,557.00	1,912.00	1,707.00	2,113.00	1,734.00	2,202.00
Periodicals per Pupil	2.75	3.78	1.62	2.04	2.31	2.73	1.42	1.97
Microforms	500.00	1,275.00	875.00	2,328.00	650.00	2,183.00	425.00	1,109.00
Microforms per Pupil	0.43	0.95	0.60	1.45	0.96	1.92	0.50	0.94
Audiovisual Resources	1,500.00	2,655.00	1,800.00	2,977.00	1,816.00	2,266.00	750.00	1,584.00
Audiovisual Resources per Pupil	1.39	2.66	1.51	2.13	1.60	2.51	0.65	1.15
Software and CD-ROM Resources	1,350.00	2,310.00	1,000.00	1,184.00	875.00	2,359.00	1,000.00	1,220.00
Software and CD-ROM Resources per Pupil	2.08	1.88	1.07	1.20	0.94	3.57	0.65	1.29
WWW-Based Resources	2,760.00	4,567.00	2,749.00	4,888.00	2,900.00	3,980.00	3,000.00	5,856.00
WWW-Based Resources per Pupil	5.06	5.77	2.46	3.57	2.97	4.33	3.16	3.30
Total Materials Expenditures (TME)	$22,050.00	$30,586.00	$22,500.00	$28,234.00	$20,955.00	$26,426.00	$25,897.00	$43,732.00
TME per Pupil	$31.86	$35.63	$18.60	$26.36	$24.03	$35.83	$27.35	$33.77

(text continued from page 508)

nificantly more than their western counterparts on videotape resources. Northeastern high schools also spent the most money per pupil, $5.06, on Web-based resources.

We always provide total media expenditures per pupil, or TME, to allow comparisons of total library expenditures from all resources—local, federal, gifts, and fund raising. The TME of $31.86 per pupil in Northeast high schools is the highest in the nation, while the TME of $18.60 in the South is the lowest. Schools in the rest of the country fall in the middle range, with a per-pupil TME of $27.35 in the West and $24.30 in the North Central region. The greatest divergence in mean and median figures—meaning the greatest variation among individual schools—is in the North Central region.

Currency of Collections

Inflation and book prices continue to rise. At the same time, educators, researchers, and the public continue to focus on reading performance. With those factors in mind, we asked librarians to estimate the currency of their collections. Respondents reported the following estimates of the numbers of out-of-date books:

- 0–10 percent of collection out of date: 32 percent of media specialists
- 11–30 percent of collection out of date: 45 percent of media specialists
- 31–70 percent of collection out of date: 21 percent of media specialists
- 71+ percent of collection out of date: 2 percent of media specialists

No analysis of this data can result in a positive view of the book collections available to students. Very large schools with large collections can probably give fairly good service with 10 percent of their books out of date, but this percentage is unacceptable in the hundreds of small schools that need to cover all subjects just as badly as larger schools. The fact that 2 percent of the schools have collections in which over two-thirds of the books are out of date is also disturbing.

Technology

As we said earlier, school libraries show continued growth in the acquisition and use of technology and electronic resources (Tables 9 and 10). More than 90 percent of respondents have computerized circulation systems, access to the Internet, e-mail, telephones, and acceptable-use policies for their computer systems and resources. A large percentage, 88 percent, reported access to the Web for searching and reference. This percentage possibly reflects the higher number of high school respondents who are providing access to the Web for searching and reference.

Resource sharing—between school libraries, between school and public libraries, and among members of regional consortia—has diminished since the last survey, as has the use of cable television. The use of broadcast television and blocking software has increased.

Table 9 / LMCs and Technology

1999–2000	Number Responding YES	Percent YES
LMC Has Online Library Catalog	499	82%
LMC Has Computerized Circulation System	555	91%
LMC Plans to Develop Online Library Catalog	52	8%
LMC Has Plans to Develop Computerized Circulation	29	6%
Additional Funds for:		
Computer Software	203	33%
Telecommunications	232	32%
CD-ROM Purchase or Lease	164	30%
Video Discs	49	8%
Technical Processing Services	109	18%
Resource Sharing	148	24%
WWW Products or Subscriptions	148	24%
LMC Uses:		
Cable TV	204	33%
Local Broadcast TV	337	55%
Closed Circuit TV	197	32%
Distance Education, 1–2 Way Audio–Video	38	6%
Distance Education, Video Conferencing	35	6%
LMC Has:		
Local Area Network	405	66%
Wide Area Network	371	61%
Computers With Modem	75	12%
Access to Telecommunications, Internet, E-mail	563	93%
CD-ROM Searching/Reference	339	56%
Access to WWW Searching/Reference	538	88%
LMC Has Access to Fax Machine:		
Yes, in LMC	153	25%
Yes, in School Only	370	61%
LMC Is Member of Resource Sharing Network	370	61%
Network Is Linked Electronically	303	50%
LMC Has Telephone	566	95%
School Has WWW Home Page	337	55%
LMC Has WWW Home Page	166	27%
School or LMC Has Acceptable-Use Policy (AUP)	577	96%
School or LMC Uses Blocking Software	418	69%
School or LMC Uses Web Portal	38	7%

For this report we also asked respondents whether they had a library home page independent of the schoolwide Web site. Fifty-five percent reported that the school has a home page, and 27 percent of librarians reported having a separate library page.

In the April 1994 survey, we began to divide schools into two groups. We described one group as high-tech schools, since their students had access to both online catalogs and automated circulation systems. The other group had one computerized system but not both. At that time, we reported that the 53 to 55 percent of those without both systems planned to provide them. In the ensuing seven years, the school-age population with access to one or both of these systems has

Table 10 / Electronic Information Resources Available in LMCs

1999–2000	Available in CD-ROM Format Only	Available on Internet or LAN	Available in Both	Total
Almanacs	14%	29%	8%	51%
eLibrary	22%	22%		
EBSCOhost	2%	31%	3%	36%
Encyclopedias	23%	29%	37%	89%
FirstSearch	14%	14%		
GaleNet	16%	16%		
InfoTrac	3%	26%	4%	33%
NetLibrary	3%	3%		
NewsBank	1%	8%	2%	11%
ProQuest	3%	22%	4%	29%
Readers' Guide	1%	5%	6%	
SIRS	8%	29%	6%	43%
State or Regional Library Databases	3%	40%	4%	47%

Table 11 / Advanced Degrees of Head Library Media Specialist

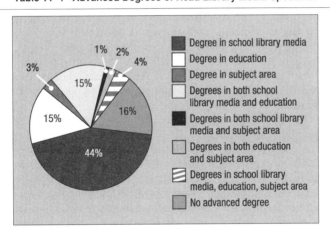

expanded greatly. For this report, only nine percent of respondents reported having neither an online catalog nor an automated circulation system. Many of those without one of these systems plan to develop them in the future.

More and more media specialists are adding electronic reference resources to their collections. Table 10 displays the percentages of schools using the most well-known resources. As might be expected, the largest number of libraries, 88 percent, uses electronic encyclopedias. One-half use almanacs. Other leading resources are periodical and resource databases, such as SIRS, EBSCOhost, and InfoTrac.

In terms of electronic resources, the biggest increase over the past two years has been in the use of state or regional electronic databases. In 1997–1998, students in 27 percent of the schools reporting had access to these databases; in 1999–2000, 47 percent of students had access. This change, and the rapid growth in the use of all kinds of technology in media centers, convinced us it was no longer appropriate to divide schools into high-tech and low-tech groups. We will provide further results on the status and use of technology in school libraries in an upcoming report.

Library Staff and Training

Information Power 2 (ALA, 1998) recommends that school libraries include at least one full-time library media specialist who holds a master's degree in librarianship. Yet, our survey shows that only 61 percent of media specialists hold a degree in school library media. As Table 11 shows, 44 percent have a library media degree, while another 17 percent have both a library media degree and a degree in a subject area or education.

We can infer from Table 11 that slightly more than one-third, or 36 percent, of respondents hold only the minimum certification required by their states of residence. Of this 36 percent, 16 per cent hold no advanced degree at all. They hold an undergraduate degree with a major or minor in school library media with teacher certification, or they hold an undergraduate degree in a subject and the few hours required by the state for school library media certification (taken as part of their degree studies or after matriculation). In all fairness, it should be pointed out that many minimally prepared school librarians would take more courses or enroll in a program for the school library advanced degree, but most state education departments don't support the graduate degree as a requirement for employment in media centers. In addition, graduate programs are not available in many parts of the country.

Salaries for media specialists continued to increase across all grade levels, with a median increase in the last two years of $2,795. But while salaries have risen, personnel levels, years of experience, and the number of support staff have remained constant over the 18 years of this series. Table 12 shows that at all grade levels, media centers are typically staffed by one full-time librarian who has a half-time clerk at the elementary and K–8 levels or a full-time clerk in a middle school or high school. While many schools report using student assistants, the median number working in the library is one, and adult volunteers still play a small role. Most librarians have worked in media centers from 12 to 15 years and have worked in schools from 18 to 20 years.

Programs and Services

At all grade levels except high school, the number of hours spent planning instruction with teachers showed a slight decrease from two years ago. Average planning time was as follows (Table 13):

Table 12 / Library Media Specialists' Experience, Salary, and Support Staff

1999–2000	Elementary n=199		Middle/Jr. High n=142		Senior High n=214		K–8, K–12, and Other n=54		Total All n=609	
	Median	Mean	Median	Mean	Median	Mean	Median	Mean	Median	Mean
No. Media Specialists in School	1.00	0.94	1.00	1.04	1.00	1.32	1.00	1.25	1.00	1.13
Years Experience in K–12 Schools	20	18	20	19	21	21	18	18	20	20
Years Experience in Library/Media	12	13	12	13	15	16	12	13	13	14
Salary of Head Media Specialist	$42,000	$42,792	$45,000	$45,979	$44,593	$44,954	$36,750	$38,227	$42,895	$43,991
Student Assistants	0.00	6.85	4.00	7.37	2.00	5.62	0.00	3.44	1.00	6.24
Support Staff/Paid Clerks	0.50	0.63	1.00	0.77	1.00	1.07	0.50	0.54	1.00	0.81
Adult Volunteers	2.00	5.97	0.00	3.58	0.00	1.16	3.00	5.20	1.00	3.66

- Elementary: 2.44 hours per week, down from 2.64
- Junior high/middle: 3.64 hours, down from 3.74
- K–8 and other: 2.5 hours, down from 2.83
- High school: media specialists reported spending almost five hours a week on planning with teachers. The increased number of high school librarians responding may account for this increase.

The little time generally reported for planning may not represent a lack of effort, especially if one considers that staffing in media centers is at an absolute minimum in the majority of schools in the United States. However, we should note that so many schools reported minimal or no planning time that we reported mean figures instead of the preferred median.

Another question raised by the data is what exactly librarians mean by planning. A total of 80 percent of media specialists reported that they collaborate with teachers (Table 15). But only 62 percent reported helping teachers develop, implement, and evaluate instruction. This discrepancy appears at all grade levels. It may

Table 13 / LMS/Teacher Instructional Planning: Activity by Grade Level

1999–2000		Mean # Hours Formal Instructional Planning	Mean # Hours Informal Instructional Planning	Mean # Hours Total Planning
Elementary	n= 199	0.64	1.80	2.44
Middle/Jr. High	n= 142	1.21	2.43	3.64
Senior High	n= 214	1.17	3.28	4.46
K–8, K–12, and Other	n= 54	0.7	1.80	2.50
Total	n= 609	0.97	2.47	3.43

Table 14 / Type of Schedule Used in Elementary LMCs and LMS-Teacher Planning

1999–2000	Flexible Schedule n=24	Combined Flex/Fixed n=84	Fixed Schedule n=85
Percent of LMS Who Regularly Plan With Teachers			
Yes	79%	82%	49%
No	21%	18%	51%
Percent of Teachers Planning With LMS			
0–15%	32%	25%	24%
16–30%	16%	32%	29%
31–70%	5%	21%	21%
More than 71%	47%	21%	26%
Mean Hours of Teacher/LMS Planning per Week			
Formal	1.00	0.94	0.27
Informal	2.79	2.23	1.11
Total Teacher–LMS Planning Hours	3.79	3.17	1.37
Mean # LMS on Staff, Full and Part Time	0.92	0.94	0.91
Mean # Support Staff, Full and Part Time	0.74	0.62	0.65

Table 15 / Comparison of LM Program Services by Grade Level

LM Program Service:	Elementary n=199	Middle/Jr. High n=142	Senior High n=214	K–8, K–12, and Other n=54	Total All n=609
1. Offers a program of curriculum integrated skills instruction	67%	61%	67%	70%	66%
2. Informally instructs students in use of resources	93%	98%	98%	91%	96%
3. Plans or conducts workshops for teachers	36%	48%	50%	35%	44%
4. Assists school curriculum committee with recommendations	52%	58%	47%	41%	51%
5. Collaborates with teachers	74%	88%	81%	78%	80%
6. Helps teachers develop, implement, and evaluate learning	55%	70%	65%	56%	62%
7. Provides teachers with information about new resources	82%	94%	92%	83%	89%
8. Provides reference assistance to students and teachers	99%	99%	99%	98%	99%
9. Helps students and teachers find and use resources outside school	66%	85%	88%	76%	79%
10. Provides interlibrary loan service for students and teachers	60%	53%	60%	43%	57%
11. Provides reading/listening/viewing guidance for students	90%	89%	76%	87%	85%
12. Helps parents realize importance of lifelong learning	68%	65%	25%	61%	49%
13. Coordinates in-school production of materials	28%	37%	33%	24%	32%
14. Coordinates video production and dissemination activities	21%	30%	23%	15%	23%
15. Coordinates cable TV, distance education, and related activities	34%	52%	44%	32%	41%
16. Coordinates school or library computer networks	40%	49%	50%	41%	46%
17. Provides access to online library catalog and circulation	80%	86%	85%	74%	82%
18. Provides Internet and online access	88%	95%	98%	87%	93%
19. Provides WWW searching and reference	79%	94%	97%	81%	89%
20. Provides electronic access to a resource sharing network	45%	51%	55%	41%	50%

relate to the inability or reluctance of media specialists to find ways to plan with teachers. Whatever the reason for the discrepancy, it's clear that assisting teachers with learning strategies and outcomes is at the heart of true collaboration.

Because the type of scheduling used in elementary school libraries can be critical to authentic learning, we also looked at librarian-teacher planning time in terms of the type of library schedule (Table 14). Seventy-nine percent of librarians with a flexible schedule report planning regularly with teachers, compared to 49 percent of those with a fixed schedule. Those media specialists working with a flexible schedule also are likely to plan with more of their teachers than those working with any other type of schedule. Total planning time is another indicator of the potential of the flexible or combined fixed/flex schedule. While media specialists in programs using fixed scheduling report 1.37 hours weekly in planning, those using flexible scheduling report almost four hours a week planning time, and those in combined programs report 3.17 hours.

Table 15 describes the types of program services provided by media specialists. Nearly all librarians (96 percent) informally instruct students in the use of resources, and 99 percent provide reference assistance to students and teachers. A large majority of media specialists (89 percent) provide teachers with information about new resources, and 89 percent help with Web searching and reference.

The 44 percent who reported planning or conducting workshops for teachers is an increase over two years ago, when one-third of media specialists said they were involved in this sort of staff development. Elementary school librarians are less likely than others to provide this service.

Librarians are increasingly involved with the development, use, and maintenance of telecommunications equipment and activities. See, for instance, the high number of respondents who reported coordinating school or library computer networks and providing access to various online resources (Table 15, items 15–20).

District-Level Leadership

In 1987, when we first asked about the presence of a district-level library media director, 40 percent of respondents said they had one. A decade later, in 1997–1998, only 33 percent said they had such leaders, and in the current study, only 30 percent of the respondents told us that they worked with a full-time, district-level media director (Table 16). Sixteen percent have access to a half-time director/consultant. Moreover, the role of the district-level media director has changed drastically in the past two decades. The functions of the position once called "supervisor" have disappeared in many places, having been replaced by an approach that stresses advice, oversight of certain aspects of the media program, and consulting, as requested by school personnel. The time that can be devoted to this position has also changed significantly. Many library directors now find themselves assigned to other administrative jobs and must oversee additional programs. While our data reflects the loss in numbers of district media directors, it does not reflect the many types of responsibilities assigned to them in addition to school media and technology.

We asked respondents to note whether they had acquired *Information Power 2* and to tell us the most valuable use they had made of the document. The four most valuable uses reported, from most to least valuable, were:

Table 16 / District Level Supervisor or Director of SLM Programs

Table 17 / Comparison of LMC and School Characteristics
by District Level Media Director Status
n=606

	With Full-Time n=185		With Part-Time n=96		Without n=325	
	count	percent	count	percent	count	percent
*Use of library media advisory committee	76	42%	23	24%	56	17%
*Availability of selection policy	158	85%	8	89%	253	79%
Book collection less than 30 percent out of date	139	78%	6	71%	244	75%
Materials budget up from last year	61	33%	31	32%	101	31%
Book budget up from last year	65	35%	24	25%	100	31%
*Added materials/supplies received from district	109	59%	54	57%	150	46%
Planning with teachers for integrated instruction	139	75%	69	72%	230	71%
Total mean hours LMS/teacher planning > 2 per week	95	51%	47	49%	143	44%
More than 30 percent of teachers plan with LMS	68	47%	29	30%	110	34%
Elementary levels have flexible scheduling	57	31%	31	32%	101	31%
Head LMS has advanced degree in library media	143	77%	69	72%	253	78%
LMS is certified in school library media	169	92%	84	88%	279	86%
*Less than 30 percent of students receive free/reduced lunch	96	52%	56	58%	196	60%
School or LMC has acceptable internet use policy	176	95%	93	98%	307	95%
School or LMC uses blocking/filter software	131	71%	74	78%	211	65%
LMC is member of resource sharing network	106	57%	62	65%	200	62%
*Added funds for resource sharing	31	17%	2	26%	91	28%
Telephone in LMC	171	92%	92	96%	301	93%
*LMC has prepaid telecommunications, Internet access	77	43%	38	39%	103	32%
*LMS has copy of IP2	148	80%	69	72%	207	64%
IP2 was used in library planning/goal setting	83	45%	4	45%	123	38%
*Statistically significant at p=.05						

- Planning individual school or district programs
- Defining student literacy standards
- Defining their roles as LMSs
- Setting goals and objectives

Conclusions

The 1999–2000 survey data offers a picture of a profession increasingly preoccupied with technology and its many demands. At the same time, the survey portrays a profession that still finds time for the main functions of the school librarian: reference specialist, teacher, and resource and instructional consultant to both teachers and students.

School librarians on the whole still find funds for books in short supply. Inflation plays havoc with book allocations, as do the growing number of elementary schools deciding to redistribute book funds by building classroom collections, a long-disproved strategy for providing for individual needs and differences. At the same time, funds for computer technologies and resources continue to grow.

The long-predicted shortage of school librarians is beginning to be widely apparent. The growth in the number of uncertified and minimally certified personnel is an expected outcome of this shortage and does not bode well for the realization of our vision of the library program as central to student achievement.

Our next survey, in 2002, will mark 20 years of data collection from wonderfully patient school library media specialists across the country. Over the years, the length of the questionnaire has stretched and stretched. There seems always to be one more thing we would like to know. We hope that media specialists continue to find the data valuable for comparison purposes and for goal setting, change, and improvement. Thank you for your participation.

Behind the Data

Survey Population

This data represents the results of a questionnaire mailed in September 1999 to 1,530 library media specialists. The respondents were selected by systematic random sampling from *School Library Journal*'s school-based subscription list covering all 50 states. After follow-up mailings to nonrespondents, we received 637 completed questionnaires. Discarding those that were incomplete, we were left with a 39.8 percent response rate, slightly higher than the rate in the 1997–1998 study. Of the total number of responses, 51, or 8.4 percent, were from private schools.

There were minimal changes in the geographic distribution of the survey, with, as in previous surveys, the largest number reporting from the South (Table 18). But noticeable differences did appear in the enrollment and grade-level distributions. Nineteen percent of the responses were from media specialists who serve 1,000 to 1,999 students, an increase of 4 percent from 1997–1998. Seven percent of responses came from schools with enrollments over 2000, compared to

Table 18 / Distribution of Respondents
by Grade Level

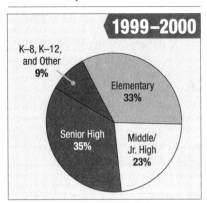

Table 19 / Distribution of Respondents
by Census Region

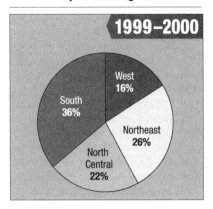

Table 20 / Distribution of Respondents
by School Enrollment

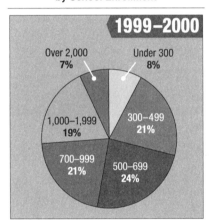

3 percent in the previous survey (Table 20). The response rates went down for schools with enrollments of 700–999 (21 percent) and 500–699 (24 percent). The latter represents a 5 percent drop. Thirty-five percent of the responses were from high schools, an increase of 10 percent over the 1997–98 survey (Table 18). Eight percent fewer elementary schools reported this year, and 9 percent of the responses were from the K–8 and other category, a 2 percent decrease from the previous study. The "other" category in the tables represents K–8 and other combinations, such as grades 7–12 and K–12.

Methodology

Each response was checked for accuracy and then coded and entered into a computer data file. Analysis was done using the Statistical Package for the Social

Sciences (SPSS). Measures of central tendency (means and medians) were produced for all of the budget collection items listed in the survey. The statistical test Chi-square was used to determine statistical significance for the category variables in Table 20.

Both means and medians are reported wherever appropriate to give a more accurate description of the data. The mean allows for comparisons with other studies that have used this measure; however, the median indicates more accurately the expenditures reported by most media specialists.

Although the mean (or average) is the descriptive statistic most commonly used in studies of this type, analysis showed an upward skew because a few respondents reported spending extremely large amounts in some categories. With data distribution like this, the few large scores inflate the mean and make it a less desirable measure. For example, Table 3 reports mean and median local expenditures per schools. In analyzing the data, we found that five schools spent under $900 for books—one of the schools spent only $100. At the other end of the scale, we found eight schools that spent more than $50,000 each on books. One of the eight spent $98,500. Thus, the median sum of $5,957 is a more reasonable figure for all schools.

Book Trade Research and Statistics

Prices of U.S. and Foreign Published Materials

Sharon G. Sullivan

Chair, ALA ALCTS Library Materials Price Index Committee

The Library Materials Price Index Committee (LMPIC) of the American Library Association's Association for Library Collections and Technical Services continues to monitor library prices for a range of library materials from sources within North America and from other key publishing centers around the world. During 2001 library materials for most categories increased at a rate greater than the U.S. Consumer Price Index (CPI), returning to trends of earlier years.

The decrease in price for books (hardcover and trade paperbacks) may be due to a change in the database from which this information was collected. A detailed explanation of this change appears with Tables 3, 6, and 7. CPI data are obtained from the Bureau of Labor Statistics Web site at http://www.bls.gov/cpi.

Some indexes have not been updated and are repeated from last year. Changes in the publishing world due to mergers and acquisitions make it more difficult to determine what is published in a foreign country by "multinational" firms. Additionally, the conversion to the Eurodollar by several countries has affected our ability to obtain information from foreign agents and wholesalers. The conversion of pricing data from national currencies to the Eurodollar makes comparison from this year to prior ones inconsistent. In other cases, the vendors were unable to provide data due to internal system migrations. The CD-ROM Price Inventory (former Table 10) is no longer being updated because the number of CD-ROM titles continues to decrease, with many of these publications migrating to Web-based publications.

	Percent Change				
Index	1996	1997	1998/1999	2000	2001
CPI	3.3	1.7	2.7	2.7	1.6
Periodicals	9.9	10.3*	10.4	9.2	8.6
Serials services	3.9	4.5*	5.6	5.3	5.8
Hardcover books	6.0	-4.4	-1.9	-2.4	n.a.
Academic books	3.6	2.1	3.8	2.0	n.a.
College books	1.8	2.7	-1.3	2.3	1.9
Mass market paperbacks	12.3	1.7	3.5	2.3	n.a.
Trade paperbacks	-1.3	1.1	6.5	-5.7	n.a.

*Payments made in 1997 for 1998 receipts.
n.a. = not available

U.S. Published Materials

Tables 1 through 9 indicate average prices and price indexes for library materials published primarily in the United States. These indexes include Periodicals (Table 1), Serials Services (Table 2), U.S. Hardcover Books (Table 3), North American Academic Books (Table 4), U.S. College Books (Table 5), U.S. Mass Market Paperback Books (Table 6), U.S. Trade Paperbacks (Table 7), U.S. Daily Newspapers and International Newspapers (Tables 8A and 8B), and U.S. Nonprint Media (Table 9).

Periodical and Serial Prices

The LMPI Committee and divine/Faxon Library Services jointly produce the U.S. Periodical Price Index (Table 1). The subscription prices shown are publishers' list prices, excluding publisher discount or vendor service charges. This report includes 2000, 2001, and 2002 data indexed to the base year of 1984. More extensive reports on the periodical price index have been published annually in the April 15 issue of *Library Journal* through 1992, and in the May issue of *American Libraries* since 1993.

Compiled by Brenda Dingley and Barbara Albee, this table shows that U.S. periodical prices, excluding Russian translations, increased by 7.9 percent from 2001 to 2002. This figure represents a 0.4 percent decrease in the overall rate of inflation from the 8.3 percent figure posted in 2001. Including the Russian translation category, the single-year increase was only slightly lower, at 7.6 percent for 2002. This figure is 1.0 percent lower than the rate of 8.6 percent for the entire sample in 2001. The multidisciplinary category of Russian translations posted the highest percentage price increase again this year (at 10.6 percent), while Sociology and Anthropology posted the highest increase of any single subject category (at 10.6 percent). The subject category Political Science, which last year had the highest increase of any single subject category, dropped to fifth place this year, with an 8.9 percent rise. No other subject category posted a double-digit increase in 2002.

Nancy Chaffin, compiler of the U.S. Serials Services Index (Table 2), notes that titles continue to experience migration from print to electronic format. As the index is built only of printed products, the e-only titles have been dropped from the various subject indexes. While some are converting to CD-ROM, there is a stronger movement toward Web-based delivery, especially in the Business category. U.S. Government Documents are also increasingly delivered only via the Web. As this trend continues, it becomes more difficult to identify new titles that are print subscriptions.

All areas of serials services saw increases in prices for 2002, with the highest in Law (up 6.8 percent) and the lowest (3.3 percent) in Business. The average increase was 5.1 percent for all subject categories. A more detailed article on serials services pricing appears in the May 2001 issue of *American Libraries*.

Book Prices

Last year significant changes occurred in Tables 3, 6, and 7 (hardcover, mass market paperbacks, and trade and other paperbacks) as a result of changes in the source of the information provided by R. R. Bowker. Catherine Barr, who compiled these tables from data supplied by Bowker, provides the following background. The three tables (3, 6, and 7) are now based on figures from Bowker's Books In Print database, a change that has resulted in a dramatic increase in title output (83 percent, or 54,448 titles between 1997 and 1998). In years past the basic data used to produce the title output and average price figures was extracted from Bowker's American Book Publishing Record database, supplemented by data from Paperbound Books In Print and by additional manual calculation. These figures reflected only those books cataloged by the Library of Congress, especially those passing through the Cataloging in Publication (CIP) program. The Books In Print database includes books that do not fall within the scope of CIP—inexpensive editions, annuals, and much of the output of small presses and self-publishers, for example—and therefore results in a more accurate portrayal of the current state of American book publishing.

The average price for hardcover books (Table 3A) decreased by $1.48 (2.37 percent) between 1999 and 2000, following a decline of $1.21 (1.9 percent) between 1998 and 1999. However, preliminary prices for 2001 showed a jump of $6.48 in the overall hardcover average price.

In the North American Academic Books index (Table 4), compiler Stephen Bosch finds that the average price increased only 2.0 percent, compared with a 3.8 percent increase the prior year. The data used for this index is provided by Baker and Taylor, Blackwell North America, and Yankee Book Peddler. The index includes paperback editions; the overall average price of materials is lower than if the index consisted only of hardbound editions.

Academic book price increases vary among subject categories. A number of categories including General Works, Military Science, and Psychology saw price decreases. Chemistry reversed last year's decrease with an increase of 8.6 percent, overtaking General Works to show the highest average price. Just the opposite is true for General Works, which posted a decrease of 12.2 percent in the wake of last year's nearly 49 percent increase. It should be noted that this category includes many reference materials and can be influenced by a few very expensive titles in any one year.

U.S. College Books (Table 5) contains information based on titles reviewed during 2000 in *Choice* magazine, a publication of the Association of College and Research Libraries. Donna Alsbury compiled this table, which shows a modest increase of 1.9 percent across all categories. However, almost the entire increase came from the Reference category, which rose 10.9 percent. With the exception of Reference books, the average price remained almost flat.

Paperback prices were mixed. Mass market paperback books (Table 6A) recorded a small increase of 13 cents (2.30 percent) between 1999 and 2000. Preliminary figures for 2001 indicated a larger increase for the year. Trade and other paperbacks (Table 7A) registered a drop of $1.86 (5.65 percent) in 2000, reversing a 6.6 percent increase between 1998 and 1999. Preliminary figures for 2001 appear to signal a steep increase in price. Additional information on hardcover and paperback output and prices can be found in the following article, "Book Title Output and Average Prices: 2000 Final and 2001 Preliminary."

(text continues on page 540)

Table 1 / U.S. Periodicals: Average Prices and Price Indexes, 2000–2002

Index Base: 1984 = 100

Subject Area	1984 Average Price	2000 Average Price	2000 Index	2001 Average Price	2001 Index	2002 Average Price	2002 Index
U.S. periodicals excluding Russian translations	$54.97	$241.54	439.4	$261.56	475.8	$282.31	513.6
U.S. periodicals including Russian translations	72.47	311.37	429.7	338.25	466.7	363.77	502.0
Agriculture	24.06	92.72	385.4	102.57	423.6	109.11	453.5
Business and economics	38.87	142.08	365.5	152.79	393.1	164.70	423.7
Chemistry and physics	228.90	1,302.79	569.2	1,407.47	614.9	1,519.83	664.0
Children's periodicals	12.21	25.14	205.9	25.52	209.0	26.56	217.5
Education	34.01	124.23	365.3	135.72	399.1	146.98	432.2
Engineering	78.70	369.23	469.2	401.32	509.9	432.88	550.0
Fine and applied arts	26.90	56.51	210.1	59.17	220.0	62.33	231.7
General interest periodicals	27.90	44.48	159.4	45.96	164.7	47.57	170.5
History	23.68	63.12	266.6	67.06	283.2	72.23	305.0
Home economics	37.15	115.57	311.1	125.77	338.5	136.69	367.9
Industrial arts	30.40	110.83	364.6	112.57	370.3	122.70	403.6
Journalism and communications	39.25	116.17	296.0	122.44	311.9	128.96	328.6
Labor and industrial relations	29.87	114.84	384.5	127.02	425.2	135.74	454.4
Law	31.31	93.44	298.4	95.40	304.7	101.56	324.4
Library and information sciences	38.85	95.78	246.5	106.31	273.6	115.98	298.5
Literature and language	23.02	55.74	242.1	60.03	260.8	64.95	282.1
Mathematics, botany, geology, general science	106.56	516.70	484.9	559.23	524.8	603.11	566.0
Medicine	125.57	663.21	528.2	726.61	578.6	789.44	628.7
Philosophy and religion	21.94	58.54	266.8	62.43	284.5	67.11	305.9
Physical education and recreation	20.54	51.87	252.5	54.11	263.4	57.15	278.2
Political science	32.43	121.62	375.0	136.59	421.2	148.77	458.7
Psychology	69.74	319.46	458.1	355.63	509.9	387.15	555.1
Russian translations	381.86	1,575.51	412.6	1,774.85	464.8	1,962.39	513.9
Sociology and anthropology	43.87	182.56	416.1	197.24	449.6	217.37	495.5
Zoology	78.35	470.43	600.4	510.53	651.6	543.96	694.3
Total number of periodicals							
Excluding Russian translations	3,731	3,729		3,729		3,729	
Including Russian translations	3,942	3,935		3,928		3,919	

For further comments, see *American Libraries*, May 2000, May 2001, and May 2002.
Compiled by Barbara Albee, divine/Faxon Library Services, and Brenda Dingley, University of Missouri, Kansas City.

Table 2 / U.S. Serial Services: Average Price and Price Indexes 2000–2002

Index Base: 1984 = 100

Subject Area	1984 Average Price	2000 Average Price	2000 Index	2001 Average Price	2001 Percent Increase	2001 Index	2002 Average Price	2002 Percent Increase	2002 Index
U.S. serial services*	$295.13	$671.94	227.7	$711.07	5.80%	240.9	$747.16	5.10%	253.2
Business	437.07	820.73	187.8	822.48	0.20	188.2	849.65	3.30	194.4
General and humanities	196.55	503.98	256.4	538.68	6.90	274.1	569.02	5.60	289.5
Law	275.23	703.56	255.6	786.39	11.8	285.7	839.65	6.80	305.1
Science and technology	295.36	866.69	293.4	924.29	6.60	312.9	975.49	5.50	330.3
Social sciences	283.82	600.06	211.4	624.62	4.10	220.1	656.54	5.10	231.3
U.S. documents	97.37	195.16	200.4	197.26	1.10	202.6	202.60	2.70	208.1
Total number of services	1,537		1,294			1,302			1,311

Compiled by Nancy J. Chaffin, Arizona State University (West) from data supplied by divine/Faxon Library Services, publishers' list prices, and library acquisitions records.

The definition of a serial service has been taken from *American National Standard for Library and Information Services and Related Publishing Practices—Library Materials—Criteria for Price Indexes* (ANSI Z39.20 - 1983).

* Excludes Wilson Index; excludes Russian translations as of 1988.

Table 3 / U.S. Hardcover Books: Average Prices and Price Indexes, 1999–2001
Index Base: 1997 = 100

Category	1997 Average Price	1999 Volumes	1999 Average Price	1999 Index	2000 Final Volumes	2000 Final Average Price	2000 Final Index	2001 Preliminary Volumes	2001 Preliminary Average Price	2001 Preliminary Index
Agriculture	$63.70	504	$55.40	87.0	563	$66.52	104.4	478	$65.38	102.6
Arts	55.99	2,293	59.31	105.9	2,447	50.31	89.9	2,243	53.29	95.2
Biography	54.78	2,227	45.20	82.5	2,017	45.31	82.7	1,961	52.29	95.5
Business	99.34	1,408	131.50	132.4	1,588	93.84	94.5	1,318	81.07	81.6
Education	85.74	1,175	59.75	69.7	1,107	62.23	72.6	994	71.18	83.0
Fiction	24.97	3,992	27.95	111.9	4,250	25.75	103.1	3,754	28.34	113.5
General works	108.87	732	153.98	141.4	639	165.39	151.9	548	155.62	142.9
History	62.81	3,841	52.25	83.2	4,137	54.01	86.0	3,422	49.72	79.2
Home economics	36.79	1,160	38.52	104.7	1,081	39.76	108.1	897	50.72	137.9
Juveniles	19.25	5,469	23.06	119.8	5,119	22.71	118.0	4,981	21.01	109.1
Language	71.90	1,035	55.92	77.8	1,143	57.27	79.7	1,026	66.99	93.2
Law	109.95	1,406	100.13	91.1	1,400	101.50	92.3	1,048	85.58	77.8
Literature	62.07	2,068	73.92	119.1	1,776	55.17	88.9	1,576	56.04	90.3
Medicine	111.88	2,758	90.03	80.5	2,845	90.32	80.7	2,315	98.97	88.5
Music	57.87	550	55.55	96.0	619	42.91	74.2	1,767	111.37	192.5
Philosophy, psychology	59.87	2,415	54.01	90.2	2,321	52.02	86.9	2,004	64.74	108.1
Poetry, drama	46.99	936	46.11	98.1	708	39.90	84.9	569	42.28	90.0
Religion	54.32	2,446	44.68	82.3	2,629	41.61	76.6	2,325	40.92	75.3
Science	103.54	4,658	94.55	91.3	5,222	90.11	87.0	4,495	99.18	95.8
Sociology, economics	79.32	6,855	62.24	78.5	6,981	66.79	84.2	6,083	97.23	122.6
Sports, recreation	46.97	1,143	38.45	81.9	1,254	40.64	86.5	1,070	42.21	89.9
Technology	133.58	3,436	100.53	75.3	3,449	102.40	76.7	2,769	93.16	69.7
Travel	44.87	602	40.31	89.8	652	40.27	89.8	559	71.48	159.3
Totals	$72.67	53,109	$62.32	85.8	53,947	$60.84	83.7	48,202	$67.32	92.6

Compiled by Catherine Barr from data supplied by the R. R. Bowker Company's Books In Print database. Final data for each year include items listed between January of that year and June of the following year with an imprint date of the specified year. Figures for 1995 to 1998, based on books recorded in Bowker's *Weekly Record* (cumulated in the *American Book Publishing Record*), are available in Table 3A.

Table 3A / U.S. Hardcover Books: Average Prices and Price Indexes, 1995–1998

Index Base: 1984 = 100

Subject Area	1984 Average Price	1995 Volumes	1995 Average Price	1995 Index	1996 Volumes	1996 Average Price	1996 Index	1997 Volumes	1997 Average Price	1997 Index	1998 Final Volumes	1998 Final Average Price	1998 Final Index
Agriculture	$34.92	392	$49.00	140.3	399	$45.11	129.2	507	$47.54	136.1	539	$42.85	122.7
Art	33.03	1,116	41.23	124.8	1,070	53.40	161.7	870	46.00	139.3	1,072	42.41	128.4
Biography	22.53	1,596	30.01	133.2	1,829	31.67	140.6	1,773	33.50	148.7	1,723	34.34	152.4
Business	26.01	972	46.90	180.3	1,005	52.62	202.3	689	52.89	203.3	800	53.27	204.8
Education	24.47	610	43.00	175.7	652	47.10	192.5	453	45.57	186.2	458	48.48	198.1
Fiction	14.74	2,345	21.47	145.7	2,915	22.89	155.3	2,882	21.41	145.2	3,132	21.92	148.7
General works	35.61	1,209	54.11	152.0	1,181	68.36	192.0	1,200	59.39	166.8	992	59.26	166.4
History	27.53	1,691	42.19	153.3	2,028	45.62	165.7	2,052	43.51	158.0	2,057	42.79	155.4
Home economics	15.70	651	22.53	143.5	655	23.39	149.0	658	23.32	148.5	636	23.29	148.3
Juvenile	10.02	3,649	14.55	145.2	3,730	15.97	159.4	2,013	15.64	156.1	2,010	15.57	155.4
Language	22.97	320	54.89	239.0	399	58.81	256.0	414	57.95	252.3	372	58.57	255.0
Law	43.88	716	73.09	166.6	827	88.51	201.7	740	89.15	203.2	761	82.40	187.8
Literature	23.57	1,302	38.49	163.3	1,575	43.28	183.6	1,299	44.89	190.5	1,248	43.94	186.4
Medicine	40.65	2,035	75.80	186.5	2,480	81.48	200.4	2,088	85.92	211.4	2,001	80.67	198.5
Music	27.79	251	43.27	155.7	253	39.21	141.1	208	43.58	156.8	254	45.14	162.4
Philosophy and psychology	29.70	1,001	45.26	152.4	1,154	48.40	163.0	949	48.06	161.8	983	50.35	169.5
Poetry and drama	26.75	567	34.96	130.7	606	34.15	127.7	568	36.76	137.4	541	36.86	137.8
Religion	17.76	1,364	34.27	193.0	1,544	36.62	206.2	1,385	40.52	228.2	1,384	33.43	188.2
Science	46.57	2,095	93.52	200.8	2,372	90.63	194.6	2,242	78.14	167.8	2,345	74.40	159.8
Sociology and economics	33.35	5,145	55.51	166.4	5,973	53.82	161.4	5,081	55.05	165.1	5,238	58.55	175.6
Sports and recreation	20.16	517	32.14	159.4	591	34.71	172.2	639	32.35	160.5	605	35.21	174.7
Technology	45.80	1,454	88.28	192.8	1,599	91.60	200.0	1,559	89.96	196.4	1,576	86.55	189.0
Travel	21.31	199	38.30	179.7	179	33.92	159.2	236	30.58	143.5	225	34.69	162.8
Total	$29.99	31,197	$47.15	157.2	35,016	$50.00	166.7	30,505	$50.22	167.5	30,952	$48.04	160.2

Compiled by Bill Robnett, California State University Monterey Bay, from data supplied by the R. R. Bowker Company. Price indexes on Tables 3A and 7A are based on books recorded in the R. R. Bowker Company's *Weekly Record* (cumulated in the *American Book Publishing Record*). Final data for each year include items listed between January of that year and June of the following year with an imprint date of the specified year. See Table 3 for more recent data.

Table 4 / North American Academic Books: Average Prices and Price Indexes 1998–2000
(Index Base: 1989 = 100)

Subject Area	LC Class	1989		1998		1999		2000			
		No. of Titles	Average Price	No. of Titles	Average Price	No. of Titles	Average Price	No. of Titles	Average Price	% Change 1999–2000	Index
Agriculture	S	897	$45.13	984	$62.75	1,001	$64.90	1,152	$69.25	6.7	153.4
Anthropology	GN	406	32.81	539	41.74	607	45.87	568	45.78	-0.2	139.5
Botany	QK	251	69.02	161	98.81	210	96.01	179	103.05	7.3	149.3
Business and economics	H	5,979	41.67	6,101	56.60	6,494	60.13	6,642	60.22	0.1	144.5
Chemistry	QD	577	110.61	494	149.54	592	132.46	515	143.81	8.6	130.0
Education	L	1,685	29.61	2,225	39.58	2,377	41.39	2,623	44.29	7.0	149.6
Engineering and technology	T	4,569	64.94	4,777	86.51	4,926	90.79	5,116	94.53	4.1	145.6
Fine and applied arts	M-N	3,040	40.72	3,402	46.98	3,655	46.21	3,955	45.84	-0.8	112.6
General works	A	333	134.65	98	94.81	131	141.20	155	124.02	-12.2	92.1
Geography	G	396	47.34	652	63.29	693	59.29	633	60.85	2.6	128.5
Geology	QE	303	63.49	184	82.31	220	87.77	229	81.05	-7.7	127.7
History	C-D-E-F	5,549	31.34	6,242	39.38	6,396	39.91	7,078	43.22	8.3	137.9
Home economics	TX	535	27.10	638	28.91	682	30.21	628	31.60	4.6	116.6
Industrial arts	TT	175	23.89	173	29.62	145	29.96	198	28.82	-3.8	120.6
Law	K	1,252	51.10	1,573	68.03	1,717	71.42	1,679	74.48	4.3	145.8
Library and information science	Z	857	44.51	630	56.66	639	57.29	608	68.44	19.5	153.8

Subject	LC class									% change	Index
Literature and language	P	10,812	24.99	10,649	33.78	11,181	34.38	11,684	35.90	4.4	143.7
Mathematics and computer science	QA	2,707	44.68	3,550	64.10	4,120	64.57	4,172	64.76	0.3	144.9
Medicine	R	5,028	58.38	5,873	71.48	6,175	73.20	5,832	74.51	1.8	127.6
Military and naval science	U-V	715	33.57	417	65.02	529	66.61	548	62.03	-6.9	184.8
Philosophy and religion	B	3,518	29.06	4,411	42.70	4,760	42.94	5,046	45.52	6.0	156.6
Physical education and recreation	GV	814	20.38	716	27.88	718	28.33	827	29.11	2.8	142.8
Physics and astronomy	QB	1,219	64.59	1,118	95.01	1,149	95.29	1,065	97.66	2.5	151.2
Political science	J	1,650	36.76	1,701	50.49	2,056	53.10	2,074	53.81	1.3	146.4
Psychology	BF	890	31.97	1,057	43.34	1,337	49.79	1,173	47.04	-5.5	147.1
Science (general)	Q	433	56.10	375	80.76	313	71.09	324	70.58	-0.7	125.8
Sociology	HM	2,742	29.36	3,630	43.00	3,815	44.99	3,886	46.53	3.4	158.5
Zoology	QH,L,P,R	1,967	71.28	1,888	84.95	1,927	86.84	1,951	86.54	-0.3	121.4
Average for all subjects		59,299	$41.69	64,258	$54.24	68,565	$56.30	70,540	$57.42	2.0	137.7

Compiled by Stephen Bosch, University of Arizona from electronic data provided by Baker and Taylor, Blackwell North America, and Yankee Book Peddler. The data represents all titles (includes hardcover, trade & paperback books, as well as annuals) treated for all approval plan customers serviced by the three vendors. Due to the merger between Yankee and Baker and Taylor, Baker and Taylor no longer services approval accounts so the B&T data represents all 2000 imprints in their database. This table covers titles published or distributed in the United States and Canada during the calendar years listed.

This index does include paperback editions. The overall average price of materials is lower than if the index consisted only of hardbound editions.

Table 5 / U.S. College Books: Average Prices and Price Indexes, 1999–2001
(Index base for all years: 1983=100. 2000 also indexed to 1999; 2001 also indexed to 2000)

Choice Subject Categories	1983 No. of Titles	1983 Avg. Price Per Title	1999 No. of Titles	1999 Avg. Price Per Title	1999 Prices Indexed to 1983	2000 No. of Titles	2000 Avg. Price Per Title	2000 Prices Indexed to 1983	2000 Prices Indexed to 1999	2001 No. of Titles	2001 Avg. Price Per Title	2001 Prices Indexed to 1983	2001 Prices Indexed to 2000
General	11	$24.91	23	$50.75	203.7	—	—	—	—	—	—	—	—
Humanities	40	$24.53	36	$45.73	186.4	43	$49.57	202.1	108.4	41	$48.69	198.5	98.2
Art and architecture	372	40.31	373	53.21	132.0	123	52.61	130.5	98.9	130	49.73	123.4	94.5
Communication	51	22.22	82	47.38	213.2	60	46.12	207.5	97.3	63	49.90	224.6	108.2
Language and literature	109	23.39	88	45.40	194.1	102	49.05	209.7	108.0	98	51.23	219.0	104.4
African and Middle Eastern [4]	—	—	26	37.94	—	25	51.31	—	135.2	30	44.89	—	87.5
Asian and Oceanian [4]	—	—	29	41.02	—	28	49.21	—	120.0	23	42.26	—	85.9
Classical	19	28.68	25	48.06	167.6	16	48.33	168.5	100.6	20	51.94	181.1	107.5
English and American	579	23.47	512	46.48	198.0	515	45.60	194.3	98.1	530	47.06	200.5	103.2
Germanic	53	20.45	41	42.90	209.8	25	50.51	247.0	117.8	42	46.39	226.8	91.8
Romance	93	20.47	89	42.43	207.3	106	46.61	227.7	109.9	86	46.80	228.6	100.4
Slavic	35	23.09	31	52.81	228.7	25	49.26	213.3	93.3	22	52.00	225.2	105.6
Performing arts	19	24.32	22	42.73	175.7	15	39.22	161.3	91.8	15	44.75	184.0	114.1
Film	67	24.81	79	48.72	196.4	110	47.60	191.8	97.7	90	50.46	203.4	106.0
Music	106	25.09	119	46.56	185.6	80	51.21	204.1	110.0	115	50.67	202.0	99.0
Theater and Dance [5]	51	23.18	43	45.01	194.2	50	47.63	205.5	105.8	53	50.94	219.8	107.0
Philosophy	155	26.27	177	47.83	182.1	155	46.43	176.7	97.1	158	45.80	174.3	98.6
Religion	196	19.33	209	38.95	201.5	149	40.37	208.9	103.6	222	37.94	196.3	94.0
Total Humanities [6]	2,038	$26.26	1,981	$46.74	178.0	1,932	$48.32	184.0	103.4	1,988	$48.05	183.0	99.4
Science/Technology	159	36.11	88	$39.94	110.6	63	$38.50	106.6	96.4	55	$43.14	119.5	112.0
History of science/technology	56	28.45	79	46.32	162.8	70	41.25	145.0	89.0	75	47.06	165.4	114.1
Astronautics/astronomy	18	27.78	34	41.74	150.2	56	35.94	129.4	86.1	57	43.96	158.3	122.3
Biology	145	39.28	103	52.95	134.8	113	55.49	141.3	104.8	129	46.98	119.6	84.7
Botany	23	31.78	86	50.75	159.7	82	59.13	186.1	116.5	75	59.21	186.3	100.1
Zoology	38	44.21	79	47.10	106.5	70	53.93	122.0	114.5	71	56.62	128.1	105.0
Chemistry	30	48.57	64	99.32	204.5	35	109.93	226.3	110.7	47	82.99	170.9	75.5
Earth science	42	35.43	63	58.86	166.1	55	66.09	186.5	112.3	59	72.64	205.0	109.9
Engineering	154	44.88	70	76.12	169.6	78	82.37	183.5	108.2	70	77.66	173.0	94.3
Health sciences	121	24.45	124	41.91	171.4	124	53.09	217.1	126.7	138	49.67	203.1	93.6
Information/computer science	63	29.48	40	43.15	146.4	35	42.53	144.3	98.6	35	53.12	180.2	124.9
Mathematics	44	32.82	70	59.17	180.3	101	59.57	181.5	100.7	84	55.91	170.4	93.9
Physics	38	34.13	38	58.97	172.8	45	47.02	137.8	79.7	57	47.71	139.8	101.5
Sports/physical education	61	18.67	53	35.98	192.7	55	37.89	202.9	105.3	47	37.73	202.1	99.6
Total Science/Technology	992	$34.77	991	$53.22	153.1	982	$55.41	159.4	104.1	999	$54.51	156.8	98.4

Social/Behavioral Sciences	173	$24.24	66	43.50	179.4	54	$41.11	169.6	94.5	86	52.42	216.2
Anthropology	98	26.68	162	51.33	192.4	147	50.91	190.8	99.2	152	50.52	189.4
Business management/labor	156	25.01	146	41.23	164.8	153	44.19	176.7	107.2	140	44.37	177.4
Economics	315	27.60	245	48.86	177.0	260	53.92	195.4	110.3	256	50.00	181.2
Education	120	20.23	204	43.74	216.2	153	43.25	213.8	98.9	162	47.61	235.3
History, geography/area studies	92	25.58	48	48.43	189.3	50	45.24	176.8	93.4	88	44.85	175.3
Africa	17	26.94	31	48.75	180.9	32	51.90	192.7	106.5	23	56.62	210.2
Ancient history	46	31.80	39	53.58	168.5	42	65.94	207.3	123.1	26	48.23	151.7
Asia and Oceania	58	25.55	61	49.95	195.5	65	49.60	194.1	99.3	80	49.27	192.8
Central and Eastern Europe [3]	—	—	44	50.76	—	54	51.21	—	100.9	61	46.41	—
Latin America and Caribbean	25	24.72	47	49.35	199.6	64	50.85	205.7	103.0	49	47.76	193.2
Middle East and North Africa	33	28.42	34	52.69	185.4	40	48.34	170.1	91.8	39	51.94	182.8
North America	274	24.42	430	39.76	162.8	431	38.11	156.1	95.8	364	40.33	165.2
United Kingdom [3]	—	—	124	52.90	—	113	53.60	—	101.3	104	55.81	—
Western Europe [3]	—	—	128	49.73	—	124	53.32	—	107.2	156	48.71	—
Political science	439	25.00	24	53.44	213.8	19	46.93	187.7	87.8	31	48.37	193.5
Comparative politics [2]	—	—	202	52.57	—	197	53.10	—	101.0	170	51.12	—
International relations [2]	—	—	137	50.28	—	142	50.74	—	100.9	160	50.78	—
Political theory [2]	—	—	59	40.08	—	50	50.78	—	126.7	55	48.90	—
U.S. politics [2]	—	—	166	42.78	—	183	45.05	—	105.3	146	42.43	—
Psychology	162	26.57	141	45.92	172.8	116	39.86	150.0	86.8	106	49.65	186.9
Sociology	244	24.38	132	47.02	192.9	156	45.63	187.2	97.0	193	50.61	207.6
Total Social/Behavioral Sciences	2,537	$25.81	2,670	$46.58	180.5	2,645	$47.31	183.3	101.6	2,647	$47.93	185.7
Total General, Humanities, Science/Technology, Social/Behavioral Sciences (excl. Reference) [6]	5,578	$27.57	5,665	$47.81	173.4	5,559	$49.10	178.1	102.7	5,634	$49.14	178.2
Reference	506	$44.75	—	—	—	—	—	—	—	—	—	—
General [1]	—	—	64	$88.00	—	93	$73.74	—	83.8	109	$84.57	—
Humanities [1]	—	—	185	97.60	—	199	89.33	—	91.5	177	94.47	—
Science/Technology [1]	—	—	73	97.50	—	91	85.67	—	87.9	82	103.90	—
Social/Behavioral	—	—	236	94.03	—	243	97.96	—	104.2	266	107.83	—
Total Reference	506	$44.75	558	$94.98	212.2	626	$89.83	200.7	94.6	634	$99.59	222.6
Grand Total (incl. Reference) [6]	6,084	$29.00	6,223	$52.04	179.5	6,185	$53.22	183.5	102.3	6,268	$54.24	187.0

(Additional final index column)

Social/Behavioral Sciences	127.5
Anthropology	99.2
Business management/labor	100.4
Economics	92.7
Education	110.1
History, geography/area studies	99.1
Africa	109.1
Ancient history	73.1
Asia and Oceania	99.3
Central and Eastern Europe [3]	90.6
Latin America and Caribbean	93.9
Middle East and North Africa	107.4
North America	105.8
United Kingdom [3]	104.1
Western Europe [3]	91.4
Political science	103.1
Comparative politics [2]	96.3
International relations [2]	100.1
Political theory [2]	96.3
U.S. politics [2]	94.2
Psychology	124.6
Sociology	110.9
Total Social/Behavioral Sciences	101.3
Total General, Humanities, Science/Technology, Social/Behavioral Sciences (excl. Reference) [6]	100.1
General [1]	114.7
Humanities [1]	105.8
Science/Technology [1]	121.3
Social/Behavioral	110.1
Total Reference	110.9
Grand Total (incl. Reference) [6]	101.9

1 Began appearing as separate sections in July 1997.
2 Began appearing as separate sections in March 1988
3 Began appearing as separate sections, replacing Europe, in July 1997.

4 Began appearing as separate sections in September 1995.
5 Separate sections for Theater and Dance combined in September 1995.
6 1983 totals include Linguistics (incorporated into Language and Literature in 1985), Non-European/Other (replaced by African and Middle Eastern and Asian and Oceanian in September 1995), and Europe (replaced by Central and Eastern Europe, United Kingdom and Western Europe in July 1997).

Compiled by Donna Alsbury, Florida Center for Library Automation.

Table 6 / Mass Market Paperbacks Average Per-Volume Prices, 1999–2001

Index Base: 1997 = 100

Category	1997 Average Prices	1999 Volumes	1999 Average Prices	1999 Index	2000 Final Volumes	2000 Final Average Prices	2000 Final Index	2001 Preliminary Volumes	2001 Preliminary Average Prices	2001 Preliminary Index
Agriculture	$7.50	10	$6.42	85.6	8	$7.48	99.7	6	$5.79	77.1
Arts	6.54	22	6.95	106.3	19	7.26	111.0	15	6.25	96.0
Biography	6.46	111	6.37	98.6	96	6.71	103.9	70	7.35	113.3
Business	6.51	14	7.61	116.9	20	8.41	129.2	64	9.63	137.1
Education	7.32	44	7.39	101.0	15	7.30	99.7	18	7.02	95.9
Fiction	5.40	4,217	5.58	103.3	4,020	5.78	107.0	4,620	5.80	106.9
General works	7.48	42	7.01	93.7	12	6.57	87.8	12	7.19	95.6
History	6.13	35	6.65	108.5	36	7.36	120.1	55	7.18	114.3
Home economics	6.89	55	6.99	101.5	48	7.07	102.6	80	7.74	112.0
Juveniles	4.69	2,653	5.12	109.2	2,358	5.21	111.1	2,247	5.37	113.1
Language	5.92	48	7.13	120.4	35	6.92	116.9	57	6.52	108.7
Law	6.69	6	6.66	99.6	5	8.77	131.1	3	6.64	99.4
Literature	6.72	137	6.49	96.6	64	6.71	99.9	71	7.03	104.6
Medicine	6.53	114	6.32	96.8	77	6.70	102.6	117	8.31	126.6
Music	7.97	25	6.64	83.3	17	7.24	90.8	5	6.77	83.4
Philosophy, psychology	6.52	216	7.20	110.4	127	7.24	111.0	190	7.54	114.1
Poetry, drama	6.41	50	6.26	97.7	39	6.09	95.0	21	5.71	88.5
Religion	6.99	136	7.48	107.0	85	8.16	116.7	159	7.47	105.9
Science	5.17	89	6.34	122.6	52	6.58	127.3	72	6.19	115.5
Sociology, economics	6.76	119	6.53	96.6	89	6.99	103.4	180	7.62	112.3
Sports, recreation	6.43	95	6.73	104.7	91	6.66	103.6	51	7.26	112.5
Technology	6.87	24	6.89	100.3	16	6.71	97.7	29	7.59	110.7
Travel	8.75	19	8.35	95.4	21	8.65	98.9	20	7.62	86.9
Totals	$5.36	8,281	$5.64	105.2	7,350	$5.77	107.7	8,162	$5.95	110.2

Compiled by Catherine Barr from data supplied by the R. R. Bowker Company's Books In Print database. Final data for each year include items listed between January of that year and June of the following year with an imprint date of the specified year. Figures for 1995 to 1998, based on books recorded in Bowker's Paperbound Books in Print, are available in Table 6A.

Table 6A / U.S. Mass Market Paperback Books: Average Prices and Price Indexes, 1995–1998
Index Base: 1984 = 100

Subject Area	1984 Average Price	1995 Average Price	1995 Volumes	1995 Index	1996 Volumes	1996 Average Price	1996 Index	1997 Final Volumes	1997 Final Average Price	1997 Final Index	1998 Preliminary Volumes	1998 Preliminary Average Price	1998 Preliminary Index
Agriculture	$2.85	$9.13	10	320.4	13	$11.59	406.7	1	$18.00	631.6	5	$16.49	578.5
Art	8.28	11.24	12	135.7	8	12.00	144.9	20	16.45	198.6	17	14.26	172.2
Biography	4.45	8.08	39	181.6	38	10.12	227.4	43	13.73	308.5	74	15.97	358.9
Business	4.92	10.81	18	219.7	19	13.25	269.3	22	17.91	364.0	24	16.29	331.1
Education	5.15	12.40	29	240.8	31	10.29	199.8	10	14.04	272.6	19	16.79	326.1
Fiction	3.03	5.51	3,680	181.8	3,569	6.25	206.3	2,950	8.51	280.9	3,150	8.45	278.9
General works	4.58	19.37	29	422.9	34	9.31	203.3	20	13.91	303.7	29	10.42	227.5
History	3.77	10.06	24	266.8	17	10.92	289.7	25	14.71	390.1	30	12.57	333.4
Home economics	4.95	8.70	43	175.8	35	8.67	175.2	72	14.61	295.1	88	14.02	283.2
Juveniles	2.31	3.99	396	172.7	288	4.25	184.0	296	6.29	272.3	295	5.98	258.9
Language	5.56	9.60	8	172.7	8	7.87	141.5	21	8.99	161.7	15	10.59	190.5
Law	5.12	9.79	5	191.2	5	10.39	202.9	12	12.28	239.9	12	12.30	240.2
Literature	3.63	8.73	47	240.5	72	9.42	259.5	68	10.64	293.1	73	10.68	294.2
Medicine	5.01	8.38	10	167.3	20	8.93	178.2	99	11.33	226.1	166	13.84	276.2
Music	5.28	24.98	3	473.1	5	20.57	389.6	7	14.38	272.3	16	14.98	283.7
Philosophy and psychology	4.38	4.83	103	110.3	108	7.58	173.1	133	14.12	322.4	160	12.15	277.4
Poetry and drama	5.11	9.70	32	189.8	28	10.88	212.9	15	10.53	206.0	27	8.61	168.5
Religion	3.87	9.39	16	242.6	16	8.93	230.7	48	13.48	348.3	56	14.77	381.7
Science	3.55	11.28	8	317.7	9	12.16	342.5	25	15.09	425.1	42	14.27	402.0
Sociology and economics	4.42	9.60	42	217.2	34	9.91	224.2	108	16.29	368.6	135	14.14	319.9
Sports and recreation	4.06	8.28	82	203.9	75	8.79	216.5	75	14.67	361.2	99	14.62	360.1
Technology	8.61	11.62	22	135.0	20	11.14	129.4	21	12.08	140.3	27	13.13	152.5
Travel	5.86	13.96	3	238.2	10	9.63	164.3	5	15.57	265.7	4	11.10	189.4
Total	$3.41	$5.85	4,661	171.6	4,462	$6.57	192.7	4,096	$9.31	273.1	4,563	$9.31	273.1

Compiled by Stephen Bosch, University of Arizona, from data supplied by the R. R. Bowker Company. Average prices of mass market paperbacks are based on listings of mass market titles in Bowker's Paperbound Books in Print. See Table 6 for more recent data.

Table 7 / U.S. Paperbacks (Excluding Mass Market): Average Prices and Price Indexes, 1999–2001

Index Base: 1997 = 100

Category	1997 Average Price	1999 Volumes	1999 Average Price	1999 Index	2000 Final Volumes	2000 Final Average Price	2000 Final Index	2001 Preliminary Volumes	2001 Preliminary Average Price	2001 Preliminary Index
Agriculture	$28.50	523	$39.26	137.8	502	$41.31	145.0	469	$35.76	125.5
Arts	27.78	2,480	26.54	95.5	2,514	26.96	97.1	2,275	29.65	106.7
Biography	19.83	1,713	19.99	100.8	1,786	19.47	98.2	1,739	18.52	93.4
Business	128.45	2,367	48.85	38.0	2,461	52.00	40.5	2,281	80.14	62.4
Education	27.41	2,189	29.18	106.5	2,257	28.43	103.7	1,946	27.43	100.1
Fiction	16.22	4,163	16.09	99.2	6,345	15.90	98.0	7,495	16.77	103.4
General works	199.57	682	40.76	20.4	667	39.84	20.0	730	129.42	64.9
History	26.24	3,610	26.05	99.3	3,758	27.24	103.8	3,705	23.77	90.6
Home economics	25.16	1,349	19.32	76.8	1,384	18.95	75.3	1,174	33.71	134.0
Juveniles	19.26	1,316	19.47	101.1	1,214	20.78	107.9	1,047	18.77	97.5
Language	28.98	1,482	30.17	104.1	1,357	26.52	91.5	1,199	26.03	89.8
Law	44.78	1,666	49.52	110.6	1,665	51.87	115.8	1,470	48.17	107.6
Literature	20.98	1,441	20.52	97.8	1,532	20.53	97.9	1,593	22.21	105.9
Medicine	47.25	3,281	44.41	94.0	3,313	35.72	75.6	3,283	38.80	82.1
Music	22.18	1,018	21.71	97.9	946	22.49	101.4	861	26.89	121.2
Philosophy, psychology	23.72	3,230	23.49	99.0	3,108	21.60	91.1	3,070	22.00	92.8
Poetry, drama	17.00	1,469	16.04	94.4	1,732	16.26	95.7	1,428	16.26	95.7
Religion	20.03	3,462	20.40	101.9	3,496	18.38	91.8	3,892	18.93	94.5
Science	48.57	3,115	49.33	101.6	3,191	40.29	83.0	3,013	38.94	80.2
Sociology, economics	31.23	7,605	39.20	125.5	7,839	41.22	132.0	6,552	36.41	116.6
Sports, recreation	23.56	2,014	22.62	96.0	2,138	20.76	88.1	2,097	20.78	88.2
Technology	69.52	5,436	59.82	86.1	5,117	56.22	80.9	4,748	100.79	145.0
Travel	20.13	2,356	21.56	107.1	2,498	22.45	111.5	2,082	22.26	110.6
Totals	$38.45	57,967	$32.93	85.6	60,820	$31.07	80.8	58,149	$36.06	93.8

Compiled by Catherine Barr from data supplied by the R. R. Bowker Company's Books In Print database. Final data for each year include items listed between January of that year and June of the following year with an imprint date of the specified year. Figures for 1995 to 1998, based on books recorded in Bowker's *Weekly Record* (cumulated in the *American Book Publishing Record*), are available in Table 7A.

Table 7A / U.S. Trade (Higher Priced) Paperback Books: Average Prices and Price Indexes, 1995–1998

Index Base: 1984 = 100

Subject Area	1984 Average Price	1995 Average Price	1995 Volumes	1995 Index	1996 Average Price	1996 Volumes	1996 Index	1997 Average Price	1997 Volumes	1997 Index	1998 Final Average Price	1998 Final Volumes	1998 Final Index
Agriculture	$17.77	$26.97	218	151.8	$20.45	248	115.1	$21.34	280	120.1	$21.04	338	118.4
Art	13.12	20.58	874	156.9	21.57	872	164.4	22.10	728	168.4	23.24	841	177.1
Biography	15.09	16.59	813	109.9	17.37	979	115.1	17.56	902	116.4	17.93	953	118.8
Business	17.10	24.24	709	141.8	26.08	687	152.5	26.50	681	155.0	30.24	602	176.8
Education	12.84	22.96	738	178.8	23.76	832	185.0	24.98	608	194.6	25.53	568	198.8
Fiction	8.95	12.71	1,275	142.0	12.35	1,852	138.0	13.09	1,708	146.2	13.49	1,610	150.7
General works	14.32	32.99	1,375	230.4	34.65	1,693	242.0	38.50	1,546	268.9	38.62	1,427	269.7
History	13.49	18.48	1,041	137.0	20.09	1,381	148.9	19.69	1,165	145.9	20.74	1233	153.7
Home economics	9.40	14.87	629	158.2	15.35	727	163.3	15.30	748	162.7	15.82	641	168.3
Juveniles	5.94	15.75	990	265.2	8.30	1,117	139.7	9.29	954	156.4	8.15	896	137.2
Language	11.61	21.58	304	185.9	21.17	427	182.3	21.94	386	189.0	22.11	399	190.4
Law	17.61	30.26	415	171.8	30.81	434	175.0	31.41	373	178.4	30.58	434	173.7
Literature	11.70	16.54	945	141.4	17.69	1,278	151.2	19.02	984	162.6	19.95	946	170.5
Medicine	15.78	27.91	1,092	176.9	27.37	1,577	173.4	27.46	1,411	174.0	26.54	1,435	168.2
Music	12.53	19.81	174	158.1	20.14	183	160.7	21.54	166	171.9	23.00	144	183.6
Philosophy and psychology	13.64	19.92	800	146.0	18.83	989	138.0	19.12	898	140.2	20.48	801	150.1
Poetry and drama	8.68	15.69	712	180.8	12.92	862	148.8	14.20	789	163.6	14.68	710	169.1
Religion	9.32	14.60	1,723	156.7	14.93	2,100	160.2	15.65	1,951	167.9	16.48	1,758	176.8
Science	16.22	33.42	874	206.0	32.95	1,134	203.1	36.42	936	224.5	36.32	1025	223.9
Sociology and economics	17.72	23.69	3,321	133.7	23.47	3,983	132.4	27.29	3,200	154.0	25.31	3,150	142.8
Sports and recreation	11.40	16.53	900	145.0	16.33	1,028	143.2	17.31	779	151.9	17.95	706	157.5
Technology	21.11	38.75	827	183.6	39.17	890	185.6	37.71	821	178.6	41.45	801	196.4
Travel	9.88	16.38	480	165.8	16.74	537	169.4	16.33	517	165.2	17.16	501	173.7
Total	$13.86	$21.71	21,229	156.6	$21.42	25,810	154.5	$22.67	22,531	163.5	$22.90	21,919	165.3

Compiled by Bill Robnett, California State University Monterey Bay, from data supplied by the R. R. Bowker Company. Price indexes on Tables 3A and 7A are based on books recorded in the R. R. Bowker Company's *Weekly Record* (cumulated in the *American Book Publishing Record*). Final data for each year include items listed between January of that year and June of the following year with an imprint date of the specified year. See Table 7 for more recent data.

(text continued from page 527)

Newspaper Prices

The indexes for U.S. (Table 8A) and international (Table 8B) newspapers showed only minor price changes. The U.S. newspaper price increase of 2.9 percent is slightly above inflation. The increase for international newspapers of 1.4 percent may reflect the weakening of the U.S. dollar during the past year against most other major currencies. Compilers Genevieve Owens and Wilba Swearingen anticipated this increase last year in light of higher postage rates. The high average costs of this material reflect the high frequency of publication and cost of timely shipment in the area of international newspapers. The figures reflect a

Table 8A / U.S. Daily Newspapers:
Average Prices and Price Indexes, 1990–2002
Index Base: 1990 = 100

Year	Average No. Titles	Price	Percent Increase	Index
1990	165	$189.58	0.0	100.0
1991	166	198.13	4.5	104.5
1992	167	222.68	12.4	117.5
1993	171	229.92	3.3	121.3
1994	171	261.91	13.9	138.2
1995	172	270.22	3.2	142.5
1996	166	300.21	11.1	158.4
1997	165	311.77	3.9	164.5
1998	163	316.60	1.5	167.0
1999	162	318.44	0.6	168.0
2000	162	324.26	1.8	171.0
2001	160	330.78	2.0	174.5
2002	158	340.38	2.9	179.5

Table 8B / International Newspapers:
Average Prices and Price Indexes, 1993–2002
Index Base: 1993 = 100

Year	Average No. Titles	Price	Percent Change	Index
1993	46	$806.91	0.0	100.0
1994	46	842.01	4.3	104.3
1995	49	942.13	11.9	116.3
1996	50	992.78	5.4	123.0
1997	53	1,029.49	3.7	127.6
1998	52	1,046.72	1.7	129.7
1999	50	1,049.13	0.2	130.0
2000	50	1,050.88	0.2	130.2
2001	50	1,038.26	-1.2	128.7
2002	49	1,052.69	1.4	130.5

Compiled by Genevieve S. Owens, Williamsburg Regional Library, and Wilba Swearingen, Louisiana State University Health Sciences Center Library, from data supplied by EBSCO Subscription Services. We thank Kathleen Born of EBSCO for her assistance with this project.

decrease of two U.S. newspapers and one international newspaper. These titles are no longer available through EBSCO on a subscription basis. Data is provided with the assistance of EBSCO subscription services.

Prices of Other Media

The U.S. nonprint media index (Table 9) does not appear this year. Those wishing historical information can find data for 1997 and 1998, indexed to a base of 1980, in the 2001 edition of the *Bowker Annual*. The database, compiled in previous years by Dana Alessi, collects information from titles reviewed in *Booklist, Library Journal, School Library Journal*, and *Video Librarian*.

The CD-ROM price inventory that formerly appeared as Table 10 was discontinued last year. As with U.S. Serials Services, many of the titles that were published in CD-ROM format have migrated to Web editions. Additionally the changes from single-workstation pricing to network pricing or site licenses made tracking of the prices for this category of material difficult to obtain.

Foreign Prices

The *Federal Reserve Bulletin* reports that in the third quarter of 2001 the dollar depreciated 4.1 percent against the yen and depreciated 7.3 percent against the euro. These are the most recent figures available prior to publication of this article. The slowdown of the U.S. economy, combined with the terrorist attacks of September 11, contributed heavily to the decline. More recent monthly data on individual currencies see a rebound of the dollar against most currencies.

Analysis of prior 2001 quarters is available at http://www.federalreserve. gov/pubs/bulletin. The adoption of the euro in January 2002 by most members of the European Community has complicated computations of the price fluctuations for foreign publications used by the compilers of the LMPIC indexes. Agents and wholesalers that supplied the data have converted to Eurodollars for ongoing operations, but not all historic data was converted. The exchange table below indicates that the Federal Reserve Board no longer tracks U.S. dollar exchange rates against individual European currencies. The exchange rates as of the end of 2001 are taken from the regional Federal Reserve Bank of St. Louis Web site (http://www.stls. frb.org/fred/data/exchange.html) for all national currencies noted.

Dates	12/31/96	12/31/97	12/31/98	12/31/99	12/31/00	12/31/01
Canada	1.3705	1.3567	1.5433	1.5375	1.5219*	1.5964*
France	5.1900	6.0190	5.5981	6.4882*	7.3022*	7.3604*
U.K.	0.5839	0.6058	0.5985	0.6014	0.6836*	0.6938*
Germany	1.5400	1.7991	1.6698	1.9345*	2.1773*	2.1946*
Japan	115.85	130.45	129.73	102.16	112.21*	127.59*
Netherlands	1.7410	2.0265	1.8816	2.1797*	2.4532*	2.4727*

* Data from the regional Federal Reserve Bank of St. Louis. Upon introduction of the euro on January 1, 1999, the Federal Reserve Board discontinued posting dollar exchange rates against the ECU and the currencies of the 11 countries participating in the European Economic and Monetary Union.

(text continues on page 546)

Table 9 / British Academic Books: Average Prices and Price Indexes, 1999–2001
Index Base: 1985 = 100; prices listed are pounds sterling

Subject Area	1985 No. of Titles	1985 Average Price	1999 No. of Titles	1999 Average Price	1999 Index	2000 No. of Titles	2000 Average Price	2000 Index	2001 No. of Titles	2001 Average Price	2001 Index
General works	29	£30.54	36	£37.84	123.9	27	£56.25	184.2	29	£35.89	117.5
Fine arts	329	21.70	387	32.78	151.1	420	34.86	160.6	427	34.93	161.0
Architecture	97	20.68	138	33.82	163.5	196	31.67	153.1	167	31.76	153.6
Music	136	17.01	129	37.00	217.5	134	54.33	319.4	143	38.71	227.6
Performing arts except music	110	13.30	151	34.08	256.2	225	29.48	221.6	204	31.32	235.5
Archaeology	146	18.80	148	42.16	224.3	218	37.15	197.6	112	41.95	223.1
Geography	60	22.74	18	50.80	223.3	55	42.13	185.3	54	42.24	185.6
History	1,123	16.92	902	33.39	197.3	968	36.21	214.0	738	32.05	189.4
Philosophy	127	18.41	228	42.12	228.8	281	47.12	255.9	283	39.52	214.7
Religion	328	10.40	401	31.11	299.1	595	29.32	281.9	588	33.06	317.9
Language	135	19.37	151	47.13	243.3	217	44.36	229.0	234	45.61	235.5
Miscellaneous humanities	59	21.71	34	37.24	171.5	36	45.83	211.1	249	38.36	176.7
Literary texts (excluding fiction)	570	9.31	325	17.16	184.3	485	15.29	164.2	548	15.79	169.6
Literary criticism	438	14.82	464	37.49	253.0	631	37.87	255.5	589	36.90	249.0
Law	188	24.64	350	52.09	211.4	521	52.40	212.7	511	55.28	224.4
Library science and book trade	78	18.69	64	34.27	183.4	77	48.43	259.1	59	35.08	187.7
Mass communications	38	14.20	92	37.30	262.7	122	32.28	227.3	113	34.53	243.2
Anthropology and ethnology	42	20.71	61	43.48	209.9	80	60.32	291.3	75	42.16	203.6
Sociology	136	15.24	205	43.35	284.4	237	43.58	286.0	265	42.80	280.8
Psychology	107	19.25	182	37.13	192.9	191	39.42	204.8	147	38.51	200.1
Economics	334	20.48	541	54.40	265.6	669	53.20	259.8	660	48.41	236.4
Political science, international relations	314	15.54	569	41.01	263.9	819	39.88	256.6	834	38.94	250.6
Miscellaneous social sciences	20	26.84	30	42.19	157.2	44	46.07	171.6	39	46.35	172.7
Military science	83	17.69	42	31.81	179.8	89	34.13	192.9	85	30.73	173.7
Sports and recreation	44	11.23	58	32.83	292.3	60	29.26	260.6	63	36.56	325.6
Social service	56	12.17	101	34.89	286.7	106	32.98	271.0	116	30.44	250.1
Education	295	12.22	316	39.25	321.2	401	34.34	281.0	385	34.97	286.2
Management and business administration	427	19.55	527	45.06	230.5	669	47.89	245.0	820	39.05	199.7
Miscellaneous applied social sciences	13	9.58	20	33.01	344.6	18	48.87	510.1	20	39.36	410.9
Criminology	45	11.45	65	40.89	357.1	79	37.71	329.3	101	34.13	298.1

Applied interdisciplinary social sciences	254	14.17	559	43.22	305.0	674	39.34	277.6	637	40.73	287.4
General science	43	13.73	28	33.24	242.1	50	37.72	274.7	53	42.89	312.4
Botany	55	30.54	39	58.60	191.9	34	61.83	202.5	42	73.10	239.4
Zoology	85	25.67	59	55.59	216.6	76	55.53	216.3	66	58.88	229.4
Human biology	35	28.91	34	46.68	161.5	50	50.41	174.4	48	53.16	183.9
Biochemistry	26	33.57	35	61.39	182.9	48	84.18	250.8	40	63.73	189.8
Miscellaneous biological sciences	152	26.64	145	53.06	199.2	186	57.77	216.9	149	59.01	221.5
Chemistry	109	48.84	125	80.17	164.1	162	80.68	165.2	123	69.55	142.4
Earth sciences	87	28.94	102	65.44	226.1	140	63.30	218.7	110	61.29	211.8
Astronomy	43	20.36	44	53.61	263.3	80	35.81	175.9	78	40.16	197.2
Physics	76	26.58	207	62.91	236.7	327	57.17	215.1	269	62.75	236.1
Mathematics	123	20.20	178	48.23	238.8	308	44.78	221.7	288	47.85	236.9
Computer sciences	150	20.14	134	39.41	195.7	364	37.48	186.1	327	38.48	191.1
Interdisciplinary technical fields	38	26.14	67	55.43	212.1	154	44.16	168.9	126	42.38	162.1
Civil engineering	134	28.68	117	65.76	229.3	130	62.65	218.4	52	75.72	264.0
Mechanical engineering	27	31.73	21	111.38	351.0	42	83.63	263.6	16	60.92	192.0
Electrical and electronic engineering	100	33.12	74	66.46	200.7	105	59.42	179.4	142	54.56	164.7
Materials science	54	37.93	73	78.51	207.0	112	88.85	234.2	74	80.12	211.2
Chemical engineering	24	40.48	42	82.74	204.4	39	76.55	189.1	27	66.00	163.0
Miscellaneous technology	217	36.33	152	64.25	176.9	282	68.34	188.1	369	58.68	161.5
Food and domestic science	38	23.75	22	73.38	309.0	42	54.72	230.4	31	46.30	194.9
Non-clinical medicine	97	18.19	154	36.93	203.0	178	37.99	208.9	220	36.96	203.2
General medicine	73	21.03	63	53.93	256.4	101	62.24	296.0	12	50.08	238.1
Internal medicine	163	27.30	188	53.45	195.8	212	64.92	237.8	30	58.69	215.0
Psychiatry and mental disorders	71	17.97	142	36.90	205.3	167	35.16	195.7	34	46.11	256.6
Surgery	50	29.37	49	72.74	247.7	69	79.34	270.1	6	62.75	213.7
Miscellaneous medicine	292	22.08	256	45.39	205.6	348	47.04	213.2	725	49.94	226.2
Dentistry	20	19.39	14	29.83	153.8	10	31.87	164.4	15	48.62	250.7
Pharmacy*	n.a.	n.a.	n.a.	n.a.	n.a.	n.a.	n.a.	n.a.	20	53.02	n.a.
Nursing	71	8.00	74	22.68	283.5	91	24.09	301.1	96	25.96	324.5
Agriculture and forestry	78	23.69	51	50.47	213.0	71	55.87	235.8	67	59.93	253.0
Animal husbandry and veterinary medicine	34	20.92	41	45.72	218.5	48	60.57	289.5	48	45.39	217.0
Natural resources and conservation	58	22.88	41	47.38	207.1	53	49.74	217.4	68	41.37	180.8
Total, all books	9,049	£19.07	10,332	£42.54	223.1	13,847	£42.99	225.4	13,423	£40.81	214.0

Compiled by Curt Holleman, Southern Methodist University, from data supplied by B. H. Blackwell and the Library and Information Statistics Unit at Loughborough University.
* New category introduced in 2001.

Table 10 / German Academic Periodical Price Index, 1999–2001

Index Base: 1990 = 100; prices in Deutsche marks

Subject	LC Class	1990 Average Price	1999 No. of Titles	1999 Average Price	1999 Percent Increase	1999 Index	2000 Final No. of Titles	2000 Final Average Price	2000 Final Percent Increase	2000 Final Index	2001 Preliminary No. of Titles	2001 Preliminary Average Price	2001 Preliminary Percent Increase	2001 Preliminary Index
Agriculture	S	DM235.11	166	DM373.87	-1.1	159.0	161	DM456.89	22.2	194.3	173	DM497.04	8.8	211.4
Anthropology	GN	112.88	16	185.17	18.5	164.0	17	192.73	4.1	170.7	17	194.08	0.7	171.9
Botany	QK	498.79	16	994.49	20.5	199.4	17	1,017.94	2.4	204.1	17	1,057.11	3.8	211.9
Business and economics	H-HJ	153.48	260	255.01	10.5	166.2	212	254.14	-0.3	165.6	238	259.12	2.0	168.9
Chemistry	QD	553.06	52	2,737.38	27.0	495.0	50	3,315.49	21.1	599.5	52	3,535.08	6.6	639.2
Education	L	70.86	57	93.76	2.4	132.3	40	108.49	15.7	153.1	41	116.28	7.2	164.1
Engineering and technology	T-TT	239.40	332	415.79	10.3	173.7	290	474.13	14.0	198.0	306	495.69	4.5	207.1
Fine and applied arts	M-N	84.15	151	112.07	3.1	133.2	136	122.15	9.0	145.2	140	121.42	-0.6	144.3
General	A	349.37	68	432.15	-0.9	123.7	53	406.95	-5.8	116.5	54	405.08	-0.5	115.9
Geography	G	90.42	23	196.95	28.7	217.8	20	214.06	8.7	236.7	21	228.21	6.6	252.4
Geology	QE	261.30	36	637.44	22.3	243.9	30	788.26	23.7	301.7	30	828.03	5.0	316.9
History	C,D,E,F	66.09	147	103.00	6.2	155.8	143	104.18	1.1	157.6	143	103.13	-1.0	156.0
Law	K	193.88	155	350.81	8.5	180.9	137	364.11	3.8	187.8	142	372.32	2.3	192.0
Library and information science	Z	317.50	44	471.68	17.3	148.6	34	275.23	-41.6	86.7	36	653.98	137.6	206.0
Literature and language	P	102.69	176	155.44	9.0	151.4	160	159.37	2.5	155.2	163	151.99	-4.6	148.0
Mathematics and computer science	QA	1,064.62	62	1,370.49	5.8	128.7	51	1,734.75	26.6	162.9	54	1,670.88	-3.7	156.9
Medicine	R	320.62	337	756.80	23.1	236.0	343	796.83	5.3	248.5	365	811.90	1.9	253.2
Military and naval science	U-V	86.38	21	126.88	27.3	146.9	21	126.12	-0.6	146.0	21	127.31	0.9	147.4
Natural history	QH	728.36	47	1,774.61	29.0	243.6	52	1,784.22	0.5	245.0	55	1,867.72	4.7	256.4
Philosophy and religion	B	65.00	195	112.67	-1.5	173.3	195	115.13	2.2	177.1	194	114.46	-0.6	176.1
Physical education and recreation	GV	81.96	41	108.70	4.9	132.6	32	115.52	6.3	140.9	32	117.65	1.8	143.5
Physics and astronomy	QB-QC	684.40	50	2,472.22	30.1	361.2	54	2,716.26	9.9	396.9	54	2,916.39	7.4	426.1
Physiology	QM-QR	962.83	13	3,264.38	23.2	339.0	14	3,700.47	13.4	384.3	14	3,883.15	4.9	403.3
Political science	J	80.67	117	105.20	0.1	130.4	107	104.08	-1.1	129.0	107	104.55	0.5	129.6
Psychology	BF	94.10	33	189.71	19.4	201.6	30	184.77	-2.6	196.4	31	197.10	6.7	209.5
Science (general)	Q	310.54	24	602.08	16.3	193.9	21	736.25	22.3	237.1	21	736.25	0.0	237.1
Sociology	HM-HX	109.61	77	147.91	1.1	134.9	66	163.41	10.5	149.1	66	164.76	0.8	150.3
Zoology	QL	161.02	25	406.68	28.6	252.6	28	521.44	28.2	323.8	30	587.21	12.6	364.7
Totals and Averages		228.40	2,741	DM472.68	17.1	207.0	2,514	DM541.27	14.5	237.0	2,617	DM567.33	4.8	248.4

Data, supplied by Otto Harrassowitz, represent periodical and newspaper titles published in Germany; prices listed in marks.
Index is compiled by Steven E. Thompson, Brown University Library.

Table 11A / Latin American Periodical Price Index, 1999–2000:
Country and Region Index

	Total Titles	Mean w/o newspapers	Index (1992 = 100)	Weighted mean w/o newspapers	Index (1992 = 100)
Country					
Argentina	151	$95.58	109	$86.53	120
Bolivia	5	46.16	106	40.37	116
Brazil	272	69.81	103	57.66	78
Caribbean	30	44.84	106	42.58	108
Chile	72	117.89	191	70.92	150
Colombia	49	83.24	181	97.57	209
Costa Rica	25	32.50	125	47.97	154
Cuba	7	46.43	131	44.69	117
Ecuador	14	64.11	184	75.49	227
El Salvador	7	45.71	241	43.08	278
Guatemala	9	158.23	207	266.53	306
Honduras	n.a.	n.a.	n.a.	n.a.	n.a.
Jamaica	18	43.33	135	65.22	206
Mexico	153	80.12	123	74.99	131
Nicaragua	7	28.22	92	29.13	94
Panama	11	32.50	122	29.03	114
Paraguay	6	19.33	122	30.85	138
Peru	45	104.06	103	92.84	84
Uruguay	20	93.39	280	59.66	182
Venezuela	37	88.64	87	78.14	165
Region					
Caribbean	55	43.75	118	49.70	135
Central America	59	53.65	148	71.16	172
South America	671	85.23	114	72.76	112
Mexico	153	80.12	123	74.99	131
Latin America	938	$80.04	119	$71.48	123

Subscription information was provided by divine/Faxon Library Services, Library of Congress, Rio Office, and the University of Texas, Austin. Index based on 1992 LAPPI mean prices. The 1998/1999 subscription prices were included in this year's index if a new subscription price was not given.
Compiled by Scott Van Jacob, University of Notre Dame.
n.a. = fewer than five subscription prices were found.

Table 11B / Latin American Periodical Price Index, 1999–2000: Subject Index

Subjects	Mean	Index (1992 = 100)	Weighted mean	Index (1992 = 100)
Social sciences	$94.69	146	$77.34	143
Humanities	46.26	123	42.08	116
Science/technology	67.99	118	73.01	130
General	87.02	86	79.59	86
Law	109.09	97	85.17	99
Newspapers	747.94	153	700.34	172
Totals w/o newspapers	80.04	95	71.48	111
Total with newspapers	$112.51	167	$82.17	142

Total titles with newspapers = 986

Total titles without newspapers = 938

(text continued from page 541)

Price indexes include British Academic Books (Table 9, formerly Table 10), German Academic Periodicals (Table 10, formerly Table 12), Dutch English-Language Periodicals (Table 13, formerly Table 14), and Latin American Periodicals (Tables 14 A and 14 B, formerly Tables 15A and 15B).

British Prices

The price index for British academic books (Table 9) is compiled by Curt Holleman from information supplied by Blackwell Book Services. The overall inflation rate for books shows a decrease of 5.1 percent. At the same time, the dollar remained strong against the British pound during 2001, experiencing a 1.5 percent increase during the year. These factors continue a trend noted in the past— that the cost for U.S. academic libraries to continue collecting British books at a pace similar to the prior year is falling.

German Prices

The price index for German Academic Books does not appear this year. Otto Harrassowitz, which provides the data, has been unable to supply prices for 1999 and more recent years due to system migration and conversion to the euro. Those wishing historical information will find data for 1996 through 1998, indexed to 1989, in the 2001 edition of the *Bowker Annual.*

The index for German Academic Periodicals (Table 10), compiled by Steven E. Thompson, is based on data provided by Otto Harrassowitz. This table is repeated from last year. Conversion to the euro has made price comparisons with previous data impractical. Final 2000 data show an overall increase of 14.5 percent in the average price of this material. Preliminary 2001 periodical prices indicate a more moderate 4.8 percent increase. Looking at final 2000 data, only General Works, Library Science, and Psychology decreased in average price by more than 1 percent. However, periodicals in many of the sciences continue to show price increases well above 10 percent and even above 20 percent, including Agriculture (up 22.2 percent), Chemistry (up 21.1 percent), Geology (up 23.7 percent), Math and Computer Science (up 26.6 percent), Science (General) (up 22.3 percent), and Zoology (up 28.2 percent). The average prices noted are in German marks, so the relative strength of the U.S. dollar over this currency may have slightly reduced the impact of these increases.

Dutch Prices

The Dutch English Language Periodical Index (former Table 13) is also omitted this year. Nijhoff, which provides this data, has found it increasing difficult to identify appropriate titles for this category. There are two reasons for this. It is hard to determine which periodicals are produced in the Netherlands, as "multinational" Dutch publishers publish all over the world. And these materials tend to be priced in different currencies, making it difficult to establish consistent prices. The sale of Nijhoff to Swets Blackwell took place during 2001.

Latin American Prices

Scott Van Jacobs compiles the Latin American Periodicals indexes (Tables 11A and 11B, former Tables 14A and 14B) with prices provided by divine/Faxon Library Services, the Library of Congress, and the University of Texas, Austin. The most recent Latin American book price index was published in 1997. A new index based on data provided by Latin American book vendors is expected to replace that index, but is not yet available.

Tables 11A and 11B are reprinted from last year as updated figures were not available in time for this publication. The weighted overall mean for Latin American periodicals including newspapers rose 8.2 percent in 1999–2000. When newspapers are not included, the increase was a modest 3 percent. However increases varied widely by region with the average price of materials from Central America rising 68.2 percent compared with an average decrease of 7.9 percent for material from Mexico. This was just the opposite of the average price trends in these two regions in 1998–1999.

Using the Price Indexes

Librarians are encouraged to monitor trends in the publishing industry and changes in economic conditions when preparing budget forecasts and projections. The ALA ALCTS Library Materials Price Index Committee endeavors to make information on publishing trends readily available by sponsoring the annual compilation and publication of price data contained in Tables 1–11. The indexes cover newly published library materials and document prices and rates of percent changes at the national and international level. They are useful benchmarks against which local costs can be compared, but because they reflect retail prices in the aggregate, they are not a substitute for cost data that reflect the collecting patterns of individual libraries, and they are not a substitute for specific cost studies.

Differences between local prices and those found in national indexes arise partially because these indexes exclude discounts, service charges, shipping and handling fees, and other costs that the library might incur. Discrepancies may also relate to a library's subject coverage; mix of titles purchased, including both current and backfiles; and the proportion of the library's budget expended on domestic or foreign materials. These variables can affect the average price paid by an individual library, although the individual library's rate of increase may not differ greatly from the national indexes.

LMPIC is interested in pursuing studies that would correlate a particular library's costs with the national prices. The committee welcomes interested parties to its meetings at ALA Annual and Midwinter conferences.

Current Library Materials Price Index Committee members are Barbara Albee, Janet Belanger, Pamela Bluh, Martha Brogan, Mae Clark, Doina Farkas, Mary Fugle, Harriet Lightman, and Sharon Sullivan (Chair). Consultants include Barbara Albee, Donna Alsbury, Catherine Barr, Ajaye Bloomstone, Stephen Bosch, Nancy Chaffin, Brenda Dingley, Virginia Gilbert, Curt Holleman, Genevieve Owens, Wilba Swearingen, Steven Thompson, and Scott van Jacob.

Book Title Output and Average Prices: 2000 Final and 2001 Preliminary Figures

Catherine Barr
Contributing Editor

Andrew Grabois
Senior Director for Publisher Relations and Content Development, R. R. Bowker

American book title output reached a new high of 122,108 titles in 2000, according to figures compiled by R. R. Bowker. This total represents an increase of 2,751 titles, or 2.30 percent, over the 119,357 titles reported for 1999, and reverses the slight decline seen in 1999. Preliminary figures for 2001 would appear to indicate continuing growth, although the effects of the downturn after the terrorist attacks of September 11 may not be fully reflected in these early data. Preliminary mass market paperback figures, however, had already registered an increase over 2000 when the preliminary data were released.

Table 1 / American Book Production, 1998–2001

| Category | All Hard and Paper | | | |
	1998 Final	1999 Final	2000 Final	2001 Preliminary
Agriculture	1,201	1,037	1,073	953
Arts	4,934	4,795	4,980	4,529
Biography	3,206	4,051	3,899	3,770
Business	3,844	3,789	4,068	3,663
Education	3,391	3,408	3,378	2,958
Fiction	11,016	12,372	14,617	15,867
General works	1,504	1,456	1,318	1,290
History	7,346	7,486	7,931	7,180
Home economics	2,518	2,564	2,513	2,151
Juveniles	9,195	9,438	8,690	8,272
Language	2,862	2,565	2,536	2,282
Law	3,007	3,078	3,070	2,519
Literature	3,784	3,646	3,371	3,240
Medicine	6,718	6,153	6,234	5,714
Music	1,398	1,593	1,582	2,633
Philosophy, psychology	5,965	5,861	5,556	5,264
Poetry, drama	3,018	2,455	2,479	2,018
Religion	6,347	6,044	6,206	6,374
Science	8,486	7,862	8,464	7,577
Sociology, economics	14,645	14,579	14,908	12,812
Sports, recreation	3,718	3,252	3,483	3,218
Technology	9,103	8,896	8,582	7,543
Travel	3,038	2,977	3,170	2,660
Totals	120,244	119,357	122,108	114,487

As explained in the 2000 edition of the *Bowker Annual*, the title output and average price figures are now compiled from Bowker's Books In Print database, resulting in a more accurate and comprehensive portrayal of American book publishing.

Output by Format and by Category

Book title output for 2000 showed a slight increase for hardcover books, a decline for mass market paperbacks, and a moderate increase in trade and other paperbacks. Hardcover output (Table 2) increased by 838 titles (1.58 percent), mass market paperback output (Table 4) declined by 931 titles (11.24 percent), reversing the 19.86 increase seen in 1999, and output of other paperbacks, including trade paperbacks (Table 5), increased by 2,853 titles (4.92 percent).

Nonfiction subject categories experienced mixed results in title output between 1999 and 2000 with equal numbers of categories rising and declining. The nonfiction categories that experienced the largest year-to-year declines in terms of titles were juveniles (children's books) with a decrease of 748 titles (7.93 percent), philosophy and psychology with a decrease of 305 titles (5.20

Table 2 / Hardcover Average Per-Volume Prices, 1999–2001

Category	1999 Prices	2000 Final			2001 Preliminary		
		Vols.	$ Total	Prices	Vols.	$ Total	Prices
Agriculture	$55.40	563	$37,449.25	$66.52	478	$31,251.33	$65.38
Arts	59.31	2,447	123,118.13	50.31	2,243	119,528.16	53.29
Biography	45.20	2,017	91,396.20	45.31	1,961	102,532.27	52.29
Business	131.50	1,588	149,015.16	93.84	1,318	106,854.92	81.07
Education	59.75	1,107	68,885.59	62.23	994	70,749.81	71.18
Fiction	27.95	4,250	109,451.56	25.75	3,754	106,380.54	28.34
General works	153.98	639	105,684.88	165.39	548	85,281.78	155.62
History	52.25	4,137	223,428.58	54.01	3,422	170,139.50	49.72
Home economics	38.52	1,081	42,976.58	39.76	897	45,491.42	50.72
Juveniles	23.06	5,119	116,245.01	22.71	4,981	104,648.04	21.01
Language	55.92	1,143	65,459.48	57.27	1,026	68,727.22	66.99
Law	100.13	1,400	142,100.21	101.50	1,048	89,685.12	85.58
Literature	73.92	1,776	97,987.02	55.17	1,576	88,326.48	56.04
Medicine	90.03	2,845	256,960.24	90.32	2,315	229,118.86	98.97
Music	55.55	619	26,559.75	42.91	1,767	196,783.10	111.37
Philosophy, psychology	54.01	2,321	120,743.53	52.02	2,004	129,740.67	64.74
Poetry, drama	46.11	708	28,251.15	39.90	569	24,058.70	42.28
Religion	44.68	2,629	109,401.74	41.61	2,325	95,135.18	40.92
Science	94.55	5,222	470,538.35	90.11	4,495	445,797.08	99.18
Sociology, economics	62.24	6,981	466,266.86	66.79	6,083	591,443.87	97.23
Sports, recreation	38.45	1,254	50,962.77	40.64	1,070	45,166.63	42.21
Technology	100.53	3,449	353,173.00	102.40	2,769	257,968.69	93.16
Travel	40.31	652	26,256.62	40.27	559	39,955.16	71.48
Totals	$62.32	53,947	$3,282,311.66	$60.84	48,202	$3,244,764.53	$67.32

percent), technology with a decrease of 314 titles (3.53 percent), and literature with a decrease of 275 titles (7.54 percent). The largest increases were registered in the categories of science (up 602 titles, or 7.66 percent), history (up 445, or 5.94 percent), sociology and economics (up 329, or 2.26 percent), and business (up 279, or 7.36 percent).

Fiction, an important measure of the overall health of the publishing industry, experienced an increase of 2,245 titles (18.15 percent) between 1999 and 2000, building on a 12.30 percent increase in the previous year. Most of this increase (2,182 titles) was seen in trade and other paperbacks, with mass market paperbacks registering a decline of 197 titles. The preliminary 2000 figures would appear to indicate a continuing increase in fiction title output, markedly in mass market and trade paperbacks.

Average Book Prices

Average book prices were mixed in 2000, with some subject categories showing price increases and others recording decreases. The overall average book price for hardcover books (Table 2) decreased by $1.48 (2.37 percent) between 1999

Table 3 / Hardcover Average Per-Volume Prices, Less Than $81, 1999–2001

Category	1999 Prices	2000 Final			2001 Preliminary		
		Vols.	$ Total	Prices	Vols.	$ Total	Prices
Agriculture	$34.98	428	$14,998.40	$35.04	359	$12,677.10	$35.31
Arts	39.50	2,186	88,133.08	40.32	2,009	82,311.70	40.97
Biography	33.65	1,859	61,748.39	33.22	1,640	52,867.33	32.24
Business	43.16	1,110	46,601.60	41.98	1,000	39,487.31	39.49
Education	42.52	918	41,876.56	45.62	826	36,360.46	44.02
Fiction	24.85	4,229	105,560.79	24.96	3,711	92,216.24	24.85
General works	41.74	370	15,219.92	41.13	312	12,255.09	39.28
History	40.46	3,717	147,662.02	39.73	3,109	123,458.06	39.71
Home economics	25.15	1,029	27,930.77	27.14	858	23,121.07	26.95
Juveniles	18.21	5,013	92,239.95	18.40	4,886	90,371.36	18.50
Language	41.93	930	39,190.76	42.14	809	35,586.08	43.99
Law	47.78	829	40,987.51	49.44	698	33,952.22	48.64
Literature	39.75	1,554	63,047.63	40.57	1,375	56,497.58	41.09
Medicine	42.44	1,678	70,079.62	41.76	1,314	56,477.78	42.98
Music	36.62	556	18,755.15	33.73	572	19,021.00	33.25
Philosophy, psychology	39.71	2,015	80,558.79	39.98	1,727	69,052.49	39.98
Poetry, drama	32.37	651	21,853.00	33.57	511	17,071.40	33.41
Religion	33.15	2,404	79,746.30	33.17	2,114	70,292.15	33.25
Science	42.72	2,917	121,606.34	41.69	2,513	105,337.26	41.92
Sociology, economics	45.07	5,635	257,172.30	45.64	4,815	219,136.55	45.51
Sports, recreation	33.42	1,182	39,327.17	33.27	996	33,552.43	33.69
Technology	44.16	1,921	89,581.04	46.63	1,672	77,226.94	46.19
Travel	31.11	606	19,496.72	32.17	511	16,870.16	33.01
Totals	$35.96	43,737	$1,583,373.81	$36.20	38,337	$1,375,199.76	$35.87

Table 4 / Mass Market Paperbacks Average Per-Volume Prices, 1999–2001

Category	1999 Prices	2000 Final			2001 Preliminary		
		Vols.	$ Total	Prices	Vols.	$ Total	Prices
Agriculture	$6.42	8	$59.84	$7.48	6	$34.74	$5.79
Arts	6.95	19	137.96	7.26	15	93.69	6.25
Biography	6.37	96	644.48	6.71	70	514.26	7.35
Business	7.61	20	168.13	8.41	64	616.43	9.63
Education	7.39	15	109.49	7.30	18	126.42	7.02
Fiction	5.58	4,020	23,245.72	5.78	4,620	26,818.05	5.80
General works	7.01	12	78.81	6.57	12	86.31	7.19
History	6.65	36	265.13	7.36	55	394.92	7.18
Home economics	6.99	48	339.22	7.07	80	619.43	7.74
Juveniles	5.12	2,358	12,284.62	5.21	2,247	12,071.20	5.37
Language	7.13	35	242.09	6.92	57	371.65	6.52
Law	6.66	5	43.83	8.77	3	19.93	6.64
Literature	6.49	64	429.33	6.71	71	499.01	7.03
Medicine	6.32	77	515.71	6.70	117	972.22	8.31
Music	6.64	17	123.10	7.24	5	33.87	6.77
Philosophy, psychology	7.20	127	919.90	7.24	190	1,433.54	7.54
Poetry, drama	6.26	39	237.34	6.09	21	119.81	5.71
Religion	7.48	85	693.46	8.16	159	1,187.39	7.47
Science	6.34	52	342.25	6.58	72	445.46	6.19
Sociology, economics	6.53	89	622.47	6.99	180	1,372.47	7.62
Sports, recreation	6.73	91	605.62	6.66	51	370.18	7.26
Technology	6.89	16	107.31	6.71	29	220.07	7.59
Travel	8.35	21	181.62	8.65	20	152.33	7.62
Totals	$5.64	7,350	$42,397.43	$5.77	8,162	$48,573.38	$5.95

and 2000, following a decline of $1.21 (1.9 percent) between 1998 and 1999. However, preliminary prices for 2001 showed an end to this downward trend, with a jump of $6.48 in the overall hardcover average price.

The overall average price for mass market paperback books (Table 4) recorded a small increase of 13 cents (2.30 percent) between 1999 and 2000. Paperbacks other than mass market (Table 5) registered a drop of $1.86 (5.65 percent), reversing a 6.6 percent increase between 1998 and 1999.

The average book prices for fiction titles, usually a closely watched barometer of book prices, were also mixed in 2000. Hardcover fiction titles fell $2.20 (7.87 percent), mass market rose 20 cents (3.58 percent), and trade and other paperbacks fell 19 cents (1.18 percent). All three formats were showing increases in the preliminary numbers for 2001.

Hardcover children's books (juveniles), which had posted average price increases of 9.3 percent in 1999 and 9.6 percent in 1998, declined 35 cents (1.52 percent) in 2000. Children's mass market paperbacks experienced a small increase of 9 cents, or 1.76 percent, while trade and other paperback children's titles registered a more significant hike of $1.31 (6.73 percent).

Most of the other subject categories recorded mixed average prices in 2000, with many categories showing year-to-year price increases and decreases, varying

Table 5 / Other Paperbacks Average Per-Volume Prices, 1999–2001

Category	1999 Prices	2000 Final			2001 Preliminary		
		Vols.	$ Total	Prices	Vols.	$ Total	Prices
Agriculture	$39.26	502	$20,737.72	$41.31	469	$16,769.99	$35.76
Arts	26.54	2,514	67,779.82	26.96	2,275	67,457.98	29.65
Biography	19.99	1,786	34,773.36	19.47	1,739	32,198.25	18.52
Business	48.85	2,461	127,983.02	52.00	2,281	182,790.19	80.14
Education	29.18	2,257	64,171.32	28.43	1,946	53,369.50	27.43
Fiction	16.09	6,345	100,901.02	15.90	7,495	125,718.94	16.77
General works	40.76	667	26,572.54	39.84	730	94,476.57	129.42
History	26.05	3,758	102,385.08	27.24	3,705	88,053.69	23.77
Home economics	19.32	1,384	26,226.00	18.95	1,174	39,577.25	33.71
Juveniles	19.47	1,214	25,224.86	20.78	1,047	19,652.18	18.77
Language	30.17	1,357	35,981.99	26.52	1,199	31,215.35	26.03
Law	49.52	1,665	86,360.62	51.87	1,470	70,812.31	48.17
Literature	20.52	1,532	31,451.11	20.53	1,593	35,385.66	22.21
Medicine	44.41	3,313	118,332.94	35.72	3,283	127,365.41	38.80
Music	21.71	946	21,274.45	22.49	861	23,154.40	26.89
Philosophy, psychology	23.49	3,108	67,126.33	21.60	3,070	67,544.63	22.00
Poetry, drama	16.04	1,732	28,156.31	16.26	1,428	23,219.53	16.26
Religion	20.40	3,496	64,273.18	18.38	3,892	73,692.04	18.93
Science	49.33	3,191	128,552.26	40.29	3,013	117,335.76	38.94
Sociology, economics	39.20	7,839	323,088.61	41.22	6,552	238,573.60	36.41
Sports, recreation	22.62	2,138	44,388.25	20.76	2,097	43,570.90	20.78
Technology	59.82	5,117	287,672.90	56.22	4,748	478,562.45	100.79
Travel	21.56	2,498	56,080.67	22.45	2,082	46,345.70	22.26
Totals	$32.93	60,820	$1,889,494.36	$31.07	58,149	$2,096,842.28	$36.06

by format. Biography, for example, shows an average price increase of 11 cents (0.24 percent) for hardcover titles, an increase of 34 cents (5.34 percent) for mass market paperback titles, and a decrease of 52 cents (2.6 percent) for other paperback titles. Religion recorded an average price decrease of $3.06 (6.85 percent) for hardcover titles, an increase of 68 cents (9.09 percent) for mass market paperback titles, and a decrease of $2.02 (9.9 percent) for other paperback titles.

Each of the 23 standard subject groups used here represents one or more specific Dewey Decimal Classification numbers, as follows: Agriculture, 630–699, 712–719; Art, 700–711, 720–779; Biography, 920–929; Business, 650–659; Education, 370–379; Fiction; General Works, 000–099; History, 900–909, 930–999; Home Economics, 640–649; Juveniles; Language, 400–499; Law, 340–349; Literature, 800–810, 813–820, 823–899; Medicine, 610–619; Music, 780–789; Philosophy, Psychology, 100–199; Poetry, Drama, 811, 812, 821, 822; Religion, 200–299; Science, 500–599; Sociology, Economics, 300–339, 350–369, 380–389; Sports, Recreation, 790–799; Technology, 600–609, 620–629, 660–699; Travel, 910–919.

Book Sales Statistics, 2001:
AAP Preliminary Estimates

Association of American Publishers

The industry estimates shown in the following table are based on the U.S. Census of Manufactures. However, book publishing is currently being transferred to the Economic Census, also called the Census of Information. Like the Census of Manufactures, this is a five-year census conducted in years ending in "2" and "7"; 1997 was a transition census with the data being collected and processed by the same government people as in prior years, but the forthcoming output will be under the auspices of the new census. Census data for 1997 had been released and were under review as this publication went to press.

Between censuses, the Association of American Publishers (AAP) estimates are "pushed forward" by the percentage changes that are reported to the AAP statistics program, and by other industry data that are available. Some AAP data are collected in a monthly statistics program, and it is largely this material that is shown in this preliminary estimate table. More detailed data are available from, and additional publishers report to, the AAP annual statistics program, and this additional data will be incorporated into Table S1 that will be published in the AAP 2001 Industry Statistics.

Readers comparing the estimated data with census reports should be aware that the U.S. Census of Manufactures does not include data on many university presses or on other institutionally sponsored and not-for-profit publishing activities, or (under SIC 2731: Book Publishing) for the audiovisual and other media materials that are included in this table. On the other hand, AAP estimates have traditionally excluded "Sunday School" materials and certain pamphlets that are incorporated in the census data. These and other adjustments have been built into AAP's industry estimates.

As in prior reports, the estimates reflect the impact of industry expansion created by new establishments entering the field, as well as nontraditional forms of book publishing, in addition to incorporating the sales increases and decreases of established firms.

It should also be noted that the Other Sales category includes only incidental book sales, such as music, sheet sales (both domestic and export, except those to prebinders), and miscellaneous merchandise sales.

The estimates include domestic sales and export sales of U.S. product, but they do not cover indigenous activities of publishers' foreign subsidiaries.

Non-rack-size Mass Market Publishing is included in Trade—Paperbound. Prior to the 1988 AAP Industry Statistics, this was indicated as Adult Trade Paperbound. It is recognized that part of this is Juvenile (estimate: 20 percent), and adjustments have been made in this respect. AAP also notes that this area includes sales through traditional "mass market paperback channels" by publishers not generally recognized as being "mass market paperback" publishers.

Table 1 / Estimated Book Publishing Industry Sales, 1992, 1997, 1999–2001
(figures in millions of dollars)

	1992	1997	1999	% Change from 1998	2000	% Change from 1999	2001 Preliminary	% Change from 2000	Compound Growth Rate 1992–2001	Compound Growth Rate 1997–2001
Trade (total)	$4,661.6	$5,774.1	$6,792.1	10.5	$6,540.8	-3.7	$6,369.9	-2.6	3.5	2.5
Adult hardbound	2,222.5	2,663.6	3,036.7	10.4	2,685.9	-11.6	2,626.5	-2.2	1.9	-0.4
Adult paperbound	1,261.7	1,731.7	2,047.2	7.3	1,900.7	-7.2	1,927.2	1.4	4.8	2.7
Juvenile hardbound	850.8	908.5	1,061.4	11.3	1,201.1	13.2	928.6	-22.7	1.0	0.5
Juvenile paperbound	326.6	470.3	646.8	23.2	753.1	16.4	887.6	17.9	11.7	17.2
Religious (total)	907.1	1,132.7	1,216.9	3.3	1,246.9	2.5	1,305.1	4.7	4.1	3.6
Bibles, testaments, hymnals, etc.	260.1	285.4	310.0	4.7	323.3	4.3	315.0	-2.6	2.2	2.5
Other religious	647.0	847.3	906.9	2.8	923.6	1.8	990.1	7.2	4.8	4.0
Professional (total)	3,106.7	4,156.4	4,720.4	6.8	5,129.5	8.7	4,739.1	-7.5	4.8	3.3
Business	490.3	768.1	909.9	6.8	n.a.	n.a.	n.a.	n.a.	n.a.	n.a.
Law	1,128.1	1,502.7	1,726.9	8.5	n.a.	n.a.	n.a.	n.a.	n.a.	n.a.
Medical	622.7	856.5	982.8	6.9	n.a.	n.a.	n.a.	n.a.	n.a.	n.a.
Technical, scientific, other prof'l	865.6	1,029.1	1,100.8	4.3	n.a.	n.a.	n.a.	n.a.	n.a.	n.a.
Book clubs	742.3	1,143.1	1,272.0	5.2	1,291.6	1.5	1,334.5	3.3	6.7	3.9
Mail order publications	630.2	521.0	412.8	-12.3	431.8	4.6	353.9	-18.0	-6.2	-9.2
Mass market paperback, rack-sized	1,263.8	1,433.8	1,552.0	2.5	1,559.2	0.5	1,546.6	-0.8	2.3	1.9
University presses	280.1	367.8	411.7	5.1	402.0	-2.4	408.2	1.5	4.3	2.6
Elementary, secondary (K–12 education)	2,080.9	3,005.4	3,424.7	3.3	3881.2	13.3	4,183.6	7.8	8.1	8.6
Higher education	2,084.1	2,669.7	3,128.8	8.3	3237.1	3.5	3,468.9	7.2	5.8	6.8
Standardized tests	140.4	191.4	218.7	6.9	234.1	7.0	250.1	6.8	6.6	6.9
Subscription reference	572.3	736.5	788.9	2.8	809.1	2.6	819.4	1.3	4.1	2.7
Other sales (incl. AV)	449.0	510.0	541.6	2.9	559.4	3.3	577.2	3.2	2.8	3.1
Total	$16,918.5	$21,641.9	$24,480.6	6.3	$25,322.7	3.4	$25,356.5	0.1	4.6	4.0

Source: Association of American Publishers

U.S. Book Exports and Imports: 2001

Catherine Barr

Contributing Editor

U.S. exports of books were valued at $1,813 million in 2001, a decrease of 8.38 percent from 2000. This decline followed increases of 3.34 percent in 2000 and 3.91 percent in 1999, according to data from the U.S. Department of Commerce. Total unit sales in 2001 were just under 1 billion, 9.81 percent below the 2000 figure.

Imports, valued at $1,634 billion, were up 3.81 percent over 2000; units imported grew by 0.82 percent.

The positions of major trading partners remained fairly stable over the 12 months, with only slight fluctuations in the rankings for most categories.

Tables 1 and 7 show U.S. exports and imports, respectively, with the percentage increase over 2000 by category. Tables 2 and 8 show exports to and imports from the 15 principal book trading partners. Tables 3 to 6 show exports of important categories by destination (mass market paperbacks; technical, scientific, and professional books; encyclopedias and serial installments; and textbooks). Tables 9 to 13 detail the sources of important categories of imports (encyclopedias and serial installments; textbooks; religious books; technical, scientific, and professional books; and mass market paperbacks).

U.S. Department of Commerce figures do not include low-value shipments. Currently, exports valued at less than $2,500 and imports valued at less than $1,250 are excluded.

Table 1 / U.S. Exports of Books: 2001

Category	Value (millions of current $)	Percent change 2000–2001	Units (millions of copies)	Percent change 2000–2001
Dictionaries and thesauruses	4.37	29.53	0.93	-12.21
Encyclopedias	16.27	-8.11	4.12	12.22
Textbooks	348.80	5.57	54.24	9.54
Religious books	82.08	19.24	75.53	12.03
Directories	39.52	-22.18	13.50	-32.42
Technical, scientific, and professional	426.79	-17.23	82.11	-14.75
Art and pictorial books	22.86	53.57	8.38	19.34
Hardcover books, n.e.s.	139.41	-1.42	39.78	-1.48
Mass market paperbacks	196.53	-12.83	110.87	-12.73
Music books	17.57	4.17	3.75	33.74
Maps, charts, atlases	2.63	21.63	0.49	51.22
All other books	515.74	-12.72	604.77	-12.55
Total, all books	1,812.57	-8.38	998.47	-9.81

n.e.s. = not elsewhere specified.
Data for individual categories may not add to totals due to statistical rounding.
Source: U.S. Department of Commerce, Bureau of the Census

Table 2 / U.S. Book Exports to 15 Principal Countries: 2001

Country	Value (millions of current $)	Percent change 2000–2001	Units (millions of copies)	Percent change 2000–2001
Canada	763.18	-3.44	491.77	-1.53
United Kingdom	256.41	-6.30	114.71	-22.55
Japan	131.52	5.38	48.65	9.4
Mexico	100.93	-13.50	87.56	-10.44
Australia	67.99	-41.79	28.11	-48.1
Singapore	49.18	-21.24	25.06	-24.63
Korea (Republic of)	38.29	1.75	18.57	4.92
Netherlands	35.51	-39.38	10.42	-31.45
Germany	34.70	-2.58	13.52	-19.19
Hong Kong	30.05	-8.50	7.52	-14.84
Taiwan	29.23	-19.90	10.18	-37.2
Brazil	19.54	13.21	7.87	28.38
Philippines	19.15	3.18	8.88	-18.83
India	16.12	10.87	9.78	7.12
South Africa	14.96	-2.73	8.83	5.37
Total, top 15 countries	1,606.76	-8.30	891.43	4.53

Source: U.S. Department of Commerce, Bureau of the Census

Table 3 / U.S. Exports of Mass Market Paperbacks (Rack-Sized), Top 15 Markets: 2001

Country	Value	Units
Canada	$89,734,281	59,059,817
United Kingdom	36,807,897	17,235,652
Australia	8,974,109	5,357,183
Germany	7,013,921	2,816,423
Korea (Republic of)	6,775,481	3,582,354
South Africa	5,776,323	1,475,262
Netherlands	5,421,234	2,819,695
Singapore	5,296,345	3,189,349
Brazil	4,886,262	3,121,678
Philippines	4,477,317	1,843,800
Taiwan	3,447,944	1,657,333
France	2,887,558	1,391,868
Argentina	2,047,657	1,276,932
Japan	1,665,203	746,786
Thailand	1,353,778	472,392

Source: U.S. Department of Commerce

Table 4 / U.S. Exports of Technical, Scientific, and Professional Books, Top 15 Markets: 2001

Country	Value	Units
Canada	$130,922,537	18,271,895
Japan	73,828,164	12,821,135
United Kingdom	34,192,241	6,327,726
Netherlands	21,942,889	2,898,390
Australia	16,376,477	2,556,842
Germany	16,296,406	1,936,945
Singapore	13,572,045	2,445,331
Mexico	12,933,910	16,147,692
Hong Kong	10,705,600	1,178,934
Belgium	9,640,491	918,233
Korea (Republic of)	7,833,864	1,730,921
Brazil	6,888,945	1,108,076
India	6,812,589	1,400,293
Ireland	5,972,224	856,012
Switzerland	5,849,754	1,000,723

Source: U.S. Department of Commerce

Table 5 / U.S. Exports of Encyclopedias and Serial Installments, Top 15 Markets: 2001

Country	Value	Units
Mexico	$3,720,290	1,647,056
Canada	2,759,261	579,554
Japan	1,430,096	308,613
Venezuela	1,338,085	296,573
United Kingdom	938,533	189,092
Argentina	831,930	183,028
Philippines	776,712	135,404
Australia	504,628	88,219
South Africa	363,100	50,767
India	300,278	48,608
Mauritius	256,980	34,900
Germany	229,555	47,809
Chile	214,284	38,824
Indonesia	200,508	34,804
Singapore	180,065	26,691

Source: U.S. Department of Commerce

Table 6 / U.S. Exports of Textbooks, Top 15 Markets: 2001

Country	Value	Units
United Kingdom	$107,353,307	18,452,353
Canada	65,588,281	6,033,213
Japan	22,981,757	2,909,964
Australia	20,987,100	4,229,219
Taiwan	15,274,935	1,821,940
Mexico	14,757,856	2,989,413
Singapore	14,060,370	2,618,113
Hong Kong	13,516,490	979,826
Korea (Republic of)	13,461,374	2,751,825
Germany	4,773,614	903,998
Philippines	4,740,142	720,876
Netherlands	3,828,010	995,831
Brazil	2,775,434	600,900
South Africa	2,110,186	1,001,328
Italy	2,013,591	405,231

Source: U.S. Department of Commerce

Table 7 / U.S. Imports of Books: 2001

Category	Value (millions of current $)	Percent change 2000–2001	Units (millions)	Percent change 2000–2001
Dictionaries and thesauruses	8.39	14.78	3.99	19.8
Encyclopedias	8.18	20.89	1.62	-0.53
Textbooks	145.34	-9.22	31.46	-7.85
Religious books	76.51	1.38	44.65	6.58
Directories	42.67	134.78	29.15	88.44
Technical, scientific, and professional	193.00	-4.38	29.29	-15.22
Art and pictorial books	39.46	13.68	13.90	11.94
Hardcover books, n.e.s.	629.82	7.93	211.00	5.85
Mass market paperbacks	61.52	-6.85	37.01	-17.57
Music books	4.21	6.86	1.01	-8.26
Atlases	14.08	11.59	6.09	-6.93
All other books	433.32	1.75	449.60	-1.52
Total, all books	1,633.84	3.81	856.89	0.82

n.e.s. = not elsewhere specified.
Data for individual categories may not add to totals due to statistical rounding.
Source: U.S. Department of Commerce, Bureau of the Census

Table 8 / U.S. Book Imports from 15 Principal Countries: 2001

Country	Value (millions of current $)	Percent change 2000–2001	Units (millions)	Percent change 2000–2001
United Kingdom	306.53	-4.25	50.54	-13.12
Canada	270.41	16.49	271.63	9.99
China	266.97	21.03	182.76	21.03
Hong Kong	229.72	2.02	121.18	-7.28
Singapore	96.63	11.41	40.59	16.10
Italy	87.78	-7.46	35.78	-17.48
Germany	52.44	-7.68	12.62	5.70
Spain	50.22	-9.35	18.45	-2.79
Japan	49.94	-15.17	12.67	-32.35
Korea (Republic of)	36.63	21.61	18.04	42.38
Belgium	28.55	5.39	9.53	3.03
France	24.87	-1.70	7.90	27.01
Netherlands	19.30	-4.46	2.50	-5.66
Mexico	19.24	-22.01	12.45	-71.43
Israel	12.95	22.63	2.64	19.46
Total, top 15 countries	1,552.18	4.27	799.28	1.00

Source: U.S. Department of Commerce, Bureau of the Census

Table 9 / U.S. Imports of Encyclopedias and Serial Installments, Top 15 Sources: 2001

Country	Value	Units
Italy	$2,906,133	513,123
Hong Kong	1,404,544	355,647
Spain	945,449	165,913
United Kingdom	549,693	49,526
Germany	406,031	69,743
Singapore	280,042	56,734
Colombia	236,331	9,352
Slovakia	211,196	49,732
Canada	210,564	96,472
Thailand	177,816	66,000
Mexico	171,204	13,791
China	128,286	35,425
Russia	120,000	2,000
United Arab Emirates	99,640	59,844
France	93,790	6,886

Source: U.S. Department of Commerce

Table 10 / U.S. Imports of Textbooks, Top 15 Sources: 2001

Country	Value	Units
United Kingdom	$67,524,981	9,500,896
Canada	16,718,604	5,105,068
Hong Kong	15,730,741	5,228,237
China	10,161,893	2,812,449
Mexico	4,902,829	605,150
Singapore	4,190,051	1,437,075
Spain	3,530,804	777,355
Italy	3,234,836	1,312,661
Germany	1,977,527	268,949
Japan	1,690,922	376,535
New Zealand	1,663,170	822,076
United Arab Emirates	1,657,654	312,052
Netherlands	1,623,522	192,256
France	1,448,096	233,347
Australia	1,336,066	239,375

Source: U.S. Department of Commerce

Table 11 / U.S. Imports of Bibles, Testaments, Prayer Books, and Other Religious Books, Top 15 Sources: 2001

Country	Value	Units
Belgium	$12,789,324	2,887,028
Korea (Republic of)	12,409,643	3,289,563
Israel	9,445,000	2,250,300
China	6,701,994	5,602,117
United Kingdom	5,823,795	2,372,670
Colombia	4,616,470	5,580,664
Hong Kong	3,421,048	3,300,735
Spain	3,027,070	954,718
Canada	2,071,352	2,401,759
Singapore	1,954,156	851,554
France	1,811,195	1,899,457
Italy	1,610,370	4,969,538
Mexico	1,411,714	1,022,278
Brazil	884,959	965,690
Germany	881,880	371,538

Source: U.S. Department of Commerce

Table 12 / U.S. Imports of Technical, Scientific, and Professional Books, Top 15 Sources: 2001

Country	Value	Units
United Kingdom	$50,048,036	4,522,413
Canada	48,335,109	7,082,172
Germany	21,940,739	2,420,433
Japan	11,306,113	1,938,726
Netherlands	10,702,734	647,361
France	6,792,064	578,988
China	6,583,829	2,931,202
Hong Kong	5,681,663	1,853,108
Mexico	3,276,952	1,415,626
Singapore	3,272,544	1,572,084
Belgium	2,943,811	56,909
Sweden	2,667,943	682,436
Italy	2,508,694	600,974
Israel	2,502,561	143,102
Korea (Republic of)	2,217,491	524,336

Source: U.S. Department of Commerce

Table 13 / U.S. Imports of Mass Market Paperbacks (Rack-Sized), Top 15 Sources: 2001

Country	Value	Units
United Kingdom	$12,015,622	4,196,834
Hong Kong	10,370,031	8,728,701
Canada	10,004,838	6,322,826
China	8,560,908	6,749,096
Singapore	3,710,471	2,259,962
Germany	3,103,297	451,491
Italy	2,647,263	1,608,656
Spain	1,859,466	2,000,451
France	1,634,627	1,404,369
Japan	1,363,539	172,909
Taiwan	1,334,445	581,423
Korea (Republic of)	1,292,505	669,891
Mexico	961,901	326,770
Australia	770,633	267,431
India	358,653	235,384

Source: U.S. Department of Commerce

Number of Book Outlets in the United States and Canada

The *American Book Trade Directory* (Information Today, Inc.) has been published since 1915. Revised annually, it features lists of booksellers, wholesalers, periodicals, reference tools, and other information about the U.S. and Canadian book markets. The data shown in Table 1, the most current available, are from the 2001–2002 edition of the directory.

The 27,992 stores of various types shown are located throughout the United States, Canada, and regions administered by the United States. "General" bookstores stock trade books and children's books in a general variety of subjects. "College" stores carry college-level textbooks. "Educational" outlets handle school textbooks up to and including the high school level. "Mail order" outlets sell general trade books by mail and are not book clubs; all others operating by mail are classified according to the kinds of books carried. "Antiquarian" dealers sell old and rare books. Stores handling secondhand books are classified as "used." "Paperback" stores have more than 80 percent of their stock in paperbound books. Stores with paperback departments are listed under the appropriate major classification ("general," "department store," "stationer," etc.). Bookstores with at least 50 percent of their stock on a particular subject are classified by subject.

Table 1 / Bookstores in the United States and Canada, 2001

Category	United States	Canada
Antiquarian General	1,566	109
Antiquarian Mail Order	523	15
Antiquarian Specialized	249	8
Art Supply Store	73	2
College General	3,445	188
College Specialized	121	10
Comics	243	24
Computer Software	964	0
Cooking	170	5
Department Store	1,986	0
Educational*	341	31
Federal Sites†	235	1
Foreign Language*	38	2
General	6,267	833
Gift Shop	388	16
Juvenile*	262	30
Mail Order General	313	18
Mail Order Specialized	714	26
Metaphysics, New Age, and Occult	248	20
Museum Store and Art Gallery	586	39
Nature and Natural History	198	6
Newsdealer	92	5

Table 1 / Bookstores in the United States and Canada, 2001 *(cont.)*

Category	United States	Canada
Office Supply	57	12
Other‡	1,980	259
Paperback§	250	13
Religious*	3,849	259
Self Help/Development	41	13
Stationer	11	16
Toy Store	112	12
Used*	594	104
Totals	25,916	2,076

* Includes Mail Order Shops for this topic, which are not counted elsewhere in this survey.

† National Historic Sites, National Monuments, and National Parks.

‡ Stores specializing in subjects or services other than those covered in this survey.

§ Includes Mail Order. Excludes used paperback bookstores, stationers, drugstores, or wholesalers handling paperbacks.

Review Media Statistics

Compiled by the staff of the *Bowker Annual*

Number of Books and Other Media
Reviewed by Major Reviewing Publications, 2000–2001

	Adult		Juvenile		Young Adult		Total	
	2000	2001	2000	2001	2000	2001	2000	2001
Appraisal[1]	12	16	450	659	228	165	690	840
Book[2]	328	281	36	44	—	—	364	325
Booklist[3]	4,601	4,772	2,750	2,884	966	996	8,317	8,652
Bulletin of the Center for Children's Books[4]	—	—	784	790	—	—	784	790
Chicago Sun Times	800	500	125	85	—	—	925	585
Chicago Tribune Sunday Book Section	n.a.	650	n.a.	275	n.a.	15	n.a.	940
Choice[5]	6,340	6,321	—	—	—	—	6,340	6,321
Horn Book Guide[6]	—	—	3,600	3,957	—	—	3,600	3,957
Horn Book Magazine	—	—	317	297	81	88	398	385
Kirkus Reviews[6]	n.a.	3,930	n.a.	2,211	—	—	n.a.	6,141
Library Journal[7]	6,073	6,237	—	—	—	—	6,073	6,237
Los Angeles Times[6]	1,380	1,050	120	150	—	—	1,500	1,200
New York Times Sunday Book Review[6]	1,923	1,600	297	155	—	—	2,220	1,755
Publishers Weekly[8]	8,145	6,745	1,919	2,249	—	—	10,064	8,994
Rapport[9]	723	980	—	—	—	—	723	980
School Library Journal[10]	293	278	3,399	3,568	—	—	4,148	4,182
Washington Post Book World	1,400	1,410	40	50	25	30	1,465	1,490

n.a.=not available

1 *Appraisal Science Books for Young People* reviews current science books for children and teenagers, plus teachers' resources for science. As of 2001, it is published online only at http://www.appraisal. neu.edu.

2 The adult figure includes 39 older titles. YA books are included in the juvenile total. *Book* also reviewed 23 audiobooks.

3 All figures are for a 12-month period from September 1, 2000, to August 31, 2001 (vol. 97). The YA total consists solely of reviews of adult books that are appropriate for young adults.

4 All figures are for 12-month period beginning September and ending July/August. The *Bulletin* also reviewed 22 professional books. YA books are included in the juvenile total.

5 All books reviewed in *Choice* are scholarly publications intended for undergraduate libraries. Total includes 317 Internet sites, 29 CD-ROMs, and 4 e-books.

6 Juvenile figures include young adult titles.

7 In addition, *LJ* reviewed 379 audiobooks, 55 magazines, 362 videos, 479 books in "Collection Development," 181 Web sites, 47 e-books, 174 online databases and CD-ROMs, and previewed 678 books in "Prepub Alert."

8 *Publishers Weekly* also reviewed 112 audiobooks and 28 e-books.

9 Total includes 310 reviews of other media, including CDs.

10 Total includes 82 books for professional reading, 75 December holiday books, 126 reference books, and 53 "Best Books." Juvenile count includes YA titles.

Part 5
Reference Information

Bibliographies

The Librarian's Bookshelf

Cathleen Bourdon, MLS

Executive Director, Reference and User Services Association, American Library Association

Most of the books on this selective bibliography were published after 1999; a few earlier titles are retained because of their continuing importance.

General Works

Alternative Library Literature, 1998/1999: A Biennial Anthology. Ed. by Sanford Berman and James P. Danky. McFarland, 2000. Paper $45.

American Library Directory, 2002–2003. 2 vols. Information Today, 2002. $299.

The Bowker Annual Library and Book Trade Almanac, 2002. Information Today, 2002. $199.

Introduction to Indexing and Abstracting. 3rd ed. By Donald and Ana Cleveland. Libraries Unlimited, 2000. $45.

Library and Information Science Annual. Vol. 7. Ed. by Bohdan S. Wynar. Libraries Unlimited, 1999. $65.

Library Literature and Information Science Index. H. W. Wilson, 1921. Also available online, 1984–.

Library Reference Center. http://www.epnet. com. Indexes 30 periodicals in librarianship for the past five years.

The Whole Library Handbook: Current Data, Professional Advice, and Curiosa About Libraries and Library Services. 3rd ed. Comp. by George Eberhart. American Library Association, 2000. Paper $40.

Academic Libraries

ARL Statistics. Association of Research Libraries. Annual. 1964–. $79.

Academic Libraries as High-Tech Gateways: A Guide to Design and Space Decisions. 2nd ed. By Richard J. Bazillion and Connie L. Braum. American Library Association, 2000. Paper $55.

Academic Library Trends and Statistics, 2000. Association of College and Research Libraries/American Library Association, 2000. 3 vols. $180.

Academic Research on the Internet: Options for Scholars and Libraries. Ed. by Helen Laurence and William Miller. Haworth Press, 2001. Paper $49.95.

Books, Bytes, and Bridges: Libraries and Computer Centers in Academic Institutions. Ed. by Larry Hardesty. American Library Association, 2000. Paper $48.

CLIP (College Library Information Packet) *Notes.* Association of College and Research Libraries/American Library Association, 1980–. Most recent volume is No. 30, 2001. $23.

Outsourcing Library Operations in Academic Libraries: An Overview of Issues and Outcomes. By Claire-Lise Benaud and Sever Bordeianu. Libraries Unlimited, 1998. $40.

Recreating the Academic Library: Breaking Virtual Ground. Ed. by Cheryl LaGuardia. Neal-Schuman, 1998. Paper $65.

SPEC Kits. Association of Research Libraries. 1973–. 10/yr. $260.

Survey of Academic and Special Libraries, 2001 Edition. Primary Research Group, 2000. $72.95.

Administration and Personnel

Advances in Library Administration and Organization. Most recent volume is No. 18. Ed. by Edward D. Garten and Delmus E. Williams. AI/Elsevier Science, 2001. $85.

Charging and Collecting Fees and Fines: A Handbook for Libraries. By Murray S. Martin and Betsy Parks. Neal-Schuman, 1998. Paper $49.95.

Coaching in the Library: A Management Strategy for Achieving Excellence. By Ruth F. Metz. American Library Association, 2001. Paper $45.

Complete Guide to Performance Standards for Library Personnel. By Carole E. Goodson. Neal-Schuman, 1997. Paper $55.

Get Them Talking: Managing Change Through Case Studies and Case Study Discussion. Ed. by Gwen Arthur. Reference and User Services Association/American Library Association, 2000. Paper $16.

Getting Political: An Action Guide for Librarians and Library Supporters. By Anne M. Turner. Neal-Schuman, 1997. Paper $45.

Interpreting and Negotiating Licensing Agreements: A Guidebook for the Library, Research and Teaching Professions. By Arlene Bielefield and Lawrence Cheeseman. Neal-Schuman, 1999. Paper $59.95.

The Library Meeting Survival Manual. By George J. Soete. Tulane Street Publications, 2000. Paper $29.95.

Library Security and Safety Handbook: Prevention, Policies and Procedures. By Bruce A. Shuman. American Library Association, 1999. Paper $42.

Management for Research Libraries Cooperation. Ed. by Sul H. Lee. Haworth Press, 2000. Paper $39.95.

Managing Overdues: A How-To-Do-It Manual for Librarians. Ed. by Patsy J. Hansel. Neal-Schuman, 1998. Paper $45.

Marketing/Planning Library and Information Services. By Darlene E. Weingand. Libraries Unlimited, 1999. $47.50.

Moving Library Collections: A Management Handbook. By Elizabeth Chamberlain Habich. Greenwood, 1998. $82.50.

Practical Strategies for Library Managers. By Joan Giesecke. American Library Association, 2000. Paper $32.

Recruiting Library Staff: A How-To-Do-It Manual for Librarians. By Kathleen Low. Neal-Schuman, 1999. Paper $45.

Staff Development: A Practical Guide. 3rd ed. Ed. by Elizabeth Fuseler Avery, Terry Dahlin, and Deborah A. Carver. American Library Association, 2001. Paper $40.

Stop Talking, Start Doing! Attracting People of Color to the Library Profession. By Gregory L. Reese and Ernestine L. Hawkins. American Library Association, 1999. Paper $30.

Using Public Relations Strategies to Promote Your Nonprofit Organization. By Ruth Ellen Kinzey. Haworth Press, 2000. $59.95.

Bibliographic Instruction/ Information Literacy

Basic Library Skills. 4th ed. By Carolyn Wolf. McFarland, 1999. Paper $24.95.

Becoming a Library Teacher. By Cheryl LaGuardia and Christine K. Oka. Neal-Schuman, 2000. Paper $49.95.

Information Literacy Toolkit: Grades Kindergarten–6; Information Literacy Toolkit: Grades 7 and Up; and *Research Projects: An Information Literacy Planner for Students.* By Jenny Ryan and Steph Capra. American Library Association, 2001. Paper with CD-ROM $45 for each toolkit, $20 for Research Project.

Library Instruction: A Peer Tutoring Model. By Susan Deese-Roberts and Kathleen Keating. Libraries Unlimited, 2000. Paper $46.

Practical Steps to the Research Process for High School. By Deborah B. Stanley. Libraries Unlimited, 1999. Paper $32.

Web-Based Instruction: A Guide for Libraries. By Susan Sharpless Smith. American Library Association, 2001. Paper $40.

Working with Faculty to Design Undergraduate Information Literacy Programs: A How-To-Do-It Manual for Librarians. By Rosemary M. Young and Stephena Harmony. Neal-Schuman, 1999. Paper $45.

Cataloging and Classification

The Concise AACR2: 1998 Revision. By Michael Gorman. American Library Association, 1999. Paper $32.

Dewey Decimal Classification, 21st Edition: A Study Manual and Number Building Guide. By Mona L. Scott. Libraries Unlimited, 1998. $47.50.

The Future of Cataloging: Insights from the Lubetzky Symposium. Ed. by Tschera Harkness Connell and Robert L. Maxwell. American Library Association, 2000. Paper $65.

Guidelines on Subject Access to Individual Works of Fiction, Drama, Etc. By the Association for Library Collections and Technical Services. American Library Association, 2000. Paper $19.

Learn Library of Congress Classification. By Helena Dittmann and Jane Hardy. Scarecrow Press, 1999. Paper $29.50.

Managing Cataloging and the Organization of Information: Philosophies, Practices and Challenges at the Onset of the 21st Century. Ed. by Ruth C. Carter. Haworth Press, 2001. Paper $39.95.

Metadata and Organizing Educational Resources on the Internet. Ed. by Jane Greenberg. Haworth Press, 2000. Paper $39.95.

Proceedings of the Bicentennial Conference on Bibliographic Control for the New Millennium: Confronting the Challenges of Networked Resources and the Web. Ed. by Ann M. Sandberg-Fox. Library of Congress, Cataloging Distribution Service, 2001. Paper $45.

Sorting Out the Web: Approaches to Subject Access. By Candy Schwartz. Ablex Publishing/Greenwood, 2001. Paper $32.95.

Standard Cataloging for Schools and Public Libraries. 3rd ed. By Sheila S. Intner and Jean Weihs. Libraries Unlimited, 2001. $45.

Wynar's Introduction to Cataloging and Classification. 9th ed. By Arlene G. Taylor. Libraries Unlimited, 2000. $65.

Children's and Young Adult Services and Materials

Bare Bones Children's Services: Tips for Public Library Generalists. By Anitra T. Steele. American Library Association, 2001. Paper $32.

Bare Bones Young Adult Services: Tips for Public Library Generalists. 2nd ed. By Renee J. Vaillancourt. American Library Association, 1999. Paper $32.

Best Books for Young Adults. 2nd ed. By Betty Carter, with Sally Estes, Linda Waddle, and the Young Adult Library Services Association. American Library Association, 2000. Paper $35.

Booktalks and Beyond: Thematic Learning Activities for Grades K–6. By Nancy J. Keane. Upstart Books, 2001. Paper $16.95.

Center for the Study of Books in Spanish for Children and Adolescents at California State University, San Marcos Web site: http://www.csusm.edu/campus_centers/csb. Lists recommended books in Spanish for youth published worldwide.

Children and Libraries: Getting It Right. By Virginia A. Walter. American Library Association, 2000. Paper $32.

Do it Right! Best Practices for Serving Young Adults in School and Public Libraries. By Patrick Jones and Joel Shoemaker. Neal-Schuman, 2001. Paper $45.

Excellence in Library Services to Young Adults. 3rd ed. By Mary K. Chelton. American Library Association, 2000. Paper $25.

Fantastic, Fun Reading Programs. By Kathryn Totten. Upstart Books/Highsmith Press, 2001. Paper $16.95.

Keep Talking That Book! Booktalks to Promote Reading, Volume III. By Carol Littlejohn and Cathlyn Thomas. Linworth Publishing, 2001. Paper $36.95.

Managing Children's Services in the Public Library. 2nd ed. By Adele M. Fasick. Libraries Unlimited, 1998. $37.

The New Books Kids Like. Ed. by Sharon Deeds and Catherine Chastain. American Library Association, 2001. Paper $32.

The Newbery and Caldecott Awards: A Guide for the Medal and Honor Books. By the Association for Library Service to Children (ALSC). American Library Association, 2001. Paper $18.

Story Programs: A Source Book of Materials. 2nd ed. By Carolyn Sue Peterson, Ann D. Fenton, and Stefani Koorey. Scarecrow Press, 2000. Paper $29.50.

Storytime Sourcebook: A Compendium of Ideas and Resources for Storytellers. 2nd ed. By Carolyn N. Cullum. Neal-Schuman, 1999. Paper $45.

A Storytime Year: A Month-To-Month Kit for Preschool Programming. By Susan M. Dailey (illus. by Nancy Carol Wagner). Neal-Schuman, 2000. Loose-leaf binder, $59.95.

VOYA Reader Two: Articles from Voice of Youth Advocates. Ed. by Dorothy M. Broderick and Mary K. Chelton. Scarecrow Press, 1998. Paper $24.50.

Collection Development

Building Electronic Library Collections: The Essential Guide to Selection Criteria and Core Subject Collections. By Diane Kovacs. Neal-Schuman, 1999. Paper $75.

Collection Evaluation Techniques: A Short, Selective, Practical, Current, Annotated Bibliography, 1990–1998. Ed. by Bonnie Strohl. Reference and User Services Association/American Library Association, 1999. Paper $16.

Coretta Scott King Award Book, 1970–1999. Ed. by Henritta M. Smith. American Library Association, 1999. Paper $32.

Creating New Strategies for Cooperative Collection Development. Ed. by Milton T. Wolf and Marjorie E. Bloss. Haworth Press, 2000. Paper $32.95.

Developing Christian Fiction Collections for Children and Adults: Selection Criteria and a Core Collection. By Barbara J. Walker. Neal-Schuman, 1998. Paper $38.50.

Guide to User Needs Assessment for Integrated Information Resource Management and Collection Development. Ed. by Dora Biblarz, Stephen Bosch, and Chris Sugnet. Scarecrow Press, 2001. Paper $17.50.

Literature in English: A Guide for Librarians in the Digital Age (Publications in Librarianship, No. 54). Ed. by Betty H. Day and William A. Wortman. Association of College and Research Libraries/American Library Association, 2000. Paper $32.

Selecting and Managing Electronic Resources: A How-To-Do-It Manual. By Vicki L. Gregory. Neal-Schuman, 2000. Paper $55.

Weeding Library Collections: Library Weeding Methods. 4th ed. By Stanley J. Slote. Libraries Unlimited, 1997. $65.

Copyright

Commonsense Copyright: A Guide for Educators and Librarians. 2nd ed. By R. S. Talab. McFarland Publishers, 1999. Paper $39.95.

Copyright Essentials for Librarians and Educators. By Kenneth D. Crews. American Library Association, 2000. Paper $45.

Copyright in Cyberspace: Questions and Answers for Librarians. By Gretchen McCord Hoffmann. Neal-Schuman, 2001. Paper $55.

Copyright Plain and Simple. 2nd ed. By Cheryl Besenjak. Career Press, 2000. Paper $12.99.

Technology and Copyright Law: A Guidebook for the Library, Research and Teaching Professions. By Arlene Bielefield and Lawrence Cheesemen. Neal-Schuman, 1997. Paper $55.

Customer Service

Assessing Service Quality: Satisfying the Expectations of Library Customers. By Peter Hernon and Ellen Altman. American Library Association, 1998. Paper $40.

Defusing the Angry Patron: A How-To-Do-It Manual for Librarians and Paraprofessionals. By Rhea Joyce Rubin. Neal-Schuman, 2000. Paper $45.

Delivering Satisfaction and Service Quality: A Customer-Based Approach for Libraries. By Peter Hernon and John R. Whitman. American Library Association, 2000. Paper $40.

Diversity in the Library: A Way of Life. Library Video Network, 2001. 20-minute video $99.

Distance Education

The Browsable Classroom: An Introduction to E-Learning. By Carolyn B. Noah and Linda W. Braun. Neal-Schuman, 2001. Paper $45.

Library Outreach, Partnerships, and Distance Education: Reference Librarians at the Gateway. Ed. by Wendi Arant and Pixey Anne Mosley. Haworth Press, 2000. Paper $24.95.

Library Services for Open and Distance Learning: The Third Annotated Bibliography. By Alexander L. Slade and Marie A. Kascus. Libraries Unlimited, 2000. $75.

Off-Campus Library Services Ed. by Anne Marie Casey. Haworth Press, 2001. Paper $49.95.

The Electronic Library

Being Analog: Creating Tomorrow's Libraries. By Walt Crawford. American Library Association, 1999. Paper $28.

Creating a Virtual Library: A How-To-Do-It Manual for Librarians. Ed. by Frederick Stielow. Neal-Schuman, 1999. Paper $55.

Digital Libraries. By William Y. Arms. MIT Press, 2000. $45.

The Evolving Virtual Library II: Practical and Philosophical Perspectives. Ed. by Laverna M. Saunders. Information Today, 1999. $39.50.

Finding Common Ground: Creating the Library of the Future Without Diminishing the Library of the Past. Ed. by Cheryl LaGuardia and Barbara A. Mitchell. Neal-Schuman, 1998. Paper $82.50.

From Gutenberg to the Global Information Infrastructure: Access to Information in the Networked World. By Christine L. Borgman. MIT Press, 2000. $42.

Innovative Use of Information Technology by Colleges. Council on Library and Information Resources, 1999. Paper $20.

Issues for Libraries and Information Science in the Internet Age. By Bruce A. Shuman. Libraries Unlimited, 2001. Paper $45.

Leading the Wired Organization: The Information Professional's Guide to Managing Technological Change. By Mark Stover. Neal-Schuman, 1999. Paper $49.95.

Strategies for Building Digitized Collections. By Abby Smith. Council on Library and Information Resources, 2001. Paper $20.

Evaluation of Library Services

An Action Plan for Outcomes Assessment in Your Library. By Peter Hernon and Robert E. Dugan. American Library Association, 2001. Paper $49.

Identifying and Analyzing User Needs: A Complete Handbook and Ready-To-Use Assessment Workbook with Disk. By Lynn Westbrook. Neal-Schuman, 2000. Paper with CD-ROM $75.

Library Evaluation: A Casebook and Can-Do Guide. Ed. by Danny P. Wallace and Connie Van Fleet. Libraries Unlimited, 2000. Paper $45.

Measuring What Matters: A Library/LRC Outcomes Assessment Manual. By Bonnie Gratch Lindauer. Learning Resources Association, 2000. Three-ring binder $79.

Statistical Methods for the Information Professional: A Practical, Painless Approach to Understanding, Using and Interpreting Statistics. By Liwen Vaughan. Information Today, 2001. $39.50.

Fund Raising

Becoming a Fundraiser: The Principles and Practice of Library Development. 2nd ed. By Victoria Steele and Stephen D. Elder. American Library Association, 2000. Paper $38.

The Funding Game: Rules for Public Library Advocacy. By Mary Anne Craft. Scarecrow Press, 1999. $35.

Fundraising and Friend-Raising on the Web. By Adam Corson-Finnerty and Laura

Blanchard. American Library Association, 1998. Paper $50.

Grantsmanship for Small Libraries and School Library Media Centers. By Sylvia D. Hall-Ellis, Doris Meyer, Frank W. Hoffman, and Ann Jerabek. Libraries Unlimited, 1999. Paper $32.50.

Legacies for Libraries: A Practical Guide to Planned Giving. By Amy Sherman Smith and Matthew D. Lehrer. American Library Association, 2000. $35.

The Librarian's Guide to Partnerships. Ed. by Sherry Lynch. Highsmith Press, 1999. Paper $19.

Government Documents

Guide to Popular U.S. Government Publications. 5th ed. By Frank W. Hoffman and Richard J. Wood. Libraries Unlimited, 1998. $38.50.

International Information: Documents, Publications and Electronic Information of International Governmental Organizations. 2nd ed. Ed. by Peter I. Hajnal. Libraries Unlimited, 1997. $120.

Introduction to United States Government Information Sources. 6th ed. By Joe Morehead. Libraries Unlimited, 1999. Paper $65.

U.S. Government on the Web: Getting the Information You Need. 2nd ed. By Peter Hernon, Robert E. Dugan, and John A. Shuler. Libraries Unlimited, 2001. Paper $45.

Health Information, Medical Librarianship

Administration and Management in Health Sciences Libraries. Ed. by Rick B. Forsman. Scarecrow Press, 2000. $55.

Health Care Resources on the Internet: A Guide for Librarians and Health Care Consumers. Ed. by M. Sandra Wood. Haworth Press, 1999. Paper $24.95.

The Medical Library Association Guide to Managing Health Care Libraries. Ed. by Ruth Holst and Sharon A. Phillips. Neal-Schuman, 2000. Paper $75.

Information Science

Intelligent Technologies in Library and Information Service Applications. By F. W. Lancaster and Amy Warner. Information Today, 2001. $39.50.

Introductory Concepts in Information Science. By Melanie J. Norton. Information Today, 2000. $39.50.

Knowledge and Knowing in Library and Information Science: A Philosophical Framework. By John M. Budd. Scarecrow Press, 2001. Paper $38.50.

Knowledge Management for the Information Professional. Ed. by T. Kanti Srikantaiah and Michael Koenig. Information Today, 2000. $44.50.

Preparing the Information Professional: An Agenda for the Future. By Sajjad ur Rehman. Greenwood, 2000. $60.

Techno-Human Mesh: The Growing Power of Information Technologies. By Cynthia K. West. Quorum Books, 2000. $62.50.

Super Searchers Go to the Source: The Interviewing and Hands-On Information Strategies of Top Primary Researchers, Online, on the Phone and in Person. By Risa Sacks. CyberAge Books/Information Today, 2001. Paper $24.95.

The Web of Knowledge: A Festschrift in Honor of Eugene Garfield. Ed. by Blaise Cronin and Helen Barsky Atkins. Information Today, 2000. $49.50.

Intellectual Freedom

Banned Books Resource Guide. Office for Intellectual Freedom/American Library Association, 2001. Paper $30.

Censorship and Selection: Issues and Answers for Schools. 3rd ed. By Henry Reichman. American Library Association, 2001. Paper $35.

IFLA/FAIFE World Report on Libraries and Intellectual Freedom. IFLA/FAIFE, 2001. Paper $10.

Intellectual Freedom and Social Responsibility in American Librarianship, 1967–1974. By Toni Samek. McFarland, 2001. $35.

Intellectual Freedom Manual. 6th ed. ALA Office for Intellectual Freedom. American Library Association, 2001. Paper $45.

Libraries and Democracy: The Cornerstones of Liberty. By Nancy Kranich. American Library Association, 2001. Paper $32.

Libraries, First Amendment, and Cyberspace: What You Need to Know. By Robert S. Peck. American Library Association, 2000. Paper $32.

Teaching Banned Books: 12 Guides for Young Readers. By Pat R. Scales. American Library Association, 2001. Paper $28.

Interlibrary Loan, Document Delivery, and Resource Sharing

Interlibrary Loan/Document Delivery and Customer Satisfaction. Ed. by Pat Weaver-Meyers, Wilbur Stolt, and Yem Fong. Haworth, 1997. Paper $49.95.

Interlibrary Loan Policies Directory. 7th ed. Ed. by Leslie R. Morris. Neal-Schuman, 2002. Paper $199.95.

Interlibrary Loan Practices Handbook. 2nd ed. By Virginia Boucher. American Library Association, 1996. Paper $45.

The Internet/Web

The Cybrarian's Manual 2. 2nd ed. By Pat Ensor. American Library Association, 2000. Paper $45.

A Digital Gift to the Nation: Fulfilling the Promise of the Digital and Internet Age. By Lawrence K. Grossman and Newton N. Minow. Brookings Institution, 2001. Paper $15.95.

Instant Web Forms and Surveys for Academic Libraries; Instant Web Forms and Surveys for Public Libraries; Instant Web Forms and Surveys for Children's/YA Services and School Libraries. By Gail Junion-Metz and Derrek L. Metz. Neal-Schuman, 2001. Paper and CD-ROM, $75 each.

The Internet Public Library Handbook. By Joseph Janes, David Carter, Annette Lagace, Michael McLennen, Sara Ryan, and Schelle Simcox. Neal-Schuman, 1999. Paper $55.

The Internet Searcher's Handbook: Locating People, Information and Software. 2nd ed. By Peter Morville, Louis Rosenfeld, Joseph Janes, and GraceAnne A. DeCandido. Neal-Schuman, 1999. Paper $49.95.

The Invisible Web: Uncovering Information Sources Search Engines Can't See. By Chris Sherman and Gary Price. CyberAge Books/Information Today, 2001. Paper $29.95.

The Librarian's Quick Guide to Internet Resources. 2nd ed. By Jenny Lynne Semenza. Highsmith Press, 2000. Paper $18.95.

Managing the Internet Controversy. Ed. by Mark Smith. Neal-Schuman, 2001. Paper $45.

Neal-Schuman Complete Internet Companion for Librarians. 2nd ed. By Allen C. Benson. Neal-Schuman, 2001. Paper and CD-ROM $79.95.

Neal-Schuman Internet Policy Handbook for Libraries. By Mark Smith. Neal-Schuman, 1999. Paper $55.

The Role and Impact of the Internet on Library and Information Services. Ed. by Lewis-Guodo Liu. Greenwood, 2001. $64.95.

Teaching the Internet in Libraries. By Rachel Singer Gordon. American Library Association, 2001. Paper $38.

Usability Assessment of Library-Related Web Sites: Methods and Case Studies. Ed. by Nicole Campbell. Library and Information Technology Association/American Library Association, 2001. Paper $25.

Usability Testing for Library Web Sites: A Hands-On Guide. By Elaina Norlin and CM! Winters. American Library Association, 2001. Paper $32.

Librarians and Librarianship

The ALA Survey of Librarian Salaries 2001. Ed. by Mary Jo Lynch. American Library Association, 2001. Paper $56.

ARL Annual Salary Survey, 2000–2001. Association of Research Libraries, 2001. Paper $100.

The Best of Times: A Personal and Occupational Odyssey. By Paul Wasserman. Omnigraphics, 2000. $35.

Diversity in Libraries: Academic Residency Programs. Ed. by Raquel V. Cogell and Cindy A. Gruwell. Greenwood, 2001. $62.50.

Handbook of Black Librarianship. 2nd ed. By E. J. Josey and Marva L. DeLoach. Scarecrow Press, 2000. $69.50.

The Information Professional's Guide to Career Development Online. By Sarah L. Nesbeitt and Rachel Singer Gordon. Information Today, 2001. Paper $29.50.

Librarians in Fiction: A Critical Bibliography. By Grant Burns. McFarland, 1998. Paper $29.95.

Librarianship—Quo Vadis? Opportunities and Dangers as We Face the New Millennium. By Herbert S. White. Libraries Unlimited, 2000. $65.

On Account of Sex: An Annotated Bibliography on the Status of Women in Librarianship, 1993–1997. Ed. by Betsy Kruger and Catherine A. Larson. Scarecrow Press, 1999. $65.

Our Enduring Values: Librarianship in the 21st Century. By Michael Gorman. American Library Association, 2000. Paper $28.

Re-Membering Libraries: Essays on the Profession. By T. D. Webb. McFarland, 2000. Paper $39.95.

What Else You Can Do With a Library Degree: Career Options for the '90s and Beyond. Ed. by Betty-Carol Sellen. Neal-Schuman, 1997. Paper $32.95.

Writing Resumes That Work: A How-To-Do-It Manual for Librarians. By Robert R. Newlen. Neal-Schuman, 1998. Paper and disk $59.

Library Automation

Directory of Library Automation Software, Systems, and Services. Ed. by Pamela Cibbarelli. Information Today, 2000. Paper $89. Published biennially.

Introduction to Automation for Librarians. 4th ed. By William Saffady. American Library Association, 1999. Paper $60.

History of Telecommunications Technology: An Annotated Bibliography. By Christopher H. Sterling and George Shiers. Scarecrow Press, 2000. $65.

Library Automation in Transitional Societies: Lessons from Eastern Europe. Ed. by Andrew Lass and Richard E. Quandt. Oxford University Press, 2000. $55.

Neal-Schuman Library Technology Companion: A Basic Guide for Library Staff. By John J. Burke. Neal-Schuman, 2000. Paper $45.

System Analysis for Librarians and Information Professions. 2nd ed. By Larry N. Osborne and Margaret Nakamura. Libraries Unlimited, 2000. Paper $50.

Writing and Updating Technology Plans: A Guidebook with Sample Plans on CD-ROM. By John M. Cohn, Ann L. Kelsey, and Keith Michael Fiels. Neal-Schuman, 1999. Paper and CD-ROM $99.95.

Library Buildings and Space Planning

Building Libraries for the 21st Century: The Shape of Information. Ed. by T. D. Webb. McFarland, 2000. $55.

Checklist of Library Building Design Considerations. 4th ed. By William W. Sannwald. American Library Association, 2001. Paper $38.

Construction from a Staff Perspective. By Williamsburg (Virginia) Regional Library. McFarland, 2001. Paper $35.

Countdown to a New Library: Managing the Building Project. By Jeannette Woodward. American Library Association, 2000. Paper $48.

First a Dream: A Community Builds a Library. By Jo Ann Ridley. Vision Books International, 2001. $35.

The Librarian's Facility Management Handbook. By Carmine J. Trotta and Marcia Trotta. Neal-Schuman, 2000. Paper $75.

When Change Is Set in Stone: An Analysis of Seven Academic Libraries Designed by Perry Dean Rogers and Partners, Architects. By Michael J. Crosbie and Damon

D. Hickey. Association of College and Research Libraries/American Library Association, 2001. $60.

Library History

American Libraries Before 1876. By Haynes McMullen. Greenwood, 2000. $67.

America's Library: The Story of the Library of Congress, 1800–2000. By James Conaway. Yale University Press, 2000. $39.95.

Carnegie Libraries Across America: A Public Legacy. By Theodore Jones. Wiley, 1997. $29.95.

Cuneiform to Computer: A History of Reference Sources. By Bill Katz. Scarecrow Press, 1998. $46.

Enrichment: A History of the Public Library in the United States in the Twentieth Century. By Lowell A. Martin. Scarecrow Press, 1998. $35.

The Evolution of the Book. By Frederick G. Kilgour. Oxford University Press, 1998. $35.

Libraries, Immigrants, and the American Experience. By Plummer Alston Jones, Jr. Greenwood, 1999. $68.

Library History Research in America: Essays Commemorating the Fiftieth Anniversary of the Library History Round Table. Ed. by Andrew B. Wertheimer and Donald G. Davis, Jr. Oak Knoll Press, 2000. $35.

OCLC 1967–1997: Thirty Years of Furthering Access to the World's Information. Ed. by K. Wayne Smith. Haworth, 1998. Paper $19.95.

Museums

Creating Web-Accessible Databases: Case Studies for Libraries, Museums, and Other Non-Profits. Ed. by Julie M. Still. Information Today, 2001. $39.50.

Museum Librarianship. 2nd ed. Esther Green Bierbaum. McFarland, 2000. Paper $39.95.

The New Museum: Selected Writings by John Cotton Dana. Ed. William A. Peniston. American Association of Museums, 1999. Paper $28.

Nonprint Materials

Cataloging of Audiovisual Materials and Other Special Materials. 4th ed. By Nancy B. Olson. Media Marketing Group, 1998. Paper $75.

Culturally Diverse Videos, Audios, and CD-ROMs for Children and Young Adults. Ed. by Irene Wood. Neal-Schuman, 1999. Paper $35.

Finding and Using Educational Videos: A How-To-Do-It Manual. By Barbara Stein, Gary Treadway, and Lauralee Ingram. Neal-Schuman, 1998. Paper $38.50.

Preservation

Avoiding Technological Quicksand: Finding a Viable Technical Foundation for Digital Preservation. By Jeff Rothenberg. Council on Library and Information Resources, 1999. Paper $20.

Digital Preservation and Metadata: History, Theory, Practice. By Susan S. Lazinger. Libraries Unlimited, 2001. Paper $55.

Getting Ready for the Nineteenth Century: Strategies and Solutions for Rare Book and Special Collections Librarians. Ed. by William E. Brown, Jr., and Laura Stalker. Association of College and Research Libraries/American Library Association, 2000. Paper $18.

Handbook for Digital Projects: A Management Tool for Preservation. Ed. by Maxine Sitts. Northeast Document Conservation Center, 2000. $38.

Library Disaster Planning and Recovery Handbook. By Camila Alire. Neal-Schuman, 2000. Paper $75.

Moving Theory Into Practice: Digital Imaging for Libraries and Archives. By Anne R. Kenney and Oya Y. Rieger. Research Libraries Group, 2000. Paper $89.

Preservation: Issues and Planning. Ed. by Paul N. Banks and Roberta Pilette. American Library Association, 2000. Paper $78.

The Storage of Art on Paper: A Basic Guide for Institutions. By Sherelyn Ogden. GLIS Publications Office, University of Illinois, 2001. Paper $8.

Public Libraries

Administration of the Small Public Library. 4th ed. By Darlene E. Weingand. American Library Association, 2001. Paper $45.

Adult Programs in the Library. By Brett W. Lear. American Library Association, 2001. Paper $40.

Civic Librarianship: Renewing the Social Mission of the Public Library. By Ronald B. McCabe. Scarecrow Press, 2001. $39.50.

Creating the Full-Service Homework Center in Your Library. By Cindy Mediavilla. American Library Association, 2001. Paper $32.

The Library Book Cart Precision Drill Team Manual. By Linda D. McCracken and Lynne Zeiher. McFarland, 2001. Paper $25.

Library Networks in the New Millennium: Top Ten Trends. Ed. by Sara Laughlin. Association of Specialized and Cooperative Library Agencies/American Library Association, 2000. Paper $25.

Model Policies for Small and Medium Public Libraries. By Jeanette Larson and Hermon Totten. Neal-Schuman, 1998. Paper $49.95.

The New Planning for Results: A Streamline Approach. By Sandra Nelson. American Library Association, 2001. Paper $55.

A Place at the Table: Participating in Community Building. By Kathleen de la Peña McCook. American Library Association, 2000. Paper $25.

Public Librarian's Human Resources Handbook. By David A. Baldwin. Libraries Unlimited, 2001. Paper $55.

Public Libraries in Africa: A Report and Annotated Bibliography. By Aissa Issak. INAS, 2000. Paper £15.

Public Library Data Service Statistical Report. Public Library Association/ALA, 2001. Paper $75.

The Public Library Service: IFLA/UNESCO Guidelines for Development. By Philip Gill on behalf of the IFLA Section on Public Libraries. K. G. Saur Verlag, 2001. $49.

Statistics and Performance Measures for Public Library Networked Services. By John Carlo Bertot, Charles R. McClure, and Joe Ryan. American Library Association, 2000. Paper $38.

Readers' Advisory

ALA's Guide to Best Reading. American Library Association, 2001. Kit $34.95. Camera-ready lists of the year's best books for children, teens, and adults.

Hooked on Horror: A Guide to Reading Interests in Horror Fiction. By Anthony J. Fonseca and June Michele Pulliam. Libraries Unlimited, 1999. $55.

The Mystery Readers' Advisory: The Librarian's Clues to Murder and Mayhem. By John Charles, Joanna Morrison, and Candace Clark. American Library Association, 2001. Paper $30.

The Reader's Advisory Guide to Genre Fiction. By Joyce G. Saricks. American Library Association, 2001. Paper $38.

Readers' Advisory Service in the Public Library. 2nd ed. By Joyce G. Saricks and Nancy Brown. American Library Association, 1997. Paper $28.

The Romance Reader's Advisory: The Librarian's Guide to Love in the Stacks. By Ann Bouricius. American Library Association, 2000. Paper $28.

The Short Story Readers' Advisory: A Guide to the Best. By Brad Hooper. American Library Association, 2000. Paper $28.

Reference Services

Digital Reference Services in the New Millennium: Planning, Management and Evaluation. Ed. by R. David Lankes, John W. Collins, III, and Abby S. Kasowitz. Neal-Schuman, 2000. Paper $65.

The Enoch Pratt Free Library Brief Guide to Reference Sources. 10th ed. Ed. by Thomas H. Patterson, John A. Damond, Jr., and Rachel Kubie. Enoch Pratt Free Library, 2001. Paper $12.

Establishing a Virtual Reference Service. By Anne Grodzins Lipow and Steve Coffman. Library Solutions Press, 2001. $125.

Evaluating Reference Services: A Practical Guide. By Jo Bell Whitlatch. American Library Association, 2000. Paper $39.

Fundamental Reference Sources. 3rd ed. By James H. Sweetland. American Library Association, 2000. $75.

Introduction to Library Public Services. 6th ed. By G. Edward Evans, Anthony J. Amodeo, and Thomas L. Carter. Libraries Unlimited, 1999. Paper $60.

New Technologies and Reference Services. Ed. by Bill Katz. Haworth Press, 2000. $39.95.

Reference and Information Services: An Introduction. 3rd ed. Ed. by Richard E. Bopp and Linda C. Smith. Libraries Unlimited, 2000. Paper $49.50.

Reference Services for the Adult Learner: Challenging Issues for the Traditional and Technological Era. Ed. by Kwasi Sarkodie-Mensah. Haworth Press, 2000. Paper $49.95.

Rethinking Reference: The Reference Librarian's Practical Guide for Surviving Constant Change. By Elizabeth Thomsen. Neal-Schuman, 1999. Paper $45.

Where to Find What: A Handbook to Reference Service. 4th ed. By James M. Hillard. Scarecrow Press, 2000. $45.

School Libraries/Media Centers

Battle of the Books and More: Reading Activities for Middle School Students. By Sybilla Cook, Frances Corcoran, and Beverley Fonnesbeck. Highsmith Press, 2000. Paper $19.95.

Curriculum Partner: Redefining the Role of the Library Media Specialist. By Carol A. Kearney. Greenwood, 2000. $39.95.

Designing a School Library Media Center for the Future. By Rolf Erikson and Carolyn Markuson. American Library Association, 2000. Paper $39.

The Information-Powered School. Ed. by Sandra Hughes-Hassell and Anne Wheelock. American Library Association, 2001. Paper $35.

Leadership in Today's School Library: A Handbook for the Library Media Specialist and the School Principal. By Patricia Potter Wilson and Josette Anne Lyders. Greenwood, 2001. $39.95.

Lessons from Library Power: Enriching Teaching and Learning. By Douglas L. Zweizig and Dianne McAfee Hopkins, with Norman Lott Webb and Gary Wehlage. Libraries Unlimited, 1999. Paper $37.50.

The Net Effect: School Library Media Centers and the Internet. Ed. by Lyn Hay and James Henri. Scarecrow Press, 1999. Paper $36.

Output Measures for School Library Media Programs. By Frances Bryant Bradburn. Neal-Schuman, 1999. Paper $49.95.

Premiere Events: Library Programs That Inspire Elementary School Patrons. By Patricia Potter Wilson and Roger Leslie. Libraries Unlimited, 2001. Paper $35.

Student Assistants in the School Library Media Center. By Therese Bissen Bard. Libraries Unlimited, 1999. Paper $30.

Serials

Developing and Managing Electronic Journal Collections: A How-To-Do-It Manual for Librarians. By Donnelyn Curtis, Virginia M. Scheschy, and Adolfo Tarango. Neal-Schuman, 2000. Paper $55.

Guide to Performance Evaluation of Serials Vendors. Association for Library Collections and Technical Services/American Library Association, 1997. Paper $15.

Making Waves: New Serials Landscapes in a Sea of Change. Ed. by Joseph C. Harmon and P. Michelle Fiander. Haworth Press, 2001. Paper $44.95.

Management of Serials in Libraries. By Thomas E. Nisonger. Libraries Unlimited, 1998. $70.

Managing Electronic Serials: Essays Based on the ALCTS Electronic Serials Institutes 1997–1999. Ed. By Pamela Bluh. Association of Library Collections and Technical Services (ALCTS)/American Library Association, 2001. Paper $38.

Serials Cataloging Handbook. By Carol Liheng and Winnie S. Chan. American Library Association, 1998. Paper $70.

Services for Special Groups

Accessible Libraries on Campus: A Practical Guide for the Creation of Disability-Friendly Libraries. Ed. by Tom McNulty. Association of College and Research Libraries/American Library Association, 1999. Paper $22.

Adaptive Technologies for Learning and Work Environments. 2nd ed. By Joseph J. Lazzaro. American Library Association, 2001. Paper $48, CD-ROM, $35.

Adult Literacy Assessment Tool Kit. By Suzanne Knell and Janet Scrogins. American Library Association, 2000. Paper $35.

American Indian Library Services in Perspective. By Elizabeth Rockefeller-MacArthur. McFarland, 1998. $32.50.

Blind to Failure. West Virginia Library Commission Television Network, 2001. 30-minute video, $25.

Choosing and Using Books with Adult New Readers. By Marguerite Crowley Weibel. Neal-Schuman, 1996. Paper $45.

The Functions and Roles of State Library Agencies. Comp. by Ethel E. Himmel and William J. Wilson. Association of Specialized and Cooperative Library Agencies/ American Library Association, 2000. Paper $20.

Guidelines for Library Services for People with Mental Retardation. American Library Association/Association of Specialized and Cooperative Library Agencies, 1999. Paper $14.

Including Families of Children with Special Needs: A How-To-Do-It Manual for Librarians. By Sandra Feinberg, Barbara Jordan, Kathleen Deerr, and Michelle Langa. Neal-Schuman, 1999. Paper $45.

Libraries Inside: A Practical Guide for Prison Librarians. Ed. by Rhea Joyce Rubin and Daniel Suvak. McFarland, 1995. $41.50.

Library Services to the Sandwich Generation and Serial Caregivers. Compiled by Linda Lucas Walling. Association of Specialized and Cooperative Library Agencies/American Library Association, 2001. Paper $20.

Literacy and Libraries: Learning from Case Studies. Ed. by GraceAnne A. DeCandido. ALA Office for Literacy and Outreach Services/American Library Association, 2001. Paper $40.

Planning for Library Services to People with Disabilities. By Rhea Rubin. Association of Specialized and Cooperative Library Agencies/American Library Association, 2001. Paper $30.

Poor People and Library Services. Ed. by Karen M. Venturella. McFarland, 1998. Paper $28.50.

The Power of Language/El Ponder de la Palabra: Selected Papers from the Second REFORMA National Conference. Ed. by Lillian Castillo-Speed. Libraries Unlimited, 2001. Paper $35.

Serving Latino Communities: A How-To-Do-It Manual for Librarians. By Camila Alire and Orlando Archibeque. Neal-Schuman, 1998. Paper $39.95.

Venture into Cultures: A Resource Book of Multicultural Materials and Programs. 2nd ed. Ed. by Olga R. Kuharets. American Library Association, 2001. Paper $38.

Technical Services

Book Repair: A How-To-Do-It Manual. 2nd ed. By Kenneth Lavender. Neal-Schuman, 2001. Paper $49.95.

Guide to Managing Approval Plans. Ed. by Susan Flood. American Library Association, 1998. Paper $18.

Introduction to Technical Services for Library Technicians. By Mary L. Kao. Haworth Press, 2001. Paper $22.95.

Library Off-Site Shelving: Guide for High-Density Facilities. Ed. by Danuta A. Nitecki and Curtis L. Kendrick. Libraries Unlimited, 2001. Paper $60.

Library Relocations and Collection Shifts. By Dennis C. Tucker. Information Today, 1999. $35.

Managing Electronic Reserves. Ed. by Jeff Rosedale. American Library Association, 2001. Paper $42.

Managing Public Access Computers: A How-To-Do-It Manual for Librarians. By Donald Barclay. Neal-Schuman, 2000. Paper $59.95.

Technical Services Today and Tomorrow. 2nd ed. Ed. by Michael Gorman. Libraries Unlimited, 1998. $45.

Understanding the Business of Library Acquisitions. 2nd ed. Ed. by Karen A. Schmidt. American Library Association, 1998. Paper $54.

Volunteers

Recruiting and Managing Volunteers in Libraries: A How-to-Do-It Manual for Librarians. By Bonnie F. McCune and Charleszine "Terry" Nelson. Neal-Schuman, 1995. Paper $45.

The Volunteer Library: A Handbook. By Linda S. Fox. McFarland, 1999. Paper $35.

Periodicals and Periodical Indexes

Acquisitions Librarian
Advanced Technology Libraries
Against the Grain
American Libraries
American Society for Information Science Journal
Behavioral and Social Sciences Librarian
Book Links
Book Report: Journal for Junior and Senior High School Librarians
Booklist
The Bottom Line
Bulletin of the Medical Library Association
Cataloging and Classification Quarterly
Catholic Library World
CHOICE
College and Research Libraries
College and Undergraduate Libraries
Collection Management
Community and Junior College Libraries
Computers in Libraries
The Electronic Library
Government Information Quarterly
Information Technology and Libraries
Information Outlook (formerly Special Libraries)
Interface
Journal of Academic Librarianship
Journal of Education for Library and Information Science
Journal of Information Ethics

Journal of Interlibrary Loan, Document Delivery and Information Supply
Journal of Library Administration
Journal of Youth Services in Libraries
Knowledge Quest
Law Library Journal
Legal Reference Services Quarterly
Libraries & Culture
Library Administration and Management
Library and Information Science Research (LIBRES)
Library Hi-Tech
Library Issues: Briefings for Faculty and Academic Administrators
Library Journal
Library Mosaics
The Library Quarterly
Library Resources and Technical Services
Library Talk: The Magazine for Elementary School Librarians
Library Technology Reports
Library Trends
MLS: Marketing Library Services
Medical Reference Services Quarterly
MultiCultural Review
MultiMedia Schools
Music Library Association Notes
Music Reference Services Quarterly
The One-Person Library
Online & CD-ROM Review
Public and Access Services Quarterly
Public Libraries
Public Library Quarterly
RBM: A Journal of Rare Books, Manuscripts, and Cultural Heritage
RSR: Reference Services Review
Reference and User Services Quarterly (formerly RQ)
Reference Librarian
Resource Sharing & Information Networks
Rural Libraries
School Library Journal
Science & Technology Libraries
Serials Librarian
Serials Review
Technical Services Quarterly
Technicalities
Today's Librarian
Unabashed Librarian
Video Librarian
Voice of Youth Advocates (VOYA)

Ready Reference

Publishers' Toll-Free Telephone Numbers and Web Sites

Publishers' toll-free telephone numbers and World Wide Web addresses play an important role in ordering, verification, and customer service. This list comes from *Literary Market Place* (Information Today, Inc.). The list is not comprehensive, and both toll-free numbers and Web addresses are subject to change. Readers may want to call for toll-free directory assistance at 800-555-1212.

A D D Warehouse
  800-233-9273
  www.addwarehouse.com
A R O Publishing Co.
  www.arobook.com
A-R Editions
  800-736-0070
  www.areditions.com
AAAI Press
  www.aaaipress.org
AANS–American Association of
  Neurological Surgeons
  www.neurosurgery.org
AAPG (American Association of Petroleum
  Geologists)
  800-364-AAPG; fax 800-898-2274
  www.aapg.org
Abacus
  800-451-4319
  www.abacuspub.com
Abaris Books
  abarisbooks.com
Abbeville Publishing Group
  800-ART-BOOK
  www.abbeville.com
Abbott, Langer & Associates
  www.abbott-langer.com
ABC-CLIO
  800-368-6868
  www.abc-clio.com
Abdo Publishing
  800-458-8399
  www.abdopub.com

ABELexpress
  800-542-9001
ABI Professional Publications
  800-551-7776
  www.abipropub.com
Abingdon Press
  800-251-3320
  www.abingdon.org
Ablex Publishing
  800-398-9985
  www.greenwood.com
Abrams & Co. Publishers
  800-227-9120; fax 800-737-3322
Harry N. Abrams
  800-345-1359
  www.abramsbooks.com
Absey & Co.
  888-412-2739
Acada Books
  888-242-6657
  www.acadabooks.com
Academic International Press
  www.ai-press.com
Academic Press
  800-321-5068
  www.academicpress.com
Academy Chicago Publishers
  800-248-7323
  www.academychicago.com
Academy of Producer Insurance Studies
  800-526-2777; fax 800-828-8454
  www.scic.com

Accent Publications
    800-708-5550; fax 800-430-0726
Acres USA
    800-355-5313
    www.acresusa.com
Acropolis Books
    800-773-9923
    www.acropolisbooks.com
ACS Publications
    800-888-9983
ACTA Publications
    800-397-2282; fax 800-397-0079
Action Publishing LLC
    800-705-7482
    www.actionpublishing.com
ACU Press
    800-444-4228
    www.acu.edu/campusoffices/acupress
Adams Media Corp.
    800-872-5627; fax 800-827-5628
    www.adamsmedia.com
Adams-Blake Publishing
    www.adams-blake.com
ADC The Map People
    www.adcmap.com
ADDAX Publishing Group
    800-598-5550
Addicus Books
    800-352-2873
    www.addicusbooks.com
Addison Wesley Higher Education Group
    www.awl.com
Adenine Press
    adeninepress.com
Adirondack Mountain Club
    800-395-8080
    www.adk.org
ADP Hollander
    800-825-0644
    www.hollander-auto-parts.com
Advance Publishing
    www.advancepublishing.com
Advantage Publishers Group
    800-284-3580; fax 800-499-3822
    www.advantagebooksonline.com
Adventure House
    www.adventurehouse.com
Adventure Publications
    800-678-7006
Adventures Unlimited Press
    www.adventuresunlimitedpress.com

Aegean Park Press
    800-736-3587
    www.aegeanparkpress.com
Aegis Publishing Group
    800-828-6961
    www.aegisbooks.com
AEI Press
    800-937-5557
    www.aei.org
Aerial Photography Services
    800-204-4910
    www.aps-1.com
Africa World Press
    800-789-1898
    africanworld.com
African American Images
    800-552-1991
    africanamericanimages.com
Agathon Press
    800-488-8040
    www.agathonpress.com
AIMS Education Foundation
    888-733-2467
    www.aimsedu.org/
Airmont Publishing Co.
    800-223-5251
AK Press Distribution
    www.akpress.org
Alaska Geographic Society
    888-255-6697
    www.akgeo.com
Alaska Native Language Center
    www.uaf.edu/anlc/
Alba House
    800-343-2522
    www.albahouse.org
Alban Institute
    800-486-1318
    www.alban.org
Alef Design Group
    800-845-0662
    www.alefdesign.com
Algonquin Books of Chapel Hill
    www.algonquin.com
Algora Publishing
    888-405-0689
    www.algora.com
ALI-ABA Committee on Continuing
    Professional Education
    800-CLE-NEWS
    www.ali-aba.org

Alicejamesbooks
www.umf.maine.edu/~ajb
All About Kids Publishing
www.aakp.com
Allied Health Publications
800-221-7374
Allworth Press
800-491-2808
www.allworth.com
Allyn & Bacon
www.ablongman.com
ALPHA Publications of America
800-528-3494; fax 800-770-4329
www.alphapublications.com
Alpine Publications
800-777-7257
www.alpinepub.com
AltaMira Press
www.altamirapress.com
Altitude Publishing Canada Ltd.
800-957-6888; fax 800-957-1477
Alyson Publications
www.alyson.com
AMACOM Books
800-250-5308
www.amacombooks.org
Frank Amato Publications
800-541-9498
www.amatobooks.com
Ambassador Books
800-577-0909
www.ambassadorbooks.com
Amboy Associates
800-448-4023
www.oshastuff.com
America West Publishers
800-729-4131; 877-726-2632
American Academy of Environmental
Engineers
www.aaee.net
American Academy of Orthopaedic Surgeons
800-626-6726
www.aaos.org
American Academy of Pediatrics
888-227-1770
www.aap.org
American Anthropological Association
www.aaanet.org
American Antiquarian Society
www.americanantiquarian.org

American Association for Vocational
Instructional Materials
800-228-4689
www.aavim.com
American Association of Blood Banks
www.aabb.org
American Association of Cereal Chemists
800-328-7560
www.scisoc.org/aacc
American Association of Colleges for
Teacher Education
www.aacte.org
American Association of Collegiate
Registrars & Admissions Officers
www.aacrao.org
American Association of Community
Colleges
800-250-6557
www.aacc.nche.edu
American Atheist Press
www.atheists.org
American Bankers Association
800-BANKERS
www.aba.com
American Bar Association
800-285-2221
www.abanet.org/abapubs
American Bible Society
800-322-4253
www.americanbible.org
American Catholic Press
www.acpress.org
American Chemical Society
800-227-5558
www.acs.org
American College
www.amercoll.edu
American College of Physician Executives
800-562-8088
www.acpe.org
American College of Surgeons
www.facs.org
American Correctional Association
800-222-5646
www.corrections.com/aca
American Council on Education
800-279-6799
www.acenet.edu
American Counseling Association
800-422-2648; fax 800-473-2329
www.counseling.org

American Diabetes Association
800-232-6733
www.diabetes.org

American Dietetic Association
www.eatright.org

American Eagle Publications
800-719-4957
www.ameaglepubs.com

American Federation of Arts
800-232-0270
www.afaweb.org

American Federation of Astrologers
888-301-7630
www.astrologers.com

American Fisheries Society
www.fisheries.org

American Foundation for the Blind (AFB
Press)
800-232-3044
www.afb.org

American Geological Institute
www.agiweb.org

American Geophysical Union
800-966-2481
www.agu.org

American Guidance Service
800-328-2560; fax 800-471-8457
www.agsnet.com

American Health Publishing Co.
800-736-7323
www.thelifestylecompany.com

American Historical Press
800-550-5750
www.theaha.org

American Indian Studies Center Publications
at UCLA
www.sscnet.ucla.edu/esp/aisc/index.html

American Industrial Hygiene Association
www.aiha.org

American Institute for CPCU & Insurance
Institute of America
800-644-2101
www.aicpcu.org

American Institute of Aeronautics &
Astronautics
800-639-2422
www.aiaa.org

American Institute of Certified Public
Accountants
888-777-7077
www.aicpa.org

American Institute of Chemical Engineers
800-242-4363
www.aiche.org/

American Institute of Ultrasound in Medicine
www.aium.org

American Judicature Society
www.ajs.org

American Law Institute
800-253-6397
www.ali.org

American Map Corp.
800-432-MAPS

American Marketing Association
800-262-1150
www.ama.org

American Mathematical Society
800-321-4267
www.ams.org

American Medical Association
800-621-8335
www.ama-assn.org

American Numismatic Society
www.amnumsoc.org

American Nurses Publishing
800-637-0323
www.nursesbooks.org

American Occupational Therapy Association
www.aota.org

American Philosophical Society
www.amphilsoc.org

American Phytopathological Society
800-328-7560
www.apsnet.org

American Printing House for the Blind
800-223-1839

American Psychiatric Publishing
800-368-5777
www.psych.org

American Psychological Association
800-374-2721
www.apa.org/books

American Public Works Association
www.apwa.net

American Quilter's Society
800-626-5420
www.aqsquilt.com

American Showcase
800-894-7469
showcase.com

American Society for Nondestructive Testing
800-222-2768
www.asnt.org

American Society for Photogrammetry &
Remote Sensing
www.asprs.org

American Society for Quality Press
800-248-1946
qualitypress.asq.org

American Society for Testing & Materials
www.astm.org

American Society for Training &
Development
800-628-2783
www.astd.org

American Society of Agricultural Engineers
www.asae.org

American Society of Agronomy
www.agronomy.org

American Society of Civil Engineers
800-548-2723
www.asce.org

American Society of Health-System
Pharmacists
www.ashp.org

American Society of Mechanical Engineers
800-843-2763
www.asme.org

American Society of Plant Taxonomists
www.sysbot.org

American Technical Publishers
800-323-3471
www.go2atp.com

American Water Works Association
www.awwa.org

Amherst Media
www.amherstmedia.com

Amirah Publishing
800-337-4287

Amsco School Publications
800-969-8398
www.amscopub.com

Anacus Press
www.anacus.com

Analytic Press
800-926-6579
www.analyticpress.com

Ancestry Publishing
800-262-3787
www.ancestry.com

Anchor Publishing, Maryland
www.antion.com

Anchorage Press Plays
applays.com

Anderson Publishing Co.
800-582-7295
www.andersonpublishing.com

Andmar Press
www.andmar.com

Andrews McMeel Publishing
www.uexpress.com

Andrews University Press
800-467-6369
www.andrewsuniversitypress.com

Angelus Press
800-966-7337; 888-855-9022
www.angeluspress.org

Anglican Book Centre
800-268-1168 (Canada only)
www.anglicanbookcentre.com

Anhinga Press
www.anhinga.org

Anker Publishing Co.
www.ankerpub.com

Ann Arbor Press
800-487-2323
www.sleepingbearpress.com

Annabooks
800-462-1042
www.annabooks.com

Anness Publishing
800-354-9657

Annual Reviews
800-523-8635
www.annualreviews.org

ANR Publications University of California
800-994-8849
anrcatalog.ucdavis.edu

Anthroposophic Press
800-856-8664; fax 800-277-9747
www.anthropress.org

Anti-Aging Press
800-SO-YOUNG

Antique Collectors Club Ltd.
800-252-5231
www.antiquecc.com

Antique Trader Books
888-457-2873
www.krause.com

AOCS Press
800-336-AOCS
www.aocs.org

AOL Time Warner Book Group
www.twbookmark.com

APDG
  800-227-9681
  www.apdg-Inc.com
Aperture
  800-929-2323
  www.aperture.org
Apex Press
  800-316-2739
  www.cipa-apex.org
APPA: The Association of Higher Education
  Facilities Officers
  www.appa.org
Appalachian Mountain Club Books
  www.outdoors.org
Appalachian Trail Conference
  888-287-8673
  www.atctrailstore.org
Applause Theatre & Cinema Books
  800-524-4425
  www.applausebooks.com
Applewood Books
  www.awb.com
Appraisal Institute
  www.appraisalinstitute.org
APS Press
  800-328-7560
  www.aps.org/press
Aqua Quest Publications
  800-933-8989
  www.aquaquest.com
Aquila Communications
  800-667-7071
  www.aquilacommunications.com
Arcade Publishing
  www.arcadepub.com
Arcadia Publishing
  888-313-2665
  www.arcadiapublishing.com
ARE Press
  888-273-3400
  www.edgarcayce.org
Ariadne Press
  ariadnepress.com
Ariel Press
  800-336-7769
Arkansas Research
  www.arkansasresearch.com
Arkham House Publishers
  www.arkhamhouse.com
Armenian Reference Books Co.
  877-504-2550
  www.vassiliansdepot.com

Arnold Publishing Ltd.
  800-563-2665
  www.arnold.ca/
Jason Aronson
  800-782-0015
  www.aronson.com
Arrow Map
  800-343-7500
  www.arrowmap.com
Arsenal Pulp Press Book Publishers
  888-600-PULP
  www.arsenalpulp.com
Art Image Publications
  800-361-2598; fax 800-559-2598
  www.artimagepublications.com
Art Institute of Chicago
  www.artic.edu/aic
Artabras
  800-ART-BOOK
  www.abbeville.com
Arte Publico Press
  800-633-2783
  www.arte.uh.edu
Artech House
  800-225-9977
  www.artechhouse.com
Artisan
  artisanbooks.com
ASCP Press
  800-621-4142
  www.ascp.org
Ashgate Publishing Co.
  www.ashgate.com
Aslan Publishing
  800-786-5427
  www.aslanpublishing.com
ASM International
  800-336-5152
  www.asminternational.org
ASM Press
  800-546-2416
  www.asmpress.org
Aspen Publishers
  800-638-8437
  www.aspenpublishers.com/
Association for Computing Machinery
  800-342-6626
  www.acm.org
Association for Supervision & Curriculum
  Development
  800-933-2723
  www.ascd.org

Association of College & Research Libraries
800-545-2433 ext. 2515
www.ala.org/acrl.html
Association of Research Libraries
www.arl.org
Association of School Business Officials
International
www.asbointl.org
Astragal Press
astragalpress.com
Astronomical Society of the Pacific
800-335-2624
ATL Press
800-835-7543
www.atlpress.com
Atlantic Publishing
800-555-4037
www.atlntc.com
Atwood Publishing
888-242-7101
www.atwoodpublishing.com
Audio Renaissance Tapes
800-452-5589
Augsburg Fortress Publishers
800-426-0115; fax 800-722-7766
augsburgfortress.org
August House Publishers
800-284-8784; fax 800-284-8784
www.augusthouse.com
Augustinian Press
800-871-9404
www.augustinian.org
Authorlink Press
www.authorlink.com
Authors Cooperative
www.authorscooperative.com
Autonomedia
www.autonomedia.org
Ava Launch
www.avalaunch.com
Avalon Publishing Group
800-788-3123
www.avalonpub.com
Ave Maria Press
800-282-1865; fax 800-282-5681
www.avemariapress.com
Avery Color Studios
800-722-9925
www.penguinputnam.com
AVKO Educational Research Foundation
www.avko.org

Avon Books
www.harpercollins.com
Avotaynu
800-286-8296
www.avotaynu.com
An Awakening Publishing Co.
800-308-4372; 888-522-9253
www.hzharris.com
Awe-Struck E-Books
www.awe-struck.net
Ayer Co.
www.scry.com/ayer
Aztex Corp.
www.aztexcorp.com

B N I Publications
800-873-6397
Backbeat Books
www.books.uemedia.com
Baen Publishing Enterprises
baen.com
Baker Books
800-877-2665; fax 800-398-3110
www.bakerbooks.com
Baker's Plays
www.bakersplays.com
Ball Publishing
www.ballpublishing.com
Ball-Stick-Bird Publications
www.ballstickbird.com
Ballantine Books
800-200-3552; fax 800-200-3552
www.randomhouse.com
The Baltimore Sun
800-829-8000 ext. 6800
www.sunspot.net
Bandanna Books
www.bandannabooks.com
The Banner of Truth
800-263-8085
www.banneroftruth.co.uk
Bantam Doubleday Dell
800-223-6834
Baptist Spanish Publishing House (d/b/a
Casa Bautista de Publicaciones)
800-755-5958
www.casabautista.org
Barbour Publishing
www.barbourbooks.com
Barefoot Books
www.barefootbooks.com

Barnes & Noble Books (Imports & Reprints)
800-462-6420
Barricade Books
800-592-6657
www.barricadebooks.com
Barron's Educational Series
800-645-3476
www.barronseduc.com
Bartleby Press
www.bartlebythepublisher.com
Basic Books
800-242-7737
www.basicbooks.com
Battelle Press
800-451-3543
www.battelle.org/bookstore
Battery Press
www.batterypress.com
Bay Books & Tapes
800-557-9463
www.baybooks.com
Baylor University Press
www.baylor.edu
Baywood Publishing Co.
800-638-7819
www.baywood.com
Be Puzzled
800-347-4818
www.areyougame.com
Beacham Publishing Corp.
800-466-9644
www.beachampublishing.com
Beacon Hill Press of Kansas City
800-877-0700
www.bhillkc.com
Beacon Press
www.beacon.org
Bear & Co.
800-932-3277
innertraditions.com
Groupe Beauchemin, Editeur Ltée
800-361-2598
Beautiful America Publishing
www.beautifulamericapub.com
Bedford/St Martin's
www.bedfordstmartins.com
Beekman Publishers
888-BEEKMAN
www.beekman.net
Thomas T. Beeler Publisher
800-818-7574
www.beelerpub.com

Begell House
www.begellhouse.com
Behrman House
www.behrmanhouse.com
Bell Springs Publishing
800-515-8050
bellsprings.com
Bellerophon Books
800-253-9943
www.bellerophonbooks.com
The Benefactory
800-729-7251
John Benjamins Publishing Co.
800-562-5666
www.benjamins.com
Bentley Publishers
800-423-4595
www.bentleypublishers.org
Bereshith Publishing
www.bereshith.com
R. J. Berg & Co.
800-638-3909
Berghahn Books
www.berghahnbooks.com
Berkeley Hills Books
888-848-7303
www.berkeleyhills.com
Berkeley Slavic Specialties
www.berkeley-slavic.com
Berkley Books
www.penguinputnam.com
Berkley Publishing Group
www.penguinputnam.com
Berkshire House Publishers
800-321-8526
www.berkshirehouse.com
Bernan
800-865-3457; fax 800-865-3450
www.bernan.com
Berrett-Koehler Publishers
www.bkconnection.com
Bess Press
800-910-2377
www.besspress.com
A. M. Best Co.
www.ambest.com
Best Publishing Co.
800-468-1055
www.diveweb.com/best
Bethany House Publishers
800-328-6109
www.bethanyhouse.com

Bethlehem Books
800-757-6831
www.bethlehembooks.com
Betterway Books
800-666-0963; 888-590-4082
Between the Lines
800-718-7201
www.btlbooks.com
Beyond Words Publishing
800-284-9673
www.beyondword.com
Bhaktivedanta Book Publishing
800-927-4152
Biblical Archaeology Society
800-221-4644
www.bib-arch.org
Biblo & Tannen Booksellers & Publishers
800-272-8778; fax 800-272-8778
Bick Publishing House
www.bickpubhouse.com
Binford & Mort Publishing
888-221-4514
Biomed
www.biomedbooks.com
BioTechniques Books
800-655-8285
www.biotechniques.com
Birch Brook Press
www.birchbrookpress.com
Birkhauser Boston
800-777-4643
www.birkhauser.com
George T. Bisel
800-247-3526
www.bisel.com
Bisk Publishing Co.
800-874-7877; fax 800-345-8273
www.bisk.com
Black Classic Press
www.blackclassic.com
Black Diamond Book Publishing
800-962-7622; fax 800-962-7622
Black Heron Press
www.blackheronpress.com
Black Rose Books
800-565-9523; fax 800-221-9985
www.web.net/blackrosebooks
Blackbirch Press
800-831-9183
www.blackbirch.com
Blacksmith Corp.
800-531-2665

Blackwell Publishers
www.blackwellpub.com
Blackwell Science
www.blackwellscience.com
John F. Blair Publisher
800-222-9796
www.blairpub.com
Blizzard Publishing
800-694-9256
www.blizzard.mb.ca/catalog
Bloomberg Press
800-388-2749 ext. 4670
www.bloomberg.com/books
Blue Book Publications
800-877-4867
www.bluebookinc.com
Blue Dolphin Publishing
800-643-0765
www.bluedolphinpublishing.com
Blue Dove Press
800-691-1008
www.bluedove.org
Blue Heron Publishing
www.teleport.com/~bhp
Blue Note Publications
800-624-0401
www.bluenotebooks.com
Blue Poppy Press
800-487-9296
www.bluepoppy.com
Bluestar Communication Corp.
800-625-8378
www.bluestar.com
Bluestocking Press
800-959-8586
www.bluestockingpress.com
Blushing Rose Publishing
800-898-2263
www.blushingrose.com
BNA Books
800-960-1220
www.bnabooks.com
Bobley Harmann Corp.
www.bobley.com
Bolchazy-Carducci Publishers
www.bolchazy.com
Bonus Books
800-225-3775
www.bonus-books.com
Book Beat Ltd.
www.thebookbeat.com

Book Network International
www.capstone.co.uk
Book Peddlers
800-255-3379
www.bookpeddlers.com
Book Publishing Co.
888-260-8458
www.bookpubco.com
Book Sales
www.booksalesusa.com
Book World/Blue Star Productions
888-472-2665
www.bluestarproductions.net
BookPartners
800-895-7323
www.bookpartners.com
Books in Motion
800-752-3199
www.booksinmotion.com
booktech.com
800-750-6229
www.booktech.com
Borealis Press Ltd.
877-829-9989
www.borealispress.com
Boson Books
www.cmonline.com/boson
Boston America Corp.
www.bostonamerica.com
Bottom Dog Press
members.aol.com/lsmithdog/bottomdog
Thomas Bouregy & Co.
800-223-5251
Eddie Bowers Publishing
800-747-2411
R. R. Bowker
888-269-5372
www.bowker.com
Boydell & Brewer
www.boydell.co.uk
Boyds Mills Press
877-512-8366
www.boydsmillspress.com
Boynton/Cook Publishers
800-541-2086
www.boyntoncook.com
Boys Town Press
800-282-6657
www.girlsandboystown.org/btpress
William K. Bradford Publishing
800-421-2009
www.wkbradford.com

BradyGAMES Publishing
800-545-5912; 800-571-5840
www.bradygames.com
Allen D. Bragdon Publishers
877-8-SMARTS
Branden Publishing Co.
800-537-7335
www.branden.com
Brandywine Press
800-345-1776
www.brandywinepress.com
Brassey's
800-775-2518
www.brasseysinc.com
Breakaway Books
800-548-4348
www.breakawaybooks.com
Breakthrough Publications
800-824-5000
www.booksonhorses.com
Breakwater Books Ltd.
800-563-3333
www.breakwater.nf.net
Nicholas Brealey Publishing
888-BREALEY
www.nbrealey-books.com
Brenner Information Group
800-811-4337
www.brennerbooks.com
Brentwood Publishers Group
800-334-8861
www.brentwoodbooks.com
Brethren Press
800-323-8039
www.brethrenpress.com
Brewers Publications
888-822-6273
www.beertown.org/BP/bp.htm
Bridge Learning Systems
800-487-9868
www.blsinc.com
Bridge-Logos Publishers
800-631-5802; fax 800-93-LOGOS
www.bridgepub.com
Bridge Publications
800-722-1733
www.bridgelogos.com
Briefings Publishing Group
800-888-2086
www.briefings.com
Brighton Publications
800-536-2665

Brightwater Publishing Company/StrataGem
Press
800-247-6553
www.BrightwaterPublishing.com
Brill Academic Publishers
800-962-4406
www.brill.nl
Bristol Publishing Enterprises
800-346-4889
www.bristolcookbooks.com
Britannica
800-323-1227
www.britannica.com
Broadman & Holman Publishers
www.broadmanholman.com
Broadway Press
800-869-6372
www.broadwaypress.com
Brooding Heron Press
www.califiabooks.com/finepress/b/blueher
on.html
Paul H. Brookes Publishing Co.
800-638-3775
www.brookespublishing.com
Brookings Institution Press
800-275-1447
www.brookings.edu
Brookline Books
800-666-2665
www.brooklinebooks.com
Brooklyn Botanic Garden
800-367-9692; fax 800-542-7567
www.bbg.org
BrownTrout Publishers
800-777-7812
www.browntrout.com
Brunner/Routledge
800-634-7064
www.brunner-routledge.com
Brunswick Publishing Corp.
www.brunswickbooks.com
Building News
888-264-2665
www.bnibooks.com
Bulfinch Press
800-759-0190
www.twbookmark.com
Bull Publishing Co.
800-676-2855
www.bullpub.com

Bureau of Business Practice
800-876-9105; 800-243-0876
www.bbpnews.com
Burford Books
www.burfordbooks.com
Burrelle's Information Services
800-631-1160; fax 800-898-6677
www.burrelles.com
Business & Legal Reports
800-727-5257
www.blr.com
Business Research Services
800-845-8420
www.sba8a.com
Business/Technology Books
www.evinfo.com
Doug Butler Enterprises
800-728-3826
Butte Publications
800-330-9791
www.buttepublications.com
Butternut & Blue
www.dealersweb.com
Butterworth-Heinemann
800-366-2665; fax 800-446-6520
www.bh.com
Butterworths Canada Ltd.
800-668-6481; fax 800-461-3275
www.butterworths.ca

C & T Publishing
800-284-1114
www.ctpub.com
CAAS Publications
800-206-CAAS
www.sscnet.ucla.edu/caas
Cadence Jazz Books
www.cadencebuilding.com
Cadmus Editions
www.cadmus-editions.com
Cahners Travel Group
www.cahners.com
California Institute of Public Affairs
www.cipahq.org
Callaway Editions
www.callaway.com
Cambridge Educational
800-468-4227
www.cambridgeeducational.com
Cambridge University Press
800-221-4512
www.cup.org

Cameron & Co.
800-779-5582
Camino Books
www.caminobooks.com
Camino E E & Book Co.
www.camino-books.com
Canada Law Book
800-263-2037
www.canadalawbook.ca
Canadian Bible Society
800-465-2425
www.canbible.ca
Canadian Institute of Chartered Accountants
800-268-3793
www.cica.ca
Canadian Museum of Civilization
800-555-5621
www.civilization.ca
Canon Law Society of America
www.clsa.org
Capital Books
800-758-3756
capital-books.com
Capital Enquiry
www.capenq.com
Capstone Press
800-747-4992; 888-262-0705
www.capstone-press.com
Captain Fiddle Publications
www.tiac.net/users/cfiddle/
Aristide D. Caratzas, Publisher
800-204-2665
www.caratzas.com
Cardweb.com
www.cardweb.com
Career Press
800-CAREER-1
www.careerpress.com
Caribe Betania Editores
800-322-7423; 800-251-4000
www.caribebetania.com
Carnegie Mellon University Press
www.cmu.edu/universitypress
Carolina Academic Press
800-489-7486
www.cap-press.com
Carolrhoda Books
800-328-4929; fax 800-332-1132
www.lernerbooks.com
Carousel Publications Ltd.
www.carousel-music.com

Carson-Dellosa Publishing Co.
www.carsondellosa.com
Carstens Publications
www.cartens-publications.com
Carswell
800-387-5164
www.carswell.com
CarTech
800-551-4754
www.cartechbooks.com
Amon Carter Museum
800-573-1933
www.cartermuseum.org
Cascade Pass
888-837-0704
www.cascadepass.com
Cason Hall & Co. Publishers
800-448-7357
www.casonhall.com
Catbird Press
800-360-2391
www.catbirdpress.com
Catholic News Publishing Co.
800-433-7771
www.graduateguide.com
Cato Institute
800-767-1241
www.cato.org
Cave Books
www.cavebooks.com
Cavendish Books
800-665-3166; fax 800-665-3167
www.cavendishbooks.ca
Caxton Press
800-657-6465
www.caxtonpress.com
CCC Publications
866-LITEUUP
CCH Canadian Ltd.
800-268-4522; fax 800-461-4131
www.cch.ca
CCH
888-224-7377
www.cch.com
CDG Books Canada
877-963-8830
Cedco Publishing Co.
800-227-6162
www.cedco.com
CEF Press
800-748-7710
www.cefonline.com

Celebrity Press
800-327-5113
Celestial Arts
800-841-BOOK
www.tenspeed.com
Center for Self Sufficiency
www.centerforselfsufficiency.com
Center for Chinese Studies (University of
Michigan)
www.umich.edu/~iinet/ccs
Center for Creative Leadership
www.ccl.org/publications
Center for East Asian Studies
www.ac.wwu.edu/~eas/publications.html
Center for Futures Education
800-966-2554
www.thectr.com
Center for Latin American Studies
www.asu.edu/clas/latin
Center for Migration Studies of New York
www.cmsny.org
Center for Strategic & International Studies
www.csis.org
Center for Thanatology Research &
Education
www.thanatology.org
Center for Urban Policy Research
www.policy.rutgers.edu/cupr
Center for Women Policy Studies
www.centerwomenpolicy.org
Centering Corp.
www.centering.org
Centerstream Publishing
www.centerstream-usa.com
Central Conference of American
Rabbis/CCAR Press
800-935-2227
www.ccarnet.org/press/
Central European University Press
www.ceupress.com
Centre Franco-Ontarien de Ressources en
Alphabetisation
888-814-4422
www.centrefora.on.ca
Chain Store Guide
800-927-9292
www.csgis.com
Chalice Press
800-366-3383
www.cbp21.com
Chaosium
www.chaosium.com

Charisma House
800-283-8494
www.charismahouse.com
CharismaLife Publishers
800-451-4598
www.charismalife.com
Charles River Media
800-382-8505
www.charlesriver.com
Charlesbridge Publishing
800-225-3214
www.charlesbridge.com
Charlton Press
800-442-6042; fax 800-442-1542
www.charltonpress.com
Chartwell Books
800-526-7257
www.booksalesusa.com
Chatelaine Press
800-249-9527
www.chatpress.com
Chatsworth Press
800-262-7367; 800-272-7367
Chelsea Green Publishing Co.
800-639-4099
www.chelseagreen.com
Chelsea House Publishers
800-848-BOOK
www.chelseahouse.com
Chelsea Publishing Co.
800-821-4267
www.ams.org
Chemical Education Resources
800-355-9983; fax 800-451-3661
www.cerlabs.com/chemlabs
Chemical Publishing Co.
800-786-3659
www.chemicalpublishing.com
Cheng & Tsui Co.
800-554-1963
www.cheng-tsui.com
Cherokee Publishing Co.
800-653-3952
Cherry Lane Music Co.
www.cherrylane.com
Chess Combination
800-354-4083
chessNIC.com
Chess Digest
800-462-3548
www.chessdigest.com

Chicago Review Press
800-888-4741
Chicago Spectrum Press
800-594-5190
www.evanstonpublishing.com
Child's Play
800-472-0099; fax 800-854-6989
www.childs-play.com
Children's Book Press
www.cbookpress.org
Children's Press
www.grolier.com
Childswork/Childsplay LLC
www.childswork.com
China Books & Periodicals
www.chinabooks.com
Chitra Publications
800-628-8244
www.quilttownusa.com
Chivers North America
800-621-0182
Chosen Books
800-877-2665
www.bakerbooks.com
Christian Literature Crusade
800-659-1240
Christian Publications
800-233-4443; fax 800-865-8799
www.christianpublications.com
Christian Schools International
800-635-8288
www.gospelcom.net/csi
Christopher Publishing House
www.cphbooks.com
Christopher-Gordon Publishers
www.christopher-gordon.com
Chronicle Books LLC
800-722-6657; fax 800-858-7787
www.chroniclebooks.com
Chronicle Guidance Publications
800-622-7284
www.chronicleguidance.com
Church Growth Institute
800-553-4769; fax 800-860-3109
www.churchgrowth.org
Cinco Puntos Press
800-566-9072
www.cincopuntos.com
Circlet Press
www.circlet.com
Cistercian Publications
www.spencerabbey.org/cistpub

City & Company
www.cityandcompany.com
City Lights Books
www.citylights.com
Clarion Books
800-225-3362
Clarity Press
800-729-6423
www.claritypress.com
Clark Publishing
800-845-1916
www.clarkpub.com
Clarkson Potter Publishers
www.randomhouse.com
Clear Light Publishers
800-253-2747
www.clearlightbooks.com
Cleis Press,
800-780-2279
www.cleispress.com
Close Up Publishing
800-765-3131
www.closeup.org
Clovernook Printing House for the Blind
clovernook.org
Clymer Publications
800-262-1954
www.intertec.com
CMP Media
800-848-5594
www.cmpbooks.com
Coaches Choice
888-229-5745
www.coacheschoiceweb.com
Cobblestone Publishing Co.
800-821-0115
www.cobblestonepub.com
Coffee House Press
www.coffeehousepress.org
Cognizant Communication Corp.
cognizantcommunication.com
Cold Spring Harbor Laboratory Press
800-843-4388
www.cshlpress.com
Cole Publishing Group
800-959-2717
Collectors Press
800-423-1848
www.collectorspress.com
College & University Professional
Association for Human Resources
www.cupahr.org

College Press Publishing Co.
800-289-3300
www.collegepress.com
Colonial Williamsburg Foundation
800-HISTORY
www.history.org
Colorado Geological Survey
www.dnr.state.co.us/geosurvey
Colorado Railroad Museum
800-365-6263
crrm.org
Columba Publishing Co.
800-999-7491
www.columbapublishing.com
Columbia Books
888-265-0600
www.columbiabooks.com
Columbia University Press
800-944-8648
www.cc.columbia.edu/cu/cup
Combined Publishing
800-418-6065
www.combinedpublishing.com
Comex Systems
800-543-6959
Common Courage Press
800-497-3207
www.commoncouragepress.com
Commonwealth Business Media
www.cbizmedia.com
Communication Creativity
www.spannet.org/cc/js
The Communication Project
800-772-7765
www.tcpnow.com
Communication Skill Builders
800-228-0752; fax 800-232-1223
www.hbtpc.com
Commuters Library
800-643-0295
Company's Coming Publishing Ltd.
800-875-7108
www.companyscoming.com
Competency Press
800-603-3779
Comprehensive Health Education Foundation
800-323-2433
www.chef.org
Computer Adaptive Technologies
www.catinc.com
Computer Curriculum Corp.
888-CCC4KIDS
www.ccclearn.com

Conari Press
800-685-9595
www.conari.com
Conciliar Press
800-967-7377
www.conciliarpress.com
Concordia Publishing House
800-325-3040
www.cph.org
Congressional Information Service
800-638-8380
www.cispubs.com
Congressional Quarterly Books
800-638-1710
www.cqpress.com
Conroca Publishing
800-521-8110
www.conrocapub.com
Consulting Psychologists Press
800-624-1765
Consumer Press
members.aol.com/bookguest
Consumertronics
www.consumertronics.net
Contemporary Publishing Co,
www.contemporarypublishing.com
Context Books
www.contextbooks.com
Continental Afrikan Publishers
www.freeyellow.com/members3/mike11
Continuing Education Press
800-547-8887 ext. 4891
extended.pdx.edu/press/
Continuing Legal Education Society of
British Columbia
800-663-0437
www.cle.bc.ca
Continuum International Publishing Group
800-561-7704
www.continuumbooks.com
Cook Communications
800-437-4337
www.cookministries.com
Copley Publishing Group
800-562-2147
www.copleycustom.com
Copper Canyon Press
www.coppercanyonpress.org
Copywriter's Council of America
www.lgroup.addr.com/cca.htm
Cormorant Books
800-387-0141; 800-387-0172
www.cormorantbooks.com

Cornell Cooperative Extension
www.cce.cornell.edu/publications/catalog.
html

Cornell Maritime Press
800-638-7641

Cornell University Press
www.cornellpress.cornell.edu

Cornell University Southeast Asia Program
Publications
www.einaudi.cornell.edu/southeastasia

Cortina Learning International
800-245-2145
www.cortinalanguages.com

Corwin Press
800-417-2466
www.corwinpress.com

Coteau Books
800-440-4471 (Canada Only)
www.coteaubooks.com

Cottonwood Press
800-864-4297
www.cottonwoodpress.com

Council for Exceptional Children
888-232-7733
www.cec.sped.org

Council for Indian Education
www.mcn.net/~cieclague

Council for Research in Values & Philosophy
800-659-9962
www.crvp.org

Council Oak Books LLC
800-247-8850
www.counciloakbooks.com

Council of State Governments
800-800-1910
www.csg.org

Council on Foreign Relations Press
www.cfr.org

Council on Social Work Education
www.cswe.org

Counterpoint Press
800-242-7737
www.perseusbooksgroup.com

Countryman Press
800-245-4151
www.countrymanpress.com

Course Technology
800-648-7450
www.course.com

La Courte Echelle
800-387-6192; fax 800-450-0391

Covenant Communications
800-662-9545
www.covenant-lds.com

Cowley Publications
800-225-1534
www.cowley.org/

Coyote Press
www.coyotepress.com

CQ Press
800-638-1710; fax 800-380-3810
www.CQPress.com

Crabtree Publishing Co.
800-387-7650; fax 800-355-7166
www.crabtree-pub.com

Craftsman Book Co.
800-829-8123
www.craftsman-book.com

Crane Hill Publishers
800-841-2682
www.cranehill.com

CRC Press LLC
800-272-7737; fax 800-643-9428
www.crcpress.com

CRC Publications
800-333-8300
www.crcpublications.org

Creating Keepsakes Books
800-815-3538
www.creatingkeepsakes.com

Creative Arts Book Co.
800-848-7789
www.creativeartsbooks.com

Creative Bound
800-287-8610
www.creativebound.com

Creative Co.
800-445-6209

Creative Homeowner
800-631-7795
www.creativehomeowner.com

Creative Publishing International
800-328-0590
www.howtobookstore.com

Creative Works Publishing
888-490-9059
cwp-books.com

Criminal Justice Press
800-914-3379
www.criminaljustice.press.com

Crisp Publications
800-442-7477
www.crisplearning.com

Crop Circle Press
www.cropcirclebooks.com
Cross Cultural Publications
800-273-6526
crossculturalpub.com
Crossing Press
800-777-1048
www.crossingpress.com
Crossquarter Publishing Group
www.crossquarter.com
Crossroad Publishing Co.
800-395-0690; fax 800-338-4550
www.crossroadpublishing.com
Crossway Books
www.crosswaybooks.org
Crown Publishing Group
800-869-2976
www.randomhouse.com
Crystal Clarity Publishers
800-424-1055
www.crystalclarity.com
Crystal Fountain Publications
www.crystalfountain.org
Crystal Productions
800-255-8629
www.crystalproductions.com
Crystal Publishers
www.crystalpub.com
CTB/McGraw-Hill
800-538-9547
www.ctb.com
Cumberland House Publishing
888-439-2665
www.cumberlandhouse.com
Curbstone Press
www.curbstone.org
Current Clinical Strategies Publishing
800-331-8227; fax 800-965-9420
www.ccspublishing.com
Current Medicine
800-427-1796
CyclopsMedia.com
www.cyclopsmedia.com
Cyclotour Guide Books
www.cyclotour.com

Da Capo Press
800-242-7737
Dalkey Archive Press/Review of
Contemporary Fiction
www.dalkeyarchive.com

Dandy Lion Publications
800-776-8032
www.dandylionbooks.com
John Daniel & Co.
800-662-8351
www.danielpublishing.com
Dante University of America Press
www.danteuniversity.org
Dark Horse Comics
800-862-0052
www.darkhorse.com
Dartnell Corp.
800-621-5463
www.dartnellcorp.com
Data Trace Publishing Co.
800-342-0454
www.datatrace.com
Davies Publishing
www.daviespublishing.com
Davies-Black Publishing
800-624-1765
www.cpp-db.com
F. A. Davis Co.
800-523-4049
DAW Books
800-526-0275
www.dawbooks.com
Dawbert Press
800-933-2923
www.dawbert.com
Dawn Horse Press
877-770-0772
www.adidam.com
Dawn Publications
800-545-7475
www.dawnpub.com
Dawn Sign Press
800-549-5350
www.dawnsign.com
DBI Books
888-457-2873
www.krause.com
dbS Productions
800-745-1581
www.dbs-sar.com
DC Comics
800-759-0190
www.dccomics.com
De Vorss & Co.
800-843-5743
www.devorss.com

Dealer's Choice Books
www.dealerschoicebooks.com
Dearborn Financial Publishing
www.dearborn.com
B. C. Decker
800-568-7281
www.bcdecker.com
Ivan R. Dee Publisher
800-462-6420; fax 800-338-4550
www.ivanrdee.com
Marcel Dekker
800-228-1160
www.dekker.com
Delittle Storyteller Co.
www.gdi.net/delittle/
Delmar
800-998-7498
www.delmar.com
Delorme Publishing Co.
www.delorme.com
Delta Systems Co.
800-323-8270; fax 800-909-9901
www.delta-systems.com
Demos Medical Publishing
800-532-8663
demosmedpub.com
Denlinger's Publishers Ltd.
www.thebookden.com
Deseret Book Co.
800-453-3876
www.deseretbook.com
Design Image Group
800-563-5455
www.designimagegroup.com
Destiny Image
800-722-6774
www.reapernet.com
Developmental Studies Center
800-666-7270
www.devstu.org
Dewey Publications
www.deweypub.com
Dharma Publishing
800-873-4276
www.dharmapublishing.com
Diablo Press
800-488-2665
www.diablopress.com
Dial Books for Young Readers
www.penguinputnam.com
Diamond Communications
800-480-3717
www.diamondbooks.com

Diamond Farm Book Publishers
800-481-1353; fax 800-305-5138
www.diamondfarm.com
DIANE Publishing Co.
800-782-3833
www.dianepublishingcentral.com
Marcel Didier
800-361-1664
www.hurtubisehmh.com
Dine College Press
www.crystal.ncc.cc.nm.us
Discipleship Publications International
888-DPI-Book
www.dpibooks.org
Discover Guides
www.readersndex.com
Discovery Enterprises Ltd.
800-729-1720
Discovery House Publishers
800-653-8333
www.gospelcom.net/rbc/dhp
Disney Press
www.disneybooks.com
Disney Publishing Worldwide
www.disneybooks.com
Dissertation.com
800-636-8329
www.dissertation.com
Do It Now Foundation
www.doitnow.org
Dog-Eared Publications
888-364-3277
www.dog-eared.com
Dogwood Press
dogwoodpress.myriad.net
Dominie Press
800-232-4570
www.dominie.com
Donning Co. Publishers
800-296-8572
www.donning.com
Doral Publishing
800-633-5385
www.doralpub.com
Dorchester Publishing Co.
800-481-9191
www.dorchesterpub.com
Dorland Healthcare Information
800-784-2332
www.dorlandhealth.com
Dorling Kindersley
877-342-5357
usstore.dk.com

Dorset House Publishing Co.
800-DHBOOKS
www.dorsethouse.com
Doubleday Broadway Publishing Group
800-223-6834
Doubleday Canada
800-668-4247
www.randomhouse.ca
Dover Publications
800-223-3130
www.doverpublications.com
Down East Enterprise
800-766-1670
www.downeastbooks.com
Dramatic Publishing Co.
800-448-7469; fax 800-344-5302
www.dramaticpublishing.com
Dufour Editions
800-869-5677
www.dufoureditions.com
Duke University Press
888-651-0124
www.dukepress.edu
Dumbarton Oaks
www.doaks.org
Dun & Bradstreet
www.dnb.com
Dunhill Publishing
www.dunhillpublishing.net
Dunwoody Press
www.dunwoodypress.com
Duquesne University Press
800-666-2211
www.dupress.duq.edu
Dustbooks
800-477-6110
www.dustbooks.com
Dutton
www.penguinputnam.com

Eagan Press
800-328-7560
www.scisoc.org/aacc/bookstore
Eakin Press
800-880-8642
www.eakinpress.com
East View Publications
800-477-1005
www.eastview.com
Eastland Press
800-453-3278; fax 800-241-3329
www.eastlandpress.com

Eckankar
800-327-5113
www.eckankar.org
ECS Publishing
800-777-1919
www.ecspub.com
EDC Publishing
800-475-4522; fax 800-747-4509
www.edcpub.com
Nellie Edge Resources
800-523-4594
www.nellieedge.com
EDGE Science Fiction & Fantasy Publishing
877-254-0115
www.edgewebsite.com
Editions Yvon Blais
800-363-3047
www.editionyvonblais.com
Editions du Phare
800-561-2371 (Canada)
Editions du Renouveau Pedagogique
800-263-3678; fax 800-643-4720
Editions Etudes Vivantes
800-267-8387
www.educalivres.com
Editions Fides
800-363-1451
Editions Griffon d'Argile
800-268-6898 (Canada only)
griffondargile.com
Editions Hurtubise HMH Ltée
800-361-1664
Editions Marie-France
800-563-6644
www.marie-france.qc.ca
Editions Phidal
800-738-7349
www.phidal.com
Editions Anne Sigier
800-463-6846 (Canada only)
www.annesigier.qc.ca
Editorial Bautista Independiente
800-398-7187
www.ebi-bmm.org
Editorial Portavoz
800-733-2607
www.kregel.com
Editorial Unilit
800-767-7726
www.editorialunilit.com
Educational Directories
800-357-6183

Educational Impressions
800-451-7450
www.edimpressions.com
Educational Insights
800-933-3277
www.edin.com
Educational Ministries
800-221-0910
www.educationalministries.com
Educational Technology Publications
800-952-2665
www.bookstoread.com/etp
Educators Progress Service
888-951-4469
www.epsbooks.com
Educators Publishing Service
800-225-5750
Edupress
800-835-7978
Wm. B. Eerdmans Publishing
800-253-7521
Elan Press
800-805-1083
www.elanpress.com/home.html
Edward Elgar Publishing
800-390-3149
www.e-elgar.com
Elsevier Science
www.elsevier.com
EMC/Paradigm Publishing
800-328-1452; fax 800-328-4564
Emerald Books
800-922-2143
www.ywampublishing.com
Emond Montgomery Publications Ltd.
888-837-0815
www.emp.on.ca
Encyclopaedia Britannica
800-323-1229
www.eb.com
Engineering Information
800-221-1044
www.ei.org
Enslow Publishers
800-398-2504
www.enslow.com
ERIC Clearinghouse on Reading,
English & Communication
800-759-4723
Lawrence Erlbaum Associates
800-9-BOOKS-9

eSchool News
800-394-0115
www.eschoolnews.com
ETC Publications
800-382-7869
Evan-Moor Educational Publishers
800-777-4362
www.evan-moor.com
Evangel Publishing House
800-253-9315
www.evangelpublishing.com
Evanston Publishing
888-BOOK-S80
www.evanstonpublishing.com
Everyday Learning Corp.
800-382-7670
www.everydaylearning.com
Evolutionary Products
800-777-4751
www.evolutionaryproducts.com
Exley Giftbooks
800-423-9539; fax 800-453-5248
Explorers Guide Publishing
800-487-6029
www.explorers-guide.com

F C & A Publishing
800-226-8024
www.fca.com
F J H Music Co.
800-262-8744
Faber & Faber
888-330-8477
Factor Press
800-304-0077
Facts on File
800-322-8755; fax 800-678-3633
www.factsonfile.com
Fairchild Books
800-932-4724
www.fairchildbooks.com
Fairview Press
800-544-8207
www.press.fairview.org
Fairwinds Press
877-913-0645
Faith & Fellowship Press
800-332-9232
www.clba.org
Faith & Life Press
800-743-2484
www2.southwind.net/~gcmc/flp

Faith Library Publications
888-258-0999
www.rhema.org
Falcon
800-582-2665
www.falcon.com
Fantagraphics Books
800-657-1100
www.fantagraphics.com
W. D. Farmer Residence Designer
800-225-7526
www.wdfarmerplans.com
FC&A Publishing
800-537-1275
Philipp Feldheim
800-237-7149
www.feldheim.com
Frederick Fell Publishers
800-771-FELL
www.fellpub.com
Fenn Publishing Co. Ltd.
800-267-3366 (Canada only); fax 800-465-3422 (Canada only)
www.hbfenn.com
Ferguson Publishing Co.
800-306-9941; fax 800-306-9942
www.fergpubco.com
Fifth House Publishers
800-387-9776; fax 800-260-9777
Filter Press LLC
888-570-2663
filterpressbooks.com
Financial Executives Research Foundation
800-680-FERF
www.fei.org/rf/default.cfm
Financial Times/Prentice Hall
800-445-1360; fax 800-445-6991
www.phptr.com
Fire Engineering Books & Videos
800-752-9764
www.pennwell-store.com
Firebird Publications
800-852-6546
Firefly Books Ltd.
800-387-5085; fax 800-565-6034
www.fireflybooks.com
First Avenue Editions
800-328-4929; fax 800-332-1132
www.lernerbooks.com
Fisherman Library
800-553-4745

Fitzhenry & Whiteside Ltd.
800-387-9776; fax 800-260-9777
www.fitzhenry.ca
Fitzroy Dearborn Publishers
800-850-8102
www.fitzroydearborn.com
Flower Valley Press
800-735-5197
www.flowervalleypress.com
Focus on the Family
800-232-6459
www.family.org
Focus Publishing/R. Pullins Co.
800-848-7236
www.pullins.com
Fodor's Travel Publications
800-733-3000
www.fodors.com
Fondo de Cultura Economica USA
800-532-3872
www.fceusa.com
Fordham University Press
800-247-6553
Forest House Publishing/HTS Books
800-394-READ
Forest of Peace Publishing
800-659-3227
www.forestofpeace.com
Formac Publishing Ltd.
800-565-1975
Forward Movement Publications
800-543-1813
www.forwardmovement.org
Walter Foster Publishing
800-426-0099
www.walterfoster.com
Foundation Center
800-424-9836
www.fdncenter.org
Foundation for Economic Education
800-452-3518
www.fee.org
Foundation Publications
800-257-6272
www.foundationpublications.com
Franciscan University Press
800-333-0381
www.franuniv.edu
Fraser Institute
800-665-3558
www.fraserinstitute.ca

Fraser Publishing Co.
877-996-3336
www.fraserbooks.com
Free Press
800-223-2345
Free Spirit Publishing
800-735-7323
www.freespirit.com
Friends United Press
800-537-8839
www.fum.org
Frog Ltd.
800-337-2665
www.northatlanticbooks.com
Front Row Experience
800-524-9091; fax 800-524-9091
www.frontrowexperience.com
Fulcrum Publishing
800-992-2908; fax 800-726-7112
www.fulcrum-books.com
Futura Publishing Co.
800-877-8761
www.futuraco.com
Future Horizons
800-489-0727
www.futurehorizons-autism.com

G W Medical Publishing
800-600-0330
www.gwmedical.com
Gage Educational Publishing
800-667-1115
www.gagelearning.com
P. Gaines Co.
800-578-3853
Gale Group
800-877-4253; fax 800-414-5043
www.galegroup.com
Gallaudet University Press
gupress.gallaudet.edu
Gallopade International
800-536-2GET; fax 800-871-2979
www.gallopade.com
Garamond Press Ltd.
800-898-9535
www.garamond.ca
Garland Publishing
www.garlandpub.com
Gareth Stevens
800-341-3569
Garrett Educational Corp.
800-654-9366

Garrett Publishing
800-333-2069
www.garrettpub.com
Gateways Books & Tapes
800-869-0658
www.gatewaysbooksandtapes.com
Graphic Arts Technical Foundation
800-910-4283
www.gatf.org
Gayot/Gault Millau
800-LE BEST 1
www.gayot.com
Gefen Books
800-477-5257
www.israelbooks.com
GEM Publications
800-290-6128
www.spacestar.com/users/gem
GemStone Press
800-962-4544
www.gemstonepress.com
Genealogical Publishing Co.
800-296-6687
www.genealogical.com
General Publishing
800-805-1083
www.genpub.com
General Store Publishing House
800-465-6072
www.gsph.com
Genesis Press
888-463-4461
www.genesis-press.com
Geological Society of America
800-472-1988
www.geosociety.org
Georgetown University Press
800-246-9606
www.georgetown.edu/publications/gup/
GIA Publications
800-442-1358
Gifted Psychology Press
877-954-4200
www.giftedpsychologypress.com
Glenbridge Publishing Ltd.
800-986-4135
www.glenbridgepublishing.com
Glencoe/McGraw-Hill
800-848-1567
www.glencoe.com
Peter Glenn Publications
888-332-6700
www.pgdirect.com

Globe Pequot Press
800-243-0495; fax 800-820-2329
www.globe-pequot.com
Golden Books Publishing Co.
800-558-3291
www.goldenbooks.com
Golden Educational Center
800-800-1791
goldened.com
Golden West Publishers
800-658-5830
Good Books
800-762-7171
www.goodbks.com
Goodheart-Willcox Publisher
800-323-0440
www.goodheartwillcox.com
Goosefoot Acres Press
800-697-4858
www.edibleweeds.bigstep.com
Christopher-Gordon Publishers
800-934-8322
Gospel Publishing House
800-641-4310
Gould Publications
800-717-7917
www.gouldlaw.com
Government Research Service
800-346-6898
Grafco Productions
888-656-1500
www.jackwboone.com
Donald M. Grant Publisher
800-476-0510
www.grantbooks.com
Grapevine Publications
800-338-4331
www.read-gpi.com
Graphic Arts Center Publishing
800-452-3032; fax 800-355-9685
www.gacpc.com
Graphic Arts Publishing
800-724-9476
Graphic Learning
800-874-0029; fax 800-737-3322
Graywolf Press
800-283-3572
www.graywolfpress.org
Great Quotations
800-354-4889
Warren H. Green
800-537-0655
www.whgreen.com

Greenhaven Press
800-877-GALE; fax 800-414-5043
www.greenhaven.com
Greenleaf Book Group LLC
800-932-5420
Greenwillow Books
800-242-7737; fax 800-822-4090
Greenwood Publishing Group
800-225-5800
www.greenwood.com
Grey House Publishing
800-562-2139
www.greyhouse.com
Greycliff Publishing Co.
800-874-4171
www.greycliff.com
Grolier
800-563-3231
www.grolier.com/
Group Publishing
800-447-1070
www.grouppublishing.com
Grove/Atlantic
800-521-0178
Grove's Dictionaries
800-221-2123
www.grovereference.com
Gryphon Editions
800-633-8911
www.gryphoneditions.com
Gryphon House
800-638-0928
www.gryphonhouse.com
Guerin Editeur Ltée
800-398-8337
www.guerin.qc.ca
Guernica Editions
800-565-9523; fax 800-221-9985
www.guernicaeditions.com
Guild Press of Indiana
800-913-9563
www.guildpress.com
Guild Publishing
800-930-1856
www.guild.com
Guilford Press
800-365-7006
www.guilford.com

H D I Publishers
800-321-7037
www.hdipub.com

Hachai Publications
  800-50-HACHAI
  www.hachai.com
Hackett Publishing Co.
  800-783-9213
  www.hackettpublishing.com
Hagstrom Map Co.
  800-432-MAPS
Hambleton Hill Publishing
  800-327-5113
  www.apgbooks.com
Alexander Hamilton Institute
  800-879-2441
  www.ahipubs.com
Hammond World Atlas Corp.
  800-526-4953
  www.hammondmap.com
Hampton-Brown Co.
  800-933-3510
Hampton Press
  800-894-8955
  www.hamptonpress.com
Hampton Roads Publishing Co.
  800-766-8009; fax 800-766-9042
  www.hrpub.com
Hancock House Publishers
  800-938-1114; fax 800-983-2262
  www.hancockhouse.com
Hanley & Belfus
  800-962-1892
  www.hanleyandbelfus.com
Hanley-Wood LLC
  800-837-0870
  www.hwbookstore.com
Hanser Gardner Publications
  800-950-8977; fax 800-953-8801
  www.hansergardner.com
Harcourt Canada Groupe Educalivres
  800-567-3671
  www.educalivres.com
Harcourt Canada Ltd.
  800-387-7278
  www.harcourtcanada.com
Harcourt College Publishers
  800-782-4479
  www.hbcollege.com
Harcourt
  800-225-5425
Harcourt Legal & Professional Publications
  800-787-8717; fax 800-433-6303
  www.gilbertlaw.com

Harcourt School Publishers
  800-225-5425
  www.harcourtschool.com
Harmonie Park Press
  800-886-3080
  harmonieparkpress.com
Harmony Books
  800-869-2976
  www.randomhouse.com
HarperCollins Publishers
  800-742-7831
  www.harpercollins.com
Harris InfoSource
  800-888-5900; fax 800-643-5997
  www.harrisinfo.com
Harrison House Publishers
  800-888-4126; fax 800-830-4126
  www.harrisonhouse.com
Hartley & Marks Publishers
  800-277-5887
Hartman Publishing
  800-999-9534; fax 800-474-6106
  www.hartmanonline.com
Harvard Business School Press
  888-500-1016
  www.hbsp.harvard.edu
Harvard Common Press
  888-657-3755
  www.harvardcommonpress.com
Harvard University Press
  800-448-2242; fax 800-962-4983
  www.hup.harvard.edu
Harvest Hill Press
  888-288-8900
Harvest House Publishers
  800-547-8979
Hastings House/Daytrips Publishers
  800-206-7822
Hatherleigh Press
  800-528-2550
  www.hatherleighpress.com
HAWK Publishing Group
  877-429-5782
The Haworth Press
  800-429-6784; fax 800-895-0582
  www.haworthpress.com
Hay House
  800-650-5115; 800-654-5126
Hayden Publishing
  800-200-7441
  www.haydenpublishing.com

Haynes Manuals
800-442-9637
www.haynes.com
Hazelden Publishing & Educational Services
800-328-0094
www.hazelden.org
HCPro
800-650-6787; fax 800-639-8511
Health Communications
800-851-9100; 800-441-5569 (order-entry)
Health for Life
800-874-5339
Health Infonet
800-446-1947
hinbooks.com
Health Professions Press
888-337-8808
www.healthpropress.com
Health Research
888-844-2386
www.healthresearchbooks.com
Hearts & Tummies Cookbook Co.
800-571-BOOK
William S. Hein & Co.
800-828-7571
www.wshein.com
Heinemann
800-541-2086
www.heinemann.com
Hemingway Western Studies Series
800-992 TEXT
www.boisestate.edu/hemingway/series.htm
Hendrickson Publishers
800-358-3111
www.hendrickson.com
Hensley Publishing
800-288-8520
www.hensleypublishing.com
Herald Press
800-245-7894
www.mph.org
Herald Publishing House
800-767-8181
www.heraldhouse.org
Heritage Books
800-398-7709; fax 800-276-1760
www.heritagebooks.com
Heritage Foundation
800-544-4843
www.heritage.org

Heritage House Publishing Co.
800-665-3302
www.heritagehouse.ca
Herodias
800-219-9116
www.herodias.com
Hewitt Homeschooling Resources
800-348-1750
hewitthomeschooling.com
Hi Willow Research & Publishing
800-873-3043
www.lmcsource.net
High Plains Press
800-552-7819
www.highplainspress.com
High Tide Press
888-487-7377; 800-698-3979
www.hightidepress.com
Highsmith Press
800-558-2110
www.hpress.highsmith.com
Hill Street Press
800-295-0365
www.hillstreetpress.com
Hillsdale College Press
800-437-2268
www.hillsdale.edu
Himalayan Institute Press
800-822-4547
www.himalayaninstitute.org
Hippocrene Books
800-809-3855
www.hippocrenebooks.com
Hi-Time Pflaum
800-543-4383; fax 800-370-4450
www.peterli.com
Hobby House Press
800-554-1447
www.hobbyhouse.com
Hogrefe & Huber Publishers
800-228-3749
www.hhpub.com
Hohm Press
800-381-2700
www.hohmpress.com
Hollywood Creative Directory
800-815-0503
www.hcdonline.com
Holmes & Meier Publishers
800-698-7781; fax 800-557-5601

Henry Holt and Co.
888-330-8477
www.henryholt.com

Holt, Rinehart and Winston
800-225-5425
www.hrw.com

Home Builder Press
800-223-2665
www.builderbooks.com

Home Planners LLC
800-322-6797
www.homeplanners.com

Homestyles Publishing & Marketing
888-626-2026
homestyles.com

Honor Books
800-678-2126
www.honorbooks.com

Hoover Institution Press
800-935-2882
www.hoover.org

Hoover's
800-486-8666
www.hoovers.com

Hope Publishing Co.
800-323-1049
www.hopepublishing.com

Horizon Books
800-233-4443
www.christianpublications.com

Horizon Publishers & Distributors
800-453-0812
www.horizonpublishers.com

Houghton Mifflin Co.
800-225-3362
www.hmco.com

House to House Publications
800-848-5892
www.dcfi.org

Howard Publishing
800-858-4109
howardpublishing.com

Howell Press
800-868-4512
www.howellpress.com

HRD Press
800-822-2801

Human Kinetics
800-747-4457
www.humankinetics.com

Humanics Publishing Group
800-874-8844
humanicspub.com

Hungry Minds
800-762-2974
www.hungryminds.com

Hunter House
800-266-5592
www.hunterhouse.com

Huntington House Publishers
800-749-4009
www.huntingtonhousebooks.com

Huntington Press Publishing
800-244-2224
www.huntingtonpress.com

Hyperion
800-759-0190

I Film Publishing
800-815-0503
www.ifilm.com

I O P Publishing
800-632-0880
bookmarkphysics.iop.org

Ibex Publishers
888-718-8188
www.ibexpub.com

IBFD Publications USA (International
Bureau of Fiscal Documentation)
800-299-6330
www.ibfd.nl

Iconografix
800-289-3504

ICS Press
800-326-0263
www.icspress.com

Idaho Center for the Book
800-992-8398
www.lili.org/icb

Ideals Children's Books
800-327-5113

IEEE Computer Society
800-272-6657
computer.org

Ignatius Press
877-320-9276; fax 800-278-3566
www.ignatius.com

Images from the Past
888-442-3204
www.ImagesfromthePast.com

Imaginart Press
800-828-1376; fax 800-737-1376
www.imaginartonline.com

ImaJinn Books
877-625-3592
www.imajinnbooks.com

Impact Publishers
800-246-7228
www.impactpublishers.com
Incentive Publications
800-421-2830
www.incentivepublications.com
Indiana Historical Society
800-447-1830
www.indianahistory.org
Indiana University Press
800-842-6796
www.indiana.edu/~iupress
Industrial Press
888-528-7852
www.industrialpress.com
Information Gatekeepers
800-323-1088
www.igigroup.com
Information Today, Inc.
www.infotoday.com
Ingenix Publishing Group
800-999-4600
www.ingenix.com
Inner Ocean Publishing
800-863-1449; fax 800-755-4118
www.innerocean.com
Inner Traditions International Ltd.
800-246-8648
www.innertraditions.com
Innisfree Press
800-367-5872
www.innisfreepress.com
Institute for International Economics
800-522-9139
www.iie.com
Institute for Language Study
800-245-2145
www.cortina-languages.com
Institute of Continuing Legal Education
877-229-4351
www.icle.org/
Institute of Psychological Research
888-382-3007
Interchange
800-669-6208; fax 800-729-0395
www.interchangeinc.com
Intercultural Press
800-370-2665
www.interculturalpress.com
Interlink Publishing Group
800-238-LINK
www.interlinkbooks.com

International Chess Enterprises
800-26-CHESS
www.insidechess.com
International Conference of Building
Officials
800-423-6587
www.icbo.org
International Foundation of Employee
Benefit Plans
888-217-5960
www.ifebp.org
International LearningWorks
800-344-0451
www.intllearningworks.com
International Linguistics Corp.
800-237-1830
www.learnables.com
International Medical Publishing
800-537-4314
www.medicalpublishing.com
International Risk Management Institute
800-827-4242
www.irmi.com
International Scholars Publications
800-462-6420
www.interscholars.com
International Society for Technology
in Education
800-336-5191
www.iste.org
International Wealth Success
800-323-0548
www.iwsmoney.com
Interpharm Press
877-295-9240
www.interpharm.com
Interstate Publishers
800-843-4774
www.interstatepublishers.com
Intertec Publishing Corp.
800-262-1954
www.intec.com
InterVarsity Press
800-843-7225
www.ivpress.com/
Interweave Press
800-272-2193
Iowa State University Press
800-862-6657
www.isupress.com
Irwin Publishing
800-263-7824
www.irwin-pub.com

ISI Books
800-526-7022
Island Press
800-828-1302
www.islandpress.org
Ivy League Press
888-IVY-PRES

J & L Lee Co.
888-665-0999
www.leebooksellers.com
Jalmar Press
800-662-9662
www.jalmarpress.com
Jameson Books
800-426-1357
Jane's Information Group
800-836-0297
www.janes.com
Janex International
800-541-2205
www.janexinternational.com
Jewish Lights Publishing
800-962-4544
www.jewishlights.com
Jewish Publication Society
800-234-3151
www.jewishpub.org
JIST Publishing
800-648-5478; fax 800-264-3763
www.jist.com
John Deere Publishing
800-522-7448
www.deere.com
Johns Hopkins University Press
800-537-5487
www.press.jhu.edu
Johnson Books
800-824-5505
www.jpcolorado.com
Jones & Bartlett Publishers
800-832-0034
www.jbpub.com
Jones McClure Publishing
800-626-6667
www.jonesmcclure.com
Bob Jones University Press
800-845-5731
www.bjup.com
Jossey-Bass
800-956-7739
josseybass.com

Joy Publishing
800-454-8228
www.joypublishing.com
Judaica Press
800-972-6201
www.judaicapress.com
Judson Press
800-458-3766
www.judsonpress.com

Kabel Publishers
800-543-3167
www.erols.com/kabelcomp/index2.html
Kaeden Corp.
800-890-7323
www.kaeden.com
Kalimat Press
800-788-4067
www.kalimat.com
Kalmbach Publishing Co.
800-558-1544
www.kalmbach.com
Kar-Ben Copies
800-4-KARBEN
www.karben.com
KC Publications
800-626-9673
www.kcpublications.com
J. J. Keller & Associates
800-327-6868; fax 800-727-7516
www.jjkeller.com
Kendall/Hunt Publishing Co.
800-228-0810; fax 800-772-9165
www.kendallhunt.com
Kennedy Information
800-531-0007
www.kennedyinfo.com
Kensington Publishing Corp.
800-221-2647
www.kensingtonbooks.com
Kent State University Press
800-247-6553
bookmasters.com/ksu-press
Key Curriculum Press
800-995-6284; fax 800-541-2442
www.keypress.com
Kids Can Press Ltd.
800-265-0884
www.kidscanpress.com
Kidsbooks
800-890-7137
www.kidsbooks.com

Kindred Productions
800-545-7322
www.mbconf.org/kindred.htm
Kingfisher
800-497-1657; fax 800-874-4027
Kinship
800-249-1109
www.kinshipny.com
Kirkbride Bible Co.
800-428-4385
www.kirkbride.com
Kluwer Law International
800-577-8118
www.kluwerlaw.com
Allen A. Knoll Publishers
800-777-7623
www.knollpublishers.com
Alfred A. Knopf
800-638-6460
Knopf Canada
800-668-4247
www.randomhouse.ca
Krause Publications
800-258-0929; 888-457-2873
www.krause.com
Kregel Publications
800-733-2607
www.kregel.com
Krieger Publishing Co.
800-724-0025
www.krieger-publishing.com
Kumarian Press
800-289-2664
www.kpbooks.com

LadybugPress
888-892-5000
www.ladybugbooks.com
LAMA Books
888-452-6244
www.lamabooks.com
Landauer Books
800-557-2144
Landes Bioscience
800-736-9948
Peter Lang Publishing
800-770-5264
www.peterlangusa.com
Langenscheidt Publishers
800-432-MAPS; 888-773-7979
www.langenscheidt.com

LangMarc Publishing
800-864-1648
Larson Publications
800-828-2197
www.lightlink.com/larson/
Laureate Press
800-946-2727
www.fencingbooks.com
Lawbook Exchange Ltd.
800-422-6686
www.lawbookexchange.com
LDA Publishers
888-388-9887
Leadership Ministries Worldwide
800-987-8790
www.outlinebible.org
Leadership Publishers
800-814-3757
Leading Edge Reports
800-866-4648
www.bta-ler.com
Learning Connection (TLC)
800-338-2282
Learning Links
800-724-2616
Learning Publications
800-222-1525
www.learningpublications.com
Learning Resources Network
800-678-5376
www.lern.org
LearningExpress
800-295-9556
www.learnatest.com
Hal Leonard Corp.
800-524-4425
www.halleonard.com
Lectorum Publications
800-853-3291
www.lectorum.com
Lederer Books
800-773-6574
messianicjewish.net
Legal Education Publishing
800-957-4670
www.legaledpub.com
Leisure Arts
800-643-8030
Lerner Publishing Group
800-328-4929; fax 800-332-1132
www.lernerbooks.com

The Letter People
800-227-9120
letterpeople.com
Lexis
800-446-3410
Liberty Fund
800-955-8335
www.libertyfund.org
Libraries Unlimited
800-237-6124
www.lu.com
Library of America
www.loa.org
Lidec
800-350-5991 (Canada only)
www.lidec.qc.ca

Mary Ann Liebert
800-654-3237
www.liebertpub.com
Liguori Publications
800-464-2555
www.liguori.org
Lindisfarne Books
800-856-8664
www.lindisfarne.org
LinguiSystems
800-776-4332
www.linguisystems.com
Linns Stamp News-Ancillary Division
800-340-9501
www.linns.com
Linworth Publishing
www.linworth.com
Lippincott Williams & Wilkins
800-638-3030
www.lww.com
Listen & Live Audio
800-653-9400
www.listenandlive.com
Literacy Institute for Education (LIFE)
866-256-3576
bknelson.com
Little, Brown
800-759-0190
www.twbookmark.com
Liturgical Press
800-858-5450; fax 800-445-5899
www.litpress.org
Liturgy Training Publications
800-933-1800; fax 800-933-7094

Living Language
800-726-0600; fax 800-659-2436
www.livinglanguage.com
Llewellyn Publications
800-843-6666
www.llewellyn.com
Loizeaux Brothers
800-526-2796
www.biblecompanion.org
London Bridge
800-805-1083; fax 800-481-6207
Lone Oak Press Ltd.
877-315-2746
www.loneoak.org
Lone Pine Publishing
800-661-9017; fax 800-424-7173
www.lonepinepublishing.com
Lonely Planet Publications
800-275-8555
www.lonelyplanet.com
Longman Publishing
www.longman.com
Longstreet Press
800-927-1488
Loompanics Unlimited
800-380-2230
www.loompanics.com
Looseleaf Law Publications
800-647-5547
www.LooseleafLaw.com
Lost Classics Book Co.
888-211-2665
www.lostclassicsbooks.com
Lotus Press
800-824-6396
www.lotuspress.com
Loyola Press
800-621-1008
www.loyolapress.org
LRP Publications
800-341-7874
www.lrp.com
LRS
800-255-5002
lrs-largeprint.com
Lucent Books
www.lucentbooks.com
Lucky Press LLC
800-345-6665
www.luckypress.com

Lyons Press
800-836-0510
www.lyonspress.com

MacAdam/Cage Publishing
866-986-7470
www.macadamcage.com

Macalester Park Publishing Co.
800-407-9078
www.mcchronicle.com

McBooks Press
888-266-5711
www.mcbooks.com

McClanahan Publishing House
800-544-6959
www.kybooks.com

McCormack's Guides
800-222-3602
www.mccormacks.com

McCutchan Publishing Corp.
800-227-1540

McDonald & Woodward Publishing Co.
800-233-8787
www.mwpubco.com

McDougal Littell
800-462-6595

McFarland & Co. Inc. Publishers
800-253-2187
www.mcfarlandpub.com

McGraw-Hill
www.mcgraw-hill.com

McGraw-Hill Children's Publishing
800-540-4663; 800-305-5571
www.mhkids.com

McGraw-Hill/Contemporary
877-226-4997

McGraw-Hill Higher Education
800-338-3987
www.mhhe.com

McGraw-Hill/Irwin
800-338-3987
www.mhhe.com

McGraw-Hill/Osborne Media
800-227-0900
www.osborne.com

McGraw-Hill Ryerson Ltd.
800-565-5758
www.mcgrawhill.ca

Andrews McMeel Publishing
800-826-4216

Macmillan Computer Publishing USA
800-545-5914
www.mcp.com

Macmillan Digital Publishing USA
800-545-5914
www.macdigital.com

Macmillan USA
800-545-5914
www.mcp.com

McPherson & Co.
800-613-8219; fax 800-613-8219
www.mcphersonco.com

Madison House Publishers
800-462-6420
www.globaldialog.com/~mhbooks

Mage Publishers
800-962-0922
www.mage.com

Magick Mirror Communications
800-356-6796
www.magickmirror.com

Maharishi University of Management Press
800-831-6523
www.mum.edu/press/welcome.html

Manhattan Publishing Co.
888-686-7066
www.manhattanpublishing.com

MapEasy
888-627-3279
www.mapeasy.com

MAR*CO Products
800-448-2197
www.marcoproducts.com

Marathon Press
800-228-0629
www.marathonpress.com

MARC Publications
800-777-7752
www.marcpublications.com

Market Data Retrieval
800-333-8802
www.schooldata.com

Marlor Press
800-669-4908

Marquette University Press
800-247-6553
www.mu.edu/mupress

Marquis Who's Who
www.marquiswhoswho.com

Marshall & Swift
800-544-2678
www.marshallswift.com

Marshall Cavendish Corp.
www.marshallcavendish.com

Martingale & Co.
800-426-3126
www.martingalepub.com
Marvin Melnyk Associates Ltd.
800-682-0029
www.meljack.com
Massachusetts Continuing Legal Education
800-966-6253
www.mcle.org
Math Teachers Press
800-852-2435
Mathematical Association of America
800-331-1622
www.maa.org
MCP Software
800-858-7674
www.macmillansoftware.com
MDRT Center for Productivity
800-879-6378
Meadowbrook Press
800-338-2232
R. S. Means Co.
800-448-8182; fax 800-632-6701
www.rsmeans.com
MedBooks
800-443-7397
www.medbooks.com
Media & Methods
800-555-5657
www.media-methods.com
Media Associates
800-373-1897
www.arkives.com
Medical Economics
800-442-6657
www.medec.com
Medical Group Management Association
888-608-5601
www.mgma.com
Medical Physics Publishing Corp.
800-442-5778
www.medicalphysics.org
Russell Meerdink Co.
800-635-6499
www.horseinfo.com
Mega Media Press
800-803-9416
www.imagetics.com
Mel Bay Publications
800-863-5229
www.melbay.com

Menasha Ridge Press
800-247-9437
www.menasharidge.com
Mercer University Press
800-637-2378 ext. 2880
www.mupress.org
Meriwether Publishing Ltd./Contemporary
Drama Service
800-937-5297; 888-594-4436
www.meriwetherpublishing.com
Merriam-Webster
800-828-1880
www.merriam-webster.com
Merryant Publishers
800-228-8958
Mesa House Publishing
888-306-0060
www.mesahouse.com
Mesorah Publications Ltd.
800-637-6724
www.mesorah.com
Metal Bulletin
800-638-2525
www.metbul.com
Metamorphous Press
800-937-7771
www.metamodels.com
MGI Management Institute
800-932-0191
www.mgi.org
Michelin Travel Publications
800-361-8236 (Canada)
www.michelin-travel.com
Michelin Travel Publications
800-423-0485; fax 800-378-7471
www.viamichelin.com
Michigan Municipal League
800-653-2483
www.mml.org
MicroMash
800-272-7277
www.micromash.net/index.htm
Micromedia Limited
800-387-2689
www.micromedia.on.ca
Microsoft Press
800-677-7377
www.microsoft.com
MidWest Plan Service
800-562-3618
www.mwpshq.org

Midwest Traditions
800-736-9189
Milady Publishing
800-998-7498
www.milady.com
Miles River Press
800-767-1501
www.milesriverpress.com
Milkweed Editions
800-520-6455
www.milkweed.org
Millbrook Press
800-462-4703
Milliken Publishing Co.
800-325-4136; fax 800-538-1319
www.millikenpub.com
Minerals, Metals & Materials Society
800-759-4867
www.tms.org/pubs/Publications.html
Minnesota Historical Society Press
800-647-7827
www.mnhs.org/mhspress
MIT Press
800-356-0343
mitpress.mit.edu
Mitchell Lane Publishers
800-814-5484
www.angelfire.com/biz/mitchelllane
MMB Music
800-543-3771
www.mmbmusic.com
Modern Curriculum Press
www.mcschool.com
Modulo Editeur
888-738-9818
www.modulo.ca
Monday Morning Books
800-255-6049; fax 800-255-6048
www.mondaymorningbooks.com
Mondia Editeurs
800-561-2371 (Canada)
Mondo Publishing
800-242-3650
www.mondopub.com
Money Market Directories
800-446-2810
www.mmdaccess.com
Monthly Review Press
800-670-9499
www.MonthlyReview.org

Moody Press
800-678-8812
www.moodypress.org
Thomas More
800-527-5030; fax 800-688-8356
Morehouse Publishing Co.
800-877-0012
www.morehousegroup.com
Morgan Kaufmann Publishers
800-745-7323; fax 800-874-6418
www.mkp.com
Morgan Quitno Corp.
800-457-0742
www.morganquitno.com
Morgan Reynolds
800-535-1504; fax 800-535-5725
www.morganreynolds.com
Morning Glory Press
888-612-8254
888-327-4362
www.morningglorypress.com
Morningside Bookshop
800-648-9710
www.morningsidebooks.com
Mosaic Press
800-932-4044
w3.one.net/~kirwin/mp.htm
Mosby
800-325-4177
www.mosby.com
Mount Olive College Press
800-653-0854
www.mountolivecollege.edu/mocpress/
mocpress.htm
Mountain n' Air Books
800-446-9696; fax 800-303-5578
Mountain Press Publishing Co.
800-234-5308
www.mountainpresspublishing.com
Mountaineers Books
800-553-4453; fax 800-568-7604
www.mountaineersbooks.org
Andrew Mowbray
800-999-4697
Moyer Bell
888-789-1945
www.moyerbell.com
Moznaim Publishing Corp.
800-364-5118
MTG Publishing
800-430-3363

Multicultural Publications
800-238-0297; fax 800-238-0297
Editions Multimondes
800-840-3029
Multnomah Publishers
800-929-0910
www.multnomahbooks.com
Municipal Analysis Services
800-488-3932
Mike Murach & Associates
800-221-5528
www.murach.com
Museum of New Mexico Press
800-249-7737; fax 800-622-8667
www.museumofnewmexico.org
Mustang Publishing Co.
800-250-8713
www.mustangpublishing.com
My Chaotic Life
800-426-0099
www.mychaoticlife.com

NAFSA: Association of International
Educators
800-836-4994
www.nafsa.org
Naiad Press
800-533-1973
www.naiadpress.ocm
Napoleon Publishing/Rendezvous Press
877-730-9052
www.transmedia95.com
National Academy Press
800-624-6242
www.nap.edu
National Association of Broadcasters
800-368-5644
www.nab.org
National Association of Secondary School
Principals
800-253-7746
www.nassp.org
National Association of Social Workers
800-638-8799
www.socialworkers.org
National Braille Press
800-548-7323
www.nbp.org
National Council of Teachers of English
800-369-6283; 877-369-6283
www.ncte.org

National Council of Teachers of Mathematics
800-235-7566
www.nctm.org
National Council on Radiation Protection
& Measurements
800-229-2652
www.ncrp.com
National Crime Prevention Council
800-627-2911
www.ncpc.org
National Geographic Society
www.nationalgeographic.com
National Golf Foundation
800-733-6006
www.ngf.org
National Institute for Trial Advocacy
800-225-6482
National Learning Corp.
800-645-6337
www.passbooks.com
National Museum of Women in the Arts
800-222-7270
www.nmwa.org
National Notary Association
800-876-6827
www.nationalnotary.org
National Publishing Co.
888-333-1863
National Register Publishing
800-521-8110
www.nationalregisterpub.com
National Science Teachers Association
800-722-NSTA
www.nsta.org
National Underwriter Co.
800-543-0874
www.nationalunderwriter.com
Natural Heritage/Natural History
800-725-9982
Naturegraph Publishers
800-390-5353
www.naturegraph.com
Naval Institute Press
800-233-8764
www.navalinstitute.org
NavPress Publishing Group
800-366-7788; fax 800-343-3902
NBM Publishing
800-886-1223
Neal-Schuman Publishers
866-672-6657
www.neal-schuman.com

E. T. Nedder Publishing
877-817-2742
nedderpublishing.com

Neibauer Press
800-322-6203
www.churchstewardship.com

Nelson Information
888-371-4575
www.nelnet.com

Nelson Thomson Learning
800-268-2222; 800-668-0671

New City Press
800-462-5980
www.newcitypress.com

New Directions Publishing Corp.
800-233-4830
www.ndpublishing.com

New Forums Press
800-606-3766
www.newforums.com

New Harbinger Publications
800-748-6273
www.newharbinger.com

New Horizon Press
800-533-7978

New Leaf Press
800-643-9535
www.newleafpress.net

New Press
800-233-4830; fax 800-458-6515
www.thenewpress.com

New Readers Press
800-448-8878
www.laubach.org

New Victoria Publishers
800-326-5297; fax 800-326-5297
www.newvictoria.com

New World Library
800-227-3900
www.newworldlibrary.com

New York Academy of Sciences
800-843-6927
www.nyas.org

New York State Bar Association
800-582-2452
www.nysba.org

New York University Press
800-996-6987
www.nyupress.nyu.edu

NeWest Press
866-796-5433
www.newestpress.com

NewLife Publications
800-235-7255; fax 800-514-7072
www.newlifepubs.com

Newmarket Press
800-669-3903
www.newmarketpress.com

Nightingale-Conant
800-572-2770; fax 800-647-9198
www.nightingale.com

Nilgiri Press
800-475-2369
www.nilgiri.org

Nimbus Publishing Ltd.
800-646-2879
www.nimbus.ns.ca

No Starch Press
800-420-7240
www.nostarch.com

Nolo.com
800-992-6656
www.nolo.com

Norman Publishing
800-544-9359
www.normanpublishing.com

North Atlantic Books
800-337-2665
www.northatlanticbooks.com

North Light Books
800-666-0963
888-590-4082

North River Press Publishing Corp.
800-486-2665; fax 800-BOOK-FAX
www.northriverpress.com

Northland Publishing Co.
800-346-3257
www.northlandpub.com

Northstone Publishing
800-299-2926
www.joinhands.com

Northwestern University Press
800-621-2736
www.nupress.nwu.edu

Jeffrey Norton Publishers
800-243-1234
www.audioforum.com

W. W. Norton & Company
800-233-4830; fax 800-458-6515
www.wwnorton.com

Nova Press
800-949-6175
www.novapress.net

Novalis Publishing
800-387-7164; fax 800-204-4140
www.novalis.ca
Nystrom
800-621-8086
www.nystromnet.com

OAG Worldwide
800-323-3537
www.oag.com
Oak Knoll Press
800-996-2556
www.oakknoll.com
Oasis Press/Hellgate Press
800-228-2275
www.psi-research.com
Ocean View Books
800-848-6222
www.probook.net/ocean.html
Oceana Publications
800-831-0758
www.oceanalaw.com
Ohio State University Foreign Language
Publications
800-678-6999
flc.ohio-state.edu
Ohio State University Press
800-621-2736; fax 800-621-8476
ohiostatepress.org
Ohio University Press
800-621-2736
Omnibus Press
800-431-7187
Omnidawn Publishing
800-792-4957
www.omnidawn.com
Omnigraphics
800-234-1340; fax 800-875-1340
www.omnigraphics.com
One Planet Publishing House
877-526-3814
www.oneplanetpublishinghouse.com
OneOnOne Computer Training
800-424-8668
www.oootraining.com
OneSource
800-333-8036
www.onesource.com
Online Training Solutions
800-854-3344
www.otsiweb.com

Open Horizons Publishing Co.
800-796-6130
www.bookmarket.com
Opis/Stalsby Directories
800-275-0950
www.opisnet.com
Optical Society of America
800-582-0416
www.osa.org
Optima Books
877-710-2196; fax 800-515-8737
optimabooks.com
Orange Frazer Press
800-852-9332
www.orangefrazer.com
Orbis Books
800-258-5838
www.orbisbooks.com
Orca Book Publishers
800-210-5277
www.orcabook.com
Orchard Books
800-433-3411
www.scholastic.com
Oregon Catholic Press
800-548-8749; fax 800-843-8181
www.ocp.org
Oregon State University Press
800-426-3797; fax 800-426-3797
osu.orst.edu/dept/press
O'Reilly & Associates
800-998-9938
Organization for Economic Cooperation
& Development
800-456-6323
www.oecdwash.org
Oryx Press
800-279-6799; fax 800-279-4663
www.oryxpress.com
Other Press LLC
877-843-6843
Our Sunday Visitor Publishing
800-348-2440
www.osv.com
Outdoor Empire Publishing
800-645-5489
The Overmountain Press
800-992-2691
www.overmtn.com
Richard C. Owen Publishers
800-336-5588
www.rcowen.com

Oxbridge Communications
800-955-0231
www.mediafinder.com
Oxford University Press Canada
800-387-8020; fax 800-665-1771
www.oup.com/ca
Oxford University Press
800-451-7556
www.oup-usa.org
Oxmoor House
800-633-4910
Ozark Publishing
800-321-5671

P & R Publishing Co.
800-631-0094
prpbooks.com
P S M J Resources
800-537-7765
www.psmj.com
Pacific Heritage Books
888-870-8878
www.wind-water.com
Pacific Press Publishing Association
800-447-7377
www.pacificpress.com
PageMill Press
888-774-7595
www.wildcatcanyon.com
Paladin Press
800-392-2400
Pangaea Publications
888-690-3320
pangaea.org
Panoptic Enterprises
800-594-4766
www.fedgovcontracts.com
Pantheon Books/Schocken Books
800-638-6460
Para Publishing
800-727-2782
www.parapublishing.com
Parabola Books
800-560-6984
www.parabola.org
Paraclete Press
800-451-5006
www.paracletepress.com
Paradigm Publications
800-873-3946
www.paradigm-pubs.com

Paradise Cay Publications
800-736-4509
www.paracay.com
Paragon House
800-447-3709; fax 800-494-0997
www.paragonhouse.com
Parenting Press
800-99-BOOKS
www.parentingpress.com
Park Place Publications
888-702-4500
www.parkplace-publications.com
Parkway Publishers
800-821-9155
www.parkwaypublishers.com
Parlay International
800-457-2752
www.parlay.com
Parthenon Publishing Group
800-735-4744
www.parthpub.com
PartMiner
800-447-4666
Pastoral Press
800-548-8749; fax 800-462-7329
Path Press
800-548-2600
Pathfinder Publishing of California
800-977-2282
www.pathfinderpublishing.com
Pathways Publishing
888-333-7284
www.pathwayspub.com
Patient-Centered Guides
800-998-9938
Patrick's Press
800-654-1052
Pauline Books & Media
800-876-4463
www.pauline.org
Paulist Press
800-218-1903; fax 800-836-3161
www.paulistpress.com
PBC International
800-527-2826
Peachtree Publishers Ltd.
800-241-0113; fax 800-875-8909
www.peachtree-online.com
Peanut Butter & Jelly Press LLC
800-408-6226; fax 800-408-6226
www.infertilitydiet.com

Pearson Custom Publishing
800-428-4466
www.pearsoned.com

Pearson Education Canada
800-567-3800; fax 800-263-7733
www.pearsoned.com

T. H. Peek Publisher
800-962-9245

Peel Productions
800-345-6665
www.peelbooks.com

Pelican Publishing Co.
800-843-1724
www.pelicanpub.com

Pencil Point Press
800-356-1299
pencilpointpress.com

Penfield Press
800-728-9998
www.penfield-press.com

Penguin Books
www.penguinputnam.com

Penguin Putnam
www.penguinputnam.com

Penhurst Books
877-496-0416
www.extremeadventurebooks.com

Pennsylvania Historical & Museum
Commission
800-747-7790
www.phmc.state.pa.us

Pennsylvania State University Press
800-326-9180
www.psupress.org

PennWell Books
800-752-9764

Penton Overseas
800-748-5804
www.pentonoverseas.com

Per Annum
800-548-1108
www.perannum.com

Peradam Press
800-241-8689; fax 800-241-8689

Perfection Learning Corp.
800-762-2999
perfectionlearning.com

Perseus Books
800-242-7737
www.perseusbooksgroup.com

Peter Pauper Press
800-833-2311
www.peterpauper.com

Peterson's
800-338-3282; fax 800-772-2465
www.petersons.com

Petroleum Extension Service
800-687-4132; fax 800-687-7839
www.utexas.edu/cee/pete

X. Peytral Publications
877-PEYTRAL
www.peytral.com

Pfeifer-Hamilton Publishers
800-247-6789
www.phpublisher.com

Phaidon Press
877-742-4366
www.phaidon.com

Phi Delta Kappa International
800-766-1156
www.pdkintl.org

Philosophical Publishing Co.
877-652-3535

Philosophy Documentation Center
800-444-2419
www.pdcnet.org

Phoenix Learning Resources
800-221-1274
www.phoenixlr.com

Phoenix Society for Burn Survivors
800-888-BURN
www.phoenix-society.org

Picasso Publications
877-250-1300
art-books.com

Pictorial Histories Publishing Co.
888-763-8350

Picture Me Books
800-762-6775
www.picture-me-books.com

Pieces of Learning
800-729-5137; fax 800-844-0455
www.peicesoflearning.com

Pilgrim Press/United Church Press
800-537-3394
pilgrimpress.com

Pineapple Press
800-746-3275
www.pineapplepress.com

Pippin Publishing Corp.
888-889-0001
www.pippinpub.com

Pitspopany Press
800-232-2931
Planetary Publications
800-372-3100
www.heartmath.com
Planning/Communications
888-366-5200
www.jobfindersonline.com
Plough Publishing House
800-521-8011
www.plough.com
Pocket Press
888-237-2110
www.pocketpressinc.com
Polestar Book Publishers
800-663-5714; fax 800-565-3770
www.raincoast.com
Police Executive Research Forum
800-202-4563
www.policeforum.org
Pomegranate Communications
800-227-1428
www.pomegranate.com
Popular Culture
800-678-8828; fax 800-678-8828
Popular Press
800-515-5118
www.bgsu.edu/offices/press/index.html
Portage & Main
800-667-9673
www.peguis.com
Porter Sargent Publishers
800-342-7470
www.portersargent.com
Possibility Press
800-566-0534
Clarkson Potter Publishers
800-869-2976
Pottersfield Press
800-NIMBUS9
Practising Law Institute
800-260-4PLI; fax 800-321-0093
www.pli.edu
Prairie Oak Press
888-833-9118
Prairie View Press
800-477-7377
Prakken Publications
800-530-9673
Precept Press
800-225-3775
www.bonus-books.com

PREP Publishing
800-533-2814
www.prep-pub.com
Presbyterian Publishing Corp.
800-227-2872; fax 800-541-5113
www.ppcpub.org
Prestel Publishing
888-463-6110
www.prestel.com
Prima Publishing
800-632-8676
www.primapublishing.com
Primedia Special Interest Publications
800-521-2885
Princeton Architectural Press
800-722-6657
www.pappress.com
Princeton Book Co. Publishers
800-220-7149
www.dancehorizons.com
Princeton Review
800-733-3000
www.randomhouse.com
Princeton University Press
800-777-4726; fax 800-999-1958
www.pup.princeton.edu
Printery House
800-889-0105
www.printeryhouse.org
PRO-ED
800-897-3202; fax 800-397-7633
www.proedinc.com
Pro Lingua Associates
800-366-4775
www.prolinguaassociates.com
Pro Quest Information & Learning
800-521-0600 (editorial)
www.bellhowell.infolearning.com
Productivity
800-394-6868; fax 800-394-6286
www.productivityinc.com
Professional Communications
800-337-9838
www.pcibooks.com
Professional Education Group
800-229-2531
www.proedgroup.com
Professional Publications
800-426-1178
www.ppi2pass.com
Professional Publishing
800-2McGraw

Professional Resource Exchange
800-443-3364
www.prpress.com
Prometheus Books
800-421-0351
www.Prometheusbooks.com
ProStar Publications
800-481-6277; fax 800-487-6277
Providence House Publishers
800-321-5692
www.providencehouse.com
Pruett Publishing Co.
800-247-8224; fax 800-527-9727
PST
800-284-7043
www.pstpub.com
Psychological Assessment Resources
800-331-8378; fax 800-727-9329
www.parinc.com
Psychological Corp & Harcourt Educational
Measurement
800-211-8378
www.hbem.com
PT Publications
800-547-4326
www.ptpublications.com
Public Affairs
800-242-7737
www.perseusbooksgroup.com
Public Utilities Reports
800-368-5001
www.pur.com
Les Publications du Quebec
800-463-2100 (Quebec only)
www.publicationsduquebec.gouv.qc.ca
Publishing Directions LLC
800-562-4357
www.strongbooks.com
Puffin Books
www.penguinputnam.com
Purple Mountain Press Ltd.
800-325-2665
www.catskill.net/purple
Purple People
866-787-7535
www.purplepeople.com
Putnam Publishing Group
800-631-8571
www.penguinputnam.com

Quail Ridge Press
800-343-1583
quailridge.com

Quality Education Data
800-525-5811
www.qeddata.com
Quality Medical Publishing
800-423-6865
www.qmp.com
Quantum Leap SLC Publications
877-571-9788
877-571-9788
www.blackamericanhandbook.com
Quest Publishing Co.
800-777-9149
home.att.net/~TheQuest
Quintessence Publishing Co.
800-621-0387
www.quintpub.com
Quixote Press
800-571-BOOK

Ragged Edge Press
888-948-6263
Rainbow Books
800-431-1579; 888-613-2665
Rainbow Publishers
800-323-7337
Rainbow Studies International
800-242-5348
www.rainbowstudies.com
Raincoast Book Distribution Ltd.
800-663-5714 (Canada only)
www.raincoast.com
RAND Corp.
www.rand.org
Rand McNally
800-333-0136
www.randmcnally.com
Random House, Canada
800-668-4247
www.randomhouse.ca
Random House Children's Books
800-200-3552
www.randomhouse.com/kids
Random House
800-726-0600
www.randomhouse.com
Rayve Productions
800-852-4890
www.rayveproductions.com
Reader's Digest Association (Canada)
800-465-0780
www.readersdigest.ca

Reader's Digest Association
800-431-1726
www.rd.com
Reader's Digest Childrens Books
800-934-0977
Reader's Digest General Books
800-431-1726
Reader's Digest USA Select Editions
800-310-6261
Record Research
800-827-9810
www.recordresearch.com
Red Sea Press
800 789-1898
www.africanworld.com
Red Wheel/Weiser
800-423-7087
www.weiserbooks.com
Redleaf Press
800-423-8309; fax 800-641-0115
www.redleafpress.org
Thomas Reed Publications
800-995-4995
www.reedsalmanac.com
Referee Books
800-733-6100
www.referee.com
Regal Books
800-446-7735; fax 800-860-3109
www.gospellight.com
Regatta Press Ltd.
800-688-2877
www.regattapress.com
Regnery Publishing
800-462-6420
www.regnery.com
Regular Baptist Press
800-727-4440; 888-588-1600
www.regularbaptistpress.org
Rei America
800-726-5337
www.americainc.com
Renaissance House
800-547-5113; fax 800-998-3103
renaissancehouse.net
Renaissance Media
800-266-2834
www.renaissancebks.com
Reprint Services Corp.
800-273-6635
Research Press
800-519-2707
www.researchpress.com

Resort Gifts Unlimited
800-266-5265; fax 800-973-6694
www.resortgifts.com
Resource Centre
800-923-0330
Resources for Christian Living
800-527-5030; fax 800-688-8356
www.rclweb.com
Fleming H. Revell
800-877-2665
www.bakerbooks.com
Review & Herald Publishing Association
800-234-7630
River City Publishing, LLC
877-408-7078
www.rivercitypublishing.com
RiverOak Publishing
866-273-2718
www.riveroakpublishing.com
Riverside Publishing Co.
800-767-8420; 800-323-9540
Rizzoli International Publications
800-522-6657
Rocky Mountain Books Ltd.
800-566-3336
www.rmbooks.com
Rocky River Publishers LLC
800-343-0686
www.rockyriver.com
Rod & Staff Publishers
800-643-1244
Rodale
800-848-4735
www.rodalepress.com
Ronsdale Press
888-879-0919
ronsdalepress.com
Rosen Publishing Group
800-237-9932
www.rosenpublishing.com
Ross Books
800-367-0930
www.rossbooks.com
Norman Ross Publishing
800-648-8850
www.nross.com
Roth Publishing
800-899-ROTH
Rough Guides
www.roughguides.com
Rough Notes Co.
800-428-4384; fax 800-321-1909

Rowman & Littlefield Publishers
800-462-6420
www.rowmanlittlefield.com

Runestone Press
800-328-4929; 800-332-1132
www.lernerbooks.com

Running Press Book Publishers
800-345-5359; fax 800-453-2884
www.runningpress.com

Russell Sage Foundation
800-524-6401
www.russellsage.org

Rutgers University Press
800-446-9323
rutgerspress.rutgers.edu

Rutledge Hill Press
800-251-4000
www.rutledgehillpress.com

RV Consumer Group
800-405-3325
www.rv.org

William H. Sadlier
800-221-5175
www.sadlier.com

Society of Automotive Engineers
877-606-7323
www.sae.org

Sagamore Publishing
800-327-5557
www.sagamorepub.com

Sage Publications
www.sagepub.com

St. Anthony Messenger Press
800-488-0488
www.AmericanCatholic.org

Saint Anthony Publishing
800-632-0123
www.ingenix.com

St. Augustine's Press
888-997-4994
www.staugustine.net

St. James Press
800-877-GALE; fax 800-414-5043
www.stjames.com

St. Martin's Press LLC
800-221-7945
www.stmartins.com

Saint Mary's Press
800-533-8095; fax 800-344-9225
www.smp.org

Saint Nectarios Press
800-643-4233
www.stnectariospress.com

Salem Press
800-221-1592
www.salempress.com

Sams Technical Publishing
800-428-SAMS; fax 800-552-3910
www.samswebsite.com

J. S. Sanders & Co.
800-462-6420; fax 800-338-4550

Sandlapper Publishing
800-849-7263

Santa Monica Press LLC
800-784-9553
www.santamonicapress.com

Santillana USA Publishing Co.
888-248-9518
www.santillanausa.com

Sarpedon Publishers
800-207-8045

Sasquatch Books
800-775-0817
www.sasquatchbooks.com

W. B. Saunders Company
800-545-2522
www.wbsaunders.com

Savage Press
800-732-3867
www.savpress.com

Scarecrow Press
800-462-6420
www.scarecrowpress.com

Scepter Publishers
800-322-8773
www.scepterpub.org

Robert Schalkenbach Foundation
800-269-9555
www.progress.org/books

Scholarly Resources
800-772-8937
www.scholarly.com

Scholastic Canada Ltd.
800-268-3848; fax 800-387-4944
www.scholastic.ca

Scholastic
www.scholastic.com

Schonfeld & Associates
800-205-0030
www.saibooks.com

School Zone Publishing Co.
800-253-0564
www.schoolzone.com

Schreiber Publishing
800-822-3213
schreibernet.com

Scott & Daughter Publishing
800-547-2688
www.workbook.com

Scott Foresman
800-535-4391
www.scottforesman.com

Scott Publications
800-458-8237

Scott Publishing Co.
800-572-6885
www.scottonline.com

Scurlock Publishing Co.
800-228-6389
www.muzzmag.com

Seal Books
800-668-4247
www.randomhouse.ca

Seal Press
800-754-0271
www.sealpress.com

Seedling Publications
877-857-7333
www.seedlingpub.com

SelectiveHouse Publishers
888-256-6399
www.selectivehouse.com

Self-Counsel Press International Ltd.
877-877-6490
www.self-counsel.com

Shambhala Publications
888-424-2329
www.shambhala.com

M. E. Sharpe
800-541-6563
www.mesharpe.com

Sheed & Ward
800-558-0580; fax 800-369-4448
www.bookmasters.com/sheed

Sheep Meadow Press
800-972-4491

Sherman Asher Publishing
888-984-2686
www.shermanasher.com

Siddha Yoga Publications
888-422-3334
www.siddhayoga.org

Sierra Press
800-745-2631
www.nationalparksusa.com

Signature Books Publishing LLC
800-356-5687
www.signaturebooks.com

Silver Moon Press
800-874-3320
www.silvermoonpress.com

Silver Pixel Press
800-394-3686
www.silverpixelpress.com

Simcha Press
800-851-9100; fax 800-424-7652
www.simchapress.com

Simon & Pierre Publishing
800-565-9523
www.dundurn.com

Simon & Schuster
800-223-2336; fax 800-943-9831
www.simonsays.com

Singular Publishing Group
800-521-8545; fax 800-774-8398
www.singpub.com

Six Strings Music Publishing
800-784-0203
www.sixstringsmusicpub.com

SkillPath Publications
800-873-7545
www.ourbookstore.com

Sky Publishing Corp.
800-253-0245
www.skypub.com

SkyLight Paths Publishing
800-962-4544
www.skylightpaths.com

Skylight Professional Development
800-348-4474
www.skylightedu.com

Slack
800-257-8290
www.slackbooks.com

Smith & Kraus
800-895-4331
www.smithkraus.com

Gibbs Smith Publisher
800-748-5439; fax 800-213-3023

M. Lee Smith Publishers
800-274-6774
www.mleesmith.com

Smyth & Helwys Publishing
800-747-3016
www.helwys.com

Snow Lion Publications
800-950-0313
www.snowlionpub.com

Society for Industrial & Applied
Mathematics
800-447-7426
www.siam.org
Society for Mining, Metallurgy
& Exploration
800-763-3132
www.smenet.org
Society of Biblical Literature
877-725-3334
www.sbl-site.org
Society of Manufacturing Engineers
800-733-4763
www.sme.org
Software Training Resources
800-419-7420
www.strmanuals.com
Sogides Ltée.
800-361-4806
sogides.com
Solano Press Books
800-931-9373
www.solano.com
Soli Deo Gloria Publications
888-266-5734
www.sdgbooks.com
Solucient
800-568-3282
www.solucient.com
Sophia Institute Press
800-888-9344
www.sophiainstitute.com
Sopris West
800-547-6747
www.sopriswest.com
Sorin Books
800-282-1865; fax 800-282-5681
www.sorinbooks.com
Sourcebooks
800-432-7444
www.sourcebooks.com
South Carolina Bar
800-768-7787
www.scbar.org
South End Press
800-533-8478
www.southendpress.org
South-Western College Publishing
800-543-0487
thomsonlearning.com
Southeast Asia Publications
888-731-9599
www.niu.edu/cseas/seap

Southern Illinois University Press
800-346-2680; fax 800-346-2681
www.siu.edu/siupress
Southern Institute Press
800-633-4891
www.intl-nlp.com
Southwest Parks & Monuments Association
888-569-SPMA
www.spma.org
Space Link Books
877-767-0057
www.spacelinkbooks.com
Spizzirri Publishing
800-322-9819
spizzirri.com
Sports Publishing
800-327-5557
www.sportspublishinginc.com
Springer-Verlag New York
800-777-4643
www.springer.de
SPS Studios
800-525-0642; fax 800-545-8573
spsstudios.com
Squarebooks
800-345-6699
fotobaron.com/squarebooks
ST Publications Book Division
800-925-1110
www.stpubs.com
Stackpole Books
800-732-3669
www.stackpolebooks.com
Standard Publishing Co.
877-867-5751
www.standardpub.com
Standard Publishing Corp.
800-682-5759
standardpublishingcorp.com
Stanford University Press
www.sup.org
Star Bright Books
800-788-4439
www.starbrightbooks.com
Starburst Publishers
800-441-1456
www.starburstpublishers.com
Starlite
800-577-2929
State Bar of Wisconsin
800-728-7788

State House Press
800-421-3378
www.statehousepress.com

State University of New York Press
800-666-2211; fax 800-688-2877
www.sunypress.edu

Statistics Canada
800-700-1033; fax 800-889-9734

Steck-Vaughn Publishers
877-578-2638
www.steck-vaughn.com

Stemmer House Publishers
800-676-7511; fax 800-645-6958
www.stemmer.com

Stenhouse Publishers
888-363-0566; fax 800-833-9164

Sterling Publishing Co.
800-367-9692

SterlingHouse Publisher
888-542-2665

Stewart, Tabori & Chang
800-932-0070

Stoddart Publishing Co.
800-805-1083
www.stoddartpub.com

Stone Bridge Press
800-947-7271

Stoneydale Press Publishing Co.
800-737-7006

Storey Books
800-793-9396
www.storey.com

Studio 4 Productions
888-782-5474
studio4productions.com

Stylus Publishing LLC
800-232-0223
styluspub.com

Sulzburger & Graham
800-366-7086
www.sgpublishing.com

Summers Press
800-743-6491
www.summerspress.com

Summit Publications
800-419-0200
www.yogs.com

Summit University Press
800-245-5445
www.hostmontana.com/supress

Summy-Birchard
800-327-7643

Sunbelt Publications
800-626-6579
www.sunbeltpub.com

Sunburst Technology
800-338-3457

Sundance Publishing LLC
800-343-8204; fax 800-456-2419
www.sundancepub.com

Surrey Books
800-326-4430
www.surreybooks.com

Swallow Press
800-621-2736; fax 800-621-8476
www.ohiou.edu/oupress/

Swedenborg Foundation Publishers
800-355-3222
www.swedenborg.com

SYBEX
800-227-2346
www.sybex.com

Synapse Information Resources
888-SYN-CHEM
www.synapseinfo.com

Syracuse University Press
800-365-8929
www.sumweb.5yr.edu/su_press

T. J. Publishers
800-999-1168

Tapestry Press Ltd.
800-535-2007
www.tapestrypress.com

Tarascon Publishing
877-929-9926
www.tarascon.com

Taschen America
888-TASCHEN
www.taschen.com

Taunton Press
800-283-7252
www.taunton.com

Taylor & Francis
www.taylorandfrancis.com

Taylor Publishing Co.
800-677-2800
www.taylorpub.com

Teach Me Tapes
800-456-4656
www.teachmetapes.com

Teacher Created Materials
800-662-4321; fax 800-525-1254
www.teachercreated.com

Teacher Ideas Press
800-237-6124
www.lu.com
Teachers & Writers Collaborative
888-266-5789
www.twc.org
Teacher's Discovery
800-521-3897
www.teachersdiscovery.com
Teachers Friend Publications
800-343-9680; fax 800-307-8176
www.teachersfriend.com
Teaching Strategies
800-637-3652
www.teachingstrategies.com
Technical Association of the Pulp & Paper
Industry
800-332-8686
www.tappi.org
Technology Training Systems
800-676-8871
www.myplantstraining.com
Technomic Publishing Co.
800-233-9936
www.techpub.com
Temple University Press
800-447-1656; fax 800-207-4442
www.temple.edu/tempress
Templegate Publishers
800-367-4844
www.templegate.com
Templeton Foundation Press
800-561-3367
www.templetonpress.org
Ten Speed Press
800-841-Book
www.tenspeed.com
Tetra Press
800-526-0650
www.tetra-fish.com
Texas A&M University Press
888-617-2421
www.tamu.edu./upress/
Texas Christian University Press
888-617-2421
www.prs.tcu.edu/prs/
Texas Tech University Press
800-832-4042
www.ttup.ttu.edu
Texas Western Press
800-488-3789
www.utep.edu/~twp

TFH Publications
800-631-2188
Thames & Hudson
800-233-4830
www.thamesandhudsonusa.com
Theosophical Publishing House
800-669-9425
www.theosophical.org
Theta Reports
800-995-1550
www.thetareports.com
Thieme Medical Publishers
800-782-3488
Thinkers' Press
800-397-7117
www.thinkerspress.com
Thinking Publications
800-225-4769; fax 800-828-8885
www.thinkingpublications.com
Charles C. Thomas Publisher Ltd.
800-258-8980
Thomas Geale Publications
800-554-5457
Thomas Nelson
800-251-4000
www.thomasnelson.com
Thomas Publications
800-840-6782
www.thomaspublications.com
Thompson Educational Publishing
800-805-1083
www.thompsonbooks.com
Gordon V. Thompson Music
800-327-7643
www.wbpdealers.com
Thomson Financial Publishing
800-321-3373
www.tfp.com
Thorndike Press
800-223-6121; fax 800-558-4676
www.mlr.com/thorndike
Through the Bible Publishers
800-284-0158
www.throughthebible.com
Tiare Publications
800-420-0579
www.tiare.com
Tide-mark Press
800-338-2508
www.tidemarkpress.com
Tidewater Publishers
800-638-7641

Timber Press
800-327-5680
www.timberpress.com

Time Being Books-Poetry in Sight & Sound
888-301-9121
www.timebeing.com

Time Life
800-621-7026

Time Warner Audio Books
www.twbookmark.com/audiobooks

Editions Pierre Tisseyre
800-643-4720

TLC Genealogy
800-858-8558

TM Publishing
888-284-8739
tomorrowschildren.com

The Toby Press LLC
800-810-7703
www.tobypress.com

Todd Publications
800-747-1056
www.toddpublications.com

TODTRI Book Publishers
800-696-7299; fax 800-696-7482

Tommy Nelson
800-251-4000

Torah Aura Productions
800-238-6724
www.torahaura.com

Totline
800-609-1735

Tower Publishing Co.
800-969-8693
www.ime.net/tower

Traders Press
800-927-8222
www.traderspress.com

Trafalgar Square
800-423-4525
www.trafalgarsquarebooks.com

Trails Illustrated/National Geographic Maps
800-962-1643; fax 800-626-8676
www.trailsillustrated.com

Trakker Maps
800-327-3108

Tralco Educational Services
888-487-2526
www.tralco.com

Transaction Publishers
888-999-6778
www.transactionpub.com

Transnational Publishers
800-914-8186
www.transnationalpubs.com

Transportation Technical Service
888-ONLY-TTS

Travelers' Tales
800-788-3123
www.travelerstales.com

Treehaus Communications
800-638-4287
www.treehaus1.com

Triad Publishing Co.
800-854-4947
www.triadpublishing.com

Tricycle Press
800-841-2665
www.tenspeed.com

Trident Press International
800-593-3662; fax 800-494-4226
www.trident-international.com

Trinity Press International
800-877-0012
www.trinitypressintl.com

TripBuilder
800-525-9745
www.tripbuilder.com

TriQuarterly Books
800-621-2736

Triumph Books
800-335-5323

Troll Communications LLC
800-526-5289
www.troll.com

Truman State University Press
800-916-6802
www2.truman.edu/tsup

Turnstone Press
800-982-6472
www.turnstonepress.com

Tuttle Publishing
800-526-2778; fax 800-FAX-TUTL
www.tuttlepublishing.com

Twenty-Third Publications
800-321-0411
www.twentythirdpublications.com

Two Thousand Three Associates
800-598-5256

Two-Can Publishing LLC
877-789-6226
two-canpublishing.com

Tyndale House Publishers
800-323-9400
www.tyndale.com

UAHC Press
888-489-UAHC
www.uahcpress.com
ULI–The Urban Land Institute
800-321-5011; fax 800-248-4585
www.uli.org
Ulysses Press
800-377-2542
www.ulyssespress.com
Unarius Academy of Science Publications
800-475-7062
www.unarius.org
Unicor Medical
800-825-7421
www.unicormed.com
Unique Publications Books & Videos
800-332-3330
www.cfwenterprises.com
United Nations Publications
800-253-9646
www.un.org/publications
United States Holocaust Memorial Museum
800-259-9998
www.ushmm.org/
United States Pharmacopeia
800-227-8772
www.usp.org
United Synagogue Book Service
800-594-5617
www.uscj.org/booksvc
Universal Radio Research
800-431-3939
University of Akron Press
877-827-7377
www.uakron.edu/uapress
University of Alaska Press
888-252-6657
University of Arizona Press
800-426-3797
www.uapress.arizona.edu
University of Arkansas Press
800-626-0090
www.uapress.com
University of British Columbia Press
877-377-9378; fax 800-668-0821
www.ubcpress.ubc.ca
University of California Press
800-822-6657
www.ucpress.edu
University of Chicago Press
800-621-2736
www.press.uchicago.edu

University of Denver Center for Teaching
International Relations Publications
800-967-2847
www.du.edu/ctir
University of Georgia Press
800-266-5842
www.uga/edu/ugapress
University of Hawaii Press
888-847-7377; fax 800-650-7811
www.uhpress.hawaii.edu
University of Healing Press
888-463-8654
www.university-of-healing.edu
University of Idaho Press
800-847-7377
www.uidaho.edu/ ~uipress
University of Illinois Press
800-545-4703
www.press.uillinois.edu
University of Iowa Press
800-621-2736; fax 800-621-8476
www.uiowa.edu/~uipress
University of Massachusetts Press
800-488-1144
www.umass.edu/umpress
University of Michigan Press
800-876-1922
www.press.umich.edu
University of Missouri Press
800-828-1894
www.system.missouri.edu/upress
University of Nebraska Press
800-755-1105; fax 800-526-2617
www.nebraskapress.un1.edu
University of Nevada Press
877-682-6657
www.nvbooks.nevada.edu
University of New Mexico Press
800-249-7737; fax 800-622-8667
University of North Carolina Press
800-848-6224; fax 800-272-6817
www.uncpress.unc.edu
University of Notre Dame Press
800-621-2736
www.undpress.nd.edu
University of Oklahoma Press
800-627-7377; fax 800-735-0476
www.ou.edu/oupress
University of Pennsylvania Museum of
Archaeology & Anthropology
800-306-1941
www.upenn.ed/museum_pubs/

University of Pennsylvania Press
800-445-9880
www.upenn.edu/pennpress
University of South Carolina Press
800-768-2500; fax 800-868-0740
www.sc.edu/uscpress/
University of Utah Press
800-773-6672
www.upress.utah.edu
University of Washington Press
800-441-4115; fax 800-669-7993
www.washington.edu/uwpress/
University of Wisconsin Press
800-621-2736; fax 800-621-8476
www.wisc.edu/wisconsinpress/
University Press of America
800-462-6420; fax 800-338-4550
University Press of Colorado
800-627-7377
University Press of Florida
800-226-3822; fax 800-680-1955
University Press of Kentucky
800-839-6855
www.uky.edu/universitypress/
University Press of Mississippi
800-737-7788
University Press of New England
800-421-1561
University Press of Virginia
877-288-6400
www.upressvirginia.edu
University Publications of America
800-638-8380
University Publishing Group
800-654-8188
Upper Room Books
800-972-0433
www.upperroom.org
URANTIA Foundation
800-525-3319
Urban Institute Press
877-UIPRESS
www.uipress.org
U.S. Conference of Catholic Bishops
800-235-8722
US Games Systems
800-544-2637
Utah Geological Survey
888-UTAH-MAP
www.ugs.state.ut.us

Utah State University Press
800-239-9974
www.usu.edu/usupress

Van der Plas Publications
877-353-1207
www.vanderplas.net
VanDam
800-UNFOLDS
www.vandam.com
Vandamere Press
800-551-7776
www.vandamere.com
Vanderbilt University Press
800-627-7377; fax 800-735-0476
www.vanderbilt.edu/vupress
Vanwell Publishing Ltd.
800-661-6136
Vault.com
888-562-8285
www.vault.com
Vida Publishers
800-843-2548
Viking
www.penguinputnam.com
Virtual Publishing Group
877-411-8744
www.ebooks2go.com
Vision Works Publishing
800-999-9551 ext. 870
Vista Publishing
800-634-2498
www.vistapubl.com
Visual Reference Publications
800-251-4545
www.visualrefernce.com
Viz Communications
800-394-3042
www.viz.com
Volcano Press
800-879-9636
www.volcanopress.com
Volt Directory Marketing Ltd.
800-677-3839; fax 800-897-2491
www.voLtd.irectory.com/vdm
Voyageur Press
800-888-9653
www.voyageurpress.com

Wadsworth Group
800-487-5510
www.wadgroup.com

J. Weston Walch Publisher
800-341-6094
www.walch.com

Waldman House Press
888-700-7333

Walker & Co.
800-289-2553; fax 800-218-9367

Wall & Emerson
877-409-4601
www.wallbooks.com

Wm. K. Walthers
800-877-7171

Warner Books
www.twbookmark.com

Warner Bros Publications
800-327-7643
www.warnerbrospublications.com

Washington State University Press
800-354-7360
www.wsu.edu/wsupress

Waterfront Books
800-639-6063
www.waterfrontbooks.com

Waterloo Music Co.
800-563-9683

Watson-Guptill Publications
800-278-8477

Wayne State University Press
800-978-7323

Wayside Publishing
888-302-2519
www.waysidepublishing.com

Weatherhill
800-437-7840; fax 800-557-5601
www.weatherhill.com

Weigl Educational Publishers Ltd.
800-668-0766
www.weigl.com

Weil Publishing Co.
800-877-9345
www.weilpublishing.com

Wesleyan Publishing House
800-493-7539; fax 800-788-3535
www.wesleyan.org

West Group
800-328-9352
www.westgroup.com

Westcliffe Publishers
800-523-3692
www.westcliffepublishers.com

Westminster John Knox Press
800-227-2872; fax 800-541-5113

Westview Press
800-242-7737
www.perseusbooksgroup.com

WH&O International
800-553-6678

Wheatherstone Press
800-980-0077

White Cliffs Media
800-359-3210
www.wc-media.com

White Cloud Press
800-380-8286; fax 800-380-8286
www.whitecloudpress.com

White Mane Publishing Co.
888-948-6263

White Wolf Publishing
800-454-9653
www.white-wolf.com

Whitehorse Press
800-531-1133
www.whitehorsepress.com

Albert Whitman & Co.
800-255-7675
www.awhitmanco.com

Whittier Publications
800-897-TEXT

Whole Person Associates
800-247-6789
www.wholeperson.com

Wide World of Maps
800-279-7654
www.maps4u.com

Michael Wiese Productions
800-379-8808
www.mwp.com

Wilderness Adventures Press
800-925-3339; fax 800-390-7558
www.wildadv.com

Wilderness Press
800-443-7227
www.wildernesspress.com

Wildlife Education Ltd.
800-992-5034
www.zoobooks.com

John Wiley & Sons Canada Ltd.
800-567-4797; fax 800-565-6802

John Wiley & Sons
800-225-5945

Williamson Publishing Co.
800-234-8791; fax 800-304-7224
www.williamsonbooks.com

Willow Creek Press
800-850-9453
www.willowcreekpress.com

H. W. Wilson
800-367-6770; fax 800-367-6770
www.hwwilson.com

Wimmer Cos./Cookbook Distribution
800-727-1034; fax 800-794-9806
www.wimmerco.com

Wind Canyon Books
800-952-7007
www.windcanyon.com

Windsor Books
800-321-5934
www.windsorpublishing.com

Wine Appreciation Guild Ltd.
800-231-9463
www.wineappreciation.com

Winslow Press
800-617-3947
www.winslowpress.com

Winters Publishing
800-457-3230; fax 800-457-3230

Wisconsin Dept of Public Instruction
800-243-8782
www.dpi.state.wi.us

Wittenborn Art Books
800-660-6403
art-books.com

WJ Fantasy
800-222-7529; fax 800-200-3000

Wood Lake Books
800-663-2775
www.joinhands.com

Woodbine House
800-843-7323
www.woodbinehouse.com

Woodbridge Press Publishing Co.
800-237-6053
www.woodbridgepress.com

Woodland Publishing
800-777-2665

Ralph Woodrow Evangelistic Assn
877-664-1549
www.ralphwoodrow.com

Wordware Publishing
800-229-4949
www.wordware.com

Workman Publishing Company
800-722-7202
www.workman.com

World Bible Publishers
800-247-5111; fax 800-822-4271
www.firstnetchristian.com

World Book
800-967-5325
www.worldbook.com

World Citizens
800-247-6553
soultosoulmedia.com

World Eagle
800-854-8273
www.worldeagle.com

World Leisure Corp.
800-292-1966

World Resources Institute
800-822-0504
www.wri.org/wri

World Scientific Publishing Co.
800-227-7562
www.wspc.com

World Trade Press
800-833-8586
www.worldtradepress.com

Worldtariff
800-556-9334
www.worldtariff.com

Wright Group/McGraw-Hill
800-523-2371; fax 800-543-7323
www.wrightgroup.com

Write Stuff Enterprises
www.writestuffbooks.com

Write Way Publishing
www.writewaypub.com

Writer's Digest Books
888-590-4082
www.writersdigest.com

Writings of Mary Baker Eddy/Publisher
www.spirituality.com

Wrox Press
www.wrox.com

Wyrick & Co.
800-227-5898

Xlibris Corp.
888-795-4274
www.xlibris.com

Yale University Press
    800-987-7323; fax 800-777-9253
    www.yale.edu/yup/
Yardbird Books
    800-622-6044
    www.yardbird.com
YMAA Publication Center
    800-669-8892
    www.ymaa.com
York Press
    800-962-2763
    www.yorkpress.com
Young People's Press
    800-231-9774
    www.youngpeoplespress.com
Yucca Tree Press
    800-383-6183
    www.yuccatree.com

YWAM Publishing
    800-922-2143
    www.ywampublishing.org

Zagat Survey
    800-333-3421
    www.zagat.com
Zaner-Bloser
    800-421-3018
    www.zaner-bloser.com
Zephyr Press
    800-232-2187
    www.zephyrpress.com
Zoland Books
    www.zolandbooks.com
Zondervan Publishing House
    800-727-1309
    www.zondervan.com

How to Obtain an ISBN

Emery Koltay

Director Emeritus
United States ISBN Agency

The International Standard Book Numbering (ISBN) system was introduced into the United Kingdom by J. Whitaker & Sons Ltd., in 1967 and into the United States in 1968 by the R. R. Bowker Company. The Technical Committee on Documentation of the International Organization for Standardization (ISO TC 46) defines the scope of the standard as follows:

> . . . the purpose of this standard is to coordinate and standardize the use of identifying numbers so that each ISBN is unique to a title, edition of a book, or monographic publication published, or produced, by a specific publisher, or producer. Also, the standard specifies the construction of the ISBN and the location of the printing on the publication.
>
> Books and other monographic publications may include printed books and pamphlets (in various bindings), mixed media publications, other similar media including educational films/videos and transparencies, books on cassettes, microcomputer software, electronic publications, microform publications, braille publications and maps. Serial publications and music sound recordings are specifically excluded, as they are covered by other identification systems. [ISO Standard 2108]

The ISBN is used by publishers, distributors, wholesalers, bookstores, and libraries, among others, in 210 countries to expedite such operations as order fulfillment, electronic point-of-sale checkout, inventory control, returns processing, circulation/location control, file maintenance and update, library union lists, and royalty payments.

Construction of an ISBN

An ISBN consists of 10 digits separated into the following parts:

1 Group identifier: national, geographic, language, or other convenient group
2 Publisher or producer identifier
3 Title identifier
4 Check digit

When an ISBN is written or printed, it should be preceded by the letters *ISBN*, and each part should be separated by a space or hyphen. In the United States, the hyphen is used for separation, as in the following example: ISBN 1-879500-01-9. In this example, 1 is the group identifier, 879500 is the publisher identifier, 01 is the title identifier, and 9 is the check digit. The group of English-speaking countries, which includes the United States, Australia, Canada, New Zealand, and the United Kingdom, uses the group identifiers 0 and 1.

The ISBN Organization

The administration of the ISBN system is carried out at three levels—through the International ISBN Agency in Berlin, Germany; the national agencies; and the publishing houses themselves. Responsible for assigning country prefixes and for coordinating the worldwide implementation of the system, the International ISBN Agency in Berlin has an advisory panel that represents the International Organization for Standardization (ISO), publishers, and libraries. The International ISBN Agency publishes the *Publishers International ISBN Directory,* which is distributed in the United States by R. R. Bowker. As the publisher of *Books In Print,* with its extensive and varied database of publishers' addresses, R. R. Bowker was the obvious place to initiate the ISBN system and to provide the service to the U.S. publishing industry. To date, the U.S. ISBN Agency has entered more than 120,000 publishers into the system.

ISBN Assignment Procedure

Assignment of ISBNs is a shared endeavor between the U.S. ISBN Agency and the publisher. The publisher is provided with an application form and an instruction sheet. After an application is received and verified by the agency, an ISBN publisher prefix is assigned, along with a computer-generated block of ISBNs. The publisher then has the responsibility to assign an ISBN to each title, to keep an accurate record of the numbers assigned by entering each title in the ISBN Log Book, and to report each title to the *Books in Print* database. One of the responsibilities of the ISBN Agency is to validate assigned ISBNs and to retain a record of all ISBNs in circulation.

ISBN implementation is very much market-driven. Wholesalers and distributors, such as Baker & Taylor, Brodart, and Ingram, as well as such large retail chains as Waldenbooks and B. Dalton recognize and enforce the ISBN system by requiring all new publishers to register with the ISBN Agency before accepting their books for sale. Also, the ISBN is a mandatory bibliographic element in the International Standard Bibliographical Description (ISBD). The Library of Congress Cataloging in Publication (CIP) Division directs publishers to the agency to obtain their ISBN prefixes.

Location and Display of the ISBN

On books, pamphlets, and other printed material, the ISBN shall be on the verso of the title leaf or, if this is not possible, at the foot of the title leaf itself. It should also appear at the foot of the outside back cover if practicable and at the foot of the back of the jacket if the book has one (the lower right-hand corner is recommended). If neither of these alternatives is possible, then the number shall be printed in some other prominent position on the outside. The ISBN shall also appear on any accompanying promotional materials following the provisions for location according to the format of the material.

On other monographic publications, the ISBN shall appear on the title or credit frames and any labels permanently affixed to the publication. If the publication is issued in a container that is an integral part of the publication, the ISBN shall be displayed on the label. If it is not possible to place the ISBN on the item or its label, then the number should be displayed on the bottom or the back of the container, box, sleeve, or frame. It should also appear on any accompanying material, including each component of a multitype publication.

Printing of ISBN in Machine-Readable Coding

In the last few years, much work has been done on machine-readable representations of the ISBN, and now all books should carry ISBNs in bar code. The rapid worldwide extension of bar code scanning has brought into prominence the 1980 agreement between the International Article Numbering, formerly the European Article Numbering (EAN), Association and the International ISBN Agency that translates the ISBN into an ISBN Bookland EAN bar code.

All ISBN Bookland EAN bar codes start with a national identifier (00–09 representing the United States), *except* those on books and periodicals. The agreement replaces the usual national identifier with a special "ISBN Bookland" identifier represented by the digits 978 for books (see Figure 1) and 977 for periodicals. The 978 ISBN Bookland/EAN prefix is followed by the first nine digits of the ISBN. The check digit of the ISBN is dropped and replaced by a check digit calculated according to the EAN rules.

Figure 1 / Printing the ISBN in Bookland/EAN Symbology

ISBN 1-879500-01-9

9 781879 500013

The following is an example of the conversion of the ISBN to ISBN Bookland/EAN:

ISBN	1-879500-01-9
ISBN without check digit	1-879500-01
Adding EAN flag	978187950001
EAN with EAN check digit	9781879500013

Five-Digit Add-On Code

In the United States, a five-digit add-on code is used for additional information. In the publishing industry, this code can be used for price information or some other specific coding. The lead digit of the five-digit add-on has been designated a currency identifier, when the add-on is used for price. Number 5 is the code for the U.S. dollar; 6 denotes the Canadian dollar; 1 the British pound; 3 the Australian dollar; and 4 the New Zealand dollar. Publishers that do not want to indicate price in the add-on should print the code 90000 (see Figure 2).

Figure 2 / Printing the ISBN Bookland/EAN Number in Bar Code with the Five-Digit Add-On Code

ISBN 0-9628556-4-2

978 = ISBN Bookland/EAN prefix
5 + Code for U.S. $
0995 = $9.95

ISBN 1-879500-01-9

90000 means no information
in the add-on code

Reporting the Title and the ISBN

After the publisher reports a title to the ISBN Agency, the number is validated and the title is listed in the many R. R. Bowker hard-copy and electronic publications, including *Books in Print, Forthcoming Books, Paperbound Books in Print, Books in Print Supplement, Books Out of Print, Books in Print Online, Books in Print Plus-CD ROM, Children's Books in Print, Subject Guide to Children's Books in Print, On Cassette: A Comprehensive Bibliography of Spoken Word Audiocassettes, Variety's Complete Home Video Directory, Software Encyclopedia, Software for Schools,* and other specialized publications.

For an ISBN application form and additional information, write to United States ISBN Agency, R. R. Bowker Company, 630 Central Ave., New Providence, NJ 07974, or call 877-310-7333. The e-mail address is ISBN-SAN@bowker.com. The ISBN Web site is at http://www.ISBN.org.

How to Obtain an ISSN

National Serials Data Program
Library of Congress

In the early 1970s the rapid increase in the production and dissemination of information and an intensified desire to exchange information about serials in computerized form among different systems and organizations made it increasingly clear that a means to identify serial publications at an international level was needed. The International Standard Serial Number (ISSN) was developed and has become the internationally accepted code for identifying serial publications. The number itself has no significance other than as a brief, unique, and unambiguous identifier. It is an international standard, ISO 3297, as well as a U.S. standard, ANSI/NISO Z39.9. The ISSN consists of eight digits in arabic numerals 0 to 9, except for the last, or check, digit, which can be an X. The numbers appear as two groups of four digits separated by a hyphen and preceded by the letters ISSN—for example, ISSN 1234-5679.

The ISSN is not self-assigned by publishers. Administration of the ISSN is coordinated through the ISSN Network, an intergovernmental organization within the UNESCO/UNISIST program. The network consists of national and regional centers, coordinated by the ISSN International Centre, located in Paris. Centers have the responsibility to register serials published in their respective countries.

Because serials are generally known and cited by title, assignment of the ISSN is inseparably linked to the key title, a standardized form of the title derived from information in the serial issue. Only one ISSN can be assigned to a title; if the title changes, a new ISSN must be assigned. Centers responsible for assigning ISSNs also construct the key title and create an associated bibliographic record.

The ISSN International Centre handles ISSN assignments for international organizations and for countries that do not have a national center. It also maintains and distributes the collective ISSN database that contains bibliographic records corresponding to each ISSN assignment as reported by the rest of the network. The database contains more than 1 million ISSNs.

In the United States, the National Serials Data Program at the Library of Congress is responsible for assigning and maintaining the ISSNs for all U.S. serial titles. Publishers wishing to have an ISSN assigned should request an application form from the program, or download one from the program's Web site, and ask for an assignment. Assignment of the ISSN is free, and there is no charge for its use.

The ISSN is used all over the world by serial publishers to distinguish similar titles from each other. It is used by subscription services and libraries to manage files for orders, claims, and back issues. It is used in automated check-in systems by libraries that wish to process receipts more quickly. Copyright centers use the ISSN as a means to collect and disseminate royalties. It is also used as an identification code by postal services and legal deposit services. The ISSN is included as a verification element in interlibrary lending activities and for union catalogs as a collocating device. In recent years, the ISSN has been incorporated into bar codes for optical recognition of serial publications and into the standards for the identification of issues and articles in serial publications.

For further information about the ISSN or the ISSN Network, U.S. libraries and publishers should contact the National Serials Data Program, Library of Congress, Washington, DC 20540-4160; 202-707-6452; fax 202-707-6333; e-mail issn@loc.gov. ISSN application forms and instructions for obtaining an ISSN are also available via the Library of Congress World Wide Web site, http://lcweb.loc.gov/issn.

Non-U.S. parties should contact the ISSN International Centre, 20 rue Bachaumont, 75002 Paris, France; telephone (33-1) 44-88-22-20; fax (33-1) 40-26-32-43; e-mail issnic@issn.org; World Wide Web http://www.ISSN.org.

How to Obtain an SAN

Emery Koltay

Director Emeritus
United States ISBN/SAN Agency

SAN stands for Standard Address Number. It is a unique identification code for addresses of organizations that are involved in or served by the book industry, and that engage in repeated transactions with other members within this group. For purposes of this standard, the book industry includes book publishers, book wholesalers, book distributors, book retailers, college bookstores, libraries, library binders, and serial vendors. Schools, school systems, technical institutes, colleges, and universities are not members of this industry, but are served by it and therefore included in the SAN system.

The purpose of SAN is to facilitate communications among these organizations, of which there are several hundreds of thousands, that engage in a large volume of separate transactions with one another. These transactions include purchases of books by book dealers, wholesalers, schools, colleges, and libraries from publishers and wholesalers; payments for all such purchases; and other communications between participants. The objective of this standard is to establish an identification code system by assigning each address within the industry a discrete code to be used for positive identification for all book and serial buying and selling transactions.

Many organizations have similar names and multiple addresses, making identification of the correct contact point difficult and subject to error. In many cases, the physical movement of materials takes place between addresses that differ from the addresses to be used for the financial transactions. In such instances, there is ample opportunity for confusion and errors. Without identification by SAN, a complex record-keeping system would have to be instituted to avoid introducing errors. In addition, it is expected that problems with the current numbering system such as errors in billing, shipping, payments, and returns, will be significantly reduced by using the SAN system. SAN will also eliminate one step in the order fulfillment process: the "look-up procedure" used to assign account numbers. Previously a store or library dealing with 50 different publishers was assigned a different account number by each of the suppliers. SAN solved this problem. If a publisher indicates its SAN on its stationery and ordering documents, vendors to whom it sends transactions do not have to look up the account number, but can proceed immediately to process orders by SAN.

Libraries are involved in many of the same transactions as book dealers, such as ordering and paying for books and charging and paying for various services to other libraries. Keeping records of transactions, whether these involve buying, selling, lending, or donations, entails similar operations that require an SAN. Having the SAN on all stationery will speed up order fulfillment and eliminate errors in shipping, billing, and crediting; this, in turn, means savings in both time and money.

History

Development of the Standard Address Number began in 1968 when Russell Reynolds, general manager of the National Association of College Stores (NACS), approached the R. R. Bowker Company and suggested that a "Standard Account Number" system be implemented in the book industry. The first draft of a standard was prepared by an American National Standards Institute (ANSI) Committee Z39 subcommittee, which was co-chaired by Russell Reynolds and Emery Koltay. After Z39 members proposed changes, the current version of the standard was approved by NACS on December 17, 1979.

The chairperson of the ANSI Z39 Subcommittee 30, which developed the approved standard, was Herbert W. Bell, former senior vice president of McGraw-Hill Book Company. The subcommittee comprised the following representatives from publishing companies, distributors, wholesalers, libraries, national cooperative online systems, schools, and school systems: Herbert W. Bell (chair), McGraw-Hill Book Company; Richard E. Bates, Holt, Rinehart and Winston; Thomas G. Brady, The Baker & Taylor Companies, Paul J. Fasana, New York Public Library; Emery I. Koltay, R. R. Bowker Company; Joan McGreevey, New York University Book Centers; Pauline F. Micciche, OCLC, Inc.; Sandra K. Paul, SKP Associates; David Gray Remington, Library of Congress; Frank Sanders, Hammond Public School System; and Peter P. Chirimbes (alternate), Stamford Board of Education.

Format

The SAN consists of six digits plus a seventh *Modulus 11* check digit; a hyphen follows the third digit (XXX-XXXX) to facilitate transcription. The hyphen is to be used in print form, but need not be entered or retained in computer systems. Printed on documents, the Standard Address Number should be preceded by the identifier "SAN" to avoid confusion with other numerical codes (SAN XXX-XXXX).

Check Digit Calculation

The check digit is based on *Modulus 11*, and can be derived as follows:

1. Write the digits of the basic number.   2 3 4 5 6 7
2. Write the constant weighting factors associated with each position by the basic number.   7 6 5 4 3 2
3. Multiply each digit by its associated weighting factor.   14 18 20 20 18 14
4. Add the products of the multiplications. $14 + 18 + 20 + 20 + 18 + 14 = 104$
5. Divide the sum by *Modulus 11* to find the remainder. $104 \div 11 = 9$ plus a remainder of 5
6. Subtract the remainder from the *Modulus 11* to generate the required check digit. If there is no remainder, generate a check digit of zero. If the check digit is 10,

generate a check digit of X to represent 10,
since the use of 10 would require an extra digit. $11 - 5 = 6$

7. Append the check digit to create the standard
    seven-digit Standard Address Number.   SAN 234-5676

SAN Assignment

The R. R. Bowker Company accepted responsibility for being the central administrative agency for SAN, and in that capacity assigns SANs to identify uniquely the addresses of organizations. No SANs can be reassigned; in the event that an organization should cease to exist, for example, its SAN would cease to be in circulation entirely. If an organization using an SAN should move or change its name with no change in ownership, its SAN would remain the same, and only the name or address would be updated to reflect the change.

The SAN should be used in all transactions; it is recommended that the SAN be imprinted on stationery, letterheads, order and invoice forms, checks, and all other documents used in executing various book transactions. The SAN should always be printed on a separate line above the name and address of the organization, preferably in the upper left-hand corner of the stationery to avoid confusion with other numerical codes pertaining to the organization, such as telephone number, zip code, and the like.

SAN Functions and Suffixes

The SAN is strictly a Standard Address Number, becoming functional only in applications determined by the user; these may include activities such as purchasing, billing, shipping, receiving, paying, crediting, and refunding. Every department that has an independent function within an organization could have a SAN for its own identification. Users may choose to assign a suffix (a separate field) to their SAN strictly for internal use. Faculty members ordering books through a library acquisitions department, for example, may not have their own separate SAN, but may be assigned a suffix by the library. There is no standardized provision for placement of suffixes. Existing numbering systems do not have suffixes to take care of the "subset" type addresses. The SAN does not standardize this part of the address. For the implementation of SAN, it is suggested that wherever applicable the four-position suffix be used. This four-position suffix makes available 10,000 numbers, ranging from 0000 to 9999, and will accommodate all existing subset numbering presently in use.

For example, there are various ways to incorporate an SAN in an order fulfillment system. Firms just beginning to assign account numbers to their customers will have no conversion problems and will simply use the SAN as the numbering system. Firms that already have an existing number system can convert either on a step-by-step basis by adopting SANs whenever orders or payments are processed on the account, or by converting the whole file by using the SAN listing provided by the SAN Agency. Using the step-by-step conversion, firms may adopt SANs as customers provide them on their forms, orders, payments, and returns.

For additional information or suggestions, please write to Diana Luongo, SAN Coordinator, ISBN/SAN Agency, R. R. Bowker Company, 630 Central Ave., New Providence, NJ 07974, call 908-771-7755, or fax 908-665-2895. The e-mail address is ISBN-SAN@bowker.com. The SAN Web site is at http://www.ISBN.org.

Distinguished Books

Notable Books of 2001

The Notable Books Council of the Reference and User Services Association, a division of the American Library Association, selected these titles for their significant contribution to the expansion of knowledge or for the pleasure they can provide to adult readers.

Fiction

Carey, Peter. *True History of the Kelly Gang.* Knopf, $25 (0-375-41084-8).

Chaon, Dan. *Among the Missing.* Ballantine, $22 (0-345-44162-1).

Davis, Lydia. *Samuel Johnson Is Indignant: Stories.* McSweeney's, $16 (0-9703355-9-8).

Everett, Percival. *Erasure: A Novel.* UP New England, $24.95 (1-58465-090-7).

Franzen, Jonathan. *The Corrections: A Novel.* Farrar, Straus and Giroux, $26 (0-374-12998-3).

Gordimer, Nadine. *The Pickup: A Novel.* Farrar, Straus and Giroux, $24 (0-374-23210-5).

MacLeod, Alistair. *Island: The Complete Stories.* Norton, $24 (0-393-05035-1).

Olds, Bruce. *Bucking the Tiger.* Farrar, Straus and Giroux, $25 (0-374-11727-6).

Sebald, W. G. *Austerlitz.* Random House, $25.95 (0-375-50483-4).

Suri, Manil. *The Death of Vishnu.* Norton, $24.95 (0-393-05042-4).

Winegardner, Mark. *Crooked River Burning.* Harcourt, $27 (0-15-100294-0).

Nonfiction

Arana, Marie. *American Chica: Two Worlds, One Childhood.* Dial, $23.95 (0-385-31962-2).

Connell, Evan. *Aztec Treasure House: New and Selected Essays.* Counterpoint, $28 (1-58243-162-0).

Elliot, Jason. *An Unexpected Light: Travels in Afghanistan.* Picador, $30 (0-312-27459-9).

Halberstam, David. *War in a Time of Peace: Bush, Clinton and the Generals.* Scribner, $28 (0-7432-0212-0).

Hallinan, Joseph T. *Going up the River: Travels in a Prison Nation.* Random House, $24.95 (0-375-50263-7).

Hessler, Peter. *River Town: Two Years on the Yangtze.* HarperCollins, $26 (0-06-019544-4).

Hillenbrand, Laura. *Seabiscuit: An American Legend.* Random House, $24.95 (0-375-50291-2).

Lerner, Barron H. *The Breast Cancer Wars: Hope, Fear and the Pursuit of a Cure in Twentieth-Century America.* Oxford, $30 (0-19-514261-6).

Martinez, Ruben. *Crossing Over: A Mexican Family on the Migrant Trail.* Metropolitan, $26 (0-8050-4908-8).

McCullough, David. *John Adams.* Simon & Schuster, $35 (0-684-81363-7).

Schlosser, Eric. *Fast Food Nation: The Dark Side of the All-American Meal.* Houghton, $25 (0-395-97789-4).

Smith, Jean Edward. *Grant.* Simon & Schuster, $35 (0-684-94926-7).

Solomon, Andrew. *The Noonday Demon: An Atlas of Depression.* Scribner, $28 (0-684-85466-X).

Poetry

Collins, Billy. *Sailing Alone Around the Room: New and Selected Poems.* Random House, $21.95 (0-375-50380-3).

Mueller, Melinda. *What the Ice Gets: Shackleton's Antarctic Expedition 1914–1916.* Van West, $14 (0-9677021-1-9).

Best Books for Young Adults

Each year a committee of the Young Adult Library Services Association (YALSA), a division of the American Library Association, compiles a list of the best fiction and nonfiction appropriate for young adults ages 12 to 18. Selected on the basis of each book's proven or potential appeal and value to young adults, the titles span a variety of subjects as well as a broad range of reading levels.

Fiction

Bell, Hilari. *A Matter of Profit.* HarperCollins, $16.95 (0-06-029513-9).

Brashares, Ann. *The Sisterhood of the Traveling Pants.* Delacorte, $14.95 (0-385-72933-2).

Brooks, Bruce. *All That Remains.* Atheneum, $16.00 (0-689-83351-2).

Card, Orson Scott. *Shadow of the Hegemon.* Tor Books, $25.95 (0-312-87651-3).

Clement-Davies, David. *Fire Bringer.* Dutton Children's Books, $19.95 (0-525-46492-1).

Color of Absence: Twelve Stories About Love and Hope. Edited by James Howe. Atheneum, $16.00 (0-689-82862-4).

Cormier, Robert. *The Rag and Bone Shop.* Delacorte, $15.95 (0-385-72962-6).

Crutcher, Chris. *Whale Talk.* HarperCollins, $16.95 (0-06-029369-1).

Ferris, Jean. *Eight Seconds.* Harcourt, $17.00 (0-15-202367-4).

Ferris, Jean. *Of Sound Mind.* Farrar, Straus and Giroux, $16.00 (0-374-35580-0).

Fleischman, Paul. *Seek.* Cricket Books, $16.95 (0-8126-4900-1).

Flinn, Alex. *Breathing Underwater.* HarperCollins, $15.95 (0-06-029198-2).

Geras, Adele. *Troy.* Harcourt, $17.00 (0-15-216492-8).

Griffin, Adele. *Amandine.* Hyperion Books for Children, $15.99 (0-7868-0618-4).

Heneghan, James. *The Grave.* Farrar, Straus and Giroux, $17.00 (0-374-32765-3).

Holm, Jennifer. *Boston Jane: An Adventure.* HarperCollins, $16.95 (0-06-028738-1).

Jenkins, A. M. *Damage.* HarperCollins, $15.95 (0-0602-9099-4).

Jimenez, Francisco. *Breaking Through.* Houghton Mifflin, $15.00 (0-618-01173-0).

Jordan, Sherryl. *Secret Sacrament.* HarperCollins, $15.95 (0-06-028904-X).

Klass, David. *You Don't Know Me.* Farrar, Straus and Giroux, $17.00 (0-374-38706-0).

Koertge, Ron. *Brimstone Journals.* Candlewick, $15.99 (0-7636-1302-9).

Les Becquets, Diane. *The Stones of Mourning Creek.* Winslow, $16.95 (1-58837-004-6).

Love and Sex: Ten Stories of Truth. Edited by Michael Cart. Simon & Schuster, $18.00 (0-689-83203-6).

Lynch, Chris. *Freewill.* HarperCollins, $15.95 (0-06-028176-6).

McCormick, Patricia. *Cut.* Front Street, $16.95 (1-886910-61-8).

McDonald, Janet. *Spellbound.* Farrar, Straus and Giroux, $16.00 (0-374-37140-7).

McDonald, Joyce. *Shades of Simon Gray.* Random House, $15.95 (0-385-32659-9).

Mikaelsen, Ben. *Touching Spirit Bear.* HarperCollins, $15.95 (0-380-97744-3).

Moriarty, Jaclyn. *Feeling Sorry for Celia.* St. Martins, $16.95 (0-312-26923-4).

Mosher, Richard. *Zazoo.* Houghton Mifflin, $16.00 (0-618-13534-0).

Na, An. *A Step from Heaven.* Front Street, $15.95 (1-886910-58-8).

Naidoo, Beverly. *The Other Side of Truth.* HarperCollins, $15.95 (0-06-029628-3).

Nix, Garth. *Lirael.* HarperCollins, $16.95 (0-06-027823-4).

Nolan, Han. *Born Blue.* Harcourt, $17.00 (0-15-201916-2).

On the Fringe. Edited by Don Gallo. Penguin Putnam, $17.99 (0-8037-2656-2).

Park, Linda Sue. *A Single Shard.* Houghton Mifflin, $15.00 (0-395-97827-0).

Peck, Richard. *Fair Weather.* Dial Books for Young Readers, $16.99 (0-8037-2516-7).

Pierce, Meredith Ann. *Treasure at the Heart of the Tanglewood.* Penguin Putnam, $16.99 (0-670-89247-5).

Pierce, Tamora. *Protector of the Small: Squire.* Random House, $15.95 (0-679-889-167).

Pratchett, Terry. *The Amazing Maurice and His Educated Rodents.* HarperCollins, $15.89 (0-06-001234-X).

Pullman, Philip. *The Amber Spyglass.* Knopf, $19.95 (0-679-87926-9).

Rees, Celia. *Witch Child.* Candlewick, $15.99 (0-7636-1421-1).

Rice, David. *Crazy Loco.* Penguin Putnam, $16.99 (0-8037-2598-1).

Ryan, Sara. *Empress of the World.* Penguin Putnam, $15.99 (0-670-89688-8).

Salisbury, Graham. *The Lord of the Deep.* Delacorte, $15.95 (0-385-72918-9).

Sanchez, Alex. *Rainbow Boys.* Simon and Schuster, $17.00 (0-689-84100-0).

Shinn, Sharon. *Summers at Castle Auburn.* Penguin Putnam, $14.95 (0-441-00803-8).

Sones, Sonya. *What My Mother Doesn't Know.* Simon & Schuster, $17.00 (0-689-84114-0).

Stratton, Allan. *Leslie's Journal.* Annick Press, $19.95 (1-55037-665-9).

Tashjian, Janet. *The Gospel According to Larry.* Henry Holt, $16.95 (0-8050-6378-1).

Taylor, Mildred. *The Land.* Penguin Putnam, $17.99 (0-8037-1950-7).

Tingle, Rebecca. *The Edge on the Sword.* Penguin Putnam, $18.99 (0-399-23580-9).

Vance, Susanna. *Sights.* Delacorte, $15.95 (0-385-32761-7).

Vande Velde, Vivian. *Being Dead.* Harcourt, $17.00. (0-15-216320-4).

Vijayaraghaven, Vineeta. *Motherland.* Soho Press, $23.00 (1-56947-217-3).

Weaver, Beth. *Rooster.* Winslow, $15.95 (1-58837-001-1).

Werlin, Nancy. *Black Mirror.* Dial Books for Young Readers, $16.99 (0-8037-2605-8).

Williams-Garcia, Rita. *Every Time a Rainbow Dies.* William Morrow, $15.95 (0-688-16245-2).

Wittlinger, Ellen. *Razzle.* Simon and Schuster, $17.00 (0-689-83565-5).

Wolff, Virginia Euwer. *True Believer.* Atheneum, $17.00 (0-689-82827-6).

Zusak, Markus. *Fighting Ruben Wolfe.* Scholastic, $15.95 (0-439-24188-X).

Nonfiction

Colton, Larry. *Counting Coup: The True Story of Basketball and Honor on the Little Big Horn.* Warner Books, $24.95 (0-446-52683-5).

Cooper, Michael. *Fighting for Honor: Japanese Americans and World War II.* Houghton Mifflin, $16.00 (0-395-91375-6).

Fisher, Antwone, with Mim Eichler Rivas. *Finding Fish.* HarperCollins, $25.00 (0-688-17699-2).

Fradin, Dennis Brindell. *Bound for the North Star: True Stories of Fugitive Slaves.* Clarion, $20.00 (0-395-97017-2).

Greenberg, Jan, and Sandra Jordan. *Vincent Van Gogh: Portrait of an Artist.* Delacorte, $14.95 (0-385-32806-0).

Heart to Heart: New Poems Inspired by 20th Century American Art. Edited by Jan Greenberg. Harry Abrams, $19.95 (0-8109-4386-7).

Hoose, Phillip. *We Were There, Too! Young People in U.S. History.* Farrar, Straus and Giroux, $26.00 (0-374-38252-2).

Kendall, Martha. *Failure Is Impossible: The History of American Women's Rights.* Lerner, $22.60 (0-82225-1744-2).

Ketchum, Liza. *Into the New Country: Eight Remarkable Women of the West.* Little, Brown, $18.95 (0-316-49597-2).

King, Daniel. *Chess: From First Moves to Checkmate.* Kingfisher, $16.95 (0-7534-5387-8).

Lawlor, Laurie. *Helen Keller: Rebellious Spirit.* Holiday House, $22.95 (0-8234-1588-0).

Lee, Bruce; selected and edited by John Little. *Bruce Lee: The Celebrated Life of the Golden Dragon.* Tuttle, $24.95 (0-8048-3230-7).

Marrin, Albert. *George Washington and the Founding of a Nation.* Dutton Children's Books, $30.00 (0-525-46481-6).

Murphy, Jim. *Blizzard: The Storm that Changed America.* Scholastic, $18.95 (0-590-67309-2).

Myers, Walter Dean. *Bad Boy: A Memoir.* HarperCollins, $15.89 (0-06-029523-6).

Myers, Walter Dean. *The Greatest: Muhammad Ali.* Scholastic, $16.95 (0-590-54342-3).

Nelson, Marilyn. *Carver: A Life in Poems.* Front Street, $16.95 (1-886910-53-7).

Orgill, Roxane. *Shout, Sister, Shout! Ten Girl Singers Who Shaped a Century.* Simon and Schuster, $18.00 (0-689-81991-9).

Owen, David. *Hidden Evidence: Forty True Crimes and How Forensic Science Helped Solve Them.* Firefly Books Ltd., $24.95 (1-55209-483-9).

Things I Have to Tell You: Poems and Writing by Teenage Girls. Edited by Betsy Franco. Candlewick, $8.99, $15.99 (0-7636-1035-6, 0-7636-0905-6).

Voices: Poetry and Art from Around the World. Edited by Barbara Brenner. National Geographic Society, $18.95 (0-7922-7071-1).

Words with Wings: A Treasury of African-American Poetry and Art. Edited by Belinda Rochelle. HarperCollins, $16.95 (0-688-16415-3).

Yell-OH Girls! Emerging Voices Explore Culture, Identity and Growing-Up Asian American. Edited by Vickie Nam. HarperCollins, $13.00 (0-06-095944-4).

Every five years, YALSA also produces a list of Outstanding Books for the College-Bound that includes books dating from the mid-19th century to the present. The most recent list appears in the 2001 edition of the *Bowker Annual.*

Quick Picks for Reluctant Young Adult Readers

The Young Adult Library Services Association, a division of the American Library Association, annually chooses a list of outstanding titles that will stimulate the interest of reluctant teen readers. This list is intended to attract teens who, for whatever reason, choose not to read.

Atwater-Rhodes, Amelia. *Shattered Mirror.* Delacorte, $9.95 (0-385-32793-5).

Bird, Isobel. Circle of Three Series. HarperCollins/Avon, paper $4.99. Vol. 1: *So Mote It Be* (0-06-447291-4); vol. 2: *Merry Meet* (0-06-447292-2); vol. 3: *Second Sight* (0-06-447293-0); vol. 4: *What the Cards Said* (0-06-447294-9); vol. 5: *In the Dreaming* (0-06-447295-7); vol. 6: *Ring of Light* (0-06-447296-5); vol. 7: *Blue Moon* (0-06-447297-3).

Black, Jonah. The Black Book (Diary of a Teenage Stud) series. HarperCollins/Avon, paper $4.99. Vol. 1: *Girls, Girls, Girls* (0-06-440798-5); vol. 2: *Stop, Don't Stop* (0-06-440799-3).

Cabot, Meg. *Princess in the Spotlight: Princess Diaries Volume II.* HarperCollins, $15.95 (0-06-029465-5); library edition $15.89 (0-06-029466-3).

Carroll, Jenny. The Mediator Series. Pocket Books, paper $4.99. Vol. 1: *Shadowland* (0-671-78791-8); vol. 2: *Ninth Key* (0-671-78798-5).

Chandler, Elizabeth. *Dark Secrets: Don't Tell.* Pocket Books, paper $4.99 (0-7434-0029-1).

David, Peter. *Spyboy: The Deadly Gourmet Affair.* Illus. Dark Horse Comics, paper $8.95 (1-56971-463-0).

Draper, Sharon M. *Darkness Before Dawn.* Simon and Schuster/Atheneum, $16 (0-689-83080-7).

Eberhardt, Thom. *Rat Boys: A Dating Experiment.* Hyperion, $15.99 (0-7868-0696-6).

Flinn, Alex. *Breathing Underwater.* HarperCollins, $15.95 (0-06-029198-2); library edition $15.89 (0-06-029199-0).

Griffin, Adele. *Amandine.* Hyperion, $15.99 (0-7868-0618-4); library edition $16.49 (0-7868-2530-8).

Groening, Matt. *Simpsons Comics Royale.* Illus. HarperCollins/HarperPerennial, paper $14.95 (0-06-093378-X).

Haddix, Margaret Peterson. *Among the Impostors.* Simon and Schuster, $16 (0-689-83904-9).

Horowitz, Anthony. *Stormbreaker.* Penguin Putnam/Philomel Books, $16.99 (0-399-23620-1).

Jemas, Bill, and Brian Michael Bendis. *Ultimate Spider-Man: Power and Responsibility.* Illus. Marvel Comics, paper $14.95 (0-7851-0786-X).

Lester, Julius. *When Dad Killed Mom.* Harcourt, $17 (0-15-216305-0).

Love and Sex: Ten Stories of Truth. Ed. by Michael Cart. Simon and Schuster, $18 (0-689-83203-6).

MacDougal, Scarlett. Have a Nice Life Series. Penguin Putnam/Alloy, paper $4.99. Vol. 1: *Start Here* (0-14-131020-0); vol. 2: *Play* (0-14-131021-9); vol. 3: *Popover* (0-14-131090-1); vol. 4: *Score* (0-14-131228-9).

Metz, Melinda. Fingerprints Series. HarperCollins/Avon, paper $4.99. Vol. 1: *Gifted Touch* (0-06-447265-5); vol. 2: *Haunted* (0-06-447266-3); vol. 3: *Trust Me* (0-06-447267-1); vol. 4: *Secrets* (0-06-447281-7).

Millar, Mark. *Ultimate X-Men: The Tomorrow People.* Illus. Marvel Comics, paper $14.95 (0-7851-0788-6).

Rennison, Louise. *On the Bright Side, I'm Now the Girlfriend of a Sex God.* HarperCollins, $15.95 (0-06-028813-2); library edition $15.89 (0-06-028872-8).

Scott, Jerry, and Jim Borgman. *Are We an "Us"? A Zits Collection Sketchbook.* Illus. Andrews McMeel, paper $10.95 (0-7407-1397-3).

Smith, Roland. *Zach's Lie.* Hyperion, $15.99 (0-7868-0617-6).

Sones, Sonya. *What My Mother Doesn't Know.* Simon and Schuster, $17 (0-689-84114-0).

Spears, Britney, and Lynne Spears. *A Mother's Gift.* Delacorte, $14.95 (0-385-72953-7).

Tiernan, Cate. Sweep Series. Penguin Putnam/Puffin, paper $4.99. Vol. 1: *Book of Shadows* (0-14-131046-4); vol. 2: *The Coven* (0-14-131047-2); vol. 3: *Blood Witch* (0-14-131111-8); vol. 4: *Dark Magick* (0-14-131112-6); vol. 5: *Awakening* (0-14-230045-4).

Zindel, Paul. *Night of the Bat.* Hyperion, $15.99 (0-7868-0340-1); library edition $16.49 (0-7868-2554-5).

Nonfiction

Angst! Teen Verses from the Edge. Ed. by Karen Tom and Kiki. Illus. Workman, paper $8.95 (0-7611-2383-0).

Beatty, Scott. *Batman: The Ultimate Guide to the Dark Knight.* Illus. Dorling Kindersley, $19.95 (0-7894-7865-X).

Blink-182: Tales from Beneath Your Mom. Ed. by Anne Hoppus. Illus. Pocket Books, paper $14.95 (0-7434-2207-4).

Chicken Soup for the Teenage Soul Letters: Letters of Life, Love, and Learning. Ed. by Jack Canfield, Mark Victor Hansen, and Kimberly Kirberger. Health Communications, library edition $24 (1-55874-805-9); paper $12.95 (1-55874-804-0).

Devito, Basil V., Jr., with Joe Layden. *WWF Wrestlemania.* Illus. HarperCollins/Regan Books, $49.95 (0-06-039387-4).

Eminem. *Angry Blonde.* Illus. HarperCollins/ReganBooks, $26 (0-06-620922-6).

Fishbein, Amy. *The Truth About Girlfriends.* HarperCollins/Parachute Press, paper $5.95 (0-06-447243-4).

Galvez, Jose. *Vatos.* Illus. Cinco Puntos Press, $19.95 (0-93817-52-0).

Genat, Robert. *Funny Cars.* Illus. MBI Publishing, paper $14.95 (0-7603-0795-4).

Genat, Robert. *Lowriders.* Illus. MBI Publishing, paper $14.95 (0-7603-0962-0).

Gottesman, Jane. *Game Face: What Does a Female Athlete Look Like?* Illus. Random House, $35 (0-375-50602-0).

Gravelle, Karen. *5 Ways to Know About You.* Illus. Walker, library edition $16.95 (0-8027-8749-5); paper $10.95 (0-8027-7586-1).

Hart, Christopher. *Manga Mania: How to Draw Japanese Comics.* Illus. Watson-

Guptill, paper $19.95 (0-8230-3035-0).

Hip Hop Divas. Illus. Crown/Three Rivers Press, paper $17.95 (0-609-80836-2).

Jackman, Ian. *TRL: The Ultimate Fan Guide.* Illus. Pocket Books, paper $12.95 (0-7434-1850-6).

Jeter, Derek. *Game Day: My Life On and Off the Field.* Ed. by Kristen Kiser. Illus. Crown/Three Rivers Press, paper $22.95 (0-609-80794-3).

Koertge, Ron. *The Brimstone Journals.* Candlewick Press, $15.99 (0-7636-1302-9).

Laurer, Joanie. *Chyna: If They Only Knew.* Illus. HarperCollins/Regan Books, $26 (0-06-039329-7).

Locker, Sari. *Sari Says: The Real Dirt on Everything from Sex to School.* HarperCollins, paper $11.95 (0-06-447306-6).

McFarlane, Evelyn and James Saywell. *If . . . Questions for Teens.* Random House/Villard Books, $9.95 (0-375-50555-5).

The Mad Gross Book. Ed. by Nick Meglin and John Ficarra. Illus. Time Warner/Mad Books, paper $9.95 (1-56389-758-X).

Masoff, Joy. *Oh, Yuck! The Encyclopedia of Everything Nasty.* Illus. Workman, paper $14.95 (0-7611-0771-1).

MTV Uncensored. Ed. by Jacob Hoye. Illus. Pocket Books, $40 (0-7434-2682-7).

Myers, Walter Dean. *The Greatest: Muhammad Ali.* Illus. Scholastic, $16.95 (0-590-54342-3).

O'Donnell, Kerri. *Inhalants and Your Nasal Passages: The Incredibly Disgusting Story.* Illus. Rosen, $25.25 (0-8239-3392-X).

Piven, Joshua, and David Borgenicht. *The Worst Case Scenario Survival Handbook: Travel.* Illus. Chronicle, paper $14.95 (0-8118-3131-0).

Shaw, Tucker. *Who Do You Think You Are? 12 Methods for Analyzing the True You.* Penguin Putnam/Alloy, paper $6.99 (0-14-131091-X).

Shaw, Tucker, and Fiona Gibb. *This Book Is About Sex.* Illus. Penguin Putnam/Alloy, paper $5.99 (0-14-131019-7).

Smith, Charles R., Jr. *Short Takes.* Illus. Penguin Putnam/Dutton, $17.99 (0-525-46454-9).

Stine, Megan. *Seventeen Trauma-Rama: Life's Most Embarrassing Moments . . . . and How to Deal.* Illus. HarperCollins/Parachute Press, paper $5.95 (0-06-440873-6).

Teen People: Real Life Diaries: Inspiring True Stories from Celebrities and Real Teens. Ed. by Linda Friedman and Dana White. HarperCollins/Avon, paper $12.95 (0-06-447329-5).

Teen People: Sex Files. HarperCollins/Avon, paper $6.95 (0-06-447319-8).

Things I Have to Tell You: Poems and Writings by Teenage Girls. Ed. by Betsy Franco. Illus. Candlewick Press, $15.99 (0-7636-0905-6); paper $8.99 (0-7636-1035-6).

Thrasher: Insane Terrain. Illus. Rizzoli/Universe, paper $27.50 (0-7893-0536-4).

Audiobooks for Young Adults

Each year a committee of the Young Adult Library Services Association, a division of the American Library Association, compiles a list of the best audiobooks for young adults ages 12 to 18. The titles are selected for their teen appeal and quality recording, and because they enhance the audience's appreciation of any written work on which the recordings may be based. While the list as a whole addresses the interests and needs of young adults, individual titles need not appeal to this entire age range but rather to parts of that range.

Bad Boy: A Memoir, by Walter Dean Myers, read by Joe Morton. Harper Audio, 4 cassettes, 5 hours (0-694-52535-9).

Borrowed Light, by Anna Fienberg, read by Rebecca Macauley. Bolinda Audio, 6 cassettes, 8 hours 15 minutes (1-74030-141-2).

Cut, by Patricia McCormick, read by Clea Lewis. Listening Library, 3 cassettes, 3 hours 59 minutes (0-8072-0523-0).

Esperanza Rising, by Pam Munoz Ryan, read by Trini Alvarado. Listening Library, 3 cassettes, 4 hours 42 minutes (0-8072-6207-2).

Give a Boy a Gun, by Todd Strasser, read by various narrators. Recorded Books, 3 cassettes, 3 hours 30 minutes (0-7887-9376-4).

The Grey King, by Susan Cooper, read by Richard Mitchley. Listening Library, 4 cassettes, 5 hours 41 minutes (0-8072-8877-2).

Homeless Bird, by Gloria Whelan, read by Sarita Choudhury. Listening Library, 2 cassettes, 3 hours 15 minutes (0-8072-8858-6).

Killing Aurora, by Helen Barnes, read by Suzi Dougherty, Bolinda Audio, 5 cassettes, 6 hours (1-74030-228-1).

The Land, by Mildred D. Taylor, read by Ruben Santiago-Hudson. Listening Library, 7 cassettes, 10 hours 56 minutes (0-8072-0619-9).

The Last Book in the Universe, by Rodman Philbrick, read by Jeremy Davies. Listening Library, 3 cassettes, 4 hours 25 minutes (0-8072-8843-8).

The Member of the Wedding, by Carson McCullers, performed by a full cast. LA Theatre Works, 2 cassettes, 1 hour 32 minutes (1-58081-206-6).

Miracle's Boys, by Jacqueline Woodson, read by Dule Hill. Listening Library, 2 cassettes, 2 hours 27 minutes (0-8072-0525-7).

Out of the Shadows, by Sue Hines, read by Caroline Lee. Bolinda Audio, 4 cassettes, 5 hours 30 minutes (1-74030-362-8).

A Series of Unfortunate Events: The Bad Beginning and The Reptile Room, by Lemony Snicket, read by Tim Curry. Listening Library, 2 cassettes each, 3 hours 17 minutes for "Book the First" and 3 hours 11 minutes for "Book the Second" (0-8072-8847-0 and 0-8072-8868-3).

Shipwreck at the Bottom of the World, by Jennifer Armstrong, read by Taylor Mali. Audio Bookshelf, 4 cassettes, 4 hours (1-883332-39-7).

The Sisterhood of the Traveling Pants, by Ann Brashares, read by Angela Goethals.

Listening Library, 4 cassettes, 6 hours 35 minutes (0-8072-0590-7).

Stargirl, by Jerry Spinelli, read by John Ritter. Listening Library, 3 cassettes, 4 hours 25 minutes (0-8072-0572-9).

Strange Objects, by Gary Crew, read by Stig Wemyss. Bolinda Audio, 4 cassettes, 5 hours 45 minutes (1-876584-82-3).

Stuck in Neutral, by Terry Trueman, read by Johnny Heller. Recorded Books, 2 cassettes, 2 hours 30 minutes (1-4025-0710-0).

Tangerine, by Edward Bloor, read by Ramon de Ocampo. Recorded Books, 8 cassettes, 10 hours (1-4025-0778-X).

Touching Spirit Bear, by Ben Mikaelsen, read by Lee Tergesen. Listening Library, 4 cassettes, 5 hours 52 minutes (0-8072-0515-X).

Walden, by Henry David Thoreau, read by William Hope. NAXOS Audiobooks, 4 cassettes, 5 hours 14 minutes (9-62634-732-5).

When Kambia Elaine Flew in from Neptune, by Lori Aurelia Williams, read by Heather Alicia Simms. Listening Library, 6 cassettes, 8 hours 31 minutes (0-8072-8850-0).

Witch Child, by Celia Rees, read by Jennifer Ehle with Carole Shelley. Listening Library, 4 cassettes, 5 hours 38 minutes (0-8072-0628-8).

Notable Children's Books

A list of notable children's books is selected each year by the Notable Children's Books Committee of the Association for Library Service to Children, a division of the American Library Association. Recommended titles are selected by children's librarians and educators based on originality, creativity, and suitability for children. [See "Literary Prizes, 2001" later in Part 5 for Caldecott, Newbery, and other award winners—*Ed.*]

Books for Younger Readers

Agee, Jon. *Milo's Hat Trick.* Michael di Capua/Hyperion Books for Children (0-7868-0902-7).

Alarcón, Francisco X. *Iguanas in the Snow.* Illus. by Maya Christina Gonzalez. Children's Book Press (0-892-39168-5).

Barton, Byron. *My Car.* Greenwillow (0-06-029625-0).

Booth, Philip. *Crossing.* Illus. by Bagram Ibatoulline. Candlewick (0-7636-1420-3).

Crews, Donald. *Inside Freight Train.* William Morrow/HarperCollins (0-688-17087-0).

Ehlert, Lois. *Waiting for Wings.* Harcourt (0-15-202608-8).

Falconer, Ian. *Olivia Saves the Circus.* Anne Schwartz Book/Atheneum (0-689-82954-X).

Falwell, Cathryn. *Turtle Splash: Countdown at the Pond.* Greenwillow/HarperCollins (0-06-029462-0).

Fraustino, Lisa Rowe. *The Hickory Chair.* Illus. by Benny Andrews. Arthur A. Levine/Scholastic (0-590-52248-5)

Graham, Bob. *"Let's Get A Pup," Said Kate.* Candlewick (0-7636-1452-1).

Henkes, Kevin. *Sheila Rae's Peppermint Stick.* Greenwillow/HarperCollins (0-06-029451-5).

Hoberman, Mary Ann. *You Read to Me, I'll Read to You: Very Short Stories to Read Together.* Illus. by Michael Emberley. Megan Tingley Books/Little Brown (0-316-36350-2).

Inkpen, Mick. *Kipper's A to Z: An Alphabet Adventure.* Red Wagon Books/Harcourt (0-15-202594-4).

Jenkins, Emily. *Five Creatures.* Illus. by Tomek Bogacki. Frances Foster Books/Farrar, Straus and Giroux (0-374-32341-0).

Little, Jean. *Emma's Yucky Brother.* Illus. by Jennifer Plecas. HarperCollins (0-06-028348-3).

Livingston, Star. *Harley.* Illus. by Molly Bang. Seastar (1-587-17048-5).

Look, Lenore. *Henry's First-Moon Birthday.* Illus. by Yumi Heo. Anne Schwartz Book/Atheneum (0-689-82294-4).

Lunge-Larsen, Lise. *The Race of the Birkebeiners.* Illus. by Mary Azarian. Houghton Mifflin (0-618-10313-9).

McKissack, Patricia C. *Goin' Someplace Special.* Illus. by Jerry Pinkney. Anne Schwartz Book/Atheneum (0-689-81885-8).

Mills, Claudia. *Gus and Grandpa at Basketball.* Illus. by Catherine Stock. Farrar, Straus and Giroux (0-374-32818-8).

Montes, Marisa. *Juan Bobo Goes to Work.* Illus. by Joe Cepeda. HarperCollins (0-688-16233-9).

Palatini, Margie. *The Web Files.* Illus. by Richard Egielski. Hyperion (0-7868-0419-X).

Ryan, Pam Muñoz. *Mice and Beans.* Illus. by Joe Cepeda. Scholastic (0-439-18303-0).

Simont, Marc. *The Stray Dog.* HarperCollins (0-06-028934-1).

Steen, Sandra, and Susan Steen. *Car Wash.* Illus. by G. Brian Karas. Putnam (0-399-23369-5).

Stevens, Janet, and Susan Stevens Crummel. *And the Dish Ran Away with the Spoon.* Illus. by Janet Stevens. Harcourt (0-15-202298-8).

Willey, Margaret. *Clever Beatrice.* Illus. by Heather Solomon. Atheneum (0-689-83254-0).

Woodson, Jacqueline. *The Other Side.* Illus. by E. B. Lewis. Putnam (0-399-23116-1).

Books for Middle Readers

Allen, Thomas B. *Remember Pearl Harbor: American and Japanese Survivors Tell Their Stories.* National Geographic (0-7922-6690-0).

Anderson, M. T. *Handel: Who Knew What He Liked.* Illus. by Kevin Hawkes. Candlewick (0-7636-1046-1).

Blumberg, Rhoda. *Shipwrecked! The True Adventures of a Japanese Boy.* Harper-Collins (0-688-17484-1).

Bruchac, Joseph. *Skeleton Man.* Harper-Collins (0-06-029075-7).

Carbone, Elisa. *Storm Warriors.* Knopf (0-375-80664-4).

Christensen, Bonnie. *Woody Guthrie: Poet of the People.* Knopf (0-375-81113-3).

Creech, Sharon. *Love That Dog.* Joanna Cotler Books/HarperCollins (0-06-029287-3).

Curlee, Lynn. *Brooklyn Bridge.* Atheneum (0-689-83183-8).

Freedman, Russell. *In the Days of the Vaqueros: America's First True Cowboys.* Clarion (0-395-96788-0).

Fritz, Jean. *Leonardo's Horse.* Illus. by Hudson Talbott. Putnam (0-399-23576-0).

Gauthier, Gail. *The Hero of Ticonderoga.* Putnam (0-399-23559-0).

Goodall, Jane. *The Chimpanzees I Love: Saving Their World and Ours.* Byron Preiss Book/Scholastic (0-439-21310-X.)

Gündisch, Karin. *How I Became an American.* Trans. by James Skofield. Cricket Books (0-8126-4875-7).

Haas, Jessie. *Runaway Radish.* Illus. by Margot Apple. Greenwillow (0-688-16688-1).

Horvath, Polly. *Everything on a Waffle.* Farrar, Straus and Giroux (0-374-32236-8).

Hoyt-Goldsmith, Diane. *Celebrating Ramadan.* Illus. by Lawrence Migdale. Holiday House (0-8234-1581-3).

Huck, Charlotte. *The Black Bull of Norroway: A Scottish Tale.* Illus. by Anita Lobel. Greenwillow/HarperCollins (0-688-16901-5).

Hurst, Carol Otis. *Rocks in His Head.* Illus. by James Stevenson. Greenwillow/HarperCollins (0-06-029403-5).

Kerley, Barbara. *The Dinosaurs of Waterhouse Hawkins: An Illuminating History of Mr. Waterhouse Hawkins, Artist and Lec-*

turer. Illus. by Brian Selznick. Scholastic (0-439-11494-2).

King-Smith, Dick. *Lady Lollipop.* Illus. by Jill Barton. Candlewick (0-7636-1269-3).

Kramer, Stephen. *Hidden Worlds: Looking Through a Scientist's Microscope.* Photographs by Dennis Kunkel. Houghton Mifflin (0-618-05546-0).

Kurlansky, Mark. *The Cod's Tale.* Illus. by S. D. Schindler. Putnam (0-399-23476-4).

McDonald, Megan. *Judy Moody Gets Famous!* Illus. by Peter Reynolds. Candlewick (0-7636-0849-1).

Macy, Sue. *Bull's Eye: A Photobiography of Annie Oakley.* National Geographic (0-7922-7008-8).

Martin, Jacqueline. *The Lamp, the Ice, and the Boat Called Fish.* Illus. by Beth Krommes. Houghton Mifflin (0-618-00341-X).

Morgenstern, Susie. *A Book of Coupons.* Trans. by Gill Rosner. Illus. by Serge Bloch. Penguin Putnam/Viking (0-670-89970-4).

Park, Linda Sue. *A Single Shard.* Clarion (0-395-97827-0).

Rumford, James. *Traveling Man: The Journey of Ibn Battuta, 1325–1354.* Houghton Mifflin (0-618-08366-9).

Ryan, Pam Muñoz. *Esperanza Rising.* Scholastic Press (0-439-12041-1).

Shreve, Susan. *Blister.* Arthur A. Levine/Scholastic (0-439-19313-3).

Wiles, Deborah. *Love, Ruby Lavender.* Gulliver Books/Harcourt (0-15-202314-3).

Yin. *Coolies.* Illus. by Chris Soentpiet. Philomel (0-399-23227-3).

Zoehfeld, Kathleen. *Dinosaur Parents, Dinosaur Young: Uncovering the Mystery of Dinosaur Families.* Illus. by Paul Carrick and Bruce Shillinglaw. Clarion (0-395-91338-1).

Books for Older Readers

Alexander, Lloyd. *The Gawgon and the Boy.* Dutton (0-525-46677-0).

Almond, David. *Heaven Eyes.* Delacorte Press (0-385-32770-6).

Bartoletti, Susan Campbell. *Black Potatoes: The Story of the Great Irish Famine,*

1845–1850. Houghton Mifflin (0-618-00271-5).

Crossley-Holland, Kevin. *The Seeing Stone.* Arthur A. Levine/Scholastic (0-439-26326-3).

Cummings, Priscilla. *A Face First.* Dutton (0-525-46522-7).

Dash, Joan. *The World at Her Fingertips: The Story of Helen Keller.* Scholastic (0-590-90715-8).

Dickinson, Peter. *The Ropemaker.* Delacorte (0-385-72921-9).

Fleischman, Paul. *Seek.* Cricket Books (0-8126-4900-1).

Greenberg, Jan (ed.). *Heart to Heart: New Poems Inspired by Twentieth-Century American Art.* Abrams (0-8109-4386-7).

Greenberg, Jan, and Sandra Jordan. *Vincent van Gogh: Portrait of an Artist.* Delacorte (0-385-32806-0).

Hesse, Karen. *Witness.* Scholastic (0-439-27199-1).

Hoose, Phillip. *We Were There, Too! Young People in U.S. History.* Farrar, Straus and Giroux (0-374-38252-2).

Jiménez, Francisco. *Breaking Through.* Houghton Mifflin (0-618-01173-0).

Lawlor, Laurie. *Helen Keller: Rebellious Spirit.* Holiday House (0-8234-1588-0).

Mosher, Richard. *Zazoo.* Clarion (0-618-13534-0).

Myers, Walter Dean. *The Greatest: Muhammad Ali.* Scholastic (0-590-54342-3).

Na, An. *A Step from Heaven.* Front Street (1-886910-58-8).

Naidoo, Beverley. *The Other Side of Truth.* HarperCollins (0-06-029628-3).

Nelson, Marilyn. *Carver: A Life in Poems.* Front Street (1-886910-53-7).

Nicholson, William. *Slaves of the Mastery.* Hyperion (0-7868-0570-6).

Rochelle, Belinda (ed.). *Words With Wings: A Treasury of African-American Poetry and Art.* Amistad/HarperCollins (0-688-16415-3).

Taylor, Mildred. *The Land.* Phyllis Fogelman/Penguin Putnam (0-8037-1950-7).

Warren, Andrea. *Surviving Hitler: A Boy in the Nazi Death Camps.* HarperCollins (0-688-17497-3).

Wolff, Virginia Euwer. *True Believer.* Atheneum (0-689-82827-6).

Books for All Ages

Janeczko, Paul (ed.). *A Poke in the I: A Collection of Concrete Poems.* Illus. by Chris Raschka. Candlewick (0-7636-0661-8).

Longfellow, Henry Wadsworth. *The Midnight Ride of Paul Revere.* Illus. by Christopher Bing. Handprint Books (1-929766-13-0).

Rappaport, Doreen. *Martin's Big Words: The Life of Dr. Martin Luther King Jr.* Illus. by Bryan Collier. Jump at the Sun/Hyperion (0-7868-0714-8).

Wiesner, David. *The Three Pigs.* Clarion (0-618-00701-6).

Williams, Vera B. *Amber Was Brave, Essie Was Smart.* Greenwillow (0-06-029460-4).

Notable Children's Videos

These titles are selected by a committee of the Association for Library Service to Children, a division of the American Library Association. Recommendations are based on originality, creativity, and suitability for young children. The members select materials that respect both children's intelligence and imagination, exhibit venturesome creativity, and encourage the interest of users.

Amelia's Moving Pictures. 22 min. Pleasant Company (1-58485-160-0). Animation. Ages 7–10. $9.99.

Ancient Greece. 24 min. Discovery Channel School (1-58738-181-8). Ages 10 and up. $49.95.

Badger's Parting Gifts. 29 min. GPN/Nebraska ETV Network and WNED-TV, Buffalo. Ages 5–10. $45.95.

Black Soul. 10 min. National Film Board of Canada. Animation. Ages 9 and up. $129.

Buttons. 14 min. Spoken Arts (0-8045-9664-6). Iconographic. Ages 8 and up. $49.95.

Christopher, Please Clean Up Your Room! 7 min. National Film Board of Canada. Animation. Ages 4–8. $139 with book.

Claude Monet. 22 min. Kiki & Associates. Animation. Ages 5 and up. $24.95.

Click, Clack, Moo: Cows That Type. 10 min. Weston Woods Studios (0-78820-764-4). Animation. Ages 3–8. $60.

Dying to Be Thin. 60 min. WGBH Boston Video (1-57807-232-8). Ages 10 and up. $19.95.

Elmo's Musical Adventure: The Story of Peter and the Wolf. 45 min. Sony Wonder (0-7389-2034-7). $12.98.

A Hunting Lesson. 13 min. National Film Board of Canada. Animation. Ages 10 and up. $129.

I, Crocodile. 10 min. Weston Woods Studios (0-78820-761-X). Iconographic. Ages 7–10. $60.

In the Small, Small Pond. 5 min. Weston Woods Studios (0-78820-767-9). Iconographic. Ages 2–6. $60.

Joseph Had a Little Overcoat. 10 min. Weston Woods Studios (0-78820-768-7). Animation. Ages 4–8. $60.

My Louisiana Sky. 90 min. Hallmark Entertainment. Ages 10 and up.

NatureWorks. 4 hours (sixteen 15-min. programs). Environmental Media. Ages 8–14. $119.95.

Nougzar in Georgia (Let's Dance! Series). 13 min. New Dimension Media (1-56353-720-6). Ages 6–12. $59 single-site, $139 multi-site.

The Old Man and the Sea. 22 min. Direct Cinema Limited (1-55974-646-7). Animation. Ages 10 and up. $95.

The Railway Children. 120 min. WGBH Boston Video (1-57807-626-9). Live action. Ages 8 and up. $19.95.

Space Case. 13 min. Weston Woods Studios (0-78820-754-7). Animation. Ages 3–8. $60.

The Spooky Book. 9 min. Spoken Arts (0-8045-9654-9). Iconographic. Ages 5–8. $49.95.

Trashy Town. 6 min. Weston Woods Studios (0-78820-760-1). Animation. Ages 2–7. $60.

Vincent van Gogh. 22 min. Kiki & Associates. Animation. Ages 5 and up. $24.95.

Wings. 7 min. Spoken Arts (0-8045-9663-8). Iconographic. Ages 6 and up. $49.95.

Notable Recordings for Children

This list of notable recordings for children was selected by the Association for Library Service to Children, a division of the American Library Association. Recommended titles, many of which are recorded books, are chosen by children's librarians and educators on the basis of their originality, creativity, and suitability.

"All Wound Up." 43 mins. Cathy Fink and Marcy Marxer, with Brave Combo, perform original and traditional songs. CD, $16.98; cassette, $10.98. Rounder Kids.

"The Bad Beginning." 3 hrs. 17 mins. Tim Curry reads the first of Lemony Snicket's *A Series of Unfortunate Events.* 2 cassettes, $23. Listening Library (0-8072-8847-0).

"Because of Winn-Dixie." 2 hrs. Performed by Cherry Jones. 2 cassettes, $23. Listening Library (0-8072-8856-X).

"Black Angels." 4 hrs. Julia Gibson narrates this story of three little angels who calm racial tension in a small town. 3 cassettes, $28. Recorded Books.

"Buttons." 14 mins. David Hyde Pierce narrates this humorous tale by Brock Cole. Cassette and book, $26.90. Spoken Arts.

"Chet Gecko—Private Eye." 2 hrs. 34 mins. Jon Cryer performs Bruce Hale's story of humorous crime-busting. 2 cassettes, $23. Listening Library (0-8072-8860-8).

"Click, Clack, Moo: Cows That Type." 7 mins. Country singer Randy Travis narrates Doreen Cronin's tale of labor trouble on the farm. Cassette and hardcover book, $24.95; cassette only, $6.95. Weston Woods.

"Country Goes Raffi." 41 mins. Raffi songs performed in a country manner. CD, $17.95; cassette, $11.95. Rounder Kids.

"Fireside Tales: More Lessons from the Animal People." 70 mins. Storyteller Dovie Thomason Sickles performs stories originating with the Iroquois Nation. CD, $14.95; cassette, $9.95. Yellow Moon Press.

"The Fledgling." 4 hrs. 30 mins. Mary Beth Hurt performs this fantasy about a little girl and a Canada goose. 3 cassettes, $30. Listening Library (0-8072-8778-4).

"Heaven Eyes." 5 hrs. 7 mins. Amanda Plummer reads this tale of three runaway orphans. 3 cassettes, $30. Listening Library (0-8072-8879-9).

"Henry Hikes to Fitchburg." 8 mins. Based on a passage from *Walden,* this fable is about two bears who set out to see who can get to Fitchburg first. Cassette and hardcover book, $24.95; cassette only, $6.95. Weston Woods.

"Henry Huggins." 2 hrs. Neil Patrick Harris reads Beverly Cleary's classic tale. 2 cassettes (0-6945-2529-4), $18; 3 CDs (0-6945-2525-1), $20. Harper Children's Audio.

"Homeless Bird." 3 hrs. 15 mins. Sarita Choudhury tells the story of a 13-year-old Indian girl in an ill-fated arranged marriage. 2 cassettes, $23. Listening Library (0-8072-8858-6).

"I, Crocodile." 9 mins. Tim Curry reads the tale of an egotistical crocodile who goes to Paris. Cassette and hardcover book, $24.95; cassette only, $6.95. Weston Woods.

"inFINity." 35 mins. Songs by Trout Fishing in America. CD, $14.98. Trout Records.

"Joseph Had a Little Overcoat." 14 mins. Simms Taback, accompanied by klezmer music, narrates his story of Joseph, who makes something from nothing again and again. Cassette and hardcover book, $25.95. Live Oak Media (0-874-99783-6).

"The King's Equal." 45 mins. Davina Porter narrates this tale of a prince who seeks a bride. Cassette, $10. Recorded Books.

"The Magician's Nephew." 4 hrs. Kenneth Branagh reads the first of C. S. Lewis's *Chronicles of Narnia.* 4 CDs (0-6945-2620-7), $27.50; 3 cassettes, (0-6945-2619-3), $24. Harper Children's Audio.

"Mama Don't Allow." 11 mins. Tom Chapin performs Thacher Hurd's bayou adventure. Cassette and paperback book, $15.95. Live Oak Media (0-87499-743-7).

"Mole Music." 8 mins. To the accompaniment of violinist Richard Auldon Clark, Jim Weiss narrates the story of avid violin student Mole. Cassette and hardcover book, $24.95. Live Oak Media (0-87499-748-8).

"Mufaro's Beautiful Daughters." 17 mins. Robin Miles narrates John Steptoe's story set in an African jungle. Cassette and paperback book, $15.95. Live Oak Media (0-87499-655-4).

"Mystery on the Docks." 10 mins. John Beach performs a spooky tale. Cassette and paperback book, $15.95. Live Oak Media (0-87499-751-8).

"Notes From a Liar and Her Dog." 5 hrs. 25 mins. Ariadne Meyers narrates this story of a middle child's search for her true self. 4 cassettes, $32. Listening Library (0-8072-0499-4).

"Over Sea, Under Stone." 7 hrs. Alex Jennings narrates Susan Cooper's novel. 6 cassettes, $40. Listening Library (0-8072-0480-3).

"The Princess Diaries." 5 hrs. 54 mins. Narrator Anne Hathaway is Mia Thermopolis in this story of a Manhattan girl who suddenly discovers that she is the Princess of Genovia. 4 cassettes, $32. Listening Library (0-8072-0514-1).

"The Reptile Room." 3hrs. 11 mins. Tim Curry performs the second installment of Lemony Snicket's *A Series of Unfortunate Events*. 2 cassettes, $23. Listening Library (0-8072-8868-3).

"The Treasure." 6 mins. Jim Weiss narrates this classic Uri Shulevitz story. Cassette and paperback book, $15.95. Live Oak Media (0-87499-754-2).

"The Ugly Duckling." 19 mins. Lynn Whitfield reads this adaptation of the Hans Christian Andersen story. Cassette and book, $24.95; cassette only, $6.95. Weston Woods.

"Witness." 2 hrs. In 1924 the citizens of a Vermont town turn against their own when the Ku Klux Klan moves in. 2 cassettes, $23; CD, $33. Listening Library.

Notable Software and Web Sites for Children

These lists are chosen by committees of the Association for Library Service to Children, a division of the American Library Association, on the basis of their originality, creativity, and suitability for young children.

Software

Disney's Magic Artist Deluxe. An introduction to creating art on a computer. Ages 5 and up. Disney Interactive. Windows/Macintosh. $29.99.

Graphmaster. Users can choose a type of graph—bar, pie, line, scatterplot or pictograph—and add new data to create a new graph for reports and presentations. Ages 9–14. Tom Snyder Productions. Windows/Macintosh. $59.95.

Harry Potter and the Sorcerer's Stone. Players enter the world of Harry Potter and Hogwarts school to play quidditch and battle evil creatures. Ages 8 and up. Electronic Arts. Windows 98, ME, XP. $29.99.

I Spy Treasure Hunt. A seaside treasure hunt develops observation, memory, and logic skills. Ages 5 and up. Scholastic. Windows/Macintosh. $29.95.

Incredible Machine: Even More Contraptions. Solving 250 puzzles and creating inventions develops skills in mechanics and problem solving. Ages 9 and up. Sierra On-Line (Vivendi). Windows/Macintosh. $29.95.

Zoombinis Mountain Rescue. The Zoombinis are trapped in a cave. Search parties are confronted with nine perilous obstacles. Ages 8 and up. Learning Company. Windows. $24.99.

Web Sites

ASPCA's Animaland
http://www.animaland.org
This child-friendly site offers interactive information on careers, animal care, and general information about animals.

Building Big
http://www.pbs.org/wgbh/buildingbig
Users explore construction by type of structure, try labs and "challenges," and read about people in engineering.

Children's Museum of Indianapolis Fun Online Page
http://www.childrensmuseum.org/funonline/funonline.html
This museum-sponsored site provides interesting information and such activities such as creating a multimedia puppet show and designing a space station.

Cool Science for Curious Kids
http://www.hhmi.org/coolscience
Created by the Howard Hughes Medical Institute, this site offers both online and offline science activities for children of all ages.

Coolmath.com
http://www.coolmath.com
A fully interactive site that allows the user to sharpen basic math skills, play math-related games, and explore new math concepts.

Lemony Snicket
http://www.lemonysnicket.com
As Lemony Snicket says, this site is filled with "dreadful images," "wretched information," and "unnerving games."

Secrets of the Lost Empires: Medieval Siege
http://www.pbs.org/wgbh/nova/lostempires/trebuchet
Users learn about life in medieval castles and how to operate a catapult. For upper elementary and middle school students.

SodaConstructor
http://sodaplay.com/constructor/index.htm
Users create a model out of digital soda straws and use their engineering skills to animate it.

Ways of Knowing Trail
http://www.brookfieldzoo.org/pagegen/wok/ways_index.html
Four children go on an environmental adventure through the Ituri Forest in central Africa.

Bestsellers of 2001

Hardcover Bestsellers: Few Surprises in the Winners' Circle

Daisy Maryles
Executive Editor, *Publishers Weekly*

Laurele Riippa
Editor, Adult Announcements, *Publishers Weekly*

Yes, the 2001 hardcover bestsellers lists are dominated by the usual chart players—veteran novelists, Oprah guests, familiar nonfiction subjects, and well-known personalities and/or prize-winning journalists.

The new nonfiction subjects, as often happens, reflect the year's headlines; this year that is most often the events and aftermath of September 11. The impact of that tragedy, combined with the softer economy, gave the strong impression that book sales for the year would plummet and set new lows. But while there was a slump for several weeks in September and early October, sales figures for the bestsellers of 2001 contradict that fear. In fact, in hardcover fiction, there were 110 titles that enjoyed annual sales of 100,000 or more last year. In 2000 the number was 109. In nonfiction, there were 123 books that sold more than 100,000 copies; the 2000 figure was 117. These tallies almost always reflect new books or books that remained on bestsellers lists from year to year. The figures do not reflect non-bestselling backlist titles.

While sales levels were down a bit in fiction, they were up substantially in nonfiction. The top 15 fiction entries did have one less player in the million-plus category (four in 2001 vs. five in 2000); still, that list bottomed out at about 625,000 copies, just a tad lower than the 638,000 in 2000. A total of 40 works of fiction each sold more than 300,000 in 2001; 39 did the same in 2000. In nonfiction, the sales levels of the top 15 books were higher—in the top spot, *The Prayer of Jabez* recorded the highest annual total ever for these year-in-review charts—and the 2001 top-15 list bottomed out at about 580,000, compared to about 475,000 in 2000.

Religion Rocks

The biggest bestseller news in 2001 was the strength of religious books, especially Christian titles. Many more books than ever before competed successfully in the general trade and continued to enjoy huge growth in the religion bookselling sector. For the first time in the history of our annual hardcover bestsellers charts, both the No. 1 fiction and No. 1 nonfiction titles come from Christian publishers.

Desecration, book No. 9 in the Left Behind apocalyptic series from Tyndale House, takes the fiction lead, with sales of more than 2.9 million copies. For the first time since 1994, John Grisham does not hold the year's lead spot, although for the first time since he began publishing blockbusters in 1991 he landed two books on the year-end charts, in the No. 2 and No. 3 spots. Book No. 8 in the

Adapted from *Publishers Weekly,* March 18, 2002

Publishers Weekly 2001 Bestsellers

FICTION

1. **Desecration** by Jerry B. Jenkins and Tim LaHaye. Tyndale (9/01) 2,969,458
2. **Skipping Christmas** by John Grisham. Doubleday (11/01)**2,093,880
3. **A Painted House** by John Grisham. Doubleday (2/01) **1,729,115
4. **Dreamcatcher** by Stephen King. Scribner (3/01) **1,287,000
5. **The Corrections** by Jonathan Franzen. Farrar, Straus & Giroux (9/01) 930,000
6. **Black House** by Stephen King and Peter Straub. Random House (9/01) 928,077
7. **The Kiss** by Danielle Steel. Delacorte (10/01) **750,000
8. **Valhalla Rising** by Clive Cussler. Putnam (8/01) 736,670
9. **A Day Late and a Dollar Short** by Terry McMillan. Viking (1/01) 718,600
10. **Violets Are Blue** by James Patterson. Little, Brown (11/01) 718,203
11. **P Is for Peril** by Sue Grafton. Putnam/Marion Wood (6/01) 644,372
12. **He Sees You When You're Sleeping** by Mary and Carol Higgins Clark. Scribner (11/01) **638,000
13. **A Common Life** by Jan Karon. Viking (4/01) 633,500
14. **Isle of Dogs** by Patricia Cornwell. Putnam (10/01) 625,202
15. **Suzanne's Diary for Nicholas** by James Patterson. Little, Brown (7/01) 624,268

NONFICTION

1. **The Prayer of Jabez** by Bruce Wilkinson. Multnomah (6/00) 8,439,540
2. **Secrets of the Vine** by Bruce Wilkinson. Multnomah (4/01) 3,023,197
3. **Who Moved My Cheese?** by Spencer Johnson. Putnam (9/98) 1,778,075
4. **John Adams** by David McCullough. Simon & Schuster (6/01) **1,452,943
5. **Guinness World Records 2002.** Guinness World Records Ltd. (9/01) 1,300,000
6. **Prayer of Jabez Devotional** by Bruce Wilkinson. Multnomah (5/01) 898,989
7. **The No Spin Zone: Confrontations with the Powerful and Famous in America** by Bill O'Reilly. Broadway (10/01) **866,000
8. **Body for Life: 12 Weeks to Mental and Physical Strength** by Bill Phillips. HarperCollins (5/99) 820,000
9. **How I Play Golf** by Tiger Woods. Warner (10/01) 770,286
10. **Jack** by Jack Welch. Warner (9/01) 724,345
11. **I Hope You Dance** by Mark D. Sanders and Tia Sillers. Rutledge Hill (11/00) 714,638
12. **Self Matters** by Phillip C. McGraw. Simon & Schuster Source (11/01) **702,914
13. **The Blue Day Book** by Bradley Trevor Greive. Andrews McMeel (3/00) 603,273
14. **The Road to Wealth** by Suze Orman. Putnam (7/01) 581,414
15. **America's Heroes: Inspiring Stories of Courage, Sacrifice and Patriotism** by the editors at SP LLC. Sports Publishing (11/01) 580,000

Note: Rankings are determined by sales figures provided by publishers; the numbers generally reflect reports of copies "shipped and billed" in calendar year 2001 and publishers were instructed to adjust sales figures to include returns through February 1, 2002. Publishers did not at that time know what their total returns would be—indeed, the majority of returns occur after that cut-off date—so none of these figures should be regarded as final net sales. (Dates in parentheses indicate month and year of publication.)

* Sales figures reflect books sold only in calendar year 2001.

** Sales figures were submitted to *PW* in confidence, for use in placing titles on the lists. Numbers shown are rounded down to the nearest 25,000 to indicate relationship to sales figures of other titles.

Left Behind series, *The Mark*, was No. 2 in 2000 and Book No. 7, *Assassins*, was No. 3 in 1999.

The bestseller record-breaker nonfiction lead title, *The Prayer of Jabez* by Bruce Wilkinson, from Multnomah, an independent publisher, sold more than eight million copies in 2001. The previous record was set in 1994 by Oprah chef Rosie Daley for *In the Kitchen with Rosie*, which sold more than 5.4 million that year. The last time a Christian title topped these annual charts was back in 1975, when Billy Graham's *Angels: God's Secret Agents* sold about 265,000 copies. Three of the top 15 in 2001 were *Jabez*-related titles, also an unprecedented achievement. Religion books fared well among the runners-up as well, and three titles—*The Christmas Box Miracle, Bringing Up Boys,* and *Traveling Light*— were among the top 30.

What's New in Blockbusters

Two John Grishams, two Stephen Kings, and two James Pattersons are among the top 15 fiction bestsellers. The other names are Danielle Steel, Clive Cussler, Terry McMillan, Sue Grafton, Mary Higgins Clark, Jan Karon, and Patricia Cornwell—all familiar and all always successful. The only new name is Jonathan Franzen; his third book, *The Corrections*, a highly touted literary novel, came close to the million mark in sales and as of mid-March had enjoyed 26 weeks on our charts. It landed in the No. 5 spot on the list shortly after publication date, riding high on excellent reviews, a movie option, and a 15-city tour. Farrar, Straus & Giroux began with a 67,500-copy printing and was quickly up to 90,000. Oprah made the book her 43rd book club pick and FSG went back to press for more copies, bringing the total to about 720,000. But Franzen was uncomfortable being an Oprah pick, and his comments got him uninvited from the usual Oprah TV appearance and book club discussion. The media gave this "dis" enormous play. Still, the book went on to win the National Book Award for fiction last year.

In nonfiction, the concept of unfortunate timing could best be exemplified by Jack Welch's *Jack*, for which Warner paid about $7 million. Laydown and opening press conference were scheduled for mid-morning September 11. Nonetheless, the book hit the list in the No. 1 position and the publisher launched it with a 1.2-million first printing; it is No. 10 on our annual chart, with sales of about 724,000.

Two nonfiction titles in the top 15 have yet to appear on a *PW* weekly list as of this writing—*The Blue Day Book* and *America's Heroes*—although both came close several times. According to their publishers, both titles enjoyed huge sales in nonbook outlets; price clubs and discounters such as Walmart and Target, to name just a few.

The Net vs. Gross Issues

Every year, we state the same disclaimers: all the calculations for this annual best-seller list are based on shipped-and-billed figures supplied by publishers for new books issued in 2001 and 2000 (a few books published earlier that continued their tenures on the 2001 weekly bestseller charts are also included). These figures reflect only 2001 domestic sales; publishers were instructed not to include book club and overseas transactions. We also asked publishers to take into account returns through February 1, 2002. None of these sales figures should be considered final net sales (and there are a lot of rumors about higher returns than usual in light of a softer economy and the September 11 tragedy, which shifted attention away from certain bestselling categories). For many of these books, especially those published in the last quarter of the year, returns are still to be calculated. Also check the charts "Fiction: Comparative Rankings" and "Nonfiction: Comparative Rankings." They show how the various bestsellers fared at the national chains, the independents, and at dot-com retailers. Note that none of the retailers in these charts represent the price clubs and discounters—outlets that move huge quantities of bestsellers.

The Fiction Runners-Up

The second tier of 2001 top-selling novels is also dominated by bestselling list veterans. In less competitive years, almost all had placed in the top 15. Three authors—Danielle Steel, Mary Higgins Clark, and James Patterson—also have titles in the top 15. There is only one debut novel in the top 30, *Cane River* by Lalita Tademy, and it owes its high rank on these charts to being one of Oprah's book club picks.

16. *On the Street Where You Live* by Mary Higgins Clark (Simon & Schuster, **610,000+)
17. *The Bonesetter's Daughter* by Amy Tan (Putnam, 608,940)
18. *Cane River* by Lalita Tademy (Warner, 587,248)
19. *1st to Die* by James Patterson. (Little, Brown, 581,211)
20. *Leap of Faith* by Danielle Steel (Delacorte, **575,000)
21. *The Villa* by Nora Roberts (Putnam, 568,385)
22. *A Bend in the Road* by Nicholas Sparks (Warner, 528,632)
23. *Lone Eagle* by Danielle Steel (Delacorte, **525,000)
24. *The Sigma Protocol* by Robert Ludlum (St. Martin's, 512,645)
25. *Midnight Bayou* by Nora Roberts (Putnam, 489,354)
26. *Chosen Prey* by John Sandford (Putnam, 477,855)
27. *One Door Away from Heaven* by Dean Koontz (Bantam, **475,000)
28. *Last Man Standing* by David Baldacci (Warner, 470,117)
29. *Scarlet Feather* by Maeve Binchy (Dutton, 419,464)
30. *Blood and Gold* by Anne Rice (Knopf, 411,761)

400,000+ Fiction Didn't Place

There were 10 novels with sales of more than 300,000 copies in 2001 that did not place in the top-30 grouping; two of these sold more than 400,000. In 2000, three books that sold over 400,000 and six that sold over 300,000 did not make the top 30.

Fiction: Comparative Rankings

How *Publishers Weekly*'s bestsellers compared with the rankings
in major chains, wholesalers, and independents

PW Rankings	Sales Outlets											
	B/N	B	W	I	HN	S	BB	H	WS	TC	AM.c	BN.c
1. Desecration	11	11	72	2	5	—	—	1	4	—	7	8
2. Skipping Christmas	1	1	1	1	1	3	18	3	1	7	1	1
3. A Painted House	2	3	2	7	—	2	45	2	2	19	2	2
4. Dreamcatcher	6	4	3	12	—	19	—	4	12	39	8	5
5. The Corrections	3	2	15	10	2	1	2	43	7	3	4	3
6. Black House	17	11	4	33	10	18	43	5	25	46	13	6
7. The Kiss	31	30	7	37	—	—	—	15	48	—	—	40
8. Valhalla Rising	15	15	9	30	3	38	—	6	3	5	20	2
9. A Day Late and a Dollar Short	14	17	13	—	—	37	—	40	22	—	—	31
10. Violets are Blue	7	7	6	23	7	40	—	14	10	—	16	7
11. P Is For Peril	18	14	20	9	—	10	—	18	16	12	17	21
12. He Sees You When You're Sleeping	26	25	11	35	—	36	—	22	—	—	—	28
13. A Common Life	13	18	21	3	—	9	—	7	42	—	15	33
14. Isle of Dogs	25	29	24	25	14	42	—	19	18	—	38	24
15. Suzanne's Diary for Nicholas	4	10	12	6	4	11	—	27	5	—	25	11

Nonfiction: Comparative Rankings

How *Publishers Weekly*'s bestsellers compared with the rankings
in major chains, wholesalers, and independents

PW Rankings	Sales Outlets											
	B/N	B	W	I	HN	S	BB	H	WS	TC	AM.c	BN.c
1. The Prayer of Jabez	1	2	1	1	5	4	38	1	2	9	2	2
2. Secrets of the Vine	5	18	15	3	27	44	—	2	5	—	21	17
3. Who Moved My Cheese?	2	1	2	2	2	3	2	3	1	2	1	1
4. John Adams	3	3	6	4	3	2	3	11	14	1	3	3
5. Guinness World Records 2002	25	42	7	—	—	43	—	21	—	—	—	—
6. The Prayer of Jabez Devotional	18	44	40	9	—	—	—	7	—	—	—	39
7. The No Spin Zone	7	6	4	15	9	13	—	5	19	—	13	11
8. Body for Life	4	4	5	6	29	17	26	4	24	5	16	6
9. How I Play Golf	14	8	14	—	—	22	—	8	37	—	18	19
10. Jack	9	5	11	25	1	1	—	34	3	4	4	5
11. I Hope You Dance	21	7	3	7	—	40	—	13	29	—	—	32
12. Self Matters	—	37	23	—	—	—	—	15	—	37	—	—
13. The Blue Day Book	—	—	8	28	—	—	—	—	49	8	—	30
14. The Road to Wealth	—	28	35	20	—	—	—	43	—	32	52	34
15. America's Heroes	—	—	—	—	—	—	—	—	—	—	—	—

BN	= Barnes & Noble	B	= Borders
W	= Waldenbooks	I	= Ingram
HN	= Hudson News	S	= Harry W. Schwartz
BB	= Book & Books	H	= Hastings
WS	= Waterstone's	TC	= Tattered Cover
AM.c	= Amazon.com	BN.c	= Barnes & Noble.com

The 400,000-plus duo are *Seven Up* by Janet Evanovich (St. Martin's) and *Jackdaws* by Ken Follett (Dutton); they were on the charts for six and seven weeks, respectively. Evanovich was one of the 14 novelists last year who hit the list in the No. 1 spot the first week out.

All the books with sales of 300,000 copies or more in 2001 enjoyed best-seller weekly runs of four weeks or more. There are two books of poetry here (quite unusual for the fiction list): *The Best Loved Poems of Jacqueline Kennedy Onassis*, selected and edited by Caroline Kennedy (Hyperion), and *Journey Through Heartsongs* by Mattie Stepanek (VSP Books). The first was on the list for 14 weeks and proves that the Kennedy name continues to have sales magic. *Journey* is by an 11-year-old boy who has a terminal illness and wanted his poetry to inspire peace and good feeling. One of his wishes was to appear on "Oprah." He did, and was invited back several times—his book sales soared.

Other 300,000-plus novels by authors familiar to national bestsellers charts are *The Fiery Cross* by Diana Gabaldon (Delacorte), *The Smoke Jumper* by Nicholas Evans (Delacorte), *Envy* by Sandra Brown (Warner), *Flesh and Blood* by Jonathan Kellerman (Random House), *Hemlock Bay* by Catherine Coulter (Putnam), and *Mercy* by Julie Garwood (Pocket).

At Fiction's 200,000+ Level

There were 15 fiction hardcovers with sales of 200,000-plus that did not make the annual top 30, two fewer than in 2000. All the books here had impressive weekly runs, with four enjoying double-digit tenure: *The Mitford Snowmen* by Jan Karon (Viking), *Back When We Were Grownups* by Anne Tyler (Knopf), *The Fourth Hand* by John Irving (Random), and *The Last Time They Met* by Anita Shreve (Little, Brown).

Books with tenures of four to eight weeks were *The Jury* by Steve Martini (Putnam), *Any Way the Wind Blows* by E. Lynn Harris (Doubleday), *Summerhouse* by Jude Deveraux (Pocket), *Lake Wobegon Summer 1956* by Garrison Keillor (Viking), *Shock* by Robin Cook (Putnam), *Edge of Danger* by Jack Higgins (Putnam), *The Woman Next Door* by Barbara Delinsky (Simon & Schuster), *Special Ops* by W. E. B. Griffin (Putnam), and *Open Season* by Linda Howard (Pocket).

Only two books in this group were on the lists for less than a month—*Portrait in Sepia* by Isabel Allende (HarperCollins) and *The Pillars of Creation* by Terry Goodkind (Tor).

A Lower Tally for 150,000+

The 16 books with sales of 150,000-plus that did not make the top-30 list is a return to the 1999 level. In 2000 there were a record 24 books with sales of 150,000. Only two in this group had yet to make an appearance on the weekly charts: *Patches of Godlight: Father Tim's Favorite Quotes* by Jan Karon (Viking) and *Good Harbor* by Anita Diamant (Scribner). Both came close on several occasions. *Patches* is one of those fiction/nonfiction hybrids—the book includes quotes by real people, but it is all in the handwriting (with notes) of fictitious Mitford rector Father Tim, made famous by bestselling novelist Jan Karon.

Viking insists that this should be in the fiction grouping; *PW* thinks not, but adhered to the publisher's wishes (as Father Tim quotes Christopher Morley: "The enemies of the truth are always awfully nice").

Only three books in the group were on our weekly lists for less than a month: *The Cat Who Smelled a Rat* by Lilian Jackson Braun (Putnam), *The Family* by Mario Puzo (ReganBooks), and *Orchid Blues* by Stuart Woods (Putnam). *Death in Holy Orders* by P. D. James (Knopf) had a 10-week run and *A Darkness More Than Night* by Michael Connelly (Little, Brown) was on the list nine times.

The other nine clocked in at more than a month but less than two. They are *Potshot* by Robert B. Parker (Putnam), *Cold Paradise* by Stuart Woods (Putnam), *Fatal Voyage* by Kathy Reichs (Scribner), *Final Target* by Iris Johansen (Bantam), *Lost & Found* by Jayne Ann Krentz (Putnam), *Star Wars: Darth Maul, Shadow Hunter* by Michael Reaves (Del Rey/LucasBooks), *A Traitor to Memory* by Elizabeth George (Bantam), *Rise to Rebellion* by Jeff Shaara (Ballantine), and *Antrax* by Terry Brooks (Del Rey).

The 125,000+ Group

This seems to be the level for debut fiction in 2001. Three of the 14 books with sales of 125,000 or more were first fiction: *The Wind Done Gone* by Alice Randall (Houghton Mifflin), *Peace Like a River* by Leif Enger (Atlantic Monthly), and *My Dream of You* by Nuala O'Faolain (Putnam). *The Wind Done Gone* (eight weeks on the charts), billed as the first-person story of Rhett Butler's black mistress, benefited from the publicity surrounding a lawsuit. O'Faolain's first book was a bestselling memoir, *Are You Somebody?* Her novel stayed seven weeks on the charts. Enger's well-reviewed book did not make the top 15 but came close several times. Two other books with sales of 125,000 that did not appear on the weekly charts were *Warrior Class* by Dale Brown (Putnam) and *The Gryphon* by Nick Bantock (Chronicle).

The other nine—all familiar names on the charts—had runs of one to four weeks each: *The Forgotten* by Faye Kellerman (Morrow), *America* by Stephen Coonts (St. Martin's), *Between Lovers* by Eric Jerome Dickey (Dutton), *Hollywood Wives—The New Generation* by Jackie Collins (Simon & Schuster), *Riley in the Morning* by Sandra Brown (Bantam), *Death in Paradise* by Robert B. Parker (Putnam), *Falling Angels* by Tracy Chevalier (Dutton), *The Skies of Pern* by Anne McCaffrey (Del Rey), and *May There Be a Road* by Louis L'Amour (Bantam).

A New Record for 100,000+

There were 25 books that sold more than 100,000 copies that did not make the top 30, a new record. In 2000 that number was 19, and the previous record was 23 in 1998. Ten titles in this group never appeared on a weekly *Publishers Weekly* list in 2001. Nine had runs of less than a month while six stayed on the list for more than a month. *Mystic River* by Dennis Lehane (Morrow) had a nine-week run, the longest in this group.

The no-shows were *Seduction by Design* by Sandra Brown (Warner), *Brazen Virtue* by Nora Roberts (Bantam), *A Woman Betrayed* by Barbara Delinsky

(Morrow), *What You Owe Me* by Bebe Moore Campbell (Putnam), *Warlock* by Wilbur Smith (St. Martin's), *To Trust a Stranger* by Karen Robards (Pocket), *The Manhattan Hunt Club* by John Saul (Ballantine), *Never Change* by Elizabeth Berg (Pocket), *The Body Artist* by Don DeLillo (Scribner), and *Looking Back* by Belva Plain (Delacorte).

Those with one- to three-week runs were *Star Wars: Cloak of Deception* by James Luceno (Del Rey/LucasBooks), *McNally's Chance* by Lawrence Sanders (Putnam), *Star Wars: The New Jedi Order, Balance Point* by Troy Denning (Del Rey/LucasBooks), *Narcissus in Chains* by Laurell K. Hamilton (Berkley), *How to Be Good* by Nick Hornby (Riverhead), *Moving Target* by Elizabeth Lowell (Morrow), *Tell No One* by Harlan Coben (Delacorte), *Blood Lure* by Nevada Barr (Putnam), and *Heart of a Warrior* by Johanna Lindsey (Morrow).

The six bestsellers with tenures of a month or more were *Blue Diary* by Alice Hoffman (Putnam), *Long Time No See* by Susan Isaacs (HarperCollins), *Dune: House Corrino* by Brian Herbert and Kevin J. Anderson (Bantam), *Hidden Passions: Secrets from the Diaries of Tabitha Lenox* (HarperEntertainment), *Mystic River* by Dennis Lehane (Morrow), and *The Surgeon* by Tess Gerritsen (Ballantine).

The Nonfiction Runners-Up

Eleven nonfiction books in this second tier enjoyed double-digit tenures on the weekly charts or appeared for three months or more on our religion charts. Two, *The Christmas Box Miracle* and *Prime Time Emeril*, never made it on a *PW* list last year; one, *Dear Mom*, appeared for a single week. These types of books often sell very well in price clubs, discount outlets, and specialty stores. History, memoirs, and inspirational tomes dominate. Two titles, *The Final Days* by Barbara Olson and *Germs* by Judith Miller et al., received a lot of media attention after September 11. Olson's tragic death in the plane that was crashed into the Pentagon got lots of coverage, and Miller was a popular "talking head" during the anthrax scare.

16. *The Wild Blue: The Men and Boys Who Flew the B-24s over Germany* by Stephen E. Ambrose (Simon & Schuster, **500,000+)

17. *Stolen Lives: Twenty Years in a Desert Jail* by Malika Oufkir and Michele Fitoussi. (Talk Miramax, 477,867)

18. *FISH! A Remarkable Way to Boost Morale and Improve Results* by Stephen C. Lundin, Harry Paul, and John Christensen. (Hyperion, 469,230)

19. *Ghost Soldiers: The Forgotten Epic Story of World War II's Most Dramatic Mission* by Hampton Sides. (Doubleday, **450,000+)

20. *The Christmas Box Miracle* by Richard Paul Evans. (Simon & Schuster, **390,000+)

21. *Theodore Rex* by Edmund Morris. (Random House, 379,142)

22. *Bringing Up Boys* by James Dobson. (Tyndale, 365,000)

23. *Crossing Over: The Stories Behind the Stories* by John Edward. (Jodere Group, 347,405)

24. *The Final Days* by Barbara Olson. (Regnery, 332,346)

25. *Germs: Biological Weapons and America's Secret War* by Judith Miller, Stephen Engelberg, and William Broad. (Simon & Schuster, **325,000)

26. *Seabiscuit: An American Legend* by Laura Hillenbrand. (Random House, 320,756)

27. *Napalm and Silly Putty* by George Carlin. (Hyperion, 319,180)

28. *Traveling Light: Releasing the Burdens You Were Never Intended to Bear* by Max Lucado. (W Publishing, 315,862)

29. *Prime Time Emeril: More TV Dinners from America's Favorite Chef* by Emeril Lagasse. (Morrow Cookbooks, 310,000)

30. *Dear Mom: Thank You for Everything* by Bradley Trevor Greive. (Andrews McMeel, 301,730)

A Higher Tally for 200,000+

Last year 27 books with sales of more than 200,000 did not make the annual top 30, a new record for this level. In 2000 the tally was 19 books; in 1999 the number was 14. Seven of these books did not appear on *PW*'s weekly charts last year: *The Lord of the Rings: The Fellowship of the Ring Visual Companion* by Jude Fisher (Houghton Mifflin), *Prescription for Nutritional Healing* by Phyllis A. Balch and James F. Balch (Avery), *Looking for Mr. Right* by Bradley Trevor Greive (Andrews McMeel), *Madonna* by Andrew Morton (St. Martin's), *War Letters* by Andrew Carroll (Scribner), *Dale Earnhardt* by the editors of the *Charlotte Observer* (Sports Publishing), and *The Prayer of Jesus* by Hank Hanegraaff (W Publishing). *Lord of the Rings* is described as a Middle-earth encyclopedia with explanations of the movie sets and special effects. Yes, Middle-earth is a fictional location, but we put this reference book in nonfiction.

Ten titles in this group enjoyed tenures of eight weeks or more on our charts: *An Album of Memories: Personal Histories from the Greatest Generation* by Tom Brokaw (Random), *Secrets of the Baby Whisperer* by Tracy Hogg and Melinda Blau (Ballantine), *Founding Brothers: The Revolutionary Generation* by Joseph J. Ellis (Knopf), *The Wisdom of Menopause* by Christiane Northrup (Bantam), *Are We Living in the End Times?* by Jerry B. Jenkins and Tim LaHaye (Tyndale), *The Universe in a Nutshell* by Stephen Hawking (Bantam), *Suzanne Somers' Eat, Cheat and Melt the Fat Away* by Suzanne Somers (Crown), *A Short Guide to a Happy Life* by Anna Quindlen (Random), *God Bless the USA* by Lee Greenwood (Rutledge Hill), and *Ice Bound: A Doctor's Incredible Battle for Survival at the South Pole* by Jerri Nielsen with Maryanne Vollers (Talk Miramax).

Four books appeared on the lists for four to eight weeks: *One Nation: America Remembers September 11, 2001* by the editors of *Life* magazine (Little, Brown), *Back to the Table: The Reunion of Food and Family* by Art Smith (Hyperion), *Fire* by Sebastian Junger (Norton), and *Foley Is Good* by Mick Foley (ReganBooks).

The other six titles had one- to three-week runs: *The Heart of the Soul: Emotional Awareness* by Gary Zukav and Linda Francis (S&S), *Holy War, Inc.* by Peter L. Bergen (Free Press), *Now, Discover Your Strengths* by Marcus Buckingham and Donald O. Clifton (Free Press), *The Lost Son: A Life in Pursuit of Justice* by Bernard B. Kerik (ReganBooks), *Past Lives, Future Healing* by Sylvia

Browne with Lindsay Harrison (Dutton), and *National Audubon Society: The Sibley Guide to Birds* by David Allen Sibley (Knopf).

Nonfiction's 150,000+

There were 18 books at this sales level that did not make the top-30 list, two more than in 2000 but five fewer than the record set in 1999. There were a number of titles in this group that became popular after September 11, especially Karen Armstrong's *Islam: A Short History*. Regnery's *Bias* is another example; it was also one of the many books reflecting strong conservative points of view that did well in the last few months of 2001.

Seven books did not appear on *PW*'s weekly lists. They were *Cosbyology: Essays and Observations from the Doctor of Comedy* by Bill Cosby (Hyperion), *At the Altar of Speed: The Fast Life and Tragic Death of Dale Earnhardt* by Leigh Montville (Doubleday), *The World Trade Center: A Tribute* by Bill Harris (Running Press/Courage), *It's True, It's True* by Kurt Angle (ReganBooks), *The Darwin Awards II* by Wendy Northcutt (Dutton), *Mars and Venus in the Workplace* by John Gray (HarperCollins), and *There's a Spiritual Solution for Every Problem* by Wayne W. Dyer (HarperCollins).

The books that did enjoy time on the weekly charts or on *PW*'s monthly religion charts were *In Harm's Way: The Sinking of the USS Indianapolis and the Extraordinary Story of Its Survivors* by Doug Stanton (Holt), *An Open Heart: Practicing the Art of Compassion* by His Holiness the Dalai Lama (Little, Brown), *Bias: A CBS Insider Exposes How the Media Distort the News* by Bernard Goldberg (Regnery), *The God Catchers: Experiencing the Manifest Presence of God* by Tommy Tenney (Nelson), *Fast Food Nation* by Eric Schlosser (Houghton Mifflin), *When You Come to a Fork in the Road, Take It!* by Yogi Berra with Dave Kaplan (Hyperion), *Life Makeovers: 52 Practical and Inspiring Ways to Improve Your Life One Week at a Time* by Cheryl Richardson (Broadway), *When Character Was King: A Story of Ronald Reagan* by Peggy Noonan (Viking), *Night Light: A Devotional for Couples* by James and Shirley Dobson (Multnomah), *Islam: A Short History* by Karen Armstrong (Modern Library), and *War in a Time of Peace* by David Halberstam (Scribner).

A Higher Tally for 125,000+

This group had 20 books that did not make our top-30 list, five more than the 2000 number. *The Art of Happiness: A Handbook for Living* by His Holiness the Dalai Lama and Howard C. Cutler (Riverhead) enjoyed a third year on our monthly hardcover religion charts, and *Wild at Heart: Discovering the Secret of a Man's Soul* by John Eldredge (Nelson) has had a five-month run on the religion list.

Eight books never appeared on a 2001 list: *Grow Younger, Live Longer* by Deepak Chopra (Harmony), *Heaven and Earth* by James Van Praagh (Simon & Schuster Source), *Financial Security in Troubled Times: What You Need to Do Now* by Ric Edelman (HarperBusiness), *Good to Great: Why Some Companies Make the Leap . . . and Others Don't* by Jim Collins (HarperBusiness), *Now Let Me Tell You What I Really Think* by Chris Matthews (Free Press), *Nickel and Dimed: On (Not) Getting By in America* by Barbara Ehrenreich (Holt/Metropolitan), *The 17 Indisputable Laws of Teamwork* by John C. Maxwell (Nelson), and *Killing Pablo: The Hunt for the World's Greatest Outlaw* by Mark Bowden (Atlantic Monthly). Also, *Q: The Autobiography of Quincy Jones* by Quincy Jones (Doubleday) made a single-week appearance.

All the others in this group had runs of a month or more on the 2001 charts: *Justice: Crimes, Trials, and Punishments* by Dominick Dunne (Crown), *French Lessons* by Peter Mayle (Knopf), *Longaberger: An American Success Story* by David H. Longaberger and Robert L. Shook (HarperBusiness), *Separation of Power* by Vince Flynn (Pocket), *The Life God Blesses* by Jim Cymbala with Stephen Sorenson (Zondervan), *The Map That Changed the World* by Simon Winchester (HarperCollins), *Living a Life That Matters: Resolving the Conflict Between Conscience and Success* by Harold S. Kushner (Knopf), *Fresh Power* by Jim Cymbala with Dean Merrill (Zondervan), and *If You Want to Walk on Water, You've Got to Get Out of the Boat* by John Ortberg (Zondervan).

The 100,000+ Circle

In 2001 a total of 28 books with sales of more than 100,000 did not place on the top-30 list—a high number, but fewer than the record set in 2000 when the tally was 36. More than half—16—did not appear on the weekly charts in 2001. Only one, *An Hour Before Daylight* by Jimmy Carter (Simon & Schuster), had a double-digit tenure, enjoying 13 weeks on the 2001 charts. *The Darwin Awards: Evolution in Action* by Wendy Northcutt (Dutton) had a nine-week run.

The other 10 titles that appeared on last year's weekly or monthly lists were *Soul Survivor: How My Faith Survived the Church* by Philip Yancey (Doubleday), *Relationship Rescue* by Phillip C. McGraw (Hyperion), *Kiss and Make-up* by Gene Simmons (Crown), *He Chose the Nails* by Max Lucado (W Publishing), *New York September 11* by Magnum Photographers (PowerHouse), *The O'Reilly Factor* by Bill O'Reilly (Broadway), *Supreme Injustice: How the High Court Highjacked Election 2000* by Alan M. Dershowitz (Oxford Univ. Press), *Meditations* by Sylvia Browne (Hay House), *It's Not About the Bike: My Journey Back to Life* by Lance Armstrong with Sally Jenkins (Putnam), and *Walking the Bible* by Bruce Feiler (Morrow).

The 16 no-shows were *Mrs. Sharp's Traditions* by Sarah Ban Breathnach (Scribner), *The Noonday Demon* by Andrew Solomon (Scribner), *Perhaps Today* by Jerry B. Jenkins and Tim LaHaye (Tyndale), *The Dirt* by Tommy Lee (ReganBooks), *My Journey* by Robert H. Schuller (Harper San Francisco), *Mother O'Mine: A Mother's Treasury* by Mary Engelbreit (Andrews McMeel), *Churchill* by Roy Jenkins (Farrar, Straus & Giroux), *Boy Meets Girl* by Joshua Harris (Multnomah), *The Kennedy Men: 1901–1963* by Laurence Leamer (Morrow), *The Naked Chef* by Jamie Oliver (Hyperion), *Shaq Talks Back* by Shaquille O'Neal (St. Martin's), *It's Only a Game* by Terry Bradshaw (Pocket), *I Love Lucy: The Official 50th Anniversary Tribute Celebrating 50 Years of Love and Laughter* by Elisabeth Edwards (Running Press), *The Botany of Desire* by Michael Pollan (Random), *Close to Shore* by Michael Capuzzo (Doubleday), and *A Cook's Tour* by Anthony Bourdain (Bloomsbury).

Paperback Bestsellers: The Paperback Game

Dermot McEvoy
Contributing Editor, *Publishers Weekly*

Daisy Maryles
Executive Editor, *Publishers Weekly*

It was the year of the Lord—*The Lord of the Rings*, that is. Not since 1997's *Titanic*—which inspired bestseller sales for at least a dozen new and backlist books—has a single film had such a strong effect on the book business. And, in fact, the sales numbers for titles connected to the film *The Lord of the Rings: The Fellowship of the Ring* were astounding, way ahead of those for *Titanic*. The books that fared the best were the titles that make up The Lord of the Ring Trilogy—*The Fellowship of the Ring, The Two Towers,* and *The Return of the King*—plus the prequel, *The Hobbit*. For several months, all four appeared on *PW*'s weekly mass market top-15 charts; combined sales in 2001 for the four Ballantine mass market editions added up to more than 5.6 million copies. The same titles in their Houghton Mifflin trade editions sold almost 4.9 million copies combined in 2001 (this also included a boxed set and a single volume of the three trilogy books). Houghton Mifflin also published two pictorial movie tie-ins—*The Lord of the Rings Official Movie Guide* and *The Lord of the Rings: The Fellowship of the Ring Photo Guide*—for a combined total of more than 360,000. All told, the very successful movie—No. 2 in box-office receipts for 2001—accounted for at least 10.8 million books sold last year.

Other than the standard mix of titles on these annual paperback bestseller lists—dominated by reprints of hardcover bestsellers, Oprah book club picks and Oprah guest authors, and all the books from the Left Behind series and a baker's dozen of Chicken Soup for the Soul titles—the newest category grouping were new and backlist books connected to the events of September 11. As the country was reeling from the terrorist attacks, there were many who were trying to comprehend the who and why, searching for books on Osama bin Laden and Islam. The Koran appeared on *PW*'s monthly religion paperback list. as did other books on Islam. New paperback reprints—Yale's *Taliban* by Ahmed Rashid and Prima's *Bin Laden: The Man Who Declared War on America* by Yossef Bodansky—were on the charts in the top spots for several weeks; also making a reappearance for a few weeks were backlist titles such as Anchor's *From Beirut to Jerusalem* by Thomas L. Friedman (1991) and Ballantine's *Jihad vs. McWorld* by Benjamin Barber (1996). Many pictorials memorializing September 11 sold well in the fall; two of the bestsellers were *September 11, 2001*, edited by Poynter Institute (Andrews McMeel) and *September 11: A Testimony* by the staff of Reuters, published by Prentice Hall/Financial Times.

Trade paperback fiction continued to be a strong category in 2001, with 22 fiction titles selling more than 500,000 copies, up from the 19 novels that achieved such strong sales in 2000. Longevity for trade bestsellers continued to be the norm—14 trade paper bestsellers had tenures of 15 weeks or more; two, *The Four Agreements* by Don Miguel Ruiz and *The Red Tent* by Anita Diament, had perfect records, not missing a single week in 2001.

In mass market, veteran bestselling novelists dominated the 2001 annual charts. And while Grisham led the charts with sales of more than three million for *A Painted House*, the prolific Nora Roberts had three two-million copy bestsellers, three in the million-plus grouping, and two under her pseudonym J. D. Robb in the 750,000-plus group. Her sales total for just this category (she had hardcover and trade bestsellers, too, in 2001) is astounding—close to 14 million last year.

Figuring 2001

Listed on the following pages are trade paperbacks and mass markets published in 2000 or 2001; the rankings are based on 2001 sales only. To qualify, trade paperback titles had to have sold more than 75,000 copies in 2001; for mass markets, sales of more than 750,000 were required. A single asterisk (*) indicates the book was published in 2000; a double asterisk (**) means the book was published earlier but either remained or reappeared on the charts in the year 2001. Those reappearances often were movie tie-ins or Oprah selections; this year, some reappeared after September 11 (these are indicated by ***). A number symbol (#) indicates that the shipped-and-billed figure was rounded down to the nearest 10,000 to indicate its relationship to sales figures of other titles. The actual figures were given to *PW* in confidence for use in placing titles on these lists.

Trade Paperbacks

1 Million+

Life Strategies. Phillip McGraw. Rep. Hyperion (1,812,714)

We Were the Mulveneys. Joyce Carol Oates. Reissue. Plume (1,550,000)

The Indwelling (Left Behind Series No. 7). Jerry B. Jenkins and Tim LaHaye. Rep. Tyndale (1,132,920)

The Lord of the Rings. J. R. R. Tolkien. Movie tie-in. Houghton Mifflin (1,061,997)

Icy Sparks. Gwyn Hyman Rubio. Rep. Penguin (1,004,231)

**The Red Tent. Anita Diamant. Rep. Picador USA (1,000,000)

Girl with a Pearl Earring. Tracy Chevalier. Rep. Plume (1,000,000)

750,000+

The Fellowship of the Rings. J. R. R. Tolkien. Movie tie-in. Houghton Mifflin (995,991)

The Mark (Left Behind Series No. 8): The Beast Rules the World. Jerry B. Jenkins and Tim LaHaye. Rep. Tyndale (972,536)

**Left Behind (Left Behind Series No. 1). Jerry B. Jenkins and Tim LaHaye. Rep. Tyndale (947,543)

Bridget Jones's Diary. Helen Fielding. Movie tie-in. Penguin (920,092)

The Hobbit. J. R. R. Tolkien. Movie tie-in. Houghton Mifflin (919,888)

Band of Brothers. Stephen E. Ambrose. Rep. Touchstone (858,700)

**The Four Agreements. Don Miguel Ruiz. Orig. Amber-Allen (850,546)

**Tribulation Force (Left Behind Series No. 2). Jerry B. Jenkins and Tim LaHaye. Rep. Tyndale (828,006)

Worst Case Scenario Survival Handbook: Travel. David Borgenicht and John Piven. Rep. Chronicle (771,785)

**Nicolae (Left Behind Series No. 3). Jerry B. Jenkins and Tim LaHaye. Rep. Tyndale (765,037)

500,000+

The Two Towers. J. R. R. Tolkien. Movie tie-in. Houghton Mifflin (744,365)

*House of Sand & Fog. Andre Dubus. Rep. Vintage (717,073)

The Return of the King. J. R. R. Tolkien. Movie tie-in. Houghton Mifflin (706,752)

**Soul Harvest (Left Behind Series No. 4).* Jerry B. Jenkins and Tim LaHaye. Rep. Tyndale (695,754)

Apollyon (Left Behind Series No. 5). Jerry B. Jenkins and Tim LaHaye. Rep. Tyndale (685,159)

Bridget Jones: The Edge of Reason. Helen Fielding. Rep. Penguin (580,309)

**Assassins (Left Behind Series No. 6).* Jerry B. Jenkins and Tim LaHaye. Rep. Tyndale (571,830)

**Rich Dad, Poor Dad.* Robert T. Kiyosaki with Sharon L. Lechter. Orig. Warner (547,713)

A Fine Balance. Rohinton Mistry. Reissue. Vintage (542,725)

**Don't Sweat the Small Stuff for Teens.* Richard Carlson. Orig. Hyperion (523,576)

A Heartbreaking Work of Staggering Genius. Dave Eggers. Rep. Vintage (512,427)

#*The Greatest Generation.* Tom Brokaw. Rep. Dell (510,000)

250,000+

The Lord of the Rings Boxed Set. J. R. R. Tolkien. Movie tie-in. Houghton Mifflin (458,806)

Prodigal Summer. Barbara Kingsolver. Rep. HarperCollins (450,000)

Chicken Soup for the Teenage Soul: On Tough Stuff. Canfield, Hansen and Kirberger. Orig. HCI (430,900)

Drowning Ruth. Christina Schwarz. Rep. Ballantine (427,602)

Chicken Soup for the Father's Soul. Canfield, Hansen and Donnelly. Orig. HCI (406,487)

**Relationship Rescue.* Phillip McGraw. Rep. Hyperion (404,346)

Chicken Soup for the Mother's Soul 2. Canfield, Hansen, Shimoff and Kline. Orig. HCI (399,448)

Me Talk Pretty One Day. David Sedaris. Rep. Little, Brown (395,149)

In the Heart of the Sea. Nathaniel Philbrick. Rep. Penguin (373,978)

Worst Case Scenario Survival Handbook: Dating and Sex. David Borgenicht and John Piven. Rep. Chronicle (370,755)

Don't Sweat the Small Stuff for Women. Kristine Carlson. Orig. Hyperion (368,962)

**Robert Ludlum's The Hades Factor.* Robert Ludlum and Gayle Lynds. Orig. St. Martin's (356,000)

Calvin and Hobbes Sunday Pages 1985–1995. Bill Watterson. Orig. Andrews McMeel (351,481)

**Don't Sweat the Small Stuff in Love.* Richard Carlson. Orig. Hyperion (342,630)

Remembering The Intimidator. Triumph Editors. Orig. Triumph (328,224)

It's Not About the Bike. Lance Armstrong with Sally Jenkins. Rep. Berkley (321,669)

**Chocolat.* Joanne Harris. Movie tie-in. Penguin (320,449)

A Queen for All Seasons. Linda Cobb. Orig. Pocket (319,834)

Little Magic. Nora Roberts. Rep. Berkley (314,249)

**Chicken Soup for the Preteen Soul.* Canfield, Hansen, Hansen and Dunlap. Orig. HCI (313,840)

Open House. Elizabeth Berg. Rep. Ballantine (312,309)

**A Man Named Dave.* Dave Pelzer. Rep. Plume (305,000)

Nothing Like It in the World. Stephen E. Ambrose. Rep. Touchstone (296,800)

The Blind Assassin. Margaret Atwood. Rep. Anchor (296,616)

4 Blondes. Candace Bushnell. Rep. Grove Atlantic (287,047)

**Chicken Soup for the Teenage Soul 3.* Canfield, Hansen and Kirberger. Orig. HCI (285,454)

Taliban. Ahmed Rashid. Rep. Yale Univ. (278,045)

The Lord of the Rings Official Movie Guide. Brian Sibley. Orig. Houghton Mifflin (276,524)

#*Flags of Our Fathers.* James Bradley with Ron Powers. Rep. Bantam (275,000)

Chicken Soup for the Veteran's Soul. Canfield, Hansen and Slagter. Orig. HCI (271,969)

Chicken Soup for the Teenage Soul Letters. Canfield, Hansen and Kirberger. Orig. HCI (269,874)

Chicken Soup for the Gardener's Soul. Canfield, Hansen, Buck, Owen, Stone and Sturgulewski. Orig. HCI (268,749)

Fortune's Rocks. Anita Shreve. Rep. Little, Brown (263,735)

Chicken Soup for the Nurse's Soul. Canfield, Hansen, Mitchell-Autio and Thieman. Orig. HCI (263,320)

Corelli's Mandolin. Louis de Bernieres. Movie tie-in. Vintage (261,313)

The Amazing Adventures of Kavalier & Clay. Michael Chabon. Rep. Picador USA (260,000)

Hungry Ocean. Linda Greenlaw. Rep. Hyperion (258,766)

100,000+

Chocolate from the Cake Mix Doctor. Anne Byrn. Orig. Workman (243,067)

The Wrinkle Cure. Nicholas Perricone, M.D. Rep. Warner (242,170)

Big Stone Gap. Adriana Trigiani. Rep. Ballantine (231,545)

Don't Sweat the Small Stuff for Men. Richard Carlson. Orig. Hyperion (231,218)

***Bin Laden: The Man Who Declared War on America.* Yossef Bodansky. Rep. Prima/Crown (225,000)

Shopgirl. Steve Martin. Rep. Hyperion (222,632)

Robert Ludlum's The Cassandra Compact. Robert Ludlum and Phillip Shelby. Orig. St. Martin's (222,000)

Courage to be Rich. Suze Orman. Rep. Riverhead (221,625)

On Writing. Stephen King. Rep. Pocket (215,080)

Galileo's Daughter. Dava Sobel. Rep. Penguin (213,287)

Chicken Soup for the Baseball Fan's Soul. Canfield, Hansen, Donnelly and LaSorda. Orig. HCI (209,309)

White Teeth. Zadie Smith. Rep. Vintage (209,028)

Rachel's Tears: The Spiritual Journey of Columbine Martyr Rachel Scott. Beth Nimmo, Darrell Scott and Steve Rabey. Orig. Thomas Nelson (208,328)

Amy and Isabelle. Elizabeth Strout. Rep. Vintage (206,294)

The Case for Faith. Lee Strobel. Orig. Zondervan (205,463)

Kitchen Confidential. Anthony Bourdain. Rep. HarperCollins (200,000)

#*Confessions of a Shopaholic.* Sophie Kinsella. Rep. Dell (200,000)

Hour Before Daylight. Jimmy Carter. Rep. Touchstone (197,800)

Closing the Gap. Jay McGraw. Orig. Fireside (196,000)

Rich Dad's Rich Kid, Smart Kid. Robert T. Kiyosaki with Sharon L. Lechter. Orig. Warner (194,031)

Bee Season. Myla Goldberg. Rep. Anchor (192,560)

Girl in Hyacinth Blue. Susan Vreeland. Rep. Penguin (189,764)

While I Was Gone. Sue Miller. Rep. Ballantine (187,384)

How to Grill. Steven Raichlen. Orig. Workman (186,130)

Where the Heart Is. Billie Letts. Movie tie-in. Warner (184,951)

Special Forces. Tom Clancy. Orig. Berkley (184,130)

Until Today! Iyanla Vanzant. Rep. Fireside (183,300)

**Mere Christianity.* C. S. Lewis. Rep. Harper San Francisco (179,827)

The Vagina Monologues. Eve Ensler. Orig. Villard (177,822)

Living Through the Meantime. Iyanla Vanzant. Orig. Fireside (176,260)

Anil's Ghost. Michael Ondaatje. Rep. Vintage (176,018)

Paris to the Moon. Adam Gopnik. Rep. Random House (175,213)

The Mists of Avalon. Marion Zimmer Bradley. Movie tie-in. Del Rey (171,576)

Windows XP for Dummies. Andy Rathbone. Orig. Wiley (166,032)

Interpreter of Maladies. Jhumpa Lahiri. Rep. Houghton Mifflin (165,054)

The 9 Steps to Financial Freedom. Suze Orman. Rep. Three Rivers (162,878)

A New Song. Jan Karon. Rep. Penguin (162,056)

J. K. Rowling: The Wizard Behind Harry Potter. Marc Shapiro. Orig. St. Martin's (161,300)

In the Line of Duty: A Tribute to New York's Finest and Bravest. Orig. HarperCollins (160,000)

Eating Well for Optimum Health. Andrew Weil. Rep. HarperCollins (160,000)

Chicken Soup for the Jewish Soul. Canfield, Hansen and Elkins. Orig. HCI (156,192)

Disobedience. Jane Hamilton. Rep. Anchor (154,779)

It's a Dog's Life, Snoopy. Charles M. Schulz. Orig. Ballantine (154,672)

Black Hawk Down. Mark Bowden. Movie tie-in. Penguin (153,049)

September 11, 2001. Poynter Institute. Orig. Andrews McMeel (150,489)

River King. Alice Hoffman. Reissue. Berkley (150,278)

#*The Greatest Generation Speaks.* Tom Brokaw. Rep. Dell (150,000)

The New New Thing. Michael Lewis. Rep. Penguin (149,066)

Adobe Photoshop 6.0 Classroom in a Book. Adobe Creative Team. Orig. Adobe (145,251)

The Dress Lodger. Sheri Holman. Rep. Ballantine (143,998)

Western Garden Book. Kathleen Brenzel. Reissue. Sunset (143,620)

Ethics for the New Millennium. Dalai Lama. Reissue. Riverhead (142,520)

Beowulf: A New Verse Translation. Seamus Heaney. Rep. Norton (142,423)

The Cashflow Quadrant. Robert T. Kiyosaki with Sharon L. Lechter. Orig. Warner (142,222)

Chicken Soup for the Golden Soul. Canfield, Hansen, Meyer, Chesser and Seeger. Orig. HCI (141,891)

The Feast of Love. Charles Baxter. Rep. Vintage (139,091)

The Nature of Good and Evil. Sylvia Browne. Orig. Hay House (136,740)

The Lexus and the Olive Tree. Thomas L. Friedman. Rep. Anchor (135,474)

The Human Stain. Phillip Roth. Rep. Vintage (135,284)

Help Yourself. Dave Pelzer. Rep. Plume (135,000)

Garfield at Large. Jim Davis. Orig. Ballantine (134,960)

The Gates of the Alamo. Stephen Harrigan. Rep. Penguin (134,269)

God Save the Sweet Potato Queens. Jill Conner Browne. Orig. Three Rivers (133,710)

Prayers. Don Miguel Ruiz with Janet Mills. Orig. Amber-Allen (130,232)

The Battle for God. Karen Armstrong. Rep. Ballantine (127,858)

***From Beirut to Jerusalem.* Thomas L. Friedman. Rep. Anchor (127,636)

The Travel Detective. Peter Greenberg. Orig. Villard (126,547)

When Did Ignorance Become a Point of View? Scott Adams. Orig. Andrews McMeel (125,309)

From Dawn to Decadence. Jacques Barzun. Rep. HarperCollins (125,000)

#*Fierce Invalids Home from Hot Climates.* Tom Robbins. Rep. Bantam

Dispatches from the Tenth Circle. Edited by Robert Siegel. Orig. Three Rivers (124,899)

The Girlfriends' Guide to Getting Your Groove Back. Vicki Iovine. Rep. Perigee (120,635)

Weber's Big Book of Grilling. Jamie Purviance. Rep. Chronicle (117,912)

BodyChange. Montel Williams and Wini Linguvic. Orig. Hay House (116,824)

Standing for Something. Gordon B. Hinckley. Rep. Three Rivers (116,695)

Bad Girls Guide to Getting What You Want. Cameron Tuttle. Rep. Chronicle (115,652)

Soul Mountain. Gao Xingjian. Rep. HarperCollins (115,000)

White Oleander. Janet Fitch. Rep. Little, Brown (114,259)

Desire of the Everlasting Hills. Thomas Cahill. Rep. Anchor (113,990)

A Beautiful Mind. Sylvia Nasar. Movie tie-in. Touchstone (113,079)

Suzanne Somers' Get Skinny on Fabulous Food. Suzanne Somers. Rep. Three Rivers (112,649)

Horse Heaven. Jane Smiley. Rep. Ballantine (112,537)

The Hours. Michael Cunningham. Rep. Picador USA (112,000)

Microsoft Windows ME for Dummies. Andy Rathbone. Orig. Wiley (111,136)

How to Know God. Deepak Chopra. Rep. Three Rivers (110,754)

Speaking with the Angel. Edited by Nick Hornby. Rep. Riverhead (108,724)

Photoshop 6 for Windows and Macintosh: Visual QuickStart Guide. Elaine Weinmann and Peter Lourekas. Orig. Peachpit (108,378)

Excuse Me While I Wag. Scott Adams. Orig. Andrews McMeel (107,870)

George W. Bushisms. Jacob Weisberg. Orig. Fireside (106,100)

Chocolate for a Women's Dreams. Kay Allenbaugh. Orig. Fireside (103,360)

Enemy at the Gates. William Craig. Movie tie-in. Penguin (103,123)

My Grandfather's Blessings. Rachael Remen, M.D. Rep. Riverhead (102,799)

*Lady & Sons, Too. Paula Deen. Orig. Villard (102,738)

*The Jumbo Duct Tape Book. Tim and Jim (The Duct Tape Guys). Orig. Workman (101,624)

75,000+

The Business Plan for the Body. Jim Karas. Orig. Three Rivers (99,366)

Lord, I Want to Be Whole: The Power of Prayer and Scripture in Emotional Healing. Stormie Omartian. Orig. Thomas Nelson (97,962)

*The Girls' Guide to Hunting and Fishing. Melissa Bank. Rep. Penguin (95,171)

*Rich Dad Guide to Investing. Robert T. Kiyosaki with Sharon L. Lechter. Orig. Warner (94,228)

Cherry. Mary Karr. Rep. Penguin (93,225)

*A Cup of Comfort. Colleen Sell. Orig. Adams Media (93,182)

America's Queen. Sarah Bradford. Rep. Penguin (92,571)

Riding in Cars with Boys. Beverly Donofrio. Movie tie-in. Penguin (92,204)

Beauty: The New Basics. Rona Berg. Orig. Workman (92,143)

Gone for Soldiers. Jeff Shaara. Rep. Ballantine (91,049)

*Gap Creek. Robert Morgan. Rep. Scribner (88,300)

*Father to Son: Life Lessons on Raising a Boy. Harry H. Harrison, Jr. Orig. Workman (88,273)

In the Fall. Jeffery Lent. Rep. Vintage (88,125)

Beloved. Toni Morrison. Movie tie-in. Plume (88,000)

*Plainsong. Kent Haruf. Rep. Vintage (87,716)

***Jihad vs. McWorld. Benjamin Barber. Rep. Ballantine (87,439)

When We Were Orphans. Kazuo Ishiguro. Rep. Vintage (86,944)

Brunelleschi's Dome. Ross King. Rep. Penguin (86,717)

*God, Creation, and Tools for Life. Sylvia Browne. Orig. Hay House (86,653)

Remembering Dale Earnhardt. Rich Wolfe. Orig. Triumph (86,322)

Boone's Lick. Larry McMurtry. Rep. Scribner Paperback Fiction (86,240)

Simpsons Comics Royale. Matt Groening. Orig. HarperCollins (86,000)

A Conspiracy of Paper. David Liss. Rep. Ballantine (85,611)

Chocolate for a Teen's Heart. Kay Allenbaugh. Orig. Fireside (85,120)

Fast Food Nation. Eric Schlosser. Rep. HarperCollins (85,000)

The Shipping News. Annie Proulx. Movie tie-in. Scribner (84,850)

*Waiting. Ha Jin. Rep. Vintage (84,618)

The Lord of the Rings: The Fellowship of the Ring Photo Guide. Edited by Alison Sage. Orig. Houghton Mifflin (84,215)

J. K. Lasser's New Tax Law Simplified. Orig. Wiley (83,193)

True History of the Kelly Gang. Peter Carey. Rep. Vintage (83,132)

The Rise of Theodore Roosevelt. Edmund Morris. Reissue. Modern Library (83,121)

Praying God's Will for Your Life: A Prayerful Walk to Spiritual Well Being. Stormie Omartian. Orig. Thomas Nelson (82,176)

River-Horse. William Least Heat-Moon. Rep. Penguin (81,999)

Midwives. Chris Bohjalian. Movie tie-in. Vintage (81,737)

Face Forward. Kevyn AuCoin. Rep. Little, Brown (81,636)

Georgiana: Duchess of Devonshire. Amanda Foreman. Rep. Modern Library (80,225)

The Family Orchard. Nomi Eve. Rep. Vintage (80,042)

Day of Infamy. Walter Lord. Reissue. Holt (80,000)

Cook Right for Your Type. Dr. Peter D'Adamo. Rep. Berkley (79,358)

The Language of Threads. Gail Tsukiama. Rep. St. Martin's (79,000)

Inca Gold. Clive Cussler. Rep. Pocket (77,904)

Chicken Soup for the Expectant Mother's Soul. Canfield, Hansen, Aubery and Mitchell. Orig. HCI (77,557)

***A History of God*. Karen Armstrong. Ballantine Rep. (77,376)

***The Koran*. Trans. by N. J. Dawood. Rep. Penguin (77,365)

Life Strategies for Teens. Jay McGraw. Orig. Fireside (77,170)

1001 Playthinks: Puzzles, Paradoxes, Illusions & Games. Ivan Moscovich. Orig. Workman (76,171)

The Camino. Shirley MacLaine. Rep. Pocket (77,022)

Landscaping With Stone. Sunset Editors. Orig. Sunset (75,719)

September 11: A Testimony. Staff of Reuters. Orig. Prentice Hall/Financial Times (75,315)

Small Miracles for Women. Yitta Halberstam and Judith Leventhal. Orig. Adams Media (75,215)

Almanacs, Atlases, and Annuals

The World Almanac And Book of Facts 2002. Edited by Ken Park. Orig. World Almanac (1,207,333)

The World Almanac And Book of Facts 2001. Edited by Ken Park. Orig. World Almanac (314,704)

The Ernst & Young Tax Guide 2002. Orig. Wiley (196,029)

J. K. Lasser's Your Income Tax 2002. Orig. Wiley (185,522)

The Best American Short Stories 2001. Edited by Barbara Kingsolver. Orig. Houghton Mifflin (123,069)

ESPN 2002 Almanac. Gerry Brown, Mike Morrison and the Editors of Information Please. Orig. Hyperion (115,854)

What Color Is Your Parachute 2002. Richard Nelson Bolles. Orig. Ten Speed (109,535)

What Color Is Your Parachute 2001. Richard Nelson Bolles. Orig. Ten Speed (97,026)

The New York Times Almanac 2002. Edited by John W. Wright. Orig. Penguin (81,096)

Mass Market

Two Million+

#*A Painted House*. John Grisham. Rep. Dell (3,000,000+)

#*Hannibal*. Thomas Harris. Movie tie-in. Dell (2,900,000)

Dance upon Air. Nora Roberts. Orig. Berkley (2,500,000)

Heaven and Earth. Nora Roberts. Orig. Berkley (2,300,000)

Bear and Dragon. Tom Clancy. Reissue. Berkley (2,200,000)

Carolina Moon. Nora Roberts. Reissue. Berkley (2,100,000)

The Lord of the Rings: The Fellowship of the Ring. J. R. R. Tolkien. Movie tie-in. Del Rey (2,042,826)

Last Precinct. Patricia Cornwell. Reissue. Berkley (2,000,000)

One Million+

#*Before I Say Goodbye*. Mary Higgins Clark. Rep. Pocket (1,870,000)

Time and Again. Nora Roberts. Orig. Silhouette (1,760,000)

Reflections and Dreams. Nora Roberts. Orig. Silhouette (1,730,000)

#*Journey*. Danielle Steel. Rep. Dell (1,700,000)

Stanislavsky Sisters. Nora Roberts. Orig. Silhouette (1,700,000)

The Hobbit. J. R. R. Tolkien. Movie tie-in. Del Rey (1,624,790)

#*Dreamcatcher*. Stephen King. Rep. Pocket (1,580,000)

#*From the Corner of His Eye*. Dean Koontz. Rep. Bantam (1,525,000)

Easy Prey. John Sandford. Reissue. Berkley (1,500,000)

#*The Wedding*. Danielle Steel. Rep. Dell (1,450,000)

Winter Solstice. Rosamunde Pilcher. Rep. St. Martin's (1,400,000)

Roses Are Red. James Patterson. Rep. Warner (1,341,251)

#*Deck the Halls*. Mary Higgins Clark and Carol Higgins. Rep. Pocket (1,320,000)

The Prometheus Deception. Robert Ludlum. Rep. St. Martin's (1,300,000)

Tom Clancy's Op-Center, Vol. VIII. Tom Clancy, Steve Pieczenik and Jeff Rovin. Orig. Berkley (1,300,000)

Atlantis Found. Clive Cussler. Reissue. Berkley (1,300,000)

Code to Zero. Ken Follett. Orig. NAL (1,300,000)

Devil's Code. John Sandford. Reissue. Berkley (1,300,000)

O Is for Outlaw. Sue Grafton. Rep. Ballantine (1,275,065)

#The House on Hope Street. Danielle Steel. Rep. Dell (1,275,000)

Dr. Death. Jonathan Kellerman. Rep. Ballantine (1,251,502)

Protect and Defend. Richard North Patterson. Rep. Ballantine (1,225,086)

Sky Is Falling. Sidney Sheldon. Rep. Warner (1,216,156)

#Heartbreaker. Julie Garwood. Rep. Pocket (1,130,000)

Tom Clancy's Net Force No. 5. Tom Clancy. Orig. Berkley (1,100,000)

Scottish Bride. Catherine Coulter. Orig. Berkley (1,100,000)

Power Plays Cold War. Tom Clancy. Orig. Berkley (1,100,000)

Riptide. Catherine Coulter. Reissue. Berkley (1,100,000)

Nightshade. John Saul. Rep. Ballantine (1,082,769)

#Temptation. Jude Deveraux. Rep. Pocket (1,050,000)

Omerta. Mario Puzo. Rep. Ballantine (1,036,591)

The Talisman. Stephen King and Peter Straub. Rep. Fawcett (1,031,349)

#Hearts in Atlantis. Stephen King. Movie tie-in. Pocket

The Switch. Sandra Brown. Rep. Warner (1,029,119)

#The Search. Iris Johansen. Rep. Bantam (1,025,00)

The Rescue. Nicholas Sparks. Rep. Warner (1,017,917)

The Lord of the Rings: The Two Towers. J. R. R. Tolkien. Movie tie-in. Del Rey (1,014,109)

Cradle and All. James Patterson. Rep. Warner (1,012,195)

#The End of the Rainbow. V. C. Andrews. Orig. Pocket (1,000,000)

750,000+

#Vineyard. Barbara Delinsky. Rep. Pocket (960,000)

The Lord of the Rings: The Return of the King. J. R. R. Tolkien. Movie tie-in. Del Rey (951,175)

Home for the Holidays. Johanna Lindsey. Rep. HarperCollins (950,000)

Seduction in Death. J. D. Robb. Orig. Berkley (950,000)

Robert Ludlum's The Hades Factor. Robert Ludlum and Gayle Lynds. Rep. St. Martin's (960,000)

Betrayal in Death. J. D. Robb. Orig. Berkley (950,000)

Wish You Well. David Baldacci. Rep. Warner (975,398)

Dawn in Eclipse Bay. Jayne Ann Krentz. Orig. Berkley (900,000)

Whispers. Dean Koontz. Reissue. Berkley (900,000)

Dr. Atkins' New Diet Revolution. Robert C. Atkins. Rep. HarperCollins (900,000)

Lost and Found. Jayne Ann Krentz. Reissue. Berkley (900,000)

Impulse. Catherine Coulter. Reissue. NAL (850,000)

Hot Six. Janet Evanovich. Rep. St. Martin's (850,000)

#Ice. V. C. Andrews. Orig. Pocket

*Cuba. Stephen Coonts. Rep. St. Martin's (840,000)

#NUMA Files 2: Blue Gold. Clive Cussler. Orig. Pocket

#Cinnamon. V. C. Andrews. Orig. Pocket (825,000)

Vittorio the Vampire. Anne Rice. Rep. Ballantine (790,079)

Angel Falls. Kristin Hannah. Rep. Ballantine (776,327)

Nothing but the Truth. John Lescroat. Orig. NAL (775,000)

#Rose. V. C. Andrews. Orig. Pocket (770,000)

#The Empty Chair. Jeffrey Deaver. Rep. Pocket (755,000)

#Honey. V. C. Andrews. Orig. Pocket (755,000)

16 Lighthouse Road. Debbie Macomber. Orig. Mira (755,000)

Children's Bestsellers: A Change in the Ranks

Diane Roback
Senior Editor, Children's Books, *Publishers Weekly*

In hardcover frontlist, there are noticeably fewer titles: only 88 titles sold more then 75,000 copies each last year, compared with 121 in 2000. However, the big standouts were Lemony Snicket's A Series of Unfortunate Events, which sky-rocketed last year (the three new titles published in 2001 sold more than a million copies combined), and the two Prayer of Jabez titles for younger readers (almost 900,000 copies sold combined). *Olivia Saves the Circus*, the followup to *Olivia*, sold almost 300,000 copies (with the first title selling slightly more, in the back-list category). And Eoin Colfer's *Artemis Fowl*, a highly anticipated first novel from Britain, sold 260,785 copies.

Hardcover backlist has the same number of titles as last year, though there is a slight decline in the number of Harry Potter titles sold: in 2000 three Potter books in this category sold 10.8 million copies, vs. 7.4 million copies in 2001, no doubt due in large part to the fact that two titles (*Prisoner* and *Sorcerer*) appeared in paperback for the first time last year.

The growing appeal of the Lemony Snicket books was apparent in this cate-gory as well: only one title was on the 2000 list—*The Bad Beginning*, at No. 80—with 122,268 copies sold. This year's list has five Lemony Snicket titles on it, for a total of just under 2.4 million copies sold.

Elsewhere in hardcover backlist, books by Dr. Seuss continued to sell, with fairly steady numbers compared with the year before. Board book editions of old (and newer) favorites were also very strong performers.

Harry Potter is the undisputed king of paperback frontlist, with six titles combining for almost 6.6 million copies sold. The number of overall titles on this list is slightly up as well: 90 paperback frontlist titles sold more than 100,000 copies in 2001, compared with 81 the previous year.

Captain Underpants hitched up his drawers and sold 930,000 copies of two new titles, reflecting the series' growing popularity. Series in general continue to be the stars in this category, with Harry and the Captain joined by Magic Tree House, Junie B. Jones, and Bob the Builder, as well as tie-ins for *Monsters, Inc.* Other paperback standouts were *The Princess Diaries* (helped by the release of the movie in August), which sold more than half a million copies, and Beverly Cleary's *Ramona's World*, with 280,012 copies sold.

There are more titles on the paperback backlist list than in 2000: 157 books sold more than 100,000 copies, compared with 135 the previous year. However, kids seem to have eaten enough soup—Chicken Soup, that is. In 2000 Chicken Soup for the Soul titles nabbed four out of the top five positions on the list, for a total of more than 11 million copies, but has only one title on the entire list this year (*Chicken Soup for the Preteen Soul*), with 906,768 copies sold.

Louis Sachar's *Holes* stayed strong in its second year of paperback release (587,889 sold last year, and 618,340 in 2000). The four backlist Captain Under-pants titles sold more than 1.6 million copies (for a combined 2001 sales total of 2.5 million for all Captain Underpants titles, new and old). And the Magic Tree

House series seemed stronger than ever, with sales of each backlist title rising at least 50 percent over the previous year.

Some sales figures were supplied to *Publishers Weekly* in confidence, for ranking purposes only.

Hardcover Frontlist

300,000+

1. *The Prayer of Jabez for Kids.* Bruce Wilkinson and Melody Carlson. Tommy Nelson (478,957)
2. *The Prayer of Jabez for Little Ones.* Bruce Wilkinson and Melody Carlson, illus. by Alexi Natchev. Tommy Nelson (415,457)
3. *The Hostile Hospital (A Series of Unfortunate Events No. 8).* Lemony Snicket, illus. by Brett Helquist. HarperCollins (363,760)
4. *The Ersatz Elevator (A Series of Unfortunate Events No. 6).* Lemony Snicket, illus. by Brett Helquist. HarperCollins (363,354)
5. *The Vile Village (A Series of Unfortunate Events No. 7).* Lemony Snicket, illus. by Brett Helquist. HarperCollins (345,292)
6. *Monsters, Inc.: Read-Aloud Storybook.* Random/Disney (324,901)
7. Disney's 5-Minute Adventure Stories. Sarah Heller. Disney (301,435)

200,000+

8. *Olivia Saves the Circus.* Ian Falconer. Atheneum/Schwartz (288,244)
9. *Ripley's Believe It or Not.* Scholastic (267,500)
10. *What's Wrong with Timmy?* Maria Shriver, illus. by Sandra Speidel. Little, Brown (264,241)
11. *Artemis Fowl.* Eoin Colfer. Talk Miramax/Hyperion (260,785)
12. *Disney's Princess Collection.* Random/Disney (258,865)
13. *I Spy Year-Round Challenger!* Jean Marzollo and Walter Wick, illus. by Wick. Cartwheel (217,000)
14. *Walt Disney's Classic Storybook.* Disney (209,977)
15. *Rainbow Fish: The Dangerous Deep.* HarperFestival (209,524)
16. *Christmas in Camelot (Magic Tree House).* Mary Pope Osborne, illus. by Sal Murdocca. Random (194,031)
17. *Disney's My Very First Winnie the Pooh: More Growing Up Stories.* Kathleen Zoehfeld, illus. by Robbin Cuddy. Disney (189,768)
18. *The Fire Engine Book.* Illus. by Tibor Gergely. Little Golden (184,835)*
19. *So You Want to Be President?* Judith St. George, illus. by David Small. Philomel (183,805)
20. *Junie B., First Grader (at last!).* Barbara Park, illus. by Denise Brunkus. Random (182,372)

*Random House acquired Golden Books in August 2001.

21. *My World.* Margaret Wise Brown, illus. by Clement Hurd. HarperCollins (167,281)

22. *The Veritas Project: Hangman's Curse.* Frank Peretti. Tommy Nelson (163,578)

23. *The Little Red Hen.* Illus. by Tibor Gergely. Little Golden (163,232)

24. *Atlantis: The Lost Empire: A Read-Aloud Storybook.* Random/Disney (159,073)

25. *The Book of Wizard Craft.* Janice Eaton Kilby. Sterling (159,000)

100,000+

26. *Dream Snow.* Eric Carle. Philomel (149,239)

27. *A Year Down Yonder.* Richard Peck. Dial (149,072)

28. *Monsters, Inc.: I'm Mike.* Random/ Disney (148,920)

29. *Rudolph the Red-Nosed Reindeer: Oh, Nose!* Dennis Shealy. Little Golden (142,845)

30. *Jan Brett's Christmas Treasury.* Jan Brett. Putnam (140,273)

31. *Taggerung.* Brian Jacques. Philomel (136,599)

32. *Complete Tales & Poems of Winnie-the-Pooh.* A. A. Milne, illus. by Ernest H. Shepard. Dutton (135,544)

33. *Castaways of the Flying Dutchman.* Brian Jacques. Philomel (133,004)

34. *Monsters, Inc.: I'm Sulley.* Random/ Disney (132,706)

35. *Baloney, Henry P.* Jon Scieszka, illus. by Lane Smith. Viking (132,631)

36. *Sheila Rae's Peppermint Stick.* Kevin Henkes. HarperCollins/Greenwillow (127,712)

37. *The Sisterhood of the Traveling Pants.* Ann Brashares. Delacorte (124,427)

38. *I Loved You Before You Were Born.* Anne Bowen, illus. by Greg Shed. HarperCollins (123,130)

39. *The Cheerios Halloween Play Book (board book).* Lee Wade. Little Simon (122,506)

40. *Princess in the Spotlight.* Meg Cabot. HarperCollins (122,282)

41. *Sleepy Time Olie.* William Joyce. HarperCollins/Geringer (121,496)

42. *The Prayer of Jabez for Young Hearts.* Bruce Wilkinson and Robert Suggs, illus. by Sergio Martinez. Tommy Nelson (119,029)

43. *Now I Know My 1, 2, 3's.* Nora Gaydos, illus. by Martin Lemelman. InnovativeKids (115,424)

44. *The Good Fight: How World War II Was Won.* Stephen E. Ambrose. Atheneum (114,583)

45. *Green Eggs and Ham (board book).* Dr. Seuss. Random (114,394)

46. *My Little Library of Early Learning.* Vincent Douglas, illus. by Warrick Schroeder. McGraw-Hill (113,000)

47. *Harry Potter and the Sorcerer's Stone: A Deluxe Pop-up Book.* Scholastic (112,000)

48. *Bob the Builder: Bob's Busy World.* Annie Auerbach, illus. by Mel Grant. Simon Spotlight (110,645)

49. *You Read to Me & I'll Read to You.* Selected by Janet Schulman. Knopf (109,553)

50. *Monsters, Inc.: Monster Fun.* Random/Disney (109,238)

51. *Baby Einstein: Neighborhood Animals.* Julie Aigner-Clark. Hyperion (109,163)

52. *My Little Library of Farm Animals.* Vincent Douglas, illus. by Warrick Schroeder. McGraw-Hill (105,000)

53. *Barbie: A Happy Holiday.* Diane Muldrow. Little Golden (104,543)

54. *Baby Einstein: See and Spy Counting.* Julie Aigner-Clark. Hyperion (103,984)

55. *Baby Einstein: See and Spy Shapes.* Julie Aigner-Clark. Hyperion (103,210)

56. *Harry Potter Hogwarts School: A Magical 3-D Carousel Pop-up.* Scholastic (103,000)

57. *My Little Library of Nursery Rhymes.* Vincent Douglas, illus. by Warrick Schroeder. McGraw-Hill (102,000)

58. *Toot & Puddle: I'll Be Home for Christmas.* Holly Hobbie. Little, Brown (101,592)

75,000+

59. *The Quiltmaker's Gift.* Jeff Brumbeau, illus. by Gail de Marcken. Scholastic (99,400)

60. *You Are My I Love You.* Maryann Cusimano, illus. by Satomi Ichikawa. Philomel (98,077)

61. *The Night Before Christmas.* Clement C. Moore, illus. by Mircea Catusanu. Little Golden (96,468)

62. *Merry Christmas, from Biscuit.* Alyssa Satin Capucilli, illus. by Pat Schories. HarperFestival (95,698)

63. *Monsters, Inc.: Welcome to Monstropolis.* Random/Disney (95,279)

64. *Chunky Safari Elephant.* Illus. by Emily Bolam. Barron's

65. *Princess Poems.* Random/Disney (93,617)

66. *Cirque du Freak.* Darren Shan. Little, Brown (91,235)

67. *Barney's C Is for Christmas.* Scholastic (90,000)

68. *Barney's ABC, 123, and More!* Scholastic (89,000)

69. *Chunky Safari Lion.* Illus. by Emily Bolam. Barron's

70. *My Little Library of Bible Stories.* Vincent Douglas, illus. by Robert Sanford. McGraw-Hill (88,000)

71. *Barney's Favorite Farm Animals.* Scholastic (87,000)

72. *Santa's Little Library of Christmas Stories.* Vincent Douglas, illus. by Robert Sanford. McGraw-Hill (86,000)

73. *Clifford's Glow-in-the-Dark Halloween.* Norman Bridwell. Cartwheel (85,000)

74. *The Water Hole.* Graeme Base. Abrams (85,000)
75. *Scooby-Doo! That's Snow Ghost.* Adapted by Molly Wigan. Little Golden (84,951)
76. *Chunky Safari Zebra.* Illus. by Emily Bolam. Barron's
77. *Bob the Builder: Bob's White Christmas.* Alison Inches, illus. by Mel Grant. Simon Spotlight (80,205)
78. *Barney Goes to the Zoo.* Scholastic (79,000)
79. *Hope Was Here.* Joan Bauer. Putnam (77,919)
80. *You Are Mine.* Max Lucado, illus. by Sergio Martinez. Crossway (77,840)
81. *There Was an Old Lady Who Swallowed a Fly.* Illus. by Pam Adams. Child's Play (77,303)
82. *Love That Dog.* Sharon Creech. HarperCollins/Cotler (76,588)
83. *Easter Bugs.* David A. Carter. Little Simon (76,073)
84. *Cassie's Runaway Kite.* Margaret Snyder, illus. by Don Williams. Random/Sesame Workshop (75,661)
85. *The Macmillan Dictionary for Children.* S&S (75,423)
86. *I'm Little and Shy. Who Am I?* Simon Lewin, illus. by Bob Berry. Random (75,413)
87. *Who's So Scary?* Random/Disney (75,371)
88. *Chunky Safari Rhino.* Illus. by Emily Bolam. Barron's

Hardcover Backlist

500,000+

1. *Harry Potter and the Prisoner of Azkaban.* J. K. Rowling. Scholastic/Levine, 1999 (960,000)
2. *Harry Potter and the Sorcerer's Stone.* J. K. Rowling. Scholastic/Levine, 1998 (890,000)
3. *The Bad Beginning (A Series of Unfortunate Events No. 1).* Lemony Snicket, illus. by Brett Helquist. HarperCollins, 1999 (732,521)
4. *Goodnight Moon (board book).* Margaret Wise Brown, illus. by Clement Hurd. HarperFestival, 1991 (625,631)
5. *The Reptile Room (A Series of Unfortunate Events No. 2).* Lemony Snicket, illus. by Brett Helquist. HarperCollins, 1999 (547,241)
6. *The Night Before Christmas.* Clement C. Moore, illus. by Bruce Whatley. HarperCollins, 1999 (545,527)
7. *Green Eggs and Ham.* Dr. Seuss. Random, 1960 (541,027)

300,000+

8. Oh, the Places You'll Go! Dr. Seuss. Random, 1990 (465,022)
9. *The Wide Window (A Series of Unfortunate Events No. 3).* Lemony Snicket, illus. by Brett Helquist. HarperCollins, 2000 (462,534)

10. *Brown Bear, Brown Bear, What Do You See? (board book)*. Bill Martin, Jr., illus. by Eric Carle. Holt, 1996 (442,000)

11. *Disney's Princess Collection*. Disney, 1999 (436,491)

12. *Guess How Much I Love You (board book)*. Sam McBratney, illus. by Anita Jeram. Candlewick, 1997 (420,854)

13. *Disney's Storybook Collection*. Disney, 1998 (420,747)

14. *If You Take a Mouse to the Movies*. Laura Numeroff, illus. by Felicia Bond. HarperCollins/Geringer, 2000 (402,751)

15. *Harry Potter and the Chamber of Secrets*. J. K. Rowling. Scholastic/Levine, 1999 (400,000)

16. *The Cat in the Hat*. Dr. Seuss. Random, 1957 (385,889)

17. *One Fish Two Fish Red Fish Blue Fish*. Dr. Seuss. Random, 1960 (362,832)

18. *The Miserable Mill (A Series of Unfortunate Events No. 4)*. Lemony Snicket, illus. by Brett Helquist. HarperCollins, 2000 (337,130)

19. *The Austere Academy (A Series of Unfortunate Events No. 5)*. Lemony Snicket, illus. by Brett Helquist. HarperCollins, 2000 (311,912)

20. *Mr. Brown Can Moo! Can You? (board book)*. Dr. Seuss. Random, 1996 (303,713)

21. *Olivia*. Ian Falconer. Atheneum/ Schwartz, 2000 (303,432)

200,000+

22. Harry Potter and the Goblet of Fire. J. K. Rowling. Scholastic/Levine, 2000 (295,000)

23. *Five Little Monkeys Jumping on the Bed (board book)*. Eileen Christelow. Clarion, 1998 (286,129)

24. *The Very Hungry Caterpillar (board book)*. Eric Carle. Philomel, 1994 (283,493)

25. *Hop on Pop*. Dr. Seuss. Random, 1963 (279,313)

26. *Are You My Mother? (board book)*. P. D. Eastman. Random, 1998 (274,766)

27. *Dr. Seuss's ABC (board book)*. Dr. Seuss. Random, 1996 (274,255)

28. *The Giving Tree*. Shel Silverstein. HarperCollins, 1964 (273,094)

29. *Where the Sidewalk Ends*. Shel Silverstein. HarperCollins, 1974 (264,629)

30. *Polar Bear, Polar Bear, What Do You Hear? (board book)*. Bill Martin, Jr., illus. by Eric Carle. Holt, 1997 (261,000)

31. *Goodnight Moon*. Margaret Wise Brown, illus. by Clement Hurd. HarperCollins, 1947 (246,114)

32. *Scooby-Doo: The Haunted Carnival*. Little Golden, 1999 (229,643)

33. *The Foot Book (board book)*. Dr. Seuss. Random, 1996 (218,390)

34. *Fox in Socks*. Dr. Seuss. Random, 1965 (216,797)

35. *Dr. Seuss's ABC*. Dr. Seuss. Random, 1960 (216,321)

36. *Disney's Animal Stories*. Disney, 2000 (209,994)

37. *Now I Know My ABCs.* Nora Gaydos, illus. by Eileen Hine. Innovative-Kids, 2000 (206,344)
38. *Are You My Mother?* P. D. Eastman. Random, 1960 (203,711)
39. *Go, Dog. Go!* P. D. Eastman. Random, 1961 (195,254)
40. *How the Grinch Stole Christmas!* Dr. Seuss. Random, 1957 (185,227)
41. *Pat the Bunny.* Dorothy Kunhardt. Golden, 1940 (183,611)
42. *Blue's Clues: Good Night Blue.* Simon Spotlight, 1999 (182,243)
43. *The Runaway Bunny.* Margaret Wise Brown, illus. by Clement Hurd. HarperCollins, 1942 (179,212)
44. *I Can Read with My Eyes Shut!* Dr. Seuss. Random, 1978 (177,278)
45. *There's a Wocket in My Pocket! (board book).* Dr. Seuss. Random, 1996 (175,839)
46. *If You Give a Mouse a Cookie.* Laura Numeroff, illus. by Felicia Bond. HarperCollins/Geringer, 1985 (173,149)
47. *The Polar Express.* Chris Van Allsburg. Houghton Mifflin, 1985 (169,503)
48. *Tootle.* Gertrude Crampton, illus. by Tibor Gergely. Little Golden, 1945 (167,585)
49. *Click, Clack, Moo.* Doreen Cronin, illus. by Betsy Lewin. S&S, 2000 (166,767)
50. *Peter Cottontail Is on His Way.* Little Golden, 2000 (165,730)
51. *The Poky Little Puppy.* Janet Sebring, illus. by Gustaf Tenggren. Little Golden, 1942 (164,313)
52. *Amelia Bedelia Treasury.* Peggy Parish. HarperCollins, 1995 (162,001)
53. *Ten Apples Up on Top! (board book).* Dr. Seuss. Random, 1998 (159,614)
54. *The Cat in the Hat Comes Back.* Dr. Seuss. Random, 1958 (159,340)
55. *The Cheerios Play Book.* Lee Wade. Little Simon, 1998 (158,348)
56. *Soft Shapes Counting.* Innovative Kids, 1999 (153,717)
57. *I Spy Treasure Hunt.* Jean Marzollo and Walter Wick, illus. by Wick. Cartwheel, 1999 (153,000)
58. *The Frog and Toad Treasury.* Arnold Lobel. HarperCollins, 1996 (153,000)
59. *The Runaway Bunny (board book).* Margaret Wise Brown, illus. by Clement Hurd. HarperCollins, 1991 (151,258)

100,000+

60. Go, Dog. Go! (board book). P. D. Eastman. Random, 1997 (149,913)
61. *Falling Up.* Shel Silverstein. HarperCollins, 1996 (147,834)
62. *Soft Shapes Colors.* Innovative Kids, 1999 (147,062)
63. *Disney's Christmas Storybook.* Disney, 2000 (142,587)
64. *If You Give a Pig a Pancake.* Laura Numeroff, illus. by Felicia Bond. HarperCollins/Geringer, 1998 (142,136)
65. *Pajama Time!* Sandra Boynton. Workman, 2000 (140,572)
66. *Barnyard Dance!* Sandra Boynton. Workman, 1993 (140,025)

67. *Soft Shapes Animals.* Innovative Kids, 1999 (139,438)
68. *The Little Engine That Could.* Watty Piper. Grosset & Dunlap, 1930 (139,072)
69. *The Saggy Baggy Elephant.* Kathryn and Bryon Jackson, illus. by Gustaf Tenggren. Little Golden, 1947 (132,814)
70. *Fire!* Beth Sycamore, illus. by Lee MacLeod. Pleasant Co./Matchbox, 2000 (131,194)
71. *The Rainbow Fish (board book).* Marcus Pfister. North-South, 1996 (129,679)
72. *If You Give a Moose a Muffin.* Laura Numeroff, illus. by Felicia Bond. HarperCollins/Geringer, 1991 (127,268)
73. *Soft Shapes Shapes.* Innovative Kids, 1999 (126,281)
74. *Once Upon a Potty—Boy.* Alona Frankel. HarperFestival, 1999 (124,546)
75. *Clifford's Schoolhouse.* Norman Bridwell. Cartwheel, 2000 (124,000)
76. *The Tawny Scrawny Lion.* Kathryn Jackson, illus. by Gustaf Tenggren. Little Golden, 1952 (123,050)
77. *A Light in the Attic.* Shel Silverstein. HarperCollins, 1981 (123,024)
78. *Scuffy the Tugboat.* Gertrude Crampton, illus. by Tibor Gergely. Little Golden, 1955 (122,990)
79. *Elmo's Big Lift-and-Look Book.* Anna Ross. Random/Sesame Workshop, 1994 (122,906)
80. *You Are Special.* Max Lucado, illus. by Sergio Martinez. Crossway, 1997 (120,861)
81. *The Sailor Dog.* Margaret Wise Brown, illus. by Garth Williams. Little Golden, 1953 (118,804)
82. *Disney's My Very First Winnie the Pooh: Growing Up Stories.* Disney, 1999 (118,706)
83. *Once Upon a Potty—Girl.* Alona Frankel. HarperFestival, 1999 (118,051)
84. *Disney's Easy-to-Read Stories.* Disney, 1999 (116,627)
85. *Hand, Hand, Fingers, Thumb (board book).* Al Perkins. Random, 1998 (115,736)
86. *Where Do Kisses Come From?* Maria Fleming. Little Golden, 2000 (115,216)
87. *Winnie the Pooh and His Friends.* Random/Disney, 1997 (114,896)
88. *The Very Lonely Firefly (board book).* Eric Carle. Philomel, 1999 (113,324)
89. *Oh, the Thinks You Can Think!* Dr. Seuss. Random, 1975 (113,081)
90. *Good Night, Gorilla (board book).* Peggy Rathmann. Putnam, 1996 (112,556)
91. *I Love You As Much . . . (board book).* Laura Krauss Melmed, illus. by Henri Sorensen. HarperFestival, 1998 (112,009)
92. *Peter Cottontail: The Great Mitten Hunt.* Little Golden, 2000 (111,733)
93. *The Cheerios Animal Play Book.* Lee Wade. Little Simon, 1999 (110,727)
94. *Disney's Winnie the Pooh: 123.* Random/Disney, 1999 (110,476)
95. *The Secret of the Old Clock (Nancy Drew No. 1).* Carolyn Keene. Grosset & Dunlap, 1930 (109,371)

96. *I Spy Spooky Night.* Jean Marzollo, illus. by Walter Wick. Cartwheel, 1996 (109,000)
97. *My First Counting Book.* Lilian Moore, illus. by Garth Williams. Little Golden, 1956 (106,485)
98. *Because of Winn-Dixie.* Kate DiCamillo. Candlewick, 2000 (106,171)
99. *Disney's Winnie the Pooh: ABC.* Random/Disney, 1999 (106,090)
100. *The Danny and the Dinosaur Treasury.* Syd Hoff. HarperCollins, 1998 (105,900)
101. *Harold's Purple Crayon Treasury.* Crockett Johnson. HarperCollins, 2000 (105,900)
102. *The Tower Treasure (Hardy Boys No. 1).* Franklin Dixon. Grosset & Dunlap, 1927 (103,799)
103. *Winnie the Pooh: The Four Seasons.* Random/Disney, 2000 (103,370)
104. *The Going to Bed Book (board book).* Sandra Boynton. Little Simon, 1982 (102,132)

Paperback Frontlist

1,000,000+

1. *Harry Potter and the Prisoner of Azkaban.* J. K. Rowling. Scholastic/ Levine (2,900,000)
2. *Harry Potter and the Sorcerer's Stone (mass market).* J. K. Rowling. Scholastic/ Levine (1,500,000)
3. *Fantastic Beasts and Where to Find Them.* Newt Scamander (aka J. K. Rowling). Scholastic/Levine (1,430,000)
4. *Quidditch Through the Ages.* Kennilworthy Whisp (aka J. K. Rowling). Scholastic/Levine (1,420,000)

300,000+

5. *Captain Underpants and the Wrath of the Wicked Wedgie Woman.* Dav Pilkey. Scholastic/Blue Sky (590,000)
6. *Harry Potter and the Sorcerer's Stone Poster Book.* Scholastic (550,000)
7. *The Princess Diaries.* Meg Cabot. HarperTrophy (510,138)
8. *Chicken Soup for the Teenage Soul: On Tough Stuff.* Jack Canfield et al. HCI (472,980)
9. *Amelia Bedelia 4 Mayor.* Herman Parish, illus. by Lynn Sweat. Harper-Trophy (384,790)
10. *Twister on Tuesday (MTH No. 23).* Mary Pope Osborne, illus. by Sal Murdocca. Random (353,997)
11. *Junie B. Jones Is a Graduation Girl.* Barbara Park, illus. by Denise Brunkus. Random/Stepping Stone (350,946)
12. *The Captain Underpants Extra-Crunchy Book O' Fun.* Dav Pilkey. Scholastic/Blue Sky (340,000)

13. *Junie B. Jones Is Captain Field Day*. Barbara Park, illus. by Denise Brunkus. Random/Stepping Stone (322,380)

200,000+

14. *Bob the Builder: Bob's Birthday*. Simon Spotlight (292,344)
15. *Earthquake in the Early Morning (MTH No. 24)*. Mary Pope Osborne, illus. by Sal Murdocca. Random/ Stepping Stone (290,575)
16. *Ramona's World*. Beverly Cleary, illus. by Alan Tiegreen. HarperTrophy (280,012)
17. *Bob the Builder: Scoop Saves the Day*. Simon Spotlight (267,562)
18. *Chicken Soup for the Teenage Soul: Letters*. Jack Canfield et al. HCI (265,555)
19. *The Showdown (Left Behind: The Kids No. 13)*. Jerry B. Jenkins and Tim LaHaye. Tyndale (252,811)
20. *Judgment Day (Left Behind: The Kids No. 14)*. Jerry B. Jenkins and Tim LaHaye. Tyndale (240,675)
21. *Monsters, Inc.* Random/Disney (228,498)
22. *Fire From Heaven (Left Behind: The Kids No. 16)*. Jerry B. Jenkins and Tim LaHaye. Tyndale (227,663)
23. *Battling the Commander (Left Behind: The Kids No. 15)*. Jerry B. Jenkins and Tim LaHaye. Tyndale (227,229)
24. *The Hobbit*. J. R. R. Tolkien. Houghton Mifflin (223,995)
25. *Bob the Builder: Wendy Helps Out*. Simon Spotlight (217,673)
26. *Bob the Builder: Dizzy's Bird Watch*. Simon Spotlight (213,739)
27. *Conversations with J. K. Rowling*. Lindsey Fraser. Scholastic (210,000)
28. *The Case of the Dog Camp Mystery (New Adventures of Mary-Kate & Ashley No. 24)*. HarperEntertainment (205,000)
29. *Monsters Inc.: M Is for Monster*. Random/Disney (202,962)
30. *Biscuit Wants to Play*. Alyssa Satin Capucilli, illus. by Pat Schories. HarperTrophy (201,923)
31. *Biscuit's New Trick*. Alyssa Satin Capucilli, illus. by Pat Schories. HarperTrophy (201,527)

100,000+

32. *Terror in the Stadium (Left Behind: The Kids No. 15)*. Jerry B. Jenkins and Tim LaHaye. Tyndale (192,854)
33. *Darkening Skies (Left Behind: The Kids No. 18)*. Jerry B. Jenkins and Tim LaHaye. Tyndale (192,628)
34. *Sealed with a Kiss (Two of a Kind No. 20)*. HarperEntertainment (190,000)
35. *Shore Thing (Two of a Kind No. 17)*. HarperEntertainment (190,000)
36. *Jimmy Neutron Boy Genius: Movie Novelization*. Marc Cerasini. Simon Spotlight (181,505)
37. *Bob the Builder: Bob's Recycling Day*. Simon Spotlight (177,240)

38. *Speak.* Laurie Halse Anderson. Puffin (177,147)
39. *The Case of the Jingle Bell Jinx (New Adventures of Mary-Kate & Ashley No. 26).* HarperEntertainment (170,000)
40. *Because of Winn-Dixie.* Kate DiCamillo. Candlewick (166,640)
41. *Surprise, Surprise! (Two of a Kind No. 19).* HarperEntertainment (165,000)
42. *Two for the Road (Two of a Kind No. 18).* HarperEntertainment (165,000)
43. *Bob the Builder: A Day at the Barn.* Simon Spotlight (162,590)
44. *Monsters Inc.: Scream Team.* Random/Disney (161,686)
45. *It's Snow Problem (Two of a Kind No. 15).* HarperEntertainment (160,000)
46. *Likes Me, Likes Me Not (Two of a Kind No. 16).* HarperEntertainment (160,000)
47. *Shrek Gag Book.* R. E. Volting. DreamWorks (155,013)
48. *The Case of the High Seas Secret (New Adventures of Mary-Kate & Ashley No. 22).* HarperEntertainment (150,000)
49. *The Case of the Logical I Ranch (New Adventures of Mary-Kate & Ashley No. 23).* HarperEntertainment (150,000)
50. *Inspector Hopper.* Doug Cushman. HarperTrophy (144,562)
51. *Shrek Movie Novelization.* Ellen Weiss. DreamWorks. (142,258)
52. *Monsters, Inc.: Employee Handbook.* Random/Disney (140,194)
53. *The Case of the Screaming Scarecrow (New Adventures of Mary-Kate & Ashley No. 25).* HarperEntertainment (140,000)
54. *Winning London (Mary Kate & Ashley Starring In No. 2).* HarperEntertainment (140,000)
55. *Good Night, Maman.* Norma Fox Mazer. HarperTrophy (139,319)
56. *Our Only May Amelia.* Jennifer L. Holm. HarperTrophy (138,530)
57. *The World Almanac for Kids 2002.* Edited by Elaine Israel. World Almanac (137,963)
58. *The Prayer of Jabez Devotions for Kids.* Bruce Wilkinson and Robert Suggs. Tommy Nelson (131,914)
59. *A Long Way from Chicago.* Richard Peck. Puffin (127,689)
60. *Jimmy Neutron Boy Genius: No Parents Day.* Annie Auerbach. (126,088)
61. *School Dance Party (Mary Kate & Ashley Starring In No. 3).* HarperEntertainment (125,000)
62. *The Case of the Game Show Mystery (New Adventures of Mary-Kate & Ashley No. 27).* HarperEntertainment (125,000)
63. *How to Train a Boy (So Little Time No. 1).* HarperEntertainment (125,000)
64. *Angus, Thongs and Full-Frontal Snogging.* Louise Rennison. HarperTempest (123,692)
65. *Clifford's Glow-in-the-Dark Christmas.* Norman Bridwell. Cartwheel (119,000)
66. *Barbie Girls Club: Let's Be Friends.* Golden (115,453)
67. *Uptown Poodle, Downtown Pups (All American Puppies No. 4).* Susan Saunders, illus. by Henry Cole. HarperTrophy (114,598)

68. *Hello, Spring!* Random/Disney (114,132)
69. *Pooh Gets a Checkup.* Random/Disney (113,935)
70. *The Copycat Fish.* Gail Donovan. North-South/Night Sky (113,613)
71. *Blue's Clues: Blue's Egg Hunt.* Simon Spotlight (111,557)
72. *A Bear-y Good Neighbor.* Random/ Disney (111,099)
73. *Barney and BJ Go to the Zoo.* Scholastic (110,000)
74. *Shrek Scratch & Stink Storybook.* DreamWorks (109,153)
75. *Welcome to My World.* Random/Disney (109,094)
76. *When Zachary Beaver Came to Town.* Kimberly Willis Holt. Dell/Yearling (107,690)
77. *Monster.* Walter Dean Myers. HarperTempest (106,962)
78. *Kida and the Crystal.* Random/Disney (106,776)
79. *Little Bill: Elephant on the Loose.* Kim Watson, illus. by Sheree Boyd. Simon Spotlight (106,223)
80. *Hidden Treasures.* Gail Donovan. North-South/Night Sky (105,565)
81. *The Good, the Bad, and the Robotic.* Random/Disney (105,513)
82. *Little Bill: A Trip to the Hospital.* Kim Watson, illus. by Mark Salisbury. Simon Spotlight (105,265)
83. *A Fishy Story.* Gail Donovan. North-South/Night Sky (104,156)
84. *Max and Emmy's Flower Power.* Random/Sesame Workshop (103,024)
85. *Rescue Mission.* Justine Korman and Ron Fontes. Random (102,439)
86. *Which Witch?* Eva Ibbotson. Puffin (101,908)
87. *Shrek Mad Libs.* Roger Price. DreamWorks (101,505)
88. *The Golden Compass.* Philip Pullman. Del Rey (101,199)
89. *Arthur's First Kiss.* Marc Brown. Random (100,911)
90. *Jimmy Neutron Boy Genius: My Book of Inventions.* Lisa Bergen. (100,540)

Paperback Backlist

300,000+

1. *Harry Potter and the Sorcerer's Stone.* J. K. Rowling. Scholastic/Levine, 1999 (2,500,000)
2. *Chicken Soup for the Preteen Soul.* Jack Canfield et al. HCI, 2000 (906,768)
3. *Harry Potter and the Chamber of Secrets.* J. K. Rowling. Scholastic/Levine, 2000 (800,000)
4. *Holes.* Louis Sachar. Dell/Yearling, 2000 (587,889)
5. *Charlotte's Web.* E. B. White, illus. by Garth Williams. HarperTrophy, 1974 (532,362)
6. *The Outsiders.* S. E. Hinton. Puffin, 1997 (523,960)
7. *Captain Underpants and the Perilous Plot of Professor Poopypants.* Dav Pilkey. Scholastic/Blue Sky, 2000 (425,000)

8. *Captain Underpants and the Attack of the Talking Toilets.* Dav Pilkey. Scholastic/Blue Sky, 1999 (411,000)

9. *The Adventures of Captain Underpants.* Dav Pilkey. Scholastic/Blue Sky (405,000)

10. *Love You Forever.* Robert Munsch, illus. by Sheila McGraw. Firefly (402,954)

11. *The Giver.* Lois Lowry. Dell/Laurel-Leaf (399,260)

12. *Captain Underpants and the Invasion of the Incredibly Naughty Cafeteria Ladies from Outer Space.* Dav Pilkey. Scholastic/Blue Sky, 1997 (384,000)

13. *Dinosaurs Before Dark (MTH No. 1).* Mary Pope Osborne, illus. by Sal Murdocca. Random/Stepping Stone, 1992 (333,373)

14. *The Vanishings (Left Behind: The Kids No. 1).* Jerry B. Jenkins and Tim LaHaye. Tyndale, 1998 (329,750)

15. *Charlie and the Chocolate Factory.* Roald Dahl, illus. by Quentin Blake. Puffin, 1998 (319,367)

200,000+

16. *Mummies in the Morning (MTH No. 3).* Mary Pope Osborne, illus. by Sal Murdocca. Random/Stepping Stone, 1993 (293,604)

17. *The Lion, the Witch and the Wardrobe.* C. S. Lewis, illus. by Pauline Baynes. HarperTrophy, 1994 (281,573)

18. *The Knight at Dawn (MTH No. 2).* Mary Pope Osborne, illus. by Sal Murdocca. Random/Stepping Stone, 1993 (269,880)

19. *Goodnight Moon.* Margaret Wise Brown, illus. by Clement Hurd. Harper-Trophy, 1977 (266,413)

20. *Where the Wild Things Are.* Maurice Sendak. HarperTrophy, 1988 (261,101)

21. *Roll of Thunder, Hear My Cry.* Mildred Taylor. Puffin, 1991 (252,272)

22. *Pirates Past Noon (MTH No. 4).* Mary Pope Osborne, illus. by Sal Murdocca. Random/Stepping Stone, 1994 (250,786)

23. *Junie B. Jones and the Stupid Smelly Bus.* Barbara Park, illus. by Denise Brunkus. Random/ Stepping Stone, 1992 (244,254)

24. *Second Chance (Left Behind: The Kids No. 2).* Jerry B. Jenkins and Tim LaHaye. Tyndale, 1998 (241,991)

25. *Junie B. Jones and Some Sneaky Peeky Spying.* Barbara Park, illus. by Denise Brunkus. Random/Stepping Stone, 1994 (237,762)

26. *Junie B. Jones and Her Big Fat Mouth.* Barbara Park, illus. by Denise Brunkus. Random/Stepping Stone, 1993 (232,310)

27. *Hatchet.* Gary Paulsen. Aladdin, 1995 (229,394)

28. *James and the Giant Peach.* Roald Dahl, illus. by Lane Smith. Puffin, 1996 (226,162)

29. *When I Get Bigger.* Mercer Mayer. Golden, 1983 (219,870)

30. *Junie B. Jones and a Little Monkey Business.* Barbara Park, illus. by Denise Brunkus. Random/Stepping Stone, 1993 (209,227)

31. *Bridge to Terabithia.* Katherine Paterson, illus. by Donna Diamond. HarperTrophy, 1987 (201,622)

100,000+

32. *The Mouse and the Motorcycle.* Beverly Cleary, illus. by Louis Darling. HarperTrophy, 1990 (191,524)
33. *Number the Stars.* Lois Lowry. Dell/Yearling, 1990 (187,455)
34. *The Magician's Nephew.* C. S. Lewis, illus. by Pauline Baynes. HarperTrophy, 1994 (185,573)
35. *A Wrinkle in Time.* Madeleine L'Engle. Dell/Yearling, 1976 (185,418)
36. *Through the Flames (Left Behind: The Kids No. 3).* Jerry B. Jenkins and Tim LaHaye. Tyndale, 1998 (184,137)
37. *Just Me in the Tub.* Mercer Mayer. Golden, 1994 (173,293)
38. *Dolphins at Daybreak (MTH No. 9).* Mary Pope Osborne, illus. by Sal Murdocca. Random/Stepping Stone, 1997 (173,291)
39. *Little House on the Prairie.* Laura Ingalls Wilder, illus. by Garth Williams. HarperTrophy, 1971 (172,678)
40. *Just Go to Bed.* Mercer Mayer. Golden, 1983 (172,537)
41. *Dolphin Freedom.* Wayne Grover, illus. by Jim Fowler. HarperTrophy, 2000 (171,844)
42. *The Care and Keeping of You.* Valorie Schaefer, illus. by Norm Bendel. Pleasant Co., 1998 (171,833)
43. *Walk Two Moons.* Sharon Creech. HarperTrophy, 1996 (169,794)
44. *Where's the Big Red Doggie?* Norman Bridwell. Cartwheel, 1998 (168,000)
45. *Little House in the Big Woods.* Laura Ingalls Wilder, illus. by Garth Williams. HarperTrophy, 1971 (167,404)
46. *Ramona the Pest.* Beverly Cleary. HarperTrophy, 1996 (166,766)
47. *Tonight on the Titanic (MTH No. 17).* Mary Pope Osborne, illus. by Sal Murdocca. Random/Stepping Stone, 1999 (166,181)
48. *Night of the Ninjas (MTH No. 5).* Mary Pope Osborne, illus. by Sal Murdocca. Random/Stepping Stone, 1995 (166,138)
49. *Stone Fox.* John Reynolds Gardiner, illus. by Marcia Sewall. HarperTrophy, 1983 (165,498)
50. *Where the Red Fern Grows.* Wilson Rawls. Bantam, 1997 (163,954)
51. *Just Me and My Dad.* Mercer Mayer. Golden, 1982 (161,236)
52. *Sarah, Plain and Tall.* Patricia MacLachlan. HarperTrophy, 1987 (159,620)
53. *Afternoon on the Amazon (MTH No. 6).* Mary Pope Osborne, illus. by Sal Murdocca. Random/Stepping Stone, 1995 (159,054)
54. *Amelia Bedelia.* Peggy Parish, illus. by Fritz Siebel. HarperTrophy, 1992 (158,599)
55. *The Trumpet of the Swan.* E. B. White, illus. by Fred Marcellino. HarperTrophy, 2000 (158,563)

56. *Stuart Little.* E. B. White, illus. by Garth Williams. HarperTrophy, 1974 (157,871)

57. *Just Me and My Mom.* Mercer Mayer. Golden, 1990 (155,482)

58. *Revolutionary War on Wednesday (MTH No. 22).* Mary Pope Osborne, illus. by Sal Murdocca. Random/ Stepping Stone, 2000 (155,271)

59. *Facing the Future (Left Behind: The Kids No. 4).* Jerry B. Jenkins and Tim LaHaye. Tyndale, 1998 (154,069)

60. *Tales of a Fourth Grade Nothing.* Judy Blume. Dell/Yearling, 1976 (152,401)

61. *Midnight on the Moon (MTH No. 8).* Mary Pope Osborne, illus. by Sal Murdocca. Random/Stepping Stone, 1996 (151,709)

62. *Junie B. Jones Has a Peep in Her Pocket.* Barbara Park, illus. by Denise Brunkus. Random/Stepping Stone, 2000 (149,320)

63. *The Cay.* Theodore Taylor. HarperTrophy, 1977 (148,386)

64. *Dingoes at Dinnertime (MTH No. 20).* Mary Pope Osborne, illus. by Sal Murdocca. Random/Stepping Stone, 2000 (147,510)

65. *Frog and Toad Are Friends.* Arnold Lobel. HarperTrophy, 1979 (147,785)

66. *Ramona Quimby, Age 8.* Beverly Cleary. HarperTrophy, 1992 (147,298)

67. *Civil War on Sunday (MTH No. 21).* Mary Pope Osborne, illus. by Sal Murdocca. Random/Stepping Stone, 2000 (146,985)

68. *Clifford's Puppy Days.* Norman Bridwell. Cartwheel, 1989 (146,000)

69. *Clifford the Big Red Dog.* Norman Bridwell. Cartwheel, 1995 (145,000)

70. *The Secret Garden Book and Charm.* Frances Hodgson Burnett, illus. by Tasha Tudor. HarperFestival (143,636)

71. *Tuck Everlasting.* Natalie Babbitt. Farrar, Straus & Giroux, 1985 (143,250)

72. *Tigers at Twilight (MTH No. 19).* Mary Pope Osborne, illus. by Sal Murdocca. Random/Stepping Stone, 1999 (142,764)

73. *Vacation Under the Volcano (MTH No. 13).* Mary Pope Osborne, illus. by Sal Murdocca. Random/Stepping Stone, 1998 (142,655)

74. *Ella Enchanted.* Gail Carson Levine. HarperTrophy, 1998 (142,603)

75. *Polar Bears Past Bedtime (MTH No. 12).* Mary Pope Osborne, illus. by Sal Murdocca. Random/Stepping Stone, 1998 (141,821)

76. *The Sign of the Beaver.* Elizabeth George Speare. Dell/Yearling, 1984 (141,358)

77. *Cassie Loves a Parade.* Random/ Sesame Workshop, 2000 (138,870)

78. *All by Myself.* Mercer Mayer. Golden, 1983 (135,678)

79. *Junie B. Jones Is (Almost) a Flower Girl.* Barbara Park, illus. by Denise Brunkus. Random/Stepping Stone, 1999 (135,616)

80. *The Westing Game.* Ellen Raskin. Puffin, 1997 (131,781)

81. *Sunset of the Sabertooth (MTH No. 7).* Mary Pope Osborne, illus. by Sal Murdocca. Random/Stepping Stone, 1996 (130,882)

82. *Danny and the Dinosaur.* Syd Hoff. HarperTrophy, 1978 (130,391)

83. *Biscuit.* Alyssa Satin Capucilli, illus. by Pat Schories. HarperTrophy, 1997 (130,362)

84. *Ghost Town at Sundown (MTH No. 10)*. Mary Pope Osborne, illus. by Sal Murdocca. Random/Stepping Stone, 1997 (129,861)

85. *Lions at Lunchtime (MTH No. 11)*. Mary Pope Osborne, illus. by Sal Murdocca. Random/Stepping Stone, 1998 (128,943)

86. *Island of the Blue Dolphins*. Scott O'Dell. Dell/Yearling, 1987 (127,650)

87. *The Watsons Go to Birmingham—1963*. Christopher Paul Curtis. Dell/Yearling, 1997 (127,566)

88. *The Horse and His Boy*. C. S. Lewis, illus. by Pauline Baynes. HarperTrophy, 1994 (127,055)

89. *Johnny Tremain*. Esther Forbes. Dell/Yearling, 1987 (125,862)

90. *Joey Pigza Swallowed the Key*. Jack Gantos. HarperTrophy, 2000 (125,094)

91. *The Boxcar Children*. Gertrude Chandler Warner. Whitman, 1989 (124,973)

92. *Go Ask Alice*. Anonymous. Aladdin, 1994 (124,942)

93. *Nicolae High (Left Behind: The Kids No. 5)*. Jerry B. Jenkins and Tim LaHaye. Tyndale, 1999 (124,767)

94. *Out of the Dust*. Karen Hesse. Scholastic, 1999 (124,000)

95. *Junie B. Jones and the Mushy Gushy Valentine*. Barbara Park, illus. by Denise Brunkus. Random/Stepping Stone, 1999 (121,980)

96. *Buffalo Before Breakfast (MTH No. 18)*. Mary Pope Osborne, illus. by Sal Murdocca. Random/Stepping Stone, 1999 (121,489)

97. *Day of the Dragon-King (MTH No. 14)*. Mary Pope Osborne, illus. by Sal Murdocca. Random/Stepping Stone, 1998 (121,488)

98. *Anne of Green Gables Book and Charm*. Lucy Maud Montgomery. Harper-Festival (121,098)

99. *Catherine, Called Birdy*. Karen Cushman. HarperTrophy, 1995 (120,883)

100. *The Witch of Blackbird Pond*. Elizabeth George Speare. Dell/Yearling, 1972 (119,978)

101. *A Little Princess Book and Charm*. Frances Hodgson Burnett, illus. by Tasha Tudor. HarperFestival (119,111)

102. *Prince Caspian*. C. S. Lewis, illus. by Pauline Baynes. HarperTrophy, 1994 (118,697)

103. *Little Bear*. Else Holmelund Minarik, illus. by Maurice Sendak. Harper-Trophy, 1978 (118,570)

104. *Teen Love: On Friendship*. Kimberly Kirberger. HCI, 2000 (118,219)

105. *WeeSing Children's Songs and Fingerplays*. Pamela Conn Beall and Susan Hagen Nipp. Price Stern Sloan, 1977 (117,487)

106. *The Lion, the Witch and the Wardrobe*. C. S. Lewis, illus. by Pauline Baynes. HarperTrophy, 1994 (117,204)

107. *Maniac Magee*. Jerry Spinelli. Little, Brown, 2000 (117,042)

108. *Julie of the Wolves*. Jean Craighead George, illus. by John Schoenherr. HarperTrophy, 1974 (116,940)

109. *Frog and Toad Together*. Arnold Lobel. HarperTrophy, 1979 (116,580)

110. *Junie B. Jones Is a Party Animal.* Barbara Park, illus. by Denise Brunkus. Random/Stepping Stone, 1997 (115,621)

111. *Hour of the Olympics (MTH No. 19).* Mary Pope Osborne, illus. by Sal Murdocca. Random/Stepping Stone, 1998 (115,412)

112. *Voyage of the Dawn Treader.* C. S. Lewis, illus. by Pauline Baynes. HarperTrophy, 1994 (114,780)

113. *The Pigman.* Paul Zindel. Bantam, 1983 (114,740)

114. *The Phantom Tollbooth.* Norton Juster, illus. by Jules Feiffer. Random, 1988 (114,553)

115. *The Underground (Left Behind: The Kids No. 6).* Jerry B. Jenkins and Tim LaHaye. Tyndale, 1999 (114,047)

116. *Junie B. Jones Smells Something Fishy.* Barbara Park, illus. by Denise Brunkus. Random/Stepping Stone, 1999 (113,621)

117. *Junie B. Jones Is a Beauty Shop Guy.* Barbara Park, illus. by Denise Brunkus. Random/Stepping Stone, 1998 (113,310)

118. *Farewell to Manzanar.* Jeanne Houston. Dell/Laurel-Leaf, 1983 (112,596)

119. *The Silver Chair.* C. S. Lewis, illus. by Pauline Baynes. HarperTrophy, 1994 (112,238)

120. *Junie B. Jones Is Not a Crook.* Barbara Park, illus. by Denise Brunkus. Random/Stepping Stone, 1997 (111,859)

121. *Just My Friend and Me.* Mercer Mayer. Golden, 1987 (111,755)

122. *Junie B. Jones and That Meanie Jim's Birthday.* Barbara Park, illus. by Denise Brunkus. Random/Stepping Stone, 1996 (111,737)

123. *Bathtime for Biscuit.* Alyssa Satin Capucilli, illus. by Pat Schories. HarperTrophy, 1999 (111,671)

124. *Sideways Stories from Wayside School.* Louis Sachar, illus. by Julie Brinckloe. HarperTrophy, 1985 (110,395)

125. *Junie B. Jones and the Yucky Blucky Fruitcake.* Barbara Park, illus. by Denise Brunkus. Random/Stepping Stone, 1995 (110,064)

126. *Clifford's Christmas.* Norman Bridwell. Cartwheel, 1984 (110,000)

127. *The Last Battle.* C. S. Lewis, illus. by Pauline Baynes. HarperTrophy, 1994 (109,841)

128. *Dear Mr. Henshaw.* Beverly Cleary, illus. by Paul O. Zelinsky. HarperTrophy, 1992 (109,507)

129. *That Was Then, This Is Now.* S. E. Hinton. Puffin, 1998 (109,299)

130. *Clifford the Firehouse Dog.* Norman Bridwell. Cartwheel, 1994 (109,000)

131. *Teen Ink 2: More Voices, More Visions.* John and Stephanie Meyers. HCI, 2000 (108,973)

132. *Just Going to the Dentist.* Mercer Mayer. Golden, 1990 (108,865)

133. *Junie B. Jones Has a Monster Under Her Bed.* Barbara Park, illus. by Denise Brunkus. Random/Stepping Stone, 1997 (108,559)

134. *Biscuit Finds a Friend.* Alyssa Satin Capucilli, illus. by Pat Schories. HarperTrophy, 1998 (107,694)

135. *The BFG.* Roald Dahl, illus. by Quentin Blake. Puffin, 1998 (107,036)

136. *Clifford Counts 1 2 3.* Norman Bridwell. Cartwheel, 1998 (107,000)

137. *Viking Ships at Sunrise (MTH No. 15).* Mary Pope Osborne, illus. by Sal Murdocca. Random/Stepping Stone, 1998 (106,856)

138. *Zak and Wheezie Clean Up.* Random/Sesame Workshop, 2000 (106,326)

139. *Frindle.* Andrew Clements. Aladdin, 1996 (105,061)

140. *Ginger Pye.* Eleanor Estes. Harcourt/Odyssey, 2000 (104,635)

141. *Catch Me, Catch Me! (Thomas the Tank Engine).* Rev. W. Awdry, illus. by Owain Bell. Random (104,405)

142. *The Secret of Platform 13.* Eva Ibbotson. Puffin, 1999 (104,221)

143. *Freckle Juice.* Judy Blume. Dell/Yearling, 1978 (103,389)

144. *The Magician's Nephew.* C. S. Lewis, illus. by Pauline Baynes. HarperTrophy (102,960)

145. *Little Engines Can Do Big Things (Thomas and the Magic Railroad).* Rev. W. Awdry, illus. by Ted Gadecki. Random (102,683)

146. *Mrs. Frisby and the Rats of NIMH.* Robert C. O'Brien. Aladdin, 1986 (102,654)

147. *Mad Libs No. 1: Original.* Robert Price and Larry Sloan. Price Stern Sloan, 1974 (102,476)

148. *Shiloh.* Phyllis Reynolds Naylor. Aladdin, 1992 (101,593)

149. *Clifford's Kitten.* Norman Bridwell. Cartwheel, 1992 (101,000)

150. *Alexander and the Terrible, Horrible, No Good, Very Bad Day.* Judith Viorst, illus. by Ray Cruz. Aladdin, 1972 (100,683)

151. *Junie B. Jones Loves Handsome Warren.* Barbara Park, illus. by Denise Brunkus. Random/Stepping Stone, 1996 (100,667)

152. *My Brother Sam Is Dead.* James and Christopher Collier. Scholastic, 1985 (100,500)

153. *Superfudge.* Judy Blume. Dell/Yearling, 1986 (100,423)

154. *A Wrinkle in Time.* Madeleine L'Engle. Dell/Laurel-Leaf, 1998 (100,216)

155. *The Grouchy Ladybug.* Eric Carle. HarperTrophy, 1996 (100,165)

156. *Amelia Bedelia and the Surprise Shower.* Peggy Parish, illus. by Barbara Siebel. HarperTrophy, 1979 (100,037)

157. *More Taste Berries for Teens.* Bettie Youngs and Jennifer Leigh Youngs. HCI, 2000 (100,000)

Literary Prizes, 2001

Gary Ink
Research Librarian, *Publishers Weekly*

Academy of American Poets Fellowship for Distinguished Poetic Achievement. *Offered by*: Academy of American Poets. *Winner*: Lyn Hejinian.

Ambassador Book Awards. To honor an exceptional contribution to the interpretation of life and culture in the United States. *Offered by*: English-Speaking Union. *Winners*: (fiction) Russell Banks for *Angel on the Roof* (HarperCollins); (poetry) Robert Haas, John Hollander, Carolyn Kizer, Nathaniel Mackey, and Marjorie Perloff for *American Poetry: The Twentieth Century* (Library of America).

American Academy of Arts and Letters Award of Merit for the Short Story. *Offered by*: American Academy of Arts and Letters. *Winner*: Frederick Busch.

American Academy of Arts and Letters Awards in Literature. *Offered by*: American Academy of Arts and Letters. *Winners*: (poetry) David Ferry, Alice Notley, Carl Phillips; (fiction) Guy Davenport, Frederic Tuten, Tobias Wolf; (creative nonfiction) Charles Mee.

American Academy of Arts and Letters. Rome Fellowship. For a one-year residency at the American Academy in Rome by a young writer of promise. *Offered by*: American Academy of Arts and Letters. *Winners*: Mark Halliday, Vincent Katz.

Barnes & Noble Discover Great New Writers Award. To honor a first novel by an American author. *Offered by*: Barnes & Noble, Inc. *Winner*: Tracy Chevalier for *Girl With a Pearl Earring* (Plume).

Mildred L. Batchelder Award. For an American publisher of a book originally published in a foreign language in a foreign country, and subsequently published in English in the United States. *Offered by*: American Library Association, Association for Library Service to Children. *Winner*: Scholastic/Levine for *Samir and Yonatan* by Daniella Carmi.

Before Columbus Foundation American Book Awards. For literary achievement by people of various ethnic backgrounds. *Offered by*: Before Columbus Foundation. *Winners*: (poetry) Diana Garcia for *When Living Was a Labor Camp* (University of Arizona); Sandra Gilbert for *Kissing the Bread* (Norton); Janet McAdams for *The Island of Lost Luggage* (University of Arizona); Carolyne Wright for *Seasons of Mangoes and Brainfire* (Lynx House); (fiction) Russell Charles Leong for *Phoenix Eyes and Other Stories* (University of Washington); Elizabeth Nunez for *Bruised Hibiscus* (Seal Press); W. S. Penn for *Killing Time with Strangers* (University of Arizona); Chris Ware for *Jimmy Corrigan: The Smartest Kid on Earth* (Pantheon); (creative nonfiction) Cheri Register for *Packinghouse Daughter* (Minnesota Historical Society); (editor/publisher award) Malcolm Margolin; (lifetime achievement) Ted Joans, Philip Whalen,Tillie Olsen.

Bellwether Prize for Literature. For a previously unpublished work of socially or politically engaged fiction. *Offered by*: Barbara Kingsolver. *Winner*: Donna M. Gershten for *Kissing the Virgin's Mouth* (HarperCollins).

Curtis Benjamin Award for Creative Publishing. *Offered by*: Association of American Publishers. *Winner*: Roger Straus.

Helen B. Bernstein Award for Excellence in Journalism. *Offered by*: New York Public Library. *Winner*: Elaine Sciolino for *Persian Mirrors* (Free Press).

James Tait Black Memorial Prizes (United Kingdom). For the best novel and the best biography of the year. *Offered by*: University of Edinburgh. *Winners*: (novel) Zadie Smith for *White Teeth* (Hamish Hamilton); (biography) Martin Amis for *Experience* (Cape).

Bollingen Prize in Poetry. To a living U.S. poet for the best collection published in the previous two years. *Offered by*: Yale

University. *Winner*: Louise Glück for *Vita Nova* (Ecco Press).

Booker Prize (United Kingdom). For the best novel written in English by a Commonwealth author. *Offered by*: Book Trust and Booker PLC. *Winner*: Peter Carey for *True History of the Kelly Gang* (Faber).

BookSense Book of the Year Awards (formerly ABBY Awards). To honor titles that members have most enjoyed handselling in the past year. *Offered by*: American Booksellers Association. *Winners*: (adult fiction) Anita Diamant for *The Red Tent* (Picador); (adult nonfiction) Ross King for *Brunelleschi's Dome* (Walker & Co.); (children's literature) Kate DiCamillo for *Because of Winn-Dixie* (Candlewick); (children's illustrated) Ian Falconer for *Olivia* (Atheneum).

Boston Globe/Horn Book Awards. For excellence in children's literature. *Offered by: Boston Globe* and *Horn Book Magazine*. *Winners*: (fiction and poetry) Marilyn Nelson for *Carver: A Life in Poems* (Front Street); (nonfiction) Joan Dash for *The Longitude Prize,* illus. by Dušan Petričić (Frances Foster Books); (picture book) Cynthia DeFelice for *Cold Feet,* illus. by Robert Andrew Parker (DK Publishing).

Witter Bynner Prize for Poetry. To support the work of emerging poets. *Offered by*: American Academy of Arts and Letters. *Winner*: Rachel Wetzsteon.

Randolph Caldecott Medal. For the artist of the most distinguished picture book. *Offered by*: American Library Association, Association for Library Service to Children. *Winner*: David Small for *So You Want to Be President?* by Judith St. George (Philomel).

John W. Campbell Award for the Best New Writer. For science fiction writing. *Offered by*: Center for the Study of Science Fiction. *Winner*: Kristine Smith.

John W. Campbell Memorial Award. For science fiction writing. *Offered by*: Center for the Study of Science Fiction. *Winner*: Poul Anderson for *Genesis* (Tor).

Carnegie Medal (United Kingdom). For the outstanding children's book of the year. *Offered by*: The Library Association. *Win-*

ner: Beverley Naidoo for *The Other Side of Truth* (Puffin).

Hayden Carruth Award. To honor a distinguished first, second, or third book by a poet. *Offered by*: Copper Canyon Press. *Winner*: Jenny Factor for *Unraveling at the Name* (Copper Canyon).

Mary Higgins Clark Award. For the book written most closely in the Mary Higgins Clark tradition. *Offered by*: Mystery Writers of America. *Winner*: Barbara D'Amato for *Authorized Personnel Only* (Forge).

Arthur C. Clarke Award (United Kingdom). For the best science fiction novel of the year. *Offered by*: British Science Fiction Association. *Winner*: China Mieville for *Perdido Street Station* (Macmillan).

David Cohen British Literature Prize (United Kingdom). To a living British poet, fiction writer, or creative nonfiction writer in recognition of an entire body of work written in English. *Winner*: Doris Lessing.

Commonwealth Writers Prize (United Kingdom). To reward and encourage new Commonwealth fiction and ensure that works of merit reach a wider audience outside their country of origin. *Offered by*: Commonwealth Institute. *Winners*: Peter Carey for *True History of the Kelly Gang* (Faber); (first novel) Zadie Smith for *White Teeth* (Hamish Hamilton).

Thomas Cook/Daily Telegraph Travel Book Award (United Kingdom). For travel writing. *Offered by*: Book Trust. *Winner*: Stanley Stewart for *In the Empire of Genghis Khan* (HarperCollins).

Crime Writers' Association Awards (United Kingdom). For the best crime writing of the year. *Offered by*: Crime Writers' Association. *Winners*: (Gold Dagger for fiction) Henning Mankell for *Sidetracked* (Harvill); (Silver Dagger for fiction) Giles Blunt for *Forty Words for Sorrow* (HarperCollins); (Gold Dagger for nonfiction) Philip Etienne and others for *The Infiltrators* (Penguin).

Alice Fay Di Castagnola Award. For a work in progress to recognize a poet in a critical stage of his or her work. *Offered by*: Poetry Society of America. *Winners*: Angie Estes, Glori Simmons.

Margaret A. Edwards Award. For lifetime contribution in writing for young adults. *Offered by*: American Library Association, Association for Library Service to Children. *Winner*: Robert Lipsyte.

T. S. Eliot Prize (United Kingdom). For poetry. *Offered by*: Poetry Book Society. *Winner*: Michael Longley for *The Weather in Japan* (Cape).

Eleanor Farjeon Award (United Kingdom). For a distinguished contribution to children's books. *Offered by*: Book Trust. *Winner*: Amelia Edwards.

Forward Poetry Prize (United Kingdom). *Offered by: The Forward. Winners*: (best collection) Sean O'Brien for *Downriver* (Picador); (best first collection) John Stammers for *Panoramic Lounge* (Picador).

Frankfurt e-Book Awards (Germany). To encourage the publishers of electronic books. *Offered by*: International e-Book Award Foundation. *Winners*: (grand award for fiction) Amitav Ghosh for *The Glass Palace* (Random House); (grand award for nonfiction) Steven Levy for *Cripto* (Penguin Putnam); (distinguished award for fiction) Eric Nisenson for *The Making of Blue* (St. Martin's); (distinguished award for nonfiction) Joyce Carol Oates for *Faithless* (HarperCollins); (technical award) Thierry Brethes/Mobipocket; (Roxanna Frost Award) *Fodor's e-book New York City Guide*.

Frost Medal for Distinguished Achievement. To recognize achievement in poetry over a lifetime. *Offered by*: Poetry Society of America. *Winner*: Sonia Sanchez.

Giller Prize (Canada). For the best novel or short story collection written in English. *Offered by*: Giller Prize Foundation. *Winner*: Richard B. Wright for *Clara Callan* (HarperFlamingo).

Golden Kite Awards. For children's book writing and illustration. *Offered by*: Society of Children's Book Writers and Illustrators. *Winners*: (fiction) Kathleen Karr for *The Boxer* (Farrar Straus & Giroux); (nonfiction) Ellen Levine for *Darkness over Denmark* (Holiday House); (picture book text) Jane Kurtz for *River Friendly, River Wild* (Simon & Schuster); (picture book illustration) David Shannon for *The Rain Came Down* (Scholastic).

Governor General's Literary Awards (Canada). For recognition of the best English-language and best French-language works by Canadian authors, illustrators, and translators published in Canada and abroad. *Offered by*: Canadian Authors Association. *Winners*: (fiction) Richard B. Wright for *Clara Callan* (HarperFlamingo); (nonfiction) Thomas Homer-Dixon for *The Ingenuity Gap* (Knopf); (poetry) George Elliott Clarke for *Execution Poems* (Gaspereau Press); (children's illustration) Mireille Levert for *Island in the Soup* (Groundwood Books); (children's text) Arthur Slade for *Dust* (HarperCollins); (translation) Fred A. Reed and David Homel for *Fairy Ring* (Talonbooks), translation of *Le Cercle de Clara* by Martine Desjardins.

Kate Greenaway Medal (United Kingdom). For children's book illustration. *Offered by*: The Library Association. *Winner*: Lauren Child for *I Will Not Ever Never Eat a Tomato* (Orchard Books).

Griffin Poetry Prizes (Canada). For excellence in poetry. *Offered by*: Griffin Trust. *Winners*: (international prize) Paul Celan for *Glottal Stop* (Wesleyan/University of New England); (Canadian prize) Anne Carson for *Men in the Off Hours* (Vintage).

Guardian Children's Fiction Prize (United Kingdom). For an outstanding children's novel. *Offered by: The Guardian. Winner*: Kevin Crossley-Holland for *The Seeing Stone* (Orion Children's Books).

Guardian First Book Prize (United Kingdom). For recognition of a first book. *Offered by: The Guardian. Winner*: Chris Ware for *Jimmy Corrigan* (Cape).

Guggenheim Literary Fellowships. For unusually distinguished achievement in the past and exceptional promise for future accomplishment. *Offered by*: Guggenheim Menorial Foundation. *Winners*: (poetry) Tom Andrews, Nick Flynn, Dorianne Laux, Marilyn Nelson, Wyatt Prunty, David Rivard, Charles Harper Webb; (fiction) Charlotte Bacon, Christopher Bram, Kathleen Cambor, Andre Dubus, III, Tom Franklin, Jessica Hagedorn, Ehud Havazelet, Brain Morton; (creative nonfiction)

Geneive Abdo, Ralph Blumenthal, George Packer, Justin Spring.

O. B. Hardison, Jr. Poetry Prize. To a U.S. poet who has published at least one book in the past five years, and has made important contributions as a teacher, and is committed to furthering the understanding of poetry. *Offered by*: Folger Shakespeare Library. *Winner*: David St. John.

Drue Heinz Literature Prize. To recognize and encourage the writing of short fiction. *Offered by*: Drue Heinz Foundation and the University of Pittsburgh. *Winner*: Brett Ellen Block for *Destination Known* (University of Pittsburgh).

Ernest Hemingway Foundation Award. For a distinguished work of first fiction by an American. *Offered by*: PEN New England. *Winner*: Akhil Sharma for *An Obedient Father* (Farrar Straus & Giroux).

Hugo Awards. For outstanding science fiction writing. *Offered by*: World Science Fiction Convention. *Winners*: (best novel) J. K. Rowling for *Harry Potter and the Goblet of Fire* (Scholastic); (best related book) Bob Eggleton and Nigel Suckling for *Greetings From Earth* (Paper Tiger); (best editor) Gardner Dozois; (best artist) Bob Eggleton.

IMPAC Dublin Literary Award (Ireland). For a book of high literary merit written in English or translated into English. *Offered by*: IMPAC Corp. and the City of Dublin. *Winner*: Alistair MacLeod for *No Great Mischief* (Vintage).

Jerusalem Prize (Israel). To a writer whose works best express the theme of freedom of the individual in society. *Offered by*: Jerusalem International Book Fair. *Winner*: Susan Sontag.

Jewish Book Awards. For contributions to Jewish literature. *Offered by*: Jewish Book Council. *Winners*: (fiction) Philip Roth for *The Human Stain* (Houghton Mifflin); (nonfiction) Samuel G. Freedman for *Jew vs. Jew* (Simon & Schuster); (children's) Howard Schwartz for *The Day the Rabbi Disappeared* (Viking); (Literary Achievement Award) Elie Wiesel.

Jewish Fiction by Emerging Writers Prize. For a first or second novel or collection of short stories by a U.S. author under 40 that explores the American Jewish experience. *Offered by*: National Foundation for Jewish Culture. *Winner*: Simone Zelitch for *Louisa* (Putnam).

Samuel Johnson Prize for Nonfiction (United Kingdom). For an outstanding work of nonfiction. *Offered by*: an anonymous donor. *Winner*: Michael Burleigh for *The Third Reich* (Macmillan).

James Jones First Novel Fellowship. For a novel-in-progress by a U.S. fiction writer who has never published a book-length work of fiction. *Offered by*: James Jones Literary Society. *Winner*: Steven Phillip Policoff.

Sue Kaufman Prize for First Fiction. For a first novel or collection of short stories. *Offered by*: American Academy of Arts and Letters. *Winner*: Akhil Sharma for *An Obedient Father* (Farrar Straus & Giroux).

Coretta Scott King Awards. For works that promote the cause of peace and brotherhood. *Offered by*: American Library Association, Social Responsibilities Round Table. *Winners*: (author award) Jacqueline Woodson for *Miracle's Boys* (Putnam); (illustrator award) Bryan Collier for *Uptown* (Holt).

Kiriyama Pacific Rim Book Prizes. For a book of fiction and a book of nonfiction that best contribute to fuller understanding among the nations and peoples of the Pacific Rim. *Offered by*: Kiriyama Pacific Rim Institute. *Winners*: (fiction) Patricia Grace for *Dogside Story* (Penguin); (nonfiction) Peter Hessler for *RiverTown* (HarperCollins).

Robert Kirsch Award. To a living author whose residence or focus is the American West and whose contributions to American letters clearly merit body-of-work recognition. *Offered by: Los Angeles Times*. *Winner*: Lawrence Ferlinghetti.

Gregory Kolovakos Award. To honor a translator, scholar, or educator whose life's work has contributed to the appreciation of Hispanic literature by English-language readers. *Offered by*: PEN American Center. *Winners*: Gregory Rabassa, Alastair Reid.

Koret Jewish Book Award. To underline the centrality of books in Jewish culture and to encourage serious readers to seek the best of Jewish books. *Offered by*: Koret Foundation. *Winner*: Philip Roth for *The Human Stain* (Houghton Mifflin).

Harold Morton Landon Translation Award. For a book of verse translated into English by a single translator. *Offered by*: Academy of American Poets. *Winners*: Clayton Eshleman for *Trilce* by Cesar Vallejo (Wesleyan University); Edward Snow for *Duino Elegies* by Rainer Maria Rilke (North Point).

Lannan Literary Awards. To recognize both established and emerging writers of poetry, fiction, and nonfiction. *Offered by*: Lannan Foundation. *Winners*: (lifetime achievement) Robert Creeley, Edward Said; (prize for cultural freedom) Mahmoud Darwish.

Ruth Lilly Poetry Prize. To a U.S. poet whose accomplishments warrant extraordinary recognition. *Offered by*: Modern Poetry Association. *Winner*: Yusef Komunyakaa.

Locus Awards. For science fiction writing. *Offered by*: Locus Publications. *Winners*: (science fiction novel) Ursula K. Le Guin for *The Telling* (Harcourt); (fantasy novel) George R. R. Martin for *A Storm of Swords* (Voyager); (first novel) Geoffrey A. Landis for *Mars Crossing* (Tor); (nonfiction) Stephen King for *On Writing* (Scribner); (art book) Cathy and Arnie Farmer for *Spectrum 7: The Best in Contemporary Fantastic Art* (Underwood Books); (collection) Michael Swanwick for *Tales of Old Earth* (North Atlantic); (anthology) Gardner Dozois, ed., for *The Year's Best Science Fiction: Seventeenth Annual Collection* (St. Martin's); (editor) Gardner Dozois; (publisher) Tor.

Los Angeles Public Library Literary Award. To recognize world leaders in the field of literature. *Offered by*: Los Angeles Public Library. *Winner*: Carlos Fuentes.

Los Angeles Times Book Prizes. To honor literary excellence. *Offered by: Los Angeles Times. Winners*: (fiction) David Means for *Assorted Fire Events* (Context Books); (first fiction) Pankaj Mishra for *The Romantics* (Anchor Books); (mystery/thriller) Val McDermid for *A Place of Execution*

(St. Martin's); (biography) William J. Cooper for *Jefferson Davis, American* (Knopf); (current interest) Frances Fitzgerald for *Way Out There in the Blue* (Simon & Schuster); (science and technology) James Le Fanu for *The Rise and Fall of Modern Medicine* (Carroll & Graf); (poetry) Gjertrud Schnackenberg for *The Throne of Labdacus* (Farrar Straus & Giroux); (history) Alice Kaplan for *The Collaborator* (University of Chicago); (young adult) Jacqueline Woodson for *Miracle's Boys* (Putnam).

McKitterick Prize (United Kingdom). For a first novel by a writer over the age of 40. *Offered by*: Society of Authors. *Winner*: Giles Waterfield for *The Long Afternoon* (Headline).

Somerset Maugham Awards (United Kingdom). For young British writers to gain experience in foreign countries. *Offered by*: Society of Authors. *Winners*: Edward Platt for *Leadville* (Picador), Ben Rice for *Pobby and the Dragon* (Cape).

Addison Metcalf Award for Literature. To a young writer of great promise. *Offered by*: American Academy of Arts and Letters. *Winner*: Dave Eggers.

James A. Michener Memorial Prize. To a writer who has published his or her first book at age 40 or over. *Offered by*: Random House. *Winner*: Richard Wertime for *Citadel on the Mountain* (Farrar Straus & Giroux).

National Arts Club Medal of Honor for Literature. *Offered by*: National Arts Club. *Winner*: Tom Wolfe.

National Book Awards. For the best books of the year published in the United States. *Offered by*: National Book Foundation. *Winners*: (fiction) Jonathan Franzen for *The Corrections* (Farrar Straus & Giroux); (nonfiction) Andrew Solomon for *The Noonday Demon* (Scribner); (poetry) Alan Dugan for *Poems Seven* (Seven Stories); (young people's) Virginia Euwer Wolff for *True Believer* (Atheneum); (Distinguished Contribution to American Letters) Arthur Miller.

National Book Critics Circle Awards. For literary excellence. *Offered by*: National Book Critics Circle. *Winners*: (fiction) Jim

Crace for *Being Dead* (Farrar Straus & Giroux); (general nonfiction) Ted Conover for *Newjack* (Random House); (biography/autobiography) Herbert P. Bix for *Hirohito and the Making of Modern Japan* (HarperCollins); (poetry) Judy Jordan for *Carolina Ghost Woods* (Louisiana State University); (criticism) Cynthia Ozick for *Quarrel & Quandary* (Knopf).

Nebula Awards. For the best science fiction and fantasy writing. *Offered by*: Science Fiction and Fantasy Writers of America. *Winners*: (best novel) Greg Bear for *Darwin's Radio* (Del Rey); (Grand Master) Philip José Farmer; (author emeritus) Robert Sheckley; (Bradbury Award) Yuri Rasovsky and Harlan Ellison.

Neustadt International Prize for Literature. To recognize a significant contribution to world literature. *Offered by: World Literature Today* and the University of Oklahoma. *Winner*: Alvaro Mutis.

John Newbery Medal. For the most distinguished contribution to literature for children. *Offered by*: American Library Association, Association for Library Service to Children. *Medal contributed by*: Daniel Melcher. *Winner*: Richard Peck for *A Year Down Yonder* (Dial Books for Young Readers).

Nobel Prize in Literature (Sweden). For the total literary output of a distinguished career. *Offered by*: Swedish Academy. *Winner*: V. S. Naipaul.

Flannery O'Connor Awards for Short Fiction. *Offered by*: PEN American Center. *Winners*: Dana Johnson for *Break Any Woman Down* (University of Georgia); Gina Ochsner for *The Necessary Grace to Fall* (University of Georgia).

Scott O'Dell Award for Historical Fiction. *Offered by: Bulletin of the Center for Children's Books,* University of Chicago. *Winner*: Janet Taylor Lisle for *The Art of Keeping Cool* (Atheneum/Jackson).

Orange Prize for Fiction (United Kingdom). For the best novel written by a woman and published in the United Kingdom. *Offered by*: Orange PLC. *Winner*: Kate Grenville for *The Idea of Perfection* (Picador).

PEN/Martha Albrand Award for the Art of the Memoir. For a first book-length memoir by a U.S. author. *Offered by*: PEN American Center. *Winner*: C. K. Williams for *Misgivings* (Farrar Straus & Giroux).

PEN Award for Poetry in Translation. *Offered by*: PEN American Center. *Winner*: Chana Block and Chana Kronfeld for *Open Closed Open* by Yehuda Amichai (Harcourt).

PEN/Book-of-the-Month Club Translation Award. For a book-length literary translation from any language into English published in the United States. *Offered by*: PEN American Center. *Winner*: Tina Nunnally for *Kristin Lavransdatter III, The Cross* by Sigrid Undset (Penguin).

PEN/Faulkner Award for Fiction. To honor the best work of fiction published by an American author. *Offered by*: PEN American Center. *Winner*: Philip Roth for *The Human Stain* (Houghton Mifflin).

PEN/Roger Klein Editorial Award. For distinguished editorial achievement. *Offered by*: PEN American Center. *Winners*: Gerlad Howard, Marian Wood.

PEN Literary Awards. For outstanding literary achievement. *Offered by*: PEN American Center. *Winners*: (career achievement) Gregory Rabassa and Alastair Reid; (visual arts) Leonard Barkan for *Unearthing the Past* (Yale University); Debora Silverman for *Van Gogh and Gaugin* (Farrar Straus & Giroux); (essay) David Quammen for *The Boilerplate Rhino* (Scribner); (first nonfiction) Charles Seife for *Zero* (Viking); (memoir) C. K. Williams for *Misgivings* (Farrar Straus & Giroux); (translation) Tina Nunnally for *Kristin Lavransdatter III, The Cross* by Sigrid Undset (Penguin); (poetry in translation) Chana Black and Chana Kronfeld for *Open Closed Open* by Yehuda Amichai (Harcourt); (working writer) Graham McNamee; (emerging poet) Richard Matthews.

PEN/ Malamud Award for Excellence in Short Fiction. To an author who has demonstrated long-term excellence in short fiction. *Offered by*: PEN American Center. *Winners*: Anne Beattie, Nathan Englander.

PEN/Joyce Osterweil Award for Poetry. To an American poet of special promise. *Offered by*: PEN American Center. *Winner*: Richard Matthews.

PEN/Spielvogel-Diamonstein Essay Award. For an outstanding book of essays by an

American writer. *Offered by*: PEN American Center. *Winner*: David Quammen for *The Boilerplate Rhino* (Scribner).

Edgar Allan Poe Awards. For outstanding mystery, crime, and suspense writing. *Offered by*: Mystery Writers of America. *Winners*: (novel) Joe R. Lansdale for *The Bottoms* (Mysterious Press); (first novel) David Liss for *A Conspiracy of Paper* (Random House); (paperback original) Mark Graham for *The Black Maria* (Avon); (fact crime) Dick Lehr and Gerard O'Neill for *Black Mass* (Public Affairs); (critical/biographical) Robert Kuhn McGregor and Ethan Lewis for *Conundrums for the Long Week-End* (Kent State University); (young adult) Elaine Marie Alphin for *Counterfeit Son* (Harcourt); (children's) Frances O'Roark Dowell for *Dovey Coe* (Atheneum); (Grand Master) Edward D. Hoch.

Michael L. Printz Award. For excellence in literature for young adults. *Offered by*: American Library Association, Association for Library Service to Children. *Winner*: David Almond for *Kit's Wilderness* (Delacorte).

Pulitzer Prizes in Letters. To honor distinguished work by American writers, dealing preferably with American themes. *Offered by*: Columbia University, Graduate School of Journalism. *Winners*: (fiction) Michael Chabon for *The Amazing Adventures of Kavalier & Clay* (Random House); (history) Joseph J. Ellis for *Founding Brothers* (Knopf); (biography/autobiography) David Levering Lewis for *W. E. B. Du Bois* (Holt); (poetry) Stephen Dunn for *Different Hours* (Norton); (general nonfiction) Herbert P. Bix for *Hirohito and the Making of Modern Japan* (HarperCollins).

Quality Paperback Book Club New Visions Award. For the most distinct and promising work of nonfiction by a new writer offered by the club each year. *Offered by*: Quality Paperback Book Club. *Winner*: Andrew Pham for *Catfish and Mandala* (St. Martin's).

Quality Paperback Book Club New Voices Award. For the most distinct and promising work of fiction by a new writer offered by the club each year. *Offered by*: Quality Paperback Book Club. *Winner*: Mark Danielewski for *The House of Leaves* (Pantheon).

Ellery Queen Award. To honor writing teams and outstanding people in the mystery publishing industry. *Offered by*: Mystery Writers of America. *Winner*: Douglas Greene, Crippen & Landru.

Raiziss/De Palchi Translation Fellowship. Biennial award given for a translation into English of modern Italian poetry, to enable an American translator to travel, study, or otherwise advance a significant work-in-progress. *Offered by*: Academy of American Poets. *Winner*: Emanuel di Pasquale for *Sharing a Trip* by Silvio Ramat.

Rea Award for the Short Story. To honor a living U.S. or Canadian writer who has made a significant contribution to the short story as an art form. *Offered by*: Dungannon Foundation. *Winner*: Alice Munro.

John Llewellyn Rhys Memorial Award (United Kingdom). For fiction. *Offered by: The Mail on Sunday. Winner*: Edward Platt for *Leadville* (Picador).

Richard and Hinda Rosenthal Foundation Award. For a work of fiction that is a considerable literary achievement though not necessarily a commercial success. *Offered by*: American Academy of Arts and Letters. *Winner*: David Ebershoff for *The Danish Girl* (Viking).

Juan Rulfo International Latin American and Caribbean Prize for Literature (Mexico). To a writer of poetry, novels, short stories, drama, or essays who is a native of Latin America or the Caribbean, and who writes in Spanish, Portuguese, or English. *Offered by*: Juan Rulfo Award Committee. *Winner*: Juan Garcia Ponce.

Sagittarius Prize (United Kingdom). For a first novel by a writer over the age of 60. *Offered by*: Society of Authors. *Winner*: Michael Richardson for *The Pig Bin* (Tindal Street).

Robert F. Sibert Award. For the most distinguished informational book for children. *Offered by*: American Library Association, Association for Library Service to Children. *Winner*: Marc Aronson for *Sir Walter Ralegh and the Quest for El Dorado* (Clarion).

Smarties Book Prizes (United Kingdom). To encourage high standards and to stimulate interest in books for children. *Offered by*: Book Trust and Nestle Rowntree. *Winners*: (ages 9–11) Eva Ibbotson for *Journey to the River Sea* (Macmillan); (ages 6–8) Emily Smith for *The Shrimp* (Young Corgi); (ages 0–5) Laurence and Catherine Anholt for *Chimp and Zee* (Frances Lincoln).

W. H. Smith Literary Award (United Kingdom). For a significant contribution to literature. *Offered by*: W. H. Smith Ltd. *Winner*: Philip Roth for *The Human Stain* (Cape).

Agnes Lynch Starrett Poetry Prize. For a first book of poetry. *Offered by*: University of Pittsburgh Press. *Winner*: Amy Quan Barry for *Asylum* (University of Pittsburgh).

Wallace Stevens Prize (formerly the Tanning Prize). To recognize outstanding and proven mastery in the art of poetry. *Offered by*: Academy of American Poets. *Winner*: Frank Bidart.

Bram Stoker Awards. For horror fiction. *Offered by*: Horror Writers Association. *Winners*: (novel) Richard Laymon for *The Traveling Vampire Show* (Cemetery Dance); (first novel) Brian Hopkins for *The Licking Valley Coon Hunters Club* (Yard Dog Press); (long fiction) Steve Rasnic Tem and Melanie Tem for *The Man on the Ceiling* (American Fantasy Press); (fiction collection) Peter Straub for *Magic Terror* (Random House); (anthology) Ellen Datlow and Terri Windling, eds., for *The Year's Best Fantasy and Horror: Thirteenth Annual Collection* (St. Martin's); (nonfiction) Stephen King for *On Writing* (Scribner); (illustrated narrative) Alan Moore for *The League of Extraordinary Gentlemen* (America's Best Comics); (work for young readers) Nancy Etchemendy for *The Power of Un* (Cricket Press); (poetry collection) Tom Piccirilli for *A Student of Hell* (Skull Job Productions); (specialty press award) Subterranean Press; (Richard Laymon Award) Judi Rohrig and Kathy Ptacek.

Templeton Prize for Progress in Religion. To honor a person judged to have contributed special insight into religion and spirituality. *Offered by*: Templeton Foundation. *Winner*: Arthur Peacocke.

Betty Trask Awards (United Kingdom). For works of a romantic or traditional nature by writers under the age of 35. *Offered by*: Society of Authors. *Winners*: (first novel) Zadie Smith for *White Teeth* (Hamish Hamilton); Justin Hill for *The Drink and Dream Teahouse* (Weidenfeld & Nicholson); Maggie O'Farrell for *After You'd Gone* (Headline); Vivien Kelly for *Take One Young Man* (Arrow); Mohsin Hamid for *Moth Smoke* (Granta): Patrick Neate for *Musungu Jim and the Great Chief Tuloko* (Penguin).

Kate Frost Tufts Discovery Award. For a first or very early book of poetry by an emerging poet. *Offered by*: Claremont Graduate School. *Winner*: Jennifer Clarvoe for *Invisible Teacher* (Fordham University).

Kingsley Tufts Poetry Award. For a book of poetry by a mid-career poet. *Offered by*: Claremont Graduate School. *Winner*: Alan Shapiro for *The Dead Alive and Busy* (University of Chicago).

Whitbread Book of the Year (United Kingdom). For literature of merit that is readable on a wide scale. *Offered by*: Booksellers Association of Great Britain. *Winner*: Philip Pullman for *The Amber Spyglass* (Scholastic).

Whitbread Literary Prizes (United Kingdom). For literature of merit that is readable on a wide scale. *Offered by*: Booksellers Association of Great Britain. *Winners*: (novel) Patrick Neate for *Twelve Bar Blues* (Viking); (first novel) Sid Smith for *Something Like a House* (Picador); (biography) Diana Souhami for *Selkirk's Island* (Weidenfeld); (poetry) Selima Hill for *Bunny* (Bloodaxe); (children's) Philip Pullman for *The Amber Spyglass* (Scholastic).

William Allen White Children's Book Awards. To encourage children to read and enjoy books. *Offered by*: Emporia State University. *Winners*: (grades 3–5) Cynthia DeFelice for *The Ghost of Fossil Glen* (Farrar Straus & Giroux); (grades 6–8) Louis Sachar for *Holes* (Yearling).

Whiting Writers Awards. For emerging writers of exceptional talent and promise. *Offered by*: Mrs. Giles Whiting Foundation.

Winners: (nonfiction) Judy Blunt, Kathleen Finneran; (fiction) Emily Carter, Matthew Klam, Akhil Sharma, Samrat Upadhyay, John Wray; (poetry) Joel Brouwer, Jason Sommer; (plays) Brighde Mullins.

Walt Whitman Award. For poetry. *Offered by*: Academy of American Poets. *Winner*: John Canaday for *The Invisible World* (Louisiana State University).

Laura Ingalls Wilder Award. For an author or illustrator whose books have made a substantial and lasting contribution to children's literature. *Offered by*: American Library Association, Association for Library Service to Children. *Winner*: Milton Meltzer.

Robert H. Winner Memorial Award. For a poem or sequence of poems characterized by a delight in language and the possibilities of ordinary life. *Offered by*: Poetry Society of America. *Winners*: Robert Franklin, Alice Jones.

L. L. Winship Award. For a book of fiction, nonfiction, or poetry by a New England author or with a New England subject. *Offered by*: PEN New England. *Winner*: Jay Wright for *Transfigurations* (Louisiana State University).

Helen and Kurt Wolf Translator's Prize. For an outstanding translation from German into English, published in the United States. *Offered by*: Goethe Institut Inter Nationes Chicago. *Winner*: Krishna Winston for *Too Far Afield* by Günter Grass (Harcourt).

World Fantasy Convention Awards. For outstanding fantasy writing. *Offered by*: World Fantasy Convention. *Winners*: (best novel) Tim Powers for *Declare* (Morrow); (best anthology) Sheree R. Thomas, ed., for *Dark Matter* (Warner Aspect); (best collection) Andy Duncan for *Beluthahatchie and Other Stories* (Golden Gryphon); (best artist) Shaun Tan; (lifetime achievement) Philip José Farmer, Frank Frazetta.

Young Lions Fiction Award. For a novel or collection of short stories by an American author under the age of 35. *Offered by*: Young Lions of New York Public Library. *Winner*: Mark Z. Danielewski for *House of Leaves* (Pantheon).

Morton Dauwen Zabel Award in Poetry. To writers of experimental and progressive tendencies. *Offered by*: American Academy of Arts and Letters. *Winner*: Paul Violi.

Charlotte Zolotow Award. For outstanding writing in a picture book. *Offered by*: Cooperative Children's Book Center, University of Wisconsin. *Winner*: Kate Banks for *The Night Worker,* illus. by Georg Hallensleben (Farrar Straus & Giroux).

Part 6
Directory of Organizations

Directory of Library and Related Organizations

Networks, Consortia, and Other Cooperative Library Organizations

This list is taken from the 2001–2002 edition of *American Library Directory* (Information Today, Inc.), which includes additional information on member libraries and primary functions of each organization.

United States

Alabama

Alabama Health Libraries Association, Inc. (ALHeLa), Univ. of Southern Alabama Medical Center Lib., 2451 Fillingim St., Mobile 36617. SAN 372-8218. Tel. 334-471-7855, fax 334-471-7857. *Pres.* Susan Williams.

Jefferson County Hospital Librarians Association, Brookwood Medical Center, 2010 Brookwood Medical Center Dr., Birmingham 35209. SAN 371-2168. Tel. 205-877-1131, fax 205-877-1189.

Library Management Network, Inc., 110 Johnston St. S.E., Decatur 35601. SAN 322-3906. Tel. 256-308-2529, fax 256-308-2533. *System Coord.* Charlotte Moncrief.

Marine Environmental Sciences Consortium, Dauphin Island Sea Lab., 101 Bienville Blvd., Dauphin Island 36528. SAN 322-0001. Tel. 334-861-2141, fax 334-861-4646, e-mail disl@disl.org. *Dir.* George Crozier.

Network of Alabama Academic Libraries, c/o Alabama Commission on Higher Education, Box 302000, Montgomery 36130-2000. SAN 322-4570. Tel. 334-242-2164, fax 334-242-0270. *Dir.* Sue Medina.

Alaska

Alaska Library Network (ALN), 344 W. 3 Ave., Suite 125, Anchorage 99501. SAN 371-0688. Tel. 907-269-6570, fax 907-269-6580, e-mail aslanc@eed.state.ak.us.

Arizona

Maricopa County Community College District Library Technical Services, 2411 W. 14 St., Tempe 85281-6942. SAN 322-0060. Tel. 480-731-8774, fax 480-731-8787. *System Coord.* Cheryl Laieski.

Arkansas

Arkansas Area Health Education Center Consortium (AHEC), Box 17006, Fort Smith 72917-7006. SAN 329-3734. Tel. 501-441-5337, fax 501-441-5339. *Dir.* Grace Anderson.

Arkansas' Independent Colleges and Universities, 1 Riverfront Place, Suite 610, North Little Rock 72114. SAN 322-0079. Tel. 501-378-0843, fax 501-374-1523. *Pres.* E. Kearney Dietz.

Northeast Arkansas Hospital Library Consortium, 223 E. Jackson, Jonesboro 72401. SAN 329-529X. Tel. 870-972-1290, fax 870-931-0839.

South Arkansas Film Coop., 301 S. Main St., Malvern 72104-3738. SAN 321-5938. Tel.

501-332-5442, fax 501-332-6679, e-mail hotspringcountylibrary@yahoo.com.

California

Area Wide Library Network (AWLNET), 2420 Mariposa St., Fresno 93721. SAN 322-0087. Tel. 559-488-3229, fax 559-488-2965. *Dir.* Sharon Vandercook.

Bay Area Library and Information Network (BAYNET), 672 Prentiss St., San Francisco 94110-6130. SAN 371-0610. Tel. 415-826-2464, e-mail infobay@baynetlibs.org.

Central Association of Libraries (CAL), 605 N. El Dorado St., Stockton 95202-1999. SAN 322-0125. Tel. 209-937-8649, fax 209-937-8292.

Consortium for Open Learning, 3841 N. Freeway Blvd., Suite 200, Sacramento 95834-1948. SAN 329-4412. Tel. 916-565-0188, fax 916-565-0189, e-mail cdl@calweb.com. *Exec. Dir.* Jerome Thompson.

Consumer Health Information Program and Services (CHIPS), County of Los Angeles Public Lib., 151 E. Carson St., Carson 90745. SAN 372-8110. Tel. 310-830-0909, fax 310-834-4097, e-mail chips@colopl.org. *Libn.* Scott Willis.

Dialog Corporation, 2440 El Camino Real, Mountain View 94040. SAN 322-0176. Tel. 650-254-7000, fax 650-254-8093.

Hewlett-Packard Library Information Network, 1501 Page Mill Rd., Palo Alto 94304. SAN 375-0019. Tel. 650-857-3091, 857-6620, fax 650-852-8187.

Kaiser Permanente Library System—Southern California Region (KPLS), Health Sciences Lib., 4647 Zion Ave., San Diego 92120. SAN 372-8153. Tel. 619-528-7323, fax 619-528-3444. *Dir.* Sheila Latus.

Metropolitan Cooperative Library System (MCLS), 3675 E. Huntington Dr., Suite 100, Pasadena 91107. SAN 371-3865. Tel. 626-683-8244, fax 626-683-8097, e-mail mclshq@mclsys.org. *Exec. Dir.* Barbara Custen.

National Network of Libraries of Medicine—Pacific Southwest Regional Medical Library (PSRML), Louise M. Darling Biomedical Lib., 12-077 Center for the Health Sciences, Box 951798, Los Angeles 90095-1798. SAN 372-8234. Tel. 310-825-1200, fax 310-825-5389, e-mail psr-nnlm@library.ucla.edu. *Dir.* Alison Bunting.

Northern California Association of Law Libraries (NOCALL), 100 1st St., Suite 100, San Francisco 94105. SAN 323-5777. Tel. 916-739-7014, fax 916-653-0952, e-mail admin@nocall.org. *Senior Libn.* Mary Parker.

Northern California Consortium of Psychology Libraries (NCCPL), California School of Professional Psychology, 1005 Atlantic, Alameda 94501. SAN 371-9006. Tel. 510-523-2300 ext. 185, fax 510-523-5943. *Dir.* Deanna Gaige.

Northern California and Nevada Medical Library Group, Box 2105, Berkeley 94704. SAN 329-4617. E-mail ncnmlg@stanford.edu.

OCLC Western Service Center, 9227 Haven Ave., Suite 260, Rancho Cucamonga 91730. SAN 370-0747. Tel. 909-941-4220, fax 909-948-9803. *Dir.* Mary Nash.

Peninsula Libraries Automated Network (PLAN), 25 Tower Rd., San Mateo 94402-4000. SAN 371-5035. Tel. 650-358-6704, fax 650-358-6706. *Database Manager* Susan Yasar.

Research Libraries Group, Inc. (RLG), 1200 Villa St., Mountain View 94041-1100. SAN 322-0206. Tel. 800-537-7546, fax 650-964-0943, e-mail bl.ric@rlg.stanford.edu. *Pres.* James Michalko.

San Bernardino, Inyo, Riverside Counties United Library Services (SIRCULS), Box 468, Riverside 92502-0468. SAN 322-0222. Tel. 909-369-7995, fax 909-784-1158, e-mail sirculs@inlandlib.org. *Exec. Dir.* Kathleen Aaron.

San Diego and Imperial Counties College Learning Resources Cooperative (SDICC-CL), Palomar College, 1140 W. Mission Rd., San Marcos 92069. SAN 375-006X. Tel. 760-744-1150 ext. 2848, fax 760-761-3500.

San Francisco Biomedical Library Network (SFBLN), H. M. Fishbon Memorial Lib., UCSF Medical Center at Mount Zion, 1600 Divisadero St., Rm. A116, San Francisco 94115. SAN 371-2125. Tel. 415-885-7378.

Santa Clarita Interlibrary Network (SCILNET), 21726 W. Placerita Canyon Rd., Santa Clarita 91321. SAN 371-8964. Tel. 661-259-3540, fax 661-222-9159. *Coord.* Janet Tillman.

Serra Cooperative Library System, 5555 Overland Ave., Bldg. 15, San Diego 92123. SAN 372-8129. Tel. 858-694-3600, fax 858-495-5905, e-mail hq@serralib.org. *System Coord.* Susan Swisher.

Smerc Library, 101 Twin Dolphin Dr., Redwood City 94065-1064. SAN 322-0265. Tel. 650-802-5655, fax 650-802-5665.

Southnet, c/o Silicon Valley Lib. System, 180 W. San Carlos St., San Jose 95113. SAN 322-4260. Tel. 408-294-2345, fax 408-295-7388, e-mail srch@ix.netcom.com.

Substance Abuse Librarians and Information Specialists (SALIS), Box 9513, Berkeley 94709-0513. SAN 372-4042. Tel. 510-642-5208, fax 510-642-7175, e-mail salis @arg.org. *Chair* Leigh Hallingby.

Colorado

American Gas Association—Library Services (AGA-LSC), c/o Excel Energy, 1225 17th St., Denver 80202. SAN 371-0890. Tel. 303-294-2620, fax 303-294-2799.

Arkansas Valley Regional Library Service System (AVRLSS), 635 W. Corona, Suite 113, Pueblo 81004. SAN 371-5094. Tel. 719-542-2156, fax 719-542-3155.

Bibliographical Center for Research, Rocky Mountain Region, Inc. (BCR), 14394 E. Evans Ave., Aurora 80014-1478. SAN 322-0338. Tel. 303-751-6277, fax 303-751-9787, e-mail admin@bcr.org. *Exec. Dir.* David Brunell.

Central Colorado Library System (CCLS), 4350 Wadsworth Blvd., Suite 340, Wheat Ridge 80033-4634. SAN 371-3970. Tel. 303-422-1150, fax 303-431-9752. *Dir.* Gordon Barhydt.

Colorado Alliance of Research Libraries, 3801 E. Florida Ave., Suite 515, Denver 80210. SAN 322-3760. Tel. 303-759-3399, fax 303-759-3363.

Colorado Association of Law Libraries, Box 13363, Denver 80201. SAN 322-4325. Tel. 303-492-7312. *Pres.* Linda Rose.

Colorado Council of Medical Librarians (CCML), Box 101058, Denver 80210-1058. SAN 370-0755. Tel. 303-450-3568, fax 303-560-4504.

Colorado Library Resource Sharing and Information Access Board, c/o Colorado State Lib., 201 E. Colfax, Denver 80203-

1799. SAN 322-3868. Tel. 303-866-6900, fax 303-866-6940. *Dir.* Brenda Bailey.

High Plains Regional Library Service System, 800 8th Ave., Suite 341, Greeley 80631. SAN 371-0505. Tel. 970-356-4357, fax 970-353-4355.

Peaks and Valleys Library Consortium, c/o Arkansas Valley Regional Lib. Service System, 635 W. Corona Ave., Suite 113, Pueblo 81004. SAN 328-8684. Tel. 719-542-2156, 546-4197, 546-4677, fax 719-546-4484.

Southwest Regional Library Service System (SWRLSS), P.O. Drawer B, Durango 81302. SAN 371-0815. Tel. 970-247-4782, fax 970-247-5087.

Three Rivers Regional Library Service System, 1001 Grand Ave., Suite 205, Glenwood Springs 81601. SAN 301-9934. Tel. 970-945-2626, fax 970-945-9396. *Dir.* Sandra Scott.

Connecticut

Capitol Area Health Consortium, 270 Farmington Ave., Suite 352, Farmington 06032-1909. SAN 322-0370. Tel. 860-676-1110, fax 860-676-1303.

Capitol Region Library Council, 599 Matianuck Ave., Windsor 06095-3567. SAN 322-0389. Tel. 860-298-5319, fax 860-298-5328, e-mail office@crlc.org.

Council of State Library Agencies in the Northeast (COSLINE), Connecticut State Lib., 231 Capitol Ave., Hartford 06106. SAN 322-0451. Tel. 860-757-6510, fax 860-757-6503.

CTW Library Consortium, Olin Memorial Lib., Wesleyan Univ., Middletown 06457-6065. SAN 329-4587. Tel. 860-685-3889, fax 860-685-2661. *Dir.* Alan Hagyard.

Eastern Connecticut Libraries (ECL), ECSU Lib. Rm. 134, 83 Windham St., Willimantic 06226. SAN 322-0478. Tel. 860-465-5001, fax 860-465-5004. *Dir.* Christine Bradley.

Hartford Consortium for Higher Education, 1800 Asylum Ave., West Hartford 06117. SAN 322-0443. Tel. 860-236-1203, fax 860-233-9723. *Exec. Dir.* Rosanne Druckman.

LEAP (Library Exchange Aids Patrons), 110 Washington Ave., North Haven 06473.

SAN 322-4082. Tel. 203-239-1411, fax 203-239-9458. *Exec. Dir.* Diana Sellers.
Libraries Online, Inc. (LION), 123 Broad St., Middletown 06457. SAN 322-3922. Tel. 860-347-1704, fax 860-346-3707. *Exec. Dir.* Edward Murray.
National Network of Libraries of Medicine New England Region (NN-LM NE Region), Univ. of Connecticut Health Center, 263 Farmington Ave., Farmington 06030-5370. SAN 372-5448. Tel. 860-679-4500, fax 860-679-1305. *Dir.* Ralph D. Arcari.
Southern Connecticut Library Council, 2911 Dixwell Ave., Suite 201, Hamden 06518-3130. SAN 322-0486. Tel. 203-288-5757, fax 203-287-0757, e-mail office@sclc.org. *Acting Dir.* Peter Ciparelli.
Western Connecticut Library Council, Inc., 530 Middlebury Rd., Suite 210B, Box 1284, Middlebury 06762. SAN 322-0494. Tel. 203-577-4010, fax 203-577-4015. *Exec. Dir.* Anita Barney.

Delaware

Central Delaware Library Consortium, Dover Public Lib., 45 S. State St., Dover 19901. SAN 329-3696. Tel. 302-736-7030, fax 302-736-5087. *Pres.* Robert S. Wetherall.
Delaware Library Consortium (DLC), Delaware Academy of Medicine, 1925 Lovering Ave., Wilmington 19806. SAN 329-3718. Tel. 302-656-6398, fax 302-656-0470. *Pres.* Gail P. Gill.
Sussex Help Organization for Resources Exchange (SHORE), Box 589, Georgetown 19947. SAN 322-4333. Tel. 302-855-7890, fax 302-855-7895.
Wilmington Area Biomedical Library Consortium (WABLC), Christiana Care Health System, Box 6001, Newark 19718. SAN 322-0508. Tel. 302-733-1116, fax 302-733-1365, e-mail ccw@christianacare.org. *Pres.* Christine Chastain-Warheit.

District of Columbia

CAPCON Library Network, 1990 M St. N.W., Suite 200, Washington 20036-3430. SAN 321-5954. Tel. 202-331-5771, fax 202-331-5788, e-mail capcon@capcon.net. *Exec. Dir.* Robert A. Drescher.
Council for Christian Colleges and Universities, 321 8th St. N.E., Washington 20002. SAN 322-0524. Tel. 202-546-8713, fax 202-546-8913, e-mail council@cccu.org. *Pres.* Robert Andringa.
District of Columbia Health Sciences Information Network (DOCHSIN), American College of Obstetrics and Gynecology Resource Center, 409 12th St. S.W., Washington 20024. SAN 323-9918. Tel. 202-863-2449.
Educational Resources Information Center (ERIC), U.S. Dept. of Education, Office of Educational Resources and Improvement, National Lib. of Education, 400 Maryland Ave., FOB-6 4th fl., Washington 20202. SAN 322-0567. Tel. 202-401-6014, fax 202-205-7759, e-mail eric@inet.ed.gov. *Dir.* Luna Levinson.
EDUCAUSE, c/o 1112 16th St. N.W., Suite 600, Washington 20036. SAN 371-487X. Tel. 202-872-4200, fax 202-872-4318.
FEDLINK (Federal Library and Information Network), c/o Federal Library and Information Center Committee (FLICC), Lib. of Congress, Washington 20540-5110. SAN 322-0761. Tel. 202-707-4800, fax 202-707-4818, e-mail flicc@loc.gov. *Exec. Dir.* Susan M. Tarr.
National Library Service for the Blind and Physically Handicapped, Library of Congress (NLS), 1291 Taylor St. N.W., Washington 20542. SAN 370-5870. Tel. 202-707-5100, fax 202-707-0712, e-mail nls@loc.gov. *Dir.* Frank Cylke.
Transportation Research Board, 2101 Constitution Ave. N.W., Washington 20418. SAN 370-582X. Tel. 202-334-2990, fax 202-334-2527. *Dir.* Barbara Post.
Veterans Affairs Library Network (VALNET), Library Division Programs Office, 810 Vermont Ave. N.W., Washington 20420. SAN 322-0834. Tel. 202-273-8522, 202-273-8523, fax 202-273-9125.
Washington Theological Consortium, 487 Michigan Ave. N.E., Washington 20017-1585. SAN 322-0842. Tel. 202-832-2675, fax 202-526-0818, e-mail wtconsort@aol.com.

Florida

Central Florida Library Cooperative (CFLC), 431 E. Horatio Ave., Suite 230, Maitland 32751. SAN 371-9014. Tel. 407-644-9050, fax 407-644-7023. *Exec. Dir.* Marta Westall.

Florida Library Information Network, c/o Bureau of Lib. and Network Services, State Lib. of Florida, R. A. Gray Bldg., Tallahassee 32399-0250. SAN 322-0869. Tel. 850-487-2651, fax 850-488-2746, e-mail library@mail.dos.state.fl.us.

Miami Health Sciences Library Consortium (MHSLC), KBI/IDM (142D), 1201 N.W. 16 St., Miami 33125-1673. SAN 371-0734. Tel. 305-355-5653, fax 954-355-4400. *Pres.* Rena Dole.

Palm Beach Health Sciences Library Consortium (PBHSLC), c/o Good Samaritan Medical Center Medical Lib., Box 3166, West Palm Beach 33402. SAN 370-0380. Tel. 561-650-6315, fax 561-650-6417.

Panhandle Library Access Network (PLAN), 5 Miracle Strip Loop, Suite 8, Panama City Beach 32407-3850. SAN 370-047X. Tel. 850-233-9051, fax 850-235-2286. *Exec. Dir.* William Conniff.

Southeast Florida Library Information Network, Inc. (SEFLIN), 100 S. Andrews Ave., Fort Lauderdale 33301. SAN 370-0666. Tel. 954-357-7345, fax 954-357-6998. *Exec. Dir.* Tom Sloan.

Southwest Florida Library Network, 24311 Walden Center Dr., Suite 100, Bonita Springs 34134. Tel. 941-948-1830, fax 941-948-1842. *Exec. Dir.* Barbara Stites.

Tampa Bay Library Consortium, Inc., 1202 Tech Blvd., Suite 202, Tampa 33619. SAN 322-371X. Tel. 813-740-3963, fax 813-628-4425.

Tampa Bay Medical Library Network (TABAMLN), Lakeland Regional Medical Center, 1324 Lakeland Hills Blvd., Lakeland 33805. SAN 322-0885. Tel. 863-687-1176, fax 863-687-1488, e-mail jan.booker@lrmc.com.

Georgia

Association of Southeastern Research Libraries (ASERL), c/o SOLINET, 1438 W. Peachtree St. N.W., Suite 200, Atlanta 30309-2955. SAN 322-1555. Tel. 404-892-0943, fax 404-892-7879. *Dir.* Amy Dykerman.

Atlanta Health Science Libraries Consortium, Wellstar Kennestone Hospital Lib., 677 Church St., Marietta 30060. SAN 322-0893. Tel. 770-793-7178, fax 770-793-7956. *Pres.* Linda Venis.

Biomedical Media, 1440 Clifton Rd. N.E., Rm. 113, Atlanta 30322. SAN 322-0931. Tel. 404-727-9797, fax 404-727-9798. *Dir.* Chuck Bogle.

Georgia Interactive Network for Medical Information (GAIN), c/o Medical Lib., School of Medicine, Mercer Univ., 1550 College St., Macon 31207. SAN 370-0577. Tel. 478-301-2515, fax 478-301-2051. *Dir.* Jan LaBeause.

Georgia Online Database (GOLD), c/o Public Lib. Services, 1800 Century Pl. N.E., Suite 150, Atlanta 30345-4304. SAN 322-094X. Tel. 404-982-3560, fax 404-982-3563. *Acting Dir.* Tom Ploeg.

Metro Atlanta Library Association (MALA), 483 James St., Lilburn 30247. SAN 378-2549. Tel. 770-431-2860, fax 770-431-2862. *Pres.* Michael Seigler.

Southeastern Library Network (SOLINET), 1438 W. Peachtree St. N.W., Suite 200, Atlanta 30309-2955. SAN 322-0974. Tel. 404-892-0943, fax 404-892-7879. *Exec. Dir.* Kate Nevins.

SWGHSLC, Colquitt Regional Medical Center Health Sciences Lib., Box 40, Moultrie 31776. SAN 372-8072. Tel. 912-890-3460, fax 912-891-9345. *Libn.* Susan Leik.

University Center in Georgia, Inc., 50 Hurt Plaza, Suite 465, Atlanta 30303-2923. SAN 322-0990. Tel. 404-651-2668, fax 404-651-1797.

Hawaii

Hawaii-Pacific Chapter of the Medical Library Association (HPAC-MLA), 1221 Punchbowl St., Honolulu 96813. SAN 371-3946. Tel. 808-536-9302, fax 808-524-6956. *Chair* Tina Okamoto.

Idaho

Boise Valley Health Sciences Library Consortium (BVHSLC), Health Sciences Lib., St. Alphonsus Regional Medical Center, Boise 83706. SAN 371-0807. Tel. 208-367-3993, fax 208-367-2702.

Canyon Owyhee Library Group, 203 E. Idaho Ave., Homedale 83628. Tel. 208-337-4613, fax 208-337-4933, e-mail stokes@sd370.k12.id.us.

Catalyst, c/o Boise State Univ., Albertsons Lib., Box 46, Boise 83707-0046. SAN

375-0078. Tel. 208-426-4024, fax 208-426-1885.

Cooperative Information Network (CIN), 8385 N. Government Way, Hayden 83835-9280. SAN 323-7656. Tel. 208-772-5612, fax 208-772-2498. *In Charge* John Hartung.

Eastern Idaho Library System, 457 Broadway, Idaho Falls 83402. SAN 323-7699. Tel. 208-529-1450, fax 208-529-1467.

Gooding County Library Consortium, c/o Gooding H.S., 1050 7th Ave. W., Gooding 83330. SAN 375-0094. Tel. 208-934-4831, fax 208-934-4347, e-mail senators@northrim.com.

Grangeville Cooperative Network, c/o Grangeville Centennial Lib., 215 W. North St., Grangeville 83530-1729. SAN 375-0108. Tel. 208-983-0951, fax 208-983-2336, e-mail granglib@lcsc.edu.

Idaho Health Information Association (IHIA), Kootenai Medical Center, W. T. Wood Medical Lib., 2003 Lincoln Way, Coeur d'Alene 83814. SAN 371-5078. Tel. 208-666-3498, fax 208-666-2854. *Dir.* Marcie Horner.

Lynx, c/o Boise Public Lib., 715 Capitol Blvd., Boise 83702-7195. SAN 375-0086. Tel. 208-384-4238, fax 208-384-4025. *In Charge* Toni Hansen.

Southeast Idaho Document Delivery Network, c/o American Falls District Lib., 308 Roosevelt St., American Falls 83211-1219. SAN 375-0140. Tel. 208-226-2335, fax 208-226-2303.

Valnet, Lewis Clark State College Lib., 500 8th Ave., Lewiston 83501. SAN 323-7672. Tel. 208-792-2227, fax 208-792-2831.

Illinois

Alliance Library System, Business Office, 845 Brenkman Dr., Pekin 61554. SAN 371-0637. Tel. 309-353-4110, fax 309-353-8281. *Exec. Dir.* Valerie Wilford.

American Theological Library Association (ATLA), 250 S. Wacker Dr., Suite 1600, Chicago 60606-5834. SAN 371-9022. Tel. 312-454-5100, fax 312-454-5505, e-mail atla@atla.com. *Exec. Dir.* Dennis Norlin.

Areawide Hospital Library Consortium of Southwestern Illinois (AHLC), c/o St. Elizabeth Hospital Health Science Lib., 211 S. 3 St., Belleville 62222. SAN 322-

1016. Tel. 618-234-2120 ext. 1181, fax 618-222-4620, e-mail campese@exl.com.

Association of Chicago Theological Schools (ACTS), McCormick Seminary, 5555 S. Woodlawn Ave., Chicago 60637. SAN 370-0658. Tel. 773-947-6300, fax 773-288-2612. *Pres.* Cynthia Campbell.

Capital Area Consortium, Decatur Memorial Library—Health Science Lib., 2300 N. Edward, Decatur 62526. Tel. 217-876-2940, fax 217-876-2945. *Coord.* Karen Stoner.

Center for Research Libraries, 6050 S. Kenwood, Chicago 60637-2804. SAN 322-1032. Tel. 773-955-4545, fax 773-955-4339. *Pres.* Bernard Reilly.

Chicago Library System (CLS), 224 S. Michigan, Suite 400, Chicago 60604. SAN 372-8188. Tel. 312-341-8500, fax 312-341-1985.

Chicago and South Consortium, Governors State University Lib., University Park 60466. SAN 322-1067. Tel. 708-534-5000 ext. 5142, fax 708-534-8454.

Consortium of Museum Libraries in the Chicago Area, c/o Morton Arboretum, Sterling Morton Lib., 4100 Illinois Rte. 53, Lisle 60532-1293. SAN 371-392X. Tel. 630-719-7932, fax 630-719-7950. *Chair* Michael Stieber.

Council of Directors of State University Libraries in Illinois (CODSULI), Univ. of Illinois at Springfield, Brookens Lib. 204A, Box 19243, Springfield 62794-9243. SAN 322-1083. Tel. 217-206-6597, fax 217-206-6354. *Chair* Sharon Hogan.

East Central Illinois Consortium, Carle Foundation Hospital Lib., 611 W. Park St., Urbana 61801. SAN 322-1040. Tel. 217-383-3011, fax 217-383-3452.

Fox Valley Health Science Library Consortium, Central DuPage Hospital Medical Lib., 25 N. Winfield Rd., Winfield 60190. SAN 329-3831. Tel. 630-681-4535, fax 630-682-0028.

Heart of Illinois Library Consortium, Galesburg Cottage Hospital, 695 N. Kellogg, Galesburg 61401. SAN 322-1113. Tel. 309-341-5106, fax 309-344-3526. *Coord.* Michael Wold.

Illinois Health Libraries Consortium, c/o Meat Industry Info. Center, National Cattleman's Beef Assn., 444 N. Michigan

Ave., Chicago 60611. SAN 322-113X. Tel. 312-670-9272, fax 312-467-9729. *Coord.* William D. Siarny, Jr.

Illinois Library Computer Systems Organization (ILCSO), Univ. of Illinois, 205 Johnstowne Centre, 502 E. John St., Champaign 61820. SAN 322-3736. Tel. 217-244-7593, fax 217-244-7596, e-mail oncall@ listserv.ilcso.uiuc.edu. *Dir.* Kristine Hammerstrand.

Illinois Library and Information Network (ILLINET), c/o Illinois State Lib., 300 S. 2nd St., Springfield 62701-1796. SAN 322-1148. Tel. 217-782-2994, fax 217-785-4326. *Dir.* Jean Wilkins.

Illinois Office of Educational Services, 2450 Foundation Dr., Suite 100, Springfield 62703-5464. SAN 371-5108. Tel. 217-786-3010, fax 217-786-3020, e-mail oesiscc@ siu.edu.

Judaica Library Network of Metropolitan Chicago (JLNMC), 618 Washington Ave., Wilmette 60091. SAN 370-0615. Tel. 847-251-0782.

Libras, Inc., Dominican Univ., River Forest 60305. SAN 322-1172. Tel. 708-524-6875 ext. 6889, fax 708-366-5360.

Metropolitan Consortium of Chicago, Weiss Memorial Hospital Medical Lib., 4646 N. Marine Dr., Chicago 60640. SAN 322-1180. Tel. 773-564-5820, fax 773-564-5821, e-mail libsch@interaccess.com. *Coord.* Syed Maghrabi.

National Network of Libraries of Medicine— Greater Midwest Region, c/o Lib. of the Health Sciences, Univ. of Illinois at Chicago, 1750 W. Polk St., M/C 763, Chicago 60612-4330. SAN 322-1202. Tel. 312-996-2464, fax 312-996-2226, e-mail gmr @uic.edu. *Dir.* Susan Jacobson.

Private Academic Libraries of Illinois (PALI), c/o Wheaton College Lib., Franklin and Irving, Wheaton 60187. SAN 370-050X. Tel. 630-752-5101, fax 630-752-5855, e-mail crflatzkehr@curf.edu. *Pres.* P. Snezek.

Quad Cities Libraries in Cooperation (QUAD-LINC), Box 125, Coal Valley 61240-0125. Tel. 309-799-3155, fax 309-799-5103. *Automation System Coord.* Mary Stewart.

Quad City Area Biomedical Consortium, Perlmutter Lib., 855 Hospital Rd., Silvis 61282. SAN 322-435X. Tel. 309-792-4360, fax 309-792-4362.

River Bend Library System (RBLS), Box 125, Coal Valley 61240-0125. SAN 371-0653. Tel. 309-799-3155, fax 309-799-7916.

Sangamon Valley Academic Library Consortium, MacMurray College, Henry Pfeiffer Lib., 447 E. College St., Jacksonville 62650. SAN 322-4406. Tel. 217-479-7110, fax 217-245-5214, e-mail mjthomas @mac.edu.

Shabbona Consortium, c/o Illinois Valley Community Hospital, 925 West St., Peru 61354. SAN 329-5133. Tel. 815-223-3300 ext. 502, fax 815-223-3394.

Upstate Consortium, c/o Menbota Community Hospital, 1315 Memorial Dr., Menbota 61342. SAN 329-3793. Tel. 815-539-7461 ext. 305.

Indiana

American Zoo and Aquarium Association (AZA-LSIG), Indianapolis Zoo, 1200 W. Washington St., Indianapolis 46222. SAN 373-0891. Tel. 317-630-5110, fax 317-630-5114.

Central Indiana Health Science Libraries Consortium, Indiana Univ. School of Medicine Lib., 975 W. Walnut, IB100, Indianapolis 46202. SAN 322-1245. Tel. 317-274-2292, fax 317-278-2349. *Pres.* Peggy Richwine.

Collegiate Consortium Western Indiana, c/o Cunningham Memorial Lib., Indiana State Univ., Terre Haute 47809. SAN 329-4439. Tel. 812-237-3700, fax 812-237-3376. *Acting Dean* Elizabeth Hine.

Evansville Area Library Consortium, 3700 Washington Ave., Evansville 47750. SAN 322-1261. Tel. 812-485-4151, fax 812-485-7564. *Coord.* E. Saltzman.

Indiana Cooperative Library Services Authority (INCOLSA), 6202 Morenci Trail, Indianapolis 46268-2536. SAN 322-1296. Tel. 317-298-6570, fax 317-328-2380.

Indiana State Data Center, Indiana State Lib., 140 N. Senate Ave., Indianapolis 46204-2296. SAN 322-1318. Tel. 317-232-3733, fax 317-232-3728.

Northeast Indiana Health Science Libraries Consortium (NEIHSL), Univ. of Saint Francis Health Sciences Lib., 2701 Spring St., Fort Wayne 46808. SAN 373-1383.

Tel. 219-434-7691, fax 219-434-7695. *Coord.* Lauralee Aven.

Northwest Indiana Health Science Library Consortium, c/o Northwest Center for Medical Education, Indiana Univ. School of Medicine, 3400 Broadway, Gary 46408-1197. SAN 322-1350. Tel. 219-980-6852, fax 219-980-6566.

Society of Indiana Archivists, University Archives, 201 Bryan Hall, Indiana Univ., Bloomington 47405. SAN 329-5508. Tel. 812-855-5897, fax 812-855-8104.

Iowa

Bi-State Academic Libraries (BI-SAL), c/o Marycrest International Univ., 1607 W. 12th St., Davenport 52804. SAN 322-1393. Tel. 319-326-9255. *Libn.* Mary Edwards.

Consortium of College and University Media Centers, Instructional Technology Center, Iowa State Univ., 1200 Comm. Bldg., Ames 50011-3243. SAN 322-1091. Tel. 515-294-1811, fax 515-294-8089, e-mail ccumc@ccumc.org. *Exec. Dir.* Don Rieck.

Dubuque (Iowa) Area Library Information Consortium, c/o Wahlert Memorial Lib., Loras College, Dubuque 52004-0178. Tel. 319-888-7009. *Pres.* Robert Klein.

Iowa Private Academic Library Consortium (IPAL), c/o Buena Vista Univ. Lib., 610 W. 4 St., Storm Lake 50588. SAN 329-5311. Tel. 712-749-2127, fax 712-749-2059.

Linn County Library Consortium, National Czech and Slovak Museum and Lib., 30 16th Ave. S.W., Cedar Rapids 52402. SAN 322-4597. Tel. 319-352-8500, fax 319-363-2209. *Pres.* David Muhlena.

Polk County Biomedical Consortium, c/o Cowles Lib., Drake Univ., 2507 University Ave., Des Moines 50311. SAN 322-1431. Tel. 515-271-4819, fax 515-271-3933. *Coord.* Claudia Frazer.

Sioux City Library Cooperative (SCLC), c/o Sioux City Public Lib., 529 Pierce St., Sioux City 51101-1203. SAN 329-4722. Tel. 712-255-2933 ext. 251, fax 712-279-6432.

State of Iowa Libraries Online Interlibrary Loan (SILO-ILL), State Lib. of Iowa, E. 12th and Grand, Des Moines 50319. SAN 322-1415. Tel. 515-281-4105, fax 515-281-6191. *State Libn.* Sharman B. Smith.

Kansas

Associated Colleges of Central Kansas, 210 S. Main St., McPherson 67460. SAN 322-1474. Tel. 620-241-5150, fax 620-241-5153.

Dodge City Library Consortium, c/o Dodge City, 1001 2nd Ave., Dodge City 67801. SAN 322-4368. Tel. 316-225-0248, fax 316-225-0252. *Pres.* Sarah Simpson.

Kansas Library Network Board, 300 S.W. 10th Ave., Rm. 343 N, Topeka 66612-1593. SAN 329-5621. Tel. 785-296-3875, fax 785-296-6650, e-mail erich@ink.org. *Exec. Dir.* Eric Hansen.

Mid-America Law School Library Consortium (MALSLC), Washburn Univ. School of Law Lib., 1700 S.W. College Ave., Topeka 66621. SAN 371-6813. Tel. 785-231-1088. *Chair* John Christensen.

Kentucky

Association of Independent Kentucky Colleges and Universities, 484 Chenault Rd., Frankfort 40601. SAN 322-1490. Tel. 502-695-5007, fax 502-695-5057. *Pres.* Gary Cox.

Eastern Kentucky Health Science Information Network (EKHSIN), c/o Camden-Carroll Lib., Morehead State Univ., Morehead 40351. SAN 370-0631. Tel. 606-783-2610, fax 606-783-5311. *Coord.* William J. DeBord.

Kentuckiana Metroversity, Inc., 200 W. Broadway, Suite 700, Louisville 40202. SAN 322-1504. Tel. 502-897-3374, fax 502-895-1647.

Kentucky Health Science Libraries Consortium, VA Medical Center, Lib. Services 142D, 800 Zorn Ave., Louisville 40206-1499. SAN 370-0623. Tel. 502-894-6240, fax 502-894-6134.

Kentucky Library Information Center (KLIC), Box 537, Frankfort 40602-0537. SAN 322-1512. Tel. 502-564-8300, fax 502-564-5773. *Dir.* Charlene Davis.

Kentucky Library Network, Inc., 300 Coffee Tree Rd., Box 537, Frankfort 40602. SAN 371-2184. Tel. 502-564-8300, fax 502-564-5773. *Pres.* William Hanson.

State Assisted Academic Library Council of Kentucky (SAALCK), c/o Steely Lib., Northern Kentucky Univ., Highland Heights

41099. SAN 371-2222. Tel. 859-572-5483, fax 859-572-6181.

Theological Education Association of Mid America (TEAM-A), c/o Southern Baptist Theological Seminary, 2825 Lexington Rd., Louisville 40280-0294. SAN 322-1547. Tel. 502-897-4807, fax 502-897-4600. *Acting Libn.* Bruce Keisling.

Louisiana

Baton Rouge Hospital Library Consortium, Earl K. Long Hospital, 5825 Airline Hwy., Baton Rouge 70805. SAN 329-4714. Tel. 504-358-1089, fax 504-358-1240. *Pres.* Eileen Stanley.

Health Sciences Library Association of Louisiana Medical Library, LSU Health Sciences Lib., 433 Bolivar St., New Orleans 70112-7021. SAN 375-0035. Tel. 504-568-6100. *Chair* Carolyn Bridgewater.

Loan SHARK, State Lib. of Louisiana, Box 131, Baton Rouge 70821. SAN 371-6880. Tel. 225-342-4918, 225-342-4920, fax 225-219-4725. *Coord.* Virginia Smith.

Louisiana Government Information Network (LaGIN), c/o State Lib. of Louisiana, Box 131, Baton Rouge 70821. SAN 329-5036. Tel. 225-342-4920, e-mail lagin@pelican. state.lib.la.us. *Coord.* Virginia Smith.

New Orleans Educational Telecommunications Consortium, 2 Canal St., Suite 2038, New Orleans 70130. SAN 329-5214. Tel. 504-524-0350, fax 504-524-0327. *Chair* Gregory M. St. L. O'Brien.

Maine

Health Science Library Information Consortium (HSLIC), 25 Pleasant St., Fort Kent 04743. SAN 322-1601. Tel. 207-743-5933 ext. 323, fax 207-973-8233. *Chair* Amy Averre.

Maryland

ERIC Processing and Reference Facility, 4483-A Forbes Blvd., Lanham 20706. SAN 322-161X. Tel. 301-497-4080, fax 301-953-0263, e-mail ericfac@inet.ed. gov. *Dir.* Donald Frank.

Library Video Network (LVN), 320 York Rd., Towson 21204. SAN 375-5320. Tel. 410-887-2090, fax 410-887-2091, e-mail lvn@bcpl.net.

Maryland Association of Health Science Librarians (MAHSL), St. Agnes Health-care, 900 Caton Ave., Baltimore 21229. SAN 377-5070. Tel. 410-368-3123.

Maryland Interlibrary Organization (MILO), c/o Enoch Pratt Free Lib., 400 Cathedral St., Baltimore 21201-4484. SAN 343-8600. Tel. 410-396-5498, fax 410-396-5837, e-mail milo@epfl.net. *Mgr.* Sharon Smith.

Metropolitan Area Collection Development Consortium (MCDAC), c/o Carrol County Public Lib., 115 Airport Dr., Westminster 21157. SAN 323-9748. Tel. 410-386-4500 ext. 144, fax 410-386-4509. *Coord.* Nancy Haile.

National Library of Medicine, MEDLARS Medical Literature Analysis and Retrieval System, 8600 Rockville Pike, Bethesda 20894. SAN 322-1652. Tel. 301-402-1076, fax 301-496-0822, e-mail custserv@ nlm.nih.gov.

National Network of Libraries of Medicine (NN-LM), National Lib. of Medicine, 8600 Rockville Pike, Rm. B1E03, Bethesda 20894. SAN 373-0905. Tel. 301-496-4777, fax 301-480-1467.

National Network of Libraries of Medicine—Southeastern Atlantic Region, Univ. of Maryland Health Sciences and Human Services Lib., 601 W. Lombard St., Baltimore 21201-1512. SAN 322-1644. Tel. 410-706-2855, fax 410-706-0099.

Regional Alcohol and Drug Abuse Resource Network (RADAR), National Clearinghouse of Alcohol and Drug Information, 11426 Rockville Pike, Suite 200, Rockville 20852-3007. SAN 377-5569. Tel. 301-468-2600, fax 301-468-2600, e-mail info@health.org. *Coord.* M. Pierce.

Washington Research Library Consortium (WRLC), 901 Commerce Dr., Upper Marlboro 20774. SAN 373-0883. Tel. 301-390-2031, fax 301-390-2020. *Exec. Dir.* Lizanne Payne.

Massachusetts

Automated Bristol Library Exchange (ABLE, Inc.), 547 W. Grove St., Box 4, Middleboro 02346. SAN 378-0074. Tel. 508-946-8600, fax 508-946-8605. *Exec. Dir.* Deborah K. Conrad.

Boston Area Music Libraries (BAML), Music Lib., Wellesley College, Wellesley 02481. SAN 322-4392. Tel. 781-283-2076, fax 781-283-3687.

Boston Biomedical Library Consortium (BBLC), c/o Percy R. Howe Memorial Lib., Forsyth Institute, 140 The Fenway, Boston 02115. SAN 322-1725. Tel. 617-262-5200 ext. 244, fax 617-262-4021. *Chair* Susan Orlando.

Boston Library Consortium, 700 Boylston St., Rm. 317, Boston 02117. SAN 322-1733. Tel. 617-262-0380, fax 617-262-0163. *Exec. Dir.* Barbara Preece.

Boston Theological Institute Library Program, 99 Brattle St., Cambridge 02138. SAN 322-1741. Tel. 617-349-3602 ext. 315, e-mail btilibrary@edswjst.org. *Coord.* Linda Ronan.

Cape Libraries Automated Materials Sharing (CLAMS), 270 Communication Way, Unit 4E-4F, Hyannis 02601. SAN 370-579X. Tel. 508-790-4399, fax 508-771-4533.

Catholic Library Association, 100 North St., Suite 224, Pittsfield 01201-5109. SAN 329-1030. Tel. 413-443-2252, fax 413-442-2252, e-mail cla@vgernet.net. *Exec. Dir.* Jean Bostley, SSJ.

Central Massachusetts Consortium of Health Related Libraries (CMCHRL), c/o Medical Lib., Univ. of Massachusetts Memorial Healthcare, 119 Belmont St., Worcester 01605. SAN 371-2133.

Consortium for Information Resources, Emerson Hospital, Old Rd. to Nine Acre Corner, Concord 01742. SAN 322-4503. Tel. 978-287-3090, fax 978-287-3651.

Cooperating Libraries of Greater Springfield (CLIC), Springfield College, 263 Alden St., Springfield 01109. SAN 322-1768. Tel. 413-748-3309, fax 413-748-3631. *Chair* Gerald Davis.

C W Mars (Central-Western Massachusetts Automated Resource Sharing), 1 Sunset Lane, Paxton 01612-1197. SAN 322-3973. Tel. 508-755-3323, fax 508-755-3721.

Fenway Libraries Online (FLO), Wentworth Inst. of Technology, 550 Huntington Ave., Boston 02115. SAN 373-9112. Tel. 617-442-2384, fax 617-442-1519.

Fenway Library Consortium, Sawyer Lib., 8 Ashburton Place, Boston 02108. SAN 327-9766. Tel. 617-573-8536, fax 617-521-3093.

Massachusetts Health Sciences Libraries Network (MAHSLIN), c/o Beverly Hospital Medical Lib., 55 Herrick St., Beverly

01915. SAN 372-8293. Tel. 978-922-3000 ext. 2920, fax 978-922-3000 ext. 2273. *Pres.* Ann Tomes.

Merrimac Interlibrary Cooperative, c/o J. V. Fletcher Lib., 50 Main St., Westford 01886. SAN 329-4234. Tel. 508-692-5555, fax 508-692-4418. *Chair* Nanette Eichell.

Merrimack Valley Library Consortium, 123 Tewksbury St., Andover 01810. SAN 322-4384. Tel. 978-475-7632, fax 978-475-7179. *Exec. Dir.* Lawrence Rungren.

Metrowest Massachusetts Regional Library System (METROWEST), 135 Beaver St., Waltham 02452. Tel. 781-398-1819, fax 781-398-1821. *Admin.* Sondra Vandermark.

Minuteman Library Network, 10 Strathmore Rd., Natick 01760-2419. SAN 322-4252. Tel. 508-655-8008, fax 508-655-1507. *Exec. Dir.* Carol Caro.

NELINET, Inc., 153 Cordaville Rd., Southborough 01772. SAN 322-1822. Tel. 508-460-7700, fax 508-460-9455. *Exec. Dir.* Arnold Hirshon.

New England Law Library Consortium, Inc., Harvard Law School Lib., Langdell Hall, Cambridge 02138. SAN 322-4244. Tel. 508-428-5342, fax 508-428-7623. *Exec. Dir.* Diane Klaiber.

North Atlantic Health Sciences Libraries, Inc. (NAHSL), Lamar Soutter Lib., Univ. of Massachusetts Medical School, 55 Lake Ave. N., Worcester 01655. SAN 371-0599. Tel. 508-856-2099, fax 508-856-5899.

North of Boston Library Exchange, Inc. (NOBLE), 26 Cherry Hill Dr., Danvers 01923. SAN 322-4023. Tel. 978-777-8844, fax 978-750-8472. *Exec. Dir.* Ronald Gagnon.

Northeast Consortium of Colleges and Universities in Massachusetts (NECCUM), Northern Essex Community College, 100 Elliott St., Haverhill 01830. SAN 371-0602. Tel. 978-556-3000. *Coord.* Marie McDonald.

Northeastern Consortium for Health Information (NECHI), Anna Jaques Hospital, Medical Lib., 25 Highland Ave., Newburyport 01950. SAN 322-1857. Tel. 978-463-1000.

Sails, Inc., 547 W. Groves St., Suite 4, Middleboro 02346. SAN 378-0058. Tel. 508-946-8600, fax 508-946-8605. *Pres.* Sharon St. Hilaire.

Southeastern Massachusetts Consortium of Health Science Libraries (SEMCO), South Shore Hospital, 55 Fogg Rd., South Weymouth 02190. SAN 322-1873. Tel. 781-340-8528, fax 781-331-0834.

Southeastern Massachusetts Cooperating Libraries (SMCL), c/o Wheaton College, Madeleine Clark Wallace Lib., Norton 02766-0849. SAN 322-1865. Tel. 508-285-8225, fax 508-286-8275.

West of Boston Network (WEBNET), Horn Lib., Babson College, Babson Park 02457. SAN 371-5019. Tel. 781-239-4308, fax 781-239-5226. *Pres.* Hope Tillman.

Western Massachusetts Health Information Consortium, c/o Holyoke Hospital Medical Lib., 575 Beech St., Holyoke 01040. SAN 329-4579. Tel. 413-534-2500 ext. 5282, fax 413-534-2710.

Worcester Area Cooperating Libraries (WACL), Gordon Lib., 100 Institute Rd., Worcester 01609. SAN 322-1881. Tel. 508-754-3964, fax 508-831-5829. *Coord.* Gladys Wood.

Michigan

Berrien Library Consortium, c/o Lake Michigan College Lib., 2755 E. Napier Ave., Benton Harbor 49022-1899. SAN 322-4678. Tel. 616-927-8605, fax 616-927-6656.

Capital Area Library Network Inc. (CALNET), Box 71, Napoleon 49261-0071. SAN 370-5927. Tel. 517-536-8667 ext. 244, fax 517-536-8030, e-mail board@calnet.mlc.lib.mi.us.

Detroit Area Consortium of Catholic Colleges, c/o Sacred Heart Seminary, 2701 Chicago Blvd., Detroit 48206. SAN 329-482X. Tel. 313-883-8500, fax 313-868-6440. *Pres.* Allen H. Vigneron.

Detroit Associated Libraries Region of Cooperation (DALROC), Detroit Public Lib., 5201 Woodward Ave., Detroit 48202. SAN 371-0831. Tel. 313-833-4835, fax 313-832-0877. *Chair* Pamela Lazar.

Kalamazoo Consortium for Higher Education (KCHE), Kalamazoo College, 1200 Academy St., Kalamazoo 49006. SAN 329-

4994. Tel. 616-337-7220, fax 616-337-7219. *Pres.* James Jones.

Lakeland Library Cooperative, 4138 Three Mile Rd. N.W., Grand Rapids 49544. SAN 308-132X. Tel. 616-559-5253, fax 616-559-4329. *Dir.* Dan Siebersma.

Library Network, 13331 Reeck Rd., Southgate 48195. SAN 370-596X. Tel. 734-281-3830, fax 734-281-1905, 734-281-1817. *Dir.* A. Deller.

Michigan Association of Consumer Health Information Specialists (MACHIS), Bronson Methodist Hospital, Health Sciences Lib., 601 John St., Box B, Kalamazoo 49007. SAN 375-0043. Tel. 616-341-8627, fax 616-341-8828.

Michigan Health Sciences Libraries Association (MHSLA), Genesys Regional Medical Center, 1 Genesys Pkwy., Grand Blanc 48439-1477. SAN 323-987X. Tel. 810-606-5261, fax 810-606-5270, e-mail glauet@com.msu.edu.

Michigan Library Consortium (MLC), 6810 S. Cedar St., Suite 8, Lansing 48911. SAN 322-192X. Tel. 517-694-4242, fax 517-694-9303, e-mail reception@mlcnet.org.

Northland Interlibrary System (NILS), 316 E. Chisholm St., Alpena 49707. SAN 329-4773. Tel. 517-356-1622, fax 517-354-3939. *Admin.* Christine Johnson.

Southeastern Michigan League of Libraries (SEMLOL), Univ. of Michigan-Dearborn, 4901 Evergreen Rd., 4063 ML, Dearborn 48128. SAN 322-4481. Tel. 313-593-3740, fax 313-577-5265. *Chair* M. Fraser.

Southern Michigan Region of Cooperation (SMROC), 415 S. Superior, Suite A, Albion 49224-2135. SAN 371-3857. Tel. 517-629-9469, fax 517-629-3812.

Southwest Michigan Library Cooperative (SMLC), 305 Oak St., Paw Paw 49079. SAN 371-5027. Tel. 616-657-4698, fax 616-657-4494. *Dir.* Alida Geppert.

Suburban Library Cooperative (SLC), 16480 Hall Rd., Clinton Township 48038. SAN 373-9082. Tel. 810-286-5750, fax 810-286-8951. *Dir.* Tammy Turgeon.

Upper Peninsula of Michigan Health Science Library Consortium, c/o Marquette General Hospital, 420 W. Magnetic, Marquette 49855. SAN 329-4803. Tel. 906-225-3429, fax 906-225-3524.

Upper Peninsula Region of Library Cooperation, Inc., 1615 Presque Isle Ave., Marquette 49855. SAN 329-5540. Tel. 906-228-7697, fax 906-228-5627.

Minnesota

Arrowhead Health Sciences Library Network, St. Luke's Hospital Lib., Duluth 55805. SAN 322-1954. Tel. 218-726-5320, fax 218-726-5181.

Capital Area Library Consortium (CALCO), c/o Minnesota Dept. of Transportation, Library MS155, 395 John Ireland Blvd., Saint Paul 55155. SAN 374-6127. Tel. 651-296-5272, fax 651-297-2354.

Central Minnesota Libraries Exchange (CMLE), Miller Center, Rm. 130-D, Saint Cloud State Univ., Saint Cloud 56301-4498. SAN 322-3779. Tel. 320-255-2950, fax 320-654-5131. *Dir.* Patricia Peterson.

Community Health Science Library, c/o Saint Francis Medical Center, 415 Oak St., Breckenridge 56520. SAN 370-0585. Tel. 218-643-7542, fax 218-643-7452. *Dir.* Karla Lovaasen.

Cooperating Libraries in Consortium (CLIC), 1619 Dayton Ave., Suite 204A, Saint Paul 55104. SAN 322-1970. Tel. 651-644-3878, fax 651-644-6258. *Exec. Dir.* Chris Olson.

METRONET, 1619 Dayton Ave., Suite 314, Saint Paul 55104. SAN 322-1989. Tel. 651-646-0475, fax 651-649-3169, e-mail info@metronet.lib.mn.us. *Exec. Dir.* Janet Fabio.

Metropolitan Library Service Agency (MELSA), 1619 Dayton Ave., No. 314, Saint Paul 55104-6206. SAN 371-5124. Tel. 651-645-5731, fax 651-649-3169, e-mail melsa@melsa.lib.mn.us.

MINITEX Library Information Network, c/o 15 Andersen Lib., Univ. of Minnesota, 222 21st Ave. S., Minneapolis 55455-0439. SAN 322-1997. Tel. 612-624-4002, fax 612-624-4508. *Dir.* William DeJohn.

Minnesota Department of Human Services Library, 444 Lafayette, Saint Paul 55155-3820. SAN 371-0750. Tel. 612-297-8708, fax 612-282-5340.

Minnesota Theological Library Association (MTLA), c/o Luther Seminary Lib., 2375 Como Ave., Saint Paul 55108. SAN 322-

1962. Tel. 651-641-3202, fax 651-641-3280. *Pres.* Mary Martin.

North Country Library Cooperative, Olcott Plaza, Suite 110, 820 N. 9 St., Virginia 55741. SAN 322-3795. Tel. 218-741-1907, fax 218-741-1907. *Dir.* Linda Wadman.

Northern Lights Library Network, 801 Jenny Ave. S.W., Perham 56573. SAN 322-2004. Tel. 218-347-6315, fax 218-347-6316, e-mail nloffice@nlln.org. *Dir.* Ruth Solie.

SMILE (Southcentral Minnesota Inter-Library Exchange), 1400 Madison Ave., Suite 622, Mankato 56001. SAN 321-3358. Tel. 507-625-7555, fax 507-625-4049, e-mail smile@tds.lib.mn.us.

Southeast Library System (SELS), 2600 19th St. N.W., Rochester 55901-0767. SAN 322-3981. Tel. 507-288-5513, fax 507-288-8697.

Southwest Area Multicounty Multitype Interlibrary Exchange (SAMMIE), BA 282, Southwest State Univ., Marshall 56258. SAN 322-2039. Tel. 507-532-9013, fax 507-532-2039. *Dir.* Robin Chaney.

Twin Cities Biomedical Consortium, c/o Health East St. Joseph's Hospital Lib., 69 W. Exchange St., Saint Paul 55102. SAN 322-2055. Tel. 651-232-3193, fax 651-232-3296. *Chair* Karen Brudvig.

Valley Medical Network, Lake Region Hospital Lib., 712 S. Cascade St., Fergus Falls 56537. SAN 329-4730. Tel. 218-736-8158, fax 218-736-8723.

Waseca Interlibrary Resource Exchange (WIRE), c/o Waseca High School, 1717 2nd St. N.W., Waseca 56093. SAN 370-0593. Tel. 507-835-5470 ext. 218, fax 507-835-1724, e-mail tlol@waseca.k12.mn.us.

West Group, Box 64526, Saint Paul 55164-0526. SAN 322-4031. Tel. 651-687-7000, fax 651-687-5614, e-mail webmaster@westgroup.com.

Mississippi

Central Mississippi Library Council (CMLC), c/o Hinds Commercial College Lib., Raymond 39154-9799. SAN 372-8250. Tel. 601-857-3255, fax 601-857-3293.

Mississippi Biomedical Library Consortium, c/o College of Veterinary Medicine, Mississippi State Univ., Box 9825, Mississippi

State 39762. SAN 371-070X. Tel. 601-325-1240, fax 601-325-1141.

Missouri

Health Sciences Library Network of Kansas City, Inc. (HSLNKC), Univ. of Missouri Health Sciences Lib., 2411 Holmes St., Kansas City 64108-2792. SAN 322-2098. Tel. 816-235-1880, fax 816-235-5194.

Kansas City Metropolitan Library and Information Network, 15624 E. 24 Hwy., Independence 64050. SAN 322-2101. Tel. 816-521-7257, fax 816-461-0966. *Exec. Dir.* Susan Burton.

Kansas City Regional Council for Higher Education, Park Univ., 8700 N.W. River Park Dr. 40, Parkville 64152-3795. SAN 322-211X. Tel. 816-741-2816, fax 816-741-1296. *Pres.* Ron Doering.

Library Systems Service, c/o Washington Univ., Bernard Becker Medical Lib., 660 S. Euclid Ave., Saint Louis 63110. SAN 322-2187. Tel. 314-362-2778, fax 314-362-0190. *Mgr.* Russ Monika.

Missouri Library Network Corporation, 8045 Big Bend Blvd., Suite 202, Saint Louis 63119-2714. SAN 322-466X. Tel. 314-918-7222, fax 314-918-7727, e-mail sms@mlnc.org.

Saint Louis Regional Library Network, 9425 Big Bend, Saint Louis 63119. SAN 322-2209. Tel. 314-965-1305, fax 314-965-4443.

Nebraska

Eastern Library System (ELS), 11929 Elm St., Suite 12, Omaha 68144. SAN 371-506X. Tel. 402-330-7884, fax 402-330-1859.

ICON, 5619 Jones St., Omaha 68106. SAN 372-8102. Tel. 402-556-6169.

Lincoln Health Sciences Library Group (LHSLG), Univ. of Nebraska, N219 Love Lib., Lincoln 68588-4100. SAN 329-5001. Tel. 402-472-2554, fax 402-472-5131.

Meridian Library System, 3519 2nd Ave., Suite B, Kearney 68847. SAN 325-3554. Tel. 308-234-2087, fax 308-234-4040, e-mail sosenga@nol.org. *Pres.* Joan Davis.

NEBASE, c/o Nebraska Lib. Commission, 1200 N St., Suite 120, Lincoln 68508-2023. SAN 322-2268. Tel. 402-471-2045, fax 402-471-2083.

Northeast Library System, 3038 33rd Ave., Columbus 68601-2334. SAN 329-5524. Tel. 402-564-1586.

Southeast Nebraska Library System, 5730 R St., Suite C-1, Lincoln 68505. SAN 322-4732. Tel. 402-467-6188, fax 402-467-6196.

Nevada

Information Nevada, Interlibrary Loan Dept., Nevada State Lib. and Archives, 100 N. Stewart St., Carson City 89701-4285. SAN 322-2276. Tel. 775-684-3325, fax 775-684-3330.

Nevada Medical Library Group (NMLG), Barton Memorial Hospital Lib., 2170 S. Ave., Box 9578, South Lake Tahoe 89520. SAN 370-0445. Tel. 530-542-3000 ext. 2903, fax 530-541-4697.

Western Council of State Libraries, Inc., Nevada State Lib. and Archives, 100 N. Stewart St., Carson City 89701. SAN 322-2314. Tel. 702-687-8315, fax 702-687-8311.

New Hampshire

Carroll County Library Cooperative, Box 240, Madison 03849. SAN 371-8999. Tel. 603-367-8545.

Hillstown Cooperative, 3 Meetinghouse Rd., Bedford 03110. SAN 371-3873. Tel. 603-472-2300, fax 603-472-2978. *Chair* Frances M. Wiggin.

Librarians of the Upper Valley Coop (LUV Coop), Box 1580, Grantham 03753. SAN 371-6856. Tel. 603-863-2172, fax 603-863-2172, e-mail dunbarlib@adelphia.net. *Dir.* Sally Allen.

Merri-Hill-Rock Library Cooperative, Box 190, Hampstead 03841-0190. SAN 329-5338. Tel. 603-329-6411. *Chair* Judi Crowley.

New Hampshire College and University Council, Libs. Committee, 116S River Rd., D4, Bedford 03110. SAN 322-2322. Tel. 603-669-3432, fax 603-623-8182. *Exec. Dir.* Thomas R. Horgan.

Nubanusit Library Cooperative, c/o Peterborough Town Lib., 2 Concord, Peterborough 03458. SAN 322-4600. Tel. 603-924-8040, fax 603-924-8041.

Scrooge and Marley Cooperative, 310 Central St., Franklin 03235. SAN 329-515X. Tel. 603-934-2911.

Seacoast Coop Libraries, North Hampton Public Lib., 235 Atlantic Ave., North Hampton 03862. SAN 322-4619. Tel. 603-964-6326, fax 603-964-1107.

New Jersey

Bergen County Cooperative Library System, 810 Main St., Hackensack 07601. SAN 322-4546. Tel. 201-489-1904, fax 201-489-4215, e-mail bccls@bccls.org. *Exec. Dir.* Robert White.

Bergen Passaic Health Sciences Library Consortium, c/o Englewood Hospital and Medical Center, Health Sciences Lib., 350 Engle St., Englewood 07631. SAN 371-0904. Tel. 201-894-3069, fax 201-894-9049, e-mail lia.sabbagh@ehmc.com.

Central Jersey Health Science Libraries Association, Saint Francis Medical Center Medical Lib., 601 Hamilton Ave., Trenton 08629. SAN 370-0712. Tel. 609-599-5068, fax 609-599-5773.

Central Jersey Regional Library Cooperative, 4400 Route 9 S., Freehold 07728-1383. SAN 370-5102. Tel. 732-409-6484, fax 732-409-6492. *Dir.* Connie Paul.

Cosmopolitan Biomedical Library Consortium, Medical Lib., East Orange General Hospital, 300 Central Ave., East Orange 07019. SAN 322-4414. Tel. 973-266-8519.

Dow Jones Interactive, Box 300, Princeton 08543-0300. SAN 322-404X. Tel. 609-520-4679, fax 609-520-4775.

Health Sciences Library Association of New Jersey (HSLANJ), Saint Michael's Medical Center, 268 Dr. Martin Luther King Blvd., Newark 07102. SAN 370-0488. Tel. 973-877-5471.

Highlands Regional Library Cooperative, 66 Ford Rd., Suite 124, Denville 07834. SAN 329-4609. Tel. 973-664-1776, fax 973-664-1780, e-mail help@hrlc.org.

INFOLINK Eastern New Jersey Regional Library Cooperative, Inc., 44 Stelton Rd., Suite 330, Piscataway 08902. SAN 371-5116. Tel. 732-752-7720, 973-673-2343, fax 732-752-7785, 973-673-2710, e-mail glr@infolink.org. *Exec. Dir.* Charles Dowlin.

Integrated Information Solutions, 600 Mountain Ave., Rm 3A-426, Murray Hill 07974.

SAN 329-5400. Tel. 908-582-4840, fax 908-582-3146, e-mail libnet@library.lucent.com.

LMX Automation Consortium, 1030 Saint George, Suite 203, Avenel 07001. SAN 329-448X. Tel. 732-750-2525, fax 732-750-9392.

Monmouth-Ocean Biomedical Information Consortium (MOBIC), Community Medical Center, 99 Hwy. 37 W., Toms River 08755. SAN 329-5389. Tel. 732-557-8117, fax 732-557-8354, e-mail rreisler@sbhcs.com.

Morris Automated Information Network (MAIN), Box 900, Morristown 07963-0900. SAN 322-4058. Tel. 973-631-5353, fax 973-631-5366.

Morris-Union Federation, 214 Main St., Chatham 07928. SAN 310-2629. Tel. 973-635-0603, fax 973-635-7827.

New Jersey Academic Library Network, c/o College of New Jersey, Roscoe L. West Lib., 2000 Pennington Rd., Box 7718, Ewing 08628-0718. SAN 329-4927. Tel. 609-771-2332, fax 609-637-5177.

New Jersey Health Sciences Library Network (NJHSN), Mountainside Hospital, Health Sciences Lib., Montclair 07042. SAN 371-4829. Tel. 973-429-6240, fax 973-680-7850, e-mail pat.regenberg@ahsys.org.

New Jersey Library Network, Lib. Development Bureau, 185 W. State St., Box 520, Trenton 08625-0520. SAN 372-8161. Tel. 609-984-3293, fax 609-984-7898.

Society for Cooperative Healthcare and Related Education (SCHARE), UMDNJ, 1776 Raritan Rd., Scotch Plains 07076. SAN 371-0718. Tel. 908-889-6410, fax 908-889-2487. *Coord.* Anne Calhoun.

South Jersey Regional Library Cooperative, Paint Works Corporate Center, 10 Foster Ave., Suite F-3, Gibbsboro 08026. SAN 329-4625. Tel. 609-346-1222, fax 609-346-2839. *Exec. Dir.* Karen Hyman.

New Mexico

New Mexico Consortium of Academic Libraries, Dean's Office, Univ. of New Mexico, Albuquerque 87131-1466. SAN 371-6872. Fax 505-277-7288.

New Mexico Consortium of Biomedical and Hospital Libraries, c/o Lovelace Medical

Lib., 5400 Gibson Blvd. S.E., Albuquerque 87108. SAN 322-449X. Tel. 505-262-7158, fax 505-262-7897.

New York

Academic Libraries of Brooklyn, Long Island Univ. Lib.—LLC 517, 1 University Plaza, Brooklyn 11201. SAN 322-2411. Tel. 718-488-1081, fax 715-780-4057. *Pres.* Constance Woo.

American Film and Video Association, Cornell Univ. Resource Center, 8 Business and Tech Park, Ithaca 14850. SAN 377-5860. Tel. 607-255-2090, fax 607-255-9946, e-mail dist_cent@cce.cornell.edu. *Audio Visual* Richard Gray.

Associated Colleges of the Saint Lawrence Valley, State Univ. of New York College at Potsdam, 200 Merritt Hall, Potsdam 13676-2299. SAN 322-242X. Tel. 315-267-3331, fax 315-267-2389. *Exec. Dir.* Anneke Larrance.

Brooklyn-Queens-Staten Island Health Sciences Librarians (BQSI), Saint John's Episcopal Hospital, South Shore Div. Medical Lib., 327 Beach 19 St., Far Rockaway 11691. SAN 370-0828. Tel. 718-869-7699, fax 718-869-8528.

Capital District Library Council for Reference and Research Resources, 28 Essex St., Albany 12206. SAN 322-2446. Tel. 518-438-2500, fax 518-438-2872, e-mail info@cdlc.org. *Exec. Dir.* Jean Sheviak.

Central New York Library Resources Council (CLRC), 3049 E. Genesee St., Syracuse 13224-1690. SAN 322-2454. Tel. 315-446-5446, fax 315-446-5590, e-mail mclane @clrc.org. *Exec. Dir.* Michael McLane.

Consortium of Foundation Libraries, c/o Carnegie Corporation of New York, 437 Madison Ave., 27th fl., New York 10022. SAN 322-2462. Tel. 212-207-6245, fax 212-754-4073, e-mail rs@carnegie.org.

Council of Archives and Research Libraries in Jewish Studies (CARLJS), 330 7th Ave., 21st fl., New York 10001. SAN 371-053X. Tel. 212-629-0500 ext. 215, fax 212-629-0508, e-mail nfjc@jewishculture.org. *Pres.* Zachary Baker.

Educational Film Library Association, c/o AV Resource Center, Cornell Univ., Business and Technology Park, Ithaca 14850.

SAN 371-0874. Tel. 607-255-2090, fax 607-255-9946, e-mail resCenter@cornell. edu. *Audio Visual* Rich Gray.

Library Consortium of Health Institutions in Buffalo, 155 Abbott Hall, SUNY at Buffalo, 3435 Main St., Buffalo 14214. SAN 329-367X. Tel. 716-829-2903, fax 716-829-2211. *Exec. Dir.* Martin E. Mutka.

Long Island Library Resources Council (LILRC), Melville Lib. Bldg., Suite E5310, Stony Brook 11794-3399. SAN 322-2489. Tel. 631-632-6650, fax 631-632-6662. *Dir.* Herbert Biblo.

Manhattan-Bronx Health Sciences Libraries Group, c/o KPR Medical Lib., 333 E. 38 St., New York 10016. SAN 322-2465. Tel. 212-856-8721, fax 212-856-8884.

Medical Library Center of New York, 5 E. 102 St., 7th fl., New York 10029. SAN 322-3957. Tel. 212-427-1630, fax 212-860-3496. *Dir.* William Self.

Medical and Scientific Libraries of Long Island (MEDLI), c/o Palmer School of Lib. and Info. Sciences, C. W. Post Campus, Long Island Univ., Brookville 11548. SAN 322-4309. Tel. 516-299-2866, fax 516-299-4168. *Pres.* Claire Joseph.

Metropolitan New York Library Council (METRO), 57 E. 11 St., 4th fl., New York 10003-4605. SAN 322-2500. Tel. 212-228-2320, fax 212-228-2598.

Middle Atlantic Region National Network of Libraries of Medicine, New York Academy of Medicine, 1216 5th Ave., New York 10029-5293. SAN 322-2497. Tel. 212-822-7396, fax 212-534-7042, e-mail rml@ nyam.org.

New York State Interlibrary Loan Network (NYSILL), c/o New York State Lib., Albany 12230. SAN 322-2519. Tel. 518-474-5129, fax 518-474-5786, e-mail ill@ nysl.nysed.gov.

North Country Reference and Research Resources Council, 7 Commerce Lane, Canton 13617. SAN 322-2527. Tel. 315-386-4569, fax 315-379-9553, e-mail info @northnet.org. *Exec. Dir.* John Hammond.

Northeast Foreign Law Cooperative Group, Fordham Univ., 140 W. 62, New York 10023. SAN 375-0000. Tel. 212-636-6913, fax 212-977-2662.

Research Library Association of South Manhattan, New York Univ., Bobst Lib., 70 Washington Sq. S., New York 10012. SAN 372-8080. Tel. 212-998-2477, fax 212-995-4366. *Coord.* Arno Kastner.

Rochester Regional Library Council (RRLC), 390 Packetts Landing, Box 66160, Fairport 14450-6160. SAN 322-2535. Tel. 716-223-7570, fax 716-223-7712, e-mail rrlc@rrlc.rochester.lib.ny.us. *Dir.* Kathleen Miller.

South Central Regional Library Council, 215 N. Cayuga St., Ithaca 14850. SAN 322-2543. Tel. 607-273-9106, fax 607-272-0740, e-mail scrlc@lakenet.org. *Exec. Dir.* Jean Currie.

Southeastern New York Library Resources Council (SENYLRC), Box 879, Highland 12528-0299. SAN 322-2551. Tel. 845-691-2734, fax 845-691-6987. *Exec. Dir.* John Shaloiko.

State University of New York-NYLINK, SUNY System Admin., State University Plaza, Albany 12246. SAN 322-256X. Tel. 518-443-5444, fax 518-432-4346, e-mail nylink@nylink.suny.edu.

United Nations System Consortium, c/o Dag Hammarskjold Lib., Rm. L-166A, United Nations, New York 10017. SAN 377-855X. Tel. 212-963-5142, fax 212-963-2608. *Coord.* Mary Cherif.

Western New York Library Resources Council, 4455 Genesee St., Box 400, Buffalo 14225-0400. SAN 322-2578. Tel. 716-633-0705, fax 716-633-1736. *Exec. Dir.* Gail Staines.

North Carolina

Cape Fear Health Sciences Information Consortium, Southeastern Regional Medical Center, 300 W. 27 St., Lumberton 28359. SAN 322-3930. Tel. 910-671-5000, fax 910-671-4143.

Consortium of South Eastern Law Libraries, Duke Univ. Law Lib., Towerview Rd. and Science Rd., Box 90361, Durham 27708-0361. SAN 372-8277. Tel. 919-613-7113, fax 919-613-7237.

Microcomputer Users Group for Libraries in North Carolina (MUGLNC), Catawba College, Salisbury 28144. Tel. 704-637-4214. *Pres.* Rodney Lippard.

Mid-Carolina Academic Library Network, Chowan College, 200 Jones Dr., Murfreesboro 27855. SAN 371-3989. Tel. 910-630-7122, fax 910-630-7119.

NC Area Health Education Centers, Health Sciences Lib., CB 7585, Univ. of North Carolina, Chapel Hill 27599-7585. SAN 323-9950. Tel. 919-962-0700, fax 919-966-5592.

North Carolina Community College System, 200 W. Jones St., Raleigh 27603-1379. SAN 322-2594. Tel. 919-733-7051, fax 919-733-0680. *Dir.* Pamela B. Doyle.

North Carolina Library and Information Network, State Lib. of NC, 4640 Mail Service Center, Raleigh 27699-4640. SAN 329-3092. Tel. 919-733-2570, fax 919-733-8748. *State Libn.* Sandra Cooper.

Northwest AHEC Library at Salisbury, c/o Rowan Regional Medical Center, 612 Mocksville Ave., Salisbury 28144. SAN 322-4589. Tel. 704-210-5069, fax 704-636-5050.

Northwest AHEC Library Information Network, Northwest Area Health Education Center—Carpenter Lib., Wake Forest Univ. School of Medicine, Medical Center Blvd., Winston-Salem 27157-1069. SAN 322-4716. Tel. 336-713-7115, fax 336-713-7028.

Unifour Consortium of Health Care and Educational Institutions, c/o Northwest AHEC Lib. at Hickory, Catawba Memorial Hospital, 810 Fairgrove Church Rd., Hickory 28602. SAN 322-4708. Tel. 828-326-3662, fax 828-326-3484. *Dir.* Stephen Johnson.

Western North Carolina Library Network (WNCLN), Univ. of North Carolina at Asheville, D. Hiden Ramsey Lib., 1 University Heights, Asheville 28804-3299. SAN 376-7205. Tel. 828-232-5095, fax 828-251-6012.

North Dakota

Dakota West Cooperating Libraries (DWCL), Mandan County Lib., Mandan 58554. SAN 373-1391.

Tri-College University Libraries Consortium, 209 Engineering Technology, North Dakota State Univ., Fargo 58105. SAN 322-2047. Tel. 701-231-8170, fax 701-231-7205.

Ohio

Central Ohio Hospital Library Consortium, Mount Carmel, 793 W. State St., Columbus 43222-1560. SAN 371-084X. Tel. 614-234-5364, fax 614-234-1257, e-mail cohsla@lists.acs.ohio-state.edu. *Pres.* Fern Cheek.

Cleveland Area Metropolitan Library System (CAMLS), 20600 Chagrin Blvd., Suite 500, Shaker Heights 44122-5334. SAN 322-2632. Tel. 216-921-3900, fax 216-921-7220, e-mail camls@oplin.lib.oh.us. *Exec. Dir.* Michael Snyder.

Columbus Area Library and Information Council of Ohio (CALICO), c/o Westerville Public Lib., 126 S. State St., Westerville 43081. SAN 371-683X. Tel. 614-882-7277, fax 614-882-5369.

Consortium of Popular Culture Collections in the Midwest (CPCCM), c/o Popular Culture Lib., Bowling Green State Univ., Bowling Green 43403-0600. SAN 370-5811. Tel. 419-372-2450, fax 419-372-7996. *Chair* Peter Berg.

Greater Cincinnati Library Consortium, 2181 Victory Pkwy., Suite 214, Cincinnati 45206-2855. SAN 322-2675. Tel. 513-751-4422, fax 513-751-0463, e-mail gclc@gclc-lib.org. *Exec. Dir.* Martha McDonald.

MOLO Regional Library System, 1260 Monroe Ave., New Philadelphia 44663-4147. SAN 322-2705. Tel. 330-364-8535, fax 330-364-8537, e-mail molo@tusco.net.

NEOUCOM Council of Associated Hospital Librarians, Ocasek Regional Medical Info. Center, Box 95, Rootstown 44272-0095. SAN 370-0526. Tel. 330-325-6611, fax 330-325-0522, e-mail lsc@neoucom.cdu.

NOLA Regional Library System, 4445 Mahoning Ave. N.W., Warren 44483. SAN 322-2713. Tel. 330-847-7744, fax 330-847-7704.

Northwest Library District (NORWELD), 181 ½ S. Main St., Bowling Green 43402. SAN 322-273X. Tel. 419-352-2903, fax 419-353-8310.

OCLC Online Computer Library Center, Inc., 6565 Frantz Rd., Dublin 43017-3395. SAN 322-2748. Tel. 614-764-6000, fax 614-764-6096, e-mail oclc@oclc.org. *Pres.* Jay Jordan.

Ohio Library and Information Network (Ohio-LINK), Ohio Lib. Info. Network, 2455 N. Star Rd., Suite 300, Columbus 43221. SAN 374-8014. Tel. 614-728-3600, fax 614-728-3600, e-mail info@ohiolink.edu. *Exec. Dir.* Thomas Sanville.

Ohio Network of American History Research Centers, Ohio Historical Society Archives/Lib., 1982 Velma Ave., Columbus 43211-2497. SAN 323-9624. Tel. 614-297-2510, fax 614-297-2546.

OHIONET, 1500 W. Lane Ave., Columbus 43221-3975. SAN 322-2764. Tel. 614-486-2966, fax 614-486-1527. *Exec. Dir.* Michael Butler.

Southwestern Ohio Council for Higher Education, 3155 Research Blvd., Suite 204, Dayton 45420-4014. SAN 322-2659. Tel. 937-258-8890, fax 937-258-8899, e-mail soche@soche.org.

Oklahoma

Greater Oklahoma Area Health Sciences Library Consortium (GOAL), VA Medical Center—Medical Lib., 921 N.E. 13 St., Oklahoma City 73104. SAN 329-3858. Tel. 405-270-0501 ext. 3688. *Pres.* Sara Hill.

Metropolitan Libraries Network of Central Oklahoma, Inc. (MetroNetwork), 131 Dean A. McGee Ave., Oklahoma City 73102. SAN 372-8137. Tel. 405-231-8602, 733-7323, fax 405-236-5219.

Oklahoma Health Sciences Library Association (OHSLA), Box 26901, Oklahoma City 73126-0901. SAN 375-0051. Tel. 405-271-2285, fax 405-271-3297.

Oregon

Chemeketa Cooperative Regional Library Service, c/o Chemeketa Community College, 4000 Lancaster Dr. N.E., Salem 97309-7070. SAN 322-2837. Tel. 503-399-5105, fax 503-589-7628, e-mail cocl@chemek.cc.or.us. *Coord.* Linda Cochrane.

Coos County Library Service District, Extended Service Office, Tioga 104, 1988 Newmark, Coos Bay 97420. SAN 322-4279. Tel. 541-888-7260, fax 541-888-7285.

Northwest Association of Private Colleges and Universities Libraries (NAPCUL), c/o

D. V. Hurst Lib.—Northwest College, 5520 108th Ave. N.E., Kirkland 98083-0579. SAN 375-5312. Tel. 425-889-5263, fax 425-889-7801. *Pres.* Nola Ware.

Orbis, 1501 Kincaid, Eugene 97403. SAN 377-8096. Tel. 541-346-3049, fax 541-346-1968, e-mail orbis@oregon.uoregon.edu.

Oregon Health Sciences Libraries Association (OHSLA), Oregon Health Science Center Lib., Box 573, Portland 97207. SAN 371-2176. Tel. 503-494-3462. *Pres.* Delores Judkins.

Portland Area Health Sciences Librarians, c/o Legacy Emanuel Lib., 2801 N. Gantenbein, Portland 97227. SAN 371-0912. Tel. 503-413-2558, fax 503-413-2544.

Southern Oregon Library Federation, c/o Klamath County Lib., 126 S. 3 St., Klamath Falls 97601. SAN 322-2861. Tel. 541-882-8894, fax 541-882-6166.

Washington County Cooperative Library Services, 111 N.E. Lincoln St., MS No 58, Hillsboro 97124-3036. SAN 322-287X. Tel. 503-846-3222, fax 503-846-3220.

Pennsylvania

Associated College Libraries of Central Pennsylvania, 400 Saint Bernadine St., Reading 19607. Tel. 717-337-6604, fax 717-337-6666. *Dean* Eugene Mitchell.

Basic Health Sciences Library Network, Latrobe Area Hospital Health Sciences Lib., 121 W. 2 Ave., Latrobe 15650-1096. SAN 371-4888. Tel. 724-537-1275, fax 724-537-1890.

Berks County Library Association (BCLA), Albright College Lib., Box 15234, Reading 19612-5234. SAN 371-0866. Tel. 610-406-9431.

Berks County Public Libraries (BCPL), Agricultural Center, 1238 County Welfare Rd., Box 520, Leesport 19533-0520. SAN 371-8972. Tel. 610-378-5260, fax 610-378-1525, e-mail bcpl@epix.net.

Central Pennsylvania Consortium, Dickinson College, Box 1773, Carlisle 17013-2896. SAN 322-2896. Tel. 717-245-1515, fax 717-245-1807, e-mail freese@dickinson.edu.

Central Pennsylvania Health Science Library Association (CPHSLA), Box 850 HS07, Hershey 17033-0850. SAN 375-5290. Tel.

717-531-4032, fax 717-531-5942, e-mail pmhall@psu.edu.

Consortium for Health Information and Library Services, 1 Medical Center Blvd., Upland 19013-3995. SAN 322-290X. Tel. 610-447-6163, fax 610-447-6164, e-mail ch1@hslc.org. *Exec. Dir.* Barbara R. Devlin.

Cooperating Hospital Libraries of the Lehigh Valley Area, Muhlenberg Hospital Center, 2545 Schoenersville Rd., Bethlehem 18017-7384. SAN 371-0858. Tel. 610-861-2237, fax 610-861-0711.

Delaware Valley Information Consortium, c/o Health Sciences Lib., St. Mary Medical Center, Langhorne-Newtown Rd., Langhorne 19047. Tel. 215-750-2012, fax 215-891-6453. *Dir.* Ann Laliotes.

Eastern Mennonite Associated Libraries and Archives (EMALA), 2215 Millstream Rd., Lancaster 17602. SAN 372-8226. Tel. 717-393-9745, fax 717-393-8751. *Chair* Edsel Burdge.

Erie Area Health Information Library Cooperative (EAHILC), Northwest Medical Center Medical Lib., 1 Spruce St., Franklin 16323. SAN 371-0564. Tel. 814-437-7000, fax 814-437-5023. *Chair* Ann L. Lucas.

Greater Philadelphia Law Library Association (GPLLA), Box 335, Philadelphia 19105. SAN 373-1375. Tel. 215-898-9013, fax 215-99-1020, e-mail gplla-l@hslc.org. *Pres.* Gregory Weyant.

Health Information Library Network of Northeastern Pennsylvania (HILNNEP), c/o Lib. and Info. Services, Moses Taylor Hospital, 745 Quincy Ave., Scranton 18510. Tel. 570-340-2125, fax 570-963-8994. *Chair* Jo-Ann Babish.

Health Sciences Libraries Consortium, 3600 Market St., Suite 550, Philadelphia 19104-2646. SAN 323-9780. Tel. 215-222-1532, fax 215-222-0416, e-mail info@hslc.org. *Exec. Dir.* Joseph C. Scorza.

Interlibrary Delivery Service of Pennsylvania (IDS), c/o Bucks County IU, No. 22, 705 Shady Retreat Rd., Doylestown 18901. SAN 322-2942. Tel. 215-348-2940 ext. 1620, fax 215-348-8315, e-mail ids@bciu.k12.pa.us. *Admin. Dir.* Beverly Carey.

Laurel Highlands Health Sciences Library Consortium, Owen Lib., Rm. 209, Univ. of Pittsburgh, Johnstown 15904. SAN 322-2950. Tel. 814-269-7280, fax 814-266-8230. *Dir.* Heather Brice.

Lehigh Valley Association of Independent Colleges, Inc., 130 W. Greenwich St., Bethlehem 18018. SAN 322-2969. Tel. 610-625-7888, fax 610-625-7891. *Exec. Dir.* Tom Tenges.

Neiu Consortium, 1200 Line St., Archbald 18403. SAN 372-817X. Tel. 717-876-9268, fax 717-876-8663.

Northeastern Pennsylvania Library Network, c/o Marywood Univ. Lib., 2300 Adams Ave., Scranton 18509-1598. SAN 322-2993. Tel. 570-348-6260, fax 570-961-4769. *Dir.* Catherine Schappert.

Northwest Interlibrary Cooperative of Pennsylvania (NICOP), Erie County Public Lib., 160 E. Front St., Erie 16507-1554. SAN 370-5862. Tel. 814-451-6920, fax 814-451-6907.

PALINET and Union Library Catalogue of Pennsylvania, 3401 Market St., Suite 262, Philadelphia 19104. SAN 322-3000. Tel. 215-382-7031, fax 215-382-0022, e-mail palinet@palinet.org. *Exec. Dir.* Bernadette Freedman.

Pennsylvania Citizens for Better Libraries (PCBL), 806 West St., Homestead 15120. SAN 372-8285. Tel. 412-461-1322, fax 412-461-1250.

Pennsylvania Community College Library Consortium, 1333 S. Prospect St., Nanticoke 18634. SAN 329-3939. Tel. 570-740-0415, fax 570-735-6130. *Exec. Dir.* Joan Johnson.

Pennsylvania Library Association, 3905 N. Front St., Harrisburg 17110. SAN 372-8145. Tel. 717-233-3113, fax 717-233-3121. *Exec. Dir.* Glenn Miller.

Philadelphia Area Consortium of Special Collections Libraries (PACSCL), Dept. of Special Collections, Bryn Mawr Lib., 101 N. Merion Ave., Bryn Mawr 19010. SAN 370-7504. Tel. 610-526-5272.

Southeastern Pennsylvania Theological Library Association (SEPTLA), c/o St. Charles Borromeo Seminary, Ryan Memorial Lib., 100 E. Wynnewood Rd., Wynnewood 19096-3012. SAN 371-0793. Tel.

610-667-3394, fax 610-664-7913, e-mail ebasemlib@ebts.edu or stcthelib@hslc.org.

State System of Higher Education Libraries Council (SSHELCO), c/o Bailey Lib., Slippery Rock Univ. of Pa, Slippery Rock 16057. Tel. 724-738-2630, fax 724-738-2661. *Dir.* Barbara Farah.

Susquehanna Library Cooperative, College Lib., Pennsylvania College of Technology, 1 College Ave., Williamsport 17701-5799. SAN 322-3051. Tel. 570-327-4523. *Chair* Mary Sieminski.

Tri-County Library Consortium, c/o New Castle Public Lib., 207 E. North St., New Castle 16101. SAN 322-306X. Tel. 724-658-6659, fax 724-658-9012. *Dir.* Susan E. Walls.

Tri-State College Library Cooperative (TCLC), c/o Rosemont College Lib., 1400 Montgomery Ave., Rosemont 19010-1699. SAN 322-3078. Tel. 610-525-0796, fax 610-525-1939, e-mail tclc@hslc.org. *Coord.* Ellen Gasiewski.

Rhode Island

Consortium of Rhode Island Academic and Research Libraries (CRIARL), Box 40041, Providence 02940-0041. SAN 322-3086. Tel. 401-863-2162, fax 401-863-1272. *Pres.* Merrily Taylor.

Cooperating Libraries Automated Network (CLAN), 600 Sandy Lane, Warwick 02886. SAN 329-4560. Tel. 401-738-2200, fax 401-736-8949. *Chair* Deborah Barchi.

Library of Rhode Island (LORI), c/o Office of Lib. and Info. Services, 1 Capitol Hill, 4th fl., Providence 02908-5870. SAN 371-6821. Tel. 401-222-2726, fax 401-222-4195.

South Carolina

Catawba-Wateree Area Health Education Consortium, 1228 Colonial Commons, Box 2049, Lancaster 29721. SAN 329-3971. Tel. 803-286-4121, fax 803-286-4165.

Charleston Academic Libraries Consortium, Trident Technical College, Learning Resources Centers, Charleston 29423. SAN 371-0769. Tel. 843-574-6095, fax 843-574-6484. *Chair* Sandra Winecoff.

Columbia Area Medical Librarians' Association (CAMLA), Professional Lib., 1800 Colonial Dr., Box 202, Columbia 29202. SAN 372-9400. Tel. 803-898-1735, fax 803-898-1712. *Coord.* Neeta N. Shah.

South Carolina AHEC, c/o Medical Univ. of SC, 171 Ashley Ave., Charleston 29425. SAN 329-3998. Tel. 843-792-4431, fax 843-792-4430. *Exec. Dir.* Sabra C. Slaughter.

South Carolina Library Network, 1500 Senate St., Box 11469, Columbia 29211-1469. SAN 322-4198. Tel. 803-734-8666, fax 803-734-8676. *State Libn.* James Johnson.

South Dakota

South Dakota Library Network (SDLN), University Sta., Box 9672, Spearfish 57799-9672. SAN 371-2117. Tel. 605-642-6835, fax 605-642-6298.

Tennessee

Association of Memphis Area Health Science Libraries (AMAHSL), c/o Univ. of Tennessee Health Sciences Lib., 877 Madison Ave., Memphis 38163. SAN 323-9802. Tel. 901-726-8862, fax 901-726-8807. *Asst. Prof., Special Collections* Richard Nollan.

Consortium of Southern Biomedical Libraries (CONBLS), Meharry Medical College, 1005 Dr. D. B. Todd Blvd., Nashville 37208. SAN 370-7717. Tel. 615-327-6728, fax 615-321-2932.

Knoxville Area Health Sciences Library Consortium (KAHSLC), Univ. of Tennessee Medical Center, 1924 Alcoa Hwy., Knoxville 37920. SAN 371-0556. Tel. 865-544-9528.

Mid-Tennessee Health Science Librarians Association, VA Medical Center, Murfreesboro 37129. SAN 329-5028. Tel. 615-867-6142, fax 615-867-5778.

Tennessee Health Science Library Association (THeSLA), Holston Valley Medical Center Health Sciences Lib., Box 238, Kingsport 37662. SAN 371-0726. Tel. 423-224-6870, fax 423-224-6014, e-mail sharon_m_brown@wellmont.org.

Tri-Cities Area Health Sciences Libraries Consortium, East Tennessee State Univ., James H. Quillen College of Medicine, Medical Lib., Box 70693, Johnson City 37614-0693. SAN 329-4099. Tel. 423-439-6252, fax 423-439-7025. *Pres.* Annis Evans.

West Tennessee Academic Library Consortium, Loden-Daniel Lib., Freed-Hardeman Univ., 158 E. Main St., Henderson 38340-2399. SAN 322-3175. Tel. 901-989-6067. *Chair* Hope Shull.

Texas

Abilene Library Consortium, 241 Pine St., Suite 15C, Abilene 79601. SAN 322-4694. Tel. 915-672-7081, fax 915-672-7084. *Exec. Dir.* Robert Gillette.

Alliance for Higher Education (AHE), 2602 Rutford Ave., Richardson 75080-1470. SAN 322-3337. Tel. 972-713-8170, fax 972-713-8209.

AMIGOS Library Services, Inc., 14400 Midway Rd., Dallas 75244-3509. SAN 322-3191. Tel. 972-851-8000, fax 972-991-6061, e-mail amigos@amigos.org. *Exec. Dir.* Bonnie Juergens.

APLIC International Census Network, c/o Population Research Center (PRC), 1800 Main Bldg., Univ. of Texas, Austin 78712. SAN 370-0690. Tel. 512-471-5514, fax 512-471-4886.

Council of Research and Academic Libraries (CORAL), Box 290236, San Antonio 78280-1636. SAN 322-3213.

Del Norte Biosciences Library Consortium, c/o Reference Dept. Lib., Univ. of Texas at El Paso, 500 W. University, El Paso 79968. SAN 322-3302. Tel. 915-747-6714, fax 915-747-5327.

Forest Trail Library Consortium, Inc. (FTLC), Tyler Junior College, Vaugun Lib., Box 9020, Tyler 75711. SAN 374-6283. Tel. 903-510-2759.

Harrington Library Consortium, Box 447, Amarillo 79178. Tel. 806-371-5135, fax 806-371-5119.

Health Library Information Network, John Peter Smith Hospital Lib., 1500 S. Main St., Fort Worth 76104. SAN 322-3299. Tel. 817-921-3431 ext. 5088, fax 817-923-0718.

Houston Area Research Library Consortium (HARLiC), c/o Houston Public Lib., 500 McKinney, Houston 77002. SAN 322-3329. Tel. 713-247-2700, fax 713-247-1266.

National Network of Libraries of Medicine—South Central Region, c/o HAM-TMC Lib., 1133 John Freeman Blvd., Houston 77030-2809. SAN 322-3353. Tel. 713-799-7880, fax 713-790-7030, e-mail nnlmscr@library.tmc.edu. *Assoc. Dir.* Renee Bougard.

Northeast Texas Library System (NETLS), 625 Austin, Garland 75040-6365. SAN 370-5943. Tel. 972-205-2566, fax 972-205-2767. *Dir.* Claire Bausch.

Piasano Consortium, Victoria College, Univ. of Houston, Victoria Lib., 2602 N. Ben Jordan, Victoria 77901-5699. SAN 329-4943. Tel. 512-573-3291, 576-3151, fax 512-788-6227. *Coord.* Joe Dahlstrom.

South Central Academic Medical Libraries Consortium (SCAMEL), c/o Lewis Lib./UNTHSC, 3500 Camp Bowie Blvd., Fort Worth 76107. SAN 372-8269. Tel. 817-735-2380, fax 817-735-5158. *Chair* Richard C. Wood.

Texas Council of State University Librarians, Univ. of Texas—Health Science Center at San Antonio, 7703 Floyd Curl Dr., San Antonio 78284-7940. SAN 322-337X. Tel. 210-567-2400, fax 210-567-2490. *Dir.* Virginia Bowden.

Texnet, Box 12927, Austin 78711. SAN 322-3396. Tel. 512-463-5406, fax 512-936-2306, e-mail rlinton@tsl.state.tx.us.

Utah

Forest Service Library Network, Rocky Mountain Research Station, 324 25th St., Ogden 84401. SAN 322-032X. Tel. 801-625-5445, fax 801-625-5129, e-mail rmrs_library@fs.fed.us.

National Network of Libraries of Medicine—Midcontinental Region, Spencer S. Eccles Health Sciences Lib., Univ. of Utah, 10 N. 1900 E., Bldg. 589, Salt Lake City 84112-5890. SAN 322-225X. Tel. 801-587-3412, fax 402-559-5482. *Dir.* Wayne Peay.

Utah Academic Library Consortium (UALC), Marriott Lib., Univ. of Utah, Salt Lake City 84112-0860. SAN 322-3418. Tel. 801-581-8558, fax 801-581-3997. *Chair* Wayne Peay.

Utah Health Sciences Library Consortium, c/o Eccles Health Science Lib., Univ. of Utah, Salt Lake City 84112. SAN 376-2246. Tel. 801-581-8771, fax 801-581-3632.

Vermont

Health Science Libraries of New Hampshire and Vermont (HSL-NH-VT), c/o Archivist, Dana Medical Lib., Univ. of Vermont, Burlington 05405. SAN 371-6864. Tel. 802-656-2200, fax 802-656-0762. *Pres.* Norma Phillips.

Vermont Resource Sharing Network, c/o Vermont Dept. of Libs., 109 State St., Montpelier 05609-0601. SAN 322-3426. Tel. 802-828-3261, fax 802-828-2199. *Dir. Lib. Services* Marjorie Zunder.

Virginia

American Indian Higher Education Consortium (AIHEC), c/o AIHEC, 121 Oronoco St., Alexandria 22314. SAN 329-4056. Tel. 703-838-0400, fax 703-838-0388, e-mail aihec@aihec.org. *Pres.* James Shanley.

Defense Technical Information Center, 8725 John J. Kingman Rd., Suite 0944, Fort Belvoir 22060-6218. SAN 322-3442. Tel. 703-767-9100, fax 703-767-9183.

Interlibrary Users Association (IUA), c/o Litton PRC, 1500 PRC Dr., McLean 22102. SAN 322-1628. Tel. 703-556-1166, fax 703-883-5071. *Pres.* Barbara Kopp.

Lynchburg Area Library Cooperative, Bedford Public Lib., 321 N. Bridge St., Bedford 24523. SAN 322-3450. Tel. 540-586-8911, fax 540-586-7280.

Lynchburg Information Online Network/LION Consortium of Virginia, 2315 Memorial Ave., Lynchburg 24503. SAN 374-6097. Tel. 434-381-6311, fax 434-381-6173. *Dir.* John Jaffe.

NASA Libraries Information System—NASA Galaxie, NASA Langley Research Center, MS 185-Technical Lib., Hampton 23681-0001. SAN 322-0788. Tel. 757-864-2392, fax 757-864-2375.

Richmond Academic Library Consortium, Richard Bland College Lib., 11301 Johnson Rd., Petersburg 23805. SAN 322-3469. Tel. 804-862-6226, fax 804-862-6125. *Pres.* Virginia Cherry.

Richmond Academic Library Consortium (RALC), J. Tyler Community College, 13101 Jefferson Davis Hwy., Chester 23831. SAN 371-3938. Tel. 804-796-4070, fax 804-796-4238. *Dir.* Arthur McKinney.

Southside Virginia Library Network (SVLN), Longwood College, 201 High St., Farmville 23909-1897. SAN 372-8242. Tel. 804-395-2633, fax 804-395-2453. *Dir.* Calvin J. Boyer.

Southwestern Virginia Health Information Librarians (SWVAHILI), Box 800722, Health System, Charlottesville 22908. SAN 323-9527. Tel. 804-799-4418, fax 804-799-2255. *Chair* Elaine Banner.

United States Army Training and Doctrine Command (TRADOC), Lib. Program Office, ATBO-FL, Bldg. 5A, Rm. 102, Fort Monroe 23651-5000. SAN 322-418X. Tel. 757-727-4096, fax 757-728-5300.

Virginia Independent College and University Library Association, c/o Mary Helen Cochran Lib., Sweet Briar College, Sweet Briar 24595. SAN 374-6089. Tel. 804-381-6139, fax 804-381-6173.

Virginia Tidewater Consortium for Higher Education, 5215 Hampton Blvd., William Spong Hall, Rm. 129, Norfolk 23529-0293. SAN 329-5486. Tel. 757-683-3183, fax 757-683-4515, e-mail lgdotolo@aol.com. *Pres.* Lawrence G. Dotolo.

Washington

Consortium for Automated Library Services (CALS), Evergreen State College Lib. L2300, Olympia 98505. SAN 329-4528. Tel. 360-866-6000 ext. 6260, fax 360-866-6790. *System Coord.* Steve Metcalf.

Inland Northwest Health Sciences Libraries (INWHSL), Box 10283, Spokane 99209-0283. SAN 370-5099. Tel. 509-324-7344, fax 509-324-7349.

Inland Northwest Library Automation Network (INLAN), Foley Center, Gonzaga Univ., Spokane 99258. SAN 375-0124. Tel. 509-323-6535, fax 509-323-5398, 509-323-5904. *Asst. Dean* Kathleen O'Connor.

National Network of Libraries of Medicine— Pacific Northwest Region (NN-LM PNR), Univ. of Washington, Box 357155, Seattle 98195-7155. SAN 322-3485. Tel. 206-543-8262, fax 206-543-2469, e-mail nnlm@u.washington.edu. *Dir.* Sherrilynne Fuller.

OCLC Lacey Product Center, 4224 6th Ave. S.E., Bldg. 3, Lacey 98503. SAN 322-3507. Tel. 360-923-4000, fax 360-923-4009.

Palouse Area Library Information Services (PALIS), c/o Neill Public Lib., 210 N. Grand Ave., Pullman 99163. SAN 375-0132. Tel. 509-334-3595, fax 509-334-6051. *Dir.* Mike Pollastro.

West Virginia

Huntington Health Science Library Consortium, Marshall Univ. Health Science Libs., 1600 Medical Center Dr., Suite 2400, Huntington 25701-3655. SAN 322-4295. Tel. 304-691-1753, fax 304-691-1766.

Mid-Atlantic Law Library Cooperative (MALLCO), West Virginia Univ., College of Law Lib., Morgantown 26501. SAN 371-0645. Tel. 304-293-7641.

Mountain States Consortium, c/o Alderson Broaddus College, Philippi 26416. SAN 329-4765. Tel. 304-457-1700, fax 304-457-6239.

Southern West Virginia Library Automation Corporation, 221 N. Kanawha St., Box 1876, Beckley 25802. SAN 322-421X. Tel. 304-255-0511, fax 304-255-9161.

Wisconsin

Fox River Valley Area Library Consortium, Moraine Park Technical College, 235 N. National Ave., Fond du Lac 54935. SAN 322-3531. Tel. 920-924-3112, fax 920-924-3117.

Fox Valley Library Council (FVLC), c/o Owls, Fox Valley Lib. Council, 225 N. Oneida St., Appleton 54911. SAN 323-9640. Tel. 920-832-6190, fax 920-832-6422. *Pres.* Craig Lahm.

Library Council of Metropolitan Milwaukee, Inc., 814 W. Wisconsin Ave., Milwaukee 53233-2309. SAN 322-354X. Tel. 414-271-8470, fax 414-286-2794.

North East Wisconsin Intertype Libraries, Inc. (NEWIL), 515 Pine St., Green Bay 54301. SAN 322-3574. Tel. 920-448-4412, fax 920-448-4420. *Coord.* Terrie Howe.

Northwestern Wisconsin Health Science Library Consortium, Wausau Hospital, 333 Pine Ridge Blvd., Wausau 54401. Tel. 715-847-2184, fax 715-847-2183.

South Central Wisconsin Health Science Library Consortium, c/o FAMHS Medical Lib., 611 Sherman Ave. E., Fort Atkinson

53538. SAN 322-4686. Tel. 920-568-5194, fax 920-568-5195.

Southeastern Wisconsin Health Science Library Consortium, Convenant Healthcare Systems Lib., 5000 W. Chambers, Milwaukee 53210. SAN 322-3582. Tel. 414-447-2194, fax 414-447-2128.

Southeastern Wisconsin Information Technology Exchange, Inc. (SWITCH), 6801 N. Yates Rd., Milwaukee 53217-3985. SAN 371-3962. Tel. 414-351-2423, fax 414-228-4146. *Exec. Dir.* Jack Fritts.

Wisconsin Area Research Center Network ARC Network, State Historical Society of Wisconsin, 816 State St., Madison 53706. SAN 373-0875. Tel. 608-264-6477, fax 608-264-6486. *Dir.* Richard Pifer.

Wisconsin Library Services, 728 State St., Rm. 464, Madison 53706-1494. SAN 322-3612. Tel. 608-263-4962, fax 608-292-6067. *Dir.* Kathryn Michaelis.

Wisconsin Valley Library Service (WVLS), 300 N. 1 St., Wausau 54403. SAN 371-3911. Tel. 715-261-7250, fax 715-261-7259. *Dir.* Heather Eldred.

Wyoming

University of Wyoming Information Network Plus, Univ. of Wyoming Libs. (UWIN Plus), 112 Coe Lib., Box 3334, Laramie 82071. SAN 371-4861. Tel. 307-766-6537, fax 307-766-3062, e-mail uwinplus@uwyo.edu. *Coord.* Mary Henning.

WYLD Network, c/o Wyoming State Lib., 2301 Capitol Ave., Cheyenne 82002-0060. SAN 371-0661. Tel. 307-777-6339, fax 307-777-6289. *State Libn.* Lesley Boughton.

Virgin Islands

VILINET (Virgin Islands Library and Information Network), c/o Division of Libs., Museums and Archives, 23 Dronningens Gade, Saint Thomas 00802. SAN 322-3639. Tel. 340-774-3407, fax 340-775-1887.

Canada

Alberta

Alberta Association of College Librarians (AACL), Northern Lakes College Lesser Slave Lake, 201 Main St. S.E., Alberta T0G 2A3. SAN 370-0763. Tel. 403-849-8671, fax 403-849-2570.

Alberta Government Libraries Council (AGLC), 10025 Jasper Ave., Box 1360, Edmonton T5J 2N3. SAN 370-0372. Tel. 780-415-0228, fax 780-422-9694.

Northern Alberta Health Libraries Association (NAHLA), 11620 168th St. N.W., Edmonton T5M 4A6. SAN 370-5951. Tel. 780-492-7948, e-mail lmychaj@nurses.ab.ca.

British Columbia

British Columbia College and Institute Library Services, Langara College Lib., 100 W. 49 Ave., Vancouver V5Y 2Z6. SAN 329-6970. Tel. 604-323-5237, fax 604-323-5544, e-mail cils@langara.bc.ca. *Dir.* Mary Epp.

Manitoba

Manitoba Government Libraries Council (MGLC), c/o 250-240 Graham Ave., Winnipeg R3C 4B3. SAN 371-6848. Tel. 204-984-0779, fax 204-983-3852, e-mail giesbrecht.john@bsc.ic.ic.gc.ca.

Manitoba Library Consortium, Inc. (MLCI), c/o Lib. Admin., Univ. of Winnipeg, 515 Pontage Ave., Winnipeg R3B 2E9. SAN 372-820X. Tel. 204-945-1413, fax 204-783-8910. *Chair* Betty Dearth.

New Brunswick

Maritimes Health Libraries Association (MHLA-ABSM), c/o Region 7 Hospital Corp., 500 Water St., Miramich E1V 3G5. SAN 370-0836. Tel. 506-623-3215, fax 506-623-3280. *Pres.* Nancy McAllister.

Nova Scotia

NOVANET, 1550 Bedford Hwy., No. 501, Bedford B4A 1E6. SAN 372-4050. Tel. 902-453-2461, fax 902-453-2369. *Exec. Dir.* William Birdsall.

Ontario

Bibliocentre, 80 Cowdray Court, Scarborough M1S 4N1. SAN 322-3663. Tel. 416-289-5151, fax 416-299-4841. *Exec. Dir.* Janice Hayes.

Canadian Agriculture Library System, Sir John Carling Bldg., 930 Carling Ave.,

Ottawa K1A 0C5. SAN 377-5054. Tel. 613-759-7068, fax 613-759-6627, e-mail cal-bca@em.agr.ca.

Canadian Association of Research Libraries/ Association des Bibliothèques de Recherche du Canada, Morisset Hall, Rm. 239, 65 University St., Ottawa K1N 9A5. SAN 323-9721. Tel. 613-562-5800 ext. 3652, fax 613-562-5195, e-mail carladm@ uottawa.ca. *Exec. Dir.* Timothy Mark.

Canadian Health Libraries Association (CHLA-ABSC), Box 94038, Toronto M4N 3R1. SAN 370-0720. Tel. 416-485-0377, fax 416-485-6877, e-mail chla@inforamp. net. *Pres.* Patrick Ellis.

Hamilton and District Health Library Network, c/o St. Joseph's Hospital, 50 Charlton Ave. E., Hamilton L8N 4A6. SAN 370-5846. Tel. 905-522-1155 ext. 3410, fax 905-540-6504. *Coord.* Jean Maragno.

Health Science Information Consortium of Toronto, c/o Gerstein Science Info. Center, Univ. of Toronto, 7 King's College Circle, Toronto M5S 1A5. SAN 370-5080. Tel. 416-978-6359, fax 416-971-2637, e-mail laurie.scott@utoronto.ca.

Information Network for Ontario Ministry of Tourism, Culture and Recreation, 400 University Ave., 4th fl., Toronto M7A 2R9. SAN 329-5605. Tel. 416-314-7342, fax 416-314-7635. *Dir.* Michael Langford.

Ontario Health Libraries Association (OHLA), Lib., Sarnia General Hospital, 220 N. Mitton St., Sarnia N7T 6H6. SAN 370-0739. Tel. 519-464-4500 ext. 5251, fax 519-464-4511.

Quicklaw Inc., 275 Sparks St., Suite 901, Ottawa K1R 7X9. SAN 322-368X. Tel. 613-238-3499, fax 613-238-7597, e-mail adingle@quicklaw.com.

Shared Library Services (SLS), South Huron Hospital, 24 Huron St. W., Exeter N0M 1S2. SAN 323-9500. Tel. 519-235-4002 ext. 249, fax 519-235-4476, e-mail shha. sls@hphp.org.

Sheridan Park Association, Lib. and Info. Science Committee (SPA-LISC), 2275 Speakman Dr., Mississauga L5K 1B1. SAN 370-0437. Tel. 905-823-6160, fax 905-823-6161, e-mail spamgr@interlog. com. *Mgr.* Cindy Smith.

Toronto Health Libraries Association (THLA), Box 94056, Toronto M4N 3R1. SAN 323-9853. Tel. 416-485-0377, fax 416-485-6877.

Toronto School of Theology, 47 Queen's Park Crescent E., Toronto M5S 2C3. SAN 322-452X. Tel. 416-978-4039, fax 416-978-7821. *Chair* Douglas Fox.

Quebec

Association des Bibliothèques de la Santé Affiliées a l'Université de Montréal (ABSAUM), c/o Health Lib., Box 6128 Sta. Downtown, Montréal H3C 3J7. SAN 370-5838. Tel. 514-343-6826, fax 514-343-2350.

Canadian Heritage Information Network (CHIN), 15 Eddy St., 4th fl., Hull K1A 0M5. SAN 329-3076. Tel. 819-994-1200, fax 819-994-9555, e-mail service@chin. gc.ca. *Libn.* Vicki Davis.

Saskatchewan

Saskatchewan Government Libraries Council (SGLC), c/o Saskatchewan Agriculture and Food Lib., 3085 Albert St., Regina S4S 0B1. SAN 323-956X. Tel. 306-787-5151, fax 306-787-0216.

National Library and Information-Industry Associations, United States and Canada

American Association of Law Libraries

Executive Director, Roger Parent
53 W. Jackson Blvd., Suite 940, Chicago, IL 60604
312-939-4764, fax 312-431-1097
World Wide Web http://www.aallnet.org

Object

The American Association of Law Libraries (AALL) is established for educational and scientific purposes. It shall be conducted as a nonprofit corporation to promote and enhance the value of law libraries to the public, the legal community, and the world; to foster the profession of law librarianship; to provide leadership in the field of legal information; and to foster a spirit of cooperation among the members of the profession. Established 1906.

Membership

Memb. 5,000+. Persons officially connected with a law library or with a law section of a state or general library, separately maintained. Associate membership available for others. Dues (Indiv., Indiv. Assoc., and Inst.) $133; (Inst. Assoc.) $256 times the number of members; (Retired) $32.50; (Student) $30; (SIS Memb.) $12 each per year. Year. July 1–June 30.

Officers

Pres. Barbara A. Bintliff, Univ. of Colorado Law Lib., CB402, Fleming Law Bldg., Rm. 190, 2405 Kittredge Loop Dr., Boulder, CO 80309-0402. Tel. 303-492-1233, fax 303-492-2707, e-mail barbara.bintliff@colorado.edu; *V.P.* Carol Avery Nicholson; *Past Pres.* Robert L. Oakley; *Secy.* Karl T. Gruben; *Treas.* Anne C. Matthewman.

Executive Board

Elmer F. Dattalo (2003), James E. Duggan (2004), Sarah G. Holterhoff (2003), Alvin M. Podboy, Jr. (2004), Maryruth Storer (2002), Cossette T. Sun (2002).

Committees

Access to Electronic Legal Information.
AALL LexisNexis Call for Papers Committee.
AALLNET (Advisory).
Annual Meeting Program.
Authentication & Preservation of Digital Law (Special).
Awards.
Bylaws.
Citation Formats.
Copyright.
Relations with Information Vendors.
Develop Performance Measurements for Law Librarians (Special)
Diversity.
Economic Study (Advisory).
Election Procedures (Special).
Executive Board Finance and Budget.
Executive Board Governance.
Executive Board Strategic Planning
Fair Business Practices (Special).
Future of Law Libraries in the Digital Age (Special).
Government Relations.
Grants.
Indexing of Periodical Literature (Advisory).
Membership and Retention.
Nominations.
Placement.
Price Index for Legal Publications.
Professional Development.
Public Relations.
Publications.
Recruitment to Law Librarianship.
Research.
Scholarships.

American Library Association

Executive Director, William R. Gordon
50 E. Huron St., Chicago, IL 60611
800-545-2433, 312-280-3215, fax 312-944-3897
World Wide Web http://www.ala.org

Object

The mission of the American Library Association (ALA) is to provide leadership for the development, promotion, and improvement of library and information services and the profession of librarianship in order to enhance learning and ensure access to information for all. Founded 1876.

Membership

Memb. (Indiv.) 58,879; (Inst.) 5,392; (Total) 64,271 (as of August 31, 2001). Any person, library, or other organization interested in library service and librarians. Dues (Indiv.) 1st year, $50; 2nd year, $75, 3rd year and later, $100; (Trustee and Assoc. Memb.) $45; (Student) $25; (Foreign Indiv.) $60; (Other) $35; (Inst.) $110 and up, depending on operating expenses of institution.

Officers (2001–2002)

Pres. John W. Berry, Exec. Dir., NILRC: A Consortium of Midwest Community Colleges, Colleges and Universities, Box 390, Sugar Grove, IL 60554. Tel. 708-366-0667, fax 708-366-0728, e-mail jberry@psinet.com; *Pres.-Elect* Maurice J. "Mitch" Freedman, Westchester Lib. System, 410 Saw Mill River Rd., Ardsley, NY 10549. Tel. 914-674-3600 ext. 223, fax 914-674-4185, e-mail freedman@wlsmail.org; *Immediate Past Pres.* Nancy C. Kranich, 334 W. 89 St., No. 4R, New York, NY 10024. Tel. 212-998-2447, e-mail nancy.kranich@nyu.edu; *Treas.* Lizbeth Bishoff, Colorado Digitization Project, Univ. of Denver, Penrose Lib., 2150 E. Evans Ave., Denver, CO 80208-2007. Tel. 303-871-2006, fax. 303-871-2290, e-mail bishoffl@concentric.net; *Exec. Dir.* William R. Gordon, ALA Headquarters, 50 E. Huron St., Chicago, IL 60611. Tel. 312-280-3215, fax 312-944-3897, e-mail wgordon@ala.org.

Executive Board

Camila A. Alire (2003), Alice M. Calabrese (2002), Julie Cummins (2002), Ken Haycock (2003), Kenton L. Oliver (2004), Mary E. "Molly" Raphael (2003), Barbara K. Stripling (2002), Patricia M. "Patty" Wong (2004).

Endowment Trustees

Martin Gomez, Rick J. Schwieterman, Carla J. Stoffle; *Exec. Board Liaison* Lizbeth Bishoff; *Staff Liaison* Gregory L. Calloway.

Divisions

See the separate entries that follow: American Assn. of School Libns.; Assn. for Lib. Trustees and Advocates; Assn. for Lib. Collections and Technical Services; Assn. for Lib. Service to Children; Assn. of College and Research Libs.; Assn. of Specialized and Cooperative Lib. Agencies; Lib. Admin. and Management Assn.; Lib. and Info. Technology Assn.; Public Lib. Assn.; Reference and User Services Assn.; Young Adult Lib. Services Assn.

Publications

ALA Handbook of Organization (ann.).
American Libraries (11 a year; memb.; organizations $60; foreign $70; single copy $6).
Book Links (6 a year; U.S. $27.95; foreign $35; single copy $6).
Booklist (22 a year; U.S. and possessions $79.95; foreign $95; single copy $6).

Round Table Chairpersons

(ALA staff liaison is given in parentheses.)
Continuing Library Education Network and Exchange. Katherine Schalk (Lorelle R. Swader).

Ethnic and Multicultural Information Exchange. Olga R. Kuharets (Satia Orange).

Exhibits. Kathy Young (Deidre Ross).

Federal and Armed Forces Libraries. Jewel Armstrong Player (Patricia May, Reginald Scott).

Gay, Lesbian, Bisexual, Transgendered. Faye A. Chadwell, Stephen E. Stratton (Satia Orange).

Government Documents. Cynthia J. Wolff (Patricia May, Reginald Scott).

Intellectual Freedom. Carrie Gardner (Don Wood).

International Relations. H. Lea Wells (Michael Dowling).

Library History. Michele V. Cloonan (Mary Jo Lynch).

Library Instruction. Linda L. Chopa (Lorelle R. Swader).

Library Research. Thomas E. Nisonger (Mary Jo Lynch).

Map and Geography. Mark A. Thomas (Danielle M. Alderson).

New Members. Dora Ho (Gerald G. Hodges).

Social Responsibilities. Frederick W. Stoss (Satia Orange).

Staff Organizations. Leon S. Bey (Lorelle R. Swader).

Support Staff Interests. Martha J. Parsons (Lorelle R. Swader).

Video. Gary P. Handman (Danielle M. Alderson).

Committee Chairpersons

(ALA staff liaison is given in parentheses.)

Accreditation (Standing). Jane Robbins (Ann L. O'Neill).

American Libraries Advisory (Standing). Patricia M. Hogan (Leonard Kniffel).

Appointments (Standing). Maurice J. Freedman (Elizabeth Dreazen, Lois Ann Gregory-Wood).

Awards (Standing). Robert Newlen. (Cheryl Malden).

Budget Analysis and Review (Standing). Patricia H. Smith (Gregory Calloway).

Chapter Relations (Standing). Kathy Ann East (Gerald G. Hodges).

Committee on Committees (Elected Council Committee). Maurice J.Freedman (Elizabeth Dreazen, Lois Ann Gregory-Wood).

Conference Committee (Standing). Ann K. Symons (Mary W. Ghikas, Deidre Ross).

Conference Program Coordinating Team, 2002. Thomas L. Wilding (Mary W. Ghikas, Deidre Ross).

Conference Program Coordinating Team, 2003. Sarah E. Hamrick (Mary W. Ghikas, Deidre Ross).

Constitution and Bylaws (Standing). Donald J. Sager (Linda Mays).

Council Orientation (Standing). Elizabeth E. Bingham (Lois Ann Gregory-Wood).

Education (Standing). E. Blanche Woolls (Lorelle R. Swader).

Election (Standing). Ernest Martin (to be appointed).

E-Rate (task force) Nancy M. Bolt (Saundra Shirley).

Human Resource Development and Recruitment (Standing). Jan E. Hayes (Lorelle R. Swader).

Information Technology Policy Advisory. Linda D. Crowe (Frederick Weingarten).

Intellectual Freedom (Standing). Margo Crist (Judith F. Krug).

International Relations (Standing). Nancy R. John (Michael Dowling).

Legislation (Standing). Sharon A. Hogan (Lynn Bradley).

Literacy and Outreach Services Advisory (Standing). Clara M. Chu (Satia Orange).

Membership (Standing). Marianne Hartzell (Gerald G. Hodges).

Membership Meeting Quorum (special presidential task force). Larry Romans (Lois Ann Gregory-Wood).

Membership Meetings (special presidential task force). Michael A. Golrick (Lois Ann Gregory-Wood).

Minority Concerns and Cultural Diversity (Standing). Rhea Brown Lawson (Sandra Rios Balderrama).

Nominating 2002 Election (Special). Barbara J. Ford (Elizabeth Dreazen).

Organization (Standing). James R. Rettig (Lois Ann Gregory-Wood).

Orientation, Training and Leadership Development. Karen E. Downing (Dorothy A. Ragsdale).

Pay Equity (Standing). E. J. Josey (Lorelle R. Swader).

Policy Monitoring (Standing). Mary Elizabeth Wendt (Lois Ann Gregory-Wood).
Professional Ethics (Standing). Charles Harmon (Beverley Becker, Judith F. Krug).
Public Awareness Advisory (Standing). Patricia Glass Schuman (Mark R. Gould).
Publishing (Standing). Marianne Burke (Donald Chatham).
Research and Statistics (Standing). Wanda V. Dole (Mary Jo Lynch).
Resolutions. Mary Augusta Thomas (Lois Ann Gregory-Wood).
Spectrum Scholarship Program (Special Presidential Task Force) Sarah Ann Long (Sandra Rios Balderrama).
Standards (Standing). Sarah M. Pritchard (Mary Jo Lynch).
Status of Women in Librarianship (Standing). Sarah Barbara Watstein (Lorelle R. Swader).
Web Advisory. Frederick J. Stielow (John Briody, Karen Muller).

Joint Committee Chairpersons

American Association of Law Libraries/American Correctional Association–ASCLA

Committee on Institution Libraries (joint). Carl Romalis (ACA).
American Federation of Labor/Congress of Industrial Organizations–ALA, Library Service to Labor Groups, RUSA. Deborah J. Schmidle (ALA); Anthony Sarmiento (AFL/CIO).
Anglo-American Cataloguing Rules Fund Trustees. Donald E. Chatham (ALA); Elizabeth Morton (Canadian Lib. Assn.); Janet Liebster (Lib. Assn.).
Anglo-American Cataloguing Rules Principals. Mary W.Ghikas (ALA).
Anglo-American Cataloguing Rules, Joint Steering Committee for Revision of. Ann Huthwaite (Australia).
Association of American Publishers–ALA. John W. Berry (ALA); to be appointed (AAP).
Association of American Publishers–ALCTS. Sheryl J.Nichin (ALCTS); Dan Lundy (AAP).
Children's Book Council–ALA. Lucille C. Thomas (ALA); Elle Teguis (CBC).
Society of American Archivists–ALA (Joint Committee on Library-Archives Relationships). To be appointed (ALA); Charlotte B. Brown. (SAA).

American Library Association
American Association of School Librarians

Executive Director, Julie A. Walker
50 E. Huron St., Chicago, IL 60611
312-280-4386, 800-545-2433 ext. 4386, fax 312-664-7459
E-mail AASL@ala.org
World Wide Web http://www.ala.org/aasl

Object

The American Association of School Librarians (AASL) is interested in the general improvement and extension of library media services for children and young people. AASL has specific responsibility for planning a program of study and service for the improvement and extension of library media services in elementary and secondary schools as a means of strengthening the educational program; evaluation, selection, interpretation, and utilization of media as they are used in the context of the school program; stimulation of continuous study and research in the library field and establishing criteria of evaluation; synthesis of the activities of all units of the American Library Association in areas of mutual concern; representation and interpretation of the need for the function of school libraries to other educational and lay groups; stimulation of professional growth, improvement of the status of school librarians, and encouragement of participation by members in appropriate type-of-activity divisions; conducting activities and projects for improvement and extension of service in the school library when such projects are beyond the scope of type-of-activity divisions, after specific approval by the ALA Council. Established in 1951 as a separate division of ALA.

Membership

Memb. 9,694. Open to all libraries, school library media specialists, interested individuals, and business firms with requisite membership in ALA.

Officers (2001–2002)

Pres. Helen R. Adams, Rosholt Public Schools, 346 W. Randolph, Rosholt, WI 54473-9547. Tel. 715-677-4011, fax 715-677-3543, e-mail hadams@coredcs.com; *Pres.-Elect* Nancy P. Zimmerman, Univ. of South Carolina, College of Lib. and Info. Science, 212 Davis College, Columbia, SC 29208. Tel. 803-777-1215, fax 803-777-7938, e-mail nzimmerman@gwm.sc.edu; *Treas./Financial Officer* Carolyn S. Hayes, Lakeshore, FL 33854; *Past Pres.* Harriet S. Selverstone, Norwalk H.S., 23 Calvin Murphy Dr., Norwalk, CT 06851-5500. Tel. 203-838-4481 ext. 214, fax 203-866-9418, e-mail hselver@aol.com.

Board of Directors

Officers; LuAnn L. Cogliser, Diane S. Durbin, Fran Roscello, Lesley S. J. Farmer, Jody Gehrig, Carol A. Gordon, Liz Gray, Bonnie J. Grimble, Jim Hayden, Betsy Losey, Toni Negro, Ann Marie Pipkin, Donna Shannon, Marilyn L. Shontz, J. Linda Williams, Julie A. Walker (ex officio).

Publications

Knowledge Quest (5 a year; memb.; nonmemb. $40). *Ed.* Debbie Abilock, Nueva School, 6565 Skyline Blvd., Hillsborough, CA 94010-6221. E-mail dabilock@pacbell.net.

School Library Media Research (nonsubscription electronic publication available to memb. and nonmemb. at http://www.ala.org/aasl/SLMR). *Ed.* Daniel Callison, School of Lib. and Info. Sciences, 10th and Jordan, Indiana Univ., Bloomington, IN 47405. E-mail callison@indiana.edu.

Committee Chairpersons

AASL/ELMS Executive Committee. Carolyn J. Lott.

AASL/Highsmith Research Grant. Nancy Everhart.

AASL/ISS Executive Committee. Leigh D. Barnett.

AASL/SPVS Executive Committee. Ann Carlson Weeks.

ABC/CLIO Leadership Grant. Neah J. Lohr.

Affiliate Assembly. Hilda Weisburg.

American Univ. Press Book Selection. Gail A. Richmond.

Annual Conference. Shirley Tastad, Ruth Toor, Merchuria Williams.

Appointments. Barbara Weathers.

Awards. Terrence E. Young, Jr.

Bylaws and Organization. Julia C. Van de Water.

Collaborative School Library Media Award. Miriam Erickson.

Distinguished School Administrator Award. Carol Diehl.

Distinguished Service Award. Jacqueline C. Mancall.

Frances Henne Award. M. Ellen Jay.

ICONnect FamiliesConnect. Sally Trexler.

ICONnect Online Courses. Marjorie Pappas.

Information Technology Pathfinder Award. Rochelle Glantz.

Institute Planning. Deborah Levitov.

Intellectual Freedom. Carrie Gardner.

Intellectual Freedom Award. Dianne McAfee Hopkins.

Knowledge Quest Editorial Board. Debbie Abilock.

Leadership Forum Planning. Gail K. Dickinson.

Legislation. Dennis J. LeLoup, Sandy Schuckett.

National Conference, 2003. Cassandra Barnett, Floyd Pentlin.

National School Library Media Program of

the Year Award. Sharon Coatney.
NCATE Guidelines Revision Task Force.
Marilyn L. Shontz.
Nominating, 2002 Election. Clara G. Hoover.
Publications. Donald C. Adcock.
Recruitment for the Profession Task Force.
Eileen E. Schroeder.
Research/Statistics. Donna Shannon.

School Librarians Workshop Scholarship.
Peggy Hallisey.
SLMR Electronic Editorial Board. Daniel J.
Callison.
Teaching for Learning Task Force. Sharon
Coatney.
Virtual Participation Task Force. Pam Berger.
Web Advisory. Sandra Jane Scroggs.

American Library Association
Association for Library Trustees and Advocates

Executive Director, Kerry Ward
50 E. Huron St., Chicago, IL 60611-2795
312-280-2161, 800-545-2433 ext. 2161, fax 312-944-7671
World Wide Web http://www.ala.org/alta

Object

The Association for Library Trustees and
Advocates (ALTA) is interested in the development of effective library service for all
people in all types of communities and in all
types of libraries; it follows that its members
are concerned, as policymakers, with organizational patterns of service, with the development of competent personnel, the provision
of adequate financing, the passage of suitable
legislation, and the encouragement of citizen
support for libraries. ALTA recognizes that
responsibility for professional action in these
fields has been assigned to other divisions of
ALA; its specific responsibilities as a division, therefore, are

1. A continuing and comprehensive educational program to enable library
   trustees to discharge their grave
   responsibilities in a manner best fitted
   to benefit the public and the libraries
   they represent
2. Continuous study and review of the
   activities of library trustees
3. Cooperation with other units within
   ALA concerning their activities relating to trustees
4. Encouraging participation of trustees
   in other appropriate divisions of ALA

5. Representation and interpretation of
   the activities of library trustees in contacts outside the library profession,
   particularly with national organizations and governmental agencies
6. Promotion of strong state and regional
   trustee organizations
7. Efforts to secure and support adequate
   library funding
8. Promulgation and dissemination of
   recommended library policy
9. Assuring equal access of information
   to all segments of the population
10. Encouraging participation of trustees
    in trustee/library activities, at local,
    state, regional, and national levels

Organized 1890. Became an ALA division in
1961.

Membership

Memb. 1,150. Open to all interested persons
and organizations. For dues and membership
year, see ALA entry.

Officers (2001–2002)

Pres. Gail Dysleski; *1st V.P./Pres.-Elect*
Dale H. Ross; *2nd V.P.* Shirley Bruursema;

Councilor Wayne Coco; *Past Pres.* G. Victor Johnson.

Board of Directors

Officers; Council Administrators: Lillian Broad, Ruth Newell, Jane Rowland, Sharon Saulmon, Carol K. Vogelman; Regional V.P.s: Gloria Aguilar, Denise Botto, Alma Denis, David H. Goldsmith, James Grayson, Beth A. Karpas, Virginia McCurdy, James A. McPherson, Francis Picart, Marguerite E. Ritchey, Donald L. Roalkvam.

Staff

Exec. Dir. Kerry Ward; *Program Officer.* Michael S. Edmonds.

Publication

The Voice (q.; memb.). *Ed.* Sharon Saulmon.

American Library Association
Association for Library Collections and Technical Services

Executive Director, Charles Wilt
50 E. Huron St., Chicago, IL 60611
800-545-2433 ext. 5030, fax 312-280-5033
E-mail cwilt@ala.org
World Wide Web http://www.ala.org/alcts

Object

The Association for Library Collections and Technical Services (ALCTS) provides leadership to the library and information community in developing principles, standards, and best practices for creating, collecting, organizing, delivering, and preserving information resources in all forms. It provides this leadership through its members by fostering educational, research, and professional service opportunities. ALCTS is committed to quality information, universal access, collaboration, and lifelong learning. ALCTS accomplishes this mission through divisional and sectional involvement including: acquisitions, cataloging and classification, collection management and development, serials, and the preservation of library materials. ALCTS has specific responsibility for:

1. Continuous study and review of the activities assigned to the division
2. Conduct of activities and projects within its area of responsibility
3. Syntheses of activities of all units within ALA that have a bearing on the type of activity represented

4. Representation and interpretation of its type of activity in contacts outside the profession
5. Stimulation of the development of librarians engaged in its type of activity, and stimulation of participation by members in appropriate type-of-library divisions
6. Planning and development of programs of study and research for the type of activity for the total profession

ALCTS will provide its members, other ALA divisions and members, and the library and information community with leadership and a program for action on the access to, and identification, acquisition, description, organization, preservation, and dissemination of information resources in a dynamic collaborative environment. In addition, ALCTS provides forums for discussion, research, and development and opportunities for learning in all of these areas. To achieve this mission, ALCTS has the following organizational goals:

1. To develop, evaluate, revise, and promote standards for creating, collecting,

organizing, delivering, and preserving information resources in all forms

2. To research, develop, evaluate, and implement best practices for creating, collecting, organizing, delivering, and preserving information resources in all forms

3. To assess the need for, sponsor, develop, administer, and promote educational programs and resources for life-long learning

4. To provide opportunities for professional development through research, scholarship, publication, and professional service

5. To create opportunities to interact and exchange information with others in the library and information communities

6. To ensure efficient use of Association resources and effective delivery of member services

Established 1957; renamed 1988.

Membership

Memb. 5,091. Any member of the American Library Association may elect membership in this division according to the provisions of the bylaws.

Executive Committee (July 2001–July 2002)

Pres. Bill Robnett, California State Univ.–Monterey, 100 Campus Center Bldg. 12, Seaside, CA 93955. Tel. 831-582-4448, fax 831-582-3354, e-mail bill_robnett@csumb.edu; *Pres.-Elect* Olivia M. A. Madison, Iowa State Univ. Lib., 302 Parks Lib., Ames, IA 50011-2140. Tel. 515-294-1443, fax 515-294-2112, e-mail omadison@iastate.edu; *Past Pres.* Carlen M. Ruschoff, Univ. of Maryland Libs., Rm. 2200, McKeldin Lib., College Park, MD 20742. Tel. 301-405-9299, fax 301-314-9971, e-mail ruschoff@deans.umd.edu; *Councilor* Ross W. Atkinson, Cornell Univ. Lib., 201 Olin Lib., Ithaca, NY 14853. Tel. 607-255-3393, fax 607-255-6788, e-mail ra13@cornell.edu; *Exec. Dir.* Charles Wilt, ALCTS, 50 E. Huron St., Chicago, IL 60611.

Tel. 312-280-5030, 800-545-2433 ext. 5030, fax 312-280-5033, e-mail cwilt@ala.org.

Address correspondence to the executive director.

Board of Directors

Officers; Suzanna H. Freeman, William A. Garrison, M. Dina Giambi, Debra Hackleman, Olivia M. A. Madison, Miriam W. Palm, Joy Paulson, Ann M. Sandberg-Fox, Karen A. Schmidt, Brian E. C. Schottlaender, Marla J. Schwartz, Jane Treadwell.

Publications

ALCTS Network News (irreg.; free). *Ed.* Shonda Russell. Subscribe via listproc@ala.org "subscribe an2 [yourname]."

ALCTS Newsletter Online (q.; free). *Ed.* Miriam W. Palm, 2185 Waverley St., Palo Alto, CA 94301. Tel./fax 650-327-8989, e-mail Miriam.Palm@stanford.edu. Posted to www.ala.org/alcts/alcts_news.

Library Resources & Technical Services (q.; memb.; nonmemb. $55). *Ed.* John M. Budd, School of Info. Science and Learning Technologies, Univ. of Missouri–Columbia, 221M Townsend Hall, Columbia, MO 65211. Tel. 573-882-3258, fax 573-884-4944, e-mail Buddj@missouri.edu.

Section Chairpersons

Acquisitions. M. Dina Giambi.
Cataloging and Classification. William A. Garrison.
Collection Management and Development. Suzanne H. Freeman.
Preservation and Reformatting. Joy Paulson.
Serials. Marla J. Schwartz.

Committee Chairpersons

Hugh C. Atkinson Memorial Award (ALCTS/ACRL/LAMA/LITA). Donald E. Riggs.
Association of American Publishers/ALCTS Joint Committee. Robert P. Holley.
Paul Banks and Carolyn Harris Preservation Award. Barbara Berger Eden.
Best of *LRTS* Award. Michael Kaplan.
Blackwell's Scholarship Award. Stephen J.

Bosch.

Budget and Finance. Olivia M. A. Madison.

Catalog Form and Function. Kevin Furniss.

Commercial Technical Services. Lynda S. Kresge.

Duplicates Exchange Union. To be appointed.

Education. Lynne C. Howarth.

Electronic Communications. Eleanor I. Cook.

Fund Raising. Pamela M. Bluh.

International Relations. D. Whitney Coe.

Leadership Development. Edward Shreeves.

Legislation. Charles W. Simpson.

Library Materials Price Index. Sharon G. Sullivan.

LRTS Editorial Board. John M. Budd.

MARBI. William W. Jones.

Media Resources. Diane L. Boehr.

Membership. Martin M. Kurth.

Networked Resources and Metadata. William Fietzer.

Nominating. Bruce Johnson.

Organization and Bylaws. Peggy Johnson, Joyce G. McDonough.

Esther J. Piercy Award Jury. October R. Ivins.

Planning. Brian E. C. Schottlaender.

President's Program. Julia C. Blixrud.

Program. Joan Swanekamp.

Publications. Bonnie MacEwan.

Publisher/Vendor Library Relations. Douglas A. Litts.

Research and Statistics. Elizabeth E. Cramer.

Discussion Groups

Authority Control in the Online Environment (ALCTS/LITA). Stephen S. Hearn.

Automated Acquisitions/In-Process Control Systems. Victoria M. Peters.

Creative Ideas in Technical Services. Edward A. Bergin, Elizabeth G. McClenney.

Electronic Resources. Maxine Sherman, Heidi Patrice Frank.

MARC Formats (ALCTS/LITA). Christine L. Mueller.

Newspaper. Robert C. Dowd.

Out of Print. Susan Frost.

Pre-Order and Pre-Catalog Searching. Elizabeth A. Lorenzen.

Role of the Professional in Academic Research Technical Service Departments. Vicki A. Grahame.

Scholarly Communications. Mahnaz K. Moshfegh, Taemin K. Park.

Serials Automation. Robert E. Pillow, Carol A. Trinchitella.

Technical Services Administrators of Medium-Sized Research Libraries. Sherida Downer.

Technical Services Directors of Large Research Libraries. Lee W. Leighton.

Technical Services in Public Libraries. Ross W. McLachlan.

Technical Services Workstations. Anaclare F. Evans.

American Library Association
Association for Library Service to Children

Executive Director, Malore I. Brown
50 E. Huron St., Chicago, IL 60611
312-280-2162, 800-545-2433 ext. 2162
E-mail mbrown@ala.org
World Wide Web http://www.ala.org/alsc

Object

Interested in the improvement and extension of library services to children in all types of libraries. Responsible for the evaluation and selection of book and nonbook materials for, and the improvement of techniques of, library services to children from preschool through the eighth grade or junior high school age, when such materials or techniques are intended for use in more than one type of library. Founded 1901.

Membership

Memb. 3,676. Open to anyone interested in library services to children. For information on dues, see ALA entry.

Address correspondence to the executive director.

Officers

Pres. Carole Fiore; *V.P./Pres.-Elect* Barbara Genco; *Past Pres.* Virginia Walter.

Directors

Carolyn Brodie, Nell Colburn, Randall Enos, Ellen Fader, Kathleen Horning, Carolyn Noah, Cynthia Richey, Kathleen Simonetta, Sue Zeigler.

Publications

Journal of Youth Services in Libraries (*JOYS*) (q.; memb.; nonmemb. $40; foreign $50).

Committee Chairpersons
Priority Group I: Child Advocacy
Consultant. Jean B. Gaffney.

Intellectual Freedom.
International Relations.
Legislation.
Library Service to Children with Special Needs.
Preschool Services and Parent Education.
Preschool Services Discussion Group.
Public Library-School Partnership Discussion Group.
School-Age Programs and Service.
Social Issues Discussion Group.

Priority Group II: Evaluation of Media
Consultant. Barbara Barstow.
Great Web Sites.
Notable Children's Books.
Notable Children's Recordings.
Notable Children's Videos.
Notable Children's Web Sites.
Notable Computer Software for Children.

Priority Group III: Professional Awards and Scholarships
Consultant. Virginia McKee.
ALSC/Book Wholesalers Summer Reading Program Grant and Reading Program.
ALSC/Econo-Clad Literature Program Award.
Arbuthnot Honor Lecture.
Louise Seaman Bechtel Fellowship.
Distinguished Service Award.
Penguin Putnam Books for Young Readers Award.
Scholarships: Melcher and Bound to Stay Bound.

Priority Group IV: Organizational Support
Consultant. Linda Perkins.
Local Arrangements.
Membership.
Nominating.
Organization and Bylaws.

Planning and Budget.
Preconference Planning.

Priority Group V: Projects and Research

Consultant. Kathy Toon.
Collections of Children's Books for Adult Research (Discussion Group).
National Planning of Special Collections.
Oral History.
Publications.
Research and Development.

Priority Group VI: Award Committees

Consultant. Jan Moltzan.
Mildred L. Batchelder Award Selection.
Pura Belpré Award.
Randolph Caldecott Award.
Andrew Carnegie Award.
John Newbery Award.
Sibert Informational Book Award.
Laura Ingalls Wilder Award.

Priority Group VII: Partnerships

Consultant Kathy East.
Liaison with National Organizations Serving Children and Youth.
National Children and Youth Membership Organizations Outreach.
Public Library-School Partnerships Discussion Group.
Quicklists Consulting Committee.

Priority Group VIII: Professional Development

Consultant Penny Markey.
Children and Technology.
Children's Book Discussion Group.
Education.
Managing Children's Services.
Managing Children's Services Discussion Group.
Storytelling Discussion Group.
Teachers of Children's Literature Discussion Group.

American Library Association
Association of College and Research Libraries

Executive Director, Mary Ellen K. Davis
50 E. Huron St., Chicago, IL 60611-2795
312-280-3248, 800-545-2433 ext. 3248, fax 312-280-2520
E-mail mdavis@ala.org
World Wide Web http://www.ala.org/acrl

Object

The Association of College and Research Libraries (ACRL) provides leadership for development, promotion, and improvement of academic and research library resources and services to facilitate learning, research, and the scholarly communication process. ACRL promotes the highest level of professional excellence for librarians and library personnel in order to serve the users of academic and research libraries. Founded 1938.

Membership

Memb. 11,297. For information on dues, see ALA entry.

Officers

Pres. Mary Reichel, univ. libn., Appalachian State Univ., Carol Grotnes Belk Lib., Boone, NC 28608. Tel. 828-262-2188, fax 828-262-3001, e-mail reichelml@appstate.edu; *Past Pres.* Betsy Wilson, assoc. dir. of libs./public services, Univ. of Washington, Box 352900, Seattle, WA 98195-2900. Tel. 206-685-1903, fax 206-685-8727, e-mail betsyw@u.washington.edu; *Pres.-Elect* Helen H. Spalding, assoc. dir. of libs., Univ. of Missouri–Kansas City, 5100 Rockhill Rd., Kansas City, MO 64110-2446. Tel. 816-235-1558, fax 816-333-5584, e-mail spaldingh@umkc.edu; *Budget and Finance Chair* Erika C. Linke, assoc. univ. libn., Hunt Lib., Carnegie Mellon Univ., 4909 Frew St., Pittsburgh, PA 15213-3890. Tel. 412-268-7800, fax 412-268-2793, e-mail Erika.linke@cmu.edu; *ACRL Councilor* Patricia A. Wand, univ. libn., American Univ., 4400 Massachusetts Ave. N.W., Washington, D.C. 20016-8046.

Board of Directors

Officers; Theresa S. Byrd, Lois H. Cherepon, Deborah B. Dancik, Paul Dumont, Barbara Baxter Jenkins, Patricia Kreitz, Robert F. Rose, Pamela Snelson.

Publications

Choice (11 a year; $220; foreign $270). *Ed.* Irving Rockwood.

Choice Reviews-on-Cards ($295; foreign $355).

ChoiceReviews.online ($250; foreign $250).

College & Research Libraries (6 a year; memb.; nonmemb. $60). *Ed.* Donald E. Riggs.

College & Research Libraries News (11 a year; memb.; nonmemb. $40). *Ed.* Stephanie D. Orphan.

Publications in Librarianship (formerly *ACRL Monograph Series*) (occasional). *Ed.* John M. Budd.

RBM: A Journal of Rare Books, Manuscripts, and Cultural Heritage (2 a year; $35). *Eds.* Lisa M. Browar, Marvin J. Taylor.

List of other publications and rates available through the ACRL office.

Committee and Task Force Chairpersons

Academic/Research Librarian of the Year Award Selection. Lynn Westbrook.

ACRL/Harvard Leadership Institute Advisory. Maureen Sullivan.

ACRL/TLT Group. Craig Gibson.

Appointments. Debra L. Gilchrist.

Hugh C. Atkinson Memorial Award. Diane J. Graves.

Budget and Finance. Erika C. Linke.

Bylaws. JoAnn Carr.

Choice Editorial Board. John D. Blackwell.

Colleagues. Charles Beard, Charles Kratz.

College and Research Libraries Editorial Board. Donald E. Riggs.

College and Research Libraries News Editorial Board. Brian Coutts.

Conference Program Planning, Atlanta (2002). Mary Reichel.

Copyright. Jeanne E. Boyle.

Council of Liaisons. Mary Ellen K. Davis.

Doctoral Dissertation Fellowship. Rena K. Fowler.

Effective Practices Review Committee. Randy Burke Hensley.

Excellence in Academic Libraries Award (Nominations). Lori Arp.

Excellence in Academic Libraries Award (Selection). Larry Hardesty.

Focus on the Future. W. Lee Hisle.

Funding and Organizational Models for Association-wide Initiatives. Nancy H. Allen, Robert F. Rose.

Government Relations. Stewart Bodner.

Information Literacy Advisory. Lisa Janicke Hinchliffe.

Institute for Information Literacy. Thomas Kirk, Julie Todaro.

Intellectual Freedom. C. James Schmidt.

International Relations. Priscilla Yu.

Samuel Lazerow Fellowship. Lynda Fuller Clendenning.

Membership. Susanna Boylston.

National Conference Executive Committee, Charlotte, 2003. Larry Hardesty.

New Publications Advisory. Susan M. Kroll.

Nominations. Janice D. Simmons-Welburn.

Orientation. Betsy Wilson.

President's Program Planning Committee, Atlanta, 2002. Don Frank, Susan M. Kroll.

Professional Development. Sally Kalin.

Publications. Jim M. Kapoun.

Publications in Librarianship Editorial Board. John M. Budd.

Racial and Ethnic Diversity. Gloria L. Rhodes.

Rare Books and Manuscripts Librarianship Editorial Board. Lisa M. Browar, Marvin J. Taylor.

Research. Tyrone Cannon.

K. G. Saur Award for Best *College and Research Libraries* Article. Norma Kobzina.

Scholarly Communications. Ray English.

Standards and Accreditation. Peter Watson-Boone.

Statistics. William Millter.

Supplemental Funding Models. Barbara Baxter Jenkins.

Discussion Group Chairpersons

Alliances for New Directions in Teaching/ Learning. Mark Horan.
Australian-Canadian-New Zealand Studies. Bradd Burningham.
Consumer and Family Studies. Priscilla C. Geahigan.
Electronic Reserves. Rebecca Martin, Leah G. McGinnis.
Electronic Text Centers. Michael S. Seadle.
Exhibits and Displays in College Libraries. Michael M. Miller.
Fee-Based Information Service Centers in Academic Libraries. Cynthia E. Mitchell.
Heads of Public Services. John A. Elsweiler, Jr.
Librarians and Information Science. Cathy D. Rentschler.
Library Development. Samuel T. Huang.
Media Resources. Jill W. Ortner.
Medium-Sized Libraries. Joann Michalak, Daniel A. Ortiz.
MLA International Bibliography. Susanna Van Sant.
Personnel Administrators and Staff Development Officers. Pat Hawthorne, Marilyn J. Mercado.
Philosophical, Religious, and Theological Studies. Harriet Lightman.
Popular Cultures. Rod Henshaw.

Research. Darrell L. Jenkins.
Sports and Recreation. Mila C. Su.
Team-Based Organizations. Robert Patrick Mitchell.
Undergraduate Librarians. Ree DeDonato.

Section Chairpersons

Afro-American Studies Librarians. Carol A. Rudisell.
Anthropology and Sociology. Anna L. De-Miller.
Arts. Mary T. Strow.
Asian, African, and Middle Eastern. Junlin Pan.
College Libraries. Lynn Scott Cochrane.
Community and Junior College Libraries. David Voros.
Distance Learning. Anne Marie Casey.
Education and Behavioral Sciences. Brian A. Quinn.
Instruction. Beth W. Woodard.
Law and Political Science. Lisa R. Stimatz.
Literatures in English. Kristine J. Anderson.
Rare Books and Manuscripts. Suzy Taraba.
Science and Technology. JoAnn DeVries.
Slavic and East European. Sandra L. Levy.
University Libraries. Julia A. Zimmerman.
Western European Studies. Barbara L. Walden.
Woman's Studies. Connie L. Phelps.

American Library Association
Association of Specialized and Cooperative Library Agencies

Executive Director, Cathleen Bourdon
50 E. Huron St., Chicago, IL 60611-2795
312-280-4398, 800-545-2433 ext. 4398, fax 312-944-8085
World Wide Web http://www.ala.org/ascla

Object

Represents state library agencies, specialized library agencies, multitype library cooperatives, and independent librarians. Within the interests of these types of library organizations, the Association of Specialized and Cooperative Library Agencies (ASCLA) has specific responsibility for:

1. Development and evaluation of goals and plans for state library agencies, specialized library agencies, and multitype library cooperatives to facilitate the implementation, improvement, and extension of library activities designed to foster improved user services, coordinating such activities with other appropriate ALA units

2. Representation and interpretation of the role, functions, and services of state library agencies, specialized library agencies, multitype library cooperatives, and independent librarians within and outside the profession, including contact with national organizations and government agencies

3. Development of policies, studies, and activities in matters affecting state library agencies, specialized library agencies, multitype library cooperatives and independent librarians relating to (a) state and local library legislation, (b) state grants-in-aid and appropriations, and (c) relationships among state, federal, regional, and local governments, coordinating such activities with other appropriate ALA units

4. Establishment, evaluation, and promotion of standards and service guidelines relating to the concerns of this association

5. Identifying the interests and needs of all persons, encouraging the creation of services to meet these needs within the areas of concern of the association, and promoting the use of these services provided by state library agencies, specialized library agencies, multitype library cooperatives and independent librarians

6. Stimulating the professional growth and promoting the specialized training and continuing education of library personnel at all levels in the areas of concern of this association and encouraging membership participation in appropriate type-of-activity divisions within ALA

7. Assisting in the coordination of activities of other units within ALA that have a bearing on the concerns of this association

8. Granting recognition for outstanding library service within the areas of concern of this association

9. Acting as a clearinghouse for the exchange of information and encouraging the development of materials, publications, and research within the areas of concern of this association

Membership

Memb. 992.

Board of Directors (2001–2002)

Pres. Jerome W. Krois; *Pres.-Elect* Ethel E. Himmel; *Past Pres.* Donna O. Dziedzic; *Dirs.-at-Large* Loretta L. Flowers, Judith A. Gibbons, Patrcia L. Owens, S. Jane Ulrich; *Div. Councilor* Marilyn M. Irwin; *Newsletter Editor* Sara G. Laughlin; *Ex Officio* Brenda M. Pacey; *Section Reps.* Christie Pearson Brandau, Jenifer O. Flaxbart, Barbara Land, Ruth J. Nussbaum, Jeannette P. Smithee.

Executive Staff

Exec. Dir. Cathleen Bourdon; *Deputy Exec. Dir.* Lillian Lewis.

Publications

Interface (q.; memb.; single copies $7). *Ed.* Sara G. Laughlin, 1616 Treadwell Lane, Bloomington, IN 47408. Tel. 812-334-8485.

Committee Chairpersons

ADA Assembly. Donna Z. Pontau.

American Correctional Association/ASCLA Joint Committee on Institution Libraries. Carl Romalis.

Awards. Jan Walsh.

Conference Program Coordination. Gordon R. Barhydt.

Legislation. Janice Ison.

Library Personnel and Education. Cheryl G. Bryan.

Membership Promotion. Marshall Alex Shore.

Organization and Bylaws. Brenda M. Pacey.

Planning and Finance, Donna O. Dziedzic, Ethel E. Himmel.

Publications. Sandra Vandermark.

Research. Barbara W. Cole.

Standards Review. John M. Day.

American Library Association
Library Administration and Management Association

Executive Director, Lorraine Olley
50 E. Huron St., Chicago, IL 60611
312-280-2156, 800-545-2433 ext. 2156, fax 312-280-5033
E-mail Lolley@ala.org, World Wide Web http://www.ala.org/lama

Object

The Library Administration and Management Association (LAMA) provides an organizational framework for encouraging the study of administrative theory, for improving the practice of administration in libraries, and for identifying and fostering administrative skill. Toward these ends, the division is responsible for all elements of general administration that are common to more than one type of library. These may include organizational structure, financial administration, personnel management and training, buildings and equipment, and public relations. LAMA meets this responsibility in the following ways:

1. Study and review of activities assigned to the division with due regard for changing developments in these activities
2. Initiating and overseeing activities and projects appropriate to the division, including activities involving bibliography compilation, publication, study, and review of professional literature within the scope of the division
3. Synthesizing the activities of other ALA units that have a bearing upon the responsibilities or work of the division
4. Representing and interpreting library administrative activities in contacts outside the library profession
5. Aiding the professional development of librarians engaged in administration and encouraging their participation in appropriate type-of-library divisions
6. Planning and developing programs of study and research in library administrative problems that are most needed by the profession

Established 1957.

Membership

Memb. 4,941.

Officers (July 2001–July 2002)

Pres. Joan R. Giesecke; *Pres.-Elect* Linda Sue Dobb; *Past Pres.* Jeanne M. Thorsen; *Dirs.-at-Large* Joyce Taylor, Eva D. Poole; *Div. Councilor* Charles E. Beard; *COLA Chair* Nicky Stanke; *Budget and Finance Chair* Arne Almquist; *Section Chairs* Shawn Tonner (BES), Chandler Jackson (FRFDS), Detrice Bankhead (HRS), Wayne Crocker (LOMS), Janifer Holt (MAES), Judith Gibbons (PRMS), Anne Edwards (SASS); *Ex officio* Marsha Stevenson, Pamela Bonnell, Teri Switzer, Myra Baughman, Judith Hunt, Marcia Schneider, Gregg Sapp, Virginia Steel, Kathryn Hammell Carpenter, Robert F. Moran, Jr.; *Exec. Dir.* Lorraine Olley.

Address correspondence to the executive director.

Publications

Library Administration and Management (q.; memb.; nonmemb. $55; foreign $65). *Ed.* Kathryn Hammell Carpenter; *Assoc. Ed.* Robert F. Moran, Jr.

LEADS from LAMA (approx. weekly; free through Internet). *Ed.* Lorraine Olley. To subscribe, send to listproc@ala.org the message *subscribe lamaleads [first name last name]*.

Committee Chairpersons

Budget and Finance. Arne J. Almquist.
Certified Public Library Administrator Certification, LAMA/PLA/ASCLA. Joyce Taylor.
Council of LAMA Affiliates. Nicky Stanke.
Cultural Diversity. Julie Alexander.

Editorial Advisory Board. Mary Augusta Thomas.
Education. Mary Genther.
Governmental Affairs. Philip Tramdack.
Leadership Development. Janice Flug.
Membership. Susan Schreiner.
National Institute Planning. Rod Henshaw.
Nominating, 2002 Elections. Deborah Carver.
Organization. Virginia Steel.
Partners. Rhonna Goodman.
President's Program 2002. Joyce Wright.
Program. Paul Anderson.
Publications. Barbara G. Preece.
Recognition of Achievement. Judith Adams-Volpe.
Research. Glenda Thornton.
Small Libraries Publications Series. Sondra Vandermark.
Special Conferences and Programs. Robert Smith.
Strategic Planning Implementation. Catherine Murray-Rust.

Section Chairpersons

Buildings and Equipment. Shawn Tonner.
Fund Raising and Financial Development. Chandler Jackson.
Human Resources. Detrice Bankhead.
Library Organization and Management. Wayne Crocker.
Measurement, Assessment, and Evaluation. Janifer Holt.
Public Relations and Marketing. Judith Gibbons.
Systems and Services. Anne Edwards.

Discussion Group Chairpersons

Assistants-to-the-Director. Marsha Stevenson.
Diversity Officers. Laura K. Blessing.
Library Storage. Thomas Schneider.
Middle Management. Lorraine Haricombe, Angela Jacobs.
Women Administrators. Elizabeth A. Avery.

American Library Association
Library and Information Technology Association

Executive Director, Mary C. Taylor
50 E. Huron St., Chicago, IL 60611
312-280-4270, 800-545-2433
World Wide Web http://www.lita.org

Object

The Library and Information Technology Association (LITA) envisions a world in which the complete spectrum of information technology is available to everyone—in libraries, at work, and at home. To move toward this goal, LITA provides a forum for discussion, an environment for learning, and a program for actions on many aspects of information technology for both practitioners and managers.

LITA educates, serves, and reaches out to its members, other ALA members and divisions, and the entire library and information community through its publications, programs, and other activities designed to promote, develop, and aid in the implementation of library and information technology. LITA is concerned with the planning, development, design, application, and integration of technologies within the library and information environment, with the impact of emerging technologies on library service, and with the effect of automated technologies on people.

Membership

Memb. 4,800.

Officers (2001–2002)

Pres. Flo Wilson; *V.P./Pres.-Elect* Pat Ensor; *Past Pres.* Sara Randall.

Directors

Officers; Karen Cook, Thomas Dowling, James R. Kennedy, Joan L. Kuklinski, George S. Machovec, Scott Muir, Colby M. Riggs; *Councilor* Barbra Higginbotham; *Bylaws and Organization* Susan Jacobson; *Exec. Dir.* Mary C. Taylor.

Publications

Information Technology and Libraries (ITAL) (q.; memb.; nonmemb. $50; single copy $15). *Ed.* Dan Marmion. For information or to send manuscripts, contact the editor. *LITA News* and Web site (http://www.lita.org). *Coord.* Martin Kalfatovic.

Committee Chairpersons

Budget Review. Sara Randall.
Bylaws and Organization. Susan Jacobson.
Committee Chair Coordinator. Michele Newberry.
Education. Catherine L. Wilkinson.
Executive. Flo Wilson.
International Relations. Carol Jones.
ITAL Editorial Board. Dan Marmion.
Leadership Development. Bonnie S. Postlethwaite.
Legislation and Regulation. Nancy W. Fleck.
LITA/Endeavor Student Writing Award. Rochelle Logan.
LITA/Gaylord Award. Rebecca A. Graham.
LITA/Geac and LITA/Christian Larew Scholarships. Alice F. Permenter.
LITA/Library Hi Tech Award. Dale Poulter.
LITA/LSSI and LITA/OCLC Minority Scholarships. Laura Galvan-Estrada.
LITA National Forum 2002. Patrick Mullin.
LITA News and Web Site. Martin Kalfatovic.
LITA/OCLC Kilgour Award. Dan Iddings.
Membership. Patricia Earnest.

Nominating. Barbra Higginbotham.
Program Planning. Jacqueline Zelman.
Publications. Thomas C. Wilson.
Regional Institutes. Lynne Lysiak.
Research. Kathleen M. Herick.
TESLA. Katharina Klemperer.
Technology and Access. Ellen Parravano.
Top Technology Trends. David Ward.
TER Board. Adriene Lim.
Web Coordinating. Martin Kalfatovic.

Interest Group Chairpersons

Interest Group Coordinator. Susan Logue.
Authority Control in the Online Environment (LITA/ALCTS). Shannon Hoffman.
Distance Learning. Tommie Wingfield.
Electronic Publishing/Electronic Journals. Lloyd Davidson.
Emerging Technologies. Samantha Yeung.
Heads of Library Technology. Byron Mayes.
Human/Machine Interface. Kevin Rundblad.
Imagineering. Jan Bridges.
Intelligent and Knowledge-Based Systems. Paul Bracke.
Internet Resources. Mary Amanda Axford.
Library Consortia/Automated Systems. Del Hamilton.
MARC Formats (LITA/ALCTS). Andrea Demsey.
Microcomputer Users. Henry Harken, Jr.
Online Catalogs. Karen J. Davis.
Open Source Systems. Jeremy Frumkin.
Secure Systems and Services. Mark Needleman.
Serials Automation (LITA/ALCTS). Carol Trinchitella.
Technical Issues of Digital Data. Lorre Smith.
Technical Services Workstations (LITA/ALCTS). Anaclare Frost Evans.
Technology and the Arts. Elizabeth E. Stewart.
Telecommunications. Frederick Fishel.

American Library Association
Public Library Association

Executive Director, Greta K. Southard
50 E. Huron St., Chicago, IL 60611
312-280-5752, 800-545-2433 ext. 5752, fax 312-280-5029
E-mail pla@ala.org
World Wide Web http://www.pla.org

Object

The Public Library Association (PLA) has specific responsibility for

1. Conducting and sponsoring research about how the public library can respond to changing social needs and technical developments

2. Developing and disseminating materials useful to public libraries in interpreting public library services and needs

3. Conducting continuing education for public librarians by programming at national and regional conferences, by publications such as the newsletter, and by other delivery means

4. Establishing, evaluating, and promoting goals, guidelines, and standards for public libraries

5. Maintaining liaison with relevant national agencies and organizations engaged in public administration and human services, such as the National Association of Counties, the Municipal League, and the Commission on Post-Secondary Education

6. Maintaining liaison with other divisions and units of ALA and other library organizations, such as the Association of American Library Schools and the Urban Libraries Council

7. Defining the role of the public library in service to a wide range of user and potential user groups

8. Promoting and interpreting the public library to a changing society through legislative programs and other appropriate means

9. Identifying legislation to improve and to equalize support of public libraries

PLA enhances the development and effectiveness of public librarians and public library services. This mission positions PLA to

- Focus its efforts on serving the needs of its members

- Address issues that affect public libraries

- Promote and protect the profession

- Commit to quality public library services that benefit the general public

To carry out its mission, PLA will identify and pursue specific goals. These goals will drive PLA's structure, governance, staffing, and budgeting, and will serve as the basis for all evaluations of achievement and performance. The following broad goals and strategies were established for PLA in 2001:

1. PLA will provide market-driven, mission-focused programs and services delivered in a variety of formats.

2. PLA will have increased its members and diversified its leadership.

3. PLA will have maximized its fiscal resources to enable the full implementation of its goals and to take full advantage of strategic opportunities.

4. PLA will be recognized as a positive, contemporary champion of public librarians and public libraries.

5. PLA will have demonstrated its leadership in developing and promoting sound public policies affecting public libraries.

6. PLA will have implemented, evaluated, and refined its structure and governance.

7. PLA will have the facilities, technology, staff, and systems required to achieve its mission.

Membership

Memb. 9,000+. Open to all ALA members interested in the improvement and expansion of public library services to all ages in various types of communities.

Officers (2001–2002)

Pres. Toni Garvey, Phoenix Public Lib., 1221 N. Central Ave., Phoenix, AZ 85004. Tel. 602-262-4735, fax 602-261-8836, e-mail tgarvey1@ci.phoenix.az.us; *V.P./Pres.-Elect* Jo Ann Pinder, Gwinnett County Public Lib., 101 Lawrenceville Hwy., Lawrenceville, GA 30045; *Past Pres.* Kay K. Runge, Public Lib. of Des Moines, 100 Locust St., Des Moines IA 50309. E-mail krunge@pldminfo.org.

Publication

Public Libraries (bi-m.; memb.; nonmemb. $50; foreign $60; single copy $10). *Managing Ed.* Kathleen Hughes, PLA, 50 E. Huron St., Chicago, IL 60611.

Cluster Chairpersons

Issues and Concerns Steering Committee. Luis Herrera.
Library Development Steering Committee. Arthur Weeks.
Library Services Steering Committee. Marilyn H. Boria.

Committee Chairs

Issues and Concerns Cluster

Intellectual Freedom. Dierdre Brennan.
Legislation. David J. Karre.
Library Confidentialty Task Force. Eileen Longsworth.
Public Policy in Public Libraries. Peter Young.

Recruitment of Public Librarians. Susan G. Calbreath.
Research and Statistics. Jeanne E. Goodrich.
Workload Measures and Staffing Patterns. Irene S. Blalock.

Library Development Cluster

Branch Libraries. Wayne Disher.
Marketing Public Libraries. Richard Chartrand.
Metropolitan Libraries. Thomas J. Alrutz.
Practical Applications of Technology in Public Libraries. Bruce Ziegman.
Public Library Systems. Steve Schaefer.
Rural Library Services. Roseanne E. Goble.
Small and Medium-Sized Libraries. Deborah A. Pawlik.
Technology in Public Libraries. Susan B. Harrison.

Library Services Cluster

Adult Lifelong Learning Services. Joe Ann Shapiro.
Audiovisual. Michael Boedicker.
Basic Education and Literarcy Services. Carol Brey.
Cataloging Needs of Public Libraries. Joanne Rita Gilmore.
Collection Management Committee. Cynthia Orr, Marsha L. Spyros.
Community Information Services. Donna Reed, Nancy Charnee.
Continuing and Independent Learning Services. Kathleen Degyansky.
Job and Career Information Services. Frances Roehm.
Resources for the Adult New Reader. Maureen O'Connor.
Services to Multicultural Populations. Joseph M. Eagan.
Services to Children, Youth, and Their Caregivers. Linda Fein.

Business Committees

2002 National Conference. Christine L. Hage.
2002 National Conference (Local Arrangements). Leslie J. Steffes.
2002 National Conference (Program). Linda Mielke, Jo Ann Pinder.
2004 National Conference. Clara Nailli Bohrer.

2004 National Conference (Program). Neel Parikh.

Awards. Peggy Sullivan.

Awards, Advancement of Literacy Award Jury. Sharman Gerdes.

Awards, Baker & Taylor Entertainment Audio/Music/Video Product Award Jury. Laura Kline.

Awards, Demco Creative Merchandising Grant Jury. Mary Kay Wallace.

Awards, Excellence in Small and/or Rural Public Library Service Award Jury. Ellen Myrick.

Awards, Highsmith Library Innovation Award Jury. Susan Baerg Epstein.

Awards, Allie Beth Martin Award Jury. Susan Hildreth.

Awards, New Leaders Travel Grant Jury. Iza Cieszynski.

Awards, Charlie Robinson Award Jury. Diane Mayo.

Budget and Finance. Eva Poole.

Bylaws and Organization. Pamela Bonnell.

Certified Public Library Administrator (PLA/LAMA/ASCLA). Anders C. Dahlgren.

Leadership Development 2003. Alan Harkness.

Membership. Claudia Sumler.

PLA Partners. Nancy Tessman.

President's Events 2003. Claudia Sumler.

Publications, Electronic Communications Advisory. Julie A. James.

Publications, PLA Monographs. Larry Neal.

Publications, *Public Libraries* Advisory. Victor Kralisz.

Publications, *Statistical Report* Advisory. Louise A. Sevold.

Publications, University Press Books for Public Libraries. Marcia Warner.

State Relations, LaDonna T. Kienitz.

Task Force on Preschool Literacy Initiatives (joint with ALSC). Harriet Henderson, Elaine Meyers.

American Library Association
Reference and User Services Association

Executive Director, Cathleen Bourdon
50 E. Huron St., Chicago, IL 60611-2795
312-280-4398, 800-545-2433 ext. 4398, fax 312-944-8085
E-mail rusa@ala.org
World Wide Web http://www.ala.org/rusa

Object

The Reference and User Services Association (RUSA) is responsible for stimulating and supporting in every type of library the delivery of reference/information services to all groups, regardless of age, and of general library services and materials to adults. This involves facilitating the development and conduct of direct service to library users, the development of programs and guidelines for service to meet the needs of these users, and assisting libraries in reaching potential users.

The specific responsibilities of RUSA are

1. Conduct of activities and projects within the association's areas of responsibility

2. Encouragement of the development of librarians engaged in these activities, and stimulation of participation by members of appropriate type-of-library divisions

3. Synthesis of the activities of all units within the American Library Association that have a bearing on the type of activities represented by the association

4. Representation and interpretation of the association's activities in contacts outside the profession

5. Planning and development of programs of study and research in these areas for the total profession

6. Continuous study and review of the association's activities

Membership

Memb. 4,934. For information on dues, see ALA entry.

Officers (July 2001–June 2002)

Pres. Carol M. Tobin; *Pres.-Elect* Cindy Stewart Kaag; *Past Pres.* Catherine R. Friedman; *Secy.* Kathy L. Tomajko.

Other Members: Dirs.-at-Large

Emily Batista, A. Craig Hawbaker, Merle L. Jacob, Elliot Jay Kanter, Kathleen M. Kluegel, David A. Tyckoson; *Councilor* Julia M. Rholes; *Ed.* Suzanne Sweeney; *Exec. Dir.* Cathleen Bourdon.

Address correspondence to the executive director.

Publications

RUSQ (q.; memb. $50, foreign memb. $60, single copies $15). *Eds.* Connie J. Van Fleet, Danny P. Wallace.

Section Chairpersons:

Business Reference and Services. Susan Riehm Goshorn.
Collection Development and Evaluation. John R. M. Lawrence.
History. James P. Niessen.
Machine-Assisted Reference. William A. McHugh.

Management and Operation of User Services. Gwen Arthur.

Committee Chairpersons

Access to Information. Rosanne M. Cordell.
AFL/CIO Joint Committee on Library Services to Labor Groups. Deborah J. Schmidle, Anthony R. Sarmiento.
Awards Coordinating. Lambrini Papangelis.
Conference Program. Kathleen M. Kluegel.
Conference Program Coordinating. Carla Rickerson.
Dartmouth Medal. Sharmon H. Kenyon.
Facts on File Grant. Jerilyn A. Marshall.
Gale Research Award for Excellence in Reference and Adult Services. Deborah Abston.
Membership. Nancy E. Bodner.
Margaret E. Monroe Library Adult Services Award. Eugenia D. Bryant.
Isadore Gilbert Mudge/R. R. Bowker Award. Danise Gianneschi Hoover.
Nominating 2002. Janice D. Simmons-Welburn.
Organization. Denise Beaubien Bennett.
Planning and Finance. Catherine R. Friedman.
Professional Competencies (ad hoc). Jo Bell Whitlatch.
Professional Development. Merle L. Jacob.
Publications. Karen A. Reinman-Sendi.
Reference Services Press Award. Julie Tharp.
John Sessions Memorial Award. Amy Tracy Wells.
Louis Shores/Oryx Press Award. Susan C. Awe.
Standards and Guidelines. Marcelle Elaine Hughes.

American Library Association
Young Adult Library Services Association

Executive Director, Julie A. Walker
50 E. Huron St., Chicago, IL 60611
312-280-4390, 800-545-2433 ext. 4390, fax 312-664-7459
E-mail yalsa@ala.org
World Wide Web http://www.ala.org/yalsa

Object

In every library in the nation, quality library service to young adults is provided by a staff that understands and respects the unique informational, educational, and recreational needs of teenagers. Equal access to information, services, and materials is recognized as a right, not a privilege. Young adults are actively involved in the library decision-making process. The library staff collaborates and cooperates with other youth-serving agencies to provide a holistic, community-wide network of activities and services that support healthy youth development. To ensure that this vision becomes a reality, the Young Adult Library Services Association (YALSA), a division of the American Library Association (ALA),

1. Advocates extensive and developmentally appropriate library and information services for young adults, ages 12 to 18

2. Promotes reading and supports the literacy movement

3. Advocates the use of information and communications technologies to provide effective library service

4. Supports equality of access to the full range of library materials and services, including existing and emerging information and communications technologies, for young adults

5. Provides education and professional development to enable its members to serve as effective advocates for young people

6. Fosters collaboration and partnerships among its individual members with the library community and other groups involved in providing library and information services to young adults

7. Influences public policy by demonstrating the importance of providing library and information services that meet the unique needs and interests of young adults

8. Encourages research and is in the vanguard of new thinking concerning the provision of library and information services for youth

Membership

Memb. 3,320. Open to anyone interested in library services and materials for young adults. For information on dues, see ALA entry.

Officers (July 2001–July 2002)

Pres. Bonnie Kunzel, Princeton (New Jersey) Public Lib. Tel. 609-924-9529, e-mail bkunzel @aol.com; *V.P/Pres.-Elect* Caryn Sipos, Three Creeks Community Lib., Vancouver, Washington. Tel. 360-571-9696, e-mail csipos @fvrl.org; *Past Pres.* Mary Arnold, Cuyahoga County Public Lib., Cleveland, Ohio. Tel. 216-475-5000, fax 216-587-7281, e-mail mjarnold@hotmail.com.

Directors

Officers; Amy Alessio (2004), Sheila B. Anderson (2004), Audra Caplan (2002), David Mowery (2002), Adela Peskorz (2002), Sara Ryan (2003); *Ex officio Chair, Budget and Finance* Mary Arnold; *Chair, Organization and Bylaws* Leslie Westbrook; *Chair, Strategic Planning* Connie Adams Bush.

Publications

Journal of Youth Services in Libraries (q.; memb.; nonmemb. $40; foreign $50). *Ed.* Lynn Hoffman.

Committee Chairpersons

AASL Institute Task Force. Jana Fine.

Adult Books for Young Adults Project. Deborah Taylor.

Best Books for Young Adults (2002). Donna McMillen.

Budget and Finance. Mary Arnold.

Conference Atlanta 2002 Local Arrangements. Brenda Hunter.

Cultural Diversity Task Force. Katherine Fitch, Susan Geye.

Division and Membership Promotion. Erminia Mina Gallo.

E-book Task Force. Douglas Uhlmann.

Margaret A. Edwards Award 2002. Mary Long.

Margaret A. Edwards Award 2003. Rosemary Chance.

Intellectual Freedom. Charles Harmon.

Legislation. Barbara Balbirer.

Media Selection and Usage. Francisca Goldsmith.

Nominating. Phyllis Fisher.

Organization and Bylaws. Leslie Westbrook.

Outreach to Young Adults with Special Needs. Naomi Angler.

Partnerships Advocating for Teens. Shawn Thrasher.

Popular Paperbacks for Young Adults. Sarah Dentan.

Michael L. Printz Award 2002. Judy Druse.

Michael L. Printz Award 2003. Joel Shoemaker.

Professional Development. Amy Ann Healey.

Program Planning Clearinghouse and Evaluation. Betty Acerra.

Publications. Jana Fine.

Publishers Liaison. Judy Nelson.

Quick Picks for Reluctant Young Adult Readers. Lora Bruggerman.

Research. Frances Jacobson.

Selected DVDs and Videos for Young Adults. Robyn Lupa.

Serving Young Adults in Large Urban Populations Discussion Group. Susan Raboy.

Strategic Planning. Connie Adams Bush.

Teaching Young Adult Literature Discussion Group. Adela Peskorz.

Technology for Young Adults. Joyce Valenza.

Teen Read Week Work Group. Stephen Crowley.

Teen Web Site Advisory Committee. Tracey Firestone.

2002 Grapic Novels Preconference. Michael Pawuk.

Youth Participation. Joanne Rosario.

American Merchant Marine Library Association

(An affiliate of United Seamen's Service)
Executive Director, Roger T. Korner
20 Exchange Place, Suite 2901, New York, NY 10005
212-269-0714, e-mail ussammla@ix.netcom.com
World Wide Web http://uss-ammla.com/ammla1.html

Object

Provides ship and shore library service for American-flag merchant vessels, the Military Sealift Command, the U.S. Coast Guard, and other waterborne operations of the U.S. government. Established 1921.

Officers (2001–2002)

Pres. Talmage E. Simpkins; *Chair, Exec. Committee* Edward R. Morgan; *V.P.s* John

M. Bowers, Capt. Timothy A. Brown, James Capo, David Cockroft, Capt. Remo Di Fiore, John Halas, Rene Lioeanjie, Michael R. McKay, George E. Murphy, S. Nakanishi, Capt. Gregorio Oca, Larry O'Toole, Michael Sacco, John J. Sweeney; *Secy.* Donald E. Kadlac; *Treas.* William D. Potts; *Gen. Counsel* John L. DeCurse, Jr.; *Community Relations Dir.* Eileen Horan; *Exec. Dir.* Roger T. Korner.

American Society for Information Science and Technology

Executive Director, Richard B. Hill
1320 Fenwick Lane, Suite 510, Silver Spring, MD 20910
301-495-0900, fax 301-495-0810, e-mail ASIS@asis.org

Object

The American Society for Information Science and Technology (ASIS&T) provides a forum for the discussion, publication, and critical analysis of work dealing with the design, management, and use of information, information systems, and information technology.

Membership

Memb. (Indiv.) 3,500; (Student) 800; (Inst.) 250. Dues (Indiv.) $115; (Student) $30; (Inst.) $650 and $800.

Officers

Pres. Donald Kraft, Louisiana State Univ.; *Pres.-Elect* Trudi Bellardo Hahn, Univ. of Maryland; *Treas.* Cecelia Preston, Preston and Lynch; *Past Pres.* Joseph Busch, Interwoven.

Address correspondence to the executive director.

Board of Directors

Dirs.-at-Large Dudee Chiang, Andrew Dillon, Raya Fidel, Abby Goodrum, Douglas Kaylor, Michael Leach, Kris Liberman, Gretchen Whitney; *Deputy Dirs.* Karen Howell, Vicki Gregory; *Exec. Dir.* Richard B. Hill.

Publications

Advances in Classification Research, Vols. 1–10. Available from Information Today, 143 Old Marlton Pike, Medford, NJ 08055.
Annual Review of Information Science and Technology. Available from Information Today.
ASIS Thesaurus of Information Science and Librarianship. Available from Information Today.
Bulletin of the American Society for Information Science. Available from ASIS.

Editorial Peer Review: Its Strengths and Weaknesses by Ann C. Weller. Available from Information Today.
Electronic Publishing: Applications and Implications. Eds. Elisabeth Logan and Myke Gluck. Available from Information Today.
Evaluating Networked Information Services: Techniques, Policy and Issues by Charles R. McClure and John Carlo Bertot. Available from Information Today.
From Print to Electronic: The Transformation of Scientific Communication. Susan Y. Crawford, Julie M. Hurd, and Ann C. Weller. Available from Information Today.
Historical Studies in Information Science. Eds. Trudi Bellardo Hahn and Michael Buckland. Available from Information Today.
Information Management for the Intelligent Organization: The Art of Environmental Scanning, 2nd edition, by Chun Wei Choo, Univ. of Toronto. Available from Information Today.
Intelligent Technologies in Library and Information Service Applications by F. W. Lancaster and Amy Warner. Available from Information Today.
Introductory Concepts in Information Science by Melanie J. Norton. Available from Information Today.
Journal of the American Society for Information Science. Available from John Wiley and Sons, 605 Third Ave., New York, NY 10016.
Knowledge Management for the Information Professional. Eds. T. Kanti Srikantaiah and Michael Koenig. Available from Information Today.
Knowledge Management: The Bibliography Compiled by Paul Burden. Available from Information Today.
Proceedings of the ASIS Annual Meetings. Available from Information Today.

Scholarly Publishing: The Electronic Frontier. Eds. Robin P. Peek and Gregory B. Newby. Available from MIT Press, Cambridge, Massachusetts.
Statistical Methods for the Information Professional by Liwen Vaughan. Available from Information Today.
Studies in Multimedia. Eds. Susan Stone and Michael Buckland. Based on the Proceedings of the 1991 ASIS Mid-Year Meeting. Available from Information Today.
The Web of Knowledge: A Festschrift in Honor of Eugene Garfield. Eds. Blaise Cronin and Helen Barsky Atkins. Available from Information Today.

Committee Chairpersons

Awards and Honors. Marianne Afifi.
Budget and Finance. George Ryerson.
Constitution and Bylaws. Norman Horrocks.
Education. June Lester.
Membership. Steven Hardin.
Standards. Mark Needleman.

American Theological Library Association

250 S. Wacker Dr., Suite 1600, Chicago, IL 60201
Tel. 800-665-2852, 312-454-5100, fax 312-454-5505
E-mail atla@atla.com
World Wide Web http://www.atla.com

Object

To bring its members into close working relationships with each other, to support theological and religious librarianship, to improve theological libraries, and to interpret the role of such libraries in theological education, developing and implementing standards of library service, promoting research and experimental projects, encouraging cooperative programs that make resources more available, publishing and disseminating literature and research tools and aids, cooperating with organizations having similar aims, and otherwise supporting and aiding theological education. Founded 1946.

Membership

Memb. (Inst.) 265; (Indiv.) 600. Membership is open to persons engaged in professional library or bibliographical work in theological or religious fields and others who are interested in the work of theological librarianship. Dues (Inst.) $75 to $750, based on total library expenditure; (Indiv.) $15 to $150, based on salary scale. Year. Sept. 1–Aug. 31.

Officers

Pres. Sharon Taylor, Andover Newton Theological School, Trask Lib., 169 Herrick Rd., Newton Centre, MA 02459. Tel. 617-964-1100 ext. 259, fax 617-965-9751, e-mail staylor@ants.ed; *V.P.* Eileen K. Saner, Associated Mennonite Biblical Seminary Lib., 3003 Benham Ave., Elkhart, IN 46517-1999. Tel. 219-296-6233, fax 219-295-0092, e-mail esaner@ambs.edu; *Secy.* Paul F. Stuehrenberg, Yale Univ. Divinity School Lib., 409 Prospect St., New Haven, CT 06511. Tel. 203-432-5292, fax 203-432-3906, e-mail paul.stuehrenberg@yale.edu; *Past Pres.* William Hook, Dir., Vanderbilt Univ. Divinity Lib., 419 21st Ave. S., Nashville, TN 37240-0007. Tel. 615-322-2865, fax 615-343-2918, e-mail hook@library.vanderbilt. edu.

Board of Directors

Officers; Milton J. "Joe" Coalter, Stephen Crocco, D. William Faupel, Bill Hook, Mary Martin, Sara Myers, Eileen K. Saner, Paul Schrodt, Susan Sponberg, Paul Stuehrenberg,

Sharon Taylor, Christine Wenderoth, *Exec. Dir.* Dennis A. Norlin; *Dir. of Electronic Products and Services* Tami Luedtke; *Dir. of Finance* Pradeep Gamadia; *Dir. of Indexes* Cameron Campbell; *Dir. of Member Services* Karen L. Whittlesey.

Publications

ATLA Indexes in MARC Format (semi-ann.).
ATLA Religion database on CD-ROM, 1949–.
Biblical Studies on CD-ROM (ann.).
Catholic Periodical and Literature Index on CD-ROM (ann.).
Index to Book Reviews in Religion (ann.).
Newsletter (q.; memb.; nonmemb. $50). *Ed.* Margaret Tacke.
Old Testament Abstracts on CD-ROM (ann.).
Proceedings (ann.; memb.; nonmemb. $50). *Ed.* Margaret Tacke.
Religion Index One: Periodicals (semi-ann.).
Religion Index Two: Multi-Author Works (ann.).
Religion Indexes: RIO/RIT/IBRR 1975– on CD-ROM.
Research in Ministry: An Index to Doctor of

Ministry Project Reports (ann.).
Latin American Subset on CD-ROM (ann.).

Committee Chairpersons and Other Officials

Annual Conference. Mitzi Budde.
Archives. Martha Smalley.
Collection Evaluation and Development. Thomas Haverly.
College and University. Noel S. McFerran.
Education. Marti Alt.
International Collaboration. Charles Willard.
Judaica. Alan Krieger.
Membership. Pat Graham.
NISO Representative. Myron Chace.
Nominating. Dorothy Tomason.
OCLC Theological User Group. Linda Umoh.
Preservation. Martha Smalley.
Professional Development. Roberta Schaafs-ma.
Public Services. Kris Veldheer.
Publication. Andy Keck.
Special Collections. Clair McCurdy.
Technical Services. Joanna Hause.
Technology. Duane Harbin.
World Christianity. William C. Miller.

Archivists and Librarians in the History of the Health Sciences

President, Suzanne Porter
Curator, History of Medicine Collections
Duke University Medical Center Library
Box 3702, Durham, NC 27710
919-660-1143

Object

This association was established exclusively for educational purposes to serve the professional interests of librarians, archivists, and other specialists actively engaged in the librarianship of the history of the health sciences by promoting the exchange of information and by improving the standards of service.

Membership

Memb. 170. Dues $15 (Americas), $21 (other countries).

Officers (May 2001–May 2002)

Pres. Suzanne Porter, Curator, History of Medicine Collections, Duke Univ. Medical Center Lib., Box 3702, Durham, NC 27710.

Tel. 919-660-1143, fax 919-681-7599, e-mail porte004@mc.duke.edu; *Secy.-Treas.* Micaela Sullivan-Fowler, Libn./Curator, Health Sciences Lib., Univ. of Wisconsin, 1305 Linden Dr., Madison, WI 53706. Tel. 608-262-2402, fax 608-262-4732; e-mail micaela@library.wisc.edu.

Publication

Watermark (q.; memb.). *Ed.* Lilli Sentz, Historical Lib., Harvey Cushing/John Hay Whitney Medical Lib., Yale Univ., 333 Cedar St., New Haven, CT 06520-8014. Tel. 203-483-8404, fax 203-483-5037, e-mail Lsentz@email.msn.com

ARMA International
(Association of Records Managers and Administrators)

Executive Director/CEO, Peter R. Hermann
4200 Somerset Dr., Suite 215, Prairie Village, KS 66208
913-341-3808, fax 913-341-3742
E-mail phermann@arma.org
World Wide Web http://www.arma.org

Object

To advance the practice of records and information management as a discipline and a profession; to organize and promote programs of research, education, training, and networking within that profession; to support the enhancement of professionalism of the membership; and to promote cooperative endeavors with related professional groups.

Membership

Annual dues $115 for international affiliation. Chapter dues vary. Membership categories are Chapter Member ($115 plus chapter dues), Student Member ($15), and Unaffiliated Member.

Officers (July 2001–June 2002)

Pres. H. Larry Eiring, Covington & Burling, 1201 Pennsylvania Ave. N.W., Box 7566, Washington, DC 20044. Tel. 202-662-6563, fax 202-662-6291, e-mail Leiring@cov.com; *Immediate Past Pres. and Board Chair* Tad C. Howington, Lower Colorado River Authority, 3701 Lake Austin Blvd., Austin, TX 78703. Tel. 512-473-4047, fax 512-473-3561, e-mail thowingt@lcra.org; *Pres.-Elect* Terrence J. Coan, Accutrac Software, Inc., 350 S. Figueroa St., Suite 141, Los Angeles, CA 90071. Tel. 213-626-3000, fax 213-229-9095, e-mail tcoan@accutrac. com; *Treas.* Juanita M. Skillman, Accutrac Software, Inc., 350 S. Figueroa St., Suite 141, Los Angeles, CA 90071. Tel. 213-626-3000, fax 213-229-9095, e-mail jskillman@accutrac.com; *Region Dirs.* Mid-Atlantic, Donna Galata; Great Lakes, Carol E. B. Choksy; Southeast, Susan A. Hubbard; Midwest/Rocky Mountain, Cheryl L. Pederson; Southwest, Susan B. Whitmire; Pacific, Helen Marie Streck; Northeast, Paul J. Singleton; Great Northwest, David P. McDermott; Canada, Gisele L. Crawford; International, Claudette E. Samuels.

Publication

Information Management Journal. Exec. Ed. J. Michael Pemberton, School of Info. Sciences, Univ. of Tennessee at Knoxville, 804 Volunteer Blvd., Knoxville, TN 37996-4330, e-mail jpembert@utkux.utcc.utk.edu.

Committee Chairpersons

Awards. H. Larry Eiring, Covington & Burling, 1201 Pennsylvania Ave. N.W., Washington, DC 20004. Tel 202-662-6563, fax 202-662-6291, e-mail Leiring@cov.com.

Canadian Legislative and Regulatory Affairs (CLARA). Rob Candy, City of Toronto, 55 John St., Sta. 1211, 21st fl., Metro Hall, Toronto, ON M5V3C6. Tel. 416-392-3994, fax 416-392-3995, e-mail rcandy@city.toronto.on.ca.

Education Development. Julie A. Gee, Michigan Dept. of Transportation, Records and Form, Box 30050, Lansing, MI 48909-7550. Tel. 517-373-9661, fax 517-373-0167, e-mail geej@state.mi.us.

Election Management. Tad C. Howington, Lower Colorado River Authority, 3701 Lake Austin Blvd., Austin, TX 78703. Tel. 512-473-4047, fax 512-473-3561, e-mail thowingt@lcra.org.

Electronic Records Management. Robert Meagher, CONDOR Consulting, Inc., 130 Albert St., Suite 419, Ottawa, ON K1P 5G4, Canada. Tel. 613-233-4962 ext. 23, fax 613-233-4249, e-mail rmeagher@istar.ca.

Financial Planning. Juanita M. Skillman, Accutrac Software, Inc., 350 S. Figueroa St., Suite 141, Los Angeles, CA 90071. Tel. 213-626-3000, fax 213-229-9095, e-mail jskillman@accutrac.com.

Industry Specific Program. Fred A. Pulzello, Morgan Stanley Dean Witter, Corporate Services, 1633 Broadway, 39th fl., New York, NY 10019. Tel. 212-537-2164, fax 212-537-3492, e-mail Fred.Pulzello@msdw.com.

International Relations. Claudette E. Samuels, Caribbean Examination Council, Records Mgt. Dept., The Garrison, St. Michael 20, Barbados. Tel. 246-436-6261, fax 246-429-5421, e-mail csamuels@cxc.org.

Publications Editorial Board. Jean K. Brown, Univ. Archives, Univ. of Delaware, Pearson Hall, Newark, DE 19716. Tel. 302-831-2750, fax 302-831-6903, e-mail jkbrown@udel.edu.

Strategic Planning. Paul J. Singleton, Bingham Dana LLP, 150 Federal St., Boston, MA 02110-1726. Tel. 617-951-8402, fax 617-951-8736, e-mail singlepj@bingham.com.

U.S. Government Relations. Emilie G. Himm, New Jersey Dept. of Transportation, Box 600, Trenton, NJ 08625-0600. Tel. 609-530-2071, fax 609-530-5719.

ARMA Educational Foundation. Deborah Marshall, Mayer, Brown & Patt, 1909 K St. N.W., Washington, DC 20006-1101. Tel. 202-263-3357, fax 202-263-3300, e-mail dmarshall@mayerbrown.com.

Standards Development. Sandra Williamson, Universal Studios, Inc., 100 Universal City Plaza, Universal City, CA 91608-1002. Tel. 818-777-2975, fax 818-866-5120, e-mail sandi.williamson@unistudio.com.

Art Libraries Society of North America

Executive Director, Elizabeth Clarke
329 March Rd., Suite 232, Box 11, Kanata, ON K2K 2E1, Canada
800-817-0621, 613-599-3074, fax 613-599-7027
E-mail arlisna@igs.net
World Wide Web http://www.arlisna.org

Object

To foster excellence in art librarianship and visual resources curatorship for the advancement of the visual arts. Established 1972.

Membership

Memb. 1,325. Dues (Inst.) $1,000; (Indiv.) $65; (Business Affiliate) $100; (Student) $40; (Retired/Unemployed) $50; (Sustaining) $250; (Sponsor) $500; (Overseas) basic plus $25. Year. Jan. 1–Dec. 31. Membership is open and encouraged for all those interested in visual librarianship, whether they be professional librarians, students, library assistants, art book publishers, art book dealers, art historians, archivists, architects, slide and photograph curators, or retired associates in these fields.

Officers (2002)

Pres. Ted Goodman, Avery Architectural and Fine Arts Lib., Columbia Univ., 1172 Amsterdam Ave., New York, NY 10027. Tel. 212-854-8407, fax 212-854-8904, e-mail goodman@columbia.edu; *V.P./Pres.-Elect* Daniel Starr, Thomas J. Watson Lib., Metropolitan Museum of Art, 1000 Fifth Ave., New York, NY 10028-1198. Tel. 212-650-2582, fax 212-570-3847, e-mail daniel.starr @metmuseum.org; *Past Pres.* Karen McKenzie, Art Gallery of Ontario, E. P. Taylor Research Lib. and Archives, 317 Dundas St. W., Toronto, ON M5T 1G4. Tel. 416-979-6660 ext. 389, fax 416-979-6602, e-mail Karen_ McKenzie@ago.net; *Secy.* Norine Duncan, Brown Univ., List Art Center, Box 1855, Providence, RI 02912. Tel. 401-863-3082, fax 401-863-9589, e-mail Norine_Duncan @Brown.edu; *Treas.* Trudy Jacoby, Trinity College, Hallden Hall, 300 Summit St., Hartford, CT 06106-3100. Tel. 860-297-2194, fax 860-297-5349, e-mail trudy.jacoby@trincoll. edu.

Address correspondence to the executive director.

Executive Board

Officers; *Regional Reps.* (Northeast) Laurie Whitehill Chong, (South) Paula Hardin, (Midwest) Ursula Kolmstetter, (West) Leslie E. Abrams, (Canada) Carole Goldsmith.

Publications

ARLIS/NA Update (bi-m.; memb.).
Art Documentation (semi-ann.; memb., subsc.).
Handbook and List of Members (ann.; memb.).
Occasional Papers (price varies).
Miscellaneous others (request current list from headquarters).

Committee Chairpersons

Cataloging (Advisory). Elizabeth O'Keefe.
Conference Planning. Ted Goodman, Ann Whiteside.
Development. Gregory Most.
Distinguished Service Award. Rosemary Haddad.
Diversity. Marilyn Russell-Bogle, Lucie Stylianopoulos.
Finance. Vacant.
International Relations. Susana Tejada.
Membership. Leslie Lowe Preston.
Gerd Muehsam Award. Paula Gabbard.
Nominating. Roger Lawson.
Professional Development. Tom Greives.
Public Policy. James Mitchell, Barbara Rockenbach.
Publications. Betsy Peck Learned.
Standards. David Austin.
Technology Education. Judy Dyki.
Travel Awards. Carole Ann Fabian.
George Wittenborn Award. Nancy Norris.

Asian/Pacific American Librarians Association

President, Tamiye Meehan
Library Director, Indian Trails Public Library District
355 S. Schoenbeck Rd., Wheeling, IL 60098
World Wide Web http://www.uic.edu/depts/lib/projects/resources/apala

Object

To provide a forum for discussing problems and concerns of Asian/Pacific American librarians; to provide a forum for the exchange of ideas by Asian/Pacific American librarians and other librarians; to support and encourage library services to Asian/Pacific American communities; to recruit and support Asian/Pacific American librarians in the library/information science professions; to seek funding for scholarships in library/information science programs for Asian/Pacific Americans; and to provide a vehicle whereby Asian/Pacific American librarians can cooperate with other associations and organizations having similar or allied interests. Founded 1980; incorporated 1981; affiliated with American Library Association 1982.

Membership

Open to all librarians and information specialists of Asian/Pacific descent working in U.S. libraries and information centers and other related organizations, and to others who support the goals and purposes of APALA. Asian/Pacific Americans are defined as those who consider themselves Asian/Pacific Americans. They may be Americans of Asian/Pacific descent, Asian/Pacific people with the status of permanent residency, or Asian/Pacific people living in the United States. Dues (Inst.) $25; (Indiv.) $20; (Students/Unemployed Librarians) $5.

Officers (July 2001–June 2002)

Pres. Tamiye Meehan, Dir., Indian Trails Public Lib. District, 355 S. Schoenbeck Rd., Wheeling, IL 60098. Tel. 847-459-4100, e-mail tmeehan@itpld.lib.il.us; *V.P./Pres.-Elect* Gerardo Abarro Colmenar; *Past Pres.* Sushila Shah; *Secy.* Janet Tom; *Treas.* Heawon Paick.

Publication

APALA Newsletter (q.). *Guest Ed.* Wilfred W. Fong, Asst. Dean, School of Lib. and Info. Science, Univ. of Wisconsin–Milwaukee, Box 11694, Milwaukee, WI 53211; *Ed.* Kenneth Yamashita, Lib. Div. Manager, Stockton-San Joaquin City Public Lib., 1209 W. Downs St., Stockton, CA 95207.

Committee Chairpersons

Constitution and Bylaws. Ben Wakashge, Abdul Miah.

Membership and Recruitment. Sunnie Kim.

Newsletter and Publications. Kenneth Yamashita.

Nominations. Sushila Shah.

Program and Local Arrangement. Gerardo Colmenar.

Publicity. Mario A. Ascencio.

Scholarship. Buenaventura Basco, Abdul Miah.

Web. Lisa Zhao.

Association for Information and Image Management (AIIM International)

President, John F. Mancini
1100 Wayne Ave., Suite 1100, Silver Spring, MD 20910
301-587-8202, fax 301-587-2711
E-mail aiim@aiim.org
World Wide Web http://www.aiim.org

European Office: Chappell House, The Green, Datchet, Berks SL3 9EH, England.
44-1753-592-769, fax 44-1753-592-770
E-mail europeinfo@aiim.org.

Object

To bring together the users and suppliers of document technologies and services. Founded 1943.

Officers

Chair Clifton W. Sink, IKON Office Solutions, 4900 Avalon Ridge Pkwy., Norcross, GA 30071-1572. Tel. 770-326-1058, fax 770-448-0350, e-mail csink@ikon.com; *V. Chair* Reynolds C. Bish, Captiva Software Corp., 10145 Pacific Heights Blvd., San Diego, CA 92121. Tel. 858-320-1001, fax 858-320-1010, e-mail bish@captivacorp.com.

Publication

e-doc Magazine (bi-m.; memb.).

Association for Library and Information Science Education

Executive Director, Maureen Thompson
703-243-4146, fax 703-435-4390
E-mail alise@drohanmgmt.com
World Wide Web http://www.alise.org

Object

The Association for Library and Information Science Education (ALISE) is devoted to the advancement of knowledge and learning in the interdisciplinary field of information studies. Established 1915.

Membership

Memb. 500. Dues (Inst.) for ALA-accredited programs, sliding scale; (International Affiliate Inst.) $125; (Indiv.) $90, retired or student $40. Year. January–December. Any library/information science school with a program accredited by the ALA Committee on Accreditation may become an institutional member. Any school that offers a graduate degree in librarianship or a cognate field but whose program is not accredited by the ALA Committee on Accreditation may become an institutional member at the lower rate. Any school outside the United States and Canada offering a program comparable to that of institutional membership may become an international affiliate institutional member. Any organizational entity wishing to support LIS education may become an associate institutional member. Any faculty member, administrator, librarian, researcher, or other individual employed full time may become a personal member. Any retired or part-time faculty member, student, or other individual employed less than full time may become a personal member at the lower rate. Any student may become a member at a lower rate.

Officers (2001–2002)

Pres. Prudence Dalrymple, Dominican Univ. E-mail pdalrymple@email.dom.edu; *V.P./ Pres.-Elect* Elizabeth Aversa, Univ. of Tennessee. E-mail aversa@utk.edu; *Secy.-Treas.* Pat Feehan, Univ. of South Carolina. E-mail PFeehan@qwm.sc.edu. *Past Pres.* James Matarazzo, Simmons College. E-mail james. matarazzo@simmons.edu.

Directors

Officers; Louise S. Robbins, Univ. of Wisconsin–Madison. E-mail LRobbins@macc. wisc.edu; Ann Curry, Univ. of British Columbia. E-mail ann.curry@ubc.ca; Diane Barlow, Univ. of Maryland. E-mail dbarlow@umd. edu; *Co-Eds.* Joseph Mika (2001), Wayne State Univ. E-mail jmika@cms.cc.wayne. edu; Ronald W. Powell (2001), Wayne State Univ. E-mail rpowell@cms.cc.wayne.edu; *Exec. Dir.* Maureen Thompson. E-mail m thomson@drohanmgmt.com.

Publications

ALISE Library and Information Science Education Statistical Report (ann.; $65).
Journal of Education for Library and Information Science (4 a year; $78; foreign $88).
Membership Directory (ann.; $55).

Committee Chairpersons

Awards and Honors. Mary Brown, Southern Connecticut State Univ.
Conference Planning. Elizabeth Aversa, Univ. of Tennessee.
Editorial Board. Joe Mika, Wayne State Univ.
Government Relations. Betty Turock, Rutgers Univ.
International Relations. Ismail Abdullahi, Clark Atlanta Univ.
LIS Education Statistical Report Project. Evelyn Daniel, Jerry Saye, Univ. of North Carolina.
Membership. Stephen Bajjaly, Univ. of South Carolina.
Nominating. Gretchen Whitney, Univ. of Tennessee.
Organization and Bylaws. Heidi Julien, Dalhousie Univ.
Recruitment. Ling Hwey Jen, Univ. of Kentucky.
Research. Rebecca Watson-Boone, CSIP.
Tellers. Sue Easun, Scarecrow Press.

Association of Academic Health Sciences Libraries

Executive Director, Shirley Bishop
2150 N. 107, Suite 205, Seattle, WA 98133
206-367-8704, fax 206-367-8777
E-mail shirley@shirleybishopinc.com

Object

The Association of Academic Health Sciences Libraries (AAHSL) is composed of the directors of libraries of 142 accredited U. S. and Canadian medical schools belonging to the Association of American Medical Colleges. Its goals are to promote excellence in academic health science libraries and to ensure that the next generation of health practitioners is trained in information-seeking skills that enhance the quality of health care delivery, education, and research. Founded 1977.

Membership

Memb. 142. Dues $1,500. Regular membership is available to nonprofit educational institutions operating a school of health sciences that has full or provisional accreditation by the Association of American Medical Colleges. Regular members shall be represented by the chief administrative officer of the member institution's health sciences library. Associate membership (and nonvoting representation) is available at $600 to organizations having an interest in the purposes and activities of the association.

Officers (2001–2002)

Pres. Rick Forsman, Charles Denison Memorial Lib., Univ. of Colorado; *Past Pres.* Ada Seltzer, Rowland Medical Lib., Univ. of Mississippi; *Pres.-Elect* David Ginn, Alumni Medical Lib., Boston Univ.; *Secy.-Treas.* Holly Shipp Buchanan, Health Sciences Center Lib., Univ. of New Mexico.

Association of Independent Information Professionals (AIIP)

7044 S. 13 St., Oak Creek, WI 53154-1429
414-766-0421, fax 414-768-8001
E-mail aiipinfo@aiip.org
World Wide Web http://www.aiip.org

Membership

Memb. 750+.

Officers (2001–2002)

Pres. Lynn Ecklund, Seek Information Service. Tel. 818-242-3090, e-mail lecklund@seekinfo.com.

Object

AIIP's members are owners of firms providing such information-related services as online and manual research, document delivery, database design, library support, consulting, writing, and publishing. The objectives of the association are

- To advance the knowledge and understanding of the information profession

- To promote and maintain high professional and ethical standards among its members

- To encourage independent information professionals to assemble to discuss common issues

- To promote the interchange of information among independent information professionals and various organizations

- To keep the public informed of the profession and of the responsibilities of the information professional

Publications

Connections (q.)
Membership Directory (ann.).
Professional Paper series.

Association of Jewish Libraries

15 E. 26 St., Rm. 1034, New York, NY 10010
212-725-5359
E-mail ajl@jewishbooks.org
World Wide Web http://www.jewishlibraries.org

Object

To promote the improvement of library services and professional standards in all Jewish libraries and collections of Judaica; to provide professional development opportunities for Judaic librarians; to promote quality Judaic literature and reference materials; to select and publicize quality Judaic children's literature; to serve as a center of dissemination of Jewish bibliographic information and guidance; to encourage the establishment of Jewish libraries and collections of Judaica; to promote publication of literature that will be of assistance to Judaic librarianship; to encourage people to enter the field of librarianship. Organized in 1965 from the merger of the Jewish Librarians Association and the Jewish Library Association.

Membership

Memb. 1,100. Dues $50; (Foreign) $75; (Student/Retired) $30; Year. July 1–June 30.

Officers (June 2000–June 2002)

Pres. Toby Rossner; *Past Pres.* David Gilner, Hebrew Union College, Cincinnati, Ohio; *V.P./Pres.-Elect* Pearl Berger, Yeshiva Univ. Libs.; *V.P., Memb.* Yossi Galron; *V.P., Publications* Laurel Wolfson; *Treas.* Leah Adler; *Recording Secy.* Gloria Jacobs; *Corresponding Secy.* Rachel Erlich.

Address correspondence to the association.

Publications

AJL Newsletter (q.). *General Ed.* Barbara Sutton, Lawrence Family Jewish Community Center, 4126 Executive Drive, San Diego, CA 92037.

Judaica Librarianship (irreg.). *Ed.* > Linda Lerman, Bobst Lib., New York Univ., 70 Washington Sq. S., New York, NY 10012.

Division Presidents

Research and Special Library. David Hirsch. Synagogue, School, and Center Libraries. Michlean Amir.

Association of Research Libraries

Executive Director, Duane E. Webster
21 Dupont Circle N.W., Suite 800, Washington, DC 20036
202-296-2296, fax 202-872-0884
E-mail arlhq@arl.org
World Wide Web http://www.arl.org

Object

The mission of the Association of Research Libraries (ARL) is to shape and influence forces affecting the future of research libraries in the process of scholarly communication. ARL's programs and services promote equitable access to and effective use of recorded knowledge in support of teaching, research, scholarship, and community service. The association articulates the concerns of research libraries and their institutions, forges coalitions, influences information policy development, and supports innovation and improvement in research library operations. ARL is a not-for-profit membership organization comprising the libraries of North American research institutions and operates as a forum for the exchange of ideas and as an agent for collective action.

Membership

Memb. 123. Membership is institutional. Dues $18,550.

Officers (Oct. 2001–Oct. 2002)

Pres. Paula Kauffman, Univ. of Illinois; *Past Pres.* Shirley Baker, Washington Univ., St. Louis; *V.P./Pres.-Elect* Fred Heath, Texas A&M.

Board of Directors

Nancy Baker, Univ. of Iowa; Shirley K. Baker, Washington Univ., St. Louis; Joseph Branin, Ohio State Univ.; Frances Groen, McGill Univ.; Fred Heath, Texas A&M; Paula Kaufmann, Univ. of Illinois; Sarah Michalak, Univ. of Utah; Paul Mosher, Univ. of Pennsylvania; Brian Schottlaender, Univ. of California–San Diego; Sarah Thomas, Cornell; Ann Wolpert, Massachusetts Inst. of Technology.

Publications

ARL: A Bimonthly Report on Research Libraries Issues and Actions from ARL, CNI, and SPARC (bi-m.).
ARL Academic Law and Medical Library Statistics (ann.).
ARL Annual Salary Survey (ann.).
ARL Preservation Statistics (ann.).
ARL Statistics (ann.).
ARL Supplementary Statistics (ann.).
Directory of Scholarly Electronic Journals and Academic Discussion Lists.
SPEC Kits (6 a year).

Committee and Work Group Chairpersons

Access to Information Resources. Sarah Thomas, Cornell.
Diversity. Stella Bentley, Auburn.
Information Policies. Sharon Hogan, Univ. of Illinois, Chicago.
Membership. Jim Neal, Johns Hopkins.
Preservation of Research Library Materials. Nancy Gwinn, Smithsonian.
Research Collections. Merrily Taylor, Brown Univ.
Research Library Leadership and Management. Joan Giesecke, Univ. of Nebraska.
Scholarly Communication. Marianne Gaunt, Rutgers.
Scholars Portal Working Group. Jerry Campbell, Univ. of Southern California.
SPARC Steering Committee. Ken Frazier, Univ. of Wisconsin.
Statistics and Measurement. Carla Stoffle, Univ. of Arizona.
Working Group on Copyright Issues. Paula Kauffman, Univ. of Illinois.

ARL Membership

Nonuniversity Libraries

Boston Public Lib., Canada Inst. for Scientific and Technical Info., Center for Research Libs., Lib. of Congress, National Agricultural Lib., National Lib. of Canada, National Lib. of Medicine, New York Public Lib., New York State Lib., Smithsonian Institution Libs.

University Libraries

Alabama, Alberta, Arizona, Arizona State, Auburn, Boston College, Boston Univ., Brigham Young, British Columbia, Brown, California–Berkeley, California–Davis, California–Irvine, California–Los Angeles, California–Riverside, California–San Diego, California–Santa Barbara, Case Western Reserve, Chicago, Cincinnati, Colorado, Colorado State, Columbia, Connecticut, Cornell, Dartmouth, Delaware, Duke, Emory, Florida, Florida State, George Washington, Georgetown, Georgia, Georgia Inst. of Technology, Guelph, Harvard, Hawaii, Houston, Howard, Illinois–Chicago, Illinois–Urbana, Indiana, Iowa, Iowa State, Johns Hopkins, Kansas, Kent State, Kentucky, Laval, Louisiana State, McGill, McMaster, Manitoba, Maryland, Massachusetts, Massachusetts Inst. of Technology, Miami (Florida), Michigan, Michigan State, Minnesota, Missouri, Montreal, Nebraska–Lincoln, New Mexico, New York, North Carolina, North Carolina State, Northwestern, Notre Dame, Ohio, Ohio State, Oklahoma, Oklahoma State, Oregon, Pennsylvania, Pennsylvania State, Pittsburgh, Princeton, Purdue, Queen's (Kingston, ON, Canada), Rice, Rochester, Rutgers, Saskatchewan, South Carolina, Southern California, Southern Illinois, Stanford, SUNY–Albany, SUNY–Buffalo, SUNY–Stony Brook, Syracuse, Temple, Tennessee, Texas, Texas A&M, Texas Tech, Toronto, Tulane, Utah, Vanderbilt, Virginia, Virginia Tech, Washington, Washington (Saint Louis, Mo.), Washington State, Waterloo, Wayne State, Western Ontario, Wisconsin, Yale, York.

Association of Vision Science Librarians

Chair 2002–2003, Maureen Watson
Ferris State University, Michigan College of Optometry Reading Rm.,
1310 Cramer Circle, Big Rapids, MI 49307-2738.
231-591-2124
E-mail watsonm@ferris.edu.

Object

To foster collective and individual acquisition and dissemination of vision science information, to improve services for all persons seeking such information, and to develop standards for libraries to which members are attached. Founded 1968.

Membership

Memb. (U.S.) 85; (Foreign) 35.

Publications

Guidelines for Vision Science Libraries.
Opening Day Book Collection—Visual Science.
Ph.D. Theses in Physiological Optics (irreg.).
Standards for Vision Science Libraries.
Union List of Vision-Related Serials (irreg.).

Meetings

Annual meeting held in December in connection with the American Academy of Optometry; midyear mini-meeting with the Medical Library Association.

Beta Phi Mu
(International Library and Information Studies Honor Society)

Executive Director, Jane Robbins
School of Information Studies, Florida State University,
Tallahassee, FL 32306-2100
850-644-3907, fax 850-644-6253
E-mail beta_phi_mu@lis.fsu.edu
World Wide Web http://www.beta-phi-mu.org

Object

To recognize high scholarship in the study of librarianship and to sponsor appropriate professional and scholarly projects. Founded at the University of Illinois in 1948.

Membership

Memb. 23,000. Open to graduates of library school programs accredited by the American Library Association who fulfill the following requirements: complete the course requirements leading to a fifth year or other advanced degree in librarianship with a scholastic average of 3.75 where A equals 4 points (this provision shall also apply to planned programs of advanced study beyond the fifth year that do not culminate in a degree but that require full-time study for one or more academic years) and in the top 25 percent of their class; receive a letter of recommendation from their respective library schools attesting to their demonstrated fitness for successful professional careers.

Officers (2001–2003)

Pres. Robert S. Martin, Dir., Institute of Museum and Lib. Services, 1100 Pennsylvania Ave. N.W., Washington, DC 20506. Tel. 202-606-4649, fax 202-606-8591, e-mail rmartin@imls.gov; *V.P./Pres.-Elect* W. Michael Havener, Univ. of Rhode Island, Grad. School of Lib. and Info. Studies, Rodman Hall, 94 W. Alumni Ave., Suite 2, Kingston, RI 02881. Tel. 401-874-4641, fax 401-874-4964, e-mail mhavener@uri.edu; *Past Pres.* Barbara Immroth, Graduate School of Lib. and Info. Science, Univ. of Texas at Austin; *Treas.* Sondra Taylor-Furbee, State Lib. of Florida, 500 S. Bronough St., Tallahassee, FL 32399. Tel. 850-487-2651, fax 850-488-2746, e-mail staylor-furbee@mail.dox.state.fl.us; *Exec. Dir.* Jane Robbins, School of Info. Studies, Florida State Univ., Tallahassee, FL 32306. Tel. 850-644-3907, fax 850-644-6253, e-mail Beta_Phi_Mu@lis.fsu.edu.

Directors

Susan M. Agent (2002), Nicholas C. Burckel (2003), Michael Carpenter (2004), Louise S. Robbins (2004), Vicky Schmarr (2003), Sue Stroyan (2002), Danny P. Wallace (2002).

Publications

Beta Phi Mu Monograph Series. Book-length scholarly works based on original research in subjects of interest to library and information professionals. Available from Greenwood Press, 88 Post Rd. W., Box 5007, Westport, CT 06881-9990.

Chapbook Series. Limited editions on topics of interest to information professionals. Call Beta Phi Mu for availability.

Newsletter. (2 a year). *Ed.* Selinda L. Stout.

Chapters

Alpha. Univ. of Illinois, Grad. School of Lib. and Info. Science, Urbana, IL 61801; *Beta.* (Inactive). Univ. of Southern California, School of Lib. Science, Univ. Park, Los Angeles, CA 90007; *Gamma.* Florida State Univ., School of Lib. and Info. Studies, Tallahassee, FL 32306; *Delta* (Inactive). Loughborough College of Further Education, School of Libnship., Loughborough, England; *Epsi-*

Ion. Univ. of North Carolina, School of Lib. Science, Chapel Hill, NC 27599; *Zeta.* Atlanta Univ., School of Lib. and Info. Studies, Atlanta, GA 30314; *Theta.* Pratt Inst., Grad. School of Lib. and Info. Science, Brooklyn, NY 11205; *Iota.* Catholic Univ. of America, School of Lib. and Info. Science, Washington, DC 20064; Univ. of Maryland, College of Lib. and Info. Services, College Park, MD 20742; *Kappa.* (Inactive). Western Michigan Univ., School of Libnship., Kalamazoo, MI 49008; *Lambda.* Univ. of Oklahoma, School of Lib. Science, Norman, OK 73019; *Mu.* Univ. of Michigan, School of Lib. Science, Ann Arbor, MI 48109; *Xi.* Univ. of Hawaii, Grad. School of Lib. Studies, Honolulu, HI 96822; *Omicron.* Rutgers Univ., Grad. School of Lib. and Info. Studies, New Brunswick, NJ 08903; *Pi.* Univ. of Pittsburgh, School of Lib. and Info. Science, Pittsburgh, PA 15260; *Rho.* Kent State Univ., School of Lib. Science, Kent, OH 44242; *Sigma.* Drexel Univ., School of Lib. and Info. Science, Philadelphia, PA 19104; *Tau.* (Inactive). State Univ. of New York at Genesee, School of Lib. and Info. Science, Genesee, NY 14454; *Upsilon.* (Inactive). Univ. of Kentucky, College of Lib. Science, Lexington, KY 40506; *Phi.* Univ. of Denver, Grad. School of Libnship. and Info. Mgt., Denver, CO 80208; *Chi.* Indiana Univ., School of Lib. and Info. Science, Bloomington, IN 47401; *Psi.* Univ. of Missouri at Columbia, School of Lib. and Info. Sciences, Columbia, MO 65211; *Omega.* (Inactive). San Jose State Univ., Div. of Lib. Science, San Jose, CA 95192; *Beta Alpha.* Queens College, City College of New York, Grad. School of Lib. and Info. Studies, Flushing, NY 11367; *Beta Beta.* Simmons College, Grad. School of Lib. and Info. Science, Boston, MA 02115; *Beta Delta.* State Univ. of New York at Buffalo, School of Info. and Lib. Studies, Buffalo, NY 14260; *Beta Epsilon.* Emporia State Univ., School of Lib. Science, Emporia, KS 66801; *Beta Zeta.* Louisiana State Univ., Grad. School of Lib. Science, Baton Rouge, LA 70803; *Beta Eta.* Univ. of Texas at Austin, Grad. School of Lib. and Info. Science, Austin, TX 78712; *Beta Theta.* (Inactive). Brigham Young Univ., School of Lib. and Info. Science, Provo, UT 84602; *Beta Iota.* Univ. of Rhode

Island, Grad. Lib. School, Kingston, RI 02881; *Beta Kappa.* Univ. of Alabama, Grad. School of Lib. Service, University, AL 35486; *Beta Lambda.* North Texas State Univ., School of Lib. and Info. Science, Denton, TX 76203; Texas Woman's Univ., School of Lib. Science, Denton, TX 76204; *Beta Mu.* Long Island Univ., Palmer Grad. Lib. School, C. W. Post Center, Greenvale, NY 11548; *Beta Nu.* Saint John's Univ., Div. of Lib. and Info. Science, Jamaica, NY 11439. *Beta Xi.* North Carolina Central Univ., School of Lib. Science, Durham, NC 27707; *Beta Omicron.* (Inactive). Univ. of Tennessee at Knoxville, Grad. School of Lib. and Info. Science, Knoxville, TN 37916; *Beta Pi.* Univ. of Arizona, Grad. Lib. School, Tucson, AZ 85721; *Beta Rho.* Univ. of Wisconsin at Milwaukee, School of Lib. Science, Milwaukee, WI 53201; *Beta Sigma.* (Inactive). Clarion State College, School of Lib. Science, Clarion, PA 16214; *Beta Tau.* Wayne State Univ., Div. of Lib. Science, Detroit, MI 48202; *Beta Upsilon.* (Inactive). Alabama A&M Univ., School of Lib. Media, Normal, AL 35762; *Beta Phi.* Univ. of South Florida, Grad. Dept. of Lib., Media, and Info. Studies, Tampa, FL 33647; *Beta Psi.* Univ. of Southern Mississippi, School of Lib. Service, Hattiesburg, MS 39406; *Beta Omega.* Univ. of South Carolina, College of Libnship., Columbia, SC 29208; *Beta Beta Alpha.* Univ. of California at Los Angeles, Grad. School of Lib. and Info. Science, Los Angeles, CA 90024; *Beta Beta Gamma.* Rosary College, Grad. School of Lib. and Info. Science, River Forest, IL 60305; *Beta Beta Delta.* Univ. of Cologne, Germany; *Beta Beta Epsilon.* Univ. of Wisconsin at Madison, Lib. School, Madison, WI 53706; *Beta Beta Zeta.* Univ. of North Carolina at Greensboro, Dept. of Lib. Science and Educational Technology, Greensboro, NC 27412; *Beta Beta Theta.* Univ. of Iowa, School of Lib. and Info. Science, Iowa City, IA 52242; *Beta Beta Iota.* State Univ. of New York, Univ. at Albany, School of Info. Science and Policy, Albany, NY 12222; *Beta Beta Kappa.* Univ. of Puerto Rico Grad. School of Info. Sciences and Technologies, San Juan, PR 00931-1906; *Pi Lambda Sigma.* Syracuse Univ., School of Info. Studies, Syracuse, NY 13210.

Bibliographical Society of America

Executive Secretary, Michele E. Randall
Box 1537, Lenox Hill Station, New York, NY 10021
212-452-2500 (tel./fax), e-mail bsa@bibsocamer.org
World Wide Web: http://www.bibsocamer.org

Object

To promote bibliographical research and to issue bibliographical publications. Organized 1904.

Membership

Memb. 1,200. Dues $50. Year. Jan.–Dec.

Officers

Pres. Hope Mayo; *V.P.* John Bidwell; *Treas.* R. Dyke Benjamin; *Secy.* Claudia Funke.

Council

Susan Allen (2003), Anne Anninger (2002), Florence Fearrington (2002), Marie E. Korey (2003), Mark Samuels Lasner (2003), Michael Winship (2002), Elizabeth Witherell (2003), David S. Zeidberg (2002).

Publication

Papers (q.; memb.). *Ed.* Trevor Howard-Hill, Thomas Cooper Lib., Univ. of South Carolina, Columbia, SC 29208. Tel./fax 803-777-7046, e-mail RalphCrane@msn.com.

Committee Chairpersons

Bibliographical Projects. Michael Winship.
Delegate to American Council of Learned Societies. Marcus McCorison.
Fellowship. David Zeidberg.
Finance. William P. Barlow.
Publications. John Bidwell.
Program. Laura A. Stalker.
Web Site. Trevor Howard-Hill.

Canadian Association for Information Science
(Association Canadienne des Sciences de l'Information)

University of Toronto, Faculty of Information Studies,
140 Saint George St., Toronto, ON M5S 3G6, Canada
416-978-7111, fax 416-971-1399

Object

To bring together individuals and organizations concerned with the production, manipulation, storage, retrieval, and dissemination of information, with emphasis on the application of modern technologies in these areas. The association is dedicated to enhancing the activity of the information-transfer process; utilizing the vehicles of research, development, application, and education; and serving as a forum for dialogue and exchange of ideas concerned with the theory and practice of all factors involved in the communication of information.

Membership

Institutions and individuals interested in information science and involved in the gathering, organization, and dissemination of information (computer scientists, documentalists, information scientists, librarians, journalists, sociologists, psychologists, linguists, administrators, and so forth) can become association members. Dues (Inst.) $165; (Personal) $75; (Student) $40.

Publication

Canadian Journal of Information and Library Science (q.; $95; outside Canada $110).

Canadian Library Association

Executive Director, Vicki Whitmell
328 Frank St., Ottawa, ON K2P 0X8
613-232-9625 ext. 306, fax 613-563-9895
E-mail vwhitmell@cla.ca
World Wide Web http://www.cla.ca

Object

To promote, develop, and support library and information services in Canada and to work in cooperation with all who share our values in order to present a unified voice on issues of mutual concern. The association offers library school scholarship and book awards, carries on international liaison with other library associations, makes representation to government and official commissions, offers professional development programs, and supports intellectual freedom. Founded in 1946, CLA is a nonprofit voluntary organization governed by an elected executive council.

Membership

Memb. (Indiv.) 2,500; (Inst.) 600. Open to individuals, institutions, and groups interested in librarianship and in library and information services. Dues (Indiv.) $175; (Inst.) $300.

Officers

Pres. Margaret Law, Assoc. Dir. of Libs., Univ. of Alberta, 1-22B Cameron Lib., Edmonton, AB T6G 2J8. Tel. 780-492-2721, e-mail margaret.law@ualberta.ca; *V.P.* Wendy Newman, CEO, Brantford Public Lib., 173 Colbourne St., Brantford, ON N3T 2G8. Tel. 519-756-2223 ext. 4, fax 519-756-4979, e-mail wnewman@brantford.library.on.ca; *Treas.* Kathryn Arbuckle, Law Libn., Univ. of Alberta, John A. Weir Memorial Law Lib., Edmonton, AB T6G 2H5. Tel. 780-492-3717, fax 780-492-7546, e-mail kathryn.arbuckle @ualberta.ca; *Past Pres.* Stan Skrzeszewski, ASM Advanced Strategic Management Consultants, 411 Rippleton Place, London, ON

N6G 1L4. Tel. 519-473-7651, fax 519-471-9945, e-mail asmstan@netcom.ca.

Publication

Feliciter: Linking Canada's Information Professionals (6 a year; newsletter).

Division Representatives

Canadian Association of College and University Libraries (CACUL). Jane E. Philipps, Head, Queen's Univ. Engineering and Science Lib., Douglas Lib., Kingston, Ontario K7L 5C4. Tel. 613-533-6846, fax 613-545-2684, e-mail phillipj@post.queensu.ca.

Canadian Association of Public Libraries (CAPL). Gina La Force, Chief Exec. Officer, Markham Public Lib., 445 Apple Creek Blvd., Suite 100, Markham, ON L3P 9X7 Tel. 905-513-7977, fax 905-513-7984, e-mail glaforce@markham.library. on.ca.

Canadian Association of Special Libraries and Information Services (CASLIS). Francesco Lai, Manager, Lib. and Info. Services, Agriculture and Agri-Food Canada (SCPFRC), 93 Stone Rd. W., Guelph, ON N1G 5C9. Tel. 519-829-2400 ext. 3126, fax 519-829-2600, e-mail laif@em.agr.ca.

Canadian Library Trustees' Association (CLTA). Ernest Neumann, Trustee, Burnaby Public Lib., 6100 Willdon Ave., Burnaby, BC V5H 4N5. Tel. 604-421-3559, fax 604-421-7883, e-mail ernest@abbeygraphics. com.

Canadian School Library Association (CSLA). Karin Paul, 4291 Caen Rd., Victoria, BC V8X 3S5. Tel. 250-479-1414, fax 250-479-5356, e-mail kepaul@islandnet.com.

Catholic Library Association

Executive Director, Jean R. Bostley, SSJ
100 North St., Suite 224, Pittsfield, MA 01201-5109
413-443-2252, fax 413-442-2252, e-mail cla@cathla.org
World Wide Web http://www.cathla.org

Object

The promotion and encouragement of Catholic literature and library work through cooperation, publications, education, and information. Founded 1921.

Membership

Memb. 1,000. Dues $45–$500. Year. July–June.

Officers (2001–2002)

Pres. Sally Anne Thompson, Pope John XXIII Catholic School Community, 16235 N. 60th St., Scottsdale, AZ 85254-7323. Tel. 480-905-0939, fax 480-905-0955, e-mail desertsat@aol.com; *V.P./Pres.-Elect* M. Dorothy Neuhofer, OSB, St. Leo Univ., Box 6665 MC 2128, Saint Leo, FL 33574-6665. Tel. 352-588-8260, fax 352-588-8484, e-mail neuhofd@saintleo.edu; *Past Pres.* Rev. Bonaventure Hayes, OFM, Christ the King Seminary, 711 Knox Rd., East Aurora, NY 1452-0607. Tel. 716-652-8940, fax 716-652-8903.

Address correspondence to the executive director.

Executive Board

Officers; Kathy Born, 1120 Hickory Lake Dr., Cincinnati, OH 45233; Mary Agnes Casey, SSJ, 462 Hillsdale St., Hillsdale, NJ 07642; Maxine C. Lucas, St. Mel School, 20874 Ventura Blvd., Woodland Hills, CA 91364; Nancy K. Schmidtmann, 149 Orchard St., Plainview, NY 11803-4718; Mary June Roggenbuck, Catholic Univ. of America, Washington, DC 20064; Cecil R. White, St. Patrick's Seminary, 320 Middlefield Rd., Menlo Park, CA 94025.

Publications

Catholic Library World (q.; memb.; nonmemb. $60). *General Ed.* Mary E. Gallagher, SSJ; *Production Ed.* Allen Gruenke.

Catholic Periodical and Literature Index (q.; $400 calendar year; abridged ed., $100 calendar year; *CPLI* on CD-ROM, inquire. *Ed.* Kathleen Spaltro.

Section Chairpersons

Academic Libraries/Library Education. Molly M. Lyons.

Archives. Mary E. Gallagher, SSJ.

Children's Libraries. Maxine C. Lucas.

High School Libraries. Annette B. Thibodeaux.

Parish/Community Libraries. Mary Catherine Blooming, HM.

Round Table Chairpersons

Bibliographic Instruction. To be appointed.

Cataloging and Classification. To be appointed.

Preservation of American Catholic Materials. To be appointed.

Committee Chairpersons

Catholic Library World Editorial. Nancy K. Schmidtmann.

Catholic Periodical and Literature Index. Cecil R. White.

Constitution and Bylaws. Sara Baron.

Elections. Eileen Franke.

Finance. M. Dorothy Neuhofer, OSB.

Grant Development. Jean R. Bostley, SSJ.

Membership Development. To be appointed.

Nominations. Julanne M. Good.

Publications. Mary E. Gallagher, SSJ.

Scholarship. Kathleen O'Leary.

Special Appointments

American Friends of the Vatican Library Board. Jean R. Bostley, SSJ.

Convention Program Coordinator. Jean R. Bostley, SSJ.

Parliamentarian. Rev. Jovian Lang, OFM.

Chief Officers of State Library Agencies

167 W. Main St., Suite 600, Lexington, KY 40507
859-231-1925, fax 859-231-1928
E-mail bdoty@amrinc.net

Object

To provide a means of cooperative action among its state and territorial members to strengthen the work of the respective state and territorial agencies, and to provide a continuing mechanism for dealing with the problems faced by the heads of these agencies, which are responsible for state and territorial library development.

Membership

Chief Officers of State Library Agencies (COSLA) is an independent organization of the men and women who head the state and territorial agencies responsible for library development. Its membership consists solely of the top library officers of the 50 states, the District of Columbia, and the territories, variously designated as state librarian, director, commissioner, or executive secretary.

Officers (2001–2002)

Pres. Keith Fiels, Dir., Bd. of Lib. Commissioners, 648 Beacon St., Boston, MA 02215.

Tel. 617-267-9400, fax 617-421-9833, e-mail keith.fiels@state.ma.us; *V.P./Pres.-Elect* Karen Crane, Dir., Alaska Libs., Archives and Museums, Box 110571, Juneau, AK 99811-0571. Tel. 907-465-2910, fax 907-465-2151, e-mail Karen_Crane@eed.state.ak.us; *Secy.* Nolan T. Yelich, Libn. of Virginia, Lib. of Virginia, 800 E. Broad St., Richmond, VA 23219. Tel. 804-692-3535, fax 804-692-3594, e-mail nyelich@lva.lib.va.us; *Treas.* J. Gary Nichols, State Libn., Maine State Lib., 64 State House Sta., Augusta, ME 04333. Tel. 207-287-5600, fax 207-287-5615, e-mail gary.nichols@state.me.us. *Dirs.* Michael Lucas, State Libn., Ohio State Lib., 274 E. 1 Ave., Columbus, OH 43201. Tel. 614-644-6863, fax 614-466-3584, e-mail mlucas@sloma.state.oh.us; Peggy D. Rudd, Dir. and Libn., Texas State Lib. and Archives Commission, Box 12927, Austin, TX 78711-2927. Tel. 512-463-5455, fax 512-463-5436, e-mail peggy.rudd@TSL.state.TX.US; *Past Pres.* C. Ray Ewick, Dir., Indiana State Lib., 140 N. Senate Ave., Indianapolis, IN 46204. Tel. 317-232-3692, fax 317-232-3728, e-mail ewick@statelib.lib.in.us.

Chinese American Librarians Association

Executive Director, Sally C. Tseng
949-824-6832, fax 949-857-1988
E-mail sctseng@uci.edu
World Wide Web http://www.cala-web.org

Object

To enhance communications among Chinese American librarians as well as between Chinese American librarians and other librarians; to serve as a forum for discussion of mutual problems and professional concerns among Chinese American librarians; to promote Sino-American librarianship and library services; and to provide a vehicle whereby Chinese American librarians may cooperate with other associations and organizations having similar or allied interests.

Membership

Memb. 770. Open to anyone who is interested in the association's goals and activities. Dues (Regular) $30; (Student/Nonsalaried) $15; (Inst.) $100; (Life) $400.

Officers

Pres. Liana Hong Zhou. E-mail zhoul@indiana.edu; *V.P./Pres.-Elect* Angela Yang. E-mail ayang@uci.edu; *Treas.* Dora Ho. E-mail doraho@yahoo.com; *Past Pres.* Yu-lan Chou. E-mail yulan_chou@yahoo.com.

Publications

Journal of Library and Information Science, (2 a year; memb.; nonmemb. $15). *Ed.* Haipeng Li. E-mail haipeng.li@oberlin.edu.
Membership Directory (memb.).
Newsletter (3 a year; memb.; nonmemb. $10). *Eds.* Sha-li Zhang. E-mail zhang@twsuvm.uc.twsu.edu; Jian Liu. E-mail jiliu@indiana.edu.

Committee Chairpersons

Awards. Amy Tsiang, Sha-li Zhang.
Constitution and Bylaws. Susana Liu.
Finance. Peter Wang.
International Relations. Cathy Yang, Priscilla Yu.
Membership. Lisa Zhao.
Public Relations/Fund-raising. Diana Wu, Esther Lee.
Publications. Zhijia Shen.
Scholarship. Dajin Sun.
Conference Program Committee. Angela Yang.
Webmaster. Shixing Wen.

Chapter Presidents

California. Xiwen Zhang.
Florida. Ying Zhang.
Greater Mid-Atlantic. Edwin Yu.
Midwest. Lisa Zhao.
Northeast. Janey Chao.
Southwest. George Teoh.

Church and Synagogue Library Association

Box 19357, Portland, OR 97280-0357
503-244-6919, 800-542-2752, fax 503-977-3734
E-mail CSLA@worldaccessnet.com
World Wide Web http://www.worldaccessnet.com/~CSLA

Object

To act as a unifying core for the many existing church and synagogue libraries; to provide the opportunity for a mutual sharing of practices and problems; to inspire and encourage a sense of purpose and mission among church and synagogue librarians; to study and guide the development of church and synagogue librarianship toward recognition as a formal branch of the library profession. Founded 1967.

Membership

Memb. 1,900. Dues (Inst.) $175; (Affiliated) $70; (Church/Synagogue) $45 ($50 foreign); (Indiv.) $25 ($30 foreign). Year. July–June.

Officers (July 2001–June 2002)

Pres. Barbara May; *Pres.-Elect* Helen Zappia; *2nd V.P.* Barbara Schroer; *Treas.* Beth Hodgson; *Admin.* Judith Janzen; *Past Pres.* JoMae Spoelhof; *Ed., Church and Synagogue Libraries* Karen Bota, 490 N. Fox Hills Dr., No. 7, Bloomfield Hills, MI 48304; *Book Review Ed.* Charles Snyder, 213 Lawn Ave., Sellersville, PA 18960.

Executive Board

Officers; committee chairpersons.

Publications

Bibliographies (1–5; price varies).
Church and Synagogue Libraries (bi-mo.; memb.; nonmemb. $35; Canada $45). *Ed.* Karen Bota.
CSLA Guides (1–17; price varies).

Committee Chairpersons

Awards. Barbara Messner.
Conference. Eloise Rayford.
Finance. Warren Livingston.
Library Services. Evelyn Pockrass.
Nominations and Elections. Judith Livingston.
Publications. Carol Campbell.

Coalition for Networked Information (CNI)

Executive Director, Clifford A. Lynch
21 Dupont Circle, Suite 800, Washington, DC 20036
202-296-5098, fax 202-872-0884
E-mail info@cni.org
World Wide Web http://www.cni.org

Mission

The Coalition for Networked Information (CNI) is an organization to advance the transformative promise of networked information technology for the advancement of scholarly communication and the enrichment of intellectual productivity.

Membership

Memb. 210. Membership is institutional. Dues $5,450. Year. July–June.

Officers (July 2001–June 2002)

Duane Webster, Exec. Dir., Association of Research Libraries; Brian Hawkins, Pres., EDUCAUSE.

Steering Committee

Richard P. West, California State Univ. (*Chair*); Shirley Baker, Washington Univ.; Gregory Crane, Tufts Univ; Nancy Eaton, Pennsylvania State Univ.; Brian Hawkins, EDUCAUSE; Charles Henry, Rice Univ.; Michael E. Lesk, National Science Foundation; Lawrence M. Levine, Dartmouth College; Clifford Lynch, CNI; Susan L. Perry, Mount Holyoke College; Donald J. Waters, Andrew Mellon Foundation; Duane Webster, ARL.

Publications

CNI-Announce (subscribe by e-mail to List proc@CNI.org)

Council on Library and Information Resources

1755 Massachusetts Ave. N.W., Suite 500, Washington, DC 20036-2124
202-939-4750, fax 202-939-4765
World Wide Web http://www.clir.org

Object

In 1997 the Council on Library Resources (CLR) and the Commission on Preservation and Access (CPA) merged and became the Council on Library and Information Resources (CLIR). The mission of the council is to identify and define the key emerging issues related to the welfare of libraries and the constituencies they serve, convene the leaders who can influence change, and promote collaboration among the institutions and organizations that can achieve change. The council's interests embrace the entire range of information resources and services from traditional library and archival materials to emerging digital formats. It assumes a particular interest in helping institutions cope with the accelerating pace of change associated with the transition into the digital environment. The council pursues this mission out of the conviction that information is a public good and has great social utility.

The term *library* is construed to embrace its traditional meanings and purposes and to encompass any and all information agencies and organizations that are involved in gathering, cataloging, storing, preserving, and distributing information and in helping users meet their information requirements.

While maintaining appropriate collaboration and liaison with other institutions and organizations, the council operates independently of any particular institutional or vested interests.

Through the composition of its board, it brings the broadest possible perspective to bear upon defining and establishing the priority of the issues with which it is concerned.

Membership of Board

CLIR's board of directors is limited to 18 members.

Officers

Chair Stanley Chodorow; *Pres.* Deanna B. Marcum. E-mail dmarcum@CLIR.org; *Treas.* Dan Tonkery.

Address correspondence to headquarters.

Publications

Annual Report.
CLIR Issues.
Technical reports.

Federal Library and Information Center Committee

Executive Director, Susan M. Tarr
Library of Congress, Washington, DC 20540-4935
202-707-4800
World Wide Web http://lcweb.loc.gov/flicc

Object

The Federal Library and Information Center Committee (FLICC) makes recommendations on federal library and information policies, programs, and procedures to federal agencies and to others concerned with libraries and information centers. The committee coordinates cooperative activities and services among federal libraries and information centers and serves as a forum to consider issues and policies that affect federal libraries and information centers, needs and priorities in providing information services to the government and to the nation at large, and efficient and cost-effective use of federal library and information resources and services. Furthermore, the committee promotes improved access to information, continued development and use of the Federal Library and Information Network (FEDLINK), research and development in the application of new technologies to federal libraries and information centers, improvements in the management of federal libraries and information centers, and relevant education opportunities. Founded 1965.

Membership

Libn. of Congress, Dir. of the National Agricultural Lib., Dir. of the National Lib. of Medicine, Dir. of the National Lib. of Educ., representatives of each of the cabinet-level executive departments, and representatives from each of the following agencies: National Aeronautics and Space Admin., National Science Foundation, Smithsonian Institution, U.S. Supreme Court, National Archives and Records Admin., Admin. Offices of the U.S. Courts, Defense Technical Info. Center, Government Printing Office, National Technical Info. Service (Dept. of Commerce), Office of Scientific and Technical Info. (Dept. of Energy), Exec. Office of the President, Dept. of the Army, Dept. of the Navy, Dept. of the Air Force, and chair of the FEDLINK Advisory Council. Fifteen additional voting member agencies shall be selected on a rotating basis by the voting members of FEDLINK. These rotating members will serve a three-year term. One representative from each of the following agencies is invited as an observer to committee meetings: General Accounting Office, General Services Admin., Joint Committee on Printing, National Commission on Libs. and Info. Science, Office of Mgt. and

Budget, Office of Personnel Mgt., and U.S. Copyright Office.

Officers

Chair James H. Billington, Libn. of Congress; *Chair Designate* Winston Tabb, Assoc. Libn. for Lib. Services, Lib. of Congress; *Exec. Dir.* Susan M. Tarr.

Address correspondence to the executive director.

Publications

Annual FLICC Forum on Federal Information Policies (summary and papers). *FEDLINK Technical Notes* (m.). *FLICC Newsletter* (q.).

Federal Publishers Committee

Chair, Glenn W. King
Bureau of the Census, Washington, DC 20233
301-457-1171, fax 301-457-4707
E-mail glenn.w.king@census.gov

Object

To foster and promote effective management of data development and dissemination in the federal government through exchange of information, and to act as a focal point for federal agency publishing.

Membership

Memb. 500. Membership is available to persons involved in publishing and dissemination in federal government departments, agencies, and corporations, as well as independent organizations concerned with federal government publishing and dissemination.

Some key federal government organizations represented are the Joint Committee on Printing, Government Printing Office, National Technical Info. Service, National Commission on Libs. and Info. Science, and the Lib. of Congress. Meetings are held monthly during business hours.

Officers

Chair Glenn W. King; *V. Chair, Programs* Sandra Smith; *Dirs.* John Ward, Pat Woods.

Publication

Guide to Federal Publishing (occasional).

Lutheran Church Library Association

Executive Director, Leanna D. Kloempken
122 W. Franklin Ave., No. 604, Minneapolis, MN 55404
612-870-3623, fax 612-870-0170
E-mail ContactUs@LCLAHQ.org
World Wide Web http://www.lclahq.org

Object

To promote the growth of church libraries by publishing a quarterly journal, *Lutheran Libraries*; furnishing recommended-book lists; assisting member libraries with technical problems; and providing workshops and meetings for mutual encouragement, guidance, and exchange of ideas among members. Founded 1958.

Membership

Memb. 1,800 churches, 250 personal. Dues $28, $40, $55, $70, $75, $100, $500, $1,000. Year. Jan.–Jan.

Officers (2001–2002)

Pres. Jeanette Johnson; *V.P.* Bonnie McLellan; *Secy.* Claudia Kolb; *Treas.* Dale Kannen.

Address correspondence to the executive director.

Directors

Sue Benich, Gerrie Buzard, Doris Engstrom, Mildred Herder, Lila Reinmuth, Helen Shoup.

Publication

Lutheran Libraries (q.; memb.; nonmemb. $30).

Board Chairpersons

Advisory. Mary Jordan.
Finance. Vernita Kennen.
Library Services. Marlys Johnson.
Publications. David Halaas.
Telecommunications. Chuck Mann.

Medical Library Association

Executive Director, Carla Funk
65 E. Wacker Pl., Suite 1900, Chicago, IL 60601
312-419-9094, fax 312-419-8950
E-mail info@mlahq.org
World Wide Web http://mlanet.org

Object

Established in 1898, the Medical Library Association (MLA) is an educational organization of 5,000 individuals and institutions in the health sciences information field. MLA is dedicated to excellence in health through access to information. Its major purposes are to serve society by improving health through the provision of information for the delivery of health care, the education of health professionals, the conduct of research, and the public's understanding of health. The foremost concern of the membership is the dissemination of quality health sciences information for use in education, research, and patient care.

Membership

Memb. (Inst.) 1,100; (Indiv.) 3,800. Institutional members are medical and allied scientific libraries. Individual members are people who are (or were at the time membership was established) engaged in professional library or bibliographic work in medical and allied scientific libraries or people who are interested in medical or allied scientific libraries. Dues (Student) $30; (Emeritus) $50; (International) $90; (Indiv.) $135; (Lifetime) $2,540; and (Inst.) $210–$495, based on the number of the library's periodical subscriptions. Members may be affiliated with one or more of MLA's 23 special-interest sections and 14 regional chapters.

Officers

Pres. Carol Jenkins, AHIP, Health Sciences Lib., Univ. of North Carolina–Chapel Hill, Box 7585, Chapel Hill, NC 27599-7585; *Pres.-Elect* Linda A. Watson, AHIP, Claude Moore Health Sciences Lib., Univ. of Virginia Health System, Box 800722, 1300 Jefferson Park Ave., Charlottesville, VA 22908-0722; *Past Pres.* J. Michael Homan, AHIP, Mayo Medical Lib., Mayo Clinic, 200 First St. S.W., Rochester, MN 55905.

Directors

Dianna Cunningham (2004), Lynn Fortney (2003), Mark Funk (2003), Nancy L. Henry (2002), Ruth Holst (2004), Linda Garr Markwell (2004), Julie McGowan (2002), Jocelyn Rankin (2002), Jean Shipman (2002).

Publications

Journal of the Medical Library Association (q.; $136).
MLA News (10 a year; $48.50).

Miscellaneous (request current list from association headquarters).

Committee Chairpersons

Awards. Bette Sydelko.
Books. Anne Prussing.
Bylaws. Patricia Thibodeau.
Continuing Education. Kathryn Nesbit.
Credentialing. Anna Beth Crabtree.
Governmental Relations. Logan Ludwig.
Grants and Scholarships. Jeanne Strausman.
Journal. T. Scott Plutchak.
Joseph Leiter NLM/MLA Lectureship. Marjorie Cahn.
Membership. Russet Hambrick.
MLANET Editorial Board. Scott Garrison.
National Program (2002). Connie Poole.
National Program (2003). Ysabel Bertolucci.
National Program (2004). M. J. Tooey.
Oral History. Jana Allcock.
Publications. Joan Dalrymple.

Ad Hoc Committee and Task Force Charges

Benchmarking Implementation. Debra Rand.
Center of Excellence in Health Information Education Initiative. Lynn Fortney.
Fixed Meeting Schedule. Frieda Weise.
Informationist Conference. Jean Shipman.
Joint MLA/AAHSLD Legislative. Lynne Siemers.
MLA/Pew Credible Information. M. J. Tooey.
Promote the Importance of Expert Searching. Ruth Holst.
Recruit the Twenty-first Century Workforce. Elizabeth Irish.

Music Library Association

8551 Research Way, Suite 180, Middleton, WI 53562
608-836-5825
World Wide Web http://www.musiclibraryassoc.org

Object

To promote the establishment, growth, and use of music libraries; to encourage the collection of music and musical literature in libraries; to further studies in musical bibliography; to increase efficiency in music library service and administration; and to promote the profession of music librarianship. Founded 1931.

Membership

Memb. 1,197. Dues (Inst.) $90; (Indiv.) $75; (Retired) $45; (Student) $35. Year. July 1–June 30.

Officers

Pres. James P. Cassaro, Univ. of Pittsburgh, Music Lib., B-30 Music Bldg., Pittsburgh, PA 15260. Tel. 412-624-4130, fax 412-624-4180, e-mail cassaro+@pitt.edu; *Past Pres.* Paula D. Matthews, Mendel Music Lib., Princeton Univ., Woolworth Center for Musical Studies, Princeton, NJ 08548. Tel. 609-258-4251, e-mail pmatthew@princeton.edu; *Rec. Secy.* Michael Colby, Catalog Dept., Shields Lib., 100 N. West Quad, Univ. of California–Davis, Davis, CA 95616-5292. Tel. 530-752-0931, fax 530-754-8785, e-mail mdcolby@ucdavis.edu; *Treas./Exec. Secy.* Laura Gayle Green, Miller Nichols Lib., Univ. of Missouri–Kansas City, 5100 Rockill Rd., Kansas City, MO 64110. Tel. 816-235-1679, fax 816-333-5584, e-mail greenlg@umkc.edu.

Members-at-Large

Allie Goudy, Western Illinois Univ.; Neil Hughes, Univ. of Georgia; Deborary Pierce, Univ. of Washington; Michael Rogan, Tufts Univ.; Leslie Troutman, Univ. of Illinois; Philip Vandermeer, Univ. of North Carolina, Chapel Hill.

Special Officers

Advertising Mgr. Susan Dearborn, 1572 Massachusetts Ave., No. 57, Cambridge, MA 02138. Tel. 617-876-0934; *Business Mgr.* Jim Zychowicz, 8551 Research Way, Suite 180, Middleton, WI 53562. Tel. 608-836-5825; *Convention Mgr.* Gordon Rowley, Box 395, Bailey's Harbor, WI 54202. Tel. 920-839-2444, e-mail baileysbreeze@itol.com; *Asst. Convention Mgr.* Don L. Roberts, Northwestern Univ. Music Lib., 1935 Sheridan Rd., Evanston, IL 60208-2300. Tel. 847-491-3434, fax 847-491-8306, e-mail droberts@nwu.edu; *Placement* Renee McBride, UCLA, A1538 Young Research Lib., Box 951575, Los Angeles, CA 90095-1575. Tel. 310-206-5853, fax 310-206-4974, e-mail rmcbride@library.ucla.edu; *Publicity* Alan Karass, College of the Holy Cross, Music Lib., Worcester, MA 01610. Tel. 508-793-2295, e-mail akarass@holycross.edu.

Publications

MLA Index and Bibliography Series (irreg.; price varies).
MLA Newsletter (q.; memb.).
MLA Technical Reports (irreg.; price varies).
Music Cataloging Bulletin (mo.; $25).
Notes (q.; indiv. $70; inst. $80).

Committee and Roundtable Chairpersons

Administration. Robert Acker, DePaul Univ.
Bibliographic Control. Matthew Wise, New York Univ.
Finance. Philip Vandermeer, Univ. of North Carolina, Chapel Hill.
Legislation. Bonna Boettcher, Bowling Green State Univ.
Membership. Sarah Dorsey, Univ. of North Carolina, Greensboro.
Preservation. Marlena Frackowski, Univ. of Arizona.
Public Libraries. Anna Seaberg, King County

Lib. System. Publications. Nancy Nuzzo, SUNY Buffalo.

Reference Sharing and Collection Development. Mark Germer, Univ. of the Arts.

National Association of Government Archives and Records Administrators

48 Howard St., Albany, NY 12207
518-463-8644, fax 518-463-8656
E-mail nagara@caphill.com
World Wide Web http://www.nagara.org

Object

Founded in 1984, the association is successor to the National Association of State Archives and Records Administrators, which had been established in 1974. NAGARA is a growing nationwide association of local, state, and federal archivists and records administrators, and others interested in improved care and management of government records. NAGARA promotes public awareness of government records and archives management programs, encourages interchange of information among government archives and records management agencies, develops and implements professional standards of government records and archival administration, and encourages study and research into records management problems and issues.

Membership

Most NAGARA members are federal, state, and local archival and records management agencies.

Officers

Pres. Jeanne Young, Board of Governors of the Federal Reserve System, 20th and C Sts. N.W., MS-56, Washington, DC 20551. Tel. 202-452-2033, fax 202-452-3819, e-mail jeanne.young@frb.gov; *V.P.* Terry B. Ellis, County Records Manager, Salt Lake County

Records Management and Archives, 2001 S. State St. N4400, Salt Lake City, UT 84190-3000. Tel. 801-468-2332, fax 801-468-3987, e-mail tellis@co.slc.ut.us; *Secy.* Robert Horton, State Archivist, Minnesota Historical Society, 345 Kellogg Blvd. W., St. Paul, MN 55102. Tel. 651-215-5866, fax 651-296-9961, e-mail robert.horton@mnhs.org; *Treas.* John Stewart, State Archivist, Alaska State Archives and Records, 141 Willoughby Ave., Juneau, AK 99801. Tel. 907-465-2275, fax 907-465-2465, e-mail john_stewart@eed.state.ak.us

Directors

Kent Carter, National Archives and Records Administration, Southwest Region; Nancy Fortna, National Archives and Records Administration, Washington, D.C.; C. Preston Huff, Library of Virginia; Kay Lanning Minchew, Troup County (Georgia) Archives; Richard Roberts, City of Hollywood (Florida); Timothy A. Slavin, Delaware Public Archives.

Publications

Clearinghouse (q.; memb.).
Crossroads (q.; memb.).
Government Records Issues (series).
Preservation Needs in State Archives (report).
Program Reporting Guidelines for Government Records Programs.

NFAIS

Executive Director, Dan Duncan
1518 Walnut St., Philadelphia, PA 19102
215-893-1561, fax 215-893-1564
E-mail nfais@nfais.org
World Wide Web http://www.NFAIS.org

Object

NFAIS (formerly National Federation of Abstracting and Information Services) is an international, nonprofit membership organization comprised of leading information providers. Its membership includes government agencies, nonprofit scholarly societies, and private-sector businesses. NFAIS serves groups that aggregate, organize, or facilitate access to information. To improve members' capabilities and to contribute to their ongoing success, NFAIS provides a forum to address common interests through education and advocacy. Founded 1958.

Membership

Memb. 50+. Full members: regular and government organizations that provide information services, primarily through organizing, compiling, and providing access to original or source materials. Examples of full members: organizations that assemble tables of contents, produce abstract and indexing services, provide library cataloging services, or generate numeric or factual compilations.

Associate members: organizations that operate or manage online information services, networks, in-house information centers, and libraries; undertake research and development in information science or systems; are otherwise involved in the generation, promotion, or distribution of information products under contract; or publish original information sources.

Corporate affiliated members: another member of the corporation or government agency must already be a NFAIS member paying full dues.

Officers (2001–2002)

Pres. Michael Dennis; *Past Pres.* Paul Ryan; *Secy.* Mary Berger; *Treas.* Kevin Bouley.

Directors

Barbara Bauldock, Linda Beebe, Terence Ford, Margie Hlava, Linda Sacks.

Staff

Exec. Dir. Dan Duncan; *Dir., Planning and Communications* Jill O'Neill; *Office Mgr.* Wendy McMillan; *Customer Service* Margaret Manson.

Publications

Beyond Boolean (1996; memb. $50; nonmemb. $75).

Careers in Electronic Information (1997; memb. $29; nonmemb. $39).

Computer Support to Indexing (1998; memb. $175; nonmemb. $235).

Flexible Workstyles in the Information Industry (1993; memb. $50; nonmemb. $75).

Guide to Careers in Abstracting and Indexing (1992; memb. $25; nonmemb. $29).

Guide to Database Distribution, 2nd ed., (1994; memb. $50; nonmemb. $75).

Impacts of Changing Production Technologies (1995; memb. $50, nonmemb. $75).

Metadiversity: The Call for Community (1999; memb./nonmemb. $39).

NFAIS Newsletter (mo.; North America $120; elsewhere $135).

National Information Standards Organization

Executive Director, Patricia R. Harris
4733 Bethesda Ave., Suite 300, Bethesda, MD 20814
301-654-2512, fax 301-654-1721
E-mail nisohq@niso.org
World Wide Web http://www.niso.org

Object

To initiate, develop, maintain, and publish technical standards for information services, libraries, publishers, and others involved in the business of the creation, storage, preservation, sharing, accession, and dissemination of information. Experts from their respective fields volunteer to lend their expertise in the development of NISO standards. The standards are approved by the consensus body of NISO's voting membership, which consists of 70+ voting members representing libraries, government, associations, and private businesses and organizations. NISO is supported by its membership and corporate grants. Formerly a committee of the American National Standards Institute (ANSI), NISO, formed in 1939, was incorporated in 1983 as a nonprofit educational organization. NISO is accredited by ANSI and serves as the U.S. Technical Advisory Group to ISO/TC 46.

Membership

Memb. 75. Open to any organization, association, government agency, or company willing to participate in and having substantial concern for the development of NISO standards.

Officers

Chair Beverly P. Lynch, Univ. of California, 3045 Moore Hall, Los Angeles, CA 90095; *V. Chair/Chair-Elect/Treas.* Jan Peterson, V.P., Content Development, Infotrieve, 10850 Wilshire Blvd., Los Angeles, CA 90024. *Secy.* Patricia R. Harris, NISO, 4733 Bethesda Ave., Suite 300, Bethesda, MD 20814; *Past Chair* Donald J. Muccino, Exec. V.P./COO, Online Computer Lib. Center, 6565 Frantz Rd., Dublin, OH 43017-0702.

Publications

Information Standards Quarterly (q.; $80; foreign $120).

NISO published standards are available free of charge as downloadable PDF files from the NISO Web site (http://www.niso.org). Standards in hard copy are available for sale on the Web site. NISO Press catalogs and the *NISO Annual Report* are available on request.

REFORMA (National Association to Promote Library Services to Latinos and the Spanish-Speaking)

President, Susana Hinojosa
218 Doe Library, University of California, Berkeley
Berkeley, CA 94720-6000

Object

Promoting library services to the Spanish-speaking for more than 28 years, REFORMA, an ALA affiliate, works in a number of areas: to promote the development of library collections to include Spanish-language and Latino-oriented materials; the recruitment of more bilingual and bicultural professionals and support staff; the development of library services and programs that meet the needs of the Latino community; the establishment of a national network among individuals who share our goals; the education of the U.S. Latino population in regard to the availability and types of library services; and lobbying efforts to preserve existing library resource centers serving the interest of Latinos.

Membership

Memb. 900. Any person who is supportive of the goals and objectives of REFORMA.

Officers

Pres. Susan Hinojosa, UC Berkeley, Berkeley, CA 94720-6000. Tel. 510-643-9347, fax 510-642-6830, e-mail shinojos@library. berkeley.edu; *Pres.-Elect* Ben Ocon, Salt Lake City Public Lib. Tel. 801-524-8287, e-mail bocon@mail.slcpl.lib.ut.us; *Past Pres.* Oralia Garza de Cortes. Tel. 512-929-7958, e-mail odgc@aol.com; *Treas.* Ramona Grijalva, Tucson Lib. Tel. 520-791-4791, e-mail Rgrijal1@ci.tucson.az.us; *Secy.* Derrie Perez, USF Lib. System. Tel. 813-974-1642, e-mail dperez@lib.usf.edu; *Newsletter Ed.* Kathryn

Blackmer Reyes; *Archivist*: Sal Guereña; *Membership Coord.* Al Milo.

Publications

REFORMA Newsletter (q.; memb.). *Ed.* Denice Adkins, Byers Branch Lib., 675 Santa Fe Dr., Denver, CO 80204. Tel. 303-571-1665, fax 303-572-4787, e-mail denice @u.arizona.edu.

Committees

Pura Belpré Award. Jean Hatfield.

Children's and Young Adult Services. Pamela Martin-Diaz, Maria Mena.

Education. Rhonda Rios-Kravitz.

Finance. Oralia Garza de Cortes.

Fund-raising. Susana Hinojosa.

Information Technology. Richard Chabran, Lily Castillo-Speed.

Joint Ethnic Caucus Conference. John Ayala, Toni Bissessar.

Librarian of the Year. Rafaela Castro.

Member at Large. Alexandra Rivera-Rule.

Mentoring Committee. Maria Champlin.

Nominations. Isabel Espinal.

Organizational Development. Paola Ferate-Soto.

Program Committee. Ben Ocon.

Public Relations. Adalin Torres-Zayas.

Scholarship. Armando Ramirez.

Meetings

General membership and board meetings take place at the American Library Association's Midwinter Meeting and Annual Conference.

RLG (Research Libraries Group)

Manager of Corporate Communications, Jennifer Hartzell
1200 Villa St., Mountain View, CA 94041-1100
650-691-2207, fax 650-964-0943
E-mail jlh@notes.rlg.org
World Wide Web http://www.rlg.org

Object

RLG (the Research Libraries Group) is a not-for-profit membership corporation of universities, archives, historical societies, national libraries, and other institutions with collections for research and learning. Rooted in collaborative work that addresses members' shared goals for these collections, RLG develops and operates cooperative programs to manage, preserve, and extend access to research library, museum, and archival holdings. Both for its members and for nonmember institutions and individuals worldwide, RLG develops and operates databases and software to serve an array of information access and management needs. RLG's main classes of information, available over the Web, are Library Resources (international union catalogs), Citation Resources (article- and chapter-level indexing), Archival Resources (full-text finding aids and archival collections cataloging), and Museum/Cultural Resources (exemplified by the new RLG Cultural Materials resource and the AMICO Library of high-quality art images and descriptions from the Art Museum Image Consortium. RLG also provides Ariel and ILL Manager PC-based document transmission and interlibrary loan software for use over the Internet. CJK, Eureka, Marcadia, and RLIN are registered trademarks of the Research Libraries Group, Inc. Ariel is a registered trademark of the Ariel Corporation used by RLG under license.

Membership

Memb. 160+. Membership is open to any nonprofit institution with an educational, cultural, or scientific mission. There are two membership categories: general and special. General members are institutions that serve a clientele of more than 5,000 faculty, academic staff, research staff, professional staff, stu-dents, fellows, or members. Special members serve a similar clientele of 5,000 or fewer.

Directors

RLG has a 19-member board of directors, comprising 12 directors elected from and by RLG's member institutions, up to six at-large directors elected by the board itself, and the president. Theirs is the overall responsibility for the organization's governance and for ensuring that it fulfills its purpose and goals. Annual board elections are held in the spring. In 2002 the board's chair is Reg Carr, director of university library services and Bodley's Librarian at Oxford University. For a current list of directors, see the Web site http://www.rlg.org/boardbio.html.

Staff

Pres. James Michalko; *Dir., Integrated Information Services* Susan Yoder; *Dir., Member Programs and Initiatives* Linda West; *Dir., Customer and Operations Support* Jack Grantham; *Dir., Computer Development* David Richards; *Dir., Finance and Administration* John Sundell.

Publications

Research Libraries Group News (2 a year; 20-page news magazine).

RLG DigiNews (bi-m.; Web-based newsletter to help keep pace with preservation uses of digitization).

RLG Focus (bi-m.; Web-based user services newsletter).

For informational, research, and user publications, see the Web site http://www.rlg.org/pub.html, or contact RLG.

NewsScan Daily (daily; cosponsored online summary of information technology news).

ShelfLife (weekly; online executive news summary for information professionals worldwide that provides context for RLG's major initiatives).

Scholarly Publishing and Academic Resources Coalition (SPARC)

Enterprise Director, Richard Johnson
21 Dupont Circle, Suite 800, Washington, DC 20036
202-296-2296, fax 202-872-0884
E-mail sparc@arl.org
World Wide Web http://www.arl.org/sparc

Mission

The Scholarly Publishing and Academic Resources Coalition (SPARC) was established as a project of the Association of Research Libraries (ARL) in 1997 to engage research institutions, libraries, and other organizations worldwide in encouraging competition in the scholarly communications marketplace. SPARC introduces new solutions to scientific journal publishing, facilitates the use of technology to expand access, and partners with publishers to provide top-quality, low-cost research to a greater audience. SPARC has been a constructive response to market dysfunctions in the scholarly communication system. It serves as a catalyst for action, helping to create systems that expand information dissemination and use in a networked digital environment while responding to the needs of scholars and academe. The SPARC agenda focuses on enhancing broad and cost-effective access to peer-reviewed scholarship and is pursued via three strategic thrusts:

- Incubation of competitive alternatives to current high-priced commercial journals and digital aggregations, implemented by publisher partnership programs and advisory services that promote competition for authors and buyers, demonstrate alternatives to the traditional journal business model, and stimulate expansion of the non-profit sector's share of overall scholarly activity

- Public advocacy of fundamental changes in the system and the culture of scholarly communication by targeted outreach to various stakeholders (for example, librarians, faculty, and editorial boards), as well as ongoing communications and public relations

activities that publicize key issues and initiatives

- Education campaigns that enhance awareness of scholarly communication issues and support expanded institutional and scholarly community roles in and control over the scholarly communication process

Building on its initial mission, SPARC is emphasizing practical initiatives that encourage development of institution-based repositories for the work of scholars, supporting scholar-led journal publishing projects, and developing new collaborative digital publishing enterprises and models.

Membership

Memb. 201, with eight affiliates. Membership is institutional. Full member dues $5,000 a year, with $7,500 purchase commitment.

Steering Committee (2002)

Chair James Neal, V.P. for Info. Services and Univ. Libn., Columbia Univ.; Cynthia Archer, Univ. Libn., York Univ.; Karyle Butcher, Deputy Vice-Provost for Info. Services, Oregon State Univ.; Kenneth Frazier, Dir. of Libs., Univ. of Wisconsin, Madison; Ray English, Dir. of Libs., Oberlin College; Sarah Michalak, Dir., Univ. of Utah Lib.; *Liaison to SPARC Europe Steering Committee* J. S. M. (Bas) Savenije, Univ. Libn., Utrecht Univ. (Netherlands).

Publications

SPARC e-news (subscribe by sending name, title, organization and e-mail address to alison@arl.org).
Declaring Independence: A Guide to Creating Community-Controlled Science Journals (http://www.arl.org/sparc/di).

Society for Scholarly Publishing

Executive Directors, Francine Butler, Jerry Bowman
10200 W. 44 Ave., Suite 304, Wheat Ridge, CO 80033
303-422-3914, fax 303-422-8894
E-mail ssp@resourcenter.com
World Wide Web http://www.sspnet.org

Object

To draw together individuals involved in the process of scholarly publishing. This process requires successful interaction of the many functions performed within the scholarly community. The Society for Scholarly Publishing (SSP) provides the leadership for such interaction by creating opportunities for the exchange of information and opinions among scholars, editors, publishers, librarians, printers, booksellers, and all others engaged in scholarly publishing.

Membership

Memb. 800. Open to all with an interest in the scholarly publishing process and dissemination of information. Dues (Indiv.) $90; (Contributing) $1,000; (Sustaining) $2,500. Year. Jan. 1–Dec. 31.

Executive Committee (2001–2002)

Pres. Bill Kasdorf, Impressions Book and Journal Services; *Pres.-Elect* Ed Barnas, Cambridge Univ. Press; *Past Pres.* Janet Fisher, MIT Press; *Secy.-Treas.* Ray Fastiggi, Rockefeller Univ. Press.

Meetings

An annual meeting is conducted in June; the location changes each year. Additionally, SSP conducts several seminars throughout the year and a Top Management Roundtable each fall.

Society of American Archivists

Executive Director, Susan E. Fox
527 S. Wells St., Fifth fl., Chicago, IL 60607
312-922-0140, fax 312-347-1452
World Wide Web: http://www.archivists.org

Object

Provides leadership to ensure the identification, preservation, and use of records of historic value. Founded 1936.

Membership

Memb. 3,600. Dues (Indiv.) $70–$170, graduated according to salary; (Assoc.) $70, domestic; (Student) $40; (Inst.) $225; (Sustaining) $440.

Officers (2001–2002)

Pres. Steve Hensen; *V.P.* Peter Hirtle; *Treas.* Elizabeth Adkins.

Council

Thomas Battle, Dana Bell-Russel, Tom Connors, Jackie Dooley, Mark Greene, David Haury, Richard Pearce-Moses, Megan Sniffin-Marinoff, Becky Tousey.

Staff

Exec. Dir. Susan E. Fox; *Meetings/Memb. Coord.* Bernice E. Brack; *Publishing Dir.* Teresa Brinati; *Dir. of Finance* Carroll Dendler; *Educ. Dirs.* Solveig Desutter, Patricia O'Hara.

Publications

American Archivist (q.; $85; foreign $90). *Ed.* Philip Eppard; *Managing Ed.* Teresa Brinati. Books for review and related correspondence should be addressed to the managing editor.

Archival Outlook (bi-m.; memb.). *Ed.* Teresa Brinati.

Software and Information Industry Association

1090 Vermont Ave. N.W., Washington, DC 20005
Tel. 202-289-7442, fax 202-289-7097
World Wide Web: http://www.siia.net

Membership

Memb. 1,200 companies. Formed January 1, 1999, through the merger of the Software Publishers Association (SPA) and the Information Industry Association (IIA). Open to companies involved in the creation, distribution, and use of software information products, services, and technologies. For details on membership and dues, see the SIIA Web site.

Staff

Pres. Kenneth Wasch. E-mail kwasch@siia.net; *Exec. V.P.* Lauren Hall. E-mail lhall@siia.net

Board of Directors

Graham Beachum, II, Edge Technology Group; Daniel Cooperman, Oracle Corp.; Elizabeth Frazee, AOL Time Warner; Edward A. Friedland, Thomson Corp.; Dale Fuller, Borland Software Corp.; Glenn Goldberg, McGraw-Hill Companies; Kathy Hurley, NetSchools Corp.; R. Douglas Kemp, Bloomberg L.P.; Kirk Loevner, InterTrust Technologies Corp.; Steve Manzo, Reed Elsevier; David E. Moran, Dow Jones; Michael Morris, Sun Microsystems; Ron Okamoto, Apple; Joel Ronning, Digital River; David H. W. Turner, Reuters Information.

Special Libraries Association

Executive Director, Roberta I. Shaffer
1700 18th St. N.W., Washington, DC 20009-2514
202-234-4700, fax 202-265-9317
E-mail sla@sla.org
World Wide Web http://www.sla.org

Object

To advance the leadership role of special librarians in putting knowledge to work in the information- and knowledge-based society. The association offers myriad programs and services designed to help its members serve their customers more effectively and succeed in an increasingly challenging environment of information management and technology.

Membership

Memb. 13,500. Dues (Sustaining) $500; (Indiv.) $125; (Student) $35. Year. July–June.

Officers (July 2001–June 2002)

Pres. Hope N. Tillman; *Pres.-Elect* William Fisher; *Treas.* Richard G. Geiger; *Chapter Cabinet Chair* Daille Pettit; *Chapter Cabinet Chair-Elect* Stephanie D. Tolson; *Div. Cabinet Chair* Susan M. Klopper; *Div. Chapter Chair-Elect* Karen Bleakley; *Past Pres.* Donna W. Scheeder.

Directors

Officers; G. Lynn Berard, Marjorie M. K. Hlava, Karen Kreizman-Reczek, Mary "Dottie" Moon, Christine De Bow Klein, David Stern.

Publications

Information Outlook (mo.) (memb., non-memb. $125/yr. *Dir. Publications* Leslie Shaver.

Committee Chairpersons

Association Office Operations. Hope Tillman.
Awards and Honors. Susan S. DiMattia
Bylaws. Dorothy McGarry.
Cataloging. Paige Andrew.
Committees. Fred Roper.
Conference Plan (2002). Ethel Salonen.
Consultation Service. Anne Abate.
Diversity Leadership Development. Tamika Barnes.
Finance. Richard Geiger.
Public Policy. Barbara Folensbee-Moore.
International Relations. Mary Dickenson.
Networking. Jill Hurst.
Nominating. Barbara Semonche.
Professional Development. Lynne McCay.
Public Relations. Linda Morgan Davis.
Research. Sharyn Ladner.
SLA Endowment Fund Grants. Mildred Lorenti.
SLA Scholarship. Judith Bernstein.
Strategic Planning. Mary "Dottie" Moon.
Student and Academic Relations. Yvonne Chandler.
Technical Standards. Marcia Lei Zeng.

Theatre Library Association

c/o The Shubert Archive, 149 W. 45 St., New York, NY 10036
212-944-3895, fax 212-944-4139
World Wide Web http://tla.library.unt.edu

Object

To further the interests of collecting, preserving, and using theater, cinema, and performing-arts materials in libraries, museums, and private collections. Founded 1937.

Membership

Memb. 500. Dues (Indiv./Inst.) $30. Year. Jan. 1–Dec. 31.

Officers

Pres. Kevin Winkler, New York Public Lib. for the Performing Arts; *V.P.* Martha S. LoMonaco, Fairfield Univ.; *Exec. Secy.* Camille Croce Dee, independent researcher; *Treas.* Paul Newman, private collector.

Executive Board

Pamela Bloom, Ann L. Ferguson, B. Donald Grose, Mary Ann Jensen, Florence M. Jumon-

ville, Brigitte J. Kueppers, Annette Marotta, Susan L. Peters, Jason Rubin, Kenneth Schlesinger, Daniel J. Watermeier, Joseph M. Yranski.; *Honorary* Paul Myers; *Historian* Louis A. Rachow; *Legal Counsel* Madeleine Nichols.

Publications

Broadside (q.; memb.). *Ed.* Ellen Truax.
Performing Arts Resources (occasional; memb.).
Membership Directory. Ed. Maryann Chach.

Committee Chairpersons

TLA/Freedley Awards. Richard Wall.
Professional Award. Nena Couch, Camille Croce Dee.
Finance. Paul Newman.
Membership. Paul Newman, Maryann Chach.
Nominating. Bob Taylor.
Programs. Kevin Winkler.
Strategic Planning. Martha S. LoMonaco.

Urban Libraries Council

President, Eleanor Jo Rodger
1603 Orrington Ave., Suite 1080, Evanston, IL 60201
847-866-9999, fax 847-866-9989
E-mail info@urbanlibraries.org
World Wide Web http://www.urbanlibraries.org

Object

To identify and make known the problems relating to urban libraries serving cities of 100,000 or more individuals, located in a Standard Metropolitan Statistical Area; to provide information on state and federal legislation affecting urban library programs and systems; to facilitate the exchange of ideas and programs of member libraries and other

libraries; to develop programs that enable libraries to act as a focus of community development and to supply the informational needs of the new urban populations; to conduct research and educational programs that will benefit urban libraries and to solicit and accept grants, contributions, and donations essential to their implementation.

ULC currently receives core funding from membership dues. Current major projects supported by grant funding from a variety of sources include: The Public Libraries as Partners in Youth Development Initiative (funded by Wallace Reader's Digest Funds), Community Partnerships for Informal Lifelong Learning (funded by a research grant from the Institute for Museum and Library Services), and the Executive Leadership Institute (funded by the Institute for Museum and Library Services, the Bill and Melinda Gates Foundation, and the W. K. Kellogg Foundation). ULC is a 501(c)(3) not-for-profit corporation based in the state of Illinois.

Membership

Membership is open to public libraries serving populations of 100,000 or more located in a Standard Metropolitan Statistical Area and to corporations specializing in library-related materials and services. Annual dues are based on the size of the library's operating budget, according to the following schedule: under $2 million to $10 million, $3,000; over $10 million, $5,000. In addition, ULC member libraries may choose Sustaining or Contributing status (Sustaining, $12,000; Contributing, $7,000). Corporate membership dues are $5,000.

Officers (2001–2002)

Chair Betty Jane Narver, Daniel J. Evans School of Public Affairs, Univ. of Washington, 324 Parrington Hall, Box 353060, Seattle, WA 98195. Tel. 206-543-0190. *Vice-Chair/Chair-Elect* Jim Fish, Dir., Baltimore County Public Lib., 320 York Rd., Towson,

MD. Tel. 410-887-6160. *Secy./Treas.* Dan Bradbury, Dir., Kansas City Public Lib., 311 E. 12 St., Kansas City, MO 64106. Tel. 816-701-3410. *Past Chair* Elliot Shelkrot, Dir., Free Lib. of Philadelphia, 1901 Vine St., Philadelphia, PA 19103-1189. Tel. 215-686-5300.

Officers serve one-year terms, members of the executive board two-year terms. New officers are elected and take office at the summer annual meeting of the council.

Executive Board

Dan Bradbury. E-mail dan@kcpl.lib.mo.us; Don Estes. E-mail dbestes@aol.com; Jim Fish. E-mail jfish@mail.bcpl.net; Diane Frankel. E-mail dfrankel@irvine.org; Toni Garvey. E-mail tgarvey@ci.phoenix.az.us; Duncan Highsmith. E-mail dhighsmith @highsmith.com; Laura Isenstein. E-mail lisenstein@ci.sat.tx.us. Marilyn Jackson. E-mail jacks088@tc.umn.edu; Jenny McCurdy. E-mail jenny.mccurdy@gbhcs.org; Michael Morand. E-mail michael.morand@ yale.edu; Donna Nicely. E-mail donna_nicely @metro.nashville.org; Eleanor Jo Rodger. E-mail ejr@urbanlibraries.org; Pamela J. Seigle. E-mail pseigle@wellesley.edu; Marsha L. Steinhardt. E-mail msteinha@courts.state. ny.us; Maurice Wheeler. E-mail mwheele@ detroit.lib.mi.us.

Key Staff

Pres. Eleanor Jo "Joey" Rodger; *Senior V.P., Admin./Member services* Bridget A. Bradley; *V.P., Program/Development.* Danielle Milam.

State, Provincial, and Regional Library Associations

The associations in this section are organized under three headings: United States, Canada, and Regional. Both the United States and Canada are represented under Regional associations.

United States

Alabama

Memb. 1,200. Term of Office. Apr. 2001–Apr. 2002. Publication. *The Alabama Librarian* (q.).

Pres. Henry Stewart, Dean, Lib. Services, Wallace Hall, Troy State Univ., Troy 36082. Tel. 334-670-3263, fax 334-670-3694, e-mail hstewart@troyst.edu; *Pres.-Elect* Paulette Williams, Teacher Resource Center, Shelby County Schools, 36 6th Ave. S.E., Alabaster 35007. Tel. 205-682-5921, fax 205-682-5925, e-mail pwilliams@shebyed.k12.AL.us; *Secy.* Juanita Owes, Montgomery Public Lib., Box 1950, Montgomery 36102. Tel. 334-240-4300, e-mail jowes@mccpl.lib.AL.us; *Treas.* Vivian White, Montgomery Public Lib., Box 1950, Montgomery 36102. Tel. 334-213-3902; *Exec. Dir.* Sara Warren. Tel. 334-262-5210, fax 334-262-5255, e-mail alala@mindspring.com.

Address correspondence to the executive director.

World Wide Web http://alala.home.mindspring.com.

Alaska

Memb. 463. Publication. *Newspoke* (bi-mo.).

Pres. Patience Frederiksen. E-mail Patience_Frederiksen@eed.state.ak.us; *V.P./Committees* Deborah Mole. E-mail afdlm2@uaa.alaska.edu; *V.P./Conference* Sherri Douglas. E-mail douglasss@ci.anchorage.sk.us; *Secy.* Freya Anderson. E-mail freya_anderson@eed.state.ak.us; *Treas.* Mary Jennings. E-mail maryj@gci.net; *Exec. Officer* Mary Jennings. E-mail exec_officer@akla.org.

Address correspondence to the secretary, Alaska Library Association, Box 81084, Fairbanks 99708. Fax 877-863-1401, e-mail akla@akla.org.

World Wide Web http://www.akla.org.

Arizona

Memb. 1,200. Term of Office. Nov. 2001–Dec. 2002. Publication. *AzLA Newsletter* (mo.).

Pres. Robert Shupe, Mohave Community College. Tel. 520-757-0802, e-mail robshu@et.mohave.cc.az.us; *Pres.-Elect* Brenda Brown, Peoria Public Lib. Tel. 623-773-7557, e-mail Brendab@peoriaaz.com; *Past Pres.* Teri Metros, Tempe Public Lib., 3500 S. Rural Rd., Tempe 85282. Tel. 480-350-5551, fax 480-380-5554, e-mail Teri_metros@tempe.gov; *Treas.* Carol Damaso, Scottsdale Public Lib. Tel. 480-312-6031, e-mail cdamaso@ci.scottsdale.az.us; *Secy.* Louis Howley, Phoenix Public Lib., Cholla Branch. Tel. 602-534-3775, e-mail lhowley@mindspring.com; *Exec. Secy.* Jean Johnson, 14449 N. 73 St., Scottsdale 85260-3133. Tel. 480-998-1954, fax 480-998-7838, e-mail meetmore@aol.com.

Address correspondence to the executive secretary.

World Wide Web http://www.azla.org.

Arkansas

Memb. 600. Term of Office. Jan.–Dec. 2002. Publication. *Arkansas Libraries* (bi-mo.).

Pres. Barbie James, Forrest City H.S., 467 Victoria St., Forrest City 72335. Tel. 870-633-1464 ext. 12, fax 870-261-1844, e-mail jamesb@fcsd.grsc.k12.ar.us; *V.P./Pres.-Elect* Dwain Gordon, Central Arkansas Lib. System, 100 Rock St. Little Rock 72201. Tel. 501-918-3053, fax 501-375-7451, e-mail dwain@cals.lib.ar.us; *Secy.-Treas.* Art Lichtenstein, Univ. of Central Arkansas, 201 Donaghey Ave., Conway 72035. Tel. 501-450-5230, fax 501-450-3234, e-mail artl@mail.uca.edu; *Exec. Dir.* Jennifer Coleman, Arkansas Lib. Assn., 9 Shackleford Plaza, Ste. 1, Little Rock 72211. Tel. 501-228-0775, fax 501-228-5535, e-mail JCole10145@aol.com.

Address correspondence to the executive director.

World Wide Web http://library.uca.edu/arla.

California

Memb. 2,500. Publication. *California Libraries* (mo., except July/Aug., Nov./Dec.).
Pres. Anne M. Turner. E-mail turner@santacruzpl.org; *V.P./Pres.-Elect* Les Kong. E-mail Lkong@wiley.csusb.edu; *Exec. Dir.* Susan E. Negreen, California Lib. Assn., 717 20th St., Ste. 200, Sacramento 95814. Tel. 916-447-8541, fax 916-447-8394, e-mail info@cla-net.org.

Address correspondence to the executive director.

World Wide Web http://www.cla-net.org.

Colorado

Memb. 1,100. Term of Office. Oct. 2001–Oct. 2002. Publication. *Colorado Libraries* (q.). *Ed.* Nancy Carter, Univ. of Colorado, Campus Box 184, Boulder 80309.
Pres. Lorena Mitchell, Plains and Peaks Regional Lib. Service System, 530 Communications Circle, No. 205, Colorado Springs 80905. Tel. 719-473-3417, e-mail Lorena mitchell@earthlink.net; *Treas.* George Jaramillo, Colorado State Univ., Fort Collins 80523-1019. E-mail gjaramil@manta.colostate.edu; *Exec. Dir.* Kathleen Sagee.

Address correspondence to the executive director at 4350 Wadsworth Blvd., Ste. 340, Wheat Ridge 80033. Tel. 303-463-6400, fax 303-431-9752, e-mail officemanager@cla-web.org.

World Wide Web http://www.cla-web.org.

Connecticut

Memb. 1,100. Term of Office. July 2001–June 2002. Publication *Connecticut Libraries* (11 a year). *Ed.* David Kapp, 4 Llynwood Dr., Bolton 06040. Tel. 203-647-0697.
Pres. Mary Engels, Middletown Lib. Service Center, 786 S. Main St., Middletown 06457. Tel. 860-344-2972; *V.P./Pres.-Elect* Karen McNulty, Avon Free Public Lib., 281 Country Club Rd., Avon 06001. Tel. 860-673-9712; *Treas.* Veronica Stevenson-Moudamane, Danbury Public Lib., Danbury 06810. Tel. 203-797-4505; *Administrator* Karen Zoller, Connecticut Lib. Assn., Box 85, Willimantic 06226. Tel. 860-465-5006, e-mail kzoller@cla.lib.ct.us.

Address correspondence to the administrator.

World Wide Web http://www.lib.uconn.edu/cla.

Delaware

Memb. 300. Term of Office. Apr. 2001–Apr. 2002. Publication. *DLA Bulletin* (3 a year).
Pres. Paula Davino, Dover Public Lib., 45 S. State St., Dover 19901. Tel. 302-736-7030, fax 302-736-5087, e-mail pauladavino@yahoo.com; *V.P./Pres.-Elect* L. Win Rosenberg, Rehoboth Beach Public Lib, 226 Rehoboth Ave., Rehoboth Beach 19971. Tel. 302-227-8044, fax 302-227-0597, e-mail wrosenberg@delaware.net; *Treas.* Nick Chiarkas, Univ. of Delaware Lib., Newark 19717-5267. Tel. 302-831-0234, fax 302-831-1046, e-mail chiarkas@udel.edu; *Secy.* John Philos, Delaware Div. of Libs., 43 S. DuPont Hwy., Dover 19901. Tel. 302-739-4748, fax 302-739-6787, e-mail jphilos@lib.de.us.

Address correspondence to the association, Box 816, Dover 19903-0816. E-mail dla@dla.lib.de.us.

World Wide Web http://www.dla.lib.de.us/aboutus.html.

District of Columbia

Memb. 600. Term of Office. Aug. 2001–Aug. 2002. Publication. *Intercom* (mo.).
Pres. Claudette Tennant, ALA Washington Office. Tel. 202-628-8410, fax 202-628-8419, e-mail ctennant@alawash.org; *V.P./Pres.-Elect* Andrea Gruhl. Tel./fax 301-596-5460, e-mail andreagruhl@aol.com; *Secy.* Barbara Conaty, Lib. of Congress. Tel. 202-707-2715, fax 202-707-0810, e-mail bcon@loc.gov; *Treas.* William F. Tuceling, U.S. General Accounting Office. Tel. 202-512-5025, fax 202-512-3373, e-mail tuceling@erols.com.

Address correspondence to the association, Box 14177, Benjamin Franklin Sta., Washington, DC 20044.

World Wide Web http://www.dcla.org.

Florida

Memb. (Indiv.) 1,343; (In-state Inst.) 131. Term of Office. July 2001–June 2002. Publication. *Florida Libraries* (bi-ann.).
Pres. Betty D. Johnson, Dupont-Ball Lib., Stetson Univ., 421 N. Woodland Blvd., Unit

8418, DeLand 32720. Tel. 904-822-7178, fax 904-740-3626, e-mail betty.johnson@stetson. edu; *V.P./Pres.-Elect* Marta Westall, Central Florida Lib. Cooperative 431 E. Horatio Ave., No. 230, Maitland 32751. Tel. 407-644-9050, fax 407-644-7023, e-mail mwestall@cflc.net; *Secy.* Rob Lenholt, DuPont Ball Lib., Stetson Univ., 421 N Woodland Blvd., Unit 841, DeLand 32720. Tel. 904-822-7181, fax 904-822-7199, e-mail rlenholt@stetson.edu; *Treas.* Sherry Carrillo, Green Lib., Florida International Univ., University Park, Miami 33199. Tel. 305-348-2463, fax 305-348-3408, e-mail carrillo@fiu.edu; *Past Pres.* Mary A. Brown, St. Petersburg Public Lib., St. Petersburg 33701. Tel. 727-893-7736, fax 727-822-6828, e-mail brownma@splib.lib.fl. us; *Exec. Secy.* Marjorie Stealey, Florida Lib. Assn., 1133 W. Morse Blvd., Winter Park 32789. Tel. 407-647-8839, fax 407-629-2502, e-mail mjs@crowsegal.com.

Address correspondence to the executive secretary.

World Wide Web http://www.flalib.org.

Georgia

Memb. 950. Term of Office. Oct. 2001–Oct. 2002. Publication. *Georgia Library Quarterly. Ed.* Susan Cooley, Sara Hightower Regional Lib., 203 Riverside Pkwy., Rome 30161. Tel. 706-236-4621, fax 706-236-4631, e-mail cooley@mail.floyd.public.lib. ga.us.

Pres. Tom Budlong, 949 Rupley Dr. N.E.; Atlanta 30306-3818. Tel 404-874-7483, e-mail tbudlong@bellsouth.net; *1st V.P./ Pres.-Elect* Gordon N. Baker, Coord. of Instructional Technology, Henry County Schools, Technical Services, 396 Tomlinson St., McDonough 30253. Tel. 770-957-6601 ext. 147, fax 678-583-4974, e-mail gnbaker@ henry.k12.ga.us; *2nd V.P.* Carol Stanley, Libn., Athens Technical College, Elbert County Campus, 1317 Athens Hwy., Elberton 30635. Tel. 706-783-2116, fax 706-783-3441, e-mail stanley@admin1.athens.tec.ga. us; *Secy.* Fred Smith, Henderson Lib., Georgia Southern Univ., Statesboro 30460-8074. Tel. 912-681-5647, fax 912-681-5034, e-mail fsmith@gasou.edu; *Treas.* Robert E. Fox, Jr., Dir. Lib. Services, Clayton College and State Univ., Box 285, Morrow 30260. Tel. 770-961-3520, fax 770-961-3712, e-mail bobfox

@mail.clayton.edu; *Past Pres.* Eddie McLeod, Chattahoochee Technical College Lib., 980 S. Cobb Dr. S.E., Marietta 30060-3300. Tel. 770-528-4422, fax 770-528-4454, e-mail emcleod@chattcollege.com; *ALA Councillor* Ann Hamilton, Georgia Southern Univ., 211 Wendwood Dr., Statesboro 30458-5075. Tel. 912-681-5115, e-mail ahamilton@gasou.edu.

Address correspondence to the president.

World Wide Web http://wwwlib.gsu.edu/ gla.

Hawaii

Memb. 320. Publications. *HLA Newsletter* (3 a year).

Pres. Vickery Lebbin. E-mail vickery@ hawaii.edu; *V.P.* Cora Nishimura. E-mail coran@lib.state.hi.us.

Address correspondence to the association, Box 4441, Honolulu 96812-4441.

World Wide Web http://www.hlaweb.org.

Idaho

Memb. 500. Term of Office. Oct. 2001–Oct. 2002.

Pres. Marlene Earnest, 15335 David St., Caldwell 83607. Tel. 208-454-9253 ext. 301, e-mail mearnest@sd139.k12.id.us; *Treas.* Pam Bradshaw, Idaho State Lib., 325 W. State St., Boise 82702. Tel. 208-334-2150, e-mail pbradsha@isl.state.id.us.

Address correspondence to the president.

World Wide Web http://www.idaho libraries.org.

Illinois

Memb. 3,000. Term of Office. July 2001–July 2002. Publication. *ILA Reporter* (bimo.).

Pres. Arthur P. Young, Univ. Libs., Northern Illinois Univ., De Kalb 60115-2868. Tel. 815-753-9801, fax 815-753-9803, e-mail ayoung@niu.edu; *V.P./Pres.-Elect* Sylvia Murphy Williams, Exec. Committee, Dundee Township Public Lib. District, 555 Barrington Ave. Dundee 60118-1422. Tel. 847-428-3661, fax 847-428-0521, e-mail smwill@ nslsilus.org; *Treas.* Tamiye Trejo Meehan, Indian Trails Public Lib. District, 355 S. Schoenbeck Rd., Wheeling 60090. Tel. 847-459-4100 ext. 202, fax 847-459-4760, e-mail tmeehan@itpld.lib.il.us; *Past Pres.* Denise M. Zielinski, DuPage Lib. System, 127 S.

First St., Geneva, IL 60134-2701. Tel. 630-232-8457, fax 630-232-0699, e-mail dzielins @dupagels.lib.il.us; *Exec. Dir.* Robert P. Doyle, 33 W. Grand Ave., Ste. 301, Chicago 60610-4306. Tel. 312-644-1896, fax 312-644-1899, e-mail ila@ila.org.

Address correspondence to the executive director.

World Wide Web http://www.ila.org.

Indiana

Memb. 3,000+. Term of Office. March 2001–April 2002. Publications. *Focus on Indiana Libraries* (11 a year), *Indiana Libraries* (s. ann.). *Ed.* Patricia Tallman.

Exec. Dir. Linda Kolb. E-mail Lkolb@ ilfonline.

Address correspondence to the Indiana Lib. Federation, 941 E. 86 St., Ste. 260, Indianapolis 46240. Tel. 317-257-2040, fax 317-257-1389, e-mail ilf@indy.net.

World Wide Web http://www.ilfonline. org.

Iowa

Memb. 1,700. Term of Office. Jan.–Dec. Publication. *The Catalyst* (bi-mo.). *Ed.* Laurie Hews.

Pres. Gina Millsap. Tel. 515-239-5632, fax 515-233-1718, e-mail gmillsap@ames. lib.ia.us; *V.P./Pres.-Elect* Betty Rogers. Tel. 319-399-8017, e-mail brogers@coe.edu; *Treas.* Laurie Hews. Tel. 515-243-2172, e-mail ialib@mcleodusa.net; *Secy.* Marilyn Murphy. Tel. 319-363-8213 ext. 1244, e-mail marilyn@mmc.mtmercy.edu.

Address correspondence to the association, 505 Fifth Ave., Ste. 823, Des Moines 50309. Tel. 515-243-2172, fax 515-243-0614, e-mail ialib@mcleoduse.net or ila@iren.net.

World Wide Web http://www.iowalibrary association.org.

Kansas

Memb. 1,200. Term of Office. July 2001–June 2002. Publications. *KLA Newsletter* (q.); *KLA Membership Directory* (ann.).

Pres. Karyl Buffington, Coffeyville Public Lib., 311 W. 10 St., Coffeyville 67337. Tel. 620-252-1370, fax 620-251-1612, e-mail kbuffington@terraworld.net; *1st V.P.* Robert Walter, Axe Lib., Pittsburg State Univ., Pittsburg 66762. Tel. 620-235-4878, fax 620-235-4090, e-mail bwalter@mail.pittstate.edu; *2nd V.P.* Debra Ludwig, Auschutz Lib., Rm. 424A, Univ. of Kansas, 1301 Hoch Auditoria Dr., Lawrence 66045. Tel. 785-864-1376, fax 785-864-5380, e-mail dlugwig@ku.ed; *Secy.* Roseanne Goble, Dodge City Public Lib., 1001 W. 2nd, Dodge City 67801. Tel. 620-225-1231, fax 620-225-0252; *Past Pres.* John Stratton, Regents Center Lib., Univ. of Kansas, Edwards Campus, 12600 Quivira Rd., Overland Park 66213-2402. Tel. 913-897-8556, e-mail jstratton@ukans.edu; *Exec. Secy.* Leroy Gattin, Hutchinson Public Lib., 901 N. Main St., Hutchinson 67501. Tel. 620-663-5441 ext. 110, fax 620-663-9506, e-mail lgatt@hplsck.org.

Address correspondence to the executive secretary.

World Wide Web http://skyways.lib.ks.us/ KLA.

Kentucky

Memb. 1,900. Term of Office. Oct. 2001–Oct. 2002. Publication. *Kentucky Libraries* (q.).

Pres. Terri Kirk, Heath H.S., 4330 Metropolis Lake Rd., West Paducah 42086. Tel. 270-744-4104, e-mail tkirk@mccracken.k12. ky.us; *V.P./Pres.-Elect* Sue Burch, Univ. of Kentucky, 122 Law Lib., Lexington 40506-0048. Tel. 859-257-5133, fax 859-323-4906, e-mail sburch@pop.uky.edu; *Secy.* Laura Davison, Southeast AHEC Lib., ARH Regional Medical Center, 100 Medical Center Dr., Hazard 41701. Tel. 606-439-6793, e-mail lcdavi01@pop.uky.edu; *Exec. Secy.* Tom Underwood, 1501 Twilight Trail, Frankfort 40601. Tel. 502-223-5322, fax 502-223-4937, e-mail kylibasn@mis.net.

Address correspondence to the executive secretary.

World Wide Web http://www.kylibasn. org.

Louisiana

Memb. (Indiv.) 1,500; (Inst.) 60. Term of Office. July 2001–June 2002. Publication. *Louisiana Libraries* (q.).

Pres. Debra Rollins. Tel. 318-448-3457, fax 318-487-0771, e-mail llapresident2002@ yahoo.com or rollins@iamerica.net; *1st V.P./Pres.-Elect* Angelles Deshautelles. Tel. 225-647-8924, fax 225-644-0063, e-mail adeshaut@pelican.state.lib.la.us; *2nd V.P.* Marilyn Hankel. Tel. 504-280-7276, fax 504-280-7277, e-mail mhankel@uno.edu; *Secy.* Barbara Royer. Tel. 337-475-5743, fax 337-475-5719, e-mail broyer@mail.mcneese.edu. *Past Pres.* David Duggar. Tel. 318-675-5472, fax 318-675-5442, e-mail ddugga@lsuhsc.edu; *Exec. Dir.* Beverly Laughlin, Louisiana Lib. Assn., 421 S. 4 St., Eunice 70535. Tel. 337-550-7890, fax 337-550-7846, e-mail la libassoc@yahoo.com.

World Wide Web http://www.llaonline.org.

Maine

Memb. 950. Term of Office. (Pres., V.P.) spring 2000–spring 2002. Publications. *Maine Entry* (q.); *Maine Memo* (mo.).

Pres. Jay Scherma, Thomas Memorial Lib., 6 Scott Dyer Rd., Cape Elizabeth. Tel. 207-799-1720, e-mail jscherma@thomas.lib.me.us; *V.P.* Anne Davis, Gardiner Public Lib., 152 Water St., Gardiner 04345. Tel. 207-582-3312, e-mail staff@gpl.lib.me.us; *Secy.* Vaughan Gagne, Wilton Free Public Lib., Box 454, 6 Goodspeed St., Wilton, ME 04294-0454. Tel. 207-645-4831, e-mail vgagne@wilton-free.lib.me.us; *Treas.* Donna Rasche, Turner Memorial Lib., 39 Second St., Presque Isle 04769-2677. Tel. 207-764-2571, fax 207-768-5756, e-mail drasche@presqueisle.lib.me.us.

Address correspondence to the association, 60 Community Dr., Augusta 04330. Tel. 207-623-8428, fax 207-626-5947.

World Wide Web http://mainelibraries.org.

Maryland

Memb. 1,300. Term of Office. July 2001–July 2002. Publications. *Happenings* (mo.), *The Crab* (q.).

Pres. Karen Trennepohl, Howard County Lib., Savage Branch, 9525 Durness La., Laurel 20723. Tel. 410-880-5990, fax 410-880-5999; *Exec. Dir.* Margaret Carty.

Address correspondence to the association, 1401 Hollins St., Baltimore 21223. Tel. 410-947-5090, fax 410-947-5089, e-mail mla@mdlib.org.

World Wide Web http://mdlib.org.

Massachusetts

Memb. (Indiv.) 950; (Inst.) 100. Term of Office. July 2001–June 2002. Publication. *Bay State Libraries* (10 a year).

Pres. James Sutton, Memorial Hall Lib., Elm Sq., Andover 01810. Tel. 978-623-8401, fax 978-623-8407, e-mail jsutton@mhl.org; *V.P./Pres.-Elect* Krista McLeod, Nevins Memorial Lib., 305 Broadway, Methuen 01844-6898. Tel. 978 686-4080, fax 978 686-8669; *Secy.* Carol Caro, Minuteman Lib. Network, 10 Strathmore Rd., Natick 01760. Tel. 508-655-8008, fax 508-655-1507, e-mail ccaro@mln.lib.ma.us; *Treas.* Patricia T. Cramer, Westfield Athenaeum, 6 Elm St., Westfield 01085-2997. Tel. 413-568-7833, fax 413-568-1558; *Past Pres.* Christine Kardokas, Worcester Public Lib., 3 Salem Sq., Worcester 01608-2074. Tel. 508-799-1726, fax 508-799-1652, e-mail ckardoka@cwmarsmail.cwmars.org; *Exec. Secy.* Barry Blaisdell, Massachusetts Lib. Assn., Countryside Offices, 707 Turnpike St., North Andover 01845. Tel. 508-686-8543, fax 508-685-9410, e-mail info@masslib.org.

Address correspondence to the executive secretary.

World Wide Web http://www.masslib.org.

Michigan

Memb. (Indiv.) 1,850; (Inst.) 375. Term of Office. July 2001–June 2002. Publication. *Michigan Librarian Newsletter* (6 a year), Michigan Library Association Forum e-journal (2 a year).

Pres. Elaine Didier, Kresge Lib., Oakland Univ., 13060 Beacon Hill Dr., Plymouth 48170-6502. Tel. 248-370-2486, fax 248-370-2474, e-mail didier@oakland.edu; *Pres.-Elect* Phyllis Jose, Oakland County Lib., 1200 N. Telegraph Rd., Pontiac 48341-0481. Tel. 248-858-0380, fax 248-858-1234, e-mail pjose@tln.lib.mi.us; *Secy.* Roger Mendel, Mideastern Michigan Lib. Coop., 503 S. Saginaw, Ste. 839, Flint 48502. Tel. 810-232-7119, fax 810-232-6639, e-mail rmendel@gfn.org; *Treas.* Leslee Niethammer, Saline District Lib., 555 N. Maple Rd., Saline 48176. Tel. 734-429-2313, fax 734-944-0600, e-mail leslee@saline.lib.mi.us; *Past Pres.* Tom Genson, Grand Rapids Public Lib., 3020 E. Fulton, Grand Rapids 49505. Tel. 616-988-5402, fax 616-988-5419, e-mail tgenson@grpl.org; *Exec. Dir.* Stephen A. Kershner, Michigan Lib. Assn., 6810 S. Cedar St., Ste. 6, Lansing 48911. Tel. 517-694-6615, fax 517-694-4330, e-mail kershner@mlc.lib.mi.us.

Address correspondence to the executive director.

World Wide Web http://www.mla.lib.mi.us.

Minnesota

Memb. 1,200. Term of Office. (Pres., Pres.-Elect) Jan.–Dec. 2002; (Treas.) Jan. 2001–Dec. 2003; (Secy.) Jan. 2000–Dec. 2002. Publication. *MLA Newsletter* (6 a year).

Pres. Chris Olson, CLIC; *Pres.-Elect* Melissa Brechon, Carver County Lib. System; *ALA Chapter Councillor* Bill Asp, Dakota County Lib.; *Secy.* Robin Chaney, SAMMIE; *Treas.* Sandy Walsh, Ramsey County Lib.; *Exec. Dir.* Alison Johnson, 1619 Dayton Ave., Ste. 314, Saint Paul 55104. Tel. 651-641-0982, fax 651-641-3169, e-mail mla@mr.net.

Address correspondence to the executive director.

World Wide Web http://www.mnlibrary association.org.

Mississippi

Memb. 700. Term of Office. Jan.–Dec. 2002. Publication. *Mississippi Libraries* (q.).

Pres. Terry S. Latour, W. B. Roberts Lib., Delta State Univ., Cleveland 38733. Tel. 662-846-4440, fax 662-846-4443, e-mail tlatour@merlin.deltast.edu; *V.P./Pres.-Elect* Prima Plauché, Hancock County Lib. System, 312 Hwy. 90, Bay St. Louis 39520-2595. Tel. 228-467-6836, fax 228-467-5503, e-mail pplauche@hancock.lib.ms.us; *Secy.* Kathleen L. Wells, Univ. of Southern Mississippi Libs., Box 5053, Hattiesburg 39406-5053. Tel. 601-266-6399, fax 601-266-6033, e-mail Kathleen.Wells@usm.edu; *Exec. Secy.* Mary Julia Anderson, Box 20448, Jackson 39289-1448. Tel. 601-352-3917, fax 601-352-4240, e-mail mla@meta3.net.

Address correspondence to the executive secretary.

World Wide Web http://www.lib.usm.edu/~mla/org/main.html.

Missouri

Memb. 825. Term of Office. Jan.–Dec. 2002. Publication. *MO INFO* (bi-mo.). *Ed.* Jean Ann McCartney.

Pres. Frances Benham, Univ. Libn., Saint Louis Univ., 3650 Lindell Blvd., St. Louis 63108. Tel. 314-9977-3102, fax 314-977-3108, e-mail benham@slu.edu; *V.P./Pres.-Elect* Karen Hicklin, Dir., Livingston County Lib., 450 Locust St., Chillicothe 64601. Tel. 660-646-0547, fax 660-646-5504, e-mail ugy001@mail.connect.more.net; *Exec. Dir.* Jean Ann McCartney, Missouri Lib. Assn., 1306 Business 63 S., Ste. B, Columbia 65201. Tel. 573-449-4627, fax 573-449-4655, e-mail jmccartn@mail.more.net.

Address correspondence to the executive director.

World Wide Web http://www.molib.org.

Montana

Memb. 600. Term of Office. July 2001–June 2002. Publication. *Montana Library Focus* (bi-mo.). *Ed.* Pam Henley, Bozeman Public Lib., 220 E. Lamme, Bozeman 59715-3579.

Pres. Renee Goss, Sidney Public Lib., 121 Third Ave. N.W., Sidney 59270. Tel. 406-482-1917, fax 406-482-4642, e-mail rgoss@mtlib.org; *V.P./Pres.-Elect* Coby Johnson, UM-Mansfield Lib., 32 Campus Dr., No. 9936, Missoula 59812-9936. Tel. 406-243-4729, fax 406-243-4067, e-mail ml_crj@selway.umt.edu; *Secy./Treas.* Kitty Field, Billings West H.S., 1334 Parkhill Dr., Billings 59102-3141. Tel. 406-655-1362, fax 406-655-3110, e-mail kfield@wtp.net; *Admin. Asst.* Karen A. Hatcher, 510 Arbor, Missoula 59802-3126. Tel. 406-243-6832 or 406-721-3347, fax 406-243-2060, e-mail khatcher@uswest.net.

Address correspondence to the administrative assistant.

Nevada

Memb. 400. Term of Office. Jan.–Dec. 2002. Publication. *Nevada Libraries* (q.).

Pres. Tom Fay, Henderson District Public Libs., 280 Water St., Henderson 89015. Tel. 702-565-8402, fax 702-565-8832, e-mail tffay@hdpl.org; *V.P./Pres.-Elect* Holly Van Valkenburgh, Nevada State Lib. and Archives. E-mail hvanvalk@clan.lib.nv.us; *Treas.* Michelle Mazzanti, e-mail mlmazzanti @hdpl.org; *Exec. Secy.* Amie Maurins. E-mail amaurins@mail.co.washoe.nv.us.

Address correspondence to the executive secretary.

World Wide Web http://www.nevada libraries.org.

New Hampshire

Memb. 700. Publication. *NHLA News* (bi-mo.).

Pres. Lesley Gaudreau, Wiggin Memorial Lib., Bunker Hill Ave., Stratham 03885. E-mail Lesley@WigginML.org; *V.P.* Rob Sargent, Franklin Public Lib., 310 Central St., Franklin 03235. E-mail library@fcgnetworks. net; *Secy.* Jennifer Bone, Keene Public Lib., 60 Winter St., Keene 03431. E-mail jbone@ ci.keene.nh.us; *Treas.* Sue McCann, Portsmouth Public Lib., 8 Islington St., Portsmouth 03801. E-mail sfmccann@lib.cityof portsmouth.com.

Address correspondence to the association, Box 2332, Concord 03302.

World Wide Web http://webster.state.nh. us/nhla.

New Jersey

Memb. 1,700. Term of Office. July 2001–June 2002. Publication. *New Jersey Libraries Newsletter* (mo.).

Pres. Leslie Burger, Princeton Public Lib., 65 Witherspoon St., Princeton 08542. Tel. 609-924-8822 ext. 253, fax 609-924-7937, e-mail burger@princetonlibrary.org; *V.P.* Karen Avenick, Camden County Lib., 203 Laurel Rd., Voorhees 08043. Tel. 856-772-1636 ext. 3328, fax 856-772-6105, e-mail karen@camden.lib.nj.us; *2nd V.P.* John Hurley, Woodbridge Public Lib., George Frederick Plaza, Woodbridge 07095. Tel. 732-634-4450 ext. 248, fax 732-636-1569, e-mail jhurley@lmxac.org; *Secy.* Michele Maiullo, Free Public Lib. of Hasbrouck Heights, 301 Division Ave., Hasbrouck Heights 07604. Tel. 201-288-0488, fax 201-288-6653, e-mail maiullo@bccls.org; *Treas.* Deborah Dennis, Moorestown Public Lib., 111 W. Second St., Moorestown 08057. Tel. 856-234-0333 ext. 3029, fax 856-778-9536, e-mail ddennis@ moorestown.lib.nj.us; *Exec. Dir.* Patricia Tumulty, New Jersey Lib. Assn., Box 1534, Trenton 08607. Tel. 609-394-8032, fax 609-394-8164, e-mail ptumulty@burlco.lib.nj.us.

Address correspondence to the executive director, Box 1534, Trenton 08607.

World Wide Web http://www.njla.org.

New Mexico

Memb. 550. Term of Office. Apr. 2001–Apr. 2002. Publication. *New Mexico Library Asso-ciation Newsletter* (6 a year). *Ed.* Lorie Mitchell. Tel. 505-887-9538, e-mail loriem 1970@hotmail.com.

Pres. Kay Krehbiel, NM Tech, Campus Sta., Socorro 87801. Tel. 505-835-5615, e-mail kkrehbie@admin.nmt.edu; *V.P.* Earl Phillips, 6050 Shadow Hills Rd., Las Cruces 88012. Tel. 505-527-6065, e-mail ephillip@ lcps.k12.nm.us; *Secy.* Clair Odenheim, Onate H.S. Lib., Las Cruces 88011. Tel. 505-527-9430, e-mail odenheim@lib.nmsu.edu; *Admin. Services* Linda O'Connell.

Address correspondence to the association, Box 26074, Albuquerque 87125. Tel. 505-899-7600, e-mail nmla@rt66.com.

World Wide Web http://lib.nmsu.edu/nmla.

New York

Memb. 3,000. Term of Office. Oct. 2001–Nov. 2002. Publication. *NYLA Bulletin* (6 a year). *Ed.* David Titus.

Pres. Carolyn Giambra. Tel. 716-626-8025, e-mail cgiambra@williamsvillek12. org; *Treas.* Mary Brown. Tel. 518-563-5190, e-mail mabrown@northnet.org; *Exec. Dir.* Susan Lehman Keitel, New York Lib. Assn., 252 Hudson Ave., Albany 12210. Tel. 518-432-6952, e-mail nyladirector@pobox.com.

Address correspondence to the executive director.

World Wide Web http://www.nyla.org.

North Carolina

Memb. 2,000. Term of Office. Oct. 2001–Oct. 2003. Publication. *North Carolina Libraries* (q.). *Ed.* Frances Bradburn, Media and Technology, N.C. Dept. of Public Instruction, 301 N. Wilmington St., Raleigh 27601-2825. Tel. 919-715-1528, fax 919-733-4762, e-mail fbradbur@dpi.state.nc.us.

Pres. Ross Holt, Randolph County Public Lib., 201 Worth St., Asheboro 27203. Tel. 336-318-6806, fax 336-318-6823, e-mail rholt@ncsl.dcr.state.nc.us; *V.P./Pres.-Elect* Pauletta Bracy, North Carolina Central Univ., SLIS, Box 19586, Durham 27707. Tel. 919-560-6485, fax 919-560-6402, e-mail pbracy @slis.nccu.edu; *Secy.* Martha Davis, 5002 Marigold Way, Greensboro 27410. Tel. 336-855-0853, e-mail mdavis92627@yahoo.com; *Treas.* Diane Kester, Dept. of Broadcasting, Libnship. and Educ. Technology, 102 Joyner E., Greenville 27858-4353. Tel. 252-328-

6621, fax 252-328-4368, e-mail kesterd@ mail.ecu.edu or Lsddkest@eastnet.ecu.edu; *Admin. Asst.* Maureen Costello, North Carolina Lib. Assn., 4646 Mail Service Center, Raleigh 27699-4646. Tel. 919-839-6252, fax 919-839-6253, e-mail ncla@mindspring.com.

Address correspondence to the administrative assistant.

World Wide Web http://www.nclaonline. org.

North Dakota

Memb. (Indiv.) 400; (Inst.) 18. Term of Office. Sept. 2001–Sept. 2002. Publication. *The Good Stuff* (q.). *Ed.* Andrea Winkjer Collin, 502 Juniper Dr., Bismarck 58501. Tel. 701-222-8714, 701-250-9404.

Pres. La Dean S. Moen, Box 908, Hettinger 58639. Tel./fax 701-567-2741, e-mail moen@sendit.nodak.edu; *Pres.-Elect* Kaaren Pupino, Thormodsgard Law Lib., Univ. of North Dakota, Centennial Dr., Box 9004, Grand Forks 58202-9004. Tel. 701-777-2486, fax 701-777-2217, e-mail Kaaren.Pupino@ thor.law.und.nodak.edu; *Secy.* Marlene Anderson, Bismarck State College Lib., Box 5587, Bismarck 58506-5587. Tel. 701-224-5578, 701-224-5551, e-mail marander@ gwmail.nodak.edu; *Treas.* Michael Safratowich, UND Health Sciences Lib., Box 9002, Grand Forks 58202-9002. Tel. 701-777-2602, fax 701-777-4790, e-mail msafrat@medicine. nodak.edu.

Address correspondence to the president.

World Wide Web http://ndsl.lib.state.nd. us/ndla.

Ohio

Memb. 3,400+. Term of Office. Jan.–Dec. Publications. *Access* (mo.); *Ohio Libraries* (q.).

Chair JoAnn Scanlon, 2335 Abington Rd., Columbus 43221. Tel. 614-486-3906, e-mail jvsohio@columbus.rr.com; *V. Chair* Meribah Mansfield, Worthington Public Lib., 820 High St., Worthington 43085-4108. Tel. 614-645-2620 ext. 239, fax 614-645-2642, e-mail meribah@worthingtonlibraries.org; *Secy.* Jack Welsh, 1805 Westover Lane, Mansfield 44906-3344. Tel. 419-529-8793, e-mail welread2@aol.com; *Treas.* Thomas Adkins, Garnet A. Wilson Public Lib. of Pike County, 207 N. Market St., Waverly 45690-1176. Tel.

740-947-4921, fax 740-947-2918, e-mail dirgaw@oplin.lib.oh.us; *Co-Exec. Secys.* Lynda Murray, Wayne Piper. E-mail lmurray @olc.org or wpiper@olc.org.

Address correspondence to the association, 35 E. Gay St., Ste. 305, Columbus 43215. Tel. 614-221-9057, fax 614-231-6234, e-mail olc@olc.org.

World Wide Web http://www.olc.org.

Oklahoma

Memb. (Indiv.) 1,050; (Inst.) 60. Term of Office. July 2001–June 2002. Publication. *Oklahoma Librarian* (bi-mo.).

Pres. Wayne Hanway. E-mail whanway@ sepl.lib.ok.us; *V.P./Pres.-Elect* Kathryn Roots Lewis. E-mail klewis@norman.k12.ok. us; *Secy.* Francine Fisk. E-mail francinefisk@utulsa.edu; *Treas.* Anne R. Hsieh. E-mail ahsieh@mls.lib.ok.us; *Exec. Dir.* Kay Boies, 300 Hardy Dr., Edmond 73013. Tel./ fax 405-348-0506, e-mail kboies@ionet.net.

Address correspondence to the executive director.

World Wide Web http://www.pioneer.lib. ok.us/ola.

Oregon

Memb. (Indiv.) 1,049. Publications. *OLA Hotline* (bi-w.), *OLA Quarterly.*

Pres. Janet Webster, Guin Lib., Oregon State Univ. Tel. 541-867-0108, e-mail Janet. Webster@orst.edu; *V.P./Pres.-Elect* Connie Bennett , Eugene Public Lib. Tel. 541-682-5363. E-mail connie.j.bennet@ci.eugene.or. us; *Secy.* Barbara O'Neill, Washington County Cooperative Lib. Services. Tel. 503-988-5577, e-mail barbarao@multcolib.org.

Address correspondence to John McCully, Professional Administrative Services. Tel. 503-370-7019, e-mail assoc@wvi.com.

World Wide Web http://www.olaweb.org.

Pennsylvania

Memb. 1,500. Term of Office. Jan.–Dec. 2002. Publication. *PaLA Bulletin* (10 a year).

Pres. Mary Elizabeth Colombo, Dir., B. F. Jones Memorial Lib., 663 Franklin Ave., Aliquippa 15001. Tel. 724-375-2900, fax 724-375-3274, e-mail bfjones@shrsys.hslc. org; *1st V.P.* Olga Conneen, Dir., Northampton Community College Lib. E-mail oconneen @northampton.edu; *2nd V.P.* Jonelle Darr,

Exec. Dir., Cumberland County Lib. System. E-mail jdarr@ccpa.net; *Exec. Dir.* Glenn R. Miller, Pennsylvania Lib. Assn., 3905 N. Front St., Harrisburg 17110. Tel. 717-233-3113, 800-622-3308 (Pennsylvania only), fax 717-233-3121, e-mail glenn@palibraries.org. Address correspondence to the executive director.

World Wide Web http://www.palibraries.org.

Rhode Island

Memb. (Indiv.) 349; (Inst.) 59. Term of Office. June 2001–June 2003. Publication. *Rhode Island Library Association Bulletin.* *Ed.* James Giles.

Pres. David Macksam, Cranston Public Lib., 140 Sockanosset Cross Rd., Cranston 02920. Tel. 401-943-9080, fax 401-946-5079, e-mail davidmm@lori.state.ri.us; *Secy.* Joyce May, Coventry Public Lib., 1672 Flat River Rd., Coventry 02816. Tel. 401-822-9100, fax 401-822-9133, e-mail mayjoyb@aol.com; *Clerk* Derryl Johnson, Marian Mohr Memorial Lib., 1 Memorial Dr., Johnston 02919. Tel. 401-231-4980, fax 401-231-4984, e-mail derryljn@lori.state.ri.us. Address correspondence to the secretary.

South Carolina

Memb. 800. Term of Office. Jan.–Dec. 2002. Publication. *News and Views.*

Pres. Jeanette Bergeron, Crumley Lutheran Archives, 4201 N. Main St., Columbia 20203. Tel. 803-787-8840, fax 803-787-8840, e-mail bergeron@conterra.com; *V.P./Pres.-Elect* Tom Gilson, Robert Scott Small Lib., College of Charleston. Tel. 843-953-8014, fax 843-953-8019, e-mail gilsont@cofc.edu; *2nd V.P.* Kathleen S. Turner, Daniel Lib., The Citadel. Tel. 843-953-7058, e-mail turnerk@citadel.edu; *Secy.* Nancy Taylor, Custom Business Research, 40 Wood Pointe Dr., No. 9, Greenville 29615. Tel. 864-235-3980, fax 864-271-7225, e-mail ntaylor@myexcel.com; *Treas.* Quincy Pugh, Richland County Public Lib., 1431 Assembly St., Columbia 29201. Tel. 803-929-3449, fax 803-929-3448, e-mail qpugh@richland.lib.sc.us; *Co-Exec. Secys.* Camille McCutcheon, USC Spartanburg. Tel. 864-503-5612, fax 864-503-5601, e-mail execsecretary@scla.org; Mark Mancuso, Lexington County Lib.,

5440 Augusta Rd., Lexington 29072. Tel. 803-808-2673, fax 803-808-2683, e-mail execsecretary@scla.org. Address correspondence to the co-executive secretaries.

World Wide Web http://www.scla.org.

South Dakota

Memb. (Indiv.) 497; (Inst.) 54. Term of Office. Oct. 2001–Oct. 2002. Publication. *Book Marks* (bi-mo.).

Pres. Ann Smith, Sioux Falls 57103. Tel. 605-367-7951, e-mail smithann@SF.K12.SD.US; *Secy.* Peggy Whalen, Brookings Public Lib., Brookings 57006; *Treas.* Mary Kraljic, South Dakota State Univ., Brookings 57007; *ALA Councillor* Joe Edelen, ID Weeks Lib., Univ. of South Dakota, Vermillion 57069; *MPLA Rep.* Suzanne Miller, SD State Lib., Pierre 57501.

Address correspondence to Brenda Standiford, Exec. Secy., SDLA, c/o Devereaux Lib., 501 E. St. Joseph St., Rapid City 57701. Tel. 605-394-1258, fax 605-394-1256, e-mail brenda.standiford@sdsmt.edu.

World Wide Web http://www.usd.edu/sdla.

Tennessee

Memb. 875. Term of Office. July 2001–July 2002. Publications. *Tennessee Librarian* (q.), *TLA Newsletter* (bi-mo.).

Pres. Faith Holdredge, Dir., Caney Fork Regional Lib., 25 Rhea St., Sparta 38583. Tel. 931-836-2209, e-mail fholdred@mail.state.tn.us; *V.P./Pres.-Elect* B. P. Ponnappa, Lib. Dir., James H. Quillen College of Medicine, ETSU, Johnson City, TN 37614. Tel. 423-439-6355, e-mail ponnappa@etsu.edu; *Treas.* Lynn T. Lilley, Lib. Media Specialist, McGavock H.S., 3150 McGavock Pkwy., Nashville 37214. Tel. 615-885-8881, e-mail LilleyL@k12tn.net; *Past Pres.* Tena Litherland, Webb School of Knoxville, Knoxville 37923. Tel. 865-291-3813, e-mail tena_litherland@webbschool.org; *Exec. Dir.* Annelle Huggins, Tennessee Lib. Assn., Box 158417, Nashville 37215-8417. Tel. 615-297-8316, fax 615-269-1807.

Address correspondence to the executive director.

World Wide Web http://www.lib.utk.edu/~tla.

Texas

Memb. 7,200. Term of Office. Apr. 2001–
Apr. 2002. Publications. *Texas Library Journal* (q.); *TLACast* (9 a year).
Pres. Herman L. Totten, Univ. of North
Texas SLIS, Denton 76205. Tel. 940-565-
3567, fax 940-565-3101, e-mail totten@lis.
admin.unt.edu; *Pres.-Elect* Barry Bishop,
Spring Branch ISD, Box 19432, Houston
77224. Tel. 713-365-5580, fax 713-365-
4330, e-mail bishopb@springbranchisd.com;
Treas. June Koelker, Texas Christian Univ.,
MCB Lib., Box 298400, Fort Worth 76129.
Tel. 817-257-7696, fax 817-481-7282, e-mail
j.koelker@tcu.edu; *Exec. Dir.* Patricia H.
Smith, 3355 Bee Cave Rd., Ste. 401, Austin
78746-6763. Tel. 512-328-1518, fax 512-
328-8852, e-mail pats@txla.org.

Address correspondence to the executive
director.

World Wide Web http://www.txla.org.

Utah

Memb. 650. Term of Office. May 2001–May
2002. Publication. *UTAH Libraries News* (bi-
mo.) (electronic at http://www.ula.org/
newsletter).
Pres. Susan Hamada, Sandy Lib., 10100 S.
Petunia Way, Sandy 84092. Tel. 801-944-
7684, fax 801-282-0943, e-mail shamada@
slco.lib.ut.us; *V.P./Pres.-Elect* Kayla Willey,
Harold B. Lee Lib., Brigham Young Univ.,
Provo 84602. Tel. 801-378-6766. E-mail
kayla_willey@byu.edu. *Treas./Exec. Secy.*
Shannon Reid.

Address correspondence to the executive
secretary, Box 970488 Orem 84097-0488.
Tel. 801-378-4433, e-mail shannon_reid@
byu.edu.

World Wide Web http://www.ula.org.

Vermont

Memb. 400. Publication. *VLA News* (6 a
year).
Pres. Trina Magi, Univ. of Vermont,
Burlington 05405. Tel. 802-656-5723, e-mail
tmagi@zoo.uvm.edu *V.P./Pres.-Elect* Karen
Lane, Aldrich Public Lib., 6 Washington,
Barre 05644. Tel. 802-476-7550, e-mail
aldrich@helicon.net; *Secy.* Daisy Benson,
Bailey/Howe Lib., Univ. of Vermont, Burlington 05405. Tel. 802-656-0636, e-mail
dsbenson@zoo.uvm.edu; *Treas.* Jane Plough-
man, Deborah Rawson Memorial Lib., 8
River Rd., Jericho 05465. Tel. 802-899-4962,
e-mail j_ploughman@yahoo.com; *Past Pres.*
Kathy Naftaly, Rutland Free Lib., 10 Court
St., Rutland 05701. Tel. 802-773-1860,
e-mail rutland_free@dol.state.vt.us.

Address correspondence to the president,
VLA, Box 803, Burlington 05402-0803.

World Wide Web http://vermontlibraries.
org.

Virginia

Memb. 1,200. Term of Office. Oct. 2001–
Oct. 2002. Publications. *Virginia Libraries*
(q.). *Co.-Eds.* Barbie Selby. Tel. 423-924-
3504, e-mail bselby@virginia.edu; Earlene
Viano. Tel. 757-727-1312, e-mail eviano@
hampton.gov; *VLA Newsletter* (10 a year).
Ed. Helen Q. Sherman, 4369 Wiltshire Place,
Dumphries 22026. E-mail hsherman@dtic.
mil.
Pres. Iza Cieszynski, Newport News Pub-
lic Lib., 2400 Washington Ave., Newport
News 23607. Tel. 757-926-8506, fax 757-
926-3563, e-mail icieszynski@nngov.com;
V.P./Pres.-Elect Morel Fry, Old Dominion
Univ., Perry Lib., Norfolk 23529-0256. Tel.
757-683-4143, fax 757-683-5767, e-mail
mfry@odu.edu; *2nd V.P.* Harriett Edmunds,
Lib. of Virginia, 800 E. Broad St., Richmond
23219. Tel. 804-692-3727, fax 804-692-
3736, e-mail hedmunds@lva.lib.va.us; *Secy.*
Janis Augustine, Salem Public Lib., 28 E.
Main St., Salem 24153. Tel. 540-375-3089,
fax 540-389-7054, e-mail jaugustine@
ci.salem.va.us; *Treas.* Andrew Morton,
Boatwright Memorial Lib., Univ. of Richmond, Richmond 23173. Tel. 804-287-6047,
fax 804-287-1840, e-mail amorton@
richmond.edu; *Exec. Dir.* Linda Hahne, Box
8277, Norfolk 23503-0277. Tel. 757-583-
0041, fax 757-583-5041, e-mail lhahne@
coastalnet.com.

Address correspondence to the executive
director.

World Wide Web http://www.vla.org.

Washington

Memb. 1,200. Term of Office. Apr. 2001–
Apr. 2003. Publications. *ALKI* (3 a year),
WLA Link (5 a year).
Pres. Carol Gill Schuyler, Kitsap Regional
Lib., 1301 Sylvan Way, Bremerton 98310-

3498. Tel. 360-405-9127, fax 360-405-9128, e-mail carol@krl.org; *V.P./Pres.-Elect* John Sheller, Federal Way 320th/KCLS, 848 S. 320, Federal Way 98003. Tel. 253-839-0257, fax 206-296-5053, e-mail jsheller@kcls.org; *Secy.* Karen Highum, UW/Suzzallo, Box 352900, Seattle 98195-2900. Tel. 206-685-3981, e-mail highum@u.washington.edu; *Treas.* Monica Weyhe, Yakima Valley Regional Lib., 102 N. 3 St., Yakima 98901. Tel. 509-452-8541 ext. 702, fax 509-575-2093, e-mail mweyhe@yvrls.lib.wa.us; *Assn. Coord.* Gail E. Willis.

Address correspondence to the association office, 4016 1st Ave. N.E., Seattle 98105-6502. Tel. 206-545-1529, 800-704-1529, fax 206-545-1543, e-mail wasla@wla.org.

World Wide Web http://www.wla.org.

West Virginia

Memb. 667. Term of Office. Dec. 2001–Nov. 2002. Publication. *West Virginia Libraries* (6 a year). *Ed.* Dottie Thomas, Ohio County Public Lib., 52 16th St., Wheeling 26003. E-mail thomas@weirton.lib.wv.us.

Pres. Sharon Saye, Bridgeport Public Lib., 1200 Johnson Ave., Bridgeport 26330. E-mail saye@bridgeportwv.com; *1st V.P./Pres.-Elect* Julie Spiegler, Kanawha County Public Lib.; *2nd V.P.* Myra Zeigler, Summers County Public Lib. E-mail zieglerm@raleigh.lib. wv.us; *Secy.* Tim Balch, Marshall University Libs. E-mail balch@marshall.edu; *Treas.* Steve Christo, Cabell County Public Lib. E-mail schristo@cabell.lib.wv.us.

Address correspondence to the president.

World Wide Web http://wvnvaxa.wvnet. edu/~wvla.

Wisconsin

Memb. 2,000. Term of Office. Jan.–Dec. 2002. Publication. *WLA Newsletter* (bi-mo.). *Pres.* Stephen Proces, Neenah Public Lib., Box 569, Neenah 54957-0569. Tel. 920-571-4722, e-mail proces@neenahlibrary.org; *Pres.-Elect* Peter Gilbert, Mudd Lib., Lawrence Univ., Box 599, Appleton 54911-5683. Tel. 920-832-6700, fax 920-832-6967, e-mail peter.j.gilbert@lawrence.edu; *Secy.* Paulette Feld, Polk Lib., UW Oshkosh, Oshkosh 54901. Tel. 920-424-7369, fax 920-424-2175, e-mail feld@uwosh.edu; *Treas.* Mich-

ael Cross, Div. for Libs., Technology, and Community Learning. Tel. 608-267-9225, fax 608-267-1052, e-mail michael.cross@ dpi.state.wi.us; *Exec. Dir.* Lisa Strand. Tel. 608-245-3640, fax 608-245-3646, e-mail strand@scls.lib.wi.us.

Address correspondence to the association, 5250 E. Terrace Dr., Ste. A1, Madison 53718-8345.

World Wide Web http://www.wla.lib.wi.us.

Wyoming

Memb. (Indiv.) 425; (Inst.) 21. Term of Office. Oct. 2001–Oct. 2002.

Pres. Trish Palluck, Wyoming State Lib., Supreme Court Bldg., Cheyenne 82002. Tel. 307-777-5913, fax 307-777-6289, e-mail Tpallu@state.wy.us; *V.P./Pres.-Elect* Kay Carlson, Northwest College, 231 W. 6 St., Powell 82435. Tel. 307-754-6527, fax 307-754-6010, e-mail carlsonk@nwc.cc.wy.us; *Exec. Secy.* Laura Grott, Box 1387, Cheyenne 82003. Tel. 307-632-7622, fax 307-638-3469, e-mail grottski@aol.com.

Address correspondence to the executive secretary.

World Wide Web http://www.wyla.org.

Canada

Alberta

Memb. 500. Term of Office. May 2001–Apr. 2002. Publication. *Letter of the LAA* (5 a year).

Pres. Rick Leech, Mgr., Provincial Court Lib. System, 5th fl. North, Law Courts, 1A Sir Winston Churchill Sq., Edmonton T5J 0R2. Tel. 780-427-3247, fax 780-427-0481, e-mail rick.leech@just.gov.ab.ca; *Exec. Dir.* Christine Sheppard, 80 Baker Crescent N.W., Calgary T2L 1R4. Tel. 403-284-5832, fax 403-282-6646, e-mail shepparc@cadvision. com.

Address correspondence to the executive director.

World Wide Web http://www.laa.ab.ca.

British Columbia

Memb. 750. Term of Office. May 2001–April 2002. Publication. *BCLA Reporter. Ed.* Ted Benson.

Pres. Carol Elder; *V.P./Pres.-Elect* Gohar Ashoughian; *Exec. Dir.* Michael Burris.

Address correspondence to the association, 150-900 Howe St., Vancouver V6Z 2M4. Tel. 604-683-5354, fax 604-609-0707, e-mail office@bcla.bc.ca.

Manitoba

Memb. 500. Term of Office. May 2001–May 2002. Publication. *Newsline* (mo.).

Pres. Mark Leggott, Univ. of Winnipeg Lib., 515 Portage Ave., Winnipeg R3B 2E9. E-mail mark.leggott@uwinnipeg.ca; *V.P./ Pres.-Elect* Janice Linton, Neil John Maclean Health Sciences Lib., Univ. of Manitoba, Winnipeg R3E 0W3. E-mail lintonjs@ms. umanitoba.ca.

Address correspondence to the association, 606-100 Arthur St., Winnipeg R3B 1H3. Tel. 204-943-4567, fax 204-942-1555.

World Wide Web http://www.mla.mb.ca/index.html.

Ontario

Memb. 3,750. Term of Office. Jan. 2002–Jan. 2003. Publications. *Access* (q.); *Teaching Librarian* (q.); *Accessola.com* (q.).

Pres. Stephen Abram, IHS Micromedia Ltd. Tel. 416-369-2594, fax 416-362-1699, e-mail sabram@micromedia.on.ca; *V.P.* To be announced; *Past Pres.* Michael Ridley, University of Guelph. Tel. 519-824-4121 ext. 2181, fax 519-824-6931, e-mail mridley@ uoguelph.ca; *Treas.* Cathi Gibson-Gates, Toronto District School Board; *Exec. Dir.* Larry Moore.

Address correspondence to the association, 100 Lombard St., Ste. 303, Toronto M5C 1M3. Tel. 416-363-3388, fax 416-941-9581; e-mail info@accessola.com.

World Wide Web http://www.accessola.org.

Quebec

Memb. (Indiv.) 125; (Inst.) 13; (Commercial) 2. Term of Office. June 2001–May 2002. Publication. *ABQ/QLA Bulletin* (3 a year).

Pres. Dorothy Cameron; *Exec. Secy.* Cheryl McDonell, Box 1095, Pointe-Claire H95 4H9. Tel. 514-421-7541, e-mail abqla@ abqla.qc.ca.

Address correspondence to the executive secretary.

World Wide Web http://www.abqla.qc.ca.

Saskatchewan

Memb. 225. Term of Office. June 2001–May 2002. Publication. *Forum* (5 a year).

Pres. Rosemary Loeffler, La Ronge Public Lib., Box 864, La Ronge S0J 1L0. E-mail R.Loeffler.SLA@pnls.sk.ca; *V.P.* Michelle Splitter, John M. Cuelenaere Lib., 125 12th St. E., Prince Albert S6V 1B7. E-mail splitter @jmc.panet.pa.sk.ca; *Exec. Dir.* Judith Silverthorne, Box 3388, Regina S4P 3H1. Tel. 306-780-9413, fax 306-780-9447, e-mail sla@pleis.lib.sk.ca.

Address correspondence to the executive director.

World Wide Web http://www.lib.sk.ca/sla.

Regional

Atlantic Provinces: N.B., Nfld., N.S., P.E.I.

Memb. (Indiv.) 193; (Inst.) 30. Term of Office. May 2001–May 2002. Publications. *APLA Bulletin* (bi-mo.), *Membership Directory and Handbook* (ann.).

Pres. Norine Hanus, Collections Libn., Robertson Lib., UPEI, Charlottetown, PE C1A 4P3. Tel. 902-566-0479, fax 902-628-4305, e-mail nhanus@upei.ca; *V.P./Pres.-Elect* Elaine MacLean, Head, Technical Services, Angus L. MacDonald Lib., St. Francis Xavier Univ., Antigonish, NS B2W 2W5. Tel. 902-867-2221, fax 902-867-5253, e-mail emalean@stfx.ca; *Secy.* Dawn Hooper, Reference Libn., Robertson Lib., Univ. of Prince Edward Island, Charlottetown, PE C1A 4P3. Tel. 902-566-0453, fax 902-628-4305, e-mail dhooper@upei.ca; *Treas.* Marnie MacGillivray, Reference and Instruction Libn., Mount Saint Vincent Univ., Halifax, NS B3J 2X4. Tel. 902-457-6200, fax 902-457-6445, e-mail marnie.macgillivray@ msvu.ca.

Address correspondence to Atlantic Provinces Lib. Assn., c/o School of Lib. and Info. Studies, Dalhousie Univ., Halifax, NS B3H 4H8.

World Wide Web http://www.stmarys.ca/partners/apla.

Mountain Plains: Ariz., Colo., Kan., Mont., Neb., Nev., N.Dak., N.M., Okla., S.Dak., Utah, Wyo.

Memb. 820. Term of Office. One year. Publications. *MPLA Newsletter* (bi-mo.), *Ed. and Adv. Mgr.* Lisa Mecklenberg Jackson, Montana Legislative Reference Center, Box 201706, Helena, MT 59620-1706. Tel. 406-444-2957, e-mail ljackson@state.mt.us; *Membership Directory* (ann.).

Pres. Debbie Iverson, Sheridan College Lib., Box 1500, Sheridan, WY 82801. Tel. 307-674-6446 ext. 6201, fax 307-674-4874, e-mail diverson@sc.cc.wy.us; *V.P./Pres.-Elect* Jean Hatfield, Johnson County Lib., Box 2933, Shawnee Mission, KS 66201-1333, e-mail hatfield@ jcl.lib.ks.us; *Exec. Secy.* Joe Edelen, I. D. Weeks Lib., Univ. of South Dakota, Vermillion, SD 57069. Tel. 605-677-6082, fax 605-677-5488, e-mail jedelen@usd.edu.

Address correspondence to the executive secretary, Mountain Plains Lib. Assn.

World Wide Web http://www.usd.edu/mpla.

New England: Conn., Maine, Mass., N.H., R.I., Vt.

Memb. (Indiv.) 1,300; (Inst.) 100. Term of Office. Nov. 2001–Oct. 2002. (Treas., Dirs., and Secy., two years). Publication. *New England Libraries* (bi-mo.). *Ed.* Patricia Holloway. E-mail holloway@crlc.org.

Pres. Cheryl Bryan, 10 Riverside Dr., Lakeville, MA 02347. Tel. 508-923-3531, fax 508-923-3539, e-mail cbryan@semls.org; *V.P./Pres.-Elect* Karen Valley, Portland Public Lib., 5 Monument Sq., Portland, ME 04101. Tel. 207-871-1716, fax 207-871-1703, e-mail valley@portland.lib.me.us; *Exec. Secy.* Barry Blaisdell, New England Lib. Assn., 14 Pleasant St., Gloucester, MA 01930. Tel. 972-282-0787, e-mail info@ nelib.org.

Address correspondence to the executive secretary.

World Wide Web http://nelib.cjweb solutions.com/index.html.

Pacific Northwest: Alaska, Idaho, Mont., Ore., Wash., Alberta, B.C.

Memb. (Active) 550; (Subscribers) 100. Term of Office. Aug. 2001–Aug. 2002. Publication. *PNLA Quarterly.*

Pres. Sandy Carlson, Kitsap Regional Lib., 1301 Sylvan Way, Bremerton, WA 98310. Tel. 360-405-9111, fax 360-405-9128, e-mail sandy@krl.org; *1st V.P./Pres.-Elect* Dan Masoni, Unalaska Public Lib., Box 610, Unalaska, AK 99685. Tel. 907-581-5060, fax 907-581-5266, e-mail akunak@ci. unalaska.ak.us; *2nd V.P.* Christine Sheppard, Lib. Assn. of Alberta, 80 Baker Crescent N.W., Calgary, AB T2L 1R4. Tel. 403-284-5818, e-mail shepparc@cadvision.com; *Secy.* Carol Reich, Hillsboro Public Lib., Hillsboro, OR 17864. Tel. 503-615-6505, e-mail carolr @ci.hillsboro.or.us; *Treas.* Robert Hook, Univ. of Idaho Lib., Moscow, ID. E-mail rdhook@uidaho.edu.

Address correspondence to the president, Pacific Northwest Lib. Assn.

World Wide Web http://www.pnla.org.

Southeastern: Ala., Ark., Fla., Ga., Ky., La., Miss., N.C., S.C., Tenn., Va., W.Va.

Memb. 500. Term of Office. Oct. 2000–Oct. 2002. Publication. *The Southeastern Librarian* (q.).

Pres. Barry Baker, Univ. of Central Florida, Box 162666, Orlando, FL 32816-2666. Tel. 407-823-2564, fax 407-823-2529, e-mail bbaker@mail.ucf.edu; *V.P./Pres.-Elect* Ann H. Hamilton, Assoc. Dean of Libs., Georgia Southern Univ., 211 Wendwood Dr., Statesboro, GA. 30458-5075. Tel. 912-681-5115, fax 912-681-0093, e-mail: ahamilton@gasou. edu; *Secy.* Sybil Boudreaux, Univ. of New Orleans, Earl K. Long Lib., Lake Front, LA 70148-2720. Tel. 504-280-1157, fax 504-280-7277, e-mail sboudrea@uno.edu; *Treas.* Glenda Neely, Univ. of Louisville, Ekstrom Lib., Louisville, KY 40292. Tel. 502-285-8741, fax 502-852-8736, e-mail glenda.neely @louisville.edu.

State and Provincial Library Agencies

The state library administrative agency in each of the U.S. states will have the latest information on its state plan for the use of federal funds under the Library Services and Technology Act (LSTA). The directors and addresses of these state agencies are listed below.

Alabama

Rebecca Mitchell, Dir., Alabama Public Lib. Service, 6030 Monticello Dr., Montgomery 36130. Tel. 334-213-3900, fax 334-213-3993, e-mail rmitchell@apls.state.al.us.

Alaska

Karen R. Crane, Dir., State Lib., Archives, and Museums, Alaska Dept. of Educ., Box 110571, Juneau 99811-0571. Tel. 907-465-2910, fax 907-465-2151, e-mail karen_crane@eed.state.ak.us.

Arizona

GladysAnn Wells, Dir., Dept. of Lib., Archives, and Public Records, State Capitol, Rm. 200, 1700 W. Washington, Phoenix 85007-2896. Tel. 602-542-4035, fax 602-542-4972, e-mail gawells@dlapr.lib.az.us.

Arkansas

Jack C. Mulkey, State Libn., Arkansas State Lib., 1 Capitol Mall, Little Rock 72201-1081. Tel. 501-682-1526, fax 501-682-1899, e-mail jmulkey@asl.lib.ar.us.

California

Kevin Starr, State Libn., California State Lib., Box 942837, Sacramento 94237-0001. Tel. 916-654-0174, fax 916-654-0064, e-mail kstarr@library.ca.gov.

Colorado

Nancy Bolt, Deputy State Libn. and Asst. Commissioner, Dept. of Educ., 201 E. Colfax Ave., Denver 80203. Tel. 303-866-6733, fax 303-866-6940, e-mail nbolt@csn.net.

Connecticut

Ken Wiggin, State Libn., Connecticut State Lib., 231 Capitol Ave., Hartford 06106. Tel. 860-757-6510, fax 860-566-8940, e-mail kwiggin@cslib.org.

Delaware

Mary Chute, Dir. and State Libn., Div. of Libs., 43 S. DuPont Hwy., Dover 19901. Tel. 302-739-4748, fax 302-739-6787, e-mail mchute@lib.de.us.

District of Columbia

Mary E. "Molly" Raphael, Dir. and State Libn., Dist. of Columbia Public Lib., 901 G St. N.W., Suite 400, Washington 20001. Tel. 202-727-1101, fax 202-727-1129, e-mail mraphael@rapgroup.com.

Florida

Barratt Wilkins, State Libn., Div. of Lib. and Info. Services, R. A. Gray Bldg., Tallahassee 32399-0250. Tel. 850-487-2651, fax 850-488-2746, e-mail bwilkins@mail.dos.state.fl.us.

Georgia

Lamar Veatch, Dir., Georgia Public Lib. Service, 1800 Century Place, Suite 150, Atlanta 30345. Tel. 404-982-3560, fax 404-982-3563, e-mail Lveatch@state.lib.ga.us.

Hawaii

Virginia Lowell, State Libn., Hawaii State Public Lib. System, 465 S. King St., Rm. B1, Honolulu 96813. Tel. 808-586-3704, fax 808-586-3715, e-mail STLIB@lib.state.hi.us.

Idaho

Charles Bolles, State Libn., Idaho State Lib., 325 W. State St., Boise 83702. Tel. 208-334-2150, fax 208-334-4016, e-mail cbolles@isl.state.id.us.

Illinois

Jean Wilkins, Dir., Illinois State Lib., 300 S. 2 St., Springfield 62701-1796. Tel. 217-782-2994, fax 217-785-4326, e-mail jwilkins@ilsos.net.

Indiana

C. Ray Ewick, Dir., Indiana State Lib., 140 N. Senate Ave., Indianapolis 46204-2296. Tel. 317-232-3692, fax 317-232-0002, e-mail ewick@statelib.lib.in.us.

Iowa

Mary Wegner, State Libn., State Lib. of Iowa, E. 12 and Grand, Des Moines 50319. Tel. 515-281-7574, e-mail Mary.Wegner@lib.state.ia.us.

Kansas

Duane Johnson, State Libn., Kansas State Lib., State Capitol, 3rd fl., Topeka 66612. Tel. 785-296-3296, fax 785-296-6650, e-mail duanej@ink.org.

Kentucky

James A. Nelson, State Libn./Commissioner, Kentucky Dept. for Libs. and Archives, 300 Coffee Tree Rd., Box 537, Frankfort 40602-0537. Tel. 502-564-8300, fax 502-564-5773, e-mail jim.nelson@kdla.net.

Louisiana

Thomas F. Jaques, State Libn., State Lib. of Louisiana, Box 131, Baton Rouge 70821-0131. Tel. 225-342-4923, fax 225-219-4804, e-mail tjaques@pelican.state.lib.la.us.

Maine

J. Gary Nichols, State Libn., Maine State Lib., 64 State House Sta., Augusta 04333-0064. Tel. 207-287-5600, fax 207-287-5615, e-mail gary.nichols@state.me.us.

Maryland

J. Maurice Travillian, Asst. State Superintendent for Libs., Div. of Lib. Development and Services, Maryland State Dept. of Educ., 200 W. Baltimore St., Baltimore 21201-2595. Tel. 410-767-0435, fax 410-333-2507, e-mail maurice0523@email.com.

Massachusetts

Keith Michael Fiels, Dir., Massachusetts Board of Lib. Commissioners, 648 Beacon St., Boston 02215. Tel. 617-267-9400, fax 617-421-9833, e-mail Keith.Fiels@state.ma.us.

Michigan

Christie Pearson Brandau, State Libn., Lib. of Michigan, 717 W. Allegan St., Box 30007, Lansing 48909. Tel. 517-373-5504, fax 517-373-4480, e-mail cbrandau@libraryofmichigan.org.

Minnesota

Joyce Swonger, Dir., Lib. Development and Services, Minnesota Dept. of Children, Families, and Learning, 1500 Hwy. 36 West, Roseville 55113. Tel. 651-582-8722, fax 651-582-8897, e-mail joyce.swonger@state.mn.us.

Mississippi

Sharman B. Smith, Exec. Dir., Mississippi Lib. Commission, 1221 Ellis Ave., Box 10700, Jackson 39289-0700. Tel. 601-961-4039, fax 601-354-6713, e-mail sharman@lc.lib.ms.us.

Missouri

Sara Parker, State Libn., Missouri State Lib., 600 W. Main, Box 387, Jefferson City 65102-0387. Tel. 573-751-2751, fax 573-751-3612, e-mail parkes@sosmail.state.mo.us.

Montana

Karen Strege, State Libn., Montana State Lib., 1515 E. 6 Ave., Box 201800, Helena 59620-1800. Tel. 406-444-3115, fax 406-444-5612, e-mail kstrege@state.mt.us.

Nebraska

Rod Wagner, Dir., Nebraska Lib. Commission, The Atrium, 1200 N St., Suite 120, Lincoln 68508-2023. Tel. 402-471-4001, fax 402-471-2083, e-mail rwagner@nlc.state.ne.us.

Nevada

Sara Jones, Dept. of Museums, Libs. and Arts, 100 N. Stewart St., Carson City 89710. Tel. 775-684-3315, fax 775-684-3311, e-mail sfjones@clan.lib.nv.us.

New Hampshire

Michael York, State Libn., New Hampshire State Lib., 20 Park St., Concord 03301-6314. Tel. 603-271-2397, fax 603-271-6826, e-mail myork@finch.nhsl.lib.nh.us.

New Jersey

Norma Blake, State Libn., Div. of State Lib., Dept. of Educ., 185 W. State St., Trenton 08625-0520. Tel. 609-292-6200, fax 609-292-2746, e-mail blake@njstatelib.org.

New Mexico

Benjamin Wakashige, State Libn., New Mexico State Lib., Aquisitions Section, 1209 Camino Carlos Rey, Santa Fe 87505. Tel. 505-476-9762, fax 505-476-9761, e-mail ben @stlib.state.nm.us.

New York

Janet M. Welch, State Libn./Asst. Commissioner for Libs., New York State Lib. Cultural Educ. Center, Albany 12230. Tel. 518-474-5930, fax 518-486-6880, e-mail jwelch2 @mail.nysed.gov.

North Carolina

Sandra M. Cooper, State Libn., State Lib. of North Carolina, 4640 Mail Service Center, Raleigh 27699-4640. Tel. 919-733-2570, fax 919-733-8748, e-mail scooper@library.dcr. state.nc.us.

North Dakota

Joe Linnertz, Acting State Libn., North Dakota State Lib., 604 E. Boulevard Ave., Dept. 250, Bismarck 58505-0800. Tel. 701-328-2492, fax 701-328-2040, e-mail jlinnert @state.nd.us.

Ohio

Michael Lucas, State Libn., State Lib. of Ohio, 274 E. 1 Ave., Columbus 43201. Tel. 614-644-6863, fax 614-466-3584, e-mail mlucas@sloma.state.ohio.us.

Oklahoma

Susan McVey, Dir., Oklahoma Dept. of Libs., 200 N.E. 18 St., Oklahoma City 73105. Tel. 405-521-2502, fax 405-525-7804, e-mail smcvey@oltn.odl.state.ok.us.

Oregon

Jim Scheppke, State Libn., Oregon State Lib., 250 Winter St. N.E., Salem 97301-3950. Tel. 503-378-4367, fax 503-588-8059, e-mail jim.b.scheppke@state.or.us.

Pennsylvania

Gary D. Wolfe, Deputy Secy. and Commissioner of Libs., Dept. of Educ., Office of Commonwealth Libs., Box 1601, Harrisburg 17105-1601. Tel. 717-787-2646, fax 717-772-3265, e-mail gwolfe@state.pa.us.

Rhode Island

Barbara F. Weaver, Chief Info. Officer, Office of Lib. and Info. Services, Rhode Island Dept. of Admin., 1 Capitol Hill, Providence 02908-5870. Tel. 401-222-4444, fax 401-222-4195, e-mail barbarawr@gw.doa. state.ri.us.

South Carolina

James B. Johnson, Jr., State Libn., South Carolina State Lib., 1500 Senate St., Box 11469, Columbia 29211. Tel. 803-734-8666, fax 803-734-8676, e-mail jim@leo.scsl.state. sc.us.

South Dakota

Suzanne Miller, State Libn., South Dakota State Lib., 800 Governors Dr., Pierre 57501-2294. Tel. 605-773-6962, fax 605-773-4950, e-mail suzanne.miller@state.sd.us.

Tennessee

Edwin S. Gleaves, State Libn./Archivist, Tennessee State Lib. and Archives, 403 Seventh Ave. N., Nashville 37243-0312. Tel. 615-741-7996, fax 615-741-6471, e-mail egleaves@mail.state.tn.us.

Texas

Peggy Rudd, Dir./State Libn., Texas State Lib. and Archives Commission, Box 12927, Capitol Sta., Austin 78711-2927. Tel. 512-463-5460, fax 512-463-5436, e-mail peggy. rudd@tsl.state.tx.us.

Utah

Amy Owen, Dir., Utah State Lib. Div., 250 N. 1950 W., Suite A, Salt Lake City 84115-7901. Tel. 801-715-6770, fax 801-715-6767, e-mail aowen@state.lib.ut.us.

Vermont

Sybil Brigham McShane, State Libn., Vermont Dept. of Libs., 109 State St., Montpelier 05609-0601. Tel. 802-828-3265, fax 802-828-2199, e-mail sybil.mcshane@dol.state.vt.us.

Virginia

Nolan T. Yelich, State Libn., Lib. of Virginia, 800 E. Broad St., Richmond 23219-3491. Tel. 804-692-3535, fax 804-692-3594, e-mail nyelich@lva.lib.va.us.

Washington

Nancy L. Zussy, State Libn., Washington State Lib., Box 42460, Olympia 98504-2460. Tel. 360-753-2915, fax 360-586-7575, e-mail nzussy@statelib.wa.gov.

West Virginia

J. D. Waggoner, Interim Secy., West Virginia Lib. Commission, 1900 Kanawha Blvd. E., Charleston 25305-0620. Tel. 304-558-2041, fax 304-558-2044, e-mail waggoner@wvlc.lib.wv.us

Wisconsin

Calvin Potter, Asst. Superintendent and Admin., Div. for Libs. and Community Learning, Dept. of Public Instruction, Box 7841, Madison 53707-7841. Tel. 608-266-2205, fax 608-267-1052, e-mail calvin.potter@dpi.state.wi.us.

Wyoming

Lesley Boughton, State Libn., State Lib. Div., Dept. of Admin. and Info., Supreme Court and State Lib. Bldg., 2301 Capitol Ave., Cheyenne 82002-0060. Tel. 307-777-7283, fax 307-777-6289, e-mail lbough@missc.state.wy.us.

American Samoa

Territorial Libn. (to be appointed), American Samoa Government, Box 997687, Pago Pago, AS 96799. Tel. 684-633-5816, fax 684-633-2126, e-mail camorales@netscape.net.

Federated States of Micronesia

Eliuel K. Pretrick, Secy., Dept. of Health, Education, and Social Affairs, FSM Div. of Educ., Box PS 70, Palikir Sta., Pohnpei, FM 96941. Tel. 691-320-2619, fax 691-320-5500, e-mail fsmhealth@mail.fm.

Guam

Christine K. Scott-Smith, Dir./Territorial Libn., Guam Public Lib. System, 254 Martyr St., Agana 96910-0254. Tel. 671-475-4753, fax 671-477-9777.

Northern Mariana Islands

Joseph McElroy, Commonwealth Libn. and Dir., Joeten-Kiyu Public Lib., Box 1092, Commonwealth of the Northern Mariana Islands, Saipan 96950. Tel. 670-235-7322, fax 670-235-7550, e-mail jklibrary@saipan.com.

Palau (Republic of)

Billy G. Kuartei, Minister of Educ., Republic of Palau, Box 189, Koror, PW 96940. Tel. 680-488-1464, fax 680-488-2830, e-mail bkuartei@palaunet.com.

Puerto Rico

Cesar Ray Hernandez, Secy. of Educ., Puerto Rico Dept. of Educ./Public Lib. Programs, Box 190759, San Juan, PR 00919-0759. Tel. 787-763-2171, fax 787-250-0275.

Republic of the Marshall Islands

Frederick deBrum, Secy., Internal Affairs, Marshall Islands, Box 629, Majuro, MH 96960. Tel. 692-625-3372, fax 692-625-3226, e-mail rmihpo@ntamar.com.

Virgin Islands

Claudette C. Lewis, Exec. Assistant Commissioner, Div. of Libs., Archives, and Museums, Cyril E. King Airport Terminal Bldg., St. Thomas, VI 00802. Tel. 340-774-3320, fax 340-775-5706.

Canada

Alberta

Punch Jackson, Dir., Strategic Info. and Libs., Alberta Community Development, 803 Standard Life Center, 10405 Jasper Ave., Edmonton T5J 4R7. Tel. 780-427-6315, fax 780-415-8594, e-mail libraries@mcd.gov.ab.ca.

British Columbia

Barbara Greeniaus, Dir., Lib. Services Branch, Ministry of Municipal Affairs, Box 9490 Sta. Prov. Govt., Victoria V8W 9N7. Tel.

250-356-1791, fax 250-953-3225, e-mail b greeniaus@hq.marh.gov.bc.ca.

Manitoba

Al Davis, Dir., Manitoba Culture, Heritage and Tourism, Public Lib. Services, Unit 200, 1525 First St., Brandon R7A 7A1. Tel. 204-726-6864, fax 204-726-6868, e-mail aldavis @gov.mb.ca.

New Brunswick

Sylvie Nadeau, Exec. Dir., New Brunswick Public Lib. Service, Box 6000, Fredericton E3B 5H1. Tel. 506-453-2354, fax 506-444-4064, e-mail Sylvie.Nadeau@gnb.ca.

Newfoundland

Shawn Tetford, Exec. Dir., Provincial Info. and Lib. Resources Board, 48 St. George's Ave., Stephenville A2N 1K9. Tel. 709-643-0901, fax 709-643-0925, e-mail shawntetford @publib.nf.ca, World Wide Web http://www. publib.nf.ca.

Northwest Territories

Sandy MacDonald, Territorial Libn., Northwest Territories Public Lib. Services, 75 Woodland Dr., Hay River X0E 1G1. Tel. 867-874-6531, fax 867-874-3321, e-mail sandy_macdonald@gov.nt.ca.

Nova Scotia

Elizabeth Armstrong, Acting Provincial Libn., Nova Scotia Provincial Lib., 3770 Kempt Rd.,

Halifax B3K 4X8. Tel. 902-424-2455, fax 902-424-0633, e-mail armstreh@gov.ns.ca.

Ontario

Michael Langford, Dir., Heritage and Libs. Branch, Ontario Government Ministry of Citizenship, Culture, and Recreation, 400 University Ave., 4th fl., Toronto M7A 2R9. Tel. 416-314-7342, fax 416-314-7635, e-mail Michael.Langford@mczcr.gov.on.ca.

Prince Edward Island

Allen Groen, Provincial Libn., P.E.I. Provincial Lib. Service, 89 Red Head Rd., Box 7500, Morell C0A 1S0. Tel. 902-961-7320, fax 902-961-7322, e-mail plshq@gov.pe.ca.

Quebec

M. André Couture, Dir., Direction des Projets Spéciaux et de la Coordination, 225 Grande Allée Est, Quebec G1R 5G5. Tel. 418-380-2304, fax 418-380-2324.

Saskatchewan

Joylene Campbell, Provincial Libn., Saskatchewan Provincial Lib., 1352 Winnipeg St., Regina S4P 3V7. Tel. 306-787-2972, fax 306-787-2029, e-mail campbell@prov.lib.sk.ca.

Yukon Territory

Linda R. Johnson, Dir., Dept. of Educ., Libs., and Archives, Box 2703, Whitehorse Y1A 2C6. Tel. 867-667-5309, fax 867-393-6253, e-mail Linda.Johnson@gov.yk.ca.

State School Library Media Associations

Alabama

Children's and School Libns. Div., Alabama Lib. Assn. Memb. 650. Publication. *The Alabama Librarian* (q.).

Co-Chairs Jane Garret, Maureen Womack; *Exec. Dir.* Sara Warren, 400 S. Union St., Suite 140, Montgomery 36104. Tel. 334-262-5210, fax 334-262-5255, e-mail allaonline@mindspring.com.

Address correspondence to the executive director.

World Wide Web http://allaonline.home.mindspring.com.

Alaska

Alaska Assn. of School Libns. Memb. 200+. Term of office. Mar. 2001–Feb. 2002. Publication. *Puffin* (3 a year).

Pres. Bob VanDerWege. E-mail rvdw@kpbsd.k12.ak.us; *Pres.-Elect* Cathy Boutin. E-mail boutinc@jsd.k12.ak.us; *Secy.* Darla Grediagin. E-mail jelinek121@aol.com; *Treas.* Karen Joynt. E-mail joynt@alaska.net; *School Lib. Coord. for Alaska State Lib.* Sue Sherif. E-mail sue_sherif@eed.state.ak.us.

World Wide Web http://www.akla.org/akasl.

Arizona

School Lib. Media Div., Arizona Lib. Assn. Memb. 500. Term of Office. Dec. 2001–Dec. 2002. Publication. *AZLA Newsletter.*

Pres. Debra LaPlante, Barcelona School, Tel. 623-842-3889, e-mail dlaplante@alhambra.k12.az.us; *Pres.-Elect* Judi Moreillon, Van Buskirk Elementary School. Tel. 520-749-8359, e-mail storypower@theriver.com.

Address correspondence to the president.

Arkansas

Arkansas Assn. of School Libns. and Media Educators. Term of Office. Jan.–Dec. 2002.

Chair Carol Ann Hart, Lee City Schools, 523 N. Forrest Ave., Marianna 72360. Tel. 870-295-7130, e-mail hartc@lhs.grsc.k12.ar.us.

Address correspondence to the chairperson.

California

California School Lib. Assn. Memb. 2,200. Publication. *CSLA Journal* (2 a year). *Ed.* Barbara Duffy.

Pres. Jeanne V. Nelson, Murrieta Valley Unified School Dist., 26396 Beckman Ct., Murrieta 92562. Tel. 909-696-1600 ext. 1027, e-mail jnelson@murrieta.k12.ca.us; *Pres.-Elect* Linda Jewett, Sacramento City Unified School Dist., 4701 Joaquin Way, Rm. 36, Sacramento 95822. Tel. 916-277-6963, e-mail Lindaje@sac-city.k12.ca.us; *Secy.* Kathryn L. Matlock, Jehue Middle School, 1500 Eucalyptus Ave., Colton 92376. Tel. 909-421-7377 ext. 1115, e-mail klweideman@earthlink.net; *Treas.* Betty Vandivier, San Diego City Schools, 12460 Creekview Dr., San Diego 92128. Tel. 858 496-8486, e-mail bvandivi@mail.sandi.net; *Office Mgr.* Carol Clayton, 717 K St., Suite 515, Sacramento 95814. Tel. 916-447-2684, e-mail csla@pacbell.net

World Wide Web http://www.schoollibrary.org.

Address correspondence to the office manager.

Colorado

Colorado Educational Media Assn. Memb. 500. Term of Office. Feb. 2001–Feb. 2002. Publication. *The Medium* (5 a year).

Pres. Judy Barnett, Colorado Springs Dist. 11. E-mail barnejm@d11.org; *Exec. Secy.* Heidi Baker.

Address correspondence to the executive secretary, CEMA, Box 22814, Denver 80222. Tel. 303-292-5434, e-mail cemacolorado@juno.com.

World Wide Web http://www.cemacolorado.org.

Connecticut

Connecticut Educational Media Assn. Memb. 550. Term of Office. July 2000–June 2002. Publications. *CEMA Update* (q.); *CEMA Gram* (mo.).

Pres. Irene Kwidzinski, 293 Pumpkin Hill Rd., New Milford 06776. Tel. 203-355-0762,

e-mail Kwidzinskii.NOR-PO@new-milford.
k12.ct.us; *V.P.* Rebecca Hickey, West Hills
Middle Magnet School, New Haven 06515.
Tel. 203-946-7367; *Past Pres.* Frances Nadeau, 440 Matthews St., Bristol 06010. Tel.
203-589-0813, e-mail nadeau@ccsu.edu.

Address correspondence to the administrative secretary.

World Wide Web http://www.ctcema.org.

Delaware

Delaware School Lib. Media Assn., Div. of
Delaware Lib. Assn. Memb. 100+. Term of
Office. Apr. 2001–Apr. 2002. Publications.
DSLMA Newsletter (irreg.); column in *DLA
Bulletin* (3 a year).

Pres. Elizabeth S. Tiffany. E-mail etiffany
@irsd.k12.de.us.

Address correspondence to the president.

World Wide Web http://www.udel.edu/
educ/slms/dslma.html.

District of Columbia

District of Columbia Assn. of School Libns.
Memb. 90+. Publication. *Newsletter* (4 a
year).

Pres. André Maria Taylor, Wheaton,
Maryland. E-mail divalibrarian2@aol.com.

Florida

Florida Assn. for Media in Education. Memb.
1,450. Term of Office. Nov. 2001–Oct. 2002.
Publication. *Florida Media Quarterly.* Ed.
Linda Miller. E-mail miller_12@firn.edu
(advertising inquiries to FAME, 320 W.
Sabal Palm Place, Suite 150, Longwood
32779. E-mail fame@amni .net).

Pres. Vic Burke. Tel. 352-671-7751, fax
352-671-7757, e-mail burke_v@firn.edu;
Pres.-Elect Kathryn "Ginger" Klega. Tel.
407-905-2400 ext. 2682, fax 407-905-2400
ext. 2703, e-mail klegag@ocps.k12.fl.us; *V.P.*
Jane Terwillegar. Tel. 561-848-6070 Fax
561-848-8633, e-mail terwillj@bellsouth.net;
Secy. Leslie Miller. Tel. 850-492-6136 ext.
233, e-mail miller3@aol.com; *Treas.* Judy
Coon. Tel. 561-564-4193, fax 561-564-4215,
e-mail judycoon11@hotmail.com; *Exec. Dir.*
Jo Sienkiewicz, AMNI Association Management Network. Tel. 407-834-6688, fax 407-
834-4747, e-mail fame@amni.net.

Address correspondence to the executive
director.

World Wide Web http://www.firn.edu/
fame.

Georgia

Georgia Lib. Media Assn. Memb. 200. Term
of Office. Jan. 2002–Jan. 2003.

Pres. Kathy Brock. E-mail kbrock@westga.
edu; *Secy.* Janice Sly; *Treas.* Susan Grigsby;
Past Pres. Melissa P. Johnston.

Hawaii

Hawaii Assn. of School Libns. Memb. 210.
Term of Office. June 2001–May 2002. Publications. *HASL Newsletter* (4 a year).

Pres. Tennye Kohatsu, Iolani School; *V.P.,
Programming* Fran Corcoran, St. Andrew's
Priory School; *V.P., Membership* Grace Omu-
ra, Kamehameha Schools. E-mail gomura@
ksbe.edu.

Address correspondence to the association,
Box 235019, Honolulu 96823. World Wide
Web http://www.k12.hi.us/~hasl.

Idaho

Educational Media Div., Idaho Lib. Assn.
Memb. 125. Term of Office. Oct. 2001–Oct.
2002. Publication. Column in *The Idaho
Librarian* (q.).

Chair Sue Bello, Capital H.S., 8055 Goddard, Boise 83704. Tel. 322-3875 ext 199,
e-mail bellos@cap1.sd01.k12.id.us.

Address correspondence to the chairperson.

Illinois

Illinois School Lib. Media Assn. Memb.
1,100. Term of Office. July 2001–June 2002.
Publications. *ISLMA News* (5 a year), *ISLMA
Membership Directory* (ann.).

Pres. Pam Storm. Tel. 217-345-2768,
e-mail pstorm@charleston.k12.il.us; *Pres.-
Elect* Katherine Oberhardt, University H.S.,
Illinois State Univ., Normal 61790-7100. Tel.
309-438-7100, fax 309-438-5250, e-mail
koberhar@ilstu.edu.; *Secy.* Marge Fashing.

World Wide Web http://www.islma.org.

Indiana

Assn. for Indiana Media Educators. Term of
Office. May 2001–Apr. 2002. Publications.

AIME News (mo.), *Indiana Media Journal* (q.).

Pres. Becky Conner, Evansville-Vanderburgh School, Evansville. E-mail rwc0604em@evsc.k12.in.us; *Pres.-Elect* Ann Abel, Maple Crest Middle School, Kokomo. E-mail aabel@kokomo.k12.in.us.

Address correspondence to the association, 1908 E. 64 St., South Drive, Indianapolis 46220. Tel. 317-257-8558, fax 317-259-4191, e-mail aime@doe.state.in.us.

World Wide Web http://www.ips.k12.in.us/telecom/manual/aime.htm.

Iowa

Iowa Educational Media Assn. Memb. 500. Term of Office. Mar. 2001–Mar. 2002. Publication. *Iowa Media Message* (4 a year). *Ed.* Becky Stover, 415 17th St. S.E., Cedar Rapids 52403.

Pres. Loretta Moon. E-mail Lmoon@po-q.iowa-falls.k12.ia.us; *V.P./Pres.-Elect* Dee Davis. E-mail ddavis@cr-cath.pvt.k12.ia.us; *Secy.* Kelly Diller. E-mail kelly.diller@uni.edu; *Treas.* Mia Beasley; *Exec. Secy.* Paula Behrendt, 2306 6th, Harlan 51537. Tel./fax 712-755-5918, e-mail paulab@harlannet.com.

Address correspondence to the executive secretary.

World Wide Web http://www.iema-ia.org.

Kansas

Kansas Assn. of School Libns. Memb. 700. Term of Office. Aug. 2001–July 2002. Publication. *KASL Newsletter* (s. ann.).

Pres. Joann Hettenbach. Tel. 785-655-2551; *Pres.-Elect* Jane Barnard. Tel. 316-776-3391; *Secy.* Marjorie Loyd. Tel. 785-271-3765; *Treas.* Martha House. Tel. 620-767-5149; *Exec. Secy.* Judith Eller, 8517 W. Northridge, Wichita 67205. Tel. 316-773-6723, e-mail judell@hotmail.com.

Address correspondence to the executive secretary.

World Wide Web http://skyways.lib.ks.us/kasl.

Kentucky

Kentucky School Media Assn. Memb. 620. Term of Office. Oct. 2001–Oct. 2002. Publication. *KSMA Newsletter* (q.).

Pres. Margaret Roberts, Scott County H.S., 1080 Cardinal Dr., Georgetown 40324. Tel. 502-863-4131 ext. 1200, e-mail mroberts@scott.k12.ky.us; *Pres.-Elect* Tammy Rich. E-mail trich@adair.k12.ky.us; *Secy.* Pat Hall, Old Mill Elementary School, 11540 Hwy. 44 E., Mount Washington 40047. Tel. 502-955-7696, e-mail pehall@bullitt.k12.ky.us; *Treas.* Lisa Hughes, Paducah Tilghman H.S., 24th and Washington Sts., Paducah 42003. Tel. 502-444-5650 ext. 2420, fax 502-444-5659, e-mail lhughes@paducah.k12.ky.us.

Address correspondence to the president.

World Wide Web http://www.kysma.org.

Louisiana

Louisiana Assn. of School Libns. Memb. 400+. Term of Office. July 2001–June 2002.

Pres. Betty Brackins, Baton Rouge Magnet H.S., 2825 Government St., Baton Rouge 70806. Tel. 225-819-2313, e-mail bbrackins@ebrschools.org; *1st V.P.* Jerilyn Woodson. Tel. 225-273-2972, e-mail jwoodson@lsvi.org; *2nd V.P.* Linda Lingefelt. Tel. 337-828-3714, e-mail llingefelt@stmary.k12.la.us; *Secy.* Jan McGee. Tel. 318-396-6495, e-mail jmcgee8038@aol.com.

Address correspondence to the association, c/o Louisiana Lib. Assn., Box 3058, Baton Rouge 70821.

World Wide Web http://www.leeric.lsu.edu/lla/lasl.

Maine

Maine School Lib. Assn. Memb. 350. Term of Office. May 2000–May 2002. Publication. *Maine Entry* (with the Maine Lib. Assn.; q.).

Pres. Nancy B. Grant, Penquis Valley Info. Center, 48 Penquis Dr., Milo 04463. Tel. 207-943-7346 ext. 212, e-mail nbgrant@ctel.net; *1st V.P.* Pam Goucher, Freeport Middle School, Freeport 04032. E-mail Pam_Goucher@coconetme.org; *Secy.* Margaret McNamee, Biddeford H.S. E-mail margaretmc@lamere.net.

Address correspondence to the president.

World Wide Web http://www.maslibraries.org.

Maryland

Maryland Educational Media Organization. Term of Office. July 2001–June 2002.

Pres. Elizabeth Harwood, Frederick Douglass H.S., Upper Marlboro 20772. E-mail eharwood@pgcps.org.

Address correspondence to the association, Box 21127, Baltimore 21228.

World Wide Web www.tcps.k12.md.us/memo/memo.html.

Massachusetts

Massachusetts School Lib. Media Assn. Memb. 700. Term of Office. June 2001–May 2002. Publication. *Media Forum* (q.).

Pres. Dorothy McQuillan, Newton South H.S. Tel. 617-552-7539, fax 617-552-7078, e-mail Dorothy_McQuillan@newton.mec.edu; *Secy.* Phyllis Robinson. Tel. 781-380-0170 ext. 1112, e-mail prob@bhs.ssec.org; *Treas.* Thelma Dakubu, Chelsea H.S. Tel. 617-889-4868, fax 617-889-8468, e-mail tdakubu@yahoo.com; *Admin. Asst.* Deb McDonald, MSLMA, Box 25, Three Rivers 01080-0025. Tel./fax 413-283-6675, e-mail mslma@samnet.net.

Address correspondence to the administrative assistant.

World Wide Web http://www.mslma.org.

Michigan

Michigan Assn. for Media in Education. Memb. 1,400. Term of Office. Jan.–Dec. 2002. Publications. *Media Spectrum* (3 a year); *MAME Newsletter* (4 a year).

Pres. Ginger Sisson, Grandville H.S., 4700 Canal S.W., Grandville 49418. Tel. 616-261-6450, fax 616-261-6501, e-mail gsisson@gpsk12.net; *Pres.-Elect* Karen Lemmons, Hutchinson Elementary, 5221 Montclair, Detroit 48213. Tel. 313-852-9912, fax 313-852-9911, e-mail camaraife@aol.com; *Secy.* Joanne Steckling; *Treas.* Susan Thornton, Ezra Eby Elementary Media Center, 220 West St., Box 308, Napoleon 49261-0308. Tel. 517-536-8667 ext. 463, fax 517-536-8109, e-mail thorntonsl@aol.com; *Past Pres.* Teri Terry, Pinckney H.S., 10255 Dexter/Pinckney Rd., Box 439, Pinckney 48169. Tel. 810-225-5531, fax 810-225-5535, e-mail t2t_51@yahoo.com; *Exec. Dir.* Roger Ashley, MAME Headquarters, 6810 S. Cedar St., Suite 8, Lansing 48911. Tel. 517-699-1717, fax 517-694-9303, e-mail AshleyMame@aol.com.

Address correspondence to the executive director.

World Wide Web http://www.mame.gen.mi.us.

Minnesota

Minnesota Educational Media Organization. Memb. 750. Term of Office. (Pres.) July 2001–July 2002. Publications. *Minnesota Media*; *ImMEDIAte*; *MEMOrandom.*

Co-Pres. Nancy Evans, 1979 40th St. N., Sartell 56377. Tel. 763-241-3505 ext. 2817, e-mail nevans@elkriver.k12.mn.us; Susan Meyer, 6530 46th Ave. S.E., St. Cloud 56304. Tel. 763-261-4501 ext. 3134, e-mail sue.meyer@becker.k12.mn.us; *Secy.* Douglas A. Howard, 613 5th St. N., New Ulm 56073. Tel. 507-359-7431, e-mail dhoward@newulm.k12.mn.us; *Treas.* Kelly Sharkey, 501 E. Main St., New Prague 56071. Tel. 612-708-1693 or 888-815-8052, e-mail ksharkey@bevcomm.net; *Admin. Asst.* Heather Hoernemann, 336 108th Ave. N.W., Coon Rapids 55448. Tel. 763-767-4755, fax 763-767-4579, e-mail hoernemann@msn.com.

World Wide Web http://memoweb.org.

Mississippi

School Section, Mississippi Lib. Assn. Memb. 1,300.

Chair Cindy Harrison. E-mail cindyjh55@hotmail.com; *V. Chair* Karen Williams.

Address correspondence to the association, c/o Mississippi Lib. Assn., Box 2044, Jackson 39289-1448. Tel. 601-352-3917, e-mail mla@meta3.net.

World Wide Web http://library.msstate.edu/mla/mla.html.

Missouri

Missouri Assn. of School Libns. Memb. 1,129. Term of Office. June 2001–May 2002. Publication. *Media Horizons* (ann.), *Connections* (q.).

Pres. Marianne Fues; *1st V.P./Pres.-Elect* Karen Vialle; *2nd V.P.* Cheryl Hoemann; *Secy.* Linda Stephenson; *Treas.* Suzanne Myers.

Address correspondence to the association, 3912 Manorwood Dr., St. Louis 63125-4335. Tel./fax 314-416-0462, e-mail masl@il.net, World Wide Web http://maslonline.org.

Montana

Montana School Lib. Media Div., Montana Lib. Assn. Memb. 200+. Term of Office. July 2001–June 2002. Publication. *FOCUS* (published by Montana Lib. Assn.) (q.).

Chair Norma Glock, Columbus Public Schools, Box 871, Columbus 59019. Tel. 406-322-5373, fax 406-322-5028, e-mail nglock@mcn.net.

World Wide Web http://www.mtlib.org/slmd/slmd.html.

Nebraska

Nebraska Educational Media Assn. Memb. 370. Term of Office. July 2001–June 2002. Publication. *NEMA News* (q.).

Pres. Glenda Willnerd, 311 Wedgewood Dr., Lincoln 68510. Tel. 402-436-1301, fax 402-436-1540, e-mail gwilln@LPS.org; *Exec. Secy.* Joie Taylor, 2301 31st St., Columbus 68601. Tel. 402-564-1781, fax 402-563-7035, e-mail jtaylor@esu7.org.

Address correspondence to the executive secretary.

World Wide Web http://nema.k12.ne.us.

Nevada

Nevada School and Children's Lib. Section, Nevada Lib. Assn. Memb. 120.

Exec. Secy. Amie Maurins. E-mail amaurins @mail.co.washoe.nv.us.

Address correspondence to the executive secretary.

New Hampshire

New Hampshire Educational Media Assn., Box 418, Concord 03302-0418. Memb. 265. Term of Office. June 2001–June 2002. Publications. *On line* (5 a year).

Pres. Gail Shea Grainger, Chesterfield School, Box 205, Chesterfield 03443. E-mail ggrainger@deweybrowse.org; *V.P./Pres.-Elect* Jean Newcomb, Fairgrounds Junior H.S., Nashua 03064. Tel 603-594-4393, e-mail newcombj@nashua.edu; *Treas.* Jeff Kent, Dewey School, 38 Liberty St., Concord 03301. Tel. 603-225-0833, e-mail jkent@csd. k12.nh.us; *Secy.* Mimi Crowley, Amherst Street School, 71 Amherst St., Nashua 03064, e-mail crowleym@nashua.edu.

Address correspondence to the president.

World Wide Web http://www.nhema.net.

New Jersey

Educational Media Assn. of New Jersey. Memb. 1,100. Term of Office. Aug. 2001–July 2003. Publications. *Bookmark* (mo).

Pres. Susan Heinis, West Essex Senior H.S., W. Greenbrook Rd., North Caldwell 07006. Tel. 973-228-1200 ext. 252, e-mail sheinis@westex.org; *Pres.-Elect* Cathie Miller, Princeton Day School, Box 75, Great Rd., Princeton 08542. Tel. 609-924-6700 ext 242, e-mail cmiller@pds.org.

Address correspondence to the president-elect.

World Wide Web http://www.emanj.org.

New Mexico

[See "New Mexico" under "State, Provincial, and Regional Library Associations" earlier in Part 6—*Ed.*].

New York

School Lib. Media Section, New York Lib. Assn., 252 Hudson St., Albany 12210. Tel. 518-432-6952, 800-252-6952. Memb. 880. Term of Office. Oct. 2001–Oct. 2002. Publications. *SLMSGram* (q.); participates in *NYLA Bulletin* (mo. except July and Aug.).

Pres. Cathie Marriott, Orchard Park Schools, 330 Baker Rd., Orchard Park 14127. Tel. 716-209-6330, fax 716-209-8191, e-mail CEMarriott@aol.com; *V.P./Pres.-Elect* Rosina Alaimo, 540 Ashland Ave., Buffalo 14222. Tel. 716-631-4860, fax 716-631-4867, e-mail Rosella@att.net; *V.P. Conferences* Patricia Shanley; *V.P. Communications* Ellen Rubin; *Secy.* Marcia Eggleston; *Treas.* Sally Koes; *Past Pres.* Erin Dinneen.

Address correspondence to the president.

World Wide Web http://www.slms-nyla.org.

North Carolina

North Carolina School Lib. Media Assn. Memb. 200. Term of Office. Oct. 2001–Oct. 2002.

Pres. Karen Gavigan, Teacher Educ. Resource Center, Univ. of North Carolina, Greensboro, Box 26171, Greensboro 27402. Tel. 336-334-4035, fax 336-334-4120, e-mail kpwg@aol.com; *V.P./Pres.-Elect* Rusty Taylor, Media Services, Wake County Public Schools, 4401 Atlantic Ave., Raleigh 27604.

Tel. 919-431-8081, fax 919-431-8077, e-mail jtaylor@wcpss.net; *Secy.* Martha Hayes, Asheville City Public Schools, 125 Hill St., Asheville 28801. Tel. 828-255-5376, fax 828-255-5589, e-mail martha.hayes@asheville.K12.nc.us; *Treas.* Diane Averett, Kerr Vance Academy, 700 Vance Academy Rd., Henderson 27536. Tel. 252-492-0018, fax 252-438-4652, e-mail daverett@kerrvance.com.

Address correspondence to the chairperson.

World Wide Web http://www.ncslma.org.

North Dakota

School Lib. and Youth Services Section, North Dakota Lib. Assn. Memb. 100. Term of Office. Sept. 2001–Sept. 2002. Publication. *The Good Stuff* (q).

Co-Chairs Susan Gessner, Minot H.S.—Magic City Campus Media Center, 1100 11th Ave. S.W., Minot 58701-4206. Tel. 701-857-4534, e-mail Susan.Gessner@sendit.nodak.edu; Melody Kuehn, Minot H.S.—Central Campus, 110 2nd Ave. S.E., Minot 58701-3983. Tel. 701-857-4641, fax 701-857-4636, e-mail Melody.Kuehn@sendit.nodak.edu.

Address correspondence to the co-chairs.

Ohio

Ohio Educational Lib. Media Assn. Memb. 1,200. Publication. *Ohio Media Spectrum* (q.).

Pres. Linda Cornette. E-mail lcornett@columbus.rr.com; *V.P.* Suellyn Stotts. E-mail stotts_suellyn@msmail.dublin.k12.oh.us; *Exec. Dir.* Ann Hanning, 1631 N.W. Professional Plaza, Columbus 43220. Tel. 614-326-1460, fax 614-459-2087, e-mail oelma@mecdc.org.

Address correspondence to the executive director.

World Wide Web http://www.oelma.org.

Oklahoma

Oklahoma Assn. of School Lib. Media Specialists. Memb. 3,000+. Term of Office. July 2001–June 2002. Publication. *Oklahoma Librarian*.

Chair Lily Kendall; *Chair-Elect* Jayme Seat; *Secy.* Joan Sizemore; *Treas.* Sue Jenk-

ins; *AASL Delegate* Buffy Edwards; *Past Chair* Sandy Austin.

Address correspondence to the chairperson, c/o Oklahoma Lib. Assn., 300 Hardy Dr., Edmond 73013. Tel. 405-348-0506.

Oregon

Oregon Educational Media Assn. Memb. 600. Term of Office. July 2001–June 2002. Publication. *INTERCHANGE.*

Pres. Jeri Petzel. E-mail jpetzel@canby.com; *Pres.-Elect* Kelly Kuntz. E-mail kelly_kuntz@beavton.k12.or.us; *Exec. Dir.* Jim Hayden, Box 277, Terrebonne 97760. Tel./fax 541-923-0675, e-mail jhayden@bendnet.com.

Address correspondence to the executive director.

World Wide Web http://www.OEMA.net.

Pennsylvania

Pennsylvania School Libns. Assn. Memb. 1,565. Term of Office. July 2001–June 2002. Publication. *Learning and Media* (q.).

Pres. Veanna Baxter. E-mail vebaxter@epix.net; *V.P./Pres.-Elect* Geneva Reeder. E-mail greeder@redrose.net; *Secy.* Judy Speedy; *Treas.* Margaret Winterhalter Foster.

Address correspondence to the president.

World Wide Web http://www.psla.org.

Rhode Island

Rhode Island Educational Media Assn. Memb. 398. Term of Office. June 2001–May 2002.

Pres. Connie Malinowski. E-mail ride0276@ride.ri.net; *V.P.* Holly Barton. E-mail bartonh@ride.ri.net; *Secy.* Sue Fleisig. E-mail suefleisig@aol.com; *Treas.* Livia Giroux. E-mail ride7572@ride.ri.net.

Address correspondence to the association, Box 762, Portsmouth 02871.

World Wide Web http://www.ri.net/RIEMA/index.html.

South Carolina

South Carolina Assn. of School Libns. Memb. 1,100. Term of Office. June 2001–May 2002. Publication. *Media Center Messenger* (4 a year).

Pres. Claudia Myers. E-mail claudiamyers@berkeley.k12.sc.us; *Pres.-Elect* Janet Boltjes. E-mail jboltjes@lexington1.net; *Secy.* Ruth Harper. E-mail rharper@clover.k12. sc.us; *Treas.* Sue Waddell. E-mail swaddell @greenville.k12.sc.us.

Address correspondence to the president.

World Wide Web http://www.scasl.net.

South Dakota

South Dakota School Lib. Media Assn., Section of the South Dakota Lib. Assn. and South Dakota Education Assn. Memb. 146. Term of Office. Oct. 2001–Oct. 2002.

Pres. Gary Linn, Box 807, Lead 57754; *Secy.-Treas.* Mary Quiett, Gettysburg School, 100 E. King Ave., Gettysburg 57442-1799.

Address correspondence to the secretary-treasurer.

Tennessee

Tennessee Assn. of School Libns. Memb. 450. Term of Office. Jan.–Dec. 2002. Publication. *Footnotes* (q.).

Pres. Janette Lambert, Pearl-Cohn H.S., 904 26th Ave. N., Nashville 37208. E-mail tasl2002@aol.com; *V.P./Pres.-Elect* Nancy Dickinson, Hillsboro Elementary School, 284 Winchester Hwy., Hillsboro 37342. E-mail fsufan@dtccom.net; *Secy.* Dorothy Hooper, Martin Luther King Magnet School, 613 17th Ave. N., Nashville 37203; *Treas.* Vicki Randolph, Springfield Middle School, 715 Fifth Ave. W., Springfield 37172. E-mail randolphv @k12tn.net.

Address correspondence to the president.

World Wide Web http://www.korrnet.org/ tasl.

Texas

Texas Assn. of School Libns. (Div. of Texas Lib. Assn.). Memb. 3,686. Term of Office. 2001–2002. Publication. *Media Matters* (3 a year).

Chair Susan Meyer, 2309 Covington, Plano 75023. E-mail pmkm@worldnet.att. net.

Address correspondence to the association, 3355 Bee Cave Rd., Suite 401, Austin 78746. Tel. 512-328-1518, fax 512-328-8852, e-mail tla@txla. org.

World Wide Web http://www.txla.org/ groups/tasl/index.html.

Utah

Utah Educational Lib. Media Assn. Memb. 390. Term of Office. Mar. 2001–Feb. 2002. Publication. *UELMA Newsletter* (4 a year).

Pres. Dennis Morgan, Riverview Junior H.S., 751 W. Tripp Lane, Murray 84123. Tel. 801-264-7406, e-mail dmorgan@rjh.mury. k12.ut.us; *Pres.-Elect* Paula Zsiray. E-mail paula.zsiray@cache.k12.ut.us; *Secy.* George Reay. E-mail greay@m.dsssd.k12.ut.us; *Exec. Dir.* Larry Jeppesen, Cedar Ridge Middle School, 65 N. 200 W., Hyde Park 84318. Tel. 435-563-6229, fax 435-563-3914, e-mail ljeppese@crms.cache.k12.ut.us.

Address correspondence to the executive director.

World Wide Web http://www.uelma.org.

Vermont

Vermont Educational Media Assn. Memb. 203. Term of Office. May 2001–May 2002. Publication. *VEMA News* (q.).

Pres. Dianne Wyllie, Lower Lib., 257 Western Ave., St. Johnsbury 05819. Tel. 802-748-8912 ext. 1180, e-mail dwyllie@ sover.net; *Pres.-Elect* Chris Varney, Hinesburg Community School, 10888 Rte. 116, Hinesburg 05461. Tel. 802-482-6288, fax 802-482-2003, e-mail varney@hcsvt.org; *Secy.* Chris Fricke; *Treas.* Bonnie Richardson.

Address correspondence to the president.

World Wide Web http://www.vemaonline. org.

Virginia

Virginia Educational Media Assn. Memb. 1,450. Term of Office. (Pres. and Pres.-Elect) Nov. 2001–Nov. 2002 (other offices 2 years in alternating years). Publication. *Mediagram* (q.).

Pres. Ann Tinsman, Massaponax H.S. E-mail atinsman@hotmail.com; *Pres.-Elect* Roxanne Mills, Chesapeake Public Schools. E-mail millsrwe@cps.k12.va.us ; *Exec. Dir.* Jean Remler. Tel./fax 703-764-0719, e-mail jremler@pen.k12.va.us.

Address correspondence to the association, Box 2743, Fairfax 22031-0743.

World Wide Web http://vema.gen.va.us.

Washington

Washington Lib. Media Assn. Memb. 1,200. Term of Office. Oct. 2001–Oct. 2002. Publications. *The Medium* (3 a year), *The Message* (2 a year).

Pres. Marie-Anne Harkness. E-mail ma harkness@attbi.com; *Pres.-Elect* Sally Lancaster. E-mail slancaster@everett.wednet. edu; *V.P.* Barbara Trimble. E-mail btrimble @cloverpark.k12.wa.us; *Treas.* Kathy Kugler. E-mail kkugler@mindspring.com; *Secy.* Kathleen Allstot. E-mail rkallstot@atnet.net.

Address correspondence to the association, Box 50194, Bellevue 98015-0194. E-mail wlma@wlma.org.

World Wide Web http://www.wlma.org.

West Virginia

West Virginia Technology, Education, and Media Specialists (WVTEAMS). Memb. 200. Term of Office. July 2001–July 2002.

Pres. Ann Skinner. E-mail spirit@access. mountain.net; *Secy.* Becky Butler. E-mail rbutler@access.k12.wv.us; *Treas.* Carla Campbell. E-mail carla4040@aol.com.

Address correspondence to the president.

World Wide Web http://www.wvteams.org.

Wisconsin

Wisconsin Educational Media Assn. Memb. 1,122. Term of Office. Apr. 2001–Apr. 2002. Publication. *Dispatch* (7 a year).

Pres. Jim Bowen. E-mail Bowenjm@ netnet.net; *Pres.-Elect* Mary Lou Zuege. E-mail mlz@mixcom.com; *Secy.* Cindy Turner. E-mail cturner@waunakee.k12.wi.us; *Treas.* Linda Nemschoff. E-mail linda_ nemschoff@neenah.k12.wi.us.

Address correspondence to the president or the secretary.

World Wide Web http://www.wemaonline. org/ab.main.cfm.

Wyoming

Section of School Library Media Personnel, Wyoming Lib. Assn. Memb. 91. Term of Office. Oct. 2001–Oct. 2002. Publications. *WLA Newsletter*; *SSLMP Newsletter*.

Chair Lisa Smith, Lib. Media Specialist, Tongue River H.S., Box 408, Dayton 83836. Tel. 306-655-2236, fax 307-655-9897, e-mail lisa@sheridank12.net; *Chair-Elect* Val Roady, Dist. Lib. Media Specialist, Big Horn County Dist. 4. E-mail roady@bgh4.k12.wy.us; *Secy.* Cheryl Davis, Lib. Media Specialist, Kelly Walsh H.S. Lib. Media Center. E-mail cheryl _davis@ncsd.k12.wy.us.

Address correspondence to the chairperson.

International Library Associations

International Association of Agricultural Information Specialists (IAALD)

c/o J. van der Burg, President
Boeslaan 55, 6703 ER Wageningen, Netherlands
Tel./fax 31-317-422820
E-mail Jvdburg@user.diva.nl
World Wide Web http://www.lib.montana.edu/~alijk/IAALD.html

Object

The association facilitates professional development of and communication among members of the agricultural information community worldwide. Its goal is to enhance access to and use of agriculture-related information resources. To further this mission, IAALD will promote the agricultural information profession, support professional development activities, foster collaboration, and provide a platform for information exchange. Founded 1955.

Membership

Memb. 600+. Dues (Inst.) US$95; (Indiv.) $35.

Officers

Pres. J. van der Burg, Boeslaan 55, 6703 ER Wageningen, Netherlands; *1st V.P.* Pamela Q. J. Andre, National Agricultural Library, USDA, Beltsville, MD 20705; *Secy.-Treas.* Margot Bellamy, c/o CAB International, Wallingford, Oxon, OX10 8DE, England. Tel. 44-1491-832111, fax 44-1491-833508.

Publications

Quarterly Bulletin of the IAALD (memb.). *World Directory of Agricultural Information Resource Centres.*

International Association of Law Libraries

Box 5709, Washington, DC 20016-1309
Tel. 804-924-3384, fax 804-924-7239
World Wide Web http://www.iall.org

Object

IALL is a worldwide organization of librarians, libraries, and other persons or institutions concerned with the acquisition and use of legal information emanating from sources other than their jurisdictions, and from multinational and international organizations.

IALL's basic purpose is to facilitate the work of librarians who must acquire, process, organize, and provide access to foreign legal materials. IALL has no local chapters but maintains liaison with national law library associations in many countries and regions of the world.

Membership

More than 800 members in more than 50 countries on five continents.

Officers (2001–2004)

Pres. Holger Knudsen (Germany); *1st V.P.* Jules Winterton (Great Britain); *2nd V.P.* Marie-Louise H. Bernal (USA); *Secy.* Ann Morrison (Canada); *Treas.* Gloria F. Chao (USA).

Board Members

Jennefer Aston (Ireland); Joan A. Brathwaite (Barbados); James Butler (Australia); Richard A. Danner (USA); Halvor Kongshavn

(Norway); Jarmila Looks (Switzerland); Lisbeth Rasmussen (Denmark); Silke A. Sahl (USA).

Publications

International Journal of Legal Information (3

a year; US$65 for individuals; $95 for institutions).

Committee Chairpersons

Communications. Richard A. Danner (USA).

International Association of Music Libraries, Archives and Documentation Centres (IAML)

c/o Alison Hall, Secretary-General
Cataloging Dept., Carleton University Library
1125 Colonel By Drive, Ottawa, ON K1S 5B6, Canada
Tel. 613 520-2600 ext. 8150, fax 613 520-2750, e-mail Alison_Hall@Carleton.ca
World Wide Web http://www.cilea.it/music/iaml/iamlhome.htm

Object

To promote the activities of music libraries, archives, and documentation centers and to strengthen the cooperation among them; to promote the availability of all publications and documents relating to music and further their bibliographical control; to encourage the development of standards in all areas that concern the association; and to support the protection and preservation of musical documents of the past and the present.

Membership

Memb. 2,000.

Board Members (2002–2004)

Pres. John H. Roberts, Music Lib., 240 Morrison Hall, Univ. of California, Berkeley, Berkeley, CA 94720. Tel. 510-642-2428, fax 510-642-8237, e-mail jroberts@library.berkeley.edu; *Past Pres.* Pamela Thompson, Royal College of Music Lib., Prince Consort Rd., London SW7 2BS, England; *Past Pres.* Veslemoy Heintz, Statens Musikbibliotek, Box 16326, S-103 26 Stockholm, Sweden; *V.P.s* Dominique Hausfater, Mediathèque Hector Berlioz, Conservatoire National Supérieur de Musique et de Danse de Paris, 209 Ave. Jean-Jaurès, F-75019 Paris, France. Tel. 33-1-40-40-46-28, fax 33-1-40-40-45-34, e-mail dhausfater@cnsmdp.fr; Ruth

Hellen, Audio Visual Services, Enfield Libs., Town Hall, Green Lane, London N13 4XD, England. Tel. 44-20-8379-2760, fax 44-20-879-2761, e-mail r-hellen@msn.com; Federica Riva, Bibliotecario del Conservatorio Sezione Musicale della Biblioteca Palatina, Nel Conservatorio di Musica Arrigo Boito, via Conservatorio 27/a, I-43100 Parma, Italy. Tel. 39-0521-381-958, fax 39-0521-200-398, e-mail f.riva@agora.it; Kirsten Voss-Eliasson, Astershaven 149, DK-2765 Smorum, Denmark. E-mail kvoss@worldonline.dk; *Secy.-Gen.* Alison Hall, Cataloging Dept., Carleton Univ. Lib., 1125 Colonel By Dr., Ottawa, ON K1S 5B6; *Treas.* Martie Severt, MCO Muziekbibliotheek, Postbus 125, NL-1200 AC Hilversum, Netherlands. E-mail m.severt@mco.nl.

Publication

Fontes Artis Musicae (4 a year; memb.). *Ed.* John Wagstaff, Music Faculty Lib., Oxford Univ., St. Aldate's, Oxford OX1 1DB, England.

Professional Branches

Archives and Documentation Centres. Judy Tsou, Univ. of Washington, Seattle, WA 98145.

Broadcasting and Orchestra Libraries. Kauko Karjalainen, Yleisradio Oy, Box 76, FIN-

00024 Yleisradio, Finland.
Libraries in Music Teaching Institutions.
Federica Riva, Bibliotecario del Conservatorio Sezione Musicale della Biblioteca Palatina, Parma, Italy.
Public Libraries. Kirsten Voss-Eliasson,
Astershaven 149, DK-2765 Smorum, Denmark.
Research Libraries. Ann Kersting, Music- und Theaterabteilung, Stadt- und Universitätsbibliothek, Bockenheimer Landstr. 134-138, D-60325 Frankfurt, Germany.

International Association of School Librarianship

Penny Moore, Executive Director
Box 34069, Dept. 962, Seattle, WA 98124-1069
Tel. 604-925-0266, fax 604-925-0566, e-mail iasl@rockland.com, and
penny.moore@xtra.co.nz
World Wide Web http://www.iasl-slo.org

Object

The objectives of the International Association of School Librarianship are to advocate the development of school libraries throughout all countries; to encourage the integration of school library programs into the instructional and curriculum development of the school; to promote the professional preparation and continuing education of school library personnel; to foster a sense of community among school librarians in all parts of the world; to foster and extend relationships between school librarians and other professionals connected with children and youth; to foster research in the field of school librarianship and the integration of its conclusions with pertinent knowledge from related fields; to promote the publication and dissemination of information about successful advocacy and program initiatives in school librarianship; to share information about programs and materials for children and youth throughout the international community; and to initiate and coordinate activities, conferences, and other projects in the field of school librarianship and information services. Founded 1971.

Membership

Memb. 850.

Officers and Executive Board

Pres. Peter Genco, USA; V.P.s; Helle Barrett, Sweden; Sandy Zinn, South Africa; James Henri, Hong Kong; Financial Officer Kathy Lemaire, United Kingdom; Dirs. Eleanor Howe, USA; Sandra Hughes, Canada; Constanza Mekis, Latin America; John Royce, North Africa/Middle East; Monica Milsson, Europe; Margaret Balfour-Awuah, Africa–Sub-Sahara; Diljit Singh, Asia; Kazuyuki Sunaga, East Asia; Elizabeth Greef, Oceania; Elizabeth Townson, International Schools.

Publications

Annual Proceedings of the International Association of School Librarianship: An Author and Subject Index to Contributed Papers, 1972–1984; $10.
Books and Borrowers; $15.
Connections: School Library Associations and Contact People Worldwide; $15.
Indicators of Quality for School Library Media Programs; $15.
International Association of School Librarianship Worldwide Directory; A Listing of Personal, Institutional and Association Members; $15.
Library Service to Isolated Schools and Communities; $8.
School Librarianship: International Perspectives and Issues; $35.
Sustaining the Vision: A Collection of Articles and Papers on Research in School Librarianship; $35.

International Association of Technological University Libraries

c/o President, Michael Breaks, Heriot-Watt Univ. Lib., Edinburgh EH14 4AS, Scotland.
Tel. 44-131-451-3570, fax 44-131-451-3164, e-mail m.l.breaks@hw.ac.uk
World Wide Web http://www.iatul.org

Object

To provide a forum where library directors can meet to exchange views on matters of current significance in the libraries of universities of science and technology. Research projects identified as being of sufficient interest may be followed through by working parties or study groups.

Membership

Ordinary, associate, sustaining, and honorary. Membership fee is 107 Euros a year, sustaining membership 500 Euros a year. Memb. 203 (in 40 countries).

Officers and Executives

Pres. Michael Breaks, Heriot-Watt Univ. Lib., Edinburgh EH14 4AS, Scotland. Tel. 44-131-451-3570, fax 44-131-451-3164, e-mail m.l.breaks@hw.ac.uk; *1st V.P.* Egbert Gerryts, Univ. of Pretoria, Merensky Lib., Academic Info. Services, Pretoria 0002, South Africa. Tel. 27-12-420-22-41, fax 27-12-342-24-53, e-mail gerrytse@ais.u.ac.za; *2nd V.P.* Gaynor Austen, Queensland Univ. of Technology, GPO Box 2434, Brisbane, Qld. 4001, Australia. Tel. 61-7-3864-2560, fax 61-7-3864-1823, e-mail g.austen@qut.edu.au; *Secy.* Judith Palmer, Radcliffe Science Lib., Oxford Univ., Parks Road, Oxford OX1 3QP, England. E-mail judith.palmer@bodley.ox.ac.uk; *Treas.* Maria Heijne, Delft Univ. of Technology Lib. (DUTL), Postbus 98, 2600 MG Delft, Netherlands. Tel. 31-15-278 56 56, fax 31-15-257 20 60, e-mail M.A.M.Heijne@library.tudelft.nl; *Past Pres.* Nancy Fjällbrant, Chalmers Univ. of Technology Lib., 412 96 Gothenburg, Sweden. Tel. 46-31-772-37-54, fax 46-31-772-37-79, e-mail nancyf@lib.chalmers.se; *Membs.* Murray Shepherd, Canada; C. Lee Jones, U.S.A.; Marianne Nordlander, Sweden.

Publications

IATUL News (q.).
IATUL Proceedings (ann.).

International Council on Archives

Joan van Albada, Secretary-General
60 Rue des Francs-Bourgeois, F-75003 Paris, France
Tel. 33-1-40-27-63-06, fax 33-1-42-72-20-65, e-mail ica@ica.org
World Wide Web http://www.ica.org

Object

To establish, maintain, and strengthen relations among archivists of all lands, and among all professional and other agencies or institutions concerned with the custody, organization, or administration of archives, public or private, wherever located. Established 1948.

Membership

Memb. c. 1,675 (representing c. 180 countries and territories).

Officers

Secy.-Gen. Joan van Albada; *Deputy Secy.-Gen.* Marcel Caya.

Publications

Comma (subscription to K. G. Saur Verlag, Ortlerstr. 8, Postfach 70 16 20, 81-373 Munich, Germany).

Guide to the Sources of the History of Nations (Latin American Series, 11 vols. pub.; African South of the Sahara Series, 20 vols. pub.; North Africa, Asia, and Oceania: 15 vols. pub.)

Guide to the Sources of Asian History (English language series (India, Indonesia, Korea, Nepal, Pakistan, Singapore), 14 vols. pub.; National Language Series (Indonesia, Korea, Malaysia, Nepal, Thailand, 6 vols. pub.; other guides, 3 vols. pub.)

International Federation for Information and Documentation (FID)

J. Stephen Parker, Executive Director
Box 90402, 2509 LK The Hague, Netherlands
Tel. 31-70-314-0671, fax 314-0667, e-mail fid@fid.nl
World Wide Web http://www.fid.nl

Object

The International Federation for Information and Documentation (FID) is an independent international nongovernmental professional association with about 350 national, institutional, corporate, and personal members in 90 countries.

It promotes, through international cooperation, research in and development of information science, information management, and documentation, which includes inter alia the organization, storage, retrieval, repackaging, dissemination, value adding, and evaluation of information, however recorded, in the fields of science, technology, industry, social sciences, arts, and humanities.

Officers

Pres. Martha B. Stone, c/o International Development Research Centre IDRC, Box 8500, Ottawa, ON K1G 3H9, Canada. Tel. 613-235-2252, fax 819-457-2359, e-mail mstone@idrc.ca.

Program

FID devotes much of its attention to corporate information; industrial, business, and finance information; information policy research; the application of information technology; information service management; the marketing of information systems and services; content analysis, for example, in the design of database systems; linking information and human resources; and the repackaging of information for specific user audiences.

Publications

FID Annual Report (ann.).
FID Directory (bienn.).
FID Review (2 a year).

FID Publications List (irreg.).
Document Delivery Survey and *ET Newsletter*.
International Forum on Information and Documentation (q.).
Proceedings of congresses; directories; bibliographies on information science, documentation, education and training, and classification research.

International Federation of Film Archives (FIAF)

Secretariat, 1 Rue Defacqz, B-1000 Brussels, Belgium
Tel. 32-2-538-3065, fax 32-2-534-4774, e-mail info@fiafnet.org
World Wide Web http://www.fiafnet.org

Object

Founded in 1938, FIAF brings together institutions dedicated to rescuing films both as cultural heritage and as historical documents. FIAF is a collaborative association of the world's leading film archives whose purpose has always been to ensure the proper preservation and showing of motion pictures. A total of 126 archives in more than 60 countries collect, restore, and exhibit films and cinema documentation spanning the entire history of film.

FIAF seeks to promote film culture and facilitate historical research, to help create new archives around the world, to foster training and expertise in film preservation, to encourage the collection and preservation of documents and other cinema-related materials, to develop cooperation between archives, and to ensure the international availability of films and cinema documents.

Officers

Pres. Ivan Trujillo Bolio; *Secy.-Gen.* Steven Ricci; *Treas.* Karl Griep; *Members* Adriano Apra, Claude Bertemes, Hong-Teak Chung, Valeria Ciompi, Stefan Droessler, Vera Gyurey, Vigdis Lian, Susan Oxtoby, Roger Smither, Paolo Cherchi Usai.

Address correspondence to Christian Dimitriu, Senior Administrator, c/o the Secretariat. E-mail info@fiafnet.org.

Publications

Journal of Film Preservation.
International Filmarchive CD-ROM.
For other FIAF publications, see the Web site http://www.fiafnet.org.

International Federation of Library Associations and Institutions (IFLA)

Box 95312, 2509 CH The Hague, Netherlands
Tel. 31-70-314-0884, fax 31-70-383-4027
E-mail IFLA@IFLA.org, World Wide Web http://www.IFLA.org

Object

To promote international understanding, cooperation, discussion, research, and development in all fields of library activity, including bibliography, information services, and the education of library personnel, and to provide a body through which librarianship can be represented in matters of international interest. Founded 1927.

Membership

Memb. (Lib. Assns.) 153; (Inst.) 1,116; (Aff.) 430; Sponsors: 34. Membs. represent 153 countries.

Officers and Governing Board

Pres. Christine Deschamps, Bibliothèque de l'Université de Paris V–René Descartes, Paris, France; *Pres.-Elect* Kay Raseroka, Univ. Lib. of Botswana, Gaborone, Botswana; *Treas.* Derek Law, Univ. of Strathclyde, Glasgow, Scotland; *Governing Board* Alex Byrne, Univ. of Technology, Sydney, Australia; Sissel Nilsen, National Lib. of Norway, Oslo Div.; Sally McCallum, Lib. of Congress, Washington, D.C.; Ellen Tise, Univ. of the Western Cape, Bellville, South Africa; Ingrid Parent, National Lib. of Canada, Ottawa; Claudia Lux, Zentral- und Landesbibliothek Berlin, Berlin, Germany; Jianzhong Wu, Shanghai Lib., Shanghai, China; Ana Maria Peruchena Zimmermann, ABGRA, Buenos Aires, Argentina; Wanda V. Dole, Washburn Univ., Topeka, Kansas; Ia McIlwaine, Dir., School of Lib., Archive, and Info. Studies, Univ. College, London, England; John Meriton, National Art Lib., Victoria and Albert Museum, London, England; Marian Koren, NBLC, The Hague, Netherlands; Mary E. Jackson, Assn. of Research Libs., Washington, D.C.; John M. Day, Gallaudet Univ. Lib., Washington,

D.C.; Winston Tabb, Lib. of Congress; Cristobal Pasadas Urena, Universidad de Granada Biblioteca, Granada, Spain; Rashidah Begun bt. Fazal Mohamed, Lib., Universiti Malaysia; *Secy.-Gen.* Ross Shimmon; *Coord. Professional Activities* Sjoerd M. J. Koopman; *IFLA Office for Universal Bibliographic Control and International MARC Program Dir.* Marie-France Plassard, Deutsche Bibliothek, Frankfurt am Main, Germany; *IFLA International Program for UAP Program Dir.* Graham Cornish, British Lib. Document Supply Centre, Boston Spa, Wetherby, West Yorkshire, England; *IFLA Office for Preservation and Conservation Program Dir.* M. T. Varlamoff, Bibliothèque Nationale de France, Paris; *IFLA Office for the Advancement of Librarianship Dir.* Birgitta Sandell, Uppsala Univ. Lib., Uppsala, Sweden; *IFLA Office for International Lending Dir.* Graham Cornish; *IFLA Committee on Copyright and Other Legal Matters Chair* Marianne Scott; *IFLA Committee on Freedom of Access to Information and Freedom of Expression (FAIFE) Chair* Alex Byrne.

Publications

IFLA Annual Report
IFLA Directory (bienn.).
IFLA Journal (6/yr.).
IFLA Professional Reports.
IFLA Publications Series.
International Cataloguing and Bibliographic Control (q.).
International Preservation News.
UAP Newsletter (s. ann.).

American Membership

American Assn. of Law Libs.; American Lib. Assn.; Art Libs. Society of North America; Assn. for Lib. and Info. Science Education; Assn. of Research Libs.; International Assn.

of Law Libs.; International Assn. of School Libns.; Medical Lib. Assn.; Special Libs. Assn. *Institutional Membs.* There are 143 libraries and related institutions that are insti-tutional members or consultative bodies and sponsors of IFLA in the United States (out of a total of 1,167), and 105 personal affiliates (out of a total of 361).

International Organization for Standardization (ISO)

ISO Central Secretariat, 1 rue de Varembé, Case Postale 56,
CH-1211 Geneva 20, Switzerland
41-22-749-0111, fax 41-22-733-3430, e-mail central@iso.org
World Wide Web http://www.iso.org

Object

Worldwide federation of national standards bodies, founded in 1947, at present comprising some 140 members, one in each country. The object of ISO is to promote the development of standardization and related activities in the world with a view to facilitating international exchange of goods and services, and to developing cooperation in the spheres of intellectual, scientific, technological, and economic activity. The scope of ISO covers international standardization in all fields except electrical and electronic engineering standardization, which is the responsibility of the International Electrotechnical Commission (IEC). The results of ISO technical work are published as International Standards.

Officers

Pres. Mario Gilberto Cortopassi, Brazil; *V.P. (Policy)* Torsten Bahke, Germany; *V.P. (Technical Management)* Ross Wraight, Australia; *Secy.-Gen.* L. D. Eicher.

Technical Work

The technical work of ISO is carried out by some 190 technical committees. These include:

ISO/TC 46–Information and documentation (Secretariat, Association Française de Normalization, 11 Ave. Francis de Pressensé, Saint-Denis La Plaine, Cedex, France). Scope: Standardization of practices relating to libraries, documentation and information centers, indexing and abstracting services, archives, information science, and publishing.

ISO/TC 37–Terminology and other languages resources (Secretariat, INFOTERM, Aichholzgasse 6/12, 1120, Vienna, Austria). Scope: Standardization of methods for creating, compiling, and coordinating terminologies.

ISO/IEC JTC 1–Information technology (Secretariat, American National Standards Institute, 25 W. 43 St., 4th fl., New York, NY 10036). Scope: Standardization in the field of information technology.

Publications

ISO Annual Report.
ISO Bulletin (mo.).
ISO Catalogue (ann.).
ISO International Standards.
ISO Management Systems (bi-mo.).
ISO Memento (ann.).
ISO Online information service on World Wide Web (http://www.iso.org).

Foreign Library Associations

The following is a selective list of regional and national library associations around the world. A more complete list can be found in *International Literary Market Place* (Information Today, Inc.).

Regional

Africa

Standing Conference of African Univ. Libs., c/o E. Bejide Bankole, Editor, *African Journal of Academic Librarianship,* Univ. of Lagos, Akoka, Yaba, Lagos, Nigeria. Tel. 1-524-968, fax 1-822-644.

The Americas

Asociación de Bibliotecas Universitarias, de Investigación e Institucionales del Caribe (Assn. of Caribbean Univ., Research, and Institutional Libs.), Box 23317, UPR Sta., San Juan, Puerto Rico 00931. Tel. 787-790-8054, fax 787-764-2311, e-mail acuril @rrpac.upr.clu.edu or acuril@coqui.net, World Wide Web http://www.acuril.rrp. upr.edu. *Exec. Secy.* Oneida R. Ortiz.

Seminar on the Acquisition of Latin American Lib. Materials, c/o *Exec. Secy.,* Laura Gutiérrez-Witt, SALALM Secretariat, Benson Latin American Collection, Sid Richardson Hall 1.109, Univ. of Texas, Austin, TX 78713. Tel. 512-495-4471, fax 512-495-4488, e-mail SandyL@mail. utexas.edu, World Wide Web http://www. lib.utexas.edu/benson/secretariat.

Asia

Congress of Southeast Asian Libns. IV (CONSAL IV), c/o *Secy.-Gen.* R. Ramachandran, CONSAL Secretariat, c/o National Lib. Board, 1 Temasek Ave., No. 06-00, Millenia Tower, Singapore 039192. Tel. 65-332-3600, fax 65-332-3616, e-mail rama@nlb.gov.sg.

The Commonwealth

Commonwealth Lib. Assn., c/o *Exec. Secy.* Norma Amenu-Kpodo, Box 144, Kingston 7, Jamaica. Tel. 876-927-2123, fax 876-927-1926. *Pres.* Elizabeth Watson.

Standing Conference on Lib. Materials on Africa, Commonwealth Secretariat, Marlborough House, Pall Mall, London SW14 5HX, England. Tel. 207-747-6564, fax 207-747-6168, e-mail scolma@hotmail.com. *Chair* Sheila Allcock.

Europe

Ligue des Bibliothèques Européennes de Recherche (LIBER) (Assn. of European Research Libs.), c/o H.-A. Koch, Universität Bremen, Postfach 330440, 28334 Bremen, Germany. Tel. 421-218-3361.

National

Argentina

Asociación de Bibliotecarios Graduados de la República Argentina (ABGRA) (Assn. of Graduate Libns. of Argentina), Tucuman 1424, 8 piso D, 1050 Buenos Aires. Tel./ fax 1-373-0571, e-mail postmaster@abgra. org.ar. *Pres.* Ana Maria Peruchena Zimmermann; *Exec. Secy.* Rosa Emma Monfasani.

Australia

Australian Lib. and Info. Assn., Box E 441, Kingston, ACT 2600. Tel. 6-285-1877, fax 6-282-2249, e-mail enquiry@alia.org.au. *Pres.* Mairead Browne; *Exec. Dir.* Jennifer Nicholson.

Australian Society of Archivists, c/o Queensland State Archives, Box 1397, Sunnybank Hills, Qld. 4109. Tel. 7-3875-8742, fax 7-3875-8764, e-mail shicks@gil.com.au, World Wide Web http://www.archives.qld. gov.au or http://www.achivenet.gov.au/ asa/asa. *Pres.* Kathryn Dan; *Secy.* Fiona Burn.

Council of Australian State Libs., c/o State Lib. of New South Wales, Macquarie St.,

Sydney, NSW. Tel. 2-9273-1414, fax 7-3846-2421. *Chair* D. H. Stephens.

Austria

Österreichische Gesellschaft für Dokumentation und Information (Austrian Society for Documentation and Info.), c/o TermNet, Simmeringer Hauptstr. 24, A-1110 Vienna. Tel. 1-7404-0280, fax 1-7404-0281, e-mail oegdi@oegdi.at, World Wide Web http://www.oegdi.at. *Pres.* Gerhard Richter.

Vereinigung Österreichischer Bibliothekarinnen und Bibliothekare (Assn. of Austrian Libns.), Universitätsbibliothek Graz, Universitätsplatz 3, A-8010 Graz. Tel. 0316-380/3101, fax 0316-384987, e-mail sigrid.reinitzer@kfunigraz.ac.at. *Pres.* Sigrid Reinitzer; *Secy.* Brigitte Schaffer.

Bangladesh

Lib. Assn. of Bangladesh, c/o Safia Kanal National Public Lib. Bldg., Shahbagh, Ramna, Dacca 1000. Tel. 2-504-269, e-mail msik@icddrb.org. *Pres.* M. Shamsul Islam Khan; *Gen. Secy.* Kh. Fazlur Rahman.

Barbados

Lib. Assn. of Barbados, Box 827E, Bridgetown. *Pres.* Shirley Yearwood; *Secy.* Hazelyn Devonish.

Belgium

Archives et Bibliothèques de Belgique/Archief- en Bibliotheekwezen in België (Archives and Libs. of Belgium), 4 Blvd. de l'Empereur, B-1000 Brussels. Tel. 2-519-5351, fax 2-519-5533. *Gen. Secy.* Wim De Vos.

Association Belge de Documentation/Belgische Vereniging voor Documentatie (Belgian Assn. for Documentation), Chaussée de Wavre 1683, Waversesteenweg, B-1160 Brussels. Tel. 2-675-5862, fax 2-672-7446, e-mail abd@synec-doc.be, World Wide Web http://www.synec-doc.be/abd-bvd. *Pres.* Evelyne Luetkens.

Association Professionnelle des Bibliothécaires et Documentalistes (Assn. of Libns. and Documentation Specialists), 7 rue des Marronniers, 5651 Thy-Le Château, Brussels. Tel. 71-614-335, fax 71-611-634, e-mail biblio.hainaut@skynet.be. *Pres.* Jean Claude Tréfois; *Secy.* Laurence Hennaux.

Vlaamse Vereniging voor Bibliotheek-, Archief-, en Documentatiewezen (Flemish Assn. of Libns., Archivists, and Documentalists), Statiestraat 179, B-2600 Berchem, Antwerp. Tel. 3-281-4457, fax 3-218-8077, e-mail marc.storms@vvbad.be, World Wide Web http://www.vvbad.be. *Pres.* Geert Puype; *Exec. Dir.* Marc Storms.

Belize

Belize Lib. Assn., c/o Central Lib., Bliss Inst., Box 287, Belize City. Tel. 2-7267. *Pres.* H. W. Young; *Secy.* Robert Hulse.

Bolivia

Asociación Boliviana de Bibliotecarios (Bolivian Lib. Assn.), c/o Biblioteca y Archivo Nacional, Calle Bolivar, Sucre. *Dir.* Gunnar Mendoza.

Bosnia and Herzegovina

Drustvo Bibliotekara Bosne i Hercegovine (Libns. Society of Bosnia and Herzegovina), Zmaja od Bosne 8B, 71000 Sarajevo. Tel./fax 71-212-435, e-mail nevenka@utic.net.ba. *Pres.* Nevenka Hajdarovic.

Botswana

Botswana Lib. Assn., Box 1310, Gaborone. Tel. 31-355-2295, fax 31-357-291, e-mail mbangiwa@noka.ub.bw. *Chair* F. M. Lamusse; *Secy.* A. M. Mbangiwa.

Brazil

Associação dos Arquivistas Brasileiros (Assn. of Brazilian Archivists), Rua da Candelária, 9-Sala 1004, Centro, Rio de Janeiro RJ 20091-020. Tel./fax 21-233-7142. *Pres.* Lia Temporal Malcher; *Secy.* Laura Regina Xavier.

Brunei Darussalam

Persatuan Perpustakaan Kebangsaan Negara Brunei (National Lib. Assn. of Brunei), c/o Language and Literature Bureau Lib., Jalan Elizabeth II, Bandar Seri Begawan. Tel. 2-235-501. *Contact* Abu Bakar Bin.

Cameroon

Association des Bibliothécaires, Archivistes, Documentalistes et Muséographes du Cameroun (Assn. of Libns., Archivists, Documentalists, and Museum Curators of Cameroon), Université de Yaoundé, Bibliothèque Universitaire, B.P. 337, Yaounde. Tel. 220-744, fax 221-320.

Canada

Bibliographical Society of Canada/La Société Bibliographique du Canada, Box 575, Postal Sta. P, Toronto, ON M5S 2T1. E-mail mcgaughe@yorku.ca, World Wide Web http://www.library.utoronto.ca/bsc. *Pres.* Peter McNally; *Secy.* Anne McGaughey.

Canadian Assn. for Info. Science/Association Canadienne de Sciences de l'Information, c/o CAIS Secretariat, Faculty of Info. Studies, Univ. of Toronto, 140 Saint George St., Toronto, ON M5S 3G6. Tel. 416-978-8876, fax 416-971-1399, e-mail caisasst@fis.utoronto.ca. *Pres.* Berndt Frohmann.

Canadian Council of Lib. Schools/Conseil Canadien des Ecoles de Bibliothéconomie, c/o Grant Campbell, Faculty of Info. and Media Studies, Univ. of Western Ontario, Middlesex College, R. 270, London, ON N6A 5B7. Tel. 519-661-2111, fax 519-661-3506, e-mail gcampbel@uwo.ca.

Canadian Lib. Assn., c/o *Exec. Dir.* Vicki Whitmell, 328 Frank St., Ottawa, ON K2P 0X8. Tel. 613-232-9625, fax 613-563-9895, e-mail vwhitmell@cla.ca. (For detailed information on the Canadian Lib. Assn. and its divisions, see "National Library and Information-Industry Associations, United States and Canada." For information on the library associations of the provinces of Canada, see "State, Provincial, and Regional Library Associations.")

Chile

Colegio de Bibliotecarios de Chile AG (Chilean Lib. Assn.), Diagonal Paraguay 383, Depto. 122 Torre 11, Santiago 3741. Tel./fax 2-222-5652, e-mail cdb@interaccesses.cl. *Pres.* Esmerelda Ramos Ramos; *Secy.* Monica Nunez.

China

China Society for Lib. Science, 39 Bai Shi Qiao Rd., Beijing 100081. Tel. 10-684-15566, ext. 5563, fax 10-684-19271. *Secy.-Gen.* Liu Xiangsheng.

Colombia

Asociación Colombiana de Bibliotecarios (Colombian Lib. Assn.), Calle 10, No. 3-16, Apdo. Aéreo 30883, Bogotá. Tel. 1-269-4219. *Pres.* Saul Sanchez Toro.

Costa Rica

Asociación Costarricense de Bibliotecarios (Costa Rican Assn. of Libns.), Apdo. 3308, San José. *Secy.-Gen.* Nelly Kopper.

Croatia

Hrvatsko Bibliotekarsko Drustvo (Croation Lib. Assn.), Ulica Hrvatske bratske zajednice b b, 10000 Zagreb. Tel. 41-616-4037, fax 41-616-4186, e-mail hbd@nsk.hr, World Wide Web http://pubwww.srce.hr/hkd. *Pres.* Dubravka Stancin-Rosic; *Secy.* Dunja Marie Gabriel.

Cuba

Lib. Assn. of Cuba, Biblioteca Nacional José Marti, Apdo. 6881, Ave. de Independencia e/20 de Mayo y Aranguren, Plaza de la Revolución, Havana. Tel. 7-708-277. *Dir.* Marta Terry González.

Cyprus

Kypriakos Synthesmos Vivliothicarion (Lib. Assn. of Cyprus), Box 1039, Nicosia. *Pres.* Costas D. Stephanov; *Secy.* Paris G. Rossos.

Czech Republic

Svaz Knihovniku Informachnich Pracovniku Ceske Republiky (Assn. of Lib. and Info. Professionals of the Czech Republic), National Lib., Klementinum 190, 11000 Prague. Tel. 2-2166-3338, fax 2-2166-3175, e-mail vit.richter@mkp.cr, World Wide Web http://www.nkp.cz. *Pres.* Vit Richter.

Denmark

Arkivforeningen (Archives Society), c/o Landsarkivet for Sjaelland, jagtvej 10,

2200 Copenhagen K K. Tel. 3139-3520, fax 3315-3239. *Pres.* Tyge Krogh; *Secy.* Charlotte Steinmark.

Danmarks Biblioteksforening (Danish Lib. Assn.), Telegrafvej 5, DK-2750 Ballerup. Tel. 4468-1466, fax 4468-1103. *Dir.* Winnie Vitzansky.

Danmarks Forskningsbiblioteksforening (Danish Research Lib. Assn.), Postboks 2149, 1016 Copenhagen K. Tel. 3393-6222, fax 3391-9596, e-mail df@kb.dk. *Pres.* Erland Kolding; *Secy.* D. Skovgaard.

Kommunernes Skolebiblioteksforening (formerly Danmarks Skolebiblioteksforening) (Assn. of Danish School Libs.), Vesterbrogade 20, DK-1620, Copenhagen V. Tel. 3325-3222, fax 3325-3223, e-mail kom skolbib@internet.dk, World Wide Web http://www.ksbk.dk. *Chief Exec.* Paul Erik Sorensen.

Dominican Republic

Asociación Dominicana de Bibliotecarios (Dominican Assn. of Libns.), c/o Biblioteca Nacional, Plaza de la Cultura, Cesar Nicolás Penson 91, Santo Domingo. Tel. 809-688-4086. *Pres.* Prospero J. Mella-Chavier; *Secy.-Gen.* V. Regús.

Ecuador

Asociación Ecuatoriana de Bibliotecarios (Ecuadoran Lib. Assn.), c/o Casa de la Cultura Ecuatoriana Benjamin Carrión, Apdo. 67, Ave. 6 de Diciembre 794, Quito. Tel. 2-528-840, 2-263-474. *Pres.* Eulalia Galarza.

Egypt

Egyptian Assn. for Lib. and Info. Science, c/o Dept. of Archives, Librarianship and Info. Science, Faculty of Arts, Univ. of Cairo, Cairo. Tel. 2-567-6365, fax 2-572-9659. *Pres.* S. Khalifa; *Secy.* Hosam El-Din.

El Salvador

Asociación de Bibliotecarios de El Salvador (El Salvador Lib. Assn.), c/o Biblioteca Nacional, 8A Avda. Norte y Calle Delgado, San Salvador. Tel. 216-312.

Asociación General de Archivistas de El Salvador (Assn. of Archivists of El Salvador),

Archivo General de la Nación, Palacio Nacional, San Salvador. Tel. 229-418.

Ethiopia

Ye Ethiopia Betemetshaft Serategnoch Mahber (Ethiopian Lib. and Info. Assn.), Box 30530, Addis Ababa. Tel. 1-518-020, fax 1-552-544. *Pres.* Mulugeta Hunde; *Secy.* Girma Makonnen.

Finland

Suomen Kirjastoseura (Finnish Lib. Assn.), Vuorkatu 22 A18, FIN-00100 Helsinki. Tel. 9-622-1399, fax 9-622-1466, e-mail fla@fla.fi. *Pres.* Kaarina Dromberg; *Secy.-Gen.* Sinikka Sipila.

France

Association des Archivistes Français (Assn. of French Archivists), 60 Rue des Francs-Bourgeois, F-75141 Paris Cedex 3. Tel. 1-40-27-60-00. *Pres.* Jean-Luc Eichenlaub; *Secy.* Jean LePottier.

Association des Bibliothécaires Français (Assn. of French Libns.), 31 Rue de Chabrol, F-75010 Paris. Tel. 1-55-33-10-30, fax 1-55-30-10-31, e-mail abf@wanadoo.fr, World Wide Web http://www.abf.asso.fr. *Pres.* Claudine Belayche; *Gen. Secy.* Marie-Martine Tomiteh.

Association des Professionnels de l'Information et de la Documentation (Assn. of Info. and Documentation Professionals), 25 rue Claude Tillier, 75012 Paris. Tel. 1-43-72-25-25, fax 1-43-72-30-41, e-mail adbs@adbs.fr, World Wide Web http://www.adbs.fr. *Pres.* Florence Wilhelm.

Germany

Arbeitsgemeinschaft der Spezialbibliotheken (Assn. of Special Libs.), c/o Forschungszentrum, Jülich GmbH, Zentralbibliothek, 52426 Jülich. Tel. 2461-61-2907, fax 2461-61-6103, e-mail e.salz@fz-juelich.de. *Chair* Rafael Ball; *Secretariat Dir.* Edith Salz.

Deutsche Gesellschaft für Informationswissenschaft und Informationspraxis eV (German Society for Info. Science and Practice), Ostbahnhofstr. 13, 60314 Frankfurt-am-Main 1. Tel. 69-430-313, fax 69-490-9096, e-mail dgd@darmstadt.gmd.de,

World Wide Web http://www.dge.de. *Pres.* Horst Neiber.

Deutscher Bibliotheksverband eV (German Lib. Assn.), Strasse des 17 Juni 114, 10623 Berlin. Tel. 30-3900-1480, fax 30-3900-1484, fax 30-3900-1484, e-mail dbv@bdbibl.de, World Wide Web http://www.bdbibl.de/bv. *Pres.* Christof Eichert.

Verband Deutscher Archivarinnen und Archivare e.V. (Assn. of German Archivists), Postfach 2119, 99402 Weimar. Tel. 03643/870-235, fax 03643/870-164, e-mail info@vda.archiv.net, World Wide Web http://www.vda.archiv.net. *Chair* Volker Wahl.

Verein der Bibliothekare und Assisten (Assn. of Libns. and Lib. Staff), Postfach 1324, 72703 Reutlingen. Tel. 7121-34910, fax 7121-300-433, e-mail bub.uba@t-online. de, World Wide Web http://www.s-linede/homepages/uba. *Pres.* Klaus Peter Bottger; *Secy.* Katharina Boulanger.

Verein der Diplom-Bibliothekare an Wissenschaftlichen Bibliotheken (Assn. of Certified Libns. at Academic Libs.), c/o Universitätsbibliothek, Am Hubland 97074, Würzburg. Tel. 221-574-7161, fax 221-574-7110. *Chair* Marianne Saule.

Verein Deutscher Bibliothekare (Assn. of German Libns.), Krummer Timpen 3-5, 48143 Münster. Tel. 251-832-4032, fax 251-832-8398. *Pres.* Klaus Hilgemann. E-mail hilgema@ui-muenster.de; *Secy.* Lydia Jungnickel.

Ghana

Ghana Lib. Assn., Box 4105, Accra. Tel. 2-668-731. *Pres.* E. S. Asiedo; *Secy.* A. W. K. Insaidoo.

Greece

Enosis Hellinon Bibliothekarion (Greek Lib. Assn.), Themistocleus 73, 10683 Athens. Tel. 1-322-6625. *Pres.* K. Xatzopoulou; *Gen. Secy.* E. Kalogeraky.

Guyana

Guyana Lib. Assn., c/o National Lib., Church St. and Ave. of the Republic, Georgetown. Tel. 2-62690, 2-62699. *Pres.* Hetty London; *Secy.* Jean Harripersaud.

Honduras

Asociación de Bibliotecarios y Archiveros de Honduras (Assn. of Libns. and Archivists of Honduras), 11a Calle, 1a y 2a Avdas., No. 105, Comayagüela DC, Tegucigalpa. *Pres.* Fransisca de Escoto Espinoza; *Secy.-Gen.* Juan Angel R. Ayes.

Hong Kong

Hong Kong Lib. Assn., GPO 10095, Hong Kong. E-mail hklib@hklib.org.hk, World Wide Web http://www.hklib.org.hk. *Pres.* Tommy Yeung.

Hungary

Magyar Könyvtárosok Egyesülete (Assn. of Hungarian Libns.), Hold u 6, H-1054 Budapest. Tel./fax 1-311-8634. *Pres.* Zoltan Ambrus; *Gen. Secy.* Katalin Haraszti.

Iceland

Bókavardafélag Islands (Icelandic Lib. Assn.), Box 1497, 121 Reykjavik. Tel. 564-2050, fax 564-3877. *Pres.* H. A. Hardarson; *Secy.* A. Agnarsdottir.

India

Indian Assn. of Special Libs. and Info. Centres, P-291, CIT Scheme 6M, Kankurgachi, Calcutta 700054. Tel. 33-334-9651. Indian Lib. Assn., c/o Mukerjee Nagar, A/40-41, Flat 201, Ansal Bldg., Delhi 110009. Tel. 11-711-7743. *Pres.* P. S. G. Kumar.

Indonesia

Ikatan Pustakawan Indonesia (Indonesian Lib. Assn.), Jalan Merdeka Selatan No. 21, Box 3624, 10002 Jakarta, Pusat. Tel. 21-342-529, fax 21-310-3554. *Pres.* S. Kartosdono.

Iraq

Iraqi Lib. Assn., c/o National Lib., Bab-el-Muaddum, Baghdad. Tel. 1-416-4190. *Dir.* Abdul Hameed Al-Alawchi.

Ireland

Cumann Leabharlann Na h-Eireann (Lib. Assn. of Ireland), 53 Upper Mount St., Dublin. Tel. 1-661-9000, fax 1-676-1628, e-mail laisec@iol.ie. *Pres.* L. Ronayne; *Hon. Secy.* Brendan Teeling.

Israel

Israel Libns. and Info. Specialists Assn., Box 238, 17 Strauss St., 91001 Jerusalem. Tel. 2-6207-2868, fax 2-625-628. *Pres.* Benjamin Schachter.

Israel Society of Special Libs. and Info. Centers, 31 Habarzel St., Ramat Ha Hayal, 69710 Tel Aviv. Tel. 3-648-0592. *Chair* Karen Sitton.

Italy

Associazione Italiana Biblioteche (Italian Lib. Assn.), C.P. 2461, I-00100 Rome A-D. Tel. 6-446-3532, fax 6-444-1139, e-mail aib@aib.it, World Wide Web http://www.aib.it. *Pres.* I. Poggiali; *Secy.* A. Paoli.

Jamaica

Jamaica Lib. Assn., Box 58, Kingston 5. Tel. 876-63310, fax 876-62188. *Pres.* P. Kerr; *Secy.* F. Salmon.

Japan

Joho Kagaku Gijutsu Kyokai (Info. Science and Technology Assn.), Sasaki Bldg., 5-7 Koisikawa 2, Bunkyo-ku, Tokyo. *Pres.* T. Gondoh; *Gen. Mgr.* Yukio Ichikawa.

Nihon Toshokan Kyokai (Japan Lib. Assn.), 1-11-14 Shinkawa, Chuo-ku, Tokyo 104 0033. Tel. 3-3523-0841, fax 3-3421-7588. *Secy.-Gen.* Reiko Sakagawa.

Senmon Toshokan Kyogikai (Japan Special Libs. Assn.), c/o National Diet Lib., 10-1 Nagata-cho, 1-chome, Chiyoda-ku, Tokyo 100. Tel. 3-3581-2331, fax 3-3597-9104. *Pres.* Kousaku Inaba; *Exec. Dir.* Fumihisa Nakagawa.

Jordan

Jordan Lib. Assn., Box 6289, Amman. Tel. 6-629-412. *Pres.* Anwar Akroush; *Secy.* Yousra Abu Ajamieh.

Kenya

Kenya Lib. Assn., Box 46031, Nairobi. Tel. 2-214-917, fax 2-336-885, e-mail jwere@ken.healthnet.org. *Chair* Jacinta Were; *Secy.* Alice Bulogosi.

Korea (Republic of)

Korean Lib. Assn., 60-1 Panpo Dong, Seo-cho-ku, Seoul. Tel. 2-535-4868, fax 2-535-5616, e-mail klanet@hitel.net *Pres.* Ki Nam Shin; *Exec. Dir.* Won Ho Jo.

Laos

Association des Bibliothécaires Laotiens (Assn. of Laotian Libns.), c/o Direction de la Bibliothèque Nationale, Ministry of Info. and Culture, B.P. 122, Vientiane. Tel. 21-212-452, fax 21-213-029, e-mail pfd-mill@pan.laos.net.la. *Dir.* Somthong.

Latvia

Lib. Assn. of Latvia, Latvian National Lib., Kr. Barona iela 14, 1423 Riga. Tel. 132-728-98-74, fax 132-728-08-51, e-mail lnb@com.latnet.lv. *Pres.* Aldis Abele.

Lebanon

Lebanese Lib. Assn., c/o American Univ. of Beirut, Univ. Lib./Serials Dept., Box 113/5367, Beirut. Tel. 1-374-374, ext. 2606. *Pres.* Fawz Abdalleh; *Exec. Secy.* Rudaynah Shoujah.

Lesotho

Lesotho Lib. Assn., Private Bag A26, Maseru. *Chair* S. M. Mohai; *Secy.* N. Taole.

Lithuania

Lithuanian Libns. Assn., Sv Ignoto G-108, LT-2600, Vilnius. Tel./fax 2-750-340, e-mail Libd@vpu.Lt, World Wide Web http://www.Lbd.Lt.

Macedonia

Bibliotekarsko Drustvo na Makedonija (Union of Libns.' Assns. of Macedonia), Box 566, 91000 Skopje. Tel. 91-212-736, fax 91-232-649, e-mail mile@nubsk.edu.mk or bmile47@yahoo.com. *Pres.* Mile Boseki; *Secy.* Poliksena Matkovska.

Malawi

Malawi Lib. Assn., Box 429, Zomba. Tel. 50-522-222, fax 50-523-225. *Chair* Joseph J. Uta; *Secy.* Vote D. Somba.

Malaysia

Persatuan Perpustakaan Malaysia (Lib. Assn. of Malaysia), Box 12545, 50782 Kuala Lumpur. Tel. 3-273-114, fax 3-273-1167. *Pres.* Chew Wing Foong; *Secy.* Leni Abdul Latif.

Mali

Association Malienne des Bibliothécaires, Archivistes et Documentalistes (Mali Assn. of Libns., Archivists, and Documentalists), c/o Bibliothèque Nationale du Mali, Ave. Kasse Keita, B.P. 159, Bamako. Tel. 224-963. *Dir.* Mamadou Konoba Keita.

Malta

Malta Lib. and Info. Assn. (MaLIA), c/o Univ. Lib., Msida MSD 06. *Secy.* Joseph R. Grima.

Mauritania

Association Mauritanienne des Bibliothécaires, Archivistes et Documentalistes (Mauritanian Assn. of Libns., Archivists, and Documentalists), c/o Bibliothèque Nationale, B.P. 20, Nouakchott. *Pres.* O. Diouwara; *Secy.* Sid'Ahmed Fall dit Dah.

Mauritius

Mauritius Lib. Assn., c/o The British Council, Royal Rd., Box 111, Rose Hill. Tel. 454-9550, fax 454-9553, e-mail bcouncil @intnet.mu, World Wide Web http://www.britishcouncil.org/mauritius. *Pres.* K. Appadoo; *Secy.* S. Rughoo.

Mexico

Asociación Mexicana de Bibliotecarios (Mexican Assn. of Libns.), Apdo. 27-651, Admin. de Correos 27, México D.F. 06760. Tel. 5-575-1135, e-mail ambac@solar.sar. net. *Pres.* Elsa M. Ramirez Leyva; *Secy.* Jose L. Almanza Morales.

Myanmar

Myanmar Lib. Assn., c/o National Lib., Strand Rd., Yangon. *Chief Libn.* U Khin Maung Tin.

Nepal

Nepal Lib. Assn., c/o National Lib., Harihar Bhawan, Pulchowk Lib., Box 2773, Kathmandu. Tel. 1-521-132. *Libn.* Shusila Dwivedi.

The Netherlands

Nederlandse Vereniging voor Beraepsbeaefenaren in de Bibliotheck-Informatie-en Kennissector (Netherlands Libns. Society), NVB-Verenigingsbureau, Plompetorengracht 11, NL-3512 CA Utrecht. Tel. 30-231-1263, fax 30-231-1830, e-mail nvbinfo @wxs.nl, World Wide Web http://www.kb.b.nl/nvb. *Pres.* J. S. N. Savenye.

New Zealand

Lib. and Info. Assn. of New Zealand, Old Wool House, Level 5, 139-141 Featherston St., Box 12-212, Wellington. Tel. 4-473-5834, fax 4-499-1480, e-mail steve@lianza.org.nz.

Nicaragua

Asociación Nicaraguense de Bibliotecarios y Profesionales a Fines (Nicaraguan Assn. of Libns.), Apdo. Postal 3257, Managua. *Exec. Secy.* Susana Morales Hernández.

Nigeria

Nigerian Lib. Assn., c/o National Lib. of Nigeria, 4 Wesley St., PMB 12626, Lagos. Tel. 1-260-0220, fax 1-631-563. *Pres.* A. O. Banjo; *Secy.* D. D. Bwayili.

Norway

Arkivarforeningen (Assn. of Archivists), c/o Riksarkivet, Folke Bernadottes Vei 21, Postboks 10, N-0807 Oslo. Tel. 22-022-600, fax 22-237-489.

Norsk Bibliotekforening (Norwegian Lib. Assn.), Malerhaugveien 20, N-0661 Oslo. Tel. 2-268-8550, fax 2-267-2368. *Dir.* Berit Aaker.

Pakistan

Pakistan Lib. Assn., c/o Pakistan Inst. of Development Economics, Univ. Campus, Box 1091, Islamabad. Tel. 51-921-4041, fax 51-921-0886, e-mail naqvizj@hotmail.com. *Pres.* Sain Malik; *Secy.-Gen.* Atta Ullah.

Panama

Asociación Panameña de Bibliotecarios
. (Panama Lib. Assn.), c/o Biblioteca Inter-
americana Simón Bolivar, Estafeta Uni-
versitaria, Panama City. *Pres*. Bexie
Rodriguez de León.

Paraguay

Asociación de Bibliotecarios del Paraguay
(Assn. of Paraguayan Libns.), Casilla 910,
2064 Asunción. *Pres*. Gloria Ondina Ortiz;
Secy. Celia Villamayor de Diaz.

Peru

Asociación de Archiveros del Perú (Peruvian
Assn. of Archivists), Archivo Central
Salaverry, 2020 Jesús Mario, Universidad
del Pacifico, Lima 11. Tel. 1-471-2277,
fax 1-265-0958, e-mail dri@u8p.edu.pe.
Pres. José Luis Abanto Arrelucea.

Asociación Peruana de Bibliotecarios (Peruvian Assn. of Libns.), Bellavista 561
Miraflores, Apdo. 995, Lima 18. Tel. 1-
474-869. *Pres*. Martha Fernandez de Lopez;
Secy. Luzmila Tello de Medina.

Philippines

Assn. of Special Libs. of the Philippines, Rm.
301, National Lib. Bldg., T. M. Kalaw St.,
Manila. Tel./fax 2-590-177. *Pres*. Zenaida
F. Lucas; *Secy*. Socorro G. Elevera.

Bibliographical Society of the Philippines,
National Lib. of the Philippines, T. M.
Kalaw St., 1000 Ermita, Box 2926, Mani-
la. Tel. 2-583-252, fax 2-502-329, e-mail
amb@max.ph.net. *Secy.-Treas*. Leticia R.
Maloles.

Philippine Libns. Assn., c/o National Lib. of
the Philippines, Rm. 301, Box 2926, T. M.
Kalaw St., Manila. Tel. 2-590-177. *Pres*.
Antonio M. Sontos; *Secy*. Rosemarie Ros-
ali.

Poland

Stowarzyszenie Bibliotekarzy Polskich (Polish Libns. Assn.), Ul. Hankiewicza 1,
02103 Warsaw. Tel. 22-823-0270, fax 22-
822-5133. *Chair* Stanislaw Czajka; *Secy.-
Gen*. Dariusz Kuzminski.

Portugal

Associação Portuguesa de Bibliotecários,
Arquivistas e Documentalistas (Portuguese
Assn. of Libns., Archivists, and Documentalists), R. Morais Soares, 43C-1 DTD,
1900-341 Lisbon. Tel. 1-815-4479, fax 1-
815-4508, e-mail badbn@mail.telepac.pt.
Pres. Ernestina de Castro.

Puerto Rico

Sociedad de Bibliotecarios de Puerto Rico
(Society of Libns. of Puerto Rico), Apdo.
22898, Universidad de Puerto Rico Sta.,
San Juan 00931. Tel. 787-764-0000, fax
787-763-5685, e-mail vtorres@upracd.upr.
clu.edu. *Pres*. Aura Jiménez de Panepinto;
Secy. Olga L. Hernández.

Romania

Asociatüia Bibliotecarilor din Bibliotecile
Publice-România (Assn. of Public Libns.
of Romania), Strada Ion Ghica 4, Sector 3,
79708 Bucharest. Tel. 1-614-2434, fax 1-
312-3381, e-mail bnr@ul.ici.ro. *Pres*.
Gheorghe-Iosif Bercan; *Secy*. Georgeta
Clinca.

Russia

Lib. Council, State V. I. Lenin Lib., Prospect
Kalinina 3, Moscow 101000. Tel. 95-202-
4656. *Exec. Secy*. G. A. Semenova.

Senegal

Association Sénégalaise des Bibliothécaires,
Archivistes et Documentalistes (Sene-
galese Assn. of Libns., Archivists, and
Documentalists), BP 3252, Dakar. Tel.
246-981, fax 242-379. *Pres*. Mariétou
Diongue Diop; *Secy*. Emmanuel Kabou.

Sierra Leone

Sierra Leone Assn. of Archivists, Libns., and
Info. Scientists, c/o Sierra Leone Lib.
Board, Box 326, Freetown. Tel. 223-848.
Pres. Deanna Thomas.

Singapore

Lib. Assn. of Singapore, c/o Bukit Merah
Central, Box 0693, Singapore 9115. *Hon.
Secy*. Siti Hanifah Mustapha.

Slovenia

Zveza Bibliotekarskih Drustev Slovenije (Lib. Assn. of Slovenia), Turjaska 1, 1000 Ljubljana. Tel. 61-200-1193, fax 61-251-3052, World Wide Web http://www.zveza-zbds.si. *Pres.* Stanislav Bahor. E-mail stanislav.bahor@nuk.uni-lj.si. *Secy.* Lijana Hubej.

South Africa

African Lib. Assn. of South Africa, c/o Lib., Univ. of the North, Private Bag X1106, Sovenga 0727. Tel. 1521-689-111, fax 1521-670-152. *Secy./Treas.* A. N. Kambule.

Spain

Asociación Española de Archiveros, Bibliotecarios, Museólogos y Documentalistas (Spanish Assn. of Archivists, Libns., Curators, and Documentalists), Recoletos 5, 28001 Madrid. Tel. 1-575-1727, fax 91-575-1727. *Pres.* Julia M. Rodrigez Barrero.

Sri Lanka

Sri Lanka Lib. Assn., Professional Center, 275/75 Bauddhaloka Mawatha, Colombo 7. Tel. 1-589-103, e-mail postmast@slla.ac.LK. *Pres.* Harrison Perera.

Swaziland

Swaziland Lib. Assn., Box 2309, Mbabane. Tel. 43101, fax 42641. *Chair* L. Dlamini; *Secy.* P. Muswazi.

Sweden

Svenska Arkivsamfundet (Swedish Assn. of Archivists), c/o Riksarkivet, Box 12541, S-10229 Stockholm. Tel. 8-737-6350, fax 8-657-9564, e-mail anna-christina.ulfsparre@riksarkivet.ra.se. *Pres.* Anna Christina Ulfsparre.

Sveriges Allmanna Biblioteksförening (Swedish Lib. Assn.), Box 3127, S-103 62 Stockholm. Tel. 8-5451-3230, fax 8-5451-3231, e-mail christina.stenberg@sab.se, World Wide Web http://www.sab.se. *Secy.-Gen.* Christina Stenberg.

Switzerland

Association des Bibliothèques et Bibliothécaires Suisses/Vereinigung Schweizerischer Bibliothekare/Associazione dei Bibliotecari Svizzeri (Assn. of Swiss Libs. and Libns.), Effingerstr. 35, CH-3008 Berne. Tel. 31-382-4240, fax 31-382-4648, e-mail bbs@bbs.ch, World Wide Web http://www.bbs.ch. *Gen. Secy.* Marianne Tschaeppat.

Schweizerische Vereinigung für Dokumentation/Association Suisse de Documentation (Swiss Assn. of Documentation), Schmidgasse 4, Postfach 601, CH-6301 Zug. Tel. 41-726-4505, fax 41-726-4509. *Pres.* S. Holláander; *Secy.* H. Schweuk.

Verein Schweizerischer Archivarinnen und Archivare (Assn. of Swiss Archivists), Archives Cantonales Vaudoises, rue de la Mouline 32, 1022 Chavanne-près-Renens. Tel. 21-316-3711, e-mail smueller@thenet.ch, World Wide Web http://www.staluzern.ch/vsa. *Pres.* Gilbert Coutaz.

Taiwan

Lib. Assn. of China, c/o National Central Lib., 20 Chungshan S. Rd., Taipei 100-01. Tel. 2-2331-2475, fax 2-2370-0899, e-mail lac@msg.ncl.edu.tw, World Wide Web http://www.lac.ncl.edu.tw. *Pres.* Huang Shih-wson; *Secy.-Gen.* Teresa Wang Chang.

Tanzania

Tanzania Lib. Assn., Box 2645, Dar es Salaam. Tel. 51-402-6121. *Chair* T. E. Mlaki; *Secy.* A. Ngaiza.

Thailand

Thai Lib. Assn., 273 Vibhavadee Rangsit Rd., Phayathai, Bangkok 10400. Tel. 2-271-2084. *Pres.* K. Chavallt; *Secy.* Karnmanee Suckcharoen.

Trinidad and Tobago

Lib. Assn. of Trinidad and Tobago, Box 1275, Port of Spain. Tel. 868-624-5075, e-mail latt@ttemail.com. *Pres.* Esahack Mohammed; *Secy.* Shamin Renwick.

Tunisia

Association Tunisienne des Documentalistes, Bibliothécaires et Archivistes (Tunisian Assn. of Documentalists, Libns., and Archivists), B.P. 380, 1015 Tunis. *Pres.* Ahmed Ksibi.

Turkey

Türk Küüphaneciler Dernegi (Turkish Libns. Assn.), Elgün Sok-8/8, 06440 Yenisehir, Ankara. Tel. 312-230-1325, fax 312-232-0453. *Pres.* A. Berberoglu; *Secy.* A. Kaygusuz.

Uganda

Uganda Lib. Assn., Box 5894, Kampala. Tel. 141-285-001, ext. 4. *Chair* Elisam Naghra; *Secy.* Charles Batembyze.

Ukraine

Ukrainian Lib. Assn., 14 Chyhorin St., Kiev 252042. Tel. 380-44-268-2263, fax 380-44-295-8296. *Pres.* Valentyna S. Pashkova.

United Kingdom

ASLIB (Assn. for Info. Management), Information House, 20-24 Old St., London EC1V 9AP, England. Fax 20-7903-0011, e-mail aslib@aslib.com, World Wide Web http://www.aslib.com. *Dir.* R. B. Bowes.

Bibliographical Society, c/o Welcome Lib., Victoria & Albert Museum, 183 Euston Rd., London NW1 2BE, England. Tel. 20-7611-7244, fax 20-7611-8703, e-mail d.pearson@welcome.ac.uk. *Hon. Secy.* David Pearson.

The Lib. Assn., 7 Ridgmount St., London WC1E 7AE, England. Tel. 20-7255-0650, fax 20-7255-0501, e-mail marketing@ LA-hq.org.uk, World Wide Web http:// www.LA-hq.org.uk. *Chief Exec.* Bob McKee.

School Lib. Assn., Unit 2, Lotmead Business Village, Lotmead Farm, Wanborough, Swindon, Wilts. SN4 0UY, England. Tel. 1793-791-787, fax 1793-791-786, e-mail info@sla.org.uk, World Wide Web http:// www.sla.org.uk. *Pres.* Frank N. Hogg; *Chief Exec.* Kathy Lemaire.

Scottish Lib. Assn., 1 John St., Hamilton ML3 7EU, Scotland. Tel. 1698-458-888, fax 1698-458-899, e-mail sla@slainte. org.uk, World Wide Web http://www. slainte.org.uk. *Dir.* Robert Craig.

Society of Archivists, 40 Northampton Rd., London EC1R 0HB, England. Tel. 20-7278-8630, fax 20-7278-2107, e-mail societyofarchivists@archives.org.uk, World Wide Web http://www.archives.

org.uk. *Exec. Secy.* P. S. Cleary.

Society of College, National & Univ. Libs. (SCONUL) (formerly Standing Conference of National and Univ. Libs.), 102 Euston St., London NW1 2HA, England. Tel. 20-7387-0317, fax 20-7383-3197. *Exec. Secy.* A. J. C. Bainton.

Welsh Lib. Assn., c/o Publications Office, Dept. of Info. and Lib. Studies, Llanbadarn Fawr, Aberystwyth, Dyfed SY23 3AS, Wales. Tel. 1970-622-174, fax 1970-622-190, e-mail hle@aber.ac.uk. *Exec. Officer* Huw Evans.

Uruguay

Agrupación Bibliotecológica del Uruguay (Uruguayan Lib. and Archive Science Assn.), Cerro Largo 1666, 11200 Montevideo. Tel. 2-400-57-40. *Pres.* Luis Alberto Musso.

Asociación de Bibliotecцólogos del Uruguay, Eduardo V. Haedo 2255, CC 1315, Box 1315, 11000 Montevideo. Tel./fax 2-499-989.

Vatican City

Biblioteca Apostolica Vaticana, 00120 Vatican City, Rome. Tel. 6-6988-3302, fax 6-6988-4795, e-mail bav@librsbk.vatlib.it. *Prefect* Don Raffaele Farina.

Venezuela

Colegio de Bibliotecólogos y Archivólogos de Venezuela (Venezuelan Lib. and Archives Assn.), Apdo. 6283, Caracas. Tel. 2-572-1858. *Pres.* Elsi Jimenez de Diaz.

Vietnam

Hôi Thu-Vien Viet Nam (Vietnamese Lib. Assn.), National Lib. of Vietnam, 31 Trang Thi, 10000 Hanoi. Tel. 4-825-2643.

Zambia

Zambia Lib. Assn., Box 32839, Lusaka. *Chair* C. Zulu; *Hon. Secy.* W. C. Mulalami.

Zimbabwe

Zimbabwe Lib. Assn., Box 3133, Harare. *Chair* Driden Kunaka; *Hon. Secy.* Albert Masheka.

Directory of Book Trade and Related Organizations

Book Trade Associations, United States and Canada

For more extensive information on the associations listed in this section, see the annual edition of *Literary Market Place* (Information Today, Inc.).

American Booksellers Assn. Inc., 828 S. Broadway, Tarrytown, NY 10591. Tel. 800-637-0037, 914-591-2665, fax 914-591-2724; World Wide Web http://www. bookweb.org. *Pres.* Neal Coonerty, Bookshop Santa Cruz, 1520 Pacific Ave., Santa Cruz, CA 95060-3903. Tel. 831-460-3224, fax 831-423-8371, e-mail neal@bookshop santacruz.com; *V.P./Secy.* Ann Christophersen, Women & Children First, 5233 N. Clark St., Chicago, IL 60640-2122. Tel. 773-769-9299, fax 773-769-6729, e-mail achristophersen@sprintmail.com; *Chief Exec. Officer* Avin Mark Domnitz.

American Institute of Graphic Arts, 164 Fifth Ave., New York, NY 10010. Tel. 212-807-1990, fax 212-807-1799, e-mail aiga@ aiga.org, World Wide Web http://www. aiga.org.

American Literary Translators Association (ALTA), Univ. of Texas–Dallas, Box 830688, Richardson, TX 75083-0688. Tel. 972-883-2093, fax 972-883-6303, e-mail ert@utdallas.edu, World Wide Web http:// www.utdallas.edu/research/cts/al membershipinformation.html. *Dir.* Rainer Schulte; *Exec. Dir.* Eileen Tollett.

American Medical Publishers Assn., 14 Fort Hill Rd., Huntington, NY 11734. Tel./fax 631-423-0075, e-mail jillrudansky-ampa@ email.msn.com, World Wide Web http:// www.ampaonline.org. *Exec. Dir.* Jill Rudansky.

American Printing History Assn., Box 4922, Grand Central Sta., New York, NY 10163-

4922. *Pres.* Martin Antonetti; *Exec. Secy.* Stephen Crook. E-mail scrook@printing history.org, World Wide Web http://www. printinghistory.org.

American Society of Indexers, 10200 W. 44 Ave., Suite 304, Wheat Ridge, Colorado 80033. Tel 303-463-2887, fax 303-422-8894, e-mail info@asindexing.org, World Wide Web http://www.asindexing.org/site. *Pres.* Diana Witt. E-mail dlwitt@concentric. net; *Exec. Dir.* Jerry Bowman.

American Society of Journalists and Authors, 1501 Broadway, Suite 302, New York, NY 10036. Tel. 212-997-0947, fax 212-768-7414, e-mail execdir@asja.org, World Wide Web http://www.asja.org. *Pres.* Jim Morrison; *Exec. Dir.* Brett Harvey.

American Society of Media Photographers, 150 N. 2 St., Philadelphia, PA 19106. Tel. 215-451-2767, fax 215-451-0880, e-mail Weisgrau@ASMP.org, World Wide Web http://www.asmp.org. *Pres.* Susan Carr; *Exec. Dir.* Richard Weisgrau.

American Society of Picture Professionals, Inc., 409 S. Washington St., Alexandria, VA 22314. Tel./fax 703-299-0219, e-mail aspp1@idsonline.com, World Wide Web http://www.aspp.com. *Exec. Dir.* Cathy Sachs. E-mail cathy@aspp.com.

American Translators Assn., 225 Reinekers Lane, Suite 590, Alexandria, VA 22314. Tel. 703-683-6100, fax 703-683-6122, e-mail ata@atanet.org, World Wide Web http://www.atanet.org. *Pres.* Thomas L. West, III; *Pres.-Elect* Scott Brennan; *Secy.*

Courtney Searls-Ridge; *Treas.* Jiri Stejskal; *Exec. Dir.* Walter W. Bacak, Jr. E-mail walter@atanet.org.

Antiquarian Booksellers Assn. of America, 20 W. 44 St., 4th fl., New York, NY 10036-6604. Tel. 212-944-8291, fax 212-944-8293, e-mail inquiries@abaa.org, World Wide Web http://www.abaa.org.

Assn. of American Publishers, 71 Fifth Ave., New York, NY 10003. Tel. 212-255-0200, fax 212-255-7007. *Pres./CEO* Patricia S. Schroeder; *Exec. V.P.* Thomas D. McKee. *Washington Office* 50 F St. N.W., Washington, DC 20001-1564. Tel. 202-347-3375, fax 202-347-3690. *V.P.s* Allan Adler, Kathryn Blough, Barbara Meredith; *Dir., Communications and Public Affairs* Judith Platt; *Exec. Dir., School Division* Stephen D. Driesler; *Chair* Robert Evanson, McGraw Hill; *V. Chair* Jane Friedman, HarperCollins.

Assn. of American Univ. Presses, 71 W. 23 St., Suite 901, New York, NY 10010. Tel. 212-989-1010, e-mail info@aaupnet.org, World Wide Web http://aaupnet.org. *Pres.* William Sisler; *Exec. Dir.* Peter Givler; *Asst. Exec. Dir./Controller* Timothy Muench. Address correspondence to the executive director.

Assn. of Authors' Representatives, Inc., Box 237201, Ansonia Sta., New York, NY 10023. Tel. 212-252-3695, e-mail aarinc@mindspring.com, World Wide Web http://aar-online.org. *Pres.* Donald Maass; *Admin. Secy.* Leslie Carroll.

Assn. of Canadian Publishers, 110 Eglinton Ave. W., Suite 401, Toronto, ON M4R 1A3. Tel. 416-487-6116, fax 416-487-8815, e-mail info@canbook.org, World Wide Web http://www.publishers.ca. *Exec. Dir.* Monique Smith. Address correspondence to the executive director.

Assn. of Educational Publishers (AEP), 510 Heron Dr., Suite 309, Logan Township, NJ 08085. Tel. 856-241-7772, fax 856-241-0709, e-mail mail@edpress.org, World Wide Web http://www.edpresss.org. *Exec. Dir.* Charlene F. Gaynor.

Assn. of Graphic Communications, 330 Seventh Ave., 9th fl., New York, NY 10001. Tel. 212-279-2100, fax 212-279-5381, World Wide Web http://www.agcomm.org.

Pres. Susan Greenwood. E-mail susie@agcomm.org.

Assn. of Jewish Book Publishers, c/o Jewish Book Council, Attn. Ari Schuchman, 10 E. 26 St., 10th fl., New York, NY 10010. Tel. 212-532-4949 ext. 452, fax 212-481-4174, e-mail owner-ajbp@shamash.org, World Wide Web http://www.avotaynu.com/ajbp. html.

Book Industry Study Group, 750 Hwy. 34, Suite 1, Matawan, NJ 07747. Tel. 732-583-0066, fax 732-583-3652, e-mail bisg-info@bisg.org, World Wide Web http://www.bisg.org.

Book Manufacturers Institute, 65 William St., Suite 300, Wellesley, MA 02481-3800. Tel. 781-239-0103, fax 781-239-0106, e-mail info@bmibook.com, World Wide Web http://www.BMIbook.com. *Pres.* William Flavell, National Publishing Co.; *V.P.* Bruce W. Smith, R. R. Donnelley & Sons Co.; *Exec. V.P./Secy.* Stephen P. Snyder. Address correspondence to the executive vice president.

Book Publicists of Southern California, 6464 Sunset Blvd., Suite 755, Hollywood 90028. Tel. 323-461-3921, fax 323-461-0917, e-mail bookpublicists@aol.com. *Pres.* Ernest Weckbaugh; *V.P.* Patricia Weckbaugh; *Treas.* Lynn Walford; *Pres. Emeritus* Irwin Zucker.

Book Publishers of Texas, 6387 B Camp Bowie No. 340, Fort Worth, TX 76116. Tel. 817-247-6016, e-mail bookpublishersoftexas@att.net, World Wide Web http://www.bookpublishersoftexas.com.

Bookbuilders of Boston, Inc., 26 Bates Way, Hanover, MA 02339-1591. Tel. 781-875-1306, fax 508-782-6926, e-mail office@bbboston.org, World Wide Web: http://www.bbboston.org. *Pres.* Lisa Flanagan, Blackwell Science; *1st V.P.* Sarah Bodden Kopec, Houghton Mifflin; *2nd V.P.* Carol Heston, Victor Graphics; *Treas.* Larry Bisso, Edwards Brothers; *Secy.* Heather Irish Valeri

Bookbuilders West, Box 7046, San Francisco, CA 94120-9727. Tel. 415-273-5790, World Wide Web http://www.bookbuilders.org; *Pres.* Mary Lou Goforth, Banta Book Group; *1st V.P.* Michele Bisson Savoy, Quebecor World; *2nd V.P.* Larry Lazapoulos, McGraw-Hill Higher Education; *Secy.* Ramona Beville, Sheriden Books; *Treas.* Michael O'Brien, GTS Companies.

Canadian Booksellers Assn.,789 Don Mills Rd., Suite 700, Toronto, ON M3C 1T5. Tel. 416-467-7883, fax 416-467-7886, e-mail enquiries@cbabook.org, World Wide Web http://www.cbabook.org. *Gen. Mgr.* Susan Dayus. E-mail sdayus@cbabook.org.

Canadian ISBN Agency, c/o Acquisitions and Bibliographic Services Branch, National Library of Canada, 395 Wellington St., Ottawa, ON K1A 0N4. Tel. 819-994-6872, fax 819-997-7517, e-mail isbn@nlc-bnc.ca.

Canadian Printing Industries Association, 75 Albert St., Suite 906, Ottawa, ON K1P 5E7. Tel. 613-236-7208, fax 613-236-8169, World Wide Web http://www.cpia-aci.ca. *Pres.* Pierre Boucher; *Chair* Steve Cropper; *V. Chair* Bob Kadis.

Catholic Book Publishers Assn. Inc., 8404 Jamesport Dr., Rockford, IL 61108. Tel. 815-332-3245, e-mail cbpa3@aol.com, World Wide Web http://cbpa.org; *Pres.* John D. Wright; *V.P.* Kay Weiss; *Secy.* Thomas R. Artz; *Treas.* Matthew Thibeau; *Exec. Dir.* Terry Wessels.

Chicago Book Clinic, 5443 N. Broadway, Suite 101, Chicago, IL 60640. Tel. 773-561-4150, fax 773-561-1343, e-mail kgboyer@ix.netcom.com, World Wide Web http://www.chicagobookclinic.org. *Pres.* Scott Hamilton; *Exec. Dir.* Kevin G. Boyer.

Children's Book Council, Inc., 12 W. 37 St., 2nd fl., New York, NY 10018-7480. Tel. 212-966-1990, fax 212-966-2073, e-mail info@CBCbooks.org, World Wide Web http://www.cbcbooks.org. *Pres.* Paula Quint; *V.P., Marketing and Publicity* JoAnn Sabatino-Falkenstein.

Copyright Society of the USA. E-mail barpan@rcn.com. *Pres.* Robert J. Bernstein; *Admin.* Barbara S. Pannone; *Secy.* Maria A. Danzilo; *Treas.* Barry Slotnick.

Council of Literary Magazines & Presses, 154 Christopher St., Suite 3C, New York, NY 10014. Tel. 212-741-9110, fax 212-741-9112, e-mail info@clmp.org, World Wide Web http://clmp.org. *Interim Exec. Dir.* Jeffrey Lependorf.

Educational Paperback Assn., *Pres.* Thomas J. Milano; *V.P.* Dick Tinder; *Treas.* Jennifer Carrico; *Exec. Secy.* Marilyn Abel, Box 1399, East Hampton, NY 11937. Tel. 212-879-6850, e-mail edupaperback@aol.com.

Evangelical Christian Publishers Assn., 1969 E. Broadway Rd., Suite 2, Tempe, AZ 85282. Tel. 480-966-3998, fax 480-966-1944, e-mail dross@ecpa.org. *Pres.* Doug Ross.

Friendship Press, 475 Riverside Dr., Suite 860, New York, NY 10115. Tel. 212-870-2896, fax 212-870-2030, World Wide Web http://www.bruno.nccusa.org.

Graphic Artists Guild, Inc., 90 John St., Suite 403, New York, NY 10038. Tel. 212-791-3400, fax 212-792-0333, e-mail execdir@gag.org, World Wide Web http://www.gag.org. *Exec. Dir.* Steve Schubert. Address correspondence to the executive director.

Great Lakes Booksellers Assn., c/o *Exec. Dir.* Jim Dana, Box 901, 208 Franklin St., Grand Haven, MI 49417. Tel. 616-847-2460, fax 616-842-0051, e-mail glba@books-glba.org, World Wide Web http://www.books-glba.org. *Pres.* Tom Lowry, Lowry's Books, Three Rivers, MI 49093; *V.P.* Dave Kaverman, Little Professor Book Company.

Guild of Book Workers, 521 Fifth Ave., New York, NY 10175. Tel. 212-292-4444, World Wide Web http://palimpsest.stanford.edu/byorg/gbw. *Memb. Secy.* Bernadette Callery. E-mail bcallery@flounder.com.

International Association of Printing House Craftsmen, Inc. (IAPHC), 7042 Brooklyn Blvd., Minneapolis, MN 55429. Tel. 800-466-4274, 612-560-1620, fax 612-560-1350, World Wide Web http://www.iaphc.org/. *Chair* Tom Blanchard. E-mail tom.blanchard@rogers.com; *V. Chair* Howard Drayson. E-mail dbmman@aol.com; *Pres./CEO* Kevin Keane. E-mail kkeane1069@aol.com.

International Standard Book Numbering U.S. Agency, 630 Central Ave., New Providence, NJ 07974. Tel. 877-310-7333, fax 908-665-2895, e-mail ISBN-SAN@bowker.com, World Wide Web http://www.ISBN.org. *Chair* Michael Cairns; *Dir.* Doreen

Gravesande; *Industrial Relations Mgr.* Don Riseborough; *SAN Mgr.* Diana Luongo.

Jewish Book Council, 15 E. 26 St., 10th fl., New York, NY 10010. Tel. 212-532-4949 ext. 297, fax 212-481-4174, e-mail carolyn hessel@jewishbooks.org. *Exec. Dir.* Carolyn Starman Hessel.

Library Binding Institute, 70 E. Lake St., Suite 300, Chicago, IL 60601. Tel. 312-704-5020, fax 312-704-5025, e-mail info @lbibinders.org, World Wide Web http:// www.lbibinders.org. *Pres.* Gary Wert; *V.P.* John Salistean; *Treas.* Jay B. Fairfield; *Exec. Dir.* Joanne Rock.

Magazine Publishers of America, Inc., 919 Third Ave., 22nd fl., New York, NY 10022. Tel. 212-872-3700, fax 212-888-4217, e-mail mpa@magazine.org, World Wide Web http://www.magazine.org. *Pres.* Nina Link. Tel. 212-872-3710; *Exec. V.P./Gen. Manager* Michael Pashby. Tel. 212-872-3750.

Midwest Independent Publishers Assn., Box 581432, Minneapolis, MN 55458-1432. Tel. 651-917-0021, World Wide Web http://www.mipa.org; *Pres.* Archie Spencer. E-mail acespencer@aol.com.

Miniature Book Society, Inc., c/o *Pres.* Neale M. Albert, 815 Park Ave., New York, NY 10021. Tel. 212-861-9093, fax 212-772-9905, e-mail nma815@aol.com; *V.P.* Jon Mayo, Box 74, North Clarendon, VT 05759. Tel. 802-773-9695, fax 802-773-1493, e-mail microbib@sover.net; *Secy.* Patricia Pistner, 10 Seagate Dr. PH 1N, Naples, FL 34103. Tel. 941-263-6005, fax 941-263-4544, e-mail pistner@mediaone. net; *Treas.* Mark Palcovic, 620 Clinton Springs Ave., Cincinnati, OH 45229-1325. Tel. 513-861-3554, fax 513-556-2113. World Wide Web http://www.mbs.org.

Minnesota Book Publishers Roundtable. *Pres.* Dorothy Molstad, Waldman House Press, 525 N. 3rd St., Minneapolis 55401. Tel. 612-341-4044, fax 612-925-3626, e-mail dendoor@aol.com; *V.P.* Jim Cihlar, Redleaf Press, 450N. Syndicate Ave., No. 5, St. Paul 55104. Tel. 651-641-6629, fax 651-645-0990, e-mail jcihlar@redleafpress. org; *Secy.* Nancy Mostad, Llewellyn Worldwide, Ltd., 84 S. Wabasha, St. Paul 55107.

Tel. 651-291-1970, fax 651-291-1908, e-mail nancym@llewellyn.com; *Treas.* Brad Vogt, Bradley & Assoc., 40214 Wallaby Rd., Rice 56367. Tel. 320-260-3594, fax 320-656-9520, e-mail bvogt@cloudnet. com. World Wide Web http://www. publishersroundtable.org. Address correspondence to the treasurer.

Mountains and Plains Booksellers Assn., 19 Old Town Sq., Suite 238, Fort Collins, CO 80524. Tel. 970-484-5856, fax 970-407-1479, e-mail lknudsen@mountainsplains. org, World Wide Web http://www. mountainsplains.org. *Exec. Dir.* Lisa Knudsen; *Pres.* Cathy Langer; *Secy./Treas.* Linda Brummett.

National Assn. for Printing Leadership, 75 W. Century Rd., Paramus, NJ 07652. Tel. 201-634-9600, fax 201-634-0324, e-mail napl@napl.org, World Wide Web http:// www.napl.org. *Pres.* I. Gregg Van Wert. E-mail gvanwert@napl.org.

National Assn. of College Stores, 500 E. Lorain St., Oberlin, OH 44074-1294. Tel. 440-775-7777, fax 440-775-4769, e-mail info @nacs.org, World Wide Web http://www. nacs.org. *Chief Exec. Officer* Brian Cartier.

National Assn. of Independent Publishers, Box 430, Highland City, FL 33846. Tel./ fax 863-648-4420, e-mail NAIP@aol.com. World Wide Web http://www.publishers report.com.

National Coalition Against Censorship (NCAC), 275 Seventh Ave., 20th fl., New York, NY 10001. Tel. 212-807-6222, fax 212-807-6245, e-mail NCAC@NCAC.org, World Wide Web http://www.ncac.org.

National Council of Churches, Rm. 850, 475 Riverside Dr., New York, NY 10115. Tel. 212-870-2385, fax 212-870-2265, e-mail news@ncccusa.org. *Gen. Secy.* Bob Edgar.

New Atlantic Independent Booksellers Assn., 2667 Hyacinth St., Westbury, NY 11590. Tel. 516-333-0681, fax 516-333-0689, e-mail info@naiba.com. *Exec. Dir.* Eileen Dengler.

New England Booksellers Assn., 1770 Massachusetts Ave., Cambridge, MA 02140. Tel. 800-466-8711, fax 617-576-3091, e-mail rusty@neba.org, World Wide Web http://www.newenglandbooks.org. *Pres.*

Linda Ramsdell; *V.P.* Susan Novotny; *Treas.* Peter Sevenair; *Exec. Dir.* Wayne A. Drugan, Jr.

New Mexico Book League, 8632 Horacio Place N.E., Albuquerque, NM 87111. Tel. 505-299-8940, fax 505-294-8032. *Ed., Book Talk* Carol A. Myers.

North American Bookdealers Exchange, Box 606, Cottage Grove, OR 97424. Tel. 541-942-7455, fax 561-258-2625, e-mail nabe @bookmarketingprofits.com, World Wide Web http://bookmarketingprofits.com. *Dir.* Al Galasso.

Northern California Independent Booksellers Assn., The Presidio, 37 Graham St., Suite 210, Box 29169, San Francisco, CA 94129. Tel. 415-561-7686, fax 415-561-7685, e-mail office@nciba.com, World Wide Web http://www.nciba.com. *Pres.* Karen Pennington; *Exec. Dir.* Hut Landon.

Pacific Northwest Booksellers Assn., 317 W. Broadway, Suite 214, Eugene, OR 97401-2890. Tel. 541-683-4363, fax 541-683-3910, e-mail info@pnba.org. *Pres.* Holly Myers, Elliott Bay Book Co., 101 S. Main St., Seattle, WA 98104-2581. Tel. 206-624-6600, fax 206-903-1601, E-mail hmyers @elliottbaybook.com; *Exec. Dir.* Thom Chambliss.

PEN American Center, Div. of International PEN, 568 Broadway, New York, NY 10012. Tel. 212-334-1660, fax 212-334-2181, e-mail pen@pen.org, World Wide Web http://www.pen.org.

Periodical and Book Assn. of America, Inc., 120 E. 34 St., Suite 7K, New York, NY 10016. Tel. 212-689-4952, fax 212-545-8328, e-mail PBAA@aol.com. *Exec. Dir.* Richard T. Browne.

Periodical Wholesalers of North America and Periodical Marketers of Canada, 1007-175 Bloor St. E., South Tower, Toronto, ON M4W 3R8. Tel. 416-968-7218, fax 416-968-6182.

Philadelphia Book Clinic, c/o *Secy.* Thomas Colaiezzi, 136 Chester Ave., Yeadon, PA 19050-3831. Tel. 610-259-7022, fax 610-394-9886.

Publishers Marketing Assn., 627 Aviation Way, Manhattan Beach, CA 90266. Tel. 310-372-2732, fax 310-374-3342, e-mail info@pma-online.org, World Wide Web http://www.pma-online.org. *Pres.* Linda Ligon, Interweave Press, Inc., 201 E. Fourth St., Loveland CO 80537-5655. Tel. 970-669-7672, fax 970-667-8317; Exec. Dir. *Jan Nathan.*

Research and Engineering Council of the Graphic Arts Industry, Inc., Box 1086, White Stone, VA 22578. Tel. 804-436-9922, fax 804-436-9511, e-mail recouncil @rivnet.net, World Wide Web http://www. recouncil.org. *Pres.* Laura Gale; *Exec. V.P./Secy.* Jeffrey White; *Exec. V.P./ Treas.* Lynn Poretta; *Managing Dir.* Ronald Mihills.

Romance Writers of America, 3707 FM 1960 W., Suite 555, Houston, TX 77068. Tel. 281-440-6885, fax 281-440-7510, e-mail info@rwanational.com, World Wide Web http://www.rwanational.com. *Pres.* Harold Lowry; *Pres.-Elect* Shirley Hailstock; *Secy.* Nancy Fraser; *Treas.* Ruth MacLean.

Science Fiction and Fantasy Writers of America, Inc., Box 877, Chestertown, MD 21620. E-mail execdir@sfwa.org, World Wide Web http://www.sfwa.org. *Pres.* Norman Spinrad; *V.P.* Sharon Lee; *Secy.* Madeleine E. Robins; *Treas.* Chuck Rothman; *Exec. Dir.* Jane Jewell.

Small Press Center, 20 W. 44 St., New York, NY 10036. Tel. 212-764-7021, fax 212-354-5365, World Wide Web http://www. smallpress.org. *Exec. Dir.* Karin Taylor.

Small Publishers Assn. of North America (SPAN), Box 1306-W, Buena Vista, CO 81211-1306. Tel. 719-395-4790, fax 719-395-8374, e-mail SPAN@SPANnet.org, World Wide Web http://www.SPANnet. org. *Exec. Dir.* Marilyn Ross.

Society of Children's Book Writers & Illustrators (SCBWI), 8271 Beverly Blvd., Los Angeles, CA 90048. Tel. 323-782-1010, fax 323-782-1892, e-mail stephenmooser @scbwi.org, World Wide Web http:// www.scbwi.org. *Pres.* Stephen Mooser; *Exec. Dir.* Lin Oliver.

Society of Illustrators (SI), 128 E. 63 St., New York, NY 10021. Tel. 212-838-2560, fax 212-838-2561, e-mail SI1901@aol. com, World Wide Web http://www.society illustrators.org.

Society of National Association Publications (SNAP), 1595 Spring Hill Rd., Suite 330, Tysons Corner, Vienna, VA 22182. Tel. 703-506-3285, fax 703-506-3266, e-mail snapinfo@snaponline.org, World Wide Web http://www.snaponline.org. *Pres.* Howard Hoskins; *V.P.* Fred Haag; *Treas.* John Grady.

Technical Assn. of the Pulp and Paper Industry, 15 Technology Pkwy. South Norcross, GA 30092; postal address Box 105113, Atlanta, GA 30348. Tel. 770-446-1400, fax 770-446-6947, World Wide Web http://www.tappi.org. *Pres.* Richard G. Barker; *Exec. Dir.* W. H. Gross.

West Coast Book People Assn., 27 McNear Dr., San Rafael, CA 94901. *Exec. Dir.* Frank G. Goodall. Tel. 415-459-1227, fax 415-459-1227, e-mail goodall27@aol.com.

Western Writers of America, Inc., c/o *Secy./Treas.* James Crutchfield, 1012 Fair St., Franklin, TN 37064. World Wide Web http://www.westernwriters.org. *Pres.* Loren D. Estleman; *V.P.* Paul Andrew Hutton.

Women's National Book Assn., 26 W. 17 St., Suite 504, New York, NY 10011. Tel. 212-727-7271, fax 212-208-4629, e-mail wnba@bookbuzz.com. *Pres.* Nancy Stewart; *Treas.* Margaret Auer; *Past Pres.* Diane Ullius.

International and Foreign Book Trade Associations

For Canadian book trade associations, see the preceding section, "Book Trade Associations, United States and Canada." For a more extensive list of book trade organizations outside the United States and Canada, with more detailed information, consult *International Literary Market Place* (Information Today, Inc.), which also provides extensive lists of major bookstores and publishers in each country.

International

Afro-Asian Book Council, 4835/24 Ansari Rd., Daryaganj, New Delhi 110-002, India. Tel. 11-326-1487, fax 11-326-7437, e-mail del.nail@axcess.net.in. *Chair* Mohiuddin Ahmed; *Secy.-Gen.* Sukumar Das; *Dir.* Abul Hasan.

Centre Régional pour la Promotion du Livre en Afrique (Regional Center for Book Promotion in Africa), Box 1646, Yaoundé, Cameroon. Tel. 22-4782/2936. *Secy.* William Moutchia.

Centro Régional para el Fomento del Libro en América Latina y el Caribe (CERLALC) (Regional Center for Book Promotion in Latin America and the Caribbean), Calle 70, No. 9-52, Apdo. Aéreo 57348, Santafé de Bogotá 2, Colombia. Tel. 1-249-5141, fax 1-255-4614, e-mail cerlalc@impsat. net.co. *Dir.* Carmen Barvo.

Federation of European Publishers, Ave. de Tervueren 204, B-1150, Brussels, Belgium. Tel. 2-770-1110, fax 2-771-2071, e-mail fep.Alemann@brutele.be. *Pres.* Michael Gill; *Dir.* Mechtild Von Alemann.

International Board on Books for Young People (IBBY), Nonnenweg 12, Postfach, CH-4055 Basel, Switzerland. Tel. 61-272-2917, fax 61-272-2757, e-mail ibby@eye. ch, ibby@ibby.org. *Dir.* Leena Maissen.

International Booksellers Federation, Rue de Grand Hospice 34A, B1000 Brussels, Belgium. Tel. 2-223-4940, fax 2-223-4941, e-mail eurobooks@skynet.be. *Pres.* Yvonne Steinberger; *Gen. Secy.* Christiane Vuidar.

International Assn. of Scientific, Technical and Medical Publishers (STM), Muurhuisen 165, 3811 EG Amersfoort, Netherlands. Tel. 33-465-6060, fax 33-465-6538, e-mail lefebvre@stm.nl, World Wide Web http:/www.stm-assoc.org. *Secy.* Lex Lefebvre.

International League of Antiquarian Booksellers, 400 Summit Ave., Saint Paul, MN 55102. Tel. 800-441-0076, 612-290-0700, fax 612-290-0646, e-mail rulon@winternet. com, World Wide Web http://www.ilab. org. *Secy. Gen.* Rob Rulon-Miller.

International Publishers Assn. (Union Internationale des Editeurs), Ave. Miremont 3, CH-1206 Geneva, Switzerland. Tel. 22-346-3018, fax 22-347-5717, e-mail secretariat@ipa-uie.org, World Wide Web http://www.ipa-uie.org. *Pres.* Pere Vicens; *Secy.-Gen.* Benoît Muller.

Seminar on the Acquisition of Latin American Library Materials, Secretariat, General Lib., Univ. of New Mexico, Albuquerque, NM 87131-1466. Tel. 505-277-5102, fax 505-277-0646. *Exec. Secy.* Sharon A. Moynahan.

National

Argentina

Cámara Argentina de Publicaciones (Argentine Publications Assn.), Lavalle 437, 6 D-Edif Adriático, 6 piso, 1047 Buenos Aires. Tel./fax 011-4394-2892. *Pres.* Agustin dos Santos.

Cámara Argentina del Libro (Argentine Book Assn.), Avda. Belgrano 1580, 4 piso, 1093 Buenos Aires. Tel. 1-4381-8383, fax 1-4381-9253. *Dir.* Norberto J. Pou.

Fundación El Libro (Book Foundation), Hipolito Yrigoyen 1628, 5 piso, 1344 Buenos Aires. Tel. 1-4374-3288, fax 1-4375-0268, e-mail fund@libro.satlink.net, World Wide Web http://www.el-libro. com.ar. *Pres.* Jorge Naveiro; *Dir.* Marta V. Diaz.

Australia

Australian and New Zealand Assn. of Antiquarian Booksellers, 69 Broadway, Nedlands, WA 6009. Tel. 8-9386-5842, e-mail anazaab@iinet.net.au, World Wide Web http://www.anzaab.com.au. *Secy.* Nicholas Dawes.

Australian Booksellers Assn., 136 Rundle Mall, Adelaide, SA 5000. Tel. 3-9663-7888, fax 3-9663-7557. *Pres.* Tim Peach; *Exec. Dir.* Celia Pollock.

Australian Publishers Assn., Ste. 59, 89 Jones St., Ultimo, NSW 2007. Tel. 2-9281-9788, fax 2-9281-1073, e-mail apa@magna.com.au, World Wide Web http://www.publishers.asn.au. *Pres.* Sandy Grant; *Exec. Dir.* Susan Bridge.

National Book Council, 71 Collins St., Melbourne, Vic. 3000. Tel. 3-663-8043, fax 3-663-8658. *Pres.* Michael G. Zifcak; *Exec. Dir.* Thomas Shapcott.

Austria

Hauptverband des Österreichischen Buchhandels (Austrian Publishers and Booksellers Assn.), Grünangergasse 4, A-1010 Vienna. Tel. 1-512-1535, fax 1-512-8482, World Wide Web http://www.buecher.at. *Pres.* Anton C. Hilscher.

Verband der Antiquare Österreichs (Austrian Antiquarian Booksellers Assn.), Grünangergasse 4, A-1010 Vienna. Tel. 1-512-1535, fax 1-512-8482, e-mail hbv-wein@austrobook.co.at. *Pres.* Hansjörg Krug.

Belarus

National Book Chamber of Belarus, 31a Very Khoruzhey St., 220002 Minsk. Tel./fax 172-769-396, e-mail palata@palata.belpak.minsk.by. *Contact* Anatoli Voronko.

Belgium

Vereniging ter Bevordering van het Vlaamse Boekwezen (Assn. for the Promotion of Dutch Language Books/Books from Flanders), Hof ter Schriecklaan 17, 2600 Berchem/Antwerp. Tel. 3-230-8923, fax 3-281-2240. *Pres.* Andre Van Halewyck; *Dir.* Dorian Van Der Brempt.

Vlaamse Boekverkopersbond (Flemish Booksellers Assn.), Hof ter Schriecklaan 17, 2600 Berchem/Antwerp. Tel. 3-239-5740, fax 3-230-8835, e-mail luc.tessens@vbvb.be. *Pres.* Herwig Staes; *Gen. Secy.* Luc Tessens.

Bolivia

Cámara Boliviana del Libro (Bolivian Booksellers Assn.), Casilla 682, Calle Capitan Ravelo No. 2116, La Paz. Tel./fax 2-327-039, e-mail cabolib@ceibo.entelnet.bo. *Pres.* Rolando S. Condori; *Secy.* Teresa G. de Alvarez.

Brazil

Cámara Brasileira do Livro (Brazilian Book Assn.), Av. Ipiranga 1267, 10 andar, 01039-907 São Paulo. Tel. 11-229-7855, fax 11-229-5258. *Gen. Mgr.* Aloysio T. Costa.

Sindicato Nacional dos Editores de Livros (Brazilian Publishers Assn.), SDS, Edif. Venancio VI, Loja 9/17, 70000 Brasilia, Brazil. Tel. 21-233-6481, fax 21-253-8502. *Pres.* Sérgio Abreu da Cruz Machado; *Exec. Secy.* Henrique Maltese.

Chile

Cámara Chilena del Libro AG (Chilean Assn. of Publishers, Distributors, and Booksellers), Casilla 13526, Santiago. Tel. 2-698-9519, fax 2-698-9226, e-mail camlibro@reuna.cl, World Wide Web http://www.camlibro.cl. *Exec. Secy.* Carlos Franz.

Colombia

Cámara Colombiana del Libro (Colombian Book Assn.), Carrera 17A, No. 37-27, Apdo. Aéreo 8998, Santafé de Bogotá. Tel. 1-288-6188, fax 1-287-3320.

Czech Republic

Svaz ceskych knihkupcu a nakladetelu (Czech Publishers and Booksellers Assn.), Jana Masaryka 56, 120 00 Prague 2. Tel. 2-2423-9003-0150, fax 2-2251-3198, e-mail sckn@mbox.vol.cz, World Wide Web http://www.sckn.cz. *Chair* Jitka Undeova.

Denmark

Danske Boghandlerforening (Danish Booksellers Assn.), Siljangade 6.3, DK 2200 Copenhagen S. Tel. 3254-2255, fax 3254-0041, e-mail ddb@bogpost.dk, World Wide Web http://www.bogguide.dk. *Pres.* Jesper Moller.

Danske Forlaeggerforening (Danish Publishers Assn.), 18/1 Kompagnistr. 1208, Copenhagen K. Tel. 3315-6688, fax 3315-6588, e-mail publassn@webpartner.dk. *Dir.* Tune Olsen.

Ecuador

Cámara Ecuatoriana del Libro, Núcleo de Pichincha, Avda. Eloy Alfaro No. 355, piso 9, Casilla 17-01, Quito. Tel. 2-553-311, fax 2-222-150, e-mail celnp@hoy.net. *Pres.* Luis Mora Ortega.

Egypt

General Egyptian Book Organization, Corniche El-Nil-Boulaq, Cairo. Tel. 2-775-371, 2-775-649, fax 2-754-213. *Chair* Ezz El Dine Ismail.

Estonia

Estonian Publishers Assn., Box 3366, EE0090 Tallinn. Tel. 2-443-937, fax 2-445-720. *Dir.* A. Tarvis.

Finland

Kirjakauppaliitto Ry (Booksellers Assn. of Finland), Eerikinkatu 15-17 D 43-44, 00100 Helsinki. Tel. 9-6859-9110, fax 9-6859-9119, e-mail toimisto@kirjakauppaliitto.fi. *Chief Exec.* Olli Eräkivi.

Suomen Kustannusyhdistys (Finnish Book Publishers Assn.), Box 177, FIN-00121 Helsinki. Tel. 9-2287-7250, fax 9-612-1226, e-mail finnpubl@skyry.pp.fi. *Dir.* Veikko Sonninen.

France

Cercle de la Librairie (Circle of Professionals of the Book Trade), 35 Rue Grégoire-de-Tours, F-75006 Paris. Tel. 1-44-41-28-00, fax 1-44-41-28-65. *Pres.* Charles Henri Flammarion.

Fédération Française des Syndicats de Libraires-FFSL (French Booksellers Assn.), 43 Rue de Châteaudun, F-75009 Paris. Tel. 1-42-82-00-03, fax 1-42-82-10-51. *Pres.* Jean-Luc Dewas.

France Edition, 115 Blvd. Saint-Germain, F-75006 Paris. Tel. 1-44-41-13-13, fax 1-46-34-63-83, e-mail info@franceedition.org, World Wide Web http://www.franceedition.org. *Chair* Liana Levi. *New York Branch* French Publishers Agency, 853 Broadway, New York, NY 10003-4703. Tel. 212-254-4520, fax 212-979-6229.

Syndicat National de la Librairie Ancienne et Moderne (National Assn. of Antiquarians and Modern Booksellers), 4 Rue Gît-le-Coeur, F-75006 Paris. Tel. 1-43-29-46-38, fax 1-43-25-41-63, e-mail slam@worldnet.fr, World Wide Web http://www.slam-livre.fr. *Pres.* Alain Marchiset.

Syndicat National de l'Edition (National Union of Publishers), 115 Blvd. Saint-Germain, F-75006 Paris. Tel. 1-44-41-40-50, fax 1-44-14-077. *Pres.* Serge Eyrolles.

Union des Libraires de France, 40 Rue Grégoire-de-Tours, F-75006 Paris. Tel./fax 1-43-29-88-79. *Pres.* Eric Hardin; *Gen. Delegate* Marie-Dominique Doumenc.

Germany

Börsenverein des Deutschen Buchhandels e.V. (Stock Exchange of German Booksellers), Postfach 100442, 60004 Frankfurt-am-Main. Tel. 69-1306-0, fax 69-1306-201. *Gen. Mgr.* Harald Heker.

Verband Deutscher Antiquare e.V. (German Antiquarian Booksellers Assn.), Kreuzgasse 2-4, Postfach 10-10-20, 50504 Cologne. Tel./fax 221-92-54-82-62, e-mail buch@antiquare.de, World Wide Web http://www.antiquare.de. *Pres.* Jochen Granier; *V.P.* Inge Utzt.

Ghana

University Bookshop (formerly West African University Booksellers Assn.), Univ. of Ghana, Box 1, Legon. Tel. 21-775-301. *Mgr.* E. H. Tonyigah.

Greece

Hellenic Federation of Publishers and Booksellers, Themistocleous 73, 10683 Athens.
Tel. 1-330-0924, fax 1-330-1617, e-mail
poev@otenet.gr. *Pres.* Georgios Dardanos.

Hungary

Magyar Könyvkiadók és Könyvterjesztök
Egyesülése (Assn. of Hungarian Publishers and Booksellers), PB 130, 1367 Budapest. Tel. 1-343-2540, fax 1-343-2541.
Pres. István Bart; *Secy.-Gen.* Péter Zentai.

Iceland

Félag Islenskra Bókaútgefenda (Icelandic
Publishers Assn.), Baronsstig 5, 101 Reykjavik. Tel. 511-8020, fax 511-5020, e-mail
baekur@mmedia.is, World Wide Web
http://www.bokautgefa.is. *Chair* Sigurdur
Svavarsson; *Gen. Mgr.* Vilborg Hardardóttir.

India

Federation of Indian Publishers, Federation
House, 18/1-C Institutional Area, JNU
Rd., Aruna Asaf Ali Marg, New Delhi
110067. Tel. 11-696-4847, 685-2263, fax
11-686-4054. *Pres.* Shri R. C. Govil; *Exec.
Secy.* S. K. Ghai.

Indonesia

Ikatan Penerbit Indonesia (Assn. of Indonesian Book Publishers), Jl. Kalipasir 32,
Jakarta 10330. Tel. 21-314-1907, fax 21-
314-6050. *Pres.* Rozali Usman; *Secy. Gen.*
Setia Dharma Majidd.

Ireland

CLÉ: The Irish Book Publishers Assn., The
Writers Centre, 19 Parnell Sq., Dublin 1.
Tel. 1-872-9090, fax 1-872-2035. *Contact*
Orla Martin.

Israel

Book and Printing Center, Israel Export Institute, 29 Hamered St., Box 50084, Tel Aviv
68125. Tel. 3-514-2916, fax 3-514-2881,
e-mail israeli@export.gov.il, World Wide
Web http://www.export.gov.il. *Dir.* Ronit
Adler.

Book Publishers Assn. of Israel, Box 20123,
Tel Aviv 67132. Tel. 3-561-4121, fax 3-
561-1996, e-mail tbpai@netvision.net.il.
Managing Dir. Amnon Ben-Shmuel.

Italy

Associazione Italiana Editori (Italian Publishers Assn.), Via delle Erbe 2, 20121 Milan.
Tel. 2-86-46-3091, fax 2-89-01-0863,
e-mail aie@aie.it, World Wide Web http://
www.aie.it. *Dir.* Ivan Cecchini.

Associazione Librai Antiquari d'Italia (Anti-
quarian Booksellers Assn. of Italy), Via
Jacopo Nardi 6, I-50132 Florence. Tel./fax
55-24-3253, e-mail alai@dada.it/alai,
World Wide Web http://www.dada.it/alai/.
Pres. Giuliano Gallini; *Secy.* Francesco
Scala.

Jamaica

Booksellers' Assn. of Jamaica, c/o Novelty
Trading Co. Ltd., Box 80, Kingston. Tel.
876-922-5883, fax 876-922-4743. *Pres.*
Keith Shervington.

Japan

Japan Assn. of International Publications
(formerly Japan Book Importers Assn.),
Chiyoda Kaikan 21-4, Nihonbashi 1-
chome, Chuo-ku, Tokyo 103. Tel. 3-32-
71-6901, fax 3-32-71-6920. *Chair* Nobuo
Suzuki.

Japan Book Publishers Assn., 6 Fukuro-
machi, Shinjuku-ku, Tokyo 162. Tel. 3-32-
68-1301, fax 3-32-68-1196. *Pres.* Takao
Watanabe; *Exec. Dir.* Toshikazu Gomi.

Kenya

Kenya Publishers Assn., c/o Phoenix Publishers Ltd., Box 18650, Nairobi. Tel. 2-22-
2309, 2-22-3262, fax 2-33-9875. *Secy.*
Stanley Irura.

Korea (Republic of)

Korean Publishers Assn., 105-2 Sagan-dong,
Jongro-gu, Seoul 110-190. Tel. 2-735-
2701, fax 2-738-5414, e-mail kpasibf@

soback.kornet.nm.kr. *Pres.* Choon Ho Na; *Secy.-Gen.* Jung Jong-Jin.

Latvia

Latvian Publishers Assn., K Barona iela 36-4, 1011 Riga. Tel. 371-728-2392, fax 371-728-0549, e-mail Lga@parks.lv. *Exec. Dir.* Dace Pugaca.

Lithuania

Lithuanian Publishers Assn., Z Sierakausko 15, 62600 Vilnius. Tel. 2-332-943, fax 2-330-519. *Pres.* Aleksandras Krasnovas.

Mexico

Cámara Nacional de la Industria Editorial Mexicana (Mexican Publishers' Assn.), Holanda No. 13, CP 04120, Mexico 21. Tel. 5-604-5338, fax 5-604-3147. *Co-Pres.* A. H. Gayosso, J. C. Cramerez.

The Netherlands

KVB (formerly Koninklijke Vereeniging ter Bevordering van de Belangen des Boekhandels) (Royal Dutch Book Trade Assn.), Postbus 15007, 1001 MA Amsterdam. Tel. 20-624-0212, fax 20-620-8871, e-mail info@kvb.nl, World Wide Web http://www.kvb.nl. *Exec. Dir.* C. Verberne.

Nederlands Uitgeversverbond (Royal Dutch Publishers Assn.), Postbus 12040, 1100 AA Amsterdam. Tel. 20-430-9150, fax 20-430-9179, e-mail info@uitgeversverbond.nl, World Wide Web http://www.uitgeversverbond.nl. *Pres.* Henk J. L. Vonhoff.

Nederlandsche Vereeniging van Antiquaren (Netherlands Assn. of Antiquarian Booksellers), Postbus 364, 3500 AJ, Utrecht. Tel. 30-231-9286, fax 30-234-3362, e-mail bestbook@wxs.nl, World Wide Web http://nvva.nl. *Pres.* F. W. Kuyper; *Secy.* Gert Jan Bestebreurtje.

Nederlandse Boekverkopersbond (Dutch Booksellers Assn.), Postbus 32, 3720 AA Bilthoven. Tel. 70-228-7956, fax 70-228-4566. World Wide Web http://www.boekbond.nl. *Pres.* W. Karssen; *Exec. Secy.* A. C. Doeser.

New Zealand

Booksellers New Zealand, Northshore Mail Center, Auckland 1. Tel. 4-472-8678, fax 4-472-8628. *Chair* Tony Moores.

Nigeria

Nigerian Publishers Assn., GPO Box 2541, Ibadan. Tel. 2-496-3007, fax 2-496-4370. *Pres.* V. Nwankwo.

Norway

Norske Bokhandlerforening (Norwegian Booksellers Assn.), Øvre Vollgate 15, 0158 Oslo 1. Tel. 22-396-800, fax 22-396-810, e-mail dnf@forleggerforeningen.no, World Wide Web http://www.bokhandler.no. *Dir.* Randi Ogrey.

Norske Forleggerforening (Norwegian Publishers Assn.), Øvre Vollgate 15, 0158 Oslo 1. Tel. 22-007-580, fax 22-333-830, e-mail dnf@forleggerforeningen.no, World Wide Web http://www.forleggerforeningen.no. *Dir.* Kristin Slordahl.

Peru

Cámara Peruana del Libro (Peruvian Publishers Assn.), Ave. Abancay cdra 4 s/n, Lima 1. Tel. 428-7630, fax 427-7331, e-mail jefatura@binape.gob.pe, World Wide Web http://www.binape.gob.pe. *Pres.* Julio César Flores Rodriguez; *Exec. Dir.* Loyda Moran Bustamente.

Philippines

Philippine Educational Publishers Assn., 84 P. Florentino St., 3008 Quezon City. Tel. 2-740-2698, fax 2-711-5702, e-mail dbuhain@cnl.net. *Pres.* D. D. Buhain.

Poland

Polskie Towarzystwo Wydawców Ksiazek (Polish Society of Book Editors), ul. Mazowiecka 2/4, 00-048 Warsaw. Tel./fax 22-826-0735. *Pres.* Janusz Fogler; *Gen. Secy.* Donat Chruscicki.

Stowarzyszenie Ksiegarzy Polskich (Assn. of Polish Booksellers), ul. Mokotowska 4/6,

00-641 Warsaw. Tel. 22-252-874. *Pres.* Tadeusz Hussak.

Portugal

Associação Portuguesa de Editores e Livreiros (Portuguese Assn. of Publishers and Booksellers), Largo de Andaluz, 16-7 Esq., 1000 Lisbon. Tel. 1-556-241, fax 1-315-3553. *Pres.* Francisco Espadinha; *Secy. Gen.* Jorge de Carvalho Sá Borges.

Russia

All-Union Book Chamber, Kremlevskaja nab 1/9, 121019 Moscow. Tel. 95-203-4653, fax 95-298-2576, e-mail chamber@aha.ru, World Wide Web http://www.bookchamber.ru. *Dir.-Gen.* Boris Lenski.

Publishers Assn., B. Nikitskaya St. 44, 121069 Moscow. Tel. 95-202-1174, fax 95-202-3989. *Contact* M. Shishigin.

Singapore

Singapore Book Publishers Assn., c/o Cannon International, 86 Marine Parade Centre, No. 03-213, Singapore 440086. Tel. 65-344-7801, fax 65-447-0897. *Pres.* Wu-Cheng Tan.

Slovenia

Zdruzenje Zaloznikov in Knjigotrzcev Slovenije Gospodarska Zbornica Slovenije (Assn. of Publishers and Booksellers of Slovenia), Dimiceva 13, 1504 Ljubljana. Tel. 386-1-58-98-277, fax 386-1-58-98-200, e-mail irena.brglez@zgs.si, World Wide Web http://www.gzs.si.

South Africa

Associated Booksellers of Southern Africa, Box 870, Bellville 7530. Tel. 21-951-2194, fax 21-951-4903. *Pres.* M. Hargraves; *Secy.* R. Stoltenkamp.

Publishers Assn. of South Africa, Box 116, 7946 St. James. Tel. 21-788-6470, fax 21-788-6469, e-mail pasa@icon.co.za, World Wide Web http://www.icon.co.za/~pasa. *Chair* Basil Van Rooyen.

Spain

Federación de Gremios de Editores de España (Federation of Spanish Publishers Assns.), Cea Bermudez 44, 28003 Madrid. Tel. 91-534-5195, fax 91-535-2625, e-mail fgee@fge.es, World Wide Web http://www.federacioneditores.org. *Pres.* Emiliano Martinez; *Exec. Dir.* Antonio Auila.

Sri Lanka

Sri Lanka Assn. of Publishers, 112 S. Mahinda Mawatha, Colombo 10. Tel. 1-695-773, fax 1-696-653, e-mail dayawansajay@hotmail.com. *Pres.* Dayawansa Jayakody.

Sudan

Sudanese Publishers Assn., c/o Institute of African and Asian Studies, Khartoum Univ., Box 321, Khartoum 11115. Tel./fax 249-11-77820.

Sweden

Svenska Förläggareföreningen (Swedish Publishers Assn.), Drottninggatan 97, S-11360 Stockholm. Tel. 8-736-1940, fax 8-736-1944, e-mail svf@forlagskansli.se. *Dir.* Kristina Ahlinder.

Switzerland

Schweizerischer Buchhändler- und Verleger-Verband (Swiss German-Language Booksellers and Publishers Assn.), Postfach 9045, 8050 Zurich. Tel. 1-318-6430, fax 1-318-6462, e-mail sbvv@swissbooks.ch, World Wide Web http://www.swissbooks.ch. *Secy.* Egon Räz.

Société des Libraires et Editeurs de la Suisse Romande (Assn. of Swiss French-Language Booksellers and Publishers), Case Postale 1215, 1001 Lausanne. Tel. 21-796-3300, fax 21-796-3311. *Dir.* Philippe Schibli.

Thailand

Publishers and Booksellers Assn. of Thailand, 320 Lat Phrao 94-aphat Pracha-u-thit Rd., Bangkok 10310. Tel. 2-559-2642, fax 2-559-2643.

Uganda

Uganda Publishers and Booksellers Assn., Box 7732, Kampala. Tel. 41-259-163, fax 41-251-160. *Contact* Martin Okia.

United Kingdom

Antiquarian Booksellers Assn., 154 Buckingham Palace Rd., London W1V 9PA, England. Tel. 20-7730-9273, fax 20-7439-3119. *Administrators* Philippa Gibson, Deborah Stratford.

Assn. of Learned and Professional Society Publishers, Sentosa Hill Rd., Fairlight, Hastings, East Sussex TN35 4AE, England. Tel. 1424-812-353, fax 181-663-3583, e-mail donovan@alpsp.demon.co. uk. *Secy.-Gen.* B. T. Donovan.

Book Trust, 45 East Hill, Wandsworth, London SW18 2QZ, England. Tel. 20-8516-2977, fax 20-8516-2978, e-mail sandra@ booktrust.org.uk, World Wide Web http:// www.booktrust.org.uk.

Educational Publishers Council, One Kingsway, London WC2B 6XF, England. Tel. 20-7565-7474, fax 20-7836-4543, e-mail mail@publishers.org.uk, World Wide Web http://www.publishers.org.uk. *Chair* Philip Walters; *Dir.* Graham Taylor.

Publishers Assn., One Kingsway, London WC2B 6XF, England. Tel. 20-7565-7474, fax 20-7836-4543, e-mail mail@publishers. org.uk, World Wide Web http://www. publishers.org.uk. *Pres.* Simon Master; *Chief Exec.* Ronnie Williams.

Scottish Book Trust, Scottish Book Centre, 137 Dundee St., Edinburgh EH11 1BG, Scotland. Tel. 131-229-3663, fax 131-228-4293, e-mail info@scottishbooktrust.com.

Scottish Publishers Assn., Scottish Book Centre, 137 Dundee St., Edinburgh EH11 1BG, Scotland. Tel. 131-228-6866, fax 131-228-3220, e-mail enquiries@scottishbooks.org, World Wide Web http://www.scottishbooks. org. *Dir.* Lorraine Fannin; *Chair* Peter Mackenzie.

Welsh Books Council (Cyngor Llyfrau Cymru), Castell Brychan, Aberystwyth, Ceredigion SY23 2JB, Wales. Tel. 1970-624-455, fax 1970-625-506, e-mail castel brychan@cllc.org.uk, World Wide Web http://www.cllc.org.uk. *Dir.* Gwerfyl Pierce Jones.

Uruguay

Cámara Uruguaya del Libro (Uruguayan Publishers Assn.), Juan D. Jackson 1118, 11200 Montevideo. Tel. 2-241-4732, fax 2-241-1860.

Venezuela

Cámara Venezolana del Libro (Venezuelan Publishers Assn.), Ave. Andrés Bello, Torre Oeste, 11 piso, Of. 112-0, Apdo. 51858, Caracas 1050-A. Tel. 2-793-1347, fax 2-793-1368. *Dir.* M. P. Vargas.

Zambia

Booksellers and Publishers Assn. of Zambia, Box 31838, Lusaka. Tel. 1-225-195, fax 1-225-282; *Exec. Dir.* Basil Mbewe.

Zimbabwe

Zimbabwe Book Publishers Assn., 12 Selous Ave., Harare Causeway, Harare. Tel 4-750-282, fax 4-751-202.

National Information Standards Organization (NISO) Standards

Information Retrieval

Z39.2-1994 (R 2001) Information Interchange Format
Z39.47-1993 (R 1998) Extended Latin Alphabet Coded Character Set for Bibliographic Use (ANSEL)
Z39.50-1995   Information Retrieval (Z39.50) Application Service Definition and Protocol Specification
Z39.53-2001   Codes for the Representation of Languages for Information Interchange
Z39.64-1989 (R 1995) East Asian Character Code for Bibliographic Use
Z39.76-1996   Data Elements for Binding Library Materials
Z39.84-2000   Syntax for the Digital Object Identifier

Library Management

Z39.7-1995*   Library Statistics
Z39.20-1999   Criteria for Price Indexes for Print Library Materials
Z39.71-1999   Holdings Statements for Bibliographic Items
Z39.73-1994 (R 2001) Single-Tier Steel Bracket Library Shelving

Preservation and Storage

Z39.32-1996   Information on Microfiche Headers
Z39.48-1992 (R 1997) Permanence of Paper for Publications and Documents in Libraries and Archives
Z39.62-2000   Eye-Legible Information on Microfilm Leaders and Trailers and on Containers of Processed Microfilm on Open Reels
Z39.66-1992 (R 1998) Durable Hard-Cover Binding for Books
Z39.74-1996   Guides to Accompany Microform Sets
Z39.77-2001   Guidelines for Information About Preservation Products
Z39.78-2000   Library Binding
Z39.79-2001   Environmental Conditions for Exhibiting Library and Archival Materials

Publishing and Information Management

Z39.9-1992 (R 2001) International Standard Serial Numbering (ISSN)
Z39.14-1997   Guidelines for Abstracts

Z39.18-1995*	Scientific and Technical Reports—Elements, Organization, and Design
Z39.19-1993 (R 1998)	Guidelines for the Construction, Format, and Management of Monolingual Thesauri
Z39.22-1989	Proof Corrections
Z39.23-1997	Standard Technical Report Number Format and Creation
Z39.26-1997	Micropublishing Product Information
Z39.41-1997	Printed Information on Spines
Z39.43-1993	Standard Address Number (SAN) for the Publishing Industry
Z39.56-1996	Serial Item and Contribution Identifier (SICI)
NISO/ANSI/ISO 12083	Electronic Manuscript Preparation and Markup
Z39.82-2001	Title Pages for Conference Publications
Z39.85-2001	Dublin Core Metadata Element Set

In Development

Bibliographic References
Book Item and Contribution Identifier
Circulation Interchange Protocol
Digital Talking Book

NISO Technical Reports

TR-01-1995	Environmental Guidelines for the Storage of Paper Records
TR-02-1997	Guidelines for Indexes and Related Information Retrieval Devices
TR-03-1999	A Guide to Alphanumeric Arrangement and Sorting of Numerals and Other Symbols

*These standards are being reviewed by NISO's Standards Development Committee or are under revision. For further information, please contact NISO, 4733 Bethesda Ave., Suite 300, Bethesda, MD 20814. Tel. 301-654-2512, fax 301-654-1721, e-mail nisohq@niso.org, World Wide Web http://www.niso.org.

Calendar, 2002–2009

The list below contains information on association meetings or promotional events that are, for the most part, national or international in scope. State and regional library association meetings are also included. To confirm the starting or ending date of a meeting, which may change after the *Bowker Annual* has gone to press, contact the association directly. Addresses of library and book trade associations are listed in Part 6 of this volume. For information on additional book trade and promotional events, see *Literary Market Place* and *International Literary Market Place*, published by Information Today, Inc., and other library and book trade publications such as *Library Journal, School Library Journal,* and *Publishers Weekly.*

2002

May

1–3	Massachusetts Library Assn.	Falmouth
1–3	Utah Library Assn.	Sandy
1–5	BookExpo America	New York
1–10	Tehran International Book Fair	Tehran, Iran
1–30	Jerusalem International Book Fair	Jerusalem, Israel
1–31	Salon del Libro	Turin, Italy
9–12	Prague International Book Fair	Prague, Czech Republic
15–19	Warsaw International Book Fair	Warsaw, Poland
17–23	Medical Library Assn.	Dallas
22–26	Bucharest International Book Fair	Bucharest, Romania
24–28	Beijing International Book Fair	Beijing, China

June

1–2	Printers Row Book Fair	Chicago
2–7	International Assn. of Technological University Libraries	Kansas City, MO
2–7	Rhode Island Library Assn.	Newport
8–13	Special Libraries Association	Los Angeles
13–19	American Library Assn. Annual Conference	Atlanta
19–22	American Theological Library Assn.	St. Paul, MN
19–22	Canadian Library Assn.	Halifax, NS
20–21	Australian Book Fair	Sydney
21–24	BookExpo Canada	Toronto
27–29	LOEX-of-the-West 2002	Eugene, OR

July 2002

17–22	Hong Kong Book Fair	Hong Kong

August

4–9	International Assn. of Music Libraries, Archives, and Documentation Centres (IAML)	Los Angeles
5–9	International Assn. of School Librarianship	Petaling Jaya, Malaysia
7–10	Pacific Northwest Library Assn.	Missoula, MT
13–16	Black Caucus of the American Library Assn./ National Conference of African American Librarians	Fort Lauderdale, FL
18–24	International Federation of Library Assns. and Institutions (IFLA) General Conference	Glasgow, Scotland
19–25	Society of American Archivists	Birmingham, AL

September

4–9	Moscow International Book Fair	Moscow, Russia
18–21	Expolit Latin America	Miami
18–21	Wyoming Library Assn.	Casper
23–30	Banned Book Week	
24–28	Illinois Library Assn.	Chicago
25–27	Minnesota Library Assn.	St. Paul
28–10/1	Arkansas Library Assn.	Little Rock
29–10/2	ARMA International	New Orleans

October

2–4	Missouri Library Assn.	Kansas City
2–5	Idaho Library Assn.	Boise
2–5	Mountain Plains Library Assn., North Dakota Library Assn., South Dakota Library Assn.	Fargo, ND
2–5	Nevada Library Assn.	Ely
2–5	Wyoming Library Assn.	Casper
3–6	Liber: International Book Fair	Barcelona, Spain
9–11	Georgia Library Assn.	Athens
9–11	Iowa Library Assn.	Des Moines
9–14	Frankfurt International Book Fair	Frankfurt, Germany
10–13	Library and Information Technology Assn. (LITA) National Forum	Houston
16–18	Mississippi Library Assn.	Hattiesburg
16–18	West Virginia Library Assn.	Pipestem
16–19	Kentucky Library Assn.	Louisville
17–18	Virginia Library Assn.	Williamsburg
20–22	New England Library Assn.	Sturbridge, MA
23–25	Nebraska Library Assn./Nebraska Educational Media Assn.	Lincoln

23–26	New York Library Assn.	Buffalo
24–26	South Carolina Library Assn./Southeastern Library Assn.	Charleston, SC
29–11/1	Michigan Library Assn.	Grand Rapids
29–11/1	Wisconsin Library Assn.	Middleton

November

6–9	American Translators Assn.	Atlanta
6–9	Illinois School Library Media Assn.	Arlington
7–9	Lutheran Church Library Assn.	Minnetonka, MN
9–12	Miami International Book Fair	Miami
10–13	Pennsylvania Library Assn.	Hershey
15–18	California Library Assn.	Sacramento

December

| 3–6 | Arizona Library Assn. | Phoenix |

2003

January

| 24–29 | American Library Assn. Midwinter Meeting | Philadelphia |

February

| 9–16 | Music Library Assn. | Austin, TX |

March

| 26–29 | Oklahoma Library Assn. | Oklahoma City |
| 31–4/4 | Texas Library Assn. | Houston |

April

2–4	Tennessee Library Assn.	Chattanooga
6–12	National Library Week	
9–11	Kansas Library Assn.	Salina
9–11	Wisconsin Educational Media Assn.	Milwaukee
10–11	Washington Library Assn.	Yakima
10–13	Assn. of College and Research Libraries	Charlotte, NC
24–26	Pennsylvania School Librarians Assn.	Hershey

June

| 2–6 | International Assn. of Technological University Libraries | Edinburgh, Scotland |
| 8–16 | Crimea 2002, "Libraries and Associations in the Transient World: New Technologies and New Forms of Cooperation" | Sudak, Crimea |

June 2003 *(cont.)*

14–18	Assn. of Jewish Libraries	Denver
18–21	American Theological Library Assn.	Portland, OR
19–25	American Library Assn. Annual Conference	Toronto, ON

August

1–9	International Federation of Library Assns. and Institutions (IFLA) General Conference	Berlin, Germany

September

23–26	North Carolina Library Assn.	Winston-Salem
25–27	North Dakota Library Assn.	Minot

October

1–4	Wyoming Library Assn.	Evanston
15–17	Iowa Library Assn.	Cedar Rapids
15–18	South Dakota Library Assn.	Sioux Falls
19–22	ARMA International	Boston
22–24	Nebraska Educational Media Assn.	Omaha
22–26	American Assn. of School Librarians	Kansas City, MO
26–28	New England Library Assn.	Manchester, NH
27–30	Wisconsin Library Assn.	Milwaukee

November

4–8	Mountain Plains Library Assn./ Nevada Library Assn. joint conference	North Lake Tahoe
5–8	American Translators Assn.	Phoenix
6–8	Illinois School Library Media Assn.	Decatur
15–17	South Dakota Library Assn.	Sioux Falls

2004

January

9–14	American Library Assn. Midwinter Meeting	San Diego

February

24–28	Public Libraries Assn.	Seattle

March

15–20	Texas Library Assn.	San Antonio

April

18–24	National Library Week

| 21–23 | Oklahoma Library Assn. | Tulsa |

June

| 24–30 | American Library Assn. Annual Conference | Orlando |

October

| 13–15 | Iowa Library Assn. | Sioux City |
| 20–22 | New England Library Assn. | Manchester, NH |

November

| 2–5 | Wisconsin Library Assn. | Lake Geneva |
| 3–6 | Illinois School Library Media Assn. | Arlington |

2005

January

| 14–19 | American Library Assn. Midwinter Meeting | Boston |

April

7–10	Assn. of College and Research Libraries	Minneapolis
10–16	National Library Week	
11–16	Texas Library Assn.	Dallas
20–23	Washington Library Assn.	Spokane

June

| 23–29 | American Library Assn. Annual Conference | Chicago |

September

| 20–23 | North Carolina Library Assn. | Winston-Salem |

October

16–18	New England Library Assn.	Worcester, MA
25–28	Wisconsin Library Assn.	Lacrosse
27–29	Illinois School Library Media Assn.	Decatur

2006

January

| 20–25 | American Library Assn. Midwinter Meeting | San Antonio |

April

| 2–8 | National Library Week | |
| 24–29 | Texas Library Assn. | Houston |

June 2006

22–28   American Library Assn. Annual Conference   New Orleans

2007
January

16–21   American Library Assn. Midwinter Meeting   Seattle

March

12–17   Texas Library Assn.   San Antonio

April

15–21   National Library Week

June

21–27   American Library Assn. Annual Conference   Washington, DC

2008
January

25–30   American Library Assn. Midwinter Meeting   Philadelphia

April

7–12   Texas Library Assn.   Dallas

June

26–27   American Library Assn. Annual Conference   Anaheim

2009
January

23–28   American Library Assn. Midwinter Meeting   Denver

April

20–25   Texas Library Assn.   Houston

July

9–15   American Library Assn. Annual Conference   Chicago

Acronyms

A

AALL. American Association of Law Libraries

AAP. Association of American Publishers

AASL. American Association of School Librarians

ABA. American Booksellers Association

ABFFE. American Booksellers Foundation for Free Expression

ACLU. American Civil Liberties Union

ACRL. Association of College and Research Libraries

AECT. Association for Educational Communications and Technology

AFFECT. Americans for Fair Electronic Commerce Transactions

AFRINUL. African Newspaper Union List Project

AIIP. Association of Independent Information Professionals

AJL. Association of Jewish Libraries

ALA. American Library Association

ALCTS. Association for Library Collections and Technical Services

ALIC. Archives Library Information Center

ALS. Academic Libraries Survey

ALSC. Association for Library Service to Children

ALTA. Association for Library Trustees and Advocates

AMMLA. American Merchant Marine Library Association

APALA. Asian/Pacific American Librarians Association

ARC. National Archives and Records Administration, Archival Research Catalog

ARL. Association of Research Libraries

ARLIS/NA. Art Libraries Society of North America

ASCLA. Association of Specialized and Cooperative Library Agencies

ASIS&T. American Society for Information Science and Technology

ATLA. American Theological Library Association

B

BEA. BookExpo America

BOAI. Budapest Open Access Initiative

BSA. Bibliographical Society of America

C

CAIS. Canadian Association for Information Science

CALA. Chinese-American Librarians Association

CAPL. Canadian Association of Public Libraries

CARL. Canadian Association of Research Libraries

CASLIS. Canadian Association of Special Libraries and Information Services

CD-ROM. Compact Disc Read-Only Memory

CDRS. Library of Congress, Collaborative Digital Reference Service

CIPA. Children's Internet Protection Act

CLA. Canadian Library Association; Catholic Library Association

CLTA. Canadian Library Trustees Association

CNI. Coalition for Networked Information

CNSLP. Canada, Canadian National Site Licensing Project

COPA. Child Online Protection Act

COPPA. Children's Online Privacy Protection Act

CORC. Cataloging and classification, Cooperative Online Resources Catalog

COSLA. Chief Officers of State Library Agencies

CPPA. Child Pornography Prevention Act

CSLA. Canadian School Library Association; Church and Synagogue Library Association

D

DFC. Digital Future Coalition

DID. Databases, ARL's Digital Initiatives Database

DLF. Digital Library Foundation

DMCA. Digital Millennium Copyright Act

DOE. Education, U.S. Department of

DSAL. Asia, Digital South Asia Library Program

E

EAD. Archives, Encoded Archival Description

EAR. National Technical Information Service, U.S. Export Administration Regulations

ECAR. EDUCAUSE Center for Applied Research

EDB. Databases, Energy Science and Technology Database

EDRS. Educational Resources Information Center, ERIC Document Reproduction Service

EMIERT. American Library Association, Ethnic and Multicultural Information Exchange Round Table

EPA. Environmental Protection Agency

ERIC. Educational Resources Information Center

F

FAFLRT. American Library Association, Federal and Armed Forces Librarians Round Table

FDLP. Government Printing Office, Federal Depository Library Program

FEDRIP. National Technical Information Service, FEDRIP (Federal Research in Progress Database)

FIAF. International Federation of Film Archives

FID. International Federation for Information and Documentation

FLICC. Federal Library and Information Center Committee

FPC. Federal Publishers Committee

G

GLBT. American Library Association, Gay, Lesbian, Bisexual, and Transgendered Round Table

GLIN. Global Legal Information Network

GODORT. American Library Association, Government Documents Round Table

GPO. Government Printing Office

GRC. National Technical Information Service, GOV.Research Center

H

HRDR. American Library Association, Human Resource Development and Recruitment

I

IAALD. International Association of Agricultural Information Specialists

IALL. International Association of Law Libraries

IAML. International Association of Music Libraries, Archives and Documentation Centres

IASL. International Association of School Librarianship

IATUL. International Association of Technological University Libraries

IDLH. Databases, Immediately Dangerous to Life or Health Concentrations Database

IFLA. International Federation of Library Associations and Institutions

IFRT. American Library Association, Intellectual Freedom Round Table

ILL. Interlibrary loan

IMLS. Institute of Museum and Library Services

ISBN. International Standard Book Number

ISCA. International Scholarly Communications Alliance

ISO. International Organization for
Standardization
ISSN. International Standard Serial Number

L

LAMA. Library Administration and
Management Association
LC. Library of Congress
LHRT. American Library Association,
Library History Round Table
LHTN. Library Hi-Tech News
LIS. Library of Congress, Legislative
Information System; Library/information
science
LITA. Library and Information Technology
Association
LJ. Library Journal
LPS. Government Printing Office (GPO),
Library Programs Service
LRRT. American Library Association,
Library Research Round Table
LSP. National Center for Education
Statistics, Library Statistics Program
LSTA. Library Services and Technology Act

M

MAGERT. American Library Association,
Map and Geography Round Table
MLA. Medical Library Association; Music
Library Association

N

NAGARA. National Association of
Government Archives and Records
Administrators
NAL. National Agricultural Library
NARA. National Archives and Records
Administration
NASTA. National Association of Textbook
Administrators
NCBI. National Center for Biotechnology
Information
NCEF. National Clearinghouse for
Educational Facilities
NCES. National Center for Education
Statistics
NCIPA. Neighborhood Children's Internet
Protection Act

NCLIS. National Commission on Libraries
and Information Science
NEA. National Endowment for the Arts
NEDRC. National Education Data Resource
Center
NEH. National Endowment for the
Humanities
NEN. National Education Network
NGS. National Geographic Society
NHES. National Center for Education
Statistics, National Household Education
Survey
NHPRC. National Archives and Records
Administration, National Historical
Publications and Records Commission
NIOSH. National Institute for Occupational
Safety and Health
NISO. National Information Standards
Organization
NLE. National Library of Education
NLM. National Library of Medicine
NMAM. National Institute for Occupational
Safety and Health, Manual of Analytical
Methods
NMRT. American Library Association, New
Members Round Table
NPG. National Institute for Occupational
Safety and Health, NIOSH Pocket Guide
to Chemical Hazards (NPG)
NTIS. National Technical Information
Service

O

OeBF. Open eBook Forum
OEBPS. E-books, Open eBook Publication
Structure

P

PLA. Public Library Association
PLoS. Public Library of Science
PRA. Presidential Records Act
PW. Publishers Weekly

R

RIAA. Recording Industry Association of
America

RPAC. Association of American Publishers, Rights and Permissions Advisory Committee

RTECS. Registry of Toxic Effects of Chemical Substances

RUSA. Reference and User Services Association

S

SAA. Society of American Archivists

SAN. Standard Address Number

SLA. Special Libraries Association

SLJ. School Library Journal

SPARC. Scholarly Publishing & Academic Resources Coalition

SRIM. National Technical Information Service, Selected Research in Microfiche

SRRT. American Library Association, Social Responsibilities Round Table

SSP. Society for Scholarly Publishing

StLA. State libraries and library agencies NCES State Library Agencies survey

T

TLA. Theatre Library Association

U

UCITA. Uniform Computer Information Transactions Act

ULC. Urban Libraries Council

USPS. Postal Service, U.S.

V

VRD. Educational Resources Information Center, Virtual Reference Desk

W

WNC. World News Connection

WTO. World Trade Organization

Y

YALSA. Young Adult Library Services Association

Index of Organizations

Please note that this index includes cross-references to the Subject Index. Many additional organizations can be found in Part 6 under the following headings: Networks, Consortia, and Cooperative Library Organizations; National Library and Information-Industry Associations, United States and Canada; State, Provincial, and Regional Library Associations; State and Provincial Library Agencies; State School Library Media Associations; International Library Associations; Foreign Library Associations; Book Trade Associations, United States and Canada; International and Foreign Book Trade Associations.

A

Abbeville Publishing, 23
Harry N. Abrams, 19
AGRICOLA (Agricultural OnLine Access), 62–63, 85
Agriculture, U.S. Department of (USDA) *see* National Agricultural Library
AGRIS (Agricultural Science and Technology database), 85
Amazon.com, 19, 24, 219, 223
American Association of Law Libraries (AALL), 731
 awards, 406
American Association of Retired Persons (AARP), 38
American Association of School Librarians (AASL), 13, 734–736
 awards, 408–409
 grants, 432
 Information Power . . ., 11–12, 13
 strategic planning, 16–17
American Booksellers Association (ABA), 157–160
 affinity programs, 160
 Book Sense, 158
 goals, 157–158
 litigation, 22, 159
 membership, 159
 Prescription for Reading, 158
 research, 159
 sales tax action, 159
American Booksellers Foundation for Free Expression (ABFFE), 160

American Civil Liberties Union (ACLU), 5
American Institute of Physics, 253
American Library Association (ALA), 123–137, 732–753
 American Libraries, 132
 @ Your Library, 125, 200
 awards, 406–418, 434
 Banned Books Week, 127
 Book Links, 133
 Booklist, 133
 conferences, 131–132, 135, 244
 Copyright Education Program, 128
 diversity/access/ education/continuous learning, 124–125
 Ethnic and Multicultural Information Exchange Round Table (EMIERT) awards, 412
 Exhibits Round Table awards, 412
 Federal and Armed Forces Librarians Round Table (FAFLRT) award, 412
 filtering software, position on, 5
 Gay, Lesbian, Bisexual, and Transgendered Round Table (GLBT), 413
 Government Documents Round Table (GODORT) awards, 134, 413
 grants, 129–130, 134–135
 Human Resource Development and Recruitment (HRDR), 136
 Intellectual Freedom Manual, 127
 Intellectual Freedom Round Table (IFRT), 126–128, 413
 leadership, 135–136
 Library Bill of Rights, 14
 library education, 6

American Library Association (ALA) *(cont.)*
  Library History Round Table (LHRT)
    awards, 414–415, 434
  Library Research Round Table (LRRT)
    awards, 415, 434
  Literacy and Libraries . . ., 137
  Map and Geography Round Table
    (MAGERT); awards, 415
  National Library Week, 125
  New Members Round Table (NMRT)
    awards, 415
  New York Times v. *Tasini*, 129
  notable books list, 643–654
  Publishing Committee, 132–134, 416
  READ posters, 133–134
  Social Responsibilities Round Table
    (SRRT); awards, 417
  TechSource, 132–133
  Teen Read Week, 133
  theme, 125–126
  Washington report, 128–129, 306
American Library Trustee Association
  (ALTA), *see* Association for Library
  Trustees and Advocates
American Merchant Marine Library Associa-
  tion (AMMLA), 753
American National Standards Institute
  (ANSI), *see* National Information
  Standards Organization
American Society for Information Science
  and Technology (ASIS&T), 754–755
  awards, 418, 435–436
American Theological Library Association
  (ATLA), 755–756
Americans for Fair Electronic Commerce
  Transactions (AFFECT), 163
Archives Library Information Center (ALIC),
  95
Archivists and Librarians in the History of
  the Health Sciences, 756–757
Art Libraries Society of North America
  (ARLIS/NA), 759
  awards, 418–419
ArtSTOR, 190
Arundel Books, 160
Asian/Pacific American Librarians Associa-
  tion (APALA), 419, 760
Association of Academic Health Sciences
  Libraries, 762–763
Association of American Publishers (AAP),
  138–156
  annual meeting, 141, 154–156
  antipiracy program, 149–150
  awards, 140
  banned books, 148
  book sales statistics, 553–554, 554(table)
  BookExpo America, 140, 145, 148
  Copyright, 141–143
  diversity, 144–145
  E-book Standards Project, 143
  education program, 145
  Enabling Technologies, 143–144
  Freedom to Read, 145–147
  Get Caught Reading promotion, 140–141,
    154
  government affairs, 139
  Higher Education, 147
  highlights, 138–139
  Intellectual Property, 155
  International, 141, 148
  International Freedom to Publish, 148–149
  International Trade Relations, 149–150
  legislative activities, 141–143, 145–147,
    312
  ONIX, 143
  Postal, 150–151
  Professional/Scholarly Publishing, 151
  public relations, 139–140
  Reading First, 152
  Rights and Permissions Advisory Commit-
    tee (RPAC), 141–142
  sales estimates, 24
  School Division, 151–154
  Trade Publishing, 154
  See also Legislation affecting publishing
Association Canadienne des Sciences de
  l'Information, *see* Canadian Associa-
  tion for Information Science
Association for Educational Communications
  and Technology (AECT); *Information
  Power . . .*, 11–12, 13
Association for Information and Image Management (AIIM International), 761
Association for Library Collections and
  Technical Services (ALCTS), 132,
  525–547, 737–739
  awards, 409
Association for Library Service to Children
  (ALSC), 740–741
  awards, 134, 409–410
  best books list, 652–654
  best films/videos list, 655
  best recordings list, 656–657
  best software list, 658

best Web sites, 658
Association for Library Trustees and Advocates (ALTA), 736–737
awards, 409
Association of College and Research Libraries (ACRL), 132, 741–743
awards, 410–412, 435
grants, 135
Association of Independent Information Professionals (AIIP), 763
Association of Jewish Libraries (AJL), 764
awards, 419–420
Association of Library and Information Science Education (ALISE), 761–762
awards, 419
Association of Research Libraries (ARL), 161–178, 765–766
access and technology, 165–167
African Newspaper Union List Project (AFRINUL), 168
collection services, 167–170
communications and external relations, 176–177
conference, 175, 177–178
Digital South Asia Library (DSAL), 170
diversity, 171–172
E-metrics project, 174–175
federal relations and information policy program, 163–165
German Resources Project, 168–169
Global Resources program, 168
grants, 171, 174, 175
Japan Journal Access Project, 169
Latin Americanist Research Resources Project, 169
LibQUAL+ project, 174–175
Management Services, Office of, 172–173
membership activities, 177–178
New Measures Initiative, 174–175
preservation activities, 170–171
publications, 177
Research and Development, Office of, 175–176
scholarly communication, 161–163
Scholars Portal Working Group, 165
Slavic Document Delivery Project, 169
Southeast Asia Indexing Project/Thai Journal Index, 170
statistics program, 173–175
See also Scholarly Publishing & Academic Resources Coalition

Association of Specialized and Cooperative Library Agencies (ASCLA), 743–744
awards, 412
Association of Vision Science Librarians, 766

B

Barnes & Noble, 22, 141, 159
Barnes & Noble Digital, 219, 222
BarnesandNoble.com, 19, 24, 219, 223
Beta Phi Mu, 767–768
awards, 420
Bibelot, 19
Bibliographical Society of America (BSA), 769
awards, 420
Books24X7, 226
Books and Books, 160
Books-A-Million, 18
Borders Group, 22, 159
WTC location, 23
R.R. Bowker, 21

C

C-Span II, Book TV, 140
Canadian Association of College and University Libraries (CACUL); awards, 420–421
Canadian Association for Information Science (CAIS), 769
Canadian Association of Public Libraries (CAPL); awards, 421
Canadian Association of Research Libraries (CARL), 163
Canadian Association of Special Libraries and Information Services (CASLIS); awards, 421
Canadian Free Speech League, 261–262
Canadian Jewish Congress, 262
Canadian Library Association (CLA), 207, 262, 770
awards, 420–421
Canadian Library Trustees Association (CLTA); awards, 421
Canadian School Library Association (CSLA); awards, 421
CAROL (Collections and Organizations Research Online), 433

Catholic Library Association (CLA),
        771–772
Center for the Book, 40–43
    awards, 41–42
    events, 43
    highlights, 40
    outreach, 40, 41, 42–43
    projects, 42
    reading promotion partners, 41
    state centers, 41–43
    themes, 40–41
Center for Education Statistics, *see* National
        Center for Education Statistics
Chief Officers of State Library Agencies
        (COSLA), 772
Chinese American Librarians Association
        (CALA), 773
    awards, 421
Chronicle Books, 158
Church and Synagogue Library Association
        (CSLA), 421, 774
Classic Media, 20
Coalition for Networked Information (CNI),
        775
Congress, U.S., *see* Legislation affecting
        information industry; Legislation
        affecting libraries; Legislation affect-
        ing publishing; Library of Congress
Council on Library and Information
        Resources (CLIR), 186–196, 775–776
    Academic Library Advisory Committee,
        193
    artifacts, role in library collections, 187
    awards, 195–196, 421, 429
    digital information
        collection development, 192
        libraries, 189–190
        preservation of, 189
        visual resources, database for, 187–188
    economics of information, 192
    The Evidence in Hand, 187
    grants, 187, 188, 189, 193
    international program, 194
    leadership, 193
    preservation awareness, 188–189
    professional development, 194
    publications, 194–195
    scholarship, resources for, 186–188
    scholarships, 195–196
    See also Digital Library Foundation; Frye
        Leadership Institute; Preservation
Crown Books, 18

D

Database Coalition, 164
Defense, U.S. Department of
    Appropriations Act; emergency postal
        funds, 321–322
    distance learning initiative, 143–144
Dice, 222
Digital Future Coalition (DFC), 163
Digital Library Foundation (DLF), 190–191
    See also THOMAS

E

E-Ink, 229
Earthweb, 222
Ebrary, 18, 222
Education, U.S. Department of (DOE)
    Appropriations Act, 317–318
    See also Educational Resources Informa-
        tion Center; Library Services and
        Technology Act
Educational Resources Information Center
        (ERIC), 113–121
    ACCESS ERIC, 115
    accessibility/usability, 113, 116
    Clearinghouses, 114, 119–121
    database changes, 115–116
    document delivery, 116
    ERIC Document Reproduction Service
        (EDRS), 107, 114–115, 116
    information sharing, 116–117
    processing and reference facility, 114
    publications/products, 117–118
    system directory, 119–121
    user services, 118(table), 118
    Virtual Reference Desk (VRD), 238, 239
EDUCAUSE Center for Applied Research
        (ECAR), 434
Elcom, 292
Elsevier, ScienceDirect, 253
Energy Science and Technology Database
        (EDB), 85–86
Environmental Protection Agency (EPA),
        268–269
European Union, LibEcon, 59

F

Federal Library and Information Center
        Committee (FLICC), 44–56, 776–777

awards, 44, 46–49
budget and finance, 47
content management, 48
education programs, 48, 50
FEDLINK, *see* FEDLINK
highlights, 44–45
membership meetings, 45–46
nominating working group, 48
personnel, 46, 48–49
preservation/binding, 49
publications, 49–50
Web site, 49
working groups, 44
Federal Publishers Committee (FPC), 777
FEDLINK, 45, 51–56
accounts receivable, 54
budget and revenue, 55
fiscal operations, 53
member services, 54
network operations, 51–52
procurement program, 52
revolving fund implementation, 55–56
training, 52
transfer-pay accounts payable services, 54–55
vendor services, 53–54
Web site, 49
Fictionwise.com, 224
1stBooks Library, 223, 224
FirstGov.gov, 308
Follett, 141
Foreign Broadcast Information Service (FBIS), 88
Franklin, eBookMan readers, 220
Frye Leadership Institute, 193

G

Gale Group; awards, 422
Bill and Melinda Gates Foundation, 196, 200–201
Gemstar, e-book, 155, 220, 226
Global Legal Information Network (GLIN), 31
Golden Books, 20
Government Printing Office (GPO), 72–82
bookstores, 81–82
cataloging developments, 74
digital archiving, 75
dissemination of government information, 271–272

Federal Depository Library Program (FDLP), 72–74, 74(table), 276, 302
GPO Access, *see* GPO Access
Library Programs Service (LPS), 72–73, 75
policy guidance, 74
sales, 80–82
state plans initiative, 74
Superintendent of Documents, 72
systems modernization, 75
GPO Access, 75–77, 271
aids/access to collections, 76–77
Ben's Guide . . ., 79–80
GPOLISTSERV, 77–80
methods of access, 78
recognition, 78–79
search engine evaluations, 77
training, 78
usage statistics, 78
user support, 79
Web pages, 76, 77
Grolier Publishing, 135
Gyricon Media, 229

H

Han Shin, 150
Harcourt General, 20
Houghton Mifflin, 20
litigation, 23
Hungry Minds, 20

I

Ibooks.com, 222
Illinois, University of; Mortenson Center, 194
Ingram, 19, 221
See also Lightning Source
Institute of Museum and Library Services (IMLS), 343–357, 427
conferences, 356–357
discretionary programs, 346
evaluation of programs, 354, 356
grants, 348–353(table), 355–356(table), 429, 431–432
National Award for Library Service, 357
National Leadership Program, 346–348, 348–353(table)
Native American Library Services Program, 346, 354, 355–356(table)

Institute of Museum and Library Services
(IMLS) *(cont.)*
Native Hawaiian Library Services Program,
346, 354
state-administered programs, 343–344,
344–345(table), 346
Web site, 357
See also Library Services and Technology
Act
International Association of Agricultural
Information Specialists (IAALD), 818
International Association of Law Libraries
(IALL), 818–819
International Association of Music Libraries,
Archives and Documentation Centres
(IAML), 819–820
International Association of School Librari-
anship (IASL), 820
International Association of Technological
University Libraries (IATUL), 821
International Council on Archives, 822
International Federation of Film Archives
(FIAF), 823
International Federation for Information and
Documentation (FID), 822–823
International Federation of Library Associa-
tions and Institutions (IFLA), 60,
197–203, 824
@ Your Library logo, 200
awards, 200–201, 422
conferences, 131, 197–201
copyright issues, 295
Libraries in a Digital Age, 198–199
membership, 201
personnel, 201–203
standards, 201
International Intellectual Property Alliance
(IIPA), 141
International Organization for Standardiza-
tion (ISO), 825
ISBN, *see* International Standard Book
Number
International Scholarly Communications
Alliance (ISCA), 162
International Society for Technology in Edu-
cation, 12
Internet/Web
ALA, 136
American Memory, 32
America's Library, 32
bibliography for librarians, 573
CAROL, 433

Center for the Book, 42
children's sites, notable, 658
Choice Reviewer site, 132
digital reference sites, 242
Document Digital Archive Pilot Project, 75
e-books, 221–222
filtering, *see* Filtering software
FirstGov.gov, 308
FLICC/FEDLINK, 49
GPO Access, 76, 77
IMLS, 357
kidSPEAK!, 160
LC site, 36
September 11 Web Archive, 29
Library Statistics Program, 100
Meeting of Frontiers, 32
NAL, 62, 63, 64–65, 68
NARA, 94
NCES, 100, 448
NLM, 66, 70
NTIS site, 308
as placement source, 361–362
portals, 242
preservation/conservation tutorial, 189
publishers' Web sites, 581–631
publishing boundaries, 249–254
PubSCIENCE, 322–323
spamming, 327
SPARC, 182, 185
terrorist attacks of 9/11 and, 249
THOMAS, 32
Web-Braille, 32
See also Children's Internet Protection Act;
Internet Tax Nondiscrimination Act;
main entries, e.g., MEDLINE
IPSOS-NPD, 159
ISBN, *see* International Standard Book Num-
ber
ITKnowledge, 226
IUniverse.com, 223

L

Library Administration and Management
Association (LAMA), 745–746
awards, 413–414
Library of Congress (LC), 27–39
acquisitions, 34
American Folklife Center
Documentary Project (9/11), 29
Save Our Sounds, 37–38
Veterans History Project, 38

arrearage reduction, 33
budget, 30
cataloging, 27, 28, 33
Collaborative Digital Reference Service
 (CDRS), 34, 238–239
collections, 33–34
Copyright Office, 32–33, 285–286
digital projects/planning, 31–32
exhibitions, 35–36
 online, 32
I Hear America Singing, 36
Integrated Library System (ILS), 33
international horizons, 32
Internet resources, 31–32
 September 11 Web Archive, 29
 Web-Braille, 32
John W. Kluge Center, 27, 28–29
Legislative Information System (LIS),
 30–31
National Book Festival, 27
National Film Registry, 38
preservation activities, 37–38
publications, 35
reference service, 34
security measures, 29, 36–37
storage, secondary, 33–34
symposia, 36
telephone numbers, 39
terrorism, response to, 29, 36–37
THOMAS, see THOMAS
See also Center for the Book; National
 Audio-Visual Conservation Center
The Library Corporation/CARL Corp.
 (TLC); YouSeeMore portal, 7
Library and Information Technology Associ-
 ation (LITA), 131–132, 746–747
awards, 414
Libris Casualty and Property Insurance, 160
Lightning Source, 221, 225
Little, Brown, 22
LSSI; Virtual Reference Desk (VRD), 238,
 239
Lutheran Church Library Association, 778

M

McGill University Libraries, 264
Medical Library Association (MLA),
 778–779
awards, 422–423
MEDLINE, 66–67
MEDLINEplus, 66–67, 68–69

Andrew W. Mellon Foundation, 190, 195,
 428–429
Mibrary, 141
Microsoft, 141
Music Library Association (MLA), 780–781

N

Napster, 6, 284, 290–291
National Agricultural Library (NAL), 61–65
 collection, 61–62
 Food Safety Research Information Office,
  64–65
 information management, 63
 interagency panel for assessment of, 65
 portals to science-based information, 63
 services, 62–63
 staffing, 62, 64
 symposium on agricultural trade, 64
 See also AGRICOLA
National Archives and Records Administration (NARA), 92–98
 administration, 98
 Archival Research Catalog (ARC), 94
 customer service, 97
 electronic access project, 94
 Fax-on-Demand, 96
 Federal Register, 96–97
 government documents, 95
 grants, 97–98
 Internet access, 94
 National Historical Publications and
  Records Commission (NHPRC), 97
 renovation and re-encasement, 95
 strategic plan, 93–94
 See also Archives Library Information Cen-
  ter
National Association of Government
 Archives and Records Administrators
 (NAGARA), 781
National Association of Textbook Adminis-
 trators (NASTA), 153
National Association to Promote Library Ser-
 vices to Latinos and the Spanish
 Speaking, see REFORMA
National Audio-Visual Conservation Center,
 33
National Center for Biotechnology Informa-
 tion (NCBI), 69
National Center for Education Statistics
 (NCES)
 academic library survey, 103–105

National Center for Education Statistics
(NCES) *(cont.)*
  Library Statistics Program (LSP), 99–107,
    443–452
    academic libraries, 103–105, 445–447,
      449
    planned data projects, 103
    public libraries survey, 99–102, 443–445,
      449
    Public Library Locator, 102
    school library media centers, 105, 449
    special libraries, 449–450
    State Library Agencies (StLA) survey,
      105–106, 447–452
  National Household Education Survey
    (NHES), 102–103
  printed/electronic products; how to obtain,
    106–107
National Clearinghouse for Educational
  Facilities (NCEF), 112
National Commission on Libraries and Infor-
  mation Science (NCLIS), 57–60
  *A Comprehensive Assessment of Public
    Information Dissemination*, 58,
    276–279
  highlights, 57–58
  international activities, 59–60
  legislative activities, 58, 302
  *Library and Information Services for Indi-
    viduals with Disabilities*, 58
  library statistics, 59
  national information activities, 58
  publications, 58
  School Librarians . . ., 58
  staffing, 57
National Education Data Resource Center
  (NEDRC), 107
National Education Network (NEN), 111
National Endowment for the Arts (NEA), 302
National Endowment for the Humanities
  (NEH), 302, 331–342
  challenge grants, 339
  education, 338–339
  federal-state partnership, 336
  grantmaking programs, 333–334
  preservation and access, 336–337
  public programs, 337
  public-private partnerships, 335–336
  research programs, 337–338
  state humanities councils, 339–342

National Federation of Abstracting and Infor-
  mation Services: *see new name*
  NFAIS
National Federation for the Blind, 153
National Geographic Society (NGS), 164,
  289–290
National Information Standards Organization
  (NISO), 240, 783
  Z39 standards, 851–852
National Institute for Occupational Safety
  and Health (NIOSH)
  Immediately Dangerous to Life or Health
    Concentrations database (IDLH), 86
  Manual of Analytical Methods (NMAM),
    86
  NIOSHTIC, 87
  Pocket Guide to Chemical Hazards (NPG),
    86
  See also Registry of Toxic Effects of
    Chemical Substances
National Institute for Standards and Technol-
  ogy, e-book conference, 8
National Library of Education (NLE),
  108–112
  activities, 108–109
  collections, 109–110
  ED Pubs, 111
  ED Reference Center, 108, 109–110
National Library of Medicine (NLM), 66–71,
  132
  administration, 71
  AnatLine, 70
  ArcticHealth, 67–68
  ClinicalTrials.gov, 67
  databases, 67–68
  Grateful Med, 66
  Lister Hill National Center for Biomedical
    Communications, 70
  Profiles in Science, 68
  PubMedCentral, 68
  research and development, 69–70
  statistics, selected, 71(table), 71
  Visible Human project, 70
  See also MEDLINE; MEDLINEplus;
    National Center for Biotechnology
    Information; National Network of
    Libraries of Medicine
National Library Service for the Blind and
  Physically Handicapped (NLS/BPH),
  27, 28
National Network of Libraries of Medicine
  (NN/LM), 69

National Science Foundation, 429
National Technical Information Service
    (NTIS), 83–92, 276
    contact numbers, 91–92
    customer services, 91
    databases, 84–87
    Davis-Bacon Wage Determination Database, 88–89
    E-Alerts, 89
    Export Administration Regulations (EAR),
        88
    Federal Computer Products Center, 90
    FEDRIP (Federal Research in Progress
        Database), 84
    FedWorld, 91
    funding, 308
    GOV.Research Center (GRC), 87–88
    historical background, 83
    National Audiovisual Center (NAC), 90
    Selected Research in Microfiche (SRIM),
        90
    Service Contract Wage Determination
        Database, 89
    subscriptions, online, 87–89, 89
netLibrary, 8, 18, 221, 226, 430
NFAIS, 782

O

OCLC (Online Computer Library Center), 75
    See also Internet/Web
Odyssey Press, 23
Olsson's Books and Records, 160
Online Lyceum, 173, 176
Open eBook Forum (OeBF), 144
OverDrive, 225

P

Packard Humanities Institute, 33–34
Penguin Putnam, 24
Pizza Hut, 158
Playboy Enterprises, 155
Postal Service, U.S. (USPS)
    pending legislation, 150–151, 305, 321–322
    See also Association of American Publishers, Postal Committee
Public Library Association (PLA), 132,
    748–750
    awards, 415–416
Public Library of Science (PLoS), 162

PubMed Central, 4
PubSCIENCE, 322–323

Q

Questia.com, 18, 221–222

R

Random House, 6, 20, 21, 222
    atRandom, 8, 18, 222
    bestsellers, 24
    litigation, 23, 227–228, 252, 289–290
Reader's Digest, 19
Reciprocal, 225
Recording Industry Association of America
    (RIAA), 142, 291
Reed Elsevier, 20, 21
Reference and User Services Association
    (RUSA), 750–751
    awards, 416–417
    notable books; adults, 643–644
REFORMA, 134, 784
Registry of Toxic Effects of Chemical Substances (RTECS), 87
Rizzoli, 19
RLG (Research Libraries Group), 785
Rodale, 19
RosettaBooks, 6, 224, 227–228, 229, 252,
    289–290
Rovia, 225

S

K.G. Saur; awards, 423
Scholarly Publishing & Academic Resources
    Coalition (SPARC), 179–185, 786
    advocacy/education, 182–183
    awards, 181
    conferences, 183
    governance, 184–185
    Internet publishing, 254
    priorities, 184
    Publisher Partnership Programs, 180–181
    SPARC Europe, 183
    Web sites, 185
Simon & Schuster, 24
SimonSaysShop.com, 222
Sirsi, iBistro, 7
Society of American Archivists (SAA),
    787–788

Society of American Archivists (SAA)
  (*cont.*)
  awards, 423
Society for Scholarly Publishing (SSP), 787
Software and Information Industry Association, 788
Special Libraries Association (SLA), 789
  awards, 423–424

T

Tattered Cover Book Store, 160
Texterity, 225
Theatre Library Association (TLA), 790
THOMAS, 32
Thomson Corporation, 20
3M, 130–131
Time Life Books, 19
Time Warner Trade Publishing, 18
  iPublish, 18, 222
Tower Books, 19
Tyndale House, 659, 661

U

Universal City Studios Inc., 291–292
University of Rochester Libraries, 430
Urban Libraries Council (ULC), 790–791
USNEI (U.S. Network for Education Information), 112

V

Vancouver Association of Chinese Canadians, 262
Verizon Communications, 134–135
Versaware, 225
Vivendi, 20
VTLS; Chameleon iPortal, 7

W

Wallace's Bookstores, 18–19
John Wiley & Sons, 20
World News Connection (WNC), 88
World Trade Organization (WTO), 294–295

X

Xlibris.com, 223

Y

Yahoo!, 146
Young Adult Library Services Association (YALSA), 752–753
  awards, 417–418
  best books list, 645–647
    audiobooks, 650–651
    for reluctant readers, 648–650

Z

Zany Brainy, 19

Subject Index

Please note that many cross-references refer to entries in the Index of Organizations.

A

Academic books, prices and price indexes, 151, 480(table), 481(table), 482(table)
British averages, 542–543(table)
foreign books, 484(table)
North American, 484(table), 527, 532–533(table)
U.S. college books, 484(table), 527, 534–535(table)
See also Association of American Publishers, Professional and Scholarly Publishing Division; Society for Scholarly Publishing; Textbooks
Academic journals, 4
Academic libraries, *see* Academic Libraries Survey; College and research libraries
Academic Libraries Survey (ALS), 103–105
Acquisitions
expenditures, 453–461
academic libraries, 456–457(table)
government libraries, 460–461(table)
public libraries, 454–455(table), 468(table), 474–475
special libraries, 458–459(table)
prices and price indexes, 480(table)
major components, 481(table), 482(table)
See also specific types of libraries, e.g., Public libraries
Adults, services for
readers' advisory; bibliography for librarians, 578
See also Literacy programs; Reference and User Services Association
African Newspaper Union List Project (AFRINUL), 168
Agencies, library, *see* Library associations and agencies
Agricultural libraries, *see* International Association of Agricultural Information

Specialists; National Agricultural Library
Agronsky, Martin, 34
Alabama
Center for the Book, 41
library associations, 792
networks and cooperative library organizations, 707
school library media associations, 810
Alaska
Information Empowered: The School Librarian as an Agent of Academic Achievement . . ., 15–16
library associations, 792
networks and cooperative library organizations, 707
school library media associations, 810
Albro, Sylvia, 28
Almanacs, bestselling, 676
American Women . . ., 35
America's Heroes, 24
Andre, Pamela Q.J., 64
Anfinsen, Christian, 68
Archives
acquisition expenditures
academic libraries, 456–457(table)
government libraries, 460–461(table)
public libraries, 454–455(table)
special libraries, 458–459(table)
electronic, 190–191
Encoded Archival Description (EAD), 194
Open Archives Initiative, 190
See also Archives Library Information Center; National Archives and Records Administration
Arizona
Internet/Web censorship issues, 146
library associations, 792
networks and cooperative library organizations, 707

Arizona *(cont.)*
school library media associations, 810
Arkansas
library associations, 792–793
networks and cooperative library organizations, 707–708
school library media associations, 810
Armed forces libraries, number of, 440, 441
Arms, William Y., 45
Ashcroft v. *Free Speech Coalition*, 147
Asia
Digital Dictionaries of South Asia Project (DDSA), 170
Digital South Asia Library Program (DSAL), 170
Southeast Asia Indexing Project, 170
Associations, *see* Book trade, associations; Information-industry associations; Library associations and agencies and names of specific associations
@ Your Library, 125, 129–130
Atlases, bestselling, 676
Audiocassettes
audiobooks, 430–431, 650–651
prices and price indexes, 473(table), 480(table), 486(table)
Audiovisual materials, 37
acquisition expenditures
academic libraries, 456–457(table)
government libraries, 460–461(table)
public libraries, 454–455(table)
special libraries, 458–459(table)
bibliography for librarians, 575
See also National Audio-Visual Conservation Center
Authors
freelance; electronic copyright, 6, 22–23, 129, 143, 164, 252, 287–290
Internet/Web publishing, 250–252
royalties, 224–225
Automation, 7
bibliography for librarians, 574
See also Computers; Networks and networking
Awards
AALL, 406
AAP, 140
AASL, 408–409
ACRL, 410–412, 436
AJL, 419–420
ALA, 134, 406–418, 434
ALCTS, 409

ALISE, 419, 436
ALSC, 409–410
ALTA, 409
APALA, 419
ARLIS/NA, 418–419
ASCLA, 412
ASIS&T, 418, 435–436
Beta Phi Mu, 420
BSA, 420
CACUL, 420–421
CALA, 421
Caldecott Medal, 697
CAPL, 421
Andrew Carnegie Medal, 697
CASLIS, 421
Center for the Book, 41–42
CLA, 420–421
CLIR, 195–196, 421
CLTA, 421
CSLA, 421
e-books, 230–231
EMIERT, 412
FAFLRT, 412
FLICC, 44, 46
Gale Group, 422
Gates, Bill and Melinda, Access to Learning, 196, 200–201
GLBT, 413
GODORT, 413
GPO Access, 78–79
IFLA, 422
IFRT, 413
IMLS, 357
Coretta Scott King, 699
LAMA, 413–414
LC, 35
LHRT, 414–415, 434
library scholarship and award recipients, 406–424
LITA, 414
literary, 696–704
LRRT, 415, 434
MAGERT, 415
MLA, 422–423
National Book Awards, 230–231, 661, 700
John Newbery Medal, 701
NMRT, 415
Nobel Prize in Literature, 701
PEN, 701
PLA, 415–416
Pulitzer Prizes in Letters, 702
RUSA, 416–417

SAA, 423
K.G. Saur, 423
SLA, 423–424
SPARC, 181
SRRT, 417
YALSA, 417–418
See also Books, best books; Grants and names of specific awards or organizations

B

Baker, Nicholson, 170
Banned Books Week, 127, 148, 160
Barksdale, Jim, 156
Bernardo, Paul, 263
Bestsellers, 158, 659–669
  almanacs, atlases, annuals, 676
  children's books
    hardcover, 679–686
    paperbacks, 686–695
  effect of terrorist attacks, 24, 670
  fiction, 660(table), 662, 663(table), 664–666
  hardcover, 659–669
  net vs. gross issues, 661–662
  nonfiction, 660(table), 663(table), 666–669
  paperback, 670–677
  religious, 659, 661
Bibliographic description, standards for, *see* National Information Standards Organization
Bibliographic instruction
  bibliography for librarians, 568–569
  See also Bibliographical Society of America; Education for librarians and librarianship; Library/information science (LIS) education
Bibliographic utilities, *see* Networks and networking; OCLC; RLG
Bibliography for librarians, 567–579
  academic libraries, 567–568
  administration/personnel, 568
  bibliographic instruction, 568–569
  cataloging/classification, 569
  children's/young adult services/materials, 569–570
  collection development, 570
  copyright, 570
  customer service, 570–571
  digital reference, 246
  distance education, 571
  electronic library, 571
  fund raising, 571–572
  general works, 567
  government documents, 81, 572
  health information/medical librarianship, 572
  history of libraries, 575
  intellectual freedom, 572–573
  interlibrary loan, 573
  Internet/Web, 573
  librarians and librarianship, 573–574
  library automation, 574
  library buildings/space planning, 574–575
  library services, evaluation of, 571
  museums, 575
  nonprint materials, 575
  periodicals and periodical indexes, 579
  preservation, 575
  public libraries, 576
  readers' advisory, 576
  reference services, 576–577
  school libraries/media centers, 577
  serials, 577
  special groups, services for, 578–579
  technical services, 578
  volunteers, 579
Billington, James H., 41
BioOne, 181, 184, 254
Biotechnology information, *see* National Center for Biotechnology Information
Blind, library services for the, 27, 28, 228
  Web-Braille, 32
  See also Instructional Materials Accessibility Act; National Federation for the Blind; National Library Service for the Blind and Physically Handicapped
Sonny Bono Copyright Term Extension Act, 165
Book Business . . . (Epstein), 215, 231
Book exports, *see* Books, exports and imports; United States, book exports
Book fairs, *see* Book trade, calendar of events, *and* names of specific countries or fairs
Book imports, *see* Books, exports and imports; United States, book imports
Book Links, 133
Book sales, 24–25
  AAP annual survey, statistics from, 553–554
    estimated book publishing industry sales, 554(table)

Book sales *(cont.)*
  bestsellers, *see* Bestsellers
  e-books, 219, 223–225
  terrorist attacks' effect on, 24, 661, 670
  See also Acquisitions, expenditures; Best-
    sellers; Book trade; Books; Book-
    stores; E-books
Book stores, *see* Bookstores
Book trade
  associations, 837–842
  international and foreign, 843–849
  calendar of events, 852–858
  See also Bestsellers; Book sales; Books;
    Foreign book trade; Publishers and
    publishing *and* names of specific
    associations
BookExpo America (BEA), 20–21, 140, 145,
    148, 159
Booklist, 133
Books
  acquisition expenditures
    academic libraries, 456–457(table)
    government libraries, 460–461(table)
    public libraries, 454–455(table)
    special libraries, 458–459(table)
  banned, *see* Banned Books Week; Censor-
    ship
  best books
    adult, 643–644
    audiobooks for young adults, 650–651
    bestsellers, *see* Bestsellers
    children's, 652–654
    for reluctant young adult readers,
      648–650
    young adult, 645–647
  bestsellers, *see* Bestsellers
  digital reference, 247–248
  e-books, *see* E-books
  exports and imports
    U.S. exports, 555(table), 555–561
    U.S. exports of technical, scientific, pro-
      fessional books, 557(table)
    U.S. exports of textbooks, 558(table)
    U.S. exports to principal countries,
      556(table)
    U.S. imports from principal countries,
      559(table)
    U.S. imports technical, scientific, profes-
      sional books, 561(table)
    See also United States, book exports *or*
      book imports
  hardcover, *see* Hardcover books

  imports, *see subhead* exports and imports;
    United States, book imports
  ISBN, *see* International Standard Book
    Number
  paperback, *see* Paperback books
  preservation and conservation, *see* Preser-
    vation
  prices and price indexes, 548–552,
    550(table)
    academic books, *see* Academic books,
      prices and price indexes
    hardcover books, *see* Hardcover books,
      prices and price indexes
    paperback books, *see* Paperback books,
      prices and price indexes
    See also names of specific countries, e.g.,
      Germany
  review media statistics, 564(table)
  scholarly, *see* Academic books, prices and
    price indexes; Association of Ameri-
    can Publishers, Professional and
    Scholarly Publishing Division
  title output, 548–552
    American book title production,
      548(table)
    See also Awards; Book sales; Bookstores;
      Center for the Book, *and* names of
      specific countries, e.g., Germany
Booksellers and bookselling, *see* Association
    of American Publishers; Book sales;
    Bookstores
Bookstores
  ABA's antitrust lawsuit, 159
  ABA's business insurance program, 160
  GPO Online Bookstores, 81–82
  online, 223–225
  September 11 terrorism and, 138
  U.S. and Canada, 562–563(table)
  See also Book sales
Boorstin, Daniel J., 40, 41
Botkin, Benjamin A., 36, 43
The Brethren (Grisham), 24
Brotherhood, 24
Budapest Open Access Initiative (BOAI),
    183
Budgets
  FLICC/FEDLINK, 47, 55
  LC, 30
  legislation, appropriations, 30, 302,
    303(table)
  LJ budget report, 3–4, 462–467
  school library media centers, 11

See also Funding for libraries
Bush administration, budget, 302
Bush, George W. (President), 30, 147
Bush, Laura (First Lady), 29, 41, 42, 43, 125

C

Caldecott Medal, 134, 697
Calendar of events, 852–858
California
  library associations, 793
  networks and cooperative library organiza-
    tions, 708–709
  school library media associations, 810
Canada
  American-Canadian librarianship, 210–212
  AMICUS, 212
  anti-terrorist legislation, 257
  associations
    book trade, 837–842
    library, 802–804, 808–809
  bookstores, 562–563(table)
  Canadian National Site Licensing Project
    (CNSLP), 211–212
  copyright reform, 209–210
  federal government policy and libraries,
    206–209
  hate crime legislation, 260, 261
  Homolka-Bernardo trials, 263
  intellectual freedom, 257–267
    access, 259–261
    historical development, 258–259
    political history, 257–258
  libraries, number of, 441–442
  networks and cooperative library organiza-
    tions, 729–730
  See also Canada Act; Canadian Association
    for Information Science; Canadian
    Library Association; Criminal Code of
    Canada
Canada Act, 259
Captain Underpants . . ., 678
Andrew Carnegie Medal, 697
Cataloging and classification
  AMICUS, 212
  bibliography for librarians, 569
  CORC (Cooperative Online Resources Cat-
    alog), 51–52
  GPO, 74
  LC activities, 27, 28, 33
  MARC, 27–28

CD-ROM (Compact Disc Read-Only Memory)
  bibliography for librarians, 575
  copyright issues, 284
  Greenberg v. *National Geographic*, 143
  prices and price indexes, 541
    academic libraries, 480(table), 486(table)
    public libraries, 473(table)
  See also Copyright and copyright law;
    Music, CD protection; Napster
Censorship, 7, 140, 145–147
  government power expanded after terrorist
    attacks, 147, 257
  on the Internet/Web, filtering, *see* Filtering
    software
  kidSPEAK!, 160
  in school libraries, 14
  See also Association of American Publish-
    ers, Freedom to Read *or* International
    Freedom to Publish Committee;
    Banned Books Week; Children's
    Internet Protection Act; Filtering soft-
    ware
Certification, library media specialists, 10, 16
Chemical hazards
  NIOSH Pocket Guide to, 86
  Registry of Toxic Effects of Chemical Sub-
    stances (RTECS), 87
Chi, Y.S., 21
Chicken Soup . . ., 678
Child Online Protection Act (COPA), 5, 146
Child Pornography Prevention Act (CPPA),
  147
Children and young adults, 24
  bibliography for librarians, 569–570
  children's books, notable, 652–654
    bestsellers, 679–686, 686–695
  children's films/video, notable, 655
  children's recordings, notable, 656–657
  children's software, notable, 658
  Internet/Web and, 326–327
    Ben's Guide to U.S. Government for
      Kids, 79–80
    kidSPEAK!, 160
    notable sites, 658
    See also Filtering software
  library services for: *see* Association for
    Library Service for Children; Chil-
    dren's Internet Protection Act; School
    library media centers and services;
    Young Adult Library Services Associ-
    ation; Young adults

Children and young adults *(cont.)*
  videos; notable, 655
  young adults; notable books for, 645–647
  See also Children's Internet Protection Act;
    Neighborhood Children's Internet
    Protection Act
Children's Internet Protection Act (CIPA), 5,
    126, 146, 305
China, 32, 33
Choice, 132
A Christmas Carol (Dickens), 34
Civil liberties, terrorism and, 3
Clancy, Tom, 21
Clifford, Clark, 34
Clinger-Cohen Act, 273
Clinton, Bill, 272, 309, 319–320
Cohen, Abby Joseph, 155
Cole, John Y., 43
Collection development
  bibliography for librarians, 570
  CLIR activities, 187, 191, 192
  digital, 191, 192
  The Evidence in Hand, 187
  NCES survey, 444, 446, 450–451
  NLE, 109–110
  rare books, 109–110
  school library media centers, 10–11
College and research libraries, 5–6
  acquisition expenditures, 456–457(table),
    480(table)
  alumni outreach, 173
  bibliography for librarians, 567–568
  Canadian, 442
  CLIR activities, 186–188
  construction, *see* Library buildings
  e-books, 230
  Internet/Web publishing, 250–252
  NCES survey, 445–447, 449
  number of, 440, 441
  prices and price indexes, 476–479
    books and serials, 477–478, 484(table),
      485(table)
    budget composition of operations,
      480(table)
    major components, 481(table), 482(table)
    non-print media/electronic services,
      478–479, 486(table)
    personnel compensation, 477, 480(table),
      481(table), 482(table), 483(table)
  reference, digital, 236–237
  research on, 427–430
  state library agencies, services, 449

  See also Academic Libraries Survey; Asso-
    ciation of College and Research
    Libraries; Association of Research
    Libraries; Council on Library and
    Information Resources; International
    Scholarly Communications Alliance;
    RLG
Collier, Bryan, 134
Collins, Billy, 36
Collins, Doug, 262
Colorado
  Center for the Book, 41–42
  *How School Librarians Help Kids Achieve
    Standards*, 15
  library associations, 793
  networks and cooperative library organiza-
    tions, 709
  school library media associations, 810
Combating Terrorism Act, 257
Computer software
  children's; notable, 658
  DECPLUS, 101
  DeCSS, 142, 291–292
  digital reference, 243–244
  e-book reader software, 220–221
  ElComSoft, 228
  filtering, *see* Filtering software
  Grateful Med, 66
  licensing, 295
  portals, 7, 165
  Universal City Studios, Inc. v. *Reimerdes*,
    142
  WINPLUS, 101
  See also Software and Information Industry
    Association
Computers
  free "speech" and, 142
  in school library media centers, 11
  software, *see* Computer software
  See also CD-ROM; DVD; Networks and
    networking
Conferences and seminars, 852–858
  AAP, 141, 143, 147, 151, 154–156
  AASL, 432
  ACRL, 132
  ALA, 131–132, 135, 244
  ALCTS, 132
  ARL, 166, 167, 175, 177
  BookExpo America (BEA), 20–21, 140,
    145, 148, 159
  CLA, 262
  CLIR, 192

DefCon, 228
FDLP, 75
FLICC, 44, 50
Frye Leadership Institute, 193
IFLA, 131, 197–201
IMLS, 356–357
Information Strategies, 243
LC, 27, 36
Library Research Seminar II, 427
LITA, 131–132
NAL, 64
National Federation for the Blind, 153
NIST, 8
PLA, 132
PSP, 151
RPAC, 141–142
Seybold, 229
SPARC, 183
VRD, 246
See also as subhead, e.g., American
    Library Association, conferences
Congressional Record, 271
Connecticut
    library associations, 793
    networks and cooperative library organiza-
        tions, 709–710
    school library media
        associations, 810–811
Conservation and preservation, *see* Preserva-
    tion
Consolidated Appropriations Act of 2001, 30
Consortia
    digital reference, 237–238
    directory, 707–730
Cooperative library organizations, 707–730
Copyright Act, 164, 287, 294–295, 310
    amendments, *see* Digital Millennium Copy-
        right Act
Copyright and copyright law
    AAP activities, 141–143, 154–155
    ALA activities, 128–129
    antipiracy activities, 149–150
    ARL activities, 163–164
    bibliography for librarians, 570
    Canadian reform, 209–210
    digital copyright, 6–7
    e-books, 227–229, 230
    Eldred v. *Ashcroft*, 286–287
    fair use, 154–155, 165, 285
    Felten v. *Recording Industry Association of
        America (RIAA)*, 142, 291

freelance authors' work, 6, 22–23, 129,
    143, 164, 252, 287–290
Greenberg v. *National Geographic*, 143
IFLA activities, 295
infringement, 23
international issues, 294–295
LC Copyright Office, 32–33
legislation, 165, 290–291
Mitchell Estate v. *Houghton Mifflin*, 23
MPAA v. *Corley*, 7
music, 6, 142, 291
New York Times v. *Tasini*, 129, 164,
    287–289
photographs, 143, 164, 289
Random House v. *RosettaBooks*, 23,
    227–228, 289–290
RPAC Copyright Primer, 142
Tasini v. *New York Times*, 6, 22–23
TEACH Act, 292–293
technology and, 284–296
term extension, 286–287
U.S. v. *Elcom and Sklyarov*, 292
See also Sonny Bono Copyright Term
    Extension Act; Digital Millennium
    Copyright Act
Cornwell, Patricia, 21
The Corrections (Franzen), 661
Criminal Code of Canada, 260, 261
Cumulated Index Medicus (CIM), 67
Customer service; bibliography for librarians,
    570–571
Cybercrime, 320–321
Cyberlibraries, 10–11

D

Databases, 164
    ARL's Digital Initiatives Database (DID),
        171
    Davis-Bacon Wage Determination, 88–89
    Energy Science and Technology (EDB),
        85–86
    FEDRIP, 84
    Immediately Dangerous to Life or Health
        Concentrations (IDLH), 86
    NCES survey, 448
    NLM, 67–68
    NTIS, 84–87
    protection; pending legislation, 293, 310
    Service Contract Wage Determination
        Database, 89
    for visual resources, 187–188

Databases *(cont.)*
See also CD-ROM; DVD; Networks and
networking *and* names of databases
Davis, Hal, 33
Delaware
library associations, 793
networks and cooperative library organiza-
tions, 710
school library media associations, 811
Democracy and the Rule of Law, 35
Desecration, 659
Dickens, Charles, 34
Digital libraries
ARL survey, 171
CLIR activities, 189–190, 191, 192
copyright issues, 6–7
IFLA activities, 198–199, 295
LC activities, 31–32, 34
legislation, pending, 326
See also Digital Library Foundation; Digital Millennium Copyright Act; Digital
reference; Electronic resources
Digital Millennium Copyright Act (DMCA),
31, 165, 216, 228, 229, 284
antidecryption provision, 7, 142, 164
First Sale Doctrine and, 285–286, 310–311
free speech issues, 291–292
scientific research and, 142–143
Digital reference, 234–246
academic libraries, 236–237
accessibility, 242
background, 234–235
bibliographies, 246
books, 247–248
confidentiality issues, 239
consortia, 237–238
defined, 235–236
evaluation strategies, 243
government, 238
information literacy and, 242
international, 238–239
journals, 247
marketing, 241–242
new technologies, 244–245
research studies, 245–246
resources, 246–248
software selection, 243–244
staffing issues, 241
standards, 239, 245
training/education, 240–241
Virtual Reference Desk, 235, 238, 239, 246
Disabled Americans, services for

ALA's Policy, 136
bibliography for librarians, 578
*Library and Information Services for Indi-
viduals with Disabilities* (NCLIS), 58
See also Blind, library services for the
District of Columbia
library associations, 793
networks and cooperative library organiza-
tions, 710
Northeast Neighborhood Library, 125
school library media associations, 811
Document delivery, *see* Interlibrary loan
(ILL)/document delivery
Double Fold (Baker), 170
DVD, copyright issues, 284, 291–292
movies, 142, 165
Dvorak, John, 229

E

E-books, 8, 144, 215–232, 430–431
AAP Standards Project, 143
authors' royalties, 6, 22–23, 129, 143, 164,
252, 287–290
awards, 230–231
copyright issues, 227–229, 230
customers, 219
fulfillment/e-commerce/digital conversion,
225
Gemstar, 155, 220, 226
independent retailers, 223–225
key viewpoints/publications, 231
libraries and, 226–227
market forecasts, 218–219
nonprofits, 230
online retailers, 219
Open eBook Publication Structure
(OEBPS), 229
print on demand, 221
publishers, traditional, 222–223
reader software, 220–221
reading devices, 220, 229–230
small/vanity presses, 223–225
standards, 229
textbooks, 230
timeline for 2001, 216–218
Web-based, 221–222
E-Government Act of 2001, 46, 128, 308
E-journals, 526
archiving program, 190–191, 428–429
E-publishing, 18–25

E-rate, *see* Telecommunications, E-rate program
Eames, Charles and Ray, 35–36
Economy, 155, 468
Education
  assessment/school improvement, 313–314
  distance education, 8, 50, 104, 143–144, 173, 310
    bibliography for librarians, 571
  Education Assessment . . ., 152
  National Household Education Survey, 102–103
  state spending, terrorism's effect on, 152
  student privacy issues, 314–315
  technology in, 12
  See also Association for Educational Communications and Technology; Department of Education Appropriations Act; Educational Resources Information Center; International Society for Technology in Education; National Education Data Resource Center; National Library of Education
Department of Education Appropriations Act, 317–318
Education for librarians and librarianship
  accredited master's programs, 371–374, 396–400
  ALA activities, 124–125
  digital reference training, 240–241
  FLICC activities, 48, 50
  grants, 135
  honor society, *see* Beta Phi Mu
  LIS education, 6
  Mortenson Center, 194
  school library media specialists, 9, 16–17, 515(table)
  See also Library/information science education
Education for publishers; AAP activities, 145
Eizenstat, Stuart, 34
The elderly, *see* Reference and User Services Association
Eldred v. *Ashcroft*, 165, 286–287
Electronic Information Access Enhancement Act, *see* GPO Access
Electronic resources
  acquisition expenditures
    academic libraries, 456–457(table)
    government libraries, 460–461(table)
    public libraries, 454–455(table)
    special libraries, 458–459(table)
  bibliography for librarians, 571
  expenditures; electronic information resources, 515(table)
  journals, *see* E-journals
  preservation activities, 170
Electronic services
  price indexes, academic libraries, 481(table), 482(table), 486(table), 487(table)
  price indexes, public libraries, 469(table), 473(table)
  See also E-books
Elementary and Secondary Education Act (ESEA), 5
  reauthorization, 301, 302, 303, 304, 312
  See also No Child Left Behind Act
Emergency Supplemental Appropriations Act for Recovery from and Response to Terrorist Attacks on the United States, 30
Employment opportunities, *see* International personnel exchanges for librarians; Placement
Encyclopedias
  U.S. exports, 557(table)
  U.S. imports, 559(table)
Epstein, Jason, 215, 222, 231
The Evidence in Hand, 187
Exchange programs, *see* International personnel exchanges for librarians

F

Faxes
  NARA Fax-on-Demand, 96
Federal depository libraries, 272, 276
  distribution, 73–74, 74(table)
  Electronic Federal Depository Library Program (FDLP), 72–73, 79
  funding, 302
  Library Programs Service (LPS), 72–73, 75
Federal Register, 270, 271
Fellowships, *see* Scholarships and fellowships
Felten v. *Recording Industry Association of America (RIAA)*, 142, 291
Fiction, *see* Awards; Bestsellers; Books, best books
Filtering software, 5, 146
First amendment legislation, *see* Censorship
First Monday, 251
Fiscal Operations Improvement Act, 45

The Floating World of Ukiyo-e, 35
Florida
  library associations, 793–794
  networks and cooperative library organizations, 710–711
  school library media associations, 811
Wendell H. Ford Government Publications Reform Act, 273
Foreign book trade, associations, 843–849
Foreign books; prices, 484(table), 541, 546
Foreign Law Briefs, 30
Foreign library associations, 826–835
  See also names of specific countries
Frankfurt Book Fair, 23
Franklin, John Hope, 28
Franzen, Jonathan, 661
Freedom of Information Act (FOIA), 268, 280
Freedom of speech, *see* Intellectual freedom
Freud, Sigmund, 36
Friedberg, Aaron, 28
Fund raising, 464(table)
  bibliography for librarians, 571–572
Funding for libraries
  budgets, projected, 463(table)
  federal, 316–317(table)
  See also Grants; Library Services and Technology Act
  school library media centers, 504–508

G

Gates, Bill and Melinda, 196
Genetic medicine, 69–70
Georgia
  AAP activities, 153
  library associations, 794
  networks and cooperative library organizations, 711
  school library media associations, 811
Germany
  German Resources Project, 166
  prices and price indexes; academic periodicals, 544(table), 546
Germs, 24
Get Caught Reading, 140–141, 154
Gone with the Wind (Mitchell), 23, 160
Government documents
  bibliography for librarians, 572
  NARA, 95
  See also American Library Association, Government Documents Round Table;

Federal depository libraries; Government Printing Office
Government information, access to, 76–77, 268–280
  A Comprehensive Assessment of Public Information Dissemination (NCLIS), 58
  Ben's Guide to U.S. Government for Kids, 79
  challenges/issues, 271–272
  digital reference, 238
  electronic dissemination, 273–279
  FirstGov, 308
  historical background, 269–271
  See also Electronic Information Access Enhancement Act; Federal depository libraries; GPO Access
Government libraries
  acquisitions expenditures, 460–461(table)
  Canadian, 442
  number of, 440, 441
Government Printing Office Electronic Information Access Enhancement Act: *see* GPO Access
Grann, Phyllis, 21–22
Grants
  AASL, 437
  ACRL, 135, 437
  ALA, 129–130, 436–438
  ALISE, 438–439
  ARL, 171, 174, 175
  ASIS&T, 438
  CLIR, 187, 188, 189, 193, 429, 439
  Bill and Melinda Gates Foundation, 196
  IMLS, 348–353(table), 429, 431–432
  legislation, pending, 327–328
  LSTA National Leadership Grants, 430
  LSTA Native American Library Services Program, 346, 354, 355–356(table)
  LSTA Native Hawaiian Library Services Program, 346, 354
  Andrew W. Mellon Foundation, 428–429
  MLA, 439
  NARA, 97–98
  NEH, 333, 336–338
  SLA, 439
  YALSA, 437–438
Great Britain, book prices and price indexes, 542–543(table), 546
Greater Victoria Public Library, 261
Green, Elizabeth, 35
Greenberg v. *National Geographic*, 143, 164

Grisham, John, 24, 659, 661

H

Hardcover books, 24
  bestsellers, 660(table), 663(table)
  children's, 679–686
  prices and price indexes, 472(table)
    averages, 530(table), 531(table)
    averages per-volume, 549(table)
Hass, Robert, 42
Hate crime legislation, 260, 261
  See also Hate Crimes Prevention Act;
      Local Law Enforcement Enhancement
      Act
Hate Crimes Prevention Act, 261
Hawaii
  library associations, 794
  LSTA Native Hawaiian Library Services
      Program, 346, 354
  networks and cooperative library organiza-
      tions, 711
  school library media associations, 811
Health information; bibliography for librari-
      ans, 572
Health sciences libraries, *see* Archivists and
      Librarians in the History of the Health
      Sciences; Association of Academic
      Health Sciences Libraries; Medical
      Library Association; National Library
      of Medicine
Hefner, Christie, 155
History of libraries; bibliography for librari-
      ans, 575
The Hobbit (Tolkien), 24
Hoffman, Dustin, 147
Homolka, Karla, 263
Hope, Bob, 35

I

Idaho
  library associations, 794
  networks and cooperative library organiza-
      tions, 711–712
  school library media associations, 811
Illinois
  library associations, 794–795
  networks and cooperative library organiza-
      tions, 712–713
  school library media associations, 811

India, 149
Indian tribes, library services to, *see* Native
      Americans, library and information
      services to
Indiana
  library associations, 795
  networks and cooperative library organiza-
      tions, 713–714
  school library media associations, 811–812
Information, access to: *see* Government
      information, access to; Information
      literacy
*Information Empowered: The School Librari-
      an as an Agent of Academic Achieve-
      ment . . .*, 15–16
Information literacy, 13, 242
Information Power . . . (AASL/AECT),
      11–12, 13, 14
Information science: *see* American Society
      for Information Science and Technol-
      ogy; Canadian Association for Infor-
      mation Science; National Commission
      on Libraries and Information Science
Information technology, *see* Library and
      Information Technology Association;
      National Commission on Libraries
      and Information Science; National
      Technical Information Service
Information-industry associations, 731–791
Instructional Materials Accessibility Act,
      152–153
Intellectual freedom
  ALA activities, 126–128
  bibliography for librarians, 572–573
  Canada versus U.S., 257–267
  DMCA and, 291–292
  Intellectual Freedom Manual, 127–128
  Lamont v. *Postmaster General*, 259
  in school library media centers, 13–14
  See also Association of American Publish-
      ers, Freedom to Read Committee *and*
      International Freedom to Publish
      Committee; Censorship; Filtering
      software
Intellectual property, 320–321
  AAP activities, 141, 155
  ARL activities, 163–164
  See also Digital Millennium Copyright Act
Intelligence Authorization Act, 309, 319–320
Interlibrary cooperation, *see* Interlibrary loan
      (ILL)/document delivery;

Interlibrary cooperation *(cont.)*
    Internet/Web; Networks and network-
        ing
Interlibrary loan (ILL)/document delivery
    ARL activities, 166, 169
    bibliography for librarians, 573
    ERIC, 116
    See also Internet/Web; Networks and net-
        working
International book trade, associations,
        843–849
International library activity
    associations, 818–825
    digital reference, 238–239
    See also International personnel exchanges
        for librarians; International Scholarly
        Communications Alliance; Librarians
        and librarianship
International personnel exchanges for librari-
        ans
    employment opportunities, 376–377
    overseas exchange programs, 377
    Russia/U.S., 30
International Standard Book Number (ISBN),
        633–636
    assignment procedure, 634
    construction, 633
    five-digit add-on code, 635–636, 636(fig-
        ure)
    location and display of, 634–635
    machine-readable coding, 635(figure)
    organization of system, 634
    reporting the title and the ISBN, 636
International Standard Serial Number (ISSN),
        637–638
Internet Freedom and Broadband Deploy-
        ment Act, 305
Internet Tax Nondiscrimination Act, 323–324
Iowa
    library associations, 795
    networks and cooperative library organiza-
        tions, 714
    school library media associations, 812
Iran, 148

J

Jack: Straight from the Gut (Welch), 23, 661
Japan
    Global Resources Program Japan Project,
        166
    Journal Access Project, 166, 169

Jefferson Library Project, 34
Jeffords, Jim (Sen.), 304
Jobs, *see* Placement
Johnson, Jim, 4
Johnson, Spencer, 24
Journalism, investigative, 145
Journals
    electronic, *see* E-journals
    PubSCIENCE, 322–323
    scholarly, 4

K

Kansas
    library associations, 795
    networks and cooperative library organiza-
        tions, 714
    school library media associations, 812
Keegstra, Jim, 260
Kentucky
    library associations, 795
    networks and cooperative library organiza-
        tions, 714–715
    school library media associations, 812
Coretta Scott King Awards, 134, 699
King, Stephen, 661
    e-books; micropayments, 252
Kissinger, Henry, 36
Kranich, Nancy, 125–126
Krashen, Stephen; *The Power of Reading*, 15
Kunitz, Stanley, 36

L

Lamont v. *Postmaster General*, 259
Lance, Keith Curry, 432
Latin America
    Latin Americanist Research Resources
        Project, 169
    periodical prices and price indexes,
        545(table), 547
Law libraries, *see* American Association of
        Law Libraries; International Associa-
        tion of Law Libraries
Leave No Child Behind Act, 152
Left Behind series, 659, 670
Legislation affecting information industry
    ARL activities, 163–165
    copyright, 165, 290–291
    U.S. v. *Elcom and Sklyarov*, 292

See also Digital Millennium Copyright Act; TEACH Act
Legislation affecting libraries, 30, 45, 301–311
  CIPA lawsuit, 126–127
  database protection, 310
  distance education, 310
  E-Government Act of 2001, 46, 308
  E-rate program, 5, 305
  Eldred v. *Ashcroft*, 165
  ESEA reauthorization, 301, 302, 303
  filtering, *see* Filtering software
  FirstGov, 308
  funding; appropriations for federal library and related programs, 302, 303(table)
  Greenberg v. *National Geographic Society*, 164
  hate crime legislation, 260, 261
    Canadian, 261–263
  Intelligence Authorization Act, 309
  New York Times v. *Tasini*, 164, 287–288
  No Child Left Behind, 301, 302
  NTIS, 308
  postal issues, 305
  Presidential Records Act, 309
  Tasini v. *New York Times*, 6, 22–23
  UCITA, 6, 293–294
  USA Patriot Act, 301, 306–307
  See also Digital Millennium Copyright Act; Library Services and Technology Act; TEACH Act; Uniform Computer Information Transactions Act
Legislation affecting publishing, 22–23, 312–330
  AAP activities, 139, 141–143, 145–147
  ABA activities, 159
  after September 11 terrorism, 152
  Ashcroft v. *Free Speech Coalition*, 147
  cybercrime, 320–321
  Department of Education Appropriations Act, 317–318
  Eldred v. *Ashcroft*, 286–287
  electronic dissemination of government information, 273–279
  ESEA reauthorization, 312
  Felten v. *Recording Industry Association of America (RIAA)*, 142
  Greenberg v. *National Geographic*, 143
  intellectual property, 320–321
  Intelligence Authorization Act, 319–320
  Internet Tax Nondiscrimination Act, 323–324

  Mitchell Estate v. *Houghton Mifflin*, 23
  National Geographic Society v. *Jerry Greenberg and Idaz Greenberg*, 289
  New York Times v. *Tasini*, 129, 143, 287–289
  postal issues, 150–151, 321–322
  PubSCIENCE, 322–323
  Random House v. *RosettaBooks*, 23, 227–228, 252
  school libraries, funding for, 316–317
  student privacy issues, 314–315
  tax-related, 329
  Universal City Studios, Inc. v. *Reimerdes*, 142
  USA Patriot Act, 318–319
  See also Children's Internet Protection Act; Digital Millennium Copyright Act; No Child Left Behind Act; Official Secrets Act; Reading Excellence Act; TEACH Act
Legislation affecting publishing non-enacted, 324–330
Legislative Branch Appropriations Act, 30
Letters of Delegates to Congress, 1774–1789, 35
Librarians and librarianship, 176
  American-Canadian, 210–212
  bibliography for librarians, 573–574
  Canadian-American, 204–206
  compensation, *see* Salaries
  exchange programs, *see* International personnel exchanges for librarians
  placement services, *see* Placement
  recruitment/retention, 144–145, 171
  research on, 427–439
  school librarianship, strategic planning for, 16–17
  school library media specialists, 9–17
  See also Council on Library and Information Resources; Education for librarians and librarianship; Library/information science (LIS) education; National Librarians Association
Librarianship as a profession, *see* Librarians and librarianship
Libraries
  acquisitions, *see* Acquisitions
  administration, *see* Library Administration and Management Association
  budget, *see* Funding for libraries
  buildings, *see* Library buildings

Libraries *(cont.)*
collections, *see* Collection development
depository, *see* Federal depository libraries
digital, *see* Digital libraries
electronic, *see* Electronic resources
funding, *see* Funding for libraries
international activity, *see* International
library activity
Internet/Web publishing and, 253–254
legislation, *see* Legislation affecting
libraries
research on, 427–439
Library administration, *see* Library Administration and Management Association
Library associations and agencies
Canadian, 729–730, 802–804, 808–809
foreign, 826–835
international, 818–825
national and Canadian, 731–791
networks and cooperative organizations,
707–730
placement sources
specialized associations and groups,
364–369
state and regional
state, 369–370, 447–452, 805–809
state and regional, 792–804
state school library media, 810–817
Library buildings, 488–502
academic
additions/renovations, 490(table),
491(table)
new, 489(table)
bibliography for librarians, 574–575
public
additions/renovations, 496–501(table)
cost summary, 502(table)
new, 492–495(table)
Library education, *see* Education for librarians and librarianship; Library/infor-
mation science (LIS) education
Library grants, *see* Grants; Legislation affecting libraries; Scholarships and fellowships
Library Hi Tech, 231
Library Hi-Tech News (LHTN), 433
Library Journal (LJ)
budget report, 3–4, 462–467
fund raising, 464(table)
funding and technology, 464–465
local progress reports, 465–467
projected, 463(table)

news report, 3–8
The Other E-Books, 231
Library management, *see* Library Administration and Management Association
Library materials, *see* Preservation; School
library media centers and services,
and names of specific countries, *and*
names of specific materials, e.g.,
Audiovisual materials
Library personnel
education, *see* Education for librarians and
librarianship; Library/information science (LIS) education
employment, search for, *see* Placement
exchange programs, *see* International personnel exchanges for librarians
See also Librarians and librarianship;
National Librarians Association;
Placement; Salaries; Staffing
Library schools, *see* Education for librarians
and librarianship; Library/information
science (LIS) education; Placement
Library services and programs
evaluation of; bibliography for librarians,
571
See also Library Services and Technology
Act; National Commission on
Libraries and Information Science,
and names of special interest groups
and specific countries
Library Services and Technology Act
(LSTA), 5, 128, 302, 430
Native American Library Services Pro-
gram, 346, 354, 355–356(table)
Native Hawaiian Library Services Program,
346, 354
See also Institute of Museum and Library
Services
Library standards, *see* International Organi-
zation for Standardization; National
Information Standards Organization
Library statistics, *see* National Center for
Education Statistics, Library Statistics
Program; Statistics
Library/information science (LIS) education,
5–6
accredited master's programs, 371–374,
396–400
distance ed programs, 8
honor society, *see* Beta Phi Mu
See also Education for librarians and librar-
ianship

Lieberman, Joseph I. (Sen.), 46, 277
Literacy programs
    AAP activities, 145–147
    ABA's Prescription for Reading, 158
    ALA activities, 133–134, 137
    Early Reading First, 304, 315–316
    LC activities, 27, 29
    Literacy and Libraries . . ., 137
    Mississippi reading initiative, 156
    Reading First, 152, 304, 315–316
    See also Center for the Book; Department
        of Education Appropriations Act; Get
        Caught Reading; Information literacy;
        Reading Excellence Act
Literary awards, *see* Awards
Local Law Enforcement Act, 261
The Lord of the Rings: The Fellowship of the
    Ring Photo Guide, 670
The Lord of the Rings Official Movie Guide,
    670
Lord of the Rings (Tolkien), 133, 670
Los Angeles Magazine, 147
Los Angeles Times, 228
Louisiana
    library associations, 795–796
    networks and cooperative library organiza-
        tions, 715
    school library media associations, 812
Lynch, Clifford, 231

M

McCain, John (Sen.), 276–278
McClintock, Barbara, 68
Maine
    library associations, 796
    networks and cooperative library organiza-
        tions, 715
    school library media associations, 812
Margulis, Lynn, 34
Maryland
    library associations, 796
    networks and cooperative library organiza-
        tions, 715
    school library media associations, 812–813
Marx, Groucho, 232
Massachusetts
    library associations, 796
    networks and cooperative library organiza-
        tions, 715–717
    school library media associations, 813
Mead, Margaret, 35

Media services, *see* School library media
    centers and services
Medical libraries, *see* Archivists and Librari-
    ans in the History of the Health Sci-
    ences; Association of Academic
    Health Sciences Librarians; Medical
    Library Association; National Library
    of Medicine
Michigan
    library associations, 796–797
    networks and cooperative library organiza-
        tions, 717–718
    school library media associations, 813
Microforms, 170
    acquisition expenditures
        academic libraries, 456–457(table)
        government libraries, 460–461(table)
        public libraries, 454–455(table)
        special libraries, 458–459(table)
    prices and price indexes, 468(table),
        473(table), 480(table), 486(table)
    See also Association for Information and
        Image Management; Association of
        Research Libraries; National Techni-
        cal Information Service, Selected
        Research in Microfiche
Minnesota
    library associations, 797
    networks and cooperative library organiza-
        tions, 718
    school library media associations, 813
Minorities
    professional recruitment, 171
    publishing, 144
    See also American Libraries Association,
        Ethnic and Multicultural Information
        Exchange Round Table; Native Amer-
        icans, library and information services
        to
Miracle's Boys (Woodson), 134
Miscellaneous Appropriations Act, 30
Mississippi
    library associations, 797
    networks and cooperative library organiza-
        tions, 718–719
    reading initiative, 156
    school library media associations, 813
Missouri
    library associations, 797
    networks and cooperative library organiza-
        tions, 719
    St. Louis Public Library, 431–432

Missouri *(cont.)*
  school library media associations, 813
Mitchell Estate v. *Houghton Mifflin*, 23
Mitchell, Margaret, 23, 160
Montana
  library associations, 797
  school library media associations, 814
Movies, reproduction of: *see* DVD
MPAA v. *Corley*, 7
Museums; bibliography for librarians, 575
Music
  CD protection, 142, 290–291
    Felten v. *Recording Industry Association of America (RIAA)*, 142
    See also Napster
  legislation, pending, 325–326
  libraries, *see* International Association of Music Libraries, Archives and Documentation Centres; Music Library Association

N

National Book Awards, 230–231, 661, 700
National Digital Information Infrastructure Program, 30
National Geographic, 164, 289–290
National Geographic Society v. *Jerry Greenberg and Idaz Greenberg*, 289
National Library Week, 125
Native Americans, library and information services to
  ArcticHealth, 67–68, 70
  bibliography for librarians, 578
  LSTA Native American Library Services Program, 346, 354, 355–356(table)
Nazi memorabilia, 146
Nebraska
  library associations, 797
  networks and cooperative library organizations, 719
  school library media associations, 814
Neighborhood Children's Internet Protection Act (NCIPA), 126
The Netherlands, periodical prices and price indexes; Dutch (English Language), 546
Networks and networking
  Collaborative Digital Reference Service, 34
  cooperative library organizations and, 245, 707–730

digital reference and, 245
electronic; publishing, 143
FEDLINK/OCLC activity, 51–52
international, *see* Internet/Web
Learning Objects Network, 143
national, *see* Internet/Web
NCES survey, 448
NELINET, 226
NEN, 111
NN/LM, 69
reference services, 240
SciDev.Net, 252–253
USNEI, 112
See also Coalition for Networked Information; Consortia, *and* names of specific networks, e.g., OCLC
Nevada
  library associations, 797
  networks and cooperative library organizations, 719
  school library media associations, 814
New Hampshire
  library associations, 798
  networks and cooperative library organizations, 719–720
  school library media associations, 814
The New Jackals, 24
New Jersey
  library associations, 798
  networks and cooperative library organizations, 720
  school library media associations, 814
New Mexico
  library associations, 798
  networks and cooperative library organizations, 720–721
  school library media associations, 814
New York
  library associations, 798
  networks and cooperative library organizations, 721–722
  NYC budget cuts after September 11, 3–4
  school library media associations, 814
New York September 11, 24
The New York Times, 7
New York Times v. *Tasini*, 129, 143, 164, 287–289
John Newbery Medal, 134, 701
Newspapers
  African Newspaper Union List Project (AFRINUL), 168
  as placement sources, 361

prices and price indexes, 472(table),
485(table)
international, averages, 540(table)
U.S. dailies, 540(table)
Nirenberg, Marshall, 68
No Child Left Behind Act, 301, 302, 304,
312–317
Nobel Prize in Literature, 701
Nonfiction books, *see* Awards; Bestsellers;
Books, best books
Nonprint materials, *see* Audiocassettes;
Audiovisual materials; CD-ROM;
DVD; Videocassettes
North Carolina
electronic procurement system, 153
library associations, 798–799
networks and cooperative library organizations, 722
school library media associations, 814–815
North Dakota
library associations, 799
networks and cooperative library organizations, 722
school library media associations, 815

O

Official Secrets Act, 309
Ohio
library associations, 799
networks and cooperative library organizations, 723
school library media associations, 815
Oklahoma
library associations, 799
networks and cooperative library organizations, 723
school library media associations, 815
*One Nation: America Remembers September
11, 2001*, 24
Open World Russian Leadership Program, 30
Oprah Book Club, 661, 670
Oregon
library associations, 799
networks and cooperative library organizations, 723–724
school library media associations, 815
Organic Letters, 4
Osgood, Charles, 156

P

A Painted House (Grisham), 24
Pakistan, 148–149
Paperback books
almanacs, atlases, annuals, 676
bestsellers, 24–25, 670–677
children's, 686–695
mass market, 676–679
trade, 24, 671–676
exports, mass market paperbacks,
556(table)
imports, mass market paperbacks,
561(table)
prices and price indexes
trade and mass market, 472(table), 527
U.S. mass market, averages, 527,
536(table), 537(table), 551(table),
552(table)
U.S. trade, averages, 527, 529(table),
538(table)
See also Association of American Publishers, Trade Publishing
Paperwork Reduction Act, 271, 278–279
Paretsky, Sara, 140
Patel, Marilyn Hall (Judge), 6
Patterson, James, 661
Peck, Richard, 134
Pelikan, Jaroslav, 28
PEN awards, 701
Pennsylvania
library associations, 799–800
networks and cooperative library organizations, 724–725
school library media associations, 815
Pentagon attack, *see* Terrorism
Periodicals and serials
acquisition expenditures
academic libraries, 456–457(table)
government libraries, 460–461(table)
public libraries, 454–455(table)
special libraries, 458–459(table)
bibliography for librarians, 577
electronic journals, *see* E-journals
exports (U.S.), 557(table)
imports (U.S.), 559(table)
prices and price indexes
academic library, 481(table), 482(table),
485(table)
Dutch, 546
German academic periodicals, 544(table)
Latin American, 545(table)

Periodicals and serials
  prices and price indexes *(cont.)*
    public library, 472(table)
    U.S., average, 526–527, 528(table),
      529(table), 540–541
  See also International Standard Serial Num-
    ber; Newspapers
Photographs, copyright issues, 143, 164, 289
Placement, 361–381, 394
  2000 U.S. graduates, 390–391(table)
    by school, 384–385(table)
    by type of organization, 386–387(table)
    job trends, 382
  ALA's Human Resource Development and
    Recruitment, 136
  diversity, 144–145
  job hunting, 380–381
  joblines, 362–363, 363(table)
  publishing, recruitment efforts, 154
  school library media specialists; creden-
    tials, 515(table), 517(table)
  sources
    federal employment information sources,
      374–375
    general and specialized jobs, 361,
      375–376
    Internet/Web, 361–362
    library and information studies programs,
      371–374
    newspapers, 361
    nonlibrary uses of information skills,
      378–379
    overseas, 376–377
    overseas exchange programs, 377
    specialized library associations and
      groups, 364–369
    state library agencies, 369–370
    state and regional library associations,
      370–371
    temp/part-time jobs, 379–380
Poe, Marshall, 231
Pornography, *see* Censorship
Postal issues, 150–151, 305
  anthrax virus, 301, 305
  emergency funds, 321–322
Harry Potter . . . (Rowling), 24, 678
The Power of Reading (Krashen), 15
The Prayer of Jabez (Wilkinson), 24, 661,
  678
Preservation
  acquisition expenditures
    academic libraries, 456–457(table)

    government libraries, 460–461(table)
    public libraries, 454–455(table)
    special libraries, 458–459(table)
  ALCTS activities, 137
  ARL activities, 170–171
  bibliography for librarians, 575
  CLIR activities, 188–189
  digital, 189
  FLICC activities, 44, 49
  grant awards, 347, 350–351(table)
  LC activities, 37–38
  NEH grants, 336–338
  NISO standards, 851
  prices and price indexes, academic
    libraries, 479, 481(table), 482(table)
  tutorial, Web-based, 189
  See also Council on Library and Informa-
    tion Resources; Digital Millennium
    Copyright Act; National Audio-Visual
    Conservation Center; Paperwork
    Reduction Act
Presidential Records Act (PRA), 309
Prices and price indexes
  books, 540–541, 548–552
  public/academic libraries, 468–487
  U.S. and foreign published materials,
    525–547
  using the price indexes, 547
  See also Academic books; Audiocassettes;
    Audiovisual materials; Books; CD-
    ROM; DVD; Hardcover books;
    Microforms; Newspapers; Paperback
    books; Periodicals and serials; Video-
    cassettes *and* names of countries
Prison libraries; bibliography for librarians,
  578
Privacy issues
  ALA activities, 127–128
  FLICC, 44
  legislation, pending, 329–330
  LJ news report, 3
  students, 314–315
  virtual reference; confidentiality, 239
Public libraries, 431–432
  acquisition expenditures, 454–455(table),
    474–475
  bibliography for librarians, 576
  Canadian, 261–263, 441–442
  construction, *see* Library buildings
  e-books and, 226–227
  funding, anticipated, 463(table)
  hate crime legislation and, 261–263

LJ budget report, 3–4, 462–467
NCES survey, 443–445, 449
number of, 440, 441
prices and price indexes, 468, 474–476
 books and serials, 472(table)
 major component subindexes, 470(table)
 non-print media and electronic services,
  472(table)
 operating expenses, 469(table),
  474(table), 475–476
 personnel compensation, 471(table)
Public Library Locator, 102
rural, 42
state library agencies, services, 449
See also Collection development; Electronic resources; Funding for libraries;
  Library buildings; Public Library
  Association, *and* specific states
Public Library of Science initiative, 4
Public schools, *see* School libraries; School
  library media centers and services
Public Security Act, 257
Publishers and publishing
 AAP activities, 138–156
 academic, 147
 antipiracy efforts, 148–150
 downsizing, 18–25
 electronic, *see* E-publishing
 government, *see* Government Printing
  Office
 international issues, 148–150
 Internet/Web publishing, 249–254
 legislation, *see* Legislation affecting publishing
 mergers and acquisitions, 20–21
 NISO standards, 851–852
 prices and price indexes, *see under* Academic books; Audiovisual materials;
  Books; CD-ROM; DVD; Hardcover
  books; Microforms; Newspapers;
  Paperback books; Periodicals and serials; Videocassettes
 Real Careers for Real People . . ., 144
 recruitment, 154
 sales, *see* Book sales
 telephone numbers, toll-free, 581–631
 terrorism and, 23–24
 Web sites, 581–631
 See also Association of American Publishers; Digital Millennium Copyright
  Act; E-books; Federal Publishers

Committee, *and* names of specific
  countries, e.g., Great Britain
Publishers Weekly (PW), 228
 bestseller lists, 24
  children's, 678–695
  hardcover, 659–669
  paperback, 670–677
 downsizing, 19
Pulitzer Prizes in Letters, 702

R

Randall, Alice, 23, 160
Random House v. *RosettaBooks*, 23,
  227–228, 252, 289–290
Readers' advisory; bibliography for librari-
  ans, 576
Recordings for children, notable, 656–657
Records management, *see* National Associa-
  tion of Government Archives and
  Records Administrators
Reed, Jack (Sen.), 304
Reference services
 bibliography for librarians, 576–577
 e-reference, *see* Digital reference
 ED Reference Center, 109–110
 LC, 34
 See also Reference and User Services
  Association
Rehabilitation Act, 44
Religious books
 increased sales after terrorist attacks, 24,
  659, 661
 U.S. imports, 560(table)
Religious libraries, *see* American Theologi-
  cal Library Association; Association
  of Jewish Libraries; Catholic Library
  Association; Church and Synagogue
  Library Association; Lutheran Church
  Library Association
Research libraries, *see* College and research
  libraries
Rhode Island
 library associations, 800
 networks and cooperative library organiza-
  tions, 725
 school library media associations, 815
Rhodes, Richard, 140, 145
Robinson, Jackie, 34, 36
Roosevelt, Theodore (U.S. President), 27
Rubin, Vera, 34

Russell, Mark, 155
Russia
The Empire that was Russia, 35
Open World Russian Leadership Program, 30
Web site, bilingual, Russian-English, 32

S

St. George, Judith, 134
Salaries, 382–395
  2000 U.S. graduates, 383(table), 390–391(table)
  average salary index, starting library positions, 388(table)
  comparisons by type of organization, 392–393(table)
  summary by region, 383(table)
  Davis-Bacon Wage Determination database, 88–89
  increase in, 382, 388–389, 394
  library media specialists, 517(table)
  library price indexes, personnel compensation, 468, 469(table), 471(table), 474, 477, 480(table), 481(table), 482(table), 483(table)
  professionals, by area of job assignment, 389(table)
  projected, 463(table)
  Service Contract Wage Determination Database, 89
Scholarly books, *see* Academic books, prices and price indexes; Association of American Publishers, Professional and Scholarly Publishing Division; Textbooks
Scholarships and fellowships
  award recipients, 406–424
  CLIR, 195–196
  Kluge Staff Fellowship, 28–29
  library scholarship sources, 401–405
School libraries, 9–17, 304, 432–433
  AAP activities, 151–154
  funding, 316–317
  School Librarians . . . (NCLIS), 58
  See also American Association of School Librarians; International Association of School Librarianship; School library media centers and services
School library media centers and services, 9–17, 432
  awards

bibliography for librarians, 577
budgets, 11, 302
certification, 16
collaboration between teachers and librarians, 11–12
collection development, 10–11, 513
computers in, 11
cyberlibraries and, 10–11
district-level leadership, 520, 521(table), 522
expenditures, 503–524, 504(table), 505(table), 506(table), 507(table), 508(table), 509(table)
  by school levels, 510–511(table)
  collection size/expenditures, by region, 508, 513
  comparison, by region, 512(table)
  electronic information resources, 515(table)
  survey population, 522–523, 523(table)
  technology, 513–516, 514(table)
funding, 504–508
Information Empowered: The School Librarian as an Agent of Academic Achievement . . ., 15–16
Information Power . . . (AASL/AECT), 11–12, 13, 14
instructional planning, 518(table)
intellectual freedom, 13–14
NCES survey, 105, 449
The Power of Reading (Krashen), 15
programs and services, 516, 518, 520
  by grade level, 519(table)
research on impact of, 14–16
staffing, 10, 16, 516, 517(table)
  credentials, 10, 515(table)
state associations, 810–817
state library agencies, services, 449
strategic planning for school librarianship, 16–17
telecommunications, discounted rates for: *see* Telecommunications, E-rate program
training, professional, 9
See also American Association of School Librarians; International Association of School Librarianship; School libraries
Schorr, Daniel, 36
Scientific research
  DMCA and, 142–143
  See also Public Library of Science

Security measures
  government information, dissemination of,
    279–280, 309
  GPO, 77, 130–131
  "homeland defense" measures, 301, 305
  on the Internet/Web, 249
  LC, 29, 36–37
  in schools, 153
  See also USA Patriot Act
Seminars, *see* Conferences and seminars
Senior citizens
  library services for, *see* Reference and User
    Services Association
September 11 attacks, *see* Terrorism
Serials, *see* Periodicals and serials
A Series of Unfortunate Events (Snicket),
    678
Dr. Seuss, 678
Shepard, Matthew, 261
Shinker, Bill, 21
Sklyarov, Dmitry, 7, 228–229, 292
Slavic Document Delivery Project, 169
Small, David, 134
Snicket, Lemony, 678
Snyder, Richard, 20
So You Want to Be President? (St. George),
    134
Sound recordings: *see* Audiocassettes;
    Audiovisual materials; CD-ROM;
    DVD
South Carolina
  budget cuts, 4
  library associations, 800
  networks and cooperative library organiza-
    tions, 725–726
  school library media associations, 815–816
South Dakota
  library associations, 800
  networks and cooperative library organiza-
    tions, 726
  school library media associations, 816
South Korea, 149–150
Spanish-speaking population, library services
    for, *see* REFORMA
Special libraries, 9–17, 432
  acquisition expenditures, 458–459(table)
  Canadian, 442
  NCES survey, 449
  number of, 440, 441
  See also Special Libraries Association, *and*
    names of specific associations, e.g.,
    Music Library Association

Staffing
  ALA, 135–136, 433–434
  bibliography for librarians, 568
  digital reference, 241
  IFLA, 201–203
  NCES survey, 444, 446, 451
  NCLIS, 57
  publishing industry, 21–22
  school library media centers, 10, 516,
    517(table)
Standard Address Number (SAN), 639–642
  assignment, 641
  check digit calculation, 640–641
  format, 640
  functions and suffixes, 641–642
  history, 640
Standards
  CLIR activities, 191
  digital reference, 239, 245
  e-books, 229
  IFLA activities, 201
  for information literacy, 13
  library, *see* Federal Library and Informa-
    tion Center Committee; International
    Standard Book Number; National
    Information Standards Organization
  Open eBook Publication Structure
    (OEBPS), 229
State humanities councils, 339–342
State libraries and library agencies, 792–804
  bibliography for librarians, 578
  FDLP state plans initiative, 74
  NCES State Library Agencies (StLA) sur-
    vey, 105, 447–452
  See also Chief Officers of State Library
    Agencies; Library associations and
    agencies; School library media centers
    and services, *and* names of specific
    states
Statistics
  ARL, 173–175
  book purchasing, 159
  GPO Access usage, 78
  LibEcon, 59
  NCES library statistics program, 99–107
  NCLIS, 59
  NLM, 71(table), 71
  review media statistics, 564(table)
  See also International Federation of Library
    Associations and Institutions; Nation-
    al Center for Education Statistics
Stein, Sidney (Judge), 6, 23

Stone, Doug, 23
Supplemental Appropriations Act of 2001, 30

T

Taliban, 24
Tarr, Susan M., 46
Tasini v. *New York Times*, 6, 22–23, 129
Taxes
  ABA's sales tax action, 159
  tax-cut legislation, 301, 328
  See also Internet Tax Nondiscrimination
    Act
TEACH (Technology, Education, and Copy-
    right Harmonization) Act, 292–293,
    310, 324
Technical services
  bibliography for librarians, 578–579
  See also Acquisitions; American Library
    Association, Resources and Technical
    Services Division; Association for
    Library Collections and Technical
    Services
Technology
  copyright and, 284–296
  digital reference and, 244–245
  in education, 12
  funding and, 464–465
  school library media centers, 513–516,
    514(table)
  See also American Society for Information
    Science and Technology; Association
    for Educational Communications and
    Technology; Electronic resources;
    International Society for Technology
    in Education
Teen Read Week, 133
Telecommunications, E-rate program, 5, 305
Telemedicine, 70–71
Telephones and telephone numbers
  LC, 39
  library joblines, 362–363, 363(table)
  publishers' (toll-free), 581–631
Tennant, Roy, 231
Tennessee
  library associations, 800
  networks and cooperative library organiza-
    tions, 726
  school library media associations, 816
Terrorism
  anthrax virus, 301
  books about, 23–24, 30

bookstores, effect on, 138, 661, 670
education spending affected by, 152
government power expanded due to, 147
information dissemination, effect on,
    279–280, 309
intellectual freedom, challenges to, 257
Internet/Web use since September 11, 249,
    269
legislation, effect on, 301, 312
postal issues, 151, 305
September 11 attacks, 3, 23–24, 29, 427
travel fears, resultant, 23
See also Emergency Supplemental Appro-
    priations Act for Recovery from and
    Response to Terrorist Attacks on the
    United States; Security; USA Patriot
    Act
Texas
  library associations, 801
  networks and cooperative library organiza-
    tions, 726–727
  school library media associations, 816
Textbooks
  education reform, 152
  electronic, 230
  "heavy backpack" problem, 153
  higher education, 147, 151
  U.S. exports of, 558(table)
  U.S. imports of, 558(table), 560(table)
  for the visually impaired, 152
  See also National Association of Textbook
    Administrators
Thai Journal Index, 170
Theological librarianship, *see* American The-
    ological Library Association; Associa-
    tion of Jewish Libraries; Catholic
    Library Association; Church and Syn-
    agogue Library Association; Lutheran
    Church Library Association
Tolkien, J.R.R., 24, 670
Toon, Malcolm, 34
Trejo, Arnulfo D., 134
Twin Towers, 24

U

Uniform Computer Information Transactions
    Act (UCITA), 6, 163, 293–294
United States
  associations, library/information-industry,
    731–791
  book exports, 555(table)

encyclopedias and serial installments, 557(table)

paperbacks, mass-market, 556(table)

technical, scientific, professional, 557(table)

textbooks, 558(table)

to principal countries, 556(table)

See also Books, exports and imports

book imports

encyclopedias and serial installments, 559(table)

from principal countries, 559(table)

paperbacks, mass market, 561(table)

religious books, 560(table)

technical, scientific, professional books, 561(table)

textbooks, 558(table), 560(table)

See also Books, exports and imports

book trade associations, 837–842

bookstores, 562–563(table)

Education, Department of, *see* Education, U.S. Department of

government information, *see* Government information, access to

libraries, number of, 440–442

postal service, *see* Postal Service, U.S.

prices and price indexes, *see under* Academic books; Audiocassettes; Audiovisual materials; Books; CD-ROM; DVD; Hardcover books; Microforms; Paperback books; Periodicals and serials; Videocassettes

published materials, *see* Government Printing Office

Universal City Studios, Inc. v. *Eric Corely et al.*, 165, 291–292

Universal City Studios, Inc. v. *Reimerdes*, 142

University libraries, *see* College and research libraries

Uptown (Collier), 134

Urban libraries, *see* Urban Libraries Council

U.S. v. *Elcom and Sklyarov*, 292

USA Patriot Act, 257, 301, 306–307, 318–319

Utah

library associations, 801

networks and cooperative library organizations, 727

school library media associations, 816

V

Vancouver Public Library, 262–263, 264

Vendor services

e-books, 226

FEDLINK, 53–54

SKU/ISBN issues, 144

Vermont

library associations, 801

networks and cooperative library organizations, 727

school library media associations, 816

Veterans History Project, 38

Videocassettes, 37

AAP, 145

bibliography for librarians, 575

children's; notable, 655

prices and price indexes

academic libraries, 480(table), 486(table)

public libraries, 469(table), 473(table)

Violence in media, 140, 145, 146

Virgin Islands, networks and cooperative library organizations, 729

Virginia

library associations, 801

networks and cooperative library organizations, 727–728

school library media associations, 816–817

Virtual Reference Desk, 235, 238, 239, 246

Visible Human Project, 70

Visual resources

test database for, 187–188

See also ArtSTOR

Visually handicapped, library services for, *see* Blind, library services for the

Vlades, Jacob, 229

Volunteers; bibliography for librarians, 579

W

Waldseemüller, Martin, 34

Warner, John (Sen.), 273

Washington, D.C., *see* District of Columbia

Washington

Information School, Univ. of Washington, 6

library associations, 801–802

networks and cooperative library organizations, 728

school library media associations, 817

Washington Post, 154

Welch, Jack, 23, 661
West Virginia
  Center for the Book, 41
  library associations, 802
  networks and cooperative library organiza-
    tions, 728
  school library media associations, 817
Who Moved My Cheese? (Johnson), 24
Wilkinson, Bruce, 661
Williams, Maurvene D., 42
The Wind Done Gone (Randall), 23, 160
Winfrey, Oprah, *see* Oprah Book Club
Wisconsin
  library associations, 802
  networks and cooperative library organiza-
    tions, 728–729
  school library media associations, 817
Woodson, Jacqueline, 134
Workforce Investment Act, 78
World Law Bulletin, 30
World Trade Center attacks, *see* Terrorism
Wyoming
  library associations, 802

  networks and cooperative library organiza-
    tions, 729
  school library media associations, 817

Y

A Year Down Yonder (Peck), 134
Young adults
  books, best books, 645–647
    audiobooks, 650–651
    reluctant readers, 648–650
  services for; bibliography for librarians,
    569–570
  Teen Read Week, 133
  See also Children and young adults; Young
    Adult Library Services Association

Z

Z39 Committee, *see* National Information
    Standards Organization, Z39 stan-
    dards
Zimbabwe, 149